BRIEF CONTENTS

CONTENTS

FIT & WELL

EIGHTH EDITION

Core Concepts and Labs in Physical Fitness and Wellness

Thomas D. Fahey
California State University, Chico

Paul M. Insel
Stanford University

Walton T. Roth
Stanford University

With Selections From

Concepts of Fitness and Wellness

A Comprehensive Lifestyle Approach
Seventh Edition

Charles Corbin
Arizona State University

William R. Corbin
Yale University

Gregory J. Welk
Iowa State University

Karen A. Welk
Mary Greeley Medical Center
Ames, Iowa

James Madison University
GKIN 100

Boston Burr Ridge, IL Dubuque, IA New York San Francisco St. Louis
Bangkok Bogotá Caracas Lisbon London Madrid
Mexico City Milan New Delhi Seoul Singapore Sydney Taipei Toronto

Fit & Well
Core Concepts and Labs in Physical Fitness and Wellness, Eight Edition
With Selections From
Concepts of Fitness and Wellness: A Comprehensive Lifestyle Approach, Seventh Edition

This book is a McGraw-Hill Learning Solutions textbook and contains select material from the following sources:
Fit & Well: Core Concepts and Labs in Physical Fitness and Wellness, Eighth Edition by Thomas D. Fahey, Paul M. Insel, and Walton T. Roth. Copyright © 2009 by The McGraw-Hill Companies, Inc.
Concepts of Fitness and Wellness: A Comprehensive Lifestyle Approach, Seventh Edition by Charles B. Corbin, Gregory J. Welk, William R. Corbin, and Karen A. Welk. Copyright © 2006, 2004, 2002, 2000, 1997, 1994 by The McGraw-Hill Companies, Inc.
Reprinted with permission of the publisher. Many custom published texts are modified versions or adaptations of our best-selling textbooks. Some adaptations are printed in black and white to keep prices at a minimum, while others are in color.

1 2 3 4 5 6 7 8 9 0 DIG DIG 0 9 8

ISBN-13: 978-0-07-728507-4
ISBN-10: 0-07-728507-7

Custom Publishing Specialist: Mark Badgett
Custom Publishing Representative: Ann Hayes
Production Editor: Nicole Baumgartner
Printer/Binder: Digital Impressions

BOXES

TAKE CHARGE

CRITICAL CONSUMER

WELLNESS CONNECTION

DIMENSIONS OF DIVERSITY

IN FOCUS

BEHAVIOR CHANGE WORKBOOK ACTIVITIES

PART 1 DEVELOPING A PLAN FOR BEHAVIOR CHANGE AND COMPLETING A CONTRACT

PART 2 OVERCOMING OBSTACLES TO BEHAVIOR CHANGE

The Behavior Change Workbook is also found in an interactive format on the *Fit and Well* Online Learning Center (www.mhhe.com/fahey).

LABORATORY ACTIVITIES

PREFACE

For today's fitness-conscious student, *Fit and Well* combines the best of two worlds. In the area of physical fitness, *Fit and Well* offers expert knowledge based on the latest findings in exercise physiology and sports medicine, along with tools for self-assessment and guidelines for becoming fit. In the area of wellness, it offers accurate, current information on today's most important health-related topics and issues, again with self-tests and guidelines for achieving wellness. To create this book, we have drawn on our combined expertise and experience in exercise physiology, athletic training, personal health, scientific research, and teaching.

OUR AIMS

Our aims in writing this book can be stated simply:

- To show students that becoming fit and well greatly improves the quality of their lives
- To show students how they can become fit and well
- To motivate students to make healthy choices and to provide them with tools for change

The first of these aims means helping students see how their lives can be enhanced by a fit and well lifestyle. This book offers convincing evidence of a simple truth: To look and feel our best, to protect ourselves from degenerative diseases, and to enjoy the highest quality of life, we need to place fitness and wellness among our top priorities. *Fit and Well* makes clear both the imprudence of our modern, sedentary lifestyle and the benefits of a wellness lifestyle.

Our second aim is to give students the tools and information they need to become fit and well. This book provides students with everything they need to create personalized fitness programs, including instructions for fitness tests, explanations of the components of fitness and guidelines for developing them, descriptions and illustrations of exercises, sample programs, and more. In addition, *Fit and Well* provides accurate, up-to-date, scientifically based information about other key topics in wellness, including nutrition, weight management, stress, cardiovascular health, cancer, drugs, alcohol, STDs, and a multitude of others.

In providing this material, we have pooled our efforts. Thomas Fahey has contributed his knowledge as an exercise physiologist, teacher, and author of numerous exercise science textbooks. Paul M. Insel and Walton T. Roth have contributed their knowledge of current topics in health as the authors of the leading personal health textbook *Core Concepts in Health.*

Because we know this expert knowledge can be overwhelming, we have balanced the coverage of complex topics with student-friendly features designed to make the book accessible. Written in a straightforward, easy-to-read style and presented in a colorful, open format, *Fit and Well* invites the student to read, learn, and remember. Boxes, labs, tables, figures, artwork, photographs, and other features add interest to the text and highlight areas of special importance.

Our third aim is to involve students in taking responsibility for their health. *Fit and Well* makes use of interactive features to get students thinking about their current levels of physical fitness and wellness. We offer students assessment tools and laboratory activities to evaluate themselves in terms of each component of physical fitness and each major wellness area, ranging from cardiorespiratory endurance and muscular strength to heart disease, cancer, and STDs.

We also show students how they can make difficult lifestyle changes by using the principles of behavior change. Chapter 1 contains a step-by-step description of this simple but powerful tool for change. The chapter not only explains the five-step process but also offers a wealth of tips for ensuring success. Behavior management aids, including personal contracts, behavior checklists, and self-tests, appear throughout the book. *Fit and Well*'s combined emphasis on self-assessment, self-development in each area of wellness, and behavior change ensures that students are inspired to become fit and well and also have the tools to do so.

When students use these tools to make significant lifestyle changes, they begin to realize that they are in charge of their health—and their lives. From this realization comes a sense of competence and personal power. Perhaps our overriding aim in writing *Fit and Well* is to convey the fact that virtually everyone has the ability to understand, monitor, and make changes in his or her levels of fitness and wellness. By making healthy choices from an early age, individuals may minimize the amount of professional medical care they will ever require. Our hope is that *Fit and Well* will help people make this exciting discovery: that they have the power to shape their future.

CONTENT AND ORGANIZATION OF THE EIGHTH EDITION

The content of *Fit and Well* is organized into 15 chapters. Chapter 1 provides an introduction to fitness and wellness and explains the principles of behavior change. Chapters 2–7 focus on the various areas of fitness. Chapter 2 provides an overview, discussing the components of fitness, the principles of physical training, and the factors involved in designing a well-rounded, personalized exercise program. Chapter 3 provides basic information on how the cardiorespiratory system functions, how the body produces energy for exercise, and how individuals can create successful cardiorespiratory fitness programs. Chapters 4, 5, and 6 look at muscular strength and endurance, flexibility and low-back health, and body composition, respectively. Chapter 7 puts it all together, describing the nature of a complete program that develops all the components of fitness. This chapter also includes complete sample exercise programs.

Chapters 8, 9, and 10 treat three key areas of wellness promotion: nutrition, weight management, and stress management, respectively. It is in these areas that individuals have some of the greatest opportunities for positive change. Chapters 11 and 12 focus on two of the most important reasons for making lifestyle changes: cardiovascular disease and cancer. Students learn the basic mechanisms of these diseases, how they are related to lifestyle, and what individuals can do to prevent them. Chapters 13 and 14 focus on other important wellness issues: addictive behaviors, including the use and abuse of tobacco, alcohol, and other drugs (Chapter 13), and sexually transmitted diseases (Chapter 14). Finally, Chapter 15 looks at four additional wellness topics: interpersonal relationships, aging, the health care system, and environmental health.

For the eighth edition, each chapter was carefully reviewed, revised, and updated. The latest information from scientific and wellness-related research is incorporated in the text, and newly emerging topics are discussed. The following list gives a sample of some of the new and updated material in the eighth edition:

- Physical activity guidelines from the CDC, ACSM, and other authorities
- Nutritional guidelines, including the 2005 Dietary Guidelines for Americans, MyPyramid, the DASH diet, and the Mediterranean diet
- American Cancer Society Nutrition and Physical Activity Guidelines for Cancer Prevention
- Occupational and financial wellness as important aspects of wellness
- Benefits of exercise for all dimensions of wellness
- Top physical and emotional health issues facing college students today
- Common food allergens and food labeling, food safety and foodborne illness, top antioxidant-containing foods, organic food and farming, and cancer-fighting phytochemicals in foods
- The increasing prevalence of overweight and obesity, along with associated health risks, contributing factors, differences by gender and ethnicity, and popular approaches to weight loss
- Diabetes, pre-diabetes, insulin resistance, and metabolic syndrome
- New prescription and OTC weight-loss drugs
- Functional leg strength tests as a measure of muscular strength (Lab 4.1)
- Gender differences in muscular strength
- Performance-enhancing drugs, their supposed effects, and their side effects
- Buying and using heart rate monitors
- Calisthenics circuit training
- Yoga for relaxation and pain relief
- Correct body posture and hand position for a computer workstation
- Cervical cancer and human papillomavirus (HPV), the new HPV vaccine, and CDC recommendations for its use
- Signs of ovarian cancer
- New smoking cessation products
- Revised emergency care guidelines for someone who is choking or experiencing cardiac arrest
- Updated nutritional content of common foods and of popular items from fast-food restaurants
- Sunscreens and sunless tanning products

Research in the areas of health and wellness is ongoing, with new discoveries, advances, trends, and theories reported nearly every week. For this reason, no wellness book can claim to have the final word on every topic. Yet, within these limits, *Fit and Well* does present the latest available information and scientific thinking on important wellness topics. Taken together, the chapters of the book provide students with a complete, up-to-date guide to maximizing their well-being, now and throughout their lives.

WEB To make sure that students have access to the most current information available, each chapter in the eighth edition is also closely tied to the Web site developed as a companion to the text. Boxes, illustrations, tables, terms, and sections of text marked with the World Wide Web icon have corresponding links and activities on the *Fit and Well* Online Learning Center (www.mhhe.com/fahey).

In addition, to help students make the best use of this text, we have updated the way much of the content is presented. We recognize that some students today may learn in different ways than students did in the past. The eighth edition offers a more streamlined approach to content, with more information "chunked" in lists and charts for greater accessibility and easier learning and retention. This edition also features a brighter, more open, and more eye-catching design to appeal to today's visually oriented student.

FEATURES OF THE EIGHTH EDITION

This edition of *Fit and Well* builds on the features that attracted and held our readers' interest in previous editions. These features are designed to help students increase their understanding of the core concepts of wellness and to make better use of the book.

Laboratory Activities

To help students apply the principles of fitness and wellness to their lives, *Fit and Well* includes **laboratory activities** for classroom use. These hands-on activities give students the opportunity to assess their current level of fitness and wellness, to create plans for changing their lifestyle to reach wellness, and to monitor their progress. They can assess their current lifestyle, for example, or their level of cardiorespiratory endurance; they can design a program to improve muscular strength, develop flexibility, or meet weight-loss goals; they can explore their risk of developing cardiovascular disease or cancer; and they can examine their attitudes and behaviors in relation to alcohol use and STDs. Many labs end with a Using Your Results section, which guides students in evaluating their scores, setting goals for change, and moving forward. Labs are found at the end of each chapter; they are perforated for easy removal. For a complete list of laboratory activities, see p. x in the table of contents.

Illustrated Exercise Sections

To ensure that students understand how to perform important exercises and stretches, *Fit and Well* includes three **illustrated exercise sections,** one in Chapter 4 and two in Chapter 5. The section in Chapter 4 covers exercises for developing muscular strength and endurance, as performed both with free weights and on weight machines. One section in Chapter 5 presents stretches for flexibility, and the other presents exercises to stretch and strengthen the lower back. Each exercise is illustrated with one or more full-color photographs showing proper technique.

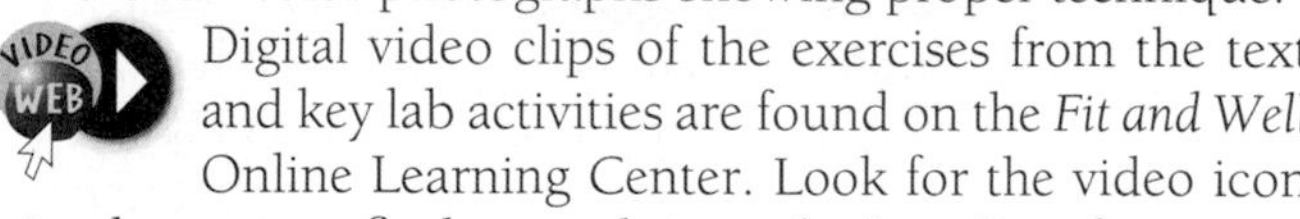

Digital video clips of the exercises from the text and key lab activities are found on the *Fit and Well* Online Learning Center. Look for the video icon in the text to find out when to look online for corresponding video clips.

Sample Programs

To help students get started, Chapter 7 offers seven complete **sample programs** designed to develop overall fitness. The programs are built around four cardiorespiratory endurance activities: walking/jogging/running, bicycling, swimming, and calisthenics circuit training. Each program includes detailed information and guidelines on equipment and technique; target intensity, duration, and frequency; calorie cost of the activity; record keeping; and adjustments to make as fitness improves. The chapter also includes general guidelines for putting together a personal fitness program: setting goals; selecting activities; setting targets for intensity, duration, and frequency; maintaining a commitment; and recording and assessing progress.

Boxes

Boxes are used in *Fit and Well* to explore a wide range of current topics in greater detail than is possible in the text itself. Boxes fall into five different categories, each marked with a special icon and label.

Take Charge boxes distill from the text the practical advice students need to apply information to their lives. By referring to these boxes, students can easily find information about such topics as making time for physical activity, deciding between walking and running, varying their activities, stretching safely, reducing the saturated and trans fats in their diets, managing anger, dealing with an alcohol emergency, protecting themselves from STDs, and many others.

Critical Consumer boxes are designed to help students develop and apply critical thinking skills, thereby enabling them to make sound choices related to health and well-being. Critical Consumer boxes provide specific guidelines for choosing exercise footwear, heart rate monitors, and home exercise equipment; using food and dietary supplement labels; evaluating Web sites and other sources of health information; choosing sunscreens, sunless tanning products, and smoking cessation products; getting an HIV test; and more.

Dimensions of Diversity boxes focus on the important theme of diversity. Most wellness issues are universal; we all need to exercise and eat well, for example. However, certain differences among people—based on gender, educational attainment, socioeconomic status, ethnicity, age, and other factors—do have important implications for wellness. Dimensions of Diversity boxes give students opportunities to identify special wellness concerns that affect them because of who they are, as individuals or as members of a group. Topics of Dimensions of Diversity boxes include differences in cardiovascular disease by gender, ethnicity, and race; gender differences in muscular strength; fitness for people with disabilities; the relationship between poverty and cancer; the healthiest ethnic foods; and others.

Wellness Connection boxes highlight important links among the different dimensions of wellness—physical, emotional, social/interpersonal, intellectual, spiritual, and environmental—and emphasize that all the dimensions must be developed for an individual to achieve optimal health and well-being. Topics include the wellness benefits of exercise, occupational wellness, yoga for relaxation and pain relief, paths to spiritual wellness, sleep, psychosocial factors contributing to cardiovascular disease, coping with cancer, and the benefits of volunteering.

In Focus boxes highlight current topics and issues of particular interest to students. These boxes focus on such topics as the wellness concerns of college students, exercise safety, classification of activity levels, diabetes, counterproductive strategies for coping with stress, glycemic index, the benefits of quitting smoking, and many others.

Vital Statistics

Vital Statistics tables and figures highlight important facts and figures in an accessible format. From tables and figures marked with the Vital Statistics label, students learn about such matters as the leading causes of death for Americans and the factors that play a part in each cause; the relationship between lifestyle and quality of life; public health achievements of the twentieth century; drug use in the United States; the effects of binge drinking on college students; routes of HIV infection; and a wealth of other information. For students who learn best when material is displayed graphically or numerically, Vital Statistics tables and figures offer a way to grasp information quickly and directly.

Common Questions Answered

Sections called **Common Questions Answered** appear at the ends of Chapters 2–14. In these student-friendly sections, the answers to frequently asked questions are presented in easy-to-understand terms. Included are such questions as, Do I need a special diet for my endurance exercise program? Will strength training improve my sports performance? Is stretching the same as warming up? Which should I eat—butter or margarine? Can stress cause headaches? Which contraceptive methods protect best against STDs? Answers to many additional questions can be found on the Online Learning Center.

Motivation Booster

Motivation Booster sections provide strategies for beginning a behavior change program and maintaining healthy new habits over time. Motivation Booster strategies focus on such key aspects of behavior change as building self-efficacy, finding role models and social support, overcoming obstacles and lapses, changing environmental cues, giving rewards, and tracking program progress. These sections appear at appropriate points throughout each chapter.

Questions for Critical Thinking and Reflection

New to the eighth edition, **Questions for Critical Thinking and Reflection** appear at appropriate points throughout the chapters. These questions are designed to prompt students to think critically about the content they have just read, relate it to their own lives, and probe a little more deeply into their own attitudes, values, and beliefs.

Tips for Today and the Future

Chapter-ending **Tips for Today and the Future** sections provide a brief distillation of the major message of each chapter, followed by suggestions for a few simple things that students can try right away and in the near future. Tips for Today and the Future are designed to encourage students and to build their confidence by giving them easy steps they can take immediately and in the next few days and weeks to improve their wellness.

Quick-Reference Appendixes

Included at the end of the book are four appendixes containing vital information in an easy-to-use format. **Appendix A, Injury Prevention and Personal Safety,** is a reference guide to preventing common injuries, whether at home, at work, at play, or on the road. It also provides information on emergency preparedness, and it includes the latest guidelines on giving emergency care when someone else's life is in danger.

Appendix B, Nutritional Content of Common Foods, allows students to assess their daily diet in terms of 11 nutrient categories, including protein, fat, saturated fat, fiber, cholesterol, and sodium. **Appendix C, Nutritional Content of Popular Items from Fast-Food Restaurants,** provides a breakdown of the nutritional content of commonly ordered menu items at popular fast-food restaurants.

Appendix D, Monitoring Your Progress, is a log that enables students to record and summarize the results of the assessment tests they complete as part of the laboratory activities. With space for preprogram and postprogram assessment results, the log provides an easy way to track the progress of a behavior change program.

Built-in Behavior Change Workbook

The built-in **Behavior Change Workbook** contains 15 separate activities that complement the lifestyle management model presented in Chapter 1. The workbook guides students in developing a successful program by walking them through each of the steps of behavior change—from choosing a target behavior to completing and signing a contract. It also includes activities to help students overcome common obstacles to behavior change. The workbook can be found on the Online Learning Center as well.

OTHER FEATURES AND LEARNING AIDS

At the beginning of each chapter, under the heading **Looking Ahead,** five or six statements preview the main points of the chapter for students and serve as learning objectives. Each chapter also opens with **Test Your Knowledge**—three multiple-choice and true-false questions, with answers. These self-quizzes facilitate learning by emphasizing key points, highlighting common misconceptions, and sparking debate. Within each chapter, important terms appear in boldface type and are defined on the same or facing page of text in a **running glossary,** helping students handle new vocabulary.

Other features and learning aids are found at the end of each chapter. **Chapter summaries** offer students a concise review and a way to make sure they have grasped the most important concepts in the chapter. **For Further Exploration** sections list recommended books, newsletters, organizations, hotlines, and Web sites.

For more on the features of the book, refer to the illustrated **User's Guide to *Fit and Well,*** found on pp. xvii–xx.

TEACHING TOOLS

Available with the eighth edition of *Fit and Well* is a comprehensive package of supplementary materials designed to enhance teaching and learning.

Instructor's Media DVD (ISBN 0-07-332568-6)

The Instructor's Media DVD includes the major electronic resources offered with the eighth edition of *Fit and Well.*

- The **Course Integrator Guide** includes learning objectives, extended chapter outlines, lists of additional resources, and many other teaching tools. It also describes all the supplements available with the text and shows how to integrate them into lectures and assignments for each chapter. For the eighth edition, the guide was prepared by Julie Lombardi, Millersville University.
- The **test bank** includes more than 1500 true-false, multiple-choice, and essay questions. The questions are available as Word files and with the **EZ Test computerized testing software.** EZ Test provides a powerful, easy-to-use test maker to create printed quizzes and exams. For secure online testing, exams created in EZ Test can be exported to WebCT, Blackboard, PageOut, and EZ Test Online. EZ Test comes with a Quick Start Guide, and, once the program is installed, users have access to a User's Manual and Flash tutorials. Additional help is available online at www.mhhe.com/eztest.
- The **PowerPoint slides** provide a lecture tool that you can alter or expand to meet the needs of your course. The slides include key lecture points and images from the text and other sources. For the eighth edition, the PowerPoint presentations were created by Andrew Shim, Indiana University of Pennsylvania. As an aid for instructors who wish to create their own presentations, a complete **image bank,** including all the illustrations from the text, is also available on the Instructor's Media DVD.

Primis Online www.mhhe.com/primis/online

Primis Online is a database-driven publishing system that allows instructors to create customized textbooks, lab manuals, or readers for their courses directly from the Primis Web site. The custom text can be delivered in print or electronic (eBook) form. A Primis eBook is a digital version of the customized text sold directly to students as a file downloadable to their computer or accessed online by password. *Fit and Well* can be customized using Primis Online.

Digital Solutions

The ***Fit and Well* Online Learning Center (www.mhhe.com/fahey)** provides many resources for both instructors and students. Instructor tools include downloadable versions of the Course Integrator Guide, the PowerPoint slides, and the computerized test bank, as well as links to professional resources. For students, there are learning objectives, self-quizzes and glossary flashcards for review, interactive Internet activities, video clips of correct training techniques, and extensive links. The Online Learning Center also includes many tools for wellness behavior change, including interactive versions of the Behavior Change Workbook.

Classroom Performance System (CPS) brings interactivity into the classroom or lecture hall. CPS is a wireless response system that gives instructors and students immediate feedback from the entire class. Each student uses a wireless response pad similar to a television remote to instantly respond to polling or quiz questions. Contact your local sales representative for more information about using CPS with *Fit and Well.*

PageOut (www.pageout.net) is a free, easy-to-use program that enables instructors to quickly develop Web sites for their courses. PageOut can be used to create a course home page, an instructor home page, an interactive syllabus that can be linked to elements in the Online Learning Center, Web links, online discussion areas, an online grade book, and much more. Instructors can combine Online Learning Center resources with popular **course-management systems.** For more information about McGraw-Hill's digital resources, including how to obtain passwords for PageOut, contact your local sales representative.

Student Resources Available with *Fit and Well*

In addition to the materials on the Online Learning Center, there are many resources available with *Fit and Well* designed to help students learn and apply key concepts.

- The **Daily Fitness and Nutrition Journal** (ISBN 0-07-332567-8) is a handy booklet that guides students in planning and tracking their fitness programs. It also helps students assess their current diet and make appropriate changes. It is available as an optional package with new copies of the text.
- The **Health and Fitness Pedometer** (ISBN 0-07-320933-3) can be packaged with copies of the text. It allows students to count their daily steps and track their level of physical activity.
- **NutritionCalc Plus** (ISBN 0-07-319532-4) is a dietary analysis program with an easy-to-use interface

that allows users to track their nutrient and food group intakes, energy expenditures, and weight control goals. It generates a variety of reports and graphs for analysis, including comparisons with the Dietary Reference Intakes. The ESHA database includes thousands of ethnic foods, supplements, fast foods, and convenience foods; users can also add foods to the database. NutritionCalc Plus is available on CD-ROM (Windows only) or in an Internet version.

- **HealthQuest 4.2** (ISBN 0-07-295117-6) is an interactive CD-ROM that helps students explore their wellness behavior. It includes tutorials, assessments, and behavior change guidance in such key areas as stress, fitness, nutrition, communicable diseases, cardiovascular disease, cancer, tobacco, alcohol, and other drugs.

Additional supplements and many packaging options are available; check with your local sales representative.

A NOTE OF THANKS

Fit and Well has benefited from the thoughtful commentary, expert knowledge, and helpful suggestions of many people. We are deeply grateful for their participation in the project.

Academic Reviewers of the Eighth Edition

Kym Atwood, University of West Florida
Motier Becque, Southern Illinois University, Carbondale
Laura Blitzer, Florida International University, Miami
Robert "BC" Charles-Liscomb, Greensboro College
Lori Clark, Chemeketa Community College
Mary Ann Erickson, Fort Lewis College
Danny Essary, East Texas Baptist University
Megan Franks, North Harris College
Steven Frierman, Hofstra University
Charlie Goehl, Elmhurst College
Jeffrey S. Hallam, University of Mississippi
Kevin Harper, University of Texas, Arlington
Robert Hess, Community College of Baltimore County at Catonsville
Stacy J. Ingraham, University of Minnesota, Minneapolis
Wayne Jacobs, LeTourneau University
Linda Jenuwine, Macomb Community College
Joe Jones, Cameron University
Heather Krueger, Concordia University
Toni LaSala, William Paterson University
Raymond Leung, University of Southern Indiana
Rosemary Lindle, University of Maryland
Karen McConnell, Pacific Lutheran University
Kathleen Meyer, Clemson University
Michelle Miller, Indiana University, Bloomington
Cenell Munford-Clark, Mount Union College
Peggy Ondrea, Columbia College
Sara Parr, Madison Area Technical College
Tim Patrick, Furman University
Charles Pelitera, Canisius College
Katherine Poole, Radford University
Kelly Quick, University of Sioux Falls
Lindsey Reider, Onondaga Community College
Misti Reisman, Tarleton State University
Amy Ries, Northeast Community College
Natalie Rose, Kennesaw State University
Phil Ryan, State University of New York, Buffalo North Campus
Rich Schroeder, De Anza College
Paula Stauf, Emory University
Martha Stephenson, San Antonio College
McKinley Thomas, Augusta State University
Iva Toler, Prince George's Community College
Gerald Walker, Fort Valley State University
Mike Webster, University of Southern Mississippi, Hattiesburg
James Zarick, High Point University

Special thanks are due to Rich Schroeder, De Anza College, for hosting the photo and video shoots for several editions and to the many students at De Anza College and California State University, Chico, who have participated in these shoots. Special thanks also go to Gary Ligouri at North Dakota State University and to the NDSU students who participated in special fitness and wellness focus groups. We are also grateful to the *Fit and Well* book team at McGraw-Hill, without whose efforts the book could not have been published. Special thanks to Chris Johnson, sponsoring editor; Kirstan Price, long-time developmental editor of this text; Tim Huddleston, developmental editor of the eighth edition; Kate Engelberg, director of development; Julia D. Akpan, developmental editor for technology; Sarah Hill, editorial coordinator; Nick Agnew, marketing manager; Chanda Feldman, production editor; Randy Hurst, production supervisor; Andrei Pasternak, design manager; Robin Mouat, art manager; Brian J. Pecko, manager, photo research; and Marty Granahan, permissions editor.

Thomas D. Fahey
Paul M. Insel
Walton T. Roth

A USER'S GUIDE TO FIT & WELL

Are you looking for ways to improve your lifestyle and become fit and well? Do you need help finding reliable wellness resources online? Would you like to boost your grade? *Fit and Well* can help you do all this and much more!

LABORATORY ACTIVITIES

These hands-on self-assessments help you determine your current level of wellness and create plans for making positive changes in your lifestyle. Lab activities are included at the end of every chapter on easy-to-use perforated pages.

FIT AND WELL ONLINE LEARNING CENTER (WWW.MHHE.COM/FAHEY)

WEB Look for the World Wide Web icon throughout the text. Elements marked with the icon have corresponding activities and links on the *Fit and Well* Online Learning Center.

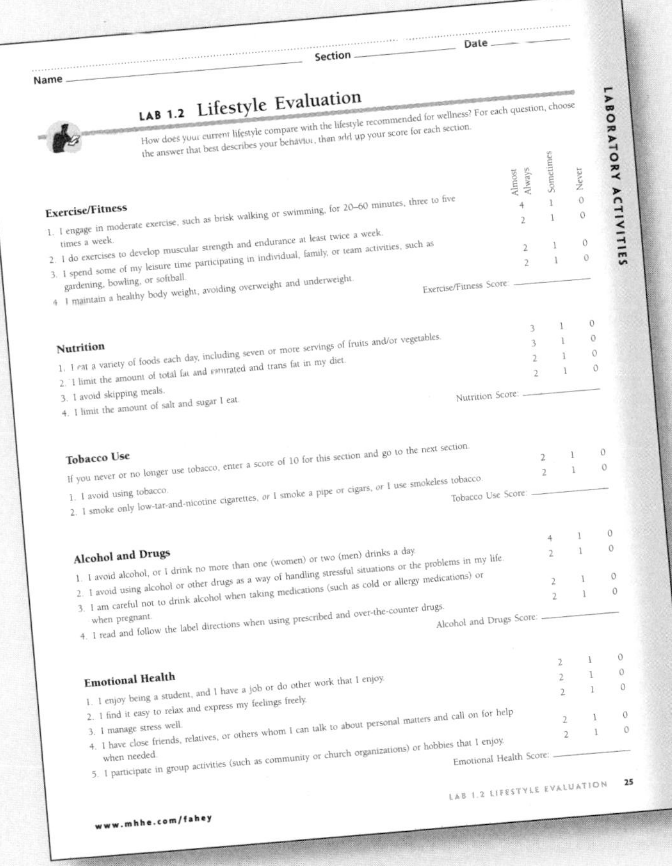

Name ______ Section ______ Date ______

LABORATORY ACTIVITIES

LAB 1.2 Lifestyle Evaluation

How does your current lifestyle compare with the lifestyle recommended for wellness? For each question, choose the answer that best describes your behavior, then add up your score for each section.

Exercise/Fitness	Almost Always	Sometimes	Never
1. I engage in moderate exercise, such as brisk walking or swimming, for 20–60 minutes, three to five times a week.	4	1	0
2. I do exercises to develop muscular strength and endurance at least twice a week.	2	1	0
3. I spend some of my leisure time participating in individual, family, or team activities, such as gardening, bowling, or softball.	2	1	0
4. I maintain a healthy body weight, avoiding overweight and underweight.	2	1	0

Exercise/Fitness Score: ______

Nutrition			
1. I eat a variety of foods each day, including seven or more servings of fruits and/or vegetables.	3	1	0
2. I limit the amount of total fat and saturated and trans fat in my diet.	3	1	0
3. I avoid skipping meals.	2	1	0
4. I limit the amount of salt and sugar I eat.	2	1	0

Nutrition Score: ______

Tobacco Use

If you never or no longer use tobacco, enter a score of 10 for this section and go to the next section.

1. I avoid using tobacco.	2	1	0
2. I smoke only low-tar-and-nicotine cigarettes, *or* I smoke a pipe or cigars, *or* I use smokeless tobacco.	2	1	0

Tobacco Use Score: ______

Alcohol and Drugs			
1. I avoid alcohol, or I drink no more than one (women) or two (men) drinks a day.	4	1	0
2. I avoid using alcohol or other drugs as a way of handling stressful situations or the problems in my life.	2	1	0
3. I am careful not to drink alcohol when taking medications (such as cold or allergy medications) or when pregnant.	2	1	0
4. I read and follow the label directions when using prescribed and over-the-counter drugs.	2	1	0

Alcohol and Drugs Score: ______

Emotional Health			
1. I enjoy being a student, and I have a job or do other work that I enjoy.	2	1	0
2. I find it easy to relax and express my feelings freely.	2	1	0
3. I manage stress well.	2	1	0
4. I have close friends, relatives, or others whom I can talk to about personal matters and call on for help when needed.	2	1	0
5. I participate in group activities (such as community or church organizations) or hobbies that I enjoy.	2	1	0

Emotional Health Score: ______

LAB 1.2 LIFESTYLE EVALUATION 25

www.mhhe.com/fahey

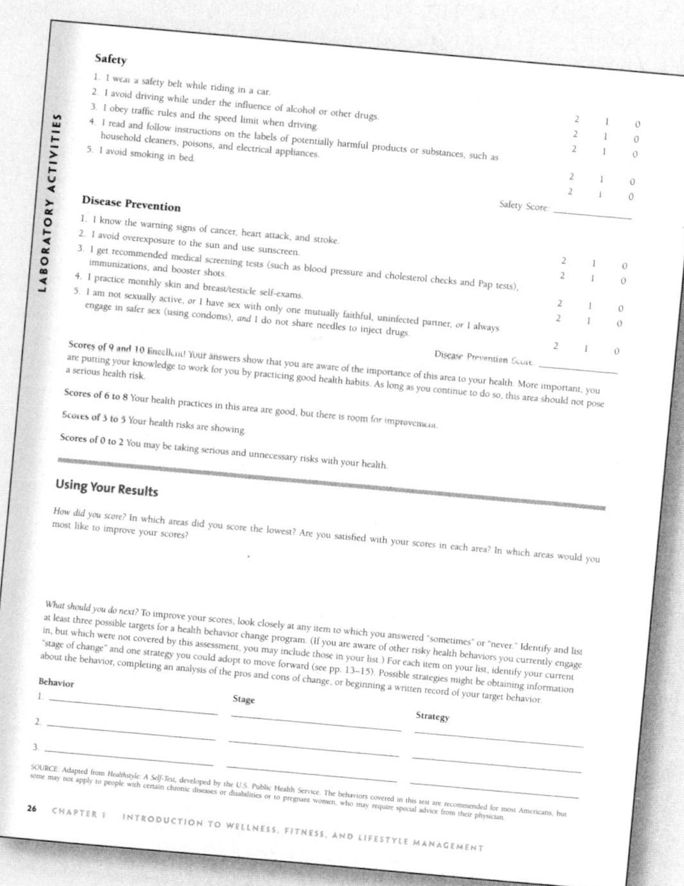

LABORATORY ACTIVITIES

Safety			
1. I wear a safety belt while riding in a car.	2	1	0
2. I avoid driving while under the influence of alcohol or other drugs.	2	1	0
3. I obey traffic rules and the speed limit when driving.	2	1	0
4. I read and follow instructions on the labels of potentially harmful products or substances, such as household cleaners, poisons, and electrical appliances.	2	1	0
5. I avoid smoking in bed.	2	1	0

Safety Score: ______

Disease Prevention			
1. I know the warning signs of cancer, heart attack, and stroke.	2	1	0
2. I avoid overexposure to the sun and use sunscreen.	2	1	0
3. I get recommended medical screening tests (such as blood pressure and cholesterol checks and Pap tests), immunizations, and booster shots.	2	1	0
4. I practice monthly skin and breast/testicle self-exams.	2	1	0
5. I am not sexually active, *or* I have sex with only one mutually faithful, uninfected partner, *or* I always engage in safer sex (using condoms), *and* I do not share needles to inject drugs.	2	1	0

Disease Prevention Score: ______

Scores of 9 and 10 Excellent! Your answers show that you are aware of the importance of this area to your health. More important, you are putting your knowledge to work for you by practicing good health habits. As long as you continue to do so, this area should not pose a serious health risk.

Scores of 6 to 8 Your health practices in this area are good, but there is room for improvement.

Scores of 3 to 5 Your health risks are showing.

Scores of 0 to 2 You may be taking serious and unnecessary risks with your health.

Using Your Results

How did you score? In which areas did you score the lowest? Are you satisfied with your scores in each area? In which areas would you most like to improve your scores?

What should you do next? To improve your scores, look closely at any item to which you answered "sometimes" or "never." Identify and list at least three possible targets for a health behavior change program. (If you are aware of other risky health behaviors you currently engage in, but which were not covered by this assessment, you may include those in your list.) For each item on your list, identify your current "stage of change" and one strategy you could adopt to move forward (see pp. 13–15). Possible strategies might be obtaining information about the behavior, completing an analysis of the pros and cons of change, or beginning a written record of your target behavior.

Behavior	Stage	Strategy
1. ______	______	______
2. ______	______	______
3. ______	______	______

SOURCE: Adapted from *Healthstyle: A Self-Test*, developed by the U.S. Public Health Service. The behaviors covered in this test are recommended for most Americans, but some may not apply to people with certain chronic diseases or disabilities or to pregnant women, who may require special advice from their physician.

26 CHAPTER 1 INTRODUCTION TO WELLNESS, FITNESS, AND LIFESTYLE MANAGEMENT

A USER'S GUIDE TO FIT & WELL

SAMPLE EXERCISE PROGRAMS

Illustrated exercise programs in Chapters 4 and 5 show proper technique for exercises and stretches that develop muscular strength and endurance, flexibility, and low-back health; video clips of the exercises can be found on the Online Learning Center. The complete sample fitness programs in Chapter 7 are built around popular endurance activities such as walking, jogging, cycling, and swimming.

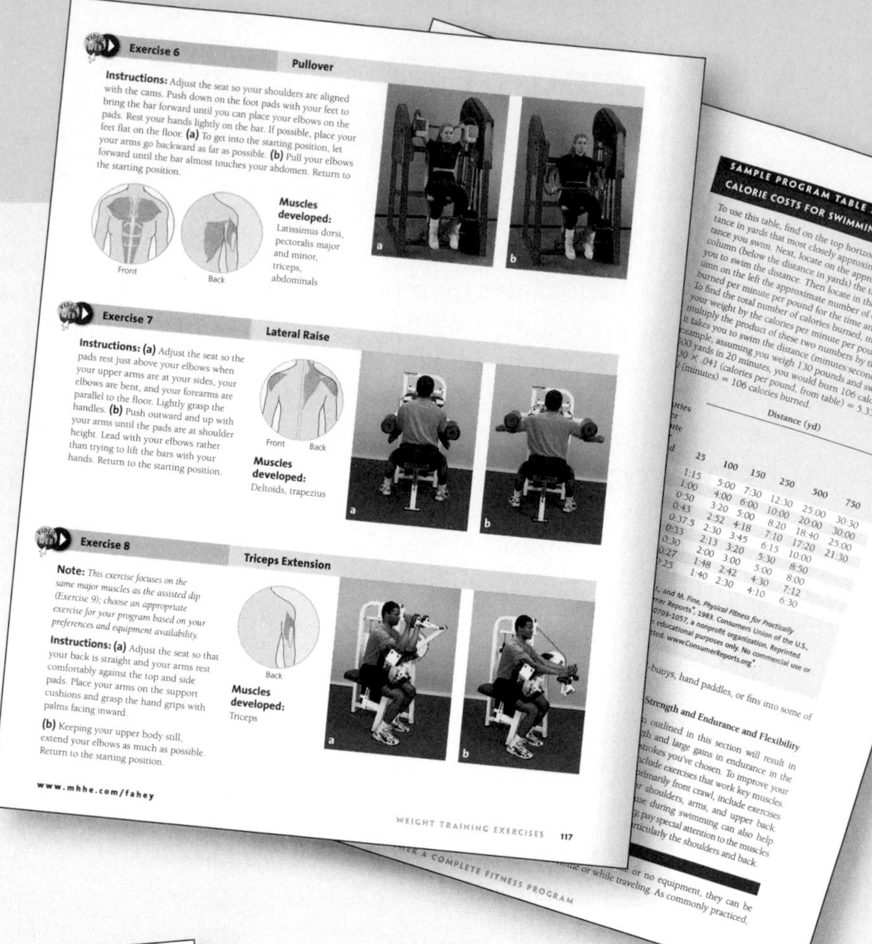

Exercise 6 — **Pullover**

Instructions: Adjust the seat so your shoulders are aligned with the cams. Push down on the foot pads with your feet to bring the bar forward until you can place your elbows on the pads. Rest your hands lightly on the bar. If possible, place your feet flat on the floor. **(a)** To get into the starting position, let your arms go backward as far as possible. **(b)** Pull your elbows forward until the bar almost touches your abdomen. Return to the starting position.

Muscles developed: Latissimus dorsi, pectoralis major and minor, triceps, abdominals

Exercise 7 — **Lateral Raise**

Instructions: (a) Adjust the seat so the pads rest just above your elbows when your upper arms are at your sides, your elbows are bent, and your forearms are parallel to the floor. Lightly grasp the handles. **(b)** Push outward and up with your arms until the pads are at shoulder height. Lead with your elbows rather than trying to lift the bars with your hands. Return to the starting position.

Muscles developed: Deltoids, trapezius

Exercise 8 — **Triceps Extension**

Note: *This exercise focuses on the same major muscles as the assisted dip (Exercise 9); choose an appropriate exercise for your program based on your preferences and equipment availability.*

Instructions: (a) Adjust the seat so that your back is straight and your arms rest comfortably against the top and side pads. Place your arms on the support cushions and grasp the hand grips with palms facing inward. **(b)** Keeping your upper body still, extend your elbows as much as possible. Return to the starting position.

Muscles developed: Triceps

www.mhhe.com/fahey

WEIGHT TRAINING EXERCISES 117

Tips for Moving Forward in the Cycle of Behavior Change

TAKE CHARGE

PRECONTEMPLATION

- *Raise your awareness.* Research your target behavior and its effects.
- *Be self-aware.* Look at the mechanisms you use to resist change, such as denial or rationalization. Find ways to counteract these mechanisms.
- *Seek social support.* Friends and family members can help you identify target behaviors and understand their impact on the people around you.
- *Identify helpful resources.* These might include exercise classes or stress-management workshops offered by your school.

CONTEMPLATION

- *Keep a journal.* A record of your target behavior and the circumstances that elicit the behavior can help you plan a change program.
- *Do a cost-benefit analysis.* Identify the costs and benefits (both current and future) of maintaining your behavior and of changing it. Costs can be monetary, social, emotional, and so on.
- *Identify barriers to change.* Knowing these obstacles can help you overcome them.
- *Engage your emotions.* Watch movies or read books about people with your target behavior. Imagine what your life will be like if you don't change.
- *Create a new self-image.* Imagine what you'll be like after changing your target behavior. Try to think of yourself in new terms right now.
- *Think before you act.* Learn why you engage in the target behavior. Determine what "sets you off," and train yourself not to act reflexively.

PREPARATION

- *Create a plan.* Include a start date, goals, rewards, and specific steps you will take to change your behavior.
- *Make change a priority.* Create and sign a contract with yourself.
- *Practice visualization and self-talk.* These techniques can help prepare you mentally for challenging situations.
- *Take short steps.* Successfully practicing your new behavior for a short time—even a single day—can boost your confidence and motivation.

ACTION

- *Monitor your progress.* Keep up with your journal entries.
- *Change your environment.* Make changes that will discourage the target behavior—for example, getting rid of snack foods or not stocking the refrigerator with beer.
- *Find alternatives to your target behavior.* Make a list of things you can do to replace the behavior.
- *Reward yourself.* Rewards should be identified in your change plan. Give yourself lots of praise, and focus on your success.
- *Involve your friends.* Tell them you want to change, and ask for their help.
- *Don't get discouraged.* Real change is difficult.

MAINTENANCE

- *Keep going.* Continue using the positive strategies that worked in earlier stages.
- *Be prepared for lapses.* Don't let slip-ups set you back.
- *Be a role model.* Once you have successfully changed your behavior, you may be able to help someone else do the same thing.

TAKE CHARGE BOXES

Take Charge boxes, found throughout the text, provide practical advice that you can apply to your everyday life.

CRITICAL CONSUMER BOXES

Critical Consumer boxes help you develop and apply critical thinking skills so you can make sound choices related to wellness. Additional resources for each Critical Consumer topic are found on the Online Learning Center.

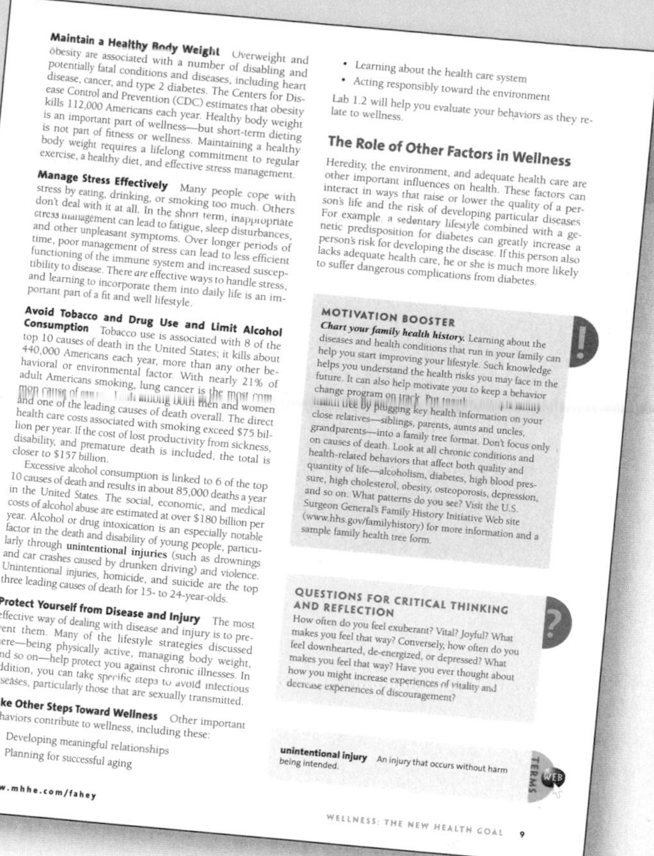

Maintain a Healthy Body Weight Overweight and obesity are associated with a number of disabling and potentially fatal conditions and diseases, including heart disease, cancer, and type 2 diabetes. The Centers for Disease Control and Prevention (CDC) estimates that obesity kills 112,000 Americans each year. Healthy body weight is an important part of wellness—but short-term dieting is not part of fitness or wellness. Maintaining a healthy body weight requires a lifelong commitment to regular exercise, a healthy diet, and effective stress management.

Manage Stress Effectively Many people cope with stress by eating, drinking, or smoking too much. Others don't deal with it at all. In the short term, inappropriate stress management can lead to fatigue, sleep disturbances, and other unpleasant symptoms. Over longer periods of time, poor management of stress can lead to less efficient functioning of the immune system and increased susceptibility to disease. There *are* effective ways to handle stress, and learning to incorporate them into daily life is an important part of a fit and well lifestyle.

Avoid Tobacco and Drug Use and Limit Alcohol Consumption Tobacco use is associated with 8 of the top 10 causes of death in the United States; it kills about 440,000 Americans each year, more than any other behavioral or environmental factor. With nearly 21% of adult Americans smoking, lung cancer is the most common cause of [illegible] among both men and women and one of the leading causes of death overall. The direct health care costs associated with smoking exceed $75 billion per year. If the cost of lost productivity from sickness, disability, and premature death is included, the total is closer to $157 billion.

Excessive alcohol consumption is linked to 6 of the top 10 causes of death and results in about 85,000 deaths a year in the United States. The social, economic, and medical costs of alcohol abuse are estimated at over $180 billion per year. Alcohol or drug intoxication is an especially notable factor in the death and disability of young people, particularly through **unintentional injuries** (such as drownings and car crashes caused by drunken driving) and violence. Unintentional injuries, homicide, and suicide are the top three leading causes of death for 15- to 24-year-olds.

Protect Yourself from Disease and Injury The most effective way of dealing with disease and injury is to prevent them. Many of the lifestyle strategies discussed here—being physically active, managing body weight, and so on—help protect you against chronic illnesses. In addition, you can take specific steps to avoid infectious diseases, particularly those that are sexually transmitted.

Take Other Steps Toward Wellness Other important behaviors contribute to wellness, including these:

- Developing meaningful relationships
- Planning for successful aging
- Learning about the health care system
- Acting responsibly toward the environment

Lab 1.2 will help you evaluate your behaviors as they relate to wellness.

The Role of Other Factors in Wellness

Heredity, the environment, and adequate health care are other important influences on health. These factors can interact in ways that raise or lower the quality of a person's life and the risk of developing particular diseases. For example, a sedentary lifestyle combined with a genetic predisposition for diabetes can greatly increase a person's risk for developing the disease. If this person also lacks adequate health care, he or she is much more likely to suffer dangerous complications from diabetes.

MOTIVATION BOOSTER

Chart your family health history. Learning about the diseases and health conditions that run in your family can help you start improving your lifestyle. Such knowledge helps you understand the health risks you may face in the future. It can also help motivate you to keep a behavior change program on track. Put [illegible] health tree by plugging key health information on your close relatives—siblings, parents, aunts and uncles, grandparents—into a family tree format. Don't focus only on causes of death. Look at all chronic conditions and health-related behaviors that affect both quality and quantity of life—alcoholism, diabetes, high blood pressure, high cholesterol, obesity, osteoporosis, depression, and so on. What patterns do you see? Visit the U.S. Surgeon General's Family History Initiative Web site (www.hhs.gov/familyhistory) for more information and a sample family health tree form.

QUESTIONS FOR CRITICAL THINKING AND REFLECTION

How often do you feel exuberant? Vital? Joyful? What makes you feel that way? Conversely, how often do you feel downhearted, de-energized, or depressed? What makes you feel that way? Have you ever thought about how you might increase experiences of vitality and decrease experiences of discouragement?

unintentional injury An injury that occurs without harm being intended.

TERMS

www.mhhe.com/fahey

WELLNESS: THE NEW HEALTH GOAL 9

MOTIVATION BOOSTER

Motivation Booster sections provide strategies for beginning a behavior change program and maintaining new healthy habits over time.

QUESTIONS FOR CRITICAL THINKING AND REFLECTION

Questions for Critical Thinking and Reflection prompt you to think critically about the information you have read and consider how it relates to your own life and experience. Some questions also ask you to reflect on your values, beliefs, and attitudes.

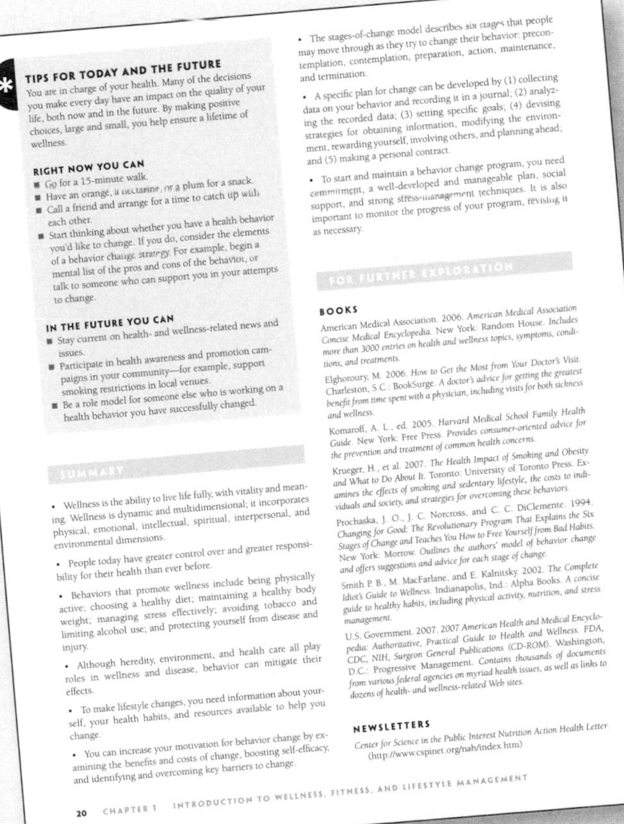

TIPS FOR TODAY AND THE FUTURE

You are in charge of your health. Many of the decisions you make every day have an impact on the quality of your life, both now and in the future. By making positive choices, large and small, you help ensure a lifetime of wellness.

RIGHT NOW YOU CAN

- Go for a 15-minute walk.
- Have an orange, a nectarine, or a plum for a snack.
- Call a friend and arrange for a time to catch up with each other.
- Start thinking about whether you have a health behavior you'd like to change. If you do, consider the elements of a behavior change strategy. For example, begin a mental list of the pros and cons of the behavior, or talk to someone who can support you in your attempts to change.

IN THE FUTURE YOU CAN

- Stay current on health- and wellness-related news and issues.
- Participate in health awareness and promotion campaigns in your community—for example, support smoking restrictions in local venues.
- Be a role model for someone else who is working on a health behavior you have successfully changed.

SUMMARY

- Wellness is the ability to live life fully, with vitality and meaning. Wellness is dynamic and multidimensional; it incorporates physical, emotional, intellectual, spiritual, interpersonal, and environmental dimensions.
- People today have greater control over and greater responsibility for their health than ever before.
- Behaviors that promote wellness include being physically active; choosing a healthy diet; maintaining a healthy body weight; managing stress effectively; avoiding tobacco and limiting alcohol use; and protecting yourself from disease and injury.
- Although heredity, environment, and health care all play roles in wellness and disease, behavior can mitigate their effects.
- To make lifestyle changes, you need information about yourself, your health habits, and resources available to help you change.
- You can increase your motivation for behavior change by examining the benefits and costs of change, boosting self-efficacy, and identifying and overcoming key barriers to change.
- The stages-of-change model describes six stages that people may move through as they try to change their behavior: precontemplation, contemplation, preparation, action, maintenance, and termination.
- A specific plan for change can be developed by (1) collecting data on your behavior and recording it in a journal; (2) analyzing the recorded data; (3) setting specific goals; (4) devising strategies for obtaining information, modifying the environment, rewarding yourself, involving others, and planning ahead; and (5) making a personal contract.
- To start and maintain a behavior change program, you need commitment, a well-developed and manageable plan, social support, and strong stress-management techniques. It is also important to monitor the progress of your program, revising it as necessary.

FOR FURTHER EXPLORATION

BOOKS

American Medical Association. 2006. *American Medical Association Concise Medical Encyclopedia.* New York: Random House. *Includes more than 3000 entries on health and wellness topics, symptoms, conditions, and treatments.*

Elghoroury, M. 2006. *How to Get the Most from Your Doctor's Visit.* Charleston, S.C.: BookSurge. *A doctor's advice for getting the greatest benefit from time spent with a physician, including visits for both sickness and wellness.*

Komaroff, A. L., ed. 2005. *Harvard Medical School Family Health Guide.* New York: Free Press. *Provides consumer-oriented advice for the prevention and treatment of common health concerns.*

Krueger, H., et al. 2007. *The Health Impact of Smoking and Obesity and What to Do About It.* Toronto: University of Toronto Press. *Examines the effects of smoking and sedentary lifestyle, the costs to individuals and society, and strategies for overcoming these behaviors.*

Prochaska, J. O., J. C. Norcross, and C. C. DiClemente. 1994. *Changing for Good: The Revolutionary Program That Explains the Six Stages of Change and Teaches You How to Free Yourself from Bad Habits.* New York: Morrow. *Outlines the authors' model of behavior change and offers suggestions and advice for each stage of change.*

Smith P. B., M. MacFarlane, and E. Kalnitsky. 2002. *The Complete Idiot's Guide to Wellness.* Indianapolis, Ind.: Alpha Books. *A concise guide to healthy habits, including physical activity, nutrition, and stress management.*

U.S. Government. 2007. *2007 American Health and Medical Encyclopedia: Authoritative, Practical Guide to Health and Wellness. FDA, CDC, NIH, Surgeon General Publications* (CD-ROM). Washington, D.C.: Progressive Management. *Contains thousands of documents from various federal agencies on myriad health issues, as well as links to dozens of health- and wellness-related Web sites.*

NEWSLETTERS

Center for Science in the Public Interest Nutrition Action Health Letter (http://www.cspinet.org/nah/index.htm)

20 CHAPTER 1 INTRODUCTION TO WELLNESS, FITNESS, AND LIFESTYLE MANAGEMENT

TIPS FOR TODAY AND THE FUTURE

Tips for Today and the Future sections, found at the end of each chapter, provide a brief summary of the major message of the chapter, followed by suggestions for a few easy steps you can try right away and in the next few weeks and months to improve your level of wellness.

FOR FURTHER EXPLORATION

For Further Exploration sections at the end of each chapter describe books, newsletters, organizations, hotlines, and Web sites that you can turn to for additional information and advice.

A USER'S GUIDE TO FIT & WELL

RUNNING GLOSSARY

Important terms appear in boldface type in the text and are defined in a running glossary on the same or facing page. A pronunciation guide to the glossary terms is found on the Online Learning Center.

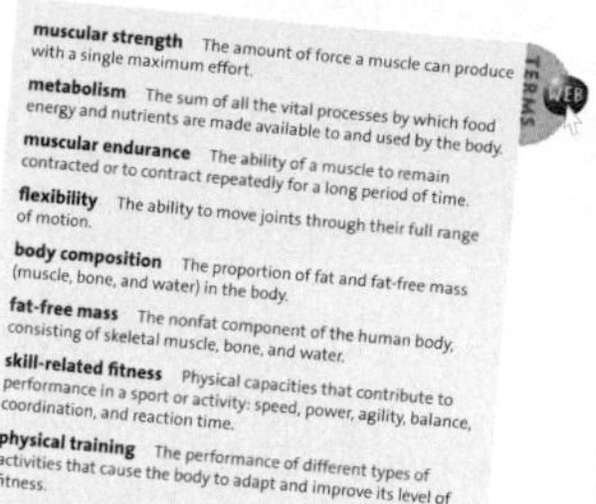

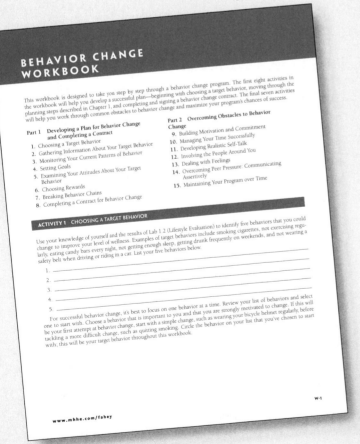

BEHAVIOR CHANGE WORKBOOK

The Behavior Change Workbook takes you step-by-step through the process of behavior change. It helps you target a specific behavior, set goals, create a plan, and overcome common obstacles to change. The Workbook is available in an interactive format on the Online Learning Center, and a printed copy is included in the full and alternate editions of the text.

LOOKING AHEAD>>>>>

AFTER READING THIS CHAPTER, YOU SHOULD BE ABLE TO:

- Describe the dimensions of wellness
- Identify the major health problems in the United States today, and discuss their causes
- Describe the behaviors that are part of a fit and well lifestyle
- Explain the steps in creating a behavior management plan to change a wellness-related behavior
- Discuss the available sources of wellness information and how to think critically about them

INTRODUCTION TO WELLNESS, FITNESS, AND LIFESTYLE MANAGEMENT

1

TEST YOUR KNOWLEDGE

1. Which of the following lifestyle factors is the leading preventable cause of death for Americans?

a. excess alcohol consumption
b. cigarette smoking
c. obesity

2. The terms *health* and *wellness* mean the same thing.

True or false?

3. Which of the following health-related issues affects the greatest number of college students each year?

a. stress
b. colds/flu/sore throat
c. sleep problems
d. concern for a friend or family member

ANSWERS

1. **b. Smoking** causes about 500,000 deaths per year; obesity is responsible for more than 100,000; and alcohol, as many as 85,000.
2. **FALSE.** Although the words are used interchangeably, they actually have different meanings. The term *health* refers to the overall condition of the body or mind and to the presence or absence of illness or injury. The term *wellness* refers to optimal health and vitality, encompassing six dimensions of well-being.
3. **a. About** 32% of college students suffer so much stress that it affects their academic performance. High stress levels affect overall health and wellness, making it important to learn effective stress-management techniques.

FIT AND WELL ONLINE LEARNING CENTER www.mhhe.com/fahey

Visit the *Fit and Well* Online Learning Center for resources that will help you get the most out of your course!

- Study and review aids include practice quizzes, glossary flashcards, chapter summaries, learning objectives, PowerPoint presentations, Common Questions Answered, student handouts, crossword puzzles, Internet activities, and links to wellness Web sites.
- Behavior change tools include a daily fitness and nutrition journal, a behavior change workbook, sample behavior change plans, and blank behavior change logs to print and use.

A college sophomore sets the following goals for herself:

- To join in new social circles and make new friends whenever possible
- To exercise every day
- To clean up trash and plant trees in blighted neighborhoods in her community

These goals may differ, but they have one thing in common. Each contributes, in its own way, to this student's health and well-being. Not satisfied merely to be free of illness, she wants more. She has decided to live actively and fully—not just to be healthy but to pursue a state of overall wellness.

WELLNESS: THE NEW HEALTH GOAL

Generations of people have viewed health simply as the absence of disease. That view largely prevails today; the word **health** typically refers to the overall condition of a person's body or mind and to the presence or absence of illness or injury. **Wellness** is a relatively new concept that expands our idea of health. Beyond the simple presence or absence of disease, wellness refers to optimal health and vitality—to living life to its fullest. Although we use the words *health* and *wellness* interchangeably, there are two important differences between them:

- Health—or some aspects of it—can be determined or influenced by factors beyond your control, such as your genes, age, and family history. For example, consider a 60-year-old man with a strong family history of prostate cancer. These factors place this man at a higher-than-average risk for developing prostate cancer himself.
- Wellness is largely determined by the decisions you make about how you live. That same 60-year-old man can reduce his risk of cancer by eating sensibly, exercising, and having regular screening tests. Even if he develops the disease, he may still rise above its effects to live a rich, meaningful life. This means choosing not only to care for himself physically but to maintain a positive outlook, keep up his relationships with others, challenge himself intellectually, and nurture other aspects of his life.

Enhanced wellness, therefore, involves making conscious decisions to control **risk factors** that contribute to disease or injury. Age and family history are risk factors you cannot control. Behaviors such as smoking, exercising, and eating a healthy diet are well within your control.

The Dimensions of Wellness

Experts have defined six dimensions of wellness:

- Physical
- Emotional
- Intellectual
- Interpersonal
- Spiritual
- Environmental

These dimensions are interrelated; each has an effect on the others. Further, the process of achieving wellness is constant and dynamic (Figure 1.1), involving change and growth. Wellness is not static; ignoring any dimension of wellness can have harmful effects on your life. The following sections briefly introduce the dimensions of wellness. Table 1.1 lists some of the specific qualities and behaviors associated with each dimension.

Physical Wellness Your physical wellness includes not just your body's overall condition and the absence of disease but your fitness level and your ability to care for yourself. The higher your fitness level (which is discussed throughout this book), the higher your level of physical wellness will be. Similarly, as you develop the ability to take care of your own physical needs, you ensure a greater level of physical wellness. To achieve optimum physical wellness, you need to make choices that will help you avoid illnesses and injuries. The decisions you make now, and the habits you develop over

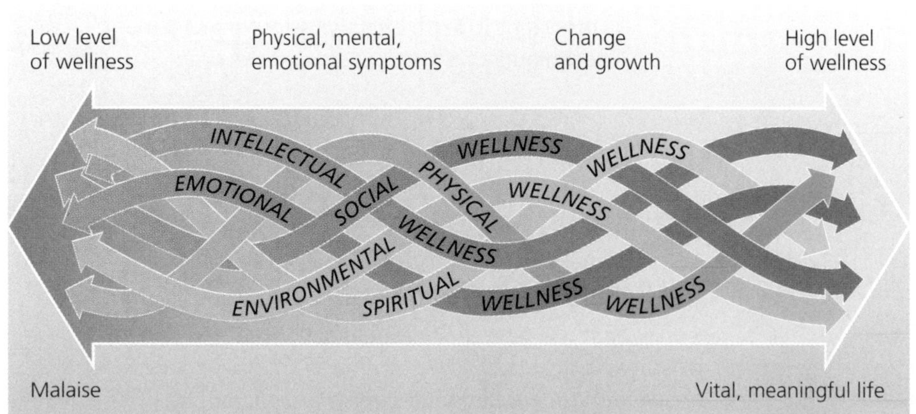

FIGURE 1.1 The wellness continuum. The concept of wellness includes vitality in six interrelated dimensions, all of which contribute to overall wellness.

Table 1.1 Examples of Qualities and Behaviors Associated with the Dimensions of Wellness

Physical	Emotional	Intellectual	Interpersonal	Spiritual	Environmental
• Eating well • Exercising • Avoiding harmful habits • Practicing safer sex • Recognizing symptoms of disease • Getting regular checkups • Avoiding injuries	• Optimism • Trust • Self-esteem • Self-acceptance • Self-confidence • Ability to understand and accept one's feelings • Ability to share feelings with others	• Openness to new ideas • Capacity to question • Ability to think critically • Motivation to master new skills • Sense of humor • Creativity • Curiosity • Lifelong learning	• Communication skills • Capacity for intimacy • Ability to establish and maintain satisfying relationships • Ability to cultivate support system of friends and family	• Capacity for love • Compassion • Forgiveness • Altruism • Joy • Fulfillment • Caring for others • Sense of meaning and purpose • Sense of belonging to something greater than oneself	• Having abundant, clean natural resources • Maintaining sustainable development • Recycling whenever possible • Reducing pollution and waste

your lifetime, will largely determine the length and quality of your life.

Emotional Wellness Your emotional wellness reflects your ability to understand and deal with your feelings. Emotional wellness involves attending to your own thoughts and feelings, monitoring your reactions, and identifying obstacles to emotional stability. Achieving this type of wellness means finding solutions to emotional problems, with professional help if necessary.

Intellectual Wellness Those who enjoy intellectual (or mental) wellness constantly challenge their minds. An active mind is essential to wellness because it detects problems, finds solutions, and directs behavior. People who enjoy intellectual wellness never stop learning; they continue trying to learn new things throughout their lifetime. They seek out and relish new experiences and challenges.

Interpersonal Wellness Your interpersonal (or social) wellness is defined by your ability to develop and maintain satisfying and supportive relationships. Such relationships are essential to physical and emotional health. Social wellness requires participating in and contributing to your community, country, and world.

Spiritual Wellness To enjoy spiritual wellness is to possess a set of guiding beliefs, principles, or values that give meaning and purpose to your life, especially in difficult times. The spiritually well person focuses on the positive aspects of life and finds spirituality to be an antidote for negative feelings such as cynicism, anger, and pessimism. Organized religions help many people develop spiritual health. Religion, however, is not the only source or form of spiritual wellness. Many people find meaning and purpose in their lives on their own—through nature, art, meditation, or good works—or with their loved ones.

Environmental Wellness Your environmental wellness is defined by the livability of your surroundings. Personal health depends on the health of the planet—from the safety of the food supply to the degree of violence in society. Your physical environment either supports your wellness or diminishes it. To improve your environmental wellness, you can learn about and protect yourself against hazards in your surroundings and work to make your world a cleaner and safer place.

Lab 1.1 will help you learn what wellness means to you and where you fall on the wellness continuum. In addition, see the box "Occupational Wellness" (p. 4) to learn about another important aspect of wellness.

New Opportunities, New Responsibilities

Wellness is a fairly new concept. A century ago, Americans considered themselves lucky just to survive to adulthood (Figure 1.2, p. 5). A child born in 1900, for example, could expect to live only about 47 years. Many people died from common **infectious diseases** (such as pneumonia, tuberculosis, or diarrhea) and poor environmental conditions (such as water pollution and poor sanitation).

Since 1900, however, life expectancy has nearly doubled, due largely to the development of vaccines and

TERMS

health The overall condition of body or mind and the presence or absence of illness or injury.

wellness Optimal health and vitality, encompassing the six dimensions of well-being.

risk factor A condition that increases one's chances of disease or injury.

infectious disease A disease that can spread from person to person; caused by microorganisms such as bacteria and viruses.

Occupational Wellness

Many experts contend that occupational (or career) wellness is a seventh dimension of wellness, in addition to the six dimensions described in this chapter. Whether or not occupational wellness appears on every list of wellness dimensions, a growing body of evidence suggests that our daily work has a considerable effect on our overall wellness.

Defining Occupational Wellness

The term *occupational wellness* refers to the level of happiness and fulfillment you gain through your work. Although high salaries and prestigious titles are nice, they alone generally do not bring about occupational wellness. An occupationally well person truly likes his or her work, feels a connection to others in the workplace, and has opportunities to learn and be challenged.

Key aspects of occupational wellness include the following:

- Enjoyable work
- Job satisfaction
- Recognition and acknowledgment from managers and colleagues
- Feelings of achievement
- Opportunities to learn and grow

An ideal job draws on your passions and interests, as well as your vocational skills, and allows you to feel that you are contributing to society in your everyday work.

Financial Wellness

Another important facet of occupational wellness is financial wellness. A person's economic situation is a key factor in his or her overall well-being. People with low socioeconomic status have higher rates of death, injury, and disease; are less likely to have access to preventive health services; and are more likely to engage in unhealthy habits.

Although money and possessions in themselves won't necessarily make you happy, financial security can contribute to your peace of mind. If you are financially secure, you can worry less about daily expenses and focus on personal interests and your future. On the other hand, money problems are a source of stress for individuals and families and are a contributing factor in many divorces and suicides.

You don't need to be rich to achieve financial wellness. Instead, you need to be comfortable with your financial situation. Financially well people understand the limits of their income and live within their means by keeping expenses in check. They know how to balance a checkbook and interpret their bank statements. The financially well person may not strive to be wealthy but at least tries to save money for the future.

Achieving Occupational Wellness

How do you achieve such wellness? Career experts suggest setting career goals that reflect your personal values. For example, a career in sales may be a good way to earn a high income but may not be a good career choice for someone whose highest values involve service to others. Such a person might find more personal satisfaction in teaching or nursing.

Aside from career choices, education is a critical factor in occupational and financial wellness. For starters, learn to manage money *before* you start making it. Classes on personal money management are available through many sources and can help you on your way to financial security, whether you dream of being wealthy or not.

antibiotics to fight infections and to public health measures to improve living conditions. Today, a different set of diseases has emerged as our major health threat, and heart disease, cancer, and stroke are now the three leading causes of death for Americans. Treating such **chronic diseases** is costly and difficult.

The good news is that people have some control over whether they develop chronic diseases. People make choices every day that increase or decrease their risks for such diseases. These **lifestyle choices** include behaviors such as smoking, diet, exercise, and alcohol use. As Tables 1.2 and 1.3 (p. 6) make clear, lifestyle factors contribute to many deaths in the United States, and people can influence their own health risks.

The global toll of preventable chronic diseases is high. The World Health Organization (WHO) reports that 4.9 million people die annually from tobacco use, 2.6 million from obesity, 4.4 million from high cholesterol, and 7.1 million from high blood pressure.

TERMS

chronic disease A disease that develops and continues over a long period of time, such as heart disease or cancer.

lifestyle choice A conscious behavior that can increase or decrease a person's risk of disease or injury; such behaviors include smoking, exercising, eating a healthy diet, and others.

The Healthy People Initiative

Wellness is a personal concern, but the U.S. government has financial and humanitarian interests in it, too. A

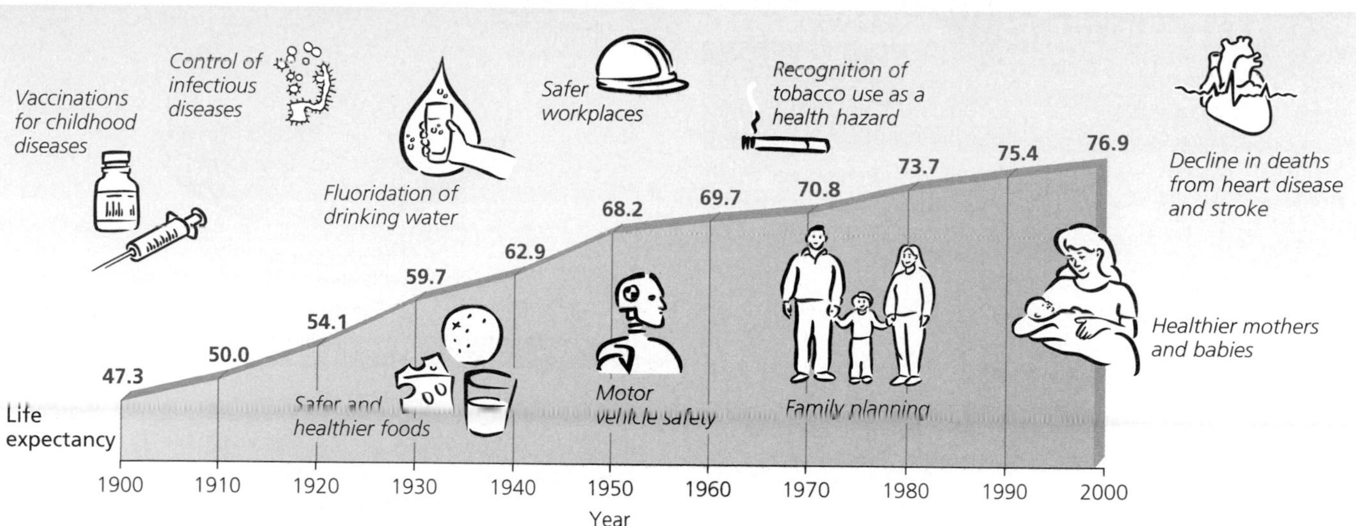

VITAL STATISTICS

FIGURE 1.2 Public health achievements of the twentieth century. During the twentieth century, public health achievements greatly improved the quality of life for Americans. A shift in the leading causes of death also occurred, with deaths from infectious diseases declining from 33% of all deaths to just 2%. Heart disease, cancer, and stroke are now responsible for more than half of all deaths among Americans.

SOURCE: National Center for Health Statistics; Centers for Disease Control and Prevention. 1999. Ten great public health achievements—United States, 1900–1999. *Morbidity and Mortality Weekly Report* 48(50): 1141.

VITAL STATISTICS

Table 1.2 Leading Causes of Death in the United States

Rank	Cause of Death	Number of Deaths	Percent of Total Deaths	Male/Female Ratio*	Lifestyle Factors
1	Heart disease	652,486	27.2	1.5	D I S A
2	Cancer	553,888	23.1	1.4	D I S A
3	Stroke	150,074	6.3	1.0	D I S A
4	Chronic lower respiratory disease	121,987	5.1	1.4	S
5	Unintentional injuries (accidents)	112,012	4.7	2.1	I S A
6	Diabetes mellitus	73,138	3.1	1.3	D I S
7	Alzheimer's disease	65,965	2.8	0.7	
8	Influenza and pneumonia	59,664	2.5	1.4	S
9	Kidney disease	42,480	1.8	1.4	D I S A
10	Septicemia (systemic blood infection)	33,373	1.4	1.2	A
11	Intentional self-harm (suicide)	32,439	1.4	4.0	A
12	Chronic liver disease and cirrhosis	27,013	1.1	2.2	A
13	Hypertension (high blood pressure)	23,076	1.0	1.0	D I S A
14	Parkinson's disease	17,989	0.8	2.3	
15	Homicide	17,357	0.7	3.7	A
	All causes	2,397,615			

Key

- D Diet plays a part
- I Inactive lifestyle plays a part
- S Smoking plays a part
- A Excessive alcohol consumption plays a part

NOTE: Although not among the overall top 15 causes of death, HIV/AIDS (approximately 13,000 deaths) is a major killer. HIV/AIDS is among the 10 leading causes of death among Americans age 15–44.

*Ratio of males to females who died of each cause. For example, for each woman who died of heart disease, 1.5 men died from the same cause.

SOURCE: National Center for Health Statistics. 2007. Deaths: Final data for 2004. ***National Vital Statistics Report*** 55 (19).

VITAL STATISTICS

Table 1.3 Actual Causes of Death Among Americans*

	Number of Deaths per Year	Percentage of Total Deaths per Year
Tobacco	440,000	18.1
Obesity**	112,000	4.6
Alcohol consumption	85,000	3.5
Microbial agents	75,000	3.1
Toxic agents	55,000	2.3
Motor vehicles	43,000	1.8
Firearms	29,000	1.2
Sexual behavior	20,000	0.8
Illicit drug use	17,000	0.7

*NOTE: Actual causes of death are defined as lifestyle and environmental factors that contribute to the leading killers of Americans. Microbial agents include bacterial and viral infections like influenza and pneumonia; toxic agents include environmental pollutants and chemical agents such as asbestos.

**The number of deaths due to obesity is an area of ongoing controversy and research. Recent estimates have ranged from 112,000 to 365,000.

SOURCES: Centers for Disease Control and Prevention. 2005. *Frequently Asked Questions About Calculating Obesity-Related Risk* (http://www.cdc.gov/PDF/Frequently_Asked_Questions_About_Calculating_Obesity-Related_Risk.pdf; retrieved December 6, 2007). Mokdad, A. H., et al. 2005. Correction: Actual causes of death in the United States, 2000. *Journal of the American Medical Association* 293(3): 293–294. Mokdad, A. H., et al. 2004. Actual causes of death in the United States, 2000. *Journal of the American Medical Association* 291(10): 1238–1245.

healthy population is the nation's source of vitality, creativity, and wealth. Poor health drains the nation's resources and raises health care costs for all.

The national Healthy People initiative aims to prevent disease and improve Americans' quality of life. Healthy People reports, published each decade since 1980, set national health goals based on 10-year agendas.

The latest report, *Healthy People 2010,* proposes two broad national goals:

- ***Increase quality and years of healthy life.*** One way to measure quality of life is to count the number of "sick days" people endure—days they can't function due to illness. About 18% of Americans take 14 or more sick days each year, a number that continually rises. Along those same lines, Americans increasingly describe their health as fair or poor rather than excellent or very good. Further, although the life expectancy of Americans has increased significantly in the past century, people can expect poor health to limit their activities and cause distress during the last 15% of their lives (Figure 1.3).
- ***Eliminate health disparities among Americans.*** Many health problems today disproportionately affect certain American populations (see the box "Wellness Issues for Diverse Populations" on p. 8). *Healthy People 2010* calls for eliminating disparities in health status, health risks, and use of preventive services among all population groups within the next decade.

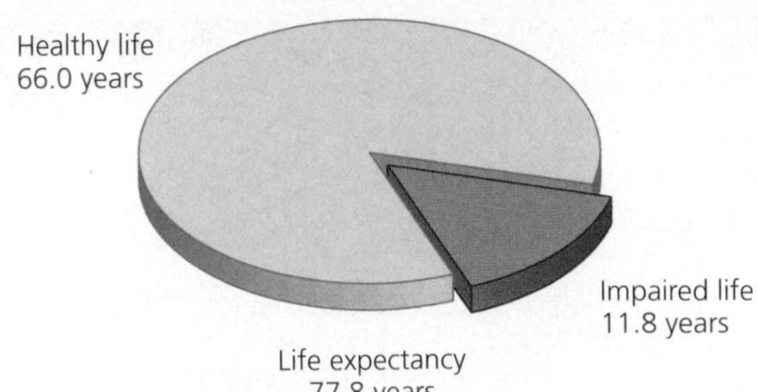

VITAL STATISTICS

FIGURE 1.3 Quantity of life versus quality of life. Years of healthy life as a proportion of life expectancy in the U.S. population.

SOURCES: National Center for Health Statistics. 2007. Deaths: Final data for 2004. *National Vital Statistics Reports.* 55(19). National Center for Health Statistics. *Healthy People* 2010; Midcourse Review. Hyattsville, Md.: Public Health Service.

Examples of individual health promotion objectives from *Healthy People 2010,* as well as estimates of how we are tracking toward the goals, appear in Table 1.4.

Behaviors That Contribute to Wellness

A lifestyle based on good choices and healthy behaviors maximizes quality of life. It helps people avoid disease, remain strong and fit, and maintain their physical and mental health as long as they live. Figure 1.4 highlights the results of just two of the research studies that have found clear links between lifestyle behaviors and the risk of developing and dying from chronic disease. The most important behaviors and habits are introduced briefly here and described in detail in later chapters.

Be Physically Active The human body is designed to work best when it is active. It readily adapts to nearly any level of activity and exertion; in fact, **physical fitness** is defined as a set of physical attributes that allow the body to respond or adapt to the demands and stress of physical effort. The more we ask of our bodies, the stronger and more fit they become. When our bodies are not kept active, however, they deteriorate. Bones lose their density, joints stiffen, muscles become weak, and cellular energy systems begin to degenerate. To be truly well, human beings must be active. Unfortunately, a **sedentary** lifestyle is common among Americans today: About one-half

TERMS

physical fitness A set of physical attributes that allow the body to respond or adapt to the demands and stress of physical effort.

sedentary Physically inactive; literally, "sitting."

Table 1.4 Selected *Healthy People 2010* Objectives

Objective	Estimate of Current Status (%)	Goal (%)
Increase the proportion of people age 18 and older who engage regularly in moderate physical activity.	30	50
Increase the proportion of people age 2 and older who consume at least 3 daily servings of vegetables, with at least one-third being dark-green or orange vegetables.	3	50
Increase the prevalence of healthy weight among people age 20 and older.	32	60
Reduce the proportion of adults 18 and older who use cigarettes.	21	12
Reduce the proportion of college students reporting binge drinking during the past 2 weeks.	39	20
Increase the proportion of adults who take protective measures to reduce the risk of skin cancer (sunscreens, sun-protective clothing, and so on).	71	85
Increase the use of safety belts by motor vehicle occupants.	82	92
Increase the number of residences with a functioning smoke alarm on every floor.	90	100
Increase the proportion of persons with health insurance.	84	100

SOURCE: National Center for Health Statistics. 2007. *DATA 2010: The Healthy People 2010 Database, October 2007 Edition* (http://wonder.cdc.gov/data2010/obj.htm; retrieved December 6, 2007).

of Americans are not regularly physically active, and about 15% are not active at all.

The benefits of physical activity are both physical and mental, immediate and long-term (Figure 1.5, p. 8). In the short term, being physically fit makes it easier to do everyday tasks, such as lifting; it provides reserve strength for emergencies; and it helps people look and feel good. In the long term, being physically fit confers protection against chronic diseases and lowers the risk of dying prematurely. Physically active individuals are less likely to develop or die from heart disease, respiratory disease, high blood pressure, cancer, osteoporosis, and type 2 diabetes (the most common form of diabetes). As they get older, they may be able to avoid weight gain, muscle and bone loss, fatigue, and other problems associated with aging.

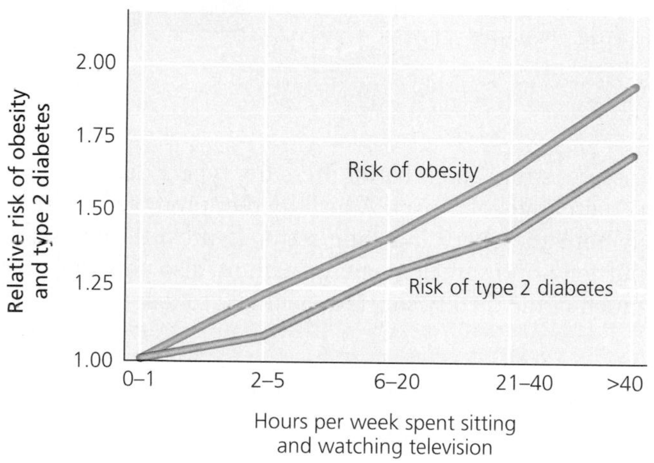

(a) Sedentary lifestyle and risk of obesity and type 2 diabetes

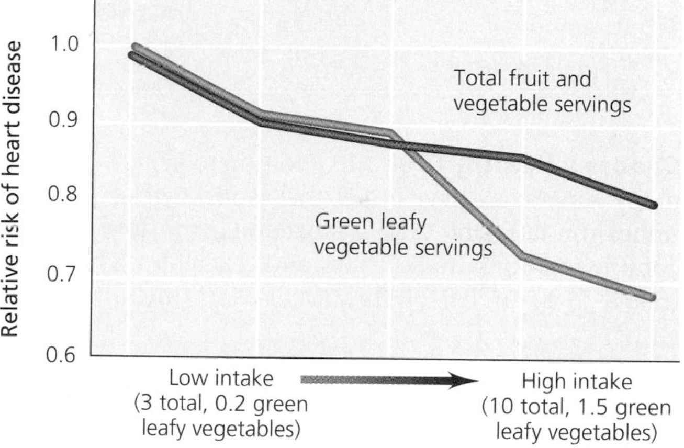

(b) Fruit and vegetable intake and risk of heart disease

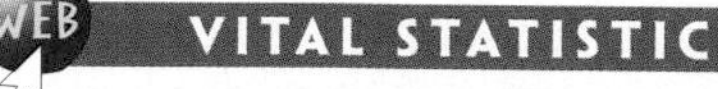

VITAL STATISTICS

FIGURE 1.4 Lifestyle and risk of chronic disease. Many research studies have found links between lifestyle behaviors and risk of chronic disease. The results of just two such studies are shown here. They indicate that (a) people who spend more time watching television are more likely to be obese and to develop type 2 diabetes and (b) people who consume more fruits and vegetables, especially leafy green vegetables, have a lower risk of heart disease.

SOURCES: (a) Hu, F. B., et al. 2003. Television watching and other sedentary behaviors in relation to risk of obesity and type 2 diabetes mellitus in women. *Journal of the American Medical Association* 289(14): 1785–1791. (b) Joshipura, K. J., et al. 2001. The effect of fruit and vegetable intake on risk for coronary heart disease. *Annals of Internal Medicine* 134(12): 1106–1114.

DIMENSIONS OF DIVERSITY

Wellness Issues for Diverse Populations

When it comes to striving for wellness, most differences among people are insignificant. We all need to exercise, eat well, and manage stress. We all need to know how to protect ourselves from heart disease, cancer, sexually transmitted diseases, and injuries.

But some of our differences—both as individuals and as members of groups—do have implications for wellness. Some of us, for example, have grown up with eating habits that increase our risk of obesity or heart disease. Some of us have inherited predispositions for certain health problems, such as osteoporosis or high cholesterol levels. These health-related differences among individuals and groups can be biological—determined genetically—or cultural—acquired as patterns of behavior through daily interactions with family, community, and society. Many health conditions are a function of biology and culture combined.

Every person is an individual with her or his own unique genetic endowment as well as unique experiences in life. However, many of these influences are shared with others of similar genetic and cultural backgrounds. Information about group similarities relating to wellness issues can be useful; for example, it can alert people to areas that may be of special concern for them and their families.

Wellness-related differences among groups can be described along several dimensions, including:

- ***Gender.*** Men and women have different life expectancies and different incidences of many diseases, including heart disease, cancer, and osteoporosis. Men have higher rates of death from injuries, suicide, and homicide; women are at greater risk for Alzheimer's disease and depression. Men and women also differ in body composition and certain aspects of physical performance.
- ***Race and ethnicity.*** A genetic predisposition for a particular health problem can be linked to race or ethnicity as a result of each group's relatively distinct history. Diabetes is more prevalent among individuals of Native American or Latino heritage, for example, and African Americans have higher rates of hypertension. Racial or ethnic groups may also vary in other ways that relate to wellness: traditional diets; patterns of family and interpersonal relationships; and attitudes toward using tobacco, alcohol, and other drugs, to name just a few.
- ***Income and education.*** Inequalities in income and education underlie many of the health disparities among Americans. People with low incomes (low *socioeconomic status,* or *SES*) and less education have higher rates of injury and many diseases, are more likely to smoke, and have less access to health care. Poverty and low educational attainment are far more important predictors of poor health than any racial or ethnic factor.

These are just some of the "dimensions of diversity"—differences among people and groups that are associated with different wellness concerns. Other factors, too, such as age, geographic location, sexual orientation, and disability, can present challenges as an individual strives for wellness. In this text, topics related to wellness and diversity are given special consideration in boxes labeled Dimensions of Diversity.

Choose a Healthy Diet In addition to being sedentary, many Americans have a diet that is too high in calories, unhealthy fats, and added sugars and too low in fiber, complex carbohydrates, fruits, and vegetables. This diet is linked to a number of chronic diseases, including heart disease, stroke, high blood pressure, type 2 diabetes, and certain kinds of cancer. A healthy diet promotes wellness in both the short and long term. It provides necessary nutrients and sufficient energy without also providing too much of the dietary substances linked to diseases.

- Increased endurance, strength, and flexibility
- Healthier muscles, bones, and joints
- Increased energy (calorie) expenditure
- Improved body composition
- More energy
- Improved ability to cope with stress
- Improved mood, higher self-esteem, and greater sense of well-being
- Improved ability to fall asleep and sleep well

- Reduced risk of dying prematurely from all causes
- Reduced risk of developing and/or dying from heart disease, diabetes, high blood pressure, and colon cancer
- Reduced risk of becoming obese
- Reduced anxiety, tension, and depression
- Reduced risk of falls and fractures
- Reduced spending for health care

FIGURE 1.5 Benefits of regular physical activity.

Maintain a Healthy Body Weight Overweight and obesity are associated with a number of disabling and potentially fatal conditions and diseases, including heart disease, cancer, and type 2 diabetes. The Centers for Disease Control and Prevention (CDC) estimates that obesity kills 112,000 Americans each year. Healthy body weight is an important part of wellness—but short-term dieting is not part of fitness or wellness. Maintaining a healthy body weight requires a lifelong commitment to regular exercise, a healthy diet, and effective stress management.

Manage Stress Effectively Many people cope with stress by eating, drinking, or smoking too much. Others don't deal with it at all. In the short term, inappropriate stress management can lead to fatigue, sleep disturbances, and other unpleasant symptoms. Over longer periods of time, poor management of stress can lead to less efficient functioning of the immune system and increased susceptibility to disease. There *are* effective ways to handle stress, and learning to incorporate them into daily life is an important part of a fit and well lifestyle.

Avoid Tobacco and Drug Use and Limit Alcohol Consumption Tobacco use is associated with 8 of the top 10 causes of death in the United States; it kills about 440,000 Americans each year, more than any other behavioral or environmental factor. With nearly 21% of adult Americans smoking, lung cancer is the most common cause of cancer death among both men and women and one of the leading causes of death overall. The direct health care costs associated with smoking exceed $75 billion per year. If the cost of lost productivity from sickness, disability, and premature death is included, the total is closer to $157 billion.

Excessive alcohol consumption is linked to 6 of the top 10 causes of death and results in about 85,000 deaths a year in the United States. The social, economic, and medical costs of alcohol abuse are estimated at over $180 billion per year. Alcohol or drug intoxication is an especially notable factor in the death and disability of young people, particularly through **unintentional injuries** (such as drownings and car crashes caused by drunken driving) and violence. Unintentional injuries, homicide, and suicide are the top three leading causes of death for 15- to 24-year-olds.

Protect Yourself from Disease and Injury The most effective way of dealing with disease and injury is to prevent them. Many of the lifestyle strategies discussed here—being physically active, managing body weight, and so on—help protect you against chronic illnesses. In addition, you can take specific steps to avoid infectious diseases, particularly those that are sexually transmitted.

Take Other Steps Toward Wellness Other important behaviors contribute to wellness, including these:

- Developing meaningful relationships
- Planning for successful aging
- Learning about the health care system
- Acting responsibly toward the environment

Lab 1.2 will help you evaluate your behaviors as they relate to wellness.

The Role of Other Factors in Wellness

Heredity, the environment, and adequate health care are other important influences on health. These factors can interact in ways that raise or lower the quality of a person's life and the risk of developing particular diseases. For example, a sedentary lifestyle combined with a genetic predisposition for diabetes can greatly increase a person's risk for developing the disease. If this person also lacks adequate health care, he or she is much more likely to suffer dangerous complications from diabetes.

MOTIVATION BOOSTER

Chart your family health history. Learning about the diseases and health conditions that run in your family can help you start improving your lifestyle. Such knowledge helps you understand the health risks you may face in the future. It can also help motivate you to keep a behavior change program on track. Put together a simple family health tree by plugging key health information on your close relatives—siblings, parents, aunts and uncles, grandparents—into a family tree format. Don't focus only on causes of death. Look at all chronic conditions and health-related behaviors that affect both quality and quantity of life—alcoholism, diabetes, high blood pressure, high cholesterol, obesity, osteoporosis, depression, and so on. What patterns do you see? Visit the U.S. Surgeon General's Family History Initiative Web site (www.hhs.gov/familyhistory) for more information and a sample family health tree form.

QUESTIONS FOR CRITICAL THINKING AND REFLECTION

How often do you feel exuberant? Vital? Joyful? What makes you feel that way? Conversely, how often do you feel downhearted, de-energized, or depressed? What makes you feel that way? Have you ever thought about how you might increase experiences of vitality and decrease experiences of discouragement?

TERMS

unintentional injury An injury that occurs without harm being intended.

But in many cases, behavior can tip the balance toward health even if heredity or environment is a negative factor. Breast cancer, for example, can run in families, but it is also associated with overweight and a sedentary lifestyle. A woman with a family history of breast cancer is less likely to die from the disease if she controls her weight, exercises, performs regular breast self-exams, and consults with her physician about mammograms.

REACHING WELLNESS THROUGH LIFESTYLE MANAGEMENT

As you consider this description of behaviors that contribute to wellness—being physically active, choosing a healthy diet, and so on—you may be doing a mental comparison with your own behaviors. If you are like most young adults, you probably have some healthy habits and some habits that place your health at risk. For example, you may be physically active and have a healthy diet but indulge in binge drinking on weekends. You may be careful to wear your seat belt in your car but smoke cigarettes or use chewing tobacco. Moving in the direction of wellness means cultivating healthy behaviors and working to overcome unhealthy ones. This approach to lifestyle management is sometimes called **behavior change.**

As you may already know from experience, changing an unhealthy habit can be harder than it looks. When you embark on a behavior change plan, it may seem like too much work at first. But as you make progress, you will gain confidence in your ability to take charge of your life. You will also experience the benefits of wellness—more energy, greater vitality, deeper feelings of appreciation and curiosity, and a higher quality of life.

In the rest of this chapter, we outline a general process for changing unhealthy behaviors that is backed by research and that has worked for many people. We also offer many specific strategies and tips for change. For additional support, work through the activities in the Behavior Change Workbook at the end of the text and on the Online Learning Center.

Getting Serious About Your Health

Before you can start changing a wellness-related behavior, you have to know that the behavior is problematic and that you *can* change it. To make good decisions, you need information about relevant topics and issues, including what resources are available to help you change.

TERMS

behavior change A lifestyle management process that involves cultivating healthy behaviors and working to overcome unhealthy ones.

target behavior An isolated behavior selected as the object for a behavior change program.

Examine Your Current Health Habits Have you considered how your current lifestyle is affecting your health today and how it will affect your health in the future? Do you know which of your current habits enhance your health and which detract from it? Begin your journey toward wellness with self-assessment: Think about your own behavior, complete the self-assessment in Lab 1.2, and talk with friends and family members about what they've noticed about your lifestyle and your health. Challenge any unrealistically optimistic attitudes or ideas you may hold—for example, "To protect my health, I don't need to worry about quitting smoking until I'm 40 years old," or "Being overweight won't put *me* at risk for diabetes." Health risks are very real, and health habits throughout life are important.

Many people start to consider changing a behavior when friends or family members express concern, when a landmark event occurs (such as turning 30), or when new information raises their awareness of risk. If you find yourself reevaluating some of your behaviors as you read this text, take advantage of the opportunity to make a change in a structured way.

Choose a Target Behavior Changing any behavior can be demanding. This is why it's a good idea to start small, by choosing one behavior you want to change—called a **target behavior**—and working on it until you succeed. Your chances of success will be greater if your first goal is simple, such as resisting the urge to snack between classes. As you change one behavior, make your next goal a little more significant, and build on your success.

Learn About Your Target Behavior Once you've chosen a target behavior, you need to learn its risks and benefits for you—both now and in the future. Ask these questions:

- How is your target behavior affecting your level of wellness today?
- What diseases or conditions does this behavior place you at risk for?
- What effect would changing your behavior have on your health?

As a starting point, use this text and the resources listed in the For Further Exploration section at the end of each chapter; see the box "Evaluating Sources of Health Information" for additional guidelines.

Find Help Have you identified a particularly challenging target behavior or mood, something like alcohol addiction, binge eating, or depression, that interferes with your ability to function or places you at a serious health risk? Help may be needed to change behaviors or conditions that are too deeply rooted or too serious for self-management. Don't be stopped by the seriousness of the

Evaluating Sources of Health Information

Believability of Health Information Sources

A 2006 survey conducted by the American College Health Association indicated that college students are smart about evaluating health information. They trust the health information they receive from health professionals and educators and are skeptical about popular information sources.

Rank	Source	Rank	Source
1	Health center staff	7	Campus peer educators
2	Health educators	8	Resident assistants/ advisers
3	Faculty/coursework		
4	Parents	9	Friends
5	Leaflets, pamphlets, flyers	10	Religious centers
		11	Internet/Web
6	Campus newspaper articles	12	Magazines
		13	Television

How smart are you about evaluating health information? Here are some tips.

General Strategies

Whenever you encounter health-related information, take the following steps to make sure it is credible:

- ***Go to the original source.*** Media reports often simplify the results of medical research. Find out for yourself what a study really reported, and determine whether it was based on good science. What type of study was it? Was it published in a recognized medical journal? Was it an animal study or did it involve people? Did the study include a large number of people? What did the authors of the study actually report?
- ***Watch for misleading language.*** Reports that tout "breakthroughs" or "dramatic proof" are probably hype. A study may state that a behavior "contributes to" or is "associated with" an outcome; this does not prove a cause-and-effect relationship.
- ***Distinguish between research reports and public health advice.*** Do not change your behavior based on the results of a single report or study. If an agency such as the National Cancer Institute urges a behavior change, however, you should follow its advice. Large, publicly funded organizations issue such advice based on many studies, not a single report.
- ***Remember that anecdotes are not facts.*** A friend may tell you he lost weight on some new diet, but individual success stories do not mean the plan is truly safe or effective. Check with your doctor before making any serious lifestyle changes.
- ***Be skeptical.*** If a report seems too good to be true, it probably is. Be wary of information contained in advertisements. An ad's goal is to sell a product, even if there is no need for it.
- ***Make choices that are right for you.*** Friends and family members can be a great source of ideas and inspiration, but you need to make health-related choices that work best for you.

Internet Resources

Online sources pose special challenges; when reviewing a health-related Web site, ask these questions:

- ***What is the source of the information?*** Web sites maintained by government agencies, professional associations, or established academic or medical institutions are likely to present trustworthy information. Many other groups and individuals post accurate information, but it is important to look at the qualifications of the people who are behind the site. (Check the home page or click the "About Us" link.)
- ***How often is the site updated?*** Look for sites that are updated frequently. Check the "last modified" date of any Web page.
- ***Is the site promotional?*** Be wary of information from sites that sell specific products, use testimonials as evidence, appear to have a social or political agenda, or ask for money.
- ***What do other sources say about a topic?*** Be cautious of claims or information that appear at only one site or come from a chat room, bulletin board, or blog.
- ***Does the site conform to any set of guidelines or criteria for quality and accuracy?*** Look for sites that identify themselves as conforming to some code or set of principles, such as those set forth by the Health on the Net Foundation or the American Medical Association. These codes include criteria such as use of information from respected sources and disclosure of the site's sponsors.

problem; many resources are available to help you solve it. On campus, the student health center or campus counseling center can provide assistance. To locate community resources, consult the yellow pages, your physician, or the Internet.

Building Motivation to Change

Knowledge is necessary for behavior change, but it isn't usually enough to make people act. Millions of people have sedentary lifestyles, for example, even though they know it's bad for their health. This is particularly true of young adults, who may not be motivated to change because they feel healthy in spite of their unhealthy behaviors (see the box "Wellness Matters for College Students" on p. 12). To succeed at behavior change, you need strong motivation.

Examine the Pros and Cons of Change Health behaviors have short-term and long-term benefits and costs. Consider the benefits and costs of an inactive lifestyle:

- Short-term, such a lifestyle allows you more time to watch TV and hang out with friends, but it leaves you less physically fit and less able to participate in recreational activities.
- Long-term, it increases the risk of heart disease, cancer, stroke, and premature death.

IN FOCUS

Wellness Matters for College Students

If you are like most college students, you probably feel pretty good about your health right now. Most college students are in their late teens or early twenties, lead active lives, have plenty of friends, and look forward to a future filled with opportunity. With all these things going for you, why shouldn't you feel good?

A Closer Look

Although most college-age people look healthy, appearances can be deceiving. Each year, thousands of students lose productive academic time to physical and emotional health problems—some of which can continue to plague them for life.

The following table shows the top 10 health issues affecting students' academic performance, according to the 2006 National College Health Assessment.

Health Issue	Students Affected (%)
Stress	32.0
Cold/flu/sore throat	26.0
Sleep problems	23.9
Concern for a friend or family member	18.0
Depression/anxiety	15.7
Relationship problems	15.6
Internet/computer game use	15.4
Death of friend or family member	8.5
Sinus infection/ear infection/bronchitis/strep throat	8.3
Alcohol use	7.3

Each of these issues is related to one or more of the six dimensions of wellness, and most can be influenced by choices students make daily. Although some troubles—such as the death of a friend—cannot be controlled, other physical and emotional concerns can be minimized by choosing healthy behaviors. For example, there are many ways to manage stress, the top health issue affecting students. By reducing unhealthy choices (such as using alcohol to relax) and by increasing healthy choices (such as using time management techniques), even busy students can reduce the impact of stress on their life.

The survey also estimated that, based on students' reporting of their height and weight, more than 30% of college students are either overweight or obese. Although heredity plays a role in determining one's weight, lifestyle is also a factor in weight and weight management. In many studies over the past few decades, a large percentage of students have reported behaviors such as these:

- Overeating
- Snacking on junk food
- Frequently eating high-fat foods
- Using alcohol and binge drinking

Clearly, eating behaviors are often a matter of choice. Although students may not see (or feel) the effects of their dietary habits today, the long-term health risks are significant. Overweight and obese persons run a higher-than-normal risk of developing diabetes, heart disease, and cancer later in life. We now know with certainty that improving one's eating habits, even a little, can lead to weight loss and improved overall health.

Other Choices, Other Problems

Students commonly make other unhealthy choices. Here are some examples from the 2006 National College Health Assessment:

- Nearly 50% of students reported that they did not use a condom the last time they had vaginal intercourse.
- About 25% of students had as many as 8 drinks the last time they partied.
- Almost 18% of students had used tobacco at least once during the past month.

What choices do you make in these situations? Remember: It's never too late to change. The sooner you trade an unhealthy behavior for a healthy one, the longer you'll be around to enjoy the benefits.

To successfully change your behavior, you must believe that the benefits of change outweigh the costs.

Carefully examine the pros and cons of continuing your current behavior and of changing to a healthier one. Focus on the effects that are most meaningful to you, including those that are tied to your personal identity and values. For example, if you see yourself as an active person who is a good role model for others, then adopting behaviors such as engaging in regular physical activity and getting adequate sleep will support your personal identity. If you value independence and control over your life, then quitting smoking will be consistent with your values and goals. To complete your analysis, ask friends and family members about the effects of your behavior on them. For example, a younger sister may tell you that your smoking habit influenced her decision to take up smoking.

The short-term benefits of behavior change can be an important motivating force. Although some people are motivated by long-term goals, such as avoiding a disease that may hit them in 30 years, most are more likely to be moved to action by shorter-term, more personal goals. Feeling better, doing better in school, improving at a sport, reducing stress, and increasing self-esteem are common short-term benefits of health behavior change. Many wellness behaviors are associated with immediate improvements in quality of life. For example, surveys of Americans have found that nonsmokers feel healthy and full of energy more days each month than do smokers, and they report fewer days of sadness and troubled sleep; the same is true when physically active people are compared with sedentary people. Over time, these types of differences add up to a substantially higher quality of life for people who engage in healthy behaviors.

You can further strengthen your motivation by raising your consciousness about your problem behavior. This will enable you to focus on the negatives of the behavior and imagine the consequences if you don't make a change. At the same time, you can visualize the positive results of changing your behavior. Ask yourself, "What do I want for myself, now and in the future?"

Boost Self-Efficacy When you start thinking about changing a health behavior, a big factor in your eventual success is whether you have confidence in yourself and in your ability to change. **Self-efficacy** refers to your belief in your ability to successfully take action and perform a specific task. Strategies for boosting self-efficacy include developing an internal locus of control, using visualization and self-talk, and obtaining encouragement from supportive people.

LOCUS OF CONTROL Who do you believe is controlling your life? Is it your parents, friends, or school? Is it "fate"? Or is it you? **Locus of control** refers to the figurative "place" a person designates as the source of responsibility for the events in his or her life. People who believe they are in control of their own lives are said to have an internal locus of control. Those who believe that factors beyond their control determine the course of their lives are said to have an external locus of control.

For lifestyle management, an internal locus of control is an advantage because it reinforces motivation and commitment. An external locus of control can sabotage efforts to change behavior. For example, if you believe that you are destined to die of breast cancer because your mother died from the disease, you may view monthly breast self-exams and regular checkups as a waste of time. In contrast, if you believe that you can take action to reduce your risk of breast cancer in spite of hereditary factors, you will be motivated to follow guidelines for early detection of the disease.

If you find yourself attributing too much influence to outside forces, gather more information about your wellness-related behaviors. List all the ways that making lifestyle changes will improve your health. If you believe you'll succeed, and if you recognize that you are in charge of your life, you're on your way to wellness.

VISUALIZATION AND SELF-TALK One of the best ways to boost your confidence and self-efficacy is to visualize yourself successfully engaging in a new, healthier behavior. Imagine yourself going for an afternoon run 3 days a week or no longer smoking cigarettes. Also visualize yourself enjoying all the short-term and long-term benefits that your lifestyle change will bring. Create a new self-image: What will you and your life be like when you become a regular exerciser or a nonsmoker?

You can also use self-talk, the internal dialogue you carry on with yourself, to increase your confidence in your ability to change. Counter any self-defeating patterns of thought with more positive or realistic thoughts: "I am a strong, capable person, and I can maintain my commitment to change." See Chapter 10 for more on self-talk.

ROLE MODELS AND OTHER SUPPORTIVE INDIVIDUALS Social support can make a big difference in your level of motivation and your chances of success. Perhaps you know people who have reached the goal you are striving for; they could be role models or mentors for you, providing information and support for your efforts. Gain strength from their experiences, and tell yourself, "If they can do it, so can I." In addition, find a buddy who wants to make the same changes you do and who can take an active role in your behavior change program. For example, an exercise buddy can provide companionship and encouragement when you might be tempted to skip your workout.

> **MOTIVATION BOOSTER**
>
> ***Find a role model.*** It can be motivating to observe people who have successfully changed their behavior. For example, watch physically active people; note what they're doing and when. If you know people who are successfully managing their weight, note their eating habits, such as food choices and portion sizes. In general, try to observe people who are similar to you in age, sex, and fitness level.

Identify and Overcome Barriers to Change Don't let past failures at behavior change discourage you; they can be a great source of information you can use to boost your chances of future success. Make a list of the problems and challenges you faced in any previous behavior change attempts; to this, add the short-term costs of behavior change that you identified in your analysis of the pros and cons of change. Once you've listed these key barriers to change, develop a practical plan for overcoming each one. For example, if you always smoke when you're with certain friends, decide in advance how you will turn down the next cigarette you are offered.

Enhancing Your Readiness to Change

The transtheoretical, or "stages of change," model has been shown to be an effective approach to lifestyle self-management. According to this model, you move through distinct stages as you work to change your target behavior.

TERMS

self-efficacy The belief in one's ability to take action and perform a specific task.

locus of control The figurative "place" a person designates as the source of responsibility for the events in his or her life.

TAKE CHARGE

Tips for Moving Forward in the Cycle of Behavior Change

PRECONTEMPLATION

- ***Raise your awareness.*** Research your target behavior and its effects.
- ***Be self-aware.*** Look at the mechanisms you use to resist change, such as denial or rationalization. Find ways to counteract these mechanisms.
- ***Seek social support.*** Friends and family members can help you identify target behaviors and understand their impact on the people around you.
- ***Identify helpful resources.*** These might include exercise classes or stress-management workshops offered by your school.

CONTEMPLATION

- ***Keep a journal.*** A record of your target behavior and the circumstances that elicit the behavior can help you plan a change program.
- ***Do a cost-benefit analysis.*** Identify the costs and benefits (both current and future) of maintaining your behavior and of changing it. Costs can be monetary, social, emotional, and so on.
- ***Identify barriers to change.*** Knowing these obstacles can help you overcome them.
- ***Engage your emotions.*** Watch movies or read books about people with your target behavior. Imagine what your life will be like if you don't change.
- ***Create a new self-image.*** Imagine what you'll be like after changing your target behavior. Try to think of yourself in new terms right now.
- ***Think before you act.*** Learn why you engage in the target behavior. Determine what "sets you off," and train yourself not to act reflexively.

PREPARATION

- ***Create a plan.*** Include a start date, goals, rewards, and specific steps you will take to change your behavior.
- ***Make change a priority.*** Create and sign a contract with yourself.
- ***Practice visualization and self-talk.*** These techniques can help prepare you mentally for challenging situations.
- ***Take short steps.*** Successfully practicing your new behavior for a short time—even a single day—can boost your confidence and motivation.

ACTION

- ***Monitor your progress.*** Keep up with your journal entries.
- ***Change your environment.*** Make changes that will discourage the target behavior—for example, getting rid of snack foods or not stocking the refrigerator with beer.
- ***Find alternatives to your target behavior.*** Make a list of things you can do to replace the behavior.
- ***Reward yourself.*** Rewards should be identified in your change plan. Give yourself lots of praise, and focus on your success.
- ***Involve your friends.*** Tell them you want to change, and ask for their help.
- ***Don't get discouraged.*** Real change is difficult.

MAINTENANCE

- ***Keep going.*** Continue using the positive strategies that worked in earlier stages.
- ***Be prepared for lapses.*** Don't let slip-ups set you back.
- ***Be a role model.*** Once you have successfully changed your behavior, you may be able to help someone else do the same thing.

It is important to determine what stage you are in now so that you can choose appropriate strategies for progressing through the cycle of change. This approach can help you enhance your readiness and intention to change. Read the following sections to determine what stage you are in for your target behavior. For ideas on changing stages, see the box "Tips for Moving Forward in the Cycle of Behavior Change."

Precontemplation People at this stage do not think they have a problem and do not intend to change their behavior. They may be unaware of the risks associated with their behavior or may deny them. They may have tried unsuccessfully to change in the past and may now think the situation is hopeless. They may also blame other people or external factors for their problems. People in the precontemplation stage believe that there are more reasons or more important reasons not to change than there are reasons to change.

Contemplation People at this stage know they have a problem and intend to take action within 6 months. They acknowledge the benefits of behavior change but are also aware of the costs of changing—to be successful, people must believe that the benefits of change outweigh the costs. People in the contemplation stage wonder about possible courses of action but don't know how to proceed. There may also be specific barriers to change that appear too difficult to overcome.

Preparation People at this stage plan to take action within a month or may already have begun to make small changes in their behavior. They may be engaging in their new, healthier behavior but not yet regularly or consistently.

They may have created a plan for change but may be worried about failing.

Action During the action stage, people outwardly modify their behavior and their environment. The action stage requires the greatest commitment of time and energy, and people in this stage are at risk for reverting to old, unhealthy patterns of behavior.

Maintenance People at this stage have maintained their new, healthier lifestyle for at least 6 months. Lapses may have occurred, but people in maintenance have been successful in quickly reestablishing the desired behavior. The maintenance stage can be as short as 6 months or as long as 5 years or more.

Termination For some behaviors, a person may reach the sixth and final stage of termination. People at this stage have exited the cycle of change and are no longer tempted to lapse back into their old behavior. They have a new self-image and total self-efficacy with regard to their target behavior.

Dealing with Relapse

People seldom progress through the stages of change in a straightforward, linear way; rather, they tend to move to a certain stage and then slip back to a previous stage before resuming their forward progress. Research suggests that most people make several attempts before they successfully change a behavior; four out of five people experience some degree of backsliding. For this reason, the stages of change are best conceptualized as a spiral, in which people cycle back through previous stages but are further along in the process each time they renew their commitment (Figure 1.6).

If you experience a lapse—a single slip—or a relapse—a return to old habits—don't give up. Relapse can be demoralizing, but it is not the same as failure; failure means stopping before you reach your goal and never changing your target behavior. During the early stages of the change process, it's a good idea to plan for relapse so you can avoid guilt and self-blame and get back on track quickly. Follow these steps:

1. ***Forgive yourself.*** A single setback isn't the end of the world, but abandoning your efforts to change could have negative effects on your life.
2. ***Give yourself credit for the progress you have already made.*** You can use that success as motivation to continue.
3. ***Move on.*** You can learn from a relapse and use that knowledge to deal with potential setbacks in the future.

MOTIVATION BOOSTER

Bombard yourself with propaganda. Put photos on your refrigerator and motivational statements on your computer screen. Talk to people who have already made the change you want to make. Train yourself to counter negative thoughts with positive ones. Frequently visualize yourself achieving your goal and enjoying its benefits. At the end of the day, review your good decisions and congratulate yourself on your successes. Even if you lapse, remind yourself that you're further along the path to change than you were before, and renew your commitment.

If relapses keep occurring or if you can't seem to control them, you may need to return to a previous stage of the behavior change process. If this is necessary, reevaluate your goals and your strategy. A different or less stressful approach may help you avoid setbacks when you try again.

Developing Skills for Change: Creating a Personalized Plan

Once you are committed to making a change, it's time to put together a plan of action. Your key to success is a well-thought-out plan that sets goals, anticipates problems, and includes rewards.

1. Monitor Your Behavior and Gather Data Keep a record of your target behavior and the circumstances surrounding it. Record this information for at least a week or

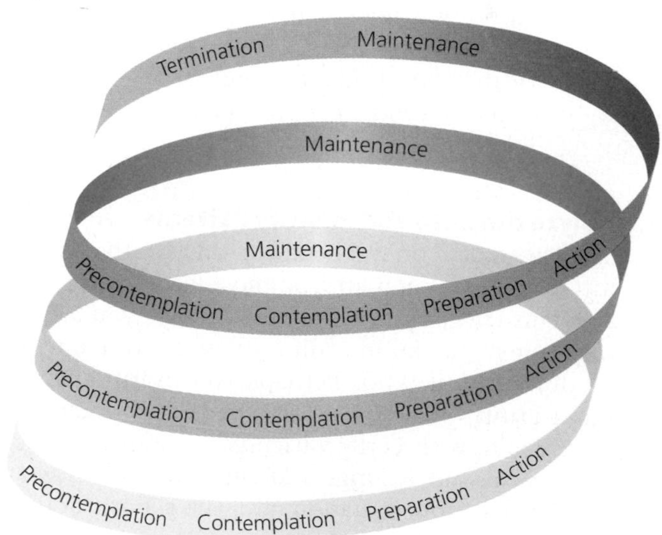

FIGURE 1.6 The stages of change: A spiral model.

SOURCE: Adapted from Prochaska, J. O., C. C. Diclemente, and J. C. Norcross. 1992. In search of how people change. *American Psychologist* 47(9): 1102–1114.

Date November 5				Day M [TU] W TH F SA SU						
Time of day	*M/S*	*Food eaten*	*Cals.*	*H*	*Where did you eat?*	*What else were you doing?*	*How did someone else influence you?*	*What made you want to eat what you did?*	*Emotions and feelings?*	*Thoughts and concerns?*
7:30	M	1 C Crispix cereal 1/2 C skim milk coffee, black 1 C orange juice	110 40 — 120	3	home	reading newspaper	alone	I always eat cereal in the morning	a little keyed up & worried	thinking about quiz in class today
10:30	S	1 apple	90	1	hall outside classroom	studying	alone	felt tired & wanted to wake up	tired	worried about next class
12:30	M	1 C chili 1 roll 1 pat butter 1 orange 2 oatmeal cookies 1 soda	290 120 35 60 120 150	2	campus food court	talking	eating w/ friends; we decided to eat at the food court	wanted to be part of group	excited and happy	interested in hearing everyone's plans for the weekend
	M/S = Meal or snack			H = Hunger rating (0–3)						

FIGURE 1.7 Sample health journal entries. Visit the Online Learning Center for examples of health journal formats focusing on other target behaviors.

two. Keep your notes in a health journal or notebook or on your computer (see the sample journal entries in Figure 1.7). Record each occurrence of your behavior, noting the following:

- What the activity was
- When and where it happened
- What you were doing
- How you felt at that time

If your goal is to start an exercise program, track your activities to determine how to make time for workouts. A blank log is provided in Activity 3 in the Behavior Change Workbook at the end of this text, and sample logs for a variety of target behaviors can be found on the Online Learning Center.

2. Analyze the Data and Identify Patterns After you have collected data on the behavior, analyze the data to identify patterns. When are you most likely to overeat? What events trigger your appetite? Perhaps you are especially hungry at midmorning or when you put off eating dinner until 9:00. Perhaps you overindulge in food and drink when you go to a particular restaurant or when you're with certain friends. Note the connections between your feelings and such external cues as time of day, location, situation, and the actions of others around you.

3. Be "SMART" About Setting Goals If your goals are too challenging, you will have trouble making steady progress and will be more likely to give up altogether. If, for example, you are in poor physical condition, it will not make sense to set a goal of being ready to run a marathon within 2 months. If you set goals you can live with, it will be easier to stick with your behavior change plan and be successful.

Experts suggest that your goals meet the "SMART" criteria; that is, your behavior change goals should be:

- *Specific:* Avoid vague goals like "eat more fruits and vegetables." Instead, state your objectives in specific terms, such as "eat 2 cups of fruit and 3 cups of vegetables every day."
- *Measurable.* Recognize that your progress will be easier to track if your goals are quantifiable, so give your goal a number. You might measure your goal in terms of time (such as "walk briskly for 20 minutes a day"), distance ("run 2 miles, 3 days per week"), or some other amount ("drink 8 glasses of water every day").
- *Attainable.* Set goals that are within your physical limits. For example, if you are a poor swimmer, it might not be possible for you to meet a short-term fitness goal by swimming laps. Walking or biking might be better options.
- *Realistic.* Manage your expectations when you set goals. For example, it may not be possible for a long-time smoker to quit cold turkey. A more realistic approach might be to use nicotine-replacement patches or gum for several weeks while getting help from a support group.
- *Time frame–specific.* Give yourself a reasonable amount of time to reach your goal, state the time

frame in your behavior change plan, and set your agenda to meet the goal within the given time frame.

Using these criteria, a sedentary person who wanted to improve his health and build fitness might set a goal of being able to run 3 miles in 30 minutes, to be achieved within a time frame of 6 months. To work toward that goal, he might set a number of smaller, intermediate goals that are easier to achieve. For example, his list of goals might look like this:

Week	Frequency (days/week)	Activity	Duration (minutes)
1	3	Walk < 1 mile	10–15
2	3	Walk 1 mile	15–20
3	4	Walk 1–2 miles	20–25
4	4	Walk 2–3 miles	25–30
5–7	3–4	Walk/run 1 mile	15–20
⋮			
21–24	4–5	Run 2–3 miles	25–30

Your environment contains powerful cues for both positive and negative lifestyle choices. Identifying and using the healthier options available to you throughout the day is a key part of a successful behavior change program.

Of course, it may not be possible to meet these goals, but you never know until you try. As you work toward meeting your long-term goal, you may find it necessary to adjust your short-term goals. For example, you may find that you can start running sooner than you thought, or you may be able to run farther than you originally estimated. In such cases, it may be reasonable to make your goals more challenging. Otherwise, you may want to make them easier in order to stay motivated.

For some goals and situations, it may make more sense to focus on something other than your outcome goal. If you are in an early stage of change, for example, your goal may be to learn more about the risks associated with your target behavior or to complete a cost-benefit analysis. If your goal involves a long-term lifestyle change, such as reaching a healthy weight, it is better to focus on developing healthy habits than to target a specific weight loss. Your goal in this case might be exercising for 30 minutes every day, reducing portion sizes, or eliminating late-night snacks.

4. Devise a Plan of Action Develop a strategy that will support your efforts to change. Your plan of action should include the following steps:

- ***Get what you need.*** Identify resources that can help you. For example, you can join a community walking club or sign up for smoking cessation program. You may also need to buy some new running shoes or nicotine-replacement patches. Get the items you need right away; waiting can delay your progress.
- ***Modify your environment.*** If there are cues in your environment that trigger your target behavior, try to control them. For example, if you normally have alcohol at home, getting rid of it can help prevent you from indulging. If you usually study with a group of friends in an environment that allows smoking, try moving to a nonsmoking area. If you always buy a snack at a certain vending machine, change your route so you don't pass by it.
- ***Control related habits.*** You may have habits that contribute to your target behavior; modifying these habits can help change the behavior. For example, if you usually plop down on the sofa while watching TV, try putting an exercise bike in front of the set so you can burn calories while watching your favorite programs.
- ***Reward yourself.*** Giving yourself instant, real rewards for good behavior will reinforce your efforts. Plan your rewards; decide in advance what each one will be and how you will earn it. Tie rewards to achieving specific goals or subgoals. For example, you might treat yourself to a movie after a week of avoiding snacks. Make a list of items or events to use as rewards; they should be special to you and preferably unrelated to food or alcohol.
- ***Involve the people around you.*** Tell family and friends about your plan, and ask them to help. To help them respond appropriately to your needs, create a specific list of dos and don'ts. For example, ask them to support you when you set aside time to exercise or avoid second helpings at dinner.
- ***Plan for challenges.*** Think about situations and people that might derail your program, and develop ways to cope with them. For example, if you think it will be hard to stick to your usual exercise program during exams, schedule short bouts of physical activity (such as a brisk walk) as stress-reducing study breaks.

5. Make a Personal Contract A serious personal contract—one that commits you to your word—can result in a higher chance of follow-through than a casual, offhand promise. Your contract can help prevent procrastination by specifying important dates and can also serve as a reminder of your personal commitment to change.

Your contract should include a statement of your goal and your commitment to reaching it. The contract should also include details, such as the following:

- The date you will start
- The steps you will take to measure your progress
- The strategies you plan to use to promote change
- The date you expect to reach your final goal

Have someone—preferably someone who will be actively helping you with your program—sign your contract as a witness.

Figure 1.8 shows a sample behavior change contract for someone who is committing to eating more fruit every day. Additional sample plans and contracts for other target behaviors can be found on the *Fit and Well* Online Learning Center, and a blank contract is included as Activity 8 in the Behavior Change Workbook and on the Online Learning Center.

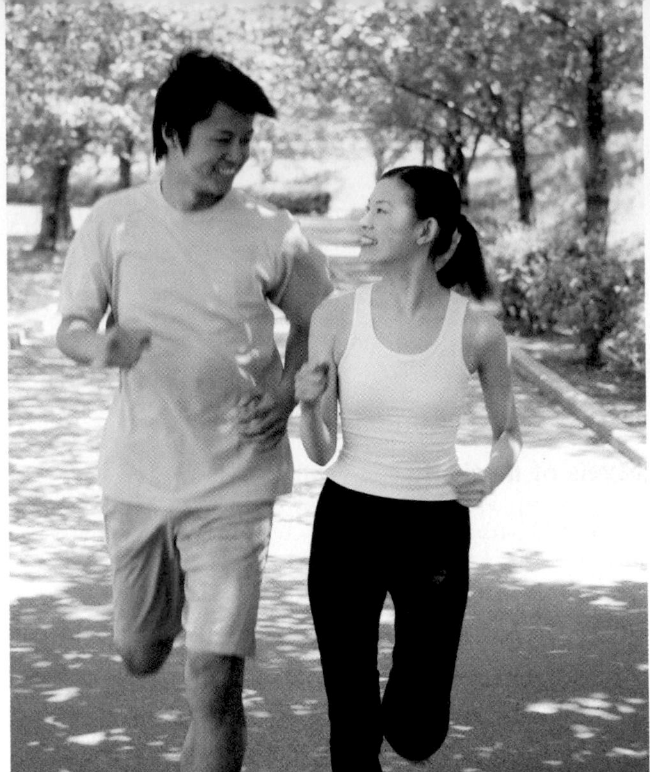

A beautiful setting and a friendly companion help make exercise a satisfying and pleasurable experience. Choosing the right activity and doing it the right way are important elements in a successful behavior change program.

Behavior Change Contract

1. I, Tammy Lau, agree to increase my consumption of fruit from 1 cup per week to 2 cups per day.
2. I will begin on 10/5 and plan to reach my goal of 2 cups of fruit per day by 12/7
3. To reach my final goal, I have devised the following schedule of mini-goals. For each step in my program, I will give myself the reward listed.

I will begin to have ½ cup of fruit with breakfast	10/5	see movie
I will begin to have ½ cup of fruit with lunch	10/26	new cd
I will begin to substitute fruit juice for soda 1 time per day	11/16	concert

My overall reward for reaching my goal will be trip to beach

4. I have gathered and analyzed data on my target behavior and have identified the following strategies for changing my behavior: Keep the fridge stocked with easy-to-carry fruit. Pack fruit in my backpack every day. Buy lunch at place that serves fruit.

5. I will use the following tools to monitor my progress toward my final goal:
Chart on fridge door
Health journal

I sign this contract as an indication of my personal commitment to reach my goal: Tammy Lau 9/28

I have recruited a helper who will witness my contract and also increase his consumption of fruit; eat lunch with me twice a week.
Eric March 9/28

FIGURE 1.8 A sample behavior change contract.

Putting Your Plan into Action

The starting date has arrived, and you are ready to put your plan into action. This stage requires commitment, the resolve to stick with the plan no matter what temptations you encounter. Remember all the reasons you have to make the change—and remember that *you* are the boss. Use all your strategies to make your plan work. Make sure your environment is change-friendly, and get as much support and encouragement from others as possible. Keep track of your progress in your health journal, and give yourself regular rewards. And don't forget to give yourself a pat on the back—congratulate yourself, notice how much better you look or feel, and feel good about how far you've come and how you've gained control of your behavior.

Staying with It

As you continue with your program, don't be surprised when you run up against obstacles; they're inevitable. In fact, it's a good idea to expect problems and give yourself time to step back, see how you're doing, and make some changes before going on. If your program is grinding to a halt, identify what is blocking your progress. It may come from one of the sources described in the following sections.

Social Influences Take a hard look at the reactions of the people you're counting on, and see if they're really supporting you. If they come up short, connect with others who will be more supportive.

A related trap is trying to get your friends or family members to change *their* behaviors. The decision to make a major behavior change is something people come to only after intensive self-examination. You may be able to influence someone by tactfully providing facts or support, but that's all. Focus on yourself. When you succeed, you may become a role model for others.

Levels of Motivation and Commitment You won't make real progress until an inner drive leads you to the stage of change at which you are ready to make a personal commitment to the goal. If commitment is your problem, you may need to wait until the behavior you're dealing with makes you unhappier or unhealthier; then your desire to change it will be stronger. Or you may find that changing your goal will inspire you to keep going. For more ideas, refer to the box "Motivation Booster" and to Activity 9 in the Behavior Change Workbook.

Choice of Techniques and Level of Effort If your plan is not working as well as you thought it would, make changes where you're having the most trouble. If you've lagged on your running schedule, for example, maybe it's because you don't like running. An aerobics class might suit you better. There are many ways to move toward your goal. Or you may not be trying hard enough. You do have to push toward your goal. If it were easy, you wouldn't need a plan.

MOTIVATION BOOSTER

Be patient with yourself. Behavior change is like many other challenges you'll encounter at school and work—it requires that you develop certain skills. Just as when you take a course in an unfamiliar subject, you shouldn't expect to master everything in your behavior change program quickly and easily or to achieve perfection. But with consistent effort, you can build your skills and achieve your goals. Think of obstacles as challenges to your skills that require effort to address but that are within your ability to manage. Thinking of behavior change in this way will help you tolerate mistakes and lapses, remain motivated, and see your behavior change program as an opportunity for personal growth and improvement.

Stress Barrier If you hit a wall in your program, look at the sources of stress in your life. If the stress is temporary, such as catching a cold or having a term paper due, you may want to wait until it passes before strengthening your efforts. If the stress is ongoing, find healthy ways to manage it (see Chapter 10). You may even want to make stress management your highest priority for behavior change.

Procrastinating, Rationalizing, and Blaming Be alert to games you might be playing with yourself, so you can stop them. Such games include the following:

- ***Procrastinating.*** If you tell yourself, "It's Friday already; I might as well wait until Monday to start," you're procrastinating. Break your plan into smaller steps that you can accomplish one day at a time.
- ***Rationalizing.*** If you tell yourself, "I wanted to go swimming today but wouldn't have had time to wash my hair afterward," you're making excuses. When you "win" by deceiving yourself, it isn't much of a victory.
- ***Blaming.*** If you tell yourself, "I couldn't exercise because Dave was hogging the elliptical trainer," you're blaming others for your own failure to follow through. Blaming is a way of taking your focus off the real problem and denying responsibility for your own actions.

Being Fit and Well for Life

Your first attempts at making behavior changes may never go beyond the contemplation or preparation stage. Those that do may not all succeed. But as you experience some success, you'll start to have more positive feelings about yourself. You may discover new physical activities and sports you enjoy; you may encounter new situations and meet new people. Perhaps you'll surprise yourself by accomplishing things you didn't think were possible—breaking a long-standing nicotine habit, competing in a race, climbing a mountain, or developing a lean, muscular body. Most of all, you'll discover the feeling of empowerment that comes from taking charge of your health. Being healthy takes extra effort, but the paybacks in energy and vitality are priceless.

Once you've started, don't stop. Assume that health improvement is forever. Take on the easier problems first, and then use what you learn to tackle more difficult problems later. When you feel challenged, remind yourself that you are creating a lifestyle that minimizes your health risks and maximizes your enjoyment of life. You *can* take charge of your health in a dramatic and meaningful way. *Fit and Well* will show you how.

QUESTIONS FOR CRITICAL THINKING AND REFLECTION

Think about the last time you made an unhealthy choice instead of a healthy one. How could you have changed the situation, the people in the situation, or your own thoughts, feelings, or intentions to avoid making that choice? What can you do in similar situations in the future to produce a different outcome?

TIPS FOR TODAY AND THE FUTURE

You are in charge of your health. Many of the decisions you make every day have an impact on the quality of your life, both now and in the future. By making positive choices, large and small, you help ensure a lifetime of wellness.

RIGHT NOW YOU CAN

- Go for a 15-minute walk.
- Have an orange, a nectarine, or a plum for a snack.
- Call a friend and arrange for a time to catch up with each other.
- Start thinking about whether you have a health behavior you'd like to change. If you do, consider the elements of a behavior change strategy. For example, begin a mental list of the pros and cons of the behavior, or talk to someone who can support you in your attempts to change.

IN THE FUTURE YOU CAN

- Stay current on health- and wellness-related news and issues.
- Participate in health awareness and promotion campaigns in your community—for example, support smoking restrictions in local venues.
- Be a role model for someone else who is working on a health behavior you have successfully changed.

SUMMARY

- Wellness is the ability to live life fully, with vitality and meaning. Wellness is dynamic and multidimensional; it incorporates physical, emotional, intellectual, spiritual, interpersonal, and environmental dimensions.
- People today have greater control over and greater responsibility for their health than ever before.
- Behaviors that promote wellness include being physically active; choosing a healthy diet; maintaining a healthy body weight; managing stress effectively; avoiding tobacco and limiting alcohol use; and protecting yourself from disease and injury.
- Although heredity, environment, and health care all play roles in wellness and disease, behavior can mitigate their effects.
- To make lifestyle changes, you need information about yourself, your health habits, and resources available to help you change.
- You can increase your motivation for behavior change by examining the benefits and costs of change, boosting self-efficacy, and identifying and overcoming key barriers to change.
- The stages-of-change model describes six stages that people may move through as they try to change their behavior: precontemplation, contemplation, preparation, action, maintenance, and termination.
- A specific plan for change can be developed by (1) collecting data on your behavior and recording it in a journal; (2) analyzing the recorded data; (3) setting specific goals; (4) devising strategies for obtaining information, modifying the environment, rewarding yourself, involving others, and planning ahead; and (5) making a personal contract.
- To start and maintain a behavior change program, you need commitment, a well-developed and manageable plan, social support, and strong stress-management techniques. It is also important to monitor the progress of your program, revising it as necessary.

FOR FURTHER EXPLORATION

BOOKS

American Medical Association. 2006. *American Medical Association Concise Medical Encyclopedia.* New York: Random House. *Includes more than 3000 entries on health and wellness topics, symptoms, conditions, and treatments.*

Elghoroury, M. 2006. *How to Get the Most from Your Doctor's Visit.* Charleston, S.C.: BookSurge. *A doctor's advice for getting the greatest benefit from time spent with a physician, including visits for both sickness and wellness.*

Komaroff, A. L., ed. 2005. *Harvard Medical School Family Health Guide.* New York: Free Press. *Provides consumer-oriented advice for the prevention and treatment of common health concerns.*

Krueger, H., et al. 2007. *The Health Impact of Smoking and Obesity and What to Do About It.* Toronto: University of Toronto Press. *Examines the effects of smoking and sedentary lifestyle, the costs to individuals and society, and strategies for overcoming these behaviors.*

Prochaska, J. O., J. C. Norcross, and C. C. DiClemente. 1994. *Changing for Good: The Revolutionary Program That Explains the Six Stages of Change and Teaches You How to Free Yourself from Bad Habits.* New York: Morrow. *Outlines the authors' model of behavior change and offers suggestions and advice for each stage of change.*

Smith P. B., M. MacFarlane, and E. Kalnitsky. 2002. *The Complete Idiot's Guide to Wellness.* Indianapolis, Ind.: Alpha Books. *A concise guide to healthy habits, including physical activity, nutrition, and stress management.*

U.S. Government. 2007. *2007 American Health and Medical Encyclopedia: Authoritative, Practical Guide to Health and Wellness. FDA, CDC, NIH, Surgeon General Publications (CD-ROM).* Washington, D.C.: Progressive Management. *Contains thousands of documents from various federal agencies on myriad health issues, as well as links to dozens of health- and wellness-related Web sites.*

NEWSLETTERS

Center for Science in the Public Interest Nutrition Action Health Letter (http://www.cspinet.org/nah/index.htm)

Consumer Reports on Health (800-234-2188;
http://www.consumerreports.org/oh/index.htm)
Harvard Health Letter (877-649-9457;
http://www.health.harvard.edu)
Harvard Men's Health Watch (877-649-9457)
Harvard Women's Health Watch (877-649-9457)
Mayo Clinic Housecall;
http://www.mayoclinic.com/health/housecall/HouseCall)
Tufts University Health & Nutrition Newsletter (800-274-7581;
http://healthletter.tufts.edu)
University of California at Berkeley Wellness Letter (800-829-9170;
http://www.wellnessletter.com)

ORGANIZATIONS, HOTLINES, AND WEB SITES

The Internet addresses listed here were accurate at the time of publication. Up-to-date links to these and many other wellness-oriented Web sites are provided on the links page of the *Fit and Well* Online Learning Center (http://www.mhhe.com/fahey).

Centers for Disease Control and Prevention. Provides a wide variety of health information.
800-311-3435
http://www.cdc.gov

Many other government sites provide health-related materials:
Federal Trade Commission: Consumer Protection—Diet, Health, and Fitness:
http://www.ftc.gov/bcp/menus/consumer/health.shtm
First Gov for Consumers—Health:
http://www.consumer.gov/health.htm
MedlinePlus: http://www.medlineplus.gov
National Institutes of Health: http://www.nih.gov

Go Ask Alice. Sponsored by the Columbia University Health Service; provides answers to student questions about stress, sexuality, fitness, and many other wellness topics.
http://www.goaskalice.columbia.edu

Healthfinder. A gateway to online publications, Web sites, support and self-help groups, and agencies and organizations that produce reliable health information.
http://www.healthfinder.gov

Healthy People 2010. Provides information on Healthy People objectives and priority areas.
http://www.healthypeople.gov

MedlinePlus: Evaluating Health Information. Provides background information and links to sites with guidelines for finding and evaluating health information on the Web.
http://www.nlm.nih.gov/medlineplus/evaluatinghealthinformation.html

National Health Information Center (NHIC). Puts consumers in touch with the organizations that are best able to provide answers to health-related questions.
800-336-4797
http://www.health.gov/nhic

National Women's Health Information Center. Provides information and answers to frequently asked questions.
800-994-9662
http://www.4woman.gov

Student Counseling Virtual Pamphlet Collection. Provides links to more than 400 pamphlets produced by different student counseling centers on a variety of wellness topics.
http://counseling.uchicago.edu/vpc

World Health Organization (WHO). Provides information about health topics and issues affecting people around the world.
http://www.who.int

The following are just a few of the many sites that provide consumer-oriented information on a variety of health issues:
Family Doctor.Org: http://www.familydoctor.org
InteliHealth: http://www.intelihealth.com
Mayo Clinic: http://www.mayoclinic.com
WebMD: http://webmd.com

The following sites provide daily health news updates:
CNN Health: http://www.cnn.com/health
MedlinePlus News: http://www.nlm.nih.gov/medlineplus/newsbydate.html
Yahoo Health News: http://news.yahoo.com/i/751

SELECTED BIBLIOGRAPHY

American Cancer Society. 2007. *Cancer Facts and Figures 2007.* Atlanta: American Cancer Society.

American College Health Association. 2007. American College Health Association National College Health Assessment Spring 2006 Reference Group Data Report (Abridged). *Journal of American College Health* 55(4): 198.

American Heart Association. 2007. *2007 Heart and Stroke Statistical Update.* Dallas: American Heart Association.

Calle, E. E., et al. 2003. Overweight, obesity, and mortality from cancer in a prospectively studied cohort of U.S. adults. *New England Journal of Medicine* 348(17): 1625–1638.

Centers for Disease Control and Prevention. 2007. Prevalence of fruit and vegetable consumption and physical activity by race/ethnicity—United States, 2005, *Morbidity and Mortality Weekly Report* 56(13): 301–304.

Centers for Disease Control and Prevention. 2007. Prevalence of heart disease—United States, 2005. *Morbidity and Mortality Weekly Report* 56(6): 113–118.

Centers for Disease Control and Prevention. 2007. QuickStats: Prevalence of selected unhealthy behavior characteristics among adults Aged ≥ 18 years, by race—National Health Interview Survey, United States, 2002–2004. *Morbidity and Mortality Weekly Report* 56(04): 79.

Centers for Disease Control and Prevention. 2005. Annual smoking-attributable mortality, years of potential life lost, and productivity losses—United States, 1997–2001. *Morbidity and Mortality Weekly Report* 54(5): 113–117.

Centers for Disease Control and Prevention. 2005. Racial/ethnic and socioeconomic disparities in multiple risk factors for heart disease and stroke, United States, 2003. *Morbidity and Mortality Weekly Report* 54(5): 113–117.

Centers for Disease Control and Prevention. 2005. Trends in leisure-time physical inactivity by age, sex, and race/ethnicity—United States, 1994–2004. *Morbidity and Mortality Weekly Report* 54(39): 991–994.

Centers for Disease Control and Prevention. 2006. Health behaviors of adults: United States, 2002–2004. *Vital and Health Statistics* 10(230).

Centers for Disease Control and Prevention, Division of Nutrition and Physical Activity. 1999. *Promoting Physical Activity: A Guide for Community Action.* Champaign, Ill.: Human Kinetics.

Douglas, K. A., et al. 1997. Results from the 1995 National College Health Risk Behavior Survey. *Journal of American College Health* 46(2): 55–56.

Gallagher, K. I., and J. M. Jakicic. 2002. Overcoming barriers to effective exercise programming. *ACSM's Health and Fitness Journal,* November/December.

Glanz, K., B. K. Rimer, and F. M. Lewis, eds. 2002. *Health Behavior and Health Education: Theory, Research, and Practice,* 3rd ed. San Francisco: Jossey-Bass.

Marcus, B. H., and L. H. Forsyth. 2003. *Motivating People to Be Physically Active*. Champaign, Ill.: Human Kinetics.

McCracken, M., et al. 2007. Health behaviors of the young adult U.S. population: Behavioral risk factor surveillance system, 2003. *Preventing Chronic Disease* 4(2): A25.

Mokdad, A. H., et al. 2005. Correction: Actual causes of death in the United States, 2000. *Journal of the American Medical Association* 293(3): 293–294.

Ritchie, S. A., and J. M. Connell. 2007. The link between abdominal obesity, metabolic syndrome and cardiovascular disease. *Nutrition, Metabolism, and Cardiovascular Diseases* 17(4): 319–326.

Seals, J. G. 2007. Integrating the transtheoretical model into the management of overweight and obese adults. *Journal of the American Academy of Nurse Practitioners* 19(2): 63–71

Sillence, E., et al. 2007. How do patients evaluate and make use of online health information? *Social Science and Medicine* 64(9): 1853–1862.

Smith, S. C. 2007. Multiple risk factors for cardiovascular disease and diabetes mellitus. *The American Journal of Medicine* 120(3 Suppl. 1): S3–S11.

National Center for Health Statistics. 2007. *Health, United States, 2006.* Hyattsville, Md.: Public Health Service.

U.S. Department of Health and Human Services. 2000. *Healthy People 2010,* 2nd ed. Washington, D.C.: DHHS.

Name ______________________ Section ______________ Date ______________

LAB 1.1 Your Wellness Profile

Consider how your lifestyle, attitudes, and characteristics relate to each of the six dimensions of wellness. Fill in your strengths for each dimension (examples of strengths are listed with each dimension). Once you've completed your lists, choose what you believe are your five most important strengths, and circle them.

Physical wellness: To maintain overall physical health and engage in appropriate physical activity (e.g., stamina, strength, flexibility, healthy body composition).

____

____

____

Emotional wellness: To have a positive self-concept, deal constructively with your feelings, and develop positive qualities (e.g., optimism, trust, self-confidence, determination, persistence, dedication).

____

____

____

Intellectual wellness: To pursue and retain knowledge, think critically about issues, make sound decisions, identify problems, and find solutions (e.g., common sense, creativity, curiosity).

____

____

____

Spiritual wellness: To develop a set of beliefs, principles, or values that gives meaning or purpose to your life; to develop faith in something beyond yourself (e.g., religious faith, service to others).

____

____

____

Interpersonal/social wellness: To develop and maintain meaningful relationships with a network of friends and family members, and to contribute to your community (e.g., friendly, good-natured, compassionate, supportive, good listener).

____

____

____

Environmental wellness: To protect yourself from environmental hazards and to minimize the negative impact of your behavior on the environment (e.g., carpooling, recycling).

____

____

____

Next, think about where you fall on the wellness continuum for each of the dimensions of wellness. Indicate your placement for each—physical, emotional, intellectual, spiritual, interpersonal/social, and environmental—by placing Xs on the continuum below.

Low level of wellness ← Physical, psychological, emotional symptoms — Change and growth → High level of wellness

Based on both your current lifestyle and your goals for the future, what do you think your placement on the wellness continuum will be in 10 years? What new health behaviors will you have to adopt to achieve your goals? Which of your current behaviors will you need to change to maintain or improve your level of wellness in the future?

Does the description of wellness given in this chapter encompass everything you believe is part of wellness for you? Write your own definition of wellness, including any additional dimensions that are important to you. Then rate your level of wellness based on your own definition.

Using Your Results

How did you score? Are you satisfied with your current level of wellness—overall and in each dimension? In which dimension(s) would you most like to increase your level of wellness?

What should you do next? As you consider possible target behaviors for a behavior change program, choose things that will maintain or increase your level of wellness in one of the dimensions you listed as an area of concern. Remember to consider health behaviors such as smoking or eating a high-fat diet that may threaten your level of wellness in the future. Below, list several possible target behaviors and the wellness dimensions that they influence.

For additional guidance in choosing a target behavior, complete the lifestyle self-assessment in Lab 1.2.

Name ______________________ Section ______________ Date ____________

LAB 1.2 Lifestyle Evaluation

How does your current lifestyle compare with the lifestyle recommended for wellness? For each question, choose the answer that best describes your behavior; then add up your score for each section.

Exercise/Fitness

	Almost Always	Sometimes	Never
1. I engage in moderate exercise, such as brisk walking or swimming, for 20–60 minutes, three to five times a week.	4	1	0
2. I do exercises to develop muscular strength and endurance at least twice a week.	2	1	0
3. I spend some of my leisure time participating in individual, family, or team activities, such as gardening, bowling, or softball.	2	1	0
4. I maintain a healthy body weight, avoiding overweight and underweight.	2	1	0

Exercise/Fitness Score: ____________

Nutrition

	Almost Always	Sometimes	Never
1. I eat a variety of foods each day, including seven or more servings of fruits and/or vegetables.	3	1	0
2. I limit the amount of total fat and saturated and trans fat in my diet.	3	1	0
3. I avoid skipping meals.	2	1	0
4. I limit the amount of salt and sugar I eat.	2	1	0

Nutrition Score: ____________

Tobacco Use

If you never or no longer use tobacco, enter a score of 10 for this section and go to the next section.

	Almost Always	Sometimes	Never
1. I avoid using tobacco.	2	1	0
2. I smoke only low-tar-and-nicotine cigarettes, *or* I smoke a pipe or cigars, *or* I use smokeless tobacco.	2	1	0

Tobacco Use Score: ____________

Alcohol and Drugs

	Almost Always	Sometimes	Never
1. I avoid alcohol, or I drink no more than one (women) or two (men) drinks a day.	4	1	0
2. I avoid using alcohol or other drugs as a way of handling stressful situations or the problems in my life.	2	1	0
3. I am careful not to drink alcohol when taking medications (such as cold or allergy medications) or when pregnant.	2	1	0
4. I read and follow the label directions when using prescribed and over-the-counter drugs.	2	1	0

Alcohol and Drugs Score: ____________

Emotional Health

	Almost Always	Sometimes	Never
1. I enjoy being a student, and I have a job or do other work that I enjoy.	2	1	0
2. I find it easy to relax and express my feelings freely.	2	1	0
3. I manage stress well.	2	1	0
4. I have close friends, relatives, or others whom I can talk to about personal matters and call on for help when needed.	2	1	0
5. I participate in group activities (such as community or church organizations) or hobbies that I enjoy.	2	1	0

Emotional Health Score: ____________

Safety

1. I wear a safety belt while riding in a car.	2	1	0
2. I avoid driving while under the influence of alcohol or other drugs.	2	1	0
3. I obey traffic rules and the speed limit when driving.	2	1	0
4. I read and follow instructions on the labels of potentially harmful products or substances, such as household cleaners, poisons, and electrical appliances.	2	1	0
5. I avoid smoking in bed.	2	1	0

Safety Score: ______________

Disease Prevention

1. I know the warning signs of cancer, heart attack, and stroke.	2	1	0
2. I avoid overexposure to the sun and use sunscreen.	2	1	0
3. I get recommended medical screening tests (such as blood pressure and cholesterol checks and Pap tests), immunizations, and booster shots.	2	1	0
4. I practice monthly skin and breast/testicle self-exams.	2	1	0
5. I am not sexually active, *or* I have sex with only one mutually faithful, uninfected partner, *or* I always engage in safer sex (using condoms), *and* I do not share needles to inject drugs.	2	1	0

Disease Prevention Score: ______________

Scores of 9 and 10 Excellent! Your answers show that you are aware of the importance of this area to your health. More important, you are putting your knowledge to work for you by practicing good health habits. As long as you continue to do so, this area should not pose a serious health risk.

Scores of 6 to 8 Your health practices in this area are good, but there is room for improvement.

Scores of 3 to 5 Your health risks are showing.

Scores of 0 to 2 You may be taking serious and unnecessary risks with your health.

Using Your Results

How did you score? In which areas did you score the lowest? Are you satisfied with your scores in each area? In which areas would you most like to improve your scores?

What should you do next? To improve your scores, look closely at any item to which you answered "sometimes" or "never." Identify and list at least three possible targets for a health behavior change program. (If you are aware of other risky health behaviors you currently engage in, but which were not covered by this assessment, you may include those in your list.) For each item on your list, identify your current "stage of change" and one strategy you could adopt to move forward (see pp. 13–15). Possible strategies might be obtaining information about the behavior, completing an analysis of the pros and cons of change, or beginning a written record of your target behavior.

Behavior	Stage	Strategy
1. ____________	____________	____________
2. ____________	____________	____________
3. ____________	____________	____________

SOURCE: Adapted from *Healthstyle: A Self-Test,* developed by the U.S. Public Health Service. The behaviors covered in this test are recommended for most Americans, but some may not apply to people with certain chronic diseases or disabilities or to pregnant women, who may require special advice from their physician.

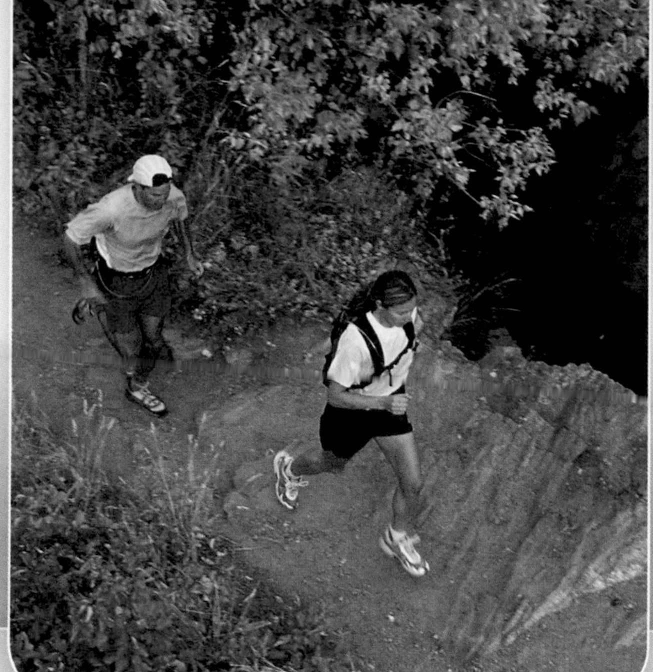

LOOKING AHEAD>>>>>

AFTER READING THIS CHAPTER, YOU SHOULD BE ABLE TO:

- Describe how much physical activity is recommended for developing health and fitness
- Identify the components of physical fitness and the way each component affects wellness
- Explain the goal of physical training and the basic principles of training
- Describe the principles involved in designing a well-rounded exercise program
- Discuss the steps that can be taken to make an exercise program safe, effective, and successful

PRINCIPLES OF PHYSICAL FITNESS 2

TEST YOUR KNOWLEDGE

1. To improve your health, you must exercise vigorously for at least 30 minutes straight, 5 or more days per week.

True or false?

2. Among American adults, about what percentage of trips of less than 1 mile long are made by walking?

a. 15%
b. 25%
c. 50%

3. If all inactive American adults became physically active, the savings in direct costs for medical care would be about _____ per year.

a. $75 million
b. $7.5 billion
c. $75 billion

ANSWERS

1. **FALSE.** Experts recommend about 30 minutes of moderate physical activity 5 or more days per week, but activity can be done in short bouts—10-minute sessions, for example—spread out over the course of the day.
2. **a.** The vast majority of short trips are made in cars. On average, Americans spend 100 minutes per day driving and 170 minutes per day watching television. Most people have many opportunities to incorporate more moderate physical activity into their daily routine.
3. **c.** People who engage in regular physical activity make fewer physician visits, use less medication, and have fewer hospital stays than physically inactive people. Nearly 25% of health care charges are linked to physical inactivity and obesity.

FIT AND WELL ONLINE LEARNING CENTER www.mhhe.com/fahey

Visit the *Fit and Well* Online Learning Center for resources that will help you get the most out of your course!

- Study and review aids include practice quizzes, glossary flashcards, chapter summaries, learning objectives, PowerPoint presentations, Common Questions Answered, student handouts, crossword puzzles, Internet activities, and links to wellness Web sites.
- Behavior change tools include a daily fitness and nutrition journal, a behavior change workbook, sample behavior change plans, and blank behavior change logs to print and use.

Any list of the benefits of physical activity is impressive. Although people vary greatly in the levels of physical fitness and performance they can ultimately achieve, the benefits of regular physical activity are available to everyone. (For more on the benefits of exercise, see the box "Exercise and Total Wellness.")

This chapter provides an overview of physical fitness. It explains how lifestyle physical activity and more formal exercise programs contribute to wellness. It also describes the components of fitness, the basic principles of physical training, and the essential elements of a well-rounded exercise program. Chapters 3–6 provide an in-depth look at each of the elements of a fitness program; Chapter 7 will help you put all these elements together into a complete, personalized program.

PHYSICAL ACTIVITY AND EXERCISE FOR HEALTH AND FITNESS

Despite the many benefits of an active lifestyle, levels of physical activity remain low for all populations of Americans (Figure 2.1). The Centers for Disease Control and Prevention (CDC) recently reported the following statistics about the physical activity levels of adult Americans:

- About 48% participate in some leisure-time physical activity, including 50% of men and 47% of women.
- Between 2001 and 2005, physical activity levels increased slightly among all age and ethnic groups, with the exception of Hispanic males.

The study also shows that education is an important factor in activity levels. For example, 54% of college graduates report doing some type of physical activity compared to 37% of high school dropouts.

Other studies show that only about 12% of Americans exercise intensively at least five times per week, and 25% do some leisure-time strength training.

Why aren't more Americans active? Possible barriers include lack of time and resources, social and environmental influences, and—most important—lack of motivation and commitment (see Lab 2.2 for more on barriers). Some people also fear injury. Although physical activity does carry some risks, the risks of inactivity are far greater. Evidence is growing that for most Americans, becoming more physically active may be the single most important lifestyle change for promoting health and well-being.

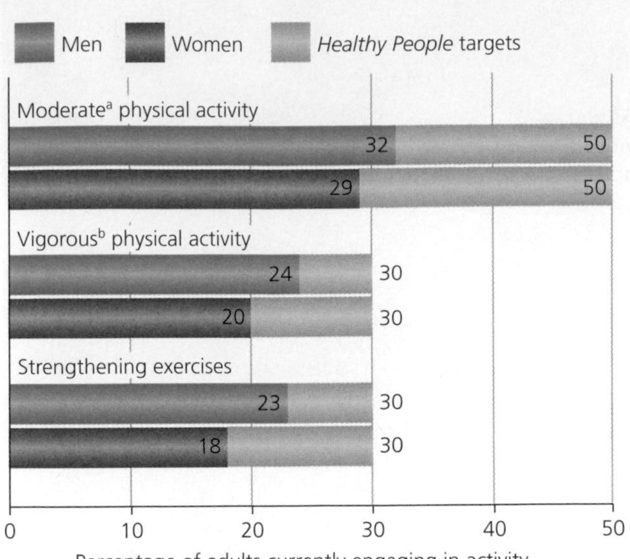

[a]Moderate physical activity for 30 or more minutes on 5 or more days per week
[b]Vigorous physical activity for 20 or more minutes on 3 or more days per week

WEB **VITAL STATISTICS**

FIGURE 2.1 Current levels of physical activity among American adults.

SOURCES: National Center for Health Statistics. 2007. *DATA2010: The Healthy People 2010 Database*, October 2007 Edition (http://wonder.cdc.gov/data2010; retrieved November 5, 2007). National Center for Health Statistics. 2006. Health Behavior of Adults: United States, 2002–04. *Vital and Health Statistics* 10 (230).

Physical Activity on a Continuum

Physical activity is any body movement carried out by the skeletal muscles and requiring energy. Different types of physical activity can be arranged on a continuum based on the amount of energy they require. Quick, easy movements such as standing up or walking down a hallway require little energy or effort; more intense, sustained activities such as cycling 5 miles or running in a race require considerably more.

Exercise refers to a subset of physical activity—planned, structured, repetitive movement of the body intended specifically to improve or maintain physical fitness. As discussed in Chapter 1, physical fitness is a set of physical attributes that allows the body to respond or adapt to the demands and stress of physical effort—to perform moderate-to-vigorous levels of physical activity without becoming overly tired. Levels of fitness depend on such physiological factors as the heart's ability to pump blood and the size of muscle fibers. These factors are a function both of genetics—a person's inborn potential for physical fitness—and of behavior—the amount of exercise a person does to improve fitness. To develop fitness, a person must perform enough physical activity to stress the body and cause long-term physiological changes.

Physical activity is essential to health and confers wide-ranging health benefits, but exercise is necessary to significantly improve physical fitness. This important distinction between physical activity, which improves health and wellness, and exercise, which improves fitness, is a key concept in understanding the guidelines discussed in this section.

Increasing Physical Activity to Improve Health and Wellness In 1996, the U.S. Surgeon General issued

Exercise and Total Wellness

As you will see throughout this chapter, an active lifestyle provides a multitude of benefits. For example, physically active adults live from 2 to 4 years longer, on average, than do sedentary adults. The benefits of regular physical activity, however, go beyond longevity. They impact quality of life across multiple dimensions of wellness.

Physical Wellness

In terms of general health, exercise increases your physical capacity so that you are better able to meet the challenges of daily life with energy and vigor. Physical activity can help you do the following:

- Generate more energy.
- Increase your stamina.
- Control your weight.
- Manage stress.
- Boost your immune system.

Over the long term, even moderate physical activity can help you avoid illnesses such as heart disease, diabetes, high blood pressure, depression, osteoporosis, and some cancers. Evidence shows that exercise can even prevent premature death from several causes.

Emotional Wellness

Exercise provides psychological and emotional benefits, contributing to your sense of competence and well-being. People who focus on staying active can also enjoy an improved self-image and a higher level of self-confidence. Such healthy self-esteem can positively affect other aspects of your life, as well. For example, a good self-image can be helpful when dealing with others or when competing.

Intellectual Wellness

Recent studies indicate that regular exercise is good for the brain—literally. One study shows that brain volume actually increases in adults who exercise regularly. Such gains in brain mass (growth or replenishment of brain matter) can improve cognitive functions and the overall health of the nervous system. Additionally, the process of mastering physical challenges—such as learning a proper golf swing—can boost intellectual fitness in the same manner as solving puzzles or engaging in other learning experiences.

Interpersonal Wellness

Joining in physical activity with a friend or a group can be a boon to your interpersonal or social wellness, too. By sharing physical challenges with others, you can make new friends, deepen your existing relationships, and build a stronger overall network of support.

Physical Activity and Health, a landmark report designed to encourage Americans to become more active. One of its findings was that people can obtain significant health benefits by including a moderate amount of physical activity on most, if not all, days of the week. This finding was echoed in the 2005 Dietary Guidelines for Americans, which recommended that all adults engage in at least 30 minutes of moderate-intensity physical activity, beyond usual activity, on most days of the week, in order to improve health. The recommendation was further refined in the publication *Physical Activity and Public Health: Updated Recommendations for Adults,* published jointly by the American College of Sports Medicine (ACSM) and the American Heart Association (AHA) in 2007. This report stated that, to promote and maintain health, adults need a minimum of 30 minutes of moderate-intensity aerobic (endurance) physical activity 5 days per week or 20 minutes of vigorous-intensity aerobic physical activity 3 days per week. Research shows that these levels of physical activity promote health and wellness in specific ways: by lowering the risk of high blood pressure, stroke, heart disease, type 2 diabetes, colon cancer, and osteoporosis and by reducing feelings of mild-to-moderate depression and anxiety.

What exactly is moderate physical activity? Activities such as brisk walking, dancing, swimming, cycling, and yard work can all count toward the daily total. The Surgeon General's report defines a moderate amount of activity as activity that uses about 150 calories of energy. Examples of activities that use about 150 calories are shown in Figure 2.2 (p. 30). You can burn the same number of calories by doing a lower-intensity activity for a longer time or higher-intensity activity for a shorter time. For more examples of light, moderate, and vigorous activities, see the box "Classifying Activity Levels" (p. 31).

The 2007 ACSM/AHA report defines moderate-intensity physical activity as activity that causes a noticeable increase in heart rate, such as a brisk walk. The report defines vigorous-intensity physical activity as activity that causes rapid breathing and a substantial increase in heart rate, as exemplified by jogging. Both the Surgeon General's report and

TERMS

physical activity Any body movement carried out by the skeletal muscles and requiring energy.

exercise Planned, structured, repetitive movement of the body intended to improve or maintain physical fitness.

Activity	Duration (min.)	
Washing a car	45–60	*Less Vigorous, More Time*
Washing windows or floors	45–60	
Volleyball	45	
Touch football	30–45	
Gardening	30–45	
Wheeling self in wheelchair	30–40	
Walking 1 3/4 miles	35 (20 min/mile)	
Shooting a basketball	30	
Bicycling 5 miles	30 (6 min/mile)	
Dancing fast	30	
Pushing a stroller 1 1/2 miles	30	
Raking leaves	30	
Walking 2 miles	30 (15 min/mile)	
Water aerobics	30	
Swimming laps	20	
Wheelchair basketball	20	
Playing a game of basketball	15–20	
Bicycling 4 miles	15 (3 3/4 min/mile)	
Jumping rope	15	
Running 1 1/2 miles	15 (10 min/mile)	
Shoveling snow	15	*More Vigorous, Less Time*
Stairwalking	15	

FIGURE 2.2 Examples of moderate amounts of physical activity. Each example uses about 150 calories.

SOURCE: Department of Health and Human Services. 1996. *Physical Activity and Health: A Report of the Surgeon General.* Atlanta: DHHS.

the ACSM/AHA report also recommend that people perform strength training exercises at least twice a week to build and maintain muscular strength and endurance.

The daily total of physical activity can be accumulated in multiple bouts of 10 or more minutes—for example, two 10-minute bike rides to and from class and a brisk 10-minute walk to the store. In this lifestyle approach to physical activity, people can choose activities that they find enjoyable and that fit into their daily routine; everyday tasks at school, work, and home can be structured to contribute to the daily activity total (see the box "Making Time for Physical Activity" on p. 32). If all Americans who are currently sedentary were to increase their lifestyle physical activity to 30 minutes per day, there would be an enormous benefit to public health and to individual well-being.

Increasing Physical Activity to Manage Weight Because two-thirds of Americans are overweight, government agencies and health organizations have also published physical activity guidelines focusing on weight management. These guidelines call for higher daily physical activity goals than the guidelines designed for more general health promotion. Table 2.1 lists recommendations for promoting health and managing weight from just a few of these organizations.

Table 2.1 Summary of Physical Activity Recommendations from Selected Leading Health Organizations

Organization	Recommendation	Purpose
Centers for Disease Control and Prevention	A minimum of 30 minutes of moderate-intensity physical activity on 5 or more days of the week	Promote health and prevent chronic disease
American College of Sports Medicine	A minimum of 30 minutes of moderate activity 5 days per week or 20 minutes of vigorous activity 3 days per week. *(The ACSM has separate guidelines for exercise programs to develop fitness; see pp. 38–41 and Table 2.2.)*	Promote health and prevent chronic disease
U.S. Surgeon General: Report on Physical Activity and Health	A minimum of 150 calories per day expended in moderate physical activity (the equivalent of about 30 minutes of brisk walking); resistance training twice a week	Promote health and prevent chronic disease
U.S. Department of Health and Human Services and U.S. Department of Agriculture: 2005 Dietary Guidelines for Americans	30 minutes of moderate-intensity exercise on most days of the week	Reduce the risk of chronic disease
	60 minutes of moderate-to-vigorous-intensity exercise on most days of the week	Manage body weight and prevent unhealthy weight gain
	60–90 minutes of moderate-intensity exercise per day	Sustain weight loss
Healthy People 2010	At least 30 minutes of moderate physical activity 5 or more days per week	Promote health and prevent chronic disease
Institute of Medicine, National Academies	At least 60 minutes of moderate physical activity per day	Promote health, prevent chronic disease, and control weight
International Association for the Study of Obesity	45–60 minutes of moderate physical activity per day	Prevent weight gain
	60–90 minutes of moderate physical activity per day	Maintain weight loss
World Health Organization	At least 30 minutes of moderate physical activity per day	Promote health, prevent chronic disease, and control weight

NOTE: See Chapter 7 for activity and exercise guidelines for people with special health concerns.

IN FOCUS

Classifying Activity Levels

Assessing your physical activity level is easier if you know how to classify different kinds of activities. Fitness experts categorize activities into the following three levels:

• *Light activity* includes the routine tasks associated with typical day-to-day life, such as vacuuming or walking to class. You probably perform dozens of light activities every day without even thinking about it. You can gain significant health benefits by turning light activities into moderate activities—by walking briskly instead of slowly, for example.

• *Moderate activity* causes your breathing and heart rate to accelerate but still allows for comfortable conversation, such as walking at 3–4 miles per hour. It is sometimes described as activity that can be performed comfortably for about 45 minutes. Raking leaves is an example of moderate physical activity, as are most occupational tasks that involve extended periods of moderate effort.

• *Vigorous activity* elevates your heart rate considerably and has other physical effects that improve your fitness level. During vigorous activity you are breathing too heavily to hold a conversation very easily. An example is walking faster than 4 miles per hour.

Here are some examples:

Light

Walking slowly
Routine tasks:
- Cooking
- Shopping

Light housework:
- Ironing
- Dusting
- Washing dishes

Light yard work or home activities:
- Pruning
- Weeding
- Plumbing

Light fitness activities:
- Light stretching or warm-up
- Swimming, slow treading

Moderate

Walking briskly
Cycling moderately on level terrain
Social dancing
Moderate housework:
- Scrubbing floors
- Washing windows

Moderate yard work or home activities:
- Planting
- Raking
- Painting
- Washing car

Fitness activities requiring moderate effort:
- Doing low-impact aerobics
- Playing Frisbee
- Swimming
- Playing tennis, doubles

Vigorous

Walking briskly uphill
Cycling on steep uphill terrain
Heavy housework:
- Moving furniture
- Carrying heavy objects upstairs

Vigorous yard work or home activities:
- Shoveling snow
- Trimming trees
- Doing construction work
- Digging

Fitness activities requiring vigorous effort:
- Running
- Doing high-impact aerobics
- Doing circuit weight training
- Swimming laps
- Playing most competitive sports

These guidelines do not conflict with those from the Surgeon General, but they do have a different emphasis. They recognize that for people who need to prevent weight gain, lose weight, or maintain weight loss, 30 minutes per day of physical activity may not be enough. Instead, they recommend 45–90 or more minutes per day of physical activity. For example, the Dietary Guidelines recommend 60 minutes of daily physical activity to manage body weight and prevent unhealthy weight gain and 60–90 minutes of daily activity to sustain weight loss. The different recommendations may seem confusing, but all major health organizations have the same message: People can improve their health by becoming more active.

Exercising to Improve Physical Fitness As mentioned earlier, moderate physical activity confers significant health and wellness benefits, especially for those who are currently sedentary and become moderately active. The Surgeon General's report, the Dietary Guidelines for Americans, and the ACSM/AHA report all conclude that people can obtain even greater health and wellness benefits by increasing the duration and intensity of physical activity. With increased activity, they will see more improvements in quality of life and greater reductions in disease and mortality risk.

More vigorous activity, as in a structured, systematic exercise program, is also needed to improve physical fitness; moderate physical activity alone is not enough. Physical fitness requires more intense movement that poses a substantially greater challenge to the body. The ACSM issued separate guidelines in 2006 for creating a formal exercise program that will develop physical fitness. These guidelines are described in detail later in the chapter.

How Much Physical Activity Is Enough?

Some experts feel that people get most of the health benefits of an exercise program simply by becoming more active over the course of the day; the amount of activity needed depends on an individual's health status and goals. Other experts feel that the activity goal set by the lifestyle approach is too low; they argue that people should exercise long enough and intensely enough to improve their body's capacity for exercise—that is, to improve physical fitness. More research is needed to clarify the health effects of different amounts of lifestyle physical activity, of

TAKE CHARGE

Making Time for Physical Activity

"Too little time" is a common excuse for not being physically active. Learning to manage your time successfully is crucial if you are to maintain a wellness lifestyle. You can begin by keeping a record of how you are currently spending your time; in your health journal, use a grid broken into blocks of 15, 20, or 30 minutes to track your daily activities. (See Activity 10 in the Behavior Change Workbook at the end of this text for a blank grid.) Then analyze your record: List each type of activity and the total time you engaged in it on a given day—for example, sleeping, 7 hours; eating, 1.5 hours; studying, 3 hours; and so on. Take a close look at your list of activities, and prioritize them according to how important they are to you, from essential to somewhat important to not important at all.

Based on the priorities you set, make changes in your daily schedule by subtracting time from some activities in order to make time for physical activity. Look particularly carefully at your leisure-time activities and your methods of transportation; these are areas where it is easy to build in physical activity. Make changes using a system of trade-offs. For example, you may choose to reduce the total amount of time you spend playing computer games, listening to the radio, and chatting on the phone in order to make time for an after-dinner bike ride or a walk with a friend. You may decide to watch 10 fewer minutes of television in the morning in order to change your 5-minute drive to class into a 15-minute walk. In making these kinds of changes in your schedule, don't feel that you have to miss out on anything you enjoy. You can get more from less time by focusing on what you are doing and by combining activities.

The following are just a few ways to incorporate more physical activity into your daily routine:

- Take the stairs instead of the elevator or escalator.
- Walk to the mailbox, post office, store, bank, or library whenever possible.
- Park your car a mile or even just a few blocks from your destination, and walk briskly.
- Do at least one chore every day that requires physical activity: Wash the windows or your car, clean your room or house, mow the lawn, or rake the leaves.
- Take study or work breaks to avoid sitting for more than 30 minutes at a time. Get up and walk around the library, your office, or your home or dorm; go up and down a flight of stairs.
- Stretch when you stand in line or watch TV.
- When you take public transportation, get off one stop early and walk to your destination.
- Go dancing instead of to a movie.
- Walk to visit a neighbor or friend rather than calling him or her on the phone. Go for a walk while you chat.
- Put your remote controls in storage; when you want to change TV or radio stations, get up and do it by hand.
- Take the dog for a walk (or an extra walk) every day.
- Play actively with children.
- If weather or neighborhood safety rule out walking outside, look for alternate locations—an indoor track, an enclosed shopping mall, or even a long hallway. Look for locations near or on the way to your campus, workplace, or residence.
- Remember, being busy isn't the same as being active. Seize every opportunity to get up and walk around. Move more and sit less.

Visit the U.S. Department of Health and Human Services Small Step Web site (www.smallstep.gov) for more ideas.

moderate-intensity versus high-intensity exercise, and of continuous versus intermittent exercise. However, there is probably some truth in both of these positions.

Regular physical activity, regardless of the intensity, makes you healthier and can help protect you from many chronic diseases. Although you get many of the health benefits of exercise simply by being more active, you obtain even more benefits when you are physically fit. In addition to long-term health benefits, fitness also significantly contributes to quality of life. Fitness can give you freedom—freedom to move your body the way you want. Fit people have more energy and better body control. They can enjoy a more active lifestyle—cycling, hiking, skiing, and so on—than their more sedentary counterparts. Even if you don't like sports, you need physical energy and stamina in your daily life and for many nonsport leisure activities—visiting museums, playing with children, gardening, and so on.

Where does this leave you? Most experts agree that some physical activity is better than none, but that more—as long as it does not result in injury—is better than some. To set a personal goal for physical activity and exercise, consider your current activity level, your health status, and your overall goals. At the very least, strive to become more active and meet the goal set by the Surgeon General's report of using about 150 calories a day in physical activity—the equivalent of about 30 minutes of moderate-intensity activity. Choose to be active whenever you can. If weight management is a concern for you, begin by achieving the goal of 30 minutes of activity per day and then try to raise your activity level further, to

QUESTIONS FOR CRITICAL THINKING AND REFLECTION

Does your current lifestyle include enough physical activity—30 minutes of moderate-intensity activity 5 or more days a week—to support health and wellness? Does your lifestyle go beyond this level to include enough vigorous physical activity and exercise to build physical fitness? What changes could you make in your lifestyle to start developing physical fitness?

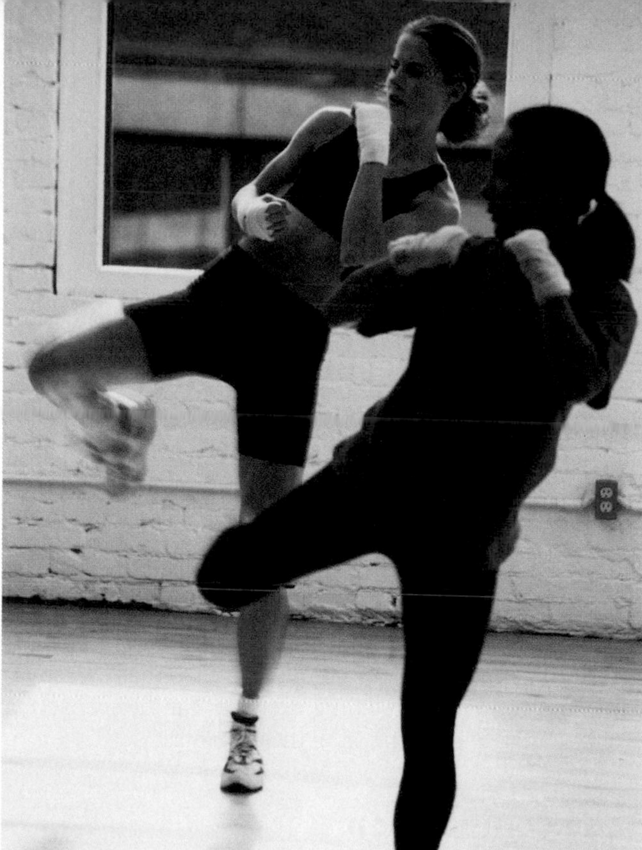

Cardiorespiratory endurance is a key component of health-related fitness. These participants in a kickboxing class are conditioning their hearts and lungs as well as gaining many other health benefits.

45–90 minutes per day or more. For even better health and well-being, participate in a structured exercise program that develops physical fitness. Any increase in physical activity will contribute to your health and well-being, now and in the future.

HEALTH-RELATED COMPONENTS OF PHYSICAL FITNESS

Some components of fitness are related to specific activities, and others relate to general health. **Health-related fitness** includes the following components:

- Cardiorespiratory endurance
- Muscular strength
- Muscular endurance
- Flexibility
- Body composition

Health-related fitness helps you withstand physical challenges and protects you from diseases.

Cardiorespiratory Endurance

Cardiorespiratory endurance is the ability to perform prolonged, large-muscle, dynamic exercise at moderate-to-high levels of intensity. It depends on such factors as the ability of the lungs to deliver oxygen from the environment to the bloodstream, the capacity of the heart to pump blood, the ability of the nervous system and blood vessels to regulate blood flow, and the capability of the body's chemical systems to use oxygen and process fuels for exercise.

When cardiorespiratory fitness is low, the heart has to work hard during normal daily activities and may not be able to work hard enough to sustain high-intensity physical activity in an emergency. As cardiorespiratory fitness improves, related physical functions also improve. For example:

- The heart pumps more blood per heartbeat.
- Resting heart rate slows.
- Blood volume increases.
- Blood supply to tissues improves.
- The body can cool itself better.
- Resting blood pressure decreases.

A healthy heart can better withstand the strains of everyday life, the stress of occasional emergencies, and the wear and tear of time.

Endurance training also improves the functioning of the chemical systems, particularly in the muscles and liver, thereby enhancing the body's ability to use energy supplied by food and to do more exercise with less effort from the oxygen transport system.

Cardiorespiratory endurance is a central component of health-related fitness because the functioning of the heart and lungs is so essential to overall good health. A person can't live very long or very well without a healthy heart. Poor cardiorespiratory fitness is linked with heart disease,

MOTIVATION BOOSTER

Track your activity. Would you be more motivated to try to increase daily physical activity if you had an easy way to monitor your level of activity? If so, consider wearing a pedometer to track the number of steps you take each day—a rough but easily obtainable reflection of daily physical activity. Wear the pedometer for a week to get a baseline average daily number of steps, and then set an appropriate goal—for example, walking 2000 additional steps each day or increasing daily steps to 10,000. Record your daily steps in a prominent location to monitor your progress and boost your motivation. Lab 2.3 includes additional advice on using a pedometer to monitor physical activity.

TERMS

health-related fitness Physical capacities that contribute to health: cardiorespiratory endurance, muscular strength, muscular endurance, flexibility, and body composition.

cardiorespiratory endurance The ability of the body to perform prolonged, large-muscle, dynamic exercise at moderate-to-high levels of intensity.

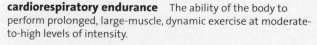

type 2 diabetes, colon cancer, stroke, depression, and anxiety. A moderate level of cardiorespiratory fitness can help compensate for certain health risks, including excess body fat: People who are lean but who have low cardiorespiratory fitness have been found to have higher death rates than people with higher levels of body fat who are otherwise fit. You can develop cardiorespiratory endurance through activities that involve continuous, rhythmic movements of large-muscle groups, such as the legs. Such activities include walking, jogging, cycling, and aerobic dancing.

Muscular Strength

Muscular strength is the amount of force a muscle can produce with a single maximum effort. It depends on such factors as the size of muscle cells and the ability of nerves to activate muscle cells. Strong muscles are important for everyday activities, such as climbing stairs, as well as for emergency situations. They help keep the skeleton in proper alignment, preventing back and leg pain and providing the support necessary for good posture. Muscular strength has obvious importance in recreational activities. Strong people can hit a tennis ball harder, kick a soccer ball farther, and ride a bicycle uphill more easily.

Muscle tissue is an important element of overall body composition. Greater muscle mass means a higher rate of **metabolism** and faster energy use. Training to build muscular strength can also help people manage stress and boost their self-confidence.

Maintaining strength and muscle mass is vital for healthy aging. Older people tend to experience a decrease in both number and size of muscle cells—a condition called *sarcopenia.* Many of the muscle cells that remain become slower, and some become nonfunctional because they lose their attachment to the nervous system. Strength training helps maintain muscle mass and function and possibly helps decrease the risk of osteoporosis (bone loss) in older people, which greatly enhances their quality of life and prevents life-threatening injuries.

Muscular Endurance

Muscular endurance is the ability to resist fatigue and sustain a given level of muscle tension—that is, to hold a muscle contraction for a long time or to contract a muscle over and over again. It depends on such factors as the size of muscle cells, the ability of muscles to store fuel, and the blood supply to muscles.

Muscular endurance is important for good posture and for injury prevention. For example, if abdominal and back muscles can't hold the spine correctly, the chances of low-back pain and back injury are increased. Good muscular endurance in the trunk muscles is more important than muscular strength for preventing back pain. Muscular endurance helps people cope with the physical demands of everyday life and enhances performance in sports and work.

QUESTIONS FOR CRITICAL THINKING AND REFLECTION

When you think about exercise, do you think of only one or two of the five components of health-related fitness, such as muscular strength or body composition? If so, where do you think your ideas come from? What role do the media play in shaping your ideas about fitness?

Flexibility

Flexibility is the ability to move the joints through their full range of motion. It depends on joint structure, the length and elasticity of connective tissue, and nervous system activity. Flexible, pain-free joints are important for good health and well-being. Inactivity causes the joints to become stiffer with age. Stiffness, in turn, often causes older people to assume unnatural body postures that can stress joints and muscles. Stretching exercises can help ensure a healthy range of motion for all major joints.

Body Composition

Body composition refers to the proportion of fat and **fat-free mass** (muscle, bone, and water) in the body. Healthy body composition involves a high proportion of fat-free mass and an acceptably low level of body fat, adjusted for age and gender. A person with excessive body fat—especially excess fat in the abdomen—is more likely to experience health problems, including heart disease, insulin resistance, high blood pressure, stroke, joint problems, type 2 diabetes, gallbladder disease, blood vessel inflammation, some types of cancer, and back pain.

The best way to lose fat is through a lifestyle that includes a sensible diet and exercise. The best way to add muscle mass is through resistance training, also known as strength training or, when weights are used, weight training. Large changes in body composition aren't necessary to improve health; even a small increase in physical activity and a small decrease in body fat can lead to substantial health improvements.

Skill-Related Components of Fitness

In addition to the five health-related components of physical fitness, the ability to perform a particular sport or activity may depend on **skill-related fitness** components such as the following:

- ***Speed***—the ability to perform a movement in a short period of time
- ***Power***—the ability to exert force rapidly, based on a combination of strength and speed
- ***Agility***—the ability to change the position of the body quickly and accurately

- ***Balance***—the ability to maintain equilibrium while moving or while stationary
- ***Coordination***—the ability to perform motor tasks accurately and smoothly using body movements and the senses
- ***Reaction and movement time***—the ability to respond and react quickly to a stimulus

Skill-related fitness tends to be sport-specific and is best developed through practice. For example, the speed, coordination, and agility needed to play basketball can be developed by playing basketball. Some fitness experts contend that some sports don't contribute to all the health-related components of physical fitness. However, engaging in sports is fun and can help you build fitness and contribute to other areas of wellness.

PRINCIPLES OF PHYSICAL TRAINING: ADAPTATION TO STRESS

The human body is very adaptable. The greater the demands made on it, the more it adjusts to meet those demands. Over time, immediate, short-term adjustments translate into long-term changes and improvements. When breathing and heart rate increase during exercise, for example, the heart gradually develops the ability to pump more blood with each beat. Then, during exercise, it doesn't have to beat as fast to meet the cells' demands for oxygen. The goal of **physical training** is to produce these long-term changes and improvements in the body's functioning. Although people differ in the maximum levels of physical fitness and performance they can achieve through training, the wellness benefits of exercise are available to everyone (see the box "Fitness and Disability" on p. 36).

Particular types and amounts of exercise are most effective in developing the various components of fitness. To put together an effective exercise program, you should first understand the basic principles of physical training, including the following:

- Specificity
- Progressive overload
- Reversibility
- Individual differences

All of these rest on the larger principle of adaptation.

Specificity—Adapting to Type of Training

To develop a particular fitness component, you must perform exercises that are specifically designed for that component. This is the principle of **specificity.** Weight training, for example, develops muscular strength but is less effective for developing cardiorespiratory endurance or flexibility. Specificity also applies to the skill-related fitness components—to improve at tennis, you must practice tennis—and to the different parts of the body—to develop stronger arms, you must exercise your arms. A well-rounded exercise program includes exercises geared to each component of fitness, to different parts of the body, and to specific activities or sports.

Progressive Overload—Adapting to Amount of Training and the FITT Principle

The body adapts to the demands of exercise by improving its functioning. When the amount of exercise (also called *overload* or *stress*) is progressively increased, fitness continues to improve. This is the principle of **progressive overload.**

The amount of overload is important. Too little exercise will have no effect on fitness (although it may improve health); too much may cause injury and problems with the body's immune system and hormone levels. The point at which exercise becomes excessive is highly individual—it occurs at a much higher level in an Olympic athlete than in a sedentary person. For every type of exercise, there is a training threshold at which fitness benefits begin to occur, a zone within which maximum fitness benefits occur, and an upper limit of safe training.

muscular strength The amount of force a muscle can produce with a single maximum effort.

metabolism The sum of all the vital processes by which food energy and nutrients are made available to and used by the body.

muscular endurance The ability of a muscle to remain contracted or to contract repeatedly for a long period of time.

flexibility The ability to move joints through their full range of motion.

body composition The proportion of fat and fat-free mass (muscle, bone, and water) in the body.

fat-free mass The nonfat component of the human body, consisting of skeletal muscle, bone, and water.

skill-related fitness Physical capacities that contribute to performance in a sport or activity: speed, power, agility, balance, coordination, and reaction time.

physical training The performance of different types of activities that cause the body to adapt and improve its level of fitness.

specificity The training principle that the body adapts to the particular type and amount of stress placed on it.

progressive overload The training principle that placing increasing amounts of stress on the body causes adaptations that improve fitness.

DIMENSIONS OF DIVERSITY

Fitness and Disability

Physical fitness and athletic achievement are not limited to the able-bodied. People with disabilities can also attain high levels of fitness and performance, as shown by the elite athletes who compete in the Paralympics. The premier event for athletes with disabilities, the Paralympics are held in the same year and city as the Olympics. The performance of these skilled athletes makes it clear that people with disabilities can be active, healthy, and extraordinarily fit; just like able-bodied athletes, athletes with disabilities strive for excellence and can serve as role models.

According to the U.S. Census Bureau, about 51 million Americans have some type of chronic disability. Some disabilities are the result of injury, such as spinal cord injuries sustained in car crashes. Other disabilities result from illness, such as the blindness that sometimes occurs as a complication of diabetes or the joint stiffness that accompanies arthritis. And some disabilities are present at birth, as in the case of congenital limb deformities or cerebral palsy.

Exercise and physical activity are as important for people with disabilities as for able-bodied individuals—if not *more* important. Being active helps prevent secondary conditions that may result from prolonged inactivity, such as circulatory or muscular problems. Currently, about 18% of people with disabilities engage in regular moderate activity.

People with disabilities don't have to be elite athletes to participate in sports and lead an active life. Some health clubs and fitness centers offer activities and events geared for people of all ages and types of disabilities. They may have modified aerobics classes, special weight training machines, classes involving mild exercise in warm water, and other activities adapted for people with disabilities. Popular sports and recreational activities include adapted horseback riding, golf, swimming, and skiing. Competitive sports are also available—for example, there are wheelchair versions of billiards, tennis, hockey, and basketball, as well as sports for people with hearing, visual, or mental impairments. For those who prefer to get their exercise at home, special videos are available geared to individuals who use wheelchairs or who have arthritis, hearing impairments, or many other disabilities.

If you have a disability and want to be more active, check with your physician about what's appropriate for you. Call your local community center, YMCA/YWCA, independent living center, or fitness center to locate facilities; look for a facility with experienced personnel and appropriate adaptive equipment. For specialized videos, check with hospitals and health associations that are geared to specific disabilities, such as the Arthritis Foundation.

SOURCES: National Center for Health Statistics. 2007. *DATA 2010: The Healthy People 2010 Database, October, 2007 Edition* (http://wonder.cdc.gov/data2010/; retrieved November 5, 2007). Steinmetz, E. 2006. *Americans with Disabilities: 2002.* Washington, D.C.: U.S. Census Bureau.

The amount of exercise needed depends on the individual's current level of fitness, the person's genetically determined capacity to adapt to training, his or her fitness goals, and the component being developed. A novice, for example, might experience fitness benefits from jogging a mile in 10 minutes, but this level of exercise would cause no physical adaptations in a trained distance runner. Beginners should start at the lower end of the fitness benefit zone; fitter individuals will make more rapid gains by exercising at the higher end of the fitness benefit zone. Progression is critical because fitness increases only if the volume and intensity of workouts increase. Exercising at the same intensity every training session will maintain fitness but will not increase it, because the training stress is below the threshold to produce adaptation.

The amount of overload needed to maintain or improve a particular level of fitness for a particular fitness component is determined through four dimensions, represented by the acronym FITT:

- *Frequency*—how often
- *Intensity*—how hard
- *Time*—how long (duration)
- *Type*—mode of activity

Chapters 3, 4, and 5 show you how to apply the FITT principle to exercise programs for cardiorespiratory endurance, muscular strength and endurance, and flexibility, respectively.

Frequency Developing fitness requires regular exercise. Optimum exercise frequency, expressed in number of days per week, varies with the component being developed and the individual's fitness goals. For most people, a frequency of 3–5 days per week for cardiorespiratory endurance exercise and 2 or more days per week for resistance and flexibility training is appropriate for a general fitness program.

An important consideration in determining appropriate exercise frequency is recovery time, which is also highly individual and depends on factors such as training experience, age, and intensity of training. For example, 24 hours of rest between highly intensive workouts that involve heavy weights or track sprints is not enough recovery time for safe and effective training; intense workouts need to be spaced out during the week to allow for sufficient recovery time. On the other hand, you can exercise every day if your program consists of moderate-intensity walking or cycling. Learn to "listen to your body"

To safely and effectively develop strength, this exerciser must overload his muscles with enough weight that his body's functioning improves but not so much weight that he becomes injured.

to get enough rest between workouts. Chapters 3–5 provide more detailed information about training techniques and recovery periods for workouts focused on different fitness components.

Intensity Fitness benefits occur when a person exercises harder than his or her normal level of activity. The appropriate exercise intensity varies with each fitness component. To develop cardiorespiratory endurance, for example, you must raise your heart rate above normal; to develop muscular strength, you must lift a heavier weight than normal; to develop flexibility, you must stretch muscles beyond their normal length.

Time (Duration) Fitness benefits occur when you exercise for an extended period of time. For cardiorespiratory endurance exercise, 20–60 minutes is recommended; exercise can take place in a single session or in several sessions of 10 or more minutes. The greater the intensity of exercise, the less time needed to obtain fitness benefits. For high-intensity exercise, such as running, 20–30 minutes is appropriate. For moderate-intensity exercise, such as walking, 45–60 minutes may be needed. High-intensity exercise poses a greater risk of injury than low-intensity exercise, so if you are a nonathletic adult, it's probably best to emphasize low- to moderate-intensity activity of longer duration.

To build muscular strength, muscular endurance, and flexibility, similar amounts of time are advisable, but these exercises are more commonly organized in terms of a specific number of repetitions of particular exercises. For resistance training, for example, a recommended program includes one or more sets of 8–12 repetitions of 8–10 different exercises that work the major muscle groups.

Type (Mode of Activity) The type of exercise in which you should engage varies with each fitness component and with your personal fitness goals. To develop cardiorespiratory endurance, you need to engage in continuous activities involving large-muscle groups—walking, jogging, cycling, or swimming, for example. Resistive exercises develop muscular strength and endurance, while stretching exercises build flexibility. The frequency, intensity, and time of the exercise will be different for each type of activity. (See pp. 38–41 for more on choosing appropriate activities for your fitness program.)

Reversibility—Adapting to a Reduction in Training

Fitness is a reversible adaptation. The body adjusts to lower levels of physical activity the same way it adjusts to higher levels. This is the principle of **reversibility.** When a person stops exercising, up to 50% of fitness improvements are lost within 2 months. However, not all fitness levels reverse at the same rate. Strength fitness is very resilient, so a person can maintain strength fitness by doing resistive exercise as infrequently as once a week. On the other hand, cardiovascular and cellular fitness reverse themselves more quickly—sometimes within just a few days or weeks. If you must temporarily curtail your training, you can maintain your fitness improvements by keeping the intensity of your workouts constant while reducing their frequency or duration.

?

QUESTIONS FOR CRITICAL THINKING AND REFLECTION

Many people who play sports have had the experience of realizing that they are not as physically gifted as a teammate or that they are never going to be in the Olympics. What can you say to encourage someone who is discouraged by this realization? What benefits of physical activity, exercise, and sports might you point out?

reversibility The training principle that fitness improvements are lost when demands on the body are lowered.

TERMS

Individual Differences—Limits on Adaptability

Anyone watching the Olympics can see that, from a physical standpoint, we are not all created equal. There are large individual differences in our ability to improve fitness, achieve a desirable body composition, and learn and perform sports skills. Some people are able to run longer distances, or lift more weight, or kick a soccer ball more skillfully than others will ever be able to, no matter how much they train. Each person responds to training at different rates; a program that works for one person may not be right for another person. There are limits on the adaptability—the potential for improvement—of any human body. The body's ability to transport and use oxygen, for example, can be improved by only about 15–30% through training. An endurance athlete must therefore inherit a large metabolic capacity in order to reach competitive performance levels. In the past few years, scientists have identified specific genes that influence body fat, strength, and endurance.

However, physical training improves fitness regardless of heredity. For the average person, the body's adaptability is enough to achieve reasonable fitness goals.

DESIGNING YOUR OWN EXERCISE PROGRAM

Physical training works best when you have a plan. A plan helps you make gradual but steady progress toward your goals. Once you've determined that exercise is safe for you, planning for physical fitness consists of assessing how fit you are now, determining where you want to be, and choosing the right activities to help you get there.

Getting Medical Clearance

People of any age who are not at high risk for serious health problems can safely exercise at a moderate intensity (60% or less of maximum heart rate) without a prior medical evaluation (see Chapter 3 for a discussion of maximum heart rate). Likewise, if you are male and under 40 or female and under 50 and in good health, exercise is probably safe for you. If you do not fit into these age groups or if you have health problems—especially high blood pressure, heart disease, muscle or joint problems, or obesity—see your physician before starting a vigorous exercise program. The Canadian Society for Exercise Physiology has developed the Physical Activity Readiness Questionnaire (PAR-Q) to help evaluate exercise safety; it is included in Lab 2.1. Completing it should alert you to any potential problems you may have. If a physician isn't sure whether exercise is safe for you, she or he may recommend an **exercise stress test** or a **graded exercise test (GXT)** to see whether you show symptoms of heart disease during exercise. For most people, however, it's far safer to exercise than to remain sedentary. For more information, see the box "Is Exercise Safe?"

WEB TERMS

exercise stress test A test usually administered on a treadmill or cycle ergometer that involves analysis of the changes in electrical activity in the heart from an electrocardiogram (EKG or ECG) taken during exercise; used to determine if any heart disease is present and to assess current fitness level.

graded exercise test (GXT) An exercise test that starts at an easy intensity and progresses to maximum capacity.

Assessing Yourself

The first step in creating a successful fitness program is to assess your current level of physical activity and fitness for each of the five health-related fitness components. The results of the assessment tests will help you set specific fitness goals and plan your fitness program. Lab 2.2 gives you the opportunity to assess your current overall level of activity and determine if it is appropriate. Assessment tests in Chapters 3–6 will help you evaluate your cardiorespiratory endurance, muscular strength, muscular endurance, flexibility, and body composition.

Setting Goals

The ultimate general goal of every health-related fitness program is the same—wellness that lasts a lifetime. Whatever your specific goals, they must be important enough to you to keep you motivated. Most sports psychologists believe that setting and achieving goals is the most effective way to stay motivated about exercise. (Refer to Chapter 1 for more on goal setting, as well as Common Questions Answered at the end of this chapter.) After you complete the assessment tests in Chapters 3–6, you will be able to set goals directly related to each fitness component, such as working toward a 3-mile jog or doing 20 push-ups. First, though, think carefully about your overall goals, and be clear about why you are starting a program.

Choosing Activities for a Balanced Program

An ideal fitness program combines a physically active lifestyle with a systematic exercise program to develop and maintain physical fitness. This overall program is shown in the physical activity pyramid in Figure 2.3. If you are currently sedentary, your goal should be to focus on activities at the bottom of the pyramid and gradually increase the amount of moderate-intensity physical activity in your daily life. Appropriate activities include

Is Exercise Safe?

Participating in exercise and sports is usually a wonderful experience that improves wellness in both the short and long term. In rare instances, however, vigorous exertion is associated with sudden death. It may seem difficult to understand that although regular exercise protects people from heart disease, it also increases the risk of sudden death.

Congenital heart defects (heart abnormalities present at birth) are the most common cause of exercise-related sudden death in people under 35. In nearly all other cases, coronary artery disease is responsible. In this condition, fat and other substances build up in the arteries that supply blood to the heart. Death can result if an artery becomes blocked or if the heart's rhythm and pumping action are disrupted. Exercise, particularly intense exercise, may trigger a heart attack in someone with underlying heart disease.

A study of jogging deaths in Rhode Island found that there was one death per 396,000 hours of jogging, or about one death per 7620 joggers per year—an extremely low risk for each individual jogger. Another study of men involved in a variety of physical activities found one death per 1.51 million hours of exercise. This 12-year study of more than 21,000 men found that those who didn't exercise vigorously were 74 times more likely to die suddenly from cardiac arrest during or shortly after exercise. It is also important to note that people are much safer exercising than engaging in many other common activities, including driving a car.

Although quite small, the risk does exist and may lead some people to wonder why exercise is considered such an important part of a wellness lifestyle. Exercise causes many positive changes in the body—in healthy people as well as those with heart disease—that more than make up for the slightly increased short-term risk of sudden death. Training slows or reverses the fatty buildup in arteries and helps protect people from deadly heart rhythm abnormalities.

People who exercise regularly have an overall risk of sudden death only about two-thirds that of nonexercisers. Active people who stop exercising can expect their heart attack risk to increase by 300%.

Obviously, someone with underlying coronary artery disease is at greater risk than someone who is free from the condition. However, many cases of heart disease go undiagnosed. The riskiest scenario may involve the middle-aged or older individual who suddenly begins participating in a vigorous sport or activity after being sedentary for a long time. This finding provides strong evidence for the recommendation that people increase their level of physical activity gradually and engage in regular, rather than sporadic, activity.

SOURCES: Thompson, P. D. 2001. Cardiovascular risks of exercise. *Physician and Sportsmedicine* 29(4). Albert, C. M., et al. 2000. Trigger of sudden death from cardiac causes by vigorous exertion. *New England Journal of Medicine* 343(19): 1355–1361.

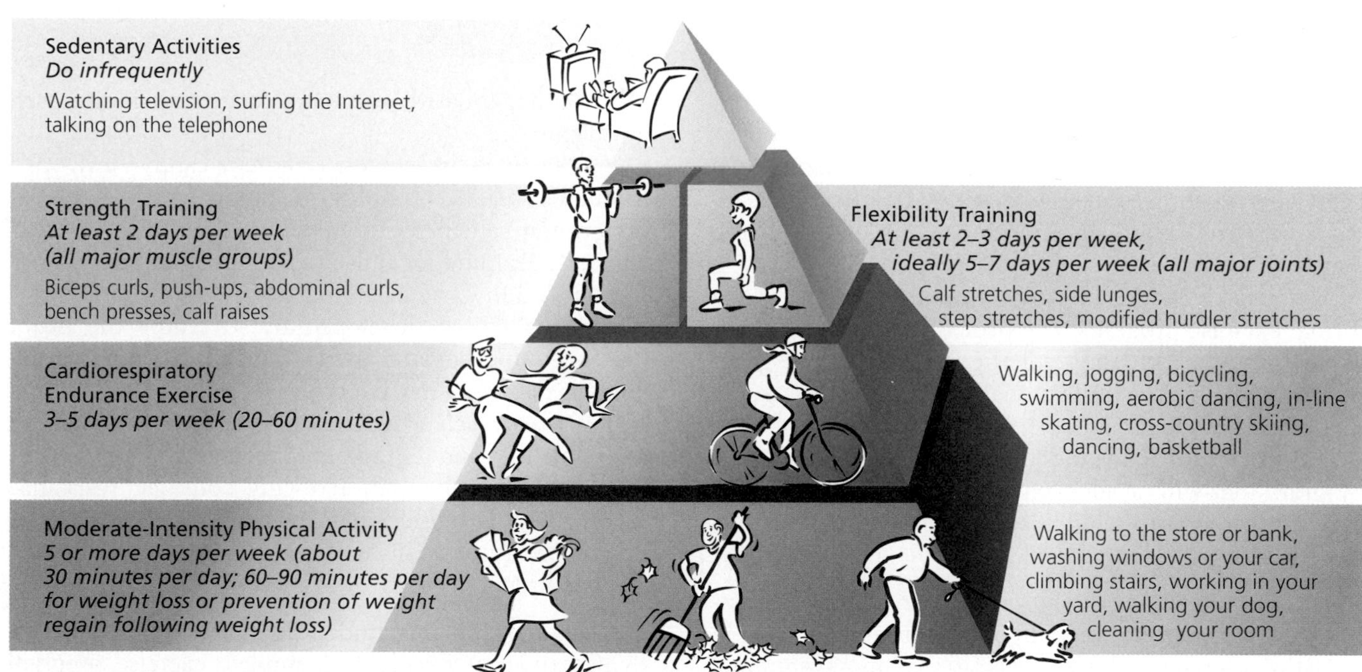

FIGURE 2.3 Physical activity pyramid. This physical activity pyramid shows the components of a balanced fitness program and emphasizes the importance of daily moderate-intensity physical activity. If you are currently sedentary, gradually increase the amount of moderate-intensity physical activity in your life. If you are already moderately active, begin a formal exercise program that includes cardiorespiratory endurance exercise, flexibility training, and strength training to help you develop all the health-related components of fitness.

Table 2.2 ACSM Exercise Recommendations for Fitness Development in Healthy Adults

Exercise to Develop and Maintain Cardiorespiratory Endurance and Body Composition	
Frequency of training	3–5 days per week.
Intensity of training	55/65–90% of maximum heart rate or 40/50–85% of heart rate reserve or maximum oxygen uptake reserve.* The lower intensity values (55–64% of maximum heart rate and 40–49% of heart rate reserve) are most applicable to individuals who are quite unfit. For average individuals, intensities of 70–85% of maximum heart rate or 60–80% of heart rate reserve are appropriate.
Time (duration) of training	20–60 total minutes of continuous or intermittent (in sessions lasting 10 or more minutes) aerobic activity. Duration is dependent on the intensity of activity; thus, low-intensity activity should be conducted over a longer period of time (30 minutes or more). Low-to-moderate-intensity activity of longer duration is recommended for nonathletic adults.
Type (mode) of activity	Any activity that uses large-muscle groups, can be maintained continuously, and is rhythmic and aerobic in nature—for example, walking-hiking, running-jogging, cycling-bicycling, cross-country skiing, aerobic dancing and other forms of group exercise, rope skipping, rowing, stair climbing, swimming, skating, and endurance game activities.
Exercise to Develop and Maintain Muscular Strength and Endurance, Flexibility, and Body Composition	
Resistance training	One set of 8–10 exercises that condition the major muscle groups, performed at least 2 days per week. Most people should complete 8–12 repetitions of each exercise to the point of fatigue; practicing other repetition ranges (for example, 3–5 or 12–15) also builds strength and endurance; for older and frailer people (approximately 50–60 and older), 10–15 repetitions with a lighter weight may be more appropriate. Multiple-set regimens will provide greater benefits if time allows. Any mode of exercise that is comfortable throughout the full range of motion is appropriate (for example, free weights, bands, or machines).
Flexibility training	Static stretches, performed for the major muscle groups at least 2–3 days per week, ideally 5–7 days per week. Stretch to the point of tightness, holding each stretch for 15–30 seconds; perform 2–4 repetitions of each stretch.

*Instructions for calculating target heart rate intensity for cardiorespiratory endurance exercise are presented in Chapter 3.

SOURCE: Adapted from American College of Sports Medicine. 2006. *ACSM's Guidelines for Exercise Testing and Prescription*, 7th ed. Philadelphia: Lippincott Williams and Wilkins.

walking briskly, climbing stairs, doing yard work, and washing your car. You don't have to exercise vigorously, but you should experience a moderate increase in your heart and breathing rates. As described earlier, your activity time can be broken up into small blocks over the course of a day.

The next two levels of the pyramid illustrate parts of a formal exercise program. The principles of this program are consistent with those of the American College of Sports Medicine, the professional organization for people involved in sports medicine and exercise science. The ACSM has established guidelines for creating an exercise program that will develop physical fitness (Table 2.2). A balanced program includes activities to develop all the health-related components of fitness:

- *Cardiorespiratory endurance* is developed by continuous rhythmic movements of large-muscle groups in activities such as walking, jogging, cycling, swimming, and aerobic dance and other forms of group exercise. Choose activities that you enjoy and that are convenient. Other popular choices are in-line skating, dancing, and backpacking. Start-and-stop activities such as tennis, racquetball, and soccer can also develop endurance if your skill level is sufficient to enable periods of continuous play. Training for cardiorespiratory endurance is discussed in Chapter 3.
- *Muscular strength and endurance* can be developed through resistance training—training with weights or performing calisthenic exercises such as push-ups and curl-ups. Training for muscular strength and endurance is discussed in Chapter 4.
- *Flexibility* is developed by stretching the major muscle groups regularly and with proper technique. Flexibility is discussed in Chapter 5.
- *Healthy body composition* can be developed through a sensible diet and a program of regular exercise. Endurance exercise is best for reducing body fat; resistance training builds muscle mass, which, to a small extent, helps increase metabolism. Body composition is discussed in Chapter 6.

Chapter 7 contains guidelines to help you choose activities and put together a complete exercise program that will suit your goals and preferences. (Refer to Figure 2.4 for a summary of the health and fitness benefits of different levels of physical activity.)

What about the tip of the activity pyramid? Although sedentary activities are often unavoidable—attending class, studying, working in an office, and so on—many

	Lifestyle physical activity	Moderate exercise program	Vigorous exercise program
Description	Moderate physical activity—an amount of activity that uses about 150 calories per day	Cardiorespiratory endurance exercise (20–60 minutes, 3–5 days per week); strength training (at least 2 days per week) and stretching exercises (2 or more days per week)	Cardiorespiratory endurance exercise (20–60 minutes, 3–5 days per week); interval training; strength training (3–4 nonconsecutive days per week); and stretching exercises (5–7 days per week)
Sample activities or program	*One of the following:* • Walking to and from work, 15 minutes each way • Cycling to and from class, 10 minutes each way • Doing yard work for 30 minutes • Dancing (fast) for 30 minutes • Playing basketball for 20 minutes	• Jogging for 30 minutes, 3 days per week • Weight training, 1 set of 8 exercises, 2 days per week • Stretching exercises, 3 days per week	• Running for 45 minutes, 3 days per week • Intervals: running 400 m at high effort, 4 sets, 2 days per week • Weight training, 3 sets of 10 exercises, 3 days per week • Stretching exercises, 6 days per week
Health and fitness benefits	Better blood cholesterol levels, reduced body fat, better control of blood pressure, improved metabolic health, and enhanced glucose metabolism; improved quality of life; reduced risk of some chronic diseases Greater amounts of activity can help prevent weight gain and promote weight loss	All the benefits of lifestyle physical activity, plus improved physical fitness (increased cardiorespiratory endurance, muscular strength and endurance, and flexibility) and even greater improvements in health and quality of life and reductions in chronic disease risk	All the benefits of lifestyle physical activity and a moderate exercise program, with greater increases in fitness and somewhat greater reductions in chronic disease risk Participating in a vigorous exercise program may increase risk of injury and overtraining

FIGURE 2.4 Health and fitness benefits of different amounts of physical activity and exercise.

people choose inactivity over activity during their leisure time. Change sedentary patterns by becoming more active whenever you can. Move more and sit less.

> **MOTIVATION BOOSTER**
>
> ***Locate resources.*** Your school and community may present challenges to making healthy lifestyle choices, but they also have resources that can help you. Find out what local resources are available and will support your efforts at change. For example, go to your school's physical education office and ask for a comprehensive listing of all the exercise and fitness facilities and courses available on your campus. Obtain the same information about facilities and classes in your neighborhood, including those offered by the city or county recreation department. What fitness facilities and/or courses fit your goals, schedule, preferences, and budget? If you can't find a local program or facility to fit your needs, check out the programs available through the President's Challenge (http://www.presidentschallenge.org).

Guidelines for Training

The following guidelines will make your exercise program more effective and successful.

Train the Way You Want Your Body to Change Stress your body so it adapts in the desired manner. To have a more muscular build, lift weights. To be more flexible, do stretching exercises. To improve performance in a particular sport, practice that sport or its movements.

Train Regularly Consistency is the key to improving fitness. Fitness improvements are lost if too much time passes between exercise sessions.

Start Slowly, and Get in Shape Gradually As Figure 2.5 (p. 42) shows, an exercise program can be divided into three phases:

- ***Beginning phase.*** The body adjusts to the new type and level of activity.
- ***Progress phase.*** Fitness increases.
- ***Maintenance phase.*** The targeted level of fitness is sustained over the long term.

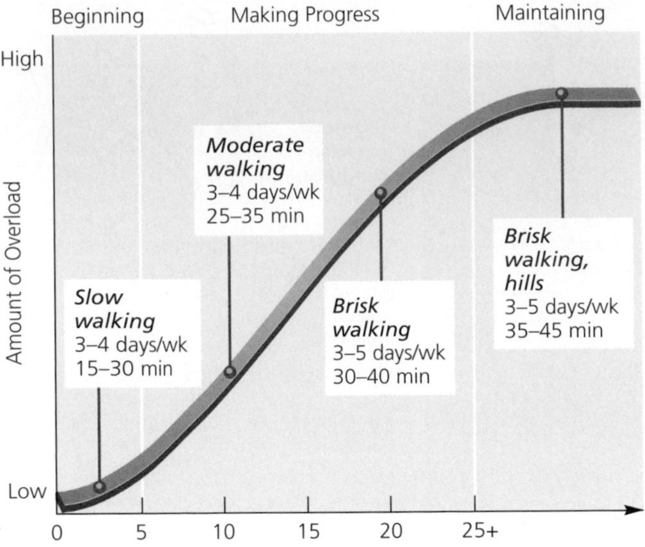

FIGURE 2.5 Progression of an exercise program. This figure shows how the amount of overload is increased gradually over time in a sample walking program. Regardless of the activity chosen, it is important that an exercise program begin slowly and progress gradually. Once you achieve the desired level of fitness, you can maintain it by exercising 3–5 days a week.

SOURCE: Progression data from American College of Sports Medicine. 2006. *ACSM's Guidelines for Exercise Testing and Prescription,* 7th ed. Philadelphia: Lippincott Williams and Wilkins.

When beginning a program, start slowly to give your body time to adapt to the stress of exercise. Choose activities carefully according to your fitness status; if you have been sedentary or are overweight, try an activity such as walking or swimming that won't jar the body or strain the joints.

As you progress, increase duration and frequency before increasing intensity. If you train too much or too intensely, you are more likely to suffer injuries or become **overtrained**, a condition characterized by lack of energy, aching muscles and joints, and decreased physical performance. Injuries and overtraining slow down an exercise program and impede motivation. The goal is not to get in shape as quickly as possible but to gradually become and then remain physically fit.

Warm Up Before Exercise Warming up can decrease your chances of injury by helping your body gradually progress from rest to activity. A good warm-up can increase muscle temperature, reduce joint stiffness, bathe the joint surfaces in lubricating fluid, and increase blood flow to the muscles, including the heart. Some studies suggest that warming up may also enhance muscle metabolism and mentally prepare you for a workout.

A warm-up should include low-intensity, whole-body movements similar to those used in the activity that will follow. For example, runners may walk and jog slowly prior to running at full speed. A tennis player might hit forehands and backhands at a low intensity before playing a vigorous set of tennis. It is important to note that a warm-up is not the same thing as a stretching workout. For safety and effectiveness, it is best to stretch *after* an endurance or strength training workout, when muscles are warm—and not as part of a warm-up. (Appropriate and effective warm-ups are discussed in greater detail in Chapters 3–5.)

Cool Down After Exercise During exercise, as much as 90% of circulating blood is directed to the muscles and skin, up from as little as 20% during rest. If you suddenly stop moving after exercise, the amount of blood returning to your heart and brain may be insufficient, and you may experience dizziness, a drop in blood pressure, or other problems. Cooling down at the end of a workout helps safely restore circulation to its normal resting condition. So don't sit or lie down or jump into the shower after exercise without cooling down first. Cool down by continuing to move at a slow pace—walking, for example—for 5–10 minutes, as your heart and breathing rate slowly return to normal. At the end of the cool-down period, do stretching exercises while your muscles are still warm. Cool down longer after intense exercise sessions.

Exercise Safely Physical activity can cause injury or even death if you don't consider safety. For example, you should always:

- Wear a helmet when biking, skiing, or rock climbing.
- Wear eye protection when playing racquetball or squash.
- Wear bright clothing when exercising on a public street.
- Walk or run with a partner in a park or on a deserted track.
- Give vehicles plenty of leeway, even when you have the right of way.

Train within your capacity because overloading your muscles and joints can lead to serious injury. Use high-quality equipment and keep it in good repair. Report broken gym equipment to the health club manager. (See Appendix A for more information on personal safety.)

Listen to Your Body and Get Adequate Rest Rest can be as important as exercise for improving fitness. Fitness reflects an adaptation to the stress of exercise. Building fitness involves a series of exercise stresses, recuperation, and adaptation leading to improved fitness, followed by further stresses. Build rest into your training

WEB TERMS

overtraining A condition caused by training too much or too intensely, characterized by lack of energy, decreased physical performance, fatigue, depression, aching muscles and joints, and susceptibility to injury.

TAKE CHARGE

Vary Your Activities

Do you have a hard time thinking of new activities to try? Check the boxes next to the activities listed here that interest you. Then look for resources and facilities on your campus or in your community.

Outdoor Exercises

- ☐ Walking
- ☐ Running
- ☐ Cycling
- ☐ Swimming
- ☐ Inline skating
- ☐ Skateboarding
- ☐ Rowing
- ☐ Horseback riding
- ☐ Hiking
- ☐ Backpacking
- ☐ Ice skating
- ☐ Fly fishing

Exercises You Can Do at Home and Work

- ☐ Desk exercises
- ☐ Calisthenics
- ☐ Gardening
- ☐ Housework
- ☐ Yard work
- ☐ Sweeping the walkway
- ☐ Exploring on foot
- ☐ Entering a walk-a-thon
- ☐ Painting the walls
- ☐ Walking the dog
- ☐ Shopping
- ☐ Running errands

Sports and Games

- ☐ Basketball
- ☐ Tennis
- ☐ Volleyball
- ☐ Golf
- ☐ Soccer
- ☐ Softball
- ☐ Water skiing
- ☐ Windsurfing
- ☐ Badminton
- ☐ Ultimate Frisbee
- ☐ Bowling
- ☐ Surfing
- ☐ Dancing
- ☐ Snow skiing
- ☐ Gymnastics

Health Club Exercises

- ☐ Weight training
- ☐ Circuit training
- ☐ Group exercise
- ☐ Treadmill
- ☐ Stationary bike
- ☐ Ski machine
- ☐ Supine bike
- ☐ Rowing machine
- ☐ Plyometrics
- ☐ Water aerobics
- ☐ Elliptical trainer
- ☐ Medicine ball
- ☐ Rope skipping
- ☐ Punching bag
- ☐ Racquetball

program, and don't exercise if it doesn't feel right. Sometimes you need a few days of rest to recover enough to train with the intensity required for improving fitness. Getting enough sleep is an important part of the recovery process. On the other hand, you can't train sporadically, either. If you listen to your body and it always tells you to rest, you won't make any progress.

Cycle the Volume and Intensity of Your Workouts To add enjoyment and variety to your program, and to further improve fitness, don't train at the same intensity during every workout. Train intensely on some days and train lightly on others. Proper management of the level of workout intensity is a key to improved physical fitness. Use cycle training, also known as periodization, to provide enough recovery for intense training: Because you trained lightly one workout, you can train harder the next. However, take care to increase the volume and intensity of your program gradually—never more than 10% per week.

Vary Your Activities Change your exercise program from time to time to keep things fresh and help develop a higher degree of fitness. The body adapts quickly to an exercise stress, such as walking, cycling, or swimming. Gains in fitness in a particular activity become more difficult with time. Varying the kinds of exercises in your program allows you to adapt to many types of exercise and develops fitness in a variety of activities. (see the box "Vary Your Activities"). Changing activities may also help reduce your risk of injury.

Try varying the type of training you do during different times of the year. During the summer, you might emphasize conditioning by jogging, playing basketball, and doing high-volume strength training exercises. During the fall, you might emphasize resistance training using more weights and fewer repetitions, gradually introducing more cardiovascular exercise into your program. In the spring, you might try a variety of activities, continue weight training, and get in great shape for the summer.

Train with a Partner Training partners can motivate and encourage each other through rough spots and help each other develop proper exercise techniques. Training with a partner can make exercising seem easier and more fun. It can also help you keep motivated and on track. For example, you may find it easy to hit the snooze button and skip a planned solo 20-minute morning walk. But would you stay in bed if you knew a friend was waiting for you? A commitment to a friend is a powerful motivator.

Train Your Mind Becoming fit requires commitment, discipline, and patience. These qualities come from understanding the importance of exercise and having clear and reachable goals. Use the lifestyle management techniques discussed in Chapter 1 to keep your program on track.

Fuel Your Activity Appropriately Good nutrition, including rehydration and resynthesis of liver and muscle carbohydrate stores, is part of optimal recuperation from exercise. Consume enough calories to support your exercise program without gaining body fat. Many studies show that consuming carbohydrates and protein before or after exercise promotes restoration of stored fuels so that you can exercise intensely again shortly. Nutrition for exercise is discussed in greater detail in Chapters 3 and 8.

Have Fun You are more likely to stick with an exercise program if it's fun. Choose a variety of activities that you enjoy. Some people like to play competitive sports, such as tennis, golf, or volleyball. Competition can boost motivation, but remember: Sports are competitive, whereas

QUESTIONS FOR CRITICAL THINKING AND REFLECTION

What kind of physical activity or exercise program would be most appropriate for you at this point in your life? If you were to start planning a program, what would be your three most important long-term goals? What would you set as short-term goals? What rewards would be meaningful to you?

training for fitness is not. Other people like more solitary activities, such as jogging, walking, or swimming. Still others like high-skill individual sports, such as skiing, surfing, or skateboarding. Many activities can help you get fit, so choose the ones you enjoy. You can also boost your enjoyment and build your social support network by exercising with friends and family.

Track Your Progress Monitoring the progress of your program can help keep you motivated and on track. Depending on the activities you've included in your program, you may track different measures of your program—minutes of jogging, miles of cycling, laps of swimming, number of push-ups, amount of weight lifted, and so on. If your program is focused on increasing daily physical activity, consider using an inexpensive pedometer to monitor the number of steps you take each day (see Lab 2.3 for more information on setting goals and monitoring activity with a pedometer). Specific examples of program monitoring can be found in the labs for Chapters 3–5 and in the Daily Fitness and Nutrition Journal.

Keep Your Exercise Program in Perspective As important as physical fitness is, it is only part of a well-rounded life. You have to have time for work and school, family and friends, relaxation and hobbies. Some people become overinvolved in exercise and neglect other parts of their lives. They think of themselves as runners, dancers, swimmers, or triathletes rather than as people who participate in those activities. Balance and moderation are the key ingredients of a fit and well life.

TIPS FOR TODAY AND THE FUTURE

Physical activity and exercise offer benefits in nearly every area of wellness. Even a low-to-moderate level of activity provides valuable health benefits. The important thing is to get moving!

RIGHT NOW YOU CAN

- Go outside and take a brisk 15-minute walk.
- Look at your calendar for the rest of the week and write in some physical activity—such as walking, running, biking, skating, swimming, hiking, or playing Frisbee—on as many days as you can. Schedule the activity for a specific time and stick to it.
- Call a friend and invite her or him to start planning a regular exercise program with you.

IN THE FUTURE YOU CAN

- Schedule a session with a qualified personal trainer who can evaluate your current fitness level and help you set personalized fitness goals.
- Create seasonal workout programs for the summer, spring, fall, and winter. Develop programs that are varied but consistent with your overall fitness goals.

SUMMARY

- Moderate daily exercise contributes substantially to good health. Even without a formal, vigorous exercise program, you can get many of the same health benefits by becoming more physically active.
- If you are already active, you benefit even more by increasing the intensity or duration of your activities.
- The five components of physical fitness most important for health are cardiorespiratory endurance, muscular strength, muscular endurance, flexibility, and body composition.
- Physical training is the process of producing long-term improvements in the body's functioning through exercise. All training is based on the fact that the body adapts to physical stress.
- According to the principle of specificity, bodies change specifically in response to the type of training received.
- Bodies also adapt to progressive overload. When you progressively increase the frequency, intensity, and time (duration) of the right type of exercise, you become increasingly fit.
- Bodies adjust to lower levels of activity by losing fitness, a principle known as reversibility. To counter the effects of reversibility, it's important to keep training at the same intensity, even if you have to reduce the number or length of sessions.
- According to the principle of individual differences, people vary in the maximum level of fitness they can achieve.
- When designing an exercise program, determine if medical clearance is needed, assess your current level of fitness, set realistic goals, and choose activities that develop all the components of fitness.
- Train regularly, get in shape gradually, warm up and cool down, maintain a structured but flexible program, exercise safely, consider training with a partner, train your mind, have fun, and keep exercise in perspective.

Q Where can I work out?

A Identify accessible and pleasant places to work out. For running, find a field or park with a soft surface. For swimming, find a pool that's open at times convenient for you. For cycling, find an area with minimal traffic and air pollution. Make sure the location is safe and convenient. If you join a health club or fitness center, follow the guidelines in the box "Choosing a Fitness Center," on p. 46.

Q What should my fitness goals be?

A Begin by thinking about your general overall goals—the benefits you want to obtain by increasing your activity level and/or beginning a formal exercise program. Examples of long-term goals include reducing your risk of chronic diseases, increasing your energy level, and maintaining a healthy body weight.

To help shape your fitness program, you need to also set specific, short-term goals based on measurable factors. These specific goals should be an extension of your overall goals—the specific changes to your current activity and exercise habits needed to achieve your general goals. In setting short-term goals, be sure to use the SMART criteria described in Chapter 1 (p. 16–17). As noted there, your goals should be **S**pecific, **M**easurable, **A**ttainable, **R**ealistic, and **T**ime frame–specific (SMART).

You need information about your current levels of physical activity and physical fitness in order to set appropriate goals. The labs in this chapter will help you determine your physical activity level—for example, how many minutes per day you engage in moderate or vigorous activity or how many daily steps you take. Using this information, you can set goals for lifestyle physical activity to help you meet your overall goals. For example, if your general long-term goals are to reduce the risk of chronic disease and prevent weight gain, the Dietary Guidelines recommend 60 minutes of moderate physical activity daily. If you currently engage in 30 minutes of moderate activity daily, then your behavior change goal would be to add 30 additional minutes of daily physical activity (or an equivalent number of additional daily steps—about 3500–4000); your time frame for the change might be 8–12 weeks.

Labs in Chapters 3–6 provide opportunities to specifically assess your fitness status for all the health-related components of fitness. The results of these assessments can guide you in setting specific fitness goals. For instance, if the labs in Chapter 4 indicate that you have good muscular strength and endurance in your lower body but poor strength and endurance in your upper body, then setting a specific goal for improving upper-body muscle fitness would be an appropriate goal—increasing the number of push-ups you can do from 22 to 30, for example. Chapters 3–6 include additional advice for setting appropriate goals.

Once you start your behavior change program, you may discover that your goals aren't quite appropriate—perhaps you were overly optimistic, or maybe you set the bar too low. There are limits to the amount of fitness you can achieve, but within the limits of your genes and health status, you can make significant improvements in fitness. Adjust your goals as needed.

Q How can I fit a workout into my day?

A Good time management is an important skill in creating and maintaining an exercise program. Choose a regular time to exercise, preferably the same time every day. Don't tell yourself you'll exercise "sometime during the day" when you have free time—that free time may never come. Schedule your workout, and make it a priority. Include alternative plans in your program to account for circumstances like bad weather or vacations. (You'll have the chance to develop strategies for successful time management in the Behavior Change Workbook at the end of the text.)

Q Where can I get help and advice about exercise?

A One of the best places to get help is an exercise class. There, expert instructors can help you learn the basics of training and answer your questions. Make sure the instructor is certified by a recognized professional organization and/or has formal training in exercise physiology. Read articles by credible experts in fitness magazines. Many of these magazines include articles by leading experts in exercise science written at a layperson's level.

A qualified personal trainer can also help you get started in an exercise program or a new form of training. Make sure this person has proper qualifications, such as a college degree in exercise physiology or physical education or ACSM, National Strength and Conditioning Association (NSCA), or American Council on Exercise (ACE) certification. Don't seek out a person for advice simply because he or she looks fit. UCLA researchers found that 60% of the personal trainers in their study couldn't pass a basic exam on training methods, exercise physiology, or biomechanics. Trainers who performed best had college degrees in exercise physiology, physical education, or physical therapy. So choose your trainer carefully and don't get caught up with fads.

Q Should I follow my exercise program if I'm sick?

A If you have a mild head cold or feel one coming on, it is probably OK to exercise moderately. Just begin slowly and see how you feel. However, if you have symptoms of a more serious illness—fever, swollen glands, nausea, extreme tiredness, muscle aches—wait until you have fully recovered before resuming your exercise program. Continuing to exercise while suffering from an illness more serious than a cold can compromise your recovery and may even be dangerous.

For more Common Questions Answered about fitness, visit the Online Learning Center.

CRITICAL CONSUMER

Choosing a Fitness Center

Fitness centers can provide you with many benefits—motivation and companionship are among the most important. A fitness center may also offer expert instruction and supervision as well as access to better equipment than you could afford on your own. There are an estimated 17,000 health clubs in the United States, serving more than 30 million members. All fitness centers, however, are not of the same overall quality. Many health facilities cater to people with very specific exercise or fitness goals. In other words, every fitness center is not for every person. If you're thinking of joining a fitness center, here are some guidelines to help you choose a club that's right for you.

Convenience

- Look for an established facility that's within 10–15 minutes of your home or work. If it's farther away, your chances of sticking to an exercise regimen start to diminish.
- Check out the facility's hours, then visit it at the time you would normally exercise. Is there adequate parking? Will you have easy access to the equipment and exercise classes you want at that time?
- If needed, ask about child-care or youth programs. What services are available, and how are they supervised?

Atmosphere

- Look around to see if there are other members who are your age and at about your fitness level. Some clubs cater to a certain age group or lifestyle, such as hard-core bodybuilders.
- If you like to exercise to music, make sure you like the music played there, both its type and volume.
- Observe how the members dress. Will you fit in, or will you be uncomfortable?
- Observe the staff. Are they easy to identify? Are they friendly and helpful?
- Check to see that the facility is clean, including showers and lockers. Make sure the facility is climate controlled, well ventilated, and well lit.

Safety

- Find out if the facility offers some type of preactivity screening as well as basic fitness testing that includes cardiovascular screening.
- Determine if personnel are trained in CPR and if there is emergency equipment such as automated external defibrillators (AEDs) on the premises. An AED can help someone with cardiac arrest.
- Ask if at least one staff member on each shift is trained in first aid.
- Find out if the club has an emergency plan in case a member has a heart attack or serious injury (many clubs do not). The facility should also have an evacuation plan, as well as established procedures for responding to other types of emergencies. All personnel should be trained in carrying out these plans.

Trained Personnel

- Determine if the personal trainers and fitness instructors are certified by a recognized professional association such as the American College of Sports Medicine (ACSM), Aerobics and Fitness Association of America (AFAA), National Strength and Conditioning Association (NSCA), or American Council on Exercise (ACE). All personal trainers are not equal; more than 100 organizations certify trainers, and few of these require much formal training. Trainers with college degrees in exercise physiology or physical education are usually the most knowledgeable.
- Find out if the club has a trained exercise physiologist on staff, such as someone with a degree in exercise physiology, kinesiology, or exercise science. If the facility offers nutritional counseling, it should employ someone who is a registered dietitian (RD) or has similar formal training.
- Ask how much experience the instructors have. Clubs may employ people because they were good athletes or look fit; by themselves, these are not good reasons to hire someone. Ideally, trainers should have both academic preparation and practical experience.

Cost

- Buy only what you need and can afford. If you want to use only workout equipment, you may not need a club that has racquetball courts and saunas.
- Check the contract. Choose the one that covers the shortest period of time possible, especially if it's your first fitness club experience. Don't feel pressured to sign a long-term contract.
- Make sure the contract permits you to extend your membership if you have a prolonged illness or go on vacation.
- Try out the club. Ask for a free trial workout, or a 1-day pass, or an inexpensive 1- or 2-week trial membership.
- Find out whether there is an extra charge for the particular services you want. Get any special offers in writing.

Effectiveness

- Tour the facility. Does it offer what the brochure says it does? Does it offer the activities and equipment you want?
- Check the equipment. A good club will have treadmills, bikes, stair-climbers, resistance machines, and weights. Make sure these machines are up-to-date and well maintained.
- Find out if new members get a formal orientation and instruction on how to safely use the equipment. Will a staff member help you develop a program that is appropriate for your current fitness level and goals?
- Make sure the facility is certified. Look for the displayed names American College of Sports Medicine (ACSM), American Council on Exercise (ACE), Aerobics and Fitness Association of America (AFAA), or International Health, Racquet, and Sportsclub Association (IHRSA).
- Don't get cheated. Check with your Better Business Bureau or Consumer Affairs office to see if others have complained about the facility.

FOR FURTHER EXPLORATION

BOOKS

American College of Sports Medicine. 2003. *ACSM Fitness Book,* 3rd ed. Champaign, Ill.: Human Kinetics. *Provides a step-by-step approach to becoming more active and developing a fitness program.*

American College of Sports Medicine. 2006. *ACSM's Guidelines for Exercise Testing and Prescription,* 7th ed. Philadelphia: Lippincott Williams and Wilkins. *Includes the ACSM guidelines for safety of exercising, a basic discussion of exercise physiology, and information about fitness testing and prescription.*

Earle, R. W., and T. R. Baechle, eds. 2004. *NSCA's Essentials of Personal Training.* Champaign, Ill.: Human Kinetics. *Comprehensive discussions of fitness testing, exercise and disease, nutrition and physical performance, and exercise prescription.*

Mayo Clinic. 2005. *Mayo Clinic Fitness for Everybody.* Rochester, Minn.: Mayo Clinic. *An illustrated guide to designing and maintaining a personalized fitness program, with hundreds of fully illustrated exercises.*

JOURNALS

ACSM Health and Fitness Journal (401 West Michigan Street, Indianapolis, IN 46202; http://www.acsm-healthfitness.org)

Physician and Sportsmedicine (4530 W. 77th Street, Minneapolis, MN 55435; many of the journal's articles are also available online at http://ww.postgradmed.com/journal.htm)

ORGANIZATIONS, HOTLINES, AND WEB SITES

American Alliance for Health, Physical Education, Recreation, and Dance (AAHPERD). A professional organization dedicated to promoting quality health and physical education programs.
800-213-7193
http://www.aahperd.org

American College of Sports Medicine (ACSM). The principal professional organization for sports medicine and exercise science. Provides brochures, publications, and audio- and videotapes.
317-637-9200
http://www.acsm.org

American Council on Exercise (ACE). Promotes exercise and fitness; the Web site features fact sheets on many consumer topics, including choosing shoes, cross-training, and steroids.
888-825-3636
http://www.acefitness.org

American Heart Association: Start! Provides practical advice for people of all fitness levels plus an online fitness diary.
http://www.heart.org/presenter.jhtml?identifier=3040778

CDC Physical Activity Information. Provides information on the benefits of physical activity and suggestions for incorporating moderate physical activity into daily life.
http://www.cdc.gov/nccdphp/dnpa/

Disabled Sports USA. Provides sports and recreation services to people with physical or mobility disorders.
http://www.dsusa.org

Health Canada's Physical Activity Guide. Offers many suggestions for incorporating physical activity into everyday life.
http://www.hc-sc.gc.ca/hl-vs/physactiv/index_e.html

International Health, Racquet, and Sportsclub Association (IHRSA): Health Clubs. Provides guidelines for choosing a health or fitness facility and links to clubs that belong to IHRSA.
http://www.healthclubs.com

MedlinePlus: Exercise and Physical Fitness. Provides links to news and reliable information about fitness and exercise from government agencies and professional associations.
http://www.nlm.nih.gov/medlineplus/exercisephysicalfitness.html

President's Council on Physical Fitness and Sports (PCPFS). Provides information on PCPFS programs and publications, including fitness guides and fact sheets.
http://www.fitness.gov
http://www.presidentschallenge.org

Shape Up America! A nonprofit organization that provides information and resources on exercise, nutrition, and weight loss.
http://www.shapeup.org

SmallStep.Gov. Provides resources for increasing activity and improving diet through small changes in daily habits.
http://www.smallstep.gov

The following provide links to sites with information on a wide variety of activities and fitness issues; evaluate commercial sites carefully.

Fitness Jumpsite: http://www.primusweb.com/fitnesspartner
NetSweat: The Internet's Fitness Resource: http://www.netsweat.com
Yahoo!Fitness: http://dir.yahoo.com/Health/Fitness

SELECTED BIBLIOGRAPHY

American College of Sports Medicine. 2007. *ACSM's Health/Fitness Facility Standards and Guidelines,* 3rd ed. Champaign, Ill.: Human Kinetics.

American College of Sports Medicine. 2006. *ACSM's Guidelines for Exercise Testing and Prescription.* Philadelphia: Lippincott Williams and Wilkins.

American College of Sports Medicine. 2006. *ACSM's Resource Manual for Guidelines for Exercise Testing and Prescription,* 5th ed. Philadelphia: Lippincott Williams and Wilkins.

American College of Sports Medicine. 1998. The recommended quantity and quality of exercise for developing and maintaining cardiorespiratory and muscular fitness, and flexibility in healthy adults. ACSM position paper. *Medicine and Science in Sports and Exercise* 30(6): 975–991.

American College of Obstetrics and Gynecology Committee on Obstetric Practice. 2002. Exercise during pregnancy and the postpartum period. Committee Opinion No. 267. *International Journal of Gynaecology and Obstetrics* 77:79–81.

American Heart Association. 2007. Resistance exercise in individuals with and without cardiovascular disease, 2007 update: A scientific statement from the American Heart Association Council on Clinical Cardiology and Council on Nutrition, Physical Activity, and Metabolism. *Circulation* 116: 572–584.

Bouchard, C., et al. 2007. *Physical Activity and Health.* Champaign, Ill.: Human Kinetics.

Centers for Disease Control and Prevention. 2005. Trends in leisure-time physical inactivity by age, sex, and race/ethnicity—United States, 1994–2004. *Morbidity and Mortality Weekly Report* 54(39): 991–994.

Centers for Disease Control and Prevention. 2007. Prevalence of regular physical activity among adults-United States, 2001 and 2005. *Morbidity and Mortality Weekly Report* 56(46): 12-9-1212

Colcombe, S. J., et al. 2006. Aerobic exercise training increases brain volume in aging humans. *The Journals of Gerontology: Series A, Biological Sciences and Medical Sciences* 61(11): 1166–1170.

Department of Health and Human Services. 1996. *Physical Activity and Health: A Report of the Surgeon General*. Atlanta: DHHS.

Dong, L., G. Block, and S. Mandel. 2004. Activities contributing to total energy expenditure in the United States: Results from the NHAPS Study. *International Journal of Behavioral Nutrition and Physical Activity* 1(4).

Ekelund, U., et al. 2007. Physical activity and metabolic risk in individuals with a family history of type 2 diabetes. *Diabetes Care* 30(2): 337–342.

Exercise for health: How much exercise is enough? ACSM works with others to avoid misunderstanding. 2003. *ACSM Fit Society Page*, Winter.

Garman, J. F., et al. 2004. Occurrence of exercise dependence in a college-aged population. *Journal of American College Health* 52(5): 221–228.

Greaney, M. L., et al. 2004. What older adults find useful for maintaining healthy eating and exercise habits. *Journal of Nutrition for the Elderly* 24: 19–35.

Haskell, W. L., et al. 2007. Physical activity and public health: Updated recommendation for adults from the American College of Sports Medicine and the American Heart Association. *Medicine & Science in Sports & Exercise* 39: 1423–1434.

Haskell, W. L., et al. 2007. Physical activity and public health in older adults: Recommendation from the American College of Sports Medicine and the American Heart Association. *Medicine & Science in Sports & Exercise* 39: 1435–1445.

Hu, F. B. 2003. Sedentary lifestyle and risk of obesity and type 2 diabetes. *Lipids* 38(2): 103–108.

Institutes of Medicine, National Academies. 2002. *Dietary Reference Intakes for Energy, Carbohydrate, Fiber, Fat, Fatty Acids, Cholesterol, Protein, and Amino Acids*. Washington, D.C.: National Academy Press.

Is easy-does-it exercise enough? 2004. *Consumer Reports on Health*, February.

Jonker, J. T., et al. 2006. Physical activity and life expectancy with and without diabetes. *Diabetes Care* 29: 38–43.

Kushi, L. H., et al. 2006. American Cancer Society guidelines on nutrition and physical activity for cancer prevention: Reducing the risk of cancer with healthy food choices and physical activity. *CA: A Cancer Journal for Clinicians* 56: 254–281.

Kruger, J., et al. 2005. Physical activity profiles of U.S. adults trying to lose weight: NHIS 1998. *Medicine and Science in Sports and Exercise* 37: 364–368.

Le Masurier, G. 2005. Walkee talkee: Answers to pedometer FAQs. *ACSM Fit Society Page*, Spring.

Lucas, J. W., J. S. Schiller, and V. Benson. 2004. Summary health statistics for U.S. adults: National Health Interview Survey, 2001. *Vital Health Statistics* 10: 1–134.

Lustyk, M. K., et al. 2004. Physical activity and quality of life: Assessing the influence of activity frequency, intensity, volume, and motives. *Behavioral Medicine* 30: 124–131.

Macfarlane, D. J., et al. 2006. Very short intermittent versus continuous bouts of activity in sedentary adults. *Preventive Medicine* 43(4): 332–336.

Malek, M. H., et al. 2002. Importance of health science education for personal fitness trainers. *Journal of Strength and Conditioning Research* 16: 19–24.

Marks, B. L., et al. Role of aerobic fitness and aging on cerebral white matter integrity. *Annals of the New York Academy of Sciences* 1097: 171–174.

Pate, R. R., et al. 1995. Physical activity and public health: A recommendation from the Centers for Disease Control and Prevention and the American College of Sports Medicine. *Journal of the American Medical Association* 273: 402–407.

President's Council on Physical Fitness and Sports. 2000. Definitions: Health, fitness, and physical activity. *Research Digest* 3(9).

Rosenbloom, C., and M. Bahns. 2006. What can we learn about diet and physical activity from master athletes? *Holistic Nursing Practice* 20(4): 161–166.

Sorensen, J. B., et al. 2007. Exercise on prescription: Trial protocol and evaluation of outcomes. *BMC Health Services Research* 7: 36.

Swain, D. P. 2005. Moderate or vigorous intensity exercise: Which is better for improving aerobic fitness? *Preventive Cardiology* 8: 55–58.

Vanhees, L., et al. 2005. How to assess physical activity? How to assess physical fitness? *European Journal of Cardiovascular Prevention and Rehabilitation* 12: 102–114.

U.S. Department of Health and Human Services and U.S. Department of Agriculture. 2005. *Dietary Guidelines for Americans, 2005*, 6th ed. Washington, D.C.: U.S. Government Printing Office.

World Health Organization/FAO Expert Consultation. 2003. *Diet, Nutrition and the Prevention of Chronic Diseases*. WHO Technical Report Series 916. Geneva: World Health Organization.

Name ________________ Section ________________ Date ________________

LAB 2.1 Safety of Exercise Participation

Physical Activity Readiness Questionnaire - PAR-Q (revised 2002)

PAR-Q & YOU

(A Questionnaire for People Aged 15 to 69)

Regular physical activity is fun and healthy, and increasingly more people are starting to become more active every day. Being more active is very safe for most people. However, some people should check with their doctor before they start becoming much more physically active.

If you are planning to become much more physically active than you are now, start by answering the seven questions in the box below. If you are between the ages of 15 and 69, the PAR-Q will tell you if you should check with your doctor before you start. If you are over 69 years of age, and you are not used to being very active, check with your doctor.

Common sense is your best guide when you answer these questions. Please read the questions carefully and answer each one honestly: check YES or NO.

YES	NO	
☐	☐	**1. Has your doctor ever said that you have a heart condition and that you should only do physical activity recommended by a doctor?**
☐	☐	**2. Do you feel pain in your chest when you do physical activity?**
☐	☐	**3. In the past month, have you had chest pain when you were not doing physical activity?**
☐	☐	**4. Do you lose your balance because of dizziness or do you ever lose consciousness?**
☐	☐	**5. Do you have a bone or joint problem (for example, back, knee or hip) that could be made worse by a change in your physical activity?**
☐	☐	**6. Is your doctor currently prescribing drugs (for example, water pills) for your blood pressure or heart condition?**
☐	☐	**7. Do you know of any other reason why you should not do physical activity?**

If you answered

YES to one or more questions

Talk with your doctor by phone or in person BEFORE you start becoming much more physically active or BEFORE you have a fitness appraisal. Tell your doctor about the PAR-Q and which questions you answered YES.

- You may be able to do any activity you want — as long as you start slowly and build up gradually. Or, you may need to restrict your activities to those which are safe for you. Talk with your doctor about the kinds of activities you wish to participate in and follow his/her advice.
- Find out which community programs are safe and helpful for you.

NO to all questions

If you answered NO honestly to all PAR-Q questions, you can be reasonably sure that you can:

- start becoming much more physically active – begin slowly and build up gradually. This is the safest and easiest way to go.
- take part in a fitness appraisal – this is an excellent way to determine your basic fitness so that you can plan the best way for you to live actively. It is also highly recommended that you have your blood pressure evaluated. If your reading is over 144/94, talk with your doctor before you start becoming much more physically active.

DELAY BECOMING MUCH MORE ACTIVE:

- if you are not feeling well because of a temporary illness such as a cold or a fever – wait until you feel better; or
- if you are or may be pregnant – talk to your doctor before you start becoming more active.

PLEASE NOTE: If your health changes so that you then answer YES to any of the above questions, tell your fitness or health professional. Ask whether you should change your physical activity plan.

Informed Use of the PAR-Q: The Canadian Society for Exercise Physiology, Health Canada, and their agents assume no liability for persons who undertake physical activity, and if in doubt after completing this questionnaire, consult your doctor prior to physical activity.

No changes permitted. You are encouraged to photocopy the PAR-Q but only if you use the entire form.

NOTE: If the PAR-Q is being given to a person before he or she participates in a physical activity program or a fitness appraisal, this section may be used for legal or administrative purposes.

"I have read, understood and completed this questionnaire. Any questions I had were answered to my full satisfaction."

NAME ________________

SIGNATURE ________________ DATE ________________

SIGNATURE OF PARENT or GUARDIAN (for participants under the age of majority) ________________ WITNESS ________________

Note: This physical activity clearance is valid for a maximum of 12 months from the date it is completed and becomes invalid if your condition changes so that you would answer YES to any of the seven questions.

Supported by: 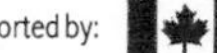  Health Canada Santé Canada

General Health Profile

To help further assess the safety of exercise for you, complete as much of this health profile as possible.

General Information

Age: __________ Total cholesterol: __________ Blood pressure: _____ /_____

Height: __________ HDL: __________ Triglycerides: __________

Weight: __________ LDL: __________ Blood glucose level: __________

Are you currently trying to _____ gain or _____ lose weight? (check one if appropriate)

Medical Conditions/Treatments

Check any of the following that apply to you, and add any other conditions that might affect your ability to exercise safely.

_____ heart disease

_____ lung disease

_____ diabetes

_____ allergies

_____ asthma

_____ depression, anxiety, or other psychological disorder

_____ eating disorder

_____ back pain

_____ arthritis

_____ other injury or joint problem: __________________

_____ substance abuse problem

_____ other: ______________________________

_____ other: ______________________________

_____ other: ______________________________

_____ Do you have a family history of cardiovascular disease (CVD) (a parent, sibling, or child who had a heart attack or stroke before age 55 for men or 65 for women)?

List any medications or supplements you are taking or any medical treatments you are undergoing. Include the name of the substance or treatment and its purpose. Include both prescription and over-the-counter drugs and supplements.

______________________________ ______________________________

______________________________ ______________________________

Lifestyle Information

Check any of the following that is true for you, and fill in the requested information.

_____ I usually eat high-fat foods (fatty meats, cheese, fried foods, butter, full-fat dairy products) every day.

_____ I consume fewer than 5 servings of fruits and vegetables on most days.

_____ I smoke cigarettes or use other tobacco products. If true, describe your use of tobacco (type and frequency): ______________________________

_____ I regularly drink alcohol. If true, describe your typical weekly consumption pattern: ______________________________

____

_____ I often feel as if I need more sleep. (I need about _____ hours per day; I get about _____ hours per day.)

_____ I feel as though stress has adversely affected my level of wellness during the past year.

Describe your current activity pattern. What types of moderate physical activity do you engage in on a daily basis? Are you involved in a formal exercise program, or do you regularly participate in sports or recreational activities?

____

____

Using Your Results

How did you score? Did the PAR-Q indicate that exercise is likely to be safe for you? Is there anything in your health profile that you think may affect your ability to exercise safely? Have you had any problems with exercise in the past?

What should you do next? If the assessments in this lab indicate that you should see your physician before beginning an exercise program, or if you have any questions about the safety of exercise for you, make an appointment to talk with your health care provider to address your concerns.

Name ______________________ Section ______________ Date ____________

LAB 2.2 Overcoming Barriers to Being Active

Barriers to Being Active Quiz

Directions: Listed below are reasons that people give to describe why they do not get as much physical activity as they think they should. Please read each statement and indicate how likely you are to say each of the following statements.

How likely are you to say this?	Very likely	Somewhat likely	Somewhat unlikely	Very unlikely
1. My day is so busy now, I just don't think I can make the time to include physical activity in my regular schedule.	3	2	1	0
2. None of my family members or friends like to do anything active, so I don't have a chance to exercise.	3	2	1	0
3. I'm just too tired after work to get any exercise.	3	2	1	0
4. I've been thinking about getting more exercise, but I just can't seem to get started.	3	2	1	0
5. I'm getting older so exercise can be risky.	3	2	1	0
6. I don't get enough exercise because I have never learned the skills for any sport.	3	2	1	0
7. I don't have access to jogging trails, swimming pools, bike paths, etc.	3	2	1	0
8. Physical activity takes too much time away from other commitments—like work, family, etc.	3	2	1	0
9. I'm embarrassed about how I will look when I exercise with others.	3	2	1	0
10. I don't get enough sleep as it is. I just couldn't get up early or stay up late to get some exercise.	3	2	1	0
11. It's easier for me to find excuses not to exercise than to go out and do something.	3	2	1	0
12. I know of too many people who have hurt themselves by overdoing it with exercise.	3	2	1	0
13. I really can't see learning a new sport at my age.	3	2	1	0
14. It's just too expensive. You have to take a class or join a club or buy the right equipment.	3	2	1	0
15. My free times during the day are too short to include exercise.	3	2	1	0
16. My usual social activities with family or friends do not include physical activity.	3	2	1	0
17. I'm too tired during the week and I need the weekend to catch up on my rest.	3	2	1	0

How likely are you to say this?	Very likely	Somewhat likely	Somewhat unlikely	Very unlikely
18. I want to get more exercise, but I just can't seem to make myself stick to anything.	3	2	1	0
19. I'm afraid I might injure myself or have a heart attack.	3	2	1	0
20. I'm not good enough at any physical activity to make it fun.	3	2	1	0
21. If we had exercise facilities and showers at work, then I would be more likely to exercise.	3	2	1	0

Scoring

- Enter the circled numbers in the spaces provided, putting the number for statement 1 on line 1, statement 2 on line 2, and so on.
- Add the three scores on each line. Your barriers to physical activity fall into one or more of seven categories: lack of time, social influence, lack of energy, lack of willpower, fear of injury, lack of skill, and lack of resources. A score of 5 or above in any category shows that this is an important barrier for you to overcome.

____ + ____ + ____ = ____________
1 8 15 Lack of time

____ + ____ + ____ = ____________
2 9 16 Social influence

____ + ____ + ____ = ____________
3 10 17 Lack of energy

____ + ____ + ____ = ____________
4 11 18 Lack of willpower

____ + ____ + ____ = ____________
5 12 19 Fear of injury

____ + ____ + ____ = ____________
6 13 20 Lack of skill

____ + ____ + ____ = ____________
7 14 21 Lack of resources

Using Your Results

How did you score? How many key barriers did you identify? Are they what you expected?

What should you do next? For your key barriers, try the strategies listed on the following pages and/or develop additional strategies that work for you. Check off any strategy that you try.

Suggestions for Overcoming Physical Activity Barriers

Lack of time

_____ Identify available time slots. Monitor your daily activities for 1 week. Identify at least three 30-minute time slots you could use for physical activity.

_____ Add physical activity to your daily routine. For example, walk or ride your bike to work or shopping, organize social activities around physical activity, walk the dog, exercise while you watch TV, park farther from your destination, etc.

_____ Make time for physical activity. For example, walk, jog, or swim during your lunch hour, or take fitness breaks instead of coffee breaks.

_____ Select activities requiring minimal time, such as walking, jogging, or stair climbing.

_____ Other: ____________________

Social influence

_____ Explain your interest in physical activity to friends and family. Ask them to support your efforts.

_____ Invite friends and family members to exercise with you. Plan social activities involving exercise.

_____ Develop new friendships with physically active people. Join a group, such as the YMCA or a hiking club.

_____ Other: ____________________

Lack of energy

_____ Schedule physical activity for times in the day or week when you feel energetic.

_____ Convince yourself that if you give it a chance, exercise will increase your energy level; then, try it.

_____ Other: ____________________

Lack of willpower

_____ Plan ahead. Make physical activity a regular part of your daily or weekly schedule and write it on your calendar.

_____ Invite a friend to exercise with you on a regular basis and write it on *both* your calendars.

_____ Join an exercise group or class.

_____ Other: ____________________

Fear of injury

_____ Learn how to warm up and cool down to prevent injury.

_____ Learn how to exercise appropriately considering your age, fitness level, skill level, and health status.

_____ Choose activities involving minimal risk.

_____ Other: ____________________

Lack of skill

_____ Select activities requiring no new skills, such as walking, jogging, or stair climbing.

_____ Exercise with friends who are at the same skill level as you are.

_____ Find a friend who is willing to teach you some new skills.

_____ Take a class to develop new skills.

_____ Other: ____________________

Lack of resources

_____ Select activities that require minimal facilities or equipment, such as walking, jogging, jumping rope, or calisthenics.

_____ Identify inexpensive, convenient resources available in your community (community education programs, park and recreation programs, worksite programs, etc.).

_____ Other: ____________________

Are any of the following additional barriers important for you? If so, try some of the strategies listed here or invent your own.

Weather conditions

_____ Develop a set of regular activities that are always available regardless of weather (indoor cycling, aerobic dance, indoor swimming, calisthenics, stair climbing, rope skipping, mall walking, dancing, gymnasium games, etc.).

_____ Look on outdoor activities that depend on weather conditions (cross-country skiing, outdoor swimming, outdoor tennis, etc.) as "bonuses"—extra activities possible when weather and circumstances permit.

_____ Other: ____________________

Travel

_____ Put a jump rope in your suitcase and jump rope.

_____ Walk the halls and climb the stairs in hotels.

_____ Stay in places with swimming pools or exercise facilities.

_____ Join the YMCA or YWCA (ask about reciprocal membership agreements).

_____ Visit the local shopping mall and walk for half an hour or more.

_____ Bring a small tape recorder and your favorite aerobic exercise tape.

_____ Other: ____________________

Family obligations

_____ Trade babysitting time with a friend, neighbor, or family member who also has small children.

_____ Exercise *with* the kids—go for a walk together, play tag or other running games, or get an aerobic dance or exercise tape for kids (there are several on the market) and exercise together. You can spend time together and still get your exercise.

_____ Hire a babysitter and look at the cost as a worthwhile investment in your physical and mental health.

_____ Jump rope, do calisthenics, ride a stationary bicycle, or use other home gymnasium equipment while the kids watch TV or when they are sleeping.

_____ Try to exercise when the kids are not around (e.g., during school hours or their nap time).

_____ Other: ____________________

Retirement years

_____ Look on your retirement as an opportunity to become more active instead of less. Spend more time gardening, walking the dog, and playing with your grandchildren. Children with short legs and grandparents with slower gaits are often great walking partners.

_____ Learn a new skill you've always been interested in, such as ballroom dancing, square dancing, or swimming.

_____ Now that you have the time, make regular physical activity a part of every day. Go for a walk every morning or every evening before dinner. Treat yourself to an exercycle and ride every day during a favorite TV show.

_____ Other: ____________________

SOURCE: CDC Division of Nutrition and Physical Activity. 1999. *Promoting Physical Activity: A Guide for Community Action.* Champaign, Ill.: Human Kinetics.

Name ______________________ Section ______________ Date ____________

LAB 2.3 Using a Pedometer to Track Physical Activity

How physically active are you? Would you be more motivated to increase daily physical activity if you had an easy way to monitor your level of activity? If so, consider wearing a pedometer to track the number of steps you take each day—a rough but easily obtainable reflection of daily physical activity.

Determine Your Baseline

Wear the pedometer for a week to obtain a baseline average daily number of steps.

	M	T	W	Th	F	Sa	Su	Average
Steps								

Set Goals

Set an appropriate goal for increasing steps. The goal of 10,000 steps per day is widely recommended, but your personal goal should reflect your baseline level of steps. For example, if your current daily steps are far below 10,000, a goal of walking 2000 additional steps each day might be appropriate. If you are already close to 10,000 steps per day, choose a higher goal. Also consider the physical activity goals in the 2005 Dietary Guidelines:

- To reduce the risk of chronic disease, aim to accumulate at least 30 minutes of moderate physical activity per day.
- To help manage body weight and prevent gradual, unhealthy weight gain, engage in 60 minutes of moderate-to-vigorous-intensity activity on most days of the week.
- To sustain weight loss, engage daily in at least 60–90 minutes of moderate-intensity physical activity.

To help gauge how close you are to meeting these time-based physical activity goals, you might walk for 10–15 minutes while wearing your pedometer to determine how many steps correspond with the time-based goals from the Dietary Guidelines.

Once you have set your overall goal, break it down into several steps. For example, if your goal is to increase daily steps by 2000, set mini-goals of increasing daily steps by 500, allowing 2 weeks to reach each mini-goal. Smaller goals are easier to achieve and can help keep you motivated and on track. Having several interim goals also gives you the opportunity to reward yourself more frequently. Note your goals below:

Mini-goal 1: ______________ Target date: ______________ Reward: ______________

Mini-goal 2: ______________ Target date: ______________ Reward: ______________

Mini-goal 3: ______________ Target date: ______________ Reward: ______________

Overall goal: ______________ Target date: ______________ Reward: ______________

Develop Strategies for Increasing Steps

What can you do to become more active? Your text includes a variety of suggestions, including walking when you do errands, getting off one stop from your destination on public transportation, parking an extra block or two away from your destination, and doing at least one chore every day that requires physical activity. If weather or neighborhood safety is an issue, look for alternative locations to walk. For example, find an indoor gym or shopping mall or even a long hallway. Check out locations that are near or on the way to your campus, workplace, or residence. If you think walking indoors will be dull, walk with friends or family members or wear headphones (if safe) and listen to music or books on tape.

Are there any days of the week for which your baseline steps are particularly low and/or it will be especially difficult because of your schedule to increase your number of steps? Be sure to develop specific strategies for difficult situations.

Below, list at least five strategies for increasing daily steps:

Track Your Progress

Based on the goals you set, fill in your goal portion of the progress chart with your target average daily steps for each week. Then wear your pedometer every day and note your total daily steps. Track your progress toward each mini-goal and your final goal. Every few weeks, stop and evaluate your progress. If needed, adjust your plan and develop additional strategies for increasing steps. In addition to the chart in this worksheet, you might also want to graph your daily steps to provide a visual reminder of how you are progressing toward your goals. Make as many copies of this chart as you need.

Week	Goal	M	Tu	W	Th	F	Sa	Su	Average
1									
2									
3									
4									

Progress Checkup

How close are you to meeting your goal? How do you feel about your program and your progress?

If needed, describe changes to your plan and additional strategies for increasing steps:

Week	Goal	M	Tu	W	Th	F	Sa	Su	Average
5									
6									
7									
8									

Progress Checkup

How close are you to meeting your goal? How do you feel about your program and your progress?

If needed, describe changes to your plan and additional strategies for increasing steps:

Week	Goal	M	Tu	W	Th	F	Sa	Su	Average
9									
10									
11									
12									

Progress Checkup

How close are you to meeting your goal? How do you feel about your program and your progress?

If needed, describe changes to your plan and additional strategies for increasing steps:

LOOKING AHEAD>>>>>

AFTER READING THIS CHAPTER, YOU SHOULD BE ABLE TO:

- Describe how the body produces the energy it needs for exercise
- List the major effects and benefits of cardiorespiratory endurance exercise
- Explain how cardiorespiratory endurance is measured and assessed
- Describe how frequency, intensity, time (duration), and type of exercise affect the development of cardiorespiratory endurance
- Explain the best ways to prevent and treat common exercise injuries

CARDIORESPIRATORY ENDURANCE 3

TEST YOUR KNOWLEDGE

1. Compared to sedentary people, those who engage in regular moderate endurance exercise are likely to

a. have fewer colds.
b. be less anxious and depressed.
c. fall asleep more quickly and sleep better.
d. be more alert and creative.

2. About how much blood does the heart pump each minute during aerobic exercise?

a. 5 quarts
b. 10 quarts
c. 20 quarts

3. During an effective 30-minute cardiorespiratory endurance workout, you should lose 1–2 pounds.

True or false?

ANSWERS

1. **ALL FOUR.** Endurance exercise has many immediate benefits that affect all the dimensions of wellness and improve overall quality of life.
2. **c.** During exercise, cardiac output increases to 20 or more quarts per minute, compared to about 5 quarts per minute at rest.
3. **FALSE.** Any weight loss during an exercise session is due to fluid loss that needs to be replaced to prevent dehydration and enhance performance. It is best to drink enough during exercise to match fluid loss in sweat (usually about 6–12 ounces every 15–20 minutes of exercise); weigh yourself before and after a workout to make sure that you are drinking enough.

FIT AND WELL ONLINE LEARNING CENTER www.mhhe.com/fahey

Visit the *Fit and Well* Online Learning Center for resources that will help you get the most out of your course!

- Study and review aids include practice quizzes, glossary flashcards, chapter summaries, learning objectives, PowerPoint presentations, Common Questions Answered, student handouts, crossword puzzles, Internet activities, and links to wellness Web sites.
- Behavior change tools include a daily fitness and nutrition journal, a behavior change workbook, sample behavior change plans, and blank behavior change logs to print and use.
- Chapter 3 resources also include three "custom chapters" that provide more in-depth information on topics of special interest—"Developing Sport and Movement Skills," "Prevention and Care of Athletic Injuries," and "The Environment and Exercise."

Cardiorespiratory endurance—the ability of the body to perform prolonged, large-muscle, dynamic exercise at moderate-to-high levels of intensity—is a key health-related component of fitness. As explained in Chapter 2, a healthy cardiorespiratory system is essential to high levels of fitness and wellness.

This chapter reviews the short- and long-term effects and benefits of cardiorespiratory endurance exercise. It then describes several tests that are commonly used to assess cardiorespiratory fitness. Finally, it provides guidelines for creating your own cardiorespiratory endurance program, one that is geared to your current level of fitness and built around activities you enjoy.

BASIC PHYSIOLOGY OF CARDIORESPIRATORY ENDURANCE EXERCISE

A basic understanding of the body processes involved in cardiorespiratory endurance exercise can help you design a safe and effective fitness program.

TERMS

cardiorespiratory system The system that circulates blood through the body; consists of the heart, blood vessels, and respiratory system.

pulmonary circulation The part of the circulatory system that moves blood between the heart and the lungs; controlled by the right side of the heart.

systemic circulation The part of the circulatory system that moves blood between the heart and the rest of the body; controlled by the left side of the heart.

venae cavae The large veins through which blood is returned to the right atrium of the heart.

atria The two upper chambers of the heart in which blood collects before passing to the ventricles; also called *auricles*.

ventricles The two lower chambers of the heart from which blood flows through arteries to the lungs and other parts of the body.

aorta The large artery that receives blood from the left ventricle and distributes it to the body.

systole Contraction of the heart.

diastole Relaxation of the heart.

blood pressure The force exerted by the blood on the walls of the blood vessels; created by the pumping action of the heart.

veins Vessels that carry blood to the heart.

arteries Vessels that carry blood away from the heart.

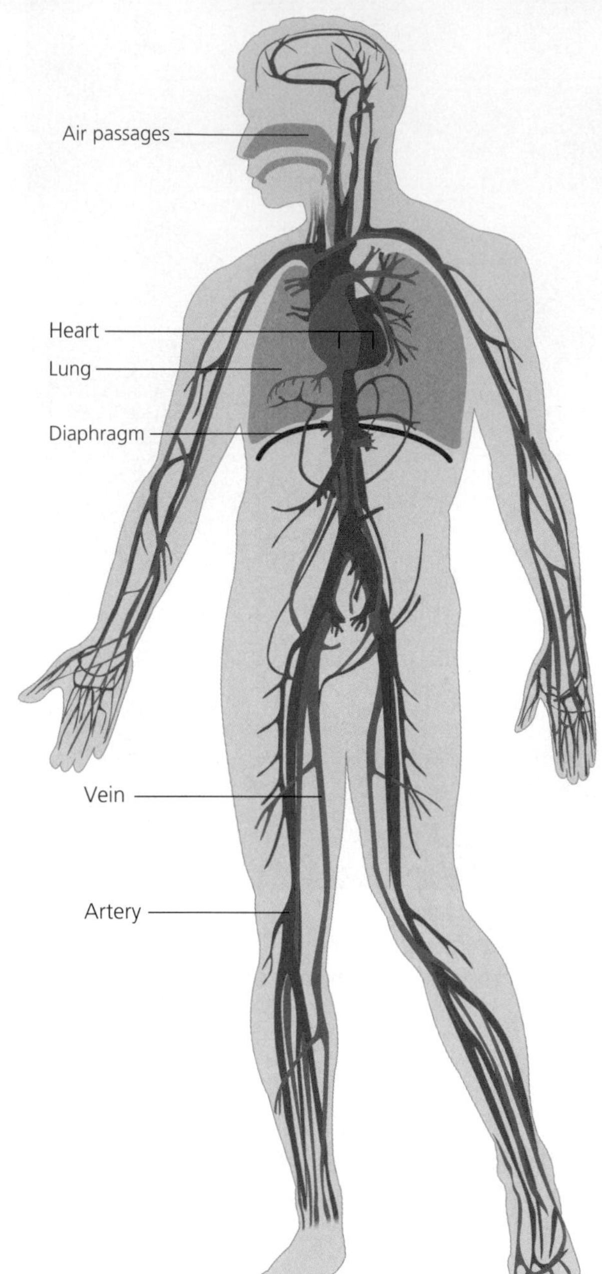

FIGURE 3.1 The cardiorespiratory system.

The Cardiorespiratory System

The **cardiorespiratory system** consists of the heart, the blood vessels, and the respiratory system (Figure 3.1). The cardiorespiratory system transports oxygen, nutrients, and other key substances to the organs and tissues that need them; it also carries waste products to where they can be used or expelled.

The Heart The heart is a four-chambered, fist-sized muscle located just beneath the sternum (breastbone). It pumps oxygen-poor blood to the lungs and oxygenated (oxygen-rich) blood to the rest of the body. Blood

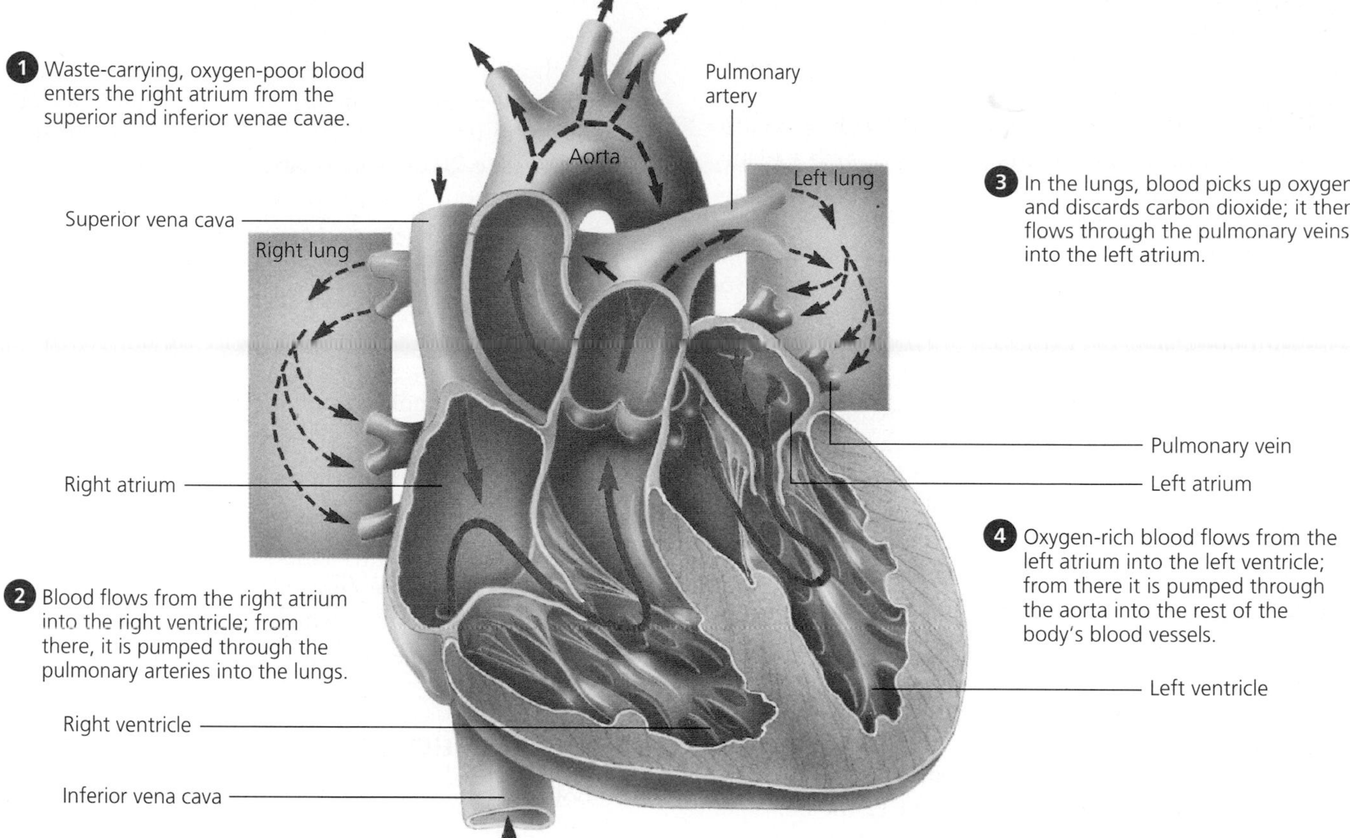

1 Waste-carrying, oxygen-poor blood enters the right atrium from the superior and inferior venae cavae.
Superior vena cava
Right lung
Aorta
Pulmonary artery
Left lung
3 In the lungs, blood picks up oxygen and discards carbon dioxide; it then flows through the pulmonary veins into the left atrium.
Pulmonary vein
Right atrium
Left atrium
4 Oxygen-rich blood flows from the left atrium into the left ventricle; from there it is pumped through the aorta into the rest of the body's blood vessels.
2 Blood flows from the right atrium into the right ventricle; from there, it is pumped through the pulmonary arteries into the lungs.
Left ventricle
Right ventricle
Inferior vena cava

FIGURE 3.2 Circulation in the heart.

actually travels through two separate circulatory systems: The right side of the heart pumps blood to the lungs in what is called **pulmonary circulation,** and the left side pumps blood through the rest of the body in **systemic circulation.**

The following steps describe the path blood follows as it travels through the cardiorespiratory system (Figure 3.2):

1. Waste-laden, oxygen-poor blood travels through large vessels, called **venae cavae,** into the heart's right upper chamber, or **atrium.**
2. After the right atrium fills, it contracts and pumps blood into the heart's right lower chamber, or **ventricle.**
3. When the right ventricle is full, it contracts and pumps blood through the pulmonary artery into the lungs.
4. In the lungs, blood picks up oxygen and discards carbon dioxide.
5. The cleaned, oxygenated blood flows from the lungs through the pulmonary veins into the heart's left atrium.
6. After the left atrium fills, it contracts and pumps blood into the left ventricle.
7. When the left ventricle is full, it pumps blood through the **aorta**—the body's largest artery—for distribution to the rest of the body's blood vessels.

The period of the heart's contraction is called **systole;** the period of relaxation is called **diastole.** During systole, the atria contract first, pumping blood into the ventricles. A fraction of a second later, the ventricles contract, pumping blood to the lungs and the body. During diastole, blood flows into the heart.

Blood pressure, the force exerted by blood on the walls of the blood vessels, is created by the pumping action of the heart; blood pressure is greater during systole than during diastole. A person weighing 150 pounds has about 5 quarts of blood, which are circulated about once every minute.

The heartbeat—the split-second sequence of contractions of the heart's four chambers—is controlled by nerve impulses. These signals originate in a bundle of specialized cells in the right atrium called the pacemaker or sinoatrial (SA) node. Unless it is speeded up or slowed down by the brain in response to such stimuli as danger or the tissues' need for more oxygen, the heart produces nerve impulses at a steady rate.

The Blood Vessels Blood vessels are classified by size and function. **Veins** carry blood to the heart; **arteries**

carry it away from the heart. Veins have thin walls, but arteries have thick elastic walls that enable them to expand and relax with the volume of blood being pumped through them.

After leaving the heart, the aorta branches into smaller and smaller vessels. The smallest arteries branch still further into **capillaries,** tiny vessels only one cell thick. The capillaries deliver oxygen and nutrient-rich blood to the tissues and pass on oxygen-poor, waste-laden blood. From the capillaries, this blood empties into small veins (*venules*) and then into larger veins that return it to the heart to repeat the cycle.

Blood pumped through the heart doesn't reach the cells of the heart, so the organ has its own network of arteries, veins, and capillaries. Two large vessels, the right and left coronary arteries, branch off the aorta and supply the heart muscle with oxygenated blood. Blockage of a coronary artery is a leading cause of heart attacks (see Chapter 11).

The Respiratory System The **respiratory system** supplies oxygen to the body, carries off carbon dioxide—a waste product of body processes—and helps regulate acid produced during metabolism. Air passes in and out of the lungs as a result of pressure changes brought about by the contraction and relaxation of the diaphragm and rib muscles; the lungs expand and contract about 12–20 times per minute. As air is inhaled, it passes through the nasal passages, the throat, larynx, trachea (windpipe), and bronchi into the lungs. The lungs consist of many branching tubes that end in tiny, thin-walled air sacs called **alveoli.**

Carbon dioxide and oxygen are exchanged between alveoli and capillaries in the lungs. Carbon dioxide passes from blood cells into the alveoli, where it is carried up and out of the lungs (exhaled). Oxygen from inhaled air is passed from the alveoli into blood cells; these oxygen-rich blood cells then return to the heart and are pumped throughout the body. Oxygen is an important component of the body's energy-producing system, so the cardiorespiratory system's ability to pick up and deliver oxygen is critical for the functioning of the body.

The Cardiorespiratory System at Rest and During Exercise At rest and during light activity, the cardiorespiratory system functions at a fairly steady pace. Your heart beats at a rate of about 50–90 beats per minute, and you take about 12–20 breaths per minute. A typical resting blood pressure in a healthy adult, measured in millimeters of mercury, is 120 systolic and 80 diastolic (120/80).

During exercise, the demands on the cardiorespiratory system increase. Body cells, particularly working muscles, need to obtain more oxygen and fuel and to eliminate more waste products. To meet these demands, your body makes the following changes:

- Heart rate increases, up to 170–210 beats per minute during intense exercise.
- The heart's **stroke volume** increases, meaning that the heart pumps out more blood with each beat.
- The heart pumps and circulates more blood per minute as a result of the faster heart rate and greater stroke volume. During exercise, this **cardiac output** increases to 20 or more quarts per minute, compared to about 5 quarts per minute at rest.
- Blood flow changes, so as much as 85–90% of the blood may be delivered to working muscles. At rest, about 15–20% of blood is distributed to the skeletal muscles.
- Systolic blood pressure increases, while diastolic blood pressure holds steady or declines slightly. A typical exercise blood pressure might be 175/65.
- To oxygenate this increased blood flow, you take deeper breaths and breathe faster, up to 40–60 breaths per minute.

All of these changes are controlled and coordinated by special centers in the brain, which use the nervous system and chemical messengers to control the process.

Energy Production

Metabolism is the sum of all the chemical processes necessary to maintain the body. Energy is required to fuel vital body functions—to build and break down tissue, contract muscles, conduct nerve impulses, regulate body temperature, and so on.

The rate at which your body uses energy—its **metabolic rate**—depends on your level of activity. At rest, you have a low metabolic rate; if you begin to walk, your metabolic rate increases. If you jog, your metabolic rate may increase more than 800% above its resting level. Olympic-caliber distance runners can increase their metabolic rate by 2000% or more.

Energy from Food The body converts chemical energy from food into substances that cells can use as fuel. These fuels can be used immediately or stored for later use. The body's ability to store fuel is critical, because if all the energy from food were released immediately, much of it would be wasted.

The three classes of energy-containing nutrients in food are carbohydrates, fats, and proteins. During digestion, most carbohydrates are broken down into the simple sugar **glucose.** Some glucose remains circulating in the blood ("blood sugar"), where it can be used as a quick source of fuel to produce energy. Glucose may also be converted to **glycogen** and stored in the liver, muscles, and kidneys. If glycogen stores are full and the body's immediate need for energy is met, the remaining glucose is converted to fat and stored in the body's fatty tissues. Excess energy from dietary fat is also stored as body fat. Protein in the diet is used primarily to build new tissue, but it can be broken down

Table 3.1 Characteristics of the Body's Energy Systems

	Energy System*		
	Immediate	**Nonoxidative**	**Oxidative**
Duration of Activity for Which System Predominates	0–10 seconds	10 seconds–2 minutes	>2 minutes
Intensity of Activity for Which System Predominates	High	High	Low to moderately high
Rate of ATP Production	Immediate, very rapid	Rapid	Slower, but prolonged
Fuel	Adenosine triphosphate (ATP), creatine phosphate (CP)	Muscle stores of glycogen and glucose	Body stores of glycogen, glucose, fat, and protein
Oxygen Used?	No	No	Yes
Sample Activities	Weight lifting, picking up a bag of groceries	400-meter run, running up several flights of stairs	1500-meter run, 30-minute walk, standing in line for a long time

*For most activities, all three systems contribute to energy production; the duration and intensity of the activity determine which system predominates.

SOURCE: Adapted from Brooks, G. A., et. al. 2005. *Exercise Physiology: Human Bioenergetics and its Applications,* 4th ed. New York: McGraw-Hill.

for energy or incorporated into fat stores. Glucose, glycogen, and fat are important fuels for the production of energy in the cells; protein is a significant energy source only when other fuels are lacking. (See Chapter 8 for more on the roles of carbohydrate, fat, and protein in the body.)

ATP: The Energy "Currency" of Cells The basic form of energy used by cells is **adenosine triphosphate,** or **ATP.** When a cell needs energy, it breaks down ATP, a process that releases energy in the only form the cell can use directly. Cells store a small amount of ATP; when they need more, they create it through chemical reactions that utilize the body's stored fuels—glucose, glycogen, and fat. When you exercise, your cells need to produce more energy. Consequently, your body mobilizes its stores of fuel to increase ATP production.

Exercise and the Three Energy Systems

The muscles in your body use three energy systems to create ATP and fuel cellular activity. These systems use different fuels and chemical processes and perform different, specific functions during exercise (Table 3.1).

The Immediate Energy System The **immediate ("explosive") energy system** provides energy rapidly but for only a short period of time. It is used to fuel activities that last for about 10 or fewer seconds—examples in sports include weight lifting and shot-putting; examples in daily life include rising from a chair or picking up a bag of groceries. The components of this energy system include existing cellular ATP stores and creatine phosphate (CP), a chemical that cells can use to make ATP. CP levels are depleted rapidly during exercise, so the maximum capacity of this energy system is reached within a few seconds. Cells must then switch to the other energy systems to restore levels of ATP and CP. (Without adequate ATP, muscles will stiffen and become unusable.)

capillaries Very small blood vessels that distribute blood to all parts of the body.

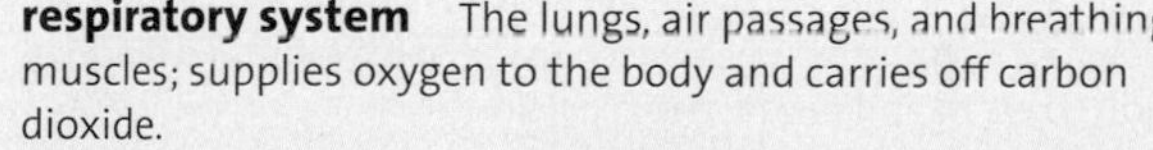

respiratory system The lungs, air passages, and breathing muscles; supplies oxygen to the body and carries off carbon dioxide.

alveoli Tiny air sacs in the lungs through whose walls gases such as oxygen and carbon dioxide diffuse in and out of blood.

stroke volume The amount of blood the heart circulates with each beat.

cardiac output The amount of blood pumped by the heart each minute; a function of heart rate and stroke volume (the amount of blood pumped during each beat).

metabolic rate The rate at which the body uses energy.

glucose A simple sugar that circulates in the blood and can be used by cells to fuel adenosine triphosphate (ATP) production.

glycogen A complex carbohydrate stored principally in the liver and skeletal muscles; the major fuel source during most forms of intense exercise. Glycogen is the storage form of glucose.

adenosine triphosphate (ATP) The energy source for cellular processes.

immediate ("explosive") energy system The system that supplies energy to muscle cells through the breakdown of cellular stores of ATP and creatine phosphate (CP).

The Nonoxidative Energy System The **nonoxidative (anaerobic) energy system** is used at the start of an exercise session and for high-intensity activities lasting for about 10 seconds to 2 minutes, such as the 400-meter run. During daily activities, this system may be called on to help you run to catch a bus or dash up several flights of stairs. The nonoxidative energy system creates ATP by breaking down glucose and glycogen. This system doesn't require oxygen, which is why it is sometimes referred to as the **anaerobic** system. The capacity of this system to produce energy is limited, but it can generate a great deal of ATP in a short period of time. For this reason, it is the most important energy system for very intense exercise.

There are two key limiting factors for the nonoxidative energy system. First, the body's supply of glucose and glycogen is limited. If these are depleted, a person may experience fatigue and dizziness, and judgment may be impaired. (The brain and nervous system rely on carbohydrates as fuel.) Second, the nonoxidative system releases substances called **hydrogen ions** that are thought to interfere with metabolism and muscle contraction, thereby causing fatigue. During heavy exercise, such as sprinting, the body produces large amounts of hydrogen ions and muscles fatigue rapidly. The anaerobic energy system also creates metabolic acids. Fortunately, exercise training increases the body's ability to cope with metabolic acid. One of these acids, called **lactic acid,** is often linked to fatigue during intense exercise. However, it is an important fuel at rest and during exercise and may actually prevent fatigue.

TERMS

nonoxidative (anaerobic) energy system The system that supplies energy to muscle cells through the breakdown of muscle stores of glucose and glycogen; also called the *anaerobic system* or the *lactic acid system* because chemical reactions take place without oxygen and produce lactic acid.

anaerobic Occurring in the absence of oxygen.

hydrogen ion A positively charged atom of hydrogen; high concentrations during exercise slow metabolism and contribute to fatigue.

lactic acid A metabolic acid resulting from the metabolism of glucose and glycogen.

oxidative (aerobic) energy system The system that supplies energy to cells through the breakdown of glucose, glycogen, fats, and amino acids; also called the *aerobic system* because chemical reactions require oxygen.

aerobic Dependent on the presence of oxygen.

mitochondria Intracellular structures containing enzymes used in the chemical reactions that convert the energy in food to a form the body can use.

maximal oxygen consumption ($\dot{V}O_{2max}$) The highest rate of oxygen consumption an individual is capable of during maximum physical effort, reflecting the body's ability to transport and use oxygen; measured in milliliters used per minute per kilogram of body weight.

The Oxidative Energy System The **oxidative (aerobic) energy system** is used during any physical activity that lasts longer than about 2 minutes, such as distance running, swimming, hiking, or even standing in line. The oxidative system requires oxygen to generate ATP, which is why it is considered an **aerobic** system. The oxidative system cannot produce energy as quickly as the other two systems, but it can supply energy for much longer periods of time. It provides energy during most daily activities.

In the oxidative energy system, ATP production takes place in cellular structures called **mitochondria.** Because mitochondria can use carbohydrates (glucose and glycogen) or fats to produce ATP, the body's stores of fuel for this system are much greater than those for the other two energy systems. The actual fuel used depends on the intensity and duration of exercise and on the fitness status of the individual. Carbohydrates are favored during more intense exercise (over 65% of maximum capacity); fats are used for mild, low-intensity activities. During a prolonged exercise session, carbohydrates are the predominant fuel at the start of the workout, but fat utilization increases over time. Fit individuals use a greater proportion of fat as fuel because increased fitness allows people to do activities at lower intensities. This is an important adaptation because glycogen depletion is one of the limiting factors for the oxidative energy system. Thus, by being able to use more fat as fuel, a fit individual can exercise for a longer time before glycogen is depleted and muscles become fatigued.

Oxygen is another limiting factor. The oxygen requirement of this energy system is proportional to the intensity of exercise—as intensity increases, so does oxygen consumption. There is a limit to the body's ability to increase the transport and use of oxygen; this limit is referred to as **maximal oxygen consumption**, or $\dot{V}O_{2max}$. $\dot{V}O_{2max}$ is influenced by genetics, fitness status (power-generating capacity and fatigue resistance), gender, and age. It depends on many factors, including the capacity of blood to carry oxygen, the rate at which oxygen is transported to the tissues, and the amount of oxygen that cells extract from the blood. $\dot{V}O_{2max}$ determines how intensely a person can perform endurance exercise and for how long, and it is considered the best overall measure of the capacity of the cardiorespiratory system. (The assessment tests described later in the chapter are designed to help you predict your $\dot{V}O_{2max}$.)

The Energy Systems in Combination Your body typically uses all three energy systems when you exercise. The intensity and duration of the activity determine which system predominates. For example, when you play tennis, you use the immediate energy system when hitting the ball, but you replenish cellular energy stores using the nonoxidative and oxidative systems. When cycling, the oxidative system predominates. However, if you must suddenly exercise intensely—ride up a steep hill, for example—the other systems become important because the oxidative system is unable to supply ATP fast enough to sustain high-intensity effort.

Physical Fitness and Energy Production Physically fit people can increase their metabolic rate substantially, generating the energy needed for powerful or sustained exercise. People who are not fit cannot respond to exercise in the same way. Their bodies are less capable of delivering oxygen and fuel to exercising muscles; they can't burn as many calories during or after exercise; and they are less able to cope with lactic acid and other substances produced during intense physical activity that contribute to fatigue. Because of this, they become fatigued more rapidly—their legs hurt and they breathe heavily walking up a flight of stairs, for example. Regular physical training can substantially improve the body's ability to produce energy and meet the challenges of increased physical activity.

In designing an exercise program, focus on the energy system most important to your goals. Because improving the functioning of the cardiorespiratory system is critical to overall wellness, endurance exercise that utilizes the oxidative energy system—activities performed at moderate-to-high intensities for a prolonged duration—is a key component of any health-related fitness program.

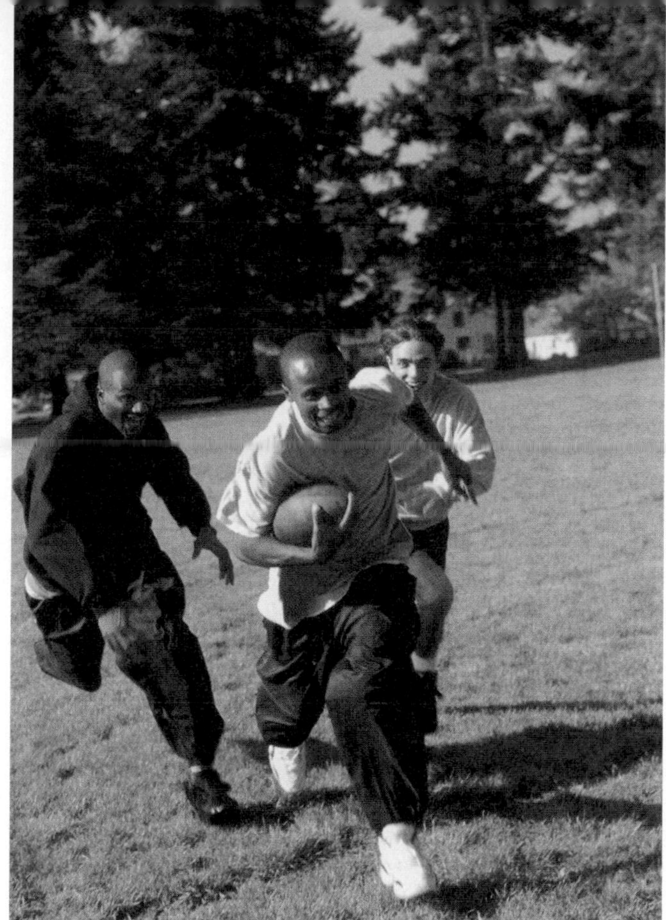

Exercise offers both long-term health benefits and immediate pleasures. Many popular sports and activities develop cardiorespiratory endurance.

QUESTIONS FOR CRITICAL THINKING AND REFLECTION

When you think about the types of physical activity you engage in during your typical day or week, which ones use the immediate energy system? The nonoxidative energy system? The oxidative energy system? How can you increase activities that use the oxidative energy system?

BENEFITS OF CARDIORESPIRATORY ENDURANCE EXERCISE

Cardiorespiratory endurance exercise helps the body become more efficient and better able to cope with physical challenges. It also lowers risk for many chronic diseases.

Improved Cardiorespiratory Functioning

Earlier in this chapter, we described some of the major changes that occur in the cardiorespiratory system when you exercise, such as increases in cardiac output and blood pressure, breathing rate, blood flow to the skeletal muscles, and sweating. In the short term, all these changes help the body respond to the challenge of exercise. When performed regularly, endurance exercise also leads to permanent adaptations in the cardiorespiratory system (Figure 3.3, p. 64). These improvements reduce the effort required to do everyday tasks and make the body better able to respond to physical challenges. This, in a nutshell, is what it means to be physically fit.

Endurance exercise enhances the heart's health by:

- Maintaining or increasing the heart's own blood and oxygen supply.
- Increasing the heart muscle's function, so it pumps more blood per beat. This improved function keeps the heart rate lower both at rest and during exercise. The resting heart rate of a fit person is often 10–20 beats per minute lower than that of an unfit person. This translates into as many as 10 million fewer beats in the course of a year.
- Strengthening the heart's contractions.
- Increasing the heart's cavity size (in young adults).
- Increasing blood volume so the heart pushes more blood into the circulatory system during each contraction.
- Reducing blood pressure.

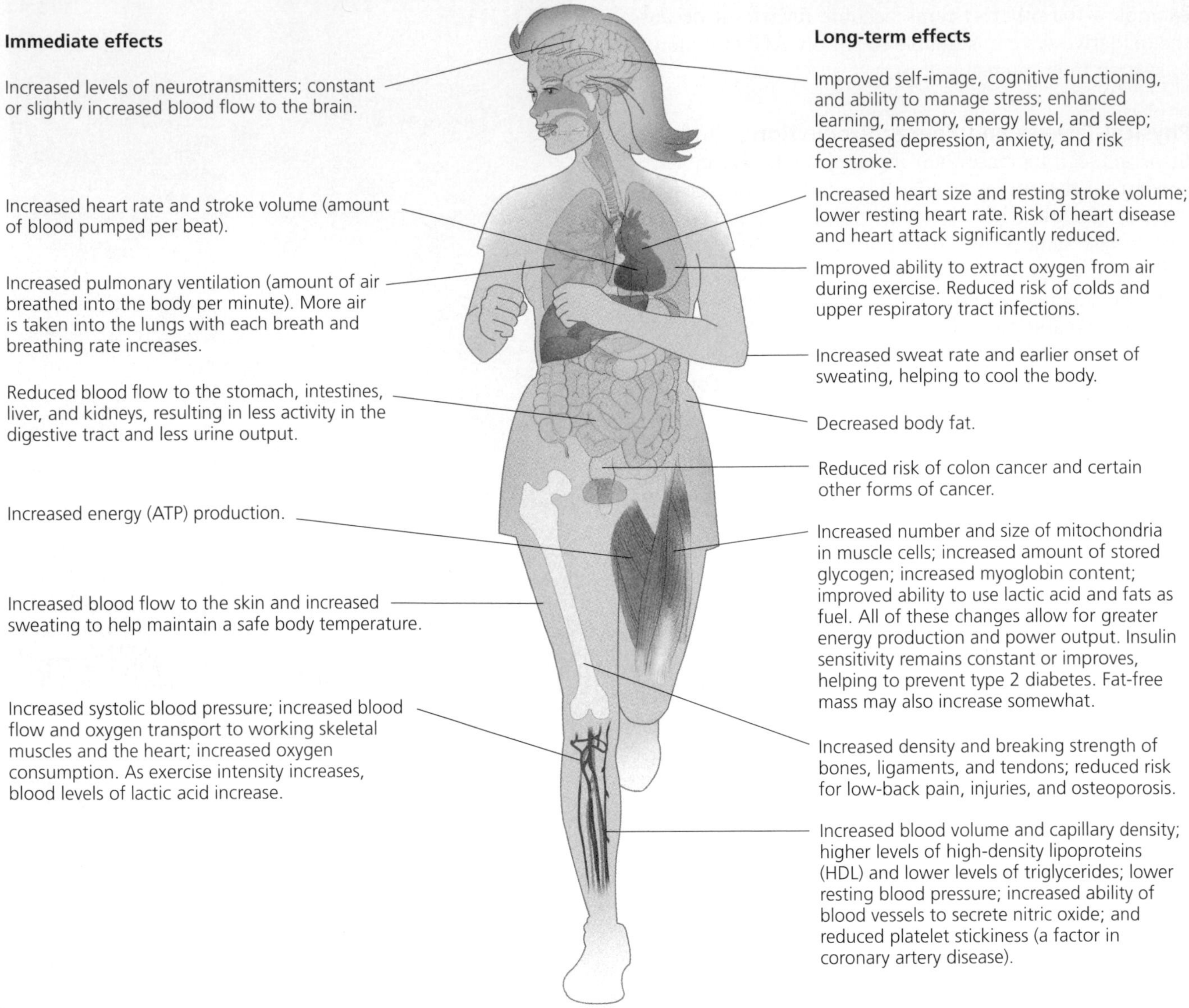

Immediate effects

Increased levels of neurotransmitters; constant or slightly increased blood flow to the brain.

Increased heart rate and stroke volume (amount of blood pumped per beat).

Increased pulmonary ventilation (amount of air breathed into the body per minute). More air is taken into the lungs with each breath and breathing rate increases.

Reduced blood flow to the stomach, intestines, liver, and kidneys, resulting in less activity in the digestive tract and less urine output.

Increased energy (ATP) production.

Increased blood flow to the skin and increased sweating to help maintain a safe body temperature.

Increased systolic blood pressure; increased blood flow and oxygen transport to working skeletal muscles and the heart; increased oxygen consumption. As exercise intensity increases, blood levels of lactic acid increase.

Long-term effects

Improved self-image, cognitive functioning, and ability to manage stress; enhanced learning, memory, energy level, and sleep; decreased depression, anxiety, and risk for stroke.

Increased heart size and resting stroke volume; lower resting heart rate. Risk of heart disease and heart attack significantly reduced.

Improved ability to extract oxygen from air during exercise. Reduced risk of colds and upper respiratory tract infections.

Increased sweat rate and earlier onset of sweating, helping to cool the body.

Decreased body fat.

Reduced risk of colon cancer and certain other forms of cancer.

Increased number and size of mitochondria in muscle cells; increased amount of stored glycogen; increased myoglobin content; improved ability to use lactic acid and fats as fuel. All of these changes allow for greater energy production and power output. Insulin sensitivity remains constant or improves, helping to prevent type 2 diabetes. Fat-free mass may also increase somewhat.

Increased density and breaking strength of bones, ligaments, and tendons; reduced risk for low-back pain, injuries, and osteoporosis.

Increased blood volume and capillary density; higher levels of high-density lipoproteins (HDL) and lower levels of triglycerides; lower resting blood pressure; increased ability of blood vessels to secrete nitric oxide; and reduced platelet stickiness (a factor in coronary artery disease).

FIGURE 3.3 Immediate and long-term effects of regular cardiorespiratory endurance exercise. When endurance exercise is performed regularly, short-term changes in the body develop into more permanent adaptations; these include improved ability to exercise, reduced risk of many chronic diseases, and improved psychological and emotional well-being.

Improved Cellular Metabolism

Regular endurance exercise improves the body's metabolism, down to the cellular level, enhancing your ability to produce and use energy efficiently. Cardiorespiratory training improves metabolism by doing the following:

- Increasing the number of capillaries in the muscles. Additional capillaries supply the muscles with more fuel and oxygen and more quickly eliminate waste products. Greater capillary density also helps heal injuries and reduce muscle aches.
- Training muscles to make the most of oxygen and fuel so they work more efficiently.
- Increasing the size of and number of mitochondria in muscle cells, increasing cells' energy capacity.
- Preventing glycogen depletion and increasing the muscles' ability to use lactic acid and fat as fuels.

Regular exercise may also help protect cells from chemical damage caused by agents called *free radicals.* (See Chapter 8 for details on free radicals and special enzymes the body uses to fight them.)

Fitness programs that best develop metabolic efficiency include both long-duration, moderately intense endurance exercise and brief periods of more intense effort. For example, climbing a small hill while jogging or cycling introduces the kind of intense exercise that leads to more efficient use of lactic acid and fats.

DIMENSIONS OF DIVERSITY

Benefits of Exercise for Older Adults

Research has shown that most aspects of physiological functioning peak when people are about 30 years old and then decline at a rate of about 0.5–1.0% per year. This decline in physical capacity is characterized by a decrease in maximal oxygen consumption, cardiac output, muscular strength, fat-free mass, joint mobility, and other factors. However, regular exercise can substantially alter the rate of decline in functional status, and it is associated with both longevity and improved quality of life.

Regular endurance exercise can improve maximal oxygen consumption in older people by up to 15–30%—the same degree of improvement seen in younger people. In fact, studies have shown that Masters athletes in their 70s have $\dot{V}O_{2max}$ values equivalent to those of sedentary 20-year-olds: At any age, endurance training can improve cardiorespiratory functioning, cellular metabolism, body composition, and psychological and emotional well-being. Older people who exercise regularly have better balance and greater bone density and are less likely than their sedentary peers to suffer injuries as a result of falls. Regular endurance training also substantially reduces the risk of many chronic and disabling diseases including heart disease, cancer, diabetes, osteoporosis, and dementia.

Other forms of exercise training are also beneficial for older adults. Resistance training is a safe and effective way to build strength and fat-free mass and can help people remain independent as they age. Lifting weights has also been shown to boost spirits in older people, perhaps because improvements in strength appear quickly and are easily applied to everyday tasks such as climbing stairs and carrying groceries. Flexibility exercises can improve the range of motion in joints and also help people maintain functional independence as they age.

It's never too late to start exercising. Even in people over 80, beginning an exercise program can improve physical functioning and quality of life. Most older adults are able to participate in moderate walking and strengthening and stretching exercises, and modified programs can be created for people with chronic conditions and other special health concerns (see Chapter 7). The wellness benefits of exercise are available to people of all ages and levels of ability.

QUESTIONS FOR CRITICAL THINKING AND REFLECTION

If you already follow an exercise program, how could you modify it to help improve your cellular metabolism? What specific activities (or changes to existing ones) could you incorporate into your program for this purpose?

Reduced Risk of Chronic Disease

Regular endurance exercise lowers your risk of many chronic, disabling diseases. It can also help people with those diseases improve their health (see the box "Benefits of Exercise for Older Adults"). The most significant health benefits occur when someone who is sedentary becomes moderately active.

Cardiovascular Diseases Sedentary living is a key contributor to **cardiovascular disease (CVD).** CVD is a general category that encompasses several diseases of the heart and blood vessels, including coronary heart disease (which can cause heart attacks), stroke, and high blood pressure. Sedentary people are significantly more likely to die of CVD than are fit individuals.

Cardiorespiratory endurance exercise lowers your risk of CVD by doing the following:

- Promoting a healthy balance of fats in the blood. High concentrations of blood fats such as cholesterol and triglycerides are linked to CVD. Exercise raises levels of "good cholesterol" (high-density lipoproteins, or HDL) and may lower levels of "bad cholesterol" (low-density lipoproteins, or LDL).
- Reducing high blood pressure, which is a contributing factor to several kinds of CVD.
- Enhancing the function of the cells that line the arteries (endothelial cells).
- Reducing inflammation.
- Preventing obesity and type 2 diabetes, both of which contribute to CVD.

Details on various types of CVD, their associated risk factors, and lifestyle factors that can reduce your risk for developing CVD are discussed in Chapter 11.

Cancer Although the findings are not conclusive, some studies have shown a relationship between increased physical activity and a reduction in a person's risk of cancer. Exercise reduces the risk of colon cancer in women, and it may reduce the risk of cancers of the breast and reproductive organs. Physical activity during the high school and college years may be particularly important

TERMS

cardiovascular disease (CVD) Disease of the heart and blood vessels.

for preventing breast cancer later in life. Exercise may also reduce the risk of pancreatic cancer and prostate cancer. See Chapter 12 for more information on various types of cancer.

Type 2 Diabetes Regular exercise helps prevent the development of type 2 diabetes, the most common form of diabetes. Exercise metabolizes (burns) excess sugar and makes cells more sensitive to the hormone insulin, which is involved in the regulation of blood sugar levels. Obesity is a key risk factor for diabetes, and exercise helps keep body fat at healthy levels. But even without fat loss, exercise improves control of blood sugar levels in many people with diabetes, and physical activity is an important part of treatment. (See Chapter 6 for more on diabetes and insulin resistance.)

Osteoporosis A special benefit of exercise, especially for women, is protection against osteoporosis, a disease that results in loss of bone density and poor bone strength. Weight-bearing exercise—particularly weight training—helps build bone during the teens and twenties. People with denser bones can better endure the bone loss that occurs with aging. With stronger bones and muscles and better balance, fit people are less likely to experience debilitating falls and bone fractures. (See Chapter 8 for more on osteoporosis.)

Deaths from All Causes Physically fit people have a reduced risk of dying prematurely from all causes, with the greatest benefits found for people with the highest levels of fitness (see Figure 3.4 for the results of one study). Poor fitness is a good predictor of premature death and is as important a risk factor as smoking, high blood pressure, obesity, and diabetes.

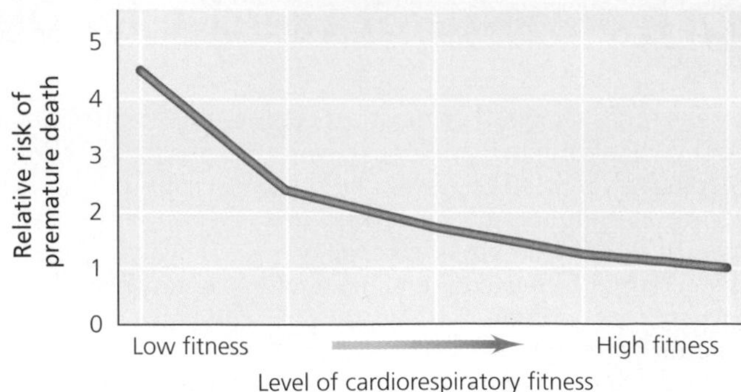

FIGURE 3.4 Cardiorespiratory fitness and risk of premature death. People with high levels of cardiorespiratory fitness have a substantially lower risk of premature death than unfit individuals.

SOURCE: Myers, J., et al. 2002. Exercise capacity and mortality among men referred for exercise testing. *New England Journal of Medicine* 346(11): 793–801.

Better Control of Body Fat

Too much body fat is linked to a variety of health problems, including CVD, cancer, and type 2 diabetes. Healthy body composition can be difficult to achieve and maintain because a diet that contains all essential nutrients can be relatively high in calories, especially for someone who is sedentary. Excess calories are stored in the body as fat. Regular exercise increases daily calorie expenditure so that a healthy diet is less likely to lead to weight gain. Endurance exercise burns calories directly and, if intense enough, continues to do so by raising resting metabolic rate for several hours following an exercise session. A higher metabolic rate means that it is easier for a person to maintain a healthy weight or to lose weight. Exercise alone cannot ensure a healthy body composition, however; as described in Chapters 6 and 9, you will lose more weight more rapidly and keep it off longer if you decrease your calorie intake and boost your calorie expenditure through exercise.

Improved Immune Function

Exercise can have either positive or negative effects on the immune system, the physiological processes that protect us from disease. Moderate endurance exercise boosts immune function, whereas overtraining (excessive training) depresses it. Physically fit people get fewer colds and upper respiratory tract infections than people who are not fit. Exercise affects immune function by influencing levels of specialized cells and chemicals involved in the immune response. In addition to regular moderate exercise, the immune system can be strengthened by eating a well-balanced diet, managing stress, and getting 7–8 hours of sleep every night.

MOTIVATION BOOSTER

Focus on benefits. Make a list of five benefits of endurance exercise that are particularly meaningful to you—reducing your risk of diabetes, for example, or being able to hike with friends. Put the list in a prominent location—on your mirror or refrigerator, for example—and use it as a motivational tool for beginning and maintaining your fitness program.

Improved Psychological and Emotional Well-Being

Most people who participate in regular endurance exercise experience social, psychological, and emotional

TERMS

endorphins Substances resembling morphine that are secreted by the brain and that decrease pain, suppress fatigue, and produce euphoria.

neurotransmitters Brain chemicals that transmit nerve impulses.

Exercise, Mood, and the Mind

Although much of the discussion of the benefits of exercise focuses on improvements to physical wellness, many people discover that the best reason to become and stay active is the boost that regular exercise provides to the nonphysical dimensions of wellness. The following are just some of the effects of regular physical activity.

- ***Reduced anxiety.*** Exercise reduces symptoms of anxiety such as worry and self-doubt both in people who are anxious most of the time (trait anxiety) and in people who become anxious in response to a particular experience (state anxiety). Exercise is associated with a lower risk for panic attacks, generalized anxiety disorder, and social anxiety disorder.
- ***Reduced depression and improved mood.*** Exercise relieves feelings of sadness and hopelessness and can be as effective as psychotherapy in treating mild-to-moderate cases of depression. Exercise improves mood and increases feelings of well-being in both depressed and nondepressed people.
- ***Improved sleep.*** Regular physical activity helps people fall asleep more easily; it also improves the quality of sleep, making it more restful.
- ***Reduced stress.*** Exercise reduces the body's overall response to all forms of stressors and helps people deal more effectively with the stress they do experience.
- ***Enhanced self-esteem, self-confidence, and self-efficacy.*** Exercise can boost self-esteem and self-confidence by providing opportunities for people to succeed and excel; it also improves body image (see Chapters 6 and 9). Sticking with an exercise program increases people's belief in their ability to be active, thereby boosting self-efficacy.
- ***Enhanced creativity and intellectual functioning.*** In studies of college students, physically active students score higher on tests of creativity than sedentary students. Exercise improves alertness and memory in the short term, and over time, exercise helps maintain reaction time, short-term memory, and nonverbal reasoning skills.
- ***Improved work productivity.*** Workers' quality of work, time-management abilities, and mental and interpersonal performance have been found to be better on days they exercise.
- ***Increased opportunities for social interaction.*** Exercise provides many opportunities for positive interaction with others.

How does exercise cause all these positive changes? A variety of mechanisms has been proposed. Physical activity stimulates the thought and emotion centers of the brain, producing improvements in mood and cognitive functioning. It increases alpha brain-wave activity, which is associated with a highly relaxed state. Exercise stimulates the release of chemicals such as **endorphins,** which may suppress fatigue, decrease pain, and produce euphoria, and phenylethylamine, which may boost energy, mood, and attention. Exercise decreases the secretion of hormones triggered by emotional stress and alters the levels of many other **neurotransmitters,** including serotonin, a brain chemical linked to mood.

Exercise also provides a distraction from stressful stimuli and an emotional outlet for feelings of stress, hostility, and aggression. Finally, exercise is a fun way to spend time!

benefits. Performing physical activities provides proof of skill mastery and self-control, thus enhancing self-image. Recreational sports provide an opportunity to socialize, have fun, and strive to excel. Endurance exercise lessens anxiety, depression, stress, anger, and hostility, thereby improving mood and boosting cardiovascular health. Regular exercise also improves sleep. For more on the wellness benefits of regular endurance exercise, see the box "Exercise, Mood, and the Mind."

ASSESSING CARDIORESPIRATORY FITNESS

The body's ability to maintain a level of exertion (exercise) for an extended time is a direct reflection of cardiorespiratory fitness. It is determined by the body's ability to take up, distribute, and use oxygen during physical activity. As explained earlier, the best quantitative measure of cardiorespiratory endurance is maximal oxygen consumption, expressed as $\dot{V}O_{2max}$, the amount of oxygen the body uses when a person reaches maximum ability to supply oxygen during exercise (measured in milliliters of oxygen used per minute for each kilogram of body weight). Maximal oxygen consumption can be measured precisely in an exercise physiology laboratory through analysis of the air a person inhales and exhales when exercising to a level of exhaustion (maximum intensity). This procedure can be expensive and time-consuming, making it impractical for the average person.

Choosing an Assessment Test

Fortunately, several simple assessment tests provide reasonably good estimates of maximal oxygen consumption (within ±10–15% of the results of a laboratory test). Three commonly used assessments are the following:

- ***The 1-mile walk test.*** This estimates your level of cardiorespiratory fitness (maximal oxygen consumption) based on the amount of time it takes you to complete

1 mile of brisk walking and your heart rate at the end of your walk. A fast time and a low heart rate indicate a high level of cardiorespiratory endurance.

- ***The 3-minute step test.*** The rate at which the pulse returns to normal after exercise is also a good measure of cardiorespiratory capacity; heart rate remains lower and recovers faster in people who are more physically fit. For the step test, you step continually at a steady rate and then monitor your heart rate during recovery.
- ***The 1.5-mile run-walk test.*** Oxygen consumption increases with speed in distance running, so a fast time on this test indicates high maximal oxygen consumption.

Lab 3.1 provides detailed instructions for each of these tests. To assess yourself, choose one of these methods based on your access to equipment, your current physical condition, and your own preference. Don't take any of these tests without checking with your physician if you are ill or have any of the risk factors for exercise discussed in Chapter 2 and Lab 2.1. Table 3.2 lists the fitness prerequisites and cautions recommended for each test.

Monitoring Your Heart Rate

Each time your heart beats, it pumps blood into your arteries; this surge of blood causes a pulse that you can feel by holding your fingers against an artery. Counting your pulse to determine your exercise heart rate is a key part of most assessment tests for maximal oxygen consumption. Heart rate can also be used to monitor exercise intensity during a workout. (Intensity is described in more detail in the next section.)

The two most common sites for monitoring heart rate are the carotid artery in the neck and the radial artery in the wrist (Figure 3.5). To take your pulse, press your index and middle fingers gently on the correct site. You may have to shift position several times to find the best place to feel your pulse. Don't use your thumb to check your pulse; it has a pulse of its own that can confuse your count. Be careful not to push too hard, particularly when taking your pulse in the carotid artery (strong

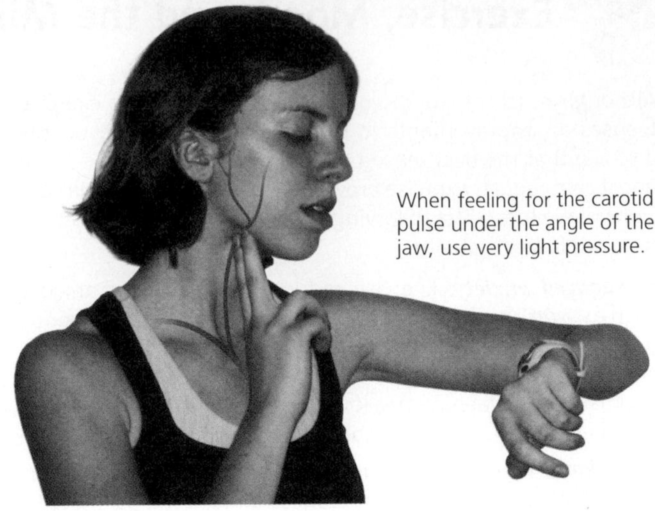

When feeling for the carotid pulse under the angle of the jaw, use very light pressure.

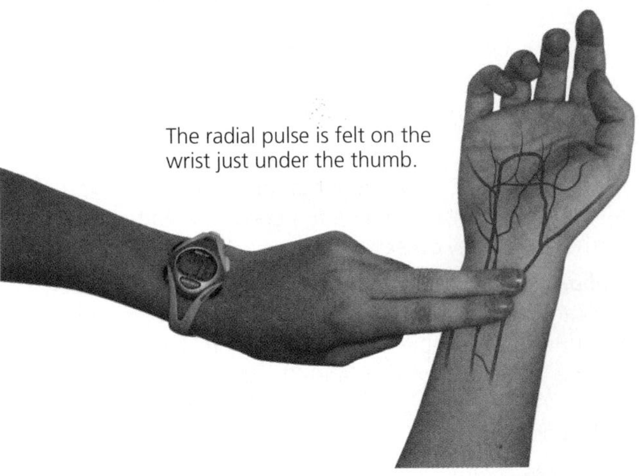

The radial pulse is felt on the wrist just under the thumb.

FIGURE 3.5 Checking your pulse. The pulse can be taken at the carotid artery in the neck (top) or at the radial artery in the wrist (bottom).

Table 3.2 Fitness Prerequisites and Cautions for the Cardiorespiratory Endurance Assessment Tests

Note: The conditions for exercise safety given in Chapter 2 apply to all fitness assessment tests. If you answered yes to any question on the PAR-Q in Lab 2.1, see your physician before taking any assessment test. If you experience any unusual symptoms while taking a test, stop exercising and discuss your condition with your instructor.

Test	Fitness Prerequisites/Cautions
1-mile walk test	Recommended for anyone who meets the criteria for safe exercise. This test can be used by individuals who cannot perform other tests because of low fitness level or injury.
3-minute step test	If you suffer from joint problems in your ankles, knees, or hips or are significantly overweight, check with your physician before taking this test. People with balance problems or for whom a fall would be particularly dangerous, including older adults and pregnant women, should use special caution or avoid this test.
1.5-mile run-walk test	Recommended for people who are healthy and at least moderately active. If you have been sedentary, you should participate in a 4- to 8-week walk-run program before taking the test. Don't take this test in extremely hot or cold weather if you aren't used to exercising under those conditions.

CRITICAL CONSUMER

Heart Rate Monitors

A heart rate monitor is an electronic device that checks the user's pulse, either continuously or on demand. These devices make it easy to monitor your heart rate before, during, and after exercise.

Wearable Monitors

Most consumer-grade monitors have two pieces—a strap that wraps around the user's chest and a wrist strap. The chest strap contains one or more small electrodes, which detect changes in the heart's electrical voltage. A transmitter in the chest strap sends this data to a receiver in the wrist strap. A small computer in the wrist strap calculates the wearer's heart rate and displays it on a small screen.

In a few low-cost monitors, the chest and wrist straps are connected together by a wire, but the most popular monitors use wireless technology to transmit data between the straps. In advanced wireless monitors, data is encoded so it cannot be read by any other monitors that may be nearby, as is often the case in a crowded gym. A one-piece (or "strapless") heart rate monitor does not include a chest strap; the wrist-worn device contains sensors that detect a pulse in the wearer's hand.

Monitors in Gym Equipment

Many pieces of workout equipment—including newer-model treadmills, stationary bikes, and elliptical trainers—feature built-in heart rate monitors. The monitor is usually mounted into the device's handles. To check your heart rate at any time while working out, simply grip the handles in the appropriate place; within a few seconds, your current heart rate will appear on the device's console.

Other Features

Heart rate monitors can do more than just check your pulse. For example, most monitors can tell you the following kinds of information:

- Highest and lowest heart rate during a session
- Average heart rate
- Target heart range, based on your age, weight, and other factors
- Time spent within the target range
- Number of calories burned during a session

Some monitors can upload their data to a computer, so information can be stored and analyzed. The analytical software can help you track your progress over a period of time or a number of workouts.

Advantages

Heart rate monitors are useful if very close tracking of heart rate is important in your program. They offer several advantages:

- They are accurate, and they reduce the risk of mistakes when checking your own pulse. (Note, however, that chest-strap monitors are considered more accurate than strapless models. If you use a monitor built into gym equipment, its accuracy will depend on how well the device is maintained.)
- They are easy to use, although a sophisticated, multifunction monitor may take some time to master.
- They do the monitoring for you, so you don't have to worry about checking your own pulse.

When shopping for a heart rate monitor, do your homework. Quality, reliability, and warranties vary. Ask personal trainers in your area for their recommendations, and look for product reviews in consumer magazines or online.

pressure on this artery may cause a reflex that slows the heart rate).

Heart rates are usually assessed in beats per minute (bpm). But counting your pulse for an entire minute isn't practical when you're exercising. And because heart rate slows rapidly when you stop exercising, it can give inaccurate results. It's best to do a shorter count—10 seconds—and then multiply the result by 6 to get your heart rate in beats per minute. (You can also use a heart rate monitor to check your pulse. See the box "Heart Rate Monitors" for more information.)

Interpreting Your Score

Once you've completed one or more of the assessment tests, use the table under "Rating Your Cardiovascular Fitness" at the end of Lab 3.1 to determine your current level of cardiorespiratory fitness. As you interpret your score, remember that field tests of cardiorespiratory fitness are not precise scientific measurements and have up to a 10–15% margin of error.

You can use the assessment tests to monitor the progress of your fitness program by retesting yourself from time to time. Always compare scores for the *same* test: Your scores on different tests may vary considerably because of differences in skill and motivation and weaknesses in the tests themselves.

QUESTIONS FOR CRITICAL THINKING AND REFLECTION

Why do you think a relatively slow resting pluse rate is a sign of good cardiorespiratory fitness? What physical conditions or attributes are reflected in your pulse rate?

DEVELOPING A CARDIORESPIRATORY ENDURANCE PROGRAM

Cardiorespiratory endurance exercises are best for developing the type of fitness associated with good health, so they should serve as the focus of your exercise program. To create a successful endurance exercise program, follow these guidelines:

- Set realistic goals.
- Set your starting frequency, intensity, and duration of exercise at appropriate levels.
- Choose suitable activities.
- Warm up and cool down.
- Adjust your program as your fitness improves.

Setting Goals

You can use the results of cardiorespiratory fitness assessment tests to set a specific oxygen consumption goal for your cardiorespiratory endurance program. Your goal should be high enough to ensure a healthy cardiorespiratory system, but not so high that it will be impossible to achieve. Scores in the fair and good ranges for maximal oxygen consumption suggest good fitness; scores in the excellent and superior ranges indicate a high standard of physical performance.

Through endurance training, an individual may be able to improve maximal oxygen consumption ($\dot{V}O_{2max}$) by about 10–30%. The amount of improvement possible depends on genetics, age, health status, and initial fitness level; people who start at a very low fitness level can improve by a greater percentage than elite athletes because the latter are already at a much higher fitness level, one that may approach their genetic physical limits. If you are tracking $\dot{V}O_{2max}$ using the field tests described in this chapter, you may be able to increase your score by more than 30% due to improvements in other physical factors, such as muscle power, which can affect your performance on the tests.

Another physical factor you can track to monitor progress is resting heart rate—your heart rate at complete rest, measured in the morning before you get out of bed and move around. Resting heart rate may decrease by as much as 10–15 beats per minute in response to endurance training. Changes in resting heart rate may be noticeable after only about 4–6 weeks of training.

You may want to set other types of goals for your fitness program. For example, if you walk, jog, or cycle as part of your fitness program, you may want to set a time or distance goal—working up to walking 5 miles in one session, completing a 4-mile run in 28 minutes, or cycling a total of 35 miles per week. A more modest goal might be to achieve the Surgeon General's minimum activity level of doing at least 30 minutes of moderate activity on most days. Although it's best to base your program on "SMART" goals, you may also want to set more qualitative goals, such as becoming more energetic, sleeping better, and improving the fit of your clothes.

MOTIVATION BOOSTER

Improve your self-talk. If you are having trouble starting a fitness program, try listening to your self-talk about exercise. Do you rationalize, make excuses, procrastinate, or avoid responsibility for your habits? This may be the case if you find yourself thinking things such as "My schedule won't allow me to exercise" or "I'll start when the weather improves." Look for ways to counter such thinking and change your habits. For example, try thinking "Lots of busy people work out, so I can find time, too," or "I can use the gym until the weather gets better." Remember: When you make excuses, the only one who loses is you.

Applying the FITT Equation

As described in Chapter 2, you can use the acronym FITT to remember key parameters of your fitness program: Frequency, Intensity, Time (duration), and Type of activity.

Frequency of Training To build cardiorespiratory endurance, you should exercise 3–5 days per week. Beginners should start with 3 and work up to 5 days per week. Training more than 5 days per week can lead to injury and isn't necessary for the typical person on an exercise program designed to promote wellness. (It is safe to do moderate-intensity activity such as walking and gardening every day.) Training fewer than 3 days per week makes it difficult to improve your fitness (unless exercise intensity is very high) or to use exercise to lose weight. In addition, you risk injury because your body never gets a chance to fully adapt to regular exercise training.

Intensity of Training Intensity is the most important factor in achieving training effects. You must exercise intensely enough to stress your body so that fitness improves. Four methods of monitoring exercise intensity are described below; choose the method that works best for you. Be sure to make adjustments in your intensity levels for environmental or individual factors. For example, on a hot and humid day or on your first day back to your program after an illness, you should decrease your intensity level.

TARGET HEART RATE ZONE One of the best ways to monitor the intensity of cardiorespiratory endurance exercise is to measure your heart rate. It isn't necessary to exercise at your maximum heart rate to improve maximal oxygen consumption. Fitness adaptations occur at lower heart rates with a much lower risk of injury.

According to the American College of Sports Medicine, your **target heart rate zone**—rates at which you should exercise to experience cardiorespiratory benefits—is between 65% and 90% of your maximum heart rate. To calculate your target heart rate zone, follow these steps:

1. Estimate your maximum heart rate (MHR) by subtracting your age from 220, or have it measured precisely by undergoing an exercise stress test in a doctor's office, hospital, or sports medicine lab. (*Note:* The formula to estimate maximum heart rate carries an error of about ±10–15 beats per minute and can be very inaccurate for some people, particularly older adults and young children. If your exercise heart rate seems inaccurate—that is, exercise within your target zone seems either too easy or too difficult—then use the perceived exertion method described in the next section or have your maximum heart rate measured precisely.)
2. Multiply your MHR by 65% and 90% to calculate your target heart rate zone. (*Note:* Very unfit people should use 55% of MHR for their training threshold.)

For example, a 19-year-old would calculate her target heart rate zone as follows:

MHR = 220 − 19 = 201

65% training intensity = 0.65 × 201 = 131 bpm

90% training intensity = 0.90 × 201 = 181 bpm

To gain fitness benefits, the young woman in our example would have to exercise at an intensity that raises her heart rate to between 131 and 181 bpm.

An alternative method for calculating target heart rate range uses **heart rate reserve**, the difference between maximum heart rate and resting heart rate. Using this method, target heart rate is equal to resting heart rate plus between 50% (40% for very unfit people) and 85% of heart rate reserve. Although some people (particularly those with very low levels of fitness) will obtain more accurate results using this more complex method, both methods provide reasonable estimates of an appropriate target heart rate zone. Formulas for both methods of calculating target heart rate are given in Lab 3.2.

If you have been sedentary, start by exercising at the lower end of your target heart rate range (65% of maximum heart rate or 50% of heart rate reserve) for at least 4–6 weeks. Fast and significant gains in maximal oxygen consumption can be made by exercising closer to the top of the range, but you may increase your risk of injury and overtraining. You *can* achieve significant health benefits by exercising at the bottom of your target range, so don't feel pressured into exercising at an unnecessarily intense level. If you exercise at a lower intensity, you can increase the duration or frequency of training to obtain as much benefit to your health, as long as you are above the 65% training threshold. (For people with a very low initial level of fitness, a lower training intensity, 55–64% of maximum heart rate or 40–49% of heart rate reserve, may be sufficient to achieve improvements in maximal oxygen consumption, especially at the start of an exercise program. Intensities of 70–85% of maximum heart rate are appropriate for average individuals.)

By monitoring your heart rate, you will always know if you are working hard enough to improve, not hard enough, or too hard. As your program progresses and your fitness improves, you will need to jog, cycle, or walk faster in order to reach your target heart rate zone. To monitor your heart rate during exercise, count your pulse while you're still moving or immediately after you stop exercising. Count beats for 10 seconds, and then multiply that number by 6 to see if your heart rate is in your target zone. Table 3.3 shows target heart rate ranges and 10-second counts based on the maximum heart rate formula.

Table 3.3 Target Heart Rate Range and 10-Second Counts

Age (years)	Target Heart Rate Range (bpm)*	10-Second Count (beats)*
20–24	127–180	21–30
25–29	124–176	20–29
30–34	121–171	20–28
35–39	118–167	19–27
40–44	114–162	19–27
45–49	111–158	18–26
50–54	108–153	18–25
55–59	105–149	17–24
60–64	101–144	16–24
65+	97–140	16–23

*Target heart rates lower than those shown here are appropriate for individuals with a very low initial level of fitness. Ranges are based on the following formula: Target heart rate = 0.65 to 0.90 of maximum heart rate, assuming maximum heart rate = 220 − age. The heart rate range values shown here correspond to ratings of perceived exertion (RPE) values of about 12–18.

TERMS

target heart rate zone The range of heart rates that should be reached and maintained during cardiorespiratory endurance exercise to obtain training effects.

heart rate reserve The difference between maximum heart rate and resting heart rate; used in one method for calculating target heart rate range.

METS One way scientists describe fitness is in terms of the capacity to increase metabolism (energy usage level) above rest. Scientists use METs to measure the metabolic cost of an exercise. One **MET** represents the body's resting metabolic rate—that is, the energy requirement of the body at rest. Exercise intensity is expressed in multiples of resting metabolic rate. For example, an exercise intensity of 2 METs is 2 times the resting metabolic rate.

METs are used to describe exercise intensities for occupational activities and exercise programs. Exercise intensities of less than 3–4 METs are considered low. Household chores and most industrial jobs fall into this category. Exercise at these intensities does not improve fitness for most people, but it will improve fitness for people with low physical capacities. Activities that increase metabolism by 6–8 METs are classified as moderate-intensity exercises and are suitable for most people beginning an exercise program. Vigorous exercise increases metabolic rate by more than 10 METs. Fast running or cycling, as well as intense play in sports like racquetball, can place people in this category. Table 3.4 lists the MET ratings for various activities.

METs are intended to be only an approximation of exercise intensity. Skill, body weight, body fat, and environment affect the accuracy of METs. As a practical matter, however, these limitations can be disregarded. METs are a good way to express exercise intensity because this system is easy for people to remember and apply.

Table 3.4 Approximate MET and Caloric Costs of Selected Activities for a 154-Pound Person

Activity	METs	Caloric Expenditure (kilocalories/min)
Rest	1	1.2
Light housework	2–4	2.4–4.8
Bowling	2–4	2.5–5
Walking	2–7	2.5–8.5
Archery	3–4	3.7–5
Dancing	3–7	3.7–8.5
Hiking	3–7	3.7–8.5
Horseback riding	3–8	3.7–10
Cycling	3–8	3.7–10
Basketball (recreational)	3–9	3.7–11
Swimming	4–8	5–10
Tennis	4–9	5–11
Fishing (fly, stream)	5–6	6–7.5
In-line skating	5–8	6–10
Skiing (downhill)	5–8	6–10
Rock climbing	5–10	6–12
Scuba diving	5–10	6–12
Skiing (cross-country)	6–12	7.5–15
Jogging	8–12	10–15

NOTE: Intensity varies greatly with effort, skill, and motivation.

SOURCE: Adapted from American College of Sports Medicine. 2006. *ACSM's Guidelines for Excercise Testing and Prescription*, 7th ed. Philadelphia: Lippincott Williams and Wilkins.

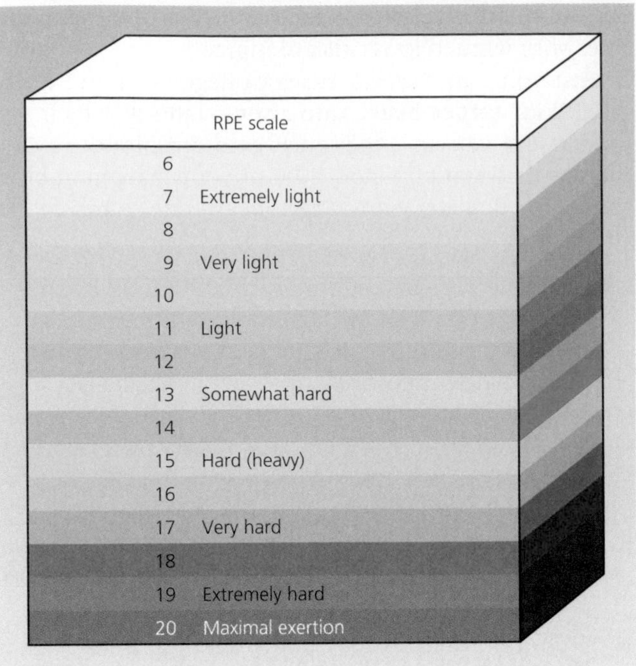

FIGURE 3.6 Ratings of perceived exertion (RPE). Experienced exercisers may use this subjective scale to estimate how near they are to their target heart rate zone. The scale was developed in the 1950s by Swedish exercise physiologist Gunnar Borg and is also known as the Borg scale.

SOURCE: *Psychology from Research to Practice* (1978), ed. H. L. Pick. Kluwer Academic/Plenum Publishing Corporation. With kind permission of Springer Science and Business Media and the author.

RATINGS OF PERCEIVED EXERTION Another way to monitor intensity is to monitor your perceived level of exertion. Repeated pulse counting during exercise can become a nuisance if it interferes with the activity. As your exercise program progresses, you will probably become familiar with the amount of exertion required to raise your heart rate to target levels. In other words, you will know how you feel when you have exercised intensely enough. If this is the case, you can use the scale of **ratings of perceived exertion (RPE)** shown in Figure 3.6 to monitor the intensity of your exercise session without checking your pulse.

To use the RPE scale, select a rating that corresponds to your subjective perception of how hard you are exercising when you are training in your target heart rate zone. If your target zone is about 135–155 bpm, exercise intensely enough to raise your heart rate to that level, and then associate a rating—for example, "somewhat hard" or "hard" (14 or 15)—with how hard you feel you are working. To reach and maintain a similar intensity in future workouts, exercise hard enough to reach what you feel is the same level of exertion. You should periodically check your RPE against your target heart rate zone to make sure it's correct. RPE is an accurate means of monitoring exercise intensity, and you may find it easier and more convenient than pulse counting.

TALK TEST Another easy method of monitoring exercise exertion—in particular, to prevent overly intense exercise—is the talk test. Although your breathing rate will increase during cardiorespiratory endurance exercise, you should not work out so intensely that you cannot speak comfortably. The talk test is an effective gauge of intensity for many types of activities.

Time (Duration) of Training A total duration of 20–60 minutes is recommended; exercise can take place in a single session or in multiple sessions lasting 10 or more minutes. The total duration of exercise depends on its intensity. To improve cardiorespiratory endurance during a low- to moderate-intensity activity such as walking or slow swimming, you should exercise for 45–60 minutes. For high-intensity exercise performed at the top of your target heart rate zone, a duration of 20 minutes is sufficient. Some studies have shown that 5–10 minutes of extremely intense exercise (greater than 90% of maximal oxygen consumption) improves cardiorespiratory endurance. However, training at high intensity, particularly during high-impact activities, increases the risk of injury. Also, because of the discomfort of high-intensity exercise, you are more likely to discontinue your exercise program. Longer-duration, low- to moderate-intensity activities generally result in more gradual gains in maximal oxygen consumption. In planning your program, start with less vigorous activities and gradually increase intensity.

Type of Activity Cardiorespiratory endurance exercises include activities that involve the rhythmic use of large-muscle groups for an extended period of time, such as jogging, walking, cycling, aerobic dancing and other forms of group exercise, cross-country skiing, and swimming. (For a discussion of the benefits of walking and running, see the box "Should I Walk or Run for Fitness?" on p. 74.) Start-and-stop sports, such as tennis and racquetball, also qualify, as long as you have enough skill to play continuously and intensely enough to raise your heart rate to target levels.

Having fun is a strong motivator; select a physical activity that you enjoy, and it will be easier to stay with your program. Exercising with a friend can also be helpful as a motivator. Consider whether you prefer competitive or individual sports and whether starting something new would be best. Other important considerations are access to facilities, expense, equipment, and the time required to achieve an adequate skill level and workout.

Warming Up and Cooling Down

It's important to warm up before every session of cardiorespiratory endurance exercise and to cool down afterward. Because the body's muscles work better when their temperature is slightly above resting level, warming up enhances performance and decreases the chance of injury. It gives the body time to redirect blood to active muscles and the heart time to adapt to increased demands. Warming up also helps spread **synovial fluid** throughout the joints, which helps protect their surfaces from injury.

As mentioned in Chapter 2, a warm-up session should include low-intensity, whole-body movements similar to those in the activity that will follow. Low-intensity movements might include walking slowly before beginning a brisk walk, hitting forehands and backhands before a tennis match, and running a 12-minute mile before progressing to an 8-minute one. An active warm-up of 5–10 minutes is adequate for most types of exercise. However, warm-up time will depend on your level of fitness, experience, and individual preferences.

If you like to stretch before exercising, experts recommend that you stretch after the active part of your warm-up, when your body temperature has been elevated (see Chapter 5). Studies have found that stretching prior to exercise can decrease performance, so some experts recommend that stretching be done *after* a workout.

Cooling down after exercise is important for returning the body to a nonexercising state. A cool-down helps maintain blood flow to the heart and brain and redirects blood from working muscles to other areas of the body; it helps prevent a large drop in blood pressure, dizziness, and other potential cardiovascular complications. A cool-down, consisting of 5–10 minutes of reduced activity, should follow every workout to allow heart rate, breathing, and circulation to return to normal. Decrease the intensity of exercise gradually during your cool-down. For example, following a running workout, begin your cool-down by jogging at half speed for 30 seconds to a minute; then do several minutes of walking, reducing your speed slowly. A good rule of thumb is to cool down at least until your heart rate

MET A unit of measure that represents the body's resting metabolic rate—that is, the energy requirement of the body at rest.

ratings of perceived exertion (RPE) A system of monitoring exercise intensity based on assigning a number to the subjective perception of target intensity.

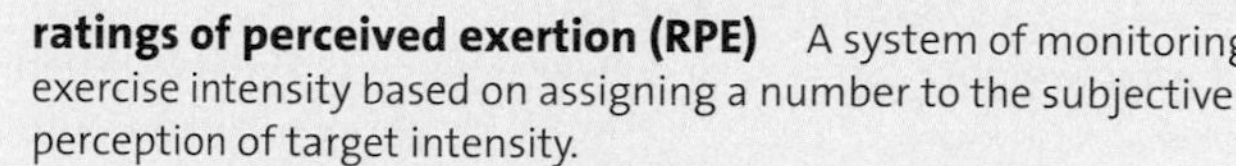

synovial fluid Fluid produced within many joints that provides lubrication and nutrients for the joints.

TAKE CHARGE

Should I Walk or Run for Fitness?

Which exercise is more beneficial for fitness—walking or running? Enthusiasts have been debating this question for years, and experts say the answer is a complicated one, at least in technical terms. Each has its advantages and drawbacks, but both walking and running can be excellent forms of exercise.

Common Benefits

Walking and running (or jogging) both allow you to burn calories and build cardiorespiratory fitness. They are both affordable, since all you need is a good pair of shoes. They are also highly accessible for most people because you can run or walk just about anywhere, as long as you choose a route that is safe.

Big Differences

As forms of exercise, the main difference between walking and running is the way they allow your body to burn calories. All things being equal, running burns more calories than walking—that is, until you factor in the duration of your exercise.

For example, if you run a mile, your body will primarily burn carbohydrates for energy because you are exercising at a relatively high intensity for a relatively short amount of time. If you walk a mile, however, your body will metabolize more fat because you are exercising for a longer amount of time. Because of walking's potential as a fat-burning exercise, some experts say that it is more effective to walk briskly for 45 minutes than to run for 20 minutes. However, running increases post-exercise metabolism more than walking, which contributes to the energy cost of exercise.

In terms of cardiorespiratory fitness, evidence varies, but experts say that brisk walking (up to a speed of about 5 mph) produces the same or better fitness benefits compared to running. Your results will depend on factors such as your age and weight, the pace at which you move, and the distance or amount of time you run or walk.

Because running and walking differ in these ways, many fitness experts say the best approach is to combine them. If your workouts include long, brisk walks interspersed with short, intense bursts of running, you can maximize your fat burning and your cardiorespiratory fitness.

The other main difference between walking and running is the risks they pose. Walking is gentler on the joints than running and carries a much lower likelihood of injury. Running is considered a high-impact form of exercise that can take a severe toll on the joints (especially the knees), ankles, and feet. Running also carries a higher risk of sudden cardiac arrest or failure, although this risk is low in healthy people who are used to running and who exercise within their limits.

How To Choose?

Instead of trying to figure out which exercise is "better," physicians and fitness authorities say you should simply do the exercise with which you are most comfortable. Here are two points that can help you decide:

- If you have been sedentary a long time or have a health problem that prevents you from running comfortably (or that might make running dangerous), then walking is probably the better option. If you are concerned that exercising might pose a risk to your health, however, talk to your physician before starting *any* kind of exercise program.
- If your exercise time is limited, running (or a combination of brisk walking and running) may suit your schedule, as it allows you to burn more calories in less time than walking. However, if you are new to running, start with a walking program and work your way into running.

See Chapter 7 for detailed information on setting up a personalized walking, running, or combination program.

drops below 100 beats per minute. Doing stretching exercises at the end of a workout is an excellent strategy: Your muscles are warm, allowing you to stretch farther with less risk of injury; in addition, there is no danger of decreased performance.

The general pattern of a safe and successful workout for cardiorespiratory fitness is illustrated in Figure 3.7.

MOTIVATION BOOSTER

Enlist support. Studies of college students have found that social support is a key factor influencing whether students exercise. Do your friends and family members actively support your fitness goals and program? If not, enlist their help and encouragement—it can make a big difference.

Building Cardiorespiratory Fitness

Building fitness is as much an art as a science. Your rate of progress will depend on your age, health status, genetics, initial level of fitness, and motivation. Your fitness improves when you overload your body. However, you must increase the intensity, frequency, and duration of exercise carefully to avoid injury and overtraining.

For the initial stage of your program, which may last anywhere from 3 to 6 weeks, exercise at the low end of your target heart rate zone. Begin with a frequency of 3–4 days per week, and choose a duration appropriate for your fitness level: 12–15 minutes if you are very unfit, 20 minutes if you are sedentary but otherwise healthy, and 30–40 minutes if you are an experienced exerciser. Use this stage of your program to allow both your body and your schedule to adjust to your new exercise routine. Once you can exercise at the upper

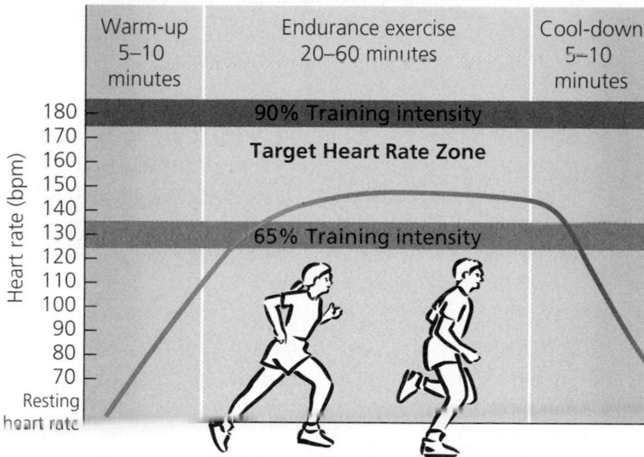

Frequency: 3–5 days per week

Intensity: 55/65–90% of maximum heart rate, 40/50–85% of heart rate reserve plus resting heart rate, or an RPE rating of about 12–18 (lower intensities—55–64% of maximum heart rate and 40–49% of heart rate reserve—are applicable to people who are quite unfit; for average individuals, intensities of 70–85% of maximum heart rate are appropriate)

Time (duration): 20–60 minutes (one session or multiple sessions lasting 10 or more minutes)

Type of activity: Cardiorespiratory endurance exercises, such as walking, jogging, biking, swimming, cross-country skiing, and rope skipping

FIGURE 3.7 The FITT principle for a cardiorespiratory endurance workout. Longer-duration exercise at lower intensities can often be as beneficial for promoting health as shorter-duration, high-intensity exercise.

Table 3.5 Sample Progression for an Endurance Program

Stage/Week	Frequency (days/ week)	Intensity* (beats/ minute)	Time (duration in minutes)
Initial stage			
1	3	120–130	15–20
2	3	120–130	20–25
3	4	130–145	20–25
4	4	130–145	25–30
Improvement stage			
5–7	3–4	145–160	25–30
8–10	3–4	145–160	30–35
11–13	3–4	150–165	30–35
14–16	4–5	150–165	30–35
17–20	4–5	160–180	35–40
21–24	4–5	160–180	35–40
Maintenance stage			
25+	3–5	160–180	20–60

*The target heart rates shown here are based on calculations for a healthy 20-year-old with a resting heart rate of 60 beats per minute; the program progresses from an initial target heart rate of 50% to a maintenance range of 70–85% of heart rate reserve.

SOURCE: Adapted from American College of Sports Medicine. 2006. *ACSM's Guidelines for Exercise Testing and Prescription,* 7th ed. Philadelphia: Lippincott Williams and Wilkins. Reprinted with permission from the publisher.

levels of frequency (4–5 days per week) and duration (30–40 minutes) without excessive fatigue or muscle soreness, you are ready to progress.

The next phase of your program is the improvement stage, lasting from 4 to 6 months. During this phase, slowly and gradually increase the amount of overload until you reach your target level of fitness (see the sample training progression in Table 3.5). Take care not to increase overload too quickly. It is usually best to avoid increasing intensity and duration during the same session or all three training variables in 1 week. Increasing duration in increments of 5–10 minutes every 2–3 weeks is usually appropriate. Signs that you are increasing overload too quickly include muscle aches and pains, lack of usual interest in exercise, extreme fatigue, and inability to complete a workout. Keep an exercise log or training diary to help you monitor your workouts and progress.

Maintaining Cardiorespiratory Fitness

You will not improve your fitness indefinitely. The more fit you become, the harder you have to work to improve. There are limits to the level of fitness you can achieve, and if you increase intensity and duration indefinitely, you are likely to become injured or overtrained. After an improvement stage of 4–6 months, you may reach your goal of an acceptable level of fitness. You can then maintain fitness by continuing to exercise at the same intensity at least 3 nonconsecutive days every week. If you stop exercising, you lose your gains in fitness fairly rapidly. If you take time off for any reason, start your program again at a lower level and rebuild your fitness in a slow and systematic way.

When you reach the maintenance stage, you may want to set new goals for your program and make some adjustments to maintain your motivation. Adding variety to your program can be a helpful strategy. Engaging in multiple types of endurance activities, an approach known as **cross-training**, can help boost enjoyment and prevent some types of injuries. For example, someone who has been jogging 5 days a week may change her program so that she jogs 3 days a week, plays tennis 1 day a week, and goes for a bike ride 1 day a week.

TERMS

cross-training Alternating two or more activities to improve a single component of fitness (for example, walking 2 days per week and swimming 2 days per week to build cardiorespiratory endurance).

TAKE CHARGE

Exercise in Hot Weather

Following a few simple principles can minimize the problems associated with exercising in the heat. To help alert people about weather conditions that could increase the risk of heat illness, the U.S. Weather Service developed the **heat index**—a measure that incorporates both temperature and relative humidity. For example, a temperature of 95 degrees combined with a relative humidity of 50% has a heat index of 107.

Prolonged exposure or physical activity when the heat index is 80–90 can cause fatigue; at a heat index of 90 or above, heat cramps, heat exhaustion, and heatstroke become more likely. Reduce and avoid exercise when the heat index is 90 or above.

A complete chart of heat index values can be found on the *Fit and Well* Online Learning Center. Local heat index information is available from the National Weather Service (http://www.weather.gov).

To avoid the risk of heat illness, follow these guidelines:

- Be in good physical condition. Exercise training can help the body adapt to heat by increasing the sweat rate.
- Use caution when exercising in extreme heat or humidity (over 80°F and/or 60% humidity).
- Slow exercise or add rest breaks to maintain your prescribed target heart rate; as you become acclimatized, you can gradually increase intensity and duration.
- Exercise in the early morning or evening, when temperatures are lowest.
- Drink 2 cups of fluids 2 hours before you begin exercising, and drink 4–8 ounces of fluid every 10–15 minutes during exercise (more frequently during high-intensity activities). Plan for regular water breaks. For an exercise session lasting longer than 60–90 minutes, choose a sports beverage that is cold (8–13°C; 46–55°F), low in sugar (less than 8 grams per 100 milliliters), and contains a small amount of electrolytes.
- During a period of hot weather, weigh yourself every day before exercising. If your weight has decreased by 3% or more from the previous day, don't exercise without first rehydrating.
- Avoid supplements and beverages containing stimulants like ephedra and caffeine when exercising in the heat; they can promote heat-induced illness. Do not use salt pills.
- Wear clothing that breathes, allowing air to circulate and cool the body. Wearing white or light colors will help by reflecting, rather than absorbing, heat. A hat can help keep direct sun off your face. Do not wear rubber, plastic, or other nonporous clothing. "Sauna suits" cause loss of body water, not fat, and don't improve body composition.
- Rest frequently in the shade.
- Slow down or stop if you begin to feel uncomfortable. Watch for the signs of heat disorders; if they occur, act appropriately.

QUESTIONS FOR CRITICAL THINKING AND REFLECTION

Suppose you want to start a new cardiorespiratory exercise program. How do your age, health status, and current level of fitness affect the kind of program you design for yourself? For the first few weeks, how often would you exercise, at what intensity (heart rate), and for how long?

EXERCISE SAFETY AND INJURY PREVENTION

Exercising safely and preventing injuries are two important challenges for people who engage in cardiorespiratory endurance exercise. This section provides basic safety guidelines that can be applied to a variety of fitness activities; visit the *Fit and Well* Online Learning Center for more detailed information about the prevention and care of exercise injuries and safe exercise in challenging environmental conditions. Chapters 4 and 5 include additional advice specific to strength training and flexibility training.

Hot Weather and Heat Stress

Human beings require a relatively constant body temperature to survive. A change of just a few degrees in body temperature can quickly lead to distress and even death. If you lose too much water or if your body temperature gets too high, you may suffer from heat stress. Problems associated with heat stress include dehydration, heat cramps, heat exhaustion, and heatstroke.

In a high-temperature environment, exercise safety depends on the body's ability to dissipate heat and maintain blood flow to active muscles. The body releases heat from exercise through the evaporation of sweat. This process cools the skin and the blood circulating near the body's surface. Sweating is an efficient process as long as the air is relatively dry. As humidity increases, however, the sweating mechanism becomes less efficient because extra moisture in the air inhibits the evaporation of sweat from the skin. This is why it takes longer to cool down in humid weather than in dry weather.

You can avoid significant heat stress by staying fit, avoiding overly intense or prolonged exercise for which you are not prepared, drinking adequate fluids before and during exercise, and wearing clothes that allow heat to dissipate. For additional tips, see the box "Exercise in Hot Weather."

Dehydration Your body needs water to carry out many chemical reactions and to regulate body temperature. Sweating during exercise depletes your body's water supply and can lead to **dehydration** if fluids aren't replaced. Although dehydration is most common in hot weather, it can occur in even comfortable temperatures if fluid intake is insufficient.

Dehydration increases body temperature and decreases sweat rate, plasma volume, cardiac output, maximal oxygen consumption, exercise capacity, muscular strength, and stores of liver glycogen. You may begin to feel thirsty when you have a fluid deficit of about 1% of total body weight.

Drinking fluids before and during exercise is important to prevent dehydration and enhance performance. Thirst receptors in the brain make you want to drink fluids, but during heavy or prolonged exercise or exercise in hot weather, thirst alone isn't a good indication of how much you need to drink. As a rule of thumb, drink at least 2 cups (16 ounces) of fluid 2 hours before exercise, and then drink enough during exercise to match fluid loss in sweat. Drink at least 1 cup of fluid for every 20–30 minutes of exercise, more in hot weather or if you sweat heavily. To determine if you're drinking enough fluid, weigh yourself before and after an exercise session—any weight loss is due to fluid loss that needs to be replaced.

Very rarely, athletes consume too much water and develop *hyponatremia,* a condition characterized by lung congestion, muscle weakness, and nervous system problems. Following the guidelines presented here can help prevent this condition.

Bring a water bottle when you exercise so you can replace your fluids when they're being depleted. For exercise sessions lasting less than 60–90 minutes, cool water is an excellent fluid replacement. For longer workouts, choose a sports drink that contains water and small amounts of electrolytes (sodium, potassium, and magnesium) and simple carbohydrates ("sugar," usually in the form of sucrose, glucose, lactate, or glucose polymers). Electrolytes, which are lost from the body in sweat, are important because they help regulate the balance of fluids in body cells and the bloodstream. The carbohydrates in typical sports drinks are rapidly digestible and can thus help maintain blood glucose levels. Choose a beverage with no more than 8 grams of simple carbohydrate per 100 milliliters. See Chapter 8 for more on diet and fluid recommendations for active people.

Heat Cramps Involuntary cramping and spasms in the muscle groups used during exercise are sometimes called **heat cramps.** While depletion of sodium and potassium from the muscles is involved with the problem, the primary cause of cramps is muscle fatigue. Children are particularly susceptible to heat cramps, but the condition can also occur in adults, even those who are fit. The best treatment for heat cramps is a combination of gentle stretching, replacement of fluid and electrolytes, and rest.

Heat Exhaustion Symptoms of **heat exhaustion** include the following:

- A rapid, weak pulse
- Low blood pressure
- Headache
- Faintness, weakness, dizziness
- Profuse sweating
- Pale face
- Psychological disorientation (in some cases)
- Normal or slightly elevated core body temperature

Heat exhaustion occurs when an insufficient amount of blood returns to the heart because so much of the body's blood volume is being directed to working muscles (for exercise) and to the skin (for cooling). Treatment for heat exhaustion includes resting in a cool area, removing excess clothing, applying cool or damp towels to the body, and drinking fluids. An affected individual should rest for the remainder of the day and drink plenty of fluids for the next 24 hours.

Heatstroke **Heatstroke** is a major medical emergency involving the failure of the brain's temperature regulatory center. The body does not sweat enough, and body temperature rises dramatically to extremely dangerous levels. In addition to high body temperature, symptoms can include the following:

- Hot, flushed skin (dry or sweaty), red face
- Chills, shivering
- Very high or very low blood pressure
- Confusion, erratic behavior
- Convulsions, loss of consciousness

A heatstroke victim should be cooled as rapidly as possible and immediately transported to a hospital. To lower body temperature, get out of the heat, remove excess

TERMS

heat index A measure of how hot it feels; the temperature that would have the same heating effect on a person as a given combination of temperature and relative humidity.

dehydration Excessive loss of body fluid.

heat cramps Sudden development of muscle spasms and pain associated with intense exercise in hot weather.

heat exhaustion Heat illness related to dehydration resulting from exertion in hot weather.

heatstroke A severe and often fatal heat illness produced by exposure to very high temperatures, especially when combined with intense exercise; characterized by significantly elevated core body temperature.

clothing, drink cold fluids, and apply cool or damp towels to the body or immerse the body in cold water.

Cold Weather

In extremely cold conditions, problems can occur if a person's body temperature drops or if particular parts of the body are exposed. If the body's ability to warm itself through shivering or exercise can't keep pace with heat loss, the core body temperature begins to drop. This condition, known as **hypothermia,** depresses the central nervous system, resulting in sleepiness and a lower metabolic rate. As metabolic rate drops, body temperature declines even further, and coma and death can result.

Frostbite—the freezing of body tissues—is another potential danger of exercise in extremely cold conditions. Frostbite most commonly occurs in exposed body parts like earlobes, fingers, and toes, and it can cause permanent circulatory damage. Hypothermia and frostbite both require immediate medical treatment.

What can you do to exercise safely in cold conditions? First of all, don't stay out in very cold temperatures for too long. Take both the temperature and the wind into account when planning your exercise session. Frostbite within 30 minutes is possible in calm conditions when the temperature is colder than −5°F or in windy conditions (30 mph) if the temperature is below 10°F. **Wind chill** values that reflect both the temperature and the wind speed are available as part of a local weather forecast and from the National Weather Service (http://www.weather.gov); a complete wind chill chart is available on the *Fit and Well* Online Learning Center.

Appropriate clothing provides insulation and helps trap warm air next to the skin. Dress in layers so you can remove them as you warm up and can put them back on if you get cold. A substantial amount of heat loss comes from the head and neck, so keep these areas covered. In subfreezing temperatures, protect the areas of your body most susceptible to frostbite—fingers, toes, ears, nose, and cheeks—with warm socks, mittens or gloves, and a cap, hood, or ski mask. Wear clothing that breathes and will wick moisture away from your skin to avoid being cooled or overheated by trapped perspiration. Many types of comfortable, lightweight clothing that provide good insulation are available. It's also important to warm up thoroughly and to drink plenty of fluids.

WEB TERMS

hypothermia Low body temperature due to exposure to cold conditions.

frostbite Freezing of body tissues characterized by pallor, numbness, and a loss of cold sensation.

wind chill A measure of how cold it feels based on the rate of heat loss from exposed skin caused by cold and wind; the temperature that would have the same cooling effect on a person as a given combination of temperature and wind speed.

Poor Air Quality

Air pollution can decrease exercise performance and negatively affect health, particularly if you have respiratory problems such as asthma, bronchitis, or emphysema, or if you smoke. The effects of smog are worse during exercise than at rest because air enters the lungs faster. Polluted air may also contain carbon monoxide, which displaces oxygen in the blood and reduces the amount of oxygen available to working muscles. In a 2007 study, the ACSM found that exercise in polluted air could decrease lung function to the same extent as heavy smoking. Symptoms of poor air quality include eye and throat irritations, difficulty breathing, and possibly headache and malaise.

Do not exercise outdoors during a smog alert or if air quality is very poor. If you have any type of cardiorespiratory difficulty, you should also avoid exertion outdoors when air quality is poor. You can avoid some smog and air pollution by exercising in indoor facilities, in parks, near water (riverbanks, lakeshores, and ocean beaches), or in residential areas with less traffic (areas with stop-and-go traffic will have lower air quality than areas where traffic moves quickly). Air quality is also usually better in the early morning and late evening, before and after the commute hours.

Exercise Injuries

Most injuries are annoying rather than serious or permanent. However, an injury that isn't cared for properly can escalate into a chronic problem, sometimes serious enough to permanently curtail the activity. It's important to learn how to deal with injuries so they don't derail your fitness program. Strategies for the care of common exercise injuries and discomforts appear in Table 3.6; some general guidelines are given below.

When to Call a Physician Some injuries require medical attention. Consult a physician for the following:

- Head and eye injuries
- Possible ligament injuries
- Broken bones
- Internal disorders: chest pain, fainting, elevated body temperature, intolerance to hot weather

Also seek medical attention for ostensibly minor injuries that do not get better within a reasonable amount of time. You may need to modify your exercise program for a few weeks to allow an injury to heal.

Managing Minor Exercise Injuries For minor cuts and scrapes, stop the bleeding and clean the wound. Treat

Table 3.6 Care of Common Exercise Injuries and Discomforts

Injury	Symptoms	Treatment
Blister	Accumulation of fluid in one spot under the skin	Don't pop or drain it unless it interferes too much with your daily activities. If it does pop, clean the area with antiseptic and cover with a bandage. Do not remove the skin covering the blister.
Bruise (contusion)	Pain, swelling, and discoloration	R-I-C-E: rest, ice, compression, elevation.
Fracture and/or dislocation	Pain, swelling, tenderness, loss of function, and deformity	Seek medical attention, immobilize the affected area, and apply cold.
Joint sprain	Pain, tenderness, swelling, discoloration, and loss of function	R-I-C-E. Apply heat when swelling has disappeared. Stretch and strengthen affected area.
Muscle cramp	Painful, spasmodic muscle contractions	Gently stretch for 15–30 seconds at a time and/or massage the cramped area. Drink fluids and increase dietary salt intake if exercising in hot weather.
Muscle soreness or stiffness	Pain and tenderness in the affected muscle	Stretch the affected muscle gently; exercise at a low intensity; apply heat. Nonsteroidal anti-inflammatory drugs, such as ibuprofen, help some people.
Muscle strain	Pain, tenderness, swelling, and loss of strength in the affected muscle	R-I-C-E; apply heat when swelling has disappeared. Stretch and strengthen the affected area.
Plantar fasciitis	Pain and tenderness in the connective tissue on the bottom of your feet	Apply ice, take nonsteroidal anti-inflammatory drugs, and stretch. Wear night splints when sleeping.
Shin splint	Pain and tenderness on the front of the lower leg; sometimes also pain in the calf muscle	Rest; apply ice to the affected area several times a day and before exercise; wrap with tape for support. Stretch and strengthen muscles in the lower legs. Purchase good-quality footwear and run on soft surfaces.
Side stitch	Pain on the side of the abdomen	Stretch the arm on the affected side as high as possible; if that doesn't help, try bending forward while tightening the abdominal muscles.
Tendinitis	Pain, swelling, and tenderness of the affected area	R-I-C-E; apply heat when swelling has disappeared. Stretch and strengthen the affected area.

injuries to soft tissue (muscles and joints) with the R-I-C-E principle: Rest, Ice, Compression, and Elevation.

- ***Rest:*** Stop using the injured area as soon as you experience pain. Avoid any activity that causes pain.
- ***Ice:*** Apply ice to the injured area to reduce swelling and alleviate pain. Apply ice immediately for 10–20 minutes, and repeat every few hours until the swelling disappears. Let the injured part return to normal temperature between icings, and do not apply ice to one area for more than 20 minutes. An easy method for applying ice is to freeze water in a paper cup, peel some of the paper away, and rub the exposed ice on the injured area. If the injured area is large, you can surround it with several bags of crushed ice or ice cubes, or bags of frozen vegetables. Place a thin towel between the bag and your skin. If you use a cold gel pack, limit application time to 10 minutes. Apply ice regularly for 36–48 hours or until the swelling is gone; it may be necessary to apply ice for a week or more if swelling persists.
- ***Compression:*** Wrap the injured area firmly with an elastic or compression bandage between icings. If the area starts throbbing or begins to change color, the bandage may be wrapped too tightly. Do not sleep with the wrap on.
- ***Elevation:*** Raise the injured area above heart level to decrease the blood supply and reduce swelling. Use pillows, books, or a low chair or stool to raise the injured area.

The day after the injury, some experts recommend also taking an over-the-counter medication such as aspirin, ibuprofen, or naproxen to decrease inflammation. To rehabilitate your body, follow the steps listed in the box "Rehabilitation Following a Minor Athletic Injury" on p. 80.

Preventing Injuries The best method for dealing with exercise injuries is to prevent them. If you choose activities for your program carefully and follow the training guidelines described here and in Chapter 2, you should be able to avoid most types of injuries. Important guidelines for preventing athletic injuries include the following:

- Train regularly and stay in condition.
- Gradually increase the intensity, duration, or frequency of your workouts.
- Avoid or minimize high-impact activities; alternate them with low-impact activities.
- Get proper rest between exercise sessions.
- Drink plenty of fluids.
- Warm up thoroughly before you exercise and cool down afterward.

TAKE CHARGE

Rehabilitation Following a Minor Athletic Injury

- Reduce the initial inflammation using the R-I-C-E principle (see text).
- After 36–48 hours, apply heat *if the swelling has completely disappeared.* Immerse the affected area in warm water or apply warm compresses, a hot water bottle, or a heating pad. As soon as it's comfortable, begin moving the affected joints slowly. If you feel pain, or if the injured area begins to swell again, reduce the amount of movement. Continue stretching and moving the affected area until you have regained normal range of motion.
- Gradually begin exercising the injured area to build strength and endurance. Depending on the type of injury, weight training, walking, and resistance training with a partner can all be effective.
- Gradually reintroduce the stress of an activity until you can return to full intensity. Don't progress too rapidly or you'll reinjure yourself. Before returning to full exercise participation, you should have a full range of motion in your joints, normal strength and balance among your muscles, normal coordinated patterns of movement (with no injury compensation movements, such as limping), and little or no pain.

- Achieve and maintain a good level of flexibility.
- Use proper body mechanics when lifting objects or executing sports skills.
- Don't exercise when you are ill or overtrained.
- Use proper equipment, particularly shoes, and choose an appropriate exercise surface. If you exercise on a grass field, soft track, or wooden floor, you are less likely to be injured than on concrete or a hard track. (For information on athletic shoes, see the box "Choosing Exercise Footwear.")
- Don't return to your normal exercise program until any athletic injuries have healed. Restart your program at a lower intensity and gradually increase the amount of overload.

QUESTIONS FOR CRITICAL THINKING AND REFLECTION

Have you ever suffered an injury while exercising? If so, how did you treat the injury? Compare your treatment with the guidelines given in this chapter. Did you do the right things? What can you do to avoid such injuries in the future?

TIPS FOR TODAY AND THE FUTURE

Regular, moderate exercise, even in short bouts spread through the day, can build and maintain cardiorespiratory fitness.

RIGHT NOW YOU CAN

- Assess your cardiorespiratory fitness by using one of the methods discussed in this chapter and in Lab 3.1.
- Do a short bout of endurance exercise: 10–15 minutes of walking, jogging, cycling, or another endurance activity.
- If you have physical activity planned for later in the day, drink some fluids now to make sure you are fully hydrated for your workout.
- Consider the exercise equipment, including shoes, you currently have on hand. If you need new equipment, start gathering the information you'll need to get the best equipment you can afford.
- Contact someone you know who engages in regular endurance exercise. Ask what strategies she or he uses to find time for exercise and to stay motivated.

IN THE FUTURE YOU CAN

- Graduate to a different, more challenging fitness assessment as your cardiorespiratory fitness improves.
- Incorporate different types of exercises into your cardiorespiratory endurance training to keep yourself challenged and motivated.

SUMMARY

- The cardiorespiratory system consists of the heart, blood vessels, and respiratory system; it picks up and transports oxygen, nutrients, and waste products.
- The body takes chemical energy from food and uses it to produce ATP and fuel cellular activities. ATP is stored in the body's cells as the basic form of energy.
- During exercise, the body supplies ATP and fuels cellular activities by combining three energy systems: immediate, for short periods of activity; nonoxidative (anaerobic), for intense activity; and oxidative (aerobic), for prolonged activity. Which energy system predominates depends on the duration and intensity of the activity.
- Cardiorespiratory endurance exercise improves cardiorespiratory functioning and cellular metabolism; it reduces the risk of chronic diseases such as heart disease, cancer, type 2 diabetes, obesity, and osteoporosis; and it improves immune function and psychological and emotional well-being.
- Cardiorespiratory fitness is measured by determining how well the cardiorespiratory system transports and uses oxygen.

(continued on p. 83)

Choosing Exercise Footwear

Footwear is perhaps the most important item of equipment for almost any activity. Shoes protect and support your feet and improve your traction. When you jump or run, you place as much as six times more force on your feet than when you stand still. Shoes can help cushion against the stress that this additional force places on your lower legs, thereby preventing injuries. Some athletic shoes are also designed to help prevent ankle rollover, another common source of injury.

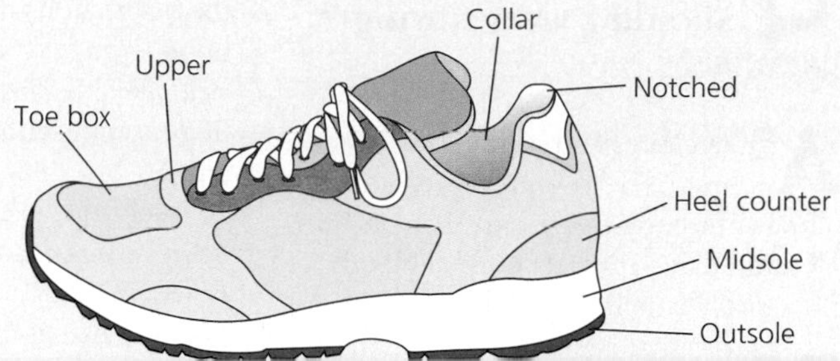

General Guidelines

When choosing athletic shoes, first consider the activity you've chosen for your exercise program. Shoes appropriate for different activities have very different characteristics. For example, running shoes typically have highly cushioned midsoles, rubber outsoles with elevated heels, and a great deal of flexibility in the forefoot. The heels of walking shoes tend to be lower, less padded, and more beveled than those designed for running. For aerobic dance, shoes must be flexible in the forefoot and have straight, nonflared heels to allow for safe and easy lateral movements. Court shoes also provide substantial support for lateral movements; they typically have outsoles made from white rubber that will not damage court surfaces.

Also consider the location and intensity of your workouts. If you plan to walk or run on trails, you should choose shoes with water-resistant, highly durable uppers and more outsole traction. If you work out intensely or have a relatively high body weight, you'll need thick, firm midsoles to avoid bottoming-out the cushioning system of your shoes.

Foot type is another important consideration. If your feet tend to roll inward excessively, you may need shoes with additional stability features on the inner side of the shoe to counteract this movement. If your feet tend to roll outward excessively, you may need highly flexible and cushioned shoes that promote foot motion. For aerobic dancers whose feet tend to roll inward or outward, mid- or high-cut shoes may be more appropriate than low-cut aerobic shoes or cross-trainers (shoes designed to be worn for several different activities). Compared to men, women have narrower feet overall and narrower heels relative to the forefoot. Most women will get a better fit if they choose shoes that are specifically designed for women's feet rather than shoes that are downsized versions of men's shoes.

Successful Shopping

For successful shoe shopping, keep the following strategies in mind:

- Shop at an athletic shoe or specialty store that has personnel trained to fit athletic shoes and a large selection of styles and sizes.
- Shop late in the day or, ideally, following a workout. Your foot size increases over the course of the day and after exercise.
- Wear socks like those you plan to wear during exercise. If you have an old pair of athletic shoes, bring them with you. The wear pattern on your old shoes can help you select a pair with extra support or cushioning in the places you need it the most.
- Ask for help. Trained salespeople know which shoes are designed for your foot type and your level of activity. They can also help fit your shoes properly.
- Don't insist on buying shoes in what you consider to be your typical shoe size. Sizes vary from shoe to shoe. In addition, foot sizes change over time, and many people have one foot that is larger or wider than the other. Try several sizes in several widths, if necessary. Don't buy shoes that are too small.
- Try on both shoes and wear them around for 10 or more minutes. Try walking on a noncarpeted surface. Approximate the movements of your activity: walk, jog, run, jump, and so on.
- Check the fit and style carefully:

  Is the toe box roomy enough? Your toes will spread out when your foot hits the ground or you push off. There should be at least one thumb's width of space from the longest toe to the end of the toe box.

  Do the shoes have enough cushioning? Do your feet feel supported when you bounce up and down? Try bouncing on your toes and on your heels.

  Do your heels fit snugly into the shoe? Do they stay put when you walk, or do they rise up?

  Are the arches of your feet right on top of the shoes' arch supports?

  Do the shoes feel stable when you twist and turn on the balls of your feet? Try twisting from side to side while standing on one foot.

  Do you feel any pressure points?

- If the shoes are not comfortable in the store, don't buy them. Don't expect athletic shoes to stretch over time in order to fit your feet properly.
- If you exercise at dawn or dusk, choose shoes with reflective sections for added visibility and safety.
- Replace athletic shoes about every 3 months or 300–500 miles of jogging or walking.

Q **What kind of clothing should I wear during exercise?**

A Exercise clothing should be comfortable, let you move freely, and allow your body to cool itself. Avoid clothing that constricts normal blood flow or is made from nylon or rubberized fabrics that prevent evaporation of perspiration. Cotton is an excellent material for facilitating the evaporation of sweat. If you sweat heavily when you exercise and find that too much moisture accumulates in cotton clothing, try fabrics containing synthetic materials such as polypropylene that wick moisture away from the skin. Socks made with moisture-wicking compounds may be particularly helpful for people whose feet sweat heavily.

A sports bra is a key piece of clothing for women. A good sports bra should be made of a breathable fabric to allow for evaporation of sweat; it should fit well and have comfortable seams and closures. Try on several styles and sizes to see what fits best, and try the jump test to make sure the bra will provide enough support for your activities. Find a bra that emphasizes function over fashion.

Q **Do I need a special diet for my endurance exercise program?**

A No. For most people, a nutritionally balanced diet contains all the energy and nutrients needed to sustain an exercise program. Don't waste your money on unnecessary supplements. (Chapter 8 has information about putting together a healthy diet.)

Q **How can I measure how far I walk or run?**

A The simplest and cheapest way to measure distance is with a pedometer, which counts your steps. A pedometer's accuracy depends on how precisely you measure your stride length; follow the instructions that come with your pedometer to set this measure. Although stride length varies among individuals, 2000 steps typically equals about 1 mile, and 10,000 steps equals about 5 miles. To track your distance and your progress using a pedometer, follow the guidelines in Lab 2.3. For advice on purchasing a pedometer that meets your needs, check consumer and fitness magazines and Web sites. More tips on using pedometers are provided on the Online Learning Center.

Q **How can I safely increase exercise intensity to build fitness?**

A For both athletes and nonathletes, it is extremely important to increase intensity very gradually and to rest between exercise sessions. If you train too hard and/or don't rest enough, you are more likely to be injured—and be discouraged from continuing with your fitness program. For endurance training, overload techniques such as interval training and wind sprints can help you build fitness quickly but also pose a greater risk of injury or overtraining. Start off with a few high-intensity bouts of exercise and build up gradually. Don't practice interval training or wind sprints more than 2–3 days per week unless you have a high fitness level.

Increase intensity or duration by about 1–3% in a single workout; rest the following day and then do your typical workout. Repeat the more difficult workout after another day of rest. Adjust your progress according to how you feel. You can't increase fitness in a few days. Be patient—with gradual increases in intensity and plenty of rest between workouts, you will be able to move to a higher level of fitness without injury.

Q **If I plan to include both cardiorespiratory endurance training and strength training in a single workout, which should I do first?**

A It depends on your goals. If your primary goal is cardiorespiratory conditioning, then do your endurance workout first. If your fitness program is focused on large gains in strength and you plan to lift relatively heavy weights, then do your strength training workout first. You are likely to make the most rapid gains in fitness in whichever activity you engage in first, when you are fresh.

Q **Is it all right to participate in cardiorespiratory endurance exercise while menstruating?**

A Yes. There is no evidence that exercise during menstruation is unhealthy or that it has negative effects on performance. If you have headaches, backaches, and abdominal pain during menstruation, you may not feel like exercising; for some women, exercise helps relieve these symptoms. Listen to your body, and exercise at whatever intensity is comfortable for you.

Q **Will high altitude affect my ability to exercise?**

A At high altitudes (above 1500 meters or about 4900 feet), there is less oxygen available in the air than at lower altitudes. High altitude doesn't affect anaerobic exercise, such as stretching and weight lifting, but it does affect aerobic activities—that is, any type of cardiovascular endurance exercise—because the heart and lungs have to work harder, even when the body is at rest, to deliver enough oxygen to body cells. The increased cardiovascular strain of exercise reduces endurance. To play it safe when at high altitudes, avoid heavy exercise—at least for the first few days—and drink plenty of water. And don't expect to reach your normal lower altitude exercise capacity.

For more Common Questions Answered about endurance training, visit the Online Learning Center. 

The upper limit of this measure is called maximal oxygen consumption, or $\dot{V}O_{2max}$.

- $\dot{V}O_{2max}$ can be measured precisely in a laboratory, or it can be estimated reasonably well through less expensive assessment tests.

- To have a successful exercise program, set realistic goals; choose suitable activities; begin slowly; always warm up and cool down; and, as fitness improves, exercise more often, longer, and/or harder.

- Intensity of training can be measured through target heart rate zone, METs, ratings of perceived exertion, or the "talk test."

- With careful attention to fluid intake, clothing, duration of exercise, and exercise intensity, endurance training can be safe in hot and cold weather conditions.

- Serious injuries require medical attention. Application of the R-I-C-E principle (rest, ice, compression, elevation) is appropriate for treating many types of muscle or joint injuries.

FOR FURTHER EXPLORATION

BOOKS

American College of Sports Medicine. 2003. *ACSM Fitness Book.* 3rd ed. Champaign, Ill.: Human Kinetics. *Includes fitness assessment tests and advice on creating a complete fitness program.*

Barough, N. 2004. *Walking for Fitness.* New York: DK. *Provides advice on putting together a walking program that matches your fitness goals.*

Beim, G., and R. Winter. 2003. *The Female Athlete's Body Book: How to Prevent and Treat Sports Injuries in Women and Girls.* New York: McGraw-Hill/Contemporary. *Provides detailed information on the prevention and treatment of athletic injuries in women and girls.*

Caron, M. 2007. *Walking for Fitness: The Beginner's Handbook.* Vancouver, B.C.: Greystone Books. *Features two complete programs for walking your way to fitness, with advice on shoes, motivation, and nutrition.*

Fenton, M. 2008. *The Complete Guide to Walking, New and Revised: For Health, Weight Loss, and Fitness.* Guilford, Conn.: Lyons Press. *Discusses walking as a fitness method and a way to avoid diseases such as diabetes.*

Gotlin, R. 2007. *Sports Injuries Guidebook.* Champaign, Ill.: Human Kinetics. *Provides information and care instructions on many types of sports-related injuries.*

Hewitt, B., ed. 2005. *New Cyclist Handbook.* Emmaus, Penn.: Rodale. *Includes information on buying and caring for a bicycle as well as on increasing fitness.*

Juba, K. 2002. *Swimming for Fitness.* New York: Lyons Press. *Provides step-by-step instructions for setting up a swimming fitness program, including advice on technique and avoiding injury and overtraining.*

Nieman, D.C. 2007. *Exercise Testing and Prescription: A Health-Related Approach,* 6th ed. New York: McGraw-Hill. *A comprehensive discussion of the effect of exercise and exercise testing and prescription.*

Noakes, T. 2003. *Lore of Running,* 4th ed. Champaign, Ill.: Human Kinetics. *Provides detailed information on physiology, training, racing, and injury prevention.*

ORGANIZATIONS AND WEB SITES

American Academy of Orthopaedic Surgeons. Provides fact sheets on many fitness and sports topics, including how to begin a program, how to choose equipment, and how to prevent and treat many types of injuries.
http://orthoinfo.aaos.org

American Heart Association. Provides information on cardiovascular health and disease, including the role of exercise in maintaining heart health and exercise tips for people of all ages.
800-AHA-USA1
http://www.americanheart.org

Dr. Pribut's Running Injuries Page. Provides information about running and many types of running injuries.
http://www.drpribut.com/sports/spsport.html

Federal Trade Commission: Consumer Protection—Diet, Health, and Fitness. Provides several brochures with consumer advice about purchasing exercise equipment.
http://www.ftc.gov/bcp/menus/consumer/health.shtm

The Human Heart. An online museum exhibit with information on the structure and function of the heart, blood vessels, and respiratory system.
http://www.fi.edu/learn/heart/index.html

MedlinePlus: Exercise and Physical Fitness. Provides links to news and reliable information about fitness from government agencies and professional associations.
http://www.nlm.nih.gov/medlineplus/exerciseandphysicalfitness.html

Physician and Sportsmedicine. Provides many articles with easy-to-understand advice about exercise injuries.
http://ww.postgradmed.com/index.html

Runner's World Online. Contains a wide variety of information about running, including tips for beginning runners, advice about training, and a shoe buyer's guide.
http://www.runnersworld.com

University of Florida: Keeping Fit. Provides useful information about fitness in a question-and-answer format; an extensive set of links is also provided.
http://www.hhp.ufl.edu/faculty/pbird/keepingfit

Women's Sports Foundation. Provides information and links about training and about many specific sports activities.
http://www.womenssportsfoundation.org

Yahoo/Recreation. Contains links to many sites with practical advice on many sports and activities.
http://dir.yahoo.com/recreation/sports

See also the listings in Chapters 2 and 11.

SELECTED BIBLIOGRAPHY

Adler, P. A., and B. L. Roberts. 2006. The use of Tai Chi to improve health in older adults. *Orthopedic Nursing* 25(2): 122–126.

American College of Sports Medicine. 2006. *ACSM's Guidelines for Exercise Testing and Prescription,* 7th ed. Philadelphia: Lippincott Williams and Wilkins.

American College of Sports Medicine. 2006. *ACSM's Resource Manual for Guidelines for Exercise Testing and Prescription,* 5th ed. Philadelphia: Lippincott Williams and Wilkins.

Brooks, G. A., et al. 2005. *Exercise Physiology: Human Bioenergetics and Its Applications,* 4th ed. New York: McGraw-Hill.

Campbell, K. L., and A. McTiernan. 2007. Exercise and biomarkers for cancer prevention studies. *The Journal of Nutrition* 137(1 Suppl.): 161S–169S.

Carnethon, M. R., et al. 2005. A longitudinal study of physical activity and heart rate recovery: CARDIA, 1987–1993. *Medicine and Science in Sports and Exercise* 37: 606–612.

Colcombe, S., et al. 2006. Aerobic exercise training increases brain volume in aging humans. *The Journals of Gerontology Series A: Biological Sciences and Medical Sciences* 61(11): 1166–1170.

Duscha, B. D., et al. 2005. Effects of exercise training amount and intensity on peak oxygen consumption in middle-age men and women at risk for cardiovascular disease. *Chest* 128(4): 2788–2793.

Federal Trade Commission. 2007. *Weightloss and Fitness* (http://www.ftc.gov/bcp/menus/consumer/health/weight.shtm; retrieved November 5, 2007).

Ferrara, C. M., et al. 2006. Effects of aerobic and resistive exercise training on glucose disposal and skeletal muscle metabolism in older men. *The Journals of Gerontology Series A: Biological Sciences and Medical Sciences* 61(5): 480–487.

Fogelholm, M. 2006. Exercise, substrate oxidation and energy balance. *International Journal of Obesity* 30(6): 1022.

Hagstromer, M., et al. 2006. The International Physical Activity Questionnaire (IPAQ): A study of concurrent and construct validity. *Public Health Nutrition* 9(6): 755–762.

Hew-Butler, T., et al. 2005. Consensus statement of the 1st International Exercise-Associated Hyponatremia Consensus Development Conference, Cape Town, South Africa, 2005. *Clinical Journal of Sports Medicine* 15(4): 208–213.

Interval training: More benefit, less fatigue. 2005. *Consumer Reports,* May.

John, E. M., P. L. Horn-Ross, and J. Koo. 2004. Lifetime physical activity and breast cancer risk in a multiethnic population. *Cancer Epidemiology, Biomarkers, and Prevention* 12(11 Pt. 1): 1143–1152.

Karavatas, S. G., and K. Tavakol. 2005. Concurrent validity of Borg's rating of perceived exertion in African-American young adults, employing heart rate as the standard. *Internet Journal of Allied Health Sciences and Practice* 3(January).

Ko, G. T., et al. 2006. A 10-week Tai-Chi program improved the blood pressure, lipid profile and SF-36 scores in Hong Kong Chinese women. *Medical Science Monitor: International Medical Journal of Experimental and Clinical Research* 12(5): CR196–CR199.

Kondo, N., et al. 2005. Association of inflammatory marker and highly sensitive C-reactive protein with aerobic exercise capacity, maximum oxygen uptake and insulin resistance in healthy middle-aged volunteers. *Circulation Journal* 69: 452–457.

Lambert, C. P., and W. J. Evans. 2005. Adaptations to aerobic and resistance exercise in the elderly. *Reviews in Endocrine and Metabolic Disorders* 6: 137–143.

Laughlin, M. H. 2004. Joseph B. Wolfe Memorial Lecture. Physical activity in prevention and treatment of coronary disease: The battle line is in exercise vascular cell biology. *Medicine and Science in Sports and Exercise* 36: 352–362.

Luebbers, P. E. 2005. Running and walking form. *ACSM Fit Society Page,* Summer.

Macfarlane, D. J., et al. 2006. Very short intermittent vs. continuous bouts of activity in sedentary adults. *Preventive Medicine* 43(4): 332–336.

National Weather Service. 2005. *Heat Index* (http://www.crh.noaa.gov/arx/heatindex.php; retrieved November 5, 2007).

Nieman, D. C. 2005. Can exercise help me sleep better? *ACSM's Health & Fitness Journal* 9(3): 6.

Nurmi-Lawton, J. A., et al. 2004. Evidence of sustained skeletal benefits from impact-loading exercise in young females. *Journal of Bone and Mineral Research* 19(2): 314–322.

Okura, T., et al. 2006. Effect of regular exercise on homocysteine concentrations: The HERITAGE Family Study. *European Journal of Applied Physiology* 98(4): 394–401.

Persinger, R., et al. 2004. Consistency of the talk test for exercise prescription. *Medicine and Science in Sports and Exercise* 36(9): 1632–1636.

Peterson, J. A. 2005. 10 common mistakes made by individuals who engage in aerobic exercises. *ACSM's Health & Fitness Journal* 9(3): 44.

Rixon K. P., et al. 2006. Analysis of the assessment of caloric expenditure in four modes of aerobic dance. *Journal of Strength and Conditioning Research* 20(3): 593–596.

Robergs, R. A., et al. 2004. Biochemistry of exercise-induced metabolic acidosis. *American Journal of Physiology: Regulatory, Integrative and Comparative Physiology* 287(3): R502–R516.

Robinson, D. L. 2007. Bicycle helmet legislation: Can we reach a consensus? *Accident Analysis and Prevention* 39(1): 86–93.

Scott, S. 2005. Combating depression with exercise. *ACSM's Health & Fitness Journal* 9(4): 31.

Shaibi, G. Q., et al. 2006. Aerobic fitness among Caucasian, African-American, and Latino youth. *Ethnic Diseases* 16(1): 120–125.

Shaw, K., et al. 2006. Exercise for overweight or obesity. *Cochrane Database of Systematic Reviews Online* Oct. 18(4): CD003817.

Slentz, C. A., et al. 2005. Inactivity, exercise, and visceral fat. STRRIDE: A randomized, controlled study of exercise intensity and amount. *Journal of Applied Physiology* 99(4): 1613–1618.

Suominen, H. 2006. Muscle training for bone strength. *Aging Clinical and Experimental Research* 18(2): 85–93.

Swain, D. P. 2005. Moderate or vigorous intensity exercise: Which is better for improving aerobic fitness? *Preventive Cardiology* 8: 55–58.

Tunceli, K., et al. 2006. Long-term effects of obesity on employment and work limitations among U.S. Adults, 1986 to 1999. *Obesity* 14(9): 1637–1646.

Wellman, N. S., et al. 2007. Eat better and move more: A community-based program designed to improve diets and increase physical activity among older Americans. *American Journal of Public Health* 97(4): 710–717.

Yamashita, S., et al. 2006. Effects of music during exercise on RPE, heart rate and the autonomic nervous system. *The Journal of Sports Medicine and Physical Fitness* 46(3): 425–430.

Name ______________ Section ______________ Date ______________

LAB 3.1 Assessing Your Current Level of Cardiorespiratory Endurance

Before taking any of the cardiorespiratory endurance assessment tests, refer to the fitness prerequisites and cautions given in Table 3.2. Choose one of the following three tests presented in this lab:

- 1-mile walk test
- 3-minute step test
- 1.5-mile run-walk test

For best results, don't exercise strenuously or consume caffeine the day of the test, and don't smoke or eat a heavy meal within about 3 hours of the test.

The 1-Mile Walk Test

Equipment

1. A track or course that provides a measurement of 1 mile
2. A stopwatch, clock, or watch with a second hand
3. A weight scale

Preparation

Measure your body weight (in pounds) before taking the test.

Body weight: ______________ lb

Instructions

1. Warm up before taking the test. Do some walking, easy jogging, or calisthenics and some stretching exercises.
2. Cover the 1-mile course as quickly as possible. Walk at a pace that is brisk but comfortable. You must raise your heart rate above 120 beats per minute (bpm).
3. As soon as you complete the distance, note your time and take your pulse for 10 seconds.

   Walking time: ______________ min ______________ sec

   10-second pulse count: ______________ beats
4. Cool down after the test by walking slowly for several minutes.

Determining Maximal Oxygen Consumption

1. Convert your 10-second pulse count into a value for exercise heart rate by multiplying it by 6.

   Exercise heart rate: ______________ (10-sec pulse count) × 6 = ______________ bpm
2. Convert your walking time from minutes and seconds to a decimal figure. For example, a time of 14 minutes and 45 seconds would be 14 + (45/60), or 14.75 minutes.

   Walking time: ______________ min + (______________ sec ÷ 60 sec/min) = ______________ min
3. Insert values for your age, gender, weight, walking time, and exercise heart rate in the following equation, where

   W = your weight (in pounds)

   A = your age (in years)

   G = your gender (male = 1; female = 0)

   T = your time to complete the 1-mile course (in minutes)

   H = your exercise heart rate (in beats per minute)

   $\dot{V}O_{2max} = 132.853 - (0.0769 \times W) - (0.3877 \times A) + (6.315 \times G) - (3.2649 \times T) - (0.1565 \times H)$

For example, a 20-year-old, 190-pound male with a time of 14.75 minutes and an exercise heart rate of 152 bpm would calculate maximal oxygen consumption as follows:

$\dot{V}O_{2max} = 132.853 - (0.0769 \times 190) - (03877 \times 20) + (6.315 \times 1) - (3.2649 \times 14.75) - (0.1565 \times 152) = 45$ *ml/kg/min*

$\dot{V}O_{2max}$ = 132.853 − (0.0769 × ____________ [weight (lb)]) − (0.3877 × ____________ [age (years)]) + (6.315 × ____________ [gender])

− (3.2649 × ____________ [walking time (min)]) − (0.1565 × ____________ [exercise heart rate (bpm)]) = __________ ml/kg/min

4. Copy this value for $\dot{V}O_{2max}$ into the appropriate place in the chart on the final page of this lab.

The 3-Minute Step Test

Equipment

1. A step, bench, or bleacher step that is 16.25 inches from ground level
2. A stopwatch, clock, or watch with a second hand
3. A metronome

Preparation

Practice stepping up onto and down from the step before you begin the test. Each step has four beats: up-up-down-down. Males should perform the test with the metronome set for a rate of 96 beats per minute, or 24 steps per minute. Females should set the metronome at 88 beats per minute, or 22 steps per minute.

Instructions

1. Warm up before taking the test. Do some walking, easy jogging, and stretching exercises.
2. Set the metronome at the proper rate. Your instructor or a partner can call out starting and stopping times; otherwise, have a clock or watch within easy viewing during the test.
3. Begin the test and continue to step at the correct pace for 3 minutes.
4. Stop after 3 minutes. Remain standing and count your pulse for the 15-second period from 5 to 20 seconds into recovery.

   15-second pulse count: __________ beats
5. Cool down after the test by walking slowly for several minutes.

Determining Maximal Oxygen Consumption

1. Convert your 15-second pulse count to a value for recovery heart rate by multiplying by 4.

   Recovery heart rate: ______________ [15-sec pulse count] × 4 = __________ bpm
2. Insert your recovery heart rate in the equation below, where

   H = recovery heart rate (in beats per minute)

   Males: $\dot{V}O_{2max} = 111.33 - (0.42 \times H)$

   Females: $\dot{V}O_{2max} = 65.81 - (0.1847 \times H)$

   For example, a man with a recovery heart rate of 162 bpm would calculate maximal oxygen consumption as follows:

   $\dot{V}O_{2max} = 111.33 - (0.42 \times 162) = 43$ *ml/kg/min*

   Males: $\dot{V}O_{2max}$ = 111.33 − (0.42 × ______________ [recovery heart rate (bpm)]) = __________ ml/kg/min

   Females: $\dot{V}O_{2max}$ = 65.81 − (0.1847 × ______________ [recovery heart rate (bpm)]) = __________ ml/kg/min
3. Copy this value for $\dot{V}O_{2max}$ into the appropriate place in the chart on the final page of this lab.

The 1.5-Mile Run-Walk Test

Equipment

1. A running track or course that is flat and provides exact measurements of up to 1.5 miles
2. A stopwatch, clock, or watch with a second hand

Preparation

You may want to practice pacing yourself prior to taking the test to avoid going too fast at the start and becoming prematurely fatigued. Allow yourself a day or two to recover from your practice run before taking the test.

Instructions

1. Warm up before taking the test. Do some walking, easy jogging, and stretching exercises.
2. Try to cover the distance as fast as possible without overexerting yourself. If possible, monitor your own time, or have someone call out your time at various intervals of the test to determine whether your pace is correct.
3. Record the amount of time, in minutes and seconds, it takes you to complete the 1.5-mile distance.

   Running-walking time: ________ min ________ sec
4. Cool down after the test by walking or jogging slowly for about 5 minutes.

Determining Maximal Oxygen Consumption

1. Convert your running time from minutes and seconds to a decimal figure. For example, a time of 14 minutes and 25 seconds would be 14 + (25/60), or 14.4 minutes.

   Running-walking time: ________ min + (________ sec ÷ 60 sec/min) = ________ min
2. Insert your running time into the equation below, where

   T = running time (in minutes)

   $\dot{V}O_{2max} = (483 \div T) + 3.5$

   For example, a person who completes 1.5 miles in 14.4 minutes would calculate maximal oxygen consumption as follows:

   $\dot{V}O_{2max} = (483 \div 14.4) + 3.5 = 37$ *ml/kg/min*

   $\dot{V}O_{2max}$ = (483 ÷ ________ (run-walk time (min))) + 3.5 = ________ ml/kg/min
3. Copy this value for $\dot{V}O_{2max}$ into the appropriate place in the chart on the final page of this lab.

Rating Your Cardiovascular Fitness

Record your $\dot{V}O_{2max}$ score(s) and the corresponding fitness rating from the table below.

Women	*Very Poor*	*Poor*	*Fair*	*Good*	*Excellent*	*Superior*
Age: 18–29	Below 31.6	31.6–35.4	35.5–39.4	39.5–43.9	44.0–50.1	Above 50.1
30–39	Below 29.9	29.9–33.7	33.8–36.7	36.8–40.9	41.0–46.8	Above 46.8
40–49	Below 28.0	28.0–31.5	31.6–35.0	35.1–38.8	38.9–45.1	Above 45.1
50–59	Below 25.5	25.5–28.6	28.7–31.3	31.4–35.1	35.2–39.8	Above 39.8
60–69	Below 23.7	23.7–26.5	26.6–29.0	29.1–32.2	32.3–36.8	Above 36.8
Men						
Age: 18–29	Below 38.1	38.1–42.1	42.2–45.6	45.7–51.0	51.1–56.1	Above 56.1
30–39	Below 36.7	36.7–40.9	41.0–44.3	44.4–48.8	48.9–54.2	Above 54.2
40–49	Below 34.6	34.6–38.3	38.4–42.3	42.4–46.7	46.8–52.8	Above 52.8
50–59	Below 31.1	31.1–35.1	35.2–38.2	38.3–43.2	43.3–49.6	Above 49.6
60–69	Below 27.4	27.4–31.3	31.4–34.9	35.0–39.4	39.5–46.0	Above 46.0

SOURCE: Ratings based on norms from The Cooper Institute of Aerobic Research, Dallas, Texas; from *The Physical Fitness Specialist Manual,* Revised 2002. Used with permission.

	$\dot{V}O_{2max}$	Cardiovascular Fitness Rating
1-mile walk test		
3-minute step test		
1.5-mile run-walk test		

Using Your Results

How did you score? Are you surprised by your rating for cardiovascular fitness? Are you satisfied with your current rating?

If you're not satisfied, set a realistic goal for improvement: ______________________

Are you satisfied with your current level of cardiovascular fitness as evidenced in your daily life—your ability to walk, run, bicycle, climb stairs, do yard work, engage in recreational activities?

If you're not satisfied, set some realistic goals for improvement, such as completing a 5K run or 25-mile bike ride:

What should you do next? Enter the results of this lab in the Preprogram Assessment column in Appendix D. If you've set goals for improvement, begin planning your cardiorespiratory endurance exercise program by completing the plan in Lab 3.2. After several weeks of your program, complete this lab again, and enter the results in the Postprogram Assessment column of Appendix D. How do the results compare? (Remember, it's best to compare $\dot{V}O_{2max}$ scores for the same test.)

SOURCES: Kline, G. M., et al. 1987. Estimation of $\dot{V}O_{2max}$ from a one-mile track walk, gender, age, and body weight. *Medicine and Science in Sports and Exercise* 19(3): 253–259. McArdle, W. D., F. I. Katch, and V. L. Katch. 1991. *Exercise Physiology: Energy, Nutrition, and Human Performance.* Philadelphia: Lea and Febiger, pp. 225–226. Brooks, G. A., and T. D. Fahey. 1987. *Fundamentals of Human Performance.* New York: Macmillan.

Name ______________________ Section ______________ Date ______________

LAB 3.2 Developing an Exercise Program for Cardiorespiratory Endurance

1. *Goals.* List goals for your cardiorespiratory endurance exercise program. Your goals can be specific or general, short or long term. In the first section, include specific, measurable goals that you can use to track the progress of your fitness program. These goals might be things like raising your cardiorespiratory fitness rating from fair to good or swimming laps for 30 minutes without resting. In the second section, include long-term and more qualitative goals, such as improving self-confidence and reducing your risk for chronic disease.

   Specific Goals: Current Status ______________________ Final Goals ______________________

   ______________________ ______________________

   ______________________ ______________________

   Other goals: ______________________

   ____

2. *Type of Activities.* Choose one or more endurance activities for your program. These can include any activity that uses large-muscle groups, can be maintained continuously, and is rhythmic and aerobic in nature. Examples include walking, jogging, cycling, group exercise such as aerobic dance, rowing, rope skipping, stair-climbing, cross-country skiing, swimming, skating, and endurance game activities such as soccer and tennis. Choose activities that are both convenient and enjoyable. Fill in the activity names on the program plan.

3. *Frequency.* On the program plan, fill in how often you plan to participate in each activity; the ACSM recommends participating in cardiorespiratory endurance exercise 3–5 days per week.

Program Plan

Type of Activity	Frequency (check ✓)							Intensity (bpm or RPE)	Time (min)
	M	T	W	Th	F	Sa	Su		

4. *Intensity.* Determine your exercise intensity using one of the following methods, and enter it on the program plan. Begin your program at a lower intensity and slowly increase intensity as your fitness improves, so select a range of intensities for your program.

   a. Target heart rate zone: Calculate target heart rate zone in beats per minute and then calculate the corresponding 10-second exercise count by dividing the total count by 6. For example, the 10-second exercise counts corresponding to a target heart rate zone of 122–180 bpm would be 20–30 beats.

   Maximum heart rate: 220 − ________ (age (yeas)) = ______ bpm

   Maximum Heart Rate Method

   65% training intensity = ____________ (maximum heart rate) bpm × 0.65 = ____________ bpm

   90% training intensity = ____________ (maximum heart rate) bpm × 0.90 = ____________ bpm

   Target heart rate zone = ____________ **to** ____________ **bpm** **10-second count =** ____________ **to** ____________

Heart Rate Reserve Method

Resting heart rate: ________ bpm (taken after 10 minutes of complete rest)

Heart rate reserve = ________ (maximum heart rate) bpm − ________ (resting heart rate) bpm = ________ bpm

50% training intensity = (________ (heart rate reserve) bpm × 0.50) + ________ (resting heart rate) bpm = ________ bpm

85% training intensity = (________ (heart rate reserve) bpm × 0.85) + ________ (resting heart rate) bpm = ________ bpm

Target heart rate zone = ________ **to** ________ **bpm** **10-second count =** ________ **to** ________

b. Ratings of perceived exertion (RPE): If you prefer, determine an RPE value that corresponds to your target heart rate range (see p. 72 and Figure 3.6).

5. *Time (Duration).* A total time of 20–60 minutes is recommended; your duration of exercise will vary with intensity. For developing cardiorespiratory endurance, higher-intensity activities can be performed for a shorter duration; lower intensities require a longer duration. Enter a duration (or a range of duration) on the program plan.

6. *Monitoring Your Program.* Complete a log like the one below to monitor your program and track your progress. Note the date on top, and fill in the intensity and time (duration) for each workout. If you prefer, you can also track other variables such as distance. For example, if your cardiorespiratory endurance program includes walking and swimming, you may want to track miles walked and yards swum in addition to the duration of each exercise session. For more extensive sets of logs, refer to the Daily Fitness and Nutrition Journal that accompanies your text.

Activity/Date												
1	Intensity											
	Time											
	Distance											
2	Intensity											
	Time											
	Distance											
3	Intensity											
	Time											
	Distance											
4	Intensity											
	Time											
	Distance											

7. *Making Progress.* Follow the guidelines in the chapter and Table 3.5 to slowly increase the amount of overload in your program. Continue keeping a log, and periodically evaluate your progress.

Progress Checkup: Week ____ of program

Goals: Original Status	Current Status
________	________
________	________
________	________

List each activity in your program and describe how satisfied you are with the activity and with your overall progress. List any problems you've encountered or any unexpected costs or benefits of your fitness program so far.

LOOKING AHEAD>>>>>

AFTER READING THIS CHAPTER, YOU SHOULD BE ABLE TO:

- Describe the basic physiology of muscles and how strength training affects muscles
- Define muscular strength and endurance, and describe how they relate to wellness
- Explain how muscular strength and endurance can be assessed
- Apply the FITT principle to create a safe and successful strength training program
- Describe the effects of supplements and drugs that are marketed to active people and athletes
- Explain how to safely perform common strength training exercises using free weights and weight machines

MUSCULAR STRENGTH AND ENDURANCE 4

TEST YOUR KNOWLEDGE

1. For women, weight training typically results in which of the following?

a. bulky muscles
b. significant increases in body weight
c. improved body image

2. To maximize strength gains, it is a good idea to hold your breath as you lift a weight.

True or false?

3. Regular strength training is associated with which of the following benefits?

a. denser bones
b. reduced risk of heart disease
c. improved body composition
d. fewer injuries

ANSWERS

1. **c.** Because the vast majority of women have low levels of testosterone, they do not develop large muscles or gain significant amounts of weight in response to a moderate weight training program. Men have higher levels of testosterone, so they can build large muscles more easily.
2. **FALSE.** Holding one's breath while lifting weights, called the Valsalva maneuver, can significantly (and possibly dangerously) elevate blood pressure; it also reduces blood flow to the heart and may cause faintness. You should breathe smoothly and normally while weight training. Some experts recommend that you exhale during the most difficult part of each exercise (the "sticking point").
3. **ALL FOUR.** Regular strength training has many benefits for lifetime wellness for both men and women.

FIT AND WELL ONLINE LEARNING CENTER www.mhhe.com/fahey

Visit the *Fit and Well* Online Learning Center for resources that will help you get the most out of your course!

- Study and review aids include practice quizzes, glossary flashcards, chapter summaries, learning objectives, PowerPoint presentations, Common Questions Answered, student handouts, crossword puzzles, Internet activities, and links to wellness Web sites.
- Behavior change tools include a daily fitness and nutrition journal, a behavior change workbook, sample behavior change plans, and blank behavior change logs to print and use.
- Chapter 4 resources also include video clips showing how to do all the exercises described and illustrated in the chapter (look for the video icon)—using free weights, weight machines, resistance bands, stability balls, and no equipment.

Muscles make up more than 40% of your body mass. You depend on them for movement, and, because of their mass, they are the site of a large portion of the energy reactions (metabolism) that take place in your body. Strong, well-developed muscles help you perform daily activities with greater ease, protect you from injury, and enhance your well-being in other ways.

As described in Chapter 2, muscular strength is the amount of force a muscle can produce with a single maximum effort; muscular endurance is the ability to resist fatigue while holding or repeating a muscular contraction. This chapter explains the benefits of strength training (also called *resistance training*) and describes methods of assessing muscular strength and endurance. It then explains the basics of weight training and provides guidelines for setting up your own strength training program.

BASIC MUSCLE PHYSIOLOGY AND THE EFFECTS OF STRENGTH TRAINING

Muscles move the body and enable it to exert force because they move the skeleton. When a muscle contracts (shortens), it moves a bone by pulling on the tendon that attaches the muscle to the bone, as shown in Figure 4.1. When a muscle relaxes (lengthens), the tension placed on the tendon is released and the bone moves back to—or closer to—its starting position.

Muscle Fibers

Muscles consist of individual muscle cells, or **muscle fibers,** connected in bundles (see Figure 4.1). A single muscle is made up of many bundles of muscle fibers and is covered by layers of connective tissue that hold the fibers together. Muscle fibers, in turn, are made up of smaller protein structures called **myofibrils.**

Strength training causes the size of individual muscle fibers to increase by increasing the number of myofibrils. Larger muscle fibers mean a larger and stronger muscle. The development of large muscle fibers is called **hypertrophy;** inactivity causes **atrophy,** the reversal of this process. In some species, muscles can increase in size through a separate process called **hyperplasia,** which involves an increase in the number of muscle fibers rather than the size of muscle fibers. In humans, hyperplasia is not thought to play a significant role in determining muscle size.

Muscle fibers are classified as slow-twitch or fast-twitch fibers according to their strength, speed of contraction, and energy source.

- **Slow-twitch fibers** are relatively fatigue-resistant, but they don't contract as rapidly or strongly as fast-twitch fibers. The principal energy system that fuels slow-twitch fibers is aerobic (oxidative). Slow-twitch muscle fibers are typically reddish in color.
- **Fast-twitch fibers** contract more rapidly and forcefully than slow-twitch fibers but fatigue more quickly. Although oxygen is important in the energy system that fuels fast-twitch fibers, they rely more on anaerobic (nonoxidative) metabolism than do slow-twitch fibers (see Chapter 3 for a discussion of energy systems). Fast-twitch muscle fibers are typically whitish in color.

Most muscles contain a mixture of slow-twitch and fast-twitch fibers. The proportion of the types of fibers varies significantly among different muscles and different individuals, and that proportion is largely fixed at birth, although fibers can contract faster or slower following a period of training or a period of inactivity. The type of fiber that acts during a particular activity depends on the type of work required. Endurance activities like jogging tend to use slow-twitch fibers, whereas strength and

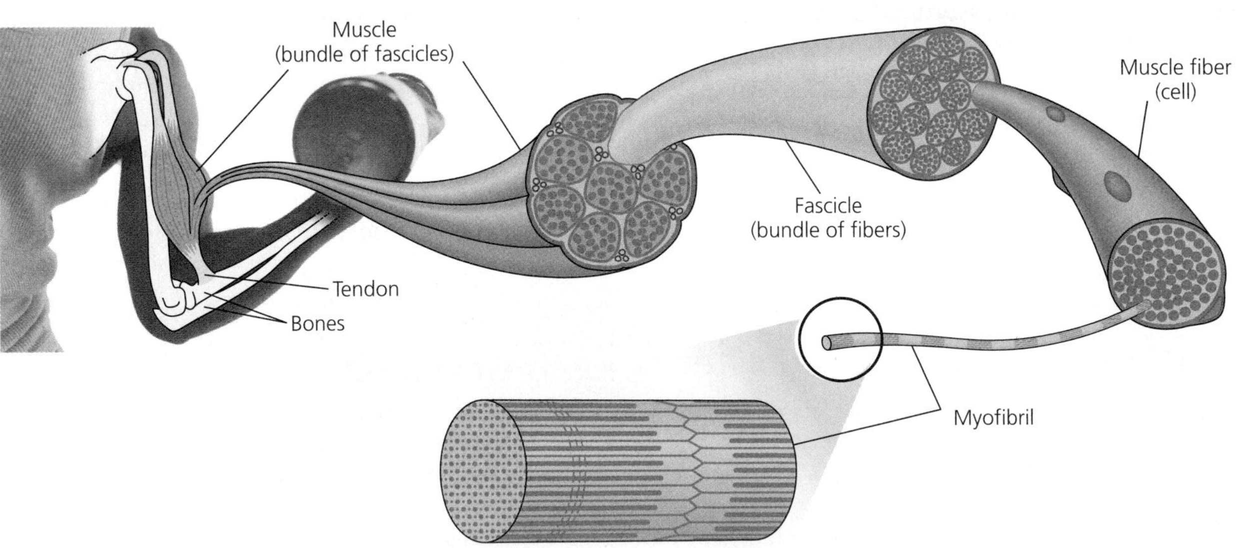

FIGURE 4.1 Components of skeletal muscle tissue.

FIGURE 4.2 Motor unit recruitment during muscle contraction. The number and size of motor units recruited for muscle contraction depends on the load (amount of resistance) and the speed of the movement. For light resistance, a small number of small motor units, made up primarily of slow-twitch fibers, are recruited. To move against heavy resistance or to move a light object very fast, a large number of motor units are recruited, including both small and large motor units. Large motor units contain a high proportion of fast-twitch fibers.

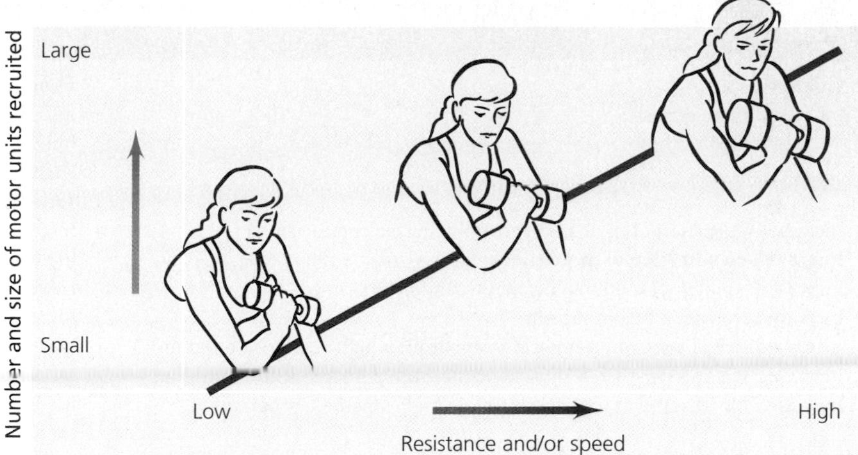

power activities like sprinting use fast-twitch fibers. Strength training can increase the size and strength of both fast-twitch and slow-twitch fibers, although fast-twitch fibers are preferentially increased.

Motor Units

To exert force, the body recruits one or more motor units to contract. A **motor unit** is made up of a nerve connected to a number of muscle fibers. The number of muscle fibers in a motor unit varies from two to hundreds. Small motor units contain slow-twitch fibers, while large motor units contain fast-twitch fibers. When a motor nerve calls on its fibers to contract, all fibers contract to their full capacity. The number of motor units recruited depends on the amount of strength required: When a person picks up a small weight, he or she uses fewer and smaller motor units than when picking up a large weight (Figure 4.2).

Strength training improves the body's ability to recruit motor units—a phenomenon called **muscle learning**—which increases strength even before muscle size increases. The physiological changes and benefits that result from strength training are summarized in Table 4.1.

BENEFITS OF MUSCULAR STRENGTH AND ENDURANCE

Enhanced muscular strength and endurance can lead to improvements in the areas of performance, injury prevention, body composition, self-image, lifetime muscle and bone health, and chronic disease prevention.

Improved Performance of Physical Activities

A person with a moderate-to-high level of muscular strength and endurance can perform everyday tasks—such as climbing stairs and carrying groceries—with ease. Increased strength can enhance your enjoyment of recreational sports by making it possible to achieve high levels of performance and to handle advanced techniques. Strength training also results in modest improvements in maximal oxygen consumption. People with poor muscle strength tire more easily and are less effective in both everyday and recreational activities.

Injury Prevention

Increased muscular strength and endurance help protect you from injury in two key ways:

- By enabling you to maintain good posture
- By encouraging proper body mechanics during everyday activities such as walking and lifting

muscle fiber A single muscle cell, usually classified according to strength, speed of contraction, and energy source.

myofibrils Protein structures that make up muscle fibers.

hypertrophy An increase in the size of muscle fibers, usually stimulated by muscular overload, as occurs during strength training.

atrophy A decrease in the size of muscle fibers.

hyperplasia An increase in the number of muscle fibers.

slow-twitch fibers Red muscle fibers that are fatigue-resistant but have a slow contraction speed and a lower capacity for tension; usually recruited for endurance activities.

fast-twitch fibers White muscle fibers that contract rapidly and forcefully but fatigue quickly; usually recruited for actions requiring strength and power.

power The ability to exert force rapidly.

motor unit A motor nerve (one that initiates movement) connected to one or more muscle fibers.

muscle learning The improvement in the body's ability to recruit motor units, brought about through strength training.

Table 4.1 Physiological Changes and Benefits from Strength Training

Change	Benefits
Increased muscle mass*	Increased muscular strength Improved body composition Higher rate of metabolism Toned, healthy-looking muscles
Increased utilization of motor units during muscle contractions	Increased muscular strength and power
Improved coordination of motor units	Increased muscular strength and power
Increased strength of tendons, ligaments, and bones	Lower risk of injury to these tissues
Increased storage of fuel in muscles	Increased resistance to muscle fatigue
Increased size of fast-twitch muscle fibers (from a high-resistance program)	Increased muscular strength and power
Increased size of slow-twitch muscle fibers (from a high-repetition program)	Increased muscular endurance
Increased blood supply to muscles (from a high-repetition program)	Increased delivery of oxygen and nutrients Increased elimination of wastes
Biochemical improvements (for example, increased sensitivity to insulin)	Enhanced metabolic health
Improved blood fat levels	Reduced risk of heart disease

*Due to genetic and hormonal differences, men will build more muscle mass than women, but both genders make about the same percent gains in strength through a good program.

Good muscle strength and, particularly, endurance in the abdomen, hips, lower back, and legs support the back in proper alignment and help prevent low-back pain, which afflicts more than 85% of Americans at some time in their lives. (Prevention of low-back pain is discussed in Chapter 5.)

Training for muscular strength and endurance also makes the **tendons, ligaments,** and cartilage cells stronger and less susceptible to injury. Resistance exercise prevents injuries best when the strength training program is gradual and progressive and builds all the major muscle groups.

Improved Body Composition

As Chapter 2 explained, healthy body composition means that the body has a high proportion of fat-free mass (primarily composed of muscle) and a relatively small proportion of fat. Strength training improves body composition by increasing muscle mass, thereby tipping the body composition ratio toward fat-free mass and away from fat.

Building muscle mass through strength training also helps with losing fat because metabolic rate is related to muscle mass: the more muscle mass, the higher the metabolic rate. A high metabolic rate means that a nutritionally sound diet coupled with regular exercise will not lead to an increase in body fat. Strength training can boost resting metabolic rate by 0–15%, depending on how hard you train. Resistance exercise also increases muscle temperature, which in turn slightly increases the rate at which you burn calories over the hours following a weight training session.

Enhanced Self-Image and Quality of Life

Strength training leads to an enhanced self-image in both men and women by providing stronger, firmer-looking muscles and a toned, healthy-looking body. Women tend to lose inches, increase strength, and develop greater muscle definition. Men tend to build larger, stronger muscles. The larger muscles in men combine with high levels of the hormone **testosterone** for a strong tissue-building effect; see the box "Gender Differences in Muscular Strength."

Because strength training involves measurable objectives (pounds lifted, repetitions accomplished), a person can easily recognize improved performance, leading to greater self-confidence and self-esteem. Strength training also improves quality of life by increasing energy, preventing injuries, and making daily activities easier and more enjoyable.

Improved Muscle and Bone Health with Aging

Research has shown that good muscular strength helps people live healthier lives. A lifelong program of regular strength training prevents muscle and nerve degeneration that can compromise the quality of life and increase the risk of hip fractures and other potentially life-threatening injuries.

In the general population, people begin to lose muscle mass after age 30, a condition called *sarcopenia*. At first they may notice that they cannot play sports as well as they could in high school. After more years of inactivity and strength loss, people may have trouble performing even the simple movements of daily life, such as walking up a flight of stairs or doing yard work. By age 75, about 25% of men and 75% of women cannot lift more than 10 pounds overhead. Although aging contributes to decreased strength, inactivity causes most of the loss. Poor strength makes it much more likely that a person will be injured during everyday activities.

DIMENSIONS OF DIVERSITY

Gender Differences in Muscular Strength

Men are generally stronger than women because they typically have larger bodies and a larger proportion of their total body mass is made up of muscle. But when strength is expressed per unit of cross-sectional area of muscle tissue, men are only 1–2% stronger than women in the upper body and about equal to women in the lower body. (Men have a larger proportion of muscle tissue in the upper body, so it's easier for them to build upper-body strength than it is for women.) Individual muscle fibers are larger in men, but the metabolism of cells within those fibers is the same in both sexes.

Two factors that help explain these disparities are testosterone levels and the speed of nervous control of muscle. Testosterone is responsible for the development of secondary sex characteristics in males (facial hair, deep voice, etc.). Testosterone also promotes the growth of muscle tissue in both males and females. Testosterone levels are about 5–10 times higher in men than in women, so men tend to have larger muscles. Also, because the male nervous system can activate muscles faster, men tend to have more power.

Some women are concerned that they will develop large muscles from strength training. Because of hormonal differences, most women do not develop big muscles unless they train intensely over many years or take anabolic steroids. Women do gain muscle and improve body composition through strength training, but they don't develop bulky muscles or gain significant amounts of weight: A study of average women who weight trained 2–3 days per week for 8 weeks found that the women gained about 1.75 pounds of muscle and lost about 3.5 pounds of fat.

Losing muscle over time is a much greater health concern for women than small gains in muscle weight, especially because any gains in muscle weight are typically more than balanced by loss of fat weight. Both men and women lose muscle mass and power as they age, but because men start out with more muscle and don't lose power as quickly, older women tend to have greater impairment of muscle function than older men. This may partially account for the higher incidence of life-threatening falls in older women.

The bottom line is that both men and women can increase strength through strength training. Women may not be able to lift as much weight as men, but pound for pound of muscle, they have nearly the same capacity to gain strength as men. Strength training is particularly beneficial for women because it helps prevent bone and muscle loss with aging and maintains fat-free weight during weight control programs.

SOURCES: Fahey, T. D. 2006. *Weight Training for Men and Women*, 6th ed. New York: McGraw-Hill. IDEA. 2006. *Fitness Tip—Why Women Need Weight Training* (http://www.ideafit.com/articles/women_training.asp; retrieved November 19, 2007). Krivickas, L. S., et al. 2001. Age and gender-related differences in maximum shortening velocity of skeletal muscle fibers. *American Journal of Physical Medicine and Rehabilitation* 80: 447–455.

As a person ages, motor nerves can become disconnected from the portion of muscle they control. By age 70, 15% of the motor nerves in most people are no longer connected to muscle tissue. Aging and inactivity also cause muscles to become slower and therefore less able to perform quick, powerful movements. Strength training helps maintain motor nerve connections and the quickness of muscles.

Osteoporosis (bone loss) is common in people over age 55, particularly postmenopausal women. Osteoporosis leads to fractures that can be life-threatening. Hormonal changes from aging account for much of the bone loss that occurs, but lack of bone mass due to inactivity and a poor diet are contributing factors. Strength training can lessen bone loss even if it is taken up later in life, and if practiced regularly, strength training may even build bone mass in postmenopausal women and older men. Increased muscle strength can also help prevent falls, which are a major cause of injury in people with osteoporosis. (Additional strategies for preventing osteoporosis are described in Chapter 8.)

MOTIVATION BOOSTER

Inspire yourself. Make a list of five benefits of muscular strength and endurance that are particularly meaningful to you—reducing your risk of back pain, for example, or improving your tennis game. Post the list in a prominent location and use it as a motivational tool for beginning and maintaining your strength training program.

TERMS

tendon A tough band of fibrous tissue that connects a muscle to a bone or other body part and transmits the force exerted by the muscle.

ligament A tough band of tissue that connects the ends of bones to other bones or supports organs in place.

testosterone The principal male hormone, responsible for the development of secondary sex characteristics and important in increasing muscle size.

QUESTIONS FOR CRITICAL THINKING AND REFLECTION

What benefits of strength training are most important to you? Are you more interested in improved physical performance? Better body composition and appearance? Long-term health benefits? How can you define your goals so they are most meaningful and motivating for you?

Prevention of Chronic Disease

Strength training helps prevent and manage both CVD and diabetes by:

- Improving glucose metabolism.
- Increasing maximal oxygen consumption.
- Reducing blood pressure.
- Increasing HDL cholesterol and reducing LDL cholesterol (in some people).

Stronger muscles reduce the demand on the heart during ordinary daily activities such as lifting and carrying objects. The benefits of resistive exercise to the heart are so great that the American Heart Association recommends that healthy adults and many low-risk cardiac patients do strength training 2–3 days per week. Resistance training is not appropriate for people with some types of heart disease.

ASSESSING MUSCULAR STRENGTH AND ENDURANCE

Muscular strength is usually assessed by measuring the maximum amount of weight a person can lift one time. This single maximum effort is called a **repetition maximum (RM).** You can assess the strength of your major muscle groups by taking the one–repetition maximum (1 RM) test for the bench press and by taking functional leg strength tests. You can measure 1 RM directly or estimate it by doing multiple repetitions with a submaximal (lighter) weight. It is best to train for at least several weeks before attempting a direct 1 RM test; once you have a baseline value, you can retest after 6–12 weeks to check your progress. Refer to Lab 4.1 for guidelines on taking these tests. For more accurate results, avoid any strenuous weight training for 48 hours beforehand.

Muscular endurance is usually assessed by counting the maximum number of **repetitions** of a muscular contraction a person can do (such as in push-ups) or the maximum amount of time a person can hold a muscular contraction (such as in the flexed-arm hang). You can test the muscular endurance of major muscle groups in your body by taking the curl-up test, the push-up test, and the squat endurance test. Refer to Lab 4.2 for complete instructions on taking these assessment tests.

CREATING A SUCCESSFUL STRENGTH TRAINING PROGRAM

Strength training develops muscular strength and endurance in the same way that endurance exercise develops cardiovascular fitness: When the muscles are stressed by a greater load than they are used to, they adapt and improve their function. The type of adaptation that occurs depends on the type of stress applied. To get the most out of your strength training program, design it to achieve maximum fitness benefits with minimum risk of injury. Before you begin, seriously consider the type and amount of training that's right for you.

Static Versus Dynamic Strength Training Exercises

Strength training exercises are generally classified as static or dynamic. Each involves a different way of using and strengthening muscles.

Static Exercise Also called **isometric** exercise, **static exercise** involves a muscle contraction without a change in the length of the muscle or the angle in the joint on which the muscle acts. In isometrics, the muscle contracts, but there is no movement. To perform an isometric exercise, a person can use an immovable object like a wall to provide resistance, or simply tighten a muscle while remaining still (for example, tightening the abdominal muscles while sitting at a desk). The spine extension and the side bridge, shown on p. 114–115, are both isometric exercises.

Static exercises are not as widely used as dynamic exercises because they don't develop strength throughout a joint's entire range of motion. However, static exercises are useful in strengthening muscles after an injury or surgery, when movement of the affected joint could delay healing. Isometrics are also used to overcome weak points in an individual's range of motion. Statically strengthening a muscle at its weakest point will allow more weight to be lifted with that muscle during dynamic exercise. Certain types of calisthenics and Pilates exercises (described in more detail later in the chapter) also involve static contractions. For maximum strength gains, hold the isometric contraction maximally for 6 seconds; do 5–10 repetitions.

Dynamic Exercise Also called **isotonic** exercise, **dynamic exercise** involves a muscle contraction with a change in the length of the muscle. (*Isotonic* means "same tension," which does not accurately describe the way muscles contract, but the term is widely used to describe

A concentric contraction.

An eccentric contraction.

dynamic exercises.) Dynamic exercises are the most popular type of exercises for increasing muscle strength and seem to be most valuable for developing strength that can be transferred to other forms of physical activity. They can be performed with weight machines, free weights, or a person's own body weight (as in curl-ups or push-ups).

There are two kinds of dynamic muscle contractions:

- A **concentric muscle contraction** occurs when the muscle applies enough force to overcome resistance and shortens as it contracts.
- An **eccentric muscle contraction** (also called a *pliometric contraction*) occurs when the resistance is greater than the force applied by the muscle and the muscle lengthens as it contracts.

For example, in an arm curl, the biceps muscle works concentrically as the weight is raised toward the shoulder and eccentrically as the weight is lowered.

CONSTANT AND VARIABLE RESISTANCE Two of the most common dynamic exercise techniques are constant resistance exercise and variable resistance exercise.

- **Constant resistance exercise** uses a constant load (weight) throughout a joint's entire range of motion. Training with free weights is a form of constant resistance exercise. A problem with this technique is that, because of differences in leverage, there are points in a joint's range of motion where the muscle controlling the movement is stronger and points where it is weaker. The amount of weight a person can lift is limited by the weakest point in the range.
- In **variable resistance exercise,** the load is changed to provide maximum load throughout the entire range of motion. This form of exercise uses machines that place more stress on muscles at the end of the range of motion, where a person has better leverage and can exert more force. The Nautilus pull-over machine is an example of a variable resistance exercise machine.

Constant and variable resistance exercises are both extremely effective for building strength and endurance.

OTHER DYNAMIC EXERCISE TECHNIQUES Athletes use four other kinds of isotonic techniques, primarily for training and rehabilitation.

- **Eccentric (pliometric) loading** involves placing a load on a muscle as it lengthens. The muscle contracts eccentrically in order to control the weight. Eccentric loading is practiced during most types of resistance training. For example, you are performing an eccentric movement as you lower the weight to your chest during a bench press in preparation for the active movement. You can also perform exercises designed specifically to overload muscle eccentrically, a technique called *negatives*.
- **Plyometrics** is the sudden eccentric loading and stretching of muscles followed by a forceful concentric contraction. An example would be the action of the lower-body muscles when jumping from a bench to the ground and then jumping back onto the bench. This type of exercise is used to develop explosive strength; it also helps build and maintain bone density.
- **Speed loading** involves moving a weight as rapidly as possible in an attempt to approach the speeds used in movements like throwing a softball or sprinting. In the bench press, for example, speed loading might involve

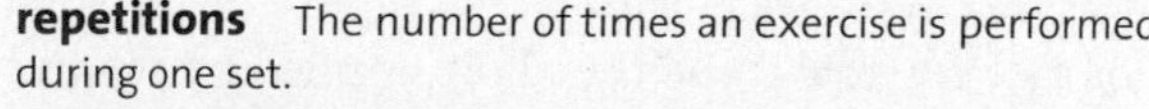

repetition maximum (RM) The maximum amount of resistance that can be moved a specified number of times.

repetitions The number of times an exercise is performed during one set.

static (isometric) exercise Exercise involving a muscle contraction without a change in the length of the muscle.

dynamic (isotonic) exercise Exercise involving a muscle contraction with a change in the length of the muscle.

concentric muscle contraction A dynamic contraction in which the muscle gets shorter as it contracts.

eccentric muscle contraction A dynamic contraction in which the muscle lengthens as it contracts; also called a *pliometric contraction*.

constant resistance exercise A type of dynamic exercise that uses a constant load throughout a joint's entire range of motion.

variable resistance exercise A type of dynamic exercise that uses a changing load, providing a maximum load throughout the joint's entire range of motion.

eccentric (pliometric) loading Loading the muscle while it is lengthening; sometimes called *negatives*.

plyometrics Rapid stretching of a muscle group that is undergoing eccentric stress (the muscle is exerting force while it lengthens), followed by a rapid concentric contraction.

speed loading Moving a load as rapidly as possible.

IN FOCUS

Exercise Machines Versus Free Weights

Exercise Machines		Free Weights	
Advantages	**Disadvantages**	**Advantages**	**Disadvantages**
• Are safe and convenient • Don't require spotters • Don't require lifter to balance bar • Provide variable resistance • Require less skill • Make it easy to move from one exercise to next • Allow easy isolation of muscles and muscle groups • Support back (on many machines)	• Have limited availability • Are inappropriate for performing dynamic movements • Allow limited number of exercises • Train muscles rather than movements • Place minimal stress on core stabilizing muscles (those in torso)	• Allow dynamic movements • Allow user to develop control of weights • Allow greater variety of exercises • Are widely available, inexpensive, and convenient for home use • Train core stabilizing muscles • Are better for building power • Are truer to real-life situations—strength transfers to daily activities	• Are not as safe • Require spotters • Require more skill • Cause more blisters and calluses

doing 5 repetitions as fast as possible using a weight that is half the maximum load you can lift. You can gauge your progress by timing how fast you can perform the repetitions. Speed loading is not recommended for most people because of the risk of injury.

- **Isokinetic** exercise involves exerting force at a constant speed against an equal force exerted by a special strength training machine. The isokinetic machine provides variable resistance at different points in the joint's range of motion, matching the effort applied by the individual while keeping the speed of the movement constant. Isokinetic exercises are excellent for building strength and endurance, but the equipment is expensive and less commonly available than other kinds of weight machines.

Comparing Static and Dynamic Exercise Static exercises require no equipment, so they can be done virtually anywhere. They build strength rapidly and are useful for rehabilitating injured joints. On the other hand, they have to be performed at several different angles for each joint to improve strength throughout the joint's entire range of motion. Dynamic exercises can be performed without equipment (calisthenics) or with equipment (weight training). They are excellent for building strength and endurance, and they tend to build strength through a joint's full range of motion. Most people develop muscular strength and endurance using dynamic exercises. Ultimately, the type of exercise a person chooses depends on individual goals, preferences, and access to equipment.

TERMS

isokinetic The application of force at a constant speed against an equal force.

spotter A person who assists with a weight training exercise done with free weights.

Weight Machines Versus Free Weights

Your muscles will get stronger if you make them work against a resistance. Resistance can be provided by free weights, by your own body weight, or by sophisticated exercise machines. Weight machines are preferred by many people because they are safe, convenient, and easy to use. You just set the resistance (usually by placing a pin in the weight stack), sit down at the machine, and start working. Machines make it easy to isolate and work specific muscles. You don't need a **spotter**—someone who stands by to assist when free weights are used—and you don't have to worry about dropping a weight on yourself.

Free weights require more care, balance, and coordination to use, but they strengthen your body in ways that are more adaptable to real life. They are also more popular with athletes for developing explosive strength for sports. Unless you are training seriously for a sport that requires a great deal of strength, training on machines is probably safer, more convenient, and just as effective as training with free weights. However, you can increase strength with either weight machines or free weights. Information listed in the box "Exercise Machines Versus Free Weights" can help you make a decision about which equipment you may prefer.

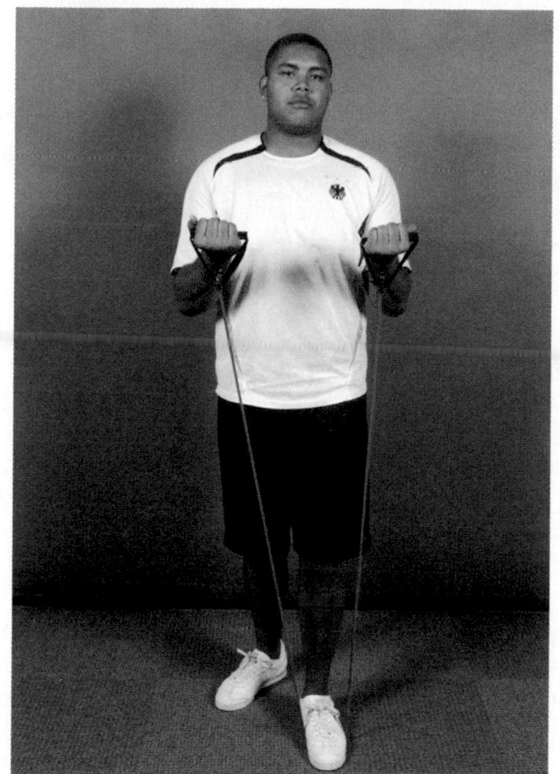

Resistance for strength training can be provided by many different techniques and types of equipment. Shown here are resistance bands (top), a stability ball (center), and a Pilates mat exercise that uses body weight for resistance.

Other Training Methods and Types of Equipment

Remember, you don't need a fitness center or expensive equipment to strength train. If you prefer to train at home or like low-cost alternatives, consider the following.

Resistance Bands Resistance or exercise bands are elastic strips or tubes of rubber material that are inexpensive, lightweight, and portable. They are available in a variety of styles and levels of resistance; some are sold with instructional guides or DVDs, and classes may be offered at fitness centers. Many free weight exercises can be adapted for resistance bands. For example, you can do biceps curls by standing on the center of the band and holding one end of the band in each hand; resistance is provided when you stretch the band to perform the curl.

Special guidelines for using resistance bands safely include examining them regularly for flaws and tears and taking care to avoid snapping the bands. Keeping a firm grip on the bands may require wrapping or looping the band; some people find bands with preformed handles easier to grasp.

Exercise (Stability) Balls The exercise or stability ball is an extra-large inflatable ball. It was originally developed for use in physical therapy but has become a popular piece of exercise equipment for use in the home or gym. It can be used to work the entire body, but it is particularly effective for working the so-called stability muscles ("the core") in the abdomen, chest, and back—muscles that are important for preventing back problems. The ball's instability forces the exerciser to use the stability muscles to balance the body—even when a person simply sits on the ball. Moves such as crunches have been found to be more effective when they are performed with an exercise ball.

When choosing a ball, make sure that your thighs are parallel to the ground when you sit on it; if you are a beginner or have back problems, choose a larger ball so that your thighs are at an angle, with hips higher than knees. Beginners should use caution until they feel comfortable with the movements and take care to avoid poor form due to fatigue.

Although stability ball exercises are generally safe, poor technique can cause falls. It is a good idea to take a class or get help from a trainer to learn proper technique and create an effective stability program.

Pilates Pilates (*pil LAH teez*) was developed by German gymnast and boxer Joseph Pilates early in the twentieth century. It often involves the use of specially designed resistance training devices, although some classes feature just mat or floor work. Pilates focuses on strengthening and stretching the core muscles in the back, abdomen, and buttocks to create a solid base of support for whole-body movement; the emphasis is on concentration, control, movement flow, and breathing. Mat exercises can be done at home, but because there are hundreds of Pilates exercises, some of them strenuous, it is best to begin with some qualified instruction. The Pilates Method Alliance (www.pilatesmethodalliance.com) offers advice on finding a qualified teacher.

No-Equipment Calisthenics You can use your own body weight as resistance for strength training. Exercises such as curl-ups, push-ups, squats, step-ups, heel raises, chair dips, and lunges can be done anywhere.

Video clips showing exercises with resistance bands, stability balls, and no equipment can be found on the Online Learning Center.

Applying the FITT Principle: Selecting Exercises and Putting Together a Program

A complete weight training program works all the major muscle groups. It usually takes about 8–10 different exercises to get a complete full-body workout. Use the FITT principle—frequency, intensity, time, and type—to set the parameters of your program.

Frequency of Exercise For general fitness, the American College of Sports Medicine (ACSM) recommends a frequency of at least two days per week for weight training. Allow your muscles at least 1 day of rest between workouts; if you train too often, your muscles won't be able to work with enough intensity to improve their fitness, and soreness and injury are more likely to result. If you enjoy weight training and want to train more often, try working different muscle groups on alternate days—a training plan called a *split routine*. For example, work your arms and upper body one day, work your lower body the next day, and then return to upper-body exercises on the third day.

Intensity of Exercise: Amount of Resistance The amount of weight (resistance) you lift in weight training exercises is equivalent to intensity in cardiorespiratory endurance training. It determines how your body will adapt to weight training and how quickly these adaptations will occur.

Choose weights based on your current level of muscular fitness and your fitness goals. Choose a weight heavy enough to fatigue your muscles but light enough for you to complete the repetitions with good form. To build strength rapidly, you should lift weights as heavy as 80% of your maximum capacity (1 RM). If you're more interested in building endurance, choose a lighter weight (perhaps 40–60% of 1 RM) and do more repetitions.

For example, if your maximum capacity for the leg press is 160 pounds, you might lift 130 pounds to build strength and 80 pounds to build endurance. For a general fitness program to develop both strength and endurance, choose a weight in the middle of this range, perhaps 70% of 1 RM. Or you can create a program that includes both higher-intensity exercise (80% of 1 RM for 8–10 repetitions) and lower-intensity exercise (60% of 1 RM for 15–20 repetitions); this routine will develop both fast-twitch and slow-twitch muscle fibers.

As noted previously, women do not have to worry about developing bulky muscles from weight training. Increases in muscle size are determined largely by testosterone levels, and college-age women have only about one-fifth the testosterone of college-age men.

Because it can be tedious and time-consuming to continually reassess your maximum capacity for each exercise, you might find it easier to choose a weight based on the number of repetitions of an exercise you can perform with a given resistance.

Time of Exercise: Repetitions and Sets To improve fitness, you must do enough repetitions of each exercise to fatigue your muscles. The number of repetitions needed to cause fatigue depends on the amount of resistance: the heavier the weight, the fewer repetitions to reach fatigue. In general, a heavy weight and a low number of repetitions (1–5) build strength and overload primarily fast-twitch fibers, whereas a light weight and a high number of repetitions (15–20) build endurance and overload primarily slow-twitch fibers (Figure 4.3).

For a general fitness program to build both strength and endurance, try to do about 8–12 repetitions of each exercise; a few exercises, such as abdominal crunches and calf raises, may require more. To avoid injury, older (approximately age 50–60 and above) and frailer people

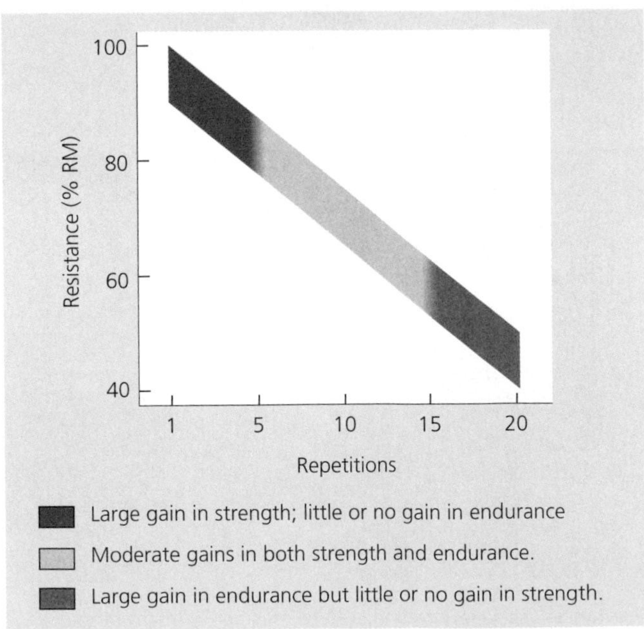

FIGURE 4.3 Training for strength versus training for endurance.

should perform more repetitions (10–15) using a lighter weight.

In weight training, a **set** refers to a group of repetitions of an exercise followed by a rest period. To develop strength and endurance for general fitness, you can make gains doing a single set of each exercise, provided you use enough resistance to fatigue your muscles. (You should just barely be able to complete the 8–12 repetitions—using good form—for each exercise.) Doing more than 1 set of each exercise will increase strength development, and most serious weight trainers do at least 3 sets of each exercise (see the section "More Advanced Strength Training Programs" for guidelines on more advanced programs).

If you perform more than 1 set of an exercise, you need to rest long enough between sets to allow your muscles to work with enough intensity to increase fitness. The length of the rest interval depends on the amount of resistance. In a program to develop a combination of strength and endurance for wellness, a rest period of 1–3 minutes between sets is appropriate; if you are lifting heavier loads to build maximum strength, rest 3–5 minutes between sets. You can save time in your workouts if you alternate sets of different exercises. Each muscle group can rest between sets while you work on other muscles.

Overtraining—doing more exercise than your body can recover from—can occur in response to heavy resistance training. Possible signs of overtraining include lack of progress or decreased performance, chronic fatigue, decreased coordination, and chronic muscle soreness. The best remedy for overtraining is rest; add more days of recovery between workouts. With extra rest, chances are you'll be refreshed and ready to train again. Adding variety to your program, as discussed later in the chapter, can also help you avoid overtraining with resistance exercise.

Type or Mode of Exercise For overall fitness, you need to include exercises for your neck, upper back, shoulders, arms, chest, abdomen, lower back, thighs, buttocks, and calves—about 8–10 exercises in all. If you are also training for a particular sport, include exercises to strengthen the muscles important for optimal performance *and* the muscles most likely to be injured. A weight training program for general fitness is presented later in this chapter, on pp. 111–119.

It is important to balance exercises between **agonist** and **antagonist** muscle groups. (When a muscle contracts, it is known as the agonist; the opposing muscle, which must relax and stretch to allow contraction by the agonist, is known as the antagonist.) Whenever you do an exercise that moves a joint in one direction, also select an exercise that works the joint in the opposite direction. For example, if you do knee extensions to develop the muscles on the front of your thighs, also do leg curls to develop the antagonistic muscles on the back of your thighs.

The order of exercises can also be important. Do exercises for large-muscle groups or for more than one joint before you do exercises that use small-muscle groups or single joints. This allows for more effective overload of the larger, more powerful muscle groups. Small-muscle groups fatigue more easily than larger ones, and small-muscle fatigue limits your capacity to overload large-muscle groups. For example, lateral raises, which work the shoulder muscles, should be performed after bench presses, which work the chest and arms in addition to the shoulders. If you fatigue your shoulder muscles by doing lateral raises first, you won't be able to lift as much weight and effectively fatigue all the key muscle groups used during the bench press.

Also, order exercises so that you work agonist and antagonist muscle groups in sequence, one after the other. For example, follow biceps curls, which work the biceps, with triceps extensions, which exercise the triceps—the antagonist muscle to the biceps.

The Warm-Up and Cool-Down

As with cardiorespiratory endurance exercise, you should warm up before every weight training session and cool down afterward (Figure 4.4). You should do both a general warm-up—several minutes of walking or easy jogging—and a warm-up for the weight training exercises you plan to perform. For example, if you plan to do 1 or more sets of 10 repetitions of bench presses with 125 pounds, you might do 1 set of 10 repetitions with 50 pounds as a warm-up. Do similar warm-up exercises for each exercise in your program.

QUESTIONS FOR CRITICAL THINKING AND REFLECTION

Considering your lifestyle and the physical activities you most commonly do, which is more important to you—muscular strength or muscular endurance? Do you think this will always be the case, or do you think your patterns of activity, exercise, recreation, and sport might change in the future? For example, are there recreational activities you would like to try out at some point in your life, such as kayaking or rock climbing?

TERMS

set A group of repetitions followed by a rest period.

agonist A muscle in a state of contraction, opposed by the action of another muscle, its *antagonist*.

antagonist A muscle that opposes the action of another muscle, its *agonist*.

Warm-up 5–10 minutes	Strength training exercises for major muscle groups (8–10 exercises)		Cool-down 5–10 minutes
	Sample program		
	Exercise	*Muscle group developed*	
	Bench press	Chest, shoulders, triceps	
	Pull-ups	Lats, biceps	
	Shoulder press	Shoulders, trapezius, triceps	
	Upright rowing	Deltoids, trapezius	
	Biceps curls	Biceps	
	Lateral raises	Shoulders	
	Squats	Gluteals, quadriceps	
	Heel raises	Calves	
	Abdominal curls	Abdominals	
	Spine extensions	Low- and mid-back spine extensors	
Start	Side bridges	Obliques, quadratus lumborum	*Stop*

Frequency: At least 2 days per week

Intensity/Resistance: Weights heavy enough to cause muscle fatigue when exercises are performed with good form for the selected number of repetitions

Time: Repetitions: 8–12 of each exercise (10–15 with a lower weight for people over age 50–60); **Sets:** 1 (doing more than 1 set per exercise may result in faster and greater strength gains); rest 1–2 minutes between exercises.

Type of activity: 8–10 strength training exercises that focus on major muscle groups

FIGURE 4.4 The FITT principle for a strength training workout.

To cool down after weight training, relax for 5–10 minutes after your workout. Although this is controversial, a few studies have suggested that including a period of postexercise stretching may help prevent muscle soreness; warmed-up muscles and joints make this a particularly good time to work on flexibility.

Getting Started and Making Progress

The first few sessions of weight training should be devoted to learning the exercises. You need to learn the movements, and your nervous system needs to practice communicating with your muscles so you can develop strength effectively. To start, choose a weight that you can move easily through 8–12 repetitions, do only 1 set of each exercise, and rest 1–2 minutes between exercises. Gradually add weight and (if you want) sets to your program over the first few weeks until you are doing 1–3 sets of 8–12 repetitions of each exercise.

Knowing how much resistance to add and when to add it is as much an art as a science. As you progress, add weight according to the "two-for-two" rule: When you can perform two additional repetitions with a given weight on two consecutive training sessions, increase the load. For example, if your target is to perform 8–10 repetitions per exercise, and you performed 12 repetitions in your previous two workouts, it would be appropriate to increase your load. If adding weight means you can do only 7 or 8 repetitions, stay with that weight until you can again complete 12 repetitions per set. If you can do only 4–6 repetitions after adding weight, or if you can't maintain good form, you've added too much and should take some off.

You can add more resistance in large-muscle exercises, such as squats and bench presses, than you can in small-muscle exercises, such as curls. For example, when you can complete 12 repetitions of squats with good form, you may be able to add 10–20 pounds of additional resistance; for curls, on the other hand, you might add only 3–5 pounds. As a general guideline, try increases of approximately 5%, which is half a pound of additional weight for each 10 pounds you are currently lifting.

You can expect to improve rapidly during the first 6–10 weeks of training: a 10–30% increase in the amount of weight lifted. Gains will then come more slowly. Your rate of improvement will depend on how hard you work and how your body responds to resistance training. There will be individual differences in the rate of improvement. Factors such as age, gender, motivation, and heredity will affect your progress.

After you achieve the level of strength and muscularity you want, you can maintain your gains by training 2–3 days per week. You can monitor the progress of your program by recording the amount of resistance and the number of repetitions and sets you perform on a workout card like the one shown in Figure 4.5.

More Advanced Strength Training Programs

The weight training program just described is sufficient to develop and maintain muscular strength and endurance for general fitness. If you have a different goal, you may need to adjust your program accordingly. As mentioned previously, performing more sets and fewer repetitions with a heavier load will cause greater increases in strength. A program designed to build strength might include 3–5 sets of 4–6 repetitions each; the load used should be heavy enough to cause fatigue with the smaller number of repetitions. Rest long enough after a set (3–5 minutes) to allow your muscles to recover and to work intensely during the next set.

Experienced weight trainers often engage in some form of cycle training, also called *periodization,* in which the exercises, number of sets and repetitions, and intensity

WORKOUT CARD FOR Sara Lopez

Exercise/Date		9/14	9/16	9/18	9/21	9/23	9/25	9/28	9/30	10/2	10/5	10/7	10/9	10/12	10/14	10/16									
Bench press	Wt.	45	45	45	50	50	50	60	60	60	60	65	65	70	70	70									
	Sets	1	1	1	1	1	1	1	1	1	1	1	1	1	1	1									
	Reps.	10	12	12	10	12	12	10	9	12	12	12	12	9	9	10									
Pull-ups (assisted)	Wt.	—	—	—	—	—	—	—	—	—	—	—	—	—	—	—									
	Sets	1	1	1	1	1	1	1	1	1	1	1	1	1	1	1									
	Reps.	5	5	5	6	6	6	7	7	7	8	8	8	9	9	10									
Shoulder press	Wt.	20	20	20	25	25	25	30	30	30	30	30	30	35	35	35									
	Sets	1	1	1	1	1	1	1	1	1	1	1	1	1	1	1									
	Reps.	10	12	12	10	12	12	8	10	9	10	12	12	10	10	10									
Upright rowing	Wt.	5	5	10	10	10	10	12	12	12	12	15	15	15	15	15									
	Sets	1	1	1	1	1	1	1	1	1	1	1	1	1	1	1									
	Reps.	12	12	8	10	11	12	9	10	12	12	8	8	8	9	10									
Biceps curls	Wt.	15	15	15	20	20	20	25	25	25	25	25	25	30	30	30									
	Sets	1	1	1	1	1	1	1	1	1	1	1	1	1	1	1									
	Reps.	10	10	10	10	12	12	8	10	10	10	12	12	9	10	12									
Lateral raise	Wt.	5	5	5	5	5	5	7.5	7.5	7.5	7.5	7.5	7.5	10	10	10									
	Sets	1	1	1	1	1	1	1	1	1	1	1	1	1	1	1									
	Reps.	8	8	10	10	12	12	8	10	10	10	12	12	8	8	9									
Squats	Wt.	—	—	—	45	45	45	55	55	55	65	65	65	75	75	75									
	Sets	1	1	1	1	1	1	1	1	1	1	1	1	1	1	1									
	Reps.	10	12	15	8	12	12	8	12	12	10	13	12	8	10	10									
Heel raises	Wt.	—	—	—	45	45	45	55	55	55	65	65	65	75	75	75									
	Sets	1	1	1	1	1	1	1	1	1	1	1	1	1	1	1									
	Reps.	15	15	15	8	12	12	10	12	12	10	12	12	10	9	12									
Abdominal curls	Wt.	—	—	—	—	—	—	—	—	—	—	—	—	—	—	—									
	Sets	1	1	1	1	1	1	1	1	1	1	1	1	1	1	1									
	Reps.	20	20	20	20	20	20	25	25	25	25	25	25	25	25	25									
Spine extensions	Wt.	—	—	—	—	—	—	—	—	—	—	—	—	—	—	—									
	Sets	1	1	1	1	1	1	1	1	1	1	1	1	1	1	1									
	Reps.	5	5	5	8	8	8	10	10	10	10	10	10	11	12	12									
Side bridge	Wt.	—	—	—	—	—	—	—	—	—	—	—	—	—	—	—									
	Sets	1	1	1	1	1	1	1	1	1	1	1	1	1	1	1									
	Seconds	60	60	60	65	65	70	70	70	70	76	75	80	80	80	80									

FIGURE 4.5 A sample workout card for a general fitness strength training program.

are varied within a workout and/or between workouts. For example, you might do a particular exercise more intensely during some sets or on some days than others; you might also vary the exercises you perform for particular muscle groups. Several sample cycle training programs are described in a Student Handout on the *Fit and Well* Online Learning Center. For more detailed information on these more advanced training techniques, consult a strength coach certified by the National Strength and Conditioning Association or another reliable source. If you decide to adopt a more advanced training regimen, start off slowly to give your body a chance to adjust and to minimize the risk of injury.

Weight Training Safety

Injuries happen in weight training. Maximum physical effort, elaborate machinery, rapid movements, and heavy weights can combine to make the weight room a dangerous place if proper precautions aren't taken. To help ensure that your workouts are safe and productive, follow the guidelines in the box "Safe Weight Training" and the following suggestions.

Use Proper Lifting Technique Every exercise has a proper technique that is important for obtaining maximum benefits and preventing injury. Your instructor or weight room attendant can help explain the specific techniques for different exercises and weight machines.

Perform exercises smoothly and with good form. The ACSM suggests a moderate rate for each repetition—a 3-second concentric contraction and a 3-second eccentric contraction. Lift or push the weight forcefully during the active phase of the lift and then lower it slowly with control. Perform all lifts through the full range of motion.

Use Spotters and Collars with Free Weights Spotters are necessary when an exercise has potential for danger; a weight that is out of control or falls can cause a serious injury. A spotter can assist you if you cannot complete a lift or if the weight tilts. A spotter can also help you move a weight into position before a lift and provide help or additional resistance during a lift. Spotting requires practice and coordination between the lifter and the spotter(s).

Collars are devices that secure weights to a barbell or dumbbell. Although people lift weights without collars,

TAKE CHARGE

Safe Weight Training

General Guidelines

- When beginning a program or trying new exercises or equipment, ask an instructor to show you how to do exercises safely and correctly.
- Lift weights from a stabilized body position; keep weights as close to your body as possible.
- Protect your back by maintaining control of your spine and avoiding dangerous positions. Don't twist your body while lifting.
- Observe proper lifting techniques and good form at all times. If you have to alter your technique to complete a repetition, you are probably lifting too much weight. Don't lift beyond the limits of your strength.
- Don't hold your breath while doing weight training exercises. Holding your breath, called the Valsalva maneuver, causes a decrease in blood returning to the heart and can make you become dizzy and faint. It can also increase blood pressure to dangerous levels. Exhale when exerting the greatest force, and inhale when moving the weight into position for the active phase of the lift. Breathe smoothly and steadily.
- Be aware of what's going on around you. Stay away from other people when they're doing exercises, and don't get distracted. If you bump into someone, you could cause an injury.
- Don't use defective equipment. Be aware of broken collars or bolts, frayed cables, broken chains, or loose cushions. Report equipment damage or malfunctions immediately.
- Don't chew gum when exercising; you could choke on the gum or bite your tongue.
- Don't exercise if you're ill, injured, or overtrained. Do not try to work through the pain.
- When returning to training after an illness or layoff, start with lighter weights than you were using before the break in training.

Free Weights

- Make sure the bar is loaded evenly on both sides and that weights are secured with collars.
- When you pick a weight up from the ground, keep your back straight and your head level. Don't bend at the waist with straight legs.
- Lift weights smoothly and slowly; don't jerk them. Control the weight through the entire range of motion. Lifting a weight too fast can increase the force output to dangerous levels.
- Do most of your lifting with your legs. Keep your hips and buttocks back. When doing standing lifts, maintain a good posture so that you protect your back. Bend at the hips, not with the spine. Feet should be shoulder-width apart, heels and balls of the feet in contact with the floor, and knees slightly bent.
- Don't bounce weights against your body during an exercise.
- When lifting barbells and dumbbells, wrap your thumbs around the bar when gripping it. You can easily drop a weight when using a "thumbless" grip.

Spotting

- Use spotters for free weights exercises in which the bar crosses the face or head (e.g., the bench press), is placed on the back (e.g., squats), or is racked in front of the chest (e.g., overhead press from the rack).
- Spotters should be at least as tall and as strong as the lifter.
- If one spotter is used, the spotter should stand behind the lifter; if two spotters are used, one spotter should stand at each end of the barbell.

- For squats with heavy resistance, use at least three spotters—one behind the lifter (hands near lifter's hips, waist, or torso) and one on each side of the bar. Squatting in a power rack will increase safety during this exercise.
- Spot dumbbell exercises at the forearms, as close to the weights as possible.
- For over-the-face and over-the-head lifts, the spotter should hold the bar with an alternate grip (one palm up and one palm down) inside the lifter's grip.
- When providing a handoff, the spotter should make sure that the lifter has control of the weight before moving away.
- Ensure good communication between spotter and lifter by agreeing on verbal signals before the exercise.
- Spotters should pay attention and be ready to act quickly to assist a person having trouble. Lifters should tell spotters to take the bar if they can no longer contribute to making the lift.

Weight Machines

- Keep away from moving weight stacks. Pay attention when you're changing weights.
- Adjust each machine for your body so that you don't have to work in an awkward position. Lock everything in place before you begin.
- Make sure the machines are clean. Carry a towel around with you, and place it on the machine where you will sit or lie down.

doing so is dangerous. It is easy to lose your balance or to raise one side of the weight faster than the other. Without collars, the weights on one side of the bar will slip off, and the weights on the opposite side will crash to the floor.

Be Alert for Injuries Report any obvious muscle or joint injuries to your instructor or physician, and stop exercising the affected area. Training with an injured joint or muscle can lead to a more serious injury. Make sure you get the necessary first aid. Even minor injuries heal faster if you use the R-I-C-E principle of treating injuries described in Chapter 3.

Consult a physician if you have any unusual symptoms during exercise or if you're uncertain whether weight training is a proper activity for you. Conditions such as heart disease and high blood pressure can be aggravated during weight training. Immediately report symptoms such as headaches; dizziness; labored breathing; numbness; vision disturbances; and chest, neck, or arm pains.

MOTIVATION BOOSTER

Graph your total workout. If you want an easy overall measure of your progress, calculate the total amount of weight you lift during each workout. For each exercise, multiply the amount of resistance by the number of repetitions and the number of sets; for example, if you do 1 set of 11 repetitions of the bench press with 60 pounds of resistance, your total for the bench press would be $1 \times 11 \times 60 = 660$ pounds. Next, add up the amounts for each exercise to get your workout total. Graph the total amount of weight lifted during each workout to measure your progress and boost your motivation.

A Caution About Supplements and Drugs

Many active people use a wide variety of nutritional supplements and drugs in the quest for improved performance and appearance. (Table 4.2 lists a selective summary of "performance aids" along with their potential side effects.) Most of these substances are ineffective and expensive, and many are dangerous (see the box "Dietary Supplements: A Consumer Dilemma" on p. 108). A balanced diet should be your primary nutritional strategy.

QUESTIONS FOR CRITICAL THINKING AND REFLECTION

Do you think athletes should be allowed to use drugs and supplements to improve their sports performance? Would you be tempted to use a banned performance-enhancing drug if you thought you could get away with it? Why or why not?

WEIGHT TRAINING EXERCISES

A general book on fitness and wellness cannot include a detailed description of all weight training exercises. Here we present a basic program for developing muscular strength and endurance for general fitness using free weights and weight machines. Instructions for each exercise are accompanied by photographs and a listing of the muscles being trained. Table 4.3 on p. 109 lists alternative and additional exercises that can be performed on various machines or with free weights. If you are interested in learning how to do these exercises, ask your instructor or coach for assistance. An illustration of the muscular system is shown in Figure 4.6 on p. 110.

Labs 4.2 and 4.3 will help you assess your current level of muscular endurance and design your own weight training program. If you want to develop strength for a particular activity, your program should contain exercises for general fitness, exercises for the muscle groups most important for the activity, and exercises for muscle groups most often injured. Regardless of the goals of your program or the type of equipment you use, your program should be structured so that you obtain maximum results without risking injury.

TIPS FOR TODAY AND THE FUTURE

You don't need a complicated or heavy training program to improve strength: Just 1 set of 8–12 repetitions of 8–10 exercises, done at least 2 days per week, is enough for general fitness.

RIGHT NOW YOU CAN

- Do a set of static (isometric) exercises. If you're sitting, try tightening your abdominal muscles as you press your lower back into the seat or work your arms by placing the palms of your hands on top of your thighs and pressing down. Hold the contraction for 6 seconds and do 5–10 repetitions; don't hold your breath.
- Think of three things you've done in the past 24 hours that would have been easier or more enjoyable if you increased your level of muscular strength and endurance. Examples might be carrying your books, climbing stairs, or playing recreational sports. Begin to visualize improvements in your quality of life that could come from increased muscular strength and endurance.

IN THE FUTURE YOU CAN

- Make an appointment with a trainer at your campus or neighborhood fitness facility. A trainer can help you put together an appropriate weight training program and introduce you to the equipment at the facility.
- Invest in an inexpensive set of free weights, a stability ball, or a resistance band. Then make a regular appointment with yourself to use your new equipment.

Table 4.2 Performance Aids Marketed to Weight Trainers

Substance	Supposed Effects	Actual Effects	Selected Potential Side Effects
Adrenal androgens, such as dehydroepiandrosterone (DHEA), androstenedione	Increased testosterone, muscle mass, and strength; decreased body fat	Increased testosterone, strength, and fat-free mass; decreased fat in older subjects (more studies needed in younger people)	Gonadal suppression, prostate hypertrophy, breast development in males, masculinization in women and children; long-term effects unknown
Amino acids	Increased muscle mass	No effects if dietary protein intake is adequate; consuming before or after training may improve performance	Minimal side effects; unbalanced amino acid intake can cause problems with protein metabolism
Amphetamines	Prevention of fatigue; increased confidence and training intensity	Increased arousal, wakefulness, and confidence; feeling of enhanced decision-making ability	Depression and fatigue (after drug wears off), extreme confusion; neural and psychological effects including aggressiveness, paranoia, hallucinations, compulsive behavior, restlessness, irritability, heart arrhythmia, high blood pressure, and chest pain
Anabolic steroids	Increased muscle mass, strength, power, psychological aggressiveness, and endurance	Increased strength, power, fat-free mass, and aggression; no effects on endurance	Liver damage and tumors, decrease in high-density lipoprotein (good cholesterol), depressed sperm and testosterone production, high blood pressure, depressed immune function, problems with sugar metabolism, psychological disturbances, gonadal suppression, liver disease, acne, breast development in males, masculinization in women and children, heart disease, thicker blood, and increased risk of cancer; steroids are controlled substances*
Beta-agonists, such as clenbuterol, salmeterol, terbutaline	Enhanced performance; prevention of muscle atrophy; increased fat-free weight; decreased body fat	Used to treat asthma, including exercise-induced asthma	Insomnia, heart arrhythmia, anxiety, anorexia, nausea, heart enlargement, heart attack (particularly if used with steroids), and heart failure
Chromium picolinate	Increased muscle mass, decreased body fat; improved blood sugar control	Well-controlled studies show no significant effect on fat-free mass or body fat	Moderate doses (50–200 µg) appear safe; higher doses may cause DNA damage and other serious effects; long-term effects unknown
Creatine monohydrate	Increased creatine phosphate levels in muscles, muscle mass, and capacity for high-intensity exercise	Increased muscle mass and performance in some types of high-intensity exercise	Minimal side effects; long-term effects unknown
Dinitrophenol (DPN)	Weight loss	Weight loss; releases food energy as heat	Increased body temperature, leading to heat injury and death; banned by the FDA
Diuretics	Promotes loss of body fluid	Promotes loss of body fluid to accentuate muscle definition; often taken with potassium supplements and very-low-calorie diets	Muscle cell destruction, low blood pressure, blood chemistry abnormalities, and heart problems
Ephedra	Decreased body fat; increased training intensity due to stimulant effect	Decreased appetite, particularly when taken with caffeine; some evidence for increased training intensity	Abnormal heart rhythms, nervousness, headache, gastrointestinal distress, and heatstroke; banned by the FDA

Table 4.2 Performance Aids Marketed to Weight Trainers *(continued)*

Substance	Supposed Effects	Actual Effects	Selected Potential Side Effects
Erythropoietin, darbepoetin	Enhanced performance during endurance events	Stimulated growth of red blood cells; enhanced oxygen uptake and endurance	Increased blood viscosity (thickness); can cause potentially fatal blood clots
Ginseng	Decreased effects of physical and emotional stress; increased oxygen consumption	Most well-controlled studies show no effect on performance	No serious side effects; high doses can cause high blood pressure, nervousness, and insomnia
Growth hormone	Increased muscle mass, strength, and power; decreased body fat	Increased muscle mass and strength; decreased fat mass; studies show no effect on muscle or exercise performance	Elevated blood sugar, high insulin levels, and carpal tunnel syndrome; enlargement of the heart and other organs; acromegaly (disease characterized by increased growth of bones in hands and face); diseases of the heart, nerves, bones, and joints; an extremely expensive controlled substance*
Human chorionic gonadotrophin (HCG)	Increased testosterone production; prevention of muscle atrophy during steroid withdrawal	Increased testosterone production	Interferes with normal testosterone regulation; banned in most sports
Beta-hydroxy beta-methylbutyrate (HMB)	Increased strength and muscle mass; decreased body fat	Some studies show increased fat-free mass and decreased fat; more research needed	No reported side effects; long-term effects unknown
Insulin	Increased muscle mass	Effectiveness in stimulating muscle growth unknown	Insulin shock (characterized by extremely low blood sugar), which can lead to unconsciousness and death
Insulin-like growth factor (IGF)	Increased muscle mass; improved cellular function	Actual effects in healthy, active people unknown	Similar to side effects of growth hormone; long-term use promotes cancer
"Metabolic-optimizing" meals for athletes	Increased muscle mass and energy supply; decreased body fat	No proven effects beyond those of balanced meals	No reported side effects; extremely expensive
Over-the-counter stimulants, such as caffeine, phenylpropanolamine (PPA)	Weight loss; improved endurance; stimulant effect	Can be used for weight control; may improve endurance; does not appear to enhance short-term maximal exercise capacity	Increased risk of heart attack and stroke in some people (in high doses); increased incidence of abnormal heart rhythm and insomnia; caffeine is addictive
Prescription appetite suppressants, such as diethylproprion, phentermine, sibutramine, rimonabant	Weight control, weight loss	Weight loss; typically prescribed only for short-term use	Restlessness, anxiety, dizziness, depression, tremors, increased urination, diarrhea, constipation, vomiting, high blood pressure, swelling of legs or ankles, insomnia, seizures, fast or irregular heartbeat, heart palpitations, blurred vision, rashes, and difficulty breathing; can be habit-forming
Protein, amino acids, polypeptide supplements	Increased muscle mass and growth hormone release; accelerated muscle development; decreased body fat	No effects if dietary protein intake is adequate; may promote protein synthesis if taken immediately before or after weight training	Can be dangerous for people with liver or kidney disease; substituting amino acid or polypeptide supplements for protein-rich food can cause nutrient deficiencies

*Possession of a controlled substance is illegal without a prescription, and physicians are not allowed to prescribe controlled substances for the improvement of athletic performance. In addition, the use of anabolic steroids, growth hormone, or any of several other substances listed in this table is banned for athletic competition.

SOURCES: Brooks, G. A., et al. 2005. *Exercise Physiology: Human Bioenergetics and Its Applications*, 4th ed. New York: McGraw-Hill. Sports-supplement dangers. 2001. *Consumer Reports*, June. U.S. National Library of Medicine, National Institutes of Health. 2007. *MedlinePlus Medical Encyclopedia* (http://www.nlm.nih.gov/medlineplus/encyclopedia.html; retrieved November 19, 2007).

CRITICAL CONSUM

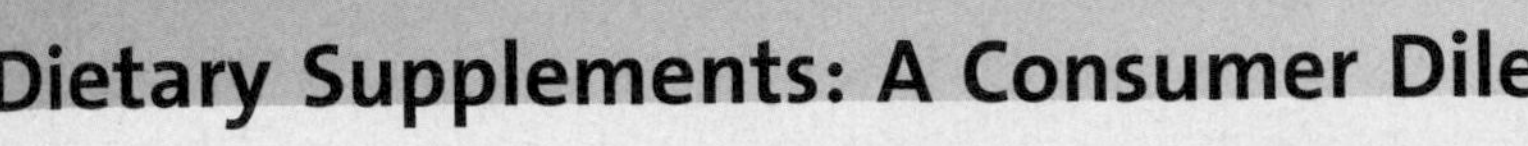

Dietary Supplements: A Consumer Dilemma

Wading through manufacturers' claims can be tricky when you are considering taking a dietary supplement. While drugs and food products undergo stringent government testing, dietary supplements can be freely marketed without testing for safety or effectiveness. There is no guarantee that advertisements about dietary supplements are accurate or true.

What's the difference between a drug—which must be approved by the Food and Drug Administration (FDA)—and a dietary supplement? In some cases, the only real difference is in how the product is marketed. Some dietary supplements are as potentially dangerous as potent prescription drugs. But because they have a different classification, dietary supplements do not have to prove they are safe and effective before being sold; the FDA can, however, take action against any unsafe supplement product after it reaches the market. This is what occurred in two high-profile cases in 2004 when the FDA acted against popular dietary supplements—androstenedione (andro) and ephedra.

Androstenedione

The male hormone testosterone is a powerful drug with many adverse effects; it is closely regulated by the FDA. Androstenedione, a hormone converted in the body to testosterone (and estrogen), was widely available without a prescription as a dietary supplement. Andro disrupts the hormonal balance of its users and can increase the risk of heart disease. Teens who take andro are at risk for early closure of bone growth centers, which could limit their adult height. (See Table 4.2 for some of andro's many other side effects.)

Advertisements for andro claimed that it would increase muscle size, strength, and performance, but there are actually few good studies of andro's effects on humans. The two best studies showed no significant difference in muscle growth and strength in andro users compared with nonusers. Most medical experts believe that andro is neither safe nor effective—yet it has been used by thousands of athletes, most of whom are unaware of the risks. In 2004, the FDA stated that andro was potentially dangerous and should not be marketed as a supplement; it ordered manufacturers to stop selling supplements containing andro.

Ephedra

Ephedra was a common ingredient of dietary supplements, often touted as an "energy booster" and a "fat burner." Because ephedra was marketed as a natural herbal product and available without a prescription, consumers assumed that it was free from serious side effects. However, the drug can cause severe high blood pressure, heart attacks, strokes, seizures, and heat illness, and it has been linked to a number of deaths. It may be especially risky in users who are dehydrated and/or fatigued or when it is combined with other stimulants such as caffeine.

Many sports organizations banned the use of ephedra because of safety concerns, and following the publication of additional studies and reports, the FDA acted to remove ephedra-containing products from the market. (Chapter 9 has more information about ephedra and other dietary supplements marketed for weight loss.)

Do You Need Supplements?

Supplement manufacturers often make glowing claims about their products, such as "Builds lean muscle fast" or "Burns fat and gives you energy." With all the hype, how can you determine if a particular supplement might be helpful? Ask yourself the following questions:

- ***Do you really need a supplement at all?*** Nutritional authorities agree that most athletes and young adults can obtain all the necessary ingredients for health and top athletic performance by eating a well-balanced diet and training appropriately. There is no dietary supplement that outperforms wholesome food and a good training regimen.
- ***Is the product safe and effective?*** The fact that a dietary supplement is available in your local store is no guarantee of safety. As described earlier, the FDA doesn't regulate supplements in the same way as drugs. The only way to determine if a supplement really works is to perform carefully controlled research on human subjects. Testimonials from individuals who claim to have benefited from the product don't count. Few dietary supplements have undergone careful human testing, so it is difficult to tell which of them may actually work.
- ***Can you be sure that the specific product is of high quality?*** There is no official agency that ensures the quality of dietary supplements. There is no guarantee that a supplement contains the desired ingredient, that dosages are appropriate, that potency is standardized, or that the product is free from contaminants. (See Chapter 8 for more information on dietary supplement labeling.)

A recent study of 12 over-the-counter brands of supplements containing androstenedione and related steroids found that 1 brand contained more and 11 brands contained less than the amount stated on the label; in addition, one brand contained a significant amount of a controlled steriod. The International Olympic Committee issued a warning to athletes based on a test of 634 different nutritional supplements: Researchers had found that 15% of the supplements tested contained unlabled substances that would cause an athlete to fail a drug test.

Many dietary supplements are ineffective and/or unsafe, but it is extremely difficult for consumers to get the information they need to make an informed decision. Reliable resources for information on dietary supplements include the FDA Center for Food Safety and Applied Nutrition (http://www.cfsan.fda. gov/~dms/supplmnt.html) and the USDA's Dietary Supplements page (http://fnic.nal.usda.gov/nal_display/index.php?info_center=4&tax_level=1&tax_subject=274).

Once you have gathered the best information you can find, consider whether the potential benefits of the supplement appear to outweigh the risks and the cost. When in doubt, it's best to avoid the product. Remember that no supplement eliminates the need for proper training, and no supplement has been shown to be safe and effective in long-term weight loss. A product that is marginally effective, not proven safe, and expensive to boot is probably not worth the money or the risk.

Table 4.3 Weight Training Exercises for Machines, Free Weights, Exercise Bands, and No Equipment

Company	Legs	Arms	Shoulders and Chest	Torso
Cybex	Hip abduction Hip adduction Leg extension Leg press Leg curl Rotary calf	Arm curl Triceps extension	Chest press Incline press Overhead press	Ab crunch Pull-down Torso rotation
Hammer	Abductor Adductor Calf H squat Iso leg curl Iso l eg extension Iso lateral leg press Leg curl Leg extension Leg press Seated calf raise	Behind-neck press Bench press Flat back chest Front military press Incline press Iso behind-neck press Iso incline press Iso wide chest Seated bicep Seated triceps	Bench press Flat back chest Iso wide chest Lateral raise Rear deltoid Rotator cuff Seated dip	Behind-neck pull-down Bilateral row Dead lift Front pull-down High row Iso pullover Low row Pullover Row Shrug
Nautilus	Calf raise Leg curl Leg extension Leg press	Biceps curl Preacher curl Triceps extension	10-degree chest 50-degree chest Bench press Incline press Lateral raise Military press Seated dip	Abdominal Compound row Hip and back Hip flexion Lat pull-down Pullover Rotary torso
Universal Gym	Abductor kick Adductor kick Calf raises (leg press) Knee extension Knee flexion Leg press	Biceps curl Dips Lat pull	Bench press Front raise Incline press Rip-up Shoulder press Upright row	Bent-over row Crunch Lat pull Pullover Pull-up Side bend
Free weights	Back squat Front squat Hack squat Leg curl Leg extension Leg press Lunges Seated calf Smith machine Step-ups	Barbell curl Dumbbell curl French curl Preacher curl	Bench press Decline press Dumbbell back raise Dumbbell flys Dumbbell front raise Dumbbell lateral raise Incline press Overhead press	Abdominal crunch Abdominal sit-ups Bent-over row Dead lift Incline lever row Lat pull-down Pullover Seated row Shrug Upright row
Exercise bands	Squats Lunges Hamstring curls Leg abduction Leg adduction Kick backs	Biceps curls Triceps extensions	Chest press Shoulder press Lateral raise Seated row	Trunk curl Reverse crunch Sit backs Back extensions Lat pull-down
Exercises without weights	Squats Overhead squats Lunges Side lunges Rear lunges Wall sits Step-ups	Isometric curls Isometric triceps extensions Chair dips 90° Bent-arm bar hang, supine grip	Push-ups Pull-ups Handstand press against wall	Curl-ups Bicycles Knee raises from bar Side bends Twists

SOURCE: Adapted from Fahey., T. D., 2007. *Basic Weight Training for Men and Women,* 6th ed. Copyright © 2007. The McGraw-Hill Companies, Inc. Reprinted with permission of The McGraw-Hill Companies, Inc.

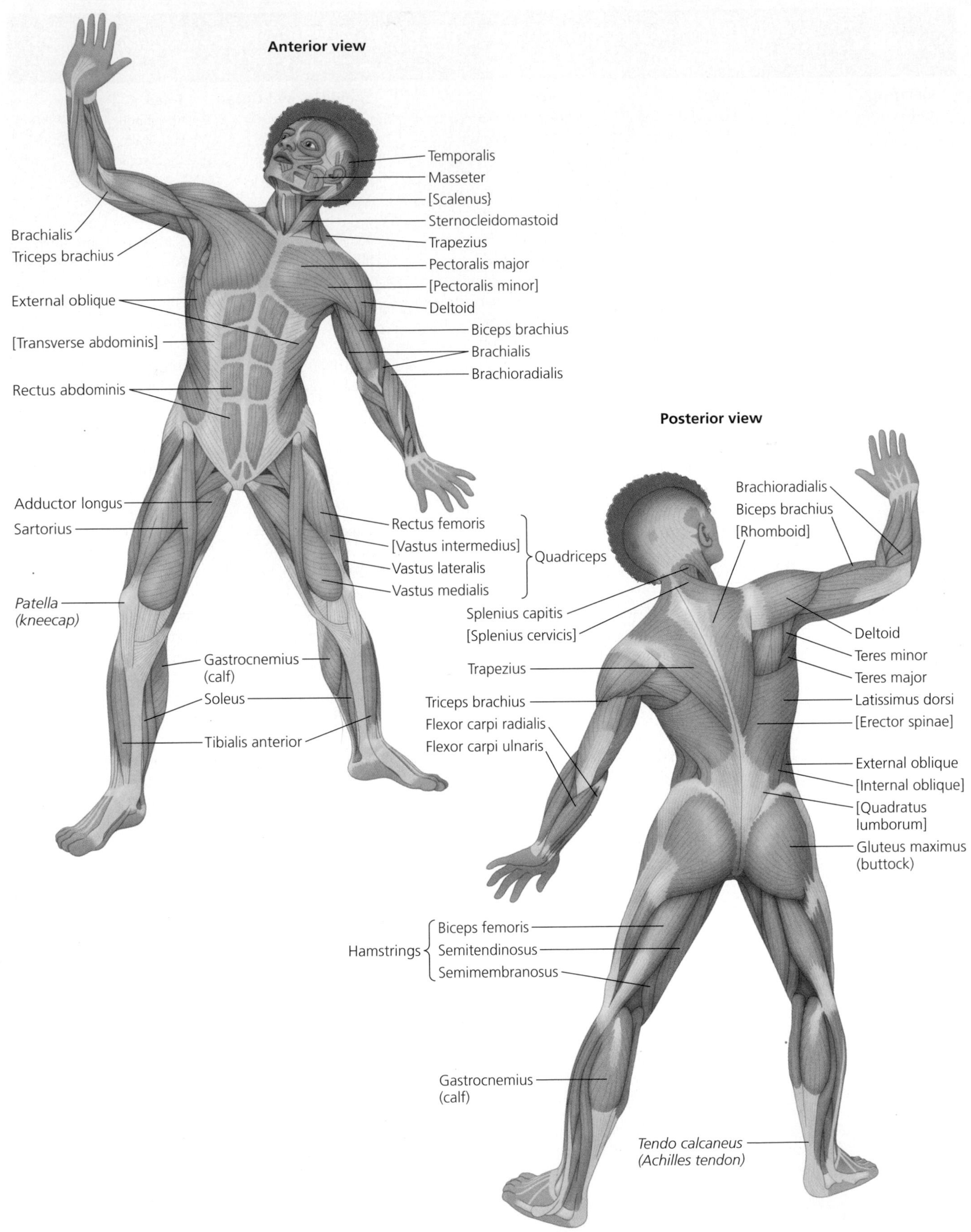

Anterior view
Temporalis
Masseter
[Scalenus}
Sternocleidomastoid
Trapezius
Pectoralis major
[Pectoralis minor]
Deltoid
Biceps brachius
Brachialis
Brachioradialis
Brachialis
Triceps brachius
External oblique
[Transverse abdominis]
Rectus abdominis
Adductor longus
Sartorius
Patella
(kneecap)
Rectus femoris
[Vastus intermedius]
Vastus lateralis
Vastus medialis
Quadriceps
Gastrocnemius
(calf)
Soleus
Tibialis anterior
Posterior view
Brachioradialis
Biceps brachius
[Rhomboid]
Splenius capitis
[Splenius cervicis]
Deltoid
Teres minor
Teres major
Trapezius
Triceps brachius
Flexor carpi radialis
Flexor carpi ulnaris
Latissimus dorsi
[Erector spinae]
External oblique
[Internal oblique]
[Quadratus
lumborum]
Gluteus maximus
(buttock)
Hamstrings
Biceps femoris
Semitendinosus
Semimembranosus
Gastrocnemius
(calf)
Tendo calcaneus
(Achilles tendon)

FIGURE 4.6 The muscular system. The muscle names enclosed in brackets refer to deep muscles.

WEIGHT TRAINING EXERCISES: FREE WEIGHTS

Exercise 1 — Bench Press

Instructions: (a) Lying on a bench on your back with your feet on the floor, grasp the bar with palms upward and hands shoulder-width apart. If the weight is on a rack, move the bar carefully from the supports to a point over the middle of your chest or slightly above it (at the lower part of the sternum). **(b)** Lower the bar to your chest. Then press it in a straight line to the starting position. Don't arch your back or bounce the bar off your chest.

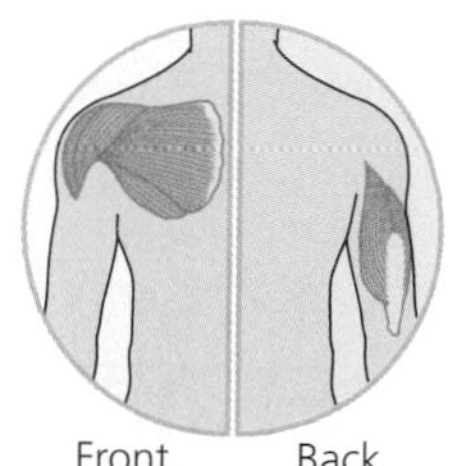

Muscles developed: Pectoralis major, triceps, deltoids

Note: *To allow an optimal view of exercise technique, a spotter does not appear in these demonstration photographs; however, spotters should be used for most exercises with free weights. Video clips illustrating spotting technique can be found on the* Fit and Well *Online Learning Center.*

Exercise 2 — Pull-Up

Assisted pull-up: (c) This is done as described for a pull-up, except that a spotter assists the person by pushing upward at the waist, hips, or legs during the exercise.

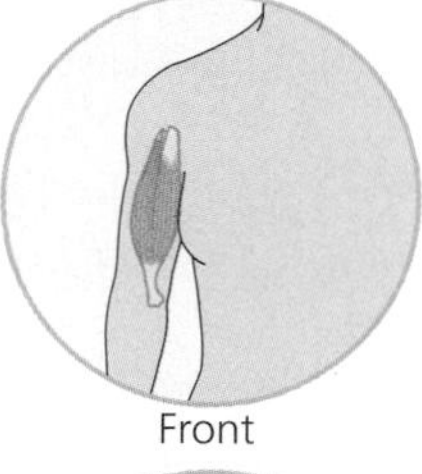

Back

Instructions: (a) Begin by grasping the pull-up bar with both hands, palms facing forward and elbows extended fully. **(b)** Pull yourself upward until your chin goes above the bar. Then return to the starting position.

Muscles developed: Latissimus dorsi, biceps

Exercise 3 — Shoulder Press (Overhead or Military Press)

Instructions: This exercise can be done standing or seated, with dumbbells or a barbell. The shoulder press begins with the weight at your chest, preferably on a rack. **(a)** Grasp the weight with your palms facing away from you. **(b)** Push the weight overhead until your arms are extended. Then return to the starting position (weight at chest). Be careful not to arch your back excessively.

If you are a more advanced weight trainer, you can "clean" the weight (lift it from the floor to your chest). The clean should be attempted only after instruction from a knowledgeable coach; otherwise, it can lead to injury.

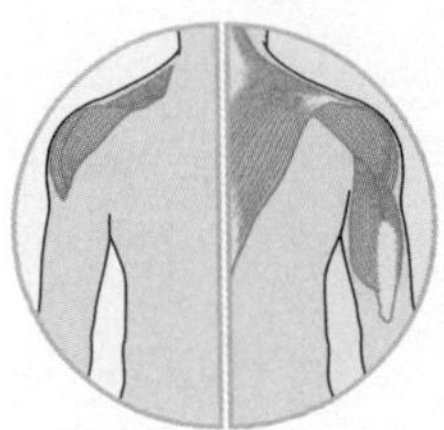

Muscles developed: Deltoids, triceps, trapezius

Exercise 4 — Upright Rowing

Instructions: From a standing position with arms extended fully, grasp a barbell with a close grip (hands about 6–12 inches apart) and palms toward the body. Raise the bar to about the level of your collarbone, keeping your elbows above bar level at all times. Return to the starting position.

This exercise can be done using dumbbells, a weighted bar (shown), or a barbell.

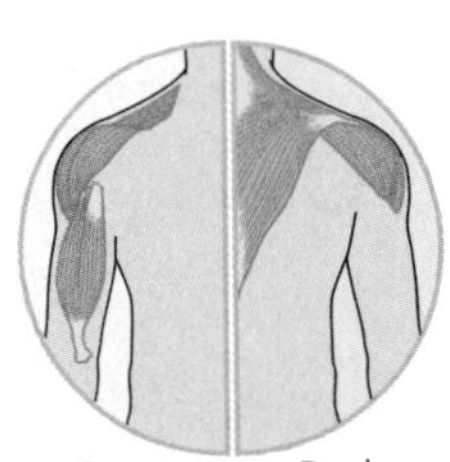

Muscles developed: Trapezius, deltoids, biceps

Exercise 5 — Biceps Curl

Instructions: (a) From a standing position, grasp the bar with your palms upward and your hands shoulder-width apart. **(b)** Keeping your upper body rigid, flex (bend) your elbows until the bar reaches a level slightly below the collarbone. Return the bar to the starting position.

This exercise can be done using dumbbells, a curl bar (shown), or a barbell; some people find that using a curl bar places less stress on the wrists.

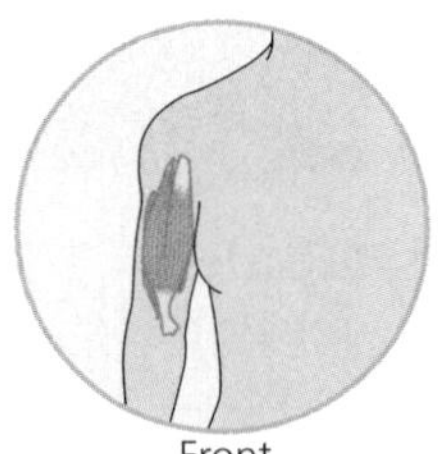

Muscles developed: Biceps, brachialis

Exercise 6 Lateral Raise

Instructions: (a) Stand with feet shoulder-width apart and a dumbbell in each hand. Hold the dumbbells parallel to each other. **(b)** With elbows slightly bent, slowly lift both weights until they reach shoulder level. Keep your wrists in a neutral position, in line with your forearms. Return to the starting position.

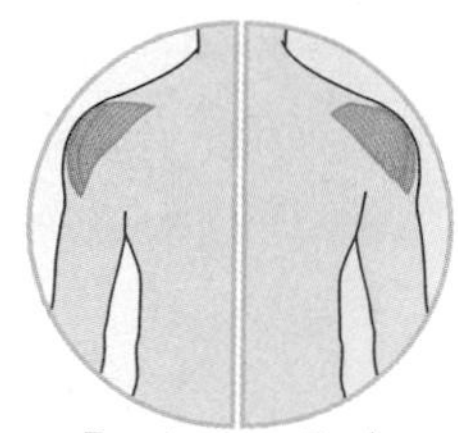

Muscles developed: Deltoids

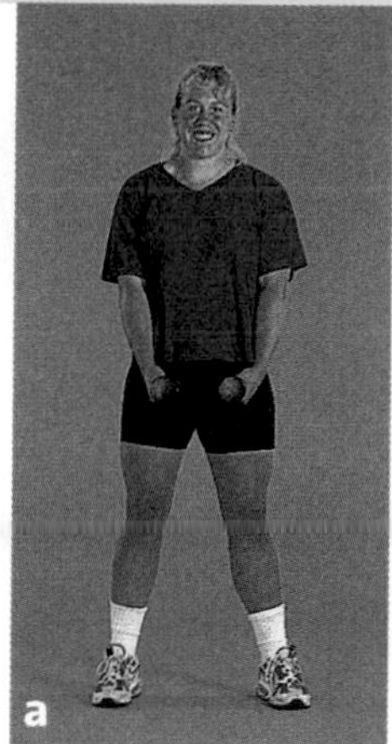

Exercise 7 Squat

Instructions: If the bar is racked, place the bar on the fleshy part of your upper back and grasp the bar at shoulder width. Keeping your back straight and head level, remove the bar from the rack and take a step back. Stand with feet slightly more than shoulder-width apart and toes pointed slightly outward. **(a)** Rest the bar on the back of your shoulders, holding it there with hands facing forward. **(b)** Keeping your head level and lower back straight and pelvis back, squat down until your thighs are below parallel with the floor. Let your thighs move laterally (outward) so that you "squat between your legs." This will help keep your back straight and keep your heels on the floor. Drive upward toward the starting position, hinging at the hips and keeping your back in a fixed position throughout the exercise.

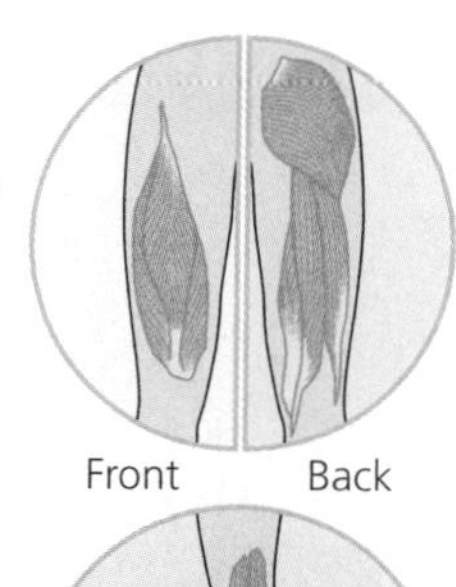

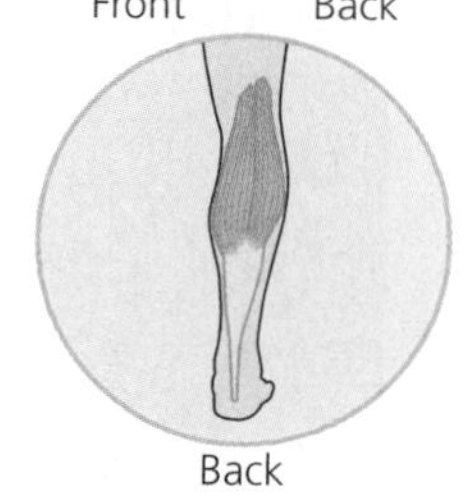

Muscles developed: Quadriceps, gluteus maximus, hamstrings, gastrocnemius

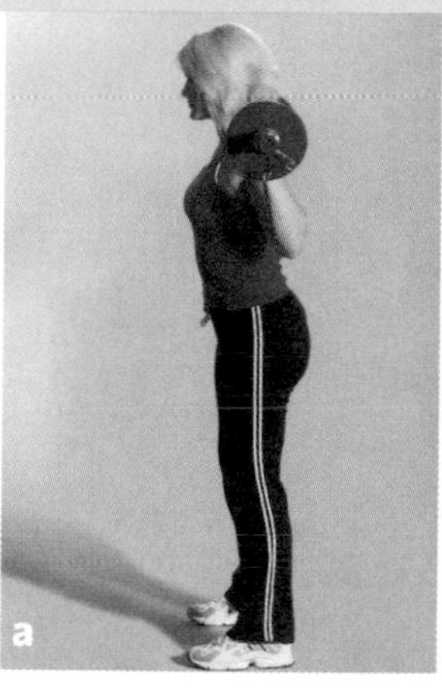

Exercise 8 Heel Raise

Instructions: Stand with feet shoulder-width apart and toes pointed straight ahead. **(a)** Rest the bar on the back of your shoulders, holding it there with hands facing forward. **(b)** Press down with your toes while lifting your heels. Return to the starting position.

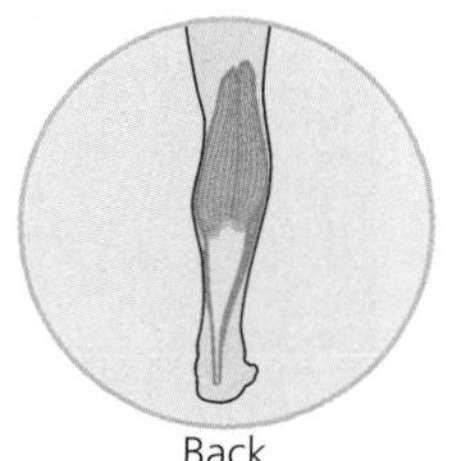

Muscles developed: Gastrocnemius, soleus

Exercise 9 — Curl-Up or Crunch

Instructions: (a) Lie on your back on the floor with your arms folded across your chest and your feet on the floor or on a bench. **(b)** Curl your trunk up and forward by raising your head and shoulders from the ground. Lower to the starting position. Focus on using your abdominal muscles rather than the muscles in your shoulders, chest, and neck.

This exercise can also be done using an exercise ball (see p. 99).

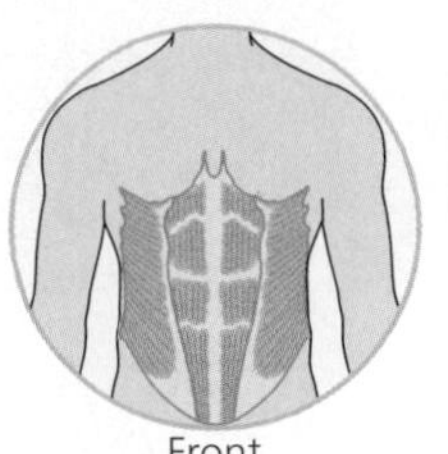

Muscles developed: Rectus abdominis, obliques

a

b

Exercise 10 — Spine Extension (Isometric Exercises)

Instructions: Begin on all fours with your knees below your hips and your hands below your shoulders.

Unilateral spine extension:

(a) Extend your right leg to the rear and reach forward with your right arm. Keep your spine neutral and your raised arm and leg in line with your torso. Don't arch your back or let your hip or shoulder sag. Hold this position for 10–30 seconds. Repeat with your left leg and left arm.

Bilateral spine extension:

(b) Extend your left leg to the rear and reach forward with your right arm. Keep your spine neutral and your raised arm and leg in line with your torso. Don't arch your back or let your hip or shoulder sag. Hold this position for 10–30 seconds. Repeat with your right leg and left arm.

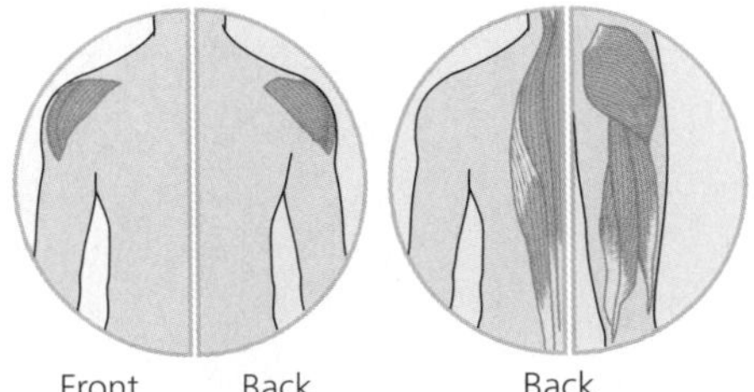

Muscles developed: Erector spinae, gluteus maximus, hamstrings, deltoids

You can make this exercise more difficult by making box patterns with your arms and legs.

a

b

Exercise 11 — Isometric Side Bridge

Instructions: Lie on the floor on your side with your knees bent and your top arm lying alongside your body. Lift your hips so that your weight is supported by your forearm and knee. Hold this position for 10 seconds, breathing normally. Repeat on the other side. Work up to a 60-second hold; perform one or more repetitions on each side.

Variation: You can make the exercise more difficult by keeping your legs straight and supporting yourself with your feet and forearm (see Lab 5.3) or with your feet and hand (with elbow straight). You can also do this exercise on an exercise ball.

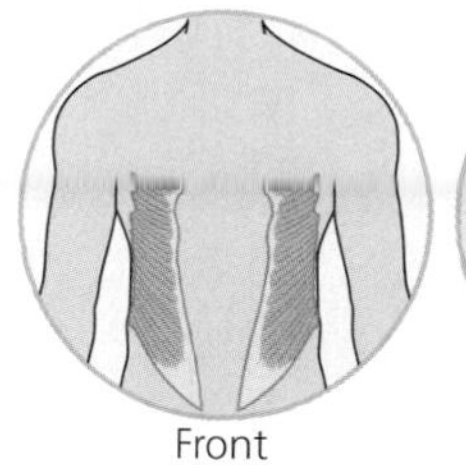

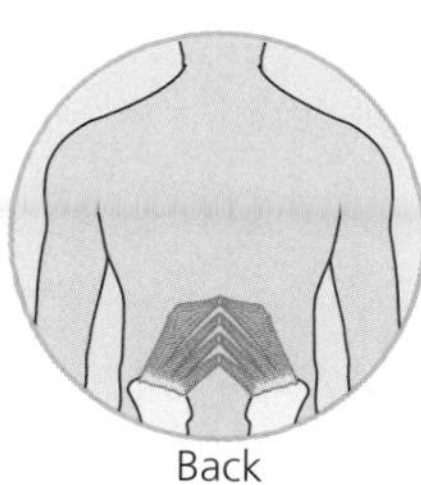

Muscles developed: Obliques, quadratus lumborum

WEIGHT TRAINING EXERCISES: WEIGHT MACHINES

Exercise 1 — Bench Press (Chest or Vertical Press)

Instructions: Sit or lie on the seat or bench, depending on the type of machine and the manufacturer's instructions. Your back, hips, and buttocks should be pressed against the machine pads. Place your feet on the floor or the foot supports.

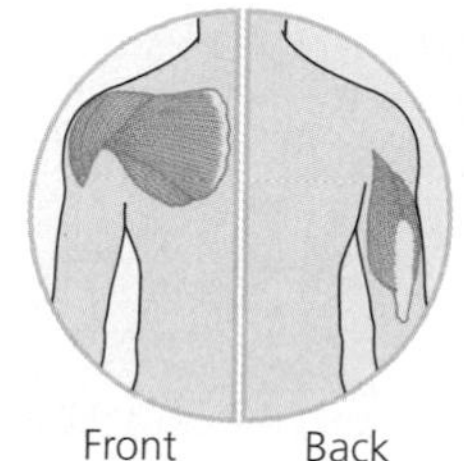

Muscles developed: Pectoralis major, anterior deltoids, triceps

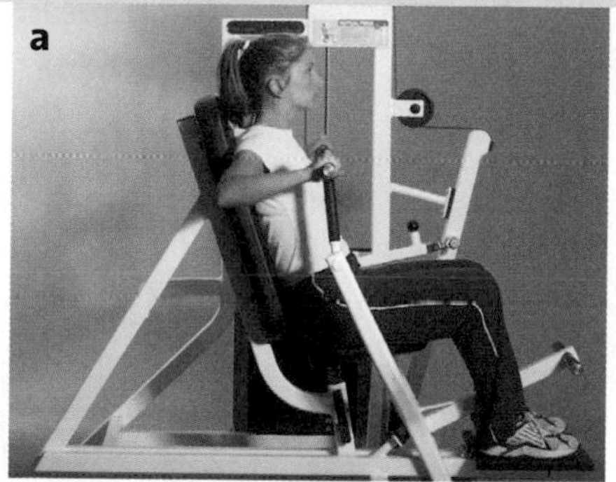

(a) Grasp the handles with your palms facing away from you; the handles should be aligned with your armpits.

(b) Push the bars until your arms are fully extended, but don't lock your elbows. Return to the starting position.

Exercise 2 — Lat Pull

Instructions: Begin in a seated or kneeling position, depending on the type of lat machine and the manufacturer's instructions.

Note: *This exercise focuses on the same major muscles as the assisted pull-up (Exercise 3); choose an appropriate exercise for your program based on your preferences and equipment availability.*

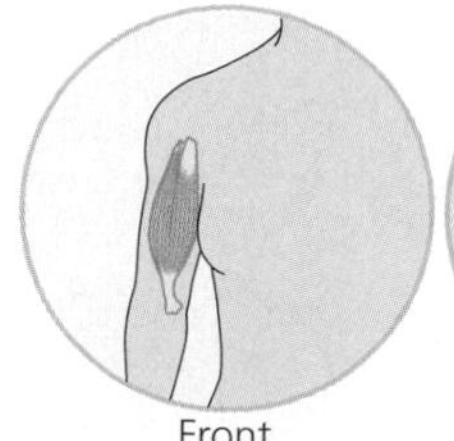

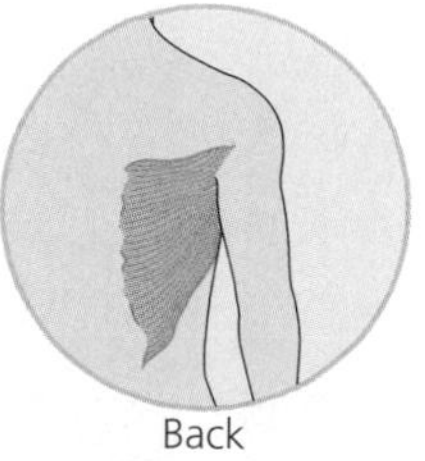

Muscles developed: Latissimus dorsi, biceps

(a) Grasp the bar of the machine with arms fully extended.

(b) Slowly pull the weight down until it reaches the top of your chest. Slowly return to the starting position.

Exercise 3 Assisted Pull-Up

Instructions: Set the weight according to the amount of assistance you need to complete a set of pull-ups—the heavier the weight, the more assistance provided.

(a) Stand or kneel on the assist platform, and grasp the pull-up bar with your elbows fully extended and your palms facing away. **(b)** Pull up until your chin goes above the bar and then return to the starting position.

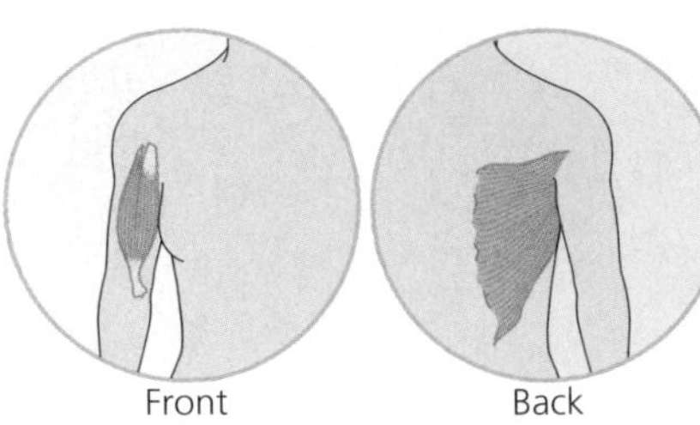

Muscles developed: Latissimus dorsi, biceps

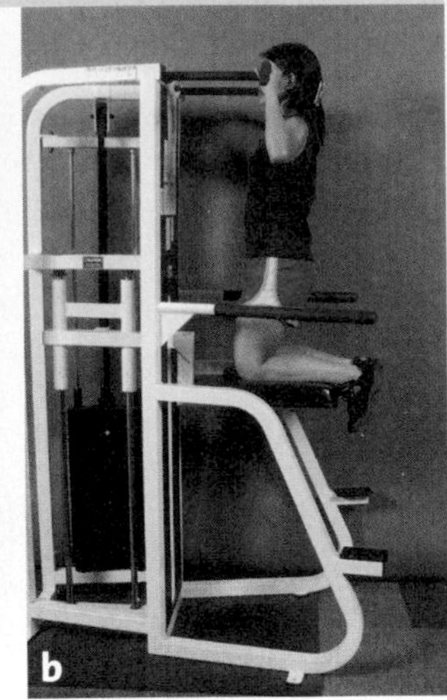

Exercise 4 Overhead Press (Shoulder Press)

Instructions: Adjust the seat so that your feet are flat on the ground and the hand grips are slightly above your shoulders.

(a) Sit down, facing away from the machine, and grasp the hand grips with your palms facing forward.

(b) Press the weight upward until your arms are extended. Return to the starting position.

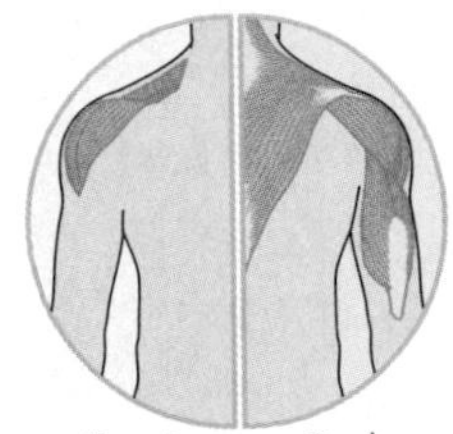

Muscles developed: Deltoids, trapezius, triceps

Exercise 5 Biceps Curl

Instructions: (a) Adjust the seat so that your back is straight and your arms rest comfortably against the top and side pads. Place your arms on the support cushions and grasp the hand grips with your palms facing up.

(b) Keeping your upper body still, flex (bend) your elbows until the hand grips almost reach your collarbone. Return to the starting position.

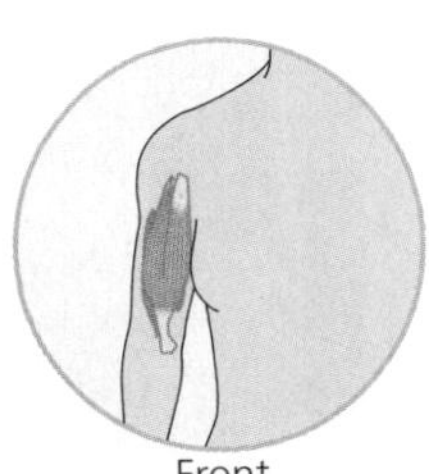

Muscles developed: Biceps, brachialis

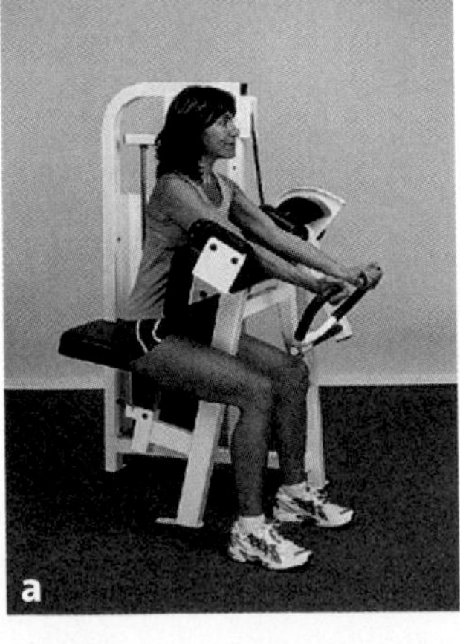

Exercise 6 Pullover

Instructions: Adjust the seat so your shoulders are aligned with the cams. Push down on the foot pads with your feet to bring the bar forward until you can place your elbows on the pads. Rest your hands lightly on the bar. If possible, place your feet flat on the floor. **(a)** To get into the starting position, let your arms go backward as far as possible. **(b)** Pull your elbows forward until the bar almost touches your abdomen. Return to the starting position.

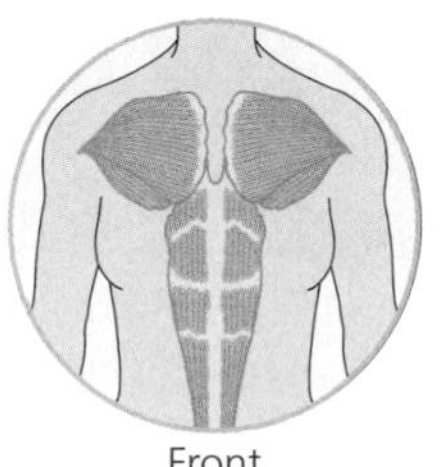

Front

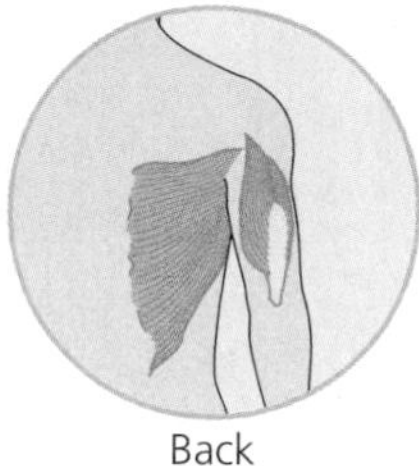

Back

Muscles developed: Latissimus dorsi, pectoralis major and minor, triceps, abdominals

a

b

Exercise 7 Lateral Raise

Instructions: (a) Adjust the seat so the pads rest just above your elbows when your upper arms are at your sides, your elbows are bent, and your forearms are parallel to the floor. Lightly grasp the handles. **(b)** Push outward and up with your arms until the pads are at shoulder height. Lead with your elbows rather than trying to lift the bars with your hands. Return to the starting position.

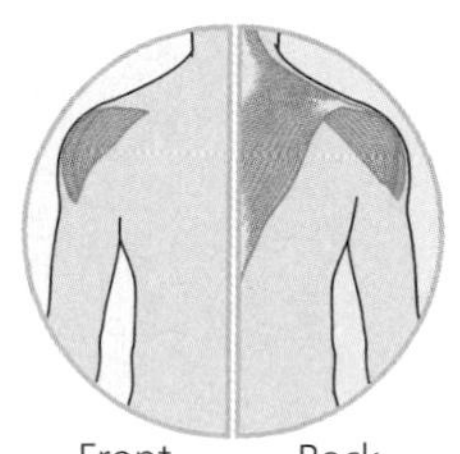

Front Back

Muscles developed: Deltoids, trapezius

a

b

Exercise 8 Triceps Extension

Note: *This exercise focuses on some of the same muscles as the assisted dip (Exercise 9); choose an appropriate exercise for your program based on your preferences and equipment availability.*

Instructions: (a) Adjust the seat so that your back is straight and your arms rest comfortably against the top and side pads. Place your arms on the support cushions and grasp the hand grips with palms facing inward.

(b) Keeping your upper body still, extend your elbows as much as possible. Return to the starting position.

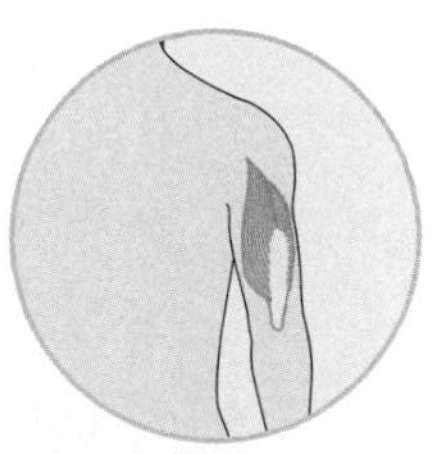

Back

Muscles developed: Triceps

a

b

Exercise 9 — Assisted Dip

Instructions: Set the weight according to the amount of assistance you need to complete a set of dips—the heavier the weight, the more assistance provided. **(a)** Stand or kneel on the assist platform with your body between the dip bar. With your elbows fully extended and palms facing your body, support your weight on your hands. **(b)** Lower your body until your upper arms are approximately parallel with the bars. Then push up until you reach the starting position.

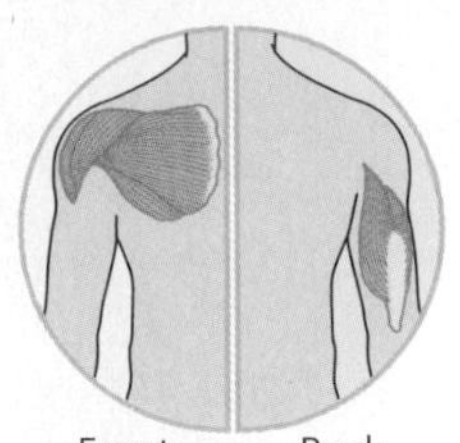

Muscles developed: Triceps, deltoids, pectoralis major

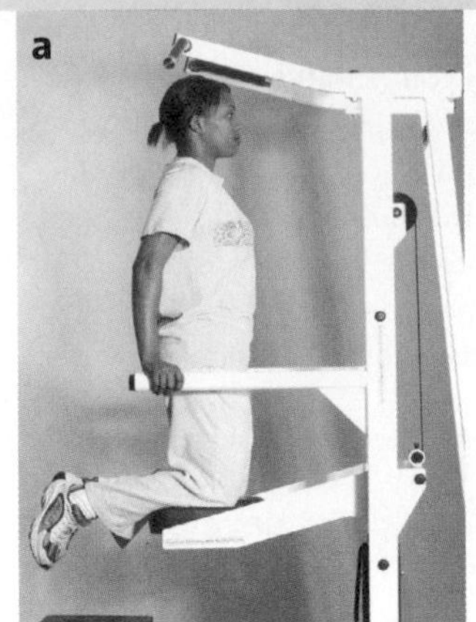

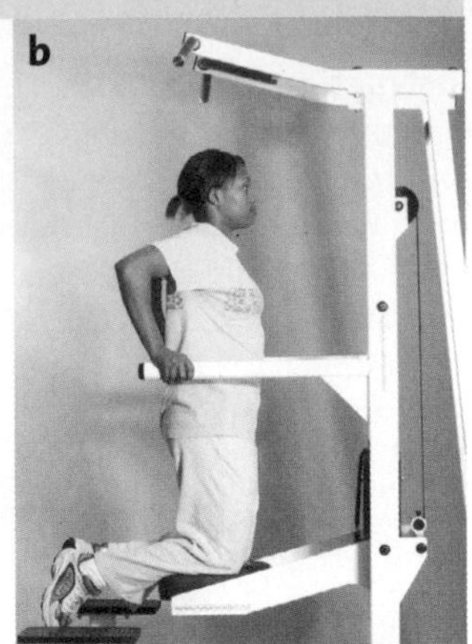

Exercise 10 — Leg Press

Instructions: Sit or lie on the seat or bench, depending on the type of machine and the manufacturer's instructions. Your head, back, hips, and buttocks should be pressed against the machine pads. Loosely grasp the handles at the side of the machine. **(a)** Begin with your feet flat on the foot platform about shoulder-width apart. Extend your legs but do not forcefully lock your knees. **(b)** Slowly lower the weight by bending your knees and flexing your hips until your knees are bent at about a 90-degree angle or your heels start to lift off the foot platform. Keep your lower back flat against the support pad. Then extend your knees and return to the starting position.

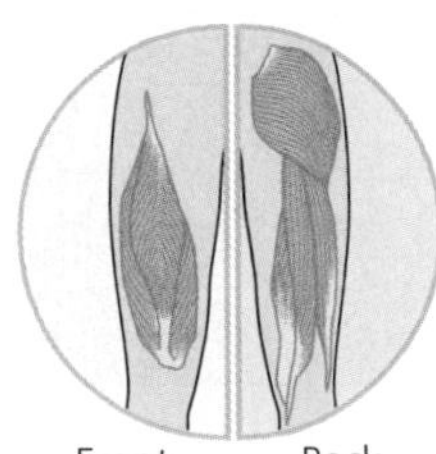

Muscles developed: Gluteus maximus, quadriceps, hamstrings

Exercise 11 — Leg Extension (Knee Extension)

Instructions: **(a)** Adjust the seat so that the pads rest comfortably on top of your lower shins. Loosely grasp the handles. **(b)** Extend your knees until they are almost straight. Return to the starting position.

Knee extensions cause kneecap pain in some people. If you have kneecap pain during this exercise, check with an orthopedic specialist before repeating it.

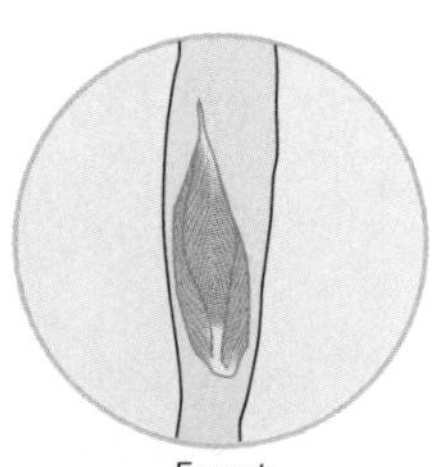

Muscles developed: Quadriceps

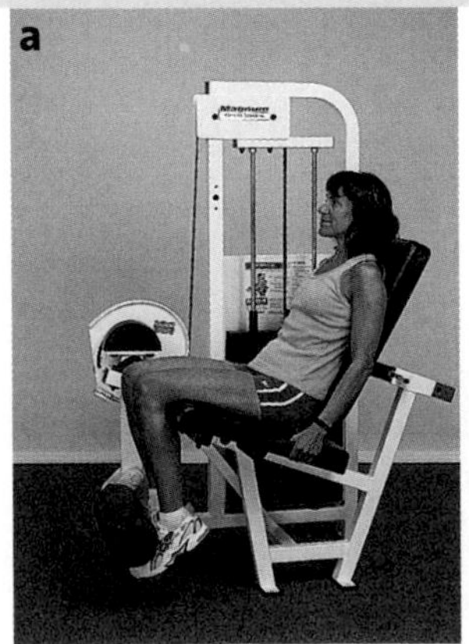

Exercise 12 Seated Leg Curl

Instructions: (a) Sit on the seat with your back against the back pad and the leg pad below your calf muscles. **(b)** Flex your knees until your lower and upper legs form a 90 degree angle. Return to the starting position.

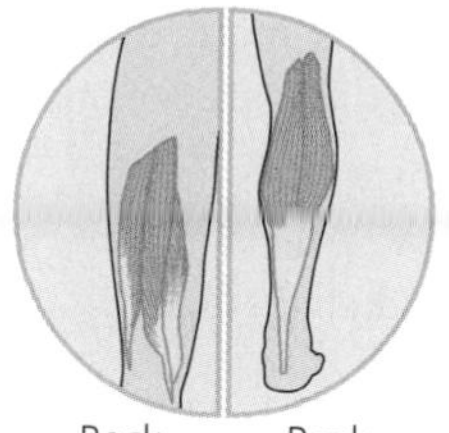

Muscles developed: Hamstrings, gastrocnemius

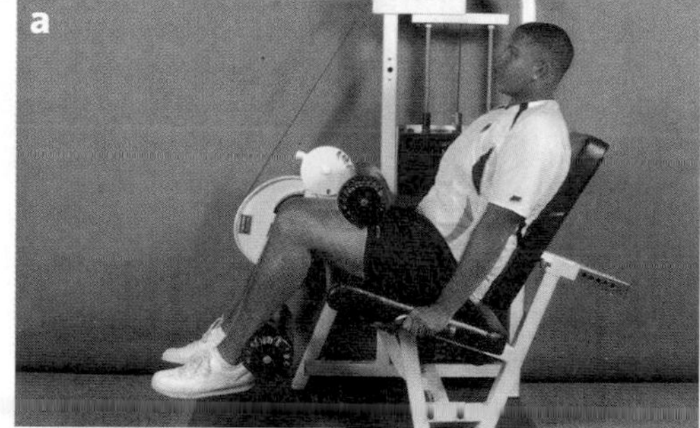

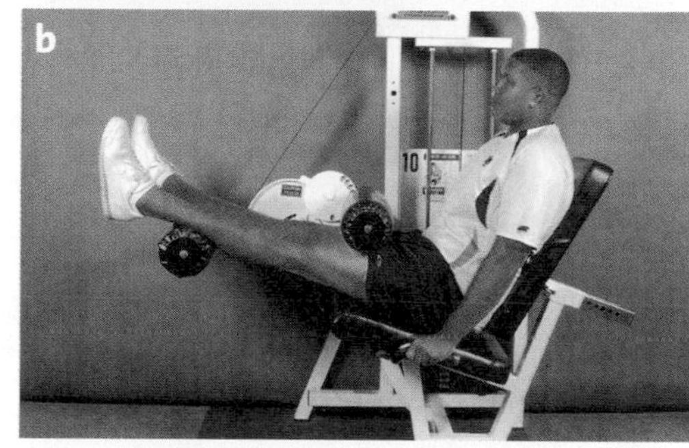

Exercise 13 Heel Raise

Instructions: (a) Stand with your head between the pads and one pad on each shoulder. The balls of your feet should be on the platform. Lightly grasp the handles. **(b)** Press down with your toes while lifting your heels. Return to the starting position. Changing the direction your feet are pointing (straight ahead, inward, and outward) will work different portions of your calf muscles.

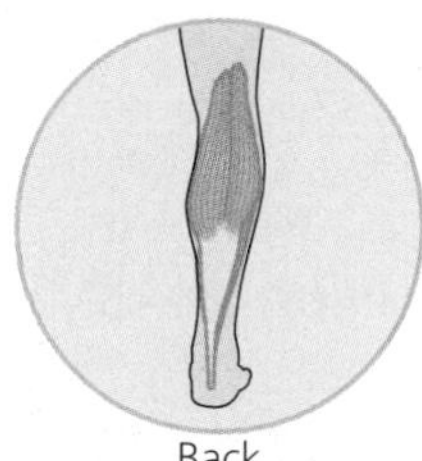

Muscles developed: Gastrocnemius, soleus

Note: Abdominal machines and low-back machines are not recommended because of injury risk. Refer to the Free Weights exercise section for appropriate exercises to strengthen the abdominal and low-back muscles. For the rectus abdominus, obliques, and transvere abdominus, perform curl-ups (Exercise 9 in the Free Weights section, p. •••), and for the erector spinae and quadratus lumborum, perform the spine extension and the isometric side bridge (Exercises 10 and 11 in the Free Weights section, p. •••).

Q Will I gain weight if I do resistance exercises?

A Your weight probably will not change significantly as a result of a general fitness program: 1 set of 8–12 repetitions of 8–10 exercises. You will increase muscle mass and lose body fat, so your weight will stay about the same. You may notice a change in how your clothes fit, however, because muscle is denser than fat. Increased muscle mass will help you control body fat. Muscle increases your metabolism, which means you burn more calories every day. If you combine resistance exercises with endurance exercises, you will be on your way to developing a healthier body composition. Concentrate on fat loss rather than weight loss.

Q Do I need more protein in my diet when I train with weights?

A No. Although there is some evidence that power athletes involved in heavy training have a higher-than-normal protein requirement, there is no reason for most people to consume extra protein. Most Americans take in more protein than they need, so even if there is an increased protein need during heavy training, it is probably supplied by the average diet. Consuming a protein-rich snack before or after training may promote muscle hypertrophy.

Q What causes muscle soreness the day or two following a weight training workout?

A The muscle pain you feel a day or two after a heavy weight training workout is caused by injury to the muscle fibers and surrounding connective tissue. Contrary to popular belief, delayed-onset muscle soreness is not caused by lactic acid buildup. Scientists believe that injury to muscle fibers causes inflammation, which in turn causes the release of chemicals that break down part of the muscle tissue and cause pain. After a bout of intense exercise that causes muscle injury and delayed-onset muscle soreness, the muscles produce protective proteins that prevent soreness during future workouts. If you don't work out regularly, you lose these protective proteins and become susceptible to soreness again.

Q Will strength training improve my sports performance?

A Strength developed in the weight room does not automatically increase your power in sports such as skiing, tennis, or cycling. Hitting a forehand in tennis and making a turn on skis are precise skills that require coordination between your nervous system and muscles. For skilled people, movements become reflex—you don't think about them when you do them. Increasing strength can disturb this coordination. Only by simultaneously practicing a sport and improving fitness can you expect to become more powerful in the skill. Practice helps you integrate your new strength with your skills, which makes you more powerful. Consequently, you can hit the ball harder in tennis or make more graceful turns on the ski slopes. (Refer to Chapter 2 for more on the concept of specificity of physical training.)

Q Will I improve faster if I train every day?

A No. Your muscles need time to recover between training sessions. Doing resistance exercises every day will cause you to become overtrained, which will increase your chance of injury and impede your progress. If your strength training program reaches a plateau, try one of these strategies:

- Train less frequently. If you are currently training the same muscle groups three or more times per week, you may not be allowing your muscles to fully recover from intense workouts.
- Change exercises. Using different exercises for the same muscle group may stimulate further strength development.
- Vary the load and number of repetitions. Try increasing or decreasing the loads you are using and changing the number of repetitions accordingly.
- Vary the number of sets. If you have been performing 1 set of each exercise, add sets.
- If you are training alone, find a motivated training partner. A partner can encourage you and assist you with difficult lifts, forcing you to work harder.

Q If I stop training, will my muscles turn to fat?

A No. Fat and muscle are two different kinds of tissue, and one cannot turn into the other. Muscles that aren't used become smaller (atrophy), and body fat may increase if caloric intake exceeds calories burned. Although the result of inactivity may be smaller muscles and more fat, the change is caused by two separate processes.

Q Should I wear a weight belt when I lift?

A Until recently, most experts advised people to wear weight belts. However, several studies have shown that weight belts do not prevent back injuries and may, in fact, increase the risk of injury by encouraging people to lift more weight than they are capable of lifting with good form. Although wearing a belt may allow you to lift more weight in some lifts, you may not get the full benefit of your program because use of a weight belt reduces the effectiveness of the workout on the muscles that help support your spine.

For more Common Questions Answered about strength training, visit the Online Learning Center. 

SUMMARY

• Hypertrophy, or increased muscle fiber size, occurs when weight training causes the number of myofibrils to increase; total muscle size thereby increases. Strength also increases through muscle learning. Most women do not develop large muscles from weight training.

• Improvements in muscular strength and endurance lead to enhanced physical performance, protection against injury, improved body composition, better self-image, improved muscle and bone health with aging, and reduced risk of chronic disease.

• Muscular strength can be assessed by determining the amount of weight that can be lifted in one repetition of an exercise; muscular endurance can be assessed by determining the number of repetitions of a particular exercise that can be performed.

• Static (isometric) exercises (contraction without movement) are most useful when a person is recovering from an injury or surgery or needs to overcome weak points in a range of motion.

• Dynamic (isotonic) exercises involve contraction that results in movement. The two most common types are constant resistance (free weights) and variable resistance (many weight machines).

• Free weights and weight machines have pluses and minuses for developing fitness, although machines tend to be safer.

• Lifting heavy weights for only a few repetitions helps develop strength. Lifting lighter weights for more repetitions helps develop muscular endurance.

• A strength training program for general fitness includes at least 1 set of 8–12 repetitions (enough to cause fatigue) of 8–10 exercises, along with warm-up and cool-down periods; the program should be carried out at least 2 days per week.

• Safety guidelines for strength training include using proper technique, using spotters and collars when necessary, and taking care of injuries.

• Supplements or drugs that are promoted as instant or quick "cures" usually don't work and are either dangerous or expensive or both.

FOR FURTHER EXPLORATION

BOOKS

Bailes, J., and J. McCloskey. 2005. *When Winning Costs Too Much: Steroids, Supplements, and Scandal in Today's Sports World.* New York: Taylor Trade. *An overview of issues relating to the use of steroids and other performance aids.*

Delavier, F. 2005. *Strength Training Anatomy,* 2nd ed. Champaign, Ill.: Human Kinetics. *Includes exercises for all major muscle groups as well as full anatomical pictures of the muscular system.* Women's Strength Training Anatomy, *a matching volume for women, was published in 2003.*

Fahey, T. D. 2007. *Basic Weight Training for Men and Women,* 6th ed. New York: McGraw-Hill. *A practical guide to developing training programs, using free weights, tailored to individual needs.*

Goldenberg, L., and P. Twist. 2007. *Strength Ball Training.* Champaign, Ill.: Human Kinetics. *A guide to incorporating exercise balls and medicine balls into a complete weight training program.*

Lethi, A., et al. 2007. *Free-Weight Training.* Berkeley, Calif.: Thunder Bay Press. *A complete guide to training with free weights, with special instructions for using weights with an exercise ball.*

Page, P. A. 2005. *Strength Band Training.* Champaign, Ill.: Human Kinetics. *Describes and illustrates more than 100 resistance band exercises, targeting every major muscle group.*

ORGANIZATIONS AND WEB SITES

American College of Sports Medicine Position Stand: Progression Models in Resistance Training for Healthy Adults. Provides an in-depth look at strategies for setting up a strength training program and making progress based on individual program goals; look for the February 2002 Position Stand.
http://www.acsm-msse.org

Exercise: A Guide from the National Institute on Aging. Provides practical advice on fitness for seniors; includes animated instructions for specific weight training exercises.
http://weboflife.ksc.nasa.gov/exerciseandaging/toc.html

Georgia State University: Strength Training. Provides information about the benefits of strength training and ways to develop a safe and effective program; also includes illustrations of a variety of exercises.
http://www.gsu.edu/~wwwfit/strength.html

Human Anatomy On-line. Provides text, illustrations, and animation about the muscular system, nerve-muscle connections, muscular contraction, and other topics.
http://www.innerbody.com/htm/body.html

Kansas State University: Nutritional Supplements for Athletes. Provides information and links to recent research findings about specific supplements.
http://www.oznet.ksu.edu/nutrition/supplements.htm

National Strength and Conditioning Association. A professional organization that focuses on strength development for fitness and athletic performance.
http://www.nsca-lift.org

Pilates Method Alliance. Provides information about Pilates and about instructor certification; includes a directory of instructors.
http://www.pilatesmethodalliance.com

United States Department of Agriculture, Food and Nutrition Information Center: Dietary Supplements page. Provides information and fact sheets about a wide variety of dietary supplements, their uses, and their effects.
http://fnic.nal.usda.gov/nal_display/index.php?info_center=4&tax_level=1&tax_subject=274

University of California, San Diego/Muscle Physiology Home Page. Provides an introduction to muscle physiology, including information about types of muscle fibers and energy cycles.
http://muscle.ucsd.edu

University of Michigan/Muscles in Action. Interactive descriptions of muscle movements.
http://www.med.umich.edu/lrc/Hypermuscle/Hyper.html

See also the listings in Chapter 2.

SELECTED BIBLIOGRAPHY

Acacio, B. D., et al. 2004. Pharmacokinetics of dehydroepiandrosterone and its metabolites after long-term daily oral administration to healthy young men. *Fertility and Sterility* 81(3): 595–604.

American College of Sports Medicine. 2006. *ACSM's Guidelines for Exercise Testing and Prescription.* Philadelphia: Lippincott Williams and Wilkins.

American College of Sports Medicine. 2006. *ACSM's Resource Manual for Guidelines for Exercise Testing and Prescription,* 5th ed. Philadelphia: Lippincott Williams and Wilkins.

American College of Sports Medicine. 2005. *News Release: Pilates Research Offers New Information on Popular Technique* (http://www.acsm.org/Content/ContentFolders/NewsReleases/2005/PILATES_RESEARCH_OFFERS_NEW_INFORMATION_ON_POPULAR_TECHNIQUE.htm; retrieved November 19, 2007).

American College of Sports Medicine. 2002. Position Stand: Progression models in resistance training for healthy adults. *Medicine and Science in Sports and Exercise* 34(2): 364–380.

Andersen, L. L., et al. 2005. The effect of resistance training combined with timed ingestion of protein on muscle fiber size and muscle strength. *Metabolism* 54: 151–156.

Anton, M. M., et al. 2006. Resistance training increases basal limb blood flow and vascular conductance in aging humans. *Journal of Applied Physiology* 101(5): 1351–1355.

Baar, K. 2006. Training for endurance and strength: Lessons from cell signaling. *Medicine and Science in Sports and Exercise* 38(11): 1939–1944.

Blazevich, A. J., et al. 2007. Lack of human muscle architectural adaptation after short-term strength training. *Muscle and Nerve* 35(1): 78–86.

Brooks, N., et al. 2006. Strength training improves muscle quality and insulin sensitivity in Hispanic older adults with type 2 diabetes. *International Journal of Medical Sciences* 4(1): 19–27.

Brooks, G. A., et al. 2005. *Exercise Physiology: Human Bioenergetics and Its Applications.* New York: McGraw-Hill.

Burt, J., et al. 2007. A comparison of once versus twice per week training on leg press strength in women. *The Journal of Sports Medicine and Physical Fitness* 47(1): 13–17.

Centers for Disease Control and Prevention. 2004. Strength training among adults aged ≥65 years. *Morbidity and Mortality Weekly Report* 53(2): 25–28.

Crews, L. 2005. Mind-body exercise: Yoga and Pilates. *ACSM Fit Society Page,* Spring.

Cribb, P. J., et al. 2007. Effects of whey isolate, creatine, and resistance training on muscle hypertrophy. *Medicine and Science in Sports and Exercise* 39(2): 298–307.

Cribb, P. J., and A. Hayes. 2006. Effects of supplement timing and resistance exercise on skeletal muscle hypertrophy. *Medicine and Science in Sports and Exercise* 38(11): 1918–1925.

Cronin, J., and B. Crewther. 2004. Training volume and strength and power development. *Journal of Science and Medicine in Sport* 7: 144–155.

Earle, R. W., and T. R. Baechle, eds. 2004. *NSCA's Essentials of Personal Training.* Champaign, Ill: Human Kinetics.

Ferguson, T. B., and D. G. Syrotuik. 2006. Effects of creatine monohydrate supplementation on body composition and strength indices in experienced resistance trained women. *Journal of Strength and Conditioning Research* 20(4): 939–946.

Field, A. E., et al. 2005. Exposure to the mass media, body shape concerns, and use of supplements to improve weight and shape among male and female adolescents. *Pediatrics* 116(2): e214–220.

Food and Drug Administration. 2006 Update. *Sales of Supplements Containing Ephedrine Alkaloids (Ephedra) Prohibited* (http://www.fda.gov/oc/initiatives/ephedra/february2004/default.htm; retrieved May 9, 2007).

Food and Drug Administration. 2004. *Questions and Answers: Androstenedione* (http://www.cfsan.fda.gov/~dms/androqa.html).

Get on the bandwagon. 2005. *University of California, Berkeley Wellness Letter,* January.

Glowacki, S. P., et al. 2004. Effects of resistance, endurance, and concurrent exercise on training outcomes in men. *Medicine and Science in Sports and Exercise* 36: 2119–2127.

Guallar-Castillon, P., et al. 2007. Waist circumference as a predictor of disability among older adults. *Obesity* (Silver Spring) 15(1): 233–244.

Hartgens, F., and H. Kuipers. 2004. Effects of androgenic-anabolic steroids in athletes. *Sports Medicine* 34: 513–554.

Haskell, W. L., et al. 2007. Physical activity and public health: updated recommendation for adults from the American College of Sports Medicine and the American Heart Association. *Circulation.* 116(9): 1081–1093.

Ibanez, J., et al. 2005. Twice-weekly progressive resistance training decreases abdominal fat and improves insulin sensitivity in older men with type 2 diabetes. *Diabetes Care* 28: 662–667.

Jurca, R., et al. 2004. Associations of muscle strength and fitness with metabolic syndrome in men. *Medicine and Science in Sports and Exercise* 36: 1301–1307.

Kemmler, W. K., et al. 2006. Predicting maximal strength in trained postmenopausal woman. *Journal of Strength and Conditioning Research* 20(4): 838–842.

Kemmler, W. K., et al. 2004. Effects of single- vs. multiple-set resistance training on maximum strength and body composition in trained postmenopausal women. *Journal of Strength and Conditioning Research* 18: 689–694.

Kraemer, W. J., et al. 2004. Changes in muscle hypertrophy in women with periodized resistance training. *Medicine and Science in Sports and Exercise* 36: 697–708.

Leyk, D., et al. 2007. Hand-grip strength of young men, women and highly trained female athletes. *European Journal of Applied Physiology* 99(4): 415–421.

Liu-Ambrose, T., et al. 2004. Resistance and agility training reduce fall risk in women aged 75 to 85 with low bone mass: A 6-month randomized, controlled trial. *Journal of the American Geriatrics Society* 52: 657–665.

Magkos, F., and S. A. Kavouras. 2004. Caffeine and ephedrine: Physiological, metabolic and performance-enhancing effects. *Sports Medicine* 34: 871–889.

Nader, G. A. 2006. Concurrent strength and endurance training: From molecules to man. *Medicine and Science in Sports and Exercise* 38(11): 1965–1970.

Peterson, J. A. 2005. 10 common mistakes made while strength training. *ACSM's Health & Fitness Journal* 9(2): 44.

Sorace, P., and T. LaFontaine, 2005. Resistance training muscle power: Design programs that work! *ACSM's Health &Fitness Journal* 9(2): 6–12.

Sosnoff, J. J., and K. M. Newell. 2006. Are age-related increases in force variability due to decrements in strength? *Experimental Brain Research* 174(1): 86–94.

Thiblin, I., and A. Petersson. 2005. Pharmacoepidemiology of anabolic androgenic steroids: A review. *Fundamental and Clinical Pharmacology* 19: 27–44.

Tsourlou, T., et al. 2006. The effects of a twenty-four-week aquatic training program on muscular strength performance in healthy elderly women. *Journal of Strength and Conditioning Research* 20(4): 811–818.

Wieser, M., and P. Haber. 2007. The effects of systematic resistance training in the elderly. *International Journal of Sports Medicine* 28(1): 59–65.

Willardson, J. M. 2006. A brief review: Factors affecting the length of the rest interval between resistance exercise sets. *Journal of Strength and Conditioning Research* 20(4): 978–984.

Willardson, J. M., and L. N. Burkett. 2005. A comparison of 3 different rest intervals on the exercise volume completed during a workout. *Journal of Strength and Conditioning Research* 19: 23–26.

Name ______________________ Section ______________ Date ____________

LAB 4.1 Assessing Your Current Level of Muscular Strength

For best results, don't do any strenuous weight training within 48 hours of any test. Use great caution when completing 1-RM tests; do not take the maximum bench press test if you have any injuries to your shoulders, elbows, back, hips, or knees. In addition, do not take these tests until you have had at least one month of weight training experience.

The Maximum Bench Press Test

Equipment

The free weights bench press test uses the following equipment:

1. Flat bench (with or without racks)
2. Barbell
3. Assorted weight plates, with collars to hold them in place
4. One or two spotters
5. Weight scale

If a weight machine is preferred, use the following equipment:

1. Universal Gym Dynamic Variable Resistance Machine
2. Weight scale

Maximum bench press test.

Preparation

Try a few bench presses with a small amount of weight so you can practice your technique, warm up your muscles, and, if you use free weights, coordinate your movements with those of your spotters. Weigh yourself and record the results.

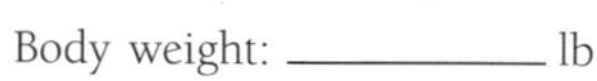

Body weight: ________ lb

Instructions

1. Use a weight that is lower than the amount you believe you can lift. For free weights, men should begin with a weight about 2/3 of their body weight; women should begin with the weight of just the bar (45 lb).
2. Lie on the bench with your feet firmly on the floor. If you are using a weight machine, grasp the handles with palms away from you; the tops of the handles should be aligned with the tops of your armpits.

   If you are using free weights, grasp the bar slightly wider than shoulder width with your palms away from you. If you have one spotter, she or he should stand directly behind the bench; if you have two spotters, they should stand to the side, one at each end of the barbell. Signal to the spotter when you are ready to begin the test by saying "1, 2, 3." On "3," the spotter should help you lift the weight to a point over your midchest (nipple line).
3. Push the bars or barbell until your arms are fully extended. Exhale as you lift. If you are using free weights, the weight moves from a low point at the chest straight up. Keep your feet firmly on the floor, don't arch your back, and push the weight evenly with your right and left arms. Don't bounce the weight on your chest.
4. Rest for several minutes, then repeat the lift with a heavier weight. It will probably take several attempts to determine the maximum amount of weight you can lift (1 RM).

   1 RM: ________ lb Check one: ________ Free weights ________ Universal ________ Other
5. If you used free weights, convert your free weights bench press score to an estimated value for 1 RM on the Universal bench press using the appropriate formula:

   Males: Estimated Universal 1 RM = (1.016 × free weights 1 RM ________ lb) + 18.41 = ________ lb

   Females: Estimated Universal 1 RM = (0.848 × free weights 1 RM ________ lb) + 21.37 = ________ lb

Rating Your Bench Press Result

1. Divide your Universal 1-RM value by your body weight.

   1 RM ____________ lb ÷ body weight ____________ lb = ____________

2. Find this ratio in the table to determine your bench press strength rating. Record the rating here and in the chart at the end of this lab.

   Bench press strength rating: ____________

Strength Ratings for the Maximum Bench Press Test

	Pounds Lifted/Body Weight (lb)					
Men	*Very Poor*	*Poor*	*Fair*	*Good*	*Excellent*	*Superior*
Age: Under 20	Below 0.89	0.89–1.05	1.06–1.18	1.19–1.33	1.34–1.75	Above 1.75
20–29	Below 0.88	0.88–0.98	0.99–1.13	1.14–1.31	1.32–1.62	Above 1.62
30–39	Below 0.78	0.78–0.87	0.88–0.97	0.98–1.11	1.12–1.34	Above 1.34
40–49	Below 0.72	0.72–0.79	0.80–0.87	0.88–0.99	1.00–1.19	Above 1.19
50–59	Below 0.63	0.63–0.70	0.71–0.78	0.79–0.89	0.90–1.04	Above 1.04
60 and over	Below 0.57	0.57–0.65	0.66–0.71	0.72–0.81	0.82–0.93	Above 0.93
Women						
Age: Under 20	Below 0.53	0.53–0.57	0.58–0.64	0.65–0.76	0.77–0.87	Above 0.87
20–29	Below 0.51	0.51–0.58	0.59–0.69	0.70–0.79	0.80–1.00	Above 1.00
30–39	Below 0.47	0.47–0.52	0.53–0.59	0.60–0.69	0.70–0.81	Above 0.81
40–49	Below 0.43	0.43–0.49	0.50–0.53	0.54–0.61	0.62–0.76	Above 0.76
50–59	Below 0.39	0.39–0.43	0.44–0.47	0.48–0.54	0.55–0.67	Above 0.67
60 and over	Below 0.38	0.38–0.42	0.43–0.46	0.47–0.53	0.54–0.71	Above 0.71

SOURCE: Based on norms from The Cooper Institute of Aerobic Research, Dallas, Texas; from *The Physical Fitness Specialist Manual,* revised 2002. Used with permission.

Predicting 1 RM from Multiple-Repetition Lifts Using Free Weights

Instead of doing the 1-RM maximum strength bench press test, you can predict your 1 RM from multiple-repetition lifts.

Instructions

1. Choose a weight you think you can bench press five times.
2. Follow the instructions for lifting the weight given in the Maximum Bench Press Test.
3. Do as many repetitions of the bench press as you can. A repetition counts only if done correctly.
4. Refer to the chart on p. 125, or calculate predicted 1 RM using the Brzycki equation:

   1 RM = *weight*/(1.0278 − [0.0278 × *number of repetitions*])

   1 RM = ____________ lb × (1.0278 − [0.0278 × ____________ repetitions]) = ____________

5. Divide your predicted 1-RM value by your body weight.

   1 RM ____________ lb ÷ body weight ____________ lb = ____________

6. Find this ratio in the table above to determine your bench press strength rating. Record the rating here and in the chart at the end of the lab.

   Bench press strength rating: ____________

RMs from the Multiple-Repetitions Bench Press Test

Weight Lifted (lb)	Repetitions											
	1	*2*	*3*	*4*	*5*	*6*	*7*	*8*	*9*	*10*	*11*	*12*
66	66	68	70	72	74	77	79	82	85	88	91	95
77	77	79	82	84	87	89	92	96	99	103	107	111
88	88	91	93	96	99	102	106	109	113	117	122	127
99	99	102	105	108	111	115	119	123	127	132	137	143
110	110	113	116	120	124	128	132	137	141	147	152	158
121	121	124	128	132	136	141	145	150	156	161	168	174
132	132	136	140	144	149	153	158	164	170	176	183	190
143	143	147	151	156	161	166	172	178	184	191	198	206
154	154	158	163	168	173	179	185	191	198	205	213	222
165	165	170	175	180	186	192	198	205	212	220	229	238
176	176	181	186	192	198	204	211	219	226	235	244	254
187	187	192	198	204	210	217	224	232	240	249	259	269
198	198	204	210	216	223	230	238	246	255	264	274	285
209	209	215	221	228	235	243	251	259	269	279	289	301
220	220	226	233	240	248	256	264	273	283	293	305	317
231	231	238	245	252	260	268	277	287	297	308	320	333
242	242	249	256	264	272	281	290	300	311	323	335	349
253	253	260	268	276	285	294	304	314	325	337	350	364
264	264	272	280	288	297	307	317	328	340	352	366	380
275	275	283	291	300	309	319	330	341	354	367	381	396
286	286	294	303	312	322	332	343	355	368	381	396	412
297	297	305	314	324	334	345	356	369	382	396	411	428
308	308	317	326	336	347	358	370	382	396	411	427	444

SOURCE: Brzycki, M. 1993. Strength testing—predicting a one-rep max from reps to fatigue. *The Journal of Physical Education, Recreation and Dance* 64: 88–90.

Functional Leg Strength Tests

The following tests assess functional leg strength using squats. Most people do squats improperly, increasing their risk of knee and back pain. Before you add weight-bearing squats to your weight training program, you should determine your functional leg strength, check your ability to squat properly, and give yourself a chance to master squatting movements. The following leg strength tests will help you in each of these areas.

These tests are progressively more difficult, so do not move to the next test until you have scored at least a 3 on the current test. On each test, give yourself a rating of 0, 1, 3, or 5, as described in the instructions that follow the fifth test.

1. *Chair Squat*

Instructions

1. Sit up straight in a chair with your back resting against the backrest and your arms at your sides. Your feet should be placed more than shoulder-width apart so that you can get them under the body.
2. Begin the motion of rising out of the chair by flexing (bending) at the hips—not the back. Then squat up using a hip hinge movement (no spine movement). Stand without rocking forward, bending your back, or using external support, and keep your head in a neutral position.

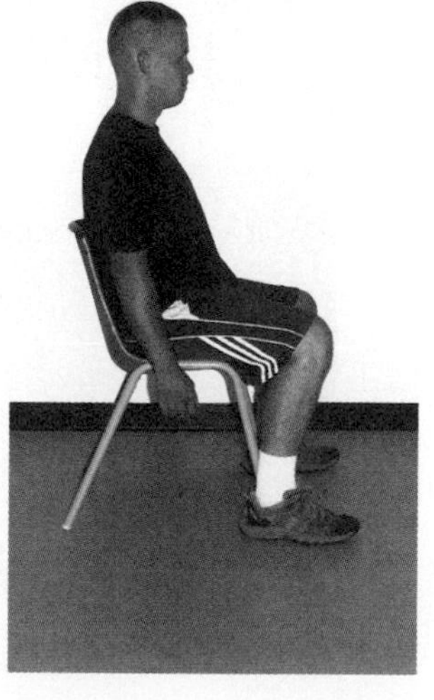

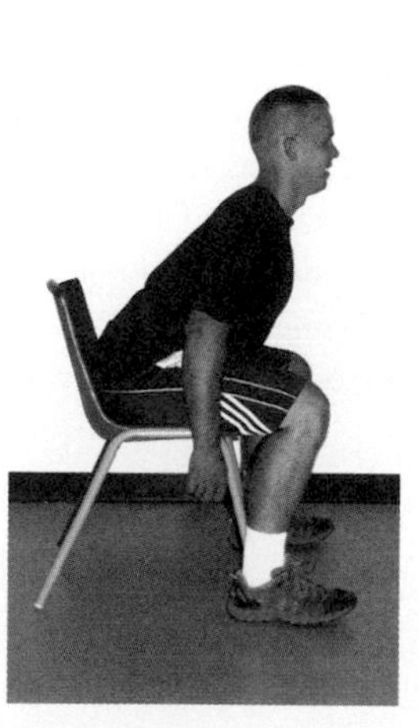

3. Return to the sitting position while maintaining a straight back and keeping your weight centered over your feet. Your thighs should abduct (spread) as you sit back in the chair. Use your rear hip and thigh muscles as much as possible as you sit.

   Do five repetitions.
   Your rating: ______________
   (See rating instructions that follow.)

2. *Single-Leg Step-Up*

Instructions

1. Stand facing a bench, with your right foot placed on the middle of the bench, right knee bent at 90 degrees, and arms at your sides.
2. Step up on the bench until your right leg is straight, maximizing the use of the hip muscles.
3. Return to the starting position. Keep your hips stable, back straight, chest up, shoulders back, and head neutral during the entire movement.

   Do five repetitions for each leg.
   Your rating: ______________
   (See rating instructions that follow.)

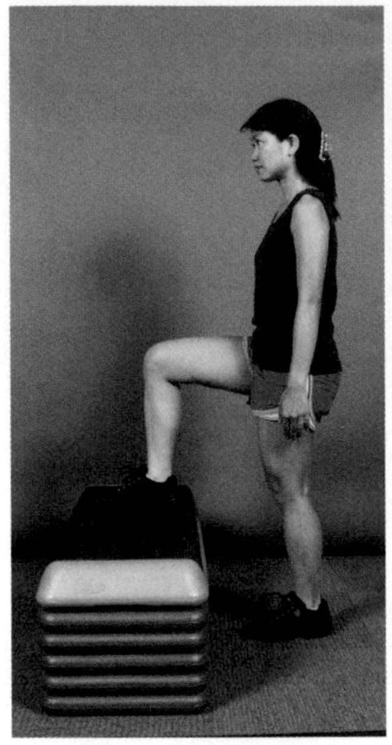

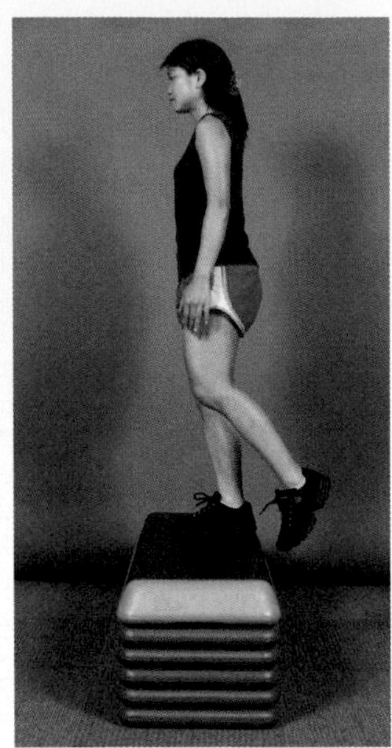

3. *Unweighted Squat*

Instructions

1. Stand with your feet placed slightly more than shoulder-width apart, toes pointed out slightly, hands on hips or across your chest, head neutral, and back straight. Center your weight over your arches or slightly behind.
2. Squat down, keeping your weight centered over your arches and actively flexing (bending) your hips until your legs break parallel. During the movement, keep your back straight, shoulders back, and chest out, and let your thighs part to the side so that you are "squatting between your legs."
3. Push back up to the starting position, hinging at the hips and not with the spine, maximizing the use of the rear hip and thigh muscles, and maintaining a straight back and neutral head position.

   Do five repetitions.
   Your rating: ______________
   (See rating instructions that follow.)

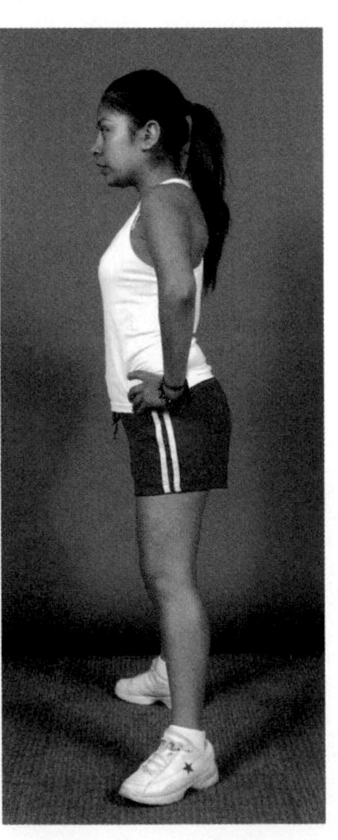

4. *Single-Leg Lunge-Squat with Rear-Foot Support*

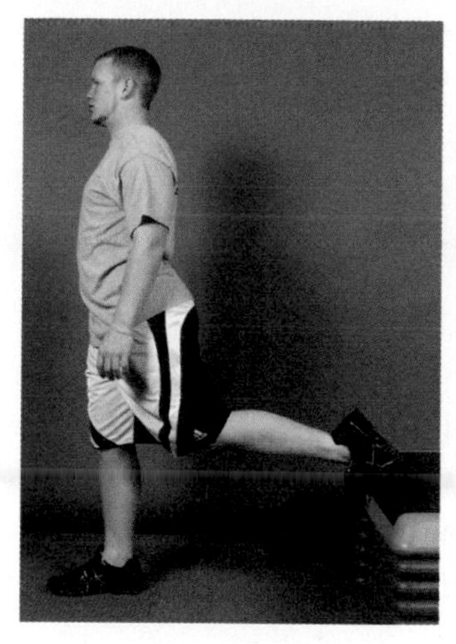

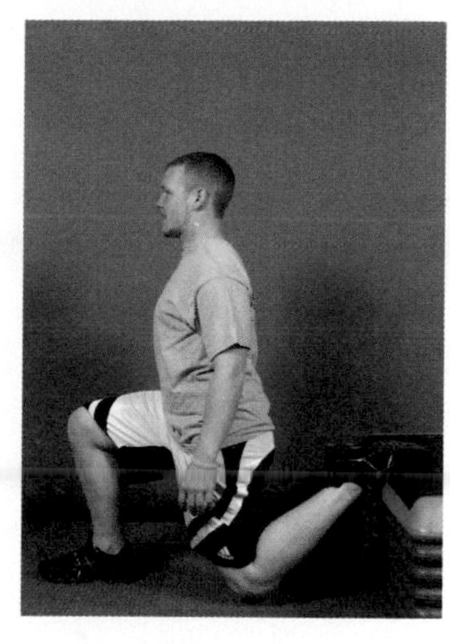

Instructions

1. Stand about 3 feet in front of a bench (with your back to the bench).
2. Place the instep of your left foot on the bench, and put most of your weight on your right leg (your left leg should be bent), with your hands at your sides.
3. Squat on your right leg until your thigh is parallel with the floor. Keep your back straight, chest up, shoulders back, and head neutral.
4. Return to the starting position.

Do three repetitions for each leg.

Your rating: ____________

(See rating instructions that follow.)

5. *Single-Leg Squat from a Bench*

Preparation

This exercise is the most difficult of the functional leg tests. Use spotters if you haven't done this exercise before or if you do not have the leg strength to perform three repetitions easily.

Instructions

1. Stand on the middle of a bench with your weight on your right leg and your arms extended in front of you. During the test, maintain a straight back and keep your weight over the arches of your feet.
2. Squat down on your right leg until your thigh is parallel with the ground, maximizing the use of your rear hip and thigh muscles. Do not rock forward on your toes or bend at the waist, and maintain a neutral head position.
3. Return to the starting position (stand up) by straightening your right hip and knee, maximizing the use of your rear hip and thigh muscles.

Perform three repetitions for each leg.

Your rating: _____

(See rating instructions that follow.)

Rating Your Functional Leg Strength Test Results

5 points: Performed the exercise properly with good back and thigh position, weight centered over the middle or rear of the foot, chest out, and shoulders back; good use of hip muscles on the way down and on the way up, with head in a neutral position throughout the movement; maintained good form during all repetitions; abducted (spread) the thighs on the way down during chair squats and double-leg squats; for single-leg exercises, showed good strength on both sides; for single-leg lunge-squat with rear-foot support, maintained straight back, and knees stayed behind toes.

3 points: Weight was forward on the toes, with some rounding of the back; used thigh muscles excessively, with little use of hip muscles; head and chest were too far forward; showed little abduction of the thighs during double-leg squats; when going down for single-leg exercises, one side was stronger than the other; form deteriorated with repetitions; for single-leg lunge-squat with rear-foot support and single-leg squat from a bench, could not reach parallel (thigh parallel with floor).

1 point: Had difficulty performing the movement, rocking forward and rounding back badly; used thigh muscles excessively, with little use of hip muscles on the way up or on the way down; chest and head were forward; on unweighted squats, had difficulty reaching parallel; and showed little abduction of the thighs; on single-leg exercises, one leg was markedly stronger than the other; could not perform multiple repetitions.

0 points: Could not perform the exercise.

Summary of Results

Maximum bench press test from either the 1-RM test or the multiple-repetition test: Weight pressed: ________ lb Rating: ________

Functional leg strength tests (0–5): Chair squat: ____________ Single-leg step-up: ____________ Unweighted squat: ____________

Single-leg lunge-squat with rear-foot support: ____________ Single-leg squat from a bench: ____________

Remember that muscular strength is specific: Your ratings may vary considerably for different parts of your body.

Using Your Results

How did you score? Are you surprised by your ratings for muscular strength? Are you satisfied with your current ratings?

If you're not satisfied, set realistic goals for improvement:

Are you satisfied with your current level of muscular strength as evidenced in your daily life—for example, your ability to lift objects, climb stairs, and engage in sports and recreational activities?

If you're not satisfied, set realistic goals for improvement:

What should you do next? Enter the results of this lab in the Preprogram Assessment column in Appendix D. If you've set goals for improvement, begin planning your strength training program by completing the plan in Lab 4.3. After several weeks of your program, complete this lab again and enter the results in the Postprogram Assessment column of Appendix D. How do the results compare?

Name ____________________ Section ____________ Date ____________

LAB 4.2 Assessing Your Current Level of Muscular Endurance

For best results, don't do any strenuous weight training within 48 hours of any test. To assess endurance of the abdominal muscles, perform the curl-up test. To assess endurance of muscles in the upper body, perform the push-up test. To assess endurance of the muscles, perform the squat endurance test.

The Curl-Up Test

Equipment

1. Four 6-inch strips of self-stick Velcro or heavy tape
2. Ruler
3. Partner
4. Mat (optional)

Preparation

Affix the strips of Velcro or long strips of tape on the mat or testing surface. Place the strips 3 inches apart.

Instructions

1. Start by lying on your back on the floor or mat, arms straight and by your sides, shoulders relaxed, palms down and on the floor, and fingers straight. Adjust your position so that the longest fingertip of each hand touches the end of the near strip of Velcro or tape. Your knees should be bent about 90 degrees, with your feet about 12–18 inches from your buttocks.
2. To perform a curl-up, flex your spine while sliding your fingers across the floor until the fingertips of each hand reach the second strip of Velcro or tape. Then return to the starting position; the shoulders must be returned to touch the mat between curl-ups, but the head need not touch. Shoulders must remain relaxed throughout the curl-up, and feet and buttocks must stay on the floor. Breathe easily, exhaling during the lift phase of the curl-up; do not hold your breath.
3. Once your partner says "go," perform as many curl-ups as you can at a steady pace with correct form. Your partner counts the curl-ups you perform and calls a stop to the test if she or he notices any incorrect form or drop in your pace.

   Number of curl-ups: ____________

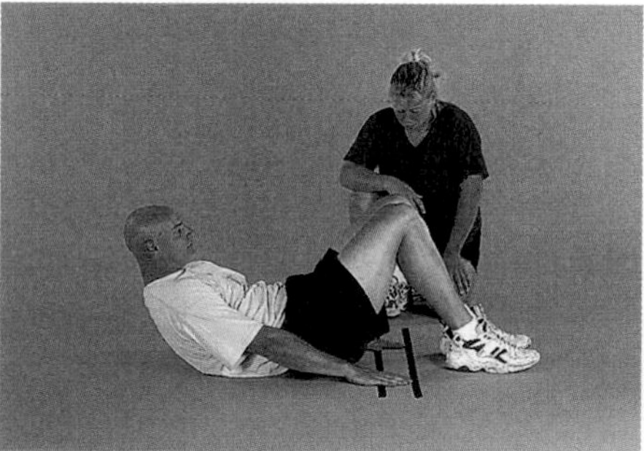

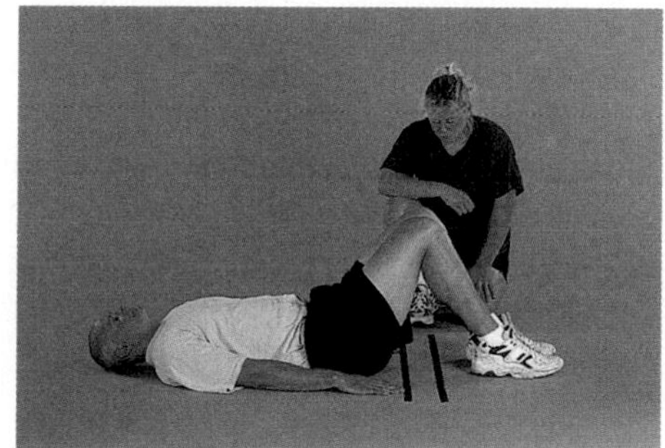

Rating Your Curl-Up Test Result

Your score is the number of completed curl-ups. Refer to the appropriate portion of the table for a rating of your abdominal muscular endurance. Record your rating below and in the summary at the end of this lab.

Rating: ____________

Ratings for the Curl-Up Test

	Number of Curl-Ups					
Men	*Very Poor*	*Poor*	*Average*	*Good*	*Excellent*	*Superior*
Age: 16–19	Below 48	48–57	58–64	65–74	75–93	Above 93
20–29	Below 46	46–54	55–63	64–74	75–93	Above 93
30–39	Below 40	40–47	48–55	56–64	65–81	Above 81
40–49	Below 38	38–45	46–53	54–62	63–79	Above 79
50–59	Below 36	36–43	44–51	52–60	61–77	Above 77
60–69	Below 33	33–40	41–48	49–57	58–74	Above 74
Women						
Age: 16–19	Below 42	42–50	51–58	59–67	68–84	Above 84
20–29	Below 41	41–51	52–57	58–66	67–83	Above 83
30–39	Below 38	38–47	48–56	57–66	67–85	Above 85
40–49	Below 36	36–45	46–54	55–64	65–83	Above 83
50–59	Below 34	34–43	44–52	53–62	63–81	Above 81
60–69	Below 31	31–40	41–49	50–59	60–78	Above 78

SOURCE: Ratings based on norms calculated from data collected by Robert Lualhati on 4545 college students, 16–80 years of age, at Skyline College, San Bruno, California. Used with permission.

The Push-Up Test

Equipment: Mat or towel (optional)

Preparation

In this test, you will perform either standard push-ups or modified push-ups, in which you support yourself with your knees. The Cooper Institute developed the ratings for this test with men performing push-ups and women performing modified push-ups. Biologically, males tend to be stronger than females; the modified technique reduces the need for upper-body strength in a test of muscular endurance. Therefore, for an accurate assessment of upper-body endurance, men should perform standard push-ups and women should perform modified push-ups. However, in using push-ups as part of a strength training program, individuals should choose the technique most appropriate for increasing their level of strength and endurance—regardless of gender.

Instructions

1. *For push-ups:* Start in the push-up position with your body supported by your hands and feet. *For-modified push-ups:* Start in the modified push-up position with your body supported by your hands and knees. *For both positions,* keep your arms and your back straight and your fingers pointed forward.

2. Lower your chest to the floor with your back straight, and then return to the starting position.
3. Perform as many push-ups or modified push-ups as you can without stopping.

   Number of push-ups: ____________ or number of modified push-ups: ____________

Rating Your Push-Up Test Result

Your score is the number of completed push-ups or modified push-ups. Refer to the appropriate portion of the table for a rating of your upper-body endurance. Record your rating below and in the summary at the end of this lab.

Rating: ____________

Ratings for the Push-Up and Modified Push-Up Tests

	Number of Push-Ups					
Men	*Very Poor*	*Poor*	*Fair*	*Good*	*Excellent*	*Superior*
Age: 18–29	Below 22	22–28	29–36	37–46	47–61	Above 61
30–39	Below 17	17–23	24–29	30–38	39–51	Above 51
40–49	Below 11	11–17	18–23	24–29	30–39	Above 39
50–59	Below 9	9–12	13–18	19–24	25–38	Above 38
60 and over	Below 6	6–9	10–17	18–22	23–27	Above 27
	Number of Modified Push-Ups					
Women	*Very Poor*	*Poor*	*Fair*	*Good*	*Excellent*	*Superior*
Age: 18–29	Below 17	17–22	23–29	30–35	36–44	Above 44
30–39	Below 11	11–18	19–23	24–30	31–38	Above 38
40–49	Below 6	6–12	13–17	18–23	24–32	Above 32
50–59	Below 6	6–11	12–16	17–20	21–27	Above 27
60 and over	Below 2	2–4	5–11	12–14	15–19	Above 19

SOURCE: Based on norms from The Cooper Institute of Aerobic Research, Dallas, Texas; from *The Physical Fitness Specialist Manual,* revised 2002. Used with permission.

The Squat Endurance Test

Instructions

1. Stand with your feet placed slightly more than shoulder width apart, toes pointed out slightly, hands on hips or across your chest, head neutral, and back straight. Center your weight over your arches or slightly behind.
2. Squat down, keeping your weight centered over your arches, until your thighs are parallel with the floor. Push back up to the starting position, maintaining a straight back and neutral head position.
3. Perform as many squats as you can without stopping.

   Number of squats: ______________

Rating Your Squat Endurance Test Result

Your score is the number of completed squats. Refer to the appropriate portion of the table for a rating of your leg muscular endurance. Record your rating below and in the summary at the end of this lab.

Rating: ______________

Ratings for the Squat Endurance Test

	Number of Squats Performed						
Men	*Very Poor*	*Poor*	*Below Average*	*Average*	*Above Average*	*Good*	*Excellent*
Age 18–25	<25	25–30	31–34	35–38	39–43	44–49	>49
26–35	<22	22–28	29–30	31–34	35–39	40–45	>45
36–45	<17	17–22	23–26	27–29	30–34	35–41	>41
46–55	<9	13–17	18–21	22–24	25–38	29–35	>35
56–65	<9	9–12	13–16	17–20	21–24	25–31	>31
65+	<7	7–10	11–14	15–18	19–21	22–28	>28
Women	*Very Poor*	*Poor*	*Below Average*	*Average*	*Above Average*	*Good*	*Excellent*
Age 18–25	<18	18–24	25–28	29–32	33–36	37–43	>43
26–35	<20	13–20	21–24	25–28	29–32	33–39	>39
36–45	<7	7–14	15–18	19–22	23–26	27–33	>33
46–55	<5	5–9	10–13	14–17	18–21	22–27	>27
56–65	<3	3–6	7–9	10–12	13–17	18–24	>24
65+	<2	2–4	5–10	11–13	14–16	17–23	>23

SOURCE: www.topendsports.com/testing/tests/home-squat.htm

Summary of Results

Curl-up test: Number of curl-ups: ______________ Rating: ______________

Push-up test: Number of push-ups: ______________ Rating: ______________

Squat endurance test: Number of squats: ______________ Rating: ______________

Remember that muscular endurance is specific: Your ratings may vary considerably for different parts of your body.

Using Your Results

How did you score? Are you surprised by your ratings for muscular endurance? Are you satisfied with your current ratings?

If you're not satisfied, set realistic goals for improvement:

Are you satisfied with your current level of muscular endurance as evidenced in your daily life—for example, your ability to carry groceries or your books, hike, and do yard work?

If you're not satisfied, set realistic goals for improvement:

What should you do next? Enter the results of this lab in the Preprogram Assessment column in Appendix D. If you've set goals for improvement, begin planning your strength training program by completing the plan in Lab 4.3. After several weeks of your program, complete this lab again and enter the results in the Postprogram Assessment column of Appendix D. How do the results compare?

Name ____________ Section ____________ Date ____________

LAB 4.3 Designing and Monitoring a Strength Training Program

1. *Set goals.* List goals for your strength training program. Your goals can be specific or general, short or long term. In the first section, include specific, measurable goals that you can use to track the progress of your fitness program—for example, raising your upper-body muscular strength rating from fair to good or being able to complete 10 repetitions of a lat pull with 125 pounds of resistance. In the second section, include long-term and more qualitative goals, such as improving self-confidence and reducing your risk for back pain.

   Specific Goals: Current Status ____________ Final Goals ____________

   ____________ ____________

   ____________ ____________

   Other goals: ____________

   ____

2. *Choose exercises.* Based on your goals, choose 8–10 exercises to perform during each weight training session. If your goal is general training for wellness, use one of the sample programs in Figure 4.4 (p. 102) and on pp. 111–119. List your exercises and the muscles they develop in your program plan.
3. *Frequency: Choose the number of training sessions per week.* Work out at least 2 nonconsecutive days per week. Indicate the days you will train in your program plan; be sure to include days of rest to allow your body to recover.
4. *Intensity: Choose starting weights.* Experiment with different amounts of weight until you settle on a good starting weight, one that you can lift easily for 10–12 repetitions. As you progress in your program, add more weight. Fill in the starting weight for each exercise in your program plan.
5. *Time: Choose a starting number of sets and repetitions.* Include at least 1 set of 8–12 repetitions of each exercise. (When you add weight, you may have to decrease the number of repetitions slightly until your muscles adapt to the heavier load.) If your program is focusing on strength alone, your sets can contain fewer repetitions using a heavier load. If you are over approximately age 50–60, your sets should contain more repetitions (10–15) using a lighter load. Fill in the starting number of sets and repetitions of each exercise in your program plan.
6. *Monitor your progress.* Use the workout card on the next page to monitor your progress and keep track of exercises, weights, sets, and repetitions.

Program Plan for Weight Training

Exercise	Muscle(s) Developed	Frequency (check ✓)							Intensity: Weight (lb)	Time	
		M	T	W	Th	F	Sa	Su		Repetitions	Sets

WORKOUT CARD FOR ______________________________

Exercise/Date																												
	Wt																											
	Sets																											
	Reps																											
	Wt																											
	Sets																											
	Reps																											
	Wt																											
	Sets																											
	Reps																											
	Wt																											
	Sets																											
	Reps																											
	Wt																											
	Sets																											
	Reps																											
	Wt																											
	Sets																											
	Reps																											
	Wt																											
	Sets																											
	Reps																											
	Wt																											
	Sets																											
	Reps																											
	Wt																											
	Sets																											
	Reps																											
	Wt																											
	Sets																											
	Reps																											
	Wt																											
	Sets																											
	Reps																											
	Wt																											
	Sets																											
	Reps																											

LOOKING AHEAD>>>>>

AFTER READING THIS CHAPTER, YOU SHOULD BE ABLE TO:

- Describe the potential benefits of flexibility and stretching exercises
- List the factors that affect the flexibility in a joint
- Explain the different types of stretching exercises and how they affect muscles
- Describe the intensity, duration, and frequency of stretching exercises that will develop the most flexibility with the lowest risk of injury
- List safe stretching exercises for major joints
- Describe how low-back pain can be prevented and managed

FLEXIBILITY AND LOW-BACK HEALTH 5

TEST YOUR KNOWLEDGE

1. Stretching exercises should be performed

a. at the start of a warm-up.
b. first thing in the morning.
c. after endurance exercise or strength training.

2. If you injure your back, it's usually best to rest in bed until the pain is completely gone.

True or false?

3. It is better to hold a stretch for a short time than to "bounce" while stretching.

True or false?

ANSWERS

1. **c.** It's best to do stretching exercises when your muscles are warm. Stretching muscles before exercise may temporarily reduce their explosive strength and interfere with neuromuscular control.
2. **FALSE.** Prolonged bed rest may actually worsen back pain. Limit bed rest to a day or less, treat pain and inflammation with cold and then heat, and begin moderate physical activity as soon as possible.
3. **TRUE.** "Bouncing" during stretching can damage your muscles. This type of stretching, called ballistic stretching, should be used only by well-conditioned athletes for specific purposes. A person of average fitness should stretch slowly, holding each stretch for 15–30 seconds.

FIT AND WELL ONLINE LEARNING CENTER www.mhhe.com/fahey

Visit the *Fit and Well* Online Learning Center for resources that will help you get the most out of your course!

- Study and review aids include practice quizzes, glossary flashcards, chapter summaries, learning objectives, PowerPoint presentations, Common Questions Answered, student handouts, crossword puzzles, Internet activities, and links to wellness Web sites.
- Behavior change tools include a daily fitness and nutrition journal, a behavior change workbook, sample behavior change plans, and blank behavior change logs to print and use.
- The Chapter 5 resources also include video clips showing how to do all the flexibility and low-back exercises described and illustrated in the chapter (look for the video icon).

Flexibility—the ability of a joint to move through its normal, full **range of motion**—is important for general fitness and wellness. Flexibility is a highly adaptable physical fitness component. It increases in response to a regular program of stretching exercises and decreases with inactivity. Flexibility is also specific: Good flexibility in one joint doesn't necessarily mean good flexibility in another. Flexibility can be increased through stretching exercises for all major joints.

This chapter describes the factors that affect flexibility and the benefits of maintaining good flexibility. It provides guidelines for assessing your current level of flexibility and putting together a successful stretching program. It also examines the common problem of low-back pain.

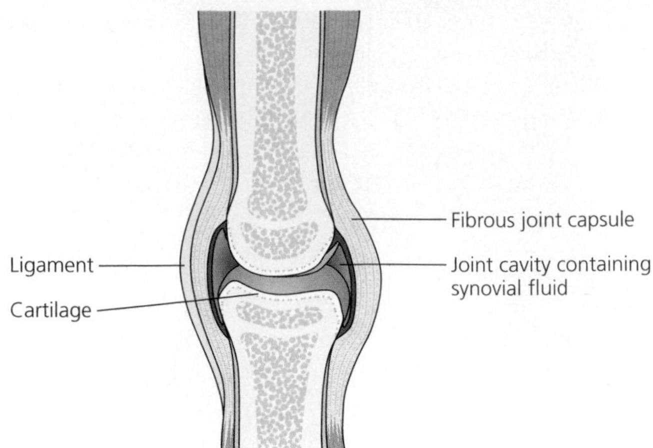

FIGURE 5.1 Basic joint structure. A moveable joint is surrounded by a fibrous joint capsule that provides support and stability. The bone surfaces within the joint are lined with cartilage and separated by synovial fluid to cushion the bones and reduce friction as the joint moves. Ligaments can be found both inside and outside the joint capsule and serve to strengthen and reinforce the joint.

TYPES OF FLEXIBILITY

There are two types of flexibility:

- *Static flexibility* is the ability to hold an extended position at one end or point in a joint's range of motion. For example, static flexibility determines how far you can extend your arm across the front of your body or out to the side. Static flexibility depends on your ability to tolerate stretched muscles, the structure of your joints, and the tightness of muscles, tendons, and ligaments.
- *Dynamic flexibility* is the ability to move a joint through its range of motion with little resistance. For example, dynamic flexibility affects your ability to pitch a ball or swing a golf club. Dynamic flexibility depends on static flexibility, but it also involves strength, coordination, and resistance to movement.

Dynamic flexibility is important for daily activities and sports. Because static flexibility is easier to measure and better researched, however, most assessment tests and stretching programs target that type of flexibility.

WHAT DETERMINES FLEXIBILITY?

The flexibility of a joint is affected by its structure, by muscle elasticity and length, and by nervous system regulation. Some factors—joint structure, for example—can't be changed. Other factors, such as the length of resting muscle fibers, can be changed through exercise; these factors should be the focus of a program to develop flexibility.

Joint Structure

The amount of flexibility in a joint is determined in part by the nature and structure of the joint (Figure 5.1). Hinge joints such as those in your fingers and knees allow only limited forward and backward movement; they lock when fully extended. Ball-and-socket joints like the hip enable movement in many different directions and have a greater range of motion. Major joints are surrounded by **joint capsules**, semielastic structures that give joints strength and stability but limit movement.

Heredity plays a part in joint structure and flexibility; for example, although everyone has a broad range of motion in the ball-and-socket hip joint, not everyone can do a split. Gender may also play a role. Some studies have found that women on average have greater flexibility in certain joints.

Muscle Elasticity and Length

Soft tissues—including skin, muscles, tendons, and ligaments—also limit the flexibility of a joint. Muscle tissue is the key to developing flexibility because it can be lengthened if it is regularly stretched. The most important component of muscle tissue related to flexibility is the connective tissue that surrounds and envelops every part of muscle tissue, from individual muscle fibers to entire muscles. Connective tissue provides structure, elasticity, and bulk and makes up about 30% of muscle mass. Two principal types of connective tissue are **collagen**—white fibers that provide structure and support—and **elastin**—yellow fibers that are elastic and flexible. Muscles contain both collagen and elastin, closely intertwined, so muscle tissue exhibits the properties of both types of fibers. A recently discovered structural protein in muscles called *titin* also has elastic properties and contributes to flexibility.

When a muscle is stretched, the wavelike elastin fibers straighten; when the stretch is relieved, they rapidly snap back to their resting position. If gently and regularly stretched, connective tissues may lengthen and flexibility may improve. Without regular stretching, the process reverses: These tissues shorten, resulting in decreased flexibility. Regular stretching may contribute to flexibility by lengthening muscle fibers through the addition of contractile units called *sarcomeres*.

The amount of stretch a muscle will tolerate is limited, and as the limits of its flexibility are reached, connective tissue becomes more brittle and may rupture if overstretched. A safe and effective program stretches muscles enough to slightly elongate the tissues but not so much that they are damaged. Research has shown that flexibility is improved best by stretching when muscles are warm (following exercise or the application of heat) and the stretch is applied gradually and conservatively. Sudden, high-stress stretching is less effective and can lead to muscle damage.

Nervous System Regulation

Nerves that send information about the muscular and skeletal systems to the nervous system are called **proprioceptors.** When these nerves detect any change in the position or force of muscles and joints, they send signals to the spine and brain, which in turn send signals back to the muscles to coordinate muscle action in ways that protect muscles and tendons from injury. They help control the speed, strength, and coordination of muscle contractions.

When a muscle is stretched (lengthened), proprioceptors detect the amount and rate of the change in muscle length. The nerves send a signal to the spinal cord, which then sends a signal back to the same muscle, triggering a muscle contraction that resists the change in muscle length. Another signal is sent to the antagonist muscle, causing it to relax, which further facilitates contraction of the stretched muscle. These reflexes occur frequently in active muscles and allow for fine control of muscle length and movement.

Small movements that only slightly stimulate these nerves cause small reflex actions. Rapid, powerful, and sudden changes in muscle length strongly stimulate the receptors and can cause large and powerful reflex muscle contractions. Thus, stretches that involve rapid, bouncy movements can be dangerous and cause injury because each bounce causes a reflex contraction, and so a muscle might be stretching at the same time it is contracting. Performing a gradual stretch and then holding it allows the proprioceptors to adjust to the new muscle length and to reduce the signals sent to the spine, thereby allowing muscles to lengthen and, over time, improving flexibility.

The stretching technique called *proprioceptive neuromuscular facilitation (PNF),* described on p. 140, takes advantage of nerve activity to improve flexibility. For example, contracting a muscle prior to stretching it can help allow the muscle to stretch farther. The advanced strength training technique called plyometrics, described in Chapter 4, also takes advantage of the patterns of nervous system action in stretching and contracting muscles.

Modifying nervous control through movement and specific exercises is the best way to improve the functional range of motion. Stretching regularly trains all of the proprioceptors to allow greater lengthening of the muscles. Proprioceptors adapt very quickly to stretching (or lack of stretching), so frequent training is beneficial for developing flexibility. It is important to note that stretching before exercising can disturb proprioceptors and interfere with motor (movement) control during exercise. This is another good reason to stretch after exercising.

BENEFITS OF FLEXIBILITY AND STRETCHING EXERCISES

Good flexibility provides benefits for the entire musculoskeletal system; it may also prevent injuries and soreness and improve performance in all physical activities.

Joint Health

Good flexibility is essential to good joint health. When the muscles and other tissues that support a joint are tight, the joint is subject to abnormal stresses that can cause joint deterioration. For example, tight thigh muscles cause excessive pressure on the kneecap, leading to pain in the knee joint. Poor joint flexibility can also cause abnormalities in joint lubrication, leading to deterioration of the sensitive cartilage cells lining the joint; pain and further joint injury can result.

Improved flexibility can greatly improve your quality of life, particularly as you get older. People tend to exercise

QUESTIONS FOR CRITICAL THINKING AND REFLECTION

Have you ever noticed that you are markedly more or less flexible than your friends or classmates? To what do you attribute these differences? Were you aware that you could increase your flexibility with a regular stretching program? Would it be meaningful to you to do so?

TERMS 

range of motion The full motion possible in a joint.

joint capsules Semielastic structures, composed primarily of connective tissue, that surround major joints.

soft tissues Tissues of the human body that include skin, fat, linings of internal organs and blood vessels, connective tissues, tendons, ligaments, muscles, and nerves.

collagen White fibers that provide structure and support in connective tissue.

elastin Yellow fibers that make connective tissue flexible.

proprioceptor A nerve that sends information about the muscular and skeletal systems to the nervous system.

less as they age, leading to loss of joint mobility. Aging also decreases the natural elasticity of muscles, tendons, and joints, resulting in stiffness. The problem is often compounded by arthritis. Good joint flexibility may prevent arthritis, and stretching may lessen pain in people who have the condition. Another benefit of good flexibility for older adults is that it increases balance and stability.

Prevention of Low-Back Pain and Injuries

Low-back pain can be related to poor spinal stability, which puts pressure on the nerves leading out from the spinal column. Strength and flexibility in the back, pelvis, and thighs may help prevent this type of back pain. However, few studies have found that trunk flexibility improves back health or reduces the risk of injury (greater spinal mobility may actually increase the risk of low-back problems in some people). Good hip and knee flexibility do protect the spine from excessive motion during the tasks of daily living.

Some studies show that poor flexibility increases the risk for injury. A general stretching program can be effective in reducing the frequency of injuries, as well as their severity. When injuries occur, flexibility exercises can be used in treatment: They reduce symptoms and help restore normal range of motion in affected joints.

Overstretching—stretching muscles to extreme ranges of motion—may decrease the stability of a joint. Although some activities, such as gymnastics and ballet, require extreme joint movements, such flexibility is not recommended for the average person. In fact, extreme flexibility may increase the risk of injury in activities such as skiing, basketball, and volleyball. As with other types of exercise, moderation is the key to safe training.

Additional Potential Benefits

- ***Relief of aches and pains.*** Studying or working in one place for a long time can make your muscles tense. Stretching helps relieve tension, so you can go back to work refreshed and effective.
- ***Relief of muscle cramps.*** Recent research suggests that exercise-related muscle cramps are caused by increased electrical activity within the affected muscle. The best treatment for muscle cramps is gentle stretching, which reduces the electrical activity and allows the muscle to relax.
- ***Improved body position and strength for sports (and life).*** Good flexibility lets you assume more efficient body positions and exert force through a greater range of motion. For example, swimmers with more flexible shoulders have stronger strokes because they can pull their arms through the water in the optimal position. Some studies also suggest that flexibility training enhances strength development.
- ***Maintenance of good posture and balance.*** Good flexibility also contributes to body symmetry and good posture. Bad posture can gradually change your body structures. Sitting in a slumped position, for example, can lead to tightness in the muscles in the front of your chest and overstretching and looseness in the upper spine, causing a rounding of the upper back. This condition, called *kyphosis,* is common in older people. It may be prevented by stretching regularly.
- ***Relaxation.*** Flexibility exercises reduce mental tension, slow your breathing rate, and reduce blood pressure.

ASSESSING FLEXIBILITY

Because flexibility is specific to each joint, there are no tests of general flexibility. The most commonly used flexibility test is the sit-and-reach test, which rates the flexibility of the muscles in the lower back and hamstrings. To assess your flexibility and identify inflexible joints, complete Lab 5.1.

CREATING A SUCCESSFUL PROGRAM TO DEVELOP FLEXIBILITY

A successful program for developing flexibility includes safe exercises executed with the most effective techniques. Your goal should be to attain normal flexibility in the major joints. Extreme flexibility causes joint instability, which can lead to pain in the back, hips, shoulders, and knees. Balanced flexibility (not too much or too little) provides

! **MOTIVATION BOOSTER**

Inspire yourself. List five benefits of flexibility and stretching exercises that are particularly meaningful to you—for example, preventing back pain and relieving neck pain from long hours of computer work. Put the list in a prominent location, and use it as a motivational tool for beginning and maintaining your stretching program.

QUESTIONS FOR CRITICAL THINKING AND REFLECTION

When you think about the health-related components of fitness, how do you rank flexibility? Is it less important to you than cardiorespiratory endurance or muscular strength? If you place a low priority on flexibility and don't include stretching in your program, why do you think this is the case? What influences have shaped your opinions—the media, teachers, coaches, peers? What can you do to increase your motivation and find time to stretch?

TAKE CHARGE

Safe Stretching

- Do stretching exercises statically. Stretch to the point of mild discomfort, hold the position for 15–30 seconds, rest for 30–60 seconds, and repeat, trying to stretch a bit farther.
- Do not stretch to the point of pain. Any soreness after a stretching workout should be mild and last no more than 24 hours. If you are sore for a longer period, you stretched too intensely.
- Relax and breathe easily as you stretch. Inhale through the nose and exhale through pursed lips during the stretch. Try to relax the muscles being stretched.
- Perform all exercises on both sides of your body.
- Increase intensity and duration gradually over time. Improved flexibility takes many months to develop.
- Stretch when your muscles are warm. Do gentle warm-up exercises such as easy jogging or calisthenics before doing a stretching routine.
- There are large individual differences in joint flexibility. Don't feel you have to compete with others during stretching workouts.
- Engage in a variety of physical activities to help you develop well-rounded functional physical fitness and allow you to perform all types of training more safely and effectively.

joint stability and facilitates smooth, economical movement patterns. You can achieve balanced flexibility by performing stretching exercises regularly and by using a variety of stretches and stretching techniques.

Applying the FITT Principle

As with the programs described for developing other health-related components of fitness, the acronym FITT can be used to remember key components of a stretching program: Frequency, Intensity, Time, and Type of exercise.

Frequency The ACSM recommends that stretching exercises be performed a minimum of 2–3 days a week, and ideally 5–7 days a week. Doing these exercises often will provide the most benefits. It's best to stretch when your muscles are warm, so try incorporating stretching into your cool-down after cardiorespiratory endurance exercise or weight training.

Never stretch when your muscles are cold; doing so can increase your risk of injury as well as limit the amount of flexibility you can develop. Although stretching before exercise is a time-honored ritual practiced by athletes in many sports, several studies have found that pre-exercise stretching decreases muscle strength and performance and disturbs neuromuscular control. If your workout involves participation in a sport or high-performance activity, you may be better off stretching after your workout; for moderate-intensity activities like walking or cycling, stretching before your workout is unlikely to impair your performance.

Intensity and Time (Duration) For each exercise, slowly stretch your muscles to the point of slight tension or mild discomfort. Hold the stretch for 15–30 seconds. As you hold the stretch, the feeling of slight tension should slowly subside; at that point, try to stretch a bit farther. Throughout the stretch, try to relax and breathe easily. Rest for about 30–60 seconds between each stretch, and do 2–4 repetitions of each stretch. A complete flexibility workout usually takes about 20–30 minutes (Figure 5.2).

Warm-up 5–10 minutes or following an endurance or strength training workout	Stretching exercises for major joints **Sample program**	
	Exercise	***Areas stretched***
	Head turns and tilts	Neck
	Towel stretch	Triceps, shoulders, chest
	Across-the-body and overhead stretches	Shoulders, upper back, back of arm
	Upper-back stretch	Upper back
	Lateral stretch	Trunk muscles
	Step stretch	Hip, front of thigh
	Side lunge	Inner thigh, hip, calf
	Inner thigh stretch	Inner thigh, hip
	Hip and trunk stretch	Trunk, outer thigh, hip, buttocks, lower back
	Modified hurdler stretch	Back of thigh, lower back
	Alternate leg stretcher	Back of thigh, hip, knee, ankle, buttocks
	Lower-leg stretch	Calf, soleus, Achilles tendon

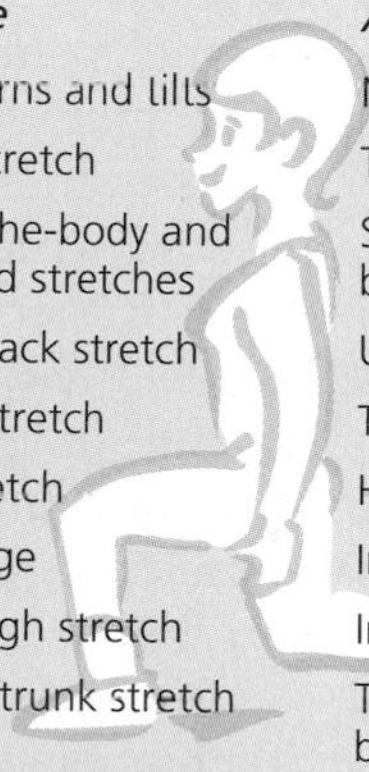

Frequency: 2–3 days per week (minimum); 5–7 days per week (ideal)

Intensity: Stretch to the point of mild discomfort, not pain

Time (duration): All stretches should be held for 15–30 seconds and performed 2–4 times

Type of activity: Stretching exercises that focus on major joints

FIGURE 5.2 The FITT principle for a flexibility program.

WEB **Types of Stretching Techniques** Stretching techniques vary from simply stretching the muscles during the course of normal activities to sophisticated methods based on patterns of muscle reflexes. Improper stretching can do more harm than good, so it's important to understand the different types of stretching exercises and how they affect the muscles. (See the box "Safe Stretching" for guidelines on creating a safe and effective stretching program.) Four common techniques are static stretches, ballistic stretches, dynamic stretches, and PNF. These techniques can be performed passively or actively.

STATIC STRETCHING In **static stretching,** each muscle is gradually stretched, and the stretch is held for 15–30 seconds. A slow stretch prompts less reaction from proprioceptors, and the muscles can safely stretch farther than usual. Static stretching is the type most often recommended by fitness experts because it's safe and effective.

The key to this technique is to stretch the muscles and joints to the point where a pull is felt, but not to the point of pain. (One note of caution: Excess static stretching can decrease joint stability and increase the risk of injury; this may be a particular concern for women, who naturally have joints that are less stable and more flexible than men.) The sample stretching program presented later in this chapter features static stretching exercises.

BALLISTIC STRETCHING In **ballistic stretching,** the muscles are stretched suddenly in a forceful bouncing movement. For example, touching the toes repeatedly in rapid succession is a ballistic stretch for the hamstrings. A problem with this technique is that the heightened activity of proprioceptors caused by the rapid stretches can continue for some time, possibly causing injuries during any physical activities that follow. Another concern is that triggering strong responses from the nerves can cause a reflex muscle contraction that makes it harder to stretch. For these reasons, ballistic stretching is usually not recommended, especially for people of average fitness.

Ballistic stretching trains the muscle dynamically, so it can be an appropriate stretching technique for some well-trained athletes. For example, tennis players stretch their hamstrings and quadriceps ballistically when they lunge for a ball during a tennis match; because this movement is part of their sport, they might benefit from ballistic training of these muscle groups.

DYNAMIC (FUNCTIONAL) STRETCHING The emphasis in **dynamic stretching** is on functionally based movements. Dynamic stretching is similar to ballistic stretching in that it includes movement, but it differs in that it does not involve rapid bouncing. Instead, dynamic stretching involves moving the joints through the range of motion used in a specific exercise or sport in an exaggerated but controlled manner; movements are fluid rather than jerky. An example of a dynamic stretch is the lunge walk, in which a person takes slow steps with an exaggerated stride length; in each step, a lunge stretch position is reached.

MOTIVATION BOOSTER

Reward yourself with stretching. If you have trouble making time for flexibility training, remember that stretching can be relaxing. Make flexibility workouts your reward after a busy day. Warm up for a few minutes, then stretch to reduce physical and mental tension. The immediate benefits may motivate you to stretch regularly.

Slow dynamic stretches can lengthen the muscles in many directions without developing high tension in the tissues; these stretches elongate the tissues and train the neuromuscular system. Because dynamic stretches are based on sports movements or movements used in daily life, they develop functional flexibility that translates well into activities.

Dynamic stretches are more challenging than static stretches; they require balance and coordination and may carry a greater risk of muscle soreness and injury. People just beginning a flexibility program might want to start off with static stretches and try dynamic stretches only after they are comfortable with static stretching techniques and have improved their flexibility. It is also a good idea to seek expert advice on dynamic stretching technique and program development.

Serious athletes may use dynamic stretches as part of their warm-up before a competitive event or a high-intensity training session in order to move their joints through the range of motion required for the activity. Functional flexibility training can also be combined with functional strength training. For example, lunge curls, which combine dynamic lunges with free weights biceps curls, stretch the hip, thigh, and calf muscles; stabilize the core muscles in the trunk; and build strength in the arm muscles. Many activities build functional flexibility and strength at the same time, including yoga, Pilates, taijiquan, Olympic weight lifting, plyometrics, stability training (including Swiss and Bosu ball exercises), medicine ball exercises, and functional training machines (for example, Life Fitness and Cybex).

PROPRIOCEPTIVE NEUROMUSCULAR FACILITATION (PNF) PNF techniques use reflexes initiated by both muscle and joint nerves to cause greater training effects. The most popular PNF stretching technique is the contract-relax stretching method, in which a muscle is contracted before it is stretched. The contraction activates proprioceptors, causing relaxation in the muscle about to be stretched. For example, in a seated stretch of calf muscles, the first step in PNF is to contract the calf muscles. The individual or a partner can provide resistance for an isometric contraction. Following a brief period of relaxation, the next step is to stretch the calf muscles by pulling the tops of the feet toward the body. A duration of 6 seconds for the contraction and 15–30 seconds for the stretch is recommended. PNF appears to be most effective if the individual pushes hard during the isometric contraction.

Another example of a PNF stretch is the contract-relax-contract pattern. In this technique, begin by contracting the muscle to be stretched and then relaxing it. Next, contract the opposing muscle (the antagonist). Finally, stretch the first muscle. For example, using this technique to stretch the hamstrings (the muscles in the back of the thigh) would require the following steps: Contract the hamstrings;

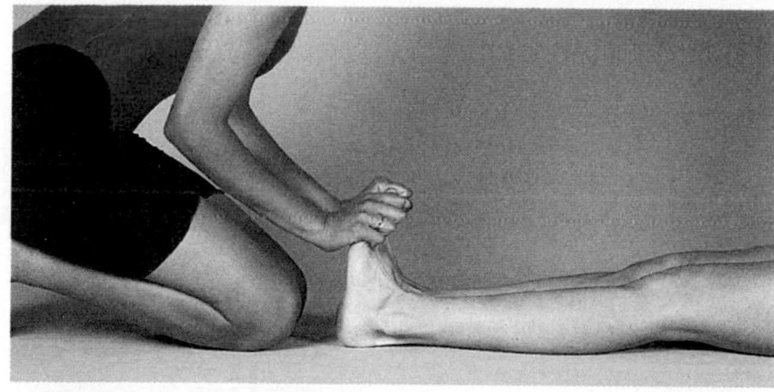

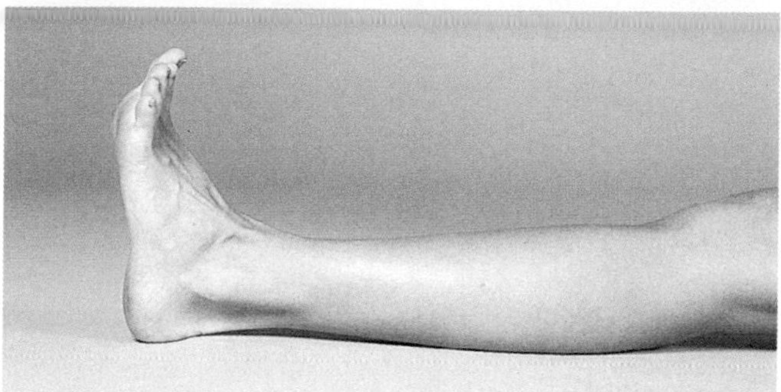

In passive stretching (top), an outside force—such as pressure exerted by another person—helps move the joint and stretch the muscles. In active stretching (bottom), the force to move the joint and stretch the muscles is provided by a contraction of the opposing muscles.

relax the hamstrings; contract the quadriceps (the muscles in the front of the thigh); stretch the hamstrings.

PNF appears to allow more effective stretching and greater increases in flexibility than static stretching, but it tends to cause more muscle stiffness and soreness. It also usually requires a partner and takes more time.

PASSIVE VERSUS ACTIVE STRETCHING Stretches can be done either passively or actively. In **passive stretching,** an outside force or resistance provided by yourself, a partner, gravity, or a weight helps your joints move through their range of motion. For example, a seated stretch of the hamstring and back muscles can be done by reaching the hands toward the feet until a pull is felt in those muscles. You can achieve a greater range of motion (a more intense stretch) using passive stretching. However, because the stretch is not controlled by the muscles themselves, there is a greater risk of injury. Communication between partners in passive stretching is important to ensure that joints aren't forced outside their normal functional range of motion.

In **active stretching,** a muscle is stretched by a contraction of the opposing muscle (the muscle on the opposite side of the limb). For example, an active seated stretch of the calf muscles occurs when a person actively contracts the muscles on the top of the shin. The contraction of this opposing muscle produces a reflex that relaxes the muscles to be stretched. The muscle can be stretched farther with a low risk of injury.

The only disadvantage of active stretching is that a person may not be able to produce enough stress (enough stretch) to increase flexibility using only the contraction of opposing muscle groups. The safest and most convenient technique is active static stretching, with an occasional passive assist. For example, you might stretch your calves both by contracting the muscles on the top of your shin and by pulling your feet toward you. This way you combine the advantages of active stretching—safety and the relaxation reflex—with those of passive stretching—greater range of motion. People who are just beginning flexibility training may be better off doing active rather than passive stretches. For PNF techniques, it is particularly important to have a knowledgeable partner.

Making Progress

As with any type of training, you will make progress and improve your flexibility if you stick with your program. Judge your progress by noting your body position while stretching. For example, note how far you can lean forward during a modified hurdler stretch. Repeat the assessment tests that appear in Lab 5.1 periodically; be sure to take the test at the same time of day each time. You will likely notice some improvement after only 2–3 weeks of a stretching program; however, attaining significant improvements will take at least 2 months. By then, you can expect flexibility increases of about 10–20% in many joints.

QUESTIONS FOR CRITICAL THINKING AND REFLECTION

Why do you think improper stretching can do more harm than good? How can stretching cause injury? Of all the types of stretching described, which ones do you think would be safest for you? Which ones appeal to you the most?

static stretching A technique in which a muscle is slowly and gently stretched and then held in the stretched position.

ballistic stretching A technique in which muscles are stretched by the force generated as a body part is repeatedly bounced, swung, or jerked.

dynamic stretching A technique in which muscles are stretched by moving joints slowly and fluidly through their range of motion in a controlled manner; also called *functional stretching.*

passive stretching A technique in which muscles are stretched by force applied by an outside source.

active stretching A technique in which muscles are stretched by the contraction of the opposing muscles.

TAKE CHARGE

Stretches to Avoid

The safe alternatives listed under each stretch are described and illustrated on pp. 143–146 as part of the complete program of safe flexibility exercises presented in this chapter.

Standing Toe Touch

Problem: Puts excessive strain on the spine.

Alternatives: Modified hurdler stretch (Exercise 10), alternate leg stretcher (Exercise 11), and lower-leg stretch (Exercise 12).

Standing Ankle-to-Buttocks Quadriceps Stretch

Problem: Puts excessive strain on the ligaments of the knee.

Alternative: Step stretch (Exercise 6).

Full Squat with Bent Back

Problem: Puts excessive strain on the ankles, knees, and spine.

Alternatives: Alternate leg stretcher (Exercise 11) and lower-leg stretch (Exercise 12).

Prone Arch

Problem: Puts excessive strain on the spine, knees, and shoulders.

Alternatives: Towel stretch (Exercise 2) and step stretch (Exercise 6).

Standing Hamstring Stretch

Problem: Puts excessive strain on the knee and lower back.

Alternatives: Modified hurdler stretch (Exercise 10) and alternate leg stretcher (Exercise 11).

Yoga Plow

Problem: Puts excessive strain on the neck, shoulders, and back.

Alternatives: Head turns and tilts (Exercise 1), across-the-body and overhead stretches (Exercise 3), and upper-back stretch (Exercise 4).

Hurdler Stretch

Problem: Turning out the bent leg can put excessive strain on the ligaments of the knee.

Alternatives: Modified hurdler stretch (Exercise 10).

Neck Circles

Problem: Puts excessive strain on the neck and cervical disks.

Alternatives: Head turns and tilts (Exercise 1).

Note: Prone leg extensions, in which a person lifts both the chest and the legs while lying on the stomach but without grabbing the ankles, should also be avoided; spine extensions (p. 152) provide a safe alternative.

Exercises to Improve Flexibility: A Sample Program

There are hundreds of exercises that can improve flexibility. Your program should include exercises that work all the major joints of the body by stretching their associated muscle groups (refer back to Figure 5.2). The exercises illustrated here are simple to do and pose a minimum risk of injury. Use these exercises to create a well-rounded program for developing flexibility. Be sure to perform each stretch using the proper technique. Hold each position for 15–30 seconds and perform 2–4 repetitions of each exercise. Avoid exercises that put excessive pressure on your joints (see the box "Stretches to Avoid"). Complete Lab 5.2 when you're ready to start your program.

Exercise 1 — Head Turns and Tilts

Instructions:

Head turns Turn your head to the right and hold the stretch. Repeat to the left.

Head tilts Tilt your head to the right and hold the stretch. Repeat to the left.

Areas stretched: Neck

Variation: Place your right palm on your right cheek; try to turn your head to the right as you resist with your hand. Repeat on the left side.

Exercise 2 — Towel Stretch

Instructions: Roll up a towel and grasp it with both hands, palms down. With your arms straight, slowly lift the towel back over your head as far as possible. The closer together your hands are, the greater the stretch.

Areas stretched: Triceps, shoulders, chest

Variation: Repeat the stretch with your arms down and the towel behind your back. Grasp the towel with your palms forward and thumbs pointing out. Gently raise your arms behind your back.

Exercise 3 — Across-the-Body and Overhead Stretches

Instructions: (a) Keeping your back straight, cross your right arm in front of your body and grasp it with your left hand. Stretch your arm, shoulders, and back by gently pulling your arm as close to your body as possible. Hold. **(b)** Bend your right arm over your head, placing your right elbow as close to your right ear as possible. Grasp your right elbow with your left hand over your head. Stretch the back of your arm by gently pulling your right elbow back and toward your head. Hold. Repeat both stretches on your left side.

Areas stretched: Shoulders, upper back, back of the arm (triceps)

a

b

Exercise 4 Upper-Back Stretch

Instructions: Stand with your feet shoulder-width apart, knees slightly bent, and pelvis tucked under. Clasp your hands in front of your body and press your palms forward.

Areas stretched: Upper back

Variation: In the same position, wrap your arms around your body as if you were giving yourself a hug.

Exercise 5 Lateral Stretch

Instructions: Stand with your feet shoulder-width apart, knees slightly bent, and pelvis tucked under. Raise one arm over your head and bend sideways from the waist. Support your trunk by placing the hand or forearm of your other arm on your thigh or hip for support. Be sure you bend directly sideways and don't move your body below the waist. Repeat on the other side.

Areas stretched: Trunk muscles

Variation: Perform the same exercise in a seated position.

Exercise 6 Step Stretch

Instructions: Step forward and flex your forward knee, keeping your knee directly above your ankle. Stretch your other leg back so that it is parallel to the floor. Press your hips forward and down to stretch. Your arms can be at your sides, on top of your knee, or on the ground for balance. Repeat on the other side.

Areas stretched: Hip, front of thigh (quadriceps)

Exercise 7 Side Lunge

Instructions: Stand in a wide straddle with your legs turned out from your hip joints and your hands on your thighs. Lunge to one side by bending one knee and keeping the other leg straight. Keep your knee directly over your ankle; do not bend it more than 90 degrees. Repeat on the other side.

Areas stretched: Inner thigh, hip, calf

Variation: In the same position, lift the heel of the bent knee to provide additional stretch. The exercise may also be performed with your hands on the floor for balance.

Exercise 8 — Inner Thigh Stretch

Instructions: Sit with the soles of your feet together. Push your knees toward the floor using your hands or forearms.

Areas stretched: Inner thigh, hip

Variation: When you first begin to push your knees toward the floor, use your legs to resist the movement. Then relax and press your knees down as far as they will go.

Exercise 9 — Hip and Trunk Stretch

Instructions: Sit with your left leg straight, right leg bent and crossed over the left knee, and right hand on the floor next to your right hip. Turn your trunk as far as possible to the right by pushing against your right leg with your left forearm or elbow. Keep your right foot on the floor. Repeat on the other side.

Areas stretched: Trunk, outer thigh and hip, buttocks, lower back

Exercise 10 — Modified Hurdler Stretch (Seated Single-Leg Hamstring)

Instructions: Sit with your left leg straight and your right leg tucked close to your body. Reach toward your left ankle as far as possible. Repeat for the other leg.

Areas stretched: Back of the thigh (hamstring), lower back

Variation: As you stretch forward, alternately flex and point the foot of your extended leg.

Exercise 11 — Alternate Leg Stretcher

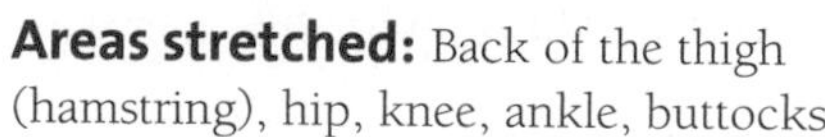

Instructions: Lie flat on your back with both legs straight. **(a)** Grasp your left leg behind the thigh, and pull in to your chest. **(b)** Hold this position, and then extend your left leg toward the ceiling. **(c)** Hold this position, and then bring your left knee back to your chest and pull your toes toward your shin with your left hand. Stretch the back of the leg by attempting to straighten your knee. Repeat for the other leg.

Areas stretched: Back of the thigh (hamstring), hip, knee, ankle, buttocks

Variation: Perform the stretch on both legs at the same time.

a

b

c

Exercise 12 Lower-Leg Stretch

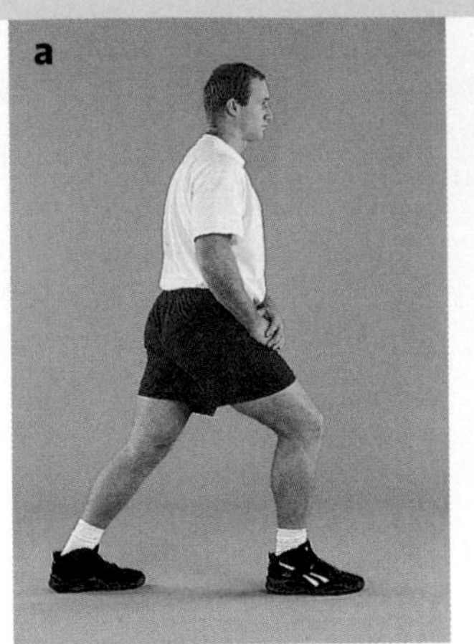

Instructions: Stand with one foot about 1–2 feet in front of the other, with both feet pointing forward. **(a)** Keeping your back leg straight, lunge forward by bending your front knee and pushing your rear heel backward. Hold. **(b)** Then pull your back foot in slightly, and bend your back knee. Shift your weight to your back leg. Hold. Repeat on the other side.

Areas stretched: Back of the lower leg (calf, soleus, Achilles tendon)

Variation: Place your hands on a wall and extend one foot back, pressing your heel down to stretch; or stand with the balls of your feet on a step or bench, and allow your heels to drop below the level of your toes.

PREVENTING AND MANAGING LOW-BACK PAIN

More than 85% of Americans experience back pain at some time in their lives. Low-back pain is the second most common ailment in the United States—headache tops the list—and the second most common reason for absences from work and visits to a physician. Low-back pain is estimated to cost as much as $50 billion a year in lost productivity, medical and legal fees, and disability insurance and compensation.

Back pain can result from sudden traumatic injuries, but it is more often the long-term result of weak and inflexible muscles, poor posture, or poor body mechanics during activities like lifting and carrying. Any abnormal strain on the back can result in pain. Most cases of low-back pain clear up within a few weeks or months, but some people have recurrences or suffer from chronic pain.

Function and Structure of the Spine

The spinal column performs many important functions in the body.

- It provides structural support for the body, especially the thorax (upper-body cavity).
- It surrounds and protects the spinal cord.
- It supports much of the body's weight and transmits it to the lower body.
- It serves as an attachment site for a large number of muscles, tendons, and ligaments.
- It allows movement of the neck and back in all directions.

The spinal column is made up of bones called **vertebrae** (Figure 5.3). The spine consists of 7 cervical vertebrae in the neck, 12 thoracic vertebrae in the upper back, and 5 lumbar vertebrae in the lower back. The 9 vertebrae at the base of the spine are fused into two sections and form the sacrum and the coccyx (tailbone). The spine has four curves: the cervical, thoracic, lumbar, and sacral curves. These curves help bring the body weight supported by the spine in line with the axis of the body.

Although the structure of vertebrae depends on their location on the spine, the different types of vertebrae share

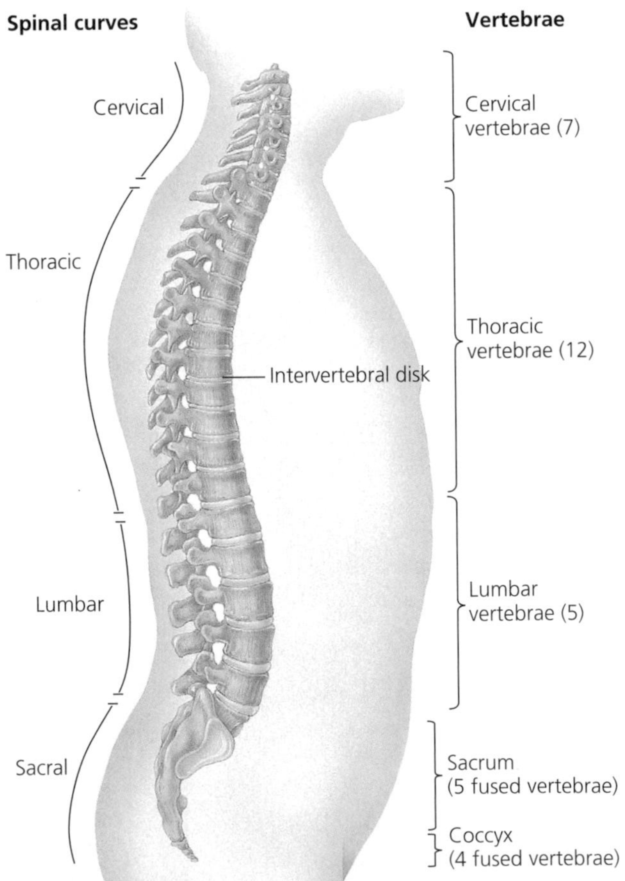

FIGURE 5.3 The spinal column. The spine is made up of five separate regions and has four distinct curves. An intervertebral disk is located between vertebrae.

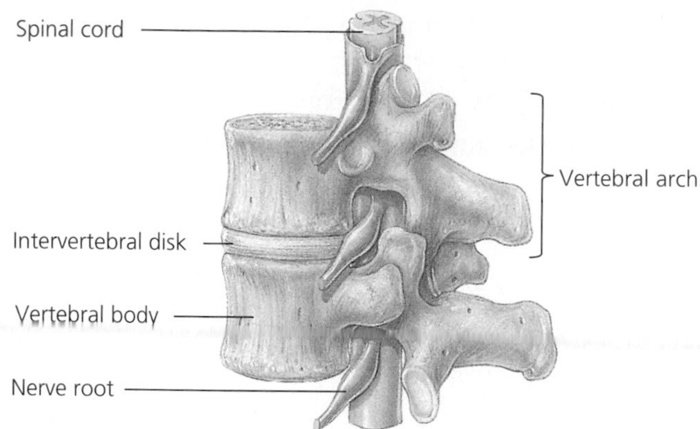

FIGURE 5.4 Vertebrae and an intervertebral disk.

common characteristics. Each consists of a body, an arch, and several bony processes (Figure 5.4). The vertebral body is cylindrical, with flattened surfaces where **intervertebral disks** are attached. The vertebral body is designed to carry the stress of body weight and physical activity. The vertebral arch surrounds and protects the spinal cord. The bony processes serve as joints for adjacent vertebrae and attachment sites for muscles and ligaments. **Nerve roots** from the spinal cord pass through notches in the vertebral arch.

Intervertebral disks, which absorb and disperse the stresses placed on the spine, separate vertebrae from each other. Disks are made up of a gel- and water-filled nucleus surrounded by a series of fibrous rings. The liquid nucleus can change shape when it is compressed, allowing the disk to absorb shock. The intervertebral disks also help maintain the spaces between vertebrae where the spinal nerve roots are located.

Core Muscle Fitness

The core muscles include those in the abdomen, pelvic floor, sides of the trunk, back, buttocks, hip, and pelvis. There are 29 of these muscles, attaching to the ribs, hips, spinal column, and other bones in the trunk of the body. As described in Chapter 4, the core muscles stabilize the spine and help transfer force between the upper body and lower body. They stabilize the midsection when you sit, stand, reach, walk, jump, twist, squat, throw, or bend. The muscles on the front, back, and sides of your trunk support your spine when you sit in a chair and fix your midsection as you use your legs to stand up. When hitting a forehand in tennis or batting a softball, most of the force is transferred from the legs and hips, across the core muscles, to the arms. Strong core muscles make movements more forceful and help prevent back pain.

During any dynamic movement, the core muscles work together; some shorten to cause movement, while others contract and hold to provide stability, lengthen to brake the movement, or send signals to the brain about the movements and positions of the muscles and bones (proprioception). When specific core muscles are weak or tired, the nervous system steps in and uses other muscles. This substitution causes abnormal stresses on the joints, decreases power, and increases the risk of injury. For example, weakness in the transverse abdominis—a muscle deep in the abdomen—creates an unstable spine and can stress muscles and joints in both the upper and lower body.

The best exercises for low-back health are whole-body exercises that force the core muscles to stabilize the spine in many different directions. The low-back exercises presented later in this chapter include several exercises that focus on the core muscles, including the step stretch (lunge), side bridges, and spine extensions. These exercises are generally safe for beginning exercisers and, with physician approval, people with some back pain. More challenging core exercises utilize stability balls or free weights. Stability ball exercises require the core muscles to stabilize the ball (and the body) while performing nearly any type of exercise. Many traditional exercises with free weights can strengthen the core muscles if you do them in a standing position. Weight machines train muscles in isolation, while exercises with free weights done while standing help train the body for real-world movements—an essential principle of core training.

Causes of Back Pain

Back pain can occur at any point along your spine; the lumbar area, because it bears the majority of your weight, is the most common site. Any movement that causes excessive stress on the spinal column can cause injury and pain. The spine is well equipped to bear body weight and the force or stress of body movements along its long axis. However, it is less capable of bearing loads at an angle to its long axis or when the trunk is flexed (bent). You do not have to carry a heavy load or participate in a vigorous contact sport to injure your back. Picking a pencil up from the floor using poor body mechanics—reaching too far out in front of you or bending over with your knees straight, for example—can also result in back pain.

Risk factors associated with low-back pain include age greater than 34 years, degenerative diseases such as arthritis or osteoporosis, a family or personal history of back pain or trauma, a sedentary lifestyle, low job satisfaction, and low socioeconomic status. Smoking increases risk because smoking appears to hasten degenerative changes in the spine. Excess body weight also increases strain on the back, and psychological stress or depression can cause

vertebrae Bony segments composing the spinal column that provide structural support for the body and protect the spinal cord.

intervertebral disk An elastic disk located between adjoining vertebrae, consisting of a gel- and water-filled nucleus surrounded by fibrous rings; serves as a shock absorber for the spinal column.

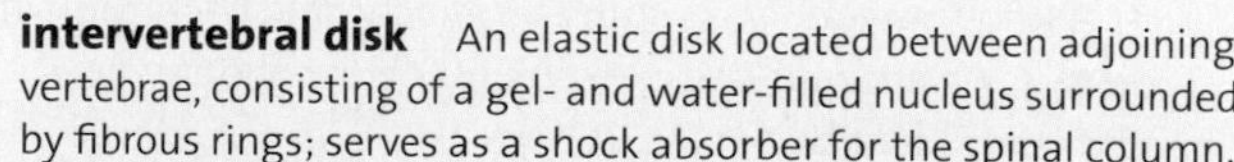

nerve root The base of each of the 31 pairs of spinal nerves that branch off the spinal cord through spaces between vertebrae.

muscle tension and back pain. Occupations and activities associated with low-back pain are those involving physically hard work, such as frequent lifting, twisting, bending, standing up, or straining in forced positions; those requiring high concentration demands (such as computer programming); and those involving vibrations affecting the entire body (such as truck driving).

Underlying causes of back pain include poor muscle endurance and strength in the core muscles; excess body weight; poor posture or body position when standing, sitting, or sleeping; and poor body mechanics when performing actions like lifting and carrying, or sports movements. Strained muscles, tendons, or ligaments can cause pain and can, over time, lead to injuries to vertebrae, intervertebral disks and surrounding muscles and ligaments.

Stress can cause disks to break down and lose some of their ability to absorb shock. A damaged disk may bulge out between vertebrae and put pressure on a nerve root, a condition commonly referred to as a *slipped disk.* Painful pressure on nerves can also occur if damage to a disk narrows the space between two vertebrae. With age, you lose fluid from the disks, making them more likely to bulge and put pressure on nerve roots. Depending on the amount of pressure on a nerve, symptoms may include numbness in the back, hip, leg, or foot; radiating pain; loss of muscle function; depressed reflexes; and muscle spasm. If the pressure is severe enough, loss of function can be permanent.

Preventing Low-Back Pain

Incorrect posture when standing, sitting, lying, and lifting is responsible for many back injuries. Strategies for maintaining good posture are presented in the box "Good Posture and Low-Back Health." Follow the same guidelines when you engage in sports or recreational activities. Maintain control over your movements, and warm up thoroughly before you exercise. Take special care when lifting weights.

The role of exercise in preventing and treating back pain is still being investigated. However, many experts recommend exercise, especially for people who have already experienced an episode of low-back pain. Regular exercise aimed at increasing muscle endurance and strength in the back and abdomen is often recommended to prevent back pain, as is lifestyle physical activity such as walking. Movement helps lubricate your spinal joints and increases muscle fitness in your trunk and legs. Other lifestyle recommendations for preventing back pain include the following:

- Lose weight, stop smoking, and reduce stress.
- Avoid sitting, standing, or working in the same position for too long. Stand up every hour or half-hour and move around. The cat stretch (p. 151) is a good exercise to perform when you take a break during a long period of sitting.
- Use a supportive seat and a medium-firm mattress. Use lumbar support when driving, particularly for long distances, to prevent muscle fatigue and pain.
- Warm up thoroughly before exercising.
- Progress gradually when attempting to improve strength or fitness.

QUESTIONS FOR CRITICAL THINKING AND REFLECTION

Do you know anyone who suffers from chronic back pain? If so, how has it affected that person's life? How about you—have you ever had back pain? Do you have any of the risk factors listed in the text? If so, what can you do to lower your risk and avoid developing chronic back problems?

Managing Acute Back Pain

Sudden back pain usually involves tissue injury. Symptoms may include pain, muscle spasms, stiffness, and inflammation. Many cases of acute back pain go away by themselves within a few days or weeks. You may be able to reduce pain and inflammation by applying cold and then heat (see Chapter 3). Begin with a cold treatment: Apply ice several times a day; once inflammation and spasms subside, you can apply heat using a heating pad or a warm bath. If the pain is bothersome, an over-the-counter, nonsteroidal anti-inflammatory medication such as ibuprofen or naproxen may be helpful; stronger pain medications and muscle relaxants are available by prescription.

Bed rest immediately following the onset of back pain may make you feel better, but it should be of very short duration. Prolonged bed rest—5 days or more—was once thought to be an effective treatment for back pain, but most physicians now advise against it because it may weaken muscles and actually worsen pain. Limit bed rest to one day and begin moderate physical activity as soon as possible. Exercise can increase muscular endurance and flexibility and protect disks from loss of fluid. Three of the back exercises discussed later in the chapter may be particularly helpful following an episode of acute back pain: curl-ups, side bridges, and spine extensions.

See your physician if acute back pain doesn't resolve within a short time. Other warning signals of a more severe problem that requires a professional evaluation include severe pain, numbness, pain that radiates down one or both legs, problems with bladder or bowel control, fever, and rapid weight loss.

Managing Chronic Back Pain

Low-back pain is considered chronic if it persists for more than 3 months. Symptoms vary—some people experience stabbing or shooting pain, and others a steady ache

Good Posture and Low-Back Health

Changes in everyday posture and behavior can help prevent and alleviate low-back pain.

- ***Lying down.*** When resting or sleeping, lie on your side with your knees and hips bent. If you lie on your back place a pillow under your knees. However, do not elevate your knees so much that the curve in your lower spine is flattened. Don't lie on your stomach. Use a medium-firm mattress.

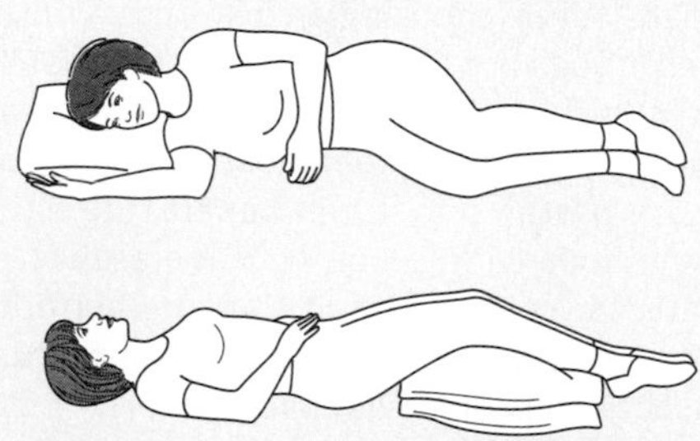

- ***Sitting at a computer.*** Sit in a slightly reclined position of 100–110 degrees, not an upright 90-degree position. Adjust your chair so your knees are slightly lower than your hips. If your back flattens as you sit, try using a lumbar roll to maintain your back's natural curvature. Place your feet flat on the floor or on a footrest. Place the monitor directly in front of you and adjust it so your eyes are level with the top of the screen; you should be looking slightly downward at the middle of the screen. Adjust the keyboard and mouse so your forearms and wrists are in a neutral position, parallel with the floor.

- ***Lifting.*** If you need to lower yourself to grasp an object, bend at the knees and hips rather than at the waist. Your feet should be about shoulder-width apart. Lift gradually, keeping your arms straight, by standing up or by pushing with your leg muscles. Keep the object close to your body. Don't twist; if you have to turn with the object, change the position of your feet.

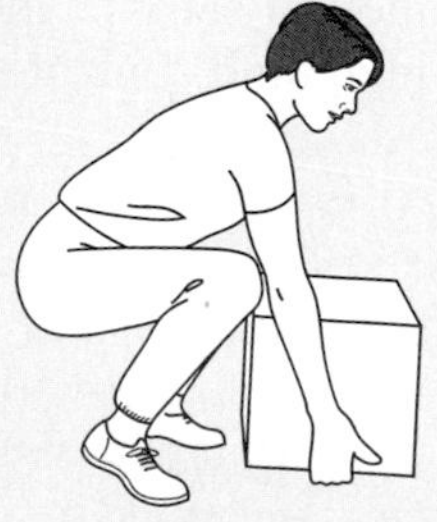

- ***Standing.*** When you are standing, a straight line should run from the top of your ear through the center of your shoulder, the center of your hip, the back of your kneecap, and the front of your ankle bone. Support your weight mainly on your heels, with one or both knees slightly bent. Try to keep your lower back flat by placing one foot on a stool. Don't let your pelvis tip forward or your back arch. Shift your weight back and forth from foot to foot. Avoid prolonged standing. (To check your posture, stand in a normal way with your back to a wall. Your upper back and buttocks should touch the wall; your heels may be a few inches away. Slide one hand into the space between your lower back and the wall. It should slide in easily but should almost touch both your back and the wall. Adjust your posture as needed, and try to hold this position as you walk away from the wall.)

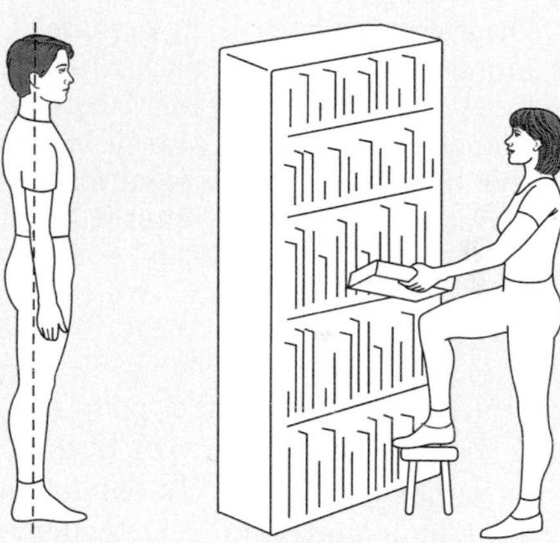

- ***Walking.*** Walk with your toes pointed straight ahead. Keep your back flat, head up and centered over your body, and chin in. Swing your arms freely. Don't wear tight or high-heeled shoes. Walking briskly is better for back health than walking slowly.

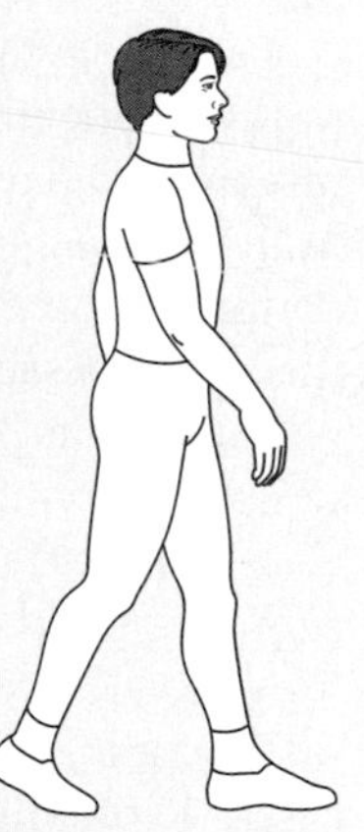

Yoga for Relaxation and Pain Relief

Certain types of exercise can provide relief from back pain, depending on the pain's underlying cause. Effective exercises stretch the muscles and connective tissue in the hips, stabilize the spine, and strengthen and build endurance in the core muscles of the back and abdomen.

Yoga may be an option for many back pain sufferers because it offers a variety of exercises that target the spine and the core muscles. Yoga is an ancient practice involving slow, gentle movements performed with controlled breathing and focused attention. Yoga practitioners slowly move into a specific posture (called an *asana*) and hold the posture for up to 60 seconds. There are hundreds of asanas, many of which are easy to do and provide good stretches.

Yoga also involves simple breathing exercises that gently stretch the muscles of the upper back while helping the practitioner focus. Yoga experts say that breathing exercises not only encourage relaxation but also clear the mind and can help relieve mild to moderate pain. Yoga enthusiasts end their workouts energized and refreshed but calm and relaxed.

Many medical professionals now recommend yoga for patients with back pain, particularly postures that involve arching and gently stretching the back, such as the cat pose (similar to the cat stretch shown on p. 151) and the child pose (shown here). These are basic asanas that most people can perform repeatedly and hold for a relatively long time.

Because asanas must be performed correctly to be beneficial, qualified instruction is recommended. For those with back pain, physicians advise choosing an instructor who is not only accomplished in yoga but also knowledgeable about back pain and its causes. Such instructors can steer students away from exercises that do more harm than good. It is especially important to choose postures that will benefit the back without worsening the underlying problem. Some asanas can aggravate an injured or painful back if they are performed incorrectly or too aggressively. In fact, a few yoga postures should not be done at all by people with back pain.

If you have back pain, see your physician to determine its cause before beginning any type of exercise program. Even gentle exercise or stretching can be bad for an already injured back, especially if the spinal disks or nerves are involved. For some back conditions, rest or therapy may be better options than exercise, at least in the short term.

accompanied by stiffness. Sometimes pain is localized; in other cases, it radiates to another part of the body. Psychological symptoms may also occur. Underlying causes of chronic back pain include injuries, infection, muscle or ligament strains, and disk herniations.

Because symptoms and causes are so varied, different people benefit from different treatment strategies, and researchers have found that many treatments have only limited benefits. Potential treatments include over-the-counter or prescription medications; exercise; physical therapy, massage, yoga, or chiropractic care; acupuncture; percutaneous electrical nerve stimulation (PENS), in which acupuncture-like needles are used to deliver an electrical current; education and advice about posture, exercise, and body mechanics; and surgery (see the box "Yoga for Relaxation and Pain Relief").

Psychological therapy may also be beneficial in some cases. Reducing emotional stress that causes muscle tension can provide direct benefits, and other therapies can help people deal better with chronic pain and its effects on their daily lives. Support groups and expressive writing are strategies that have been found beneficial for people with chronic pain and other conditions.

Exercises for the Prevention and Management of Low-Back Pain

The tests in Labs 5.3 and 5.4 can help you assess low-back muscular endurance and posture. The exercises that follow are designed to help you maintain a healthy back by stretching and strengthening the major muscle groups that affect the back—the abdominal muscles, the muscles along your spine and sides, and the muscles of your hips and thighs. If you have back problems, check with your physician before beginning any exercise program. Perform the exercises slowly and progress very gradually. Stop and consult your physician if any exercise causes back pain. General guidelines for back exercise programs include the following:

- Do low-back exercises at least 3 days per week; many experts recommend that back exercises be done daily.
- Emphasize muscular endurance rather than muscular strength—endurance is more protective.
- Don't do spine exercises involving a full range of motion early in the morning because your disks have a high fluid content early in the day and injuries may occur as a result.
- Engage in regular endurance exercise such as cycling or walking in addition to performing exercises that specifically build muscular endurance and flexibility. Brisk walking with a vigorous arm swing may help relieve back pain. Start with fast walking if your core muscles are weak or you have back pain. After you get in shape, integrate other endurance activities that you enjoy—jogging, cycling, treadmill, elliptical trainer, or stair-climber.
- Be patient and stick with your program. Increased back fitness and pain relief may require as long as 3 months of regular exercise.

LOW-BACK EXERCISES

Exercise 1 Cat Stretch

Instructions: Begin on all fours with your knees below your hips and your hands below your shoulders. Slowly and deliberately move through a cycle of extension and flexion of your spine. **(a)** Begin by slowly pushing your back up and dropping your head slightly until your spine is extended (rounded). **(b)** Then slowly lower your back and lift your chin slightly until your spine is flexed (relaxed and slightly arched). *Do not press at the ends of the range of motion.* Stop if you feel pain. Do 10 slow, continuous cycles of the movement.

Target: Improved flexibility, relaxation, and reduced stiffness in the spine

a

b

Exercise 2 Step Stretch *(See Exercise 6 in the flexibility program, p. 144.)*

Instructions: Hold each stretch for 15–30 seconds and do 2–4 repetitions on each side.

Target: Improved flexibility, strength, and endurance in the muscles of the hip and the front of the thigh

Exercise 3 Alternate Leg Stretcher *(See Exercise 11 in the flexibility program, p. 145.)*

Instructions: Hold each stretch for 15–30 seconds and do 2–4 repetitions on each side.

Target: Improved flexibility in the back of the thigh, hip, knee, and buttocks

Exercise 4 Trunk Twist

Instructions: Lie on your side with top knee bent, lower leg straight, lower arm extended out in front of you on the floor, and upper arm at your side. Push down with your upper knee while you twist your trunk backward. Try to get your shoulders and upper body flat on the floor, turning your head as well. Return to the starting position, and then repeat on the other side. Hold the stretch for 15–30 seconds and do 2–4 repetitions on each side.

Target: Improved flexibility in the lower back and sides

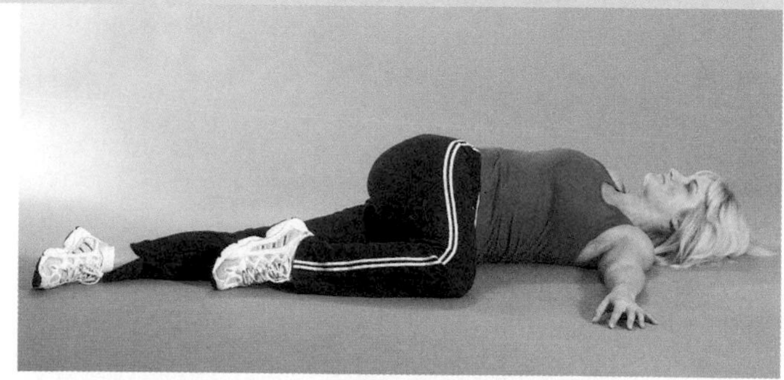

Exercise 5 Curl-Up

Instructions: Lie on your back with one or both knees bent and arms crossed on your chest or hands under your lower back. Maintain a neutral spine. Tuck your chin in and slowly curl up, one vertebra at a time, as you use your abdominal muscles to lift your head first and then your shoulders. Stop when you can see your knees and hold for 5–10 seconds before returning to the starting position. Do 10 or more repetitions.

Target: Improved strength and endurance in the abdomen

Variation: Add a twist to develop other abdominal muscles. When you have curled up so that your shoulder blades are off the floor, twist your upper body so that one shoulder is higher than the other; reach past your knee with your upper arm. Hold and then return to the starting position. Repeat on the opposite side. Curl-ups can also be done using an exercise ball (see p. 99).

Exercise 6 Isometric Side Bridge

(See Exercise 11 in the free weights program in Chapter 4, p. 114.)

Instructions: Hold the bridge position for 10 seconds, breathing normally. Work up to a 60-second hold. Perform one or more repetitions on each side.

Target: Increased strength and endurance in the muscles along the sides of the abdomen

Variation: You can make the exercise more difficult by keeping your legs straight and supporting yourself with your feet and forearm (see Lab 5.3) or with your feet and hand (with elbow straight).

Exercise 7 Spine Extensions

(See Exercise 10 in the free weights program in Chapter 4, p. 113.)

Instructions: Hold each position for 10–30 seconds. Begin with one repetition on each side, and work up to several repetitions.

Target: Increased strength and endurance in the back, buttocks, and back of the thighs

Variation: If you have experienced back pain in the past or if this exercise is difficult for you, do the exercise with both hands on the ground rather than with one arm lifted. You can make this exercise more difficult by doing it balancing on an exercise ball. Find a balance point on your chest while lying face down on the ball with one arm and the opposite leg on the ground. Tense your abdominal muscles while reaching and extending with one arm and reaching and extending with the opposite leg. Repeat this exercise using the other arm and leg.

Exercise 8 Wall Squat (Phantom Chair)

Instructions: Lean against a wall and bend your knees as though you are sitting in a chair. Support your weight with your legs. Begin by holding the position for 5–10 seconds. Squeeze your gluteal muscles together as you do the exercise. Build up to 1 minute or more. Perform one or more repetitions.

Target: Increased strength and endurance in the lower back, thighs, and abdomen

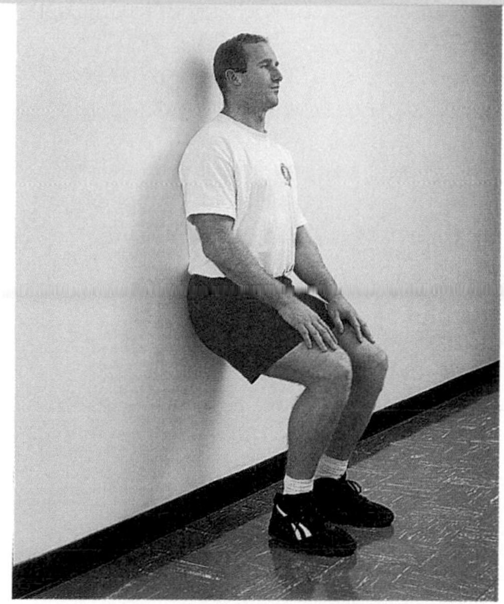

Exercise 9 Pelvic Tilt

Instructions: Lie on your back with knees bent and arms extended to the side. Tilt your pelvis under and try to flatten your lower back against the floor. Tighten your buttock and abdominal muscles while you hold this position for 5–10 seconds. Don't hold your breath. Work up to 10 repetitions of the exercise. Pelvic tilts can also be done standing or leaning against a wall. *Note:* Although this is a popular exercise with many therapists, some experts question the safety of pelvic tilts. Stop if you feel pain in your back at any time during the exercise.

Target: Increased strength and endurance in the abdomen and buttocks

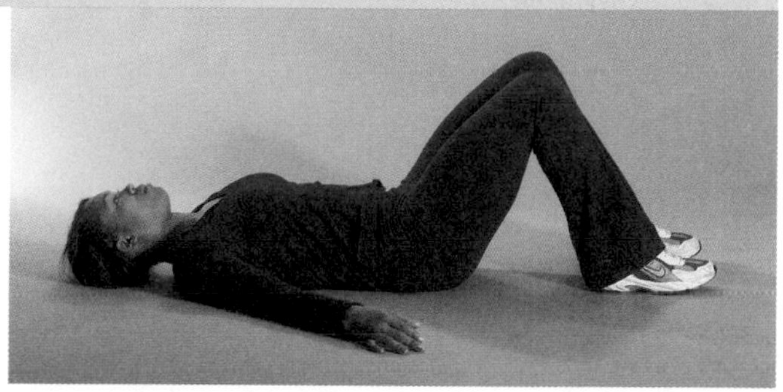

Exercise 10 Back Bridge

Instructions: Lie on your back with knees bent and arms extended to the side. Tuck your pelvis under, contract your gluteal muscles, and then lift your tailbone, buttocks, and lower back from the floor. Hold this position for 5–10 seconds with your weight resting on your feet, arms, and shoulders, and then return to the starting position. Work up to 10 repetitions of the exercise.

Target: Increased strength and endurance in the hips and buttocks

COMMON QUESTIONS ANSWERED

Q Is stretching the same as warming up?

A No. They are two distinct activities. A warm-up is light exercise that involves moving the joints through the same motions used during the activity; it increases body temperature so your metabolism works better when you're exercising at high intensity. Stretching increases the movement capability of your joints, so you can move more easily with less risk of injury. It is best to stretch at the end of your aerobic or weight training workout, when your muscles are warm. Warmed muscles stretch better than cold ones and are less prone to injury.

Q How much flexibility do I need?

A This question is not always easy to answer. If you're involved in a sport such as gymnastics, figure skating, or ballet, you are often required to reach extreme joint motions to achieve success. However, nonathletes do not need to reach these extreme joint positions. In fact, too much flexibility may, in some cases, create joint instability and increase your risk of injury. As with other types of fitness, moderation is the key. You should regularly stretch your major joints and muscle groups but not aspire to reach extreme flexibility.

Q Can I stretch too far?

A Yes. As muscle tissue is progressively stretched, it reaches a point where it becomes damaged and may rupture. The greatest danger occurs during passive stretching when a partner is doing the stretching for you. It is critical that your stretching partner not force your joint outside its normal functional range of motion.

Q Can physical training limit flexibility?

A Weight training, jogging, or any physical activity will decrease flexibility if the exercises are not performed through a full range of motion. When done properly, weight training increases flexibility. However, because of the limited range of motion used during the running stride, jogging tends to compromise flexibility. It is important for runners to do flexibility exercises for the hamstrings and quadriceps regularly.

Q Does stretching affect muscular strength?

A Several recent studies have found that stretching decreases strength, power, and motor control following the stretch. This is one reason some experts suggest that people not stretch as part of their exercise warm-up. It is important to warm up before any workout by engaging in 5–10 minutes of light exercise such as walking or slow jogging. Flexibility training increases muscle strength over time.

For more Common Questions Answered about flexibility and low-back health, visit the Online Learning Center.

* TIPS FOR TODAY AND THE FUTURE

To improve and maintain your flexibility, perform stretches that work the major joints at least twice a week.

RIGHT NOW YOU CAN

- Stand up and stretch—do either the upper-back stretch or the across-the-body stretch shown in the chapter.
- Practice the recommended sitting and standing postures suggested in the chapter. If needed, adjust your chair or find something to use as a footrest.

IN THE FUTURE YOU CAN

- Build up your flexibility by incorporating more sophisticated stretching exercises into your routine.
- Increase the frequency of your flexibility workouts to 5 or more days per week.
- Increase the efficiency of your workouts by adding stretching exercises to the cool-down period of your endurance or strength workouts.

SUMMARY

- Flexibility, the ability of joints to move through their full range of motion, is highly adaptable and specific to each joint.
- Range of motion can be limited by joint structure, muscle inelasticity, and proprioceptor activity.
- Developing flexibility depends on stretching the elastic tissues within muscles regularly and gently until they lengthen. Overstretching can make connective tissue brittle and lead to rupture.
- Signals sent between muscle and tendon nerves and the spinal cord can enhance flexibility.
- The benefits of flexibility include preventing abnormal stresses that lead to joint deterioration and possibly reducing the risk of injuries and low-back pain.
- Stretches should be held for 15–30 seconds; perform 2–4 repetitions. Flexibility training should be done a minimum of

2–3 days per week (ideally, 5–7 days per week), preferably following activity, when muscles are warm.

- Static stretching is done slowly and held to the point of mild tension; ballistic stretching consists of bouncing stretches and can lead to injury. Dynamic stretching involves moving joints slowly and fluidly through their range of motion. Proprioceptive neuromuscular facilitation uses muscle receptors in contracting and relaxing a muscle.

- Passive stretching, using an outside force in moving muscles and joints, achieves a greater range of motion (and has a higher injury risk) than active stretching, which uses opposing muscles to initiate a stretch.

- The spinal column consists of vertebrae separated by intervertebral disks. It provides structure and support for the body and protects the spinal cord. The core muscles stabilize the spine and transfer force between the upper and lower body.

- Acute back pain can be treated as a soft tissue injury, with cold treatment followed by application of heat (once swelling subsides); prolonged bed rest is not recommended. A variety of treatments have been suggested for chronic back pain, including regular exercise, physical therapy, acupuncture, education, and psychological therapy.

- In addition to good posture, proper body mechanics, and regular physical activity, a program for preventing low back pain includes exercises that develop flexibility, strength, and endurance in the muscle groups that affect the lower back.

FOR FURTHER EXPLORATION

BOOKS

Alter, M. J. 2004. *Science of Flexibility*, 3rd ed. Champaign, Ill.: Human Kinetics. *An extremely well-researched book that discusses the scientific basis of stretching exercises and flexibility.*

Anderson, B., and J. Anderson. 2003. *Stretching*, 20th anniv. ed. Bolinas, Calif.: Shelter Publications. *A best-selling exercise book, updated with more than 200 stretches for 60 sports and activities.*

Blahnik, J. 2004. *Full-Body Flexibility.* Champaign, Ill.: Human Kinetics. *Presents a blend of stretching techniques derived from sports training, martial arts, yoga, and Pilates.*

McGill, S. 2006. *Ultimate Back Fitness and Performance, 3rd ed*. Waterloo, Canada: Backfit Pro. *Written by one of the premier researchers in the world on back biomechanics and back pain; describes mechanisms of back pain and exercises and movement patterns for preventing it.*

Nelson, A. G., et al. 2006. *Stretching Anatomy*. Champaign, Ill.: Human Kinetics. *A guide to stretching that features highly detailed illustrations of the muscles that are affected by each exercise.*

ORGANIZATIONS AND WEB SITES

American Academy of Orthopaedic Surgeons. Provides information about a variety of joint problems.
http://orthoinfo.aaos.org

CUErgo: Cornell University Ergonomics Web Site. Provides information about how to arrange a computer workstation to prevent back pain and repetitive strain injuries, as well as other topics related to ergonomics.
http://ergo.human.cornell.edu

Exercise: A Guide from the National Institute on Aging. Gives practical advice on fitness for seniors; includes animated instructions for specific flexibility exercises.
http://weboflife.ksc.nasa.gov/exerciseandaging/toc.html

Georgia State University: Flexibility. Provides information about the benefits of stretching and ways to develop a safe and effective program; includes illustrations of stretches.
http://www.gsu.edu/~wwwfit/flexibility.html

MedlinePlus Interactive Tutorial: How to Prevent Back Pain. An interactive, illustrated tutorial of the causes and prevention of back pain.
http://www.nlm.nih.gov/medlineplus/tutorials/howtopreventbackpain/htm/index.htm

NIH Back Pain Fact Sheet. Provides basic information on the prevention and treatment of back pain.
http://www.ninds.nih.gov/disorders/backpain/backpain.htm

Southern California Orthopedic Institute. Provides information on a variety of orthopedic problems, including back injuries; also has illustrations of spinal anatomy.
http://www.scoi.com

Stretching and Flexibility. Provides information on the physiology of stretching and different types of stretching exercises.
http://www.ifafitness.com/stretch/index.html

See also the listings for Chapters 2 and 4.

SELECTED BIBLIOGRAPHY

American College of Sports Medicine. 2006. *ACSM's Guidelines for Exercise Testing and Prescription*. Philadelphia: Lippincott Williams and Wilkins.

American College of Sports Medicine. 2006. *ACSM's Resource Manual for Guidelines for Exercise Testing and Prescription*, 5th ed. Philadelphia: Lippincott Williams and Wilkins.

Anton, M. M., et al. 2006. Resistance training increases basal limb blood flow and vascular conductance in aging humans. *Journal of Applied Physiology* 101(5): 1351–1355.

Barnett, A. 2006. Using recovery modalities between training sessions in elite athletes: Does it help? *Sports Medicine* 36(9): 781–796.

Barr, K. P., M. Griggs, and T. Cadby. 2005. Lumbar stabilization: Core concepts and current literature. Part 1. *American Journal of Physical Medicine and Rehabilitation* 84(6): 473–480.

Beach, T. A., et al. 2005. Effects of prolonged sitting on the passive flexion stiffness of the in vivo lumbar spine. *Spine Journal* 5(2): 145–154.

Castellani, J. W., et al. 2006. American College of Sports Medicine position stand: Prevention of cold injuries during exercise. *Medicine and Science in Sports and Exercise* 38(11): 2012–2029.

Davis, D. S., et al. 2005. The effectiveness of three stretching techniques on hamstring flexibility using consistent stretching parameters. *Journal of Strength and Conditioning Research* 19(1): 27–32.

Faigenbaum, A. D., et al. 2006. Dynamic warm-up protocols, with and without a weighted vest, and fitness performance in high school female athletes. *Journal of Athletic Training* 41(4): 357–363.

Fong, D. T., et al. 2007. A systematic review on ankle injury and ankle sprain in sports. *Sports Medicine* (Auckland, New Zealand) 37(1): 73–94.

Friedrich, M., et al. 2005. Long-term effect of a combined exercise and motivational program on the level of disability of patients with chronic low back pain. *Spine* 30(9): 995–1000.

Gajdosik, R. L., et al. 2005. Effects of an eight-week stretching program on the passive-elastic properties and function of the calf muscles of older women. *Clinical Biomechanics* 20(9): 973–983.

Guidetti, L., et al. 2007. Effect of warm up on energy cost and energy sources of a ballet dance exercise. *European Journal of Applied Physiology* 99(3): 275–281.

Hakkinen, A., et al. 2005. Effects of home strength training and stretching versus stretching alone after lumbar disk surgery: A randomized study with a 1-year follow-up. *Archives of Physical Medicine and Rehabilitation* 86(5): 865–870.

Hart, L. 2005. Effect of stretching on sport injury risk: A review. *Clinical Journal of Sports Medicine* 15(2): 113.

Haskell, W. L., et al. 2007. Physical activity and public health: updated recommendation for adults from the American College of Sports Medicine and the American Heart Association. *Circulation*. 116(9): 1081–1093.

Hayden, J. A., M. W. van Tulder, and G. Tomlinson. (2005). Systematic review: Strategies for using exercise therapy to improve outcomes in chronic low back pain. *Annals of Internal Medicine* 142(9): 776–785.

Hurwitz, E. L., H. Morgenstern, and C. Chiao. 2005. Effects of recreational physical activity and back exercises on low back pain and psychological distress: Findings from the UCLA Low Back Pain Study. *American Journal of Public Health* 95(10): 1817–1824.

Kuramoto, A. M. 2006. Therapeutic benefits of Tai Chi exercise: Research review. *Wisconsin Medical Journal* 105(7): 42–46.

Liu-Ambrose, T. Y., et al. 2005. Both resistance and agility training reduce back pain and improve health-related quality of life in older women with low bone mass. *Osteoporosis International*, 9 February [Epub ahead of print].

Malina, R. M. 2006. Weight training in youth-growth, maturation, and safety: An evidence-based review. *Clinical Journal of Sport Medicine* 16(6): 478–487.

Manek, N. J., and A. J. MacGregor. 2005. Epidemiology of back disorders: Prevalence, risk factors, and prognosis. *Current Opinion in Rheumatology* 17(2): 134–140.

Mortimer, M., et al. 2006. Low back pain in a general population. Natural course and influence of physical exercise—a 5-year follow-up of the Musculoskeletal Intervention Center–Norrtalje Study. *Spine* 31(26): 3045–3051.

National Institute of Arthritis and Musculoskeletal and Skin Diseases. 2005. *Back Pain*. NIH Publication No. 05-5285.

Nelson, A. G., et al. 2005. Acute effects of passive muscle stretching on sprint performance. *Journal of Sports Science* 23(5): 449–454.

Newton, R. U., et al. 2006. Determination of functional strength imbalance of the lower extremities. *Journal of Strength and Conditioning Research* 20(4): 971–977.

Nieman, D. C. 2007. *Exercise Testing and Prescription: A Health-Related Approach*, 6th ed. New York: McGraw-Hill.

Park, D. Y., and L. Chou. 2006. Stretching for prevention of Achilles tendon injuries: A review of the literature. *Foot and Ankle International* 27(12): 1086–1095.

Reilly, T., et al. 2006. Thermoregulation in elite athletes. *Current Opinion in Clinical Nutrition and Metabolic Care* 9(6): 666–671.

Shrier, I. 2004. Does stretching improve performance? A systematic and critical review of the literature. *Clinical Journal of Sports Medicine* 14(5): 267–273.

Thacker, S. B., et al. 2004. The impact of stretching on sports injury risk: A systematic review of the literature. *Medicine and Science in Sports and Exercise* 36(3): 371–378.

Topolski, T. D., et al. 2006. The Rapid Assessment of Physical Activity (RAPA) among older adults. *Preventing Chronic Disease* 3(4): A118.

Vibe Fersum, K. 2006. Spinal manipulation and exercise was better than ultrasound and exercise for patients with chronic low back pain. *The Australian Journal of Physiotherapy* 52(4): 306.

Woolstenhulme, M. T., et al. 2006. Ballistic stretching increases flexibility and acute vertical jump height when combined with basketball activity. *Journal of Strength and Conditioning Research* 20(4): 799–803.

Name ______ Section ______ Date ______

LAB 5.1 Assessing Your Current Level of Flexibility

Part I Sit-and-Reach Test

Equipment

Use a modified Wells and Dillon flexometer or construct your own measuring device using a firm box or two pieces of wood about 30 centimeters (12 inches) high attached at right angles to each other. Attach a metric ruler to measure the extent of reach. With the low numbers of the ruler toward the person being tested, set the 26-centimeter mark of the ruler at the footline of the box. (Individuals who cannot reach as far as the footline will have scores below 26 centimeters; those who can reach past their feet will have scores above 26 centimeters.) Most studies show no relationship between performance on the sit-and-reach test and the incidence of back pain.

Preparation

Warm up your muscles with a low-intensity activity such as walking or easy jogging. Then perform slow stretching movements.

Instructions

1. Remove your shoes and sit facing the flexibility measuring device with your knees fully extended and your feet flat against the device about 10 centimeters (4 inches) apart.
2. Reach as far forward as you can, with palms down, arms evenly stretched, and knees fully extended; hold the position of maximum reach for about 2 seconds.
3. Perform the stretch 2 times, recording the distance of maximum reach to the nearest 0.5 centimeters: ______ cm

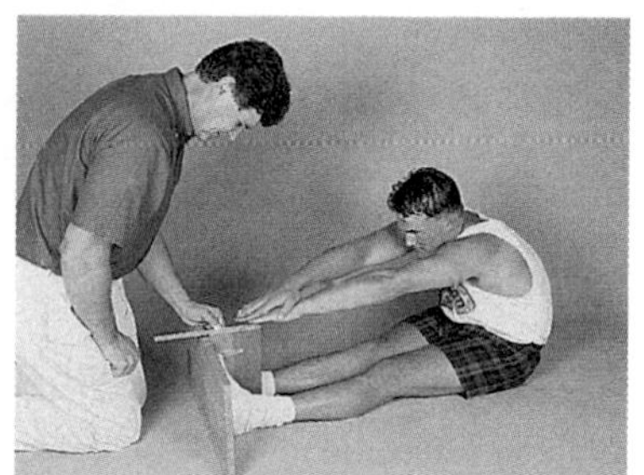

Rating Your Flexibility

Find the score in the table below to determine your flexibility rating. Record it here and on the final page of this lab.

Rating: ______

Ratings for Sit-and-Reach Test

	Rating/Score (cm)*				
Men	*Needs Improvement*	*Fair*	*Good*	*Very Good*	*Excellent*
Age: 15–19	Below 24	24–28	29–33	34–38	Above 38
20–29	Below 25	25–29	30–33	34–39	Above 39
30–39	Below 23	23–27	28–32	33–37	Above 37
40–49	Below 18	18–23	24–28	29–34	Above 34
50–59	Below 16	16–23	24–27	28–34	Above 34
60–69	Below 15	15–19	20–24	25–32	Above 32
Women					
Age: 15–19	Below 29	29–33	34–37	38–42	Above 42
20–29	Below 28	28–32	33–36	37–40	Above 40
30–39	Below 27	27–31	32–35	36–40	Above 40
40–49	Below 25	25–29	30–33	34–37	Above 37
50–59	Below 25	25–29	30–32	33–38	Above 38
60–69	Below 23	23–26	27–30	31–34	Above 34

*Footline is set at 26 cm.

SOURCE: *The Canadian Physical Activity, Fitness & Lifestyle Approach: CSEP-Health & Fitness Program's Health-Related Appraisal and Counselling Strategy,* 3rd edition, 2003. Reprinted with permission from the Canadian Society for Exercise Physiology.

Part II Range-of-Motion Assessment

This portion of the lab can be completed by doing visual comparisons or by measuring joint range of motion with a goniometer or other instrument.

Equipment

1. A partner to do visual comparisons or to measure the range of motion of your joints. (You can also use a mirror to perform your own visual comparisons.)
2. For the measurement method, you need a goniometer, flexometer, or other instrument to measure range of motion.

Preparation

Warm up your muscles with some low-intensity activity such as walking or easy jogging.

Instructions

On the following pages, the average range of motion is illustrated and listed quantitatively for some of the major joints. Visually assess the range of motion in your joints, and compare it to that shown in the illustrations. For each joint, note (with a check mark) whether your range of motion is above average, average, or below average and in need of improvement. Average values for range of motion are given in degrees for each joint in the assessment. You can also complete the assessment by measuring your range of motion with a goniometer, flexometer, or other instrument. If you are using this measurement method, identify your rating (above average, average, or below average) and record your range of motion in degrees next to the appropriate category. Although the measurement method is more time-consuming, it allows you to track the progress of your stretching program more precisely and to note changes within the broader ratings categories (below average, above average).

Record your ratings on the following pages and on the chart on the final page of this lab. (Ratings were derived from several published sources.)

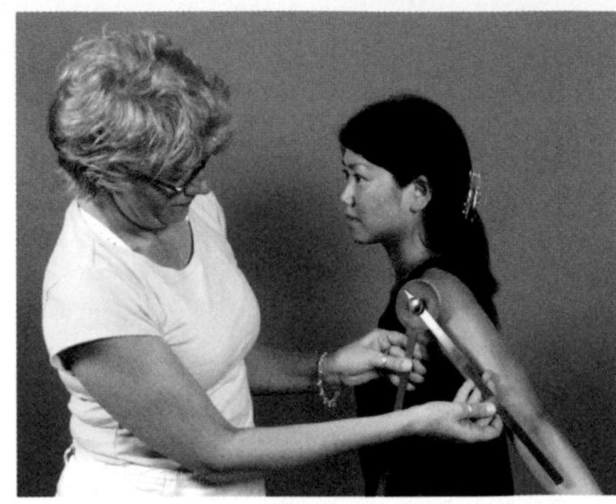

Assessment of range of motion using a goniometer.

1. Shoulder Abduction and Adduction

For each position and arm, check one of the following; fill in degrees if using the measurement method.

Shoulder abduction—raise arm up to the side.

Right	*Left*	
_______	_______	Below average/needs improvement
_______	_______	Average (92–95°)
_______	_______	Above average

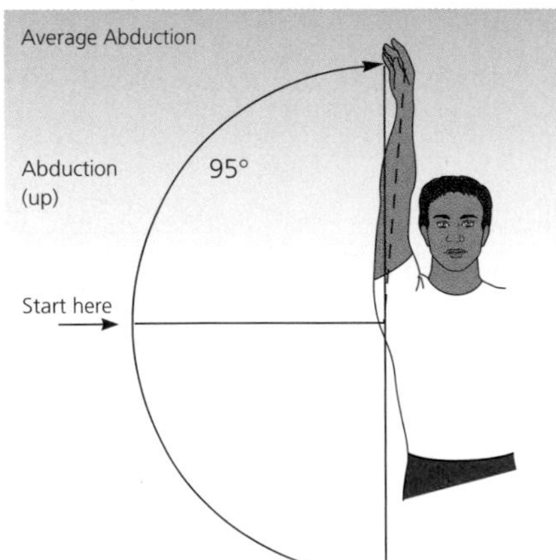

Shoulder adduction—move arm down and in front of body.

Right	*Left*	
_______	_______	Below average/needs improvement
_______	_______	Average (124–127°)
_______	_______	Above average

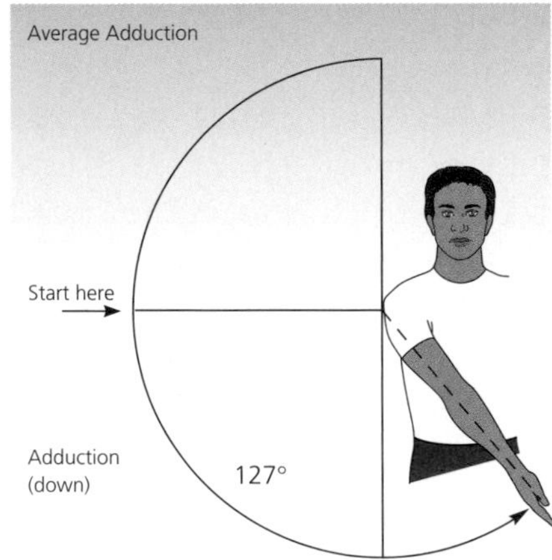

2. Shoulder Flexion and Extension

For each position and arm, check one of the following; fill in degrees if using the measurement method.

Shoulder flexion—raise arm up in front of the body.

Right	*Left*	
______	______	Below average/needs improvement
______	______	Average (92–95°)
______	______	Above average

Shoulder extension—move arm down and behind the body.

Right	*Left*	
______	______	Below average/needs improvement
______	______	Average (145–150°)
______	______	Above average

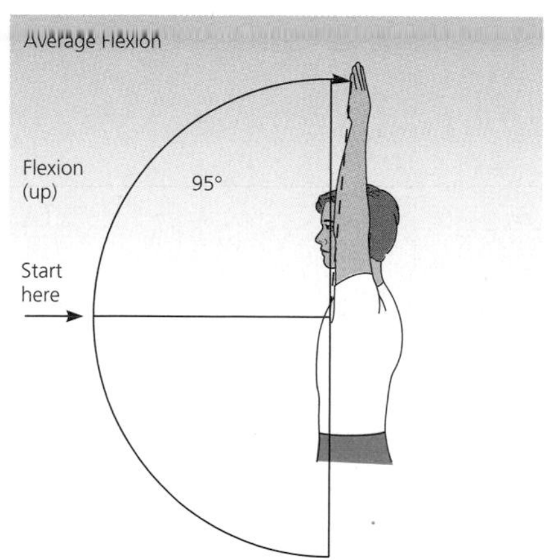

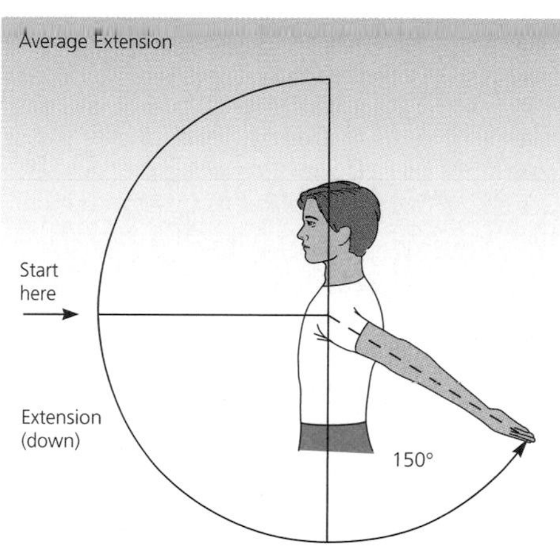

3. Trunk/Low-Back Lateral Flexion

Bend directly sideways at your waist. To prevent injury, keep your knees slightly bent, and support your trunk by placing your hand or forearm on your thigh. Check one of the following for each side; fill in degrees if using the measurement method.

Right	*Left*	
______	______	Below average/needs improvement
______	______	Average (36–40°)
______	______	Above average

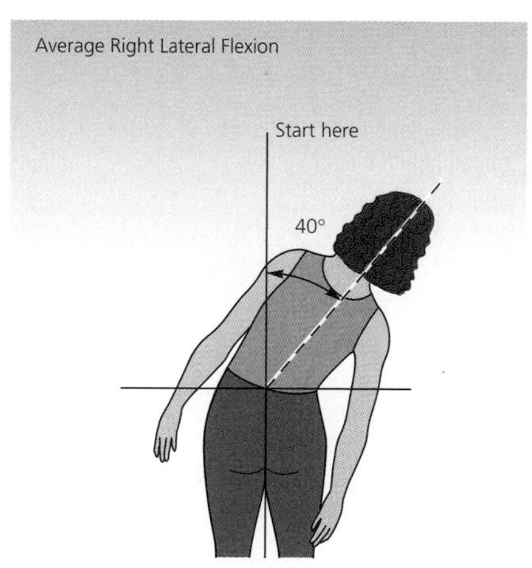

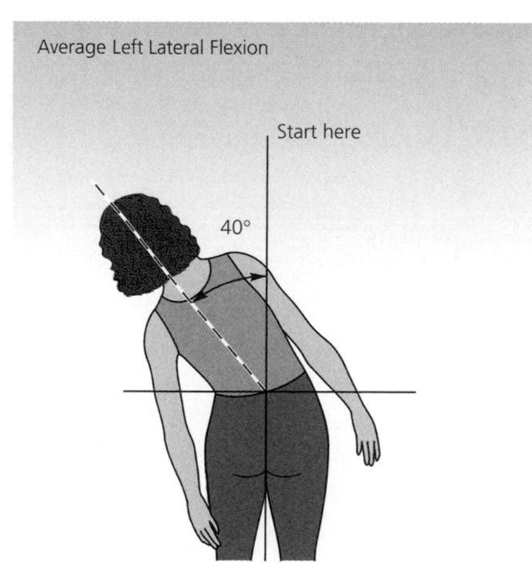

LABORATORY ACTIVITIES

4. Hip Abduction

Raise your leg to the side at the hip. Check one of the following for each leg; fill in degrees if using the measurement method.

Right	*Left*	
_______	_______	Below average/needs improvement
_______	_______	Average (40–45°)
_______	_______	Above average

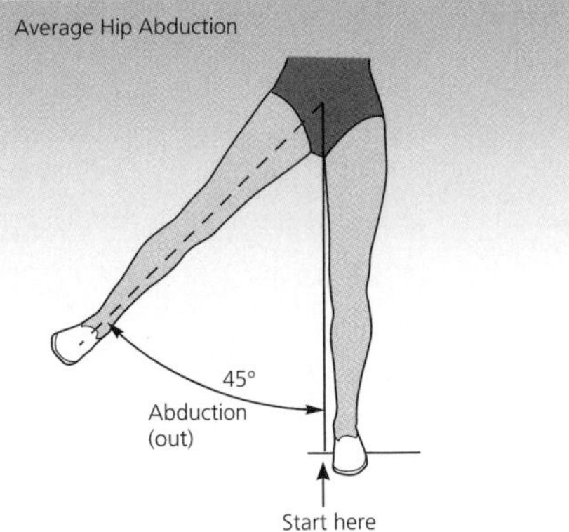

5. Hip Flexion (Bent Knee)

With one leg flat on the floor, bend the other knee and lift the leg up at the hip. Check one of the following for each leg; fill in degrees if using the measurement method.

Right	*Left*	
_______	_______	Below average/needs improvement
_______	_______	Average (121–125°)
_______	_______	Above average

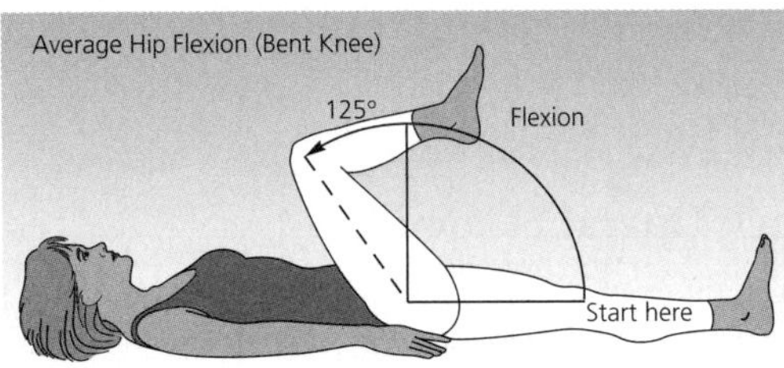

6. Hip Flexion (Straight Leg)

With one leg flat on the floor, raise the other leg at the hip, keeping both legs straight. Take care not to put excess strain on your back. Check one of the following for each leg; fill in degrees if using the measurement method.

Right	*Left*	
_______	_______	Below average/needs improvement
_______	_______	Average (79–81°)
_______	_______	Above average

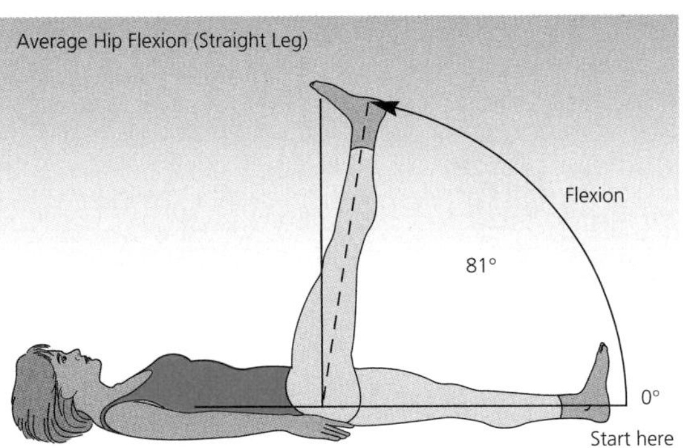

7. Ankle Dorsiflexion and Plantar Flexion

For each position and foot, check one of the following; fill in degrees if using the measurement method.

Ankle dorsiflexion—pull your toes toward your shin.

Right	*Left*	
______	______	Below average/needs improvement
______	______	Average (9–13°)
______	______	Above average

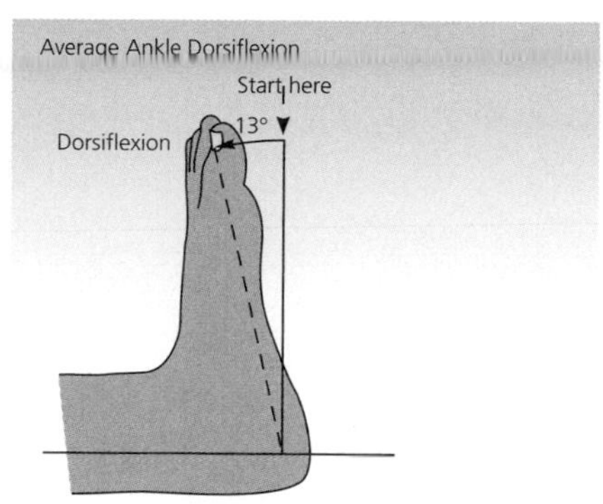

Plantar flexion—point your toes.

Right	*Left*	
______	______	Below average/needs improvement
______	______	Average (50–55°)
______	______	Above average

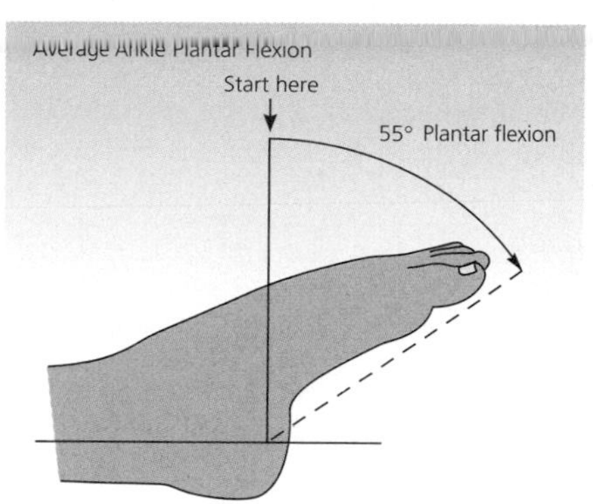

Rating Your Flexibility

Sit-and-reach test: Score: ______________ cm Rating: ______________

Range-of-Motion Assessment

Identify your rating for each joint on each side of the body. If you used the comparison method, put check marks in the appropriate categories; if you measured range of motion, enter the degrees for each joint in the appropriate category.

		Right			Left		
Joint/Assessment		Below Average	Average	Above Average	Below Average	Average	Above Average
1. Shoulder abduction and adduction	Abduction						
	Adduction						
2. Shoulder flexion and extension	Flexion						
	Extension						
3. Trunk/low-back lateral flexion	Flexion						
4. Hip abduction	Abduction						
5. Hip flexion (bent knee)	Flexion						
6. Hip flexion (straight leg)	Flexion						
7. Ankle dorsiflexion and plantar flexion	Dorsiflexion						
	Plantar flexion						

Using Your Results

How did you score? Are you surprised by your ratings for flexibility? Are you satisfied with your current ratings?

If you're not satisfied, set a realistic goal for improvement:

Are you satisfied with your current level of flexibility as expressed in your daily life—for example, your ability to maintain good posture and move easily and without pain?

If you're not satisfied, set some realistic goals for improvement:

What should you do next? Enter the results of this lab in the Preprogram Assessment column in Appendix D. If you've set goals for improvement, begin planning your flexibility program by completing the plan in Lab 5.2. After several weeks of your program, complete this lab again and enter the results in the Postprogram Assessment column of Appendix D. How do the results compare?

Name ______________________ Section ______________ Date ______________

LAB 5.2 Creating a Personalized Program for Developing Flexibility

1. *Goals.* List goals for your flexibility program. On the left, include specific, measurable goals that you can use to track the progress of your fitness program. These goals might be things like raising your sit-and-reach score from fair to good or your bent-leg hip flexion rating from below average to average. On the right, include long-term and more qualitative goals, such as reducing your risk for back pain.

   Specific Goals: Current Status ______________________ Final Goals ______________________

   ______________________ ______________________

   ______________________ ______________________

   Other goals: ______________________

   ____

2. *Exercises.* The exercises in the program plan below are from the general stretching program presented in Chapter 5. You can add or delete exercises depending on your needs, goals, and preferences. For any exercises you add, fill in the areas of the body affected.
3. *Frequency.* A minimum frequency of 2–3 days per week is recommended; 5–7 days per week is ideal. You may want to do your stretching exercises the same days you plan to do cardiorespiratory endurance exercise or weight training, because muscles stretch better following exercise, when they are warm.
4. *Intensity.* All stretches should be done to the point of mild discomfort, not pain.
5. *Time/duration.* All stretches should be held for 15–30 seconds. (PNF techniques should include a 6-second contraction followed by a 10–30-second assisted stretch.) All stretches should be performed 2–4 times.

Program Plan for Flexibility

Exercise	Areas Stretched	Frequency (check ✔)						
		M	T	W	Th	F	Sa	Su
Head turns and tilts	Neck							
Towel stretch	Triceps, shoulders, chest							
Across-the-body and overhead stretches	Shoulders, upper back, back of the arm							
Upper-back stretch	Upper back							
Lateral stretch	Trunk muscles							
Step stretch	Hip, front of thigh							
Side lunge	Inner thigh, hip, calf							
Inner thigh stretch	Inner thigh, hip							
Trunk rotation	Trunk, outer thigh and hip, lower back							
Modified hurdler stretch	Back of the thigh, lower back							
Alternate leg stretcher	Back of the thigh, hip, knee, ankle, buttocks							
Lower-leg stretch	Back of the lower leg							

You can monitor your program using a chart like the one on the next page.

Flexibility Program Chart

Fill in the dates you perform each stretch, the number of seconds you hold each stretch (should be 15–30), and the number of repetitions of each (should be 2–4). For an easy check on the duration of your stretches, count "one thousand one, one thousand two," and so on. You will probably find that over time you'll be able to hold each stretch longer (in addition to being able to stretch farther).

Exercise/Date																				
	Duration																			
	Reps																			
	Duration																			
	Reps																			
	Duration																			
	Reps																			
	Duration																			
	Reps																			
	Duration																			
	Reps																			
	Duration																			
	Reps																			
	Duration																			
	Reps																			
	Duration																			
	Reps																			
	Duration																			
	Reps																			
	Duration																			
	Reps																			
	Duration																			
	Reps																			
	Duration																			
	Reps																			
	Duration																			
	Reps																			
	Duration																			
	Reps																			
	Duration																			
	Reps																			
	Duration																			
	Reps																			
	Duration																			
	Reps																			
	Duration																			
	Reps																			

Name ______________________ Section ______________ Date ______________

LAB 5.3 Assessing Muscular Endurance for Low-Back Health

The three tests in this lab evaluate the muscular endurance of major spine-stabilizing muscles.

Side Bridge Endurance Test

Equipment

1. Stopwatch or clock with a second hand
2. Exercise mat
3. Partner

Preparation

Warm up your muscles with some low-intensity activity such as walking or easy jogging. Practice assuming the side bridge position described below.

Instructions

1. Lie on the mat on your side with your legs extended. Place your top foot in front of your lower foot for support. Lift your hips off the mat so that you are supporting yourself on one elbow and your feet (see photo). Your body should maintain a straight line. Breathe normally; don't hold your breath.
2. Hold the position as long as possible. Your partner should keep track of the time and make sure that you maintain the correct position. Your final score is the total time you are able to hold the side bridge with correct form—from the time you lift your hips until your hips return to the mat.
3. Rest for 5 minutes and then repeat the test on the other side. Record your times here and on the chart at the end of the lab. Right side bridge time: __________ sec   Left side bridge time: __________ sec

Trunk Flexors Endurance Test

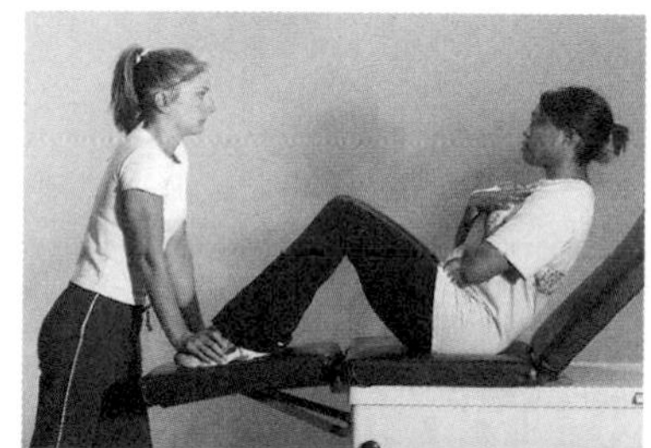

Equipment

1. Stopwatch or clock with a second hand
2. Exercise mat or padded exercise table
3. Two helpers
4. Jig angled at 60 degrees from the floor or padded bench (optional)

Preparation

Warm up with some low-intensity activity such as walking or easy jogging.

Instructions

1. To start, assume a sit-up posture with your back supported at an angle of 60 degrees from the floor; support can be provided by a jig, a padded bench, or a spotter (see photos). Your knees and hips should both be flexed at 90 degrees, and your arms should be folded across your chest with your hands placed on the opposite shoulders. Your toes should be secured under a toe strap or held by a partner.
2. Your goal is to hold the starting position (isometric contraction) as long as possible after the support is pulled away. To begin the test, a helper should pull the jig or other support back about 10 centimeters (4 inches). The helper should keep track of the time; if a spotter is acting as your support, she or he should be ready to support your weight as soon as your torso begins to move back. Your final score is the total time you are able to hold the contraction—from the time the support is removed until any part of your back touches the support. Remember to breathe normally throughout the test.
3. Record your time here and on the chart at the end of the lab. Trunk flexors endurance time: __________ sec

Back Extensors Endurance Test

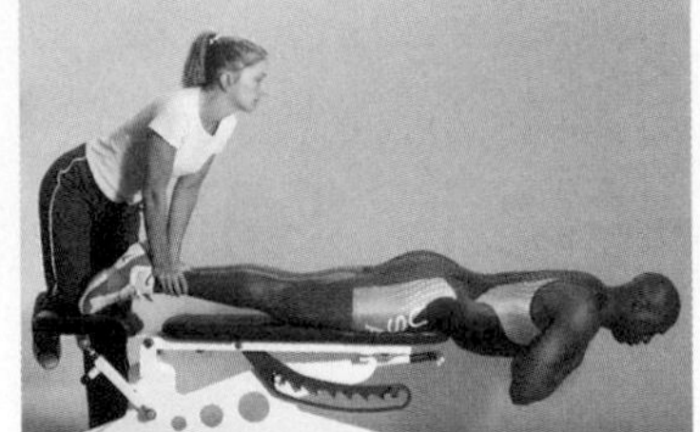

Equipment

1. Stopwatch or clock with a second hand
2. Extension bench with padded ankle support or any padded bench
3. Partner

Preparation

Warm up with some low-intensity activity such as walking or easy jogging.

Instructions

1. Lie face down on the test bench with your upper body extending out over the end of the bench and your pelvis, hips, and knees flat on the bench. Your arms should be folded across your chest with your hands placed on the opposite shoulders. Your feet should be secured under a padded strap or held by a partner.
2. Your goal is to hold your upper body in a straight horizontal line with your lower body as long as possible. Keep your neck straight and neutral; don't raise your head and don't arch your back. Breathe normally. Your partner should keep track of the time and watch your form. Your final score is the total time you are able to hold the horizontal position—from the time you assume the position until your upper body drops from the horizontal position.
3. Record your time here and on the chart below. Back extensors endurance time: __________ sec

Rating Your Test Results for Muscular Endurance for Low-Back Health

The table below shows mean endurance test times for healthy young college students with a mean age of 21 years. Compare your scores with the times shown in the table. (If you are older or have suffered from low-back pain in the past, these ratings are less accurate; however, your time scores can be used as a point of comparison.)

Mean Endurance Times (sec)

	Right side bridge	Left side bridge	Trunk flexors	Back extensors
Men	95	99	136	161
Women	75	78	134	185

SOURCE: From S. M. McGill, 2002, *Low Back Disorders: Evidence-Based Prevention and Rehabilitation,* page 227, table 12.1. © 2002 by Stuart McGill. Reprinted with permission from Human Kinetics (Champaign, IL).

Right side bridge: __________ sec — Rating (above mean, at mean, below mean): __________

Left side bridge: __________ sec — Rating (above mean, at mean, below mean): __________

Trunk flexors: __________ sec — Rating (above mean, at mean, below mean): __________

Back extensors: __________ sec — Rating (above mean, at mean, below mean): __________

Using Your Results

How did you score? Are you surprised by your scores for the low-back tests? Are you satisfied with your current ratings?

If you're not satisfied, set a realistic goal for improvement. The norms in this lab are based on healthy young adults, so a score above the mean may or may not be realistic for you. Instead, you may want to set a specific goal based on time rather than rating; for example, set a goal of improving your time by 10%. Imbalances in muscular endurance have been linked with back problems, so if your rating is significantly lower for one of the three tests, you should focus particular attention on that area of your body.

Goal:

What should you do next? Enter the results of this lab in the Preprogram Assessment column in Appendix D. If you've set a goal for improvement, begin a program of low-back exercises such as that suggested in this chapter. After several weeks of your program, complete this lab again and enter the results in the Postprogram Assessment column of Appendix D. How do the results compare?

Name ______________________ Section ______________ Date ______________

LAB 5.4 Posture Evaluation

For each row, have a partner record the point total that corresponds to the illustration that most closely matches your posture. Use a plumb line to help make an accurate assessment of your posture.

5 points	3 points	1 point	Your Score
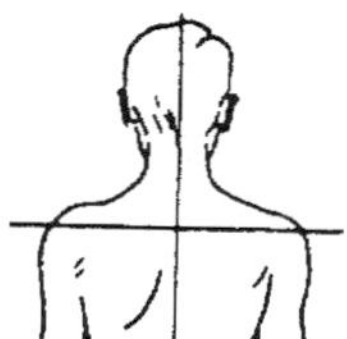 Head erect (gravity line passes directly through center)	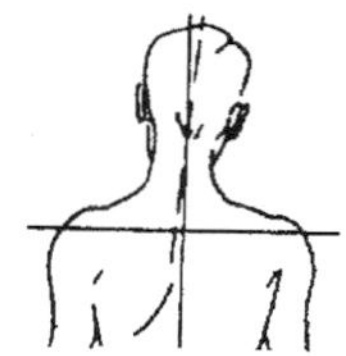 Head twisted or turned to one side slightly	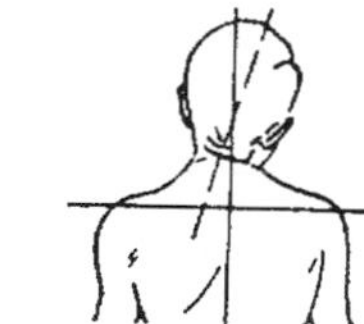 Head twisted or turned to one side markedly	______
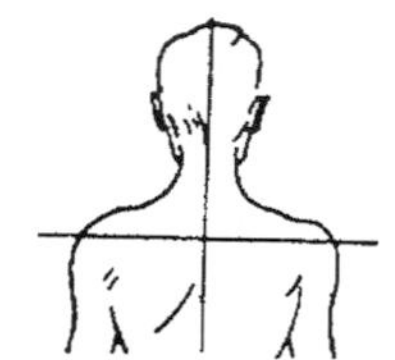 Shoulders level (horizontally)	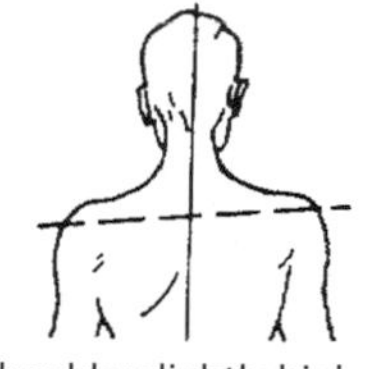 One shoulder slightly higher than other	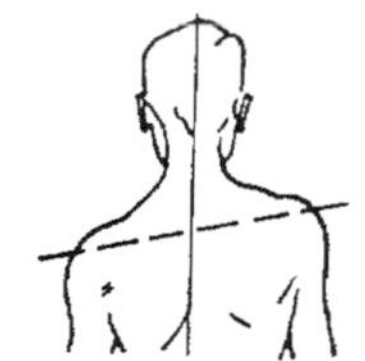 One shoulder markedly higher than other	______
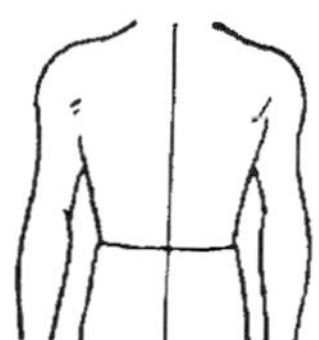 Spine straight	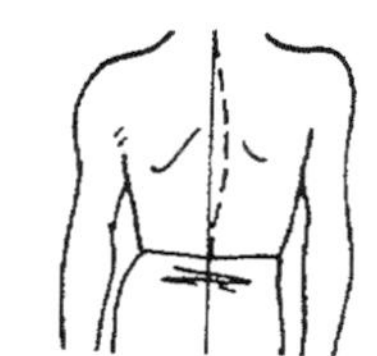 Spine slightly curved laterally	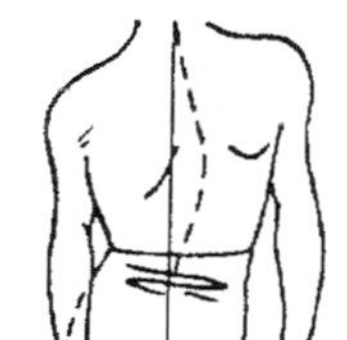 Spine markedly curved laterally	______
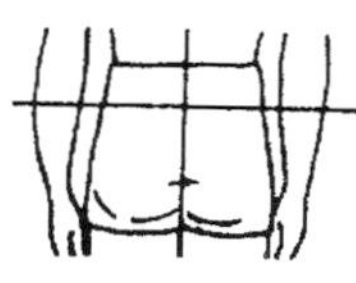 Hips level (horizontally)	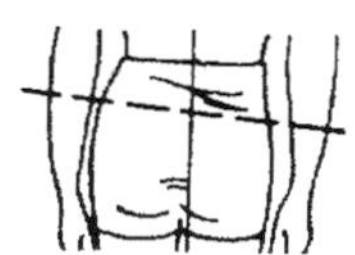 One hip slightly higher	 One hip markedly higher	______
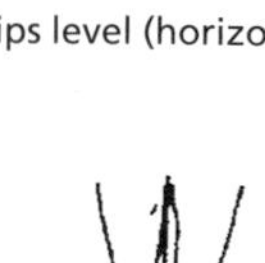 Feet pointed straight ahead	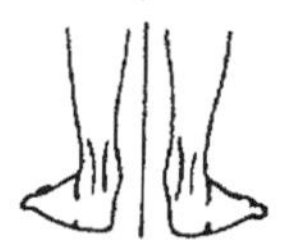 Feet pointed out	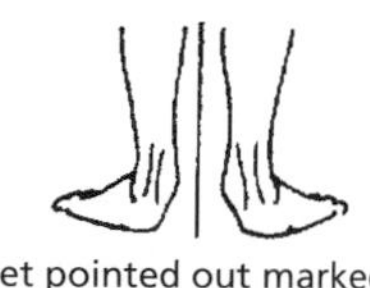 Feet pointed out markedly; ankles sag in (pronation)	______
 Arches high	 Arches lower; feet slightly flat	 Arches low; feet markedly flat	

5 points	3 points	1 point	Your Score
Neck erect, chin in, head in balance directly above shoulders	Neck slightly forward, chin slightly out	Neck markedly forward, chin markedly out	______
Chest elevated (breast-bone farthest forward part of body)	Chest slightly depressed	Chest markedly depressed (flat)	______
Shoulders centered	Shoulders slightly forward	Shoulders markedly forward (shoulder blades protruding in rear)	______
Upper back normally rounded	Upper back slightly more rounded	Upper back markedly rounded	______
Trunk erect	Trunk inclined slightly to rear	Trunk inclined markedly to rear	______
Abdomen flat	Abdomen protruding	Abdomen protruding and sagging	______
Lower back normally curved	Lower back slightly hollow	Lower back markedly hollow	______

Total Score (from both pages) (Scores should be between 13 and 65.) ______

If your posture needs improvement, review the information in the box on good posture and low-back health on p. 149. If you scored "1 point" for any item in the evaluation, you may want to consider seeing a physician; professional advice, physical therapy, orthotic devices, or other therapies may help you improve your posture.

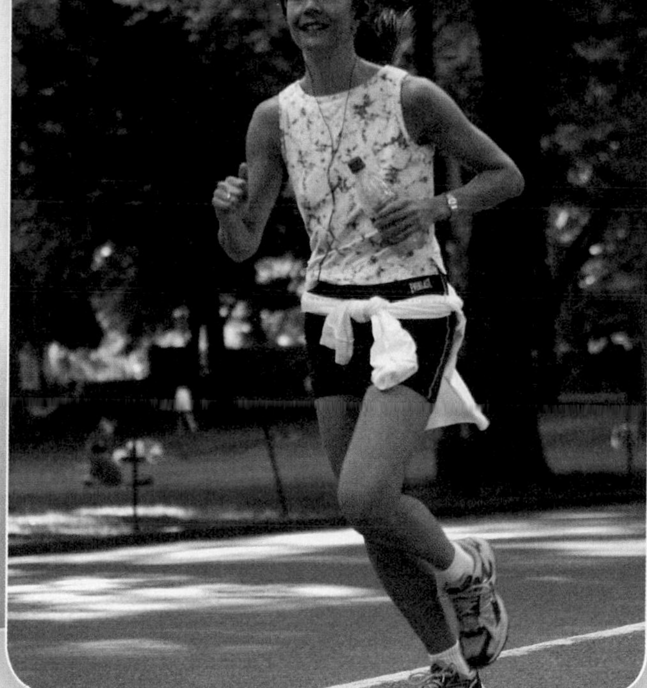

LOOKING AHEAD>>>>>

AFTER READING THIS CHAPTER, YOU SHOULD BE ABLE TO:

- Define fat-free mass, essential fat, and nonessential fat, and describe their functions in the body
- Explain how body composition affects overall health and wellness
- Describe how body mass index, body composition, and body fat distribution are measured and assessed
- Explain how to determine recommended body weight and body fat distribution

BODY COMPOSITION 6

TEST YOUR KNOWLEDGE

1. **Exercise helps reduce the risks associated with overweight and obesity even if it doesn't result in improvements in body composition.**

   True or false?

2. **Which of the following is the most significant risk factor for the most common type of diabetes (type 2 diabetes)?**
   a. smoking
   b. low-fiber diet
   c. overweight or obesity
   d. inactivity

3. **In women, excessive exercise and low energy (calorie) intake can cause which of the following?**
   a. unhealthy reduction in body fat levels
   b. amenorrhea (absent menstruation)
   c. bone density loss and osteoporosis
   d. muscle wasting and fatigue

ANSWERS

1. **TRUE.** Regular physical activity provides protection against the health risks of overweight and obesity. It lowers the risk of death for people who are overweight or obese as well as for those at a normal weight.
2. **c.** All four are risk factors for diabetes, but overweight/obesity is the most significant. It's estimated that 90% of cases of type 2 diabetes could be prevented if people adopted healthy lifestyle behaviors. About 18 million Americans have type 2 diabetes, and more than 6 million of those with diabetes don't know it.
3. **ALL FOUR.** Very low levels of body fat, and the behaviors used to achieve them, have serious health consequences for both men and women.

FIT AND WELL ONLINE LEARNING CENTER www.mhhe.com/fahey

Visit the *Fit and Well* Online Learning Center for resources that will help you get the most out of your course!

- Study and review aids include practice quizzes, glossary flashcards, chapter summaries, learning objectives, PowerPoint presentations, Common Questions Answered, student handouts, crossword puzzles, Internet activities, and links to wellness Web sites.
- Behavior change tools include a daily fitness and nutrition journal, a behavior change workbook, sample behavior change plans, and blank behavior change logs to print and use.

Body composition, the body's relative amounts of fat and fat-free mass, is an important component of fitness for health and wellness. People whose body composition is optimal tend to be healthier, to move more efficiently, and to feel better about themselves. They also have a lower risk of many chronic diseases.

Unfortunately, many people don't succeed in their efforts to obtain a fit and healthy body because they set unrealistic goals and emphasize short-term weight loss rather than the permanent changes in lifestyle that lead to fat loss and a healthy body composition. Successful management of body composition requires the long-term, consistent coordination of many aspects of a wellness program. However, even in the absence of changes in body composition, an active lifestyle can improve wellness (see the box "Body Composition and the Benefits of Physical Activity").

This chapter focuses on defining and measuring body composition. The aspects of lifestyle that affect body composition are discussed in detail in other chapters: physical activity and exercise in Chapters 2–5 and 7, nutrition in Chapter 8, weight management in Chapter 9, and stress management in Chapter 10.

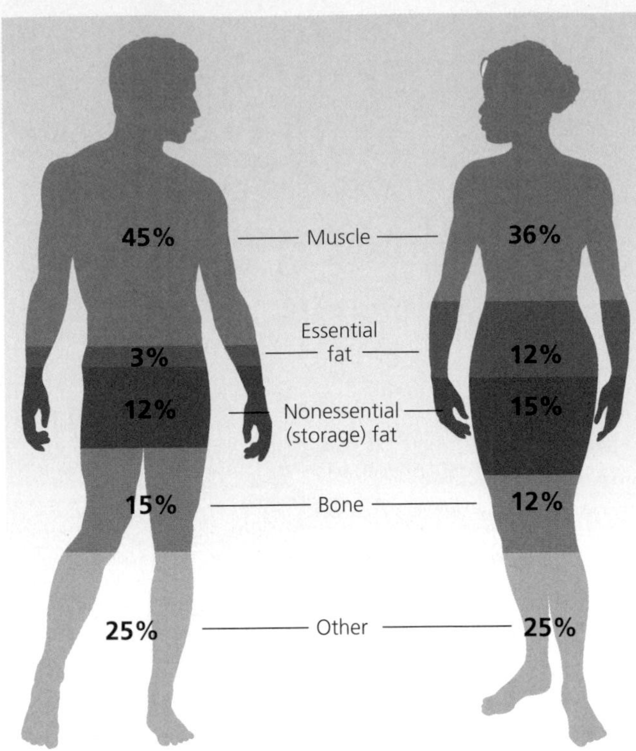

FIGURE 6.1 Body composition of a typical man and woman, 20–24 years old.

SOURCE: Adapted from Brooks, G. A., et al. 2005. *Exercise Physiology: Human Bioenergetics and Its Applications,* 4th ed. New York: McGraw-Hill.

WHAT IS BODY COMPOSITION, AND WHY I S IT IMPORTANT?

The human body can be divided into fat-free mass and body fat. Fat-free mass is composed of all the body's nonfat tissues: bone, water, muscle, connective tissue, organ tissues, and teeth. Body fat includes both essential and nonessential (storage) body fats (Figure 6.1).

- **Essential fat** includes lipids (or fats) incorporated into the nerves, brain, heart, lungs, liver, and mammary glands. These fat deposits, crucial for normal body functioning, make up 3–5% of total body weight in men and 8–12% in women. (The larger percentage in women is natural and healthy and is due to fat deposits in the breasts, uterus, and other gender-specific sites.)
- **Nonessential (storage) fat** is extra fat or fat reserves stored in the body. Nonessential fat exists primarily within fat cells, or **adipose tissue,** often located just below the skin (subcutaneous fat) and around major organs (visceral fat).

In general, when the amount of fat in the body changes, fat cells increase or decrease in size (rather than in number). The amount of storage fat depends on many factors, including gender, age, heredity, metabolism, diet, and activity level. Excess storage fat is usually the result of consuming more energy (as food) than is expended (in metabolism and physical activity).

TERMS

essential fat The fat in the body necessary for normal body functioning.

nonessential (storage) fat Extra fat or fat reserves stored in the body.

adipose tissue Connective tissue in which fat is stored.

percent body fat The percentage of total body weight that is composed of fat.

overweight Characterized by a body weight above a recommended range for good health; ranges are set through large-scale population surveys.

obese Severely overweight, characterized by an excessive accumulation of body fat; overfat. Obesity may also be defined in terms of some measure of total body weight.

Overweight and Obesity Defined

Some of the most commonly used methods of assessing and classifying body composition are described later in this chapter. Some methods are based on body fat, and others on total body weight. Methods based on total body weight are less accurate than those based on body fat, but they are commonly used because body weight is easier to measure than body fat.

In the past, many people relied on height/weight tables (which were based on insurance company mortality statistics) to determine whether they were at a healthy

Body Composition and the Benefits of Physical Activity

Does physical activity have benefits aside from the help it provides in managing weight and improving body composition? Yes! Physical activity is important for health even if it produces no changes in body composition—that is, even if a person remains overweight or obese. Physical inactivity operates as a risk factor for health problems independently of body composition; conversely, physical activity confers benefits no matter what a person weighs.

Obesity is linked to many serious diseases and physical problems, including cardiovascular disease, diabetes, certain cancers, and premature death. Regular physical activity and exercise block many of the destructive effects of obesity. For example, they improve blood pressure, blood glucose levels, cholesterol levels, and body fat distribution, and they lower the risk of cardiovascular disease, diabetes, and premature death. Although physical activity and exercise produce these improvements quickly in some people and slowly in others, due to genetic differences, the improvements do occur. Physical activity is particularly important for the many Americans who have metabolic syndrome or pre-diabetes, both characterized by insulin resistance.

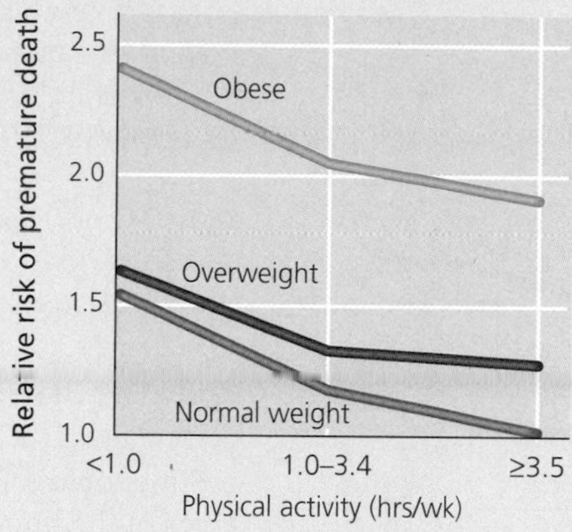

Relationship among amount of activity, body weight, and risk of premature death.

In short, while it is best to have a healthy level of body fat and an active lifestyle, physical activity is important regardless of body composition. Physical activity reduces the risk of health problems and mortality for people of all levels of body fat (see figure).

Which is more important in combating the adverse health effects of obesity—physical activity or physical fitness? Many studies suggest that both are important; the more active and fit you are, the lower your risk of having health problems and dying prematurely. Of the two, however, physical *activity* appears to be more important for health than physical *fitness*. The message: No matter what your current body composition, it helps to get up and move.

SOURCES: Hu, F. B., et al. 2004. Adiposity compared with physical activity in predicting mortality among women. *New England Journal of Medicine* 351(26): 2694–2703. Blair, S. N., Y. Cheng, and J. S. Holder. 2001. Is physical activity or physical fitness more important in defining health benefits? *Medicine and Science in Sports and Exercise* 33(Suppl.): 379–399.

weight. Such tables, however, can be highly inaccurate for some people. Because muscle tissue is denser and heavier than fat, a fit person can easily weigh more than the recommended weight on a height/weight table. For the same reason, an unfit person may weigh less than the table's recommended weight.

When looking at body composition, the most important consideration is the proportion of the body's total weight that is fat—the **percent body fat.** For example, two women may both be 5 feet, 5 inches tall and weigh 130 pounds. But one woman may have only 15% of her body weight as fat, whereas the other woman could have 34% body fat. Although neither woman is overweight by most standards, the second woman is overfat. Too much body fat (not total weight) has a negative effect on health and well-being. Just as the amount of body fat is important, so is its location on your body. Visceral fat is more harmful to health than subcutaneous fat.

Overweight is usually defined as total body weight above the recommended range for good health (as determined by large-scale population surveys). **Obesity** is defined as a more serious degree of overweight. The cutoff point for obesity may be set in terms of percent body fat or in terms of some measure of total body weight.

MOTIVATION BOOSTER

Change the cues in your environment. If you keep unhealthy snacks in your kitchen or desk drawers, replace them with healthier choices. Place your exercise clothes where you can see them. Put motivating notes in visible places around your home.

Prevalence of Overweight and Obesity Among Americans

By any measure, Americans are getting fatter. Since 1960, the average weight among adult men has increased from 166 to 191 pounds; among women, from 140 to 164 pounds. The prevalence of obesity has increased from about 13% in 1960 to about 32% today, and more than 66% of American adults are now overweight (Figure 6.2).

Possible explanations for this increase include more time spent in sedentary work and leisure activities, fewer short trips on foot and more by automobile, fewer daily gym classes for students, more meals eaten outside the home, greater consumption of fast food, increased portion sizes, and increased consumption of soft drinks and convenience foods. According to the

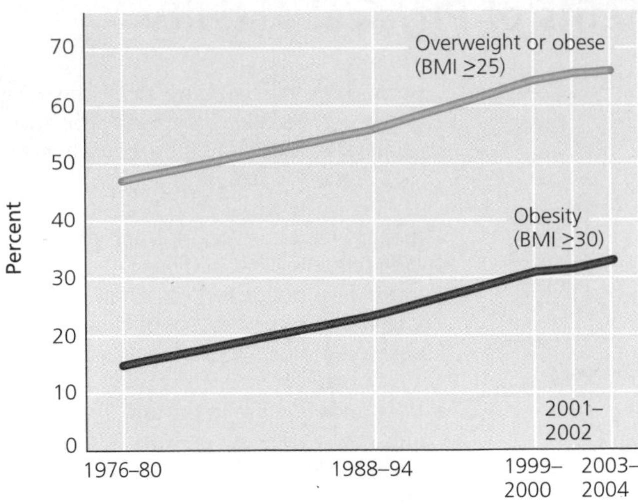

VITAL STATISTICS

FIGURE 6.2 Prevalence of overweight and obesity among American adults age 20–74.

SOURCE: National Center for Health Statistics. 2006. *2003–2004 National Health and Nutrition Examination Survey (NHANES).* Hyattsville, Md.: National Center for Health Statistics.

USDA, average calorie intake among Americans increased by more than 500 calories per day between 1970 and 2003. Further, the CDC says that nearly 40% of adult Americans are physically inactive and get no exercise at all.

Excess Body Fat and Wellness

As rates of overweight and obesity increase, so do the problems associated with them. Obesity reduces life expectancy by 10–20 years, causes more than 100,000 premature deaths each year, and costs the United States more than $117 billion annually.

Risk of Chronic Disease and Premature Death Obese people have an overall mortality rate almost twice that of nonobese people, and even mild to moderate overweight is associated with a substantial increase in the risk of heart disease and diabetes. Many overweight and obese people—especially those who are sedentary and eat a poor diet—suffer from a group of symptoms called *metabolic syndrome* (or insulin resistance syndrome). Symptoms include a resistance to the effects of insulin, high blood pressure, high blood glucose levels, abnormal blood fat levels (high triglycerides and low HDLs, or "good" cholesterol), and fat deposits in the abdominal region. Metabolic syndrome increases the risk of heart disease up to three times in men and six times in women. Scientists estimate that nearly 25% of the U.S. population has metabolic syndrome.

Obesity is also associated with increased risk of death from many types of cancer. Other health problems associated with obesity include hypertension, impaired immune function, gallbladder and kidney diseases, skin problems, sleep and breathing disorders, erectile dysfunction, pregnancy complications, back pain, arthritis, and other bone and joint disorders.

Of particular note is the strong association between excess body fat and diabetes mellitus: Obese people are more than three times as likely as nonobese people to develop diabetes, and the incidence of diabetes among Americans has increased dramatically as the rate of obesity has climbed (see the box "Diabetes").

Body Fat Distribution and Health The distribution of body fat is also an important indicator of health. Men and postmenopausal women tend to store fat in the upper regions of their bodies, particularly in the abdominal area (the "apple shape"). Premenopausal women usually store fat in the hips, buttocks, and thighs (the "pear shape"). Excess fat in the abdominal area increases risk of several diseases, including high blood pressure, diabetes, early-onset heart disease, stroke, certain cancers, and mortality. The reason for this increase in risk is not entirely clear, but it appears that abdominal fat is more easily mobilized and sent into the bloodstream, increasing disease-related blood fat levels.

The risks from body fat distribution are usually assessed by measuring waist circumference. Waist circumference can be used to measure abdominal obesity (an indicator of disease risk) and to monitor changes in body composition over time. More research is needed to determine the precise degree of risk associated with specific values for waist measurement. However, a total waist measurement of more than 40 inches for men and more than 35 inches for women is associated with a significantly increased risk of disease.

Performance of Physical Activities Too much body fat makes physical activity difficult because moving the body through everyday activities means working harder and using more energy. In general, overfat people are less fit than others and don't have the muscular strength, endurance, and flexibility that make normal activity easy. Because exercise is more difficult, they do less of it, depriving themselves of an effective way to improve body composition.

Emotional Wellness and Self-Image Obesity can affect psychological as well as physical wellness. Being perceived as fat can be a source of ridicule, ostracism, and sometimes discrimination from others; it can contribute to psychological problems such as depression, anxiety, and low self-esteem.

The popular image of the "ideal" body has changed greatly in the past 50 years, evolving from slightly plump to unhealthily thin. The ideal body—as presented by the media—is an unrealistic goal for most Americans. This is because one's ability to change body composition depends on heredity as well as diet and exercise (see the box "Exercise, Body Image, and Self-Esteem" on p. 174).

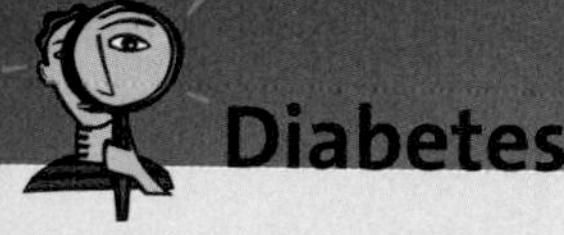

Diabetes

Diabetes mellitus is a disease that causes a disruption of normal metabolism. The pancreas, a long, thin organ located behind the stomach, normally secretes the hormone insulin, which stimulates cells to take up glucose (blood sugar) to produce energy. In a person with diabetes, this process is disrupted, causing a buildup of glucose in the bloodstream. Over the long term, diabetes is associated with kidney failure, nerve damage, circulation problems, retinal damage and blindness, and increased rates of heart attack, stroke, and hypertension. The incidence of diabetes among Americans has increased dramatically as the rate of obesity has climbed. Diabetes is currently the sixth leading cause of death in the United States.

Types of Diabetes

About 21 million Americans (7% of the population) have one of two major forms of diabetes. About 5–10% of people with diabetes have the more serious form, known as *type 1 diabetes*. In this type of diabetes, the pancreas produces little or no insulin, so daily doses of insulin are required. (Without insulin, a person with type 1 diabetes can lapse into a coma.) Type 1 diabetes usually strikes before age 30.

The remaining 90–95% of Americans with diabetes have *type 2 diabetes*. This condition can develop slowly, and about a third of affected individuals are unaware of their condition. In type 2 diabetes, the pancreas doesn't produce enough insulin, cells are resistant to insulin, or both. This condition is usually diagnosed in people over age 40, although there has been a tenfold increase in type 2 diabetes in children in the past two decades. About one-third of people with type 2 diabetes must take insulin; others may take medications that increase insulin production or stimulate cells to take up glucose.

A third type of diabetes occurs in about 7% of women during pregnancy. *Gestational diabetes* usually disappears after pregnancy, but over 50% of women who experience it develop type 2 diabetes.

The term *pre-diabetes* describes blood glucose levels that are higher than normal but not high enough for a diagnosis of full-blown diabetes. About 54 million Americans have pre-diabetes, and most people with the condition will develop type 2 diabetes unless they adopt preventive lifestyle measures.

The major factors involved in the development of diabetes are age, obesity, physical inactivity, a family history of diabetes, and lifestyle. Excess body fat reduces cell sensitivity to insulin, and insulin resistance is almost always a precursor of type 2 diabetes. Ethnic background also plays a role. African Americans and Hispanics are 55% more likely than non-Hispanic whites to develop type 2 diabetes; more than 20% of Hispanics over age 65 have diabetes. Native Americans also have a higher-than-average incidence of diabetes. The American Diabetes Association's Web site (http://www.diabetes.org) includes an interactive diabetes risk assessment.

Treatment

There is no cure for diabetes, but it can be successfully managed by keeping blood sugar levels within safe limits through diet, exercise, and, if necessary, medication. Blood sugar levels can be monitored using a home test, and close control of glucose levels can significantly reduce the rate of serious complications. Nearly 90% of people with type 2 diabetes are overweight when diagnosed, and an important step in treatment is to lose weight. Even a small amount of exercise and weight loss can be beneficial. People with diabetes should obtain carbohydrates from whole grains, fruits, vegetables, and low-fat dairy products; carbohydrates and monounsaturated fat together should provide 60–70% of total daily calories. Regular exercise and a healthy diet are often sufficient to control type 2 diabetes.

Prevention

It is estimated that 90% of cases of type 2 diabetes could be prevented if people adopted healthy lifestyle behaviors, including regular physical activity, a moderate diet, and modest weight loss. For people with pre-diabetes, lifestyle measures are more effective than medication for delaying or preventing the development of diabetes. Studies of people with pre-diabetes show that a 5–7% weight loss can lower diabetes onset by nearly 60%. Exercise (endurance and/or strength training) makes cells more sensitive to insulin and helps stabilize blood glucose levels; it also helps keep body fat at healthy levels.

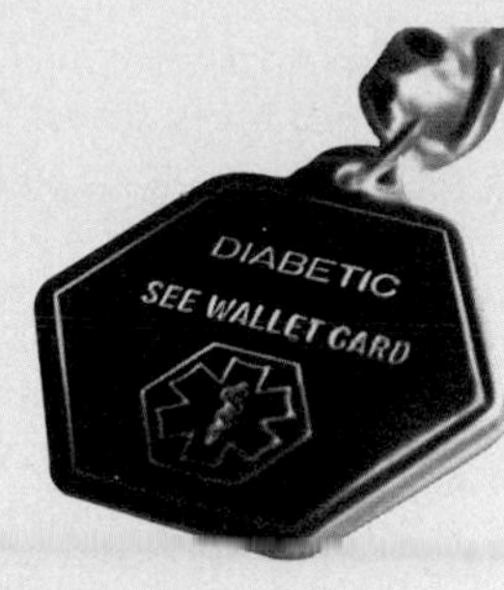

Eating a moderate diet to help control body fat is perhaps the most important dietary recommendation for the prevention of diabetes. However, the composition of the diet may also be important. Studies have linked diets low in fiber and high in sugar, refined carbohydrates, saturated fat, red meat, and high-fat dairy products to increased risk of diabetes; diets rich in whole grains, fruits, vegetables, legumes, fish, and poultry may be protective. Specific foods linked to higher diabetes risk include regular (nondiet) cola beverages, white bread, white rice, french fries, processed meats (bacon, sausage, hot dogs), and sugary desserts.

Warning Signs and Testing

Be alert for the warning signs of diabetes:

- Frequent urination
- Extreme hunger or thirst
- Unexplained weight loss
- Extreme fatigue
- Blurred vision
- Frequent infections
- Cuts and bruises that are slow to heal
- Tingling or numbness in the hands and feet
- Generalized itching, with no rash

The best way to avoid complications is to recognize these symptoms and get early diagnosis and treatment. Type 2 diabetes is often asymptomatic in the early stages, however, and major health organizations now recommend routine screening for people over age 45 and anyone younger who is at high risk, including anyone who is obese.

Screening involves a blood test to check glucose levels after either a period of fasting or the administration of a set dose of glucose. A fasting glucose level of 126 mg/dl or higher indicates diabetes; a level of 100–125 mg/dl indicates pre-diabetes. If you are concerned about your risk for diabetes, talk with your physician about being tested.

Exercise, Body Image, and Self-Esteem

If you gaze into the mirror and wish you could change the way your body looks, consider getting some exercise—not to reshape your contours but to firm up your body image and enhance your self-esteem. In one study, 82 adults completed a 12-week aerobic exercise program (using cycle ergometry) and had 12 months of follow-up. Compared with the control group, the participants not only improved their fitness but also benefited psychologically in tests of mood, anxiety, and self-concept. These same physical and psychological benefits were still significant at the 1-year follow-up.

One reason for the findings may be that people who exercise regularly often gain a sense of mastery and competence that enhances their self-esteem and body image. In addition, exercise contributes to a more toned look, which many adults prefer. Research suggests that physically active people are more comfortable with their bodies and their image than sedentary people are. In one workplace study, 60 employees were asked to complete a 36-session stretching program whose main purpose was to prevent muscle strains at work. At the end of the program, besides the significant increase by all participants in measurements of flexibility, their perceptions of their bodies improved, as did their overall sense of self-worth.

Similar results were obtained in a Norwegian study, in which 219 middle-aged people at risk for heart disease were randomly assigned to one of four groups: diet, diet plus exercise, exercise, and no intervention. The greater the participation of individuals in the exercise component of the program, the higher their scores in perceived competence/self-esteem and coping.

SOURCES: DiLorenzo, T. M., et al. 1999. Long-term effects of aerobic exercise on psychological outcomes. *Preventive Medicine* 28(1): 75–85. Sorensen, M., et al. 1999. The effect of exercise and diet on mental health and quality of life in middle-aged individuals with elevated risk factors for cardiovascular disease. *Journal of Sports Science* 17(5): 369–377. Moore, T. M. 1998. A workplace stretching program. *AAOHN Journal* 46(12): 563–568.

Most people should have the goal of developing a fit, healthy-looking body. The key to achieving this "look" is adopting a balance of proper nutrition and exercise and shedding unrealistic expectations about body composition—expectations that can negatively effect self-image and even lead to eating disorders and other problems.

Problems Associated with Very Low Levels of Body Fat

Though not as prevalent a problem as overweight or obesity, having too little body fat is also dangerous. Essential fat is necessary for the functioning of the body, and health experts generally view too little body fat—less than 8–12% for women and 3–5% for men—as a threat to health and well-being. Extreme leanness is linked with reproductive, circulatory, and immune system disorders and with premature death. Extremely lean people may experience muscle wasting and fatigue. They are also more likely to have eating disorders, which are described in more detail in Chapter 9. For women, an extremely low percentage of body fat is associated with **amenorrhea** and loss of bone mass (see the box "The Female Athlete Triad").

QUESTIONS FOR CRITICAL THINKING AND REFLECTION

How do you view your own body composition? Where do you think you've gotten your ideas about how your body should look and perform? In light of what you've learned in this chapter, do the ideals and images promoted in our culture seem reasonable? Do they seem healthy?

ASSESSING BODY MASS INDEX, BODY COMPOSITION, AND BODY FAT DISTRIBUTION

Like many people, you may weigh yourself from time to time on a scale in your bathroom, at the gym, or at a doctor's office. Although a scale can tell your total weight, it can't reveal whether a fluctuation in weight is due to a change in muscle, body water, or fat. Most importantly, a scale can't differentiate between overweight and overfat.

There are a number of simple, inexpensive ways to estimate healthy body weight and healthy body composition that are more accurate than the bathroom scale. These assessments can provide you with information about the health risks associated with your current body weight and body composition. They can also help you establish reasonable goals and set a starting point for current and future decisions about weight loss and weight gain.

Calculating Body Mass Index

Body mass index (BMI) is a measure of body weight that is useful for classifying the health risks of body weight if you don't have access to more sophisticated methods. Though more accurate than height-weight tables, body

DIMENSIONS OF DIVERSITY

The Female Athlete Triad

While obesity is at epidemic levels in the United States, many girls and women strive for unrealistic thinness in response to pressure from peers and a society obsessed with appearance. This quest for thinness has led to an increasingly common, underreported condition called the **female athlete triad.**

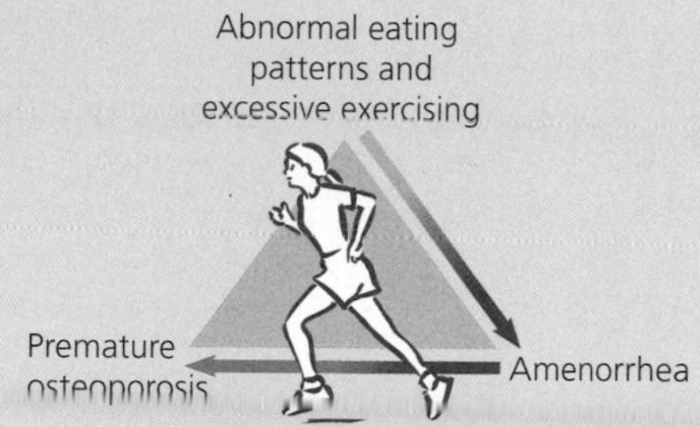

The triad consists of three interrelated disorders: abnormal eating patterns (and excessive exercising), followed by lack of menstrual periods (amenorrhea), followed by decreased bone density (premature osteoporosis). Left untreated, the triad can lead to decreased physical performance, increased incidence of bone fractures, disturbances of heart rhythm and metabolism, and even death.

Abnormal eating is the event from which the other two components of the triad flow. Abnormal eating ranges from moderately restricting food intake, to binge eating and purging (bulimia), to severely restricting food intake (anorexia nervosa). Whether serious or relatively mild, eating disorders prevent women from consuming enough calories to meet their bodies' needs.

Disordered eating, combined with intense exercise and emotional stress, can suppress the hormones that control the menstrual cycle. If the menstrual cycle stops for three consecutive months, the condition is called amenorrhea. Prolonged amenorrhea can lead to osteoporosis; bone density may erode to the point that a woman in her 20s will have the bone density of a woman in her 60s. Women with osteoporosis have fragile, easily fractured bones. Some researchers have found that even a few missed menstrual periods can decrease bone density.

All physically active women and girls have the potential to develop one or more components of the female athlete triad; for example, it is estimated that 5–20% of women who exercise regularly and vigorously may develop amenorrhea. But the triad is most prevalent among athletes who participate in certain sports: those in which appearance is highly important, those that emphasize a prepubertal body shape, those that require contour-revealing clothing for competition, those that require endurance, and those that use weight categories for participation. Such sports include gymnastics, figure skating, swimming, distance running, cycling, cross-country skiing, track, volleyball, rowing, horse racing, and cheerleading.

The female athlete triad can be life-threatening, and health professionals are taking it seriously. Typical signs of the eating disorders that trigger the condition are extreme weight loss, dry skin, loss of hair, brittle fingernails, cold hands and feet, low blood pressure and heart rate, swelling around the ankles and hands, and weakening of the bones. Female athletes who have repeated stress fractures may be suffering from the condition. Early intervention is the key to stopping this series of interrelated conditions. Unfortunately, once the condition has progressed, long-term consequences, especially bone loss, are unavoidable. Teenagers may need only to learn about good eating habits; college-age women with a long-standing problem may require intensive psychological counseling.

SOURCES: Beals, K. A., and N. L. Meyer. 2007. Female athlete triad update. *Clinics in Sports Medicine* 26(1): 69–89. Brunet, M. 2005. Female athlete triad. *Clinics in Sports Medicine* 24(3): 623–636. Art: Adapted from Yeager, K. K., et al. 1993. The female athlete triad: Disordered eating, amenorrhea, osteoporosis. *Medicine and Science in Sports and Exercise* 25:775–777. Reprinted by permission of Lippincott Williams and Wilkins.

mass index is also based on the concept that weight should be proportional to height. BMI is a fairly accurate measure of the health risks of body weight for average (nonathletic) people, and it is easy to calculate and rate. Researchers frequently use BMI in conjunction with waist circumference in studies that examine the health risks associated with body weight.

Because BMI doesn't distinguish between fat weight and fat-free weight, however, it can be inaccurate for some groups. For example, athletes who weight train have more muscle mass than average people and may be classified as overweight by the BMI scale; because their "excess" weight is in the form of muscle, however, it is healthy. Further, BMI is not particularly useful for tracking changes in body composition—gains in muscle mass and losses of fat. Women are likely to have more body fat for a given BMI than men. If you are an athlete, a serious weight trainer, or a person of short stature, do not use BMI as your primary means of assessing whether your current weight is healthy; instead, try one of the methods described in the next section for estimating percent body fat.

BMI is calculated by dividing your body weight (expressed in kilograms) by the square of your height (expressed in meters). The following example is for a

TERMS

amenorrhea Absent or infrequent menstruation, sometimes related to low levels of body fat and excessive quantity or intensity of exercise.

body mass index (BMI) A measure of relative body weight correlating highly with more direct measures of body fat, calculated by dividing total body weight (in kilograms) by the square of body height (in meters).

female athlete triad A condition consisting of three interrelated disorders: abnormal eating patterns (and excessive exercising) followed by lack of menstrual periods (amenorrhea) and decreased bone density (premature osteoporosis).

Table 6.1 Body Mass Index (BMI) Classification and Disease Risk

Classification	BMI (kg/m^2)	Obesity Class	Disease Risk Relative to Normal Weight and Waist Circumference*: Men ≤ 40 in. (102 cm) Women ≤ 35 in. (88 cm)	> 40 in. (102 cm) > 35 in. (88 cm)
Underweight**	<18.5		—	—
Normal[†]	18.5–24.9		—	—
Overweight	25.0–29.9		Increased	High
Obesity	30.0–34.9	I	High	Very high
	35.0–39.9	II	Very high	Very high
Extreme obesity	≥40.0	III	Extremely high	Extremely high

*Disease risk for type 2 diabetes, hypertension, and cardiovascular disease. The waist circumference cutoff points for increased risk are 40 inches (102 cm) for men and 35 inches (88 cm) for women.

**Research suggests that a low BMI can be healthy in some cases, as long as it is not the result of smoking, an eating disorder, or an underlying disease process. A BMI of 17.5 or less is sometimes used as a diagnostic criterion for the eating disorder anorexia nervosa.

†Increased waist circumference can also be a marker for increased risk, even in persons of normal weight.

SOURCE: Adapted from National Heart, Lung, and Blood Institute. 1998. *Clinical Guidelines on the Identification, Evaluation, and Treatment of Overweight and Obesity in Adults: The Evidence Report.* Bethesda, Md.: National Institutes of Health.

person who is 5 feet, 3 inches tall (63 inches) and weighs 130 pounds:

1. Divide body weight in pounds by 2.2 to convert weight to kilograms:

   $130 \div 2.2 = 59.1$

2. Multiply height in inches by 0.0254 to convert height to meters:

   $63 \times 0.0254 = 1.6$

3. Multiply the result of step 2 by itself to get the square of the height measurement:

   $1.6 \times 1.6 = 2.56$

4. Divide the result of step 1 by the result of step 3 to determine BMI:

   $59.1 \div 2.56 = 23$

An alternative equation, based on pounds and inches, is

$$BMI = [weight / (height \times height)] \times 703$$

Space for your own calculations can be found in Lab 6.1, and a complete BMI chart appears in Lab 6.2.

Under guidelines from the National Institutes of Health (NIH), a person is classified as overweight if he or she has a BMI of 25 or above and obese if he or she has a BMI of 30 or above (Table 6.1). More than 60% of American adults have a BMI of 25 or above. At high values of BMI (over 25), the risk of arthritis, diabetes, hypertension, endometrial cancer, and other disorders increases substantially. The increased risk of type 2 diabetes at even fairly low values of BMI, especially among women, is of particular concern (Figure 6.3).

In classifying the health risks associated with overweight and obesity, the NIH guidelines consider body fat distribution and other disease risk factors in addition to BMI. As described earlier, excess fat in the abdomen is of greater concern than excess fat in other areas. Methods of assessing body fat distribution are discussed later in the chapter; the NIH guidelines use measurement of waist

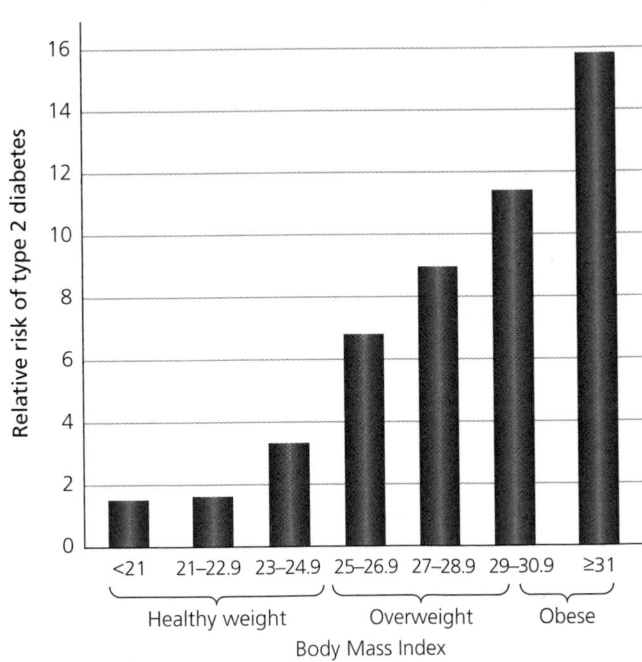

FIGURE 6.3 Body mass index (BMI) and risk of type 2 diabetes in women. The risk of diabetes goes up even for women at the high end of the healthy BMI range, but it is extremely high in overweight and obese women.

SOURCE: Hankinson, S. E., et al. 2001. *Healthy Women, Healthy Lives: A Guide to Preventing Disease from the Landmark Nurses' Health Study.* New York: Simon and Schuster.

circumference (see Table 6.1). At a given level of overweight, people with a large waist circumference and/or additional disease risk factors are at greater risk for health problems. For example, a man with a BMI of 27, a waist circumference of more than 40 inches, and high blood pressure is at greater risk for health problems than another man who has a BMI of 27 but has a smaller waist circumference and no other risk factors.

Thus, optimal BMI for good health depends on many factors; if your BMI is 25 or above, consult a physician for help in determining a healthy BMI for you. Despite its widespread use, BMI does have limitations. Although it is good for large population studies, it is less useful for measuring changes in body composition in individuals.

Estimating Percent Body Fat

Assessing body composition involves estimating percent body fat. The only method for directly measuring the percentage body weight that is fat is autopsy—the dissection and chemical analysis of the body. However, there are indirect techniques that can provide an estimate of percent body fat. One of the most accurate is underwater weighing. Other techniques include skinfold measurements, the Bod Pod, bioelectrical impedance analysis, and dual-energy X-ray absorptiometry.

All of these methods have a margin of error, so it is important not to focus too much on precise values. For example, underwater weighing has a margin of error of about ±3%, meaning that if a person's percent body fat is actually 17%, the test result may be between 14% and 20%. The results of different methods may also vary, so if you plan to track changes in body composition over time, be sure to use the same method each time to perform the assessment. Table 6.2 provides estimated ranges for healthy percent body fat.

Table 6.2 Percent Body Fat Classification, by Age and Sex

	Percent Body Fat (%)		
	20–39 Years	40–59 Years	60–79 Years
Women			
Essential*	8–12	8–12	8–12
Low/athletic**	13–20	13–22	13–23
Recommended	21–32	23–33	24–35
Overfat†	33–38	34–39	36–41
Obese†	≥39	≥40	≥42
Men			
Essential*	3–5	3–5	3–5
Low/athletic**	6–7	6–10	6–12
Recommended	8–19	11–21	13–24
Overfat†	20–24	22–27	25–29
Obese†	≥25	≥28	≥30

Note: The cutoffs for recommended, overfat, and obese ranges in this table are based on a study that linked BMI classifications from the National Institutes of Health with predicted percent body fat (measured using dual energy X-ray absorptiometry).

*Essential body fat is necessary for the basic functioning of the body.

**Percent body fat in the low/athletic range may be appropriate for some people as long as it is not the result of illness or disordered eating habits.

†Health risks increase as percent body fat exceeds the recommended range.

SOURCES: Gallagher, D., et al. 2000. Healthy percentage body fat ranges: An approach for developing guidelines based on body mass index. *American Journal of Clinical Nutrition* 72: 694–701. American College of Sports Medicine. 2006. *ACSM's Resource Manual for Guidelines for Exercise Testing and Prescription*, 5th ed. Philadelphia: Lippincott Williams and Wilkins.

Underwater Weighing In hydrostatic (underwater) weighing, an individual is submerged and weighed under water. The percentages of fat and fat-free weight are calculated from body density. Muscle has a higher density and fat a lower density than water (1.1 grams per cubic centimeter for fat-free mass, 0.91 gram per cubic centimeter for fat, and 1 gram per cubic centimeter for water). Therefore, fat people tend to float and weigh less under water, and lean people tend to sink and weigh more under water. Most university exercise physiology departments or sports medicine laboratories have an underwater weighing facility. If you want an accurate assessment of your body composition, find a place that does underwater weighing.

Skinfold Measurements Skinfold measurement is a simple, inexpensive, and practical way to assess body composition. Skinfold measurements can be used to assess body composition because equations can link the thickness of skinfolds at various sites to percent body fat calculations from more precise laboratory techniques.

Skinfold assessment typically involves measuring the thickness of skinfolds at several different sites on the body. You can sum up the skinfold values as an indirect measure of body fatness. For example, if you plan to create a fitness (and dietary change) program to improve body composition, you can compare the sum of skinfold values over time as an indicator of your program's progress and of improvements in body composition. You can also plug your skinfold values into equations like those in Lab 6.1 that predict percent body fat. When using these equations, however, it is important to remember that they have a fairly substantial margin of error (±4% if performed by a skilled technician)—so don't focus too much on specific values. The sum represents only a relative measure of body fatness.

Skinfolds are measured with a device called a **caliper,** which is a pair of spring-loaded, calibrated jaws. High-quality calipers are made of metal and have parallel jaw surfaces and constant spring tension. Inexpensive plastic calipers are also available; to ensure accuracy, plastic calipers should be spring-loaded and have metal jaws. Refer to Lab 6.1 for instructions on how to take skinfold measurements.

Taking accurate measurements with calipers requires patience, experience, and considerable practice. It's best to take several measurements at each site (or have several different people take each measurement) to help ensure accuracy. Be sure to take the measurements in the exact location called for in the procedure. Because the amount of water in your body changes during the day, skinfold measurements taken in the morning and evening often differ. If you repeat the measurements in the future to track changes in your body composition, measure skinfolds at approximately the same time of day.

The Bod Pod The Bod Pod, a small chamber containing computerized sensors, measures body composition by air displacement rather than water displacement; the technical name of the technique is *plethysmography.* It determines the percentage of fat by calculating how much air is displaced by the person sitting inside the chamber. The Bod Pod has an error rate of about ±2–4% in determining percent body fat.

Bioelectrical Impedance Analysis (BIA) The BIA technique works by sending a small electrical current through the body and measuring the body's resistance to it. Fat-free tissues, where most body water is located, are good conductors of electrical current, whereas fat is not. Thus, the amount of resistance to electrical current is related to the amount of fat-free tissue in the body (the lower the resistance, the greater the fat-free mass) and can be used to estimate percent body fat.

Bioelectrical impedance analysis has an error rate of about ±4–5%. To reduce error, follow the manufacturer's instructions carefully and avoid overhydration or underhydration (more or less body water than normal). Because measurement varies with the type of BIA analyzer, use the same instrument to compare measurements over time.

Advanced Techniques: DEXA and TOBEC Dual-energy X-ray absorptiometry (DEXA) works by measuring

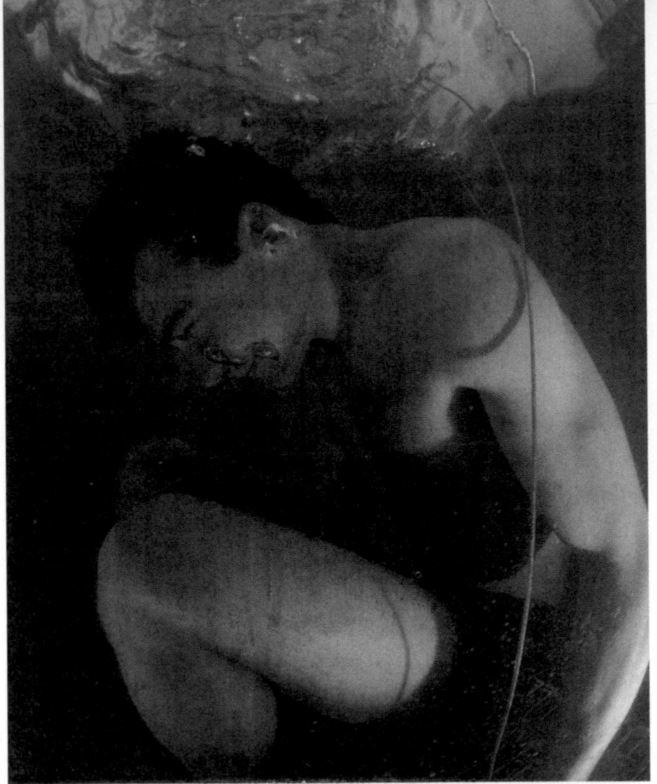

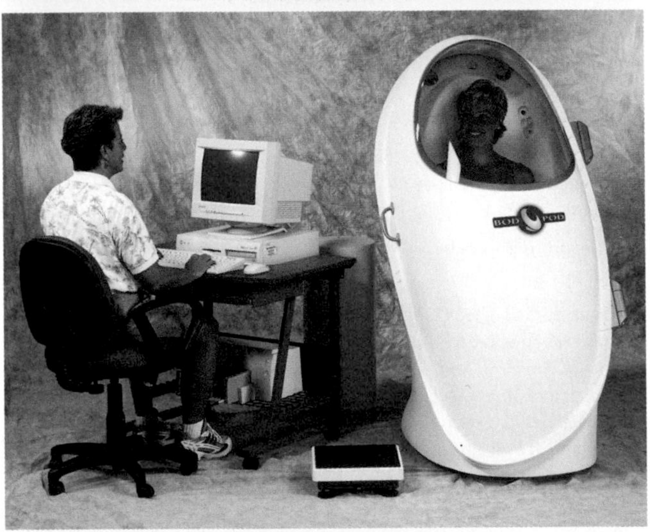

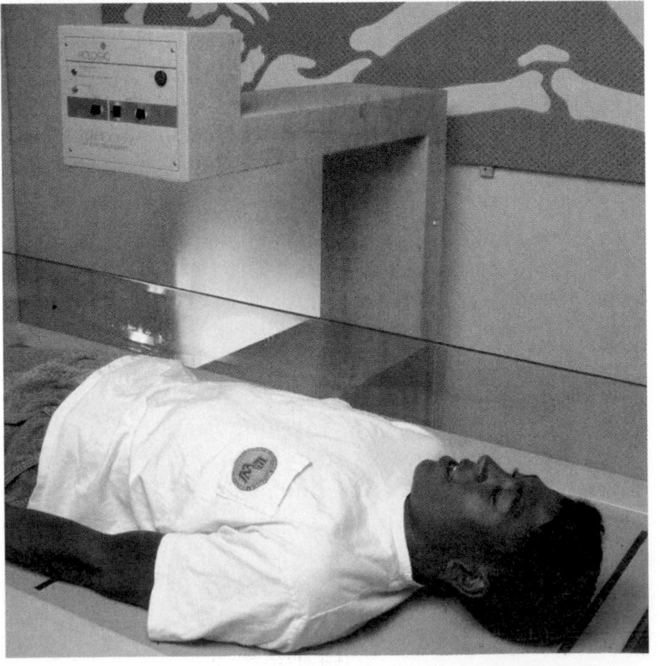

In underwater weighing (top), percent body fat is calculated from body density; muscle has a higher density than water, so people with more muscle weigh relatively more under water. The Bod Pod (middle) measures air displacement, which can be used to calculate percent body fat. DEXA (bottom) uses high- and low-energy X-ray beams to measure fat and lean tissue.

QUESTIONS FOR CRITICAL THINKING AND REFLECTION

Calculate your BMI using the formula given in the chapter, and compare it with the BMIs of several of your classmates. Do the results surprise you? How well do you think BMI reflects body composition? Why do you think it is such a commonly used measure?

MOTIVATION BOOSTER

Monitor your progress—your way. If changing your body composition is a goal, choose a method of monitoring your progress that works for you. For some people, weighing themselves frequently is discouraging and actually reduces their motivation. In some cases, it even promotes eating disorders. For other people, though, weighing is highly motivating and keeps their program on track. If weighing doesn't work for you, use another measure of progress, such as the amount of physical activity you incorporate into your day. Changing your body composition is a long-term process, so work toward short-term goals and focus on what is motivating for you.

the tissue absorption of high- and low-energy X-ray beams; studies thus far indicate that it has an error rate of about ±2%. Total body electrical conductivity (TOBEC) estimates lean body mass by passing a body through a magnetic field. Some fitness centers and sports medicine research facilities offer these body composition assessment techniques.

Assessing Body Fat Distribution

Researchers have studied many different methods for measuring body fat distribution. Two of the simplest to perform are waist circumference measurement and waist-to-hip ratio calculation. In the first method, you measure your waist circumference; in the second, you divide your waist circumference by your hip circumference. Waist circumference has been found to be a better indicator of abdominal fat than waist-to-hip ratio. More research is needed to determine the precise degree of risk associated with specific values for these two assessments of body fat distribution. However, as noted earlier, a total waist measurement of more than 40 inches (102 cm) for men and 35 inches (88 cm) for women and a waist-to-hip ratio above 0.94 for young men and 0.82 for young women are associated with a significantly increased risk of heart disease and diabetes. Lab 6.1 shows you how to measure your body fat distribution.

SETTING BODY COMPOSITION GOALS

If assessment tests indicate that fat loss would be beneficial for your health, your first step is to establish a goal. You can use the ratings in Table 6.1 or Table 6.2 to choose a target value for BMI or percent body fat (depending on which assessment you completed).

Make sure your goal is realistic and will ensure good health. Genetics limits your capacity to change your body composition, and few people can expect to develop the body of a fashion model or competitive bodybuilder. However, you can improve your body composition through a program of regular exercise and a healthy diet. If your body composition is in or close to the recommended range, you may want to set a lifestyle goal rather than a specific percent body fat or BMI goal. For example, you might set a goal of increasing your daily physical activity from 20 to 60 minutes or beginning a program of weight training, and then let any improvements in body composition occur as a secondary result of your primary target (physical activity). Remember, a lifestyle that includes regular exercise may be more important for health than trying to reach any ideal weight.

If you are significantly overfat or if you have known risk factors for disease (such as high blood pressure or high cholesterol), consult your physician to determine a body composition goal for your individual risk profile. For people who are obese, small losses of body weight (5–15%) over a 6–12 month period can result in significant health improvements.

Once you've established a body composition goal, you can then set a target range for body weight. Although body weight is not an accurate method of assessing body composition, it's a useful method for tracking progress in a program to change body composition. If you're losing a small or moderate amount of weight and exercising, you're probably losing fat while building muscle mass. Lab 6.2 will help you determine a range for recommended body weight.

Using percent body fat or BMI will generate a fairly accurate target body weight for most people. However, it's best not to stick rigidly to a recommended body weight calculated from any formula; individual genetic, cultural, and lifestyle factors are also important. Decide whether the body weight that the formulas generate for you is realistic, meets all your goals, is healthy, *and* is reasonable for you to maintain.

TERMS

caliper A pressure-sensitive measuring instrument with two jaws that can be adjusted to determine thickness.

MAKING CHANGES IN BODY COMPOSITION

Chapter 9 includes specific strategies for losing or gaining weight and improving body composition. In general, lifestyle should be your focus—regular physical activity, endurance exercise, strength training, and a moderate energy intake. Making significant cuts in food intake in order to lose weight and body fat is a difficult strategy to maintain; focusing on increased physical activity is a better approach for many people. In studies of people who have lost weight and maintained the loss, physical activity was the key to long-term success.

You can track your progress toward your target body composition by checking your body weight regularly. Also, focus on how much energy you have and how your clothes fit.

To get a more accurate idea of your progress, you should directly reassess your body composition occasionally during your program: Body composition changes as weight changes. Losing a lot of weight usually includes losing some muscle mass no matter how hard a person exercises, partly because carrying less weight requires the muscular system to bear a smaller burden. (Conversely, a large gain in weight without exercise still causes some gain in muscle mass because muscles are working harder to carry the extra weight.)

TIPS FOR TODAY AND THE FUTURE

A wellness lifestyle can lead naturally to a body composition that is healthy and appropriate for you.

RIGHT NOW YOU CAN

- Find out what types of body composition assessment techniques are available at facilities on your campus or in your community.
- Do 15 minutes of physical activity—walk, jog, bike, swim, or climb stairs.
- Drink a glass of water instead of a soda, and include a high-fiber food such as whole-grain bread or cereal, popcorn, apples, berries, or beans in your next snack or meal.

IN THE FUTURE YOU CAN

- Think about your image of the ideal body type for your sex. Consider where your idea comes from, whether you use this image to judge your own body, and whether it is a realistic goal for you. Write down five positive things about your body.
- Be aware of media messages (especially visual images) that make you feel embarrassed or insecure about your body. Remind yourself that these messages are usually designed to sell a product; they should not form the basis of your body image.

SUMMARY

- The human body is composed of fat-free mass (which includes bone, muscle, organ tissues, and connective tissues) and body fat (essential and nonessential).
- Having too much body fat has negative health consequences, especially in terms of cardiovascular disease and diabetes. Distribution of fat is also a significant factor in health.
- A fit and healthy-looking body, with the right body composition for a particular person, develops from habits of proper nutrition and exercise.
- Measuring body weight is not an accurate way to assess body composition because it does not differentiate between muscle weight and fat weight.
- Body mass index (calculated from weight and height measurements) can help classify the health risks associated with overweight. BMI is sometimes inaccurate, however, particularly in muscular people.
- Techniques for estimating percent body fat include underwater weighing, skinfold measurements, the Bod Pod, bioelectrical impedance analysis, DEXA, and TOBEC.
- Body fat distribution can be assessed through waist measurement or the waist-to-hip ratio.
- Recommended body composition and weight can be determined by choosing a target BMI or target body fat percentage. Keep heredity in mind when setting a goal, and focus on positive changes in lifestyle.

FOR FURTHER EXPLORATION

BOOKS

Bray, G. A., and C. A. Bray. 2002. *An Atlas of Obesity and Weight Control.* London: CRC Press. *Provides detailed information about assessment, classification, and treatment of obesity.*

Heyward, V. H. 2006. *Advanced Fitness Assessment and Exercise Prescription,* 5th ed. Champaign, Ill.: Human Kinetics. *Detailed coverage of assessing body composition, fitness, flexibility, and other aspects of fitness.*

Lean, M., et al. 2007. *ABC of Obesity.* Boston: Blackwell Publishing Limited. *Examines the impact of obesity on the average person's life and discusses some of the most current options for preventing and treating obesity.*

Nathan, D. M., and L. Delahanty. 2006. *Beating Diabetes: A Harvard Medical School Book.* New York: McGraw-Hill. *Provides information on identifying and changing lifestyle behaviors that contribute to the development and worsening of diabetes.*

ORGANIZATIONS AND WEB SITES

American Diabetes Association. Provides information, a free newsletter, and referrals to local support groups; the Web site includes an online diabetes risk assessment.
800-342-2383
http://www.diabetes.org

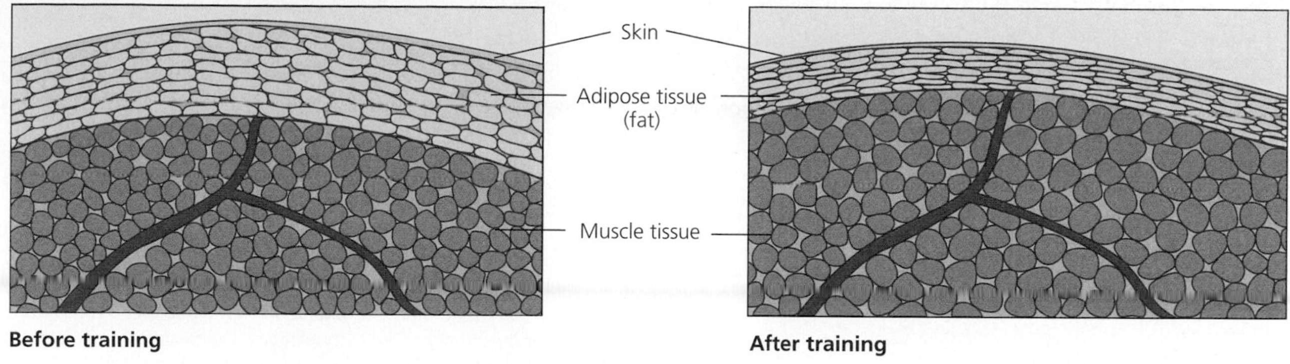

Effects of exercise on body composition. Endurance exercise and strength training reduce body fat and increase muscle mass.

Q Is spot reducing effective?

A Spot reducing refers to attempts to lose body fat in specific parts of the body by doing exercises for those parts. Danish researchers have shown that fat use increases in adipose tissue surrounding active muscle, but it is not known if short-term fat use helps reduce fat in specific sites. Most studies show that spot-reducing exercises contribute to fat loss only to the extent that they burn calories. The best way to reduce fat in any specific area is to create an overall negative energy balance: Take in less energy (food) than you use up through exercise and metabolism.

Q How does exercise affect body composition?

A Cardiorespiratory endurance exercise burns calories, thereby helping create a negative energy balance. Weight training does not use many calories and therefore is of little use in creating a negative energy balance. However, weight training increases muscle mass, which maintains a high metabolic rate (the body's energy level) and helps improve body composition. To minimize body fat and increase muscle mass, thereby improving body composition, combine cardiorespiratory endurance exercise and weight training (see figure).

Q Are people who have a desirable body composition physically fit?

A Having a healthy body composition is not necessarily associated with overall fitness. For example, many bodybuilders have very little body fat but have poor cardiorespiratory capacity and flexibility. Some athletes, such as NFL linemen, weigh 300 pounds or more; they have to lose the weight when they retire if they don't want to jeopardize their health.To be fit, you must rate high on all the components of fitness.

Q What is liposuction, and will it help me lose body fat?

A Suction lipectomy, popularly known as liposuction, has become the most popular type of elective surgery in the world. The procedure involves removing limited amounts of fat from specific areas. Typically, no more than 2.5 kilograms (5.5 pounds) of adipose tissue is removed at a time. The procedure is usually successful if the amount of excess fat is limited and skin elasticity is good. The procedure is most effective if integrated into a program of dietary restriction and exercise. Side effects include infection, dimpling, and wavy skin contours. Liposuction has a death rate of 1 in 5000 patients, primarily from pulmonary thromboembolism (a blood clot in the lungs) or fat embolism (circulatory blockage caused by a dislodged piece of fat). Other serious complications include shock, bleeding, and impaired blood flow to vital organs.

Q What is cellulite, and how do I get rid of it?

A Cellulite is the name commonly given to ripply, wavy fat deposits that collect just under the skin. The "cottage cheese" appearance stems from the breakdown of tissues supporting the fat. These rippling fat deposits are really the same as fat deposited anywhere else in the body. The only way to control them is to create a negative energy balance—burn up more calories than are taken in. There are no creams or lotions that will rub away surface (subcutaneous) fat deposits, and spot reducing is also ineffective. The solution is sensible eating habits and exercise.

For more Common Questions Answered about body composition, visit the Online Learning Center. 

Methods of Body Composition Analysis Tutorials. Provides information about body composition assessment techniques, including underwater weighing, BIA, and DEXA.

http://nutrition.uvm.edu/bodycomp

National Heart, Lung, and Blood Institute. Provides information on the latest federal obesity standards and a BMI calculator.

http://www.nhlbi.nih.gov/about/oei/index.htm

National Institute of Diabetes and Digestive and Kidney Diseases Weight-Control Information Network. Provides information about adult obesity: how it is defined and assessed, the risk factors associated with it, and its causes.

877-946-4627

http://win.niddk.nih.gov

USDA Food and Nutrition Information Center: Weight and Obesity. Provides links to recent reports and studies on the issue of obesity among Americans.

http://www.nal.usda.gov/fnic/reports/obesity.html

See also the listings for Chapters 2, 8, and 9.

SELECTED BIBLIOGRAPHY

American College of Sports Medicine. 2006. *ACSM's Resource Manual for Guidelines for Exercise Testing and Prescription,* 5th ed. Philadelphia: Lippincott Williams and Wilkins.

Anderson, D. E. 2007. Reliability of air displacement plethysmography. *Journal of Strength and Conditioning Research* 21(1): 169–172.

Bigaard, J., et al. 2005. Waist circumference and body composition in relation to all-cause mortality in middle-aged men and women. *International Journal of Obesity and Related Metabolic Disorders* 29: 778–784.

Centers for Disease Control and Prevention. 2005. *Frequently Asked Questions About Calculating Obesity-Related Risk* (http://www.cdc.gov/pdf/frequently_asked_questions_about_calculating_obesity-related_risk.pdf; retrieved May 21, 2007).

Centers for Disease Control and Prevention. 2005. National Diabetes Fact Sheet (http://www.cdc.gov/diabetes/pubs/general.htm; retrieved May 21, 2007).

Ekelund, U., S. J. Griffin, and N. J. Wareham. 2007. Physical activity and metabolic risk in individuals with a family history of type 2 diabetes. *Diabetes Care* 30(2): 337–342.

Flegal, K. M., et al. 2007. Cause-specific excess deaths associated with underweight, overweight, and obesity. *Journal of the American Medical Association* 298 (17): 2028–2037.

Frisard, M. I., F. L. Greenway, and J. P. Delany. 2005. Comparison of methods to assess body composition changes during a period of weight loss. *Obesity Research* 13: 845–854.

Gale, C. R., et al. 2007. Grip strength, body composition, and mortality. *International Journal of Epidemiology* 36(1): 228–235.

Green, J. S., et al. 2004. The effects of exercise training on abdominal visceral fat, body composition, and indicators of the metabolic syndrome in postmenopausal women with and without estrogen replacement therapy: The HERITAGE family study. *Metabolism* 53: 1192–1196.

Guida, B., et al. 2007. Bioelectrical impedance analysis and age-related differences of body composition in the elderly. *Nutrition, Metabolism, and Cardiovascular Disease* 17(3): 175–180.

Holten, M. K., et al. 2004. Strength training increases insulin-mediated glucose uptake, GLUT4 content, and insulin signaling in skeletal muscle in patients with type 2 diabetes. *Diabetes* 53(2): 294–305.

Houston, D. K., et al. 2007. The association between weight history and physical performance in the Health, Aging and Body Composition Study. *International Journal of Obesity.* (Epub ahead of print.)

Hussey, J., et al. 2007. Relationship between the intensity of physical activity, cardiorespiratory fitness and body composition in 7–10-year-old Dublin children. *British Journal of Sports Medicine* 41(5): 311–316.

Janiszewski, P. M., and R. Ross. 2007. Physical activity in the treatment of obesity: Beyond body weight reduction. *Applied Physiology, Nutrition, and Metabolism* 32(3): 512–522.

Joyner, M. J. 2005. Muscle strength, body composition, hormones, and aging. *Exercise and Sport Sciences Reviews* 33: 61–62.

Krakauer, J. C., et al. 2004. Body composition profiles derived from dual-energy X-ray absorptiometry, total body scan, and mortality. *Preventive Cardiology* 7: 109–115.

Liu, J., T. J. Wade, and H. Tan. 2007. Cardiovascular risk factors and anthropometric measurements of adolescent body composition: A cross-sectional analysis of the Third National Health and Nutrition Examination Survey. *International Journal of Obesity* 31(1): 59–64.

Malina, R. M. 2007. Body composition in athletes: Assessment and estimated fatness. *Clinics in Sports Medicine* 26(1): 37–68.

Mattsson, S., and B. J. Thomas. 2006. Development of methods for body composition studies. *Physics in Medicine and Biology* 51(13): R203–228.

Ode, J. J., et al. 2007. Body mass index as a predictor of percent fat in college athletes and nonathletes. *Medicine and Science in Sports and Exercise* 39(3): 403–409.

Plank, L. D. 2005. Dual-energy X-ray absorptiometry and body composition. *Current Opinion in Clinical Nutrition and Metabolic Care* 8: 305–309.

Redman, L. M., et al. 2007. Effect of calorie restriction with or without exercise on body composition and fat distribution. *Journal of Clinical Endocrinology and Metabolism* 92(3): 865–872.

Stookey, J. D., L. S. Adair, and B. M. Popkin. 2005. Do protein and energy intakes explain long-term changes in body composition? *Journal of Nutrition, Health and Aging* 9: 5–17.

Varady, K., et al. 2007. Validation of hand-held bioelectrical impedance analysis with magnetic resonance imaging for the assessment of body composition overweight women. *American Journal of Human Biology* 19(3): 429–433.

Wong, S. L., et al. 2004. Cardiorespiratory fitness is associated with lower abdominal fat independent of body mass index. *Medicine and Science in Sports and Exercise* 36(2): 286–291.

Zhu, S., et al. 2005. Lifestyle behaviors associated with lower risk of having the metabolic syndrome. *Metabolism* 53(11): 1503–1511.

Name ______ Section ______ Date ______

LAB 6.1 Assessing Body Mass Index and Body Composition

Body Mass Index

Equipment

1. Weight scale
2. Tape measure or other means of measuring height

Instructions

Measure your height and weight, and record the results. Be sure to record the unit of measurement.

Height: ______ Weight: ______

Calculating BMI (see also the shortcut chart of BMI values in Lab 6.2)

1. Convert your body weight to kilograms by dividing your weight in pounds by 2.2.
   Body weight ______ lb ÷ 2.2 lb/kg = body weight ______ kg
2. Convert your height measurement to meters by multiplying your height in inches by 0.0254.
   Height ______ in. × 0.0254 m/in. = height ______ m
3. Square your height measurement.
   Height ______ m × height ______ m = height ______ m^2
4. BMI equals body weight in kilograms divided by height in meters squared (kg/m^2).
   Body weight ______ (from step 1) kg ÷ height ______ (from step 3) m^2 = BMI ______ kg/m^2

Rating Your BMI

Refer to the table for a rating of your BMI. Record the results below and on the final page of this lab.

Classification	BMI (kg/m^2)
Underweight	<18.5
Normal	18.5–24.9
Overweight	25.0–29.9
Obesity (I)	30.0–34.9
Obesity (II)	35.0–39.9
Extreme obesity (III)	≥40.0

(See complete version of table on p. 176 for additional information.)

BMI ______ kg/m^2

Classification (from table) ______

Skinfold Measurements

Equipment

1. Skinfold calipers
2. Partner to take measurements
3. Marking pen (optional)

Instructions

1. *Select and locate the correct sites for measurement.* All measurements should be taken on the right side of the body with the subject standing. Skinfolds are normally measured on the natural fold line of the skin, either vertically or at a slight angle. The skinfold measurement sites for males are chest, abdomen, and thigh; for females, triceps, suprailium, and thigh. If the person taking skinfold measurements is inexperienced, it may be helpful to mark the correct sites with a marking pen.

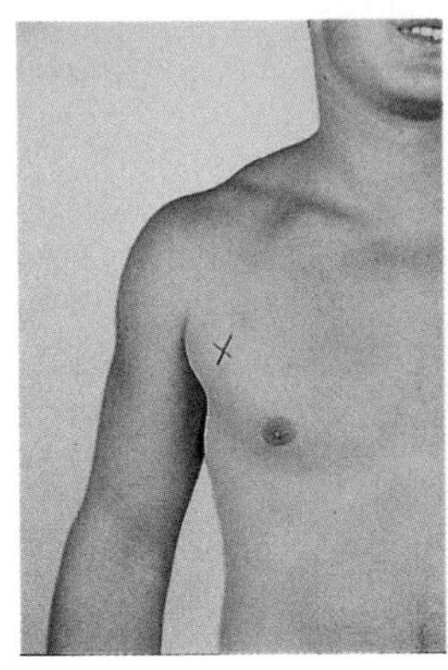

(a) Chest

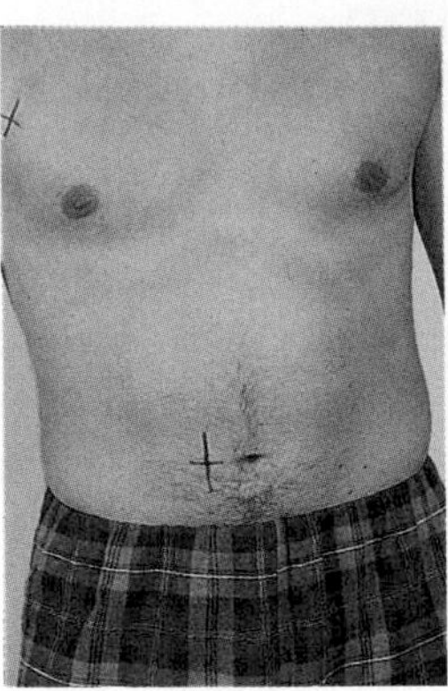

(b) Abdomen

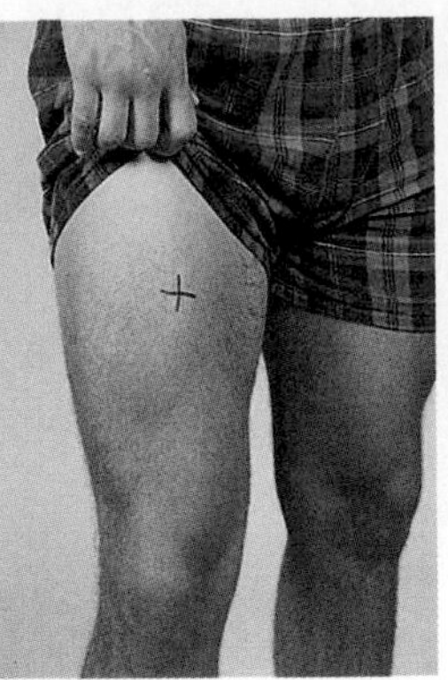

(c) Thigh

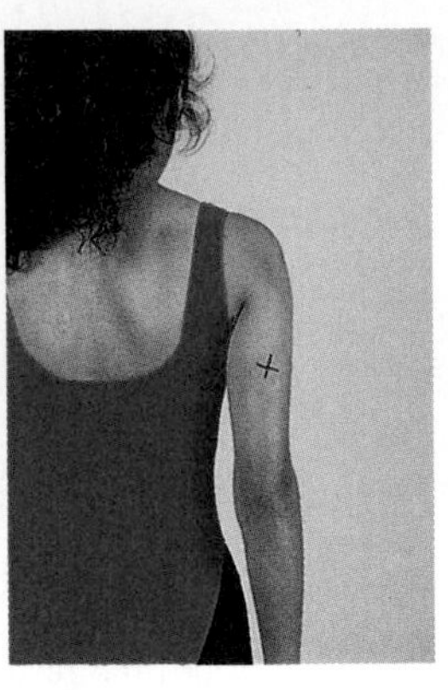

(d) Triceps

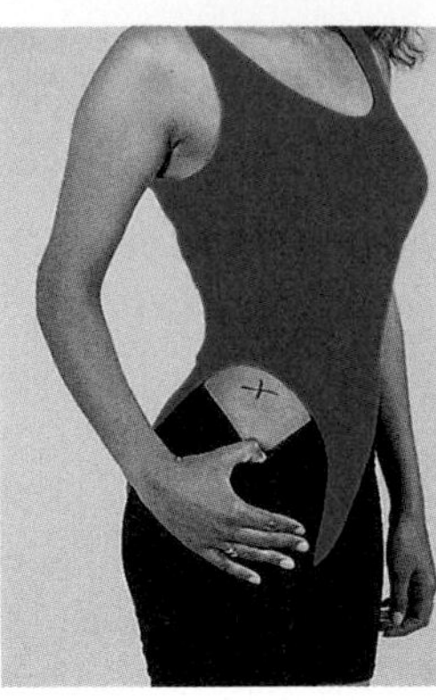

(e) Suprailium

(a) Chest. Pinch a diagonal fold halfway between the nipple and the shoulder crease. *(b) Abdomen.* Pinch a vertical fold about 1 inch to the right of the umbilicus (navel). *(c) Thigh.* Pinch a vertical fold midway between the top of the hipbone and the kneecap. *(d) Triceps.* Pinch a vertical skinfold on the back of the right arm midway between the shoulder and elbow. The arm should be straight and should hang naturally. *(e) Suprailium.* Pinch a fold at the top front of the right hipbone. The skinfold here is taken slightly diagonally according to the natural fold tendency of the skin.

2. *Measure the appropriate skinfolds.* Pinch a fold of skin between your thumb and forefinger. Pull the fold up so that no muscular tissue is included; don't pinch the skinfold too hard. Hold the calipers perpendicular to the fold and measure the skinfold about 0.25 inch away from your fingers. Allow the tips of the calipers to close on the skinfold and let the reading settle before marking it down. Take readings to the nearest half-millimeter. Continue to repeat the measurements until two consecutive measurements match, releasing and repinching the skinfold between each measurement. Make a note of the final measurement for each site.

Time of day of measurements: ____________

Men		*Women*	
Chest: ____________	mm	Triceps: ____________	mm
Abdomen: ____________	mm	Suprailium: ____________	mm
Thigh: ____________	mm	Thigh: ____________	mm

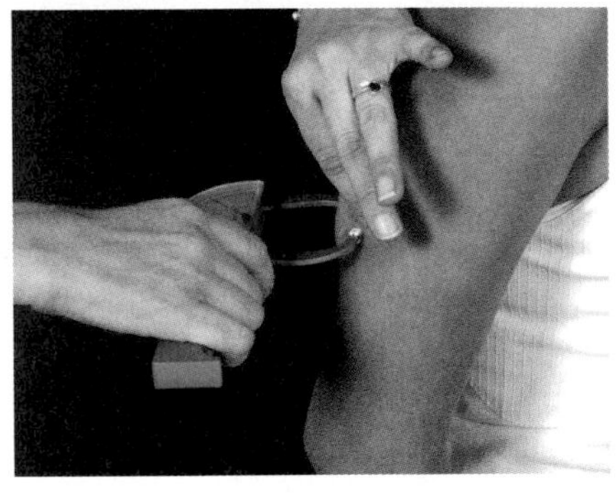

Determining Percent Body Fat

Add the measurements of your three skinfolds. Use this sum as a point of comparison for future assessments and/or find the percent body fat that corresponds to your total in the appropriate table. For example, a 19-year-old female with measurements of 16 mm, 19 mm, and 22 mm would have a skinfold sum of 57 mm; according to the table on p. 185, her percent body fat is 22.7.

Sum of three skinfolds: ____________ mm Percent body fat: ____________ %

Percent Body Fat Estimate for Women: Sum of Triceps, Suprailium, and Thigh Skinfolds

Sum of Skinfolds (mm)	Age								
	Under 22	*23–27*	*28–32*	*33–37*	*38–42*	*43–47*	*48–52*	*53–57*	*Over 57*
23–25	9.7	9.9	10.2	10.4	10.7	10.9	11.2	11.4	11.7
26–28	11.0	11.2	11.5	11.7	12.0	12.3	12.5	12.7	13.0
29–31	12.3	12.5	12.8	13.0	13.3	13.5	13.8	14.0	14.3
32–34	13.6	13.8	14.0	14.3	14.5	14.8	15.0	15.3	15.5
35–37	14.8	15.0	15.3	15.5	15.8	16.0	16.3	16.5	16.8
38–40	16.0	16.3	16.5	16.7	17.0	17.2	17.5	17.7	18.0
41–43	17.2	17.4	17.7	17.9	18.2	18.4	18.7	18.9	19.2
44–46	18.3	18.6	18.8	19.1	19.3	19.6	19.8	20.1	20.3
47–49	19.5	19.7	20.0	20.2	20.5	20.7	21.0	21.2	21.5
50–52	20.6	20.8	21.1	21.3	21.6	21.8	22.1	22.3	22.6
53–55	21.7	21.9	22.1	22.4	22.6	22.9	23.1	23.4	23.6
56–58	22.7	23.0	23.2	23.4	23.7	23.9	24.2	24.4	24.7
59–61	23.7	24.0	24.2	24.5	24.7	25.0	25.2	25.5	25.7
62–64	24.7	25.0	25.2	25.5	25.7	26.0	26.7	26.4	26.7
65–67	25.7	25.9	26.2	26.4	26.7	26.9	27.2	27.4	27.7
68–70	26.6	26.9	27.1	27.4	27.6	27.9	28.1	28.4	28.6
71–73	27.5	27.8	28.0	28.3	28.5	28.8	29.0	29.3	29.5
74–76	28.4	28.7	28.9	29.2	29.4	29.7	29.9	30.2	30.4
77–79	29.3	29.5	29.8	30.0	30.3	30.5	30.8	31.0	31.3
80–82	30.1	30.4	30.6	30.9	31.1	31.4	31.6	31.9	32.1
83–85	30.9	31.2	31.4	31.7	31.9	32.2	32.4	32.7	32.9
86–88	31.7	32.0	32.2	32.5	32.7	32.9	33.2	33.4	33.7
89–91	32.5	32.7	33.0	33.2	33.5	33.7	33.9	34.2	34.4
92–94	33.2	33.4	33.7	33.9	34.2	34.4	34.7	34.9	35.2
95–97	33.9	34.1	34.4	34.6	34.9	35.1	35.4	35.6	35.9
98–100	34.6	34.8	35.1	35.3	35.5	35.8	36.0	36.3	36.5
101–103	35.3	35.4	35.7	35.9	36.2	36.4	36.7	36.9	37.2
104–106	35.8	36.1	36.3	36.6	36.8	37.1	37.3	37.5	37.8
107–109	36.4	36.7	36.9	37.1	37.4	37.6	37.9	38.1	38.4
110–112	37.0	37.2	37.5	37.7	38.0	38.2	38.5	38.7	38.9
113–115	37.5	37.8	38.0	38.2	38.5	38.7	39.0	39.2	39.5
116–118	38.0	38.3	38.5	38.8	39.0	39.3	39.5	39.7	40.0
119–121	38.5	38.7	39.0	39.2	39.5	39.7	40.0	40.2	40.5
122–124	39.0	39.2	39.4	39.7	39.9	40.2	40.4	40.7	40.9
125–127	39.4	39.6	39.9	40.1	40.4	40.6	40.9	41.1	41.4
128–130	39.8	40.0	40.3	40.5	40.8	41.0	41.3	41.5	41.8

SOURCE: Jackson, A. S., and M. L. Pollock. 1985. Practical assessment of body composition. *The Physician and Sportsmedicine* 13(5): 76–90, Tables 6 & 7, pp. 86, 87.

Percent Body Fat Estimate for Men: Sum of Chest, Abdomen, and Thigh Skinfolds

Sum of Skinfolds (mm)	Age								
	Under 22	23–27	28–32	33–37	38–42	43–47	48–52	53–57	Over 57
8–10	1.3	1.8	2.3	2.9	3.4	3.9	4.5	5.0	5.5
11–13	2.2	2.8	3.3	3.9	4.4	4.9	5.5	6.0	6.5
14–16	3.2	3.8	4.3	4.8	5.4	5.9	6.4	7.0	7.5
17–19	4.2	4.7	5.3	5.8	6.3	6.9	7.4	8.0	8.5
20–22	5.1	5.7	6.2	6.8	7.3	7.9	8.4	8.9	9.5
23–25	6.1	6.6	7.2	7.7	8.3	8.8	9.4	9.9	10.5
26–28	7.0	7.6	8.1	8.7	9.2	9.8	10.3	10.9	11.4
29–31	8.0	8.5	9.1	9.6	10.2	10.7	11.3	11.8	12.4
32–34	8.9	9.4	10.0	10.5	11.1	11.6	12.2	12.8	13.3
35–37	9.8	10.4	10.9	11.5	12.0	12.6	13.1	13.7	14.3
38–40	10.7	11.3	11.8	12.4	12.9	13.5	14.1	14.6	15.2
41–43	11.6	12.2	12.7	13.3	13.8	14.4	15.0	15.5	16.1
44–46	12.5	13.1	13.6	14.2	14.7	15.3	15.9	16.4	17.0
47–49	13.4	13.9	14.5	15.1	15.6	16.2	16.8	17.3	17.9
50–52	14.3	14.8	15.4	15.9	16.5	17.1	17.6	18.2	18.8
53–55	15.1	15.7	16.2	16.8	17.4	17.9	18.5	19.1	19.7
56–58	16.0	16.5	17.1	17.7	18.2	18.8	19.4	20.0	20.5
59–61	16.9	17.4	17.9	18.5	19.1	19.7	20.2	20.8	21.4
62–64	17.6	18.2	18.8	19.4	19.9	20.5	21.1	21.7	22.2
65–67	18.5	19.0	19.6	20.2	20.8	21.3	21.9	22.5	23.1
68–70	19.3	19.9	20.4	21.0	21.6	22.2	22.7	23.3	23.9
71–73	20.1	20.7	21.2	21.8	22.4	23.0	23.6	24.1	24.7
74–76	20.9	21.5	22.0	22.6	23.2	23.8	24.4	25.0	25.5
77–79	21.7	22.2	22.8	23.4	24.0	24.6	25.2	25.8	26.3
80–82	22.4	23.0	23.6	24.2	24.8	25.4	25.9	26.5	27.1
83–85	23.2	23.8	24.4	25.0	25.5	26.1	26.7	27.3	27.9
86–88	24.0	24.5	25.1	25.7	26.3	26.9	27.5	28.1	28.7
89–91	24.7	25.3	25.9	26.5	27.1	27.6	28.2	28.8	29.4
92–94	25.4	26.0	26.6	27.2	27.8	28.4	29.0	29.6	30.2
95–97	26.1	26.7	27.3	27.9	28.5	29.1	29.7	30.3	30.9
98–100	26.9	27.4	28.0	28.6	29.2	29.8	30.4	31.0	31.6
101–103	27.5	28.1	28.7	29.3	29.9	30.5	31.1	31.7	32.3
104–106	28.2	28.8	29.4	30.0	30.6	31.2	31.8	32.4	33.0
107–109	28.9	29.5	30.1	30.7	31.3	31.9	32.5	33.1	33.7
110–112	29.6	30.2	30.8	31.4	32.0	32.6	33.2	33.8	34.4
113–115	30.2	30.8	31.4	32.0	32.6	33.2	33.8	34.5	35.1
116–118	30.9	31.5	32.1	32.7	33.3	33.9	34.5	35.1	35.7
119–121	31.5	32.1	32.7	33.3	33.9	34.5	35.1	35.7	36.4
122–124	32.1	32.7	33.3	33.9	34.5	35.1	35.8	36.4	37.0
125–127	32.7	33.3	33.9	34.5	35.1	35.8	36.4	37.0	37.6

SOURCE: Jackson, A. S., and M. L. Pollock. 1985. Practical assessment of body composition. *The Physician and Sportsmedicine* 13(5): 76–90, Tables 6 & 7, pp. 86, 87.

Rating Your Body Composition

Refer to the chart to rate your percent body fat. Record it below and in the chart at the end of this lab.

Rating: ___________

Percent Body Fat Classification

	Percent Body Fat (%)		
	20–39 Years	*40–59 Years*	*60–79 Years*
Women			
Essential*	8–12	8–12	8–12
Low/athletic**	13–20	13–22	13–23
Recommended	21–32	23–33	24–35
Overfat†	33–38	34–39	36–41
Obese†	≥39	≥40	≥42

	Percent Body Fat (%)		
	20–39 Years	*40–59 Years*	*60–79 Years*
Men			
Essential*	3–5	3–5	3–5
Low/athletic**	6–7	6–10	6–12
Recommended	8–19	11–21	13–24
Overfat†	20–24	22–27	25–29
Obese†	≥25	≥28	≥30

Note: The cutoffs for recommended, overfat, and obese ranges in this table are based on a study that linked body mass index classifications from the National Institutes of Health with predicted percent body fat (measured using dual-energy X-ray absorptiometry).

*Essential body fat is necessary for the basic functioning of the body.

**Percent body fat in the low/athletic range may be appropriate for some people as long as it is not the result of illness or disordered eating habits.

†Health risks increase as percent body fat exceeds the recommended range.

SOURCES: Gallagher, D., et al. 2000. Healthy percentage body fat ranges: An approach for developing guidelines based on body mass index. *American Journal of Clinical Nutrition* 72: 694–701. American College of Sports Medicine. 2006. *ACSM's Resource Manual for Guidelines for Exercise Testing and Prescription,* 5th ed. Philadelphia: Lippincott Williams and Wilkins.

Other Methods of Assessing Percent Body Fat

If you use a different method, record the name of the method and the result below and in the chart at the end of this lab. Find your body composition rating on the chart above.

Method used: ______________ Percent body fat: ______________ % Rating (from chart above): ______________

Waist Circumference and Waist-to-Hip Ratio

Equipment

1. Tape measure
2. Partner to take measurements

Preparation

Wear clothes that will not add significantly to your measurements.

Instructions

Stand with your feet together and your arms at your sides. Raise your arms only high enough to allow for taking the measurements. Your partner should make sure the tape is horizontal around the entire circumference and pulled snugly against your skin. The tape shouldn't be pulled so tight that it causes indentations in your skin. Record measurements to the nearest millimeter or one-sixteenth of an inch.

Waist. Measure at the smallest waist circumference. If you don't have a natural waist, measure at the level of your navel.
Waist measurement: ___________

Hip. Measure at the largest hip circumference. Hip measurement: ___________

Waist-to-Hip Ratio: You can use any unit of measurement (for example, inches or centimeters) as long as you're consistent. Waist-to-hip ratio equals waist measurement divided by hip measurement.

Waist-to-hip ratio: ___________ ÷ ___________ = ___________
(waist measurement) (hip measurement)

Determining Your Risk

The table below indicates values for waist circumference and waist-to-hip ratio above which the risk of health problems increases significantly. If your measurement or ratio is above either cutoff point, put a check on the appropriate line below and in the chart at the end of this lab.

Waist circumference: ____________ (✓ high risk) Waist-to-hip ratio: ____________ (✓ high risk)

Body Fat Distribution

Cutoff Points for High Risk

	Waist Circumference	*Waist-to-Hip Ratio*
Men	More than 40 in. (102 cm)	More than 0.94
Women	More than 35 in. (88 cm)	More than 0.82

SOURCES: National Heart, Lung, and Blood Institute. 1998. *Clinical Guidelines on the Identification, Evaluation, and Treatment of Overweight and Obesity in Adults: The Evidence Report.* Bethesda, Md.: National Institutes of Health. Heyward, V. H., and D. R. Wagner. 2004. *Applied Body Composition Assessment,* 2nd ed. Champaign, Ill.: Human Kinetics.

Rating Your Body Composition

Assessment	*Value*	*Classification*
BMI	____________ kg/m^2	____________
Skinfold measurements or alternative method of determining percent body fat Specify method: ____________	____________ % body fat	____________
Waist circumference Waist-to-hip ratio	____________ in. or cm ____________ (ratio)	____________ (✓ high risk) ____________ (✓ high risk)

Using Your Results

How did you score? Are you surprised by your ratings for body composition and body fat distribution? Are your current ratings in the range for good health? Are you satisfied with your current body composition? Why or why not?

If you're not satisfied, set a realistic goal for improvement:

What should you do next? Enter the results of this lab in the Preprogram Assessment column in Appendix D. If you've determined that you need to improve your body composition, set a specific goal by completing Lab 6.2, and then plan your program using the labs in Chapters 8 and 9. You can also refer to the weight management section of the Daily Fitness and Nutrition Journal on the Online Learning Center. After several weeks or months of an exercise and/or dietary change program, complete this lab again and enter the results in the Postprogram Assessment column of Appendix D. How do the results compare?

Name ______________________ Section ______________ Date ______________

LAB 6.2 Setting Goals for Target Body Weight

This lab is designed to help you set body weight goals based on a target BMI or percent body fat. If the results of Lab 6.1 indicate that a change in body composition would be beneficial for your health, you may want to complete this lab to help you set goals.

Remember, though, that a wellness lifestyle—including a balanced diet and regular exercise—is more important for your health than achieving any specific body weight, BMI, or percent body fat. You may want to set goals for improving your diet and increasing physical activity and let your body composition change as a result. If so, use the labs in Chapters 3, 4, 8, and 9 as your guides.

Equipment

Calculator (or pencil and paper for calculations)

Preparation

Determine percent body fat and/or calculate BMI as described in Lab 6.1. Keep track of height and weight as measured for these calculations.

Height: __________ Weight: __________

Instructions: Target Body Weight from Target BMI

Use the chart below to find the target body weight that corresponds to your target BMI. Find your height in the left column, and then move across the appropriate row until you find the weight that corresponds to your target BMI. Remember, BMI is only an indirect measurement of body composition. It is possible to improve body composition without any significant change in weight. For example, a weight training program may result in increased muscle mass and decreased fat mass without any change in overall weight. For this reason, you may want to set alternative or additional goals, such as improving the fit of your clothes or decreasing your waist measurement.

	<18.5 Underweight		18.5–24.9 Normal						25–29.9 Overweight					30–34.9 Obesity (Class I)					35–39.9 Obesity (Class II)					≥40 Extreme Obesity
BMI	17	18	19	20	21	22	23	24	25	26	27	28	29	30	31	32	33	34	35	36	37	38	39	40
Height	Body Weight (pounds)																							
4' 10"	81	86	91	96	101	105	110	115	120	124	129	134	139	144	148	153	158	163	168	172	177	182	187	192
4' 11"	84	89	94	99	104	109	114	119	124	129	134	139	144	149	154	159	163	168	173	178	183	188	193	198
5'	87	92	97	102	108	113	118	123	128	133	138	143	149	154	159	164	169	174	179	184	190	195	200	205
5' 1"	90	95	101	106	111	117	122	127	132	138	143	148	154	159	164	169	175	180	185	191	196	201	207	212
5' 2"	93	98	104	109	115	120	126	131	137	142	148	153	159	164	170	175	181	186	191	197	202	208	213	219
5' 3"	96	102	107	113	119	124	130	136	141	147	153	158	164	169	175	181	186	192	198	203	209	215	220	226
5' 4"	99	105	111	117	122	128	134	140	146	152	157	163	169	175	181	187	192	198	204	210	216	222	227	233
5' 5"	102	108	114	120	126	132	138	144	150	156	162	168	174	180	186	192	198	204	210	216	222	229	235	241
5' 6"	105	112	118	124	130	136	143	149	155	161	167	174	180	186	192	198	205	211	217	223	229	236	242	248
5' 7"	109	115	121	128	134	141	147	153	160	166	173	179	185	192	198	204	211	217	224	230	236	243	249	256
5' 8"	112	118	125	132	138	145	151	158	165	171	178	184	191	197	204	211	217	224	230	237	244	250	257	263
5' 9"	115	122	129	136	142	149	156	163	169	176	183	190	197	203	210	217	224	230	237	244	251	258	264	271
5' 10"	119	126	133	139	146	153	160	167	174	181	188	195	202	209	216	223	230	237	244	251	258	265	272	279
5' 11"	122	129	136	143	151	158	165	172	179	187	194	201	208	215	222	230	237	244	251	258	265	273	280	287
6'	125	133	140	148	155	162	170	177	184	192	199	207	214	221	229	236	243	251	258	266	273	280	288	295
6' 1"	129	137	144	152	159	167	174	182	190	197	205	212	220	228	235	243	250	258	265	273	281	288	296	303
6' 2"	132	140	148	156	164	171	179	187	195	203	210	218	226	234	242	249	257	265	273	281	288	296	304	312
6' 3"	136	144	152	160	168	176	184	192	200	208	216	224	232	240	248	256	264	272	280	288	296	304	312	320
6' 4"	140	148	156	164	173	181	189	197	206	214	222	230	238	247	255	263	271	280	288	296	304	312	321	329

SOURCE: Ratings from the National Heart, Lung, and Blood Institute. 1998. *Clinical Guidelines on the Identification, Evaluation, and Treatment of Overweight and Obesity in Adults.* Bethesda, Md.: National Institutes of Health.

Current BMI: ____________ Target BMI: ____________ Target body weight (from chart): ____________

Alternative/additional goals: ____

____

Note: You can calculate target body weight from target BMI more precisely by using the following formula: (1) convert your height measurement to meters, (2) square your height measurement, (3) multiply this number by your target BMI to get your target weight in kilograms, and (4) convert your target weight from kilograms to pounds:

1. Height ____________ in. × 0.0254 m/in. = height ____________ m
2. Height ____________ m × height ____________ m = ____________ m^2
3. Target BMI ____________ × height ____________ m^2 = target weight ____________ kg
4. Target weight ____________ kg × 2.2 lb/kg = target weight ____________ lb

Instructions: Target Body Weight from Target Body Fat Percentages

Use the formula below to determine the target body weight that corresponds to your target percent body fat.

Current percent body fat: ____________ Target percent body fat: ____________

Formula	*Example: 180-lb male, current percent body fat of 24%, goal of 21%*
1. To determine the fat weight in your body, multiply your current weight by percent body fat (determined through skinfold measurements and expressed as a decimal).	180 lb × 0.24 = 43.2 lb
2. Subtract the fat weight from your current weight to get your current fat-free weight.	180 lb − 43.2 lb = 136.8 lb
3. Subtract your target percent body fat from 1 to get target percent fat-free weight.	1 − 0.21 = 0.79
4. To get your target body weight, divide your fat-free weight by your target percent fat-free weight.	136.8 lb ÷ 0.79 = 173 lb

Note: Weight can be expressed in either pounds or kilograms, as long as the unit of measurement is used consistently.

1. Current body weight ____________ × percent body fat ____________ = fat weight ____________
2. Current body weight ____________ − fat weight ____________ = fat-free weight ____________
3. 1 − target percent body fat ____________ = target percent fat-free weight ____________
4. Fat-free weight ____________ ÷ target percent fat-free weight ____________ = target body weight ____________

Setting a Goal

Based on these calculations and other factors (including heredity, individual preference, and current health status), select a target weight or range of weights for yourself.

Target body weight: ____________

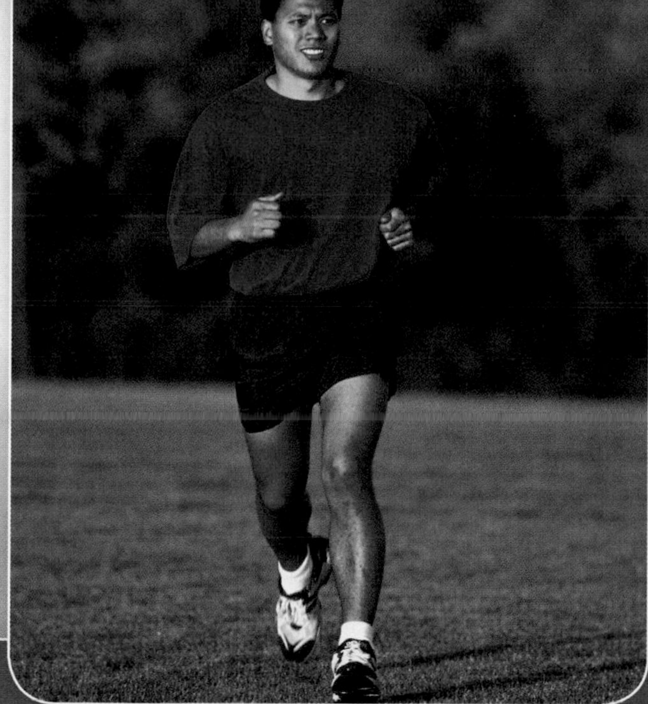

LOOKING AHEAD>>>>>

AFTER READING THIS CHAPTER, YOU SHOULD BE ABLE TO:

- Explain the steps for putting together a successful personal fitness program
- Describe strategies that can help you maintain a fitness program over the long term
- Tailor a fitness program to accommodate special health concerns and different life stages

PUTTING TOGETHER A COMPLETE FITNESS PROGRAM 7

TEST YOUR KNOWLEDGE

1. Which exercise will allow you to burn the greatest number of calories per pound, if performed vigorously?

a. aerobic dance
b. swimming
c. bicycling

2. Falling asleep in a boring class means a person needs more sleep.

True or false?

3. Exercise is not recommended for people with asthma or diabetes.

True or false?

ANSWERS

1. **b.** Of the three activities, swimming has the potential to burn 0.088 calories per pound of body weight, per minute of activity, when performed vigorously.
2. **TRUE.** A fully rested person may become bored during an uninteresting or monotonous event but will not fall asleep. Daytime sleepiness is a sign of inadequate sleep, which negatively affects health and athletic performance.
3. **FALSE.** Although special precautions may be needed, people with many types of chronic conditions can exercise safely and enjoy significant health benefits. Regular exercise reduces the risks of acute asthma attacks and improves insulin sensitivity.

FIT AND WELL ONLINE LEARNING CENTER www.mhhe.com/fahey

Visit the *Fit and Well* Online Learning Center for resources that will help you get the most out of your course!

- Study and review aids include practice quizzes, glossary flashcards, chapter summaries, learning objectives, PowerPoint presentations, Common Questions Answered, student handouts, crossword puzzles, Internet activities, and links to wellness Web sites.
- Behavior change tools include a daily fitness and nutrition journal, a behavior change workbook, sample behavior change plans, and blank behavior change logs to print and use.

Understanding the physiological basis and wellness benefits of health-related physical fitness, as explained in Chapters 1–6, is the first step toward creating a well-rounded exercise program. The next challenge is to combine activities into a program that develops all the fitness components and maintains motivation. This chapter presents a step-by-step procedure for creating and maintaining a well-rounded program. At the end of this chapter, you'll find sample programs based on popular activities. The structure these programs provide can be helpful if you're beginning an exercise program for the first time.

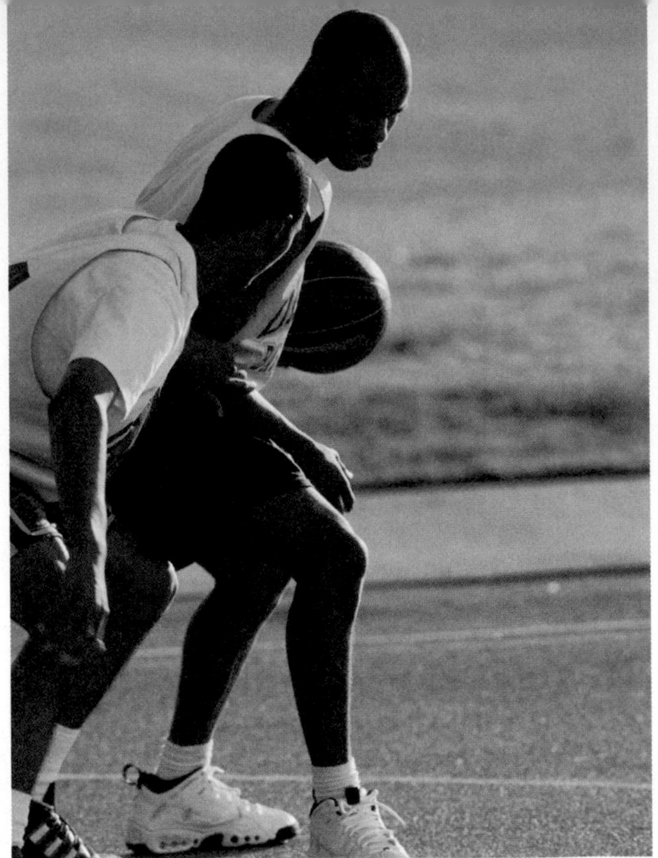

An overall fitness program includes activities to develop all the components of physical fitness.

DEVELOPING A PERSONAL FITNESS PLAN

If you're ready to create a complete fitness program based on the activities you enjoy most, begin by preparing the program plan and contract in Lab 7.1. By carefully developing your plan and signing a contract, you'll increase your chances of success. The step-by-step procedure outlined here will guide you through the steps of Lab 7.1 to create an exercise program that's right for you. Refer to Figure 7.1 for a sample personal fitness program plan and contract.

If you'd like additional help in setting up your program, choose one of the sample programs at the end of this chapter. Sample programs are provided for walking/jogging/running, cycling, swimming, and calisthenics circuit training; they include detailed instructions for starting a program and developing and maintaining fitness.

1. Set Goals

Ask yourself, "What do I want from my fitness program?" Develop different types of goals—general and specific, long term and short term. General or long-term goals might include things like lowering your risk for chronic disease, improving posture, having more energy, and improving the fit of your clothes.

It's a good idea to also develop some specific, short-term goals based on measurable factors. Specific goals might be:

- Raising $\dot{V}O_{2max}$ by 10%.
- Reducing the time it takes you to jog 2 miles from 22 minutes to 19 minutes.
- Increasing the number of push-ups you can do from 15 to 25.
- Lowering your BMI from 26 to 24.5.

Having specific goals will allow you to track your progress and enjoy the measurable changes brought about by your fitness program. Finally, break your specific goals into several smaller steps (mini-goals), such as those shown in Figure 7.1.

Physical fitness assessment tests are essential to determining your goals. They help you decide which types of exercise you should emphasize, and they help you understand the relative difficulty of attaining specific goals. If you have health problems, such as high blood pressure, heart disease, obesity, or serious joint or muscle disabilities, see your physician before taking assessment tests. Measure your progress by taking these tests about every 3 months.

You'll find it easier to stick with your program if you choose goals that are both important to you and realistic. Remember that heredity, your current fitness level, and other individual factors influence the amount and rate of improvement and the ultimate level of fitness you can expect to reach through physical training. Fitness improves most quickly during the first 6 months of an exercise program. After that, gains come more slowly and usually require a higher-intensity program. Don't expect to improve indefinitely: Improve your fitness to a reasonable target level, and then train consistently to maintain it. Sometimes you may lose fitness—due to illness, injury, missed workouts, or a vacation—so you must begin again at a lower level. Developing fitness is a dynamic process that involves gains and losses. Even if you lose ground occasionally, stay with your program, and you'll be able to achieve your goals.

A. I Tracie Kaufman (name) am contracting with myself to follow a physical fitness program to work toward the following goals:

Specific or short-term goals

1. Improving cardiorespiratory fitness by raising my $\dot{V}O_{2max}$ from 34 to 37 ml/kg/min
2. Improving upper body muscular strength and endurance rating from fair to good
3. Improving body composition (from 28% to 25% body fat)
4. Improving my tennis game (hitting 20 playable shots in a row against the ball machine)

General or long-term goals

1. Developing a more positive attitude about myself
2. Improving the fit of my clothes
3. Building and maintaining bone mass to reduce my risk of osteoporosis
4. Increasing my life expectancy and reducing my risk for diabetes and heart disease

B. **My program plan is as follows:**

Activities	Components (Check X) CRE	MS	ME	F	BC	Time	Frequency (Check X) M	Tu	W	Th	F	S	S	Intensity*
Swimming	X	X	X	X	X	35min	X		X		X			140–170 bpm
Tennis	X	X	X	X	X	90min						X		RPE= 13–16
Weight training		X	X	X	X	30min		X		X		X		see Lab 4-3
Stretching				X		25min	X		X		X	X		—

*List your target heart rate range or an RPE value if appropriate.

C. My program will begin on Sept. 21 My program includes the following schedule of mini-goals. For each step in my program, I will give myself the reward listed.

Mini-goal	Date	Reward
Completing 2 full weeks of program (mini-goal 1)	Oct. 5	movie with friends (reward)
$\dot{V}O_{2max}$ of 35 ml/kg/min (mini-goal 2)	Nov. 2	new CD (reward)
Completing 10 full weeks of program (mini-goal 3)	Nov. 30	new sweater (reward)
Percent body fat of 27% (mini-goal 4)	Dec. 22	weekend away (reward)
$\dot{V}O_{2max}$ of 36 ml/kg/min (mini-goal)	Jan. 18	new CD (reward)

D. My program will include the addition of physical activity to my daily routine (such as climbing stairs or walking to class):

1. Walking to and from campus job
2. Taking the stairs to dorm room instead of elevator
3. Bicycling to the library instead of driving
4. Doing one active chore a day
5.

E. I will use the following tools to monitor my program and my progress toward my goals:

I'll use a chart that lists the number of laps and minutes I swim and the charts for strength and flexibility from Labs 4-3 & 5-2.

I sign this contract as an indication of my personal commitment to reach my goal.

Tracie Kaufman (your signature) Sep. 10

I have recruited a helper who will witness my contract and

swim with me three days per week
(list any way your helper will participate in your program)

Russell Walker (witness's signature) Sep. 10

FIGURE 7.1 A sample personal fitness program plan and contract.

Table 7.1 A Summary of Sports and Fitness Activities

This table classifies sports and activities as high (H), moderate (M), or low (L) in terms of their ability to develop each of the five components of physical fitness: cardiorespiratory endurance (CRE), muscular strength (MS), muscular endurance (ME), flexibility (F), and body composition (BC). The skill level needed to obtain fitness benefits is noted: Low (L) means little or no skill is required to obtain fitness benefits; moderate (M) means average skill is needed to obtain fitness benefits; and high (H) means much skill is required to obtain fitness benefits. The fitness prerequisite, or conditioning needs of a beginner, is also noted: Low (L) means no fitness prerequisite is required, moderate (M) means some preconditioning is required, and high (H) means substantial fitness is required. The last two columns list the calorie cost of each activity when performed moderately and vigorously. To determine how many calories you burn, multiply the value in the appropriate column by your body weight and then by the number of minutes you exercise. Work up to using 300 or more calories per workout.

	Components							Approximate Calorie Cost (cal/lb/min)	
Sports and Activities	CRE	MS*	ME*	F*	BC	Skill Level	Fitness Prerequisite	Moderate	Vigorous
Aerobic dance	H	M	H	H	H	L	L	.046	.062
Backpacking	H	M	H	M	H	L	M	.032	.078
Badminton, skilled, singles	H	M	M	M	H	M	M	—	.071
Ballet (floor combinations)	M	M	H	H	M	M	L	—	.058
Ballroom dancing	M	L	M	L	M	M	L	.034	.049
Baseball (pitcher and catcher)	M	M	H	M	M	H	M	.039	—
Basketball, half court	H	M	H	M	H	M	M	.045	.071
Bicycling	H	M	H	M	H	M	L	.049	.071
Bowling	L	L	L	L	L	L	L	—	—
Calisthenic circuit training	H	M	H	M	H	L	L	—	.060
Canoeing and kayaking (flat water)	M	M	H	M	M	M	M	.045	—
Cheerleading	M	M	M	M	M	M	L	.033	.049
Elliptical exercise	H	M	H	M	H	L	L	.049	.070
Fencing	M	M	H	H	M	M	L	.032	.078
Field hockey	H	M	H	M	H	M	M	.052	.078
Folk and square dancing	M	L	M	L	M	L	L	.039	.049
Football, touch	M	M	M	M	M	M	M	.049	.078
Frisbee, ultimate	H	M	H	M	H	M	M	.049	.078
Golf (riding cart)	L	L	L	M	L	L	L	—	—
Handball, skilled, singles	H	M	H	M	H	M	M	—	.078
Hiking	H	M	H	L	H	L	M	.051	.073
Hockey, ice and roller	H	M	H	M	H	M	M	.052	.078
Horseback riding	M	M	M	L	M	M	M	.052	.065
Interval circuit training	H	H	H	M	H	L	L	—	.062
Jogging and running	H	M	H	L	H	L	L	.060	.104
Judo	M	H	H	M	M	M	L	.049	.090
Karate	H	M	H	H	H	L	M	.049	.090

*Ratings are for the muscle groups involved.

2. Select Activities

If you have already chosen activities and created separate program plans for different fitness components in Chapters 3–5, you can put those plans together into a single program. It's usually best to include exercises to develop each of the health-related components of fitness.

- Cardiorespiratory endurance is developed by activities such as walking, cycling, and aerobic dance that involve continuous rhythmic movements of large-muscle groups like those in the legs (see Chapter 3).
- Muscular strength and endurance are developed by training against resistance (see Chapter 4).
- Flexibility is developed by stretching the major muscle groups (see Chapter 5).
- Healthy body composition can be developed by combining a sensible diet and a program of regular exercise, including cardiorespiratory endurance exercise to burn calories and resistance training to build muscle mass (see Chapter 6).

Table 7.1 rates many popular activities for their ability to develop each of the health-related components of fitness. Check the ratings of the activities you're considering to make sure the program you put together will develop all fitness components and help you achieve your goals. One strategy is to select one activity for each component of

Table 7.1 A Summary of Sports and Fitness Activities *(continued)*

Sports and Activities	Components: CRE	MS*	ME*	F*	BC	Skill Level	Fitness Prerequisite	Approximate Calorie Cost (cal/lb/min): Moderate	Vigorous
Lacrosse	H	M	H	M	H	H	M	.052	.078
Modern dance (moving combinations)	M	M	H	H	M	L	L	—	.058
Orienteering	H	M	H	L	H	L	M	.049	.078
Outdoor fitness trails	H	M	H	M	H	L	L	—	.060
Popular dancing	M	L	M	M	M	M	L	—	.049
Racquetball, skilled, singles	H	M	M	M	H	M	M	.049	.078
Rock climbing	M	H	H	H	M	H	M	.033	.033
Rope skipping	H	M	H	L	H	M	M	.071	.095
Rowing	H	H	H	H	H	L	L	.032	.097
Rugby	H	M	H	M	H	M	M	.052	.097
Sailing	L	L	M	L	L	M	L	—	—
Skating, ice, roller, and in-line	M	M	H	M	M	H	M	.049	.095
Skiing, alpine	M	H	H	M	M	H	M	.039	.078
Skiing, cross-country	H	M	H	M	H	M	M	.049	.104
Soccer	H	M	H	M	H	M	M	.052	.097
Squash, skilled, singles	H	M	M	M	H	M	M	.049	.078
Stretching	L	L	L	H	L	L	L	—	—
Surfing (including swimming)	M	M	M	M	M	H	M	—	.078
Swimming	H	M	H	M	H	M	L	.032	.088
Synchronized swimming	M	M	H	H	M	H	M	.032	.052
Table tennis	M	L	M	M	M	M	L	—	.045
Tennis, skilled, singles	H	M	M	M	H	M	M	—	.071
Volleyball	M	L	M	M	M	M	M	—	.065
Walking	H	L	M	L	H	L	L	.029	.048
Water polo	H	M	H	M	H	H	M	—	.078
Water skiing	M	M	H	M	M	H	M	.039	.055
Weight training	L	H	H	H	M	L	L	—	—
Wrestling	H	H	H	H	H	H	H	.065	.094
Yoga	L	L	M	H	L	H	L	—	—

*Ratings are for the muscle groups involved.

SOURCE: Kusinitz, I., and M. Fine, *Physical Fitness for Practically Everybody,* Consumer Reports® 1983. Consumers Union of the U.S., Inc., Yonkers, NY 10703-1057, a nonprofit organization. Reprinted with permission for educational purposes only. No commercial use or reproduction permitted. www.ConsumerReports.org®.

fitness—bicycling, weight training, and stretching, for example. Another strategy applies the principle of cross-training, using several different activities to develop a particular fitness component—aerobics classes, swimming, and volleyball for cardiorespiratory endurance, for example. Cross-training is discussed in the next section.

If you select activities that support your commitment rather than activities that turn exercise into a chore, the right program will be its own incentive for continuing. Consider the following factors in making your choices.

- ***Fun and interest.*** Your fitness program is much more likely to be successful if you choose activities that you enjoy doing. Start by considering any activities you currently engage in and enjoy. Often you can modify your current activities to fit your fitness program. It is a good idea to try a new activity for a while before committing to it.
- ***Your current skill and fitness level.*** Although many activities are appropriate for beginners, some sports and activities require a moderate level of skill to obtain fitness benefits. For example, a beginning tennis player will probably not be able to sustain rallies long enough to develop cardiorespiratory endurance. Refer to the skill level column in Table 7.1 to determine the level of skill needed for full participation in the activities you're considering. If your current skill level doesn't meet the requirement, you may want to begin your program with a different activity. For example, a beginning tennis player may be better off adhering to a walking program while improving his or her tennis game—or practicing with a ball machine to guarantee steady activity. To build skill for a particular

Choosing Home Exercise Equipment

CRITICAL CONSUMER

A home gym can be as simple as a stability ball or as complex as a computerized weight training machine. Regardless, it's best to make sure that your equipment is appropriate for your current needs and will continue to challenge you as your fitness increases. Most importantly, your home exercise equipment should be safe.

Before buying any piece of exercise equipment, consider the following:

- ***Your fitness goals.*** Make sure the device will help you work on your targeted fitness components. Remember, however, that no single device can "do it all," even though some manufacturers and sellers make such claims. Machines are typically designed for either cardiorespiratory or strength training.
- ***Your motivation to use the device.*** If you aren't sure whether you'll use the equipment regularly, don't buy it. Instead, try using one regularly at a gym for a few weeks. A try-out period can help you decide whether the device is right for you.
- ***Quality.*** Look for product reviews in magazines and online. The Federal Trade Commission provides good general advice on shopping for exercise equipment (www.ftc.gov). A personal trainer may be able to give you recommendations, especially if he or she is not involved in selling equipment. Do not buy a device unless you are sure it is well made. Using low-quality equipment increases your risk of injury.
- ***Your space requirements.*** Will a treadmill take up your entire living room? Make sure you have enough space to accommodate the device. If necessary, look for equipment that folds up or breaks down to occupy less space between uses.

The most popular types of home equipment for aerobic exercise are treadmills, stationary bikes, cross-country ski machines, stair climbers, and elliptical trainers. When trying out such devices, make sure they support your weight without giving. They should accommodate your full range of motion and should operate smoothly and quietly.

Shop for equipment at a store that specializes in selling such devices. The store should have a highly trained staff and should be able to repair your equipment if it breaks (a real problem with mechanized devices such as treadmills). The staff should be able to tell you all about the equipment's features and warranty.

activity, consider taking a class or getting some instruction from a coach or fellow participant.

Your current fitness level may also limit the activities that are appropriate for your program. For example, if you have been inactive, a walking program would be more appropriate than a jogging program. Activities in which participants control the intensity of effort—walking, cycling, and swimming, for example—are more appropriate for a beginning fitness program than sports and activities that are primarily "other paced"—soccer, basketball, and tennis, for example. Refer to the fitness prerequisite column of Table 7.1 to determine the minimum level of fitness required for participation in the activities you're considering. However, staying active is the most important thing. If you like to play tennis but don't like to take walks or jog, then play tennis.

- ***Time and convenience.*** Unless exercise fits easily into your daily schedule, you are unlikely to maintain your program over the long term. As you consider activities, think about whether a special location or facility is required. Can you participate in the activity close to your residence, school, or job? Are the necessary facilities open and available at times convenient to you (see Lab 7.2)? Do you need a partner or a team to play? Can you participate in the activity year-round, or will you need to find an alternative during the summer or winter? Would a home treadmill make you more likely to exercise regularly?
- ***Cost.*** Some sports and activities require equipment, fees, or some type of membership investment. If you are on a tight budget, limit your choices to activities that are inexpensive or free. Investigate the facilities on your campus, which you may be able to use at little or no cost. Many activities require no equipment beyond an appropriate pair of shoes (see the box "Choosing Exercise Footwear," in Chapter 3 for more information). For tips on evaluating exercise equipment, see the box "Choosing Home Exercise Equipment."
- ***Special health needs.*** If you have special exercise needs due to a particular health problem, choose activities that will conform to your needs and enhance your ability to cope. If necessary, consult your physician about how best to tailor an exercise program to your particular needs and goals. Guidelines and safety tips for exercisers with common chronic conditions are provided later in the chapter.

QUESTIONS FOR CRITICAL THINKING AND REFLECTION

Consider the list of physical activities and sports in Table 7.1. For which ones do you have the necessary fitness prerequisite (rated low, moderate, or high)? Given your current fitness and skill level, which ones could you reasonably incorporate into your exercise program?

3. Set a Target Frequency, Intensity, and Time (Duration) for Each Activity

The next step is to apply the FITT principle and set a starting frequency, intensity, and time (duration) for each type of activity you've chosen (see the summary in Figure 7.2 and the sample in Figure 7.1). Refer to the calculations and plans you completed in Chapters 3–5.

	Cardiorespiratory endurance training	Strength training	Flexibility training
Frequency	3–5 days per week	At least 2 days per week	2–3 days per week (minimum); 5–7 days per week (ideal)
Intensity	55/65–90% of maximum heart rate	Sufficient resistance to fatigue muscles	Stretch to the point of tension
Time	20–60 minutes in sessions lasting 10 minutes or more	8–12 repetitions of each exercise, 1 or more sets	2–4 repetitions of each exercise, held for 15–30 seconds
Type	Continuous rhythmic activities using large muscle groups	Resistance exercises for all major muscle groups	Stretching exercises for all major joints

FIGURE 7.2 A summary of the FITT principle for the health-related components of fitness.

Cardiorespiratory Endurance Exercise An appropriate frequency for cardiorespiratory endurance exercise is 3–5 times per week. For intensity, note your target heart rate zone or RPE value. Your target total workout time (duration) should be about 20–60 minutes, depending on the intensity of the activity (shorter durations are appropriate for high-intensity activities, longer durations for activities of more moderate intensity). You can exercise in a single session or in multiple sessions of 10 or more minutes.

One way to check whether the total duration you've set is appropriate is to use the **calorie costs** given in Table 7.1. Your goal should be to work up to burning about 300 calories per workout; beginners should start with a calorie cost of about 100–150 calories per workout. Calculate the calorie cost of your activities by multiplying the appropriate factor from Table 7.1 by your body weight and the duration of your workout. For example, walking at a moderate pace burns about 0.029 calorie per minute per pound of body weight. A person weighing 150 pounds could begin her exercise program by walking for 30 minutes, burning about 130 calories. Once her fitness improves, she might choose to start cycling for her cardiorespiratory endurance workouts. Cycling at a moderate pace has a higher calorie cost than walking (0.049 calorie per minute per pound), and if she cycled for 40 minutes, she would burn the target 300 calories during her workout.

Muscular Strength and Endurance Training A frequency of at least 2 nonconsecutive days per week for strength training is recommended. As described in Chapter 4, a general fitness strength training program includes 1 or more sets of 8–12 repetitions of 8–10 exercises that work all major muscle groups. For intensity, choose a weight that is heavy enough to fatigue your muscles but not so heavy that you cannot complete the full number of repetitions with proper form.

Flexibility Training Stretches should be performed when muscles are warm at least 2–3 days per week (5–7 days per week is ideal). Stretches should be performed for all major muscle groups. For each exercise, stretch to the point of slight tension or mild discomfort, and hold the stretch for 15–30 seconds; do 2–4 repetitions of each exercise.

4. Set Up a System of Mini-Goals and Rewards

To keep your program on track, set up a system of goals and rewards. Break your specific goals into several steps, and set a target date for each step. For example, if one of the goals of an 18-year-old male student's program is to improve upper-body strength and endurance, he could use the push-up test in Lab 4.2 to set intermediate goals. If he can currently perform 15 push-ups (for a rating of "very poor"), he might set intermediate goals of 17, 20, 25, and 30 push-ups (for a final rating of "fair"). By allowing several weeks between mini-goals and specifying rewards,

MOTIVATION BOOSTER

Add music. To add variety and enjoyment to your workouts and to boost your motivation, try exercising to music. Researchers have found that working out to music can boost mood and even keep people working out longer and harder without feeling like they are expending extra effort. Just make sure that music provides a safe distraction and doesn't increase your risk of injury; for example, don't wear headphones while walking, jogging, or cycling on the street.

TERMS

calorie cost The amount of energy used to perform a particular activity, usually expressed in calories per minute per pound of body weight.

he'll be able to track his progress and reward himself as he moves toward his final goal. Reaching a series of small goals is more satisfying than working toward a single, more challenging, goal that may take months to achieve. Realistic goals, broken into achievable mini-goals, can boost your chances of success. For more on choosing appropriate rewards, see Chapter 1 and Activity 4 in the Behavior Change Workbook at the end of the text.

5. Include Lifestyle Physical Activity in Your Program

As described in Chapter 2, daily physical activity is an important part of a fit and well lifestyle. As part of your fitness program plan, specify ways to be more active during your daily routine. You may find it helpful to first use your health journal to track your activities for several days. Review the records in your journal, identify routine opportunities to be more active, and add these to your program plan in Lab 7.1.

6. Develop Tools for Monitoring Your Progress

A record that tracks your daily progress will help remind you of your ongoing commitment to your program and give you a sense of accomplishment. Figure 7.3 shows you how to create a general program log and record the activity type, frequency, and times (durations). Or, if you wish, complete specific activity logs like those in Labs 3.2, 4.3, and 5.2 in addition to, or instead of, a general log. Post your log in a place where you'll see it often as a reminder and as an incentive for improvement. If you have specific, measurable goals, you can also graph your weekly or monthly progress toward your goal (Figure 7.4). To monitor the overall progress of your fitness program, you may choose to reassess your cardiorespiratory endurance, muscular strength and endurance, flexibility, and body composition every 3 months or so during the improvement phase of your program. Because the results of different fitness tests vary, be sure to compare results for the same assessments over time.

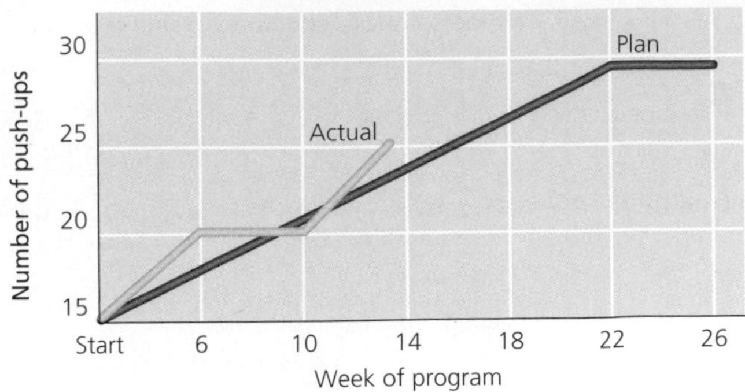

FIGURE 7.4 A sample program progress chart.

7. Make a Commitment

Your final step in planning your program is to make a commitment by signing a contract. Find a witness for your contract—preferably one who will be actively involved in your program. Keep your contract in a visible spot to remind you of your commitment.

PUTTING YOUR PLAN INTO ACTION

Once you've developed a detailed plan and signed your contract, you are ready to begin your fitness program. Refer to the specific training suggestions provided in Chapters 2–5 for advice on beginning and maintaining your program. Many people find it easier to plan a program than to put their plan into action and stick with it over time. For that reason, adherence to healthy lifestyle programs has become an important area of study for psychologists and health researchers. The guidelines below and in the next section reflect research into strategies that help people succeed in sticking with an exercise program.

- ***Start slowly and increase fitness gradually.*** Overzealous exercising can result in discouraging discomforts and injuries. Your program is meant to last a lifetime. The important first step is to break your established pattern of inactivity. Be patient and realistic. Once your body has adjusted to your starting level of exercise, slowly increase

Name Tracie Kaufman

Enter time, distance, or another factor (such as heart rate or perceived exertion) to track your progress.

Activity/Date	M	Tu	W	Th	F	S	S	Weekly Total	M	Tu	W	Th	F	S	S	Weekly Total
1 Swimming	800 yd		725 yd		800 yd			2325 yd	800 yd		800 yd		850 yd			2450 yd
2 Tennis						90 min		90 min						95 min		95 min
3 Weight Training		X		X		X				X		X			X	
4 Stretching	X		X		X	X			X			X	X	X	X	

FIGURE 7.3 A sample program log.

the amount of overload. Small increases are the key—achieving a large number of small improvements will eventually result in substantial gains in fitness. It's usually best to increase duration and frequency before increasing intensity.

- ***Find an exercise buddy.*** The social side of exercise is an important factor for many regular exercisers. Working out with a friend will make exercise more enjoyable and increase your chances of sticking with your program. Find an exercise partner who shares your goals and general fitness level.
- ***Ask for support from others.*** You have a much greater chance of exercising consistently if you have the support of important people in your life, such as parents, spouse, partner, and friends. Talk with them about your program, and let them know the importance of exercise and wellness in your life. Exercise is not a frivolous pursuit you follow after your work is finished. Rather, it is a critical component of your day (just like sleeping and eating). Good communication will help others become more supportive of and enthusiastic about the time you spend on your wellness program.
- ***Vary your activities.*** You can make your program more fun over the long term if you participate in a variety of activities that you enjoy. You can also add interest using strategies such as varying the routes you take when walking, running, biking, or in-line skating; finding a new tennis or racquetball partner; changing your music for aerobic dance; or switching to a new volleyball or basketball court.

Varying your activities, a strategy known as cross-training, has other benefits. It can help you develop balanced, total-body fitness. For example, by alternating running with swimming, you build both upper- and lower-body strength. Cross-training can thus prepare you for a wider range of activities and physical challenges. It can also reduce the risk of injury and overtraining because the same muscles, bones, and joints are not continuously subjected to the stresses of the same activity. Cross-training can be done either by choosing different activities on different days or by alternating activities within a single workout.

- ***Cycle the duration and intensity of your workouts.*** Olympic athletes use a technique called periodization of training, meaning that they vary the duration and intensity of their workouts. Sometimes they exercise very intensely; other times they train lightly or rest. You can use the same technique to improve fitness more quickly and make your training program more varied and enjoyable. For example, if your program consists of walking, weight training, and stretching, pick one day a week for each activity to train a little harder or longer than you normally do. If you usually walk 2 miles in 16 minutes per mile, increase the pace to 15 minutes per mile once a week. If you lift weights twice a week, train more intensely during one of the workouts by using more resistance or performing multiple sets.
- ***Adapt to changing environments and schedules.*** Most people are creatures of habit and have trouble adjusting to change. Don't use bad weather or a new job as an excuse to give up your exercise program. If you walk in the summer, put on a warm coat and walk in the winter. If you can't go out because of darkness, join a gym and walk on a treadmill.
- ***Expect fluctuations and lapses.*** On some days, your progress will be excellent, but on others, you'll barely be able to drag yourself through your scheduled activities. Don't let off-days or lapses discourage you or make you feel guilty. Instead, feel a renewed commitment to your fitness program (see the box "Getting Your Fitness Program Back on Track").
- ***Choose other healthy lifestyle behaviors.*** Exercise provides huge benefits for your health, but other behaviors are also important. Choose a nutritious diet, and avoid harmful habits like smoking and overconsumption of alcohol. Don't skimp on sleep, which has a mutually beneficial relationship with exercise. Physical activity improves sleep, and adequate sleep can improve physical performance (see the box "Sleep").

EXERCISE GUIDELINES FOR PEOPLE WITH SPECIAL HEALTH CONCERNS

Regular, appropriate exercise is safe and beneficial for many people with chronic conditions or other special health concerns. In fact, for many people with special health concerns, the risks associated with *not* exercising are far greater than those associated with a moderate program of regular exercise.

QUESTIONS FOR CRITICAL THINKING AND REFLECTION

How do you typically deal with setbacks? For example, if you have trouble getting motivated to study for exams, what strategies do you use to get back on track? Could those strategies work for keeping your fitness program moving forward? If so, how?

MOTIVATION BOOSTER

Track improvements. In addition to tracking the basic progress of your fitness program, you may find that directly monitoring some of your program's benefits can help keep you motivated and on track. For example, try tracking your energy level. Develop a point scale (1–10 or 1–20), record a value for your energy level each day, and graph the results. Most people find that increasing physical activity quickly boosts their energy level.

Getting Your Fitness Program Back on Track

TAKE CHARGE

Lapses are a normal part of any behavior change program. The important point is to move on and avoid becoming discouraged. Try again and keep trying. Know that continued effort will lead to success.

- Don't judge yourself too harshly. Some people make faster gains in fitness than others. Focus on the improvements you've already made from your program and how good you feel after exercise—both physically and mentally.
- Visualize what it will be like to reach your goals. Keep these images in mind as an incentive to stick with your program.
- Use your exercise journal to identify thoughts and behaviors that are causing noncompliance. Devise strategies to combat these problematic patterns. If needed, make additional changes in your environment or find more social support. For example, call a friend to walk with you, or keep exercise clothes in your car or backpack.
- Make changes in your plan and reward system to help renew your enthusiasm for and commitment to your program. Try changing fitness activities or your exercise schedule. Build in more opportunities to reward yourself.
- Plan ahead for difficult situations. Think about what circumstances might make it tough to keep up your fitness routine. Develop strategies to increase your chances of sticking with your program. For example, figure out ways to continue your program during vacation, travel, bad weather, and so on.
- If you're in a bad mood or just don't feel like exercising, remind yourself that physical activity is probably the one thing you can do that will make you feel better. Even if you can only do half your scheduled workout, you'll boost your energy, improve your mood, and help keep your program on track.

The fitness recommendations for the general population presented in this text can serve as a general guideline for any exercise program. For people with special health concerns, however, certain precautions and monitoring may be required. Anyone with special health concerns should consult a physician before beginning an exercise program. The following sections list guidelines and cautions for some common conditions.

Arthritis

- Begin an exercise program as early as possible in the course of the disease.
- Warm up thoroughly before each workout to loosen stiff muscles and lower the risk of injury.
- For cardiorespiratory endurance exercise, avoid high-impact activities that may damage arthritic joints; consider swimming, water walking, or another type of exercise in a warm pool.
- Strength train the whole body; pay special attention to muscles that support and protect affected joints (for example, build quadriceps, hamstring, and calf strength for the knee). Start with small loads and build intensity gradually.
- Perform flexibility exercises daily to maintain joint mobility.

Asthma

- Exercise regularly. Acute attacks are more likely if you exercise only occasionally.
- Carry medication during workouts and avoid exercising alone. Use your inhaler as recommended by your physician.
- Warm up and cool down slowly to reduce the risk of acute attacks.
- When starting an exercise program, choose self-paced endurance activities, especially those involving **interval training** (short bouts of exercise followed by a rest period). Increase the intensity of cardiorespiratory endurance exercise gradually.
- Educate yourself about circumstances that may trigger an asthma attack, and act accordingly. For example, cold, dry air can trigger or worsen an attack. Pollen, dust, and polluted air can also trigger an attack. To avoid attacks in dry air, drink water before, during, and after a workout to moisten your airways. In cold weather, cover your mouth with a mask or scarf to warm and humidify the air you breathe. Also, avoid outdoor activities during pollen season or when the air is polluted or dusty.

Diabetes

- Don't begin an exercise program unless your diabetes is under control and you have discussed exercise safety with your physician. Because people with diabetes have an increased risk for heart disease, an exercise stress test may be recommended.
- Don't exercise alone. Wear a bracelet identifying yourself as having diabetes.
- If you take insulin or another medication, adjust the timing and amount of each dose as needed. Work with your physician and check your blood sugar levels regularly so you can learn to balance your energy intake and output and your medication dosage.

WELLNESS CONNECTION

Sleep

The majority of Americans suffer from chronic sleep deprivation. Most of us get between one-half and two fewer hours of sleep each night than we need in order to be fully alert during the day.

Many people view sleep as a luxury or a waste of time, but sleep is absolutely essential for life and health.

- When deprived of sleep for many days, humans and other animals become ill and even die.
- Less extreme sleep deprivation over a long time makes people more vulnerable to a variety of illnesses, including CVD, diabetes, high blood pressure, and psychological disorders.
- Sleep deprivation has been linked to weight gain.
- Inadequate sleep depresses the immune system, making people more vulnerable to infection.
- Lack of sleep affects learning, memory, and attention span, all critical to academic performance.
- Athletes who don't get enough sleep cannot perform at their peak because fatigue slows reaction time and reduces endurance.

Drowsiness is a factor in at least 100,000 auto crashes each year; it impairs driving ability as much as alcohol use. Many of us think that no matter how tired we may be, we can force ourselves to be alert, but we can't. People who are sleep deprived may think they are wide awake but often fall asleep at the wheel for brief periods without even realizing it.

College students are particularly vulnerable to sleep deprivation and poor quality of sleep. Most students lead hectic lives as they juggle studies, work, socializing, and family obligations. Students who live in dormitories are often awakened by nighttime noise. Partying, especially if alcohol and other drugs are used, further disrupts sleep. Financial necessity dictates that many students work part-time or even full-time. There are only so many hours in the day, and many working students find it nearly impossible to get enough sleep to function well in school or at work. To make matters worse, teens and young adults actually need more sleep than older individuals—more than 9 hours of sleep a night—to be well rested.

How do you know if you're getting enough sleep? If you need an alarm to get yourself up every morning, rather than awakening naturally at the appropriate time, chances are you are significantly sleep deprived. Another clue is if you fall asleep within just a few minutes of getting into bed, or if you fall asleep during the day when you don't intend to, such as during lectures or while reading or watching TV.

Sleep you need but don't get is referred to as "sleep debt." Whenever you get less sleep than your body requires, you add to your sleep debt. Week after week, sleep debt can build, leaving you chronically groggy.

If you have a large sleep debt, sleeping in a few extra hours on the weekends won't solve the problem, although it can help a bit. The real solution is to make sleep a priority in your daily life. Remember that the time you spend sleeping will pay for itself in increased productivity. For example, if you go to bed one hour earlier instead of trying to study when you're half awake, you are likely to get the work done in a fraction of the time when you're more alert the next day.

- To prevent abnormally rapid absorption of injected insulin, inject it over a muscle that won't be exercised, and wait at least an hour before exercising.
- Check blood sugar levels before, during, and after exercise, and adjust your diet or insulin dosage as needed. Have high-carbohydrate foods on hand during a workout. Avoid exercise if your blood sugar level is above 250 mg/dl, and ingest carbohydrates prior to exercise if your blood sugar level is below 100 mg/dl.
- Don't lift heavy weights. Straining can damage blood vessels. Instead, perform a higher number of repetitions (15–20) using a lighter load.
- If you have poor circulation or numbness in your extremities, check your skin regularly for blisters and abrasions, especially on your feet. Avoid high-impact activities and wear comfortable shoes.
- For maximum benefit and minimum risk, choose low-to-moderate-intensity activities.

Heart Disease and Hypertension

- Check with your physician about exercise safety before increasing your activity level.
- Exercise at moderate rather than high intensity. Keep your heart rate below the level at which abnormalities appear on an exercise stress test.
- Warm up and cool down gradually, with sessions lasting at least 10 minutes each.
- Monitor your heart rate during exercise, and stop if you experience dizziness or chest pain.
- If your physician has prescribed it, carry nitroglycerin with you during exercise. If you are taking beta-blockers for hypertension, use RPE rather than heart

TERMS

interval training A training technique that alternates exercise intervals with rest intervals or intense exercise intervals with low-to-moderate intervals.

rate to monitor exercise intensity (beta-blockers reduce heart rate). Exercise at an RPE level of "fairly light" to "somewhat hard"; your breathing should be unlabored, and you should be able to talk.

- Don't hold your breath when exercising. Doing so can cause sudden, steep increases in blood pressure. Take special care during weight training; don't lift heavy loads. Exhale during the exertion phase of lifts.
- Increase exercise frequency, intensity, and time very gradually.

Obesity

- For maximum benefit and minimum risk, begin by choosing low-to-moderate-intensity activities. Increase intensity slowly as your fitness improves. Studies of overweight people show that exercising at moderate-to-high intensities causes more fat loss than training at low intensities.
- Follow the 2005 Dietary Guidelines recommending that people who want to lose weight or maintain lost weight exercise moderately 60 minutes or more every day. To get the benefit of 60 minutes of exercise, you can exercise all at once or divide your total activity time into sessions of 10, 20, or 30 minutes.
- Choose non- or low-weight-bearing activities such as swimming, water exercises, cycling, or walking. Low-impact activities are less likely to lead to joint problems or injuries.
- Stay alert for symptoms of heat-related problems during exercise (see Chapter 3). Obese people are vulnerable to heat intolerance.

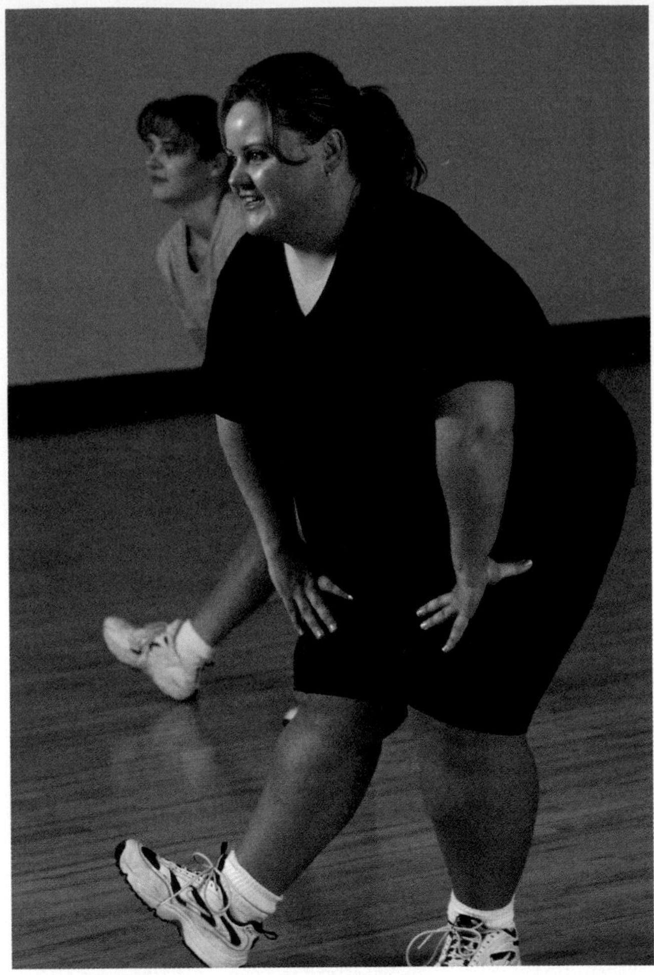

Low-impact activities like walking are a good choice for people who are overweight because they can provide a good workout and are less likely than high-impact activities to cause joint problems or injuries.

- Ease into an exercise program and increase overload gradually. Increase time and frequency of exercise before increasing intensity.
- Include strength training in your fitness program to build or maintain muscle mass.
- Try to include as much lifestyle physical activity in your daily routine as possible.

MOTIVATION BOOSTER

Join with others. If you have a special health concern and have hesitated to become more active, one helpful strategy is to take a class or join an exercise group specifically designed for your condition. Many health centers and support groups sponsor specially tailored activity programs. Such a class can provide you with both expert advice and exercise partners who share your concerns and goals.

QUESTIONS FOR CRITICAL THINKING AND REFLECTION

Do you have a special physical condition that poses an obstacle to exercising, such as asthma? How have you dealt with this condition in the past? If the condition has prevented you from exercising, how might you deal with it so you can exercise regularly? If necessary, consult with your physician to find ways to exercise despite impediments.

Osteoporosis

- For cardiorespiratory endurance activities, exercise at the maximum intensity that causes no significant discomfort. If possible, choose low-impact weight-bearing activities to help safely maintain bone density (see Chapter 8 for more strategies for building and maintaining bone density).
- To prevent fractures, avoid any activity or movement that stresses the back or carries a risk of falling.
- Include weight training in your exercise program to improve strength and balance and reduce the risk of falls and fractures. Avoid lifting heavy loads.

Exercise guidelines for people with disabilities are discussed in Chapter 2 and for people with low-back pain in Chapter 5.

EXERCISE GUIDELINES FOR LIFE STAGES

A fitness program may also need to be adjusted to accommodate the requirements of different life stages.

Children and Adolescents

Lack of physical activity has led to alarming increases in overweight and obesity in children and adolescents. If you have children or are in a position to influence children, keep these guidelines in mind:

- Provide opportunities for children and adolescents to exercise every day. Minimize sedentary activities, such as watching television. Children and adolescents should aim for at least 60 minutes of moderate activity most, but preferably all, days.
- During family outings, choose dynamic activities. For example, go for a walk or park away from a mall and then walk to the stores.
- For children younger than 12, emphasize skill development and fitness rather than excellence in competitive sports. For adolescents, combine participation and training in lifetime sports with traditional, competitive sports.
- Make sure children are developmentally capable of participating in an activity. For example, catching skills are difficult for young children because their nervous system is not developed enough to fully master the skill. When teaching a child to catch a ball, start with a large ball and throw it from a short range. Gradually increase the complexity of the skill once the child has mastered the simpler skill.
- Make sure children get plenty of water when exercising in the heat. Make sure they are dressed properly when exercising in the cold.

Pregnant Women

Exercise is important during pregnancy, but women should be cautious because some types of exercise can pose increased risk to the mother and the unborn child. The following guidelines are consistent with the recommendations of the American College of Obstetrics and Gynecology:

- See your physician about possible modifications needed for your particular pregnancy.
- Continue mild-to-moderate exercise routines at least three times a week. (For most women, this means maintaining an exercise heart rate of 100–160 beats per minute.) Avoid exercising vigorously or to exhaustion, especially in the third trimester. Monitor exercise intensity by assessing how you feel rather than by monitoring your heart rate; RPE levels of 11–13 are appropriate.
- Favor non- or low-weight-bearing exercises such as swimming or cycling over weight-bearing exercises, which can carry increased risk of injury.
- Avoid exercise in a supine position—lying on your back—after the first trimester. This position restricts blood flow to the uterus. Also avoid prolonged periods of motionless standing.
- Avoid exercise that could cause loss of balance, especially in the third trimester, and exercise that might injure the abdomen, stress the joints, or carry a risk of falling (such as contact sports, vigorous racquet sports, skiing, and in-line skating).
- Avoid activities involving extremes in barometric pressure, such as diving and mountain climbing.
- Especially during the first trimester, drink plenty of fluids and exercise in well-ventilated areas to avoid heat stress.
- Do 3–5 sets of 10 Kegel exercises daily. These exercises involve tightening the muscles of the pelvic floor for 5–15 seconds. Kegel exercises are thought to help prevent incontinence (involuntary loss of urine) and speed recovery after giving birth.
- After giving birth, resume prepregnancy exercise routines gradually, based on how you feel.

Older Adults

Older people readily adapt to endurance exercise and strength training. Exercise principles are the same as for younger people, but some specific guidelines apply:

- Include the three basic types of exercise—resistance, endurance, and flexibility.
- For strength training, follow ACSM recommendations that older adults use a lighter weight and perform more (10–15) repetitions than young adults.
- Drink plenty of water and avoid exercising in excessively hot or cold environments. Wear clothes that speed heat loss in warm environments and that prevent heat loss in cold environments.
- Warm up slowly and carefully. Increase intensity and duration of exercise gradually.
- Cool down slowly, continuing very light exercise until the heart rate is below 100.
- To help prevent soft tissue pain, do static stretching after a normal workout.

Sample fitness programs begin on p. 206.

COMMON QUESTIONS ANSWERED

Q Should I exercise every day?

A Some daily exercise is beneficial, and health experts recommend that you engage in at least 30 minutes of moderate physical activity at least 5 days per week. Back experts suggest that you also do back pain prevention exercises daily. However, if you train intensely every day without giving yourself a rest, you will likely get injured or become overtrained. When strength training, for example, rest at least 48 hours between workouts before exercising the same muscle group. For cardiorespiratory endurance exercise, rest or exercise lightly the day after an intense or lengthy workout. Balancing the proper amount of rest and exercise will help you feel better and improve your fitness faster.

Q If exercise is so good for my health, why hasn't my physician ever mentioned to me?

A A recent study by the American College of Sports Medicine (ACSM) suggests that most people would benefit from getting a physician's advice about exercising. According to the study, 65% of patients said they would be more interested in exercising if their physicians suggested it. About 40% of physicians said they talk to their patients about exercise.

To encourage physicians and patients to talk more often about exercise and its benefits, the ACSM and the American Medical Association (AMA) have launched the Exercise is Medicine program. The program advises physicians to give more guidance to patients about exercise and suggests that everyone try to exercise at least 5 days each week. For more information on the program, visit www.exerciseismedicine.org.

For more Common Questions Answered about developing and maintaining a fitness program, visit the Online Learning Center.

TIPS FOR TODAY AND THE FUTURE

A complete fitness program includes activities to build and maintain cardiorespiratory endurance, muscular strength and endurance, and flexibility.

RIGHT NOW YOU CAN

- Get a journal to track your daily physical activity and exercise routine.
- Put away your remote control devices—every bit of physical activity can benefit your health.
- Set up your next workout with your training partner.
- Plan to go to bed 15 minutes earlier than usual.

IN THE FUTURE YOU CAN

- Create a schedule that incorporates your workouts into your daily routine. Each week, update the schedule for the upcoming week.
- Learn more about the importance of sleep to good health. If you consistently have trouble sleeping, consult with your physician about seeing a sleep specialist or undergoing a sleep evaluation.

SUMMARY

- Steps for putting together a complete fitness program include (1) setting realistic goals, (2) selecting activities to develop all the health-related components of fitness, (3) setting a target frequency, intensity, and time (duration) for each activity, (4) setting up a system of mini-goals and rewards, (5) making lifestyle physical activity a part of the daily routine, (6) developing tools for monitoring progress, and (7) making a commitment.
- In selecting activities, consider fun and interest, your current skill and fitness levels, time and convenience, cost, and any special health concerns.
- Keys to beginning and maintaining a successful program include starting slowly, increasing intensity and duration gradually, finding a buddy, varying the activities and intensity of the program, and expecting fluctuations and lapses.
- Regular exercise is appropriate and beneficial for people with special health concerns or in particular stages of life; program modifications may be necessary for safety.

FOR FURTHER EXPLORATION

BOOKS, ORGANIZATIONS, AND WEB SITES

American Academy of Orthopaedic Surgeons. Provides information about injuries, treatment, and rehabilitation along with exercise guidelines for people with bone, muscle, and joint pain.
http://www.aaos.org

American College of Obstetricians and Gynecologists. Provides guidelines for promoting a healthy pregnancy and postpartum recovery, including exercise during pregnancy.
http://www.acog.org

American Diabetes Association. Promotes diabetes education, research, and advocacy; includes guidelines for diet and exercise for people with diabetes.
http://www.diabetes.org

American Heart Association. Includes information on fitness for kids as well as diet, exercise, fitness, and weight management for adults.

http://www.heart.org

For additional listings, see Chapters 2–6.

SELECTED BIBLIOGRAPHY

American College of Obstetrics and Gynecology Committee on Obstetric Practice. 2006. *Women's Health: Exercise and Fitness* (http://www.acog.org/publications/patient_education/bp045.cfm; retrieved May 25, 2007).

American College of Sports Medicine. 2006. *ACSM's Guidelines for Exercise Testing and Prescription,* 7th ed. Philadelphia: Lippincott Williams and Wilkins.

American College of Sports Medicine. 2006. *ACSM's Resource Manual for Guidelines for Exercise Testing and Prescription,* 5th ed. Philadelphia: Lippincott Williams and Wilkins.

Bianchi, C., et al. 2007. Treating the metabolic syndrome. *Expert Review of Cardiovascular Therapy* 5(3): 491–506.

Brunet, S., et al. 2005. For the patient: Exercise is important to preventing and controlling type 2 diabetes. *Ethnicity and Disease* 15: 353–354.

Centers for Disease Control and Prevention. 2007. Prevalence of actions to control high blood pressure—20 states, 2005. *Morbidity and Mortality Weekly Report* 56(17): 420–423.

Hogan, M. 2005. Physical and cognitive activity and exercise for older adults: A review. *International Journal of Aging and Human Development* 60: 95–126.

Hu, G., et al. 2007. Epidemiological studies of exercise in diabetes prevention. *Applied Physiology, Nutrition and Metabolism* 32(3): 583–595.

Lee, S., et al. 2005. Exercise without weight loss is an effective strategy for obesity reduction in obese individuals with and without type 2 diabetes. *Journal of Applied Physiology* 99: 1220–1225.

Morris, S. N., and N. R. Johnson. 2005. Exercise during pregnancy: A critical appraisal of the literature. *Journal of Reproductive Medicine* 50: 181–188.

National Sleep Foundation. 2007. *2007 Sleep in America Poll: Summary of Findings.* Washington, D.C.: WBA Market Research.

Nelson, T. F., et al. 2007. Disparities in Overweight and Obesity Among U.S. College Students. *American Journal of Health Behavior* 31(4): 363–373.

Riebe, D., et al. 2005. Long-term maintenance of exercise and healthy eating behaviors in overweight adults. *Preventive Medicine* 40: 769–778.

Vorona, R. D., et al. 2005. Overweight and obese patients in a primary care population report less sleep than patients with a normal body mass index. *Archives of Internal Medicine* 165(1): 25–30.

SAMPLE PROGRAMS FOR POPULAR ACTIVITIES

Sample programs based on four different types of cardiorespiratory activities—walking/jogging/running, bicycling, swimming, and calisthenics circuit training—are presented below. Each sample program includes regular cardiorespiratory endurance exercise, resistance training, and stretching. To choose a sample program, first compare your fitness goals with the benefits of the different types of endurance exercise featured in the sample programs (see Table 7.1). Identify the programs that meet your fitness needs. Next, read through the descriptions of the programs you're considering, and decide which will work best for you based on your present routine, the potential for enjoyment, and adaptability to your lifestyle. If you choose one of these programs, complete the personal fitness program plan in Lab 7.1, the same as if you had created a program from scratch.

No program will produce enormous changes in your fitness level in the first few weeks. Give your program a fair chance. Follow the specifics of the program for 3–4 weeks. Then, if the exercise program doesn't seem suitable, make adjustments to adapt it to your particular needs. But retain the basic elements of the program that make it effective for developing fitness.

GENERAL GUIDELINES

The following guidelines can help make the activity programs more effective for you.

- ***Frequency and time.*** To experience training effects, exercise for 20–60 minutes at least three times a week.

- ***Intensity.*** To work effectively for cardiorespiratory endurance training or to improve body composition, raise your heart rate into its target zone. Monitor your pulse or use rates of perceived exertion to monitor your intensity.

  If you've been sedentary, begin very slowly. Give your muscles a chance to adjust to their increased workload. It's probably best to keep your heart rate below target until your body has had time to adjust to new demands. At first you may not need to work very hard to keep your heart rate in its target zone, but as your cardiorespiratory endurance improves, you will probably need to increase intensity.

- ***Interval training.*** Some of the sample programs involve continuous activity. Others rely on interval training, which calls for alternating a relief interval with exercise (walking after jogging, for example, or coasting after biking uphill). Interval training is an effective way to achieve progressive overload: When your heart rate gets too high, slow down to lower your pulse rate until you're at the low end of your target zone. Interval training can also prolong the total time you spend in exercise and delay the onset of fatigue.

- ***Resistance training and stretching guidelines.*** For the resistance training and stretching parts of the program, remember the general guidelines for safe and effective exercise. For resistance training, follow these guidelines:

- Train at least 2 nonconsecutive days per week.

- Perform 1 or more sets of 8–12 repetitions of 8–10 exercises.

- Include exercises that work all the major muscle groups: neck, shoulders, chest, arms, upper and lower back, abdomen, thighs, and calves.

For stretching, follow these guidelines:

- Stretch at least 2–3 days per week (ideally, 5–7 days per week), when muscles are warm.

- Stretch to the point of mild discomfort, not pain, and hold the stretch for 15–30 seconds.

- Perform each stretch 2–4 times.

- Stretch all the major muscle groups.

- ***Warm-up and cool-down.*** Begin each exercise session with a 10-minute warm-up. Begin your activity at a slow pace, and work up gradually to your target heart rate. Always slow down gradually at the end of your exercise session to bring your system back to its normal state. It's a good idea to do stretching exercises to increase your flexibility after cardiorespiratory exercise or strength training because your muscles will be warm and ready to stretch.

- ***Record keeping.*** After each exercise session, record your daily distance or time on a progress chart.

WALKING/JOGGING/RUNNING SAMPLE PROGRAM

Walking, jogging, and running are the most popular forms of training for people who want to improve cardiorespiratory endurance; they also improve body composition and muscular endurance of the legs. It's not always easy to distinguish among these three endurance activities. For clarity and consistency, we'll consider walking to be any on-foot exercise of less than 5 miles per hour, jogging any pace between 5 and 7.5 miles per hour, and running any pace faster than that. Table 1 divides walking, jogging, and running into nine categories, with rates of speed (in both miles per hour and minutes per mile) and calorie costs for each. The faster your pace or the longer you exercise, the more calories you burn. The greater the number of calories burned, the higher the potential training effects of these activities. Tables 2 and 3 contain sample walking/jogging programs by time and distance.

Equipment and Technique

These activities require no special skills, expensive equipment, or unusual facilities. Comfortable clothing, well-fitted walking or running shoes, and a stopwatch or ordinary watch with a second hand are all you need.

SAMPLE PROGRAM TABLE 1
CALORIE COSTS FOR WALKING/JOGGING/RUNNING

This table gives the calorie costs of walking, jogging, and running for slow, moderate, and fast paces. Calculations for calorie costs are approximate and assume a level terrain. A hilly terrain would result in higher calorie costs. To get an estimate of the number of calories you burn, multiply your weight by the calories per minute per pound for the speed at which you're doing the activity, and then multiply that by the number of minutes you exercise.

	Speed		
Activity	Miles per Hour	Minutes: Seconds per Mile	Calories per Minute per Pound
Walking			
Slow	2.0	30:00	.020
	2.5	24:00	.023
Moderate	3.0	20:00	.026
	3.5	17:08	.029
Fast	4.0	15:00	.037
	4.5	13:20	.048
Jogging			
Slow	5.0	12:00	.060
	5.5	11:00	.074
Moderate	6.0	10:00	.081
	6.5	9:00	.088
Fast	7.0	8:35	.092
	7.5	8:00	.099
Running			
Slow	8.5	7:00	.111
Moderate	9.0	6:40	.116
Fast	10.0	6:00	.129
	11.0	5:30	.141

SOURCE: Kusinitz, I., and M. Fine, *Physical Fitness for Practically Everybody,* Consumer Reports®, 1983. Consumers Union of the U.S., Inc., Yonkers, NY 10703-1057, a nonprofit organization. Reprinted with permission for educational purposes only. No commercial use or reproduction permitted. www.ConsumerReports.org®.

Developing Cardiorespiratory Endurance

The four variations of the basic walking/jogging/running sample program that follow are designed to help you regulate the intensity, duration, and frequency of your program. Use the following guidelines to choose the variation that is right for you.

- *Variation 1: Walking (starting).* Choose this program if you have medical restrictions, are recovering from illness or surgery, tire easily after short walks, are obese, or have a sedentary lifestyle, and if you want to prepare for the advanced walking program to improve cardiorespiratory endurance, body composition, and muscular endurance.
- *Variation 2: Advanced walking.* Choose this program if you already can walk comfortably for 30 minutes and if you want to develop and maintain cardiorespiratory fitness, a lean body, and muscular endurance.
- *Variation 3: Preparing for a jogging/running program.* Choose this program if you already can walk comfortably for 30 minutes and if you want to prepare for the jogging/running program to improve cardiorespiratory endurance, body composition, and muscular endurance.
- *Variation 4: Jogging/running.* Choose this program if you already can jog comfortably without muscular discomfort, if you already can jog for 15 minutes without stopping or 30 minutes with brief walking intervals within your target heart rate range, and if you want to develop and maintain a high level of cardiorespiratory fitness, a lean body, and muscular endurance.

Variation 1: Walking (Starting)

FIT—frequency, intensity, and time: Walk at first for 15 minutes at a pace that keeps your heart rate below your target zone. Gradually increase to 30-minute sessions. The distance you travel will probably be 1–2 miles. At the beginning, walk every other day. You can gradually increase to daily walking if you want to burn more calories (helpful if you want to change body composition).

Calorie cost: Work up to using 90–135 calories in each session (see Table 1). To increase calorie costs to the target level, walk for a longer time or for a longer distance rather than sharply increasing speed.

At the beginning: Start at whatever level is most comfortable. Maintain a normal, easy pace, and stop to rest as often as you need to. Never prolong a walk past the point of comfort. When walking with a friend (a good motivation), let a comfortable conversation be your guide to pace.

As you progress: Once your muscles have become adjusted to the exercise program, increase the duration of your sessions—but by no more than 10% each week. Increase your intensity only enough to keep your heart rate just below your target. When you're able to walk 1.5 miles in 30 minutes, using 90–135 calories per session, you should consider moving on to Variation 2 or 3. Don't be discouraged by a lack of immediate progress, and don't try to speed things up by overdoing. Remember that pace and heart rate can vary with the terrain, the weather, and other factors.

Variation 2: Advanced Walking

FIT—frequency, intensity, and time: Start at a pace at the lower end of your target heart rate zone, and begin soon afterward to increase your pace. This might boost your heart rate into the upper levels of your target zone, which is fine for brief periods. But don't overdo the intervals of fast walking. Slow down after a short time to drop your pulse rate. Vary your pattern to allow for intervals of slow, medium, and fast walking. Walk at first for 30 minutes and gradually increase your walking time until eventually you reach 60 minutes, all the while maintaining your target heart rate. The distance you walk will probably be 2–4 miles. Walk at least every other day.

SAMPLE PROGRAM TABLE 2

WALKING/JOGGING PROGRESSION BY TIME

This table is based on a walking interval of 3.75 miles per hour, measured in seconds, and a jogging interval of 5.5 miles per hour, measured in minutes:seconds. The combination of the two intervals equals a single set. In the Number of Sets column, the higher figure represents the maximum number of sets to be completed.

	Walk Interval (sec)	Jog Interval (min:sec)	Number of Sets	Total Distance (mi)	Total Time (min:sec)
Stage 1	:60	:30	10–15	1.0–1.7	15:00–22:30
Stage 2	:60	:60	8–13	1.2–2.0	16:00–26:00
Stage 3	:60	2:00	5–19	1.3–2.3	15:00–27:00
Stage 4	:60	3:00	5–7	1.6–2.4	16:00–28:00
Stage 5	:60	4:00	3–6	1.5–2.7	15:00–30:00

SOURCE: Kusinitz, I., and M. Fine, *Physical Fitness for Practically Everybody,* Consumer Reports®, 1983. Consumers Union of the U.S., Inc., Yonkers, NY 10703-1057, a nonprofit organization. Reprinted with permission for educational purposes only. No commercial use or reproduction permitted. www.ConsumerReports.org®.

SAMPLE PROGRAM TABLE 3

WALKING/JOGGING PROGRESSION BY DISTANCE

This table is based on a walking interval of 3.75 miles per hour, measured in yards, and a jogging interval of 5.5 miles per hour, also measured in yards. The combination of the two intervals equals a single set. (One lap around a typical track is 440 yards.)

	Walk Interval (yd)	Jog Interval (yd)	Number of Sets	Total Distance (mi)	Total Time (min:sec)
Stage 1	110	55	11–21	1.0–2.0	15:00–28:12
Stage 2	110	110	16	2.0	26:56
Stage 3	110	220	11	2.0	26:02
Stage 4	110	330	8	2.0	24:24
Stage 5	110	440	7	2.2	26:05
Stage 6	110	440	8	2.5	29:49

SOURCE: Kusinitz, I., and M. Fine, *Physical Fitness for Practically Everybody,* Consumer Reports®, 1983. Consumers Union of the U.S., Inc., Yonkers, NY 10703-1057, a nonprofit organization. Reprinted with permission for educational purposes only. No commercial use or reproduction permitted. www.ConsumerReports.org®.

Calorie cost: Work up to using about 200–350 calories in each session (see Table 1).

At the beginning: Begin by walking somewhat faster than you did in Variation 1. Check your pulse to make sure you keep your heart rate within your target zone. Slow down when necessary to lower your heart rate when going up hills or when extending the duration of your walks.

As you progress: As your heart rate adjusts to the increased workload, gradually increase your pace and your total walking time. Gradually lengthen the intervals of fast walking and shorten the relief intervals of slow walking, always maintaining target heart rate. Eventually, you will reach the fitness level you would like to maintain. To maintain that level of fitness, continue to burn the same amount of calories in each session.

Vary your program by changing the pace and distance walked or by walking routes with different terrains and views. Gauge your progress toward whatever calorie goal you've set by using Table 1.

Variation 3: Preparing for a Jogging/Running Program

FIT—frequency, intensity, and time: Start by walking at a moderate pace (3–4 miles per hour or 15–20 minutes per mile). Staying within your target heart rate zone, begin to add brief intervals of slow jogging (5–6 miles per hour or 10–12 minutes per mile). Keep the walking intervals constant at 60 seconds or at 110 yards, but gradually increase the jogging intervals until eventually you jog 4 minutes for each minute of walking. You'll probably cover between 1.5 and 2.5 miles. Each exercise session should last 15–30 minutes. Exercise every other day. If your goals include changing body composition and you want to exercise more frequently, walk on days you're not jogging.

Calorie cost: Work up to using 200–350 calories in each session (see Table 1).

At the beginning: Start slowly. Until your muscles adjust to jogging, you may need to exercise at less than your target heart rate. At the outset, expect to do two to four times as much walking as jogging, and even more if you're relatively inexperienced. Be guided by how comfortable you feel—and by your heart rate—in setting the pace for your progress. Follow the guidelines presented in Chapter 3 for exercising in hot or cold weather. Drink enough liquids to stay adequately hydrated, particularly in hot weather. In addition, use the proper running technique, described below.

- Run with your back straight and your head up. Look straight ahead, not at your feet. Shift your pelvis forward and tuck your buttocks in.
- Hold your arms slightly away from your body. Your elbows should be bent so that your forearms are parallel to the ground. You may cup your hands, but do not clench your fists. Allow your arms to swing loosely and rhythmically with each stride.
- Let your heel hit the ground first in each stride. Then roll forward onto the ball of your foot and push off for the next stride. If you find this difficult, you can try a more flat-footed style, but don't land on the balls of your feet.
- Keep your steps short by allowing your foot to strike the ground in line with your knee. Keep your knees bent at all times.
- Breathe deeply through your mouth. Try to use your abdominal muscles rather than just your chest muscles to take deep breaths.
- Stay relaxed.

As you progress: Adjust your ratio of walking to jogging to keep within your target heart rate zone as much as possible. When you have progressed to the point at which most of your 30-minute session is spent jogging, consider moving on to Variation 4. To find a walking/jogging progression that suits you, refer to Tables 2 and 3 (one uses time, the other distance). Which one you choose will depend, to some extent, on where you work out. If you have access to a track or can use a measured distance with easily visible landmarks to indicate yardage covered, you may find it convenient to use distance as your organizing principle. If you'll be using parks, streets, or woods, time intervals (measured with a watch) would probably work better. The progressions in Tables 2 and 3 are not meant to be rigid; they are guidelines to help you develop your own rate of progress. Let your progress be guided by your heart rate, and increase your intensity and duration only to achieve your target zone.

Variation 4: Jogging/Running

FIT—frequency, intensity, and time: The key is to exercise within your target heart rate zone. Most people who sustain a continuous jog/run program will find that they can stay within their target heart rate zone with a speed of 5.5–7.5 miles per hour (8–11 minutes per mile). Start by jogging steadily for 15 minutes. Gradually increase your jog/run session to a regular 30–60 minutes (or about 2.5–7 miles). Exercise at least every other day. Increasing frequency by doing other activities on alternate days will place less stress on the weight-bearing parts of your lower body than will a daily program of jogging/running.

Calorie cost: Use about 300–750 calories in each session (see Table 1).

At the beginning: The greater number of calories you burn per minute makes this program less time-consuming for altering body composition than the three other variations in the walking/jogging/running program.

As you progress: If you choose this variation, you probably already have a moderate-to-high level of cardiorespiratory fitness. To stay within your target heart rate zone, increase your distance or both pace and distance as needed. Add variety to your workouts by varying your route, intensity, and duration. Alternate short runs with long runs. If you run for 60 minutes one day, try running for 30 minutes the next session. Or try doing sets that alternate hard and easy intervals—even walking, if you feel like it. You can also try a road race now and then, but be careful not to do too much too soon.

Developing Muscular Strength and Endurance and Flexibility

Walking, jogging, and running provide muscular endurance workouts for your lower body; they also develop muscular strength of the lower body to a lesser degree. If you'd like to increase your running speed and performance, you might want to focus your program on lower-body exercises. (Don't neglect upper-body strength, however; it is important for overall wellness.) For flexibility, pay special attention to the hamstrings and quadriceps, which are not worked through their complete range of motion during walking or jogging.

BICYCLING SAMPLE PROGRAM

Bicycling can also lead to large gains in physical fitness. For many people, cycling is a pleasant and economical alternative to driving and a convenient way to build fitness.

Equipment and Technique

Cycling has its own special array of equipment, including headgear, lighting, safety pennants, and special shoes. The bike is the most expensive item, ranging from about $100 to well over $1000. Avoid making a large investment until you're sure you'll use your bike regularly. While investigating what the marketplace has to offer, rent or borrow a bike. Consider your intended use of the bike. Most cyclists who are interested primarily in fitness are best served by a sturdy 10-speed rather than a mountain bike or sport bike. Stationary cycles are good for rainy days and areas that have harsh winters.

Clothing for bike riding shouldn't be restrictive or binding, nor should it be so loose-fitting or so long that it might get caught in the chain. Clothing worn on the upper body should be comfortable but not so loose that it catches the wind and slows you down. Always wear a helmet to help prevent injury in case of a fall or crash. Wearing glasses or goggles can protect the eyes from dirt, small objects, and irritation from wind.

To avoid saddle soreness and injury, choose a soft or padded saddle, and adjust it to a height that allows your legs to almost reach full extension while pedaling. Make certain the saddle doesn't put too much pressure on sensitive areas. Wear a pair of well-padded gloves if your hands tend to become numb while riding or if you begin to develop blisters or calluses. To prevent backache and neck strain, warm up thoroughly and periodically shift the position of your hands on the handlebars and your body in the saddle. Keep your arms relaxed and don't lock your elbows. To protect your knees from strain, pedal with your feet pointed straight ahead or very slightly inward, and don't pedal in high gear for long periods.

Bike riding requires a number of precise skills that practice makes automatic. If you've never ridden before, consider taking a course. In fact, many courses are not just for beginners. They'll help you develop skills in braking, shifting, and handling emergencies, as well as teach you ways of caring for and repairing your bike. For safe cycling, follow these rules:

- Always wear a helmet.
- Keep on the correct side of the road. Bicycling against traffic is usually illegal and always dangerous.
- Obey all traffic signs and signals.
- On public roads, ride in single file, except in low-traffic areas (if the law permits). Ride in a straight line; don't swerve or weave in traffic.
- Be alert; anticipate the movements of other traffic and pedestrians. Listen for approaching traffic that is out of your line of vision.
- Slow down at street crossings. Check both ways before crossing.
- Use hand signals—the same as for automobile drivers—if you intend to stop or turn. Use audible signals to warn those in your path.
- Maintain full control. Avoid anything that interferes with your vision. Don't jeopardize your ability to steer by carrying anything (including people) on the handlebars.
- Keep your bicycle in good shape. Brakes, gears, saddle, wheels, and tires should always be in good condition.
- See and be seen. Use a headlight at night and equip your bike with rear reflectors. Use side reflectors on pedals, front and rear. Wear light-colored clothing or use reflective tape at night; wear bright colors or use fluorescent tape by day.
- Be courteous to other road users. Anticipate the worst and practice preventive cycling.
- Use a rear-view mirror.

Developing Cardiorespiratory Endurance

Cycling is an excellent way to develop and maintain cardiorespiratory endurance and a healthy body composition.

FIT—frequency, intensity, and time: If you've been inactive for a long time, begin your cycling program at a heart rate that is 10–20% below your target zone. Beginning cyclists should pedal at about 80–100 revolutions per minute; adjust the gear so that you can pedal at that rate easily. Your bicycle may display different types of useful information, including speed, distance traveled, heart rate, altitude, and revolutions per minute, and it may provide a cadence signal to help you maintain your pace. Once you feel at home on your bike, try 1 mile at a comfortable speed, and then stop and check your heart rate. Increase your speed gradually until you can cycle at 12–15 miles per hour (4–5 minutes per mile), a speed fast enough to bring most new cyclists' heart rate into their target zone. Allow your pulse rate to be your guide: More highly fit individuals may need to ride faster to achieve their target heart rate. Cycling for at least 20 minutes three times a week will improve your fitness.

Calorie cost: Use Table 4 to determine the number of calories you burn during each outing. You can increase the number of calories burned by cycling faster or for a longer time (it's usually better to increase distance than to add speed).

At the beginning: It may require several outings to get the muscles and joints of your legs and hips adjusted to this new activity. Begin each outing with a 10-minute warm-up. When your muscles are warm, stretch your hamstrings and your back and neck muscles. Until you become a skilled cyclist, select routes with the fewest hazards and avoid heavy automobile traffic.

As you progress: Interval training is also effective with bicycling. Simply increase your speed for periods of 4–8 minutes or for specific distances, such as 1–2 miles. Then coast for 2–3 minutes. Alternate the speed intervals and slow intervals for a total of 20–60 minutes, depending on your level of fitness. Hilly terrain is also a form of interval training.

Developing Muscular Strength and Endurance and Flexibility

Bicycling develops a high level of endurance and a moderate level of strength in the muscles of the lower body. If one of your goals is to increase your cycling speed and performance, be sure to include exercises for the quadriceps, hamstrings, and buttocks muscles in your strength training program. For flexibility, pay special attention to the hamstrings and quadriceps, which are not worked through their complete range of motion during bike riding, and to the muscles in your lower back, shoulders, and neck.

SAMPLE PROGRAM TABLE 4

CALORIE COSTS FOR BICYCLING

This table gives the approximate calorie costs per pound of body weight for cycling from 5 to 60 minutes for distances of .50 mile up to 15 miles on a level terrain. To use the table, find on the horizontal line the time most closely approximating the number of minutes you cycle. Next, locate on the vertical column the approximate distance in miles you cover. The figure at the intersection represents an estimate of the calories used per minute per pound of body weight. Multiply this figure by your body weight. Then multiply the product of these two figures by the number of minutes you cycle to get the total number of calories burned. For example, assuming you weigh 154 pounds and cycle 6 miles in 40 minutes, you would burn 260 calories: 154 × .042 (calories per pound, from table) = 6.5 × 40 (minutes) = 260 calories burned.

	Time (min)											
Distance (mi)	5	10	15	20	25	30	35	40	45	50	55	60
.50	.032											
1.00	.062	.032										
1.50		.042	.032									
2.00		.062	.039	.032								
3.00			.062	.042	.036	.032						
4.00				.062	.044	.039	.035	.032				
5.00				.097	.062	.045	.041	.037	.035	.032		
6.00					.088	.062	.047	.042	.039	.036	.034	.032
7.00						.081	.062	.049	.043	.040	.038	.036
8.00							.078	.062	.050	.044	.041	.039
9.00								.076	.062	.051	.045	.042
10.00								.097	.074	.062	.051	.045
11.00									.093	.073	.062	.052
12.00										.088	.072	.062
13.00											.084	.071
14.00												.081
15.00												.097

SOURCE: Kusinitz, I., and M. Fine, *Physical Fitness for Practically Everybody,* Consumer Reports®, 1983. Consumers Union of the U.S., Inc., Yonkers, NY 10703-1057, a nonprofit organization. Reprinted with permission for educational purposes only. No commercial use or reproduction permitted. www.ConsumerReports.org®.

SWIMMING SAMPLE PROGRAM

Swimming is excellent for developing all-around fitness. Because water supports the body weight of the swimmer, swimming places less stress than weight-bearing activities on joints, ligaments, and tendons and tends to cause fewer injuries.

Equipment and Safety Guidelines

Aside from having access to a swimming pool, the only equipment required for a swimming program is a swimsuit and a pair of swimming goggles (that fit and do not leak) to protect the eyes from irritation in chlorinated pools. Following these few simple rules can help keep you safe and healthy during your swimming sessions:

- Swim only in a pool with a qualified lifeguard on duty.
- Always walk carefully on wet surfaces.
- Dry your ears well after swimming. If you experience the symptoms of swimmer's ear (itching, discharge, or even a partial hearing loss), consult your physician. If you swim while recovering from swimmer's ear, protect your ears with a few drops of lanolin on a wad of lamb's wool.
- To avoid back pain, try not to arch your back excessively when you swim.
- Be courteous to others in the pool.

If you swim in a setting other than a pool with a lifeguard, remember the following important rules:

- Don't swim beyond your skill and endurance limits.
- Avoid being chilled: don't swim in water colder than 70°F.
- Never drink alcohol before going swimming.
- Never swim alone.

Developing Cardiorespiratory Endurance

Any one or any combination of common swimming strokes—front crawl stroke, breaststroke, backstroke, butterfly stroke, sidestroke, or elementary backstroke—can help develop and maintain cardiorespiratory fitness. (Swimming may not be as helpful as walking, jogging, or cycling for body fat loss.)

FIT—frequency, intensity, and time: Because swimming is not a weight-bearing activity and is not done in an upright position, it elicits a lower heart rate per minute. Therefore, you'll need to adjust your target heart rate zone. To calculate your target heart rate for swimming, use this formula:

Maximum swimming heart rate (MSHR) = 205 − age
Target heart rate zone = 65 − 90% of MSHR

For example, a 19-year-old would calculate her target heart rate zone for swimming as follows:

MSHR = 205 − 19 = 186 bpm
65% intensity 0.65 × 186 = 121 bpm
90% intensity 0.90 × 186 = 167 bpm

Base your duration of swimming on your intensity and target calorie costs. Swim at least three times a week.

Calorie cost: Calories burned while swimming are the result of the pace: how far you swim and how fast (Table 5). Work up to using at least 300 calories per session.

At the beginning: If you are an inexperienced swimmer, invest in the time and money for instruction. You'll make more rapid gains in fitness if you learn correct swimming technique. If you've been sedentary and haven't done any swimming for a long time, begin your program with 2–3 weeks, three times a week, of leisurely swimming at a pace that keeps your heart rate 10–20% below your target zone. Start swimming laps of the width of the pool if you can't swim the length. To keep your heart rate below target, take rest intervals as needed. Swim one lap, then rest 15–90 seconds as needed. Start with 10 minutes of swim/rest intervals and work up to 20 minutes. How long it takes will depend on your swimming skills and muscular fitness.

As you progress: Gradually increase the duration, or the intensity, or both duration and intensity of your swimming to raise your heart rate to a comfortable level within your target zone. Gradually increase your swimming intervals and decrease your rest intervals as you progress. Once you can swim the length of the pool at a pace that keeps your heart rate on target, continue swim/rest intervals for 20 minutes. Your rest intervals should be 30–45 seconds. You may find it helpful to get out of the pool during your rest intervals and walk until you've lowered your heart rate. Next, swim two laps of the pool length per swim interval and continue swim/rest intervals for 30 minutes. For the 30-second rest interval, walk (or rest) until you've lowered your heart rate. Gradually increase the number of laps you swim consecutively and the total duration of your session until you reach your target calorie expenditure and fitness level. But take care not to swim at too fast a pace: It can raise your heart rate too high and limit your ability to sustain your swimming. Alternating strokes can rest your muscles and help prolong your swimming time. A variety of strokes will also let you work more muscle groups. You can also vary your program by incorporating kick boards, pull-buoys, hand paddles, or fins into some of your workouts.

SAMPLE PROGRAM TABLE 5

CALORIE COSTS FOR SWIMMING

To use this table, find on the top horizontal row the distance in yards that most closely approximates the distance you swim. Next, locate on the appropriate vertical column (below the distance in yards) the time it takes you to swim the distance. Then locate in the first column on the left the approximate number of calories burned per minute per pound for the time and distance. To find the total number of calories burned, multiply your weight by the calories per minute per pound. Then multiply the product of these two numbers by the time it takes you to swim the distance (minutes:seconds). For example, assuming you weigh 130 pounds and swim 500 yards in 20 minutes, you would burn 106 calories: 130 × .041 (calories per pound, from table) = 5.33 × 20 (minutes) = 106 calories burned.

Calories per Minute per Pound	Distance (yd)					
	25	100	150	250	500	750
.033	1:15	5:00	7:30	12:30	25:00	30:30
.041	1:00	4:00	6:00	10:00	20:00	30:00
.049	0:50	3:20	5:00	8:20	18:40	25:00
.057	0:43	2:52	4:18	7:10	17:20	21:30
.065	0:37.5	2:30	3:45	6:15	10:00	
.073	0:33	2:13	3:20	5:30	8:50	
.081	0:30	2:00	3:00	5:00	8:00	
.090	0:27	1:48	2:42	4:30	7:12	
.097	0:25	1:40	2:30	4:10	6:30	

SOURCE: Kusinitz, I., and M. Fine, *Physical Fitness for Practically Everybody*, Consumer Reports®, 1983. Consumers Union of the U.S., Inc., Yonkers, NY 10703-1057, a nonprofit organization. Reprinted with permission for educational purposes only. No commercial use or reproduction permitted. www.ConsumerReports.org®.

Developing Muscular Strength and Endurance and Flexibility

The swimming program outlined in this section will result in moderate gains in strength and large gains in endurance in the muscles used during the strokes you've chosen. To improve your swimming performance, include exercises that work key muscles. For example, if you swim primarily front crawl, include exercises to increase strength in your shoulders, arms, and upper back. (Training the muscles you use during swimming can also help prevent injuries.) For flexibility, pay special attention to the muscles you use during swimming, particularly the shoulders and back.

CALISTHENICS CIRCUIT-TRAINING SAMPLE PROGRAM

Calisthenics are rhythmic exercises that typically develop muscular strength, muscular endurance, and flexibility. Because calisthenic exercises require little or no equipment, they can be performed at home or while traveling. As commonly practiced, such exercises do not constitute a well-rounded fitness program because they do not develop cardiorespiratory endurance. However, a calisthenics program based on circuit training can be the basis of a complete fitness program.

Circuit training is a system of organizing a series of exercises that are performed consecutively. Exercises for different muscle groups follow one another, providing a well-rounded workout and helping to delay the onset of fatigue. When you have performed all the exercises in this model program, you will have completed one circuit; a workout consists of three trips around the circuit. By performing the exercises continuously and not resting between exercises or circuits, you can develop the cardiorespiratory endurance component of fitness. In addition, some of the individual exercises, such as jumping jacks or running in place, develop cardiorespiratory endurance.

Equipment

To time your exercises (which is required only once, when you create your work description), you need a clock or watch with a second hand. If you plan to perform calisthenics regularly, it's a good idea to get a pair of cross-training athletic shoes. Choose an exercise area that is well ventilated and comfortable, with enough room for you to do the exercises without interference. You may want to perform the floor exercises (such as curl-ups) on an exercise mat or a nonskid rug.

Technique

To perform a complete calisthenics cross-training circuit, you need to be able to perform the following exercises smoothly.

- ***Arm circles.*** Stand with your feet shoulder-width apart and your knees slightly bent. Maintain good posture to protect the lower back. Hold your arms out to the side at shoulder height with palms up. Rotate your arms forward in a circular motion. Keep your shoulders down. Halfway through the time limit or work description, reverse the direction of your circles.

- ***Jumping jacks.*** Start with your feet together and your hands at your sides. Jump into a straddle position and clap your hands over your head. Then jump back to the starting position and lower your arms to your sides. Always land with your knees slightly bent. Land on the balls of your feet and then press your heels down. If you prefer a low-impact movement, step to the side into the straddle position and then step back into the starting position; alternate legs.

- ***Push-ups.*** Depending on your level of muscular strength and endurance, you can perform either standard push-ups or modified push-ups. For standard push-ups, begin with your body supported by your hands and feet; for modified push-ups, begin with your body supported by your hands and knees. Lower your chest to the floor with your back straight and your fingers pointed forward. Return to the starting position. (See Lab 4.2, p. 130.)

- ***Squats.*** Stand with feet shoulder-width apart and toes pointed slightly outward. Keeping your head up and lower back straight, squat down until your thighs are approximately parallel with the floor. Don't let your knees extend out in front of your toes. Hold this position for about 2 seconds. Return to the starting position. (See Lab 4.1, p. 126, and Lab 4.2, p. 131.)

- ***Curls-ups.*** Lie on your back on the floor with your arms folded across your chest, knees bent, and feet on the floor. Curl your trunk up and forward by raising your head and shoulders from the ground. Lower to the starting position. (See Lab 4.2, p. 129.)

Alternative instructions (performing curl-ups this way provides better protection for the back during the exercise): Lie on your back on a mat with one knee bent and foot flat on the floor. Place your hands under your lower back and maintain a neutral spine (don't flatten your back to the mat). Curl up as far as possible by contracting the rectus abdominis muscle ("6-pack muscle") rather than your neck and shoulder muscles. As fitness improves, do the exercise with arms folded on your chest. Eventually, place your hands lightly on your forehead, but do not pull on your head and neck.

- ***Side leg raises.*** Lie on your right side, with your right arm extended flat along the floor in front of your body. Bend your right knee, keeping your knee and thigh in line with your torso. Place your left hand on the floor in front of your chest for balance. Keeping your left leg straight, foot flexed, and toes and knee facing forward (not up), lift your leg 1–2 feet off the floor. Then lower it to the starting position. Do half of your total repetitions on this side, and then do the same number of repetitions on the other side.

- ***Heel raises.*** Stand with your feet shoulder-width apart and your toes pointed slightly outward. Press down with your toes while lifting your heels. Return to the starting position. Do not bounce. (See Exercise 8 in the free weights portion of the Weight Training Exercises in Chapter 4, p. 113.)

- ***Upper-back flies.*** Stand with your feet 1½–2 times shoulder-width apart and your knees slightly bent. Keeping your back straight, lean forward at the hips until your torso is diagonal to the floor. Let your arms hang forward, with elbows slightly bent and hands fisted. Leading with your elbows, open your arms to the side and pull your shoulder blades together. Return to the starting position. Lift your arms smoothly and with resistance; do not bounce or swing them.

- ***Lunges.*** Begin with your feet shoulder-width apart and your hands at your sides or resting on your shoulders. Step forward onto your right foot until your right thigh is almost parallel to the floor. Your right knee should be directly above your right ankle and should not push out in front of your toes. Bend your left knee and drop it directly below your torso in line with your left ankle; your lower left leg should be about parallel to the floor. (See Exercise 6 in the Flexibility Exercises in Chapter 5, p. 144.) Return to the starting position, using the gluteal muscles to push off the floor. Contract the abdominals to relieve pressure on your knees and lower back. Alternate legs. (*Note:* Do not perform lunges if you have knee problems.)

- ***Back bridges.*** Lie on your back with knees bent and arms extended to the side. Tuck your pelvis under and then lift your tailbone, buttocks, and lower back from the floor. Hold for 5–10 seconds, with your weight resting on your feet, arms, and shoulders. Return to the starting position. (See Exercise 10 in the Low Back Exercises in Chapter 5, p. 153.)

• ***Spine extension.*** Start on your hands and knees, with your knees below your hips and your hands below your shoulders. Simultaneously raise and straighten your right arm and left leg until they are in line with your spine. Hold this position for 30 seconds. Do not raise either the arm or the leg above spine level (that is, don't arch your back). Return to the starting position and immediately repeat the movement with the left arm and right leg. Do not raise your arms and legs excessively or increase the low back curve by tilting the pelvis. (See Exercise 10 in the free weights portion of the Weight Training Exercises in Chapter 4, p. 114.)

• ***Side bridges.*** Lie on your side with your knees bent and your top arm lying alongside your body. Lift your hips so that your weight is supported by your forearm and knees. (See Exercise 11 in the free weights portion of the Weight Training Exercises in Chapter 4, p. 115). Hold the position for 10 seconds, breathing normally. Repeat on the other side. As you increase fitness, make the exercise more difficult by doing it with straight legs and supporting yourself with your feet and forearm or with your feet and hand (arm extended, elbow straight). (See Lab 5.3, p. 165.) Hold your spine straight—don't let it sag during the exercise.

• ***Running in place.*** Run with your knees lifted and land with the ball of your foot first. Follow through by pressing your heel to the floor. If you prefer a low-impact movement, march in place, lifting your knees high. (When you count repetitions of running or marching, count alternate steps.)

Developing Cardiorespiratory Endurance

Calisthenics can help develop cardiorespiratory fitness provided the intensity is moderate to intense. Maximize the cardiorespiratory benefits by moving rapidly between exercises and doing each movement vigorously.

FIT—frequency, intensity, and time: Do the workout 3–5 days per week. Exercise intensely enough to raise your heart rate into the target zone: 65–90% of maximum heart rate or an RPE of 12–18. (If you have been inactive for a long time, start out at a heart rate that is 10–20% below your target zone.) Exercise at an intensity that allows you to comfortably carry on a conversation. Begin by doing the calisthenics circuit one time. As you gain fitness, build up gradually until you can complete 3 circuits (see "As you progress," p. 215).

Calorie cost: To estimate the number of calories you burn, first determine the amount of time it takes to complete a circuit, multiply the calories per minute per pound (.060) by your weight, then multiply that figure by the number of minutes you need to complete one circuit of exercises. For example, assuming you weigh 145 pounds and complete a circuit in 15 minutes, you would burn 131 calories per circuit: 145 × .060 (calories per pound for vigorous training) = 8.7 × 15 (minutes) = 131 calories burned. To burn more calories, increase your repetitions, work faster, and/or work longer.

At the beginning: Before doing your first full calisthenic workout, you need to set up a work description—the number of repetitions of each exercise you will perform in each circuit. To do this, determine the maximum number of repetitions of each exercise you can perform in the time listed in the following table.

For example, count the maximum number of arm circles you can do in 30 seconds, and record that number in the "Max" column. Rest fully between exercises to obtain true maximums. Once you have filled in the "Max" column, write half of this number in the "Work Description" column labeled "1/2 Max." Once you have completed this step, you no longer have to worry about timing the individual exercises.

			Work Description						
Exercise	Time	Max	½ Max	Date: ______	Date: ______	Date: ______	Date: ______	Date: ______	Date: ______
Arm circles	30 sec								
Jumping jacks	1 min								
Push-ups	1 min								
Squats	1 min								
Curl-ups	1 min								
Side leg raises	1 min								
Heel raises	30 sec								
Upper-back flies	30 sec								
Lunges	1 min								
Back bridges	1 min								
Spine extensions	1 min								
Side bridges	1 min								
Run in place	3 min								

After your work description is set up, perform each circuit as follows:

- Warm up before you begin the circuit by doing some walking, jogging, or easy calisthenics. When you are ready to begin, note your starting time.
- Perform the exercises in order, each for the number of repetitions in the "1/2Max" column. Time no longer matters for each exercise; just work steadily.
- Monitor your intensity by checking your heart rate or monitoring your rating of perceived exertion (RPE). Do not rest between exercises unless your heart rate or RPE goes above your target zone.
- Complete three trips around the circuit. In the progress chart below, write the date and total time the three circuits took.
- Cool down.

Progress Chart

Date											
Time											

As you progress: When you can perform three circuits in 20 minutes, increase the number of repetitions (the work description) of each exercise by one-quarter of the present work description. For example, if your current work description for push-ups is 20 repetitions, your new work description will be 25. Record the date and the new work description values in the program plan table.

Developing Muscular Strength and Endurance and Flexibility

If you perform a full range of calisthenic exercises (as described in this program), you can develop muscular strength and endurance in all the major muscle groups of your body. Your gains, however, will not be as significant as those from weight training using free weights or machines (unless you add arm or leg weights to increase resistance). To develop flexibility, stretch during your cool-down, when your muscles are warm.

Name ______________________ Section ______________ Date ______________

LAB 7.1 A Personal Fitness Program Plan and Contract

A. I, ______________________ (name), am contracting with myself to follow a physical fitness program to work toward the following goals:

Specific or short-term goals (include current status for each):

1. ______________________
2. ______________________
3. ______________________
4. ______________________

General or long-term goals:

1. ______________________
2. ______________________
3. ______________________
4. ______________________

B. My program plan is as follows:

Activities	Components (Check ✓)					Frequency (Check ✓)							Intensity*	Time (duration)
	CRE	MS	ME	F	BC	M	Tu	W	Th	F	Sa	Su		

*Conduct activities for achieving CRE goals in your target range for heart rate or RPE.

C. My program will begin on ______________ (date). My program includes the following schedule of mini-goals. For each step in my program, I will give myself the reward listed.

______________________ (mini-goal 1) ______________ (date) ______________ (reward)

______________________ (mini-goal 2) ______________ (date) ______________ (reward)

______________________ (mini-goal 3) ______________ (date) ______________ (reward)

______________________ (mini-goal 4) ______________ (date) ______________ (reward)

______________________ (mini-goal 5) ______________ (date) ______________ (reward)

LABORATORY ACTIVITIES

D. My program will include the addition of physical activity to my daily routine (such as climbing stairs or walking to class):

1. ____________________

2. ____________________

3. ____________________

4. ____________________

5. ____________________

E. I will use the following tools to monitor my program and my progress toward my goals:

____
(list any charts, graphs, or journals you plan to use)

____

____

I sign this contract as an indication of my personal commitment to reach my goal.

____________________ ____________
(your signature) (date)

I have recruited a helper who will witness my contract and ____________________

____
(list any way your helper will participate in your program)

____

____________________ ____________
(witness's signature) (date)

LAB 7.2 Getting to Know Your Fitness Facility

To help create a successful training program, take time to learn more about the fitness facility you plan to use.

Basic Information

Name and location of facility: ______

Hours of operation: ______

Times available for general use: ______

Times most convenient for your schedule: ______

Can you obtain an initial session or consultation with a trainer to help you create a program? ______ yes ______ no

If so, what does the initial planning session involve? ______

Are any of the staff certified? Do any have special training? If yes, list/describe: ______

What types of equipment are available for the development of cardiorespiratory endurance? Briefly list/describe: ______

Are any group activities or classes available? If so, briefly describe: ______

What types of weight training equipment are available for use? ______

Yes	No	
______	______	Is there a fee for using the facility? If so, how much? $ ______
______	______	Is a student ID required for access to the facility?
______	______	Do you need to sign up in advance to use the facility or any of the equipment?
______	______	Is there typically a line or wait to use the equipment during the times you use the facility?
______	______	Is there a separate area with mats for stretching and/or cool-down?
______	______	Do you need to bring your own towel?
______	______	Are lockers available? If so, do you need to bring your own lock? ______ yes ______ no
______	______	Are showers available? If so, do you need to bring your own soap and shampoo? ______ yes ______ no
______	______	Is drinking water available? (If not, be sure to bring your own bottle of water.)

What other amenities, such as vending machines or saunas, are available at the facility? Briefly list/describe: ______

Information About Equipment

Fill in the specific equipment and exercise(s) that you can use to develop cardiorespiratory endurance and each of the major muscle groups. For cardiorespiratory endurance, list the type(s) of equipment and a sample starting workout: frequency, intensity, time, and other pertinent information (such as a setting for resistance or speed). For muscular strength and endurance, list the equipment and exercises, and indicate the order in which you'll complete them during a workout session (see p. 103 for suggestions on order of weight training exercises).

Cardiorespiratory Endurance Equipment

Equipment	Sample Starting Workout

Muscular Strength and Endurance Equipment

Order	Muscle Groups	Equipment	Exercise(s)
	Neck		
	Chest		
	Shoulders		
	Upper back		
	Front of arms		
	Back of arms		
	Buttocks		
	Abdomen		
	Lower back		
	Front of thighs		
	Back of thighs		
	Calves		
	Other:		
	Other:		

LOOKING AHEAD>>>>>

AFTER READING THIS CHAPTER, YOU SHOULD BE ABLE TO:

- List the essential nutrients and describe the functions they perform in the body
- Describe the guidelines that have been developed to help people choose a healthy diet, avoid nutritional deficiencies, and protect themselves from diet-related chronic diseases
- Discuss nutritional guidelines for vegetarians and for special population groups
- Explain how to use food labels and other consumer tools to make informed choices about foods
- Put together a personal nutrition plan based on affordable foods that you enjoy and that will promote wellness, today and in the future

NUTRITION 8

TEST YOUR KNOWLEDGE

1. **It is recommended that all adults consume 2–3 half-cup servings of fruits and vegetables every day.**
   True or false?
2. **Candy is the leading source of added sugars in the American diet.**
   True or false?
3. **Which of the following is not a whole grain?**
   a. brown rice
   b. wheat flour
   c. popcorn

ANSWERS

1. **FALSE.** For someone consuming 2000 calories, 2½ cups of vegetables and 2 cups of fruit are recommended—a total of 9 half-cup servings. Most Americans fail to meet this goal; half of all the vegetables we do eat are potatoes—and half of those are french fried.
2. **FALSE.** Regular (nondiet) sodas are the leading source of added sugars and calories, with an average of 55 gallons consumed per person per year. Each 12-ounce soda supplies about 10 teaspoons of sugar, or nearly 10% of the calories in a 2000-calorie diet.
3. **b.** Unless labeled "whole wheat," wheat flour is processed to remove the bran and germ and is not a whole grain.

FIT AND WELL ONLINE LEARNING CENTER www.mhhe.com/fahey

Visit the *Fit and Well* Online Learning Center for resources that will help you get the most out of your course!

- Study and review aids include practice quizzes, glossary flashcards, chapter summaries, learning objectives, PowerPoint presentations, Common Questions Answered, student handouts, crossword puzzles, Internet activities, and links to wellness Web sites.
- Behavior change tools include a daily fitness and nutrition journal, a behavior change workbook, sample behavior change plans, and blank behavior change logs to print and use.

In your lifetime, you will spend about 6 years eating—about 70,000 meals and 60 tons of food. What you eat affects your energy level, well-being, and overall health (see the box "Eating Habits and Total Wellness"). Of particular concern is the connection between lifetime nutritional habits and risk of the major chronic diseases, including heart disease, cancer, stroke, and diabetes. Choosing foods that provide adequate amounts of the nutrients you need while limiting the substances linked to disease should be an important part of your daily life. The food choices you make will significantly influence your health—both now and in the future.

Choosing a healthy diet that supports maximum fitness and protects against disease is a two-part process. First, you have to know which nutrients are necessary and in what amounts. Second, you have to translate those requirements into a diet consisting of foods you like to eat that are both available and affordable. Once you have an idea of what constitutes a healthy diet for you, you may need to make adjustments in your current diet to bring it into line with your goals.

This chapter explains the basic principles of **nutrition.** It introduces the six classes of essential nutrients, and examines their role in the functioning of the body. It also provides different sets of guidelines that you can use to design a healthy diet plan. Finally, it offers practical tools and advice to help you apply the guidelines to your life. Diet is an area of your life in which you have almost total control. Using your knowledge and understanding of nutrition to create a healthy diet plan is a significant step toward wellness.

> **MOTIVATION BOOSTER**
>
> ***Write it down.*** A nutrition journal can be a useful tool for evaluating and improving your diet. The very act of recording everything you eat may improve your dietary habits—you'll find yourself thinking before you eat and avoiding some unhealthy choices so you don't have to record them. A nutrition journal can significantly boost your awareness of both your food choices and your portion sizes. Keeping a journal also reinforces your commitment, and it can help you maintain your motivation to change your eating habits.

TERMS

nutrition The science of food and how the body uses it in health and disease.

essential nutrients Substances the body must get from food because it cannot manufacture them at all or fast enough to meet its needs. These nutrients include proteins, fats, carbohydrates, vitamins, minerals, and water.

digestion The process of breaking down foods in the gastrointestinal tract into compounds the body can absorb.

macronutrients Essential nutrients required by the body in relatively large amounts.

micronutrients Essential nutrients required by the body in minute amounts.

kilocalorie A measure of energy content in food; 1 kilocalorie represents the amount of heat needed to raise the temperature of 1 liter of water 1°C; commonly referred to as *calorie.*

NUTRITIONAL REQUIREMENTS: COMPONENTS OF A HEALTHY DIET

When you think about your diet, you probably do so in terms of the foods you like to eat—a turkey sandwich and a glass of milk or black beans and rice. What's important for your health, though, are the nutrients contained in those foods. Your body requires proteins, fats, carbohydrates, vitamins, minerals, and water—about 45 **essential nutrients.** The word *essential* in this context means that you must get these substances from food because your body either is unable to manufacture them at all or cannot do so fast enough to meet your physiological needs. The six classes of nutrients, along with their functions and major sources, are listed in Table 8.1.

Nutrients are released into the body by the process of **digestion,** which breaks food down into compounds that the gastrointestinal tract can absorb and the body can use (Figure 8.1, p. 224). A diet containing adequate amounts of all essential nutrients is vital because various nutrients provide energy, build and maintain body tissues, and regulate body functions. Some essential nutrients are needed by the body in relatively large amounts. These **macronutrients** include protein, fat, and carbohydrate. **Micronutrients,** such as vitamins and minerals, are required in much smaller amounts.

The energy in foods is expressed as **kilocalories.** One kilocalorie represents the amount of heat it takes to raise the temperature of 1 liter of water 1°C. A person needs about 2000 kilocalories a day to meet his or her energy needs. People usually refer to kilocalories as *calories,* which is a much smaller energy unit: 1 kilocalorie contains 1000 calories. This chapter uses the familiar word *calorie* to stand for the larger energy unit; you'll also find *calorie* used on food labels.

Of the six classes of essential nutrients, three supply energy:

- Fat = 9 calories per gram
- Protein = 4 calories per gram
- Carbohydrate = 4 calories per gram

Alcohol, though not an essential nutrient, also supplies energy, providing 7 calories per gram. (One gram equals a little less than 0.04 ounce.) The high caloric content of fat is one reason experts often advise against high fat consumption; most of us do not need the extra calories to meet energy needs. Regardless of their source, calories consumed in excess of energy needs can be converted to fat and stored in the body.

WELLNESS CONNECTION

Eating Habits and Total Wellness

Healthy eating does more than nourish your body—it enhances your ability to enjoy life to the fullest by improving overall wellness, both physical and mental. One study examined a group of adults who followed a healthy eating plan for 4 years. At the end of this period, the study subjects were more confident with their food choices and more satisfied with their lives in general than their peers who did not make any dietary changes. The reverse is also true—when people overeat, they often have feelings of guilt, anger, discouragement, and even self-loathing. Out-of-control eating can erode self-confidence and lead to depression.

Can individual foods affect the way we feel? Limited scientific evidence points to some correlation between certain foods and one's mood. Many people, especially women, seem to crave chocolate when they feel slightly depressed. Studies show that chocolate, in small quantities, may indeed give you a lift. Sugary foods tend to temporarily raise serotonin levels in the brain, which can improve mood (serotonin is a neurotransmitter associated with a calm, relaxed state). The fat found in chocolate acts to increase endorphins, brain chemicals that reduce pain and increase feelings of well-being. Chocolate also contains a variety of other less studied chemicals that may have a positive impact on mood.

A commonly held belief about the connection between food and the mind is that eating sugary foods makes people (especially children) hyperactive. Parents often comment on the wild behavior observed at parties and festive events where lots of sweets are consumed. However, several carefully controlled studies showed no correlation between behavior and the consumption of sugary foods. Researchers speculate that high-sugar foods tend to be eaten at birthday parties and other exciting occasions when children tend to be highly stimulated regardless of what they eat.

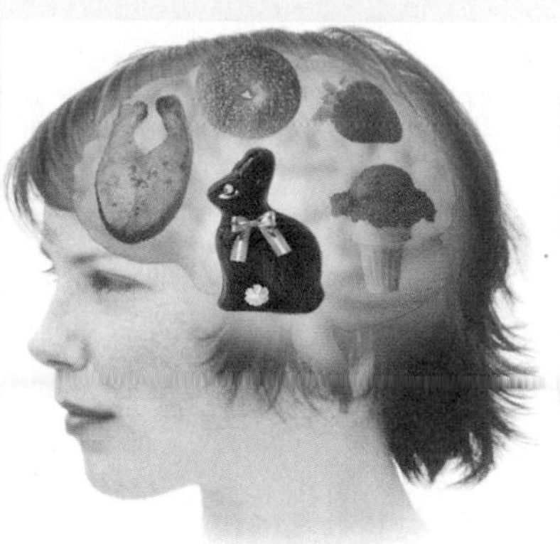

Some recent research shows that eating certain carbohydrate-rich foods, such as a plain baked potato or a bagel with jelly, can have a temporary calming effect. This effect is most pronounced when rapidly digestible carbohydrates are consumed alone, with no fats or proteins in the meal. The practical implications of this research are uncertain.

If you are looking for a mental boost, some scientists think that eating a meal consisting primarily of protein-rich foods may be helpful. Some researchers think that eating protein-rich foods could increase the synthesis of certain neurotransmitters, which can speed reaction time and increase alertness. Whether this really works, especially in well-nourished individuals who have not been lacking these nutrients to begin with, remains to be seen. In the meantime, it wouldn't hurt, and might even help, to include some protein in the meal you eat prior to your next big exam.

What we know about how food affects mood remains limited. But evidence points to the commonsense conclusion that enjoying reasonable portions of a variety of healthy and tasty foods is a great way to optimize your physical and mental health.

Table 8.1 The Six Classes of Essential Nutrients

Nutrient	Function	Major Sources
Proteins (4 calories/gram)	Form important parts of muscles, bone, blood, enzymes, some hormones, and cell membranes; repair tissue; regulate water and acid-base balance; help in growth; supply energy	Meat, fish, poultry, eggs, milk products, legumes, nuts
Carbohydrates (4 calories/gram)	Supply energy to cells in brain, nervous system, and blood; supply energy to muscles during exercise	Grains (breads and cereals), fruits, vegetables, milk
Fats (9 calories/gram)	Supply energy; insulate, support, and cushion organs; provide medium for absorption of fat-soluble vitamins	Animal foods, grains, nuts, seeds, fish, vegetables
Vitamins	Promote (initiate or speed up) specific chemical reactions within cells	Abundant in fruits, vegetables, and grains; also found in meat and dairy products
Minerals	Help regulate body functions; aid in growth and maintenance of body tissues; act as catalysts for release of energy	Found in most food groups
Water	Makes up 50–70% of body weight; provides medium for chemical reactions; transports chemicals; regulates temperature; removes waste products	Fruits, vegetables, liquids

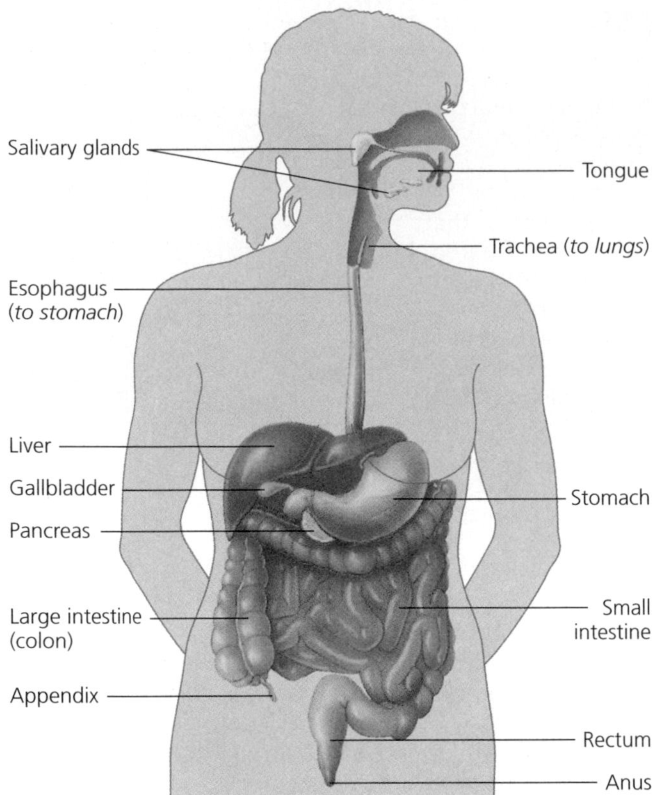

FIGURE 8.1 The digestive system. Food is partially broken down by being chewed and mixed with saliva in the mouth. After traveling to the stomach via the esophagus, food is broken down further by stomach acids. As food moves through the digestive tract, it is mixed by muscular contractions and broken down by chemicals. Most absorption of nutrients occurs in the small intestine, aided by secretions from the pancreas, gallbladder, and intestinal lining. The large intestine reabsorbs excess water; the remaining solid wastes are collected in the rectum and excreted through the anus.

Simply meeting energy needs is not enough, however; our bodies need adequate amounts of all the essential nutrients to grow and function properly. Practically all foods contain mixtures of nutrients, although foods are commonly classified according to their predominant nutrients. For example, spaghetti is considered a carbohydrate food although it contains small amounts of other nutrients. Let's take a closer look at the functions and sources of the six classes of nutrients.

Proteins—The Basis of Body Structure

Proteins form important parts of the body's main structural components: muscles and bones. Proteins also form important parts of blood, enzymes, cell membranes, and some hormones. As mentioned earlier, protein can also provide energy at 4 calories per gram of protein weight.

Amino Acids The building blocks of proteins are called **amino acids.** Twenty common amino acids are found in food; 9 of these are essential: histidine, isoleucine, leucine, lysine, methionine, phenylalanine, threonine, tryptophan, and valine. The other 11 amino acids can be produced by the body as long as the necessary components are supplied by foods.

Complete and Incomplete Proteins Individual protein sources are considered "complete" if they supply all the essential amino acids in adequate amounts and "incomplete" if they do not. Meat, fish, poultry, eggs, milk, cheese, and soy provide complete proteins. Incomplete proteins, which come from plant sources such as **legumes** and nuts, are good sources of most essential amino acids but are usually low in one or two.

Combining two vegetable proteins, such as wheat and peanuts in a peanut butter sandwich, allows each vegetable protein to make up for the amino acids missing in the other protein. The combination yields a complete protein. It was once believed that vegetarians had to "complement" their proteins at each meal in order to receive the benefit of a complete protein. It is now known, however, that proteins consumed throughout the course of the day can complement each other to form a pool of amino acids from which the body can draw to produce the necessary proteins. Vegetarians should include a variety of vegetable protein sources in their diets to make sure they get all the essential amino acids in adequate amounts. (Healthy vegetarian diets are discussed later in the chapter.)

Recommended Protein Intake Adequate daily intake of protein for adults is 0.8 gram per kilogram (0.36 gram per pound) of body weight, corresponding to 50 grams of protein per day for someone who weighs 140 pounds and 65 grams of protein for someone who weighs 180 pounds. This amount of protein is easily obtained from popular foods: 3 ounces of lean meat, poultry, or fish or ½ cup of tofu contains about 20–25 grams of protein; 1 cup of legumes such as pinto and kidney beans, 15–20 grams; 1 cup of milk or yogurt or 1½ ounces of cheese, 8–12 grams; and cereals, grains, nuts, and vegetables, about 2–4 grams of protein per serving.

Most Americans meet or exceed the protein intake needed for adequate nutrition. Protein consumed beyond what the body needs can be synthesized into fat for energy storage or burned for energy requirements. Consuming somewhat above our needs is not harmful, but it does contribute fat to the diet because protein-rich foods are often fat-rich as well. A very high protein intake can strain the kidneys and lead to dehydration.

A fairly broad range of protein intake is associated with good health. In 2002, the Food and Nutrition Board released recommendations for the balance of energy sources in a healthful diet. These recommendations, called Acceptable Macronutrient Distribution Ranges (AMDRs), are based on ensuring adequate intake of essential nutrients while also reducing the risk of chronic diseases like heart disease and cancer. The AMDR for protein for adults is 10–35% of total daily calories. The average American diet includes about 15–16% of total daily calories as protein. (See Chapter 9 for more information about high-protein diets advocated for weight loss.)

Fats—Essential in Small Amounts

Fats, also known as *lipids,* are the most concentrated source of energy, at 9 calories per gram. The fats stored in your body represent usable energy, help insulate your body, and support and cushion your organs. Fats in the diet help your body absorb fat-soluble vitamins and add flavor and texture to foods. Fats are the major fuel for the body during periods of rest and light activity. Two fats—linoleic acid and alpha-linolenic acid—are essential to the diet; they are key regulators of such body functions as the maintenance of blood pressure and the progress of a healthy pregnancy.

Types and Sources of Fats Most of the fats in food are in the form of triglycerides, which are composed of a glycerol molecule (an alcohol) plus three fatty acids. A fatty acid is made up of a chain of carbon atoms with oxygen attached at the end and hydrogen atoms attached along the length of the chain. Fatty acids differ in the length of their carbon atom chains and in their degree of saturation (the number of hydrogens attached to the chain). If every available bond from each carbon atom in a fatty acid chain is attached to a hydrogen atom, the fatty acid is said to be **saturated** (Figure 8.2). If not all the available bonds are taken up by hydrogens, the carbon atoms in the chain will form double bonds with each other. Such fatty acids are called *unsaturated fats.* If there is only one double bond, the fatty acid is called **monounsaturated.** If there are two or more double bonds, the fatty acid is called **polyunsaturated.** The essential fatty acids—linoleic and alpha-linolenic acids—are both polyunsaturated. The different types of fatty acids have different characteristics and different effects on your health.

Food fats are often composed of both saturated and unsaturated fatty acids; the dominant type of fatty acid determines the fat's characteristics. Food fats containing large amounts of saturated fatty acids are usually solid at room temperature; they are generally found naturally in animal products. The leading sources of saturated fat in the American diet are red meats (hamburger, steak, roasts), whole milk, cheese, and hot dogs and lunch meats. Food fats containing large amounts of monounsaturated and polyunsaturated fatty acids are usually from plant sources and are liquid at room temperature. Olive, canola, safflower, and peanut oils contain mostly monounsaturated fatty acids. Corn, soybean, and cottonseed oils contain mostly polyunsaturated fatty acids.

There are some notable exceptions to these generalizations. When unsaturated vegetable oils undergo the process of **hydrogenation**, a mixture of saturated and unsaturated fatty acids is produced. Hydrogenation turns many of the double bonds in unsaturated fatty acids into single bonds, increasing the degree of saturation and producing a more solid fat from a liquid oil. Hydrogenation also changes some unsaturated fatty acids into **trans fatty acids (trans fats),** unsaturated fatty acids with an atypical shape that affects their behavior in the body. Food manufacturers use hydrogenation to increase the stability of an oil so it can be reused for deep frying; to improve the texture of certain foods (to make pastries and pie crusts flakier, for example); and to extend the shelf life of foods made with oil. Hydrogenation is also used to transform liquid vegetable oils into margarine or shortening.

Glycerol — Fatty acids

Saturated fatty acid (no double bonds between carbon atoms)

Monounsaturated fatty acid (one double bond between carbon atoms)

Polyunsaturated fatty acid (two or more double bonds between carbon atoms)

FIGURE 8.2 Chemical structures of saturated and unsaturated fatty acids. This example of a triglyceride consists of a molecule of glycerol with three fatty acids attached. Fatty acids can differ in the length of their carbon chains and their degree of saturation.

TERMS

protein An essential nutrient; a compound made of amino acids that contains carbon, hydrogen, oxygen, and nitrogen.

amino acids The building blocks of proteins.

legumes Vegetables such as peas and beans that are high in fiber and are also important sources of protein.

saturated fat A fat with no carbon-carbon double bonds; usually solid at room temperature.

monounsaturated fat A fat with one carbon-carbon double bond; liquid at room temperature.

polyunsaturated fat A fat containing two or more carbon-carbon double bonds; liquid at room temperature.

hydrogenation A process by which hydrogens are added to unsaturated fats, increasing the degree of saturation and turning liquid oils into solid fats. Hydrogenation produces a mixture of saturated fatty acids and standard and trans forms of unsaturated fatty acids.

trans fatty acid (trans fat) A type of unsaturated fatty acid produced during the process of hydrogenation; trans fats have an atypical shape that affects their chemical activity.

Many baked and fried foods are prepared with hydrogenated vegetable oils, so they can be relatively high in saturated and trans fatty acids. Leading sources of trans fats in the American diet are deep-fried fast foods such as french fries and fried chicken (typically fried in vegetable shortening rather than oil); baked and snack foods such as pot pies, cakes, cookies, pastries, doughnuts, and chips; and stick margarine. In general, the more solid a hydrogenated oil is, the more saturated and trans fats it contains; for example, stick margarines typically contain more saturated and trans fats than do tub or squeeze margarines. Small amounts of trans fatty acids are also found naturally in meat and milk.

Hydrogenated vegetable oils are not the only plant fats that contain saturated fats. Palm and coconut oils, although derived from plants, are also highly saturated. Yet fish oils, derived from an animal source, are rich in polyunsaturated fats.

Fats and Health Different types of fats have very different effects on health. Many studies have examined the effects of dietary fat intake on blood **cholesterol** levels and the risk of heart disease. Saturated and trans fatty acids raise blood levels of **low-density lipoprotein (LDL),** or "bad" cholesterol, thereby increasing a person's risk of heart disease. Unsaturated fatty acids, on the other hand, lower LDL. Monounsaturated fatty acids, such as those found in olive and canola oils, may also increase levels of **high-density lipoproteins (HDL),** or "good" cholesterol, providing even greater benefits for heart health. Saturated fats have been found to impair the ability of HDLs to prevent inflammation of the blood vessels, one of the key factors in vascular disease; they have also been found to reduce the ability of the blood vessels to react normally to stress. In large amounts, trans fatty acids may lower HDL. Thus, to reduce the risk of heart disease, it is important to choose unsaturated fats instead of saturated and trans fats. (See Chapter 11 for more on cholesterol.)

Most Americans consume more saturated fat than trans fat (12% versus 2–4% of total daily calories). However, health experts are particularly concerned about trans fats

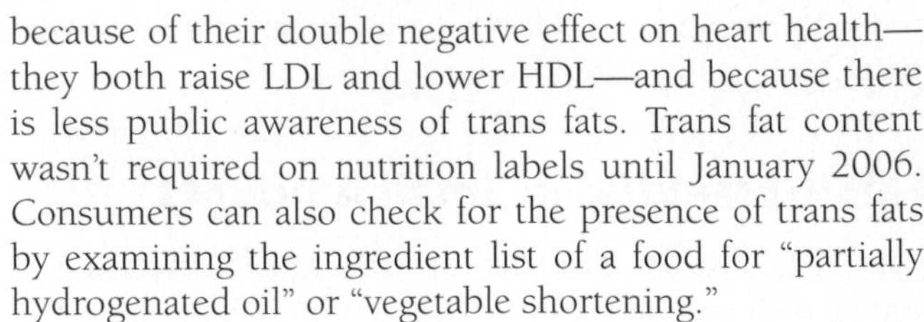

because of their double negative effect on heart health—they both raise LDL and lower HDL—and because there is less public awareness of trans fats. Trans fat content wasn't required on nutrition labels until January 2006. Consumers can also check for the presence of trans fats by examining the ingredient list of a food for "partially hydrogenated oil" or "vegetable shortening."

For heart health, it's important to limit your consumption of both saturated and trans fats. The best way to reduce saturated fat in your diet is to lower your intake of meat and full-fat dairy products (whole milk, cream, butter, cheese, ice cream). To lower trans fats, decrease your intake of deep-fried foods and baked goods made with hydrogenated vegetable oils; use liquid oils for cooking; and favor tub or squeeze margarines over stick margarines. Remember, the softer or more liquid a fat is, the less saturated and trans fat it is likely to contain.

Although saturated and trans fats pose health hazards, other fats are beneficial. Monounsaturated fatty acids, as found in avocados, most nuts, and olive, canola, peanut, and safflower oils, improve cholesterol levels and may help protect against some cancers. **Omega-3 fatty acids,** a form of polyunsaturated fat found primarily in fish, may be even more healthful. An omega-3 fatty acid has its endmost double bond three carbons from the end of the fatty acid chain. (The polyunsaturated fatty acid shown in Figure 8.2 is an omega-3 form.) Omega-3s and the compounds the body makes from them have a number of heart-healthy effects: They reduce the tendency of blood to clot, inhibit inflammation and abnormal heart rhythms, and reduce blood pressure and risk of heart attack and stroke in some people. Because of these benefits, nutritionists recommend that Americans increase the proportion of omega-3s in their diet by eating fish two or more times a week. Salmon, tuna, trout, mackerel, herring, sardines, and anchovies are all good sources of omega-3s; lesser amounts are found in plant foods, including dark green leafy vegetables; walnuts; flaxseeds; and canola, walnut, and flaxseed oils.

Another form of polyunsaturated fat, omega-6 fatty acid, has its endmost double bond at the sixth carbon atom. Most of the polyunsaturated fats currently consumed by Americans are omega-6s, primarily from corn oil and soybean oil. Foods rich in omega-6s are important because they contain the essential nutrient linoleic acid. However, some nutritionists recommend that people reduce the proportion of omega-6s they consume in favor of omega-3s. To make this adjustment, use canola oil rather than corn oil in cooking, and check for corn, soybean, or cottonseed oil in products such as mayonnaise, margarine, and salad dressing.

In addition to its effects on heart disease risk, dietary fat can affect health in other ways. Diets high in fatty red meat are associated with an increased risk of certain forms of cancer, especially colon cancer. A high-fat diet can also make weight management more difficult. Because fat is a concentrated source of calories (9 calories per gram versus

TERMS

cholesterol A waxy substance found in the blood and cells and needed for cell membranes, vitamin D, and hormone synthesis.

low-density lipoprotein (LDL) Blood fat that transports cholesterol to organs and tissues; excess amounts result in the accumulation of fatty deposits on artery walls.

high-density lipoprotein (HDL) Blood fat that helps transport cholesterol out of the arteries, thereby protecting against heart disease.

omega-3 fatty acids Polyunsaturated fatty acids commonly found in fish oils that are beneficial to cardiovascular health; the endmost double bond occurs three carbons from the end of the fatty acid chain.

	Type of Fatty Acid	Found In[a]	Possible Effects on Health
Keep Intake Low	SATURATED	Animal fats (especially fatty meats and poultry fat and skin) Butter, cheese, and other high-fat dairy products Palm and coconut oils	Raises total cholesterol and LDL cholesterol levels Increases risk of heart disease May increase risk of colon and prostate cancers
	TRANS	French fries and other deep-fried fast foods Stick margarines, shortening Packaged cookies and crackers Processed snacks and sweets	Raises total cholesterol and LDL cholesterol levels Lowers HDL cholesterol levels May increase risk of heart disease and breast cancer
Choose Moderate Amounts	MONOUNSATURATED	Olive, canola, and safflower oils Avocados, olives Peanut butter (without added fat) Many nuts, including almonds, cashews, pecans, and pistachios	Lowers total cholesterol and LDL cholesterol levels May reduce blood pressure and lower triglyceride levels (a risk factor for CVD) May reduce risk of heart disease, stroke, and some cancers
	POLYUNSATURATED (two groups)[b]		
	Omega-3 fatty acids	Fatty fish, including salmon, white albacore tuna, mackerel, anchovies, and sardines Lesser amounts in walnut, flaxseed, canola, and soybean oils; tofu; walnuts; flaxseeds; and dark green leafy vegetables	Reduces blood clotting and inflammation and inhibits abnormal heart rhythms Lowers triglyceride levels (a risk factor for CVD) May lower blood pressure in some people May reduce risk of fatal heart attack, stroke, and some cancers
	Omega-6 fatty acids	Corn, soybean, and cottonseed oils (often used in margarine, mayonnaise, and salad dressing)	Lowers total cholesterol and LDL cholesterol levels May lower HDL cholesterol levels May reduce risk of heart disease May slightly increase risk of cancer if omega-6 intake is high and omega-3 intake is low

[a] Food fats contain a combination of types of fatty acids in various proportions; for example, canola oil is composed mainly of monounsaturated fatty acids (62%) but also contains polyunsaturated (32%) and saturated (6%) fatty acids. Food fats are categorized here according to their predominant fatty acid.

[b] The essential fatty acids are polyunsaturated: Linoleic acid is an omega-6 fatty acid and alpha-linolenic acid is an omega-3 fatty acid.

FIGURE 8.3 Types of fatty acids and their possible effects on health. The health effects of dietary fats are still being investigated. In general, nutritionists recommend that we consume a diet moderate in fat overall and that we substitute unsaturated fats for saturated and trans fats. Monounsaturated fats and omega-3 polyunsaturated fats may be particularly good choices for promoting health. Eating lots of fat of any type can provide excess calories because all types of fats are rich sources of energy (9 calories per gram).

4 calories per gram for protein and carbohydrate), a high-fat diet is often a high-calorie diet that can lead to weight gain. In addition, there is some evidence that calories from fat are more easily converted to body fat than calories from protein or carbohydrate.

Although more research is needed on the precise effects of different types and amounts of fat on overall health, a great deal of evidence points to the fact that most people benefit from lowering their overall fat intake to recommended levels and choosing unsaturated fats instead of saturated and trans fats. The types of fatty acids and their effects on health are summarized in Figure 8.3.

Recommended Fat Intake To meet the body's need for essential fats, adult men need about 17 grams per day of linoleic acid and 1.6 grams per day of alpha-linolenic acid; women need 12 grams of linoleic acid and 1.1 grams of alpha-linolenic acid. It takes only 3–4 teaspoons (15–20 grams) of vegetable oil per day incorporated into your diet to supply the essential fats. Most Americans consume sufficient amounts of the essential fats; limiting unhealthy fats is a much greater health concern.

As with protein, a range of levels of fat intake is associated with good health; the AMDR for total fat is 20–35% of total calories. Although more difficult for consumers to monitor, AMDRs have also been set for omega-6 fatty acids (5–10%) and omega-3 fatty acids (0.6–1.2%) as part of total fat intake. Because any amount of saturated and trans fat increases the risk of heart disease, the Food and Nutrition Board recommends that saturated and trans fat intake be kept as low as possible; most fat in a healthy diet should be unsaturated. American adults currently consume about 33% of total calories as fat, including 11–12% of calories as saturated fat and 2–4% as trans fat.

For advice on setting individual intake goals, see the box "Setting Intake Goals for Protein, Fat, and Carbohydrate." To determine how close you are to meeting these intake goals for fat, keep a running total over the course

TAKE CHARGE

Setting Intake Goals for Protein, Fat, and Carbohydrate

Goals have been established by the Food and Nutrition Board to help ensure adequate intake of the essential amino acids, fatty acids, and carbohydrate. The daily goals for adequate intake for adults are as follows:

	Men	Women
Protein	56 grams	46 grams
Fat: Linoleic acid	17 grams	12 grams
Alpha-linolenic acid	1.6 grams	1.1 grams
Carbohydrate	130 grams	130 grams

Protein intake goals can be calculated more specifically by multiplying your body weight in kilograms by 0.8 or your body weight in pounds by 0.36. (Refer to the Nutrition Resources section at the end of the chapter for information for specific age groups and life stages.)

To meet your daily energy needs, you need to consume more than the minimally adequate amounts of the energy-providing nutrients listed above, which alone supply only about 800–900 calories. The Food and Nutrition Board provides additional guidance in the form of Acceptable Macronutrient Distribution Ranges (AMDRs). These ranges can help you balance your intake of energy-providing nutrients in ways that ensure adequate intake and reduce the risk of chronic disease.

The AMDRs for protein, total fat, and carbohydrate are as follows:

Protein	10–35% of total daily calories
Total fat	20–35% of total daily calories
Carbohydrate	45–65% of total daily calories

To set individual goals, begin by estimating your total daily energy (calorie) needs; if your weight is stable, your current energy intake is the number of calories you need to maintain your weight at your current activity level. Next, select percentage goals for protein, fat, and carbohydrate. You can allocate your total daily calories among the three classes of macronutrients to suit your preferences; just make sure that the three percentages you select total 100% and that you meet the minimum intake goals listed. Two samples reflecting different total energy intake and nutrient intake goals are shown in the table below.

To translate your percentage goals into daily intake goals expressed in calories and grams, multiply the appropriate percentages by total calorie intake, and then divide the results by the corresponding calories per gram. For example, a fat limit of 35% applied to a 2200-calorie diet would be calculated as follows: 0.35 × 2200 = 770 calories of total fat; 770 ÷ 9 calories per gram = 86 grams of total fat. (Remember that fat has 9 calories per gram and that protein and carbohydrate have 4 calories per gram.)

Two Sample Macronutrient Distributions

		Sample 1		Sample 2	
Nutrient	AMDR	Individual Goals	Amounts for a 1600-Calorie Diet	Individual Goals	Amounts for a 2800-Calorie Diet
Protein	10–35%	15%	240 calories = 60 grams	20%	560 calories = 140 grams
Fat	20–35%	30%	480 calories = 53 grams	20%	560 calories = 62 grams
Carbohydrate	45–65%	55%	880 calories = 220 grams	60%	1680 calories = 420 grams

Source: Food and Nutrition Board, Institute of Medicine, National Academies, 2002. *Dietary Reference Intakes: Energy, Carbohydrates, Fiber, Fat, Fatty Acids, Cholesterol, Protein, and Amino Acids*, Washington, D.C., National Academies Press. Reprinted with permission from *Dietary Reference Intakes for Energy, Carbohydrate, Fiber, Fat, Fatty Acids, Cholesterol, Protein, and Amino Acids (Macronutrients)*. Copyright © 2003 by the National Academy of Sciences. Courtesy of the National Academies Press, Washington, D.C.

of the day. For prepared foods, food labels list the number of grams of fat, protein, and carbohydrate; the breakdown for many foods and popular fast-food items can be found in Appendixes B and C. Nutrition information is also available in many grocery stores, in published nutrition guides, and online (see For Further Exploration at the end of the chapter). By checking these resources, you can keep track of the total grams of fat, protein, and carbohydrate you eat and assess how close your current diet is to the recommended intake goals.

In reducing fat intake to recommended levels, the emphasis should be on lowering saturated and trans fats (see Figure 8.3). You can still eat high-fat foods, but it makes sense to limit the size of your portions and to balance your intake with low-fat foods. For example, peanut butter is high in fat, with 8 grams (72 calories) of fat in each 90-calorie tablespoon. Two tablespoons of peanut butter eaten on whole-wheat bread and served with a banana, carrot sticks, and a glass of nonfat milk makes a nutritious lunch—high in protein and carbohydrate, relatively low in total and saturated fat (500 calories, 18 grams of total fat, 4 grams of saturated fat). Four tablespoons of peanut butter on high-fat crackers with potato chips, cookies, and whole milk is a less healthy combination (1000 calories, 62 grams of total fat, 15 grams of saturated fat). So although it's important to evaluate individual food items for their fat content, it is more important to look at them in the context of your overall diet.

Carbohydrates—An Ideal Source of Energy

Carbohydrates are needed in the diet primarily to supply energy to body cells. Some cells, such as those in the brain and other parts of the nervous system and in the blood, use only carbohydrates for fuel. During high-intensity exercise, muscles also get most of their energy from carbohydrates.

Simple and Complex Carbohydrates Carbohydrates are classified into two groups: simple and complex. Simple carbohydrates contain only one or two sugar units in each molecule; they include sucrose (table sugar), fructose (fruit sugar, honey), maltose (malt sugar), and lactose (milk sugar). Providing much of the sweetness in foods, they are found naturally in fruits and milk and are added to soft drinks, fruit drinks, candy, and sweet desserts. There is no evidence that any one type of simple sugar is more nutritious than any other.

Complex carbohydrates consist of chains of many sugar molecules; they include starches and most types of dietary fiber. Starches are found in a variety of plants, especially grains (wheat, rye, rice, oats, barley, millet), legumes (dried beans, peas, lentils), and tubers (potatoes, yams). Most other vegetables contain a mix of starches and simple carbohydrates. Fiber is found in fruits, vegetables, and grains.

During digestion in the mouth and small intestine, your body breaks down starches and double sugars into single sugar molecules, such as **glucose**, for absorption. Once the glucose is in the bloodstream, the pancreas releases insulin, which allows cells to take up glucose and use it for energy. The liver and muscles also take up glucose and store it in the form of a starch called **glycogen.** The muscles use glucose from glycogen as fuel during endurance events or long workouts. Carbohydrates consumed in excess of the body's energy needs can be changed into fat and stored. Whenever calorie intake exceeds calorie expenditure, fat storage can lead to weight gain. This is true whether the excess calories come from carbohydrates, proteins, fat, or alcohol.

Refined Carbohydrates Versus Whole Grains Complex carbohydrates can be further divided between refined, or processed, carbohydrates and unrefined carbohydrates, or whole grains. Before they are processed, all grains are **whole grains,** consisting of an inner layer of germ, a middle layer called the endosperm, and an outer layer of bran (Figure 8.4). During processing, the germ and bran are often removed, leaving just the starchy endosperm. The refinement of whole grains transforms whole-wheat flour into white flour, brown rice into white rice, and so on.

Refined carbohydrates usually retain all the calories of their unrefined counterparts, but they tend to be much lower in fiber, vitamins, minerals, and other beneficial compounds. Many refined grain products are enriched or fortified with vitamins and minerals, but often the nutrients lost in processing are not replaced. Unrefined carbohydrates tend to take longer to chew and digest than refined ones; they also enter the bloodstream more slowly. This slower digestive pace tends to make people feel full sooner and for a longer period, lessening the chance that they will overeat. Also, a slower rise in blood glucose levels following consumption of complex carbohydrates may help in the prevention and management of diabetes. Whole grains are also high in dietary fiber. Consumption of whole grains has been linked to reduced risk for heart disease, diabetes, high blood pressure, stroke, and certain forms of cancer. For all these reasons, whole grains are recommended over those that have been refined. This does not mean that you should never eat refined carbohydrates such as white bread or white rice; it simply means that whole-wheat bread, brown rice, and other whole grains are healthier choices. See the box "Choosing More Whole-Grain Foods" for tips on increasing your intake of whole grains.

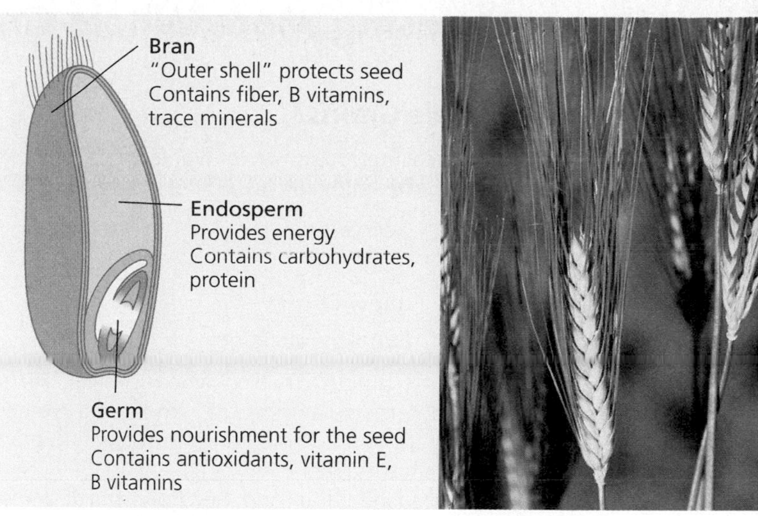

FIGURE 8.4 The parts of a whole grain kernel.

Glycemic Index Insulin and glucose levels rise and fall following a meal or snack containing any type of carbohydrate. Some foods cause a quick and dramatic rise in glucose and insulin levels; others have a slower, more moderate effect. A food that has a rapid effect on blood glucose levels is said to have a high **glycemic index.**

TERMS

carbohydrate An essential nutrient; sugars, starches, and dietary fiber are all carbohydrates.

glucose A simple sugar that is the body's basic fuel.

glycogen An animal starch stored in the liver and muscles.

whole grain The entire edible portion of a grain such as wheat, rice, or oats, including the germ, endosperm, and bran.

glycemic index A measure of how the ingestion of a particular food affects blood glucose levels.

TAKE CHARGE

Choosing More Whole-Grain Foods

What Are Whole Grains?

The first step in increasing your intake of whole grains is to correctly identify them. The following are whole grains:

whole wheat	whole-grain corn
whole rye	popcorn
whole oats	brown rice
oatmeal	whole-grain barley

Other choices include bulgur (cracked wheat), millet, kasha (roasted buckwheat kernels), quinoa, teff, wheat and rye berries, amaranth, graham flour, whole-grain kamut, whole-grain spelt, and whole-grain triticale.

Wheat flour, unbleached flour, enriched flour, and degerminated corn meal are not whole grains. Wheat germ and wheat bran are also not whole grains, but they are the constituents of wheat typically left out when wheat is processed and so are healthier choices than regular wheat flour, which typically contains just the endosperm.

Reading Food Packages to Find Whole Grains

To find packaged foods rich in whole grains, read the list of ingredients and check for special health claims related to whole grains. *The first item on the list of ingredients should be one of the whole grains listed above.* In addition, the FDA allows manufacturers to include special health claims for foods that contain 51% or more whole-grain ingredients. Such products may contain a statement such as the following on their packaging: "Rich in whole grain," "Made with 100% whole grain," or "Diets rich in whole-grain foods may help reduce the risk of heart disease and certain cancers." However, many whole-grain products will not carry such claims.

Incorporating Whole Grains into Your Daily Diet

- ***Bread.*** Look for sandwich breads, bagels, English muffins, buns, and pita breads with a whole grain listed as the first ingredient.
- ***Breakfast cereals.*** Look for whole-grain cereals, which include oatmeal, muesli, shredded wheat, and some types of raisin bran, bran flakes, wheat flakes, toasted oats, and granola.
- ***Rice.*** Choose brown rice or rice blends that include brown rice.
- ***Pasta.*** Look for whole-wheat, whole-grain kamut, or whole-grain spelt pasta.
- ***Tortillas.*** Choose whole-wheat or whole-corn tortillas.
- ***Crackers and snacks.*** Look for varieties of crackers made from whole grains, including some flatbreads or crispbreads, woven wheat crackers, and rye crackers. Other whole-grain snack possibilities include popcorn, popcorn cakes, brown rice cakes, whole-corn tortilla chips, and whole-wheat fig cookies. Be sure to check food labels for fat content, as many popular snacks are also high in fat.
- ***Mixed-grain dishes.*** Combine whole grains with other foods to create healthy mixed dishes such as tabouli; soups made with hulled barley or wheat berries; and pilafs, casseroles, and salads made with brown rice, whole-wheat couscous, kasha, millet, wheat bulgur, and quinoa.

If your grocery store doesn't carry these items, try your local health food store.

Research findings have been mixed, but some studies have found that a meal containing high-glycemic-index foods may increase appetite; over the long term, diets rich in high-glycemic-index foods are linked to increased risk of diabetes and heart disease in some people. High-glycemic-index foods do not, as some popular diets claim, directly cause weight gain beyond the calories they contain.

Attempting to base food choices on glycemic index is a difficult task, however. Although unrefined complex carbohydrates and high-fiber foods tend to have a low glycemic index, patterns are less clear for other types of foods and do not follow a simple distinction such as that of simple versus complex carbohydrates. For example, some fruits with fairly high levels of simple carbohydrates have only a moderate effect on blood glucose levels, whereas white rice, potatoes, and white bread, which are rich in complex carbohydrates, have a high glycemic index. Watermelon has a glycemic index more than twice that of strawberries, and the glycemic index of a banana changes dramatically as it ripens. The acid and fat content of a food also affect glycemic index—the more acidic and higher in fat a food is, the lower its effect on glucose levels. Other factors that affect the body's response to carbohydrates include the way foods are combined and prepared and the fitness status of the individual.

This complexity is one reason major health organizations have not issued specific guidelines for glycemic index. For people with particular health concerns, glycemic index may be an important consideration; however, it should not be the sole criterion for food choices. For example, ice cream has a much lower glycemic index than brown rice or carrots—but that doesn't make it a healthier choice overall. Glycemic index and its effects on appetite and heart health are discussed further in Chapters 9 and 11. For now, remember that most unrefined grains, fruits, vegetables, and legumes are rich in nutrients and have a low-to-moderate glycemic index. Choose a variety of vegetables daily, and avoid heavy consumption of white potatoes. Limit foods that are high in added sugars but provide few other nutrients. Some studies have singled out regular soda, with its large dose of rapidly absorbable sugar, as specifically linked to increased diabetes risk.

Recommended Carbohydrate Intake On average, Americans consume 200–300 grams of carbohydrate per day, well above the 130 grams needed to meet the body's requirement for essential carbohydrate. A range of intakes is associated with good health, and experts recommend that adults consume 45–65% of total daily calories as carbohydrate, about 225–325 grams of carbohydrate for someone consuming 2000 calories per day. The focus should be on consuming a variety of foods rich in complex carbohydrates, especially whole grains.

Health experts offer separate guidelines for intake of added sugars as part of total carbohydrate consumption. The Food and Nutrition Board set an AMDR for added sugars of 25% or less of total daily calories, but many health experts recommend a substantially lower intake. Guidelines released by the World Health Organization in 2003 suggested a limit of 10% of total daily calories from added sugars. Limits set by the USDA in 2005 are even lower, with a maximum of about 8 teaspoons (32 grams) suggested for someone consuming 2000 calories per day. Foods high in added sugar are generally high in calories and low in nutrients and fiber, thus providing "empty" calories. To reduce your intake of added sugars, limit soft drinks, candy, sweet desserts, and sweetened fruit drinks. The simple carbohydrates in your diet should come from food sources in which they are found naturally—including fruits, which are excellent sources of vitamins and minerals—and from low-fat or fat-free milk and other dairy products, which are high in protein and calcium.

Athletes in training can especially benefit from high-carbohydrate diets (60–70% of total daily calories), which enhance the amount of carbohydrates stored in their muscles (as glycogen) and therefore provide more carbohydrate fuel for use during endurance events or long workouts. In addition, high-glycemic-index carbohydrates consumed during prolonged athletic events can help fuel muscles and extend the availability of the glycogen stored in muscles. Caution is in order, however, because overconsumption of carbohydrates can lead to feelings of fatigue and underconsumption of other nutrients.

Fiber—A Closer Look

Fiber is the term given to nondigestible carbohydrates provided mainly by plants. Instead of being digested, like starch, fiber passes through the intestinal tract and provides bulk for feces in the large intestine, which in turn facilitates elimination. In the large intestine, some types of fiber are broken down by bacteria into acids and gases, which explains why consuming too much fiber can lead to intestinal gas. Because humans cannot digest fiber, it is not a source of carbohydrate in the diet; however, the consumption of fiber is necessary for good health.

Types of Dietary Fiber The Food and Nutrition Board has defined two types of fiber: dietary fiber and functional fiber. **Dietary fiber** refers to nondigestible carbohydrates and lignin that are present naturally in plants such as grains, legumes, and vegetables. **Functional fiber** refers to nondigestible carbohydrates that have been either isolated from natural sources or synthesized in a lab and then added to a food product or supplement. **Total fiber** is the sum of dietary and functional fiber.

Fibers have different properties that lead to different physiological effects in the body. **Soluble (viscous) fiber** slows the body's absorption of glucose and binds cholesterol-containing compounds in the intestine, lowering blood cholesterol levels and reducing the risk of cardiovascular disease. **Insoluble fiber** binds water, making the feces bulkier and softer so they pass more quickly and easily through the intestines.

Both kinds of fiber contribute to disease prevention. A diet high in soluble fiber can help people manage diabetes and high blood cholesterol levels. A diet high in insoluble fiber can help prevent a variety of health problems, including constipation, hemorrhoids, and **diverticulitis.** Some studies have linked diets high in fiber-rich fruits, vegetables, and grains with a lower risk of some kinds of cancer; however, it is unclear whether fiber or other food components are responsible for this reduction in risk.

Sources of Dietary Fiber All plant foods contain some dietary fiber, but fruits, legumes, oats (especially oat bran), and barley are particularly rich in it. Wheat (especially wheat bran), cereals, grains, and vegetables are all good sources of insoluble fiber. Psyllium, which is often added to cereals or used in fiber supplements and laxatives, improves intestinal health and also helps control glucose and cholesterol levels. The processing of packaged foods can remove fiber, so it's important to depend on fresh fruits and vegetables and foods made from whole grains as sources of dietary fiber.

Recommended Intake of Dietary Fiber To reduce the risk of chronic disease and maintain intestinal health, the Food and Nutrition Board recommends a daily fiber intake of 38 grams for adult men and 25 grams for adult

dietary fiber Nondigestible carbohydrates and lignin that are intact in plants.

functional fiber Nondigestible carbohydrates either isolated from natural sources or synthesized; these may be added to foods and dietary supplements.

total fiber The total amount of dietary fiber and functional fiber in the diet.

soluble (viscous) fiber Fiber that dissolves in water or is broken down by bacteria in the large intestine.

insoluble fiber Fiber that does not dissolve in water and is not broken down by bacteria in the large intestine.

diverticulitis A digestive disorder in which abnormal pouches form in the walls of the intestine and become inflamed.

women. Americans currently consume about half this amount. Fiber should come from foods, not supplements, which should be used only under medical supervision.

To increase the amount of fiber in your diet, try the following:

- Choose breads, crackers, and cereals that list whole grain first in the ingredient list: Whole-wheat flour, whole-grain oats, and whole-grain rice are whole grains; wheat flour is not. Choose a breakfast cereal with 5 or more grams of fiber per serving.
- Eat whole, unpeeled fruits rather than drinking fruit juice. Top cereals, yogurt, and desserts with berries, apple slices, or other fruit.
- Include legumes in soups and salads. Combine raw vegetables with pasta, rice, or beans in salads.
- Substitute bean dip for cheese-based or sour cream–based dips or spreads. Use raw vegetables rather than chips for dipping.

Vitamins—Organic Micronutrients

Vitamins are organic (carbon-containing) substances required in very small amounts to regulate various processes within living cells (Table 8.2). Humans need 13 vitamins. Four are fat-soluble (A, D, E, and K), and nine are water-soluble (C and the eight B-complex vitamins: thiamin, riboflavin, niacin, vitamin B-6, folate, vitamin B-12, biotin, and pantothenic acid). Solubility affects how a vitamin is absorbed, transported, and stored in the body. The water-soluble vitamins are absorbed directly into the bloodstream, where they travel freely; excess water-soluble vitamins are removed by the kidneys and excreted in urine. Fat-soluble vitamins require a more complex absorptive process; they are usually carried in the blood by special proteins and are stored in the liver and in fat tissues rather than excreted.

Functions of Vitamins Many vitamins help chemical reactions take place. They provide no energy to the body directly but help unleash the energy stored in carbohydrates, proteins, and fats. Vitamins are critical in the production of red blood cells and the maintenance of the nervous, skeletal, and immune systems. Some vitamins act as **antioxidants,** which help preserve healthy cells in the body. Key vitamin antioxidants include vitamin E, vitamin C, and the vitamin A precursor beta-carotene. (Antioxidants are described later in the chapter.)

Sources of Vitamins The human body does not manufacture most of the vitamins it requires and must obtain them from foods. Vitamins are abundant in fruits, vegetables, and grains. In addition, many processed foods, such as flour and breakfast cereals, contain added vitamins. A few vitamins are made in certain parts of the body: The skin makes vitamin D when it is exposed to sunlight, and intestinal bacteria make vitamin K. Nonetheless, you still need to get vitamin D and vitamin K from foods.

Vitamin Deficiencies and Excesses If your diet lacks sufficient amounts of a particular vitamin, characteristic symptoms of deficiency develop (see Table 8.2). For example, vitamin A deficiency can cause blindness, and vitamin B-6 deficiency can cause seizures. Vitamin deficiency diseases are most often seen in developing countries; they are relatively rare in the United States because vitamins are readily available from our food supply. However, intakes below recommended levels can have adverse effects on health even if they are not low enough to cause a deficiency disease. For example, low intake of folate increases a woman's chance of giving birth to a baby with a neural tube defect (a congenital malformation of the central nervous system). Low intake of folate and vitamins B-6 and B-12 has been linked to increased heart disease risk. Many Americans consume less-than-recommended amounts of vitamins A, C, D, and E.

Extra vitamins in the diet can be harmful, especially when taken as supplements. High doses of vitamin A are toxic and increase the risk of birth defects, for example. Vitamin B-6 can cause irreversible nerve damage when taken in large doses. Megadoses of fat-soluble vitamins are particularly dangerous because the excess will be stored in the body rather than excreted, increasing the risk of toxicity. Even when supplements are not taken in excess, relying on them for an adequate intake of vitamins can be problematic: There are many substances in foods other than vitamins and minerals, and some of these compounds may have important health effects. Later in the chapter, we discuss specific recommendations for vitamin intake and when a supplement is advisable. For now, keep in mind that it's best to obtain most of your vitamins from foods rather than supplements.

The vitamins and minerals in vegetables can be easily lost or destroyed during storage or cooking. To retain their value, eat or process vegetables immediately after buying them. If you can't do this, then store them in a cool place, covered to retain moisture—either in the refrigerator (for a few days) or in the freezer (for a longer term). To reduce nutrient losses during food preparation, minimize the amount of water used and the total cooking time. Develop a taste for a crunchier texture in cooked vegetables. Baking, steaming, broiling, grilling, and microwaving are all good methods of preparing vegetables.

WEB TERMS

vitamins Organic substances needed in small amounts to help promote and regulate chemical reactions and processes in the body.

antioxidant A substance that protects against the breakdown of body constituents by free radicals; actions include binding oxygen, donating electrons to free radicals, and repairing damage to molecules.

Table 8.2	Facts About Vitamins			
Vitamin	**Important Dietary Sources**	**Major Functions**	**Signs of Prolonged Deficiency**	**Toxic Effects of Megadoses**
Fat-Soluble				
Vitamin A	Liver, milk, butter, cheese, fortified margarine; carrots, spinach, and other orange and deep green vegetables and fruits	Maintenance of vision, skin, linings of the nose, mouth, digestive and urinary tracts, immune function	Night blindness; dry, scaling skin; increased susceptibility to infection; loss of appetite; anemia; kidney stones	Liver damage, miscarriage and birth defects, headache, vomiting and diarrhea, vertigo, double vision, bone abnormalities
Vitamin D	Fortified milk and margarine, fish oils, butter, egg yolks (sunlight on skin also produces vitamin D)	Development and maintenance of bones and teeth; promotion of calcium absorption	Rickets (bone deformities) in children; bone softening, loss, fractures in adults	Kidney damage, calcium deposits in soft tissues, depression, death
Vitamin E	Vegetable oils, whole grains, nuts and seeds, green leafy vegetables, asparagus, peaches	Protection and maintenance of cellular membranes	Red blood cell breakage and anemia, weakness, neurological problems, muscle cramps	Relatively nontoxic, but may cause excess bleeding or formation of blood clots
Vitamin K	Green leafy vegetables; smaller amounts widespread in other foods	Production of proteins essential for blood clotting and bone metabolism	Hemorrhaging	None reported
Water-Soluble				
Biotin	Cereals, yeast, egg yolks, soy flour, liver; widespread in foods	Synthesis of fat, glycogen, and amino acids	Rash, nausea, vomiting, weight loss, depression, fatigue, hair loss	None reported
Folate	Green leafy vegetables, yeast, oranges, whole grains, legumes, liver	Amino acid metabolism, synthesis of RNA and DNA, new cell synthesis	Anemia, weakness, fatigue, irritability, shortness of breath, swollen tongue	Masking of vitamin B-12 deficiency
Niacin	Eggs, poultry, fish, milk, whole grains, nuts, enriched breads and cereals, meats, legumes	Conversion of carbohydrates, fats, and proteins into usable forms of energy	Pellagra (symptoms include diarrhea, dermatitis, inflammation of mucous membranes, dementia)	Flushing of skin, nausea, vomiting, diarrhea, liver dysfunction, glucose intolerance
Pantothenic acid	Animal foods, whole grains, broccoli, potatoes; widespread in foods	Metabolism of fats, carbohydrates, and proteins	Fatigue, numbness and tingling of hands and feet, gastrointestinal disturbances	None reported
Riboflavin	Dairy products, enriched breads and cereals, lean meats, poultry, fish, green vegetables	Energy metabolism; maintenance of skin, mucous membranes, nervous system structures	Cracks at corners of mouth, sore throat, skin rash, hypersensitivity to light, purple tongue	None reported
Thiamin	Whole-grain and enriched breads and cereals, organ meats, lean pork, nuts, legumes	Conversion of carbohydrates into usable forms of energy, maintenance of appetite and nervous system function	Beriberi (symptoms include muscle wasting, mental confusion, anorexia, enlarged heart, nerve changes)	None reported
Vitamin B-6	Eggs, poultry, fish, whole grains, nuts, soybeans, liver, kidney, pork	Metabolism of amino acids and glycogen	Anemia, convulsions, cracks at corners of mouth, dermatitis, nausea, confusion	Neurological abnormalities and damage
Vitamin B-12	Meat, fish, poultry, fortified cereals	Synthesis of blood cells; other metabolic reactions	Anemia, fatigue, nervous system damage, sore tongue	None reported
Vitamin C	Peppers, cruciferous vegetables, spinach, citrus fruits, strawberries, tomatoes, potatoes, other fruits and vegetables	Maintenance and repair of connective tissue, bones, teeth, cartilage; promotion of healing; aid in iron absorption	Scurvy, anemia, reduced resistance to infection, loosened teeth, joint pain, poor wound healing, hair loss, poor iron absorption	Urinary stones in some people, acid stomach from ingesting supplements in pill form, nausea, diarrhea, headache, fatigue

SOURCES: Food and Nutrition Board, Institute of Medicine. 2006. *Dietary Reference Intakes: The Essential Guide to Nutrient Requirements.* Washington, D.C.: National Academies Press. The complete Dietary Reference Intake reports are available from the National Academies Press (http://www.nap.edu). Shils, M. E., et al., eds. 2005. *Modern Nutrition in Health and Disease,* 10th ed. Baltimore: Lippincott Williams and Wilkins.

Minerals—Inorganic Micronutrients

Minerals are inorganic (non-carbon-containing) elements you need in small amounts to help regulate body functions, aid in the growth and maintenance of body tissues, and help release energy (Table 8.3). There are about 17 essential minerals. The major minerals, those that the body needs in amounts exceeding 100 milligrams, include calcium, phosphorus, magnesium, sodium, potassium, and chloride. The essential trace minerals, those that you need in minute amounts, include copper, fluoride, iodine, iron, selenium, and zinc.

Characteristic symptoms develop if an essential mineral is consumed in a quantity too small or too large for good health. The minerals most commonly lacking in the American diet are iron, calcium, magnesium, and

Table 8.3 Facts About Selected Minerals

Mineral	Important Dietary Sources	Major Functions	Signs of Prolonged Deficiency	Toxic Effects of Megadoses
Calcium	Milk and milk products, tofu, fortified orange juice and bread, green leafy vegetables, bones in fish	Formation of bones and teeth; control of nerve impulses, muscle contraction, blood clotting	Stunted growth in children, bone mineral loss in adults; urinary stones	Kidney stones, calcium deposits in soft tissues, inhibition of mineral absorption, constipation
Fluoride	Fluoridated water, tea, marine fish eaten with bones	Maintenance of tooth and bone structure	Higher frequency of tooth decay	Increased bone density, mottling of teeth, impaired kidney function
Iodine	Iodized salt, seafood, processed foods	Essential part of thyroid hormones, regulation of body metabolism	Goiter (enlarged thyroid), cretinism (birth defect)	Depression of thyroid activity, hyperthyroidism in susceptible people
Iron	Meat and poultry, fortified grain products, dark green vegetables, dried fruit	Component of hemoglobin, myoglobin, and enzymes	Iron-deficiency anemia, weakness, impaired immune function, gastrointestinal distress	Nausea, diarrhea, liver and kidney damage, joint pains, sterility, disruption of cardiac function, death
Magnesium	Widespread in foods and water (except soft water); especially found in grains, legumes, nuts, seeds, green vegetables, milk	Transmission of nerve impulses, energy transfer, activation of many enzymes	Neurological disturbances, cardiovascular problems, kidney disorders, nausea, growth failure in children	Nausea, vomiting, diarrhea, central nervous system depression, coma; death in people with impaired kidney function
Phosphorus	Present in nearly all foods, especially milk, cereal, peas, eggs, meat	Bone growth and maintenance, energy transfer in cells	Impaired growth, weakness, kidney disorders, cardiorespiratory and nervous system dysfunction	Drop in blood calcium levels, calcium deposits in soft tissues, bone loss
Potassium	Fruits and vegetables, especially leafy greens, cantaloupe, bananas, mushrooms, potatoes	Basic functioning of cells, water balance, acid-base balance	Elevated blood pressure, bone mineral loss, kidney stones, increased salt sensitivity, cardiac arrhythmia, muscle weakness	Cardiac arrhythmia and arrest, gastrointestinal discomfort
Selenium	Seafood, meat, eggs, whole grains	Defense against oxidative stress; regulation of thyroid hormone action	Muscle pain and weakness, heart disorders	Hair and nail brittleness and loss, nausea and vomiting, weakness, irritability
Sodium	Salt, soy sauce, fast food, processed foods, especially lunch meats, canned soups and vegetables, salty snacks, processed cheese	Body water balance, acid-base balance, nerve function	Muscle weakness, loss of appetite, nausea, vomiting; deficiency rarely seen	Increased blood pressure (even at fairly low levels of intake), renal stones, edema
Zinc	Whole grains, meat, eggs, liver, seafood (especially oysters)	Synthesis of proteins, RNA, and DNA; wound healing; immune response; ability to taste	Growth failure, loss of appetite, impaired taste acuity, skin rash, impaired immune function, poor wound healing	Vomiting, impaired immune function, decline in blood HDL levels, impaired copper absorption

SOURCES: Food and Nutrition Board, Institute of Medicine. 2006. *Dietary Reference Intakes: The Essential Guide to Nutrient Requirements.* Washington, D.C.: National Academies Press. The complete Dietary Reference Intake reports are available from the National Academies Press (http://www.nap.edu). Shils, M. E., et al., eds. 2005. *Modern Nutrition in Health and Disease,* 10th ed. Baltimore: Lippincott Williams and Wilkins.

Eating for Healthy Bones

TAKE CHARGE

Osteoporosis is a condition in which the bones become dangerously thin and fragile over time. An estimated 10 million Americans over age 50 have osteoporosis, and another 34 million are at risk. Women account for about 80% of osteoporosis cases. Most bone mass is built by age 18. After bone density peaks between ages 25 and 35, bone mass is slowly lost over time. To prevent osteoporosis, the best strategy is to build as much bone as possible during your youth and then do everything you can to maintain it as you age. Up to 50% of bone loss is determined by controllable lifestyle factors. Key nutrients include the following:

- ***Calcium.*** Consuming an adequate amount of calcium is important throughout life to build and maintain bone mass. Milk, yogurt, and calcium-fortified orange juice, bread, and cereals are all good sources.
- ***Vitamin D.*** Vitamin D is necessary for bones to absorb calcium; a daily intake of 5 micrograms is recommended for adults age 19–50. Vitamin D can be obtained from foods and is manufactured by the skin when exposed to sunlight. Candidates for vitamin D supplements include people who don't eat many foods in vitamin D; those who don't expose their face, arms, and hands to the sun (without sunscreen) for 5–15 minutes a few times each week; and people who live north of an imaginary line roughly between Boston and the Oregon–California border (the sun is weaker in northern latitudes).
- ***Vitamin K.*** Vitamin K promotes the synthesis of proteins that help keep bones strong. Broccoli and leafy green vegetables are rich in vitamin K.
- ***Other nutrients.*** Other nutrients that may play an important role in bone health include vitamin C, magnesium, potassium, manganese, zinc, copper, and boron.

On the flip side, there are several dietary substances that may have a *negative* effect on bone health, especially if consumed in excess: alcohol, sodium, caffeine, and retinol (a form of vitamin A). Drinking lots of soda, which often replaces milk in the diet and which is high in phosphorus (a mineral that may interfere with calcium absorption), has been shown to increase the risk of bone fracture in teenage girls.

The effect of protein intake on bone mass depends on other nutrients: Protein helps build bone as long as calcium and vitamin D intake are adequate; but if intake of calcium and vitamin D is low, high protein intake can lead to bone loss.

As described in earlier chapters, weight-bearing aerobic exercise helps maintain bone mass throughout life, and strength training improves bone density, muscle mass, strength, and balance. Drinking alcohol only in moderation, refraining from smoking, and managing depression and stress are also important for maintaining strong bones. For people who do develop osteoporosis, a variety of medications are available to treat the condition.

potassium. Focus on good food choices for these nutrients (see Table 8.3). Lean meats are rich in iron; low-fat or fat-free dairy products are excellent choices for calcium. Plant foods such as whole grains and leafy vegetables are good sources of magnesium. Potassium-rich foods include spinach and other leafy greens, cantaloupe, bananas, mushrooms, and white and sweet potatoes. Iron-deficiency **anemia** is a problem in some age groups, and researchers fear poor calcium intakes in childhood are sowing the seeds for future **osteoporosis,** especially in women. See the box "Eating for Healthy Bones" to learn more.

Water—Vital but Often Ignored

Water is the major component in both foods and the human body: You are composed of about 50–60% water. Your need for other nutrients, in terms of weight, is much less than your need for water. You can live up to 50 days without food but only a few days without water.

Water is distributed all over the body, among lean and other tissues and in blood and other body fluids. Water is used in the digestion and absorption of food and is the medium in which most of the chemical reactions take place within the body. Some water-based fluids, such as blood, transport substances around the body; other fluids serve as lubricants or cushions. Water also helps regulate body temperature.

Water is contained in almost all foods, particularly in liquids, fruits, and vegetables. The foods and fluids you consume provide 80–90% of your daily water intake; the remainder is generated through metabolism. You lose water each day in urine, feces, and sweat and through evaporation from your lungs.

As described in Chapter 3, severe dehydration causes weakness and can lead to death. However, most people maintain a healthy water balance by consuming beverages at meals and drinking fluids in response to thirst. In 2004, the Food and Nutrition Board set levels of adequate water intake to maintain hydration; all fluids, including those containing caffeine, can count toward your total daily fluid intake. Water and other beverages typically make up about 80% of your fluid intake; the remainder comes from foods, especially fruits and vegetables. Men need to consume about 3.7 total liters of water, with 3.0 liters (about 13 cups) coming from beverages; women need

TERMS

minerals Inorganic compounds needed in small amounts for the regulation, growth, and maintenance of body tissues and functions.

anemia A deficiency in the oxygen-carrying material in the red blood cells.

osteoporosis A condition in which the bones become thin and brittle and break easily.

QUESTIONS FOR CRITICAL THINKING AND REFLECTION

Experts say that two of the most important factors in a healthy diet are eating the "right" kinds of carbohydrates and eating the "right" kinds of fats. Based on what you've read so far in this chapter, which are the "right" carbohydrates and the "right" fats? How would you say your own diet stacks up when it comes to carbs and fats?

2.7 total liters, with 2.2 liters (about 9 cups) coming from beverages. (See Table 1 in the Nutrition Resources section at the end of the chapter for recommendations for specific age groups.) If you exercise vigorously or live in a hot climate, you need to consume additional fluids to maintain a balance between water consumed and water lost. (See p. 250 for more on the fluid needs of athletes and active people.)

Other Substances in Food

There are many substances in food that are not essential nutrients but that may influence health.

Antioxidants When the body uses oxygen or breaks down certain fats or proteins as a normal part of metabolism, it gives rise to substances called **free radicals.** Environmental factors such as cigarette smoke, exhaust fumes, radiation, excessive sunlight, certain drugs, and stress can increase free radical production. A free radical is a chemically unstable molecule that reacts with fats, proteins, and DNA, damaging cell membranes and mutating genes. Free radicals have been implicated in aging, cancer, cardiovascular disease, and other degenerative diseases like arthritis.

Antioxidants found in foods can help protect the body by blocking the formation and action of free radicals and repairing the damage they cause. Some antioxidants, such as vitamin C, vitamin E, and selenium, are also essential nutrients; others, such as carotenoids, found in yellow, orange, and dark green leafy vegetables, are not. Researchers recently identified the top antioxidant-containing foods and beverages as blackberries, walnuts, strawberries, artichokes, cranberries, brewed coffee, raspberries, pecans, blueberries, cloves, grape juice, unsweetened baking chocolate, sour cherries, and red wine. Also high in antioxidants are Brussels sprouts, kale, cauliflower, and pomegranates.

Phytochemicals Antioxidants fall into the broader category of **phytochemicals,** substances found in plant foods that may help prevent chronic disease. Researchers have just begun to identify and study all the different compounds found in foods, and many preliminary findings are promising. For example, certain substances found in soy foods may help lower cholesterol levels. Sulforaphane, a compound isolated from broccoli and other **cruciferous vegetables,** may render some carcinogenic compounds harmless. Allyl sulfides, a group of chemicals found in garlic and onions, appear to boost the activity of cancer-fighting immune cells. Further research on phytochemicals may extend the role of nutrition to the prevention and treatment of many chronic diseases.

To increase your intake of phytochemicals, eat a variety of fruits and vegetables rather than relying on supplements. Like many vitamins and minerals, isolated phytochemicals may be harmful if taken in high doses. In addition, it is likely that their health benefits are the result of chemical substances working in combination. The role of phytochemicals in disease prevention is discussed further in Chapters 11 and 12.

NUTRITIONAL GUIDELINES: PLANNING YOUR DIET

Various tools have been created by scientific and government groups to help people design healthy diets. The **Dietary Reference Intakes (DRIs)** are standards for nutrient intake designed to prevent nutritional deficiencies and reduce the risk of chronic disease. **Dietary Guidelines for Americans** have been established to promote health and reduce the risk for major chronic diseases through diet and physical activity. Further guidance symbolized by **MyPyramid** provides daily food intake patterns that meet the DRIs and are consistent with the Dietary Guidelines for Americans.

Dietary Reference Intakes (DRIs)

The Food and Nutrition Board establishes dietary standards, or recommended intake levels, for Americans of all ages. The current set of standards, called Dietary Reference Intakes (DRIs), is relatively new, having been introduced in 1997. The DRIs are frequently reviewed and are updated as new nutrition-related information becomes available. The DRIs present different categories of nutrients in easy-to-read table format. An earlier set of standards, called the Recommended Dietary Allowances (RDAs), focused on preventing nutritional deficiency diseases such as anemia. The DRIs have a broader focus because recent research has looked not just at the prevention of nutrient deficiencies but also at the role of nutrients in promoting optimal health and preventing chronic diseases such as cancer, osteoporosis, and heart disease.

The DRIs include standards for both recommended intakes and maximum safe intakes. The recommended intake of each nutrient is expressed as either a Recommended Dietary Allowance (RDA) or as Adequate Intake (AI). An AI is set when there is not enough information available to set an RDA value; regardless of the type of standard used, however, the DRI represents the best available estimate of intake for optimal health. The Tolerable Upper Intake Level (UL) sets the maximum daily intake by a healthy person that is unlikely to cause health problems. For example, the RDA for calcium for an 18-year-old female is 1300 milligrams per day; the UL is 2500 milligrams per day.

Because of a lack of data, ULs have not been set for all nutrients. This does not mean that people can tolerate long-term intakes of these vitamins and minerals above recommended levels. Like all chemical agents, nutrients can produce adverse effects if intakes are excessive. There is no established benefit from consuming nutrients at levels above the RDA or AI. The DRIs can be found in the Nutrition Resources section at the end of the chapter. For more information, visit the Web site of the Food and Nutrition Board (see For Further Exploration at the end of the chapter).

Should You Take Supplements? The aim of the DRIs is to guide you in meeting your nutritional needs primarily with food, rather than with vitamin and mineral supplements. This goal is important because recommendations have not yet been set for some essential nutrients. Many supplements contain only nutrients with established recommendations, so using them to meet nutrient needs can leave you deficient in other nutrients. Supplements also lack potentially beneficial phytochemicals that are found only in whole foods. Most Americans can get most of the vitamins and minerals they need by consuming a varied, nutritionally balanced diet.

The question of whether to take supplements is a serious one. Some vitamins and minerals are dangerous when ingested in excess, as described in Tables 8.2 and 8.3. Large doses of particular nutrients can also cause health problems by affecting the absorption of other vitamins and minerals. For all these reasons, you should think carefully about whether to take high-dose supplements; consider consulting a physician or registered dietitian.

In setting the DRIs, the Food and Nutrition Board recommended supplements of particular nutrients for the following groups:

- Women who are capable of becoming pregnant should take 400 micrograms (mg) per day of folic acid (the synthetic form of the vitamin folate) from fortified foods and/or supplements in addition to folate from a varied diet. Research indicates that this level of folate intake will reduce the risk of neural tube defects. (This defect occurs early in pregnancy, before most women know they are pregnant; therefore, the recommendation for folate applies to all women of reproductive age rather than only to pregnant women.) Since 1998, enriched breads, flours, corn meals, rice, noodles, and other grain products have been fortified with small amounts of folic acid. Folate is found naturally in green leafy vegetables, legumes, oranges and orange juice, and strawberries.
- People over age 50 should consume foods fortified with vitamin B-12, B-12 supplements, or a combination of the two in order to meet the majority of the DRI of 2.4 milligrams of B-12 daily. Up to 30% of people over 50 may have problems absorbing protein-bound B-12 in foods. Vitamin B-12 in supplements and fortified foods is more readily absorbed and can help prevent a deficiency.

Because of the oxidative stress caused by smoking, the Food and Nutrition Board also recommends that smokers consume 35 milligrams *more* vitamin C per day than the DRI intake level set for their age and sex (for adults, recommended daily vitamin C intakes for nonsmokers are 90 mg for men and 75 mg for women). However, supplements are not usually needed because this extra vitamin C can easily be obtained from foods. For example, 1 cup of orange juice has about 100 milligrams of vitamin C.

Supplements may also be recommended in other cases. Women with heavy menstrual flows may need extra iron to compensate for the monthly loss. Older people, people with dark skin, and people exposed to little sunlight may need extra vitamin D from vitamin D–fortified foods and/or supplements. Some vegetarians may need supplemental calcium, iron, zinc, and vitamin B-12, depending on their food choices. Newborns need a single dose of vitamin K, which must be administered under the direction of a physician. People who consume few calories, who have certain diseases, or who take certain medications may need specific vitamin and mineral supplements; such supplement decisions must be made by a physician because some vitamins and minerals counteract the actions of certain medications.

free radical An electron-seeking compound that can react with fats, proteins, and DNA, damaging cell membranes and mutating genes in its search for electrons; produced through chemical reactions in the body and by exposure to environmental factors such as sunlight and tobacco smoke.

phytochemical A naturally occurring substance found in plant foods that may help prevent and treat chronic diseases such as heart disease and cancer; *phyto* means "plant."

cruciferous vegetables Vegetables of the cabbage family, including cabbage, broccoli, brussels sprouts, kale, and cauliflower; the flower petals of these plants form the shape of a cross, hence the name.

Dietary Reference Intakes (DRIs) An umbrella term for four types of nutrient standards: Adequate Intake (AI), Estimated Average Requirement (EAR), and Recommended Dietary Allowance (RDA) set levels of intake considered adequate to prevent nutrient deficiencies and reduce the risk of chronic disease; Tolerable Upper Intake Level (UL) sets the maximum daily intake that is unlikely to cause health problems.

Dietary Guidelines for Americans General principles of good nutrition intended to help prevent certain diet-related diseases; published by the U.S. Department of Health and Human Services and the USDA.

MyPyramid A food-group plan that provides practical advice to ensure a balanced intake of the essential nutrients.

For many Americans, general dietary changes needed to meet dietary guidelines include consuming more fruits, whole grains, and dark green vegetables. Most fats in the diet should be unsaturated, like those found in fish and nuts.

In deciding whether to take a vitamin and mineral supplement, consider whether you already regularly consume a fortified breakfast cereal. Many breakfast cereals contain almost as many nutrients as a vitamin pill. If you decide to take a supplement, choose a balanced formulation that contains 50–100% of the Daily Value for vitamins and minerals. Avoid supplements containing large doses of particular nutrients. (See p. 250 for more on choosing and using supplements.)

Daily Values Because the DRIs are too cumbersome to use as a basis for food labels, the U.S. Food and Drug Administration developed another set of dietary standards, the **Daily Values.** The Daily Values are based on several different sets of guidelines and include standards for fat, cholesterol, carbohydrate, dietary fiber, and selected vitamins and minerals. The Daily Values represent appropriate intake levels for a 2000-calorie diet. The percent Daily Value shown on a food label shows how well that food contributes to your recommended daily intake. Food labels are described in detail later in the chapter.

Dietary Guidelines for Americans

To provide general guidance for choosing a healthy diet, the U.S. Department of Agriculture (USDA) and the U.S. Department of Health and Human Services (DHHS) have jointly issued Dietary Guidelines for Americans, most recently in 2005. These guidelines are intended for healthy children age 2 and older and adults of all ages. Key recommendations include the following:

- Consume a variety of nutrient-dense foods within and among the basic food groups, while staying within energy needs.
- Control calorie intake to manage body weight.
- Be physically active every day.
- Increase daily intake of foods from certain groups: fruits and vegetables, whole grains, and fat-free or low-fat milk and milk products.
- Choose fats wisely for good health, limiting intake of saturated and trans fats.
- Choose carbohydrates wisely for good health, limiting intake of added sugars.
- Choose and prepare foods with little salt, and consume potassium-rich foods.
- If you drink alcoholic beverages, do so in moderation.
- Keep foods safe to eat.

Following these guidelines promotes health and reduces risk for chronic diseases, including heart disease, cancer, diabetes, stroke, osteoporosis, and obesity. Each of the recommendations in the 2005 Dietary Guidelines for Americans is supported by an extensive review of scientific and medical evidence. What follows is a brief summary of the guidelines.

Adequate Nutrients Within Calorie Needs Many people consume more calories than they need while failing to meet recommended intakes for all nutrients. Meeting the DRIs provides a foundation not only for current health but also for reducing chronic disease risk. Many adults don't get enough calcium, potassium, fiber, magnesium, and vitamins A, C, and E; many children don't get enough calcium, potassium, fiber, magnesium, and vitamin E. Most people need to choose meals and snacks that are high in nutrients but low to moderate in calories.

Two eating plans that translate nutrient recommendations into food choices are the USDA's MyPyramid and the DASH eating plan. MyPyramid is described in detail in the next section (pp. 242–246); the DASH plan appears in the Nutrition Resources section at the end of the chapter. You can obtain all the nutrients and other substances you need by choosing the recommended number of daily servings from basic food groups and following the advice about selecting nutrient-dense foods within the groups. Following these plans would mean that many Americans would have to make some general dietary changes:

- Eat more dark green vegetables, orange vegetables, legumes, fruits, whole grains, and low-fat and fat-free milk and milk products.
- Eat less refined grains, saturated fat, trans fat, cholesterol, added sugars, and calories.

Your nutrients should come primarily from foods that contain not only the essential vitamins and minerals but also hundreds of naturally occurring substances that may benefit health, such as antioxidants. Situations in which a supplement might be recommended were described earlier in the chapter.

For maximum nutrition, it is important to consume foods from all the food groups daily and to consume a variety of nutrient-dense foods within the groups. Nutrient-dense foods are those that provide substantial amounts of vitamins and minerals and relatively few calories. Americans currently consume many foods and beverages that are low in nutrient density, making it difficult or impossible to meet nutrient needs without overconsuming calories. Selecting nutrient-dense foods—low-fat forms of foods in each group and those free of added sugars—allows you to meet your nutrient needs without overconsuming calories and unhealthy food components such as saturated and trans fats.

People's food choices can be affected by individual and cultural preferences, moral beliefs, the cost and availability of food, and food intolerances and allergies, but healthy eating is possible no matter how foods are prepared or combined. If you avoid most or all foods from any of the major food groups, be sure to get enough nutrients from the other groups. MyPyramid can be applied to vegetarian diets.

Weight Management Overweight and obesity are a major public health problem in the United States. Calorie intake and physical activity work together to influence body weight. Most Americans need to reduce calorie intake, increase their level of physical activity, and make wiser food choices. Many adults gain weight slowly over time, but even small changes in behavior can help avoid weight gain.

Evaluate your body weight in terms of body mass index (BMI), a measure of relative body weight that also takes height into account (see Chapter 6 for instructions on how to determine your BMI). If your current weight is healthy, aim to avoid weight gain. Do so by increasing physical activity and making small cuts in calorie intake. Choose nutrient-dense foods and sensible portion sizes. Avoiding weight gain is easier than losing weight. For example, for most adults, a reduction of 50–100 calories per day may prevent gradual weight gain, whereas a reduction of 500 calories or more per day may be needed initially for weight loss.

Monitoring weight regularly helps people know if they need to adjust their food intake or physical activity to maintain a healthy weight. Those who need to lose weight should aim for slow, steady weight loss by decreasing calorie intake, maintaining adequate nutrient intake, and increasing physical activity. In terms of macronutrient intake, use the AMDR ranges described earlier in the chapter for dietary planning; within these healthy ranges, total calorie intake is what counts for weight management rather than specific percentages of particular macronutrients.

Physical Activity As described earlier, regular physical activity improves fitness, helps manage weight, promotes psychological well-being, and reduces risk of heart disease, high blood pressure, cancer, and diabetes. Become active if you are inactive, and maintain or increase physical activity if you are already active. The amount of daily physical activity recommended for you depends on your current health status and goals.

- To reduce the risk of chronic disease, aim to accumulate at least 30 minutes (adults) or 60 minutes (children) of moderate physical activity—the equivalent of brisk walking at a pace of 3–4 miles per hour—beyond your usual activity at work, home, and school. Greater health benefits can be obtained by engaging in more vigorous activity or activity of longer duration.
- To help manage body weight and prevent gradual, unhealthy weight gain, engage in 60 minutes of moderate-to-high-intensity activity on most days of the week.
- To sustain weight loss in adulthood, engage daily in at least 60–90 minutes of moderate physical activity.

You can do the activity all at once or spread it out over several 10-minute or longer bouts during the day; choose activities you enjoy and can do regularly. You can boost fitness by engaging in exercises specifically designed for the health-related fitness components: cardiorespiratory endurance exercises, stretching exercises for flexibility, and resistance training for muscular strength and endurance.

Food Groups to Encourage Many Americans do not consume the recommended amounts of fruits, vegetables, whole grains, and low-fat or fat-free milk products—all of which have health benefits.

FRUITS AND VEGETABLES Fruits and vegetables are important sources of dietary fiber, vitamins, and minerals. For a 2000-calorie diet, about 4½ cups or the equivalent (9 servings) of fruits and vegetables each day is recommended. Eat a variety of fruits—fresh, frozen, canned, or dried—rather than fruit juice for most of your fruit choices. For vegetables, choose a variety of colors and kinds. Eat more of the following types of vegetables:

- Dark green vegetables, such as broccoli, kale, and other dark leafy greens
- Orange vegetables, such as carrots, sweet potatoes, pumpkin, and winter squash
- Legumes, such as pinto beans, kidney beans, black beans, garbanzo beans, split peas, and lentils

Other fruits and vegetables that are important sources of nutrients of concern include tomatoes and tomato products, red sweet peppers, cabbage and other cruciferous vegetables, bananas, citrus fruits, berries, and melons. See the discussion of MyPyramid for more advice on choosing fruits and vegetables.

Daily Values A simplified version of the RDAs used on food labels; also included are values for nutrients with no established RDA.

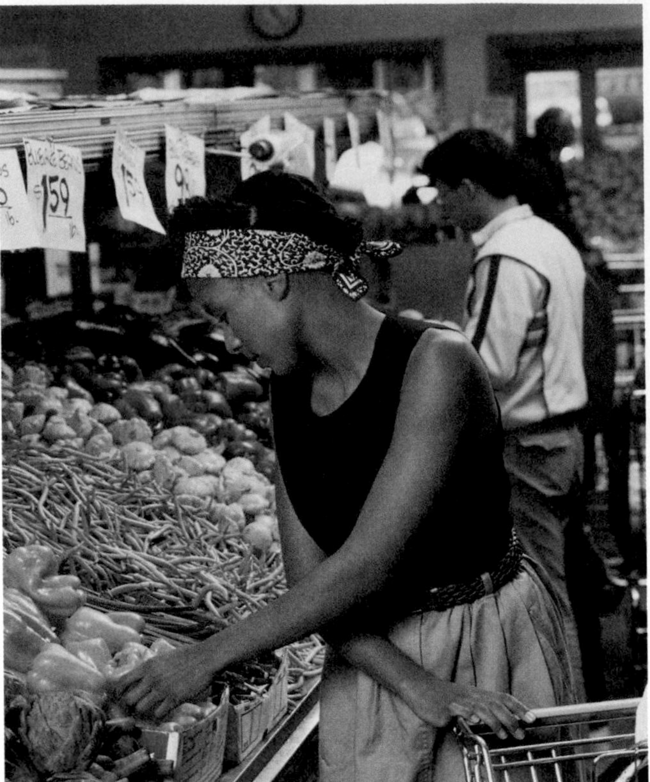

Brightly colored fruits and vegetables provide a broad range of vitamins and minerals and are excellent daily choices.

WHOLE GRAINS Whole grains provide more fiber and nutrients than refined grains, and intake of whole grains reduces the risk of chronic disease and helps with weight maintenance. For a 2000-calorie diet, 6 ounce-equivalents (6 servings) of grains each day are recommended; at least half of these servings should be whole grains. (One ounce is about 1 slice of bread, 1 cup of breakfast cereal flakes, or ½ cup of cooked pasta or rice.) The remaining grain servings should be from enriched or whole-grain products.

LOW-FAT AND FAT-FREE MILK AND MILK PRODUCTS Milk and other dairy products are important sources of calcium and other nutrients. Regular consumption of milk and milk products can reduce the risk of low bone mass throughout life. Choosing low-fat and fat-free dairy products helps to control calorie intake and reduce intake of saturated fat and cholesterol. For adults, the equivalent of 3 cups daily of fat-free or low-fat milk or milk products is recommended; 1½ ounces of cheese is the equivalent of 1 cup of milk. Yogurt and lactose-free milk are options for people who are lactose intolerant, as is use of the enzyme lactase prior to the consumption of milk products. For individuals who avoid all milk products, nondairy calcium sources include fortified cereals and beverages, tofu prepared with calcium sulfate, leafy green vegetables, soybeans, and certain types of fish.

Fats Fats and oils provide the essential fatty acids needed for a healthy diet, but, as described earlier in the chapter, the type and amount of fats consumed can make a difference for health. A diet low in saturated fat, trans fat, and cholesterol helps keep blood cholesterol low and reduces the risk for heart disease; a diet containing omega-3 fats from fish also reduces the risk for heart disease. Goals for fat intake for most adults are as follows:

Total fat: 20–35% of total daily calories

Saturated fat: Less than 10% of total daily calories

Trans fat: As little as possible

Cholesterol: Less than 300 mg per day

Most fats in the diet should come from sources of unsaturated fats, such as fish, nuts, and vegetable oils. When selecting and preparing meat, poultry, dry beans, and milk or milk products, make choices that are lean, low-fat, or fat-free. To reduce trans fat intake, limit intake of foods made with hydrogenated vegetable oils. Refer to the box "Reducing the Saturated and Trans Fats in Your Diet" for additional specific suggestions.

Cholesterol is found only in animal foods. If you need to reduce your cholesterol intake, limit your intake of foods that are particularly high in cholesterol, including egg yolks, dairy fats, certain shellfish, and liver and other organ meats; watch your serving sizes of animal foods. Food labels list the fat and cholesterol content of foods.

Two servings per week of fish rich in heart-healthy omega-3 fatty acids are also recommended for people at high risk for heart disease. However, for certain groups, intake limits are set for varieties of fish that may contain mercury (see p. 255 for more information). Fish rich in omega-3 fatty acids include salmon, mackerel, and trout.

Carbohydrates Carbohydrates are an important energy source in a healthy diet. Foods rich in carbohydrates may also be rich in dietary fiber. Fruits, vegetables, whole grains, and fat-free or low-fat milk can provide the recommended amount of carbohydrate. Choose fiber-rich foods often—for example, whole fruits, whole grains, and legumes.

People who consume foods and beverages high in added sugars tend to consume more calories but smaller amounts of vitamins and minerals than those who limit their intake of added sugars. A food is high in sugar if one of the following appears first or second in the list of ingredients or if several are listed: sugar (any type, including beet, brown, invert, raw, and cane), corn syrup or sweetener, fruit juice concentrate, honey, malt syrup, molasses, syrup, cane juice or dextrose, fructose, glucose, lactose, maltose, or sucrose.

To reduce added sugar consumption, cut back on soft drinks, candies, sweet desserts, fruit drinks, and other foods high in added sugars. Watch out for specialty coffee drinks, chai tea, smoothies, and sports drinks, which can contain hundreds of extra calories from sugar. Drink water rather than sweetened drinks, and don't let sodas and other sweets crowd out more nutritious foods, such as low-fat milk. Regular soda is the leading source of both

Reducing the Saturated and Trans Fats in Your Diet

Your overall goal is to limit total fat intake to no more than 35% of total calories. Favor unsaturated fats over saturated and trans fats.

- Be moderate in your consumption of foods high in fat, including fast foods, commercially prepared baked goods and desserts, deep-fried food, meat, poultry, nuts and seeds, and regular dairy products.
- When you eat high-fat foods, limit your portion sizes, and balance your intake with other foods that are low in fat.
- Choose lean cuts of meat, and trim any visible fat from meat before and after cooking. Remove skin from poultry before or after cooking.
- Drink fat-free or low-fat milk instead of whole milk, and use lower-fat milk in puddings, soups, and baked products. Substitute plain low-fat yogurt, blender-whipped low-fat cottage cheese, or buttermilk for sour cream.
- Use vegetable oil instead of butter or margarine. Use tub or squeeze margarine instead of stick margarine. Look for margarines that are free of trans fats. Minimize intake of coconut or palm oil.
- Season vegetables, seafood, and meats with herbs and spices rather than with creamy sauces, butter, or margarine.
- Use olive oil and lemon juice on salad, or use a yogurt-based salad dressing instead of mayonnaise or sour cream dressings.
- Steam, boil, bake, or microwave vegetables, or stir-fry them in a small amount of vegetable oil.
- Roast, bake, or broil meat, poultry, or fish so that fat drains away as the food cooks.
- Use a nonstick pan for cooking so that added fat will be unnecessary; use a vegetable spray for frying. Kitchen stores sell non-aerosol spray bottles to use with regular cooking oils.
- Chill broths from meat or poultry until the fat becomes solid. Spoon off the fat before using the broth.
- Substitute egg whites for whole eggs when baking; limit the number of egg yolks when scrambling eggs.
- Choose fruits as desserts most often.
- Eat a low-fat vegetarian main dish at least once a week.

added sugars and calories in the American diet; it provides little in the way of nutrients except sugar (Figure 8.5). The 10 teaspoons of sugar in a 12-ounce soda can exceed the recommended daily limit for added sugars for someone consuming 2000 calories per day; for more on added sugar limits, see the discussion of MyPyramid.

Nutrient	Recommended Daily Intake*	Orange Juice	Low-Fat (1%) Milk	Regular Cola	Bottled Iced Tea
Calories	2000 calories	168 calories	150 calories	152 calories	150 calories
Carbohydrate	300 g	40.5 g	18 g	38 g	37.5 g
Added sugars	32 g			38 g	34.5 g
Fat	65 g		3.9 g		
Protein	55 g		12 g		
Calcium	1000 mg	33 mg	450 mg	11 mg	
Potassium	4700 mg	15% 710 mg	12% 570 mg	4 mg	
Vitamin A	700 μg	4% 30 μg	31% 216 μg		
Vitamin C	75 mg	145.5 mg	3.6 mg		
Vitamin D	5 μg		3.7 μg		
Folate	400 μg	160 μg	20 μg		

*Recommended intakes and limits appropriate for a 20-year-old woman consuming 2000 calories per day.

FIGURE 8.5 Nutrient density of 12-ounce portions of selected beverages. The four beverages shown have approximately the same number of calories in a 12-ounce serving. However, regular cola and iced tea provide few nutrients besides added sugars; both contain more than the total daily recommended limit of added sugars (about 8 teaspoons). Orange juice is rich in potassium, vitamin C, and folate; low-fat milk is an excellent source of protein, calcium, potassium, vitamin A, and vitamin D. (Color bars represent percentage of recommended daily intake or limit for each nutrient.)

Keep your teeth and gums healthy by limiting consumption of sweet or starchy foods between meals and by brushing and flossing regularly; drinking fluoridated water also reduces the risk of dental caries (decay).

Sodium and Potassium Many people can reduce their chance of developing high blood pressure or lower already elevated blood pressure by consuming less salt; reducing blood pressure lowers the risk for stroke, heart disease, and kidney disease. Salt is made up of the minerals sodium and chloride, and although both of these minerals are essential for normal body function, we need only small amounts (1500 mg per day for adults). Most Americans consume much more salt than they need. The goal is to reduce sodium intake to less than 2300 milligrams per day, the equivalent of about 1 teaspoon of salt. Certain groups, including people with hypertension, African Americans, and older adults, benefit from an even lower sodium intake of no more than 1500 milligrams per day.

Salt is found mainly in processed and prepared foods; smaller amounts may also be added during cooking or at the table. To lower your intake of salt, choose fresh or plain frozen meat, poultry, seafood, and vegetables most often; these are lower in salt than processed forms are. Check and compare the sodium content in processed foods, including frozen dinners, cheeses, soups, salad dressings, sauces, and canned mixed dishes. Add less salt during cooking and at the table, and limit your use of high-sodium condiments like soy sauce, ketchup, mustard, pickles, and olives. Use lemon juice, herbs, and spices instead of salt to enhance the flavor of foods.

Along with lowering salt intake, increasing potassium intake helps lower blood pressure. Fruits, vegetables, and most milk products are available in forms that contain no salt, and many of these are sources of potassium. Potassium-rich foods include leafy green vegetables, sweet and white potatoes, winter squash, soybeans, tomato sauce, bananas, peaches, apricots, cantaloupes, and orange juice.

Alcoholic Beverages Alcoholic beverages supply calories but few nutrients. Drinking in moderation—that is, no more than one drink per day for women and no more than two drinks per day for men—is associated with mortality reduction among some groups, primarily males age 45 and over and women age 55 and over. Among younger people, alcohol use provides little if any health benefit, and heavy drinking is associated with motor vehicle injuries and deaths, liver disease, stroke, violence, and other health problems.

People who should not drink at all include individuals who cannot restrict their drinking to moderate levels; women who are pregnant or breastfeeding or who may become pregnant; children and adolescents; people with specific health conditions; individuals who plan to drive or operate machinery or engage in any activity that requires attention, skill, or coordination; and individuals taking prescription or over-the-counter medications that can interact with alcohol. If you choose to drink alcoholic beverages, do so sensibly and moderately, preferably with meals. Never drink in situations in which it may put you or others at risk.

Food Safety Safe foods are those that pose little risk from harmful bacteria, viruses, parasites, toxins, or chemical or physical contaminants. Foodborne diseases affect about 76 million Americans each year. Actions by consumers can reduce the occurrence of foodborne illness significantly. It is especially important to be careful with perishable foods such as poultry, meats, eggs, shellfish, milk products, and fresh fruits and vegetables. Refer to the section on foodborne illness (pp. 254–255) for specific food safety tips.

USDA's MyPyramid

When the first USDA daily food guide was published, in 1916, it emphasized the importance of getting enough calories from fats and sugars to support daily activity. Today, the guidelines stress the importance of limiting fats and sugars to control calorie intake. Many Americans are familiar with the USDA Food Guide Pyramid, the food guidance system that was first released in 1992. Since the initial release of the Pyramid, scientists have updated both nutrient recommendations (the DRIs) and the Dietary Guidelines for Americans. So, as the 2005 Dietary Guidelines were prepared, the USDA reassessed its overall food guidance system and released MyPyramid in April 2005 (Figure 8.6).

A variety of experts have proposed other food-group plans. Some of these address perceived shortcomings in the USDA plans, and some adapt the basic 1992 Pyramid to special populations. Two alternative food plans appear in the Nutrition Resources section at the end of the chapter: the DASH eating plan and the Harvard Healthy Eating Pyramid. The USDA Center for Nutrition Policy and Promotion (www.usda.gov/cnpp) has more on alternative food plans for special populations such as young children, older adults, and people choosing particular ethnic diets. MyPyramid is available in Spanish, and there is a special adaptation of MyPyramid for children age 6–11, called MyPyramid for Kids.

Another food plan that has received attention in recent years is the Mediterranean diet, which emphasizes vegetables, fruits, and whole grains; daily servings of beans, legumes, and nuts; moderate consumption of fish, poultry, and dairy products; and the use of olive oil over other types of fat, especially saturated fat. The Mediterranean diet has been associated with lower rates of heart disease and cancer, and a 2006 study found a link between the diet and a greatly reduced risk of Alzheimer's disease.

Key Messages of MyPyramid The new MyPyramid symbol (see Figure 8.6) has been developed to remind

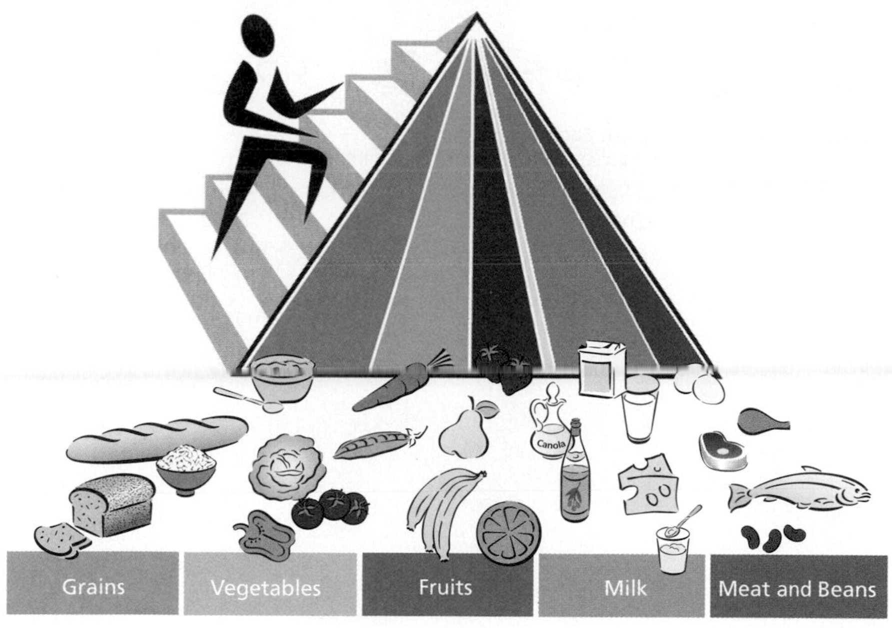

FIGURE 8.6 USDA's MyPyramid. The USDA food guidance system, called MyPyramid, can be personalized based on an individual's sex, age, and activity level; visit MyPyramid.gov to obtain a food plan appropriate for you. MyPyramid contains five main food groups plus oils (yellow band). Key consumer messages include the following:

- Grains: Make half your grains whole.
- Vegetables: Vary your veggies.
- Fruits: Focus on fruits.
- Oils: Know your fats.
- Milk: Get your calcium-rich foods.
- Meat and Beans: Go lean with protein.

SOURCE: U.S. Department of Agriculture. 2005. *MyPyramid* (http://mypyramid.gov; retrieved May 27, 2007).

consumers to make healthy food choices and to be active every day. Key messages include the following:

- *Personalization* is represented by the person on the steps and the MyPyramid.gov site, which includes individualized recommendations, interactive assessments of food intake and physical activity, and tips for success.
- *Daily physical activity*, represented by the person climbing the steps, is important for maintaining a healthy weight and reducing the risk of chronic disease.
- *Moderation* of food intake is represented by the narrowing of each food group from bottom to top.
- *Proportionality* is represented by the different widths of the food group bands. The widths provide a general guide for how much food a person should choose from each group.
- *Variety* is represented by the six color bands representing the five food groups of MyPyramid and oils. Foods from all groups are needed daily for good health.
- *Gradual improvement* is a good strategy; people can benefit from taking small steps to improve their diet and activity habits each day.

The MyPyramid chart in Figure 8.7 shows the food intake patterns recommended for different levels of calorie intake; Table 8.4 provides guidance for determining an appropriate calorie intake for weight maintenance. Use the table to identify an energy intake that is about right for you; then refer to the appropriate column in Figure 8.7. You can also get a personalized version of MyPyramid recommendations by visiting MyPyramid.gov. Each food group is described briefly in the following sections. Many Americans have trouble identifying serving sizes, so recommended daily intakes from each group are now given in terms of cups and ounces; see the box "Judging Portion Sizes" for additional advice.

Grains Foods from this group are usually low in fat and rich in complex carbohydrates, dietary fiber (if grains are unrefined), and many vitamins and minerals, including thiamin, riboflavin, iron, niacin, folic acid (if enriched or fortified), and zinc. Someone eating 2000 calories a day should include 6 ounce-equivalents each day, with half of those servings from whole grains such as whole-grain bread, whole-wheat pasta, high-fiber cereal, and brown rice. The following count as 1 ounce-equivalent:

- 1 slice of bread
- 1 small (2½-inch diameter) muffin
- 1 cup ready-to-eat cereal flakes
- ½ cup cooked cereal, rice, grains, or pasta
- 1 6-inch tortilla

Choose foods that are typically made with little fat or sugar (bread, rice, pasta) over those that are high in fat and sugar (croissants, chips, cookies, doughnuts).

Vegetables Vegetables contain carbohydrates, dietary fiber, vitamin A, vitamin C, folate, potassium, and other nutrients. They are also naturally low in fat. In a 2000-calorie diet, 2½ cups (5 servings) of vegetables should be included daily. Each of the following counts as ½ cup or equivalent (1 serving) of vegetables:

- ½ cup raw or cooked vegetables
- 1 cup raw leafy salad greens
- ½ cup vegetable juice

Because vegetables vary in the nutrients they provide, it is important to consume a variety of types of vegetables to

Daily Amount of Food from Each Group

Food group amounts shown in cups (c) or ounce-equivalents (oz-eq), with number of daily servings (srv) shown in parentheses; vegetable subgroup amounts are per week

Calorie level	1600	1800	2000	2200	2400	2600	2800	3000
Grains	5 oz-eq	6 oz-eq	6 oz-eq	7 oz-eq	8 oz-eq	9 oz-eq	10 oz-eq	10 oz-eq
Whole grains	3 oz-eq	3 oz-eq	3 oz-eq	3.5 oz-eq	4 oz-eq	4.5 oz-eq	5 oz-eq	5 oz-eq
Other grains	2 oz-eq	3 oz-eq	3 oz-eq	3.5 oz-eq	4 oz-eq	4.5 oz-eq	5 oz-eq	5 oz-eq
Vegetables	2 c (4 srv)	2.5 c (5 srv)	2.5 c (5 srv)	3c (6 srv)	3 c (6 srv)	3.5 c (7 srv)	3.5 c (7 srv)	4 c (8 srv)
Dark green	2 c/wk	3 c/wk	3 c/wk	3 c/wk	3 c/wk	3 c/wk	3 c/wk	3 c/wk
Orange	1.5 c/wk	2 c/wk	2 c/wk	2 c/wk	2 c/wk	2.5 c/wk	2.5 c/wk	2.5 c/wk
Legumes	2.5 c/wk	3 c/wk	3 c/wk	3 c/wk	3 c/wk	3.5 c/wk	3.5 c/wk	3.5 c/wk
Starchy	2.5 c/wk	3 c/wk	3 c/wk	6 c/wk	6 c/wk	7 c/wk	7 c/wk	9 c/wk
Other	5.5 c/wk	6.5 c/wk	6.5 c/wk	7 c/wk	7 c/wk	8.5 c/wk	8.5 c/wk	10 c/wk
Fruits	1.5 c (3 srv)	1.5 c (3 srv)	2 c (4 srv)	2 c (4 srv)	2 c (4 srv)	2 c (4 srv)	2.5 c (5 srv)	2.5 c (5 srv)
Milk	3 c	3 c	3 c	3 c	3 c	3 c	3 c	3 c
Lean meat and beans	5 oz-eq	5 oz-eq	5.5 oz-eq	6 oz-eq	6.5 oz-eq	6.5 oz-eq	7 oz-eq	7 oz-eq
Oils	5 tsp	5 tsp	6 tsp	6 tsp	7 tsp	8 tsp	8 tsp	10 tsp

The discretionary calorie allowances shown below are the calories remaining at each level after nutrient-dense foods in each food group are selected. Those trying to lose weight may choose not to use discretionary calories. For those wanting to maintain weight, discretionary calories may be used to increase the amount of food from each food group; to consume foods that are not in the lowest fat form or that contain added sugars; to add oil, fat, or sugars to foods; or to consume alcohol. The amounts below show how discretionary calories may be divided between solid fats and added sugars.

Discretionary calories	132	195	267	290	362	410	426	512
Solid fats	11 g	15 g	18 g	19 g	22 g	24 g	24 g	29 g
Added sugars	12 g (3 tsp)	20 g (5 tsp)	32 g (8 tsp)	38 g (9 tsp)	48 g (12 tsp)	56 g (14 tsp)	60 g (15 tsp)	72 g (18 tsp)

FIGURE 8.7 MyPyramid food intake patterns. To determine an appropriate amount of food from each group, find the column with your approximate daily energy intake. That column lists the daily recommended intake from each food group. Visit MyPyramid.gov for a personalized intake plan and for intakes for other calorie levels.

SOURCE: U.S. Department of Health and Human Services and U.S. Department of Agriculture. 2005. *Dietary Guidelines for Americans, 2005, Appendix A. Eating Patterns* (http://www.health.gov/dietaryguidelines/dga2005/document/html/appendixA.htm; retrieved May 27, 2007).

obtain maximum nutrition. Many Americans consume only a few types of vegetables, with white potatoes (baked or served as french fries) being the most popular. To help boost variety, MyPyramid recommends servings from five different subgroups within the vegetables group; choose vegetables from several subgroups each day. (For clarity, Figure 8.7 shows servings from the subgroups in terms of weekly consumption.)

- Dark green vegetables like spinach, chard, collards, bok choy, broccoli, kale, romaine lettuce, and turnip and mustard greens
- Orange and deep yellow vegetables like carrots, winter squash, sweet potatoes, and pumpkin
- Legumes like pinto beans, kidney beans, black beans, lentils, chickpeas, soybeans, split peas, and

TAKE CHARGE

Judging Portion Sizes

Studies have shown that most people underestimate the size of their food portions, in many cases by as much as 50%. If you need to retrain your eye, try using measuring cups and spoons and an inexpensive kitchen scale when you eat at home. With a little practice, you'll learn what the difference between 3 and 8 ounces of chicken or meat is, and what a half-cup of rice really looks like. For quick estimates, use the following equivalents:

- 1 teaspoon of margarine = the tip of your thumb
- 1 ounce of cheese = your thumb, four dice stacked together, or an ice cube
- 3 ounces of chicken or meat = a deck of cards or an audiocassette tape.
- 1 cup of pasta = a small fist or a tennis ball
- ½ cup of rice or cooked vegetables = an ice cream scoop or one-third of a can of soda
- 2 tablespoons of peanut butter = a Ping-Pong ball or large marshmallow
- 1 medium potato = a computer mouse
- 1–2-ounce muffin or roll = a plum or large egg
- 2-ounce bagel = a hockey puck or yo-yo
- 1 medium fruit (apple or orange) = a baseball
- ¼ cup nuts = a golf ball
- Small cookie or cracker = a poker chip

tofu; legumes can be counted as servings of vegetables *or* as alternatives to meat

- Starchy vegetables like corn, green peas, and white potatoes
- Other vegetables: tomatoes, bell peppers (red, orange, yellow, or green), green beans, and cruciferous vegetables like cauliflower are good choices

Table 8.4 MyPyramid Daily Calorie Intake Levels

Age (years)	Sedentary*	Moderately Active**	Active†
Child			
2–3	1000	1000–1400	1000–1400
Female			
4–8	1200–1400	1400–1600	1400–1800
9–13	1400–1600	1600–2000	1800–2200
14–18	1800	2000	2400
19–30	1800–2000	2000–2200	2400
31–50	1800	2000	2200
51+	1600	1800	2000–2200
Male			
4–8	1200–1400	1400–1600	1600–2000
9–13	1600–2000	1800–2200	2000–2600
14–18	2000–2400	2400–2800	2800–3200
19–30	2400–2600	2600–2800	3000
31–50	2200–2400	2400–2600	2800–3000
51+	2000–2200	2200–2400	2400–2800

*A lifestyle that includes only the light physical activity associated with typical day-to-day life.

**A lifestyle that includes physical activity equivalent to walking about 1.5–3 miles per day at 3–4 miles per hour (30–60 minutes a day of moderate physical activity), in addition to the light physical activity associated with typical day-to-day life.

†A lifestyle that includes physical activity equivalent to walking more than 3 miles per day at 3–4 miles per hour (60 or more minutes a day of moderate physical activity), in addition to the light physical activity associated with typical day-to-day life.

SOURCE: U.S. Department of Agriculture, 2005. *MyPyramid Food Intake Pattern Calorie Levels* (http://www.mypyramid.gov/downloads/mypyramid_calorie_levels.pdf; retrieved May 27, 2007).

Fruits Fruits are rich in carbohydrates, dietary fiber, and many vitamins, especially vitamin C. For someone eating a 2000-calorie diet, 2 cups (4 servings) of fruits are recommended daily. The following each count as ½ cup or equivalent (1 serving) of fruit:

- ½ cup fresh, canned, or frozen fruit
- ½ cup fruit juice (100% juice)
- 1 small whole fruit
- ¼ cup dried fruit

Good choices from this group are citrus fruits and juices, melons, pears, apples, bananas, and berries. Choose whole fruits often—they are higher in fiber and often lower in calories than fruit juices. Fruit *juices* typically contain more nutrients and less added sugar than fruit *drinks*. Choose canned fruits packed in 100% fruit juice or water rather than in syrup.

Milk This group includes all milk and milk products, such as yogurt, cheeses (except cream cheese), and dairy desserts, as well as lactose-free and lactose-reduced products. Foods from this group are high in protein, carbohydrate, calcium, riboflavin, and vitamin D (if fortified). Those consuming 2000 calories per day should include 3 cups of milk or the equivalent daily. Each of the following counts as the equivalent of 1 cup:

- 1 cup milk or yogurt
- ½ cup ricotta cheese
- 1½ ounces natural cheese
- 2 ounces processed cheese

Cottage cheese is lower in calcium than most other cheeses; ½ cup is equivalent to ¼ cup milk. Ice cream is also lower in calcium and higher in sugar and fat than many other dairy products; one scoop counts as ⅓ cup milk. To limit calories and saturated fat in your diet, it is best to choose servings of low-fat and fat-free items from this group.

Meat and Beans This group includes meat, poultry, fish, dry beans and peas, eggs, nuts, and seeds. These foods provide protein, niacin, iron, vitamin B-6, zinc, and thiamin; the animal foods in the group also provide vitamin B-12. For someone consuming a 2000-calorie diet, 5½ ounce-equivalents is recommended. Each of the following counts as equivalent to 1 ounce:

- 1 ounce cooked lean meat, poultry, or fish
- ¼ cup cooked dry beans (legumes) or tofu
- 1 egg
- 1 tablespoon peanut butter
- ½ ounce nuts or seeds

One egg at breakfast, ½ cup of pinto beans at lunch, and a 3-ounce (cooked weight) hamburger at dinner would add up to the equivalent of 6 ounces of lean meat for the day. To limit your intake of fat and saturated fat, choose lean cuts of meat and skinless poultry, and watch your serving sizes carefully. Choose at least one serving of plant proteins, such as black beans, lentils, or tofu, every day.

Oils The oils group represents the oils that are added to foods during processing or cooking or at the table; oils and soft margarines include vegetable oils and soft vegetable oil table spreads that have no trans fats. These are major sources of vitamin E and unsaturated fatty acids, including the essential fatty acids. For a 2000-calorie diet, 6 teaspoons of oils per day are recommended. One teaspoon is the equivalent of the following:

- 1 teaspoon vegetable oil or soft margarine
- 1 tablespoon salad dressing or light mayonnaise

Foods that are mostly oils include nuts, olives, avocados, and some fish. The following portions include about 1 teaspoon of oil: 8 large olives, ⅙ medium avocado, ½ tablespoon peanut butter, and ⅓ ounce roasted nuts. Food labels can help you identify the type and amount of fat in various foods.

Discretionary Calories, Solid Fats, and Added Sugars The suggested intakes from the basic food groups in MyPyramid assume that nutrient-dense foods are selected from each group; nutrient-dense foods are those that are fat-free or low-fat and that contain no added sugars. If this pattern is followed, then a small amount of additional calories can be consumed—the *discretionary calorie allowance*. Figure 8.7 shows the discretionary calorie allowance at each calorie level in MyPyramid.

People who are trying to lose weight may choose not to use discretionary calories. For those wanting to maintain weight, discretionary calories may be used to increase the amount of food from a food group; to consume foods that are not in the lowest fat form or that contain added sugars; to add oil, fat, or sugars to foods; or to consume alcohol. The amounts shown in Figure 8.7 show how discretionary calories may be divided between solid fats and added sugars. The values for additional fat target no more than 30% of total calories from fat and less than 10% of calories from saturated fat. Examples of discretionary solid fat calories include higher-fat meats such as sausages or chicken with skin, whole milk instead of fat-free milk, and foods topped with butter. For example, 1 cup of whole milk has 60 calories more than 1 cup of fat-free milk; these 60 calories would be counted as discretionary calories.

As described earlier in the chapter, added sugars are the sugars added to foods and beverages in processing or preparation, not the naturally occurring sugars in fruits or milk. The suggested amounts of added sugars may be helpful limits for including some sweetened foods or beverages in the daily diet without exceeding energy needs or underconsuming other nutrients. For example, in a 2000-calorie diet, MyPyramid lists 32 grams (8 teaspoons) for discretionary intake of added sugars. In the American diet, added sugars are often found in sweetened beverages (regular soda, sweetened teas, fruit drinks), dairy products (ice cream, some yogurts), and grain products (bakery goods). For example, a 20-ounce regular soda has 260 calories from added sugars that would be counted as discretionary calories. The current American diet includes higher-than-recommended levels of sugar intake.

Remember, the amounts listed in Figure 8.7 for solid fats and added sugars assume that you select nutrient-dense foods from the major food groups; don't just add fats and sugars to your diet. The average American diet is overich in foods that contain relatively large amounts of added sugars and fats and that are low in essential nutrients (Table 8.5). To control weight and obtain adequate amounts of essential nutrients, it is important to choose nutrient-dense foods for most of your daily servings.

Table 8.5 Top Ten Sources of Calories in the American Diet

Food	Percent of Total Calories
Regular soft drinks	7.1
Cake, sweet rolls, doughnuts, pastries	3.6
Hamburgers, cheeseburgers, meatloaf	3.1
Pizza	3.1
Potato chips, corn chips, popcorn	2.9
Rice	2.7
Rolls, buns, English muffins, bagels	2.7
Cheese or cheese spread	2.6
Beer	2.6
French fries, fried potatoes	2.2

SOURCE: Block, G. 2004. Foods contributing to energy intake in the US: Data from NHANES III and NHANES 1999–2000. *Journal of Food Composition and Analysis* 17(2004): 439–447.

MOTIVATION BOOSTER

Make a list of pros and cons. Eating well can be a challenge when you're surrounded by fast, convenient, unhealthy choices. Make a list of the short- and long-term pros and cons of your current diet and your goal diet (see Chapter 1 for tips on completing this kind of analysis). Then make a list called "Advantages of Change," and include the pros of your goal diet and the cons of your current diet. Keep this list handy to help you deal with challenging situations.

The Vegetarian Alternative

Some people choose a diet with one essential difference from the diets we've already described: Foods of animal origin (meat, poultry, fish, eggs, milk) are eliminated or restricted. Many do so for health reasons; vegetarian diets tend to be lower in saturated fat, cholesterol, and animal protein and higher in complex carbohydrates, dietary fiber, folate, vitamins C and E, carotenoids, and phytochemicals. Some people adopt a vegetarian diet out of concern for the environment, for financial considerations, or for reasons related to ethics or religion.

Types of Vegetarian Diets There are various vegetarian styles; the wider the variety of the diet eaten, the easier it is to meet nutritional needs. **Vegans** eat only plant foods. **Lacto-vegetarians** eat plant foods and dairy products. **Lacto-ovo-vegetarians** eat plant foods, dairy products, and eggs. According to some polls, about 5 million American adults never eat meat, poultry, or fish and fall into one of these three groups. Others can be categorized as **partial vegetarians, semivegetarians,** or **pescovegetarians**; these individuals eat plant foods, dairy products, eggs, and usually a small selection of poultry, fish, and other seafood. Many other people choose vegetarian meals frequently but are not strictly vegetarian. Including some animal protein (such as dairy products) in a mostly vegetarian diet makes planning easier, but it is not necessary.

A Food Plan for Vegetarians MyPyramid can be adapted for use by vegetarians with only a few key modifications. For the meat and beans group, vegetarians can focus on the nonmeat choices of dry beans (legumes), nuts, seeds, eggs, and soy foods like tofu (soybean curd) and tempeh (a cultured soy product). Vegans and other vegetarians who do not consume any dairy products must find other rich sources of calcium (see the following list). Fruits, vegetables, and whole grains are healthy choices for people following all types of vegetarian diets.

A healthy vegetarian diet emphasizes a wide variety of plant foods. Although plant proteins are generally incomplete, choosing a variety of plant foods will supply all of the essential amino acids. Choosing minimally processed and unrefined foods will maximize nutrient value and provide ample dietary fiber. Daily consumption of a variety of plant foods in amounts that meet total energy needs can provide all needed nutrients except vitamin B-12 and possibly vitamin D. Strategies for obtaining these and other nutrients of concern include the following:

- *Vitamin B-12* is found naturally only in animal foods; if dairy products and eggs are limited or avoided, B-12 can be obtained from fortified foods such as ready-to-eat cereals, soy beverages, meat substitutes, and special yeast products, or from supplements.
- *Vitamin D* can be obtained by spending 5–15 minutes a day in the sun, by consuming vitamin D–fortified products like ready-to-eat cereals and soy or rice milk, or by taking a supplement.
- *Calcium* is found in legumes, tofu processed with calcium, dark-green leafy vegetables, nuts, tortillas made from lime-processed corn, fortified orange juice, soy milk, bread, and other foods.
- *Iron* is found in whole grains, fortified bread and breakfast cereals, dried fruits, leafy green vegetables, nuts and seeds, legumes, and soy foods. The iron in plant foods is more difficult for the body to absorb than the iron from animal sources; consuming a good source of vitamin C with most meals is helpful because vitamin C improves iron absorption.
- *Zinc* is found in whole grains, nuts, legumes, and soy foods.

It takes a little planning and common sense to put together a good vegetarian diet. If you are a vegetarian or are considering becoming one, devote some extra time and thought to your diet. It's especially important to eat as wide a variety of foods as possible to ensure that all your nutritional needs are satisfied. Consulting with a registered dietitian will make your planning easier. Vegetarian diets for children, teens, and pregnant and lactating women warrant professional guidance.

Dietary Challenges for Special Population Groups

MyPyramid and the Dietary Guidelines for Americans provide a basis that everyone can use to create a healthy

TERMS

vegan A vegetarian who eats no animal products at all.

lacto-vegetarian A vegetarian who includes milk and cheese products in the diet.

lacto-ovo-vegetarian A vegetarian who eats no meat, poultry, or fish, but does eat eggs and milk products.

partial vegetarian, semivegetarian, or **pescovegetarian** A vegetarian who includes eggs, dairy products, and small amounts of poultry and seafood in the diet.

diet. However, some population groups face special dietary challenges.

Women Women tend to be smaller and to weigh less than men, meaning they have lower energy needs and so need fewer calories. Because of this, women may have more difficulty getting adequate amounts of all the essential nutrients and need to focus on nutrient-dense foods. Two nutrients of special concern are calcium and iron, minerals for which many women fail to meet the RDAs. Low calcium intake may be linked to the development of osteoporosis in later life. The *Healthy People 2010* report sets a goal of increasing from 40% to 75% the proportion of women age 20–49 who meet the dietary recommendation for calcium. Nonfat and low-fat dairy products and fortified cereal, bread, and orange juice are good choices.

Iron is also a concern: Menstruating women have higher iron requirements than other groups, and a lack of iron in the diet can lead to iron-deficiency anemia. Lean red meat, leafy green vegetables, and fortified breakfast cereals are good sources of iron. As discussed earlier, all women capable of becoming pregnant should consume adequate folate or folic acid from fortified foods and/or supplements.

Men Men are seldom thought of as having nutritional deficiencies because they generally have high-calorie diets. However, many men have a diet that does not follow recommended food intake patterns and that includes more red meat and fewer fruits, vegetables, and grains than recommended. This dietary pattern is linked to heart disease and some types of cancer. A high intake of calories can lead to weight gain in the long term if a man's activity level decreases as he ages. Men should use MyPyramid as a basis for their overall diet and focus on increasing their consumption of fruits, vegetables, and grains to obtain vitamins, minerals, dietary fiber, and phytochemicals.

The "Fruits and Veggies Matter" program was created by the Centers for Disease Control and Prevention (CDC) and partner agencies to promote increased intake of fruits and vegetables. For strategies and guidelines for consuming more fruits and vegetables, visit http://www.fruitsandveggiesmatter.gov.

College Students Foods that are convenient for college students are not always the healthiest choices. However, it is possible to make healthy eating both convenient and affordable (see the tips in the box "Eating Strategies for College Students"). Two settings of concern often found on college campuses are buffet-style dining halls and fast-food restaurants. Both may offer foods that are low in nutrient density—and in very large portions. While no foods are entirely "bad," consuming moderate portions of a wide variety of foods is critical for a healthy diet.

Older Adults As people age, they tend to become less active, so they require fewer calories to maintain their weight. At the same time, the absorption of nutrients tends to be lower in older adults because of age-related changes in the digestive tract. Thus, they must consume nutrient-dense foods to meet their nutritional requirements. As discussed earlier, foods fortified with vitamin B-12 and/or B-12 supplements are recommended for people over age 50. Because constipation is a common problem, consuming foods high in dietary fiber and obtaining adequate fluids are important goals.

Athletes Key dietary concerns for athletes are meeting increased energy and fluid requirements for training and making healthy food choices throughout the day.

ENERGY INTAKE Individuals engaged in vigorous training programs expend more energy (calories) than sedentary and moderately active individuals and may have energy needs ranging from 2000 to more than 6000 calories per day. For athletes, the American Dietetic Association recommends a diet with 60–65% of calories coming from carbohydrates, 10–15% from protein, and no more than 30% from fat. Athletes for whom maintaining low body weight and body fat is important—such as gymnasts, skaters, and wrestlers—should consume adequate calories and nutrients and avoid falling into unhealthy patterns of eating. The combination of low levels of body fat, high physical activity, disordered eating habits—and, in women, amenorrhea—is associated with stress fractures and other injuries and with osteoporosis. (The female athlete triad was discussed in Chapter 6; see Chapter 9 for more on eating disorders.)

CARBOHYDRATE Endurance athletes involved in competitive events lasting longer than 90 minutes may benefit from increasing carbohydrate intake to 65–70% of total calories; this increase should come in the form of complex, rather than simple, carbohydrates. High carbohydrate intake builds and maintains muscle glycogen stores, resulting in greater endurance and delayed fatigue during competitive events. Some endurance athletes engage in "carbohydrate loading"—a practice that involves increasing carbohydrate intake in the days before a competition. Before exercise, the ACSM recommends that an active adult or athlete consume a meal or snack that is relatively high in carbohydrates, moderate in protein, and low in fat. Soon after exercise, particularly following a strenuous competition or training session, a mixed meal containing carbohydrates, protein, and fat should be consumed to replace muscle glycogen and provide amino acids for building and repairing muscle tissue. Consuming some simple carbohydrates immediately after exercise can help replenish glycogen stores in the liver and muscles.

PROTEIN For endurance athletes, the ACSM recommends a protein intake of 1.2–1.4 grams of protein per kilogram (0.55–0.64 gram per pound) of body weight per day, up from the standard DRI of 0.8 gram per kilogram (0.36 gram per pound); for athletes engaged in heavy strength

TAKE CHARGE

Eating Strategies for College Students

General Guidelines

- Eat slowly and enjoy your food. Set aside a separate time to eat. Don't eat while you study.
- Eat a colorful, varied diet. The more colorful your diet is, the more varied and rich in fruits and vegetables it will be. Don't limit your vegetable choices to french fries, which are typically high in saturated and trans fats.
- Consider nutrient density in your food choices, and avoid large servings of foods that provide calories but few essential nutrients. Spend your daily calorie budget wisely.
- Check out the labels and ingredient lists of foods you commonly eat so that you are aware of their general nutrient profile.
- Eat breakfast. You'll have more energy in the morning and be less likely to grab an unhealthy snack later on. Whole-grain cereals or whole-grain toast are excellent breakfast choices.
- Choose healthy snacks—fruits, vegetables, grains, and cereals—as often as you can.
- Drink water more often than soft drinks or other sweetened beverages. Rent a mini-refrigerator for your dorm room, and stock up on healthy beverages.
- Pay attention to portion sizes. Read food labels carefully, and take special note of serving sizes and the total number of servings in the package. You may find that your favorite bottled drinks and packaged snack foods provide multiple servings and that you are consuming more calories, fat, and added sugars than you realize.

Eating in the Dining Hall

- Choose a meal plan that includes breakfast—and don't skip it.
- Accept that dining hall food is not going to be as good as home cooking. Find dishes that you like that are nutritious.
- If menus are posted or distributed, decide what you want to eat before getting in line and stick to your choices. Consider what you plan to do and eat for the rest of the day before making your choices.
- Ask for large servings of vegetables and small servings of meat and other high-fat main dishes. Build your meals around grains and vegetables.
- Choose whole grains.
- Choose leaner poultry, fish, or bean dishes rather than high-fat meats and fried entrees.
- Ask that gravies and sauces be served on the side; limit your intake.
- Choose broth-based or vegetable soups rather than cream soups.
- At the salad bar, load up on leafy greens, beans, and fresh vegetables. Avoid mayonnaise-coated salads (macaroni salad, potato salad), bacon, croutons, and high-fat dressings. Put dressing on the side; dip your fork into it rather than pouring it over the salad.
- Drink nonfat milk, water, mineral water, or 100% fruit juice rather than heavily sweetened fruit drinks, whole milk, soft drinks, or beer.
- Choose fruit for dessert rather than pastries, cookies, or cakes.

Eating in Fast-Food Restaurants

- Most fast-food chains can provide a brochure with a nutritional breakdown of the foods on the menu. Ask for it and identify the healthiest options. (See also the information in Appendix C.)
- Order small single burgers with no cheese instead of double burgers with many toppings.
- Ask for items to be prepared without mayonnaise, tartar sauce, sour cream, or other high-fat sauces. Ketchup, mustard, and fat-free mayonnaise or sour cream are available at many fast-food restaurants.
- Choose whole-grain buns or bread for burgers, hot dogs, and sandwiches.
- Choose chicken items made from chicken breast, not processed chicken.
- Order vegetable pizzas without extra cheese.
- If you order french fries or onion rings, get the smallest size and/or share them with a friend. Better yet, get a salad or a fruit cup instead.

Fast-food meals are a health concern. A large cheeseburger, large order of fries, and large (32 oz) nondiet soda may provide about 1600 calories, 75 grams of fat, and 30 teaspoons of added sugars. If you have a fast-food meal, balance it with healthy, nutrient-rich foods during the rest of the day.

Eating on the Run

Are you chronically short of time? Pack these items for a quick snack or meal: fresh or dried fruit, fruit juices, raw fresh vegetables, plain bagels, bread sticks, whole-wheat fig bars, low-fat cheese sticks or cubes, low-fat crackers or granola bars, nonfat or low-fat yogurt, snack-size cereal boxes, pretzels, rice or corn cakes, plain popcorn, soup (if you have access to a microwave), or water.

training, protein needs may be as high as 1.6–1.7 grams per kilogram (0.73–0.77 gram per pound) of body weight. This level of protein intake is easily obtainable from foods, however. A 160-pound athlete consuming 3500 calories per day needs to obtain only 12% of total calories as protein to achieve the upper end of the range for endurance athletes. The average American diet includes about 16% of total calories as protein, and a balanced high-carbohydrate, moderate-protein, moderate-fat diet can provide the nutrients athletes need.

There is no evidence that consuming supplements containing vitamins, minerals, protein, or specific amino acids will build muscle or improve sports performance. Strength and muscle are built with exercise, not extra protein, and carbohydrates provide the fuel needed for muscle-building exercise. Strenuous physical activity does increase the need for protein and some vitamins and minerals; however, the increased energy intake of athletes more than compensates for this increased need.

FLUIDS Moderately active people should consume adequate fluids as described earlier in the chapter. People who exercise heavily and/or live in a hot climate need to consume additional fluids to maximize performance and prevent heat illness. For a strenuous endurance event, prepare yourself the day before by drinking plenty of fluids. On the day of the event, the ACSM recommends that you consume 14–22 ounces (400–600 ml) of fluid about 2 hours before exercise, and then 6–12 ounces (150–350 ml) of fluid every 15–20 minutes during exercise—or as much of this amount as you can tolerate. Afterward, drink enough to replace lost fluids—16–24 ounces for every pound of weight lost. (Weight loss during a workout or athletic event comes primarily from fluid loss through sweat; as described in Chapter 3, checking your weight can help you monitor your fluid balance.)

Water is a good choice for fluid replacement for workouts and events lasting less than 60–90 minutes, especially if you are trying to avoid the additional calories in many other beverages. However, for workouts or events lasting longer, a sports drink can be a good choice. These contain water, electrolytes, and carbohydrates. The advantage of sports drinks is that they can provide you with some extra energy (in the form of rapidly digestible carbohydrates that help maintain blood glucose levels) and replace electrolytes like sodium that are lost in sweat.

People with Special Health Concerns Many Americans have special health concerns that affect their dietary needs. For example, women who are pregnant or breastfeeding require extra calories, vitamins, and minerals. People with diabetes benefit from a well-balanced diet that is low in simple sugars, high in complex carbohydrates, and relatively rich in monounsaturated fats. People with high blood pressure need to limit their sodium consumption and control their weight. If you have a health problem or concern that may require a special diet, discuss your situation with a physician or registered dietitian.

QUESTIONS FOR CRITICAL THINKING AND REFLECTION

What factors influence your food choices—convenience, cost, availability, habit? Do you ever consider nutritional content or nutritional recommendations like the Dietary Guidelines for Americans or MyPyramid? If not, how big a change would it be for you to think of nutritional content first when choosing food? Is it something you could do easily?

NUTRITIONAL PLANNING: MAKING INFORMED CHOICES ABOUT FOOD

Knowing about nutrition is a good start to making sound choices about food. It also helps if you can interpret food labels, understand food additives, and avoid foodborne illnesses.

Reading Food Labels

Food labels can help you apply the principles of MyPyramid and the Dietary Guidelines for Americans. Since 1994, all processed foods regulated by either the FDA or the USDA have included standardized nutrition information on their labels. Every food label shows serving sizes and the amount of fat, saturated fat, trans fat, cholesterol, protein, dietary fiber, and sodium in each serving. To make intelligent choices about food, learn to read and understand food labels (see the box "Using Food Labels"). The FDA's Web site features an interactive tutorial on reading food labels; to use this online tool, visit http://www.cfsan.fda.gov/~ear/hwm/labelman.html.

Because most meat, poultry, fish, fruits, and vegetables are not processed, they were not covered by the 1994 law. You can get information on the nutrient content of these items from basic nutrition books, registered dietitians, nutrient analysis computer software, the Web, and the companies that produce or distribute these foods. Also, supermarkets often have posters or pamphlets listing the nutrient contents of these foods. In Lab 8.3, you compare foods using the information on their labels.

Reading Dietary Supplement Labels

Dietary supplements include vitamins, minerals, amino acids, herbs, enzymes, and other compounds. Although dietary supplements are often thought of as safe and natural, they contain powerful bioactive chemicals that have the potential for harm. About one-quarter of all pharmaceutical drugs are derived from botanical sources, and even essential vitamins and minerals can have toxic effects if consumed in excess.

In the United States, supplements are not legally considered drugs and are not regulated the way drugs are. Before they are approved by the FDA and put on the market, drugs undergo clinical studies to determine safety, effectiveness, side effects and risks, possible interactions with other substances, and appropriate dosages. The FDA does not authorize or test dietary supplements, and supplements are not required to demonstrate either safety or

Using Food Labels

Food labels are designed to help consumers make food choices based on the nutrients that are most important to good health. In addition to listing nutrient content by weight, the label puts the information in the context of a daily diet of 2000 calories that includes no more than 65 grams of fat (approximately 30% of total calories). For example, if a serving of a particular product has 13 grams of fat, the label will show that the serving represents 20% of the daily fat allowance. If your daily diet contains fewer or more than 2000 calories, you need to adjust those calculations accordingly.

Food labels contain uniform serving sizes. This means that if you look at different brands of salad dressing, for example, you can compare calories and fat content based on the serving amount. (Food label serving sizes may be larger or smaller than MyPyramid serving size equivalents, however.) Regulations also require that foods meet strict definitions if their packaging includes the terms *light, low-fat,* or *high-fiber* (see below). Health claims such as "good source of dietary fiber" or "low in saturated fat" on packages are signals that those products can wisely be included in your diet. Overall, the food label is an important tool to help you choose a diet that conforms to MyPyramid and the Dietary Guidelines.

Selected Nutrient Claims and What They Mean

- ***Healthy.*** A food that is low in fat, is low in saturated fat, has no more than 360–480 mg of sodium and 60 mg of cholesterol, *and* provides 10% or more of the Daily Value for vitamin A, vitamin C, protein, calcium, iron, or dietary fiber.
- ***Light or lite.*** 33% fewer calories or 50% less fat than a similar product.
- ***Reduced or fewer.*** At least 25% less of a nutrient than a similar product; can be applied to fat ("reduced fat"), saturated fat, cholesterol, sodium, and calories.
- ***Extra or added.*** 10% or more of the Daily Value per serving when compared to what a similar product has.
- ***Good source.*** 10–19% of the Daily Value for a particular nutrient per serving.
- ***High, rich in, or excellent source of.*** 20% or more of the Daily Value for a particular nutrient per serving.
- ***Low calorie.*** 40 calories or less per serving.
- ***High fiber.*** 5 g or more of fiber per serving.
- ***Good source of fiber.*** 2.5–4.9 g of fiber per serving.
- ***Fat-free.*** Less than 0.5 g of fat per serving.
- ***Low-fat.*** 3 g of fat or less per serving.
- ***Saturated fat-free.*** Less than 0.5 g of saturated fat and 0.5 g of trans fatty acids per serving.
- ***Low saturated fat.*** 1 g or less of saturated fat per serving and no more than 15% of total calories.
- ***Cholesterol-free.*** Less than 2 mg of cholesterol and 2 g or less of saturated fat per serving.
- ***Low cholesterol.*** 20 mg or less of cholesterol and 2 g or less of saturated fat per serving.
- ***Low sodium.*** 140 mg or less of sodium per serving.
- ***Very low sodium.*** 35 mg or less of sodium per serving.
- ***Lean.*** Cooked seafood, meat, or poultry with less than 10 g of fat, 4.5 g or less of saturated fat, and less than 95 mg of cholesterol per serving.
- ***Extra lean.*** Cooked seafood, meat, or poultry with less than 5 g of fat, 2 g of saturated fat, and 95 mg of cholesterol per serving.

Note: As of June 2005, the FDA had not yet defined nutrient claims relating to carbohydrates, so foods labeled low- or reduced-carbohydrate do not conform to any approved standard.

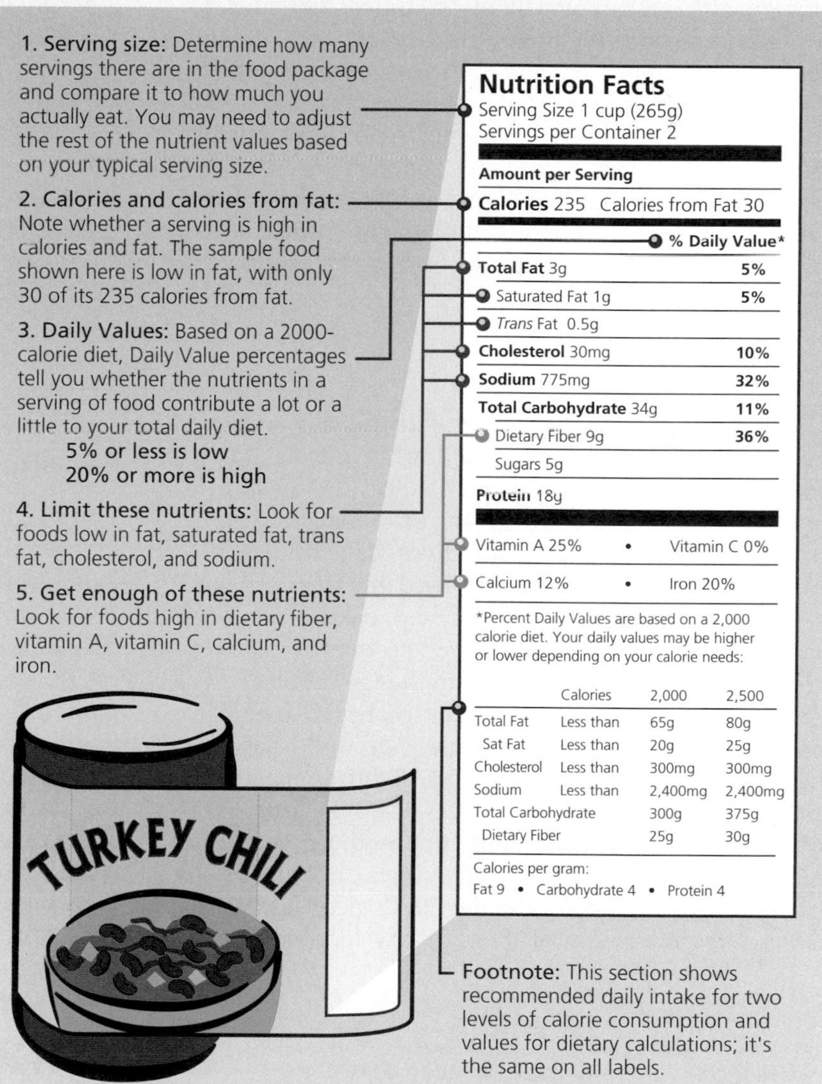
1. Serving size: Determine how many servings there are in the food package and compare it to how much you actually eat. You may need to adjust the rest of the nutrient values based on your typical serving size.
2. Calories and calories from fat: Note whether a serving is high in calories and fat. The sample food shown here is low in fat, with only 30 of its 235 calories from fat.
3. Daily Values: Based on a 2000-calorie diet, Daily Value percentages tell you whether the nutrients in a serving of food contribute a lot or a little to your total daily diet.
5% or less is low
20% or more is high
4. Limit these nutrients: Look for foods low in fat, saturated fat, trans fat, cholesterol, and sodium.
5. Get enough of these nutrients: Look for foods high in dietary fiber, vitamin A, vitamin C, calcium, and iron.
Nutrition Facts
Serving Size 1 cup (265g)
Servings per Container 2
Amount per Serving
Calories 235 Calories from Fat 30
% Daily Value*
Total Fat 3g 5%
Saturated Fat 1g 5%
Trans Fat 0.5g
Cholesterol 30mg 10%
Sodium 775mg 32%
Total Carbohydrate 34g 11%
Dietary Fiber 9g 36%
Sugars 5g
Protein 18g
Vitamin A 25% • Vitamin C 0%
Calcium 12% • Iron 20%
*Percent Daily Values are based on a 2,000 calorie diet. Your daily values may be higher or lower depending on your calorie needs:
Calories 2,000 2,500
Total Fat Less than 65g 80g
Sat Fat Less than 20g 25g
Cholesterol Less than 300mg 300mg
Sodium Less than 2,400mg 2,400mg
Total Carbohydrate 300g 375g
Dietary Fiber 25g 30g
Calories per gram:
Fat 9 • Carbohydrate 4 • Protein 4
TURKEY CHILI
Footnote: This section shows recommended daily intake for two levels of calorie consumption and values for dietary calculations; it's the same on all labels.

effectiveness before they are marketed. Although dosage guidelines exist for some of the compounds in dietary supplements, dosages for many are not well established.

Many ingredients in dietary supplements are classified by the FDA as "generally recognized as safe," but some have been found to be dangerous on their own or to interact with prescription or over-the-counter drugs in dangerous ways. Garlic supplements, for example, can cause bleeding if taken with anticoagulant (blood-thinning) medications. Even products that are generally considered safe can have side effects—St. John's wort, for example, increases the skin's sensitivity to sunlight and may decrease the effectiveness of oral contraceptives, drugs used to treat HIV infection, and many other medications.

There are also key differences in this way drugs and supplements are manufacture: FDA-approved medications are standardized for potency, and quality control and proof of purity are required. Dietary supplement manufacture is not as closely regulated, and there is no guarantee that a product even contains a given ingredient, let alone in the appropriate amount. The potency of herbal supplements can vary widely due to differences in growing and harvesting conditions, preparation methods, and storage. Contamination and misidentification of plant compounds are also potential problems.

In an effort to provide consumers with more reliable and consistent information about supplements, the FDA has developed labeling regulations. Labels similar to those found on foods are now required for dietary supplements; for more information, see the box "Using Dietary Supplement Labels".

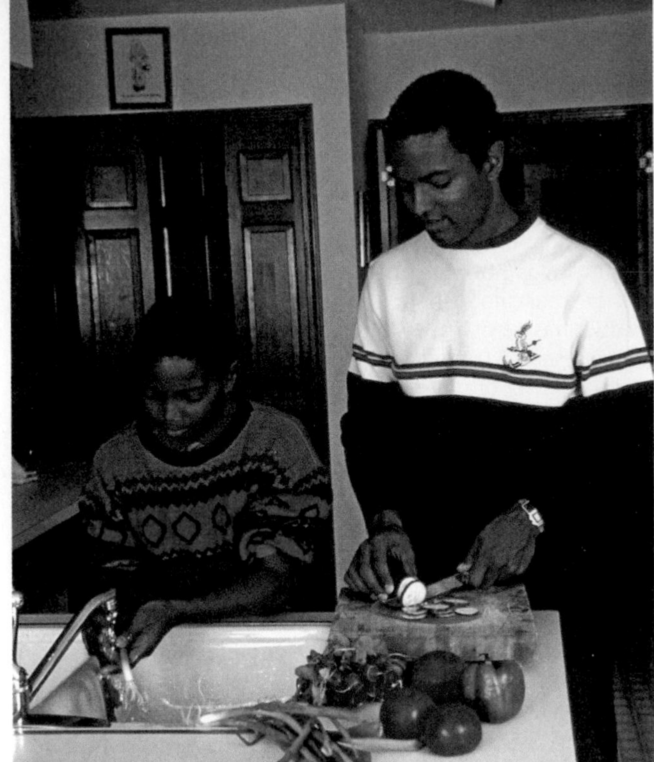

Careful food handling greatly reduces the risk of foodborne illness. Helpful strategies include washing hands and all fruits and vegetables, using separate cutting boards for meat and for foods that will be eaten raw, cooking meat thoroughly, and refrigerating leftovers promptly.

Food Additives

Today, some 2800 substances are intentionally added to foods for one or more of the following reasons: (1) to maintain or improve nutritional quality, (2) to maintain freshness, (3) to help in processing or preparation, or (4) to alter taste or appearance. Additives make up less than 1% of our food. The most widely used are sugar, salt, and corn syrup; these three, plus citric acid, baking soda, vegetable colors, mustard, and pepper, account for 98% by weight of all food additives used in the United States.

Food additives pose no significant health hazard to most people because the levels used are well below any that could produce toxic effects. Two additives of potential concern for some people are sulfites, used to keep vegetables from turning brown, and monosodium glutamate (MSG), used as a flavor enhancer. Sulfites can cause severe reactions in some people, and the FDA strictly limits their use and requires clear labeling on any food containing sulfites. MSG may cause some people to experience episodes of sweating and increased blood pressure. If you have any sensitivity to an additive, check food labels when you shop and ask questions when you eat out.

TERMS

pathogen A microorganism that causes disease.

Foodborne Illness

Many people worry about additives or pesticide residues in their food. However, a greater threat to the safety of the food supply comes from microorganisms that cause foodborne illnesses. Raw or undercooked animal products, such as chicken, hamburger, and oysters, pose the greatest risk for contamination. The CDC estimates that 76 million Americans become sick each year as a result of foodborne illness, 325,000 are hospitalized, and 5000 die. In most cases, foodborne illness produces acute gastroenteritis, characterized by diarrhea, vomiting, fever, and weakness. People often mistake foodborne illness for a bout of the flu. Although the effects of foodborne illness are usually not serious, some groups, such as children and older people, are at risk for severe complications, including rheumatic diseases, kidney failure, seizures, blood poisoning, and death.

Causes of Foodborne Illnesses Most cases of foodborne illness are caused by **pathogens**, disease-causing microorganisms that contaminate food, usually from

Using Dietary Supplement Labels

Since 1999, specific types of information have been required on the labels of dietary supplements. In addition to basic information about the product, labels include a "Supplement Facts" panel, modeled after the "Nutrition Facts" panel used on food labels (see the figure). Under the Dietary Supplement Health and Education Act (DSHEA) and food labeling laws, supplement labels can make three types of health-related claims:

- *Nutrient-content claims,* such as "high in calcium," "excellent source of vitamin C," or "high potency." The claims "high in" and "excellent source of" mean the same as they do on food labels. A "high potency" single-ingredient supplement must contain 100% of its Daily Value; a "high potency" multi-ingredient product must contain 100% or more of the Daily Value of at least two-thirds of the nutrients present for which Daily Values have been established.
- *Health claims,* if they have been authorized by the FDA or another authoritative scientific body. The association between adequate calcium intake and lower risk of osteoporosis is an example of an approved health claim. Since 2003, the FDA has also allowed so-called *qualified* health claims for situations in which there is emerging but as yet inconclusive evidence for a particular claim. Such claims must include qualifying language such as "scientific evidence suggests but does not prove."
- *Structure-function claims,* such as "antioxidants maintain cellular integrity" or "this product enhances energy levels." Because these claims are not reviewed by the FDA, they must carry a disclaimer (see the sample label).

Tips for Choosing and Using Dietary Supplements

- Check with your physician before taking a supplement. Many are not meant for children, older people, women who are pregnant or breastfeeding, people with chronic illnesses or upcoming surgery, or people taking prescription or OTC medications.
- Follow the cautions, instructions for use, and dosage given on the label.
- Look for the USP verification mark on the label, indicating that the product meets minimum safety and purity standards developed under the Dietary Supplement Verification Program by the United States Pharmacopeia (USP). The USP mark means that the product (1) contains the ingredients stated on the label, (2) has the declared amount and strength of ingredients, (3) will dissolve effectively, (4) has been screened for harmful contaminants, and (5) has been manufactured using safe, sanitary, and well-controlled procedures. The Natural Products Association has a self-regulatory testing program for its members; other, smaller associations and labs, including ConsumerLab.Com, also test and rate dietary supplements.
- Choose brands made by nationally known food and drug manufacturers or "house brands" from large retail chains. Due to their size and visibility, such sources are likely to have higher manufacturing standards.
- If you experience side effects, discontinue use of the product and contact your physician. Report any serious reactions to the FDA's MedWatch monitoring program (1-800-FDA-1088; http://www.fda.gov/medwatch).

For More Information About Dietary Supplements

ConsumerLab.Com: http://www.consumerlab.com

Food and Drug Administration: http://cfsan.fda.gov/~dms/ supplmnt.html

National Institutes of Health, Office of Dietary Supplements: http://dietary-supplements.info.nih.gov

Natural Products Association: http://www.naturalproductsassoc.org

U.S. Department of Agriculture: http://www.nal.usda.gov/fnic/etext/000015.html

U.S. Pharmacopeia: http://www.usp.org/uspverified

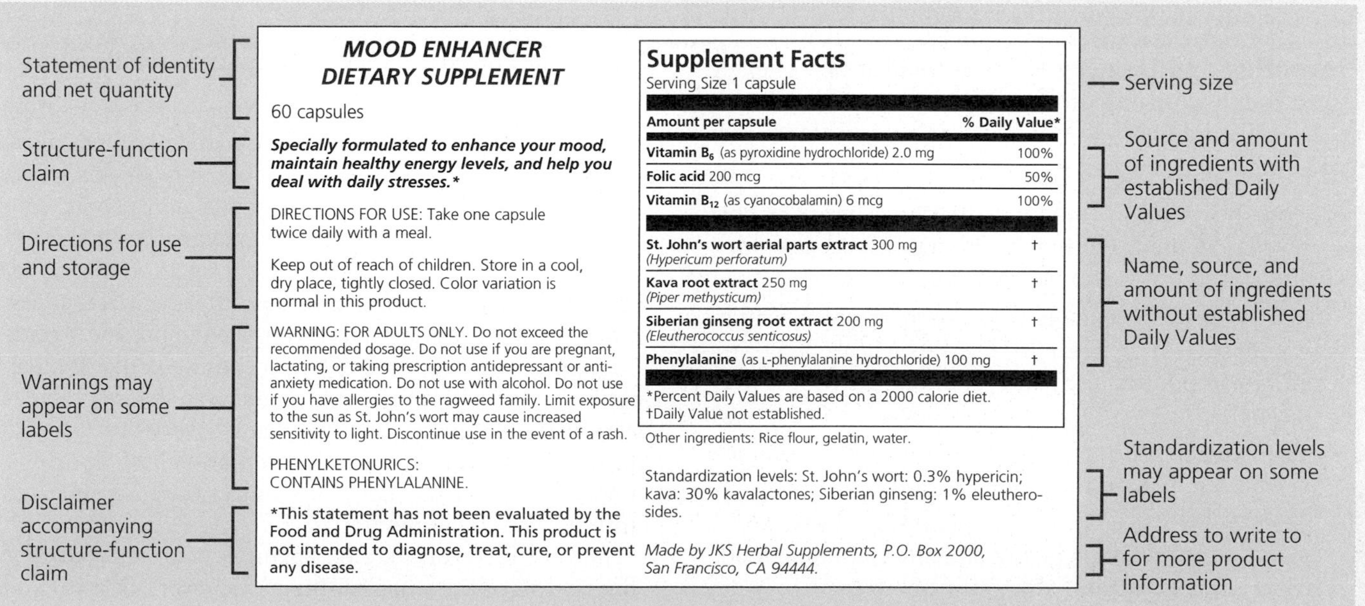
Statement of identity and net quantity
MOOD ENHANCER DIETARY SUPPLEMENT
60 capsules
Structure-function claim
Specially formulated to enhance your mood, maintain healthy energy levels, and help you deal with daily stresses.*
Directions for use and storage
DIRECTIONS FOR USE: Take one capsule twice daily with a meal.
Keep out of reach of children. Store in a cool, dry place, tightly closed. Color variation is normal in this product.
Warnings may appear on some labels
WARNING: FOR ADULTS ONLY. Do not exceed the recommended dosage. Do not use if you are pregnant, lactating, or taking prescription antidepressant or anti-anxiety medication. Do not use with alcohol. Do not use if you have allergies to the ragweed family. Limit exposure to the sun as St. John's wort may cause increased sensitivity to light. Discontinue use in the event of a rash.
PHENYLKETONURICS: CONTAINS PHENYLALANINE.
Disclaimer accompanying structure-function claim
*This statement has not been evaluated by the Food and Drug Administration. This product is not intended to diagnose, treat, cure, or prevent any disease.
Supplement Facts
Serving Size 1 capsule
Serving size
Amount per capsule | % Daily Value*
Vitamin B6 (as pyroxidine hydrochloride) 2.0 mg | 100%
Folic acid 200 mcg | 50%
Vitamin B12 (as cyanocobalamin) 6 mcg | 100%
Source and amount of ingredients with established Daily Values
St. John's wort aerial parts extract 300 mg (Hypericum perforatum) †
Kava root extract 250 mg (Piper methysticum) †
Siberian ginseng root extract 200 mg (Eleutherococcus senticosus) †
Phenylalanine (as L-phenylalanine hydrochloride) 100 mg †
Name, source, and amount of ingredients without established Daily Values
*Percent Daily Values are based on a 2000 calorie diet.
†Daily Value not established.
Other ingredients: Rice flour, gelatin, water.
Standardization levels: St. John's wort: 0.3% hypericin; kava: 30% kavalactones; Siberian ginseng: 1% eleutherosides.
Standardization levels may appear on some labels
Made by JKS Herbal Supplements, P.O. Box 2000, San Francisco, CA 94444.
Address to write to for more product information

improper handling. The threats are numerous and varied; among them are the sometimes deadly *Escherichia coli (E. coli)* O157:H7 in meat and water; *Salmonella* in eggs, on vegetables, and on poultry; *Vibrio* in shellfish; *Cyclospora* and hepatitis A virus on fruit; *Cryptosporidium* in drinking water; *Campylobacter jejuni* in meat and poultry; and *Listeria monocytogenes* in lunch meats, sausages, and hot dogs.

You can't tell by taste, smell, or sight whether a food is contaminated. In 2003, *Consumer Reports* tested 484 chickens purchased in grocery stores and found that half were contaminated with *Campylobacter* and/or *Salmonella.* Although pathogens are usually destroyed during cooking, the U.S. government is taking steps to bring down levels of contamination by improving national testing and surveillance. Raw meat and poultry products are now sold with safe-handling and -cooking instructions, and all packaged, unpasteurized fresh fruit and vegetable juices carry warnings about potential contamination. It is important to note that while foodborne illness outbreaks associated with food-processing plants make headlines, most cases of illness trace back to poor food handling in the home or in restaurants.

A potential threat from food is bovine spongiform encephalopathy (BSE), or "mad cow disease," a fatal degenerative neurological disease caused by an abnormal protein that forms deposits in the brain. A variant form of this disease, known as Creutzfeldt-Jakob disease (CJD), is believed to be caused by eating beef contaminated with central nervous system tissue from BSE-infected cows. To date, there have been about 150 confirmed cases worldwide of CJD among the hundreds of thousands of people who may have consumed BSE-contaminated products. In December 2003, the first BSE-infected cow was identified in the United States. Although the USDA states that the risk to human health from BSE is extremely low, additional steps are being taken to prevent the BSE protein from entering the food supply; visit the USDA Web site for more information (www.usda.gov).

Preventing and Treating Foodborne Illness The key to protecting yourself from foodborne illness is to handle, cook, and store foods in ways that prevent bacteria from spreading and multiplying:

- Don't buy food in containers that leak, bulge, or are severely dented. Refrigerated foods should be cold, and frozen foods should be solid.
- Refrigerate perishable items as soon as possible after purchase. Use or freeze fresh meats within 3–5 days and fresh poultry, fish, and ground meat within 1–2 days.
- Thaw frozen food in the refrigerator or in the microwave oven, not on the kitchen counter.
- Thoroughly wash your hands with warm, soapy water for 20 seconds before and after handling food, especially raw meat, fish, poultry, or eggs.
- Make sure counters, cutting boards, dishes, and other equipment are thoroughly cleaned before and after use. If possible, use separate cutting boards for meat and for foods that will be eaten raw, such as fruits and vegetables. Wash dishcloths and kitchen towels frequently.
- Thoroughly rinse and scrub fruits and vegetables with a brush, if possible, or peel off the skin.
- Cook foods thoroughly, especially beef, poultry, fish, pork, and eggs. Cooking kills most microorganisms, as long as an appropriately high temperature is reached. The USDA now recommends that consumers, especially high-risk individuals, use a food thermometer to verify that hamburgers are cooked to 160°F. When eating out, order red meat cooked "well done."
- Cook stuffing separately from poultry; or wash poultry thoroughly, stuff immediately before cooking, and transfer the stuffing to a clean bowl immediately after cooking.
- Refrigerate foods at or below 40°F and freeze at or below 0°F. Do not leave cooked or refrigerated foods, such as meats or salads, at room temperature for more than 2 hours. Use refrigerated leftovers within 3–4 days.
- Don't eat raw animal products, including raw eggs in Caesar salad, hollandaise sauce, or eggnog. Use only pasteurized milk and juice, and look for pasteurized eggs, which are now available in some states.
- Cook eggs until they're firm, and fully cook foods containing eggs. Store eggs in the coldest part of the refrigerator, not on the door, and use them within 3–5 weeks.
- Because of possible contamination with *E. coli* O157:H7 and *Salmonella,* avoid raw sprouts, or eat sprouts only after submerging them in boiling water for 10 seconds.
- According to the USDA, "When in doubt, throw it out."

Additional precautions are recommended for people at particularly high risk for foodborne illness—pregnant women, young children, older persons, and people with weakened immune systems or certain chronic illnesses. If you are a member of one of these groups, don't eat or drink any of the following products: unpasteurized juices; raw sprouts; raw (unpasteurized) milk and products made from unpasteurized milk; raw or undercooked meat, poultry, eggs, fish, and shellfish; and soft cheeses such as feta, Brie, Camembert, or blue-veined varieties. It's also important to avoid ready-to-eat foods such as hot dogs, luncheon meats, and cold cuts unless they are reheated until they are steaming hot.

If you think you may be having a bout of foodborne illness, drink plenty of clear fluids to prevent dehydration and rest to speed recovery. To prevent further contamination, wash your hands often and always before handling food until you recover. A fever higher than 102°F, blood in the stool, or dehydration deserves a physician's evaluation, especially if the symptoms persist for more than 2–3 days. In cases of suspected botulism—characterized by symptoms such as double vision, paralysis, dizziness, and vomiting—consult a physician immediately.

Irradiated Foods

Food irradiation is the treatment of foods with gamma rays, X-rays, or high-voltage electrons to kill potentially harmful pathogens, including bacteria, parasites, insects, and fungi that cause foodborne illness. It also reduces spoilage and extends shelf life. Even though irradiation has been generally endorsed by agencies such as the World Health Organization, the Centers for Disease Control and Prevention, and the American Medical Association, few irradiated foods are currently on the market due to consumer resistance and skepticism. Studies haven't conclusively identified any harmful effects of food irradiation, and newer methods of irradiation involving electricity and X-rays do not require the use of any radioactive materials. Studies indicate that when consumers are given information about the process of irradiation and the benefits of irradiated foods, most want to purchase them.

All primary irradiated foods (meat, vegetables, and so on) are labeled with the flowerlike radura symbol and a brief information label; spices and foods that are merely ingredients do not have to be labeled. It is important to remember that although irradiation kills most pathogens, it does not completely sterilize foods. Proper handling of irradiated foods is still critical for preventing foodborne illness.

Environmental Contaminants and Organic Foods

Contaminants are present in the food-growing environment, but few of them ever enter the food and water supply in amounts sufficient to cause health problems. Environmental contaminants include various minerals, antibiotics, hormones, pesticides, and industrial chemicals. Safety regulations attempt to keep our exposure to contaminants at safe levels, but monitoring is difficult, and many substances (such as pesticides) persist in the environment long after being banned from use.

Organic Foods Some people who are concerned about pesticides and other environmental contaminants choose to buy foods that are **organic.** To be certified as organic, foods must meet strict production, processing, handling, and labeling criteria. Organic crops must meet limits on pesticide residues; for meat, milk, eggs, and other animal products to be certified organic, animals must be given organic feed and access to the outdoors and may not be given antibiotics or growth hormones. The use of genetic engineering, ionizing radiation, and sewage sludge is prohibited. Products can be labeled "100% organic" if they contain all organic ingredients and "organic" if they contain at least 95% organic ingredients; all such products may carry the USDA organic seal. A product with at least 70% organic ingredients can be labeled "made with organic ingredients" but cannot use the USDA seal.

Foods that are organic may not be chemical-free, however. They may be contaminated with pesticides used on neighboring lands or on foods transported in the same train or truck. However, they tend to have lower levels of pesticide residues than conventionally grown crops. Some experts recommend that consumers who want to buy organic fruits and vegetables spend their money on those that carry higher pesticide residues than their conventional counterparts (the "dirty dozen"): apples, bell peppers, celery, cherries, imported grapes, nectarines, peaches, pears, potatoes, red raspberries, spinach, and strawberries. Experts also recommend buying organic beef, poultry, eggs, dairy products, and baby food. Fruits and vegetables that carry little pesticide residue whether grown conventionally or organically include asparagus, avocadoes, bananas, broccoli, cauliflower, corn, kiwi, mangoes, onions, papaya, pineapples, and peas. All foods are subject to strict pesticide limits; the debate about the health effects of small amounts of residue is ongoing.

Whether or not organic foods are better for your health, organic farming is better for the environment. It helps maintain biodiversity of crops and replenish Earth's resources; it is also less likely to degrade soil, contaminate water, or expose farm workers to toxic chemicals. As multinational food companies get into the organic food business, however, consumers who want to support environmentally friendly farming methods should look for foods that are not only organic but locally grown.

Guidelines for Fish Consumption A specific area of concern has been possible mercury contamination in fish. Overall, fish and shellfish are healthy sources of protein, omega-3 fats, and other nutrients; prudent choices can minimize the risk of any possible negative health effects. High mercury concentrations are most likely to be found in predator fish—large fish that eat smaller fish. Mercury can cause brain damage to fetuses and young children. In

food irradiation The treatment of foods with gamma rays, X-rays, or high-voltage electrons to kill potentially harmful pathogens and increase shelf life.

organic A designation applied to foods grown and produced according to strict guidelines limiting the use of pesticides, nonorganic ingredients, hormones, antibiotics, genetic engineering, irradiation, and other practices.

TERMS

QUESTIONS FOR CRITICAL THINKING AND REFLECTION

Have you ever taken a dietary supplement, such as St. John's wort for mild depression or echinacea or zinc for a cold? If so, who or what influenced your decision to use this product? Did you do any research before taking it? Did you read the label on the package? Do you think the product had the desired effect?

MOTIVATION BOOSTER

Get organized. Do you choose fast food or packaged snacks because they are quick and convenient? Instead, take the time to find healthier foods, restaurants, and menu items to substitute for the unhealthy ones. Identify convenient and healthy snacks that you can keep in the refrigerator (such as fruit salad or cut-up vegetables); locate inexpensive but healthy food sources or restaurants near your campus or home; and identify healthy items on the menus of your favorite restaurants. Make lists of these healthier choices and keep them handy for those times when you're tempted by less healthy ones.

2004, the FDA and Environmental Protection Agency (EPA) released an advisory with specific guidelines for certain groups. To reduce exposure to the harmful effects of mercury, women who are or who may become pregnant and nursing mothers should follow these guidelines:

- Do not eat shark, swordfish, king mackerel, or tilefish.
- Eat up to 12 ounces a week of a variety of fish and shellfish that is lower in mercury, such as shrimp, canned light tuna, salmon, pollock, and catfish. Limit consumption of albacore tuna to 6 ounces per week.
- Check advisories about the safety of recreationally caught fish from local lakes, rivers, and coastal areas; if no information is available, limit consumption to 6 ounces per week.

The same FDA/EPA guidelines apply to children, although they should consume smaller servings.

Some experts have also expressed concern about the presence of toxins such as PCBs in farmed fish, especially farmed salmon. Although no federal guidelines have been set, some researchers suggest that consumers limit themselves to 8 ounces of farmed salmon per month. Fish should be labeled with its country of origin and whether it is wild or farmed; most canned salmon is wild.

A PERSONAL PLAN: APPLYING NUTRITIONAL PRINCIPLES

Based on your particular nutrition and health status, there probably is an ideal diet for you, but no single type of diet provides optimal health for everyone. Many cultural dietary patterns can meet people's nutritional requirements (see the box "Ethnic Foods"). Customize your food plan based on your age, gender, weight, activity level, medical risk factors—and, of course, personal tastes.

Assessing and Changing Your Diet

The first step in planning a healthy diet is to examine what you currently eat. Labs 8.1 and 8.2 help you analyze your current diet and compare it with optimal dietary goals. (This analysis can be completed using Appendix B, a nutritional analysis software program, or one of several Web sites.)

To put your plan into action, use the behavioral self-management techniques and tips described in Chapter 1. If you identify several changes you want to make, focus on one at a time. You might start, for example, by substituting nonfat or low-fat milk for whole milk. When you become used to that, you can try substituting whole-wheat bread for white bread. The information on eating behavior in Lab 8.1 will help you identify and change unhealthy patterns of eating.

Staying Committed to a Healthy Diet

Beyond knowledge and information, you also need support in difficult situations. Keeping to your plan is easiest when you choose and prepare your own food at home. Advance planning is the key: mapping out meals and shopping appropriately, cooking in advance when possible, and preparing enough food for leftovers. A tight budget does not necessarily make it more difficult to eat healthy meals. It makes good health sense and good budget sense to use only small amounts of meat and to have a few meatless meals each week.

In restaurants, keeping to food plan goals becomes somewhat more difficult. Portion sizes in restaurants tend to be larger than MyPyramid serving size equivalents, but by remaining focused on your goals, you can eat only part of your meal and take the rest home for a meal later in the week. Don't hesitate to ask questions when you're eating in a restaurant. Most restaurant personnel are glad to explain how menu selections are prepared and to make small adjustments, such as serving salad dressings and sauces on the side so they can be avoided or used sparingly.

Strategies like these are helpful, but small changes cannot change a fundamentally high-fat, high-calorie meal into a moderate, healthful one. Often, the best advice is to bypass a large steak with potatoes au gratin for a flavorful but low-fat entree. Many of the selections offered in ethnic restaurants are healthy choices (refer to the box on ethnic foods for suggestions).

Ethnic Foods

There is no one ethnic diet that clearly surpasses all others in providing people with healthful foods. However, every diet has its advantages and disadvantages, and within each cuisine, some foods are better choices. The dietary guidelines described in this chapter can be applied to any ethnic cuisine. For additional guidance, refer to the table below.

	Choose More Often	Choose Less Often
CHINESE	Dishes that are steamed, poached (jum), boiled (chu), roasted (kow), barbecued (shu), or lightly stir-fried Hoisin sauce, oyster sauce, wine sauce, plum sauce, velvet sauce, or hot mustard Fresh fish and seafood, skinless chicken, tofu Mixed vegetables, Chinese greens Steamed rice, steamed spring rolls, soft noodles	Fried wontons or egg rolls Crab rangoon Crispy (Peking) duck or chicken Sweet-and-sour dishes made with breaded and deep-fried meat, poultry, or fish Fried rice Fried or crispy noodles
FRENCH	Dishes prepared au vapeur (steamed), en brochette (skewered and broiled), or grillé (grilled) Fresh fish, shrimp, scallops, or mussels or skinless chicken, without sauces Clear soups	Dishes prepared à la crème (in cream sauce), au gratin or gratinée (baked with cream and cheese), or en croûte (in pastry crust) Drawn butter, hollandaise sauce, and remoulade (mayonnaise-based sauce)
GREEK	Dishes that are stewed, broiled, or grilled, including shish kabobs (souvlaki) Dolmas (grape leaves) stuffed with rice Tzatziki (yogurt, cucumbers, and garlic) Tabouli (bulgur-based salad) Pita bread, especially whole wheat	Moussaka, saganaki (fried cheese) Vegetable pies such as spanakopita and tyropita Baba ghanoush (eggplant and olive oil) Deep-fried falafel (chickpea patties) Gyros stuffed with ground meat Baklava
INDIAN	Dishes prepared masala (curry), tandoori (roasted in a clay oven), or tikke (pan roasted); kabobs Raita (yogurt and cucumber salad) and other yogurt-based dishes and sauces Dal (lentils), pullao or pilau (basmati rice) Chapati (baked bread)	Ghee (clarified butter) Korma (meat in cream sauce) Samosas, pakoras (fried dishes) Molee and other coconut milk–based dishes Poori, bhatura, or paratha (fried breads)
ITALIAN	Pasta primavera or pasta, polenta, risotto, or gnocchi with marinara, red or white wine, white or red clam, or light mushroom sauce Dishes that are grilled or prepared cacciatore (tomato-based sauce), marsala (broth and wine sauce), or piccata (lemon sauce) Cioppino (seafood stew) Vegetable soup, minestrone or fagioli (beans)	Antipasto (cheese, smoked meats) Dishes that are prepared alfredo, frito (fried), crema (creamed), alla panna (with cream), or carbonara Veal scaloppini Chicken, veal, or eggplant parmigiana Italian sausage, salami, and prosciutto Buttered garlic bread Cannoli
JAPANESE	Dishes prepared nabemono (boiled), shabu shabu (in boiling broth), mushimono (steamed), nimono (simmered), yaki (broiled), or yakimono (grilled) Sushi or domburi (mixed rice dish) Steamed rice or soba (buckwheat), udon (wheat), or rice noodles	Tempura (battered and fried) Agemono (deep fried) Katsu (fried pork cutlet) Sukiyaki Fried tofu
MEXICAN	Soft corn or wheat tortillas Burritos, fajitas, enchiladas, soft tacos, and tamales filled with beans, vegetables, or lean meats Refried beans, nonfat or low-fat; rice and beans Ceviche (fish marinated in lime juice) Salsa, enchilada sauce, and picante sauce Gazpacho, menudo, or black bean soup Fruit or flan for dessert	Crispy, fried tortillas Dishes that are fried, such as chile relleños, chimichangas, flautas, and tostadas Nachos and cheese, chili con queso, and other dishes made with cheese or cheese sauce Guacamole, sour cream, and extra cheese Refried beans made with lard Fried ice cream
THAI	Dishes that are barbecued, sautéed, broiled, boiled, steamed, braised, or marinated Sàté (skewered and grilled meats) Fish sauce, basil sauce, chili or hot sauces Bean thread noodles, Thai salad	Coconut milk soup Peanut sauce or dishes topped with nuts Mee-krob (crispy noodles) Red, green, and yellow curries, which typically contain coconut milk

SOURCES: National Heart, Lung and Blood Institute. 2006. *Guidelines on Overweight and Obesity: Electronic Textbook* (http://www.nhlbi.nih.gov/guidelines/obesity/e_txtbk/appndx/6a3b.htm; retrieved May 27, 2007). Duyff, R. L. 2006. *The American Dietetic Association's Complete Food and Nutrition Guide,* 2nd ed. Hoboken, N.J.: Wiley.

QUESTIONS FOR CRITICAL THINKING AND REFLECTION

What is the least healthy food you eat every day (either during meals or as a snack)? Identify at least one substitute that would be healthier but just as satisfying.

Knowledge of food and nutrition is essential to the success of your program. The information provided in this chapter should give you the tools you need to design and implement a diet that promotes long-term health and well-being. If you need additional information or have questions about nutrition, be sure the source you consult is reliable.

TIPS FOR TODAY AND THE FUTURE

Opportunities to improve your diet present themselves every day, and small changes add up.

RIGHT NOW YOU CAN

- Substitute a healthy snack for an unhealthy one.
- Drink a glass of water and put a bottle of water in your backpack for tomorrow.
- Plan to make healthy selections when you eat out, such as steamed vegetables instead of french fries or salmon instead of steak.

IN THE FUTURE, YOU CAN

- Visit the MyPyramid Web site at www.mypyramid.gov and use the online tools to create a personalized nutrition plan and begin tracking your eating habits.
- Learn to cook healthier meals. There are hundreds of free Web sites and low-cost cookbooks that provide recipes for healthy dishes.

SUMMARY

- The six classes of nutrients are carbohydrates, proteins, fats, vitamins, minerals, and water.
- The nutrients essential to humans are released into the body through digestion. Nutrients in foods provide energy, measured in kilocalories (commonly called calories); build and maintain body tissues; and regulate body functions.
- Protein, an important component of body tissue, is composed of amino acids; nine are essential to good health. Foods from animal sources provide complete proteins; plants provide incomplete proteins.
- Fats, a major source of energy, also insulate the body and cushion the organs; 3–4 teaspoons of vegetable oil per day supply the essential fats. For most people, dietary fat intake should be 20–35% of total calories, and unsaturated fats should be favored over saturated and trans fats.
- Carbohydrates provide energy to the brain, nervous system, and blood and to muscles during high-intensity exercise. Naturally occurring simple carbohydrates and unrefined complex carbohydrates should be favored over added sugars and refined carbohydrates.
- Fiber includes plant substances that are impossible for the human body to digest. It helps reduce cholesterol levels and promotes the passage of wastes through the intestines.
- The 13 essential vitamins are organic substances that promote specific chemical and cell processes and act as antioxidants. The 17 known essential minerals are inorganic substances that regulate body functions, aid in growth and tissue maintenance, and help in the release of energy from food. Deficiencies in vitamins and minerals can cause severe symptoms over time, but excess doses are also dangerous.
- Water aids in digestion and food absorption, allows chemical reactions to take place, serves as a lubricant or cushion, and helps regulate body temperature.
- Foods contain other substances, such as phytochemicals, that may not be essential nutrients but that may protect against chronic diseases.
- The Dietary Reference Intakes, Dietary Guidelines for Americans, and MyPyramid food guidance system provide standards and recommendations for getting all essential nutrients from a varied, balanced diet and for eating in ways that protect against chronic disease.
- The Dietary Guidelines for Americans advise us to consume a variety of foods while staying within calorie needs; manage body weight through calorie control and regular physical activity; eat more fruits, vegetables, whole grains, and reduced-fat dairy products; choose fats and carbohydrates wisely; eat less salt and more potassium; be moderate with alcohol intake; and handle foods safely.
- Choosing foods from each group in MyPyramid every day helps ensure the appropriate amounts of necessary nutrients.
- A vegetarian diet requires special planning but can meet all human nutritional needs.
- Different population groups, such as college students and athletes, face special dietary challenges and should plan their diets to meet their particular needs.
- Consumers can get help applying nutritional principles by reading the standardized labels that appear on all packaged foods and on dietary supplements.
- Although nutritional basics are well established, no single diet provides wellness for everyone. Individuals should focus on their particular needs and adapt general dietary principles to meet them.

FOR FURTHER EXPLORATION

For reliable nutrition advice, talk to a faculty member in the nutrition department on your campus, a registered dietitian (RD), or your physician. Many large communities have a telephone service called Dial a Dietitian. By calling this number, you can receive free nutrition information from an RD.

Experts on quackery suggest that you steer clear of anyone who puts forth any of the following false statements: Most diseases are caused primarily by faulty nutrition, large doses of vitamins are effective against many diseases, hair analysis can be used to determine a person's nutritional state, or a computer-scored nutritional deficiency test is a basis for prescribing vitamins. Any practitioner—licensed or not—who sells supplements in his or her office should be thoroughly scrutinized.

BOOKS

Duyff, R. L. 2006. *ADA Complete Food and Nutrition Guide,* 3rd ed. Hoboken, N.J.: Wiley. *An excellent review of current nutrition information.*

Insel, P., R. E. Turner, and D. Ross. 2006. *Discovering Nutrition,* 2nd ed. Sudbury, Mass.: Jones and Bartlett. *A comprehensive review of major concepts in nutrition.*

Nestle, M. 2007. *What to Eat.* New York: North Point Press. *A nutritionist examines the marketing of food and explains how to interpret food-related information while shopping.*

Selkowitz, A. 2005. *The College Student's Guide to Eating Well on Campus,* rev. ed. Bethesda, Md.: Tulip Hill Press. *Provides practical advice for students, including how to make healthy choices when eating in a dorm or restaurant and how to stock a first pantry.*

Wardlaw, G. M., and A. M. Smith. 2006. *Perspectives in Nutrition,* 7th ed. New York: McGraw-Hill. *An easy-to-understand review of major concepts in nutrition.*

Warshaw, H. 2006. *What to Eat When You're Eating Out.* Alexandria, Vir.: American Diabetes Association. *A registered dietician explains how to eat well when dining in restaurants; designed especially for those trying to manage their weight or a chronic condition such as diabetes.*

NEWSLETTERS

Environmental Nutrition (800-424-7887; http://www.environmentalnutrition.com)

Nutrition Action Health Letter (202-332-9110; http://www.cspinet.org/nah)

Tufts University Health and Nutrition Letter (800-274-7581; http://www.healthletter.tufts.edu)

ORGANIZATIONS, HOTLINES, AND WEB SITES

American Dietetic Association. Provides a wide variety of educational materials on nutrition.
800-877-1600
http://www.eatright.org

American Heart Association: Delicious Decisions. Provides basic information about nutrition, tips for shopping and eating out, and heart-healthy recipes.
http://www.deliciousdecisions.org

FDA Center for Food Safety and Applied Nutrition. Offers information and interactive tools about topics such as food labeling, food additives, dietary supplements, and foodborne illness.
http://www.cfsan.fda.gov

Food Safety Hotlines. Provide information on the safe purchase, handling, cooking, and storage of food.
888-SAFEFOOD (FDA)
800-535-4555 (USDA)

Fruits and Veggies Matter. Hosted by a partnership of the CDC, DHHS, and National Cancer Institute; promotes the consumption of fruits and vegetables every day.
http://www.fruitsandveggiesmatter.gov

Gateways to Government Nutrition Information. Provides access to government resources relating to food safety, including consumer advice and information on specific pathogens.
http://www.nutrition.gov
http://www.foodsafety.gov

Harvard School of Public Health: Nutrition Source. Provides advice on interpreting news on nutrition; an overview of the Healthy Eating Pyramid, an alternative to the basic USDA pyramid; and suggestions for building a healthy diet.
http://www.hsph.harvard.edu/nutritionsource

International Food Information Council. Provides information on food safety and nutrition for consumers, journalists, and educators.
http://www.ific.org

MedlinePlus: Nutrition. Provides links to information from government agencies and major medical associations on a variety of nutrition topics.
http://www.nlm.nih.gov/medlineplus/nutrition.html

MyPyramid. Provides personalized dietary plans and interactive food and activity tracking tools.
http://www.mypyramid.gov

National Academies' Food and Nutrition Board. Provides information about the Dietary Reference Intakes and related guidelines.
http://www.iom.edu/CMS/3788.aspx

National Institutes of Health: Osteoporosis and Related Bone Diseases—National Resource Center. Provides information about osteoporosis prevention and treatment; includes a special section on men and osteoporosis.
http://www.osteo.org

National Osteoporosis Foundation. Provides information on the causes, prevention, detection, and treatment of osteoporosis.
http://www.nof.org

USDA Center for Nutrition Policy and Promotion. Click on the Healthy Eating Index for an assessment of Americans' diets and a comparison with the Dietary Guidelines and the Food Guide Pyramid.
http://www.cnpp.usda.gov

USDA Food and Nutrition Information Center. Provides a variety of materials relating to the Dietary Guidelines, food labels, Food Guide Pyramid, MyPyramid, and many other topics.
http://www.nal.usda.gov/fnic

Vegetarian Resource Group. Provides information and links for vegetarians and people interested in learning more about vegetarian diets.
http://www.vrg.org

Q Which should I eat—butter or margarine?

A Both butter and margarine are concentrated sources of fat, containing about 11 grams of fat and 100 calories per tablespoon. Butter is higher in saturated fat, which raises levels of artery-clogging LDL ("bad" cholesterol). Each tablespoon of butter has about 8 grams of saturated fat; margarine has about 2. Butter also contains cholesterol, which margarine does not.

Margarine, on the other hand, contains trans fat, which not only raises LDL but lowers HDL ("good" cholesterol). A tablespoon of stick margarine contains about 2 grams of trans fat. Butter contains a small amount of trans fat as well. Although butter has a combined total of saturated and trans fats that is twice that of stick margarine, the trans fat in stick margarine may be worse for you. Clearly, you should avoid both butter and stick margarine. To solve this dilemma, remember that softer is better. The softer or more liquid a margarine or spread is, the less hydrogenated it is and the less trans fat it contains. Tub and squeeze margarines contain less trans fat than stick margarines; some margarines are modified to be low-trans or trans-free and are labeled as such. Vegetable oils are an even better choice for cooking and for table use (such as olive oil for dipping bread) because most are low in saturated fat and completely free of trans fats.

Q MyPyramid recommends such large amounts of vegetables and fruit. How can I possibly eat that many servings without gaining weight?

A First, consider your typical portion sizes—you may be closer to meeting the recommendations than you think. Many people consume large servings of foods and underestimate the size of their portions. For example, a large banana may contain the equivalent of a cup of fruit, or half the recommended daily total for someone consuming 2000–2600 calories per day. Likewise, a medium baked potato (3-inch diameter) or an ear of corn (8-inch length) counts as a cup of vegetables. Use a measuring cup or a food scale for a few days to train your eye to accurately estimate food portion sizes. The MyPyramid.gov Web site includes charts of portion-size equivalents for each food group.

If an analysis of your diet indicates that you need to increase your overall intake of fruits and vegetables, look for healthy substitutions. If you are like most Americans, you are consuming more than the recommended number of calories from added sugars and solid fats; trim some of these calories to make room for additional servings of fruits and vegetables. Your beverage choices may be a good place to start. Do you routinely consume regular sodas, sweetened bottled teas or fruit drinks, or whole milk? One regular 12-ounce soda contains the equivalent of about 150 calories of added sugars; one 8-ounce glass of whole milk provides about 75 calories as discretionary fats. Substituting water, diet soda, or low-fat milk would free up calories for additional servings of fruits and vegetables. A half-cup of carrots, tomatoes, apples, or melon has only about 25 calories; you could consume 6 cups of these foods for the calories in one can of regular soda. Substituting lower-fat condiments for such full-fat items as butter, mayonnaise, and salad dressing is another good way to trim calories to make room for additional servings of nutrient-rich fruits and vegetables.

Also consider your portion sizes and/or the frequency with which you consume foods high in discretionary calories: You may not need to eliminate a favorite food—instead, just cut back. For example, cut your consumption of fast-food fries from four times a week to once a week, or reduce the size of your ice cream dessert from a cup to half a cup. Treats should be consumed appropriately—infrequently, and in small amounts.

For additional help on improving food choices to meet dietary recommendations, visit the MyPyramid.gov Web site and the family-friendly chart of "Go, Slow, and Whoa" foods at the site for the National Heart, Lung, and Blood Institute (www.nhlbi.nih.gov/health/public/heart/obesity/wecan/downloads/gswtips.pdf).

Q What exactly are genetically modified foods? Are they safe? How can I recognize them on the shelf, and how can I know when I'm eating them?

A Genetic engineering involves altering the characteristics of a plant, animal, or microorganism by adding, rearranging, or replacing genes in its DNA; the result is a genetically modified (GM) organism. New DNA may come from related species or organisms or from entirely different types of organisms.

You can find nutrient breakdowns of individual food items at the following sites:

Nutrition Analysis Tools and System (NATS)
http://nat.crgq.com

USDA Nutrient Data Laboratory
http://www.ars.usda.gov/ba/bhnrc/ndl

See also the resources listed in Chapters 9, 11, and 12.

SELECTED BIBLIOGRAPHY

A guide to the best and worst drinks. 2006. *Consumer Reports on Health*, July, 8–9.

Aldana, S. G., et al. 2005. Effects of an intensive diet and physical activity modification program on the health risks of adults. *Journal of the American Dietetic Association* 105(3): 371–381.

American College of Sports Medicine. 2007. American College of Sports Medicine position stand: Exercise and fluid replacement. *Medicine and Science in Sports and Exercise* 39(2): 377–390.

Many GM crops are already grown in the United States: About 75% of the current U.S. soybean crop has been genetically modified to be resistant to an herbicide used to kill weeds, and about a third of the U.S. corn crop carries genes for herbicide resistance or to produce a protein lethal to a destructive type of caterpillar. Products made with GM organisms include juice, soda, nuts, tuna, frozen pizza, spaghetti sauce, canola oil, chips, salad dressing, and soup.

The potential benefits of GM foods cited by supporters include improved yields overall and in difficult growing conditions, increased disease resistance, improved nutritional content, lower prices, and less use of pesticides. Critics of biotechnology argue that unexpected effects may occur: Gene manipulation could elevate levels of naturally occurring toxins or allergens, permanently change the gene pool and reduce biodiversity, and produce pesticide-resistant insects through the transfer of genes. In 2000, a form of GM corn approved for use only in animal feed was found to have commingled with other varieties of corn and to have been used in human foods; this mistake sparked fears of allergic reactions and led to recalls. Opposition to GM foods is particularly strong in Europe; in many developing nations that face food shortages, responses to GM crops have tended to be more positive.

In April 2000, the National Academy of Sciences released a report stating that there is no proof that GM food on the market is unsafe but that changes are needed to better coordinate regulation of GM foods and to assess potential problems.

Labeling has been another major concern. Surveys indicate that the majority of Americans want to know if their foods contain GM organisms. However, under current rules, the FDA requires special labeling only when a food's composition is changed significantly or when a known allergen is introduced. For example, soybeans that contain a gene from a peanut would have to be labeled because peanuts are a common allergen. The only foods guaranteed not to contain GM ingredients are those certified as organic.

Q How can I tell if I'm allergic to a food?

A A true food allergy is a reaction of the body's immune system to a food or food ingredient, usually a protein. This immune reaction can occur within minutes of ingesting the food, resulting in symptoms such as hives, diarrhea, difficulty breathing, or swelling of the lips or tongue. The most severe response is a systemic reaction called anaphylaxis, which involves a potentially life-threatening drop in blood pressure. Food allergies affect only about 2% of the adult population and about 4–6% of infants. Just eight foods account for more than 90% of the food allergies in the United States: cow's milk, eggs, peanuts, tree nuts (walnuts, cashews, and so on), soy, wheat, fish, and shellfish. Food manufacturers are now required to state the presence of these eight allergens in plain language in the list of ingredients on food labels.

Many people who believe they have food allergies may actually suffer from a food intolerance, a much more common source of adverse food reactions that typically involves problems with metabolism rather than with the immune system. The body may not be able to adequately digest a food or the body may react to a particular food compound. Food intolerances have been attributed to lactose (milk sugar), gluten (a protein in some grains), tartrazine (yellow food coloring), sulfite (a food additive), MSG, and the sweetener aspartame. Although symptoms of a food intolerance may be similar to those of a food allergy, they are typically more localized and not life-threatening. Many people with food intolerance can safely and comfortably consume small amounts of the food that affects them.

If you suspect you have a food allergy or intolerance, a good first step is to keep a food diary. Note everything you eat or drink, any symptoms you develop, and how long after eating the symptoms appear. Then make an appointment with your physician to go over your diary and determine if any additional tests are needed. People at risk for severe allergic reactions must diligently avoid trigger foods and carry medications to treat anaphylaxis.

For more Common Questions Answered about nutrition, visit the Online Learning Center.

American Heart Association. 2006. *Our 2006 Diet and Lifestyle Recommendations* (http://www.americanheart.org/presenter.jhtml?identifier=851; retrieved May 28, 2007).

Block, G. 2004. Foods contributing to energy intake in the US: Data from NHANES III and NHANES 1999–2000. *Journal of Food Composition and Analysis* 17(2004): 439–447.

Burke, L. M. 2007. Nutrition strategies for the marathon: Fuel for training and racing. *Sports Medicine* 37(4–5): 344–347.

Centers for Disease Control and Prevention. 2007. *Nutrition for Everyone* (http://www.cdc.gov/nccdphp/dnpa/nutrition/nutrition_for_everyone/index.htm; retrieved May 28, 2007).

Chun, O. K., et al. 2007. Estimated dietary flavonoid intake and major food sources of U.S. adults. *The Journal of Nutrition* 137(5): 1244–1252.

Clifton, P. M., J. B. Keogh, and M. Noakes. 2004. Trans fatty acids in adipose tissue and the food supply are associated with myocardial infarction. *Journal of Nutrition* 134: 874–879.

Ervin, R. B., et al. 2004. Dietary intake of selected minerals for the United States Population: 1999–2000. *Advance Data from Vital and Health Statistics*, 341.

Food and Drug Administration. 2004. *Fact Sheet: Carbohydrates* (http://www.fda.gov/oc/initiatives/obesity/factsheet.html; retrieved May 28, 2007).

Food and Nutrition Board, Institute of Medicine. 2005. *Dietary Reference Intakes for Water, Potassium, Sodium, Chloride, and Sulfate*. Washington, D.C.: National Academies Press.

Food and Nutrition Board, Institute of Medicine. 2005. *Dietary Reference Intakes for Energy, Carbohydrate, Fiber, Fat, Fatty Acids, Cholesterol, Protein, and Amino Acids*. Washington, D.C.: National Academies Press.

Hanley, D. A., and K. S. Davison. 2005. Vitamin D insufficiency in North America. *Journal of Nutrition* 135(2): 332–337.

Harvard School of Public Health, Department of Nutrition. 2007. *The Nutrition Source: Knowledge for Healthy Eating* (http://www.hsph.harvard.edu/nutritionsource/; retrieved May 28, 2007).

Hites, R. A., et al. 2004. Global assessment of organic contaminants in farmed salmon. *Science* 303(5655): 226–229.

Houston, D. K., et al. 2005. Dairy, fruit, and vegetable intakes and functional limitations and disability in a biracial cohort. *American Journal of Clinical Nutrition* 81(2): 515–522.

Kranz, S., et al. 2005. Adverse effect of high added sugar consumption on dietary intake in American preschoolers. *Journal of Pediatrics* 46(1): 105–111.

Krebs-Smith, S. M., and P. Kris-Etherton. 2007. How does MyPyramid compare to other population-based recommendations for controlling chronic disease? *Journal of the American Dietetic Association* 107(5): 830–837.

Ma, Y., et al. 2005. Association between dietary carbohydrates and body weight. *American Journal of Epidemiology* 161(4): 359–367.

Nanney, M. S., et al. 2004. Rationale for a consistent "powerhouse" approach to vegetable and fruit messages. *Journal of the American Dietetic Association* 104(3): 352–356.

National Academy of Sciences, Institute of Medicine, Food and Nutrition Board. 2006. *Dietary Reference Intakes: Recommended Intakes for Individuals* (http://www.iom.edu/Object.File/Master/7/300/Webtablemacro.pdf; retrieved May 28, 2007).

Opotowsky, A. R., et al. 2004. Serum vitamin A concentration and the risk of hip fracture among women 50 to 74 years old in the United States. *American Journal of Medicine* 117(3): 169–174.

U.S. Department of Agriculture. 2007. *Bovine Spongiform Encephalopathy* (http://www.fas.usda.gov/dlp/bse/bse.html; retrieved May 28, 2007).

U.S. Department of Agriculture. 2007. *Inside the Pyramid* (http://www.mypyramid.gov/pyramid/index.html; retrieved May 28, 2007).

U.S. Department of Health and Human Services and U.S. Department of Agriculture. 2005. *Dietary Guidelines for Americans 2005* (http://www.health.gov/dietaryguidelines/dga2005/document/; retrieved May 28, 2007).

U.S. Department of Health and Human Services and U.S. Department of Agriculture. 2005. Finding your way to a healthier you: Based on the Dietary Guidelines for Americans. *Home and Garden Bulletin* No. 232-CP.

Vartanian, L. R., et al. 2007. Effects of soft drink consumption on nutrition and health: A systematic review and meta-analysis. *American Journal of Public Health* 97(4): 667–675.

Nutrition Resources

Table 1 Dietary Reference Intakes (DRIs): Recommended Levels for Individual Intake

Life Stage	Group	Biotin (µg/day)	Choline (mg/day)[a]	Folate (µg/day)[b]	Niacin (mg/day)[c]	Pantothenic Acid (mg/day)	Riboflavin (mg/day)	Thiamin (mg/day)	Vitamin A (µg/day)[d]	Vitamin B-6 (mg/day)	Vitamin B-12 (µg/day)	Vitamin C (mg/day)[e]	Vitamin D (µg/day)[f]	Vitamin E (mg/day)[g]
Infants	0–6 months	5	125	65	2	1.7	0.3	0.2	400	0.1	0.4	40	5	4
	7–12 months	6	150	80	4	1.8	0.4	0.3	500	0.3	0.5	50	5	5
Children	1–3 years	8	200	**150**	**6**	2	**0.5**	**0.5**	**300**	**0.5**	**0.9**	**15**	5	**6**
	4–8 years	12	250	**200**	**8**	3	**0.6**	**0.6**	**400**	**0.6**	**1.2**	**25**	5	**7**
Males	9–13 years	20	375	**300**	**12**	4	**0.9**	**0.9**	**600**	**1.0**	**1.8**	**45**	5	**11**
	14–18 years	25	550	**400**	**16**	5	**1.3**	**1.2**	**900**	**1.3**	**2.4**	**75**	5	**15**
	19–30 years	30	550	**400**	**16**	5	**1.3**	**1.2**	**900**	**1.3**	**2.4**	**90**	5	**15**
	31–50 years	30	550	**400**	**16**	5	**1.3**	**1.2**	**900**	**1.3**	**2.4**	**90**	5	**15**
	51–70 years	30	550	**400**	**16**	5	**1.3**	**1.2**	**900**	**1.7**	**2.4**[h]	**90**	10	**15**
	>70 years	30	550	**400**	**16**	5	**1.3**	**1.2**	**900**	**1.7**	**2.4**[h]	**90**	15	**15**
Females	9–13 years	20	375	**300**	**12**	4	**0.9**	**0.9**	**600**	**1.0**	**1.8**	**45**	5	**11**
	14–18 years	25	400	**400**[i]	**14**	5	**1.0**	**1.0**	**700**	**1.2**	**2.4**	**65**	5	**15**
	19–30 years	30	425	**400**[i]	**14**	5	**1.1**	**1.1**	**700**	**1.3**	**2.4**	**75**	5	**15**
	31–50 years	30	425	**400**[i]	**14**	5	**1.1**	**1.1**	**700**	**1.3**	**2.4**	**75**	5	**15**
	51–70 years	30	425	**400**[i]	**14**	5	**1.1**	**1.1**	**700**	**1.5**	**2.4**[h]	**75**	10	**15**
	>70 years	30	425	**400**	**14**	5	**1.1**	**1.1**	**700**	**1.5**	**2.4**[h]	**75**	15	**15**
Pregnancy	≤18 years	30	450	**600**[j]	**18**	6	**1.4**	**1.4**	**750**	**1.9**	**2.6**	**80**	5	**15**
	19–30 years	30	450	**600**[j]	**18**	6	**1.4**	**1.4**	**770**	**1.9**	**2.6**	**85**	5	**15**
	31–50 years	30	450	**600**[j]	**18**	6	**1.4**	**1.4**	**770**	**1.9**	**2.6**	**85**	5	**15**
Lactation	≤18 years	35	550	**500**	**17**	7	**1.6**	**1.4**	**1200**	**2.0**	**2.8**	**115**	5	**19**
	19–30 years	35	550	**500**	**17**	7	**1.6**	**1.4**	**1300**	**2.0**	**2.8**	**120**	5	**19**
	31–50 years	35	550	**500**	**17**	7	**1.6**	**1.4**	**1300**	**2.0**	**2.8**	**120**	5	**19**
Tolerable Upper Intake Levels for Adults (19–70)			*3500*	*1000*[k]	*35*[k]				*3000*	*100*		*2000*	*50*	*1000*[k]

Note: The table includes values for the type of DRI standard—Adequate Intake (AI) or Recommended Dietary Allowance (RDA)—that has been established for that particular nutrient and life stage; RDAs are shown in **bold type.** The final row of the table shows the Tolerable Upper Intake Levels (ULs) for adults; refer to the full DRI report for information on other ages and life stages. A UL is the maximum level of daily nutrient intake that is likely to pose no risk of adverse effects. There is insufficient data to set ULs for all nutrients, but this does not mean that there is no potential for adverse effects; source of intake should be from food only to prevent high levels of intake of nutrients without established ULs. In healthy individuals, there is no established benefit from nutrient intakes above the RDA or AI.

[a]Although AIs have been set for choline, there are few data to assess whether a dietary supply of choline is needed at all stages of the life cycle, and it may be that the choline requirement can be met by endogenous synthesis at some of these stages.

[b]As dietary folate equivalents (DFE): 1 DFE = 1 µg food folate = 0.6 µg folate from fortified food or as a supplement consumed with food = 0.5 µg of a supplement taken on an empty stomach.

[c]As niacin equivalents (NE): 1 mg niacin = 60 mg tryptophan.

Table 1 Dietary Reference Intakes (DRIs): Recommended Levels for Individual Intake *(continued)*

Life Stage	Group	Vitamin K (μg/day)	Calcium (mg/day)	Chromium (μg/day)	Copper (μg/day)	Fluoride (mg/day)	Iodine (mg/day)	Iron (mg/day)[l]	Magnesium (mg/day)	Manganese (mg/day)	Molybdenum (μg/day)	Phosphorus (mg/day)	Selenium (μg/day)	Zinc (mg/day)[m]
Infants	0–6 months	2.0	210	0.2	200	0.01	110	0.27	30	0.003	2	100	15	2
	7–12 months	2.5	270	5.5	220	0.5	130	11	75	0.6	3	275	20	3
Children	1–3 years	30	500	11	340	0.7	90	7	80	1.2	17	460	20	3
	4–8 years	55	800	15	440	1	90	10	130	1.5	22	500	30	5
Males	9–13 years	60	1300	25	700	2	120	8	240	1.9	34	1250	40	8
	14–18 years	75	1300	35	890	3	150	11	410	2.2	43	1250	55	11
	19–30 years	120	1000	35	900	4	150	8	400	2.3	45	700	55	11
	31–50 years	120	1000	35	900	4	150	8	420	2.3	45	700	55	11
	51–70 years	120	1200	30	900	4	150	8	420	2.3	45	700	55	11
	>70 years	120	1200	30	900	4	150	8	420	2.3	45	700	55	11
Females	9–13 years	60	1300	21	700	2	120	8	240	1.6	34	1250	40	8
	14–18 years	75	1300	24	890	3	150	15	360	1.6	43	1250	55	9
	19–30 years	90	1000	25	900	3	150	18	310	1.8	45	700	55	8
	31–50 years	90	1000	25	900	3	150	18	320	1.8	45	700	55	8
	51–70 years	90	1200	20	900	3	150	8	320	1.8	45	700	55	8
	>70 years	90	1200	20	900	3	150	8	320	1.8	45	700	55	8
Pregnancy	≤18 years	75	1300	29	1000	3	220	27	400	2.0	50	1250	60	13
	19–30 years	90	1000	30	1000	3	220	27	350	2.0	50	700	60	11
	31–50 years	90	1000	30	1000	3	220	27	360	2.0	50	700	60	11
Lactation	≤18 years	75	1300	44	1300	3	290	10	360	2.6	50	1250	70	14
	19–30 years	90	1000	45	1300	3	290	9	310	2.6	50	700	70	12
	31–50 years	90	1000	45	1300	3	290	9	320	2.6	50	700	70	12
Tolerable Upper Intake Levels for Adults (19–70)			*2500*		*10,000*	*10*	*1100*	*45*	*350*[k]	*11*	*2000*	*4000*	*400*	*40*

[d]As retinol activity equivalents (RAEs): 1 RAE = 1 μg retinol, 12 μg β-carotene, or 24 μg α-carotene or β-cryptoxanthin. Preformed vitamin A (retinol) is abundant in animal-derived foods; provitamin A carotenoids are abundant in some dark yellow, orange, red, and deep-green fruits and vegetables. For preformed vitamin A and for provitamin A carotenoids in supplements, IRE = 1 RAE; for provitamin A carotenoids in foods, divide the REs by 2 to obtain RAEs. The UL applies only to preformed vitamin A.

[e]Individuals who smoke require an additional 35 mg/day of vitamin C over that needed by nonsmokers; nonsmokers regularly exposed to tobacco smoke should ensure they meet the RDA for vitamin C.

[f]As cholecalciferol: 1 μg cholecalciferol = 40 IU vitamin D. DRI values are based on the absence of adequate exposure to sunlight.

[g]As α-tocopherol. Includes naturally occurring RRR-α-tocopherol and the 2R-stereoisomeric forms from supplements; does not include the 2S-stereoisomeric forms from supplements.

[h]Because 10–30% of older people may malabsorb food-bound B-12, those over age 50 should meet their RDA mainly with supplements or foods fortified with B-12.

[i]In view of evidence linking folate intake with neural tube defects in the fetus. It is recommended that all women capable of becoming pregnant consume 400 μg from supplements or fortified foods in addition to consuming folate from a varied diet.

[j]It is assumed that women will continue consuming 400 μg from supplements or fortified food until their pregnancy is confirmed and they enter prenatal care, which ordinarily occurs after the end of the periconceptional period—the critical time for formation of the neural tube.

[k]The UL applies only to intake from supplements, fortified foods, and/or pharmacological agents and not to intake from foods.

[l]Because the absorption of iron from plant foods is low compared to that from animal foods, the RDA for strict vegetarians is approximately 1.8 times higher than the values established for omnivores (14 mg/day for adult male vegetarians; 33 mg/day for premenopausal female vegetarians). Oral contraceptives (OCs) reduce menstrual blood losses, so women taking them need less daily iron; the RDA for premenopausal women taking OCs is 10.9 mg/day. For more on iron requirements for other special situations, refer to *Dietary Reference Intakes for Vitamin A, Vitamin K, Arsenic, Boron, Chromium, Copper, Iodine, Iron, Manganese, Molybdenum, Nickel, Silicon, Vanadium, and Zinc* (visit http://www.nap.edu for the complete report).

[m]Zinc absorption is lower for those consuming vegetarian diets so the zinc requirement for vegetarians is approximately twofold greater than for those consuming a nonvegetarian diet.

Table 1 Dietary Reference Intakes (DRIs): Recommended Levels for Individual Intake *(continued)*

Life Stage	Group	Potassium (g/day)	Sodium (g/day)	Chloride (g/day)	Carbohydrate RDA/AI (g/day)	Carbohydrate AMDR[o] (%)	Total Fiber RDA/AI (g/day)	Total Fat AMDR[o] (%)	Linoleic Acid RDA/AI (g/day)	Linoleic Acid AMDR[o] (%)	Alpha-linolenic Acid RDA/AI (g/day)	Alpha-linolenic Acid AMDR[o] (%)	Protein[n] RDA/AI (g/day)	Protein[n] AMDR[o] (%)	Water[p] (L/day)
Infants	0–6 months	0.4	0.12	0.18	60	ND[q]	ND	[r]	4.4	ND[q]	0.5	ND[q]	9.1	ND[q]	0.7
	7–12 months	0.7	0.37	0.57	95	ND[q]	ND	[r]	4.6	ND[q]	0.5	ND[q]	13.5	ND[q]	0.8
Children	1–3 years	3.0	1.0	1.5	130	45–65	19	30–40	7	5–10	0.7	0.6–1.2	13	5–20	1.3
	4–8 years	3.8	1.2	1.9	130	45–65	25	25–35	10	5–10	0.9	0.6–1.2	19	10–30	1.7
Males	9–13 years	4.5	1.5	2.3	130	45–65	31	25–35	12	5–10	1.2	0.6–1.2	34	10–30	2.4
	14–18 years	4.7	1.5	2.3	130	45–65	38	25–35	16	5–10	1.6	0.6–1.2	52	10–30	3.3
	19–30 years	4.7	1.5	2.3	130	45–65	38	20–35	17	5–10	1.6	0.6–1.2	56	10–35	3.7
	31–50 years	4.7	1.5	2.3	130	45–65	38	20–35	17	5–10	1.6	0.6–1.2	56	10–35	3.7
	51–70 years	4.7	1.3	2.0	130	45–65	30	20–35	14	5–10	1.6	0.6–1.2	56	10–35	3.7
	>70 years	4.7	1.2	1.8	130	45–65	30	20–35	14	5–10	1.6	0.6–1.2	56	10–35	3.7
Females	9–13 years	4.5	1.5	2.3	130	45–65	26	25–35	10	5–10	1.0	0.6–1.2	34	10–30	2.1
	14–18 years	4.7	1.5	2.3	130	45–65	26	25–35	11	5–10	1.1	0.6–1.2	46	10–30	2.3
	19–30 years	4.7	1.5	2.3	130	45–65	25	20–35	12	5–10	1.1	0.6–1.2	46	10–35	2.7
	31–50 years	4.7	1.5	2.3	130	45–65	25	20–35	12	5–10	1.1	0.6–1.2	46	10–35	2.7
	51–70 years	4.7	1.3	2.0	130	45–65	21	20–35	11	5–10	1.1	0.6–1.2	46	10–35	2.7
	>70 years	4.7	1.2	1.8	130	45–65	21	20–35	11	5–10	1.1	0.6–1.2	46	10–35	2.7
Pregnancy	≤18 years	4.7	1.5	2.3	175	45–65	28	20–35	13	5–10	1.4	0.6–1.2	71	10–35	3.0
	19–30 years	4.7	1.5	2.3	175	45–65	28	20–35	13	5–10	1.4	0.6–1.2	71	10–35	3.0
	31–50 years	4.7	1.5	2.3	175	45–65	28	20–35	13	5–10	1.4	0.6–1.2	71	10–35	3.0
Lactation	≤18 years	5.1	1.5	2.3	210	45–65	29	20–35	13	5–10	1.3	0.6–1.2	71	10–35	3.8
	19–30 years	5.1	1.5	2.3	210	45–65	29	20–35	13	5–10	1.3	0.6–1.2	71	10–35	3.8
	31–50 years	5.1	1.5	2.3	210	45–65	29	20–35	13	5–10	1.3	0.6–1.2	71	10–35	3.8
Tolerable Upper Intake Level for Adults (19–70)			2.3	3.6											

[n]Daily protein recommendations are based on body weight for reference body weights. To calculate for a specific body weight, use the following values: 1.5 g/kg for infants, 1.1 g/kg for 1–3 years, 0.95 g/kg for 4–13 years, 0.85 g/kg for 14–18 years, 0.8 g/kg for adults, and 1.1 g/kg for pregnant (using prepregnancy weight) and lactating women.

[o]Acceptable Macronutrient Distribution Range (AMDR), expressed as a percent of total daily calories, is the range of intake for a particular energy source that is associated with reduced risk of chronic disease while providing intakes of essential nutrients. If an individual consumes in excess of the AMDR, there is a potential for increasing the risk of chronic diseases and/or insufficient intakes of essential nutrients.

[p]Total water intake from fluids and food.

[q]Not determinable due to lack of data of adverse effects in this age group and concern with regard to lack of ability to handle excess amounts. Source of intake should be from food only to prevent high levels of intake.

[r]For infants, Adequate Intake of total fat is 31 grams/day (0–6 months) and 30 grams per day (7–12 months) from breast milk and, for infants 7–12 months, complementary food and beverages.

Source: Food and Nutrition Board, Institute of Medicine, National Academies. 2004. *Dietary Reference Intakes Tables* (http://www.iom.edu/file.asp?id = 21372; retrieved June 1, 2007). The complete Dietary Reference Intake reports are available from the National Academy Press (http://www.nap.edu).

Nutrition Resources

Food groups	1600 calories	2000 calories	2600 calories	3100 calories	Serving sizes and notes
	Number of servings per day (or per week, as noted)				
Grains	6	6–8	10–11	12–13	1 slice bread, 1 oz dry cereal, ½ cup cooked rice, pasta, or cereal; choose whole grains
Vegetables	3–4	4–5	5–6	6	1 cup raw leafy vegetables, ½ cup cooked vegetables, ½ cup vegetable juice
Fruits	4	4–5	5–6	6	½ cup fruit juice, 1 medium fruit, ¼ cup dried fruit, 1/2 cup fresh, frozen, or canned fruit
Low-fat or fat-free dairy foods	2–3	2–3	3	3–4	1 cup milk; 1 cup yogurt, 1-½ oz cheese; choose fat-free or lowfat types
Meat, poultry, fish	3–6	6 or less?	6	6–9	1 oz cooked meats, poultry, or fish: select only lean; trim away visible fats; broil, roast, or boil instead of frying; remove skin from poultry
Nuts, seeds, legumes	3 servings per week	4–5 servings per week	1	1	⅓ cup or 1-½ oz nuts, 2 Tbsp or ½ oz seeds, ½ cup cooked dry beans/peas, 2 Tbsp peanut butter
Fats and oils	2	2–3	3	4	1 tsp soft margarine; 1 Tbsp low-fat mayonnaise, 2 Tbsp light salad dressing, 1 tsp vegetable oil; DASH has 27% of calories as fat (low in saturated fat)
Sweets	0	5 servings/ week or less	2	2	1 Tbsp sugar, 1 Tbsp jelly or jam, ½ cup sorbet, 1 cup lemonade; sweets should be low in fat

FIGURE 1 The DASH Eating Plan. SOURCE: National Institutes of Health, National Heart, Lung, and Blood Institute. 2006. *Your Guide to Lowering Your Blood Pressure with DASH: How Do I Make the Dash?* (http://www.nhlbi.nih.gov/health/public/heart/hbp/dash/how_make_dash html; retrieved May 27, 2007).

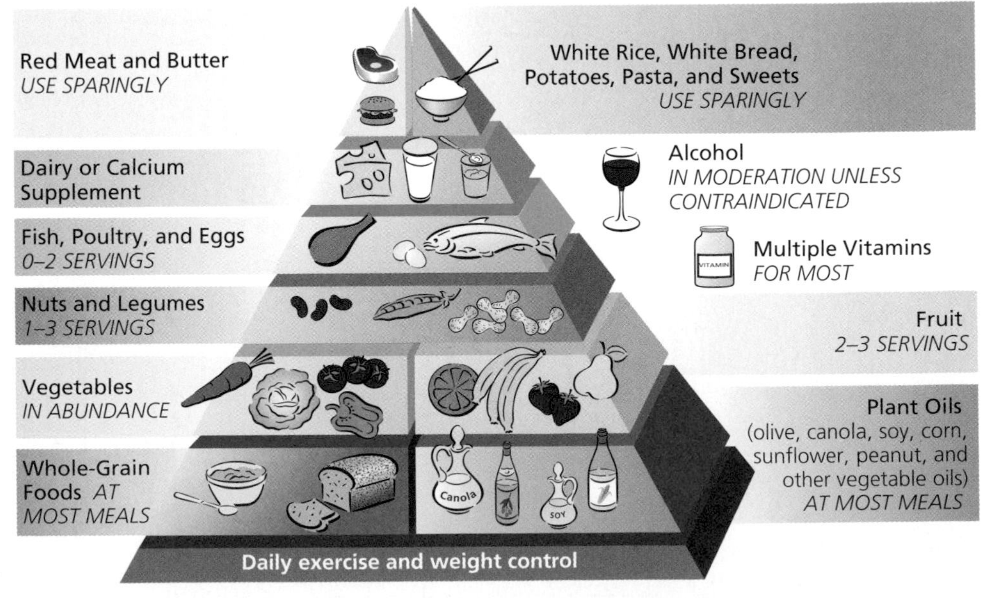

FIGURE 2 Healthy Eating Pyramid. The Healthy Eating Pyramid is an alternative food-group plan developed by researchers at the Harvard School of Public Health; this pyramid reflects many major research studies that have looked at the relationship between diet and long-term health. The Healthy Eating Pyramid differentiates between the various dietary sources of fat, protein, and carbohydrates, and it emphasizes whole grains, vegetable oils, fruits and vegetables, nuts, and dried peas and beans.

SOURCE: Reprinted by permission of Simon & Schuster Adult Publishing Group from *Eat, Drink, and Be Healthy: The Harvard Medical School Guide to Healthy Eating* by Walter C. Willett, M.D. Copyright © 2001 by the President and Fellows of Harvard College.

Name ______________________ Section ______________ Date ______________

LAB 8.1 Your Daily Diet Versus MyPyramid

Make three photocopies of the worksheet in this lab and use them to keep track of everything you eat for 3 consecutive days. Break down each food item into its component parts, and list them separately in the column labeled "Food." Then enter the portion size you consumed in the correct food-group column. For example, a turkey sandwich might be listed as follows: whole-wheat bread, 2 oz-equiv of whole grains; turkey, 2 oz-equiv of meat/beans; tomato, $\frac{1}{3}$ cup other vegetables; romaine lettuce, $\frac{1}{4}$ cup dark green vegetables; 1 tablespoon mayonnaise dressing, 1 teaspoon oils. It can be challenging to track values for added sugars and, especially, oils and fats, but use food labels and the information in Appendix B to be as accurate as you can. MyPyramid.gov has additional guidelines for counting discretionary calories.

For vegetables, enter your portion sizes in both the "Total" column and the column corresponding to the correct subgroup; for example, the spinach in a spinach salad would be entered under "Dark Green" and carrots would be entered under "Orange." For the purpose of this 3-day activity, you will compare only your total vegetable consumption against MyPyramid guidelines; as described in the chapter, vegetable subgroup recommendations are based on weekly consumption. However, it is important to note which vegetable subgroups are represented in your diet; over a 3-day period, you should consume several servings from each of the subgroups.

This activity can also be completed online using the Pyramid Tracker program at the MyPyramid.gov Web site.

Date: ______________

	Grains (oz-eq)		Vegetable (cups)										Discretionary Calories	
Food	Whole	Other	Total	*Dark Green*	*Orange*	*Legume*	*Starchy*	*Other*	Fruits (cups)	Milk (cups)	Meat/ Beans (oz-eq)	Oils (tsp)	Solid Fats (g)	Added Sugars (g/tsp)
Daily TOTAL														

Next, average your daily intake totals for the 3 days and enter them in the chart below. For example, if your three daily totals for the fruit group were 1 cup, 1½ cups, and 2 cups, your average daily intake would be 1½ cups. Fill in the recommended intake totals that apply to you from Figure 8.6 and Table 8.4.

MyPyramid Food Group	Recommended Daily Amounts or Limits	Your Actual Average Daily Intake
Grains (total)	oz-eq	oz-eq
Whole grains	oz-eq	oz-eq
Other grains	oz-eq	oz-eq
Vegetables (total)	cups	cups
Fruits	cups	cups
Milk	cups	cups
Meat and beans	oz-eq	oz-eq
Oils	tsp	tsp
Solid fats	g	g
Added sugars	g/tsp	g/tsp

Using Your Results

How did you score? How close is your diet to that recommended by MyPyramid? Are you surprised by the actual amount of food you're consuming from each food group or from added sugars and solid fats?

What should you do next? If the results of the assessment indicate that you could boost your level of wellness by improving your diet, set realistic goals for change. Do you need to increase or decrease your consumption of any food groups? List any areas of concern below, along with a goal for change and strategies for achieving the goal you've set. If you see that you are falling short in one food group, such as fruits or vegetables, but have many foods that are rich in discretionary calories from solid fats and added sugars, you might try decreasing those items in favor of an apple, a bunch of grapes, or some baby carrots. Think carefully about the reasons behind your food choices. For example, if you eat doughnuts for breakfast every morning because you feel rushed, make a list of ways to save time to allow for a healthier breakfast.

Problem: ____________________

Goal: ____________________

Strategies for change: ____________________

Problem: ____________________

Goal: ____________________

Strategies for change: ____________________

Problem: ____________________

Goal: ____________________

Strategies for change: ____________________

Enter the results of this lab in the Preprogram Assessment column in Appendix D. If you've set goals and identified strategies for change, begin putting your plan into action. Additional dietary tracking grids are available on the Online Learning Center. After several weeks of your program, complete this lab again and enter the results in the Postprogram Assessment column of Appendix D. How do the results compare?

Name ______________________ Section ______________ Date ______________

LAB 8.2 Dietary Analysis

You can complete this activity using either a nutrition analysis software program or the food composition data in Appendix B and the charts printed below. Information about the nutrient content of foods is also available online; see the For Further Exploration section for recommended Web sites. (This lab asks you to analyze one day's diet. For a more complete and accurate assessment of your diet, analyze the results from several different days, including a weekday and a weekend day.)

DATE ______________________ DAY: M Tu W Th F Sa Su

Food	Amount	Calories	Protein (g)	Carbohydrate (g)	Dietary fiber (g)	Fat, total (g)	Saturated fat (g)	Cholesterol (mg)	Sodium (mg)	Vitamin A (RE)	Vitamin C (mg)	Calcium (mg)	Iron (mg)
Recommended totals*			10–35%	45–65%	25–38 g	20–35%	<10%	≤300 mg	≤2300 mg	RE	mg	mg	mg
Actual totals**		cal	g / %	g / %	g	g / %	g / %	mg	mg	RE	mg	mg	mg

*Fill in the appropriate DRI values for vitamin A, vitamin C, calcium, and iron from Table 1 in the Nutrition Resources section.

**Total the values in each column. To calculate the percentage of total calories from protein, carbohydrate, fat, and saturated fat, use the formula on p. 272. Protein and carbohydrate provide 4 calories per gram; fat provides 9 calories per gram. For example, if you consume a total of 270 grams of carbohydrates and 2000 calories, your percentage of total calories from carbohydrates would be (270 g × 4 cal/g) ÷ 2000 cal = 54%. Do not include data for alcoholic beverages in your calculations. Percentages may not total 100% due to rounding.

Using Your Results

How did you score? How close is your diet to that recommended by the Dietary Guidelines, Dietary Reference Intakes, and other guidelines? Are you surprised by any of the results of this assessment?

What should you do next? Enter the results of this lab in the Preprogram Assessment column in Appendix D. If your daily diet meets all the recommended intakes, congratulations—and keep up the good work. If the results of the assessment pinpoint areas of concern, then work with your food record on the previous page to determine what changes you could make to meet all the guidelines. Make changes, additions, and deletions until it conforms to all or most of the guidelines. Or, if you prefer, start from scratch to create a day's diet that meets the guidelines. Use the chart below to experiment and record your final, healthy sample diet for one day. Then put what you learned from this exercise into practice in your daily life. After several weeks of your program, complete this lab again and enter the results in the Postprogram Assessment column of Appendix D. How do the results compare?

DATE ______________________________ DAY: M Tu W Th F Sa Su

Food	Amount	Calories	Protein (g)	Carbohydrate (g)	Dietary fiber (g)	Fat, total (g)	Saturated fat (g)	Cholesterol (mg)	Sodium (mg)	Vitamin A (RE)	Vitamin C (mg)	Calcium (mg)	Iron (mg)
Recommended totals			10–35%	45–65%	25–38 g	20–38%	<10%	≤300 mg	≤2300 mg	RE	mg	mg	mg
Actual totals		cal	g / %	g / %	g	g / %	g / %	mg	mg	RE	mg	mg	mg

Name ______________________ Section ______________ Date ____________

LAB 8.3 Informed Food Choices

Part I Using Food Labels

Choose three food items to evaluate. You might want to select three similar items, such as regular, low-fat, and nonfat salad dressing, or three very different items. Record the information from their food labels in the table below.

Food Items			
Serving size			
Total calories	cal	cal	cal
Total fat—grams	g	g	g
—% Daily Value	%	%	%
Saturated fat—grams	g	g	g
—% Daily Value	%	%	%
Trans fat—grams	g	g	g
Cholesterol—milligrams	mg	mg	mg
—% Daily Value	%	%	%
Sodium—milligrams	mg	mg	mg
—% Daily Value	%	%	%
Carbohydrates (total)—grams	g	g	g
—% Daily Value	%	%	%
Dietary fiber—grams	g	g	g
—% Daily Value	%	%	%
Sugars—grams	g	g	g
Protein—grams	g	g	g
Vitamin A—% Daily Value	%	%	%
Vitamin C—% Daily Value	%	%	%
Calcium—% Daily Value	%	%	%
Iron—% Daily Value	%	%	%

How do the items you chose compare? You can do a quick nutrient check by totaling the Daily Value percentages for nutrients you should limit (total fat, cholesterol, sodium) and the nutrients you should favor (dietary fiber, vitamin A, vitamin C, calcium, iron) for each food. Which food has the largest percent Daily Value sum for nutrients to limit? For nutrients to favor?

Food Items			
Calories	cal	cal	cal
% Daily Value total for nutrients to limit (total fat, cholesterol, sodium)	%	%	%
% Daily Value total for nutrients to favor (fiber, vitamin A, vitamin C, calcium, iron)	%	%	%

Part II Evaluating Fast Food

Use the information from Appendix C, "Nutritional Content of Popular Items from Fast-Food Restaurants," to complete the chart on this page for the last fast-food meal you ate. Add up your totals for the meal. Compare the values for fat, protein, carbohydrate, cholesterol, and sodium content for each food item and for the meal as a whole with the levels suggested by the Dietary Guidelines for Americans. Calculate the percent of total calories derived from fat, saturated fat, protein, and carbohydrate using the formulas given.

If you haven't recently been to one of the restaurants included in the appendix, fill in the chart for any sample meal you might eat. If some of the food items you selected don't appear in Appendix C, ask for a nutrition information brochure when you visit the restaurant, or check out online fast-food information: Arby's (http://www.arbysrestaurant.com), Burger King (http://www.burgerking.com), Domino's Pizza (http://www.dominos.com), Jack in the Box (http://www.jackinthebox.com), KFC (http://www.kfc.com), McDonald's (http://www.mcdonalds.com), Subway (http://www.subway.com), Taco Bell (http://www.tacobell.com), Wendy's (http://www.wendys.com).

	Dietary Guidelines	FOOD ITEMS						Total**
Serving size (g)		g	g	g	g	g	g	g
Calories		cal	cal	cal	cal	cal	cal	cal
Total fat—grams		g	g	g	g	g	g	g
—% calories*	20–35%	%	%	%	%	%	%	%
Saturated fat—grams		g	g	g	g	g	g	g
—% calories*	<10%	%	%	%	%	%	%	%
Protein—grams		g	g	g	g	g	g	g
—% calories*	10–35%	%	%	%	%	%	%	%
Carbohydrate—grams		g	g	g	g	g	g	g
—% calories*	45–65%	%	%	%	%	%	%	%
Cholesterol†	100 mg	mg	mg	mg	mg	mg	mg	mg
Sodium†	800 mg	mg	mg	mg	mg	mg	mg	mg

*To calculate the percent of total calories from each food energy source (fat, carbohydrate, protein), use the following formula:

$$\frac{\text{(number of grams of energy source)} \times \text{(number of calories per gram of energy source)}}{\text{(total calories in serving of food item)}}$$

(*Note:* Fat and saturated fat provide 9 calories per gram; protein and carbohydrate provide 4 calories per gram.) For example, the percent of total calories from protein in a 150-calorie dish containing 10 grams of protein is

$$\frac{\text{(10 grams of protein)} \times \text{(4 calories per gram)}}{\text{(150 calories)}} = \frac{40}{150} = 0.27\text{, or 27\% of total calories from protein}$$

**For the Total column, add up the total grams of fat, carbohydrate, and protein contained in your sample meal and calculate the percentages based on the total calories in the meal. (Percentages may not total 100% due to rounding.) For cholesterol and sodium values, add up the total number of milligrams.

†Recommended daily limits of cholesterol and sodium are divided by 3 here to give an approximate recommended limit for a single meal.

LOOKING AHEAD>>>>>

AFTER READING THIS CHAPTER, YOU SHOULD BE ABLE TO:

- Explain the health risks associated with overweight and obesity
- Explain the factors that may contribute to a weight problem, including genetic, physiological, lifestyle, and psychosocial factors
- Describe lifestyle factors that contribute to weight gain and loss, including the role of food choices, exercise, and emotional factors
- Identify and describe the symptoms of eating disorders and the health risks associated with them
- Design a personal plan for successfully managing body weight

WEIGHT MANAGEMENT 9

TEST YOUR KNOWLEDGE

1. About what percentage of American adults are overweight?

a. 15%
b. 35%
c. 65%

2. People who are overweight get less sleep than people who are at a healthy body weight.

True or false?

3. Which of the following eating disorders is most common among Americans?

a. anorexia
b. bulimia
c. binge-eating disorder

ANSWERS

1. **c.** About 66% of American adults are overweight, including more than 31% who are obese. The rate of obesity among adults has increased more than 75% since 1990.
2. **TRUE.** It is unclear whether there is a cause-and-effect relationship between lack of sleep and increased body weight, but insufficient sleep may affect hormones, metabolism, and appetite. Adequate sleep may also help prevent eating in response to feelings of stress and low energy.
3. **c.** A 2007 study reported that binge eating is more common than either anorexia or bulimia, affecting 3.5% of women and 2% of men. Binge-eating disorder is associated with severe obesity and may be a factor in the dramatic rise in obesity among Americans in recent decades.

FIT AND WELL ONLINE LEARNING CENTER www.mhhe.com/fahey

Visit the *Fit and Well* Online Learning Center for resources that will help you get the most out of your course!

- Study and review aids include practice quizzes, glossary flashcards, chapter summaries, learning objectives, PowerPoint presentations, Common Questions Answered, student handouts, crossword puzzles, Internet activities, and links to wellness Web sites.
- Behavior change tools include a daily fitness and nutrition journal, a behavior change workbook, sample behavior change plans, and blank behavior change logs to print and use.

Achieving and maintaining a healthy body weight is a serious public health challenge in the United States and a source of distress for many Americans. Under standards developed by the National Institutes of Health, only 34% of American adults are at a healthy weight: About 66% of American adults are overweight, including more than 31% who are obese (Table 9.1). The rate of obesity has more than doubled since 1960, and it continues to rise. If current rates of weight gain continue, *all* American adults will be overweight by 2030. Rates of obesity among children are also increasing, with more than 17% of 2- to 19-year-olds now classified as overweight.

Controlling body weight is really a matter of controlling body fat. As explained in Chapter 6, the most important consideration for health is not total weight but body composition—the proportion of fat to fat-free mass. Many people who are "overweight" are also "overfat," and the health risks they face are due to the latter condition. Although this chapter uses the common terms *weight management* and *weight loss,* the goal for wellness is to adopt healthy behaviors and achieve an appropriate body composition, not to conform to rigid standards of total body weight. Chapter 6 includes a variety of methods for assessing body composition.

Although not completely understood, managing body weight is not a mysterious process. The "secret" is balancing calories consumed with calories expended in daily activities—in other words, eating a moderate diet and getting regular physical activity. Unfortunately, this formula is not as exciting as the latest fad diet or "scientific breakthrough" that promises a slim body without effort. Many people fail in their efforts to manage their weight because they emphasize short-term weight loss rather than permanent changes in lifestyle. Dieting is not part of a wellness lifestyle. Successful weight management requires the long-term coordination of many aspects of a wellness lifestyle, including proper nutrition, adequate physical activity, and stress management. The goal is the adoption of healthy and sustainable habits that maximize energy and well-being and reduce the risk of chronic diseases.

Body image is a related area of concern. More and more people are becoming unhappy with their bodies and obsessed with their weight. In recent surveys, more than half of Americans have stated that they are dissatisfied with their weight; only about 10% report being completely satisfied with their bodies. Dissatisfaction with body weight and shape is associated with dangerous eating patterns such as binge eating or self-starvation and with eating disorders.

TERMS

resting metabolic rate (RMR) The energy required (in calories) to maintain vital body functions, including respiration, heart rate, body temperature, and blood pressure, while the body is at rest.

VITAL STATISTICS

Table 9.1 Weight of Americans Age 20 and Older

Group	Percent Overweight	Percent Obese
Both sexes	66.0	31.4
All races, male	70.5	29.5
All races, female	61.6	33.2
White, male	71.0	30.2
White, female	57.6	30.7
African American, male	67.0	30.8
African American, female	79.6	51.1
Latino, male	74.6	29.1
Latino, female	73.0	39.4
Percent of poverty level		
Below 100%:	63.4	33.7
100%–less than 200%:	66.2	33.6
200% or greater:	66.1	30.0

SOURCE: National Center for Health Statistics. 2006. *Health, United States, 2006, with Chartbook on Trends in the Health of Americans.* Hyattsville, Md.: National Center for Health Statistics.

This chapter explores the factors that contribute to the development of overweight and obesity as well as to eating disorders. It also takes a closer look at weight management through lifestyle and suggests specific strategies for reaching and maintaining a healthy weight.

HEALTH IMPLICATIONS OF OVERWEIGHT AND OBESITY

As rates of overweight and obesity have risen in the United States, so has the prevalence of the health conditions associated with overweight—including a more than 33% rise in the rate of type 2 diabetes in just the past decade. It's estimated that inactivity and overweight account for more than 100,000 premature deaths annually in the United States, second only to tobacco-related deaths. More than $75 billion per year is spent treating obesity-related health problems.

Obesity is one of six major controllable risk factors for heart disease; it also increases risk for other forms of cardiovascular disease (CVD), hypertension, certain forms of cancer, diabetes, gallbladder disease, respiratory problems, joint diseases, skin problems, impaired immune function, and sleep disorders. Obese people have an overall mortality rate almost twice that of nonobese people.

Gaining weight over the years has also been found dangerous; in one study, women who gained more than 22 pounds since they were 18 years old had a sevenfold increase in the risk of heart disease. Many studies have confirmed that overweight and obesity shorten lives.

IN FOCUS

Factors That May Contribute to Weight Gain

Along with the physiological issues described in this chapter, researchers are studying whether the following factors cause weight gain in some people.

Fat Cells

The amount of fat the body can store is a function of the number and size of its fat cells. These cells are like tiny containers that can expand to hold body fat; when the cells fill up, the body makes more of them so it can store more fat. Some people are born with an above-average number of fat cells and have the potential for storing more body fat. Overeating at critical times, such as in childhood, may cause the body to increase its number of fat cells. Some experts contend that having more or larger fat cells creates biological pressure to eat, in order to fill all the cells. So far, this theory has not been borne out by research.

Weight Cycling

It has been hypothesized that repeatedly losing and regaining weight, known as *weight cycling* or *yo-yo dieting*, can be harmful to health and to weight-loss efforts. According to this theory, weight cycling makes the body more efficient at extracting and storing calories from food. Thus, with each successive diet, it becomes harder to lose weight. Most studies, however, have not supported this idea.

Carbohydrate Craving

Many researchers think that carbohydrate craving may cause overeating and lead to overweight. Animal studies suggest that consuming carbohydrates increases serotonin levels in the brain, inducing calmness. People with low levels of serotonin thus might crave and consume carbohydrates because their mood and energy level improve after eating foods like bread or pasta. Research on this theory has so far been inconclusive.

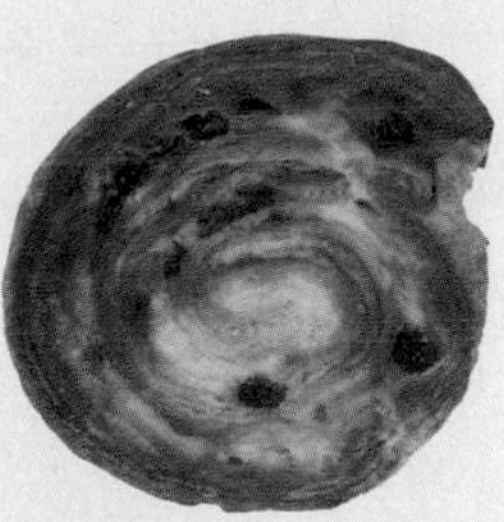

Several popular diets are based on the idea that "carbs" in general or foods with high glycemic index can cause weight gain (see Chapter 8 for information about glycemic index). There is no real data that eating carbs increases appetite or body weight beyond the effects of the calories contained in the foods. Instead of focusing on carbohydrates, people who need to manage their weight should pay attention to their overall calorie intake and choose healthy sources of carbohydrates.

In sum, although physiological differences may play a part in weight gain, the bottom line is that lifestyle choices account for most of the differences in body composition among individuals.

At the same time, even modest weight loss can have a significant positive impact on health. A weight loss of just 5–10% in obese individuals can reduce the risk of weight-related health conditions and increase life expectancy.

FACTORS CONTRIBUTING TO EXCESS BODY FAT

Several factors determine body weight and composition. These factors can be grouped into genetic, physiological, lifestyle, and psychosocial factors.

Genetic Factors

Estimates of the genetic contribution to obesity vary widely, from about 25% to 40% of an individual's body fat. More than 300 genes have been linked to obesity, but their actions are still under study. Genes influence body size and shape, body fat distribution, and metabolic rate. Genetic factors also affect the ease with which weight is gained as a result of overeating and where on the body extra weight is added. If both parents are obese, their children have an 80% risk of being obese; children with one obese parent face a 40% risk of becoming obese. In studies that compared adoptees and their biological parents, the weights of the adoptees were found to be more like those of the biological parents than the adoptive parents, indicating a strong genetic link.

Research thus suggests a genetic component in the determination of body weight. However, hereditary influences must be balanced against the contribution of environmental factors. Not all children of obese parents become obese, and normal-weight parents can have overweight children. In a study comparing men born and raised in Ireland with their biological brothers who lived in the United States, the American men were found to weigh, on average, 6% more than their Irish brothers. Environmental factors like diet and exercise are probably responsible for this difference. Thus, the *tendency* to develop obesity may be inherited, but the expression of this tendency is affected by environmental influences.

Physiological Factors

Metabolism is a key physiological factor in the regulation of body fat and body weight; hormones also play a role. A few other physiological factors have been proposed as causes for weight gain; see the box "Factors That May Contribute to Weight Gain" for more information.

Metabolism and Energy Balance Metabolism is the sum of all the vital processes by which food energy and nutrients are made available to and used by the body. The largest component of metabolism, **resting metabolic rate (RMR)**, is the energy required to maintain vital body functions, including respiration, heart rate, body temperature, and blood pressure, while the body is at rest. As

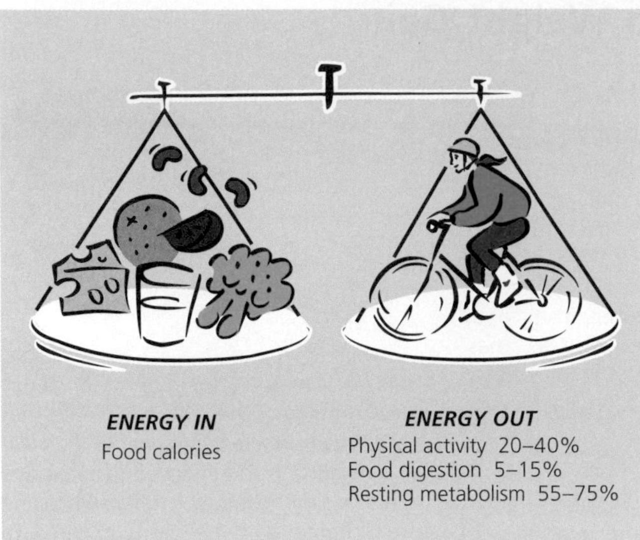

FIGURE 9.1 The energy-balance equation. To maintain your current weight, you must burn up as many calories as you take in as food each day.

shown in Figure 9.1, RMR accounts for about 55–75% of daily energy expenditure. The energy required to digest food accounts for an additional 5–15% of daily energy expenditure. The remaining 20–40% is expended during physical activity.

Both heredity and behavior affect metabolic rate. Men, who have a higher proportion of muscle mass than do women, have a higher RMR (muscle tissue is more metabolically active than fat). Also, some individuals inherit a higher or lower RMR than others. A higher RMR means that a person burns more calories while at rest and can therefore take in more calories without gaining weight.

Exercise has a positive effect on metabolism. When people exercise, they slightly increase their RMR—the number of calories their bodies burn at rest. They also increase their muscle mass, which is associated with a higher metabolic rate. The exercise itself also burns calories, raising total energy expenditure. The higher the energy expenditure, the more the person can eat without gaining weight. Weight loss or gain also affects metabolic rate. When a person loses weight, both RMR and the energy required to perform physical tasks decrease. The reverse occurs when weight is gained. One of the reasons exercise is so important during a weight-loss program is that exercise, especially resistance training, helps maintain muscle mass and metabolic rate.

The energy-balance equation is the key to weight management. If you burn the same amount of energy as you take in (a neutral energy balance), your weight remains constant. If you consume more calories than you expend (a positive energy balance), your weight increases. If you burn more calories than you consume (a negative energy balance), your weight decreases.

To create a negative energy balance and lose weight and body fat, you can increase the amount of energy you burn by increasing your level of physical activity and/or decrease the amount of energy you take in by consuming fewer calories.

WEB TERMS

binge eating A pattern of eating in which normal food consumption is interrupted by episodes of high consumption.

Hormones Hormones clearly play a role in the accumulation of body fat, especially for women. Hormonal changes at puberty, during pregnancy, and at menopause contribute to the amount and location of body fat. For example, during puberty, hormones cause the development of secondary sex characteristics, including larger breasts, wider hips, and a fat layer under the skin. This addition of body fat at puberty is normal and healthy.

One hormone thought to be linked to obesity is leptin. Secreted by the body's fat cells, leptin is carried to the brain, where it appears to let the brain know how big or small the body's fat stores are. With this information, the brain can regulate appetite and metabolic rate accordingly. Researchers hope to use leptin and other hormones to develop treatments for obesity based on appetite control; however, as most of us will admit, hunger is often *not* the primary reason we overeat. Cases of obesity based solely or primarily on hormone abnormalities do exist, but they are rare.

Lifestyle Factors

Genetic and physiological factors may increase the risk for excess body fat, but they are not sufficient to explain the increasingly high rate of obesity seen in the United States. The gene pool has not changed dramatically in the past 40 years, during which time the rate of obesity among Americans has doubled. Clearly, other factors are at work—particularly lifestyle factors such as increased energy intake and decreased physical activity.

Eating Americans have access to an abundance of highly palatable and calorie-dense foods, and many people have eating habits that contribute to weight gain. Most overweight adults will admit to eating more than they should of high-fat, high-sugar, high-calorie foods. Americans eat out more frequently now than in the past, and we rely more heavily on fast food and packaged convenience foods. Restaurant and convenience food portion sizes tend to be large, and the foods themselves are more likely to be high in fat, sugar, and calories and low in nutrients. A 2004 study found that one-third of American children eat fast food on any given day, and children who eat fast food consume almost 200 more calories per day than those who don't. In addition, studies of adults have found that the more people eat out, the more calories they consume, especially when they choose a fast-food restaurant.

Studies have also consistently found that people underestimate portion sizes by as much as 25%. When participants in one study were asked to report their food intake over the previous 24 hours, the majority underestimated their actual intake by about 600 calories. Many Americans may be unaware of how many calories they actually consume each day.

According to the Centers for Disease Control and Prevention (CDC), the average calorie intake by Americans has increased by about 300 calories per day since 1970. Even small increases in energy intake make a difference. For example, 150 additional calories per day, the amount of calories in one can of soda or beer, can translate into a 15-pound weight gain in one year (3500 calories corresponds to 1 pound of body fat). Compared to 1970, Americans today consume significantly more carbohydrates (about 65 more grams per day), slightly more fat, and about the same amount of protein. These additional carbohydrate calories come not from the fruits, vegetables, and whole grains recommended by health experts but rather from salty snacks, soft drinks, pizza, and sweet desserts.

Physical Activity Activity levels among Americans are declining, beginning in childhood and continuing throughout life. Most adults drive to work, sit all day, and then relax in front of the TV at night. During leisure time, both children and adults surf the Internet, play video games, or watch TV rather than bicycle, participate in sports, or just do yard work or chores around the house. One study found that 60% of the incidence of overweight can be linked to excessive television viewing. On average, Americans exercise 15 minutes per day and watch 170 minutes of TV and movies.

Psychosocial Factors Many people have learned to use food as a means of coping with stress and negative emotions. Eating can provide a powerful distraction from difficult feelings—loneliness, anger, boredom, anxiety, shame, sadness, inadequacy. It can be used to combat low moods, low energy levels, and low self-esteem. When eating becomes the primary means of regulating emotions, **binge eating** or other unhealthy eating patterns can develop.

QUESTIONS FOR CRITICAL THINKING AND REFLECTION

Is anyone in your family overweight? If so, can you identify factors that have contributed to this weight problem, such as heredity, eating patterns, or psychosocial factors? Has the person tried to address the problem? How was the issue handled in your family? What did family members do that helped the situation or made it worse?

MOTIVATION BOOSTER

Take a positive approach. To help keep your attitude positive and your commitment strong, state your weight management goals and strategies positively. Don't base your program on denying yourself foods or activities. Focus on what you *are* eating and on physical activities you enjoy. View occasional hunger as a positive sign that your body is using the fuel you're providing. Practice positive self-talk, and give yourself lots of rewards and encouragement.

Obesity is strongly associated with socioeconomic status. The prevalence of obesity goes down as income level goes up. More women than men are obese at lower income levels, but men are somewhat more obese at higher levels. These differences may reflect the greater sensitivity and concern for a slim physical appearance among upper-income women, as well as greater access to information about nutrition and to low-fat and low-calorie foods. It may also reflect the greater acceptance of obesity among certain ethnic groups, as well as different cultural values related to food choices.

In some families and cultures, food is used as a symbol of love and caring. It is an integral part of social gatherings and celebrations. In such cases, it may be difficult to change established eating patterns because they are linked to cultural and family values.

ADOPTING A HEALTHY LIFESTYLE FOR SUCCESSFUL WEIGHT MANAGEMENT

When all the research is assessed, it becomes clear that most weight problems are lifestyle problems. Looking at these problems in a historical context reveals why fad diets and other quick-fix approaches are not effective in reversing overweight. About 100 years ago, Americans consumed a diet very different from today's diet and got much more exercise as well. Americans now eat more calories, fat, and refined sugars and fewer complex carbohydrates. Americans today also get far less exercise than their great-grandparents did. Walking, bicycling, and farm and manual labor have all declined, resulting in a decrease in daily energy expenditure of about 200 calories.

Permanent weight loss is not something you start and stop. You need to adopt healthy behaviors that you can maintain throughout your life. Lifestyle factors that are critical for successful long-term weight management include diet and eating habits, physical activity and exercise, an ability to think positively and manage your emotions effectively, and the coping strategies you use to deal with the stresses and challenges in your life.

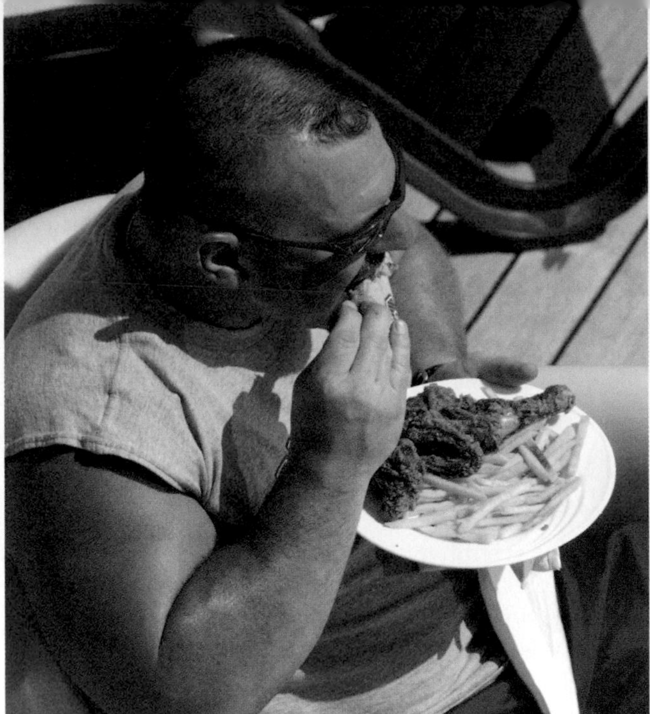

Large portions make it difficult to consume a moderate diet and manage weight. Most people significantly underestimate the amount of food they eat.

Diet and Eating Habits

In contrast to "dieting," which involves some form of food restriction and self-deprivation, "diet" refers to your daily food choices. Everyone has a diet, but not everyone is dieting. It's important to develop a diet that you enjoy and that enables you to maintain a healthy body composition.

Use MyPyramid or DASH as the basis for planning a healthy diet (see Chapter 8); choose the healthiest options within each food group. For weight management, you may need to pay special attention to total calories, portion sizes, energy density, fat and carbohydrate intake, and eating habits.

Total Calories MyPyramid suggests approximate daily energy intakes based on gender, age, and activity level (see Table 8.4). However, the precise number of calories needed to maintain weight will vary from individual to individual based on heredity, fitness status, level of physical activity, and other factors. It may be more important to focus on individual energy balance than on a general recommendation for daily calorie intake. To calculate your approximate daily caloric needs, complete Lab 9.1.

The best approach for weight loss is probably combining an increase in physical activity with moderate calorie restriction. Don't go on a crash diet. You need to consume enough food to meet your need for essential nutrients. Also, to maintain weight loss, you will probably have to maintain some degree of the calorie restriction you used to lose the weight. Therefore, it is important that you adopt a level of food intake that you can live with over the long term. For most people, maintaining weight loss is more difficult than losing the weight in the first place. To identify weight-loss goals and ways to meet them, complete Lab 9.2.

Portion Sizes Overconsumption of total calories is closely tied to portion sizes. Many Americans are unaware that the portion sizes of packaged foods and of foods served at restaurants have increased in size, and most of us significantly underestimate the amount of food we eat. One 2006 study found that the larger the meal, the greater the underestimation of calories. Limiting portion sizes is critical for weight management. For many people, concentrating on portion sizes is also a much easier method of monitoring and managing total food intake than counting calories.

To counteract portion distortion, weigh and measure your food at home for a few days every now and then. In addition, check the serving sizes listed on packaged foods. With practice, you'll learn to judge portion sizes more accurately. When eating out, try to order the smallest-sized items on the menu. When a small isn't small enough, take some home or share it with a friend. Resist the offer to supersize your portions; it may seem like a good deal, but you'll end up with calories you don't need. See Chapter 8 and the Online Learning Center for more information and hints on choosing appropriate portion sizes.

Energy (Calorie) Density Experts also recommend that you pay attention to *energy density*—the number of calories per ounce or gram of weight in a food. Studies suggest that it isn't consumption of a certain amount of fat or calories in food that reduces hunger and leads to feelings of fullness and satisfaction; rather, it is consumption of a certain weight of food. Foods that are low in energy density have more volume and bulk—that is, they are relatively heavy but have few calories. For example, for the same 100 calories, you could consume 20 baby carrots or 4 pretzel twists; you are more likely to feel full after eating the serving of carrots because it weighs 10 times that of the serving of pretzels (10 ounces versus 1 ounce).

Fresh fruits and vegetables, with their high water and fiber content, are low in energy density, as are whole-grain foods. Fresh fruits contain fewer calories and more fiber than fruit juices or drinks. Meat, ice cream, potato chips, croissants, crackers, and low-fat cakes and cookies are examples of foods high in energy density. Strategies for lowering the energy density of your diet include the following:

- Eat fruit with breakfast and for dessert.
- Add extra vegetables to sandwiches, casseroles, stir-fry dishes, pizza, pasta dishes, and fajitas.
- Start meals with a bowl of broth-based soup; include a green salad or fruit salad.
- Snack on fresh fruits and vegetables rather than crackers, chips, or other energy-dense snack foods.

- Limit serving sizes of energy-dense foods such as butter, mayonnaise, cheese, chocolate, fatty meats, croissants, and snack foods that are fried, are high in added sugars (including reduced-fat products), or contain trans fat.

Fat Calories Although some fat is needed in the diet to provide essential nutrients, you should avoid overeating fatty foods, especially those high in saturated and trans fats. There is some evidence that fat calories are more easily converted to body fat than calories from protein or carbohydrate. Limiting fat in the diet can also help you limit your total calories. As described in Chapter 8, fat should supply 20–35% of your average total daily calories, which translates into no more than 78 grams of fat in a 2000-calorie diet each day. Most of the fat in your diet should be in the form of unsaturated fats from plant and fish sources. Saturated and trans fats should be limited for weight control and disease prevention. In 2006, the American Heart Association recommended limiting trans fats to less than 1% of total calories. Foods high in unhealthy fats include full-fat dairy products, fatty meats, stick margarine, deep-fried foods, and other processed and fast foods.

As Chapter 8 made clear, moving toward a diet strong in whole grains and fresh fruits and vegetables, and away from a reliance on meat, processed foods, and fast foods is an effective approach to reducing saturated and trans fat consumption. In fact, a vegetarian—or even vegan—diet may be the solution for many people who need to greatly reduce their calories from fat. A recent study of overweight women showed that those who followed a strict vegetarian diet lost nearly twice as much weight as women who followed a standard low-cholesterol diet. Watch out for processed foods labeled "fat-free" or "reduced-fat" because they may be high in calories (see the box "Evaluating Fat and Sugar Substitutes" on p. 280). In addition, researchers have found that many Americans compensate for a lower-fat diet by consuming more calories overall. A low-fat diet that is high in calories will not lead to weight loss.

Carbohydrate Most experts agree that people should consume about 45–65% of total daily calories as carbohydrate. Food rich in whole grains and fiber are typically lower in calorie density, saturated fat, and added sugars and may promote feelings of satiety (fullness)—all characteristic features of a successful dietary pattern for weight management. They also help maintain normal blood glucose and insulin levels and reduce the risk of heart disease and diabetes. For weight management and overall health, choose a diet rich in complex carbohydrates from whole grains (Figure 9.2), vegetables, and fruits, and be moderate in your consumption of starchy vegetables like white potatoes and corn. Watch out especially for sweetened, high-calorie beverages. A 2007 analysis of government dietary data showed that Americans consume 22% of their daily calories in beverages, especially soft drinks. Many people overlook these liquid calories and don't try to compensate for them, perhaps because they find them less filling than calories from solid food.

Nutrition Facts
Serving Size 1 cup (59g)
Servings per Container about 10

Amount per Serving	Cereal	Cereal with 1/2 cup Fat Free Milk
Calories	190	230
Calories from Fat	10	10
	% Daily Value**	
Total Fat 1g*	2%	2%
Saturated Fat 0g	0%	0%
Trans Fat 0g		
Polyunsaturated Fat 0.5g		
Monounsaturated Fat 0g		
Cholesterol 0mg	0%	0%
Sodium 775mg	13%	32%
Potassium 330mg	9%	15%
Total Carbohydrate 32g	15%	11%
Dietary Fiber 8g	32%	32%
Soluble Fiber 1g		
Sugars 4g		
Other Carbohydrate 19g		
Protein 4g		

Vitamin A	15%	20%
Vitamin C	2%	2%
Calcium	2%	15%
Iron	60%	60%
Vitamin D	10%	25%
Thiamin	25%	30%
Riboflavin	25%	35%
Niacin	25%	25%
Vitamin B6	[illegible]	25%
Folic Acid	50%	50%
Vitamin B12	25%	35%
Phosphorus	20%	30%
Magnesium	25%	30%
Zinc	15%	20%
Copper	15%	15%

*Amount in Cereal. One half cup fat free milk contributes an additional 40 calories, 65mg sodium, 200mg potassium, 6g total carbohydrate (6g sugars), and 4g protein.
*Percent Daily Values are based on a 2,000 calorie diet. Your daily values may be higher or lower depending on your calorie needs:

	Calories	2,000	2,500
Total Fat	Less than	65g	80g
Sat Fat	Less than	20g	25g
Cholesterol	Less than	300mg	300mg
Sodium	Less than	2,400mg	2,400mg
Potassium		3,500mg	3,500mg
Total Carbohydrate		300g	375g
Dietary Fiber		25g	30g

INGREDIENTS: WHOLE WHEAT FLOUR, RAISINS, CORN SYRUP, SALT, MALTED BARLEY FLOUR.
VITAMINS AND MINERALS: REDUCED IRON, NIACINAMIDE, ZINC OXIDE (SOURCE OF ZINC), VITAMIN B_6, VITAMIN A PALMITATE, RIBOFLAVIN (VITAMIN B_2), THIAMIN MONONITRATE (VITAMIN B_1), FOLIC ACID, VITAMIN B_{12}, VITAMIN D.
MAY CONTAIN TRACES OF SOY.

FIGURE 9.2 High-fiber, low-calorie breakfast cereal. Many breakfast cereals are excellent sources of fiber, complex carbohydrates, and essential nutrients and are low in fat and cholesterol.

Protein Most Americans get enough protein to meet their nutritional needs. Some studies have found that increasing protein intake somewhat—while cutting calories from fat—helps people feel less hungry. If you decide to increase your protein intake, stay within the recommended intake range of 10–35% of total daily calories, and favor plant sources of protein rather than high-fat animal products.

Eating Habits Equally important to weight management is eating small, frequent meals—4–5 meals per day, including breakfast and snacks—on a dependable, regular schedule. Skipping meals leads to excessive hunger; feelings of deprivation; and increased vulnerability to binge eating or snacking on high-calorie, high-fat, or sugary foods. Establish a regular pattern of eating, and set some rules governing food choices. Rules governing breakfast might be these, for example: Choose a sugar-free, high-fiber cereal with nonfat milk and fruit most of

CRITICAL CONSUMER

Evaluating Fat and Sugar Substitutes

Foods made with fat and sugar substitutes are often promoted for weight loss. But just what are fat and sugar substitutes? And can they really contribute to weight management?

Fat Substitutes

A variety of substances are used to replace fats in processed foods and other products. Some contribute calories, protein, fiber, and/or other nutrients; others do not. Fat replacers can be classified into three general categories:

- *Carbohydrate-based fat replacers* include starch, fibers, gums, cellulose, polydextrose, and fruit purees. They are found in dairy and meat products, baked goods, salad dressing, and many other prepared foods. Newer types such as Oatrim, Z-trim, and Nu-trim are made from types of dietary fiber that may actually lower cholesterol levels. Carbohydrate-based fat replacers contribute 0–4 calories per gram.
- *Protein-based fat replacers* are typically made from milk, egg whites, soy, or whey; trade names include Simplesse, Dairy-lo, and Supro. They are used in cheese, sour cream, mayonnaise, margarine spreads, frozen desserts, salad dressings, and baked goods. These substances contribute 1–4 calories per gram.
- *Fat-based fat replacers* include glycerides, olestra, and other types of fatty acids. Some of these compounds are not absorbed well by the body and so provide fewer calories per gram (5 calories compared with the standard 9 for fats); others are impossible for the body to digest and so contribute no calories at all. Olestra, marketed under the trade name Olean and used in fried snack foods, is an example of the latter type of compound. Concerns have been raised about the safety of olestra because it reduces the absorption of fat-soluble nutrients and certain antioxidants and because it causes gastrointestinal distress in some people.

Nonnutritive Sweeteners and Sugar Alcohols

Sugar substitutes are often referred to as nonnutritive sweeteners because they provide no calories or essential nutrients. The FDA has approved five types of nonnutritive sweeteners for use in the United States: acesulfame-K (Sunett, Sweet One), aspartame (NutraSweet, Equal, NatraTaste), saccharin (Sweet 'N Low), sucralose (Splenda), and neotame. They are used in beverages, desserts, baked goods, yogurt, chewing gum, and products such as toothpaste, mouthwash, and cough syrup. Another sweetener, stevia, is an extract of a South American shrub; it is classified as a dietary supplement and so is not regulated by the FDA.

Sugar alcohols are made by altering the chemical form of sugars extracted from fruits and other plant sources; they include erythritol, isomalt, lactitol, maltitol, mannitol, sorbitol, and xylitol. Sugar alcohols provide 0.2–2.5 calories per gram, compared to 4 calories per gram in standard sugar. They have typically been used to sweeten sugar-free candies but are now being added to many sweet foods (candy, cookies, and so on) promoted as low-carbohydrate products, often combined with other sweeteners. Sugar alcohols are digested in a way that can create gas, cramps, and diarrhea if they are consumed in large amounts—more than about 10 grams in one meal.

Fat and Sugar Substitutes in Weight Management

Whether fat and sugar substitutes help you achieve and maintain a healthy weight depends on your eating and activity habits. The increase in the availability of fat-free and sugar-free foods in the United States has *not* been associated with a drop in calorie consumption. When evaluating foods containing fat and sugar substitutes, consider these issues:

- ***Is the food lower in calories or just lower in fat?*** Reduced-fat foods often contain extra sugar to improve the taste and texture lost when fat is removed, so such foods may be as high or even higher in total calories than their fattier counterparts.
- ***Are you choosing foods with fat and/or sugar substitutes instead of foods you typically eat or in addition to foods you typically eat?*** If you consume low-fat, no-sugar-added ice cream instead of regular ice cream, you may save calories. But if you add such ice cream to your daily diet simply because it is lower in fat and sugar, your overall calorie consumption—and your weight—may increase.
- ***How many foods containing fat and sugar substitutes do you consume each day?*** Although the FDA has given at least provisional approval to all the fat and sugar substitutes currently available, health concerns about some of these products linger. One way to limit any potential adverse effects is to read labels and monitor how much of each product you consume.
- ***Is an even healthier choice available?*** Many of the foods containing fat and sugar substitutes are low-nutrient snack foods. Fruits, vegetables, and whole grains are healthier snack choices.

the time; have a hard-boiled egg no more than three times a week; save pancakes and waffles for special occasions. For effective weight management, it is better to consume the majority of calories during the day rather than in the evening.

Decreeing some foods off-limits generally sets up a rule to be broken. The better rule is "everything in moderation." No foods need to be entirely off-limits, though some should be eaten judiciously.

PHYSICAL ACTIVITY AND EXERCISE

Regular physical activity is another important lifestyle factor in weight management. Physical activity and exercise burn calories and keep the metabolism geared to using food for energy instead of storing it as fat. Making significant cuts in food intake in order to lose weight is a difficult strategy to maintain; increasing your physical activity is a much better strategy. Regular physical activity also protects against weight gain and is essential for maintaining weight loss.

Physical Activity All physical activity will help you manage your weight. The first step in becoming more active is to incorporate more physical activity into your daily life. If you are currently sedentary, start by accumulating 30 minutes or more of moderate-intensity physical activity—walking, gardening, doing housework, and so on—on most, or preferably all, days of the week, for a total of 150 minutes or more per week. Even a small increase in activity level can help maintain your current weight or help you lose a moderate amount of weight (Table 9.2). In fact, research suggests that fidgeting—stretching, squirming, standing up, and so on—may help prevent weight gain in some people. If you simply walked around during TV commercials while watching 2 hours of prime-time programming, you'd accumulate more than 30 minutes of physical activity. Short bouts of activity spread throughout the day can produce many of the same health benefits as continuous physical activity.

If you are overweight and want to lose weight, or if you are trying to maintain a lower weight following weight loss, a greater amount of physical activity can help. Researchers have found that people who lose weight and don't regain it typically burn about 2800 calories per week in physical activity—the equivalent of about 1 hour of brisk walking per day. The 2005 Dietary Guidelines for Americans recommend at least 60 minutes of daily physical activity to avoid slow weight gain in adulthood, and at least 60–90 minutes of activity to lose weight or maintain weight loss.

Exercise Once you become more active every day, begin a formal exercise program that includes cardiorespiratory endurance exercise, resistance training, and stretching exercises. (See Chapter 7 for advice on creating a complete, personalized exercise program.) Moderate-intensity endurance exercise, if performed frequently for a relatively long duration, can burn a significant number of calories. Endurance training also increases the rate at which your body uses calories after your exercise session is over—burning an additional 5–180 extra calories, depending on the intensity of exercise. Resistance training builds muscle mass, and more muscle translates into a higher metabolic rate. Resistance training can also help you maintain your muscle mass during a period of weight loss, helping you avoid the significant drop in RMR associated with weight loss.

Regular physical activity, maintained throughout life, makes weight management easier. The sooner you establish good habits, the better. The key to success is making exercise an integral part of a lifestyle you can enjoy now and will enjoy in the future.

Table 9.2 Calorie Costs of Selected Physical Activities*

To determine how many calories you burn when you engage in a particular activity, multiply the calorie multiplier given below by your body weight (in pounds) and then by the number of minutes you exercise.

Activity	Cal/lb/ min	× Body weight	× min	= Total Calories
Cycling (13 mph)	.071	_____	____	_____
Dancing (popular)	.049	_____	____	_____
Digging	.062	_____	____	_____
Driving a car	.020	_____	____	_____
Doing housework	.029	_____	____	_____
Painting a house	.034	_____	____	_____
Shoveling snow	.052	_____	____	_____
Sitting quietly	.009	_____	____	_____
Sleeping and resting	.008	_____	____	_____
Standing quietly	.012	_____	____	_____
Typing or writing	.013	_____	____	_____
Walking briskly (4.5 mph)	.048	_____	____	_____

***See Chapter 7 for the energy costs of fitness activities.**

SOURCE: Adapted from Kusinitz, I., and M. Fine. 1995. *Your Guide to Getting Fit*, 3rd ed. Mountain View, Calif.: Mayfield.

Thoughts and Emotions

The way you think about yourself and your world influences, and is influenced by, how you feel and how you act. In fact, research on people who have a weight problem indicates that low self-esteem and the negative emotions that accompany it are significant problems. People with low self-esteem mentally compare the actual self to an internally held picture of the "ideal self," an image based on perfectionistic goals and beliefs about how they and others should be. The more these two pictures differ, the larger the impact on self-esteem and the more likely the presence of negative emotions.

Besides the internal picture we carry of ourselves, all of us carry on a internal dialogue about events happening to us and around us. This **self-talk** can be either self-deprecating or positively motivating, depending on our beliefs and attitudes. Having realistic beliefs and goals and engaging in positive self-talk and problem solving support a healthy lifestyle. (Chapter 10 and Activity 11 in the Behavior Change Workbook at the end of the text include strategies for developing realistic self-talk.)

self-talk A person's internal comments and discussion; instrumental in shaping self-image.

MOTIVATION BOOSTER

Be aware of your choices. Your environment may not always support your efforts at weight management, but you are in charge of your own behavior. Weight management is about choice. You have many opportunities to make positive choices about food and physical activity every day. Keep a journal to help raise your awareness of the choices you are making. Watch out for automatic eating or eating in response to emotions rather than hunger; think before you eat, and ask yourself why you are eating now and why you are choosing certain foods. View daily energy intake as a personal budget that you get to spend however you choose each day. Strategies like these can help build your sense of confidence and control and improve your chance of long-term success.

QUESTIONS FOR CRITICAL THINKING AND REFLECTION

Have you ever used food as an escape, when you were stressed out or distraught? Were you aware of what you were doing at the time? How can you avoid using food as a coping mechanism in the future?

Coping Strategies

Appropriate coping strategies help you deal with the stresses of life; they are also an important lifestyle factor in weight management. One strategy that many people adopt for coping is eating. (Others may cope by turning to drugs, alcohol, smoking, or gambling.) Those who overeat might use food to alleviate loneliness or to serve as a pickup for fatigue, as an antidote to boredom, or as a distraction from problems. Some people even overeat to punish themselves for real or imagined transgressions.

Those who recognize that they are using food in these ways can analyze their eating habits with fresh eyes. They can consciously attempt to find new coping strategies and begin to use food appropriately—to fuel life's activities, to foster growth, and to bring pleasure, *not* to manage stress. For a summary of the components of weight management through healthy lifestyle choices, see the box "Lifestyle Strategies for Successful Weight Management."

APPROACHES TO OVERCOMING A WEIGHT PROBLEM

Each year, Americans spend more than $40 billion on various weight-loss plans and products. If you are overweight, you may already be planning how to go about losing weight and keeping it off. You have many options.

Doing It Yourself

If you need to lose weight, focus on adopting the healthy lifestyle described throughout this book. The "right" weight for you will naturally evolve, and you won't have to diet. Combine modest cuts in energy intake with exercise, and avoid very-low-calorie diets. (In general, a low-calorie diet should provide 1200–1500 calories per day.) By achieving a negative energy balance of 250–1000 calories per day, you'll produce the recommended weight loss of ½–2 pounds per week. Realize that most low-calorie diets cause a rapid loss of body water at first. When this phase passes, weight loss declines. As a result, people are often misled into believing that their efforts are not working. They give up, not realizing that smaller losses later in the diet are actually better than the initial big losses, because later loss is mostly fat loss, whereas initial loss was primarily fluid. For someone who is overweight, reasonable weight loss is 8–10% of body weight over 6 months.

For many Americans, maintaining weight loss is a bigger challenge than losing weight. Most weight lost during a period of dieting is regained. When planning a weight-management program, you need to include strategies that you can maintain over the long term, both for food choices and for physical activity. Weight management is a lifelong project. A registered dietitian or nutritionist can recommend an appropriate plan for you when you want to lose weight on your own. For more tips on losing weight on your own, refer to the section later in the chapter on creating an individual weight-management plan.

Diet Books

Many people who try to lose weight by themselves fall prey to one or more of the dozens of diet books on the market. Although some books contain useful advice and motivational tips, most make empty promises. Here are some guidelines for evaluating and choosing a diet book:

- Reject books that advocate an unbalanced way of eating, such as a high-carbohydrate-only diet or a low-carbohydrate, high-protein diet. Also reject books promoting a single food, such as cabbage or grapefruit.
- Reject books that claim to be based on a "scientific breakthrough" or to have the "secret" to success.
- Reject books that use gimmicks, like matching eating to blood type, hyping insulin resistance as the single cause of obesity, combining foods in special ways to achieve weight loss, rotating levels of calories, or purporting that a weight problem is due to food allergies, food sensitivities, yeast infections, or hormone imbalances.
- Reject books that promise quick weight loss or that limit the selection of foods.
- Accept books that advocate a balanced approach to diet plus exercise and offer sound nutrition advice.

TAKE CHARGE

Lifestyle Strategies for Successful Weight Management

Food Choices

- Follow the recommendations in MyPyramid for eating a moderate, varied diet. Focus on making good choices from each food group.
- Favor foods with a *low energy density* and a *high nutrient density.*
- Check food labels for serving sizes, calories, and nutrient levels.
- Watch for hidden calories. Reduced-fat foods often have as many calories as their full-fat versions. Fat-based condiments like butter, margarine, mayonnaise, and salad dressings provide about 100 calories per tablespoon; added sugars such as jams, jellies, and syrup are also packed with calories.
- Drink fewer calories in the form of soda, fruit drinks, sports drinks, alcohol, and specialty coffees and teas.
- For problem foods, try eating small amounts under controlled conditions. Go out for a scoop of ice cream, for example, rather than buying half a gallon for your freezer.

Planning and Serving

- Keep a log of what you eat. Before you begin your program, your log will provide a realistic picture of your current diet and what changes you can make. Once you start your program, a log will keep you focused on your food choices and portion sizes. Track the food eaten, your hunger level, the circumstances (location, other activities), outside influences (environment, other people), and your thoughts and emotions.
- Eat 4–5 meals/snacks daily, *including breakfast*, to distribute calories throughout your day. In studies, people who eat breakfast consume fewer calories overall over the course of the day. Fix more meals yourself and eat out less often. Keep low-calorie snacks on hand to combat the "munchies": baby carrots, popcorn, and fresh fruits and vegetables are good choices.
- When shopping, make a list and stick to it. Don't shop when you're hungry. Avoid aisles that contain problem foods.
- Consume the majority of your daily calories during the day, not in the evening.
- Pay special attention to portion sizes. Use measuring cups and spoons and a food scale to become more familiar with appropriate portion sizes.
- Serve meals on small plates and in small bowls to help you eat smaller portions without feeling deprived.
- Eat only in specifically designated spots. Remove food from other areas of your home.
- When you eat, just eat—don't do anything else, such as reading or watching TV.
- Avoid late-night eating, a behavior specifically associated with weight gain among college students.
- Eat slowly. It takes time for your brain to get the message that your stomach is full. Take small bites and chew food thoroughly. Pay attention to every bite, and enjoy your food. Between bites, try putting your fork or spoon down and taking sips of a beverage.
- When you're done eating, remove your plate. Cue yourself that the meal is over; drink a glass of water, suck on a mint, chew gum, or brush your teeth.

Special Occasions

- When you eat out, choose a restaurant where you can make healthy food choices. Ask the server not to put bread and butter on the table before the meal, and request that sauces and salad dressings be served on the side. If portion sizes are large, take half your food home for a meal later in the week. Don't choose supersized meals.
- If you cook a large meal for friends, send leftovers home with your guests.
- If you're eating at a friend's, eat a little and leave the rest. Don't eat to be polite; if someone offers you food you don't want, thank the person and decline firmly.
- Take care during the winter holidays. Research indicates that people gain less than they think during the winter holidays (about a pound) but that the weight isn't lost during the rest of the year, leading to slow, steady weight gain.

Physical Activity and Stress Management

- Increase your level of daily physical activity. If you have been sedentary for a long time or are seriously overweight, increase your level of activity slowly. Start by walking 10 minutes at a time, and work toward 30–60 minutes or more of moderate physical activity per day.
- Begin a formal exercise program that includes cardiorespiratory endurance exercise, strength training, and stretching.
- Develop techniques for handling stress. Try walking, or use a relaxation technique. Practice positive self-talk. Get adequate sleep. (See Chapter 10 for more on stress management.)
- Develop strategies for coping with nonhunger cues to eat, such as boredom, sleepiness, or anxiety. Try calling a friend, taking a shower, or reading a magazine.
- Tell family members and friends that you're changing your eating and exercise habits. Ask them to be supportive.

Visit the Small Steps site for more tips (www.smallstep.gov).

There are many plans and supplements promoted for weight loss, but few have any research supporting their effectiveness for long-term weight management. Developing lifelong healthy eating and exercise habits is the best approach for achieving and maintaining a healthy body composition.

Many diets cause weight loss if maintained; the real difficulty is finding a safe and healthy pattern of food choices and physical activity that results in long-term maintenance of a healthy body weight and reduced risk of chronic disease (see the box "Is Any Diet Best for Weight Loss?"). In addition to the health concerns associated with some diets recommended by popular books, researchers have found low long-term success rates for many diets—again reinforcing the idea that weight management is a lifelong project that requires commitment to reasonable eating and exercise habits. Research into diet and exercise strategies for weight loss is ongoing, so you can expect to hear about further findings that may help you make informed decisions about your own weight-management program. Worksheets for evaluating diet books and commercial weight-loss plans can be found on the Online Learning Center.

Dietary Supplements and Diet Aids

The number of dietary supplements and other weight-loss aids on the market has also increased in recent years. Promoted in advertisements, magazines, direct mail campaigns, and infomercials and on Web sites, these products typically promise a quick and easy path to weight loss. Most of these products are marketed as dietary supplements and so are subject to fewer regulations than over-the-counter (OTC) medications. A 2002 report from the Federal Trade Commission stated that more than half of advertisements for weight-loss products made representations that are likely to be false. In addition, use of OTC products doesn't help in the adoption of lifestyle behaviors that can help people achieve and maintain a healthy weight over the long term.

The bottom line on nonprescription diet aids is, Caveat emptor (Let the buyer beware). There is no quick and easy way to lose weight. The most effective approach is to develop healthy diet and exercise habits and to make them a permanent part of your lifestyle. The following sections describe some commonly marketed OTC products for weight loss.

Formula Drinks and Food Bars Canned diet drinks, powders used to make shakes, and diet food bars and snacks are designed to achieve weight loss by substituting for some or all of a person's daily food intake. However, most people find it difficult to use these products for long periods, and muscle loss and other serious health problems may result if they are used as the sole source of nutrition for an extended period. Use of such products sometimes results in rapid short-term weight loss, but the weight is typically regained because users don't learn to change their eating and lifestyle behaviors.

Herbal Supplements As described in Chapter 8, herbs are marketed as dietary supplements, so there is little information about effectiveness, proper dosage, drug interactions, and side effects. In addition, labels may not accurately reflect the ingredients and dosages present, and safe manufacturing practices are not guaranteed. For example, the substitution of a toxic herb for another compound during the manufacture of a Chinese herbal weight-loss preparation caused more than 100 cases of kidney damage and cancer among users in Europe.

In 2004, the FDA banned the sale of ephedra (*ma huang*), stating that it presented a significant and unreasonable risk to human health. The ban has withstood legal appeals and remains in place. Ephedrine, the active ingredient in ephedra, is structurally similar to amphetamine and was widely used in weight-loss supplements. It may suppress appetite, but adverse effects have included elevated blood pressure, panic attacks, seizures, insomnia, and increased risk of heart attack or stroke, particularly when combined with another stimulant, such as caffeine. The synthetic stimulant phenylpropanolamine was banned in 2000 for similar reasons. Other herbal stimulants still on the market are described in Table 9.3 (p. 286).

Other Supplements Fiber is another common ingredient in OTC diet aids, promoted for appetite control. However, dietary fiber acts as a bulking agent in the large intestine, not the stomach, so it doesn't have a pronounced effect on appetite. In addition, many diet aids contain only 3 or fewer grams of fiber, which does not contribute much toward the recommended daily intake

CRITICAL CONSUMER

Is Any Diet Best for Weight Loss?

Experts agree that reducing calorie intake promotes weight loss. However, many popular weight-loss plans include a special hook and promote specific food choices and macronutrient (protein, fat, carbohydrate) combinations as best for weight loss. Research findings have been mixed, but two points are clear. Total calorie intake matters, and the best diet is probably the one you can stick with.

Low-Carbohydrate Diets

Some low-carb diets advocate fewer than 10% of total calories from carbohydrates, compared to the 45–65% recommended by the Food and Nutrition Board. Some suggest daily carbohydrate intake below the 130 grams needed to provide essential carbohydrates in the diet. Small studies have found that low-carbohydrate diets can help with short-term weight loss and be safe for relatively short periods of time—although unpleasant effects such as bad breath, constipation, and headache are fairly common.

Some low-carb diets tend to be very high in protein and saturated fat and low in fiber, whole grains, vegetables, and fruits (and thus lack some essential nutrients). Diets high in protein and saturated fat have been linked to an increased risk of heart disease, high blood pressure, and cancer. Other low-carb diets, though still emphasizing protein, limit saturated fats, allow most vegetables after an initial period, and advocate switching to "healthy carbs." These diets are healthier than the more extreme versions.

Low-Fat Diets

Many experts advocate diets that are relatively low in fat, high in carbohydrates, and moderate in protein. Critics of these diets blame them for rising rates of obesity and note that very-low-fat, very-high-carbohydrate diets can increase triglyceride levels and reduce levels of good (HDL) cholesterol in some people. These negative effects can be counteracted with moderate-intensity exercise, however, and low-fat diets combined with physical activity can be safe and effective for many people.

Few experts take the position that low-fat, high-carbohydrate diets, apart from overall diet and activity patterns, are responsible for the increase in obesity among Americans. However, the debate has highlighted the importance of total calorie intake and the quality of carbohydrate choices. A low-fat diet is not a license to consume excess calories, even in low-fat foods.

How Do Popular Diets Measure Up?

In one recent study, obese people on a very-low-carbohydrate, high-fat diet lost more weight over a 6-month period than people following a moderate-fat diet. After a year, however, the difference in weight loss between the two groups was no longer significant, and the dropout rate from both groups was high.

A 2005 study followed participants in four popular diets that emphasize different strategies—Weight Watchers (restricted portion sizes and calories), Atkins (low-carbohydrate, high-fat), Zone (relatively high protein, moderate fat and carbohydrate), and Ornish (very low fat). Each of these diets modestly reduced body weight and heart disease risk factors. There was no significant difference in weight loss at 1 year among the diets, and the more closely people adhered to each diet, the more weight they lost. Dropout rates were high—about 50% for Atkins and Ornish and 35% for Weight Watchers and Zone.

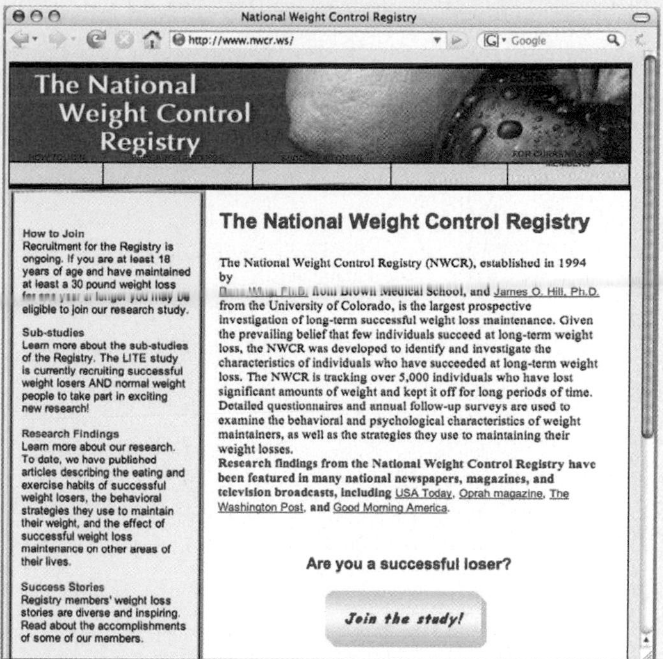

Energy Balance Counts: The National Weight Control Registry

Future research may determine that certain macronutrient patterns are somewhat more helpful for disease reduction in people with particular risk profiles. In terms of weight loss, however, such differences among diets are likely overshadowed by the importance of total calorie intake and physical activity. Important lessons about energy balance can be drawn from the National Weight Control Registry, an ongoing study of people who have lost significant amounts of weight and kept it off. The average participant in the registry has lost 71 pounds and kept the weight off for more than 5 years. Nearly all participants use a combination of diet and exercise to manage their weight. Most consume diets moderate in calories and relatively low in fat and fried foods; they monitor their body weight and their food intake frequently. Participants engage in an average of 60 minutes of moderate physical activity daily. The National Weight Control Registry study illustrates that to lose weight and keep it off, you must decrease daily calorie intake and/or increase daily physical activity—and continue to do so over your lifetime.

SOURCES: Battle of the diet books II. 2006. *Nutrition Action Healthletter,* July/August. Dansinger, M. L., et al. 2005. Comparison of the Atkins, Ornish, Weight Watchers, and Zone diets for weight loss and heart disease risk reduction. *Journal of the American Medical Association* 293(1): 43–53. Hays, N. P., et al. 2004. Effects of an ad libitum low-fat, high-carbohydrate diet on body weight, body composition, and fat distribution in older men and women. *Archives of Internal Medicine* 164(2): 210–217. Hill, J., and R. Wing. 2003. The National Weight Control Registry. *Permanente Journal* 7(3): 34–37. Bravata, D. M., et al. 2003. Efficacy and safety of low-carbohydrate diets. *Journal of the American Medical Association* 289: 1837–1850. Foster, G. D., et al. 2003. A randomized trial of low-carbohydrate diet for obesity. *New England Journal of Medicine* 348: 2082–2090.

Table 9.3	Ingredients Commonly Found in Weight-Loss Products		
Common Name	**Use/Claim**	**Evidence/Efficacy**	**Safety Issues**
Bitter orange extract (*Citrus aurantium*)	CNS stimulant	Limited evidence	Highly concentrated extracts may increase blood pressure; should not be used by people with cardiac problems
Caffeine	CNS stimulant: increases fat metabolism	Amplifies effects of ephedra	Generally considered safe; caution advised in caffeine-sensitive individuals
Garcinia cambogia	May interfere with fat metabolism or suppress appetite	Inconclusive evidence	Short-term use (<12 weeks) generally considered safe when used as directed
Green tea extract	Diuretic; increases metabolism	Limited evidence	Generally considered safe
Guarana	CNS stimulant; diuretic	Few clinical trials	Same as for caffeine; overdose can cause painful urination, abdominal spasms, and vomiting
Senna, cascara, aloe, buckthorn berries	Stimulant, laxative	Not effective for weight loss	Chronic use decreases muscle tone in large intestine, causes electrolyte imbalances, and leads to dependence on laxatives
Tea, kola, dandelion, bucho, uva-ursi, damiana, juniper	Diuretic	Not effective for weight loss	Chronic use can cause possible electrolyte imbalance in some people
Yerba mate	Stimulant, laxative, diuretic	Limited evidence	Long-term use as beverage may increase risk of oral cancer

SOURCE: Adapted from Leslie, K. K. 2003. Herbal weight-loss products: Effective and appropriate? *Today's Dietician* 5(8).

of 25–38 grams. Other popular dietary supplements include conjugated linoleic acid, carnitine, chromium, pyruvate, calcium, B vitamins, chitosan, and a number of products labeled "fat absorbers," "fat blockers," or "starch blockers." Research has not found these products to be effective, and many have potentially adverse side effects.

Weight-Loss Programs

Weight-loss programs come in a variety of types, including noncommercial support organizations, commercial programs, Web sites, and clinical programs.

Noncommercial Weight-Loss Programs Noncommercial programs such as TOPS (Take Off Pounds Sensibly) and Overeaters Anonymous (OA) mainly provide group support. They do not advocate any particular diet, but they do recommend seeking professional advice for creating an individualized diet and exercise plan. Like Alcoholics Anonymous, OA is a 12-step program with a spiritual orientation that promotes abstinence from compulsive overeating. These types of programs are generally free. Your physician or a registered dietitian can also provide information and support for weight loss.

Commercial Weight-Loss Programs Commercial weight-loss programs typically provide group support, nutrition education, physical activity recommendations, and behavior modification advice. Some also make available packaged foods to assist in following dietary advice. A 2005 study evaluated major commercial weight-loss programs—including Weight Watchers, NutriSystem, Jenny Craig, and L A Weight Loss—for 12 weeks or more with a 1-year follow-up assessment. Results showed Weight Watchers to be the only moderately priced commercial program with a mean loss of 5% of initial weight.

A responsible and safe weight-loss program should have the following features:

- The recommended diet should be safe and balanced, include all the food groups, and meet the DRIs for all nutrients. Physical activity and exercise should be strongly encouraged.
- The program should promote slow, steady weight loss averaging ½–2 pounds per week. (There may be rapid weight loss initially due to fluid loss.)
- If a participant plans to lose more than 20 pounds, has any health problems, or is taking medication on a regular basis, the program should offer physician evaluation and monitoring. The staff of the program should include qualified counselors and health professionals.
- The program should include plans for weight maintenance after the weight-loss phase is over.
- The program should provide information on all fees and costs, including those of supplements and prepackaged foods, as well as data on risks and expected outcomes of participating in the program.

You should also consider whether a program fits your lifestyle and whether you are truly ready to make a commitment to it. A strong commitment and a plan for maintenance are especially important because studies indicate that only 10–15% of program participants maintain their weight loss; the rest gain back all or more than they had lost. One study of participants found that regular exercise was the best predictor of maintaining weight loss, and frequent television viewing was the best predictor of weight gain.

Online Weight-Loss Programs A recent addition to the weight-loss program scene is the Internet-based program. Most such Web sites offer a cross between self-help and group support through chat rooms, bulletin boards, and e-newsletters. Many sites offer online self-assessment for diet and physical activity habits as well as a meal plan; some provide access to a staff professional for individualized help. Many are free, but some charge a small weekly or monthly fee.

Preliminary research suggests that this type of program provides an alternative to in-person diet counseling and can lead to weight loss for some people. Studies found that people who logged on more frequently tended to lose more weight; weekly online contact in terms of behavior therapy proved most successful for weight loss. The criteria used to evaluate commercial programs can also be applied to Internet-based programs. In addition, make sure a program offers member-to-member support and access to staff professionals.

Clinical Weight-Loss Programs Medically supervised clinical programs are usually located in a hospital or other medical setting. Designed to help those who are severely obese, these programs typically involve a closely monitored very-low-calorie diet. The cost of a clinical program is usually high, but insurance often covers part of the fee.

Prescription Drugs

For a medicine to cause weight loss, it must reduce energy consumption, increase energy expenditure, and/or interfere with energy absorption. The medications most often prescribed for weight loss are appetite suppressants that reduce feelings of hunger or increase feelings of fullness. Appetite suppressants usually work by increasing levels of catecholamine or serotonin, two brain chemicals that affect mood and appetite.

All prescription weight-loss drugs have potential side effects. Those that affect catecholamine levels, including phentermine (Ionamin, Obenix, Fastin, and Adipex-P), diethylpropion (Tenuate), and mazindol (Sanorex), may cause sleeplessness, nervousness, and euphoria. Sibutramine (Meridia) acts on both the serotonin and catecholamine systems; it may trigger increases in blood pressure and heart rate. Headaches, constipation or diarrhea, dry mouth, and insomnia are other side effects.

Most appetite suppressants are approved by the FDA only for short-term use. Two drugs, however, are approved for longer-term use: sibutramine and orlistat (Xenical). Sibutramine's safety and efficacy record is good, but regular monitoring of blood pressure is required during therapy. Orlistat lowers calorie consumption by blocking fat absorption in the intestines; it prevents about 30% of the fat in food from being digested. Similar to the fat substitute olestra, orlistat also reduces the absorption of fat-soluble vitamins and antioxidants. Therefore, taking a vitamin supplement is highly recommended if taking orlistat. Side effects include diarrhea, cramping, and other gastrointestinal problems if users do not follow a low-fat diet. In 2007, the FDA approved Orlistat for over-the-counter use by adults 18 years and over.

A new drug, rimonabant (Acomplia) has been used successfully in Europe and is now awaiting FDA approval for use in the United States. Rimonabant suppresses appetite by acting on certain brain receptors. Studies show that rimonabant may lead to greater weight loss than other drugs and may help users keep weight off for a longer time. Side effects include mild diarrhea, dizziness, and nausea.

All of these medications work best in conjunction with behavior modification. Appetite suppressants produce modest weight loss—about 5–22 pounds above the loss expected with nondrug obesity treatments. Individuals respond differently, however, and some experience more weight loss than others. Weight loss tends to level off or reverse after 4–6 months on a medication, and many people regain the weight they've lost when they stop taking the drug.

Side effects and risks are other concerns. In 1997, the FDA removed from the market two prescription weight-loss drugs, fenfluramine (Pondimin) and dexfenfluramine (Redux), after their use was linked to potentially life-threatening heart valve problems. (Fenfluramine was used most often in combination with phentermine, an off-label combination referred to as "fen/phen.") It appears that people who took these drugs over a long period or at high dosages are at greatest risk for problems, but the FDA recommends that anyone who has taken either of these drugs be examined by a physician.

Prescription weight-loss drugs are not for people who just want to lose a few pounds. The latest federal guidelines advise people to try lifestyle modification for at least 6 months before trying drug therapy. Prescription drugs are recommended only in certain cases: for people who have been unable to lose weight with nondrug options and who have a BMI over 30 (or over 27 if two or more additional risk factors such as diabetes and high blood pressure are present).

Surgery

About 5% of Americans are severely obese, meaning they have a BMI of 40 or higher or are 100 pounds or

QUESTIONS FOR CRITICAL THINKING AND REFLECTION

Why do you think people continue to buy into fad diets and weight-loss gimmicks, even though they are constantly reminded that the key to weight management is lifestyle change? Have you ever tried a fad diet or dietary supplement? If so, what were your reasons for trying it? What were the results?

more over recommended weight. Severe obesity is a serious medical condition that is often complicated by other health problems such as diabetes, sleep disorders, heart disease, and arthritis. Surgical intervention may be necessary as a treatment of last resort. According to a National Institutes of Health Consensus Conference, gastric bypass surgery may be recommended for patients with a BMI greater than 40, or greater than 35 with obesity-related illnesses. Due to the increasing prevalence of severe obesity, surgical treatment of obesity is growing worldwide. Obesity-related health conditions, as well as risk of premature death, generally improve after surgical weight loss. Surgery is not without risks, however, and is generally appropriate only for people with severe obesity-related health problems.

Gastric bypass surgery modifies the gastrointestinal tract by changing either the size of the stomach or the way the intestine drains, thereby reducing food intake. The two most common surgeries are the Roux-en-Y gastric bypass and the vertical banded gastroplasty (VGB/Lap-Band). Potential complications from surgery include nutritional deficiencies, fat intolerance, nausea, vomiting, and reflux; as many as 10–20% of patients may require follow-up surgery to address complications. Weight loss from surgery generally ranges between 40% and 70% of total body weight over the course of a year. The key to success is to have adequate follow-up and to stay motivated so that life behaviors and eating patterns are changed permanently.

The surgical technique of liposuction involves the removal of small amounts of fat from specific locations. Liposuction is not a method for treating obesity.

Psychological Help

Many people can lose weight simply by increasing their physical activity level and moderately restricting total calories, especially fat calories. When concern about body weight and shape have developed into an eating disorder, professional help is recommended. A therapist should have experience in weight management, body image issues, eating disorders, addictions, and abuse issues. Your physician may be able to provide a referral.

BODY IMAGE

The collective picture of the body as seen through the mind's eye, **body image** consists of perceptions, images, thoughts, attitudes, and emotions. A negative body image is characterized by dissatisfaction with the body in general or some part of the body in particular.

Severe Body Image Problems

Poor body image can cause significant psychological distress. A person can become preoccupied by a perceived defect in appearance, thereby damaging self-esteem and interfering with relationships. Adolescents and adults who have a negative body image are more likely to diet restrictively, eat compulsively, or develop some other form of disordered eating.

When dissatisfaction becomes extreme, the condition is called body dysmorphic disorder (BDD). BDD affects about 2% of Americans, males and females in equal numbers; BDD usually begins before age 18 but can begin in adulthood. Sufferers are overly concerned with physical appearance, often focusing on what they perceive to be slight "flaws" of the face or head. Individuals with BDD may spend hours every day thinking about their flaws and looking at themselves in mirrors; they may desire and seek repeated cosmetic surgeries. BDD is related to obsessive-compulsive disorder and can lead to depression, social phobia, and suicide if left untreated. Medication and therapy can help people with BDD.

In some cases, body image may bear little resemblance to fact. A person with the eating disorder anorexia nervosa typically has a severely distorted body image—she believes herself to be fat even when she has become emaciated (see the next section for more on anorexia). Distorted body image is also a hallmark of **muscle dysmorphia,** a disorder experienced by some bodybuilders in which they see themselves as small and out of shape despite being very muscular. People with muscle dysmorphia may let obsessive bodybuilding interfere with their work and relationships. They may also use steroids and other potentially dangerous muscle-building drugs.

To assess your body image, complete the body image self-test in Lab 9.3.

Acceptance and Change

There are limits to the changes that can be made to body weight and body shape, both of which are influenced by heredity. Knowing when the limits to healthy change have been reached—and learning to accept those limits—is crucial for overall wellness. Women in particular tend to measure self-worth in terms of their appearance; when they don't measure up to an unrealistic cultural ideal, they see themselves as defective, and

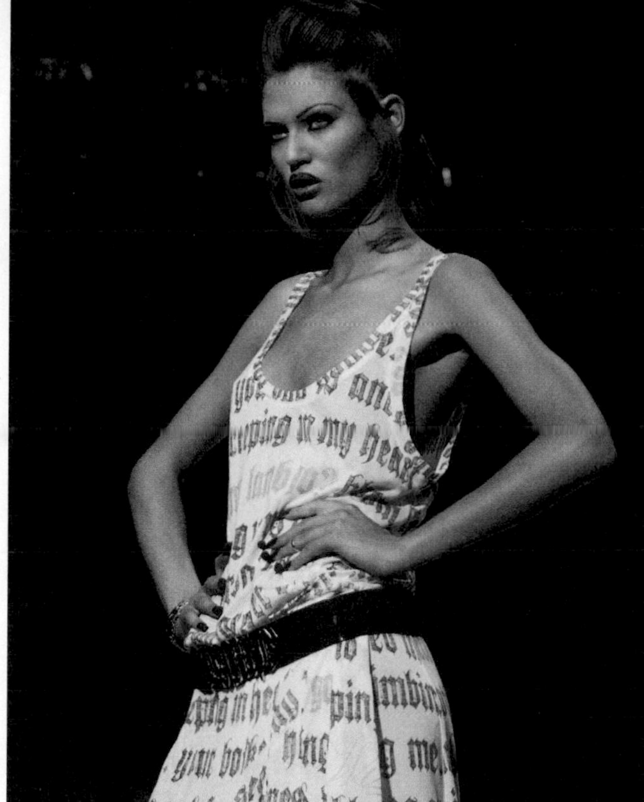

The image of the ideal body promoted by the fashion and fitness industries doesn't reflect the wide range of body shapes and sizes that are associated with good health. An overconcern with body image can contribute to low self-esteem and the development of eating disorders.

their self-esteem falls. The result can be negative body image, disordered eating, or even a full-blown eating disorder (see the box "Gender, Ethnicity, and Body Image" on p. 290).

Weight management needs to take place in a positive and realistic atmosphere. For an obese person, losing as few as 10 pounds can reduce blood pressure and improve mood. The hazards of excessive dieting and overconcern about body weight need to be countered by a change in attitude. A reasonable weight must take into account a person's weight history, social circumstances, metabolic profile, and psychological well-being.

EATING DISORDERS

Problems with body weight and weight control are not limited to excessive body fat. A growing number of people, especially adolescent girls and young women, experience **eating disorders,** characterized by severe disturbances in eating patterns and eating-related behavior. The major eating disorders are anorexia nervosa, bulimia nervosa, and binge-eating disorder. Eating disorders affect about 10 million American females and 1 million males. Many more people have abnormal eating habits and attitudes about food that, although not meeting the criteria for a full-blown eating disorder, do disrupt their lives (see the box "Borderline Disordered Eating" on p. 291). To assess your eating habits, complete Lab 9.3.

Although many different explanations for the development of eating disorders have been proposed, they share one central feature: a dissatisfaction with body image and body weight. Such dissatisfaction is created by distorted thinking, including perfectionistic beliefs, unreasonable demands for self-control, and excessive self-criticism. Dissatisfaction with body weight leads to dysfunctional attitudes about eating, such as fear of fat, preoccupation with food, and problematic eating behaviors. Eating disorders are classified as mental disorders.

Anorexia Nervosa

A person with **anorexia nervosa** does not eat enough food to maintain a reasonable body weight. A BMI of 17.5 or less is sometimes used as a diagnostic criterion for anorexia. Anorexia affects 1% of Americans, or about 3 million people, 95% of them female. Although it can occur later, anorexia typically develops between ages 12 and 18. People with anorexia have an intense fear of gaining weight or becoming fat. Their body image is distorted so that, even when emaciated, they think they are fat. People with anorexia may engage in compulsive behaviors or rituals that help them keep from eating; they also commonly use vigorous and prolonged physical activity to reduce body weight. Although they may express a great interest in food, their diet becomes more and more extreme.

Anorexics are typically introverted, emotionally reserved, and socially insecure. Their entire sense of self-esteem may be tied up in their evaluation of their body shape and weight.

Anorexia nervosa has been linked to a variety of medical complications, including disorders of the cardiovascular, gastrointestinal, and endocrine systems. Because of

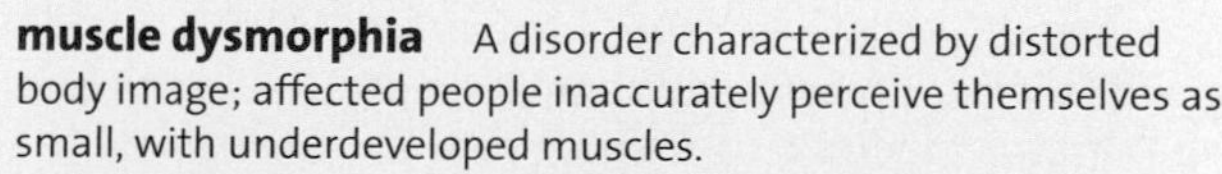

body image The mental representation a person holds about her or his body at any given moment in time, consisting of perceptions, images, thoughts, attitudes, and emotions about the body.

muscle dysmorphia A disorder characterized by distorted body image; affected people inaccurately perceive themselves as small, with underdeveloped muscles.

eating disorder A serious disturbance in eating patterns or eating-related behavior, characterized by a negative body image and concerns about body weight or body fat.

anorexia nervosa An eating disorder characterized by a refusal to maintain body weight at a minimally healthy level and an intense fear of gaining weight or becoming fat; self-starvation.

DIMENSIONS OF DIVERSITY

Gender, Ethnicity, and Body Image

Body Image and Gender

Women are much more likely than men to be dissatisfied with their bodies, often wanting to be thinner than they are. In one study, only 30% of eighth-grade girls reported being content with their bodies, while 70% of their male classmates expressed satisfaction with their looks. Girls and women are much more likely than boys and men to diet, develop eating disorders, and be obese.

One reason that girls and women are dissatisfied with their bodies is that they are influenced by the media—particularly advertisements and women's fashion magazines. Most teen girls report that the media influence their idea of the perfect body and their decision to diet. In a study of adult women, viewing pictures of thin models in magazines had an immediate negative effect on their mood. In another study, 68% of female college students felt worse about their own appearance after looking through women's magazines. Some 75% of normal-weight women think they are overweight.

It is important to note that the image of the "perfect" woman presented in the media is often unrealistic and even unhealthy. In a review of BMI data for Miss America pageant winners since 1922, researchers noted a significant decline in BMI over time, with an increasing number of recent winners having BMIs in the "underweight" category. The average fashion model is 4–7 inches taller and more than 25 pounds lighter than the average American woman. Most fashion models are thinner than 98% of American women.

Our culture may be promoting an unattainable masculine ideal as well. Researchers studying male action figures such as GI Joe from the past 40 years noted that they have become increasingly muscular. A recent Batman action figure, if projected onto a man of average height, would result in someone with a 30-inch waist, 57-inch chest, and 27-inch biceps. Such media messages can be demoralizing; although not as commonly, boys and men also suffer from body image problems.

Body Image and Ethnicity

Although some groups espouse thinness as an ideal body type, others do not. In many traditional African societies, for example, full-figured women's bodies are seen as symbols of health, prosperity, and fertility. African American teenage girls have a much more positive body image than white girls; in one survey, two-thirds of them defined beauty as "the right attitude," whereas white girls were more preoccupied with weight and body shape. Nevertheless, recent evidence indicates that African American women are as likely to engage in disordered eating behavior, especially binge eating and vomiting, as their Latina, Native American, and white counterparts. This finding underscores the complex nature of eating disorders and body image.

Avoiding Body Image Problems

To minimize your risk of developing a body image problem, keep the following strategies in mind:

- Focus on healthy habits and good physical health.
- Focus on good psychological health, and put concerns about physical appearance in perspective. Your worth as a human being does not depend on how you look.
- Practice body acceptance. You can influence your body size and type through lifestyle to some degree, but the basic fact is that some people are genetically designed to be bigger or heavier than others.
- Find things to appreciate in yourself besides an idealized body image. Men and women whose self-esteem is based primarily on standards of physical attractiveness can find it difficult to age gracefully. Those who can learn to value other aspects of themselves are more accepting of the physical changes that occur naturally with age.
- View eating as a morally neutral activity—eating dessert isn't "bad" and doesn't make you a bad person. Healthy eating habits are an important part of a wellness lifestyle, but the things you really care about and do are more important in defining who you are.
- Don't judge yourself or others based on appearance. Watch your attitudes toward people of differing body sizes and shapes, and don't joke about someone's body type. Take people seriously for what they say and do, not for their appearance. Body size is just one external characteristic; there are millions of happy and successful people who just also happen to have a weight problem.
- See the beauty and fitness industries for what they are. Realize that one of their goals is to prompt dissatisfaction with yourself so that you will buy their products.

Borderline Disordered Eating

For every person diagnosed with a full-blown eating disorder, there are many more who don't meet all the criteria but who have eating problems that significantly disrupt their lives. People with borderline disordered eating have some symptoms of eating disorders—for example, excessive dieting or occasional bingeing or purging—but do not meet the full diagnostic criteria for anorexia, bulimia, or binge-eating disorder.

Meaningful statistics about borderline disordered eating are hard to come by, in part because it is difficult to define exactly when eating habits cross the line between normal and disordered. However, many experts feel that the majority of Americans, particularly women, have at least some unhealthy attitudes and behaviors in relation to food and self-image. Concerns about weight and dieting are so common as to be considered culturally normal for many Americans.

Ideally, our relationship to food should be a happy one. The biological urge to satisfy hunger is one of our most basic drives, and eating is associated with many pleasurable sensations. For some of us, food triggers pleasant memories of good times, family, holidays, and fun. But for too many people, food is a source of anguish rather than pleasure. Eating results in feelings of guilt and self-loathing rather than satisfaction, causing tremendous disruption in the lives of the affected individuals. And experts estimate that as many as one-quarter of people with borderline disordered eating will eventually develop a full eating disorder.

How do you know if you have disordered eating habits? When thoughts about weight and food dominate your life, you have a problem. If you're convinced that your worth as a person hinges on how you look and how much you weigh, it's time to get help. We've all overeaten at a delicious holiday meal, but if you habitually eat until your stomach hurts, and if you feel guilty after a meal or a snack, you may have borderline disordered eating. Self-induced vomiting or laxative use after meals, even if only once in a while, is reason for concern. Do you feel compelled to overexercise to compensate for what you've eaten? Do you routinely restrict your food intake and sometimes eat nothing in an effort to feel more in control? These are all danger signs and could mean that you are developing a serious problem.

What can you do if you suspect you have an eating problem? Don't try to go it alone. Eating problems tend to become worse when you cloak them in secrecy. Nearly all colleges have counselors and medical personnel who can help you or refer you to a specialist if needed. If you are intimidated about asking for help, an easy first step is to learn more about eating problems online; several reliable Web sites are listed in For Further Exploration.

extreme weight loss, females with anorexia often stop menstruating. When body fat is virtually gone and muscles are severely wasted, the body turns to its organs in a desperate search for protein. Death can occur from heart failure caused by electrolyte imbalances. About 1 in 10 women with anorexia dies of starvation, cardiac arrest, or other medical complications—one of the highest death rates for any psychiatric disorder. Depression is also a serious risk, and about half the fatalities relating to anorexia are suicides.

Bulimia Nervosa

A person with **bulimia nervosa** engages in recurrent episodes of binge eating followed by **purging.** Although bulimia usually begins in adolescence or young adulthood, it has recently begun to emerge at increasingly younger (11–12 years) and older (40–60 years) ages. Research suggests that about 5% of college-age women have bulimia.

During a binge, a bulimic person may consume anywhere from 1000 to 60,000 calories within a few hours. This is followed by an attempt to get rid of the food by purging, usually by vomiting or using laxatives or diuretics. During a binge, people with bulimia feel as though they have lost control and cannot stop or limit how much they eat. Some binge and purge only occasionally; others do so many times every day. Binges may be triggered by a major life change or other stressful event. Binge eating and purging may become a way of dealing with difficult feelings such as anger and disappointment.

The binge-purge cycle of bulimia places a tremendous strain on the body and can have serious health effects, including tooth decay, esophageal damage and chronic hoarseness, menstrual irregularities, depression, liver and kidney damage, and cardiac arrhythmia. Bulimia is often difficult to recognize because bulimics conceal their eating habits and usually maintain a normal weight, although they may experience fluctuations of 10–15 pounds.

Binge-Eating Disorder

Binge-eating disorder is the most prevalent eating disorder among Americans, affecting 3.5% of women and 2%

bulimia nervosa An eating disorder characterized by recurrent episodes of binge eating and then purging to prevent weight gain.

purging The use of vomiting, laxatives, excessive exercise, restrictive dieting, enemas, diuretics, or diet pills to compensate for food that has been eaten and that the person fears will produce weight gain.

binge-eating disorder An eating disorder characterized by binge eating and a lack of control over eating behavior in general.

If Someone You Know Has Anorexia or Bulimia . . .

TAKE CHARGE

Secrecy and denial are two hallmarks of eating disorders, so it can be hard to know if someone has anorexia or bulimia. Signs that someone may have anorexia include sudden weight loss, excessive dieting or exercise, guilt or preoccupation with food or eating, frequent weighing, fear of becoming fat despite being thin, and baggy or layered clothes to conceal weight loss. Signs that someone may have bulimia include excessive eating without weight gain, secretiveness about food (stealing, hiding, or hoarding food), self-induced vomiting (bathroom visits during or after a meal), swollen glands or puffy face, erosion of tooth enamel, and use of laxatives, diuretics, or diet pills to control weight.

If you decide to approach a friend with your concerns, here are some tips to follow:

- Find out about treatment resources in your community (see the For Further Exploration section for suggestions). You may want to consult a professional at your school clinic or counseling center about the best way to approach the situation.
- Arrange to speak with your friend in a private place, and allow enough time to talk.
- Express your concerns, with specific observations of your friend's behavior. Expect him or her to deny or minimize the problem and possibly to become angry with you. Stay calm and nonjudgmental, and continue to express your concern.
- Avoid giving simplistic advice about eating habits. Listen if your friend wants to talk, and offer your support and understanding. Give your friend the information you found about where he or she can get help, and offer to go along.
- If the situation is an emergency—if your friend has fainted, for example, or attempted suicide—call 911 for help immediately.
- If you are upset about the situation, consider talking to someone yourself. The professionals at the clinic or counseling center are there to help you. Remember, you are not to blame for another person's eating disorder.

of men, according to a 2007 report. It is characterized by uncontrollable eating without any compensatory purging behaviors. Common eating patterns are eating more rapidly than normal, eating until uncomfortably full, eating when not hungry, and preferring to eat alone. Uncontrolled eating is usually followed by weight gain and feelings of guilt, shame, and depression. Many people with binge-eating disorder mistakenly see rigid dieting as the only solution to their problem, but this usually causes feelings of deprivation and a return to overeating.

QUESTIONS FOR CRITICAL THINKING AND REFLECTION

Do you know someone you suspect may be suffering from an eating disorder? Does the advice in this chapter seem helpful to you? Do you think you could follow it? Why or why not? Have you ever engaged in disordered eating patterns yourself? If so, can you identify your reasons for doing so?

Compulsive overeaters rarely eat because of hunger. Instead, they use food to cope with stress, conflict, and other difficult emotions or to provide solace or entertainment. Binge eaters are almost always obese, so they face all the health risks associated with obesity. In addition, binge eaters may have higher-than-average rates of depression and anxiety.

Treating Eating Disorders

The treatment of eating disorders must address both problematic eating behaviors and the misuse of food to manage stress and emotions. Treatment for anorexia nervosa first involves averting a medical crisis by restoring adequate body weight; then the psychological aspects of the disorder can be addressed. The treatment of bulimia nervosa or binge-eating disorder involves first stabilizing the eating patterns, then identifying and changing the patterns of thinking that lead to disordered eating. Treatment usually involves a combination of psychotherapy, medication, and medical management. Friends and family members often want to know what they can do to help; for suggestions, see the box "If Someone You Know Has Anorexia or Bulimia . . ."

People with milder patterns of disordered eating may benefit from getting a nutrition checkup with a registered dietitian. A professional can help determine appropriate body weight and calorie intake and offer advice on how to budget calories into a balanced, healthy diet.

CREATING AN INDIVIDUAL WEIGHT-MANAGEMENT PLAN

Here are some strategies for creating a program of weight management that will last a lifetime.

Assess Your Motivation and Commitment

Before starting your weight-management program, take a fresh look within and assess your motivation and commitment. The point is not only to achieve success but also to guard against frustration, negative changes in self-esteem, and the sense of failure that attends broken resolutions or yo-yo dieting. Think about the reasons you want to lose weight. Self-focused reasons, such as to feel good about yourself or to have a greater sense of well-being,

MOTIVATION BOOSTER

Develop new skills. As with any behavior change, you may need to develop new skills to reach your goals—skills like reading food labels, shopping more carefully, finding healthy recipes, cooking different types of meals, keeping a food journal, making special requests in restaurants, and raising your awareness of cues and triggers in your environment. Try mastering some of these skills through a behavior change program. Developing new skills will increase your confidence, self-efficacy, and motivation.

can often lead to success. Trying to lose weight for others or out of concern for how others view you is a poor foundation for a weight-management program. Make a list of your reasons for wanting to manage your weight, and post it in a prominent place.

Set Reasonable Goals

Choose a goal weight or body fat percentage that is both healthy and reasonable. Refer to the calculations you completed in Lab 6.2 to arrive at a goal. Subdivide your long-term goal into a series of short-term goals. Be willing to renegotiate your final goal as your program moves along.

Assess Your Current Energy Balance

To lose the recommended ½–2 pounds a week, you need to create a negative energy balance of between 1750 and 7000 calories a week, or 250–1000 calories a day. (No diet should reduce calorie intake below 1500 a day for men or 1200 a day for women.) Complete Labs 9.1 and 9.2 to assess your current daily energy needs and to develop strategies for achieving a negative energy balance that will lead to gradual, moderate weight loss. (See p. 295 for guidelines for altering your energy balance to *gain* weight.)

Increase Your Level of Physical Activity

To generate a negative energy balance, it's usually best to exercise more rather than eat less. One reason is that dieting reduces RMR, whereas exercise raises it. Furthermore, studies have shown that being physically fit is even more important than weight loss in reducing your mortality risk (see Chapter 6). The key is keeping fit with moderate exercise.

(Table 9.2 lists the calorie costs of selected physical activities; refer to Table 7.1 for the calorie costs of different types of sports and fitness activities.)

Make Changes in Your Diet and Eating Habits

If you can't generate a large enough negative calorie balance solely by increasing physical activity, you may want to supplement exercise with some dietary strategies. Don't think of this as "going on a diet"; your goal is to make small changes in your diet that you can maintain for a lifetime. Don't try skipping meals, fasting, or adopting a very-low-calorie diet. These strategies seldom work, and they can have negative effects on your ability to manage your weight and on your overall health. Instead, try monitoring calories or simply cutting portion sizes. Refer back to the box "Lifestyle Strategies for Successful Weight Management" for suggestions.

Put Your Plan into Action

Be systematic in your efforts to change your behavior, both what you eat and how you exercise. Many of those who are successful at controlling their weight track their progress, enlist the support of others, and think positively.

Write Daily Write down everything you eat, including how many calories it contains. (See Figure 1.6 for one example of a food journal.) Researchers have found that writing down the food choices you make every day increases your commitment and helps you stick to your diet, especially during high-risk times such as holidays, parties, and family gatherings. Writing every day also serves as a reminder to you that losing weight is important.

Besides tracking what you eat, keep track of your formal exercise program and other daily physical activities so you can begin increasing either their intensity or duration. People who succeed in their health program expend lots of energy in physical activity—according to one study, an average of 2700 calories a week. Popular activities are walking, cycling, aerobic dance, and stair climbing.

Get Others to Help Enlist friends and family members to help, and give them specific suggestions about what you would find helpful. You might, for instance, ask someone to leave you an encouraging voice mail once a day or twice a week, or ask someone to send you reminders by e-mail. Besides asking for regular moral support, find a buddy to work out with you regularly and to be there as an emergency support.

Think Positively Give yourself lots of praise and rewards. Think about your accomplishments each day, and congratulate yourself. You can write these positive thoughts in your food journal. If you do slip, stay objective and don't waste time on self-criticism. If you are keeping a journal, you can see the slip for what it is—an easily contained lapse rather than a catastrophic relapse that ends in your losing confidence and control. Remember that as weight loss slows, the weight loss at this slower rate is more permanent than earlier, more dramatic, losses.

TIPS FOR TODAY AND THE FUTURE

Many approaches work, but the simplest formula for weight management is moderate food intake coupled with regular exercise.

RIGHT NOW YOU CAN

- Assess your weight-management needs. Do you need to gain weight, lose weight, or stay at your current weight?
- List five things you can do to add more physical activity (not exercise) to your daily routine.
- Identify the foods you regularly eat that may be sabotaging your ability to manage your weight.

IN THE FUTURE YOU CAN

- Make an honest assessment of your current body image. Is it accurate and fair, or is it unduly negative and unhealthy? If your body image presents a problem, consider getting professional advice on how to view yourself realistically.
- Keep track of your energy needs to determine whether your energy-balance equation is correct. Use this information as part of your long-term weight-management efforts.

SUMMARY

- Excess body weight increases the risk of numerous diseases, particularly cardiovascular disease, cancer, and diabetes.
- Although genetic factors help determine a person's weight, the influence of heredity can be overcome.
- Physiological factors involved in the regulation of body weight and body fat include metabolic rate and hormones.
- Energy-balance components that an individual can control are calories taken in and calories expended in physical activity.
- Nutritional guidelines for weight management and wellness include controlling consumption of total calories, unhealthy fats and carbohydrates, and protein; monitoring portion sizes and calorie density; increasing consumption of whole grains, fruits, and vegetables; and developing an eating schedule based on decision rules.
- Activity guidelines for weight control emphasize engaging in moderate-intensity physical activity for 150 minutes or more per week; regular, prolonged endurance exercise and weight training can burn a significant number of calories while maintaining muscle mass.
- The sense of well-being that results from a well-balanced diet can reinforce commitment to weight control; improve self-esteem; and lead to realistic, as opposed to negative, self-talk. Successful weight management results in not using food as a way to cope with stress.
- In cases of extreme obesity, weight loss requires medical supervision; in less extreme cases, people can set up individual programs, perhaps getting guidance from reliable books, or they can get help by joining a formal weight-loss program.
- Dissatisfaction with body image and body weight can lead to physical problems and serious eating disorders, including anorexia nervosa, bulimia nervosa, and binge-eating disorder.
- A successful personal plan assesses motivation, sets reasonable and healthy goals, and emphasizes increased activity rather than decreased calories.

FOR FURTHER EXPLORATION

BOOKS

Critser, G. 2004. *Fat Land: How Americans Became the Fattest People in the World.* Boston: Mariner Books. *A look at the many factors in American life that have contributed to the increase in obesity rates.*

Dillon, E. 2006. *Issues That Concern You: Obesity.* New York: Greenhaven Press. *A collection of perspectives on the causes of obesity, its management, and its impact on individuals and society.*

Gaesser, G. A., and K. Katrina. 2006. *It's the Calories, Not the Carbs.* Victoria, B.C.: Trafford. *Provides a detailed look at the facts behind successful weight loss by shunning fad diets and practicing sound energy balance.*

Hensrud, D. D. 2006. *Mayo Clinic Healthy Weight for Everyone.* Rochester, Minn.: Mayo Clinic. *Provides guidelines for successful weight management.*

Herzog, D. B., et al. 2007. *Unlocking the Mystery of Eating Disorders.* New York: McGraw-Hill. *Describes the symptoms and known causes of eating disorders, and provides strategies for dealing with them.*

Ihde, G. M. 2006. *Considering Weight-Loss Surgery: The Facts You Need to Know for a Healthy Recovery.* Victoria, B.C.: Trafford. *An easy-to-read guide to the benefits and risks of weight-loss surgery.*

ORGANIZATIONS AND WEB SITES

FDA Information About Losing Weight and Maintaining a Healthy Weight. Includes guidelines for a variety of weight-loss strategies and special tips for using food labels to aid in weight management.
http://www.cfsan.fda.gov/~dms/wh-wght.html

Federal Trade Commission (FTC): Consumer Information. Provides advice for evaluating advertising about weight-loss products.
http://www.ftc.gov/bcp/conline/edcams/fitness/coninfo.html

Frontline: Fat. Information from a PBS Frontline special that looked at how society, genetics, and biology have influenced our relationship with food and at current problems with obesity and eating disorders.
http://www.pbs.org/wgbh/pages/frontline/shows/fat

MedlinePlus: Obesity and Weight Loss. Provides reliable information from government agencies and key professional associations.
http://www.nlm.nih.gov/medlineplus/obesity.html
http://www.nlm.nih.gov/medlineplus/weightcontrol.html

Q How can I safely gain weight?

A Just as for losing weight, a program for weight gain should be gradual and should include both exercise and dietary changes. The foundation of a successful and healthy program for weight gain is a combination of strength training and a high-carbohydrate, high-calorie diet. Strength training will help you add weight as muscle rather than fat.

Energy balance is also important in a program for gaining weight. You need to consume more calories than your body requires in order to gain weight, but you need to choose those extra calories wisely. Fatty, high-calorie foods may seem like an obvious choice, but consuming additional calories as fat can jeopardize your health and your weight-management program. A diet high in fat carries health risks, and your body is more likely to convert dietary fat into fat tissue than into muscle mass. A better strategy is to consume additional calories as complex carbohydrates from whole grains, fruits, and vegetables. A diet for weight gain should contain about 60–65% of total daily calories from carbohydrates. You probably do not need to be concerned with protein: Although protein requirements increase when you exercise, the protein consumption of most Americans is already well above the DRI.

In order to gain primarily muscle weight instead of fat, a gradual program of weight gain is your best bet. Try these strategies for consuming extra calories:

- Don't skip any meals.
- Add two or three snacks to your daily eating routine.
- Try a sports drink or supplement that has at least 60% of calories from carbohydrates, as well as significant amounts of protein, vitamins, and minerals. (But don't use supplements to replace meals, because they don't contain all food components.)

Q How can I achieve a "perfect" body?

A The current cultural ideal of an ultra-toned, ultrafit body is impossible for most people to achieve. A reasonable goal for body weight and body shape must take into account your heredity, weight history, social circumstances, metabolic rate, and psychological well-being. Don't set goals based on movie stars or fashion models. Modern photographic techniques can make people look much different on film or in magazines than they do in person. Many of these people are also genetically endowed with body shapes that are impossible for most of us to emulate. The best approach is to work with what you've got. Adopting a wellness lifestyle that includes regular exercise and a healthy diet will naturally result in the best possible body shape for you. Obsessively trying to achieve unreasonable goals can lead to problems such as eating disorders, overtraining, and injuries.

For more Common Questions Answered about weight management, visit the Online Learning Center. 

National Heart, Lung, and Blood Institute (NHLBI): Aim for a Healthy Weight. Provides information and tips on diet and physical activity, as well as a BMI calculator.
http://www.nhlbi.nih.gov/health/public/heart/obesity/lose_wt

National Institute of Diabetes and Digestive and Kidney Diseases (NIDDK). Health Information: Nutrition and Obesity. Provides information and referrals for problems related to obesity, weight control, and nutritional disorders.
877-946-4627
http://www.niddk.nih.gov/health/nutrit/nutrit.htm

Partnership for Healthy Weight Management. Provides information on evaluating weight-loss programs and advertising claims.
http://www.consumer.gov/weightloss

SmallStep.gov. Provides resources for increasing activity and improving diet through small changes in daily habits.
http://www.smallstep.gov

U.S. Consumer Gateway: Health—Dieting and Weight Control. Provides links to government sites with advice on evaluating claims about weight-loss products and programs.
http://www.consumer.gov/health.htm

WHO: Obesity and Overweight. Provides information on WHO's global strategy on diet and physical activity.
http://www.who.int/dietphysicalactivity

There are also many resources for people concerned about body image and eating disorders:

Something Fishy Website on Eating Disorders
http://www.something-fishy.org

MedlinePlus: Eating Disorders
http://www.nlm.nih.gov/medlineplus/eatingdisorders.html

National Association of Anorexia Nervosa and Associated Disorders
847-831-3438
http://www.anad.org

National Eating Disorders Association
800-931-2237
http://www.nationaleatingdisorders.org

Women's Body Image and Health
http://www.4woman.gov/bodyimage

See also the listings in Chapters 1, 6, and 8.

SELECTED BIBLIOGRAPHY

Adams, K. F., et al. 2006. Overweight, obesity, and mortality in a large prospective cohort of persons 50 to 71 years old. *New England Journal of Medicine* 355(8): 763–778.

American Dietetic Association. 2006. *Evidence Based Guidelines: Adult Weight Management* (http://www.eatright.org; retrieved May 30, 2007).

Baker, B. 2006. Weight loss and diet plans. *American Journal of Nursing* 106(6): 52–59.

Behn, A., and E. Ur. 2006. The obesity epidemic and its cardiovascular consequences. *Current Opinions in Cardiology* 21(4): 353–360.

Beverages total 22% of US calories—but who's counting? 2007. *Tufts Health & nutrition Letter,* March.

Bowman, S. A., et al. 2004. Effects of fast-food consumption on energy intake and diet quality among children in a national household survey. *Pediatrics* 113(1 Pt. 1): 112–118.

Centers for Disease Control and Prevention. 2004. Trends in intake of energy and macronutrients—United States, 1971–2000. *Morbidity and Mortality Weekly Report* 53(4): 80–82.

Centers for Disease Control and Prevention. 2006. *Diabetes Care.* Atlanta: U.S. Department of Health and Human Services, Centers for Disease Control and Prevention.

Dong, L., G. Block, and S. Mandel. 2004. Activities contributing to total energy expenditure in the United States: Results from the NHAPS Study. *International Journal of Behavioral Nutrition and Physical Activity* 1(4).

Farshchi, H. R., M. A. Taylor, and I. A. Macdonald. 2005. Deleterious effects of omitting breakfast on insulin sensitivity and fasting lipid profiles in healthy lean women. *American Journal of Clinical Nutrition* 81(2): 388–396.

Graves, B. S., and R. L. Welsh. 2004. Recognizing the signs of body dysmorphic disorder and muscle dysmorphia. *ACSM's Health & Fitness Journal,* January/February.

Graves, M. M. 2005. Weighing in on losing weight. *ACSM Fit Society Page,* Spring.

Haller, C. A., N. L. Benowitz, and P. Jacob. 2005. Hemodynamic effects of ephedra-free weight-loss supplements in humans. *American Journal of Medicine* 118(9): 998–1003.

Hudson, J. I., et al. 2007. The prevalence and correlates of eating disorders in the National Comorbidity Survey Replication. *Biological Psychiatry* 61(3): 348–358.

Hu, F. B., et al. 2004. Adiposity as compared with physical activity in predicting mortality among women. *New England Journal of Medicine* 351(26): 2694–2703.

Hutchinson, D. M., and R. M. Rapee. 2007. Do friends share similar body image and eating problems? The role of social networks and peer influences in early adolescence. *Behavior Research and Therapy* 45(7): 1557–1577.

Janiszewski, P. M., and R. Ross. 2007. Physical activity in the treatment of obesity: Beyond body weight reduction. *Applied Physiology, Nutrition and Metabolism* 32(3): 512–522.

Leone, J. E., and J. V. Fetro. 2007. Perceptions and attitudes toward androgenic-anabolic steroid use among two age categories: A qualitative study. *Journal of Strength and Conditioning Research* 21(2): 532–537.

Ma, Y., et al. 2005. Association between dietary carbohydrates and body weight. *American Journal of Epidemiology* 161(4): 359–367.

Meunning, P., et al. 2006. Gender and the burden of disease attributable to obesity. *American Journal of Public Health* 96(9): 1662–1668.

Narayan, K. M., et al. 2007. Effect of BMI on lifetime risk for diabetes in the U.S. *Diabetes Care* 30(6): 1562–1566.

Nicklas, B. J., et al. 2004. Association of visceral adipose tissue with incident myocardial infarction in older men and women. *American Journal of Epidemiology* 160(8): 741–749.

Ogden, C. L., et al. 2007. The epidemiology of obesity. *Gastroenterology* 132(6): 2087–2102.

Pereira, M. A., et al. 2005. Fast-food habits, weight gain, and insulin resistance (the CARDIA study): 15-year prospective analysis. *Lancet* 365(9453): 36–42.

Ritchie, S. A., and J. M. Connell. 2007. The link between abdominal obesity, metabolic syndrome and cardiovascular disease. *Nutrition, Metabolism, and Cardiovascular Diseases* 17(4): 319–326.

Schulze, M. B., et al. 2004. Sugar-sweetened beverages, weight gain, and incidence of type 2 diabetes in young and middle-aged women. *Journal of the American Medical Association* 292(8): 927–934.

Sweeteners can sour your health. 2005. *Consumer Reports on Health,* January.

Tsai, A. G., and T. A. Wadden. 2005. Systematic review: An evaluation of major commercial weight loss programs in the United States. *Annals of Internal Medicine* 142(1): 56–66.

U.S. Department of Health and Human Services. 2005. *Dietary Guidelines for Americans* (http://www.healthierus.gov/dietaryguidelines; retrieved November 26, 2007).

Vorona, R. D., et al. 2005. Overweight and obese patients in a primary care population report less sleep than patients with a normal body mass index. *Archives of Internal Medicine* 165: 25–30.

Weigle, D. S., et al. 2005. A high-protein diet induces sustained reductions in appetite, ad libitum caloric intake, and body weight despite compensatory changes in diurnal plasma leptin and ghrelin concentrations. *American Journal of Clinical Nutrition* 82(1): 42–48.

Wong, S. L., et al. 2004. Cardiorespiratory fitness is associated with lower abdominal fat independent of body mass index. *Medicine and Science in Sports and Exercise* 36(2): 286–291.

LAB 9.1 Calculating Daily Energy Needs

Part I Estimating Current Energy Intake from a Food Record

If your weight is stable, your current daily energy intake is the number of calories you need to consume to maintain your weight at your current activity level. If you completed Lab 8.2, you should have a record of your current energy intake; if you didn't complete the lab, keep a careful and complete record of everything you eat for one day, and then total the calories in all the foods and beverages you consumed. (This calculation can be done by hand or by using a nutrition analysis software program or Web site; for example, visit MyPyramid.gov and click on MyPyramid Tracker.) Record your total energy intake below:

Current energy intake (from food record): ______ calories per day

Part II Estimating Daily Energy Requirements Using Food and Nutrition Board Formulas

Many people underestimate the size of their food portions, and so energy goals based on estimates of current calorie intake from food records can be inaccurate. You can also estimate your daily energy needs using the formulas listed below. To use the appropriate formula for your sex, you'll need to plug in the following:

- Age (in years)
- Weight (in pounds)
- Height (in inches)
- Physical activity coefficient (PA) from the table below.

To help estimate your physical activity level, consider the following guidelines: Someone who typically engages in 30 minutes of moderate-intensity activity, equivalent to walking 2 miles in 30 minutes, in addition to the activities involved in maintaining a sedentary lifestyle, is considered "low active", someone who typically engages in the equivalent of 90 minutes of moderate-intensity activity is rated as "active." You might find it helpful to refer back to Lab 2.2 to estimate your physical activity level.

Physical Activity Level	Physical Activity Coefficient (PA)	
	Men	*Women*
Sedentary	1.00	1.00
Low active	1.12	1.14
Active	1.27	1.27
Very active	1.54	1.45

Estimated Daily Energy Requirement for Weight Maintenance in Men

864 − (9.72 × age) + (PA × [(6.39 × weight) + (12.78 × height)])

1. 9.72 × ______ age (years) = ______
2. 864 − ______ result from step 1 = ______ *[result may be a negative number]*
3. 6.39 × ______ weight (pounds) = ______
4. 12.78 × ______ height (inches) = ______
5. ______ result from step 3 + ______ result from step 4 = ______
6. ______ PA (from table) × ______ result from step 5 = ______
7. ______ result from step 2 + ______ result from step 6 = ______ calories per day

Estimated Daily Energy Requirement for Weight Maintenance in Women

387 − (7.31 × age) + (PA × [(4.91 × weight) + (16.78 × height)])

1. 7.31 × ________ age (years) = ________
2. 387 − ________ result from step 1 = ________ *[result may be a negative number]*
3. 4.91 × ________ weight (pounds) = ________
4. 16.78 × ________ height (inches) = ________
5. ________ result from step 3 + ________ result from step 4 = ________
6. ________ PA (from table) × ________ result from step 5 = ________
7. ________ result from step 2 + ________ result from step 6 = ________ calories per day

Daily energy needs for weight maintenance (from formula): ________ calories/day

Part III Determining an Individual Daily Energy Goal for Weight Maintenance

If you calculated values for daily energy needs based on both methods, examine the two values. Some difference is likely—people tend to underestimate their food intake and overestimate their level of physical activity—but if the two values are very far off, check your food record and your physical activity estimate for accuracy, and make any necessary adjustments. For an individualized estimate of daily calorie needs, average the two values:

Daily energy needs = (food record result ________ calories/day + formula result ________ calories/day)

÷ 2 ________ calories/day

Using Your Results

How did you score? Are you surprised by the value you calculated for your approximate daily energy needs? If so, is the value higher or lower than you expected?

What should you do next? Enter the results of this lab in the Preprogram Assessment column in Appendix D. If you wish to change your energy balance to lose weight, complete Lab 9.2 to set goals and develop specific strategies for change. (If your goal is weight gain, see p. 295 for basic guidelines.) One of the best ways to tip your energy balance toward weight loss is to increase your daily physical activity. If you include increases in activity as part of your program, then you can use the results of this lab to chart changes in your daily energy expenditure (and needs). Look for ways to increase the amount of time you spend in physical activity, thus increasing your physical activity coefficient. After several weeks of your program, complete this lab again, and enter the results in the Postprogram Assessment column of Appendix D. How do the results compare? Did your program for boosting physical activity show up as an increase in your daily energy expenditure and need?

SOURCE: Estimating Daily Energy Requirements Using Food and Nutrition Board Formulas Part II: Reprinted with permission from *Dietary Reference Intakes for Energy, Carbohydrate, Fiber, Fat, Fatty Acids, Cholesterol, Protein, and Amino Acids (Macronutrients)*. Copyright © 2002 by the National Academy of Sciences. Courtesy of the National Academies Press, Washington, D.C.

Name ________________________ Section ______________ Date ____________

LAB 9.2 Identifying Weight-Loss Goals and Ways to Meet Them

Negative Calorie Balance

Complete the following calculations to determine your weekly and daily negative calorie balance goals and the number of weeks to achieve your target weight.

Current weight __________ lb − target weight (from Lab 6.2) __________ lb
= total weight to lose __________ lb

Total weight to lose __________ lb ÷ weight to lose each week __________ lb
= time to achieve target weight __________ weeks

Weight to lose each week __________ lb × 3500 cal/lb = weekly negative calorie balance __________ cal/week

Weekly negative calorie balance __________ cal/week ÷ 7 days/week
= daily negative calorie balance __________ cal/day

To keep your weight-loss program on schedule, you must achieve the daily negative calorie balance by either decreasing your calorie consumption (eating less) or increasing your calorie expenditure (being more active). A combination of the two strategies will probably be most successful.

Changes in Activity Level

Adding a few minutes of exercise every day is a good way of expending calories. Use the calorie costs for different activities listed in Table 7.1 and Table 9.2 to plan ways for raising your calorie expenditure level.

Activity	Duration	Calories Used
	Total calories expended:	

Changes in Diet

Look closely at your diet from one day, as recorded in Lab 8.2. Identify ways to cut calorie consumption by eliminating certain items or substituting lower-calorie choices. Be realistic in your cuts and substitutions; you need to develop a plan you can live with.

Food Item	Substitute Food Item	Calorie Savings
	Total calories cut:	

Total calories expended __________ + **total calories cut** __________ = **total negative calorie balance** __________

Have you met your required negative energy balance? If not, revise your dietary and activity changes to meet your goal.

Common Problem Eating Behaviors

For each of the groups of statements that appear below, check those that are true for you. If you check several statements for a given pattern or problem, it will probably be a significant factor in your weight-management program. One possible strategy for dealing with each type of problem is given. For those eating problems you identify as important, add your own ideas to the strategies listed.

1. _____ I often skip meals.

   _____ I often eat a number of snacks in place of a meal.

   _____ I don't have a regular schedule of meal and snack times.

   _____ I make up for missed meals and snacks by eating more at the next meal.

   Problem: Irregular eating habits

   Possible solutions:

   - Write out a plan for each day's meals in advance. Carry it with you and stick to it.
   - ______________________________
   - ______________________________

2. _____ I eat more than one sweet dessert or snack each day.

   _____ I usually snack on foods high in calories and fat (chips, cookies, ice cream).

   _____ I drink regular (not sugar-free) soft drinks.

   _____ I choose types of meat that are high in fat.

   _____ I consume more than one alcoholic beverage a day.

   Problem: Poor food choices

   Possible solutions:

   - Keep a supply of raw fruits and vegetables handy for snacks.
   - ______________________________
   - ______________________________

3. _____ I always eat everything on my plate.

   _____ I often go back for seconds and thirds.

   _____ I take larger helpings than most people.

   _____ I eat up leftovers instead of putting them away.

   Problem: Portion sizes too large

   Possible solutions:

   - Measure all portions with a scale or measuring cup.
   - ______________________________
   - ______________________________

Name ______________________ Section ______________ Date ______________

LAB 9.3 Checking for Body Image Problems and Eating Disorders

LABORATORY ACTIVITIES

Assessing Your Body Image

	Never	Sometimes	Often	Always
1. I dislike seeing myself in mirrors.	0	1	2	3
2. When I shop for clothing, I am more aware of my weight problem, and consequently I find shopping for clothes somewhat unpleasant.	0	1	2	3
3. I'm ashamed to be seen in public.	0	1	2	3
4. I prefer to avoid engaging in sports or public exercise because of my appearance.	0	1	2	3
5. I feel somewhat embarrassed about my body in the presence of someone of the other sex.	0	1	2	3
6. I think my body is ugly.	0	1	2	3
7. I feel that other people must think my body is unattractive.	0	1	2	3
8. I feel that my family or friends may be embarrassed to be seen with me.	0	1	2	3
9. I find myself comparing myself with other people to see if they are heavier than I am.	0	1	2	3
10. I find it difficult to enjoy activities because I am self-conscious about my physical appearance.	0	1	2	3
11. Feeling guilty about my weight problem occupies most of my thinking.	0	1	2	3
12. My thoughts about my body and physical appearance are negative and self-critical.	0	1	2	3
Now add up the number of points you have circled in each column: _____	0	+ _____	+ _____	+ _____

Score Interpretation

The lowest possible score is 0, and this indicates a positive body image. The highest possible score is 36, and this indicates an unhealthy body image. A score higher than 14 suggests a need to develop a healthier body image.

SOURCE: Nash, J. D. 1997. *The New Maximize Your Body Potential.* Palo Alto, Calif.: Bull Publishing. Reprinted with permission from Bull Publishing.

Eating Disorder Checklist

	Always	Very Often	Often	Sometimes	Rarely	Never
1. I like eating with other people.	0	0	0	1	2	3
2. I like my clothes to fit tightly.	0	0	0	1	2	3
3. I enjoy eating meat.	0	0	0	1	2	3
4. I have regular menstrual periods.	0	0	0	1	2	3
5. I enjoy eating at restaurants.	0	0	0	1	2	3
6. I enjoy trying new rich foods.	0	0	0	1	2	3
7. I prepare foods for others, but do not eat what I cook.	3	2	1	0	0	0
8. I become anxious prior to eating.	3	2	1	0	0	0
9. I am terrified about being overweight.	3	2	1	0	0	0
10. I avoid eating when I am hungry.	3	2	1	0	0	0
11. I find myself preoccupied with food.	3	2	1	0	0	0
12. I have gone on eating binges where I feel that I may not be able to stop.	3	2	1	0	0	0
13. I cut my food into small pieces.	3	2	1	0	0	0

	Always	Very Often	Often	Sometimes	Rarely	Never
14. I am aware of the calorie content of foods that I eat.	3	2	1	0	0	0
15. I particularly avoid foods with a high carbohydrate content (bread, potatoes, rice, etc.).	3	2	1	0	0	0
16. I feel bloated after meals.	3	2	1	0	0	0
17. I feel others would prefer me to eat more.	3	2	1	0	0	0
18. I vomit after I have eaten.	3	2	1	0	0	0
19. I feel extremely guilty after eating.	3	2	1	0	0	0
20. I am preoccupied with a desire to be thinner.	3	2	1	0	0	0
21. I exercise strenuously to burn off calories.	3	2	1	0	0	0
22. I weigh myself several times a day.	3	2	1	0	0	0
23. I wake up early in the morning.	3	2	1	0	0	0
24. I eat the same foods day after day.	3	2	1	0	0	0
25. I think about burning up calories when I exercise.	3	2	1	0	0	0
26. Other people think I am too thin.	3	2	1	0	0	0
27. I am preoccupied with the thought of having fat on my body.	3	2	1	0	0	0
28. I take longer than others to eat my meals.	3	2	1	0	0	0
29. I take laxatives.	3	2	1	0	0	0
30. I avoid foods with sugar in them.	3	2	1	0	0	0
31. I eat diet foods.	3	2	1	0	0	0
32. I feel that food controls my life.	3	2	1	0	0	0
33. I display self-control around foods.	3	2	1	0	0	0
34. I feel that others pressure me to eat.	3	2	1	0	0	0
35. I give too much time and thought to food.	3	2	1	0	0	0
36. I suffer from constipation.	3	2	1	0	0	0
37. I feel uncomfortable after eating sweets.	3	2	1	0	0	0
38. I engage in dieting behavior.	3	2	1	0	0	0
39. I like my stomach to be empty.	3	2	1	0	0	0
40. I have the impulse to vomit after meals.	3	2	1	0	0	0
Now add up the number of points in each column for statements 1 through 40: _____	_____ +	_____ +	_____ +	_____ +	_____ +	_____

Score Interpretation

The possible range is 0–120. A score higher than 50 suggests an eating disorder. A score between 30 and 50 suggests a borderline eating disorder. A score less than 30 is within the normal range. Among those with normal eating habits, the average score is 15.4.

SOURCE: Garner, D. M., Omstead, M., Polivy, J., Development and Validation of a Multidimensional Eating Disorder Inventory for Anorexia Nervosa and Bulimia. *International Journal of Eating Disorders* 2: 15–33, 1983.

Using Your Results

How did you score? Are you surprised by your scores? Do the results of either assessment indicate that you may have a problem with body image or disordered eating?

What should you do next? If your results are borderline, consider trying some of the self-help strategies suggested in the chapter. If body image or disordered eating is a significant problem for you, get professional advice; a physician, therapist, and/or registered dietitian can help. Make an appointment today.

LOOKING AHEAD>>>>>

AFTER READING THIS CHAPTER, YOU SHOULD BE ABLE TO:

- Explain what stress is and how people react to it—physically, emotionally, and behaviorally
- Describe the relationship between stress and disease
- List common sources of stress
- Describe techniques for preventing and managing stress
- Put together a plan for successfully managing the stress in your life

STRESS 10

TEST YOUR KNOWLEDGE

1. Which of the following events can cause stress?

a. taking out a loan
b. failing a test
c. graduating from college
d. watching a hockey game

2. Moderate exercise can stimulate which of the following?

a. analgesia (pain relief)
b. birth of new brain cells
c. relaxation

3. Which of the following can be a result of chronic stress?

a. violence
b. heart attack
c. stroke

ANSWERS

1. **ALL FOUR.** Stress-producing factors can be pleasant or unpleasant and can include physical challenges and goal achievement as well as events that are perceived as negative.
2. **ALL THREE.** Regular exercise is linked to improvement in many dimensions of wellness.
3. **ALL THREE.** Chronic—or ongoing—stress can last for years. People who suffer from long-term stress may ultimately become violent toward themselves or others. They also run a greater than normal risk for certain ailments, especially cardiovascular disease.

FIT AND WELL ONLINE LEARNING CENTER www.mhhe.com/fahey

Visit the *Fit and Well* Online Learning Center for resources that will help you get the most out of your course!

- Study and review aids include practice quizzes, glossary flashcards, chapter summaries, learning objectives, PowerPoint presentations, Common Questions Answered, student handouts, crossword puzzles, Internet activities, and links to wellness Web sites.
- Behavior change tools include a daily fitness and nutrition journal, a behavior change workbook, sample behavior change plans, and blank behavior change logs to print and use.

Like the term *fitness*, *stress* is a word many people use without really understanding its precise meaning. Stress is popularly viewed as an uncomfortable response to a negative event, which probably describes *nervous tension* more than the cluster of physical and psychological responses that actually constitute stress. In fact, stress is not limited to negative situations; it is also a response to pleasurable physical challenges and the achievement of personal goals. Whether stress is experienced as pleasant or unpleasant depends largely on the situation and the individual. Because learning effective responses to stress can enhance psychological health and help prevent a number of serious diseases, stress management is an important component in any wellness program.

This chapter explains the physiological and psychological reactions that make up the stress response and describes how these reactions can be risks to good health. The chapter also presents ways of managing stress with a personal program or with the help of others.

TERMS

stressor Any physical or psychological event or condition that produces stress.

stress response The physical and emotional changes associated with stress.

stress The collective physiological and emotional responses to any stimulus that disturbs an individual's homeostasis.

autonomic nervous system The branch of the nervous system that controls basic body processes; consists of the sympathetic and parasympathetic divisions.

parasympathetic division A division of the autonomic nervous system that moderates the excitatory effect of the sympathetic division, slowing metabolism and restoring energy supplies.

sympathetic division A division of the autonomic nervous system that reacts to danger or other challenges by almost instantly accelerating body processes.

norepinephrine A neurotransmitter released by the sympathetic nervous system onto target tissues to increase their function in the face of increased activity; when released by the brain, causes arousal (increased attention, awareness, and alertness); also called *noradrenaline*.

endocrine system The system of glands, tissues, and cells that secrete hormones into the bloodstream to influence metabolism and other body processes.

hormone A chemical messenger produced in the body and transported in the bloodstream to target cells or organs for specific regulation of their activities.

cortisol A steroid hormone secreted by the cortex (outer layer) of the adrenal gland; also called *hydrocortisone*.

epinephrine A hormone secreted by the medulla (inner core) of the adrenal gland that affects the functioning of organs involved in responding to a stressor; also called *adrenaline*.

endorphins Brain secretions that have pain-inhibiting effects.

fight-or-flight reaction A defense reaction that prepares an individual for conflict or escape by triggering hormonal, cardiovascular, metabolic, and other changes.

WHAT IS STRESS?

In common usage, the term *stress* refers to two different things: situations that trigger physical and emotional reactions, *and* the reactions themselves. This text uses the more precise term **stressor** for a situation that triggers physical and emotional reactions and the term **stress response** for those reactions. A first date and a final exam are examples of stressors; sweaty palms and a pounding heart are symptoms of the stress response. We'll use the term **stress** to describe the general physical and emotional state that accompanies the stress response. So, a person taking a final exam experiences stress.

Physical Responses to Stressors

Imagine a near miss: As you step off the curb, a car careens toward you. With just a fraction of a second to spare, you leap safely out of harm's way. In that split second of danger and in the moments following it, you experience a predictable series of physical reactions. Your body goes from a relaxed state to one prepared for physical action to cope with a threat to your life.

Two systems in your body are responsible for your physical response to stressors: the nervous system and the endocrine system. Through rapid chemical reactions affecting almost every part of your body, you are primed to act quickly and appropriately in time of danger.

Actions of the Nervous System The nervous system consists of the brain, spinal cord, and nerves. Part of the nervous system is under voluntary control, as when you tell your arm to reach for a chocolate. The part that is not under conscious supervision—for example, the part that controls the digestion of the chocolate—is the **autonomic nervous system.** In addition to digestion, it controls your heart rate, breathing, blood pressure, and hundreds of other involuntary functions.

The autonomic nervous system consists of two divisions:

- The **parasympathetic division** is in control when you are relaxed; it aids in digesting food, storing energy, and promoting growth.
- The **sympathetic division** is activated during times of arousal, including exercise, and when there is an emergency, such as severe pain, anger, or fear.

Sympathetic nerves use the neurotransmitter **norepinephrine** to exert their actions on nearly every organ, sweat gland, blood vessel, and muscle to enable your body to handle an emergency. In general, the sympathetic division commands your body to stop storing energy and to use it in response to a crisis.

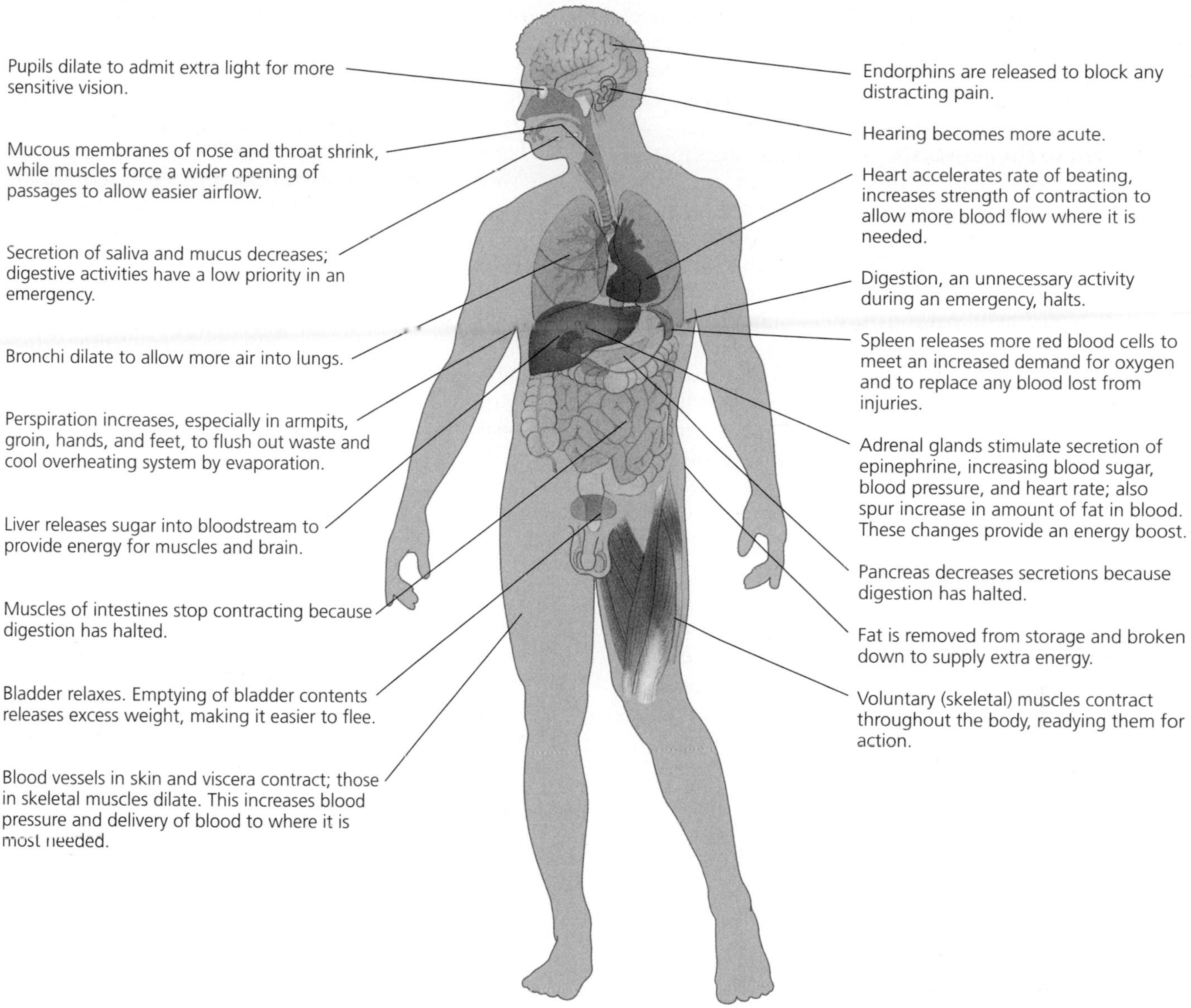

Pupils dilate to admit extra light for more sensitive vision.

Mucous membranes of nose and throat shrink, while muscles force a wider opening of passages to allow easier airflow.

Secretion of saliva and mucus decreases; digestive activities have a low priority in an emergency.

Bronchi dilate to allow more air into lungs.

Perspiration increases, especially in armpits, groin, hands, and feet, to flush out waste and cool overheating system by evaporation.

Liver releases sugar into bloodstream to provide energy for muscles and brain.

Muscles of intestines stop contracting because digestion has halted.

Bladder relaxes. Emptying of bladder contents releases excess weight, making it easier to flee.

Blood vessels in skin and viscera contract; those in skeletal muscles dilate. This increases blood pressure and delivery of blood to where it is most needed.

Endorphins are released to block any distracting pain.

Hearing becomes more acute.

Heart accelerates rate of beating, increases strength of contraction to allow more blood flow where it is needed.

Digestion, an unnecessary activity during an emergency, halts.

Spleen releases more red blood cells to meet an increased demand for oxygen and to replace any blood lost from injuries.

Adrenal glands stimulate secretion of epinephrine, increasing blood sugar, blood pressure, and heart rate; also spur increase in amount of fat in blood. These changes provide an energy boost.

Pancreas decreases secretions because digestion has halted.

Fat is removed from storage and broken down to supply extra energy.

Voluntary (skeletal) muscles contract throughout the body, readying them for action.

FIGURE 10.1 The fight-or-flight reaction. In response to a stressor, the autonomic nervous system and the endocrine system cause changes that prepare the body to deal with an emergency.

Actions of the Endocrine System During stress, the sympathetic nervous system triggers the **endocrine system.** This system of glands, tissues, and cells helps control body functions by releasing **hormones** and other chemical messengers into the bloodstream to influence metabolism and other body processes. These chemicals act on a variety of targets throughout the body. Along with the nervous system, the endocrine system prepares the body to respond to a stressor.

The Two Systems Together How do both systems work together in an emergency? Let's go back to your near collision with a car. Both reflexes and higher cognitive areas in your brain quickly make the decision that you are facing a threat—and your body prepares to meet the danger. Chemical messages and actions of sympathetic nerves cause the release of key hormones, including **cortisol** and **epinephrine.** These hormones trigger the physiological changes shown in Figure 10.1, including these:

- Heart and respiration rates accelerate to speed oxygen through the body.
- Hearing and vision become more acute.
- The liver releases extra sugar into the bloodstream to boost energy.
- Perspiration increases to cool the skin.
- The brain releases **endorphins**—chemicals that can inhibit or block sensations of pain—in case you are injured.

Taken together, these almost-instantaneous physical changes are called the **fight-or-flight reaction.** They give you the heightened reflexes and strength you need to dodge the car or deal with other stressors. Although these physical changes may vary in intensity, the same basic set of physical reactions occurs in response to any type of stressor—positive or negative, physical or psychological.

The Return to Homeostasis Once a stressful situation ends, the parasympathetic division of your autonomic nervous system takes command and halts the stress response. It restores **homeostasis,** a state in which blood pressure, heart rate, hormone levels, and other vital functions are maintained within a narrow range of normal. Your parasympathetic nervous system calms your body down, slowing a rapid heartbeat, drying sweaty palms, and returning breathing to normal. Gradually, your body resumes its normal "housekeeping" functions, such as digestion and temperature regulation. Damage that may have been sustained during the fight-or-flight reaction is repaired. The day after you narrowly dodge the car, you wake up feeling fine. In this way, your body can grow, repair itself, and acquire reserves of energy. When the next crisis comes, you'll be ready to respond—instantly—again.

The Fight-or-Flight Reaction in Modern Life The fight-or-flight reaction is a part of our biological heritage, and it's a survival mechanism that has served humans well. In modern life, however, it is often absurdly inappropriate. Many of the stressors we face in everyday life do not require a physical response—for example, an exam, a mess left by a roommate, or a stop light. The fight-or-flight reaction prepares the body for physical action regardless of whether such action is a necessary or appropriate response to a particular stressor.

Emotional and Behavioral Responses to Stressors

The physical response to a stressor may vary in intensity from person to person and situation to situation, but we all experience a similar set of physical changes—the fight-or-flight reaction. There is, however, a great deal of variation in the way people view and react to potential stressors. For example, you may feel confident about taking exams but be nervous about talking to people you don't know, while your roommate may love challenging social situations but may be very nervous about taking tests. Many factors, some external and some internal, help explain these differences.

Your cognitive (mental) appraisal of a potential stressor strongly influences how you view it. Two factors that can reduce the magnitude of the stress response are successful prediction and the perception of control. For instance, receiving course syllabi at the beginning of the term allows you to predict the timing of major deadlines and exams. Having this predictive knowledge also allows you to exert some control over your study plans and can thus help reduce the stress caused by exams.

Cognitive appraisal is highly individual and strongly related to emotions. The facts of a situation—Who? What? Where? When?—typically are evaluated fairly consistently from person to person. Evaluation with respect to personal outcome, however, varies: What does this mean for me? Can I do anything about it? Will it improve or worsen? If an individual perceives a situation as exceeding her or his ability to cope, the result can be negative emotions and an inappropriate stress response. If, on the other hand, a person perceives a situation as a challenge that is within her or his ability to manage, more positive and appropriate responses are likely. A certain amount of stress, if coped with appropriately, can help promote optimal performance (Figure 10.2).

Effective and Ineffective Responses Common emotional responses to stressors include anxiety, depression, and fear. Although emotional responses are determined in part by inborn personality or temperament, we often can moderate or learn to control them. Coping techniques are discussed later in the chapter.

Behavioral responses to stressors—controlled by the **somatic nervous system**, which manages our conscious

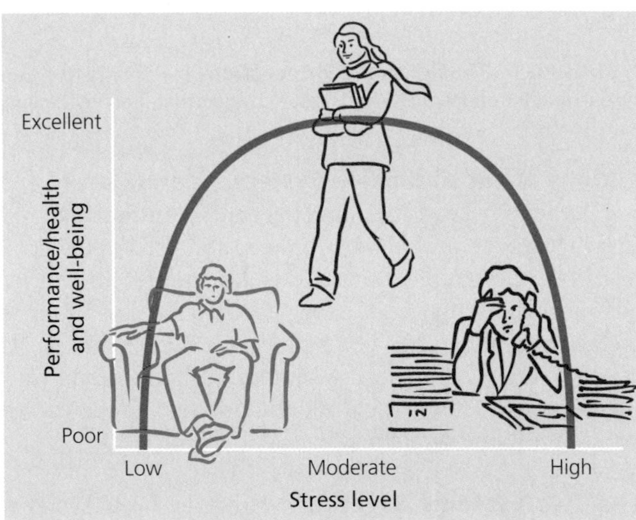

FIGURE. 10.2 Stress level, performance, and well-being. A moderate level of stress challenges individuals in a way that promotes optimal performance and well-being. Too little stress, and people are not challenged enough to improve; too much stress, and the challenges become stressors that can impair physical and emotional health.

WEB TERMS

homeostasis A state of stability and consistency in an individual's physiological functioning.

somatic nervous system The branch of the peripheral nervous system that governs motor functions and sensory information, largely under conscious control.

personality The sum of behavioral, cognitive, and emotional tendencies.

actions—are entirely under our control. Effective behavioral responses such as talking, laughing, exercising, meditating, learning time-management skills, and becoming more assertive can promote wellness and enable us to function at our best. Ineffective behavioral responses to stressors include overeating, expressing hostility, and using tobacco, alcohol, or other drugs.

Let's consider the individual variations demonstrated by two students, David and Amelia, responding to the same stressor—the first exam of the semester. David enters the exam with a feeling of dread and, as he reads the exam questions, responds to his initial anxiety with more anxiety. The more emotionally upset he gets, the less he can remember and the more anxious he becomes. Soon he's staring into space, imagining what will happen if he fails the course. Amelia, on the other hand, takes a deep breath to relax before she reads the questions, wills herself to focus on the answers she knows, and then goes back over the exam to deal with those questions she's not sure of. She leaves the room feeling calm, relaxed, and confident that she has done well.

As this simple example shows, avoiding destructive responses to stress and adopting effective and appropriate ones can have a direct effect on well-being.

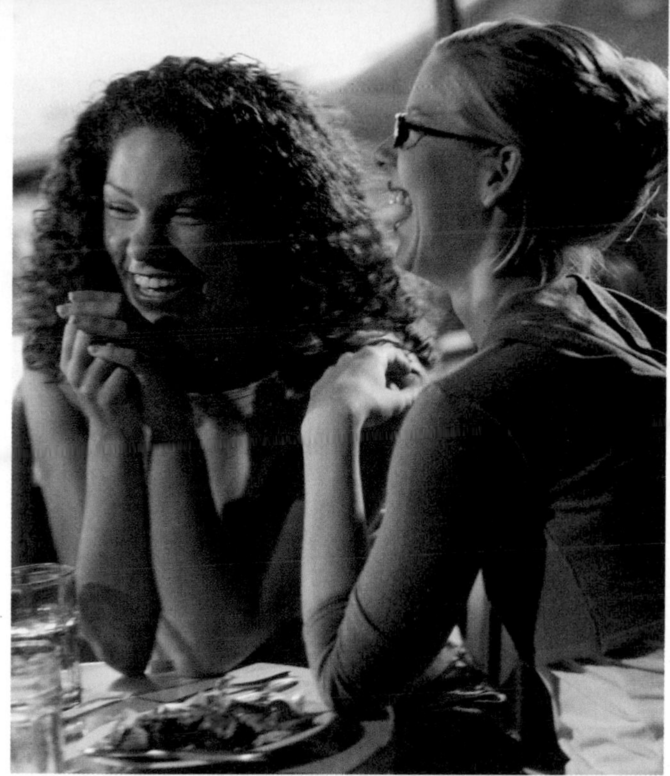

A person's emotional and behavioral responses to stressors depend on many different factors, including personality, gender, and cultural background. Research suggests that women are more likely than men to respond to stressors by seeking social support, a pattern referred to as tend-and-befriend.

Personality and Stress Some people seem to be nervous, irritable, and easily upset by minor annoyances; others are calm and composed even in difficult situations. Scientists remain unsure just why this is or how the brain's complex emotional mechanisms work. But **personality**, the sum of cognitive, behavioral, and emotional tendencies, clearly affects how people perceive and react to stressors. To investigate the links among personality, stress, and overall wellness, researchers have looked at different constellations of characteristics, or "personality types."

- ***Type A.*** People with Type A personality are described as ultracompetitive, controlling, impatient, aggressive, and even hostile. Type A people have a higher perceived stress level and more problems coping with stress. They react explosively to stressors and are upset by events that others would consider only annoyances. Studies indicate that certain characteristics of the Type A pattern—anger, cynicism, and hostility—increase the risk of heart disease.
- ***Type B.*** The Type B personality is relaxed and contemplative. Type B people are less frustrated by daily events and more tolerant of the behavior of others.
- ***Type C.*** The Type C personality is characterized by anger suppression, difficulty expressing emotions, feelings of hopelessness and despair, and an exaggerated response to minor stressors. This heightened response may impair immune functions.

Studies of Type A and C personalities suggest that expressing your emotions is beneficial but that habitually expressing exaggerated stress responses or hostility is unhealthy.

Researchers have also looked for personality traits that enable people to deal more successfully with stress. One such trait is "hardiness," a particular form of optimism. People with a hardy personality view potential stressors as challenges and opportunities for growth and learning, rather than as burdens. Hardy people perceive fewer situations as stressful, and their reaction to stressors tends to be less intense. They are committed to their activities, have a sense of inner purpose and an inner locus of control, and feel at least partly in control of their lives.

You probably can't change your basic personality, but you can change your typical behaviors and patterns of thinking, and you can use positive stress-management techniques like those described later in the chapter.

QUESTIONS FOR CRITICAL THINKING AND REFLECTION

Think of the last time you faced a significant stressor. How did you respond? List the physical, emotional, and behavioral reactions you felt. Did these responses help you deal with the stress, or did they interfere with your efforts to handle it?

Gender and Stress Our gender role—the activities, abilities, and behaviors our culture expects of us based on our sex—can affect our experience of stress. Some

Table 10.1 Symptoms of Excess Stress

Physical Symptoms	Emotional Symptoms	Behavioral Symptoms
Dry mouth	Anxiety or edginess	Crying
Excessive perspiration	Depression	Disrupted eating habits
Frequent illnesses	Fatigue	Disrupted sleeping habits
Gastrointestinal problems	Hypervigilance	Harsh treatment of others
Grinding of teeth	Impulsiveness	Problems communicating
Headaches	Inability to concentrate	Sexual problems
High blood pressure	Irritability	Social isolation
Pounding heart	Trouble remembering things	Increased use of tobacco, alcohol, or other drugs
Stiff neck or aching lower back		

behavioral responses to stressors, such as crying or openly expressing anger, may be deemed more appropriate for one gender than the other.

Strict adherence to gender roles can limit one's response to stress and can itself become a source of stress. Adherence to traditional gender roles can also affect the perception of a stressor. For example, if a man derives most of his sense of self-worth from his work, retirement may be a more stressful life change for him than for a woman whose self-image is based on several different roles.

Although both men and women experience the fight-or-flight physiological response to stress, women are more likely to respond behaviorally with a pattern of "tend-and-befriend"—nurturing friends and family and seeking social support and social contacts. Rather than becoming aggressive or withdrawing from difficult situations, women are more likely to act to create and enhance their social networks in ways that reduce stress.

Past Experiences Past experiences can profoundly influence the evaluation of a potential stressor. Consider someone who has had a bad experience giving a speech in the past. He or she is much more likely to perceive an upcoming speech as stressful than someone who has had positive public speaking experiences. Effective behavioral responses, such as preparing carefully and visualizing oneself giving a successful speech, can help overcome the effects of negative past experiences.

The Stress Experience as a Whole

Physical, emotional, and behavioral responses to stressors are intimately interrelated. The more intense the emotional response, the stronger the physical response. Effective behavioral responses can lessen stress; ineffective ones only worsen it. Sometimes people have such intense responses to stressors or such ineffective coping techniques that they need professional help. (Table 10.1 lists some symptoms of excess stress.) More often, however, people can learn to handle stressors on their own.

STRESS AND WELLNESS

According to the American Psychological Association, 43% of adult Americans suffer health problems related to stress. The role of stress in health and disease is complex, and much remains to be learned. However, mounting evidence suggests that stress can increase vulnerability to numerous ailments. Several related theories have been proposed to explain the relationship between stress and disease.

The General Adaptation Syndrome

Biologist Hans Selye was one of the first scientists to develop a comprehensive theory of stress and disease. Based on his work in the 1930s and 1940s, Selye coined the term **general adaptation syndrome (GAS)** to describe what he believed is a universal and predictable response pattern to all stressors. He recognized that stressors could be pleasant, such as attending a party, or unpleasant, such as a bad grade. He called stress triggered by a pleasant stressor **eustress** and stress triggered by an unpleasant stressor **distress.** The sequence of physical responses associated with GAS (Figure 10.3) is the same for both eustress and distress and occurs in three stages:

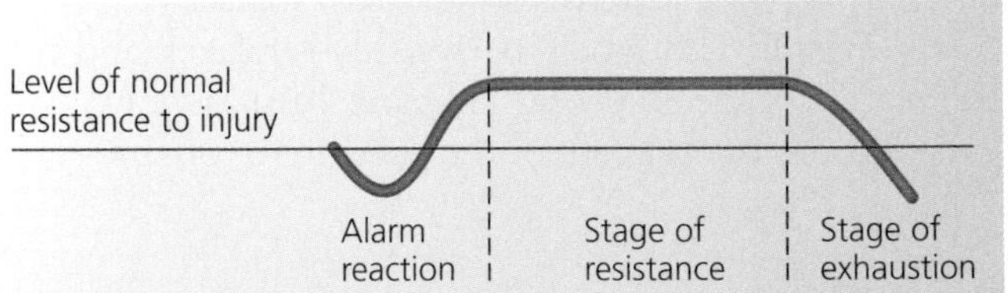

FIGURE 10.3 The general adaptation syndrome. Selye observed a predictable sequence of responses to stress. During the alarm phase, a lower resistance to injury is evident. With continued stress, resistance to injury is actually enhanced. With prolonged exposure to repeated stressors, exhaustion sets in, with a return of low resistance levels.

- *Alarm.* The alarm stage includes the complex sequence of events brought on by the fight-or-flight reaction. During this stage, the body is more susceptible to disease or injury because it is geared up to deal with a crisis. A person in this phase may experience headaches, indigestion, anxiety, and disrupted sleeping and eating patterns.
- *Resistance.* Selye theorized that with continued stress, the body develops a new level of homeostasis in which it is more resistant to disease and injury than normal. During the resistance stage, a person can cope with normal life and added stress.
- *Exhaustion.* Both the mobilization of forces during the alarm reaction and the maintenance of homeostasis during the resistance stage require a considerable amount of energy. If a stressor persists, or if several stressors occur in succession, general exhaustion results. This is not the sort of exhaustion people complain of after a long, busy day. It's a life-threatening type of physiological exhaustion characterized by such symptoms as distorted perceptions and disorganized thinking.

Allostatic Load

While Selye's model of GAS is still viewed as a key contribution to modern stress theory, some aspects of it are now discounted. For example, increased susceptibility to disease after repeated or prolonged stress is now thought to be due to the effects of the stress response itself rather than to a depletion of resources (Selye's exhaustion stage). In particular, long-term overexposure to stress hormones such as cortisol has been linked with health problems. High cortisol levels are associated, for example, with metabolic syndrome.

The long-term wear and tear of the stress response is called the **allostatic load.** An individual's allostatic load depends on many factors, including genetics, life experiences, and emotional and behavioral responses to stressors. A high allostatic load may be due to frequent stressors, poor adaptation to common stressors, an inability to shut down the stress response, or imbalances in the stress response of different body systems. High allostatic load has been linked with heart disease, high blood pressure, obesity, and reduced brain and immune system functioning. In other words, when your allostatic load exceeds your ability to cope, you are more likely to get sick.

QUESTIONS FOR CRITICAL THINKING AND REFLECTION

Have you ever been so stressed that you felt ill in some way? If so, what were your symptoms? How did you handle them? Did the experience affect the way you reacted to other stressful events?

Psychoneuroimmunology

One of the most fruitful areas of current research into the relationship between stress and disease is **psychoneuroimmunology (PNI).** PNI is the study of the interactions among the nervous system, the endocrine system, and the immune system. The underlying premise of PNI is that stress, through the actions of the nervous and endocrine systems, impairs the immune system and thereby affects health.

Researchers have discovered a complex network of connections between the nervous and endocrine systems and the immune system. We have already seen the profound physical effects of the hormones and other chemical messengers released during the stress response. These compounds also influence the immune system by affecting the number and efficiency of immune system cells, or lymphocytes.

The nervous, endocrine, and immune systems share other connections. Scientists have identified hormonelike substances called neuropeptides that appear to translate emotions into physiological events. Neuropeptides are produced and received by both brain and immune cells, so that the brain and the immune system share a biochemical "language," which also happens to be the language of emotions. The biochemical changes accompanying particular emotions can strongly influence the functioning of the immune system.

Links Between Stress and Specific Conditions

Although much remains to be learned, it is clear that people who have unresolved chronic stress in their lives or who handle stressors poorly are at risk for a wide range of health problems. In the short term, the problem might just be a cold, a stiff neck, or a stomachache. Over the long term, the problems can be more severe, such as cardiovascular disease or impairment of the immune system.

Cardiovascular Disease The stress response profoundly affects the cardiovascular system. During the stress response, heart rate increases and blood vessels constrict, causing blood pressure to rise. Chronic high blood pressure

TERMS

general adaptation syndrome (GAS) A pattern of stress responses consisting of three stages: alarm, resistance, and exhaustion.

eustress Stress resulting from a pleasant stressor.

distress Stress resulting from an unpleasant stressor.

allostatic load The long-term negative impact of the stress response on the body.

psychoneuroimmunology (PNI) The study of the interactions among the nervous, endocrine, and immune systems.

TAKE CHARGE

Overcoming Insomnia

Most people can overcome insomnia by discovering the cause of poor sleep and taking steps to remedy it. Insomnia that lasts for more than 6 months and interferes with daytime functioning requires consultation with a physician. Sleeping pills are not recommended for chronic insomnia because they can be habit-forming; they also lose their effectiveness over time.

If you're bothered by insomnia, try the following:

- Determine how much sleep you need to feel refreshed the next day, and don't sleep longer than that.
- Go to bed at the same time every night and, more importantly, get up at the same time every morning, 7 days a week, regardless of how much sleep you got. Don't nap during the day.
- Exercise regularly, but end your workout at least 3 hours before bedtime. Your metabolism needs time to slow down after exercise.
- Avoid tobacco and caffeine late in the day, and alcohol before bedtime (it causes disturbed, fragmented sleep).
- If you take any medications (prescription or not), ask your doctor or pharmacist if they interfere with sleep.
- Have a light snack before bedtime; you'll sleep better if you're not hungry.
- Use your bed only for sleep. Don't eat, read, study, or watch television in bed.
- Establish a relaxing bedtime routine that helps you unwind and lets your brain know it's time to go to sleep. Read, listen to music, or practice a relaxation technique. Don't lie down in bed until you're sleepy.
- If you don't fall asleep in 15–30 minutes, or if you wake up and can't fall asleep again, get out of bed, leave the room if possible, and do something monotonous until you feel sleepy. Try distracting yourself with imagery instead of counting sheep; imagine yourself on a pleasant vacation or enjoying some beautiful scenery.
- If sleep problems persist, ask your doctor for a referral to a sleep specialist in your area. You may be a candidate for a sleep study—an overnight evaluation of your sleep pattern that can uncover many sleep-related disorders.

is a major cause of atherosclerosis, a disease in which the lining of the blood vessels becomes damaged and caked with fatty deposits. These deposits can block arteries, causing heart attacks and strokes (see Chapter 11).

Recent research suggests that certain types of emotional responses increase a person's risk of cardiovascular disease. "Hot reactors," people who exhibit extreme increases in heart rate and blood pressure in response to emotional stressors, may face an increased risk of cardiovascular problems.

Altered Functioning of the Immune System PNI research helps explain how stress affects the immune system. Some of the health problems linked to stress-related changes in immune function include vulnerability to colds and other infections, asthma and allergy attacks, susceptibility to cancer, and flare-ups of chronic diseases such as genital herpes and HIV infection.

Other Health Problems Many other health problems may be caused or worsened by excessive stress, including the following:

- Digestive problems such as stomachaches, diarrhea, constipation, irritable bowel syndrome, and ulcers
- Tension headaches and migraines
- Insomnia and fatigue (see the box "Overcoming Insomnia")
- Injuries, including on-the-job injuries caused by repetitive strain
- Menstrual irregularities, impotence, and pregnancy complications
- Psychological problems, including depression, anxiety, panic attacks, eating disorders, and post-traumatic stress disorder (PTSD), which afflicts people who have suffered or witnessed severe trauma

COMMON SOURCES OF STRESS

Being able to recognize potential sources of stress is an important step in successfully managing the stress in your life.

Major Life Changes

Any major change in your life that requires adjustment and accommodation can be a source of stress. Early adulthood and the college years are associated with many significant changes, such as moving out of the family home. Even changes typically thought of as positive—graduation, job promotion, marriage—can be stressful.

Clusters of life changes, particularly those that are perceived negatively, may be linked to health problems in some people. Personality and coping skills, however, are important moderating influences. People with a strong support network and a stress-resistant personality are less likely to become ill in response to life changes than people with fewer resources.

Daily Hassles

Although major life changes are undoubtedly stressful, they seldom occur regularly. Researchers have proposed

Even a joyful occasion can be a source of stress, especially if it involves a major life change.

that minor problems—life's daily hassles, such as losing your keys or wallet—can be an even greater source of stress because they occur much more often.

People who perceive hassles negatively are likely to experience a moderate stress response every time they are faced with one. Over time, this can take a significant toll on health. Studies indicate that for some people, daily hassles contribute to a general decrease in overall wellness.

College Stressors

College is a time of major changes and minor hassles. For many students, college means being away from home and family for the first time. Nearly all students share stresses like the following:

- ***Academic stress.*** Exams, grades, and an endless workload await every college student but can be especially troublesome for young students just out of high school.
- ***Interpersonal stress.*** Most students are more than just students; they are also friends, children, employees, spouses, parents, and so on. Managing relationships while juggling the rigors of college life can be daunting, especially if some friends or family are less than supportive.
- ***Time pressures.*** Class schedules, assignments, and deadlines are an inescapable part of college life. But these time pressures can be drastically compounded for students who also have a job and/or family responsibilities.
- ***Financial concerns.*** The majority of college students need financial aid not just to cover the cost of tuition but to survive from day to day while in school. For many, college life isn't possible without a job, and the pressure to stay afloat financially competes with academic and other stressors.
- ***Worries about the future.*** As college life comes to an end, students face the reality of life after college. This means thinking about a career, choosing a place to live, and leaving the friends and routines of school behind.

Job-Related Stressors

Americans rate their jobs as one of the key sources of stress in their lives. Tight schedules and overtime leave less time to exercise, socialize, and engage in other stress-proofing activities. More than one-third of Americans report that they always feel rushed, and nearly half say they would give up a day's pay for a day off. Worries about job performance, salary, and job security and interactions with bosses, coworkers, and customers can contribute to stress. High levels of job stress are also common for people who are left out of important decisions relating to their jobs. When workers are given the opportunity to shape how their jobs are performed, job satisfaction goes up and stress levels go down.

If job-related (or college-related) stress is severe or chronic, the result can be burnout, a state of physical, mental, and emotional exhaustion. Burnout occurs most often in highly motivated and driven individuals who come to feel that their work is not recognized or that they are not accomplishing their goals. People in the helping professions—teachers, social workers, caregivers, police officers, and so on—are also prone to burnout. For some people who suffer from burnout, a vacation or leave of absence may be appropriate. For others, a reduced work schedule, better communication with superiors, or a change in job goals may be necessary. Improving time-management skills can also help.

Interpersonal and Social Stressors

Although social support is a key buffer against stress, your interactions with others can themselves be a source of stress. Your relationships may change as you develop new interests and as the course of your life changes.

The community and society in which you live can also be major sources of stress. Social stressors include prejudice and discrimination. You may feel stress as you try to relate to people of other ethnic or socioeconomic groups. If you are a member of a minority ethnic group, you may feel pressure to assimilate into mainstream society. If English is not your first language, you face the added burden of conducting many daily activities in a language with which you may not be completely comfortable.

Counterproductive Strategies for Coping with Stress

IN FOCUS

College students develop a variety of habits in response to stress—some of them ineffective and even unhealthy. Here are a few unhealthy coping techniques to avoid:

- ***Alcohol.*** A few drinks might make you feel at ease, and getting drunk may help you forget the stress in your life—but any relief alcohol provides is temporary. Binge drinking and excessive alcohol consumption are not effective ways to handle stress, and using alcohol to deal with stress puts you at risk for all the short- and long-term problems associated with alcohol abuse.

- ***Tobacco.*** The nicotine in cigarettes and other tobacco products can make you feel relaxed and may even increase your ability to concentrate. Tobacco, however, is highly addictive, and smoking causes cancer, heart disease, sexual problems, and many other health problems. Tobacco use is the leading preventable cause of death in the United States.

- ***Other drugs.*** Altering your body chemistry to cope with stress is a strategy with many pitfalls. Caffeine, for example, raises cortisol levels and blood pressure and can disrupt sleep. Marijuana can elicit panic attacks with repeated use, and some research suggests that it heightens the body's stress response.

- ***Binge eating.*** Eating can induce relaxation, which reduces stress. Eating as a means of coping with stress, however, may lead to weight gain and to binge eating, a risky behavior associated with eating disorders.

There is one other problem with these methods of fighting stress; that is, none of them addresses the actual cause of the stress in your life. To combat stress in a healthy way, learn some of the stress-management techniques described in this chapter.

Other Stressors

Environmental stressors—external conditions or events that cause stress—include loud noises, unpleasant smells, industrial accidents, violence, and natural disasters. (See Appendix A for preparation and coping strategies for large-scale disasters.) Internal stressors are found within ourselves. We put pressure on ourselves to reach personal goals and then evaluate our progress and performance. Physical and emotional states such as illness and exhaustion are also internal stressors.

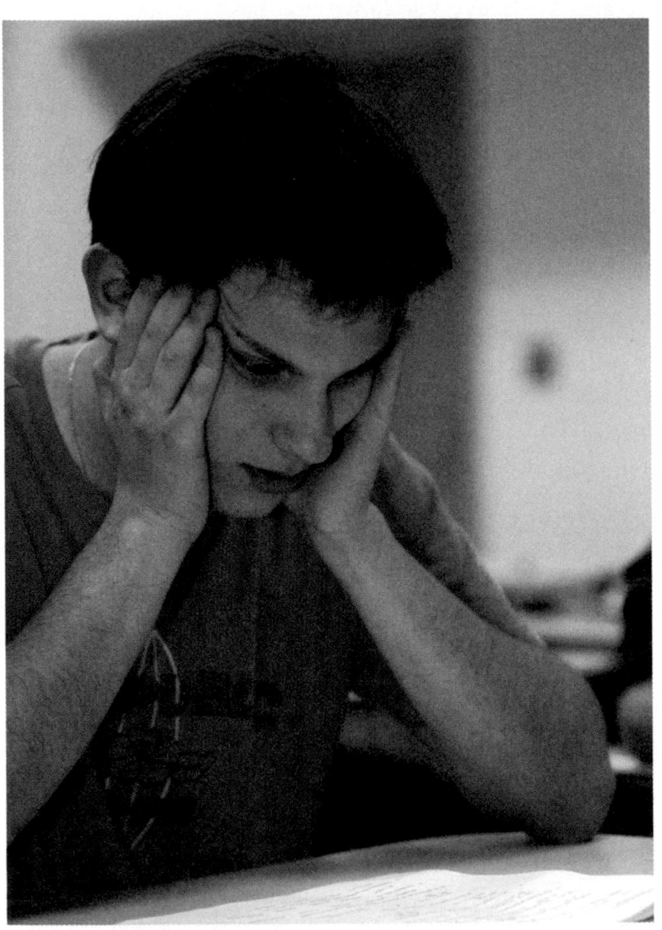

College students face a host of stressors, not the least of which is the pressure to perform academically.

QUESTIONS FOR CRITICAL THINKING AND REFLECTION

What are the top two or three stressors in your life right now? Are they new to your life—as part of your college experience—or are they stressors you've experienced in the past? Do they include both positive and negative experiences (eustress and distress)?

MOTIVATION BOOSTER

Review your day. Set aside a few minutes at the end of each day to review the progress of your behavior change program. Think back over the course of the day and take note of your accomplishments—the positive choices you made and the challenges you overcame. Then set a plan for the next day. This end-of-day review gives you the opportunity to engage in positive self-talk, and it can help you keep your behavior change program on track.

MANAGING STRESS

What can you do about all this stress? A great deal. By pursuing a wellness lifestyle—being physically active, eating well, getting enough sleep, and so on—and by learning simple ways to identify and moderate individual stressors, you can control the stress in your life. (There are also some stress-management practices you should avoid; see the box "Counterproductive Strategies for Coping with Stress.")

Exercise

One study found that taking a long walk can be effective at reducing anxiety and blood pressure. Another study showed that a brisk walk of as little as 10 minutes' duration can leave people feeling more relaxed and energetic for up to 2 hours. Regular exercise has even more benefits. Researchers have found that people who exercise regularly react with milder physical stress responses before, during, and after exposure to stressors and that their overall sense of well-being increases as well. Although even light exercise can have a beneficial effect, an integrated fitness program can have a significant impact on stress. People who took three brisk 45-minute walks a week for 3 months reported that they perceived fewer daily hassles. Their sense of wellness also increased.

These findings are not surprising because, as described earlier, the stress response mobilizes energy resources and readies the body for physical emergencies. If you experience stress and do not physically exert yourself, you are not completing the energy cycle. You may not be able to exercise while your daily stressors occur—during class, for example, or while sitting in a traffic jam—but you can be active later in the day. Physical activity allows you to expend the nervous energy you have built up and trains your body to more readily return to homeostasis after stressful situations.

One warning: For some people, exercise can become just one more stressor in a highly stressed life. People who exercise compulsively risk overtraining, a condition characterized by fatigue, irritability, depression, and diminished athletic performance. An overly strenuous exercise program can even make a person sick by compromising immune function. (For the details of a safe and effective exercise program, refer to Chapter 7.)

Nutrition

A healthy, balanced diet can help you cope with stress. In addition, eating wisely will enhance your feelings of self-control and self-esteem. Avoiding or limiting caffeine is also important in stress management. Although one or two cups of coffee a day probably won't hurt you, caffeine is a mildly addictive stimulant that leaves some people jittery, irritable, and unable to sleep; consuming caffeine during stressful situations can raise blood pressure and increase levels of cortisol. (For more on sound nutrition and for advice on evaluating dietary supplements, many of which are marketed for stress, see Chapter 8.)

Sleep

Lack of sleep can be both a cause and an effect of excess stress. Without sufficient sleep, our mental and physical processes steadily deteriorate. We get headaches, feel irritable, are unable to concentrate, forget things, and may be more susceptible to illness. Lack of sleep can also raise levels of stress hormones throughout the day. Fatigue and sleep deprivation are major factors in many fatal car, truck, and train crashes. Adequate sleep, on the other hand, improves mood, fosters feelings of competence and self-worth, and supports optimal mental and emotional functioning. Make time in your schedule to get enough sleep; if insomnia is a problem for you, refer back to the tips in the box "Overcoming Insomnia."

Social Support

Sharing fears, frustrations, and joys makes life richer and seems to contribute to the well-being of body and mind. One study of college students living in overcrowded apartments, for example, found that those with a strong social support system were less distressed by their cramped quarters than were the loners who navigated life's challenges on their own. Other studies have shown that married people live longer than single people and have lower death rates from a wide range of conditions. And people infected with HIV remain symptom-free longer if they have a strong social support network. For more on developing and maintaining your social network, see the box "Building Social Support" on p. 314.

Communication

How do you communicate your wishes and needs to others? Communicating in an assertive way that respects the rights of others as well as your own rights can prevent potentially stressful situations from getting out of control.

Some people have trouble either telling others what they need or saying no to the needs of others. They may suppress their feelings of anger, frustration, and resentment, and they may end up feeling taken advantage of or suffering in unhealthy relationships. At the other extreme are people who express anger openly and directly by being verbally or physically aggressive or indirectly by making critical, hurtful comments to others. Their abusive behavior pushes other people away, so they also have problems with relationships.

Better communication skills can help everyone form and maintain healthy relationships. If you typically suppress your feelings, you might want to take an assertiveness training course that can help you identify and change your patterns of communication. If you have trouble controlling your anger, you can benefit from learning anger management strategies; see the box "Dealing with Anger" on p. 315.

Striving for Spiritual Wellness

Spiritual wellness is associated with greater coping skills and higher levels of overall wellness. It is a very personal wellness component, and there are many ways to develop it (see the box "Paths to Spiritual Wellness" on p. 316). Researchers have linked spiritual wellness to longer life expectancy, reduced risk of disease, faster recovery, and

Building Social Support

Meaningful connections with others can play a key role in stress management and overall wellness. A sense of isolation can lead to chronic stress, which in turn can increase one's susceptibility to temporary illnesses like colds and to chronic illnesses like heart disease. Although the mechanism isn't clear, social isolation can be as significant to mortality rates as factors like smoking, high blood pressure, and obesity.

There is no single best pattern of social support that works for everyone. However, research suggests that having a variety of types of relationships may be important for wellness. Here are some tips for strengthening your social ties:

- ***Foster friendships.*** Keep in regular contact with your friends. Offer respect, trust, and acceptance, and provide help and support in times of need. Express appreciation for your friends.
- ***Keep your family ties strong.*** Stay in touch with the family members you feel close to. If your family doesn't function well as a support system for its members, create a second "family" of people with whom you have built meaningful ties.
- ***Get involved with a group.*** Do volunteer work, take a class, attend a lecture series, or join a religious group. These types of activities can give you a sense of security, a place to talk about your feelings or concerns, and a way to build new friendships. Choose activities that are meaningful to you and that include direct involvement with other people.

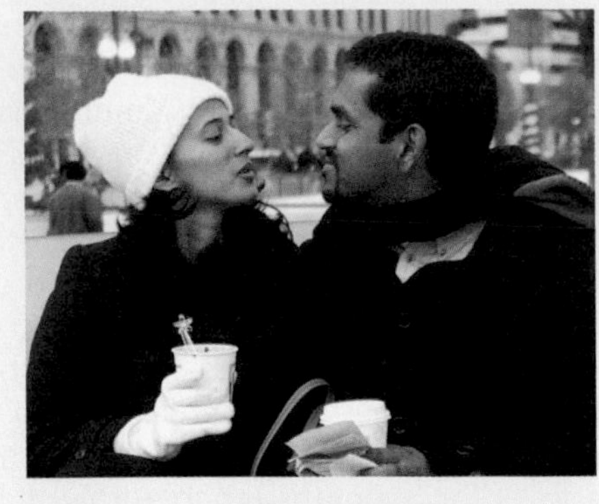

- ***Build your communication skills.*** The more you share your feelings with others, the closer the bonds between you will become. When others are speaking, be a considerate and attentive listener.

SOURCE: Friends Can Be Good Medicine. 1998. As found in the *Mind/Body Newsletter* 7(1): 3–6.

improved emotional health. Although spirituality is difficult to study, and researchers aren't sure how or why spirituality seems to improve health, several explanations have been offered.

- *Social support.* Attending religious services or participating in volunteer organizations helps people feel that they are part of a community with similar values and promotes social connectedness and caring.
- *Healthy habits.* Some of the paths to spiritual wellness may encourage healthy behaviors, such as eating a vegetarian diet or consuming less meat and alcohol, and may discourage harmful habits like smoking.
- *Positive attitude.* Spirituality can give a person a sense of meaning and purpose in life, and these qualities create a more positive attitude in the person, which in turn helps her or him cope with life's challenges.
- *Moments of relaxation.* Spiritual practices such as prayer, meditation, and immersion in artistic activities can reduce stress by eliciting the relaxation response.

Spirituality provides an ethical path to personal fulfillment that includes connectedness with self, others, and a higher power or larger reality. Spiritual wellness can make you more aware of your personal values and can help clarify them. Without an awareness of personal values, you might be driven by immediate desires and the passing demands of others. Living according to values means considering your options carefully before making a choice, choosing between options without succumbing to outside pressures that oppose your values, and making a choice and acting on it rather than doing nothing.

Lab 10.3 includes exercises designed to help you build spiritual wellness.

Confiding in Yourself Through Writing

Keeping a diary is analogous to confiding in others, except that you are confiding in yourself. This form of coping with severe stress may be especially helpful for those who are shy or introverted and find it difficult to open up to others. Although writing about traumatic and stressful events may have a short-term negative effect on mood, over the long term, stress is reduced and positive changes in health occur. A key to promoting health and well-being through journaling is to write about your emotional responses to stressful events. Set aside a special time each day or week to write down your feelings about stressful events in your life.

Time Management

Learning to manage your time can be crucial to coping with everyday stressors. Overcommitment, procrastination, and even boredom are significant stressors for many people. Along with gaining control of nutrition and exercise to maintain a healthy energy balance, time management is an important element in a wellness program. Try these strategies for improving your time-management skills:

- *Set priorities.* Divide your tasks into three groups: essential, important, and trivial. Focus on the first two, and ignore the third.

TAKE CHARGE

Dealing with Anger

Anger is a natural response to something we perceive as an injustice, a betrayal, an insult, or some other wrong—whether real or imagined. We may respond physically with faster heart and breathing rates, muscle tension, trembling, a knot in the stomach, or a red face. When anger alerts us that something is wrong, it is a useful emotion that can lead to constructive change. When anger leads to loss of control and to aggression, it causes problems.

According to current popular wisdom, it's healthy to express your feelings, including anger. However, research has shown that people who are overtly hostile are at higher risk for heart disease and heart attacks than calmer people. In addition, expressing anger in thoughtless or out-of-control ways can damage personal and professional relationships.

People who experience rage or explosive anger are particularly at risk for negative repercussions. Some of these people may have intermittent explosive disorder, characterized by aggressiveness that is impulsive and out of proportion to the stimulus. Explosive anger renders people temporarily unable to think straight or act in their own best interests. Counseling can help very angry people learn how to manage their anger.

In dealing with anger, it is important to distinguish between a reasonable degree of self-assertiveness and a gratuitous expression of aggression. When you are *assertive*, you stand up for your own rights at the same time that you respect the rights of others. When you are *aggressive*, you violate the rights of others.

Managing Your Own Anger

What are the best ways to handle anger? If you find yourself in a situation where you are getting angry, answer these questions:

- Is the situation important enough to get angry about?
- Are you truly justified in getting angry?
- Is expressing your anger going to make a positive difference?

If the answer to all these questions is yes, then calm, assertive communication may be appropriate. Use "I" statements to express your feelings ("I would like . . . ," "I feel . . ."), and listen respectfully to the other person's point of view. Don't attack verbally or make demands; try to negotiate a constructive, mutually satisfying solution.

If you answer no to any of the questions, try to calm yourself. First, reframe the situation by thinking about it differently. Try these strategies:

- Don't take it personally—maybe the driver who cut you off simply didn't see you.
- Look for mitigating factors—maybe the classmate who didn't say hello was preoccupied with money concerns.
- Practice empathy—try to see the situation from the other person's point of view.
- Ask questions—clarify the situation by asking what the other person meant. Avoid defensiveness.
- Focus on the present—don't let this situation trigger thoughts of past incidents that you perceive as similar.

Second, calm your body down.

- Use the old trick of counting to 10 before you respond.
- Concentrate on your breathing, and take long, slow breaths.
- Imagine yourself in a beautiful, peaceful place.
- If needed, take a longer cooling-off period by leaving the situation until your anger has subsided.

Dealing with Other People's Anger

If someone you are with becomes very angry, try these strategies:

- Respond asymmetrically—remain calm. Don't get angry in response.
- Apologize if you think you are to blame. (Don't apologize if you don't think you are to blame.)
- Validate the other person by acknowledging that he or she has some reason to be angry. However, don't accept verbal abuse.
- Focus on the problem and ask what can be done to alleviate the situation.
- If the person cannot be calmed, disengage from the situation, at least temporarily. After a time-out, attempts at rational problem solving may be more successful.

Warning Signs of Violence

Violence is never acceptable. The following behaviors over a period of time suggest the potential for violence:

- A history of making threats and engaging in aggressive behavior
- Drug or alcohol abuse
- Gang membership
- Access to or fascination with weapons
- Feelings of rejection or aloneness; the feeling of constantly being disrespected; victimization by bullies
- Withdrawal from usual activities and friends; poor school performance
- Failure to acknowledge the rights of others

The following are immediate warning signs of violence:

- Daily loss of temper or frequent physical fighting
- Significant vandalism or property damage
- Increased risk-taking behavior; increased drug or alcohol abuse
- Threats or detailed plans to commit acts of violence
- Pleasure in hurting animals
- The presence of weapons

Don't spend time with someone who shows these warning signs of violence. Don't carry a weapon or resort to violence to protect yourself. Ask someone in authority or an experienced professional for help.

Paths to Spiritual Wellness

Spiritual wellness means different things to different people. For many, it involves developing a set of guiding beliefs, principles, or values that give purpose and meaning to life. It helps people achieve a sense of wholeness within themselves and in their relationships with others. Spiritual wellness influences people on an individual level, as well as on a community level, where it can bond people together through compassion, love, forgiveness, and self-sacrifice.

There are many paths to spiritual wellness. One of the most common in our society is organized religion. The major religions provide paths for transforming the self in ways that can lead to greater happiness and serenity and reduce feelings of anxiety and hopelessness. For example, in Christianity, salvation means turning away from the selfish ego and to God's sovereignty and grace, where a joy is found that frees the believer from anxious self-concern and despair. *Islam* is the word for a kind of self-surrender leading to peace with God. Buddhism teaches how to detach oneself from selfish desire, leading to compassion for the suffering of others and freedom from fear-engendering illusions. Judaism emphasizes the social and ethical redemption the Jewish community can experience if it follows the laws of God.

Religions teach specific techniques for achieving these transformations of the self: prayer, both in groups and in private; meditation; the performance of rituals and ceremonies symbolizing religious truths; and good works and service to others. Religious organizations also usually offer social and material support to members who might otherwise be isolated.

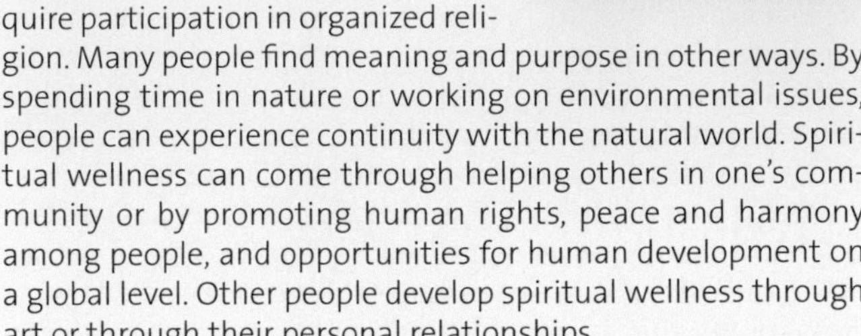

Spiritual wellness does not require participation in organized religion. Many people find meaning and purpose in other ways. By spending time in nature or working on environmental issues, people can experience continuity with the natural world. Spiritual wellness can come through helping others in one's community or by promoting human rights, peace and harmony among people, and opportunities for human development on a global level. Other people develop spiritual wellness through art or through their personal relationships.

How would you define spiritual wellness and its role in your life? What beliefs and practices do you associate with your sense of spiritual wellness? To achieve overall well-being, it is important to take time out to consider what you can do to help your spiritual side flourish.

- ***Schedule tasks for peak efficiency.*** You've undoubtedly noticed you're most productive at certain times of the day (or night). Schedule as many of your tasks for those hours as you can, and stick to your schedule.
- ***Set realistic goals and write them down.*** Attainable goals spur you on. Impossible goals, by definition, cause frustration and failure. Fully commit yourself to achieving your goals by putting them in writing.
- ***Budget enough time.*** For each project you undertake, calculate how long it will take to complete. Then tack on another 10–15%, or even 25%, as a buffer.
- ***Break up long-term goals into short-term ones.*** Instead of waiting for or relying on large blocks of time, use short amounts of time to start a project or keep it moving.
- ***Visualize the achievement of your goals.*** By mentally rehearsing your performance of a task, you will be able to reach your goal more smoothly.
- ***Keep track of the tasks you put off.*** Analyze the reasons you procrastinate. If the task is difficult or unpleasant, look for ways to make it easier or more fun. For example, if you find the readings for one of your classes particularly difficult, choose an especially nice setting for your reading, and then reward yourself each time you complete a section or chapter.
- ***Consider doing your least-favorite tasks first.*** Once you have the most unpleasant ones out of the way, you can work on the tasks you enjoy more.

Managing the many commitments of adult life—including work, school, and relationships—can sometimes feel overwhelming and produce a great deal of stress. Time-management skills, including careful scheduling with a date book or handheld computer, can help people cope with busy days.

- ***Consolidate tasks when possible.*** For example, try walking to the store so that you run your errands and exercise in the same block of time.
- ***Identify quick transitional tasks.*** Keep a list of 5- to 10-minute tasks you can do while waiting or between other tasks, such as watering your plants, doing the dishes, or checking a homework assignment.
- ***Delegate responsibility.*** Asking for help when you have too much to do is no cop-out; it's good time management. Just don't delegate the jobs you know you should do yourself.
- ***Say no when necessary.*** If the demands made on you don't seem reasonable, say no—tactfully, but without guilt or apology.
- ***Give yourself a break.*** Allow time for play—free, unstructured time when you can ignore the clock. Don't consider this a waste of time. Play renews you and enables you to work more efficiently.
- ***Avoid your personal "time sinks."*** You can probably identify your own time sinks—activities like watching television, surfing the Internet, or talking on the phone that consistently use up more time than you anticipate and put you behind schedule. Some days, it may be best to avoid problematic activities altogether; for example, if you have a big paper due, don't sit down for a 5-minute TV break if it is likely to turn into a 2-hour break. Try a 5-minute walk if you need to clear your head.
- ***Stop thinking or talking about what you're going to do, and just do it!*** Sometimes the best solution for procrastination is to stop waiting for the right moment and just get started. You will probably find that things are not as bad as you feared, and your momentum will keep you going.

For more help with time management, complete Activity 10 in the Behavior Change Workbook.

Cognitive Techniques

Certain thought patterns and ways of thinking, including ideas, beliefs, and perceptions, can contribute to stress and have a negative impact on health. But other habits of mind, if practiced with patience and consistency, can help break unhealthy thought patterns. Below are some suggestions for changing destructive thinking:

- Monitor your self-talk and attempt to minimize hostile, critical, suspicious, and self-deprecating thoughts (see the box "Realistic Self-Talk").
- Modify your expectations; they often restrict experience and lead to disappointment. Try to accept life as it comes.
- Live in the present; clear your mind of old debris and fears so you can enjoy life as it is now.
- Go with the flow. Accept what you can't change; forgive faults; be flexible.

MOTIVATION BOOSTER

Learn to solve problems. Feeling confident about your ability to tackle new challenges can help keep you motivated and on track in your behavior change program. Building the skill of problem solving is important for nearly every type of behavior change program, and it also helps in stress management. When faced with a new challenge, try the following systematic approach:

1. Define the problem in one or two sentences.
2. Identify the causes of the problem.
3. List a number of possible solutions; don't stop with just the most obvious one.
4. Weigh the positive and negative consequences of each possible solution.
5. Make a decision—choose a solution.
6. Make a list of what you will need to do to act on your decision.
7. Begin to carry out your list; if you're unable to act immediately, temporarily turn to other things.
8. Evaluate the outcome and revise your approach if necessary.

Cultivating your sense of humor is another key cognitive stress-management technique. Even a fleeting smile produces changes in your autonomic nervous system that can lift your spirits. Hearty laughter triggers the release of endorphins, and after a good laugh, your muscles go slack and your pulse and blood pressure dip below normal; you are relaxed. Try keeping a humor journal filled with funny things you and others say, including slips of the tongue. Collect funny and clever sayings and cartoons that make you smile; add them to your journal. Watch comedies on television and at the movies, especially those that make you laugh out loud. In a study of college students, those who watched an episode of *Seinfeld* prior to giving an impromptu speech were less anxious and had a lower heart rate than those who didn't watch the program.

Relaxation Techniques

First identified and described by Herbert Benson of Harvard Medical School, the **relaxation response** is a physiological state characterized by a feeling of warmth and quiet mental alertness. This state is the opposite of the fight-or-flight response. When the relaxation response is triggered by a relaxation technique, heart rate, breathing,

TERMS

relaxation response A physiological state characterized by a feeling of warmth and quiet mental alertness.

TAKE CHARGE

Realistic Self-Talk

Do your patterns of thinking make events seem worse than they truly are? Do negative beliefs about yourself become self-fulfilling prophecies? Substituting realistic self-talk for negative self-talk can help you build and maintain self-esteem and cope better with the challenges in your life. Here are some examples of common types of distorted, negative self-talk, along with suggestions for more accurate and rational responses.

Cognitive Distortion	Negative Self-Talk	Realistic Self-Talk
Focusing on negatives	School is so discouraging—nothing but one hassle after another.	School is pretty challenging and has its difficulties, but there certainly are rewards. It's really a mixture of good and bad.
Expecting the worst	Why would my boss want to meet with me this afternoon if not to fire me?	I wonder why my boss wants to meet with me. I guess I'll just have to wait and see.
Overgeneralizing	[*After getting a poor grade on a paper*] Just as I thought—I'm incompetent at everything.	I'll start working on the next paper earlier. That way, if I run into problems, I'll have time to consult with the TA.
Minimizing	I won the speech contest, but none of the other speakers was very good. I wouldn't have done as well against stiffer competition.	It may not have been the best speech I'll ever give, but it was good enough to win the contest. I'm really improving as a speaker.
Blaming others	I wouldn't have eaten so much last night if my friends hadn't insisted on going to that restaurant.	I overdid it last night. Next time I'll make different choices.
Expecting perfection	I should have scored 100% on this test. I can't believe I missed that one problem through a careless mistake.	Too bad I missed one problem through carelessness, but overall I did very well on this test. Next time I'll be more careful.

SOURCE: Adapted from Schafer, W. 1999. *Stress Management for Wellness*, 4th ed. Copyright © 2000. Reprinted with permission of Wadsworth, a division of Thomson Learning: www.thomsonrights.com.

and metabolism slow down; blood flow to the brain and skin increases; and brain waves shift from an alert beta rhythm to a relaxed alpha rhythm.

The techniques described in this section and in the box "Stress-Management Techniques from Around the World" are among the most popular techniques and the easiest to learn. All these techniques take practice, so it may be several weeks before the benefits become noticeable in everyday life.

Progressive Relaxation In this simple relaxation technique, you tense, then relax the muscles of the body one by one. Also known as deep muscle relaxation, this technique addresses the muscle tension that occurs when the body is experiencing stress. Consciously relaxing tensed muscles sends a message to other body systems to reduce the stress response.

To practice progressive relaxation, begin by inhaling as you contract your right fist. Then exhale as you release your fist. Repeat. Contract and relax your right bicep. Repeat. Do the same using your left arm. Then, working from forehead to feet, contract and relax other muscles. (A complete script for progressive relaxation is included on the Online Learning Center.) Repeat each contraction at least once, inhaling as you tense and exhaling as you relax. To speed up the process, tense and relax more muscles at one time—for example, both arms simultaneously. With practice you'll be able to relax quickly simply by clenching and releasing only your fists.

Visualization Visualization, also known as imagery, is so effective in enhancing sports performance that it has become part of the curriculum at training camps for U.S. Olympic athletes. This same technique can be used to induce relaxation, to help change habits, and to improve performance on an exam, on stage, or on a playing field.

To practice visualization, imagine yourself floating on a cloud, sitting on a mountaintop, or lying in a meadow. Try to identify all the perceptible qualities of the environment—sight, sound, temperature, smell, and so on. Your body will respond as if your imagery were real. (A complete sample script for imagery is included on the Online Learning Center.)

An alternative is to close your eyes and imagine a deep purple light filling your body. Then change the color into a soothing gold. As the color lightens, so should your distress. Imagery can also enhance performance: Visualize yourself succeeding at a task that worries you.

Deep Breathing Your breathing pattern is closely tied to your stress level. Deep, slow breathing is associated

Stress-Management Techniques from Around the World

Techniques for managing stress by inducing the relaxation response have been developed in many cultures over the centuries. One such technique is yoga, described in Chapter 5. Two other techniques that have become popular in the United States are meditation and taijiquan.

Meditation

At its most basic level, meditation, or self-reflective thought, involves quieting or emptying the mind to achieve deep relaxation. Some practitioners of meditation view it on a deeper level as a means of focusing concentration, increasing self-awareness, and bringing enlightenment to their lives. Meditation has been integrated into the practices of several religions—Buddhism, Hinduism, Confucianism, Taoism—but it is not a religion itself, nor does its practice require any special knowledge, belief, or background.

There are two general styles of meditation, centered on different ways of quieting the mind. In exclusive meditation, one focuses on a single word or thought, eliminating all others. In inclusive meditation, the mind is allowed to wander uncontrolled from thought to thought, but one observes the thoughts in a detached way, without judgment or emotion. Exclusive meditation tends to be easier to learn. Here is a simple, practical technique for eliciting the relaxation response using exclusive meditation:

1. Pick a word, phrase, or object to focus on. You can choose a word or phrase that has a deep meaning for you, but any word or phrase will work. In Zen meditation, the word *mu* (literally, "absolutely nothing") is often used. Some meditators prefer to focus on their breathing.
2. Sit comfortably in a quiet place. Close your eyes if you're not focusing on an object.
3. Relax your muscles.
4. Breathe slowly and naturally. If you're using a focus word or phrase, silently repeat it each time you exhale. If you're using an object, focus on it as you breathe.
5. Keep your attitude passive. Disregard thoughts that drift in.
6. Continue for 10–20 minutes once or twice a day.
7. After you've finished, sit quietly for a few minutes with your eyes closed, then open. Then stand up.

Allow relaxation to occur at its own pace; don't force it. Don't be surprised if you can't tune your mind out for more than a few seconds at a time. It's nothing to get angry about. The more you ignore the intrusions, the easier it will become. If you want to time your session, peek at a watch or clock occasionally, but don't set a jarring alarm.

The technique works best on an empty stomach, before a meal or about 2 hours after eating. Avoid times of day when you're tired, unless you want to fall asleep.

Although you'll feel refreshed even after the first session, it may take a month or more to get noticeable results. Be patient. Eventually, the relaxation response become so natural that it occurs spontaneously or on demand when you sit quietly for a few moments.

Taijiquan

A martial art that developed in China, taijiquan (pronounced "tie jee choo-en" and often called simply "tai chi") has become a popular form of exercise in the United States. Its movements, called forms, resemble a slow, graceful dance that mimics animals such as the snake and the crane. At its core is the Taoist belief that good health results from balanced *chi*, an energy force that surrounds and permeates all things. The forms, which can be practiced almost anywhere, are performed to help balance the body's chi to promote health and spiritual growth. The goal is to become calm and centered and to conserve and concentrate energy. Taijiquan's slow, graceful movements reinforce the idea of moving *with* rather than *against* the stressors of everyday life. Researchers have found that taijiquan is an appropriate activity for people of all ages and that it helps older adults safely boost their level of physical functioning.

The practice of taijiquan promotes relaxation and concentration as well as the development of body awareness, balance, muscular strength and endurance, and flexibility. It usually takes some time and practice to reap the stress-management benefits of taijiquan, and it's best to begin with qualified instruction.

SOURCES: Douglas, B. 2005. *The Complete Idiot's Guide to T'ai Chi and QiGong*. Indianapolis, Ind.: Alpha Books. Miller, O. H. 2004. *Essential Yoga*. San Francisco: Chronicle Books. Seaward, B. L. 2005. *Managing Stress: Principles and Strategies for Health and Well Being*, 5th ed. Boston: Jones and Bartlett.

with relaxation. Rapid, shallow, often irregular breathing occurs during the stress response. With practice, you can learn to slow and quiet your breathing pattern, thereby also quieting your mind and relaxing your body. Try one of the breathing techniques described in the box "Breathing for Relaxation" for on-the-spot tension relief, as well as for long-term stress reduction.

Listening to Music Music can relax us. It influences pulse, blood pressure, and the electrical activity of muscles. Listening to soothing, lyrical music can lessen depression, anxiety, and stress levels. To experience the stress-management benefits of music, set aside a period of at least 15 minutes to listen quietly. Choose music you enjoy and selections that make you feel relaxed.

TAKE CHARGE

Breathing for Relaxation

Controlled breathing can do more than just help you relax. It can also help control pain, anxiety, and other conditions that lead to or are related to stress. There are many methods of controlled breathing. Two of the most popular are belly breathing and tension-release breathing.

Belly Breathing

1. Lie on your back and relax.
2. Place one hand on your chest and the other on your abdomen. Your hands will help you gauge your breathing.
3. Take in a slow, deep breath through your nose and into your belly. Your abdomen should rise significantly (check with your hand); your chest should rise only slightly. Focus on filling your abdomen with air.
4. Exhale through your mouth, gently pushing out the air from your abdomen.

Tension-Release Breathing

1. Lie down or sit in a chair and get comfortable.
2. Take a slow, deep breath into your abdomen. Inhale through your nose. Try to visualize the air moving to every part of your body. As you breathe in, say to yourself, "Breathe in relaxation."
3. Exhale through your mouth. Visualize tension leaving your body. Say to yourself, "Breathe out tension."

There are many variations on these techniques. For example, sit in a chair and raise your arms, shoulders, and chin as you inhale; lower them as you exhale. Or slowly count to 4 as you inhale, then again as you exhale.

Many yoga experts suggest breathing rhythmically, in time with your own heartbeat. Relax and listen closely for the sensation of your heart beating, or monitor your pulse while you breathe. As you inhale, count to 4 or 8 in time with your heartbeat, then repeat the count as you exhale. Breathing in time with soothing music can work well, too.

Experts suggest inhaling through the nose and exhaling through the mouth. Breathe slowly, deeply, and gently. To focus on breathing gently, imagine a candle burning a few inches in front of you. Try to exhale softly enough to make the candle's flame flicker, not hard enough to blow it out.

Practice is important, too. Perform your chosen breathing exercise 2 or more times daily, for 5–10 minutes per session.

SOURCES: Duke University. 2005. *Breathing for Relaxation* (http://www.hr.duke.edu/sos/breathing.html; retrieved June 12, 2007); LIFE Center, Rehabilitation Institute of Chicago. *Pain: Breathing for Relaxation* (http://lifecenter.ric.org/content/2996/; retrieved June 12, 2007).

Other Techniques

Other stress-management techniques, such as biofeedback, hypnosis and self-hypnosis, and massage, require a partner or professional training or assistance. As with the relaxation techniques presented, all take practice, and it may be several weeks before the benefits are noticeable.

Biofeedback Biofeedback helps people reduce their response to stress by enabling them to become more aware of their level of physiological arousal. In biofeedback, some measure of stress—perspiration, heart rate, skin temperature, or muscle tension—is mechanically monitored, and feedback is given using sound (a tone or music), light, or a meter or dial. With practice, people begin to exercise conscious control over their physiological stress responses. The point of biofeedback training is to develop the ability to transfer the skill to daily life without the use of electronic equipment. Biofeedback initially requires the help of a therapist, stress counselor, or technician.

Hypnosis and Self-Hypnosis Hypnosis, a mental focusing technique that can profoundly affect the body, has been a part of healing since ancient times. Today, hypnosis is being used to help correct eating disorders, help people stop smoking, alleviate cancer pain, and hasten recovery from surgery. Hypnosis has been likened to a state of extreme concentration, in which a person becomes oblivious of his or her surroundings. A pioneer of medical hypnosis describes hypnosis as an "attentive perception and concentration, which leads to controlled imagination." Using that controlled imagination lets participants choose to feel something other than anxiety or stress or pain. Hypnosis works well for the subset of people who respond easily to being hypnotized. That same subset can be trained in self-hypnosis.

Massage Massage, the manipulation of the body's tissues, is known to subdue the stress response, diminish depression, and even increase alertness, though no one knows exactly how. Massage has been found to be helpful in managing a variety of conditions. For example, it can help premature infants gain weight, and it improves lung function and lessens anxiety in people with asthma. Massage has also been used successfully with men who have HIV to strengthen their immune systems and significantly reduce their anxiety.

GETTING HELP

You can use the principles of behavioral self-management described in Chapter 1 to create a stress-management program tailored specifically to your needs. The starting

QUESTIONS FOR CRITICAL THINKING AND REFLECTION

What percentage of your daily stress is time-related? How effective are your time management skills? Identify one thing you can start doing right now to manage your time better, and describe how you can apply it to one aspect of your daily routine.

point of a successful program is to listen to your body. When you learn to recognize the stress response and the emotions and thoughts that accompany it, you'll be in a position to take charge of how you handle stress. Labs 10.1 and 10.2 can guide you in identifying and finding ways to cope with stress-inducing situations.

If you feel you need guidance beyond the information in this text, excellent self-help guides can be found in bookstores or the library; helpful Web sites are listed in For Further Exploration at the end of the chapter. Some people also find it helpful to express their feelings in a journal. Grappling with a painful experience in this way provides an emotional release and can help you develop more constructive ways of dealing with similar situations in the future.

Peer Counseling and Support Groups

If you still feel overwhelmed despite efforts to manage your stress, you may want to seek outside help. Peer counseling, often available through the student health center or counseling center, is usually staffed by volunteer students with special training that emphasizes maintaining confidentiality. Peer counselors can steer those seeking help to appropriate campus and community resources or just offer sympathetic listening.

Support groups are typically organized around a particular issue or problem: All group members might be entering a new school, reentering school after an interruption, struggling with single parenting, experiencing eating disorders, or coping with particular kinds of trauma. Simply voicing concerns that others share can relieve stress.

Professional Help

Psychotherapy, especially a short-term course of sessions, can also be tremendously helpful in dealing with stress-related problems. Not all therapists are right for all people, so it's a good idea to shop around for a compatible psychotherapist with reasonable fees. (See the box "Choosing and Evaluating Mental Health Professionals" on p. 322.)

Is It Stress or Something More Serious?

Most of us have periods of feeling down when we become pessimistic, anxious, less energetic, and less able to enjoy life. Such feelings and thoughts can be normal responses to the ordinary challenges of life. Symptoms that may indicate a more serious problem that requires professional help include the following:

- Depression, anxiety, or other emotional problems begin to interfere seriously with school or work performance or in getting along with others.
- Suicide is attempted or is seriously considered.
- Symptoms such as hallucinations, delusions, incoherent speech, or loss of memory occur.
- Alcohol or drugs are used to the extent that they impair normal functioning; finding or taking drugs occupies much of the week; or reducing the dosage leads to psychological or physical withdrawal symptoms.

Depression is of particular concern because severe depression is linked to suicide, one of the leading causes of death among college students. In some cases, depression, like severe stress, is a clear-cut reaction to a specific event, such as losing a loved one or failing in school or work. In other cases, no trigger event is obvious. Symptoms of depression include the following:

- Negative self-concept
- Pervasive feelings of sadness and hopelessness
- Loss of pleasure in usual activities
- Poor appetite and weight loss
- Insomnia or disturbed sleep
- Restlessness or fatigue
- Thoughts of worthlessness and guilt
- Trouble concentrating or making decisions
- Thoughts of death or suicide

Not all of these symptoms are present in everyone who is depressed, but most do experience a loss of interest or pleasure in their usual activities. Warning signs of suicide include expressing the wish to be dead, revealing contemplated suicide methods, increasing social withdrawal and isolation, and exhibiting a sudden, inexplicable lightening of mood (which can indicate the person has finally decided to commit suicide). If you are severely depressed or know someone who is, expert help from a mental health professional is essential. Most communities and many colleges have hotlines and/or health services and counseling centers that can provide help. The National Suicide Prevention Lifeline can be reached at 1-800-273-TALK. Treatments for depression and many other psychological disorders are highly effective.

TERMS

depression A mood disorder characterized by loss of interest, sadness, hopelessness, loss of appetite, disturbed sleep, and other physical symptoms.

CRITICAL CONSUMER

Choosing and Evaluating Mental Health Professionals

College students are usually in a good position to find convenient, affordable mental health care. Larger schools typically have both health services that employ psychiatrists and psychologists and counseling centers staffed by professionals and peer counselors. Resources in the community may include a school of medicine, a hospital, and a variety of professionals who work independently. It's a good idea to get recommendations from physicians, clergy, friends who have been in therapy, or community agencies rather than to pick a name at random.

Financial considerations are also important. Find out how much different services will cost and what your health insurance will cover. If you're not adequately covered by a health plan, don't let that stop you from getting help; investigate low-cost alternatives on campus and in your community. The cost of treatment is linked to how many therapy sessions will be needed, which in turn depends on the type of therapy and the nature of the problem. Psychological therapies focusing on specific problems may require 8 or 10 sessions at weekly intervals. Therapies aiming for psychological awareness and personality change can last months or years.

Deciding whether a therapist is right for you will require meeting the therapist in person. Before or during your first meeting, find out about the therapist's background and training:

- Does she or he have a degree from an appropriate professional school and a state license to practice?
- Has she or he had experience treating people with problems similar to yours?
- How much will therapy cost?

You have a right to know the answers to these questions and should not hesitate to ask them. After your initial meeting, evaluate your impressions:

- Does the therapist seem like a warm, intelligent person who would be able to help you and is interested in doing so?
- Are you comfortable with the personality, values, and beliefs of the therapist?
- Is he or she willing to talk about the techniques in use? Do these techniques make sense to you?

If you answer yes to these questions, this therapist may be satisfactory for you. If you feel uncomfortable—and you're not in need of emergency care—it's worthwhile to set up one-time consultations with one or two others before you make up your mind. Take the time to find someone who feels right for you.

Later in your treatment, evaluate your progress:

- Are you being helped by the treatment?
- If you are displeased, is it because you aren't making progress or because therapy is raising difficult, painful issues you don't want to deal with?
- Can you express dissatisfaction to your therapist? Such feedback can improve your treatment.

If you're convinced your therapy isn't working or is harmful, thank your therapist for her or his efforts and find another.

TIPS FOR TODAY AND THE FUTURE

For the stress you can't avoid, develop a range of stress-management techniques and strategies.

RIGHT NOW YOU CAN

- Practice deep breathing for 5–10 minutes.
- Visualize a relaxing, peaceful place and imagine yourself experiencing it as vividly as possible. Stay there as long as you can.
- Do some stretching exercises, such as those described in Chapter 5.
- Get out your datebook and schedule what you'll be doing the rest of today and tomorrow. Pencil in a short walk and a conversation with a friend.

IN THE FUTURE YOU CAN

- Take a class or workshop that can help you overcome a source of stress, such as one in assertiveness training or time management.
- Find a way to build relaxing time into every day. Just 15 minutes of meditation, stretching, or massage can induce the relaxation response.

SUMMARY

- Stress is the collective physiological and emotional response to any stressor. Physiological responses to stressors are the same for everyone.
- The autonomic nervous system and the endocrine system are responsible for the body's physical response to stressors. The sympathetic nervous system mobilizes the body and activates key hormones of the endocrine system, causing the fight-or-flight reaction. The parasympathetic system returns the body to homeostasis.
- Behavioral responses to stress are controlled by the somatic nervous system and fall under a person's conscious control.
- The general adaptation syndrome model and research in psychoneuroimmunology contribute to our understanding of the links between stress and disease. People who have many stressors in their lives or who handle stress poorly are at risk for cardiovascular disease, impairment of the immune system, and many other problems.
- Potential sources of stress include major life changes, daily hassles, college- and job-related stressors, and interpersonal and social stressors.

COMMON QUESTIONS ANSWERED

Q Are there any relaxation techniques I can use in response to an immediate stressor?

A Yes. Try the deep breathing techniques described in the chapter, and try some of the following to see which work best for you:

- Do a full-body stretch while standing or sitting. Stretch your arms out to the sides and then reach them as far as possible over your head. Rotate your body from the waist. Bend over as far as is comfortable for you.
- Do a partial session of progressive muscle relaxation. Tense and then relax some of the muscles in your body. Focus on the muscles that are stiff or tense. Shake out your arms and legs.
- Take a short, brisk walk (3–5 minutes). Breathe deeply.
- Engage in realistic self-talk about the stressor. Mentally rehearse dealing successfully with the stressor. As an alternative, focus your mind on some other activity.
- Briefly reflect on something personally meaningful. In one study of college students, researchers found that self-reflection on important personal values prior to a stressful task reduces the hormonal response to the stressor.

Q Can stress cause headaches?

A Stress is one possible cause of the most common type of headache, the tension headache. About 90% of headaches are tension headaches, characterized by a dull, steady pain, usually on both sides of the head. It may feel as though a band of pressure is tightening around the head, and the pain may extend to the neck and shoulders. Acute tension headaches may last from hours to days, while chronic tension headaches may occur almost every day for months or even years. Stress, poor posture, and immobility are leading causes of tension headaches. There is no cure, but the pain can be relieved with over-the-counter painkillers; many people also try such therapies as massage, relaxation, hot or cold showers, and rest. Stress is also one possible trigger of migraine headaches, which are typically characterized by throbbing pain (often on one side of the head), heightened sensitivity to light and noise, visual disturbances such as flashing lights, nausea, and fatigue.

If your headaches are frequent, keep a journal with details about the events surrounding each one. Are your tension headaches associated with late nights, academic deadlines, or long periods spent sitting at a computer? Are migraines associated with certain foods, stress, fatigue, specific sounds or odors, or (in women) menstruation? If you can identify the stressors or other factors that are consistently associated with your headaches, you can begin to gain more control over the situation. If you suffer persistent tension or migraine headaches, consult your physician.

For more Common Questions Answered about stress, visit the Online Learning Center.

- Positive ways of managing stress include regular exercise, good nutrition, support from other people, clear communication, spiritual wellness, effective time management, cognitive techniques, and other relaxation techniques.
- If a personal program for stress management doesn't work, peer counseling, support groups, and psychotherapy are available.

FOR FURTHER EXPLORATION

BOOKS

Blonna, R. 2007. *Coping with Stress in a Changing World.* 4th ed. New York: McGraw-Hill. *A comprehensive guide to stress management that includes separate chapters on college stressors and spirituality.*

Greenberg, J. 2008. *Comprehensive Stress Management,* 10th ed. New York: McGraw-Hill. *Provides a clear explanation of the physical, psychological, sociological, and spiritual aspects of stress, and offers numerous stress-management techniques.*

Kabat-Zinn, J. 2005. *Coming to Our Senses: Healing Ourselves and the World Through Mindfulness.* New York: Hyperion. *Explores the connections among mindfulness, health, and our physical and spiritual well-being.*

Pennebaker, J. W. 2004. *Writing to Heal: A Guided Journal for Recovering from Trauma and Emotional Upheaval.* Oakland, Calif.: New Harbinger Press. *Provides information about using journaling to cope with stress.*

Sapolsky, R. M. 2004. *Why Zebras Don't Get Ulcers.* 3rd ed. New York: Owl Books. *Describes the links between stress and disease in addition to strategies for stress management.*

Webster, R. 2006. *Creative Visualization for Beginners.* Woodbury, Minn.: Llewellyn Worldwide. *An introduction to imagery and visualization techniques and their use for relaxation and goal achievement.*

ORGANIZATIONS AND WEB SITES

American Psychiatric Association: Healthy Minds, Healthy Lives. Provides information on mental wellness developed especially for college students.
http://www.healthyminds.org/collegementalhealth.cfm

American Psychological Association. Provides information on stress management and psychological disorders.
800-374-2721; 800-964-2000 (referrals)
http://www.apa.org; http://helping.apa.org

Association for Applied Psychophysiology and Biofeedback. Provides information about biofeedback and referrals to certified biofeedback practitioners.

http://www.aapb.org

Benson-Henry Institute for Mind Body Medicine. Provides information about stress management and relaxation techniques.

http://www.mbmi.org

Medical Basis for Stress. Includes information on recognizing stress and on the physiological basis of stress, self-assessments for stress levels, and techniques for managing stress.

http://www.teachhealth.com

National Institute of Mental Health (NIMH). Offers information about stress and stress management as well as other aspects of psychological health, including anxiety, depression, and eating disorders.

866-615-6464

http://www.nimh.nih.gov

National Institute for Occupational Safety and Health (NIOSH). Provides information and links on job stress.

http://www.cdc.gov/niosh/topics/stress

National Sleep Foundation. Provides information about sleep and how to overcome sleep problems such as insomnia and jet lag; brochures are available from the Web site or via fax.

http://www.sleepfoundation.org

Student Counseling Virtual Pamphlet Collection. Links to online pamphlets from student counseling centers at colleges and universities across the country; topics include stress, sleep, and time management.

http://counseling.uchicago.edu/vpc

SELECTED BIBLIOGRAPHY

Abbott, R. B., et al. 2007. A randomized controlled trial of Tai Chi for tension headaches. *Evidence Based Complementary and Alternative Medicine* 4(1): 107–113.

American Psychological Association. 2005. *Facts & Statistics.* (http://www.apahelpcenter.org/articles/topic.php?id=6; retrieved May 31, 2007).

American Psychological Association. 2005. *The Different Kinds of Stress.* (http://www.apahelpcenter.org/articles/article.php?id=21; retrieved May 31, 2007).

American Psychological Association. 2005. *Learning to Deal with Stress* (http://helping.apa.org/articles/article.php?id=71; retrieved May 31, 2007).

Barnes, V. A., et al. 2004. Impact of meditation on resting and ambulatory blood pressure and heart rate in youth. *Psychosomatic Medicine* 66(6): 909–914.

Bernardi, L., C. Porta, and P. Sleight. 2005. Cardiovascular, cerebrovascular and respiratory changes induced by different types of music in musicians and non-musicians: The importance of silence. *Heart,* epub Sept 30.

Bovier, P. A., E. Chamot, and T. V. Perneger. 2004. Perceived stress, internal resources, and social support as determinants of mental health among young adults. *Quality of Life Research* 13(1): 161–170.

Creswell, J. D., et al. 2005. Affirmation of personal values buffers neuroendocrine and psychological stress responses. *Psychological Science* 16(11): 846–851.

Deshmukh, V. D. 2006. Neuroscience of meditation. *Scientific World Journal* 16(6): 2239–2253.

Ditzen, B., et al. 2007. Effects of different kinds of couple interaction on cortisol and heart rate responses to stress in women. *Psychoneuroendocrinology* 32(5): 565–574.

Grewen, K. M., et al. 2005. Effects of partner support on resting oxytocin, cortisol, norepinephrine, and blood pressure before and after warm partner contact. *Psychosomatic Medicine* 67(4): 531–538.

Hamilton, N. A., et al. 2007. Sleep and the affective response to stress and pain. *Health Psychology* 26(3): 288–295.

Heerey, E. A., and A. M. Kring. 2007. Interpersonal consequences of social anxiety. *Journal of Abnormal Psychology* 116(1): 125–134.

Kivlighan, K. T., D. A. Granger, and A. Booth. 2005. Gender differences in testosterone and cortisol response to competition. *Psychoneuroendocrinology* 30(1): 58–71.

Koenig, H. G., L. K. George, and P. Titus. 2004. Religion, spirituality, and health in medically ill hospitalized older patients. *Journal of the American Geriatrics Society* 52(4): 554–562.

Lee, S. H., et al. 2007. Effectiveness of a meditation-based stress management program as an adjunct to pharmacotherapy in patients with anxiety disorder. *Journal of Psychosomatic Research* 62(2): 189–195.

Mayo Foundation for Medical Education and Research. 2006. *Stress: Unhealthy response to the pressures of life.* (http://www.mayoclinic.com/health/stress/SR00001; retrieved May 31, 2007).

Meier-Ewert, H. K., et al. 2004. Effect of sleep loss on C-reactive protein, an inflammatory marker of cardiovascular risk. *Journal of the American College of Cardiology* 43: 678–683.

Miller, G. E., et al. 2004. Psychological stress and antibody response to influenza vaccination. *Psychosomatic Medicine* 66(2): 215–223.

Pennebaker, J. W. 2004. *Writing to Heal: A Guided Journal for Recovering from Trauma and Emotional Upheaval.* Oakland, Calif.: New Harbinger Press.

Redwood, S. K., and M. H. Pollak. 2007. Student-led stress management program for first-year medical students. *Teaching and Learning Medicine* 19(1): 42–46.

Rothwell, J. D. 2004. *In the Company of Others: An Introduction to Communication,* 2nd ed. New York: McGraw-Hill.

Schoonman, G. G., et al. 2007. Is stress a trigger factor for migraine? *Psychoneuroendocrinology* 32(5): 532–538.

Segerstrom, S. C., and G. E. Miller. 2004. Psychological stress and the human immune system: A meta-analytic study of 30 years of inquiry. *Psychological Bulletin* 130: 601–630.

Steptoe, A., et al. 2004. Loneliness and neuroendocrine, cardiovascular, and inflammatory stress responses in middle-aged men and women. *Psychoneuroendocrinology* 29(5): 593–611.

Warr, D. J., et al. 2007. Money, stress, jobs: Residents' perceptions of health-impairing factors in poor neighborhoods. *Health & Place* 13(3): 743–756.

Name ______________________ Section ______________ Date ______________

LAB 10.1 Identifying Your Stress Level and Key Stressors

How Stressed Are You?

To help determine how much stress you experience on a daily basis, answer the following questions.

How many of the symptoms of excess stress in the list below do you experience frequently? ____________

Symptoms of Excess Stress

Physical Symptoms	*Emotional Symptoms*	*Behavioral Symptoms*
Dry mouth	Anxiety or edginess	Crying
Excessive perspiration	Depression	Disrupted eating habits
Frequent illnesses	Fatigue	Disrupted sleeping habits
Gastrointestinal problems	Hypervigilance	Harsh treatment of others
Grinding of teeth	Impulsiveness	Problems communicating
Headaches	Inability to concentrate	Sexual problems
High blood pressure	Irritability	Social isolation
Pounding heart	Trouble remembering things	Increased use of tobacco, alcohol, or other drugs
Stiff neck or aching lower back		

Yes No

_____ _____ 1. Are you easily startled or irritated?
_____ _____ 2. Are you increasingly forgetful?
_____ _____ 3. Do you have trouble falling or staying asleep?
_____ _____ 4. Do you continually worry about events in your future?
_____ _____ 5. Do you feel as if you are constantly under pressure to produce?
_____ _____ 6. Do you frequently use tobacco, alcohol, or other drugs to help you relax?
_____ _____ 7. Do you often feel as if you have less energy than you need to finish the day?
_____ _____ 8. Do you have recurrent stomachaches or headaches?
_____ _____ 9. Is it difficult for you to find satisfaction in simple life pleasures?
_____ _____ 10. Are you often disappointed in yourself and others?
_____ _____ 11. Are you overly concerned with being liked or accepted by others?
_____ _____ 12. Have you lost interest in intimacy or sex?
_____ _____ 13. Are you concerned that you do not have enough money?

Experiencing some stress-related symptoms or answering yes to a few questions is normal. However, if you experience a large number of stress symptoms or you answered yes to a majority of the questions, you may be experiencing a high level of stress. Take time out to develop effective stress-management techniques. Many coping strategies that can aid you in dealing with college stressors are described in this chapter. Additionally, your school's counseling center can provide valuable support.

LABORATORY ACTIVITIES

Weekly Stress Log

Now that you are familiar with the signals of stress, complete the weekly stress log to map patterns in your stress levels and identify sources of stress. Enter a score for each hour of each day according to the ratings listed below.

	A.M.							P.M.												
	6	7	8	9	10	11	12	1	2	3	4	5	6	7	8	9	10	11	12	*Average*
Monday																				
Tuesday																				
Wednesday																				
Thursday																				
Friday																				
Saturday																				
Sunday																				
Average																				

Ratings: 1 = No anxiety; general feeling of well-being
2 = Mild anxiety; no interference with activity
3 = Moderate anxiety; specific signal(s) of stress present
4 = High anxiety; interference with activity
5 = Very high anxiety and panic reactions; general inability to engage in activity

To identify daily or weekly patterns in your stress level, average your stress rating for each hour and each day. For example, if your scores for 6:00 A.M. are 3, 3, 4, 3, and 4, with blanks for Saturday and Sunday, your 6:00 A.M. rating would be 17 ÷ 5, or 3.4 (moderate to high anxiety). Then calculate an average weekly stress score by averaging your daily average stress scores. Your weekly average will give you a sense of your overall level of stress.

Using Your Results

How did you score? How high are your daily and weekly stress scores? Are you surprised by your score for average stress level?

Are you satisfied with your stress rating? If not, set a specific goal:

What should you do next? Enter the results of this lab in the Preprogram Assessment column in Appendix D. If you've set a goal for improvement, begin by using your log to look for patterns and significant time periods in order to identify key stressors in your life. Below, list any stressors that caused you a significant amount of discomfort this week; these can be people, places, events, or recurring thoughts or worries. For each, enter one strategy that would help you deal more successfully with the stressor; examples of strategies might include practicing an oral presentation in front of a friend or engaging in positive self-talk.

Next, begin to put your strategies into action. In addition, complete Lab 10.2 to help you incorporate lifestyle stress-management techniques into your daily routine.

Name ______________________ Section ______________ Date ______________

LAB 10.2 Stress-Management Techniques

Part I Lifestyle Stress Management

For each of the areas listed in the table below describe your current lifestyle as it relates to stress management. For example, do you have enough social support? How are your exercise and nutrition habits? Is time management a problem for you? For each area, list two ways that you could change your current habits to help you manage your stress. Sample strategies might include calling a friend before a challenging class, taking a short walk before lunch, and buying and using a datebook to track your time.

	Current lifestyle	Lifestyle change #1	Lifestyle change #2
Social support system			
Exercise habits			
Nutrition habits			
Time-management techniques			
Self-talk patterns			
Sleep habits			

LABORATORY ACTIVITIES

Part II Relaxation Techniques

Choose two relaxation techniques described in this chapter (progressive relaxation, visualization, deep breathing, meditation, taijiquan, massage, listening to music). If a taped recording is available for progressive relaxation or visualization, these techniques can be performed by your entire class as a group. Sample scripts for progressive relaxation and imagery can be found on the Online Learning Center.

List the techniques you tried.

1. ____________________

2. ____________________

How did you feel before you tried these techniques?

____

____

____

What did you think or how did you feel during each of the techniques you tried?

1. ____________________

____

____

2. ____________________

____

____

How did you feel after you tried these techniques?

____

____

____

LAB 10.3 Developing Spiritual Wellness

To develop spiritual wellness, it is important to take time out to think about what gives meaning and purpose to your life and what actions you can take to support the spiritual dimension of your life.

Look Inward

This week, spend some quiet time alone with your thoughts and feelings. Slow the pace of your day, remove your watch, turn your phone or pager off, and focus on your immediate experience. Try one of the following activities or develop another that is meaningful to you and that contributes to your sense of spiritual well-being.

- ***Spend time in nature.*** Experience continuity with the natural world by spending solitary time in a natural setting. Watch the sky (day or night), a sunrise, or a sunset; listen to waves on a shore or wind in the trees; feel the breeze on your face or raindrops on your skin; smell the grass, brush, trees, or flowers. Open all your senses to the beauty of nature.
- ***Experience art, architecture, or music.*** Spend time with a work of art or architecture or a piece of music. Choose one that will awaken your senses, engage your emotions, and challenge your understanding. Take a break and then repeat the experience to see how your responses change the second time.
- ***Express your creativity.*** Set aside time for a favorite activity, one that allows you to express your creative side. Sing, draw, paint, play a musical instrument, sculpt, build, dance, cook, garden—choose an activity in which you will be so engaged that you will lose track of time. Strive for feelings of joy and exhilaration.
- ***Engage in a personal spiritual practice.*** Pray, meditate, do yoga, chant. Choose a spiritual practice that is familiar to you or try one that is new. Tune out the outside world and turn your attention inward, focusing on the experience.

In the space below, describe the personal spiritual activity you tried and how it made you feel—both during the activity and after.

Reach Out

Spiritual wellness can be a bond among people and can promote values such as altruism, forgiveness, and compassion. Try one of the following spiritual activities that involve reaching out to others.

- ***Share writings that inspire you.*** Find two writings that inspire, guide, and comfort you—passages from sacred works, poems, quotations from literature, songs. Share them with someone else by reading them aloud and explaining what they mean to you.
- ***Practice kindness.*** Spend a day practicing small acts of personal kindness for people you know as well as for strangers. Compliment a friend, send a card, let someone go ahead of you in line, pick up litter, do someone else's chores, help someone with packages, say please and thank you, smile.
- ***Perform community service.*** Foster a sense of community by becoming a volunteer. Find a local nonprofit group and offer your time and talent. Mentor a youth, work at a food bank, support a literacy project, help build low-cost housing, visit seniors in a nursing home. You can also work on national or international issues by writing letters to your elected representatives and other officials.

In the space below, describe the spiritual activity you performed and how it made you feel—during the activity and after. Include details about the writings you chose or the acts of kindness or community service you performed.

Keep a Journal

One strategy for continuing on the path toward spiritual wellness is to keep a journal. Use a journal to record your thoughts, feelings, and experiences; to jot down quotes that engage you; to sketch pictures and write poetry about what is meaningful to you. Begin your spirituality journal today.

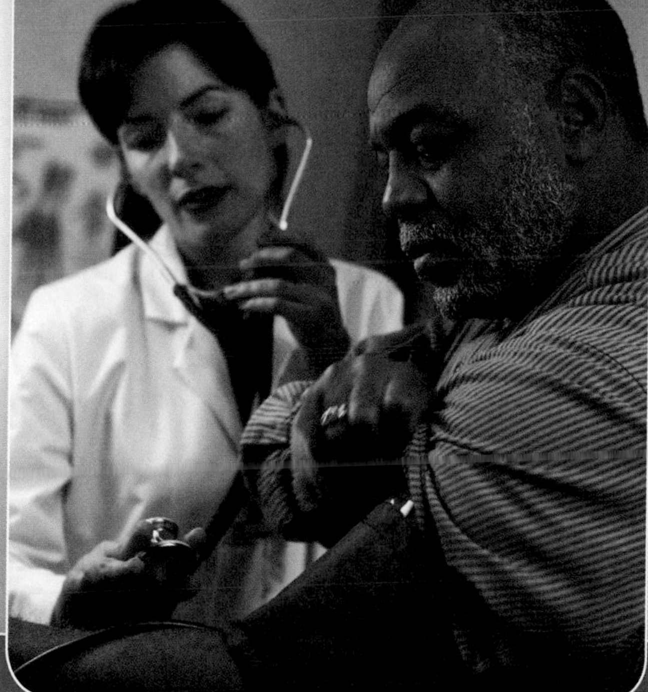

LOOKING AHEAD>>>>>

AFTER READING THIS CHAPTER, YOU SHOULD BE ABLE TO:

- Describe the controllable and uncontrollable risk factors associated with cardiovascular disease
- Discuss the major forms of cardiovascular disease and how they develop
- List the steps you can take now to lower your personal risk of developing cardiovascular disease

CARDIOVASCULAR HEALTH 11

TEST YOUR KNOWLEDGE

1. **Women are about as likely to die of cardiovascular disease as they are to die of breast cancer.**
   True or false?
2. **On average, how much earlier does heart disease develop in people who don't exercise regularly than in people who do?**
   a. 6 months
   b. 2 years
   c. 6 years
3. **Which of the following foods would be a good choice for promoting heart health?**
   a. whole grains
   b. salmon
   c. bananas

ANSWERS

1. **FALSE.** Cardiovascular disease kills far more. Among American women, nearly 1 in 3 deaths is due to CVD and about 1 in 30 is due to breast cancer. In addition, more women than men die each year from cardiovascular disease.
2. **c.** Both aerobic exercise and strength training significantly improve cardiovascular health.
3. **ALL THREE.** Whole grains (whole wheat, oatmeal, rye, barley, and brown rice), foods with omega-3 fatty acids (salmon), and foods high in potassium and low in sodium (bananas) all improve cardiovascular health.

FIT AND WELL ONLINE LEARNING CENTER www.mhhe.com/fahey

Visit the *Fit and Well* Online Learning Center for resources that will help you get the most out of your course!

- Study and review aids include practice quizzes, glossary flashcards, chapter summaries, learning objectives, PowerPoint presentations, Common Questions Answered, student handouts, crossword puzzles, Internet activities, and links to wellness Web sites.
- Behavior change tools include a daily fitness and nutrition journal, a behavior change workbook, sample behavior change plans, and blank behavior change logs to print and use.

Cardiovascular disease (CVD) affects nearly 80 million Americans and is the leading cause of death in the United States. CVD claims one life every 36 seconds—about 2400 Americans every day. According to the American Heart Association (AHA), CVD was the underlying cause of 36% of all American deaths in 2004, claiming nearly 872,000 lives. CVD is largely attributable to our way of life. Too many Americans are overweight and sedentary, smoke cigarettes, manage stress ineffectively, have uncontrolled high blood pressure or high cholesterol levels, and don't know the signs of CVD.

Not all risk factors for CVD are controllable—some people have an inherited tendency toward high cholesterol levels, for example—but many are within your control.

This chapter explains the major forms of CVD, including hypertension, atherosclerosis, and stroke. It also considers the factors that put people at risk for CVD. Most important, it explains the steps you can take to protect your heart and promote cardiovascular health throughout your life.

RISK FACTORS FOR CARDIOVASCULAR DISEASE

Researchers have identified a variety of factors associated with an increased risk of developing CVD. They are grouped into two categories: major risk factors and contributing risk factors. Some major risk factors, such as diet, exercise habits, and use of tobacco, are linked to controllable aspects of lifestyle and can therefore be changed. Others, such as age, sex, and heredity, are beyond an individual's control. (You can evaluate your personal CVD risk factors in Part I of Lab 11.1.)

Major Risk Factors That Can Be Changed

The American Heart Association has identified six major risk factors for CVD that can be changed. These are tobacco use, high blood pressure, unhealthy blood cholesterol levels, physical inactivity, obesity, and diabetes. Most

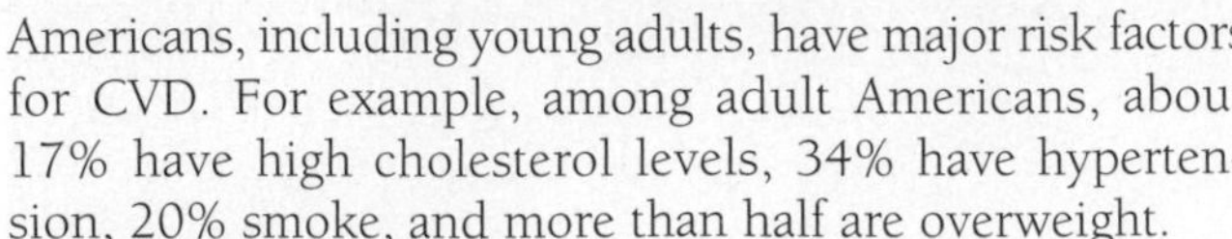

Americans, including young adults, have major risk factors for CVD. For example, among adult Americans, about 17% have high cholesterol levels, 34% have hypertension, 20% smoke, and more than half are overweight.

Tobacco Use About one in five deaths from CVD can be attributed to smoking. People who smoke a pack of cigarettes a day have twice the risk of heart attack as nonsmokers; smoking two or more packs a day triples the risk. When smokers have heart attacks, they are two to four times more likely than nonsmokers to die from them. Cigarette smoking also doubles the risk of stroke.

Smoking harms the cardiovascular system in several ways:

- It damages the lining of arteries.
- It reduces the level of high-density lipoproteins (HDL), or "good" cholesterol.
- It raises the levels of triglycerides and low-density lipoproteins (LDL), or "bad" cholesterol.
- Nicotine increases blood pressure and heart rate.
- The carbon monoxide in cigarette smoke displaces oxygen in the blood, reducing the oxygen available to the body.
- Smoking causes **platelets** to stick together in the blood stream, leading to clotting.
- Smoking speeds the development of fatty deposits in the arteries.

You don't have to smoke to be affected. The risk of death from coronary heart disease increases up to 30% among people exposed to environmental tobacco smoke (ETS)—also known as "secondhand smoke." Researchers estimate that as many as 35,000 nonsmokers die from CVD each year as a result of exposure to ETS. A 2006 Surgeon General's Report concluded that there is no safe level of exposure to ETS.

High Blood Pressure High blood pressure, or **hypertension,** is a risk factor for many forms of cardiovascular disease, including heart attacks and strokes, and is itself considered a form of CVD. As explained in Chapter 3, blood pressure, the force exerted by the blood on the vessel walls, is created by the pumping action of the heart. When the heart contracts (systole), blood pressure increases. When the heart relaxes (diastole), pressure decreases. Short periods of high blood pressure—such as in response to excitement or exertion—are normal, but chronic high blood pressure is a health risk.

Blood pressure is measured with a stethoscope and an instrument called a *sphygmomanometer.* It is expressed as two numbers—for example, 120 over 80—and measured in millimeters of mercury. The first and larger number is the systolic blood pressure; the second is the diastolic blood pressure. A normal blood pressure reading for a healthy adult is below 120 systolic over 80 diastolic; CVD risk increases when blood pressure rises above this level.

TERMS

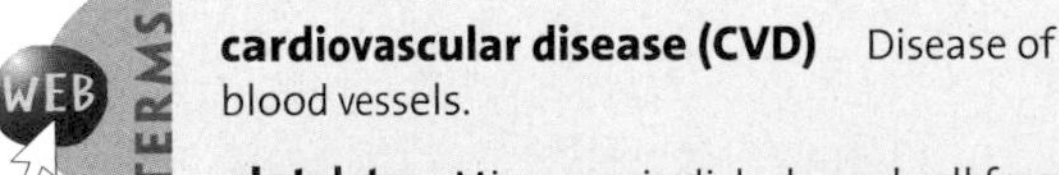

cardiovascular disease (CVD) Disease of the heart and blood vessels.

platelets Microscopic disk-shaped cell fragments in the blood that activate on contact with foreign objects and release chemicals necessary for the formation of blood clots.

hypertension Sustained abnormally high blood pressure.

atherosclerosis Cardiovascular disease in which the inner layers of artery walls are made thick and irregular by deposits of a fatty substance; the internal channels of the arteries thus become narrowed, and blood supply is reduced.

lipoproteins Blood fats formed in the liver that carry cholesterol throughout the body.

Table 11.1 Blood Pressure Classification for Healthy Adults

Category*	Systolic (mm Hg)		Diastolic (mm Hg)
Normal**	below 120	and	below 80
Prehypertension	120–139	or	80–89
Hypertension†			
Stage 1	140–159	or	90–99
Stage 2	160 and above	or	100 and above

*When systolic and diastolic pressure fall into different categories, the higher category should be used to classify blood pressure status.

**The risk of death from heart attack and stroke begins to rise when blood pressure is above 115/75.

†Based on the average of two or more readings taken at different physician visits. In persons over 50, systolic blood pressure greater than 140 is a much more significant CVD risk factor than diastolic blood pressure.

SOURCE: *The Seventh Report of the Joint National Committee on Prevention, Detection, Evaluation, and Treatment of High Blood Pressure.* 2003. Bethesda, Md.: National Heart, Lung, and Blood Institute. National Institutes of Health (NIH Publication No. 03-5233).

High blood pressure in adults is defined as equal to or greater than 140 over 90 (Table 11.1).

High blood pressure results from an increased output of blood by the heart or from increased resistance to blood flow in the arteries. The latter condition can be caused by the constriction of smooth muscle surrounding the arteries or by **atherosclerosis,** a disease process that causes arteries to become clogged and narrowed. High blood pressure also scars and hardens arteries, making them less elastic and further increasing blood pressure. When a person has high blood pressure, the heart must work harder than normal to force blood through the narrowed and stiffened arteries, straining both the heart and arteries. Eventually, the strained heart weakens and tends to enlarge, which weakens it even more.

High blood pressure is often called a silent killer, because it usually has no symptoms. A person may have high blood pressure for years without realizing it. But, during that time, it damages vital organs and increases the risk of heart attack, congestive heart failure, stroke, kidney failure, and blindness.

Hypertension is common, occurring in nearly one in three adults. Its incidence rises dramatically with increasing age; however, it can occur among children and young adults. Overall, about 34% of adults have hypertension and 30% have prehypertension. In most cases, hypertension cannot be cured, but it can be controlled. The key to avoiding complications is to have your blood pressure tested at least once every 2 years (more often if you have other CVD risk factors).

Lifestyle changes are recommended for everyone with prehypertension and hypertension. These changes include weight reduction, regular physical activity, a healthy diet, and moderation of alcohol consumption. The DASH diet, described in Chapter 8, is recommended; it emphasizes fruits, vegetables, and whole grains—foods that are rich in potassium and fiber, both of which may reduce blood pressure. Sodium restriction is also helpful. The 2005 Dietary Guidelines for Americans recommend restricting sodium consumption to less than 2300 milligrams (about 1 teaspoon of salt) per day. People with hypertension, African Americans, and middle-aged and older adults should aim to consume no more than 1500 milligrams of sodium per day. Adequate potassium intake is also important. For people whose blood pressure isn't adequately controlled with lifestyle changes, medication is prescribed.

Recent research has shed new light on the importance of lowering blood pressure to improve cardiovascular health. Death rates from CVD begin to rise when blood pressure is above 115 over 75, well below the traditional 140 over 90 cutoff for hypertension. People with blood pressures in the prehypertension range are at increased risk of heart attack and stroke as well as at significant risk of developing full-blown hypertension.

Unhealthy Cholesterol Levels Cholesterol is a fatty, waxlike substance that circulates through the bloodstream and is an important component of cell membranes, sex hormones, vitamin D, the fluid that coats the lungs, and the protective sheaths around nerves. Adequate cholesterol is essential for the proper functioning of the body. Excess cholesterol, however, can clog arteries and increase the risk of CVD (Figure 11.1, p. 334). Our bodies obtain cholesterol in two ways: from the liver, which manufactures it, and from the foods we eat.

GOOD VERSUS BAD CHOLESTEROL Cholesterol is carried in the blood by protein-lipid packages called **lipoproteins.** Low-density lipoproteins (LDLs) shuttle cholesterol from the liver to the organs and tissues that require it. LDL is known as "bad" cholesterol because if there is more than the body can use, the excess is deposited in the blood vessels. LDL that accumulates and becomes trapped in artery walls may be oxidized by free radicals, speeding inflammation and damage to artery walls and increasing the likelihood that an artery will become blocked, causing a heart attack or stroke. High-density lipoproteins (HDLs), or "good" cholesterol, shuttle unused cholesterol back to the liver for recycling.

RECOMMENDED BLOOD CHOLESTEROL LEVELS The risk for CVD increases with higher blood cholesterol levels, especially LDL. The National Cholesterol Education Program (NCEP) recommends testing at least once every 5 years for all adults, beginning at age 20. The recommended test is a lipoprotein profile that measures total cholesterol, LDL cholesterol, HDL cholesterol, and triglycerides (another blood fat). In general, high LDL, total cholesterol, and triglyceride levels and low HDL levels are associated with a higher risk for CVD; lowering LDL, total cholesterol,

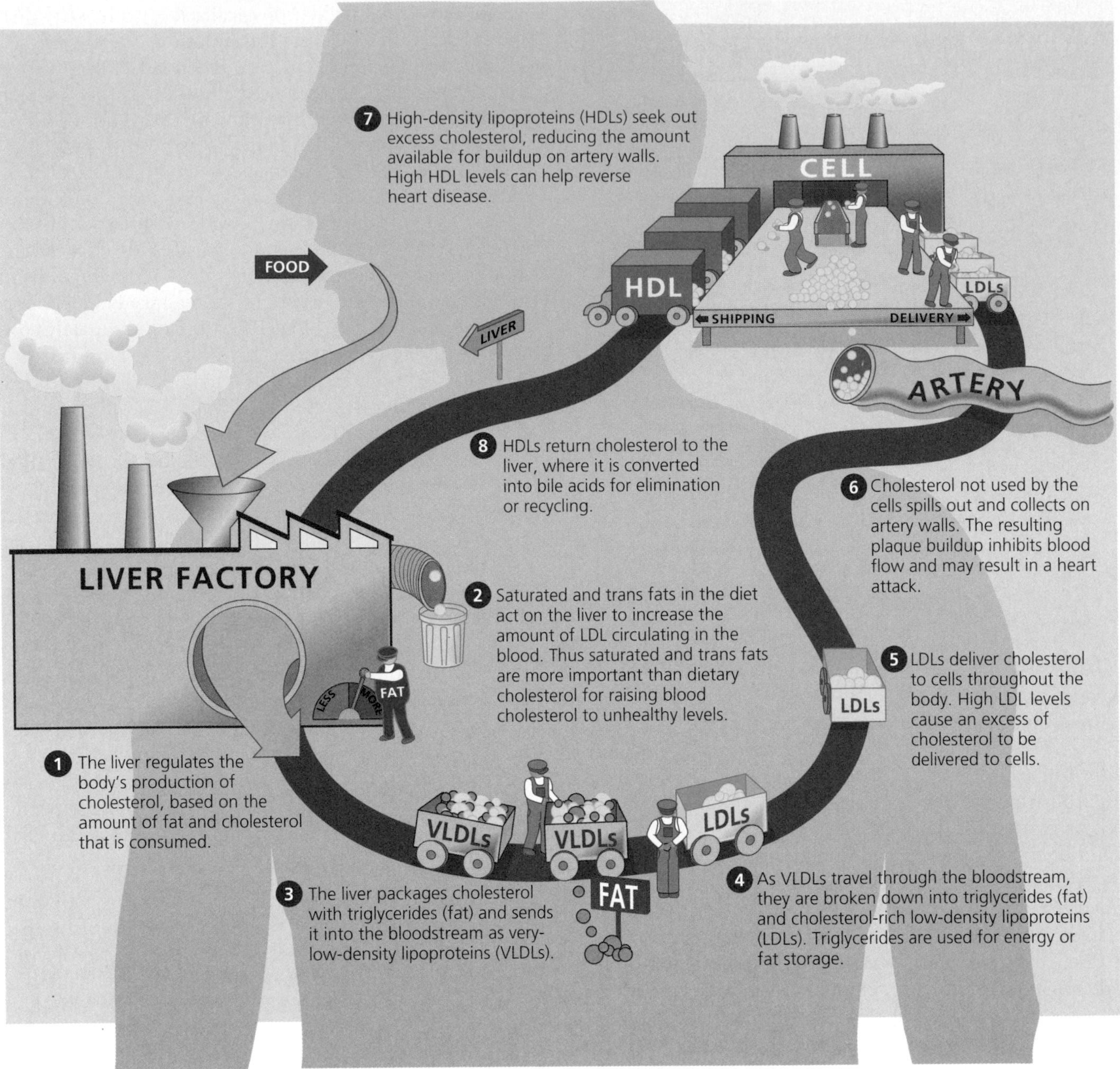

7 High-density lipoproteins (HDLs) seek out excess cholesterol, reducing the amount available for buildup on artery walls. High HDL levels can help reverse heart disease.
CELL
HDL
LDLs
SHIPPING
DELIVERY
FOOD
LIVER
ARTERY
8 HDLs return cholesterol to the liver, where it is converted into bile acids for elimination or recycling.
6 Cholesterol not used by the cells spills out and collects on artery walls. The resulting plaque buildup inhibits blood flow and may result in a heart attack.
LIVER FACTORY
2 Saturated and trans fats in the diet act on the liver to increase the amount of LDL circulating in the blood. Thus saturated and trans fats are more important than dietary cholesterol for raising blood cholesterol to unhealthy levels.
LESS
MORE
FAT
LDLs
5 LDLs deliver cholesterol to cells throughout the body. High LDL levels cause an excess of cholesterol to be delivered to cells.
1 The liver regulates the body's production of cholesterol, based on the amount of fat and cholesterol that is consumed.
VLDLs
VLDLs
LDLs
FAT
3 The liver packages cholesterol with triglycerides (fat) and sends it into the bloodstream as very-low-density lipoproteins (VLDLs).
4 As VLDLs travel through the bloodstream, they are broken down into triglycerides (fat) and cholesterol-rich low-density lipoproteins (LDLs). Triglycerides are used for energy or fat storage.

FIGURE 11.1 Travels with cholesterol.

and triglycerides can lower risk. Raising HDL is important because a high HDL level seems to offer protection from CVD even in cases where total cholesterol is high, especially for women.

As shown in Table 11.2, LDL levels below 100 mg/dl (milligrams per deciliter) and total cholesterol levels below 200 mg/dl are desirable. An estimated 105 million American adults—more than 48% of the adult population—have total cholesterol levels of 200 mg/dl or higher. The CVD risk associated with elevated cholesterol levels also depends on other factors. For example, an above optimal level of LDL would be of more concern for an individual who also smokes and has high blood pressure than for an individual without these additional CVD risk factors.

IMPROVING CHOLESTEROL LEVELS Your primary goal should be to reduce your LDL to healthy levels. Important dietary changes for reducing LDL levels include choosing unsaturated fats instead of saturated and trans fats and increasing fiber intake. Decreasing your intake of saturated and trans fats is particularly important because they promote the production and excretion of cholesterol by the liver. Exercising regularly and eating more fruits, vegetables, fish and whole grains also help. Many experts believe that cholesterol-lowering foods may be most effective when eaten in combination rather than separately. You can raise your HDL levels by exercising regularly, losing weight if you are overweight, quitting smoking, and altering the amount and type of fat you consume.

Table 11.2 Cholesterol Guidelines

Total cholesterol (mg/dl)	
Less than 200	Desirable
200–239	Borderline high
240 or more	High
LDL cholesterol (mg/dl)	
Less than 100	Optimal
100–129	Near optimal/above optimal
130–159	Borderline high
160–189	High
190 or more	Very high
HDL cholesterol (mg/dl)	
Less than 40	Low (undesirable)
60 or more	High (desirable)
Triglycerides (mg/dl)	
Less than 150	Normal
150–199	Borderline high
200–499	High
500 or more	Very high

SOURCE: Expert Panel on Detection, Evaluation, and Treatment of High Blood Cholesterol in Adults. 2001. Executive Summary of the Third Report of the National Cholesterol Education Program (NCEP) Expert Panel on Detection, Evaluation, and Treatment of High Blood Cholesterol in Adults (Adult Treatment Panel III). *Journal of the American Medical Association* 285(19).

Physical Inactivity An estimated 40–60 million Americans are so sedentary that they are at high risk for developing CVD. Exercise is thought to be the closest thing we have to a magic bullet against heart disease. It lowers CVD risk by helping to decrease blood pressure and resting heart rate, increase HDL levels, maintain desirable weight, improve the condition of the blood vessels, and prevent or control diabetes. One study found that women who accumulated at least 3 hours of brisk walking each week cut their risk of heart attack and stroke by more than half. (See Chapter 3 for more information on the physical and psychological effects of cardiorespiratory exercise.)

Obesity The risk of death from CVD is two to three times higher in obese people (BMI $\geq$ 30) than it is in lean people (BMI 18.5–24.9), and for every 5-unit increment of BMI, a person's risk of death from coronary heart disease increases by 30%. Excess weight increases the strain on the heart by contributing to high blood pressure and high cholesterol. It can also lead to diabetes, another CVD risk factor (see the next section). As discussed in Chapter 6, distribution of body fat is also significant: Fat that collects in the abdomen is more dangerous than fat that collects around the hips. Obesity in general, and abdominal obesity in particular, is significantly associated with narrowing of the coronary arteries, even in young adults in their 20s. A sensible diet and regular exercise are the best ways to achieve and maintain a healthy body weight. For someone who is overweight, even modest weight reduction can reduce CVD risk by lowering blood pressure, improving cholesterol levels, and reducing diabetes risk.

Stress and social isolation can increase risk of cardiovascular disease. A strong social support network improves both heart health and overall wellness.

Diabetes As described in Chapter 6, diabetes is a disorder in which the metabolism of glucose is disrupted, causing a buildup of glucose in the bloodstream. People with diabetes are at increased risk for CVD, partly because elevated blood glucose levels can damage the lining of arteries, making them more vulnerable to atherosclerosis; diabetics also often have other risk factors, including hypertension, obesity, unhealthy cholesterol and triglyceride levels, and platelet and blood coagulation abnormalities. Even people whose diabetes is under control face an increased risk of CVD; therefore, careful control of other risk factors is critical for people with diabetes. People with prediabetes also face a significantly increased risk of CVD.

Contributing Risk Factors That Can Be Changed

Various other CVD risk factors can be changed, including triglyceride levels, psychological and social factors, and drug use.

High Triglyceride Levels Triglycerides are blood fats that are absorbed from food and manufactured by the body. High triglyceride levels are a reliable predictor of heart disease, especially if associated with other risk factors, such as low HDL levels, obesity, and diabetes. Factors contributing to elevated triglyceride levels include excess body fat, physical inactivity, cigarette smoking, type 2 diabetes, excess alcohol intake, very-high-carbohydrate diets, and certain diseases and medications. A full lipid

Psychosocial Factors That Contribute to CVD

Risk for CVD is affected by more than diet and exercise—it's also affected by a person's attitudes, emotions, and persistent patterns of behavior. For the most part, these are risk factors that people have some control over and that can be changed.

- ***Stress.*** Excessive stress can strain the heart and blood vessels over time and contribute to CVD. A full-blown stress response causes blood vessels to constrict and blood pressure to rise. Blood platelets become more likely to cluster, possibly enhancing the formation of artery-clogging clots. Stress can trigger abnormal heart rhythms, with potentially fatal consequences. People sometimes also adopt unhealthy habits such as smoking or overeating as a means of dealing with severe stress.
- ***Chronic hostility and anger.*** Certain traits in the hard-driving Type A personality—hostility, cynicism, and anger—are associated with increased risk of heart disease. People with a quick temper, a persistently hostile outlook, and a cynical, mistrusting attitude toward life experience the stress response more intensely and frequently than do more relaxed, trusting individuals. When they encounter the irritations of daily life, their blood pressure rises, their blood vessels constrict, and their level of stress hormones increases much more than is the case for their relaxed counterparts. Over time, these effects may damage arteries and promote CVD. In a 10-year study of young adults age 18–30, those with high hostility levels were more than twice as likely to develop coronary artery calcification (a marker of early atherosclerosis) as those with low hostility levels. If you have high levels of hostility (complete the self-assessment in Lab 11.1), refer to Chapter 10 for ways to manage stress and handle anger.
- ***Suppressed psychological distress.*** Consistently suppressing anger and other negative emotions may also be hazardous to a healthy heart. People who hide psychological distress tend to have a higher rate of heart disease than people who experience similar distress but share it with others. People with so-called Type D personalities tend to be pessimistic, negative, and unhappy and to suppress these feelings.
- ***Depression and anxiety.*** Both mild and severe depression are linked to an increased risk of CVD. Researchers have also found a strong association between anxiety disorders and an increased risk of death from heart disease, particularly sudden death from heart attack.
- ***Social isolation.*** People with little social support are at higher risk of dying from CVD than people with close ties to others. Studies suggest that religious commitment has a positive effect on heart health, perhaps because of the strong community provided by church membership. A strong social support network is a major antidote to stress. Friends and family members can also promote and support a healthy lifestyle.
- ***Low socioeconomic status.*** Low socioeconomic status and low educational attainment also increase risk for CVD, probably because of a variety of factors, including lifestyle, response to stress, and access to health care.

profile should include testing and evaluation of triglyceride levels (see Table 11.2).

For people with borderline high triglyceride levels, increased physical activity, reduced intake of sugars and starches, and weight reduction can help bring levels down into the healthy range; for people with high triglycerides, drug therapy may be needed. Limiting alcohol use and quitting smoking are also helpful.

MOTIVATION BOOSTER

Plan for stress. Psychological distress impacts quality of life, raises the risk of some chronic diseases, and is a key factor in lapses during a behavior change program. When people are stressed and upset, they are more likely to eat unhealthy foods, restart a smoking habit, drink too much alcohol, or engage in other unhealthy coping strategies. No matter what your target behavior, plan ahead for how you'll handle difficult times while sticking with your behavior change program. Make a list of positive strategies you can use to reduce stress and cope with difficult emotions—for example, a short walk, a phone call to a friend, a massage, or a time-out with a favorite piece of music. Keep your list handy as a "prescription" for help when you feel stressed or overwhelmed.

Psychological and Social Factors Many of the psychological and social factors that influence other areas of wellness are also important risk factors for CVD. They include chronic stress, chronic hostility and anger, lack of social support, and others. For more on this topic, see the box "Psychosocial Factors That Contribute to CVD."

Alcohol and Drugs Drinking too much alcohol raises blood pressure and can increase the risk of stroke and heart failure. Stimulant drugs, particularly cocaine, can also cause serious cardiac problems, including heart attack, stroke, and sudden cardiac death. Injection drug use can cause infection of the heart and stroke.

Major Risk Factors That Can't Be Changed

A number of major risk factors for CVD cannot be changed: heredity, aging, being male, and ethnicity.

Family History (Heredity) Multiple genes contribute to the development of CVD and its risk factors. Having an unfavorable set of genes increases your risk, but risk is modifiable by lifestyle factors such as whether you smoke, exercise, or eat a healthy diet. People who inherit a tendency for CVD are not destined to develop it, but they may have to work harder than other people to prevent it.

Aging Of the nearly 80 million adult Americans with CVD, almost 50% are over age 65. For people over 55, the incidence of stroke more than doubles in each successive decade. However, even people in their 30s and 40s, especially men, can have heart attacks.

Being Male Although CVD is the leading killer of both men and women in the United States, men face a greater risk of heart attack than women, especially earlier in life. Until age 55, men also have a greater risk of hypertension than women. The incidence of stroke is higher for males than females until age 65. Estrogen production, which is highest during the childbearing years, may protect premenopausal women against CVD (see the box "Gender, Ethnicity, and CVD").

Ethnicity Death rates from heart disease vary among ethnic groups in the United States, with African Americans having much higher rates of hypertension, heart disease, and stroke than other groups. Figure 11.2 shows how rates of CVD compare among non-Hispanic whites, blacks, and Mexican Americans in the United States. Asian Americans historically have had far lower rates of CVD than white Americans. However, cholesterol levels among Asian Americans appear to be rising, presumably because of the adoption of a high-fat American diet.

Possible Risk Factors Currently Being Studied

In recent years, several other possible risk factors for cardiovascular disease have been identified.

High levels of a substance called C-reactive protein (CRP), which is released into the bloodstream during the inflammatory response, may be a marker for a substantially elevated risk for heart attack and stroke. CRP may be released when an artery is injured by smoking, cholesterol, infectious agents, or other factors. Lifestyle changes and certain drugs can reduce CRP levels. Statin drugs, widely prescribed to lower cholesterol, also decrease inflammation; this may be one reason that statin drugs seem to lower CVD risk even in people with normal blood lipid levels.

Elevated blood levels of homocysteine, an amino acid that may damage the lining of blood vessels, are also associated with an increased risk of CVD. Men generally have higher homocysteine levels than women, as do individuals with diets low in folic acid, vitamin B-12, and vitamin B-6. Most people can lower homocysteine levels easily by adopting a healthy diet rich in fruits, vegetables, and grains.

High levels of a specific type of LDL called lipoprotein(a), or Lp(a), may be a risk factor for coronary heart disease (CHD), especially when associated with high LDL or low HDL levels. Lp(a) levels have a strong genetic component and are difficult to treat. LDL particles differ in size and density, and people with a high proportion of small, dense LDL particles—a condition called LDL pattern B—also appear to be at greater risk for CVD. Exercise, a low-fat diet, and certain lipid-lowering drugs may help lower CVD risk in people with LDL pattern B.

Several infectious agents, including *Chlamydia pneumoniae, cytomegalovirus,* and *Helicobacter pylori,* have also been identified as possible risk factors. Infections may damage arteries and lead to chronic inflammation. Another marker for higher risk is fibrinogen, a protein involved in blood clotting.

Certain CVD risk factors are often found in a cluster referred to as *metabolic syndrome* or *insulin resistance syndrome.* As described in Chapter 6, symptoms of metabolic syndrome include abdominal obesity, high triglycerides, low HDL cholesterol, high blood pressure, and high blood glucose levels. Weight control, physical activity, and a diet rich in unsaturated fats and fiber are recommended for people with metabolic syndrome (see the box "Carbohydrates, Glycemic Index, and Heart Health").

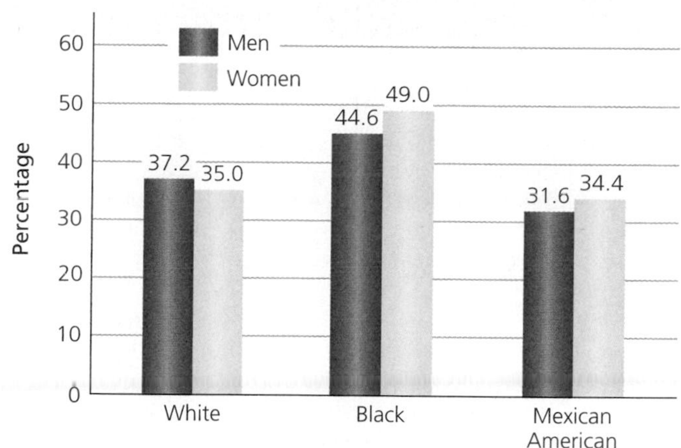

FIGURE 11.2 Percentage of adult Americans with cardiovascular disease.

SOURCE: American Heart Association. 2007. *Heart Disease and Stroke Statistics—2007 Update.* Dallas Tex.: American Heart Association.

QUESTIONS FOR CRITICAL THINKING AND REFLECTION

What risk factors do you have for cardiovascular disease? Which ones are factors you have control over, and which are factors you can't change? If you have risk factors you cannot change (such as a family history of CVD), were you aware that you can make lifestyle adjustments to reduce your risk? Do you think you will make them? Why or why not?

Gender, Ethnicity, and CVD

DIMENSIONS OF DIVERSITY

CVD is the leading cause of death for all Americans, but significant differences exist between men and women and between white Americans and African Americans in the incidence, diagnosis, and treatment of this deadly disease.

CVD in Women

CVD has been thought of as a "man's disease," but it actually kills more women than men. Polls indicate that women vastly underestimate their risk of dying of a heart attack and overestimate their risk of dying of breast cancer. In reality, nearly 1 in 3 women dies of CVD, while 1 in 30 dies of breast cancer. For women, CVD typically does not develop until after age 50.

The hormone estrogen, produced naturally by a woman's ovaries until menopause, improves blood lipid concentrations and other CVD risk factors. For several decades, many U.S. physicians encouraged menopausal women to take hormone replacement therapy (HRT) to relieve menopause symptoms and presumably to reduce their risk of CVD. However, some studies found that HRT may actually *increase* a woman's risk for heart disease and other health problems, including breast cancer. Some newer studies have found a reduced risk of CVD in women who start HRT in the early stages of menopause, suggesting that outcomes may depend on several factors, including the timing of hormone use. The U.S. Preventive Services Task Force and the American Heart Association currently recommend that HRT not be used to protect against CVD.

When women do have heart attacks, they are more likely than men to die within a year. One reason is that since they develop heart disease at older ages, they are more likely to have other health problems that complicate treatment. Women also have smaller hearts and arteries than men, possibly making diagnosis and surgery more difficult.

In addition, medical personnel appear to evaluate and treat women less aggressively than men. Women presenting with CVD are just as likely as men to report chest pain, but they are also likely to report non-chest-pain symptoms, which may obscure their diagnosis. These symptoms include fatigue, weakness, shortness of breath, nausea, vomiting, and pain in the abdomen, neck, jaw, and back. A woman who experiences these symptoms should be persistent in seeking accurate diagnosis and appropriate treatment.

Careful diagnosis of cardiac symptoms is also key in avoiding unnecessary invasive procedures in cases of stress cardiomyopathy ("broken heart syndrome"), which occurs much more commonly in women than in men. In this condition, hormones and neurotransmitters associated with a severe stress response stun the heart, producing heart-attack-like symptoms and decreased pumping function of the heart, but no damage to the heart muscle. Typically, the condition reverses quickly.

Women should be aware of their CVD risk factors and consult with a physician to assess their risk and determine the best way to prevent CVD.

CVD in African Americans

African Americans also have a different experience of CVD than do white men. Blacks are at substantially higher risk for death from CVD. The rate of hypertension among African Americans is among the highest of any group in the world. Blacks tend to develop hypertension at an earlier age than whites, and their average blood pressure is much higher. They also have a higher risk of stroke, have strokes at younger ages, and have more significant stroke-related disabilities. Some experts recommend that blacks be treated with antihypertensive drugs at an earlier stage—when blood pressure reaches 130/80 rather than the typical 140/90 cutoff for hypertension.

Possible genetic and biological factors in this CVD profile include heightened sensitivities to salt and a physiologically different response to stress, which can lead to high blood pressure and other CVD risk factors. Sickle-cell disease, a genetic disorder that occurs mainly in blacks, can contribute to CVD. Low income is another factor and is associated with reduced access to adequate health care, insurance, and information about prevention. Discrimination may also play a role, both by increasing stress and by affecting treatment by physicians and hospitals.

Although these factors are important, some evidence favors lifestyle explanations for the higher CVD rate among African Americans. For example, black New Yorkers born in the South have a much higher CVD risk than those born in the Northeast. (Researchers speculate that some lifestyle risk factors for CVD, including smoking and a high-fat diet, may be more common in the South.) People with low incomes, who are disproportionately black, tend to smoke more, use more salt, and exercise less than those with higher incomes. In addition, according to the National Center for Health Statistics, four-fifths of black women and two-thirds of black men are overweight.

The general preventive strategies recommended for all Americans may be particularly critical for African Americans. In addition, researchers have identified several dietary factors that may be of special importance for blacks. Studies have found that diets high in potassium and calcium improve blood pressure in African Americans.

Exercise is especially important because it increases insulin sensitivity even if it doesn't produce weight loss.

TERMS

plaque A deposit of fatty (and other) substances on the inner wall of the arteries.

MAJOR FORMS OF CARDIOVASCULAR DISEASE

Collectively, the various forms of CVD kill more Americans than the next four leading causes of death combined. The financial burden of CVD, including the costs of medical treatments and lost productivity, exceeds $400 billion

Carbohydrates, Glycemic Index, and Heart Health

Research indicates that eating a diet rich in carbohydrates with low glycemic index (GI) values reduces the risk of developing type 2 diabetes and coronary heart disease, especially among people who are overweight or who have metabolic syndrome. As described in Chapter 8, glycemic index is a measure of how a particular food affects blood glucose levels. A food with a high glycemic index is digested quickly, causing a rapid spike in blood glucose (and then a rapid fall); a food with a low glycemic index is digested more slowly, causing a more gradual change in blood glucose. Low-GI foods take longer to digest, so you feel full longer. Hunger tends to return quickly after you eat high-GI foods.

You might expect physicians and nutritionists to recommend that we choose foods based on their glycemic index, but it turns out that glycemic index is not a straightforward, easy-to-use measure. Rapidly digestible starchy or sugary foods like white bread, white potatoes, and sweets tend to have relatively high GIs, but so do healthy foods like carrots, raisins, and bananas. The GI of a food can change depending on how the food is prepared, how ripe the food is, and how GI is measured.

The effect of a food on your blood glucose levels also depends on how much of it you eat; for example, carrots have a relatively high GI, but the total amount of carbohydrate in one serving is very small (a food's GI multiplied by the carbohydrate content of a serving is its glycemic load). Eating a single serving (one-half cup) of raw carrots does not raise your blood glucose levels very much, despite carrots' high GI. (The GI and glycemic load values for some common foods are listed in a student handout for Chapter 8 on the Online Learning Center.) To make matters even more complicated, GI refers to the effect of a single food on blood sugar levels; estimating the effect of an entire meal is much more difficult.

Given all of these complexities, it seems that the best approach is to use glycemic index as a general tool. Avoiding high-GI carbohydrates and eating more low-GI carbohydrates supports good health, especially if you have a family history of diabetes or heart disease, are overweight, or have some of the symptoms of metabolic syndrome. High-GI carbohydrates include soft drinks, white potatoes (including french fries), white bread, sweets, and refined cereals. Low-GI carbohydrates include whole grains, nonstarchy vegetables, and fruits. If this advice sounds familiar, it's because the same diet provides good nutrition, promotes weight control, and protects you against diabetes and heart disease.

annually. Although the main forms of CVD are interrelated and have elements in common, we treat them separately here for the sake of clarity. Hypertension, which is both a major risk factor and a form of CVD, was described earlier in the chapter.

Atherosclerosis

Atherosclerosis is a form of arteriosclerosis, or thickening and hardening of the arteries. In atherosclerosis, arteries become narrowed by deposits of fat, cholesterol, and other substances. The process begins when the cells lining the arteries (endothelial cells) become damaged, probably through a combination of factors such as smoking, high blood pressure, and deposits of oxidized LDL particles. The body's response to this damage results in inflammation and changes in the artery lining. Deposits, called **plaques,** accumulate on artery walls; the arteries lose their elasticity and their ability to expand and contract, restricting blood flow. Once narrowed by a plaque, an artery is vulnerable to blockage by blood clots (Figure 11.3). Atherosclerosis often begins in childhood and has no early symptoms.

If the heart, brain, and/or other organs are deprived of blood and the oxygen it carries, the effects of atherosclerosis

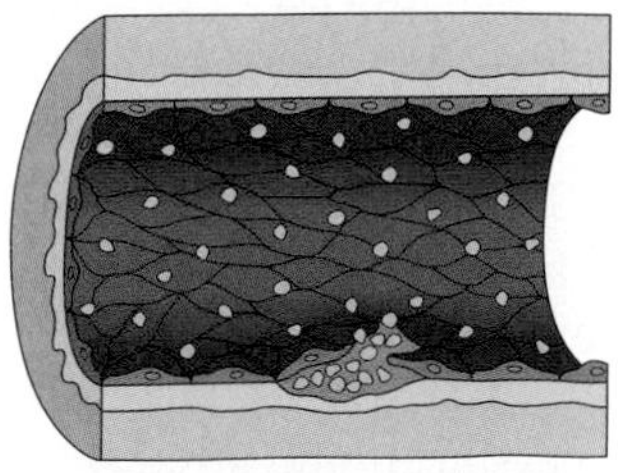

Plaque buildup begins when endothelial cells lining the arteries are damaged by smoking, high blood pressure, oxidized LDL, and other causes; excess cholesterol particles collect beneath these cells.

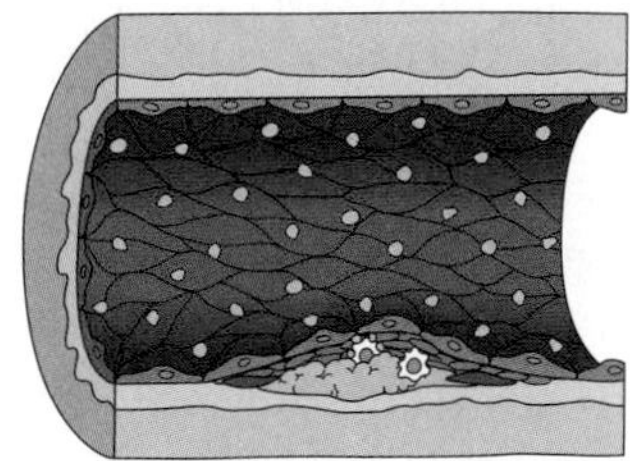

In response to the damage, platelets and other types of cells collect at the site; a fibrous cap forms, isolating the plaque within the artery wall. An early-stage plaque is called a fatty streak.

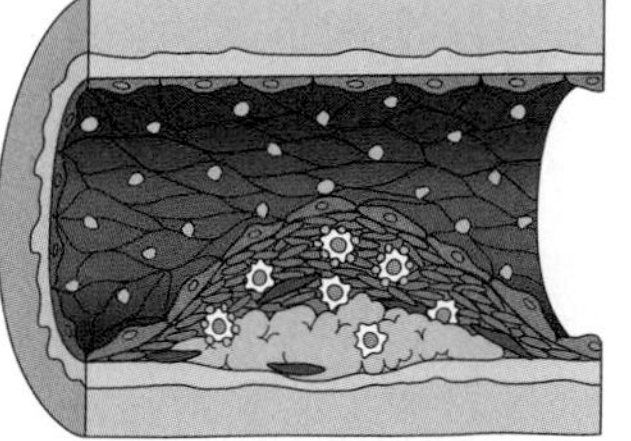

Chemicals released by cells in and around the plaque cause further inflammation and buildup; an advanced plaque contains LDL, white blood cells, connective tissue, smooth muscle cells, platelets, and other compounds.

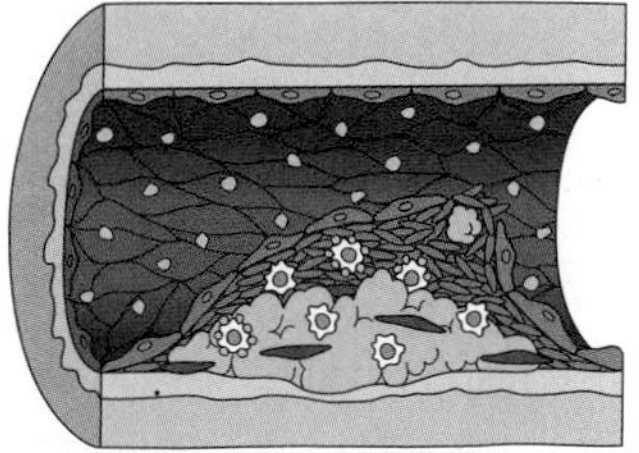

The narrowed artery is vulnerable to blockage by clots. The risk of blockage and heart attack rises if the fibrous cap cracks (probably due to destructive enzymes released by white blood cells within the plaque).

FIGURE 11.3 Stages of plaque development.

can be deadly. Coronary arteries, which supply the heart with blood, are particularly susceptible to plaque buildup, a condition called **coronary heart disease (CHD)**, or coronary artery disease. The blockage of a coronary artery causes a heart attack. If a cerebral artery (leading to the brain) is blocked, the result is a stroke. The main risk factors for atherosclerosis are cigarette smoking, physical inactivity, high levels of blood cholesterol, high blood pressure, and diabetes.

Heart Disease and Heart Attacks

Although a **heart attack**, or *myocardial infarction (MI)*, may come without warning, it is usually the end result of a long-term disease process. The heart requires a steady supply of oxygen-rich blood to function properly (Figure 11.4). If one of the coronary arteries that supplies blood to the heart becomes blocked, a heart attack results. A heart attack caused by a blood clot is called a coronary thrombosis. During a heart attack, part of the heart muscle (myocardium) may die from lack of blood flow.

Chest pain called **angina pectoris** is a signal that the heart isn't getting enough oxygen to supply its needs. Although not actually a heart attack, angina—felt as an extreme tightness in the chest and heavy pressure behind the breastbone or in the shoulder, neck, arm, hand, or back—is a warning that the heart is overloaded.

If the electrical impulses that control heartbeat are disrupted, the heart may beat too quickly, too slowly, or in an irregular fashion, a condition known as **arrhythmia.** The symptoms of arrhythmia range from imperceptible to severe and even fatal. **Sudden cardiac death,** also called cardiac arrest, is most often caused by an arrythmia called ventricular fibrillation, a kind of "quivering" of the ventricle that makes it ineffective in pumping blood. If ventricular fibrillation continues for more than a few minutes, it is generally fatal. Cardiac defibrillation, in which an electrical shock is delivered to the heart, can jolt the heart into a more efficient rhythm.

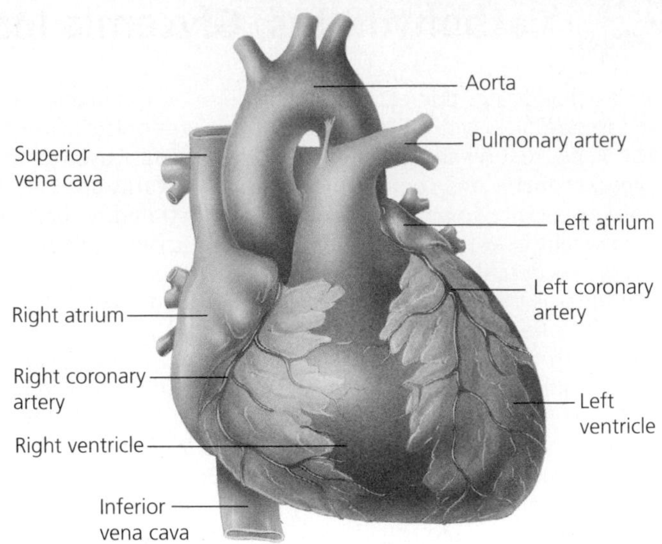

FIGURE 11.4 Blood supply to the heart. Blood is supplied to the heart from the right and left coronary arteries, which branch off the aorta. If a coronary artery becomes blocked by plaque buildup or a blood clot, a heart attack occurs; part of the heart muscle may die due to lack of oxygen.

Remember that not all heart attacks involve sharp chest pain; women, in particular, are more likely to have different symptoms—shortness of breath, weakness, unusual fatigue, cold sweat, dizziness, and nausea. If symptoms of heart trouble occur, it is critical to contact the emergency medical service or go immediately to the nearest hospital or clinic with a 24-hour emergency cardiac facility (see the box "What to Do in Case of a Heart Attack, Stroke, or Cardiac Arrest"). An additional step recommended by many experts is to chew and swallow one adult aspirin tablet (325 mg); aspirin has an immediate anticlotting effect. If someone having a heart attack gets to the emergency room quickly enough, a clot-dissolving agent can be injected to dissolve a clot in the coronary artery, reducing the amount of damage to the heart muscle.

Physicians have a variety of diagnostic tools and treatments for heart disease. A patient may undergo a stress or exercise test, in which he or she runs on a treadmill or pedals a stationary cycle while being monitored with an electrocardiogram (ECG or EKG). Certain characteristic changes in the heart's electrical activity while it is under stress can reveal particular heart problems, such as restricted blood flow to the heart muscle. Tools that allow the physician to visualize a patient's heart and arteries include magnetic resonance imaging (MRI), electron-beam computed tomography (EBC), echocardiograms, and angiograms.

If tests indicate a problem or if a person has already had a heart attack, several treatments are possible. Along with a low-fat diet, regular exercise, and smoking cessation, many patients are also advised to take aspirin daily to reduce clotting and inflammation. (Low-dose aspirin therapy appears

TERMS

coronary heart disease (CHD) Heart disease caused by hardening of the arteries that supply oxygen to the heart muscle; also called *coronary artery disease.*

heart attack Damage to, or death of, heart muscle, sometimes resulting in a failure of the heart to deliver enough blood to the body; also known as *myocardial infarction (MI).*

angina pectoris A condition in which the heart muscle does not receive enough blood, causing severe pain in the chest and often in the left arm and shoulder.

arrhythmia An irregularity in the force or rhythm of the heartbeat.

sudden cardiac death A nontraumatic, unexpected death from sudden cardiac arrest, most often due to arrhythmia; in most instances, victims have underlying heart disease.

stroke An impeded blood supply to some part of the brain resulting in the destruction of brain cells; also called *cerebrovascular accident (CVA).*

TAKE CHARGE

What to Do in Case of a Heart Attack, Stroke, or Cardiac Arrest

Heart Attack

Some heart attacks are sudden and intense, but most heart attacks start slowly, with mild pain or discomfort. Often people affected aren't sure what's wrong and wait too long before getting help. Here are signs that can mean a heart attack is happening:

- ***Chest discomfort.*** Most heart attacks involve discomfort in the center of the chest that lasts more than a few minutes, or that goes away and comes back. It can feel like uncomfortable pressure, squeezing, fullness, or pain.
- ***Discomfort in other areas of the upper body.*** Symptoms can include pain or discomfort in one or both arms, the back, neck, jaw, or stomach.
- ***Shortness of breath.*** This may occur with or without chest discomfort.
- ***Other signs.*** These may include breaking out in a cold sweat, nausea, vomiting, or lightheadedness.

If you or someone you're with has chest discomfort, especially with one or more of the other signs, don't wait more than 5 minutes before seeking help.

Calling 911 is almost always the fastest way to get lifesaving treatment. Emergency medical services (EMS) staff can begin treatment when they arrive—up to an hour sooner than if someone gets to the hospital by car. The staff are also trained to revive someone whose heart has stopped. Patients with chest pain who arrive by ambulance usually receive faster treatment at the hospital, too.

If you can't access EMS, have someone drive you to the hospital right away. If you're the one having symptoms, don't drive yourself unless you have absolutely no other option.

Stroke

The American Stroke Association identifies these as the warning signs of stroke:

- Sudden numbness or weakness of the face, arm, or leg, especially on one side of the body
- Sudden confusion, trouble speaking or understanding
- Sudden trouble seeing in one or both eyes
- Sudden trouble walking, dizziness, or loss of balance or coordination
- Sudden, severe headache with no known cause

If you or someone with you has one or more of these signs, immediately call 911 or EMS so an ambulance (ideally with advanced life support) can be sent for you. Also, check the time so you'll know when the first symptoms appeared. It's very important to take immediate action. If given within 3 hours of the start of symptoms, a clot-busting drug can reduce long-term disability from the most common type of stroke.

Cardiac Arrest

Cardiac arrest strikes suddenly and without warning. Here are the signs:

- Sudden loss of responsiveness. No response to gentle shaking. No movement or coughing.
- No normal breathing. The victim does not take a normal breath for several seconds.
- No signs of circulation. No pulse or blood pressure.

If cardiac arrest occurs, call 911 and begin CPR immediately. If an automated external defibrillator (AED) is available and someone trained to use it is nearby, involve her or him.

SOURCE: American Heart Association, 2005. Heart Attack, Stroke, and Cardiac Arrest Warning Signs. Reproduced with permission. www.americanheart.org.

to help prevent first and second heart attacks in men over age 45, second heart attacks in women over age 45, and first heart attacks and strokes in women over age 65.) Prescription drugs can also help reduce the strain on the heart. Balloon angioplasty, a common surgical treatment, involves threading a catheter with an inflatable balloon tip through a coronary artery until it reaches the area of blockage; the balloon is then inflated, flattening the plaque and widening the arterial opening. Many surgeons permanently implant coronary stents—flexible stainless steel tubes—to prop the artery open and prevent reclogging after angioplasty. In coronary bypass surgery, healthy blood vessels are grafted to coronary arteries to bypass blockages.

Stroke

For brain cells to function as they should, they must have a continuous and ample supply of oxygen-rich blood. If brain cells are deprived of blood for more than a few minutes, they die. A **stroke**, also called a cerebrovascular accident (CVA), occurs when the blood supply to the brain is cut off. Prompt treatment of stroke can greatly decrease the risk of permanent disability.

A stroke may be caused by a blood clot that blocks an artery (ischemic stroke) or by a ruptured blood vessel (hemorrhagic stroke). Ischemic strokes, which account for 80% of all strokes, are often caused by atherosclerosis or certain types of arrhythmia; hemorrhagic strokes may occur if there is a weak spot in an artery wall or following a head injury. The interruption of the blood supply to any area of the brain prevents the nerve cells there from functioning—and in some cases, causing death. Nerve cells control sensation and most body movements; depending on the area of the brain affected, a stroke may cause paralysis, walking disability, speech impairment, or memory loss. Of the 700,000 or more Americans who

MOTIVATION BOOSTER

Imagine CVD. Many people, especially young adults, have trouble motivating themselves to improve their health habits to avoid a chronic disease that won't cause symptoms for another 20–30 years. If chronic disease prevention is one of your goals, one strategy for making your goal more powerful and real is to use imagery to engage your emotions. Imagine in detail what you'd like your life to be when you are 65; then imagine how your quality of life will be diminished if you have heart disease. Do research or talk to someone affected by CVD if you need more information; watch a relevant television program or film or read a book. Finding out more about your own personal risk factors can also help; if you haven't had your blood pressure or cholesterol levels checked recently, make an appointment today.

QUESTIONS FOR CRITICAL THINKING AND REFLECTION

Has anyone you know ever had a heart attack? If so, was the onset gradual or sudden? Were appropriate steps taken to help the person (for example, call 911, give CPR, or use an AED)? Do you feel comfortable dealing with a cardiac emergency? If not, what can you do to improve your readiness?

have strokes each year, nearly one-third die within a year; those who survive usually have some lasting disability.

Effective treatment requires the prompt recognition of symptoms and correct diagnosis of the type of stroke that has occurred. Treatment may involve the use of clot-dissolving and antihypertensive drugs. Even if brain tissue has been damaged or destroyed, nerve cells in the brain can make new pathways, and some functions can be taken over by other parts of the brain.

Congestive Heart Failure

The heart's pumping mechanism can be damaged by a number of conditions, including high blood pressure, heart attack, atherosclerosis, viral infections, **rheumatic fever,** and birth defects. When the heart cannot maintain its regular pumping rate and force, fluids begin to back up. When extra fluid seeps through capillary walls, edema (swelling) results, usually in the legs and ankles, but sometimes in other parts of the body as well. Fluid can collect in the lungs and interfere with breathing, particularly when a person is lying down. This condition is called *pulmonary edema,* and the entire process is known as **congestive heart failure.** Treatment includes reducing the workload on the heart, modifying salt intake, and using drugs that help the body eliminate excess fluid.

PROTECTING YOURSELF AGAINST CARDIOVASCULAR DISEASE

You can take several important steps right now to lower your risk of developing CVD (Figure 11.5). Reducing CVD risk factors when you are young can pay off with many extra years of life and health.

Eat a Heart-Healthy Diet

For most Americans, changing to a heart-healthy diet involves cutting total fat intake, substituting unsaturated

Do More

- Eat a diet rich in fruits, vegetable, whole grains, and low-fat or fat-free dairy products. Eat 5–9 servings of fruits and vegetables each day.
- Eat several servings of high-fiber foods each day.
- Eat 2 or more servings of fish per week; try a few servings of nuts and soy foods each week.
- Choose insaturated fats rather than saturated and trans fats.
- Be physically active; do both aerobic exercise and strength training on a regular basis.
- Achieve and maintain a healthy weight.
- Develop effective strategies for handling stress and anger. Nurture old friendships and family ties, and make new friends; pay attention to your spiritual side.
- Obtain recommended screening tests and follow your physician's recommendations.

Do Less

- Don't use tobacco in any form: cigarettes, spit tobacco, cigars and pipes, bidis and clove cigarettes.
- Avoid exposure to environmental tobacco smoke.
- Limit consumption of fats, especially trans fats and saturated fats.
- Limit consumption of salt to no more than 2300 mg of sodium per day (1500 mg if you have or are at high risk for hypertension).
- Avoid excessive alcohol consumption—no more than one drink per day for women and two drinks per day for men.
- Limit consumption of cholesterol, added sugars, and refined carbohydrates.
- Avoid excess stress, anger, and hostility.

FIGURE 11.5 Strategies for reducing your risk of cardiovascular disease.

fats for saturated and trans fats, and increasing intake of whole grains and fiber.

Decreased Fat and Cholesterol Intake The National Cholesterol Education Program (NCEP) recommends that all Americans over age 2 adopt a diet in which total fat consumption is no more than 30% of total daily calories, with no more than one-third of those fat calories (10% of total daily calories) coming from saturated fat. For people with heart disease or high LDL levels, the NCEP recommends a total fat intake of 25–35% of total daily calories and a saturated fat intake of less than 7% of total calories. This higher total fat allowance is helpful for people who also have high triglyceride and low HDL levels. The American Heart Association now recommends that no more than 7% of daily calories come from saturated fats; this recommendation applies to everyone.

Saturated fat is found in animal products, palm and coconut oil, and hydrogenated vegetable oils, which are also high in trans fats. Saturated and trans fats influence the production and excretion of cholesterol by the liver, so decreasing intake of these fats is the most important dietary change you can make to improve cholesterol levels. Animal products contain cholesterol as well as saturated fat, and the NCEP recommends that most Americans limit dietary cholesterol intake to no more than 300 milligrams per day; for people with heart disease or high LDL levels, the suggested daily limit is 200 milligrams.

Increased Fiber Intake Fiber traps the bile acids the liver needs to manufacture cholesterol and carries them to the large intestine, where they are excreted. It also slows the production of proteins that promote blood clotting. Fiber may interfere with the absorption of dietary fat and may also help you cut total food intake because foods rich in fiber tend to be filling. To obtain the recommended 25–38 grams of dietary fiber a day, choose a diet rich in whole grains, fruits, and vegetables. Good sources of fiber include oatmeal, some breakfast cereals, barley, legumes, and most fruits and vegetables.

Decreased Sodium Intake and Increased Potassium Intake The recommended limit for sodium intake is 2300 milligrams per day; for population groups at special risk, including those with hypertension, middle-aged and older adults, and African Americans, the recommended limit is 1500 milligrams per day. To limit sodium intake, read food labels carefully, and avoid foods particularly high in sodium; foods that are fresh, less processed, and less sodium-dense are good choices. Adequate potassium intake is also important in control of blood pressure. Good food sources include leafy green vegetables like spinach and beet greens, root vegetables like white and sweet potatoes, vine fruits like cantaloupe and honeydew melon, winter squash, bananas, many dried fruits, and tomato sauce.

Alcohol Moderate alcohol consumption may lower the risk of CHD among men over 45 and women over 55. (Moderate means no more than one drink per day for women and two drinks per day for men.) For most people under age 45, however, the risks of alcohol use probably outweigh any health benefit. If you drink, do so moderately, with food, and at times when drinking will not put you or others at risk.

Dash A dietary plan that reflects many of the suggestions described here was released as part of a study called Dietary Approaches to Stop Hypertension (DASH). This is the DASH diet plan:

- 6–8 servings a day of grains and grain products
- 4–5 servings a day of vegetables
- 4–5 servings a day of fruits
- 2–3 servings a day of low-fat or nonfat dairy products
- 6 or fewer 1-ounce servings a day of meats, poultry, and fish
- 4–5 servings a *week* of nuts, seeds, and legumes
- 2–3 servings a day of added fats, oils, and salad dressings
- 5 or fewer servings a *week* of snacks and sweets

The DASH diet is consistent with the dietary recommendations for lowering your risk for cancer, osteoporosis, and heart disease. (See Chapter 8 and the Online Learning Center for more information on DASH.)

Exercise Regularly

You can significantly reduce your risk of CVD with a moderate amount of physical activity. Accumulate at least 30–60 minutes of moderate-intensity physical activity each day through such activities as brisk walking and stair climbing. A formal exercise program can provide even greater benefits. The information in Chapters 2–7 can help you create and implement a complete exercise program that meets your needs for fitness and prevention of chronic disease.

Avoid Tobacco

Remember: The number one risk factor for CVD that you can control is smoking. If you smoke, quit. If you

rheumatic fever A disease, mainly of children, characterized by fever, inflammation, and pain in the joints; often damages the heart muscle, a condition called *rheumatic heart disease.*

congestive heart failure A condition resulting from the heart's inability to pump out all the blood that returns to it. Blood backs up in the veins leading to the heart, causing an accumulation of fluid in various parts of the body.

Q I know what foods to avoid to prevent CVD, but are there any foods I should eat to protect myself from CVD?

A The most important dietary change for CVD prevention is a negative one: cutting back on foods high in saturated and trans fat. However, certain foods can be helpful. The positive effects of unsaturated fats, soluble fiber, and alcohol on heart health were discussed earlier in the chapter. Other potentially beneficial foods include those rich in the following:

- ***Omega-3 fatty acids.*** Found in fish, shellfish, and some nuts and seeds, omega-3 fatty acids reduce clotting and inflammation and may lower the risk of fatal arrhythmia.
- ***Folic acid, vitamin B-6, and vitamin B-12.*** These vitamins may affect CVD risk by lowering homocysteine levels; see Table 8.2 for a list of food sources.
- ***Plant stanols and sterols.*** Plant stanols and sterols, found in some types of trans-free margarines and other products, reduce the absorption of cholesterol in the body and help lower LDL levels.
- ***Soy protein.*** Replacing some animal protein with soy protein can lower LDL cholesterol. Soy-based foods include tofu, tempeh, and soy-based beverages.
- ***Calcium.*** Diets rich in calcium may help prevent hypertension and possibly stroke by reducing insulin resistance and platelet aggregation. Low-fat and fat-free dairy products are rich in calcium; refer to Chapter 8 for other sources.

Q The advice I hear from the media about protecting myself from CVD seems to be changing all the time. What am I supposed to believe?

A Health-related research is now described in popular newspapers and magazines rather than just medical journals, meaning that more and more people have access to the information. Researchers do not deliberately set out to mislead or confuse people. However, news reports may oversimplify the results of research studies, leaving out some of the qualifications and questions the researchers present with their findings. In addition, news reports may not differentiate between a preliminary finding and a result that has been verified by a large number of long-term studies. And researchers themselves must strike a balance between reporting promising preliminary findings to the public, thereby allowing people to act on them, and waiting 10–20 years until long-term studies confirm (or disprove) a particular theory.

Although you cannot become an expert on all subjects, there are some strategies you can use to assess the health advice that appears in the media; see the box "Evaluating Health News" on p. 346.

Q What's a heart murmur, and is it dangerous?

A A heart murmur is an extra or altered heart sound heard during a routine medical exam. The source is often a problem with one of the heart valves that separate the chambers of the heart. Congenital defects and certain infections can cause abnormalities in the valves. The most common heart valve disorder is mitral valve prolapse (MVP), which occurs in about 4% of the population. MVP is characterized by a "billowing" of the mitral valve, which separates the left ventricle and left

don't, don't start. The majority of people who start don't believe they will become hooked, but most do. If you live or work with people who smoke, encourage them to quit—for their sake and yours. If you find yourself breathing in smoke, take steps to prevent or stop this exposure. Quitting smoking will significantly reduce your CVD risk, but studies show that smoking and exposure to ETS may permanently increase the rate of plaque formation in arteries.

Know and Manage Your Blood Pressure

Currently, only about 34% of Americans with hypertension have their blood pressure under control. If you have no CVD risk factors, have your blood pressure measured at least once every 2 years; yearly tests are recommended if you have other risk factors. If your blood pressure is high, follow your physician's advice on lowering it.

Know and Manage Your Cholesterol Levels

Everyone age 20 and over should have a lipoprotein profile—which measures total cholesterol, HDL, LDL, and triglyceride levels—at least once every 5 years. Your goal for LDL depends in part on how many of the following major risk factors you have: cigarette smoking, high blood pressure, low HDL cholesterol (less than 40 mg/dl), a family history of heart disease, and age above 45 years for men and 55 years for women. (An HDL level of 60 mg/dl or higher is protective and removes one risk factor from your total count of risk factors.)

If you have two or fewer risk factors, the NCEP sets an LDL goal of less than 160 mg/dl. If your LDL is above that level, begin the "Therapeutic Lifestyle Changes," or TLC, recommended by the NCEP, including weight management, increased physical activity, and the TLC diet, which suggests total fat intake of 25–35% of total daily calories, saturated fat intake less than 7% of daily calories, and, for some people, atrium, during ventricular contraction; in some cases, blood leaks from the ventricle into the atrium. Most people with MVP have no symptoms; they have the same ability to exercise and live as long as people without MVP.

MVP can be confirmed with echocardiography. Treatment is usually unnecessary, although surgery may be needed in the rare cases where leakage through the faulty valve is severe. Experts disagree over whether patients with MVP should take antibiotics prior to dental procedures, a precautionary step used to prevent bacteria, which may be dislodged into the bloodstream during some types of dental and surgical procedures, from infecting the defective valve. Most often, only those patients with significant blood leakage are advised to take antibiotics.

Although MVP usually requires no treatment, more severe heart valve disorders can impair blood flow through the heart. Treatment depends on the location and severity of the problem. More serious defects may be treated with surgery to repair or replace a valve.

Q How does stress contribute to cardiovascular disease?

A With stress, the brain tells the adrenal glands to secrete cortisol and other hormones and neurotransmitters, which in turn activate the sympathetic nervous system—causing the fight-or-flight response. This response increases heart rate and blood pressure so that more blood is distributed to the heart and other muscles in anticipation of physical activity. Blood glucose concentrations and cholesterol also increase to provide a source of energy, and the platelets become activated so that they will be more likely to clot in case of injury. Such a response can be adaptive if you're being chased by a hungry lion but may be more detrimental than useful if you're sitting at a desk taking an exam or feeling frustrated by a task given to you by your work supervisor.

If you are healthy, you can tolerate the cardiovascular responses that take place during stress, but if you already have CVD, stress can lead to adverse outcomes such as abnormal heart rhythms, heart attacks, and sudden cardiac death. It has long been known that an increase in heart rhythm problems and deaths is associated with acute mental stress. For example, the rate of potentially life-threatening arrhythmias in patients who already had underlying heart disease doubled during the month after the September 11 terrorist attacks; this increase was not limited to people in close proximity to Manhattan.

Because avoiding all stress is impossible, having healthy mechanisms to cope with it is your best defense. Instead of adopting unhealthy habits such as smoking, drinking, or overeating to deal with stress, try healthier coping techniques such as exercising, getting enough sleep, and talking to family and friends.

For more Common Questions Answered about heart health, visit the Online Learning Center.

10–25 grams per day of soluble fiber and 2 grams per day of plant stanols and sterols. If your LDL level is 190 mg/dl or higher, medication may also be recommended.

If you have two or more risk factors for heart disease, the NCEP sets an LDL goal of less than 130 mg/dl. If your LDL level is 130 or above, you should begin TLC. Depending on other factors, your physician may also suggest drug therapy.

If you have CVD or diabetes, your goal for LDL is less than 100 mg/dl or, for very-high-risk patients, 70 mg/dl. TLC is recommended for all people in this risk category, and a variety of medications is available to lower LDL and improve other blood fat levels.

QUESTIONS FOR CRITICAL THINKING AND REFLECTION

Do you know what your blood pressure and cholesterol levels are, on average? If not, is there a reason you don't know? Is there something preventing you from getting this information about yourself? How can you motivate yourself to have these easy but important health checks?

Develop Ways to Handle Stress and Anger

To reduce the psychological and social risk factors for CVD, develop effective strategies for handling the stress in your life. Shore up your social support network, and, if anger and hostility are problems for you, try some of the techniques described in Chapter 10 for managing stress and anger.

Know Your Risk Factors

Know your CVD risk factors and follow your physician's advice for testing, lifestyle changes, and any drug treatments. If you are at moderate to high risk for CVD, consult a physician about taking small doses of aspirin (50–325 mg per day).

CRITICAL CONSUMER

Evaluating Health News

Americans face an avalanche of health information from newspapers, magazines, books, and television programs. It's not always easy to decide what to believe. The following questions can help you evaluate health news:

- ***Is the report based on research or on an anecdote?*** Information or recommendations based on one or more carefully designed research studies have more validity than one person's experiences.
- ***What is the source of the information?*** A study in a respected publication has been reviewed by editors and other researchers in the field—people who are in a position to evaluate the merits of the study and its results. Information put forth by government agencies and national research organizations is also usually considered fairly reliable.
- ***How big was the study?*** A study that involves many subjects is more likely to yield reliable results than a study involving only a few people. Another indication that a finding is meaningful is if several different studies yield the same results.
- ***Who were the people involved in the study?*** Research findings are more likely to apply to you if you share important characteristics with the subjects of the study. For example, the results of a study on men over age 50 who smoke may not be particularly meaningful for a 30-year-old nonsmoking woman. Even less applicable are studies done in test tubes or on animals.
- ***What kind of study was it?*** Epidemiological studies involve observation or interviews in order to trace the relationships among lifestyle, physical characteristics, and diseases. Although epidemiological studies can suggest links, they cannot establish cause-and-effect relationships. Clinical or interventional studies involve testing the effects of different treatments on groups of people who have similar lifestyles and characteristics. They are more likely to provide conclusive evidence of a cause-and-effect relationship. The best interventional studies share the following characteristics:
    - ***Controlled.*** A group of people who receive the treatment is compared with a matched group who do not receive the treatment.
    - ***Randomized.*** The treatment and control groups are selected randomly.
    - ***Double-blind.*** Researchers and participants are unaware of who is receiving the treatment.
    - ***Multicenter.*** The experiment is performed at more than one institution.
- ***What do the statistics really say?*** First, are the results described as "statistically significant"? If a study is large and well designed, its results can be deemed statistically significant, meaning there is less than a 5% chance that the findings resulted from chance. Second, are the results stated in terms of relative or absolute risk? Many findings are reported in terms of *relative risk,* how a particular treatment or condition affects a person's disease risk. Consider the following examples of relative risk:
    - According to some estimates, taking estrogen without progesterone can increase a postmenopausal woman's risk of dying from endometrial cancer by 233%.
    - Giving antiviral medication to HIV-infected pregnant women reduces prenatal transmission of HIV by 90%.

  The first of these two findings seems far more dramatic than the second—until one also considers *absolute risk,* the actual risk of the illness in the population being considered. The absolute risk of endometrial cancer is 0.3%; a 233% increase based on the effects of estrogen raises it to 1%, a change of 0.7%. Without treatment, about 25% of infants born to HIV-infected women will be infected with HIV; with treatment, the absolute risk drops to about 2%, a change of 23%. Because the absolute risk of an HIV-infected mother passing the virus to her infant is so much greater than a woman's risk of developing endometrial cancer (25% compared with 0.3%), a smaller change in relative risk translates into a much greater change in absolute risk.
- ***Is new health advice being offered?*** If the media report new guidelines for health behavior or medical treatment, examine the source. Government agencies and national research foundations usually consider a great deal of evidence before offering health advice. Above all, use common sense, and check with your physician before making a major change in your health habits based on news reports.

TIPS FOR TODAY AND THE FUTURE

Risk factors for cardiovascular disease fall into two categories—those you can do something about, such as physical activity and levels of stress, and those you can't, such as age and ethnicity. Because cardiovascular disease is a long-term process that can begin when you're young, it's important to develop heart-healthy habits early in life.

RIGHT NOW YOU CAN

- Make an appointment to have your blood pressure and cholesterol levels checked.
- List the key stressors in your life, and decide what to do about the ones that bother you most.
- Plan to replace one high-glycemic-index carbohydrate in your diet with a low-glycemic-index item—for example, replace a doughnut with a bowl of whole-grain cereal or a cup of yogurt with fruit.

IN THE FUTURE YOU CAN

- Track your eating habits for one week, then compare them to the DASH eating plan; make adjustments to bring your diet closer to the DASH recommendations.
- Sign up for a class in cardiopulmonary resuscitation (CPR). A CPR certification equips you with valuable life-saving skills you can use to help someone who is choking, having a heart attack, or experiencing cardiac arrest.

SUMMARY

- The major controllable risk factors for CVD are smoking, hypertension, unhealthy cholesterol levels, a sedentary lifestyle, obesity, and diabetes.
- Contributing factors for CVD that can be changed include high triglyceride levels, inadequate stress management, a hostile personality, depression, anxiety, lack of social support, poverty, and alcohol and drug use.
- Major risk factors for CVD that can't be changed are heredity, aging, being male, and ethnicity.
- Hypertension weakens the heart and scars and hardens arteries, causing resistance to blood flow. It is defined as blood pressure equal to or higher than 140 over 90.
- Atherosclerosis is a progressive hardening and narrowing of arteries that can lead to restricted blood flow and even complete blockage.
- Heart attacks, strokes, and congestive heart failure are the results of a long-term disease process; hypertension and atherosclerosis are usually involved.
- Reducing heart disease risk involves eating a heart-healthy diet, exercising regularly, avoiding tobacco, managing blood pressure and cholesterol levels, handling stress and anger, and knowing your risk factors.

FOR FURTHER EXPLORATION

BOOKS

Moore, T., et al. 2003. *The DASH Diet for Hypertension.* New York: Pocket Books. *Provides background information and guidelines for adopting the DASH diet; also includes recipes.*

Nelson, M. E., and A. Lichtenstein. 2006. *Strong Women, Strong Hearts.* New York: Perigree Trade. *Gives lifestyle advice for women to prevent heart disease.*

Phibbs, B. 2007. *The Human Heart: A Basic Guide to Heart Disease.* Philadelphia: Lippincott Williams and Wilkins. *Provides information about heart disease, treatments, and recovery for patients and their families.*

Romaine, D. S., and O. S. Randall. 2005. *The Encyclopedia of Heart and Heart Disease.* New York: Facts on File. *Includes entries on the functioning of the cardiovascular system, types and causes of heart disease, and prevention and treatment.*

ORGANIZATIONS AND WEB SITES

American Heart Association. Provides information on hundreds of topics relating to the prevention and control of CVD. Special guidelines for women can be found in the section on the "Go Red for Women" campaign.
800-AHA-USA1
http://www.americanheart.org (general information)
http://www.deliciousdecisions.org (dietary advice)
http://www.goredforwomen.org

The Human Heart: An On-Line Exploration. An online museum exhibit containing information on the structure and function of the heart, how to monitor your heart's health, and how to maintain a healthy heart.
http://www.fi.edu/learn/heart/index.html

MedlinePlus: Blood, Heart and Circulation Topics. Provides links to reliable sources of information on cardiovascular health.
http://www.nlm.nih.gov/medlineplus/bloodheartandcirculation.html

National Cholesterol Education Program (NCEP): Cholesterol Counts for Everyone. Provides information on cholesterol for people with heart disease and people who want to prevent heart disease.
http://rover.nhlbi.nih.gov/chd

National Heart, Lung, and Blood Institute. Provides information on a variety of topics relating to cardiovascular health and disease, including cholesterol, smoking, obesity, and hypertension.
http://www.nhlbi.nih.gov
http://rover.nhlbi.nih.gov/chd

National Stroke Association. Provides information and referrals for stroke victims and their families; the Web site has a stroke risk assessment.
800-STROKES
http://www.stroke.org

See also the listings for Chapters 9 and 10.

SELECTED BIBLIOGRAPHY

American Heart Association. 2007. *Heart Disease and Stroke Statistics—2007 Update.* Dallas: American Heart Association.

Centers for Disease Control and Prevention. 2005. Differences in disability among black and white stroke survivors. *Morbidity and Mortality Weekly Report* 54(1): 3–9.

Cooper, R. S., et al. 2005. An international comparative study of blood pressure in populations of European vs. African descent. *BMC Medicine* 3(1): 2.

Erkkila, A. T., et al. 2005. Cereal fiber and whole-grain intake are associated with reduced progression of coronary-artery atherosclerosis in postmenopausal women with coronary artery disease. *American Heart Journal* 150(1): 94–101.

Forman, J. P., et al. 2005. Folate intake and risk of incident hypertension among U.S. women. *Journal of the American Medical Association* 292(3): 320–329.

Grundy, S. M., et al. 2005. Diagnosis and management of the metabolic syndrome: An American Heart Association/National Heart, Lung, and Blood Institute Scientific Statement. *Circulation* 112(17): 2735–2752.

Gurfinkel, E. P., et al. 2007. Invasive vs. non-invasive treatment in acute coronary syndromes and prior bypass surgery. *International Journal of Cardiology* 119(1): 65–72.

Hu, G., et al. 2005. Leisure time, occupational, and commuting physical activity and the risk of stroke. *Stroke* 36(9): 1994–1999.

Matthews, C. E., et al. 2007. Influence of exercise, walking, cycling, and overall nonexercise physical activity on mortality in Chinese women. *American Journal of Epidemiology* 165(12): 1343–1350.

Meadows, M. 2005. Brain attack: A look at stroke prevention and treatment. *FDA Consumer,* March/April.

Mosca, L., et al. 2004. Evidence-based guidelines for cardiovascular disease prevention in women. *Circulation* 109: 672–693.

Mukamal, K. J., et al. 2005. Alcohol and risk of ischemic stroke in men: The role of drinking patterns and usual beverage. *Annals of Internal Medicine* 142(1): 11–19.

Müller, D., et al. 2006. How sudden is sudden cardiac death? *Circulation* 114(11): 1146–1150.

Narayan, K. M., et al. 2007. Effect of BMI on lifetime risk for diabetes in the U.S. *Diabetes Care* 30(6): 1562–1566.

Nissen, S. E., et al. 2005. Statin therapy, LDL cholesterol, C-reactive protein, and coronary artery disease. *New England Journal of Medicine* 352(1): 29–38.

Olson, M. B., et al. 2005. Hostility scores are associated with increased risk of cardiovascular events in women undergoing coronary angiography. *Psychosomatic Medicine* 67(4): 546–552.

Qureshi, A. I., et al. 2005. Cigarette smoking among spouses: Another risk factor for stroke in women. *Stroke* 36(9): e74–76.

Rho, R. W., and R. L. Page. 2007. The Automated External Defibrillator. *Journal of Cardiovascular Electrophysiology* 18: 1–4.

Ridker, P. M., et al. 2005. A randomized trial of low-dose aspirin in the primary prevention of cardiovascular disease in women. *New England Journal of Medicine* 352(13): 1293–1304.

Sui, X., et al. 2007. Cardiorespiratory fitness and the risk of nonfatal cardiovascular disease in women and men with hypertension. *American Journal of Hypertension* 20(6): 608–615.

Turhan, H., et al. 2005. High prevalence of metabolic syndrome among young women with premature coronary artery disease. *Coronary Artery Disease* 16(1): 37–40.

Wang, X., et al. 2007. Efficacy of folic acid supplementation in stroke prevention: A meta-analysis. *Lancet* 369(9576): 1876–1882.

Willingham, S. A., and E. S. Kilpatrick. 2005. Evidence of gender bias when applying the new diagnostic criteria for myocardial infarction. *Heart* 91(2): 237–238.

Wittstein, I. S., et al. 2005. Neurohumoral features of myocardial stunning due to sudden emotional stress. *New England Journal of Medicine* 352(6): 539–548.

Name ______________________________ Section ____________________ Date ________________

LAB 11.1 Cardiovascular Health

Part I CVD Risk Assessment

Your chances of suffering a heart attack or stroke before age 55 depend on a variety of factors, many of which are under your control. To help identify your risk factors, circle the response for each risk category that best describes you.

1. Sex and Age
   - 0 Female age 55 or younger; male age 45 or younger
   - 2 Female over age 55; male over age 45
2. Heredity/Family History
   - 0 Neither parent suffered a heart attack or stroke before age 60.
   - 3 One parent suffered a heart attack or stroke before age 60.
   - 7 Both parents suffered a heart attack or stroke before age 60.
3. Smoking
   - 0 Never smoked
   - 3 Quit more than 2 years ago and lifetime smoking is less than 5 pack-years*
   - 6 Quit less than 2 years ago and/or lifetime smoking is greater than 5 pack-years*
   - 8 Smoke less than 1/2 pack per day
   - 13 Smoke more than 1/2 pack per day
   - 15 Smoke more than 1 pack per day
4. Environmental Tobacco Smoke
   - 0 Do not live or work with smokers
   - 2 Exposed to ETS at work
   - 3 Live with smoker
   - 4 Both live and work with smokers
5. Blood Pressure
   (If available, use the average of the last three readings.)
   - 0 120/80 or below
   - 1 121/81–130/85
   - 3 Don't know blood pressure
   - 5 131/86–150/90
   - 9 151/91–170/100
   - 13 Above 170/100
6. Total Cholesterol
   - 0 Lower than 190
   - 1 190–210
   - 2 Don't know
   - 3 211–240
   - 4 241–270
   - 5 271–300
   - 6 Over 300
7. HDL Cholesterol
   - 0 Over 60 mg/dl
   - 1 55–60
   - 2 Don't know HDL
   - 3 45–54
   - 5 35–44
   - 7 25–34
   - 12 Lower than 25
8. Exercise
   - 0 Exercise three times a week
   - 1 Exercise once or twice a week
   - 2 Occasional exercise less than once a week
   - 7 Rarely exercise
9. Diabetes
   - 0 No personal or family history
   - 2 One parent with diabetes
   - 6 Two parents with diabetes
   - 9 Type 2 diabetes
   - 13 Type 1 diabetes
10. Body Mass Index (kg/m^2)
    - 0 <23.0
    - 1 23.0–24.9
    - 2 25.0–28.9
    - 3 29.0–34.9
    - 5 35.0–39.9
    - 7 ≥40
11. Stress
    - 0 Relaxed most of the time
    - 1 Occasionally stressed and angry
    - 2 Frequently stressed and angry
    - 3 Usually stressed and angry

Scoring

Total your risk factor points. Refer to the list below to get an approximate rating of your risk of suffering an early heart attack or stroke.

Score	*Estimated Risk*
Less than 20	Low risk
20–29	Moderate risk
30–45	High risk
Over 45	Extremely high risk

*Pack-years can be calculated by multiplying the number of packs you smoked per day by the number of years you smoked. For example, if you smoked a pack and a half a day for 5 years, you would have smoked the equivalent of $1.5 \times 5 = 7.5$ pack-years.

Part II Hostility Assessment

Are you too hostile? To help answer that question, Duke University researcher Redford Williams, M.D., has devised a short self-test. It's not a scientific evaluation, but it does offer a rough measure of hostility. Are the following statements true or false for you?

1. I often get annoyed at checkout cashiers or the people in front of me when I'm waiting in line.
2. I usually keep an eye on the people I work or live with to make sure they do what they should.
3. I often wonder how homeless people can have so little respect for themselves.
4. I believe that most people will take advantage of you if you let them.
5. The habits of friends or family members often annoy me.
6. When I'm stuck in traffic, I often start breathing faster and my heart pounds.
7. When I'm annoyed with people, I really want to let them know it.
8. If someone does me wrong, I want to get even.
9. I'd like to have the last word in any argument.
10. At least once a week, I have the urge to yell at or even hit someone.

According to Williams, five or more "true" statements suggest that you're excessively hostile and should consider taking steps to mellow out.

Using Your Results

How did you score? (1) What is your CVD risk assessment score? Are you surprised by your score?

Are you satisfied with your CVD risk rating? If not, set a specific goal:

(2) What is your hostility assessment score? Are you surprised by the result?

Are you satisfied with your hostility rating? If not, set a specific goal:

What should you do next? Enter the results of this lab in the Preprogram Assessment column in Appendix D. (1) If you've set a goal for the overall CVD risk assessment score, identify a risk area that you can change, such as smoking, exercise, or stress. Then list three steps or strategies for changing the risk area you've chosen.
Risk area:
Strategies for change:

(2) If you've set a goal for the hostility assessment score, begin by keeping a log of your hostile responses. Review the anger management strategies in Chapter 10, and select several that you will try to use to manage your angry responses. Strategies for anger management:

Next, begin to put your strategies into action. After several weeks of a program to reduce CVD risk or hostility, do this lab again and enter the results in the Postprogram Assessment column of Appendix D. How do the results compare?

SOURCES: CVD risk assessment from Insel, P. M., and W. T. Roth. 2008. *Core Concepts in Health,* 10th ed. update. Copyright © 2008 The McGraw-Hill Companies, Inc. Reprinted with permission of The McGraw-Hill Companies, Inc. Hostility quiz from *Life Skills,* by Virginia Williams and Redford Williams. New York: Times Books. Reprinted by permission of the authors.

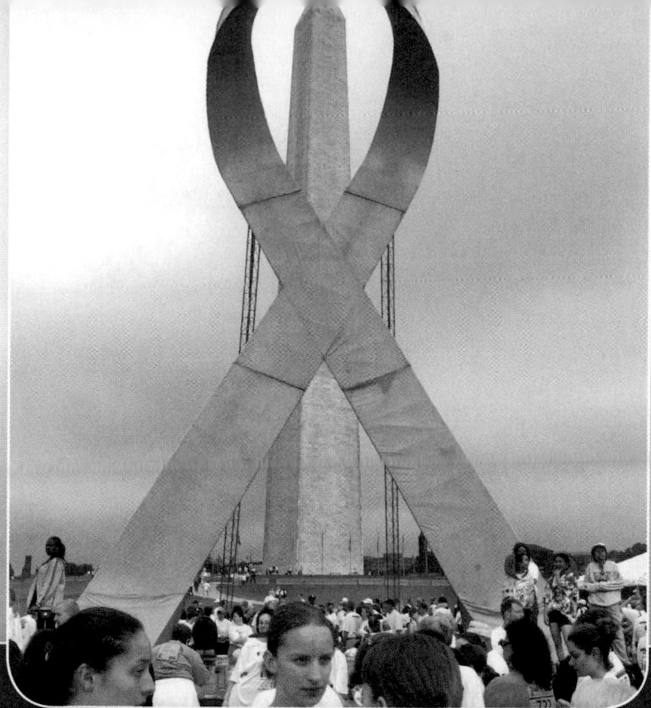

LOOKING AHEAD>>>>>

AFTER READING THIS CHAPTER, YOU SHOULD BE ABLE TO:

- Explain what cancer is and how it spreads
- List and describe common cancers—their risk factors, signs and symptoms, treatments, and approaches to prevention
- Discuss some of the causes of cancer and ways they can be avoided or minimized
- Describe the signs and symptoms of cancer in its early stages
- List specific actions you can take to lower your risk of cancer

CANCER 12

TEST YOUR KNOWLEDGE

1. Eating which of these foods may help prevent cancer?

a. chili peppers
b. broccoli
c. oranges

2. Testicular cancer is the most common cancer in men under age 30.

True or false?

3. The use of condoms during sexual intercourse can prevent cancer in women.

True or false?

ANSWERS

1. **ALL THREE.** These and many other fruits and vegetables are rich in phytochemicals, naturally occurring substances that may have anticancer effects.
2. **TRUE.** Although rare, testicular cancer is the most common cancer in men under age 30. Regular self-exams may aid in its detection.
3. **TRUE.** The primary cause of cervical cancer is infection with the human papillomavirus (HPV), a sexually transmitted pathogen. The use of condoms can prevent HPV infection.

FIT AND WELL ONLINE LEARNING CENTER www.mhhe.com/fahey

Visit the *Fit and Well* Online Learning Center for resources that will help you get the most out of your course!

- Study and review aids include practice quizzes, glossary flashcards, chapter summaries, learning objectives, PowerPoint presentations, Common Questions Answered, student handouts, crossword puzzles, Internet activities, and links to wellness Web sites.
- Behavior change tools include a daily fitness and nutrition journal, a behavior change workbook, sample behavior change plans, and blank behavior change logs to print and use.

Cancer is the second most common cause of death, after heart disease. In the United States, cancer is responsible for 1 in 4 deaths, claiming 1500 lives every day. Evidence indicates that more than half of all cancers in the United States could be prevented by simple changes in lifestyle. Tobacco use is responsible for about one-third of all cancer deaths (Figure 12.1). Diet and exercise, including their relationship with obesity, account for another one-third of cancer deaths. Your behavior now will determine your cancer risk in the future.

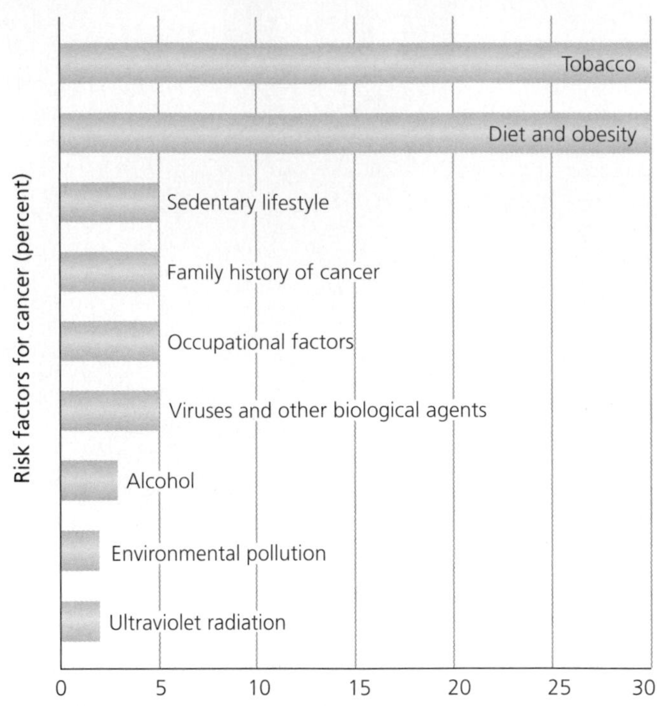

WEB VITAL STATISTICS

FIGURE 12.1 Percentage of all cancer deaths linked to risk factors.

SOURCE: Harvard Center for Cancer Prevention. 1996. Harvard Reports on Cancer Prevention. Vol. 1: Human Causes of Cancer. *Cancer Causes and Control* 7(Suppl. 1).

WHAT IS CANCER?

Cancer is the abnormal, uncontrolled growth of cells, which, if left untreated, can ultimately cause death.

Benign Versus Malignant Tumors

Most cancers take the form of tumors, although not all tumors are cancerous. A **tumor** is simply a mass of tissue that serves no physiological purpose. It can be benign, like a wart, or malignant, like most lung cancers.

Benign tumors are made up of cells similar to the surrounding normal cells and are enclosed in a membrane that prevents them from penetrating neighboring tissues. They are dangerous only if their physical presence interferes with body functions.

The term **malignant tumor** (or *neoplasm*) is synonymous with cancer. A malignant tumor is capable of invading surrounding structures, including blood vessels, the **lymphatic system**, and nerves. It can also spread to distant sites via the blood and lymphatic circulation. A few cancers, like leukemia (cancer of the blood) do not produce a mass but still have the fundamental property of rapid, uncontrolled growth of cells.

Every case of cancer begins as a change in a cell that allows it to grow and divide when it should not. A malignant cell divides without regard for normal control mechanisms and gradually produces a mass of abnormal cells, or a tumor. It takes about a billion cells to make a mass the size of a pea, so a single tumor cell must go through many divisions, often taking years, before the tumor grows to a noticeable size. Eventually, a tumor produces a sign or symptom that is detected. In an accessible location, a tumor may be felt as a lump. In less accessible locations, a tumor may be noticed only after considerable growth has taken place and may then be detected only by an indirect symptom—for instance, a persistent cough or unexplained bleeding or pain.

How Cancer Spreads: Metastasis

Metastasis, the spreading of cancer cells, occurs because cancer cells do not stick to each other as strongly as normal cells do and therefore may not remain at the site of the *primary tumor,* the original location. They break away and can pass through the lining of lymph or blood vessels to invade nearby tissue. They can also drift to distant parts of the body, where they establish new colonies of cancer cells. This traveling and seeding process is called metastasizing, and the new tumors are secondary tumors, or metastases.

This ability of cancer cells to metastasize makes early cancer detection critical. To control the cancer, every cancerous cell must be removed. Once cancer cells enter either the lymphatic system or the bloodstream, it is extremely difficult to stop their spread.

COMMON CANCERS

Each year, more than 1.4 million people are diagnosed with cancer, and about 560,000 die (Figure 12.2). These statistics exclude the more than 1 million cases of the easily curable types of skin cancer. At current U.S. rates, nearly 1 in 2 men and more than 1 in 3 women will develop cancer at some point in their lives. There are now more than 10 million Americans alive who have a history of cancer.

A discussion of all types of cancer is beyond the scope of this book. In this section, we look at the most common cancers and their causes, prevention, and treatment.

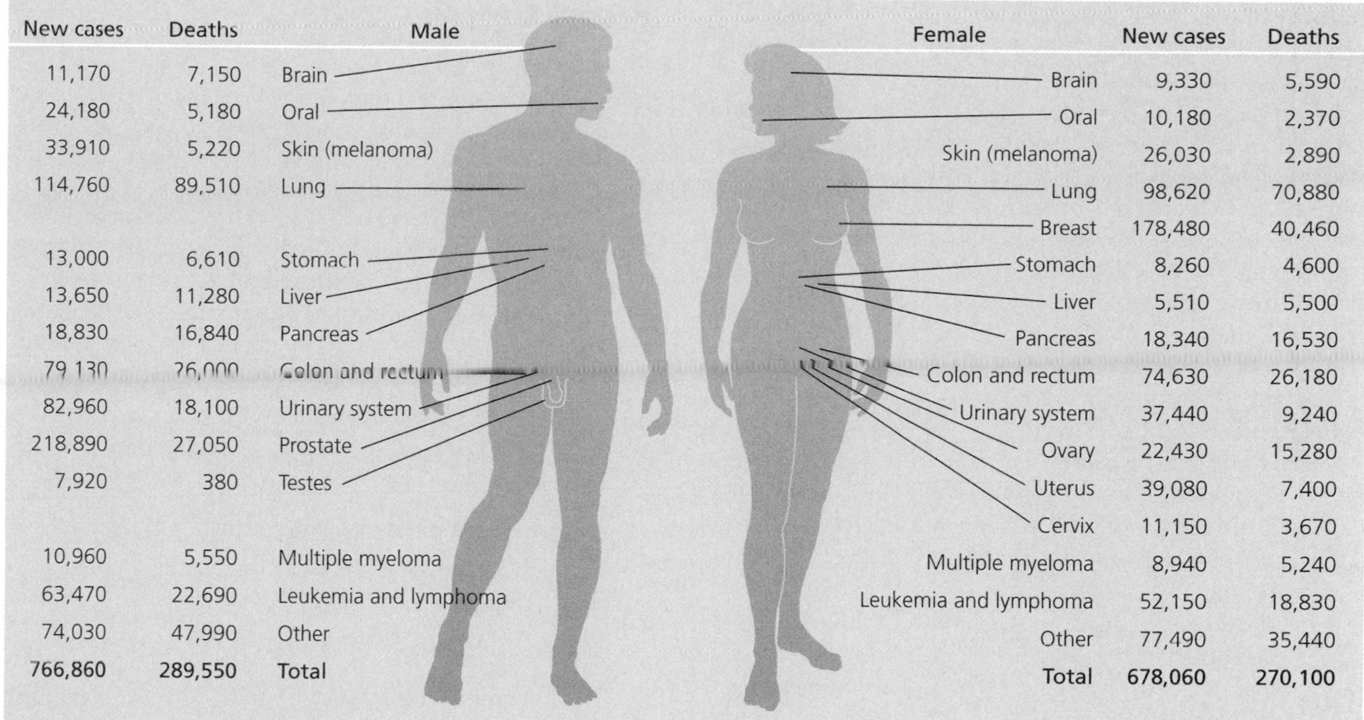

New cases	Deaths	Male
11,170	7,150	Brain
24,180	5,180	Oral
33,910	5,220	Skin (melanoma)
114,760	89,510	Lung
13,000	6,610	Stomach
13,650	11,280	Liver
18,830	16,840	Pancreas
79,130	26,000	Colon and rectum
82,960	18,100	Urinary system
218,890	27,050	Prostate
7,920	380	Testes
10,960	5,550	Multiple myeloma
63,470	22,690	Leukemia and lymphoma
74,030	47,990	Other
766,860	**289,550**	**Total**

Female	New cases	Deaths
Brain	9,330	5,590
Oral	10,180	2,370
Skin (melanoma)	26,030	2,890
Lung	98,620	70,880
Breast	178,480	40,460
Stomach	8,260	4,600
Liver	5,510	5,500
Pancreas	18,340	16,530
Colon and rectum	74,630	26,180
Urinary system	37,440	9,240
Ovary	22,430	15,280
Uterus	39,080	7,400
Cervix	11,150	3,670
Multiple myeloma	8,940	5,240
Leukemia and lymphoma	52,150	18,830
Other	77,490	35,440
Total	**678,060**	**270,100**

VITAL STATISTICS

FIGURE 12.2 Cancer cases and deaths by site and sex.

SOURCE: American Cancer Society. 2007. *Cancer Facts and Figures, 2007.* Atlanta: American Cancer Society.

Lung Cancer

Lung cancer is the most common cause of cancer death in the United States; it is responsible for about 160,000 deaths each year. Since 1987, lung cancer has surpassed breast cancer as the leading cause of cancer death in women.

The chief risk factor for lung cancer is tobacco smoke, which accounts for 87% of lung cancer deaths. When smoking is combined with exposure to other environmental **carcinogens,** such as asbestos particles, the risk of cancer can be multiplied by a factor of 10 or more. Quitting substantially reduces risk, but ex-smokers remain at higher risk than those who never smoked. And the smoker is not the only one at risk. Long-term exposure to environmental tobacco smoke (ETS), or secondhand smoke, also increases risk for lung cancer. ETS causes about 3000 lung cancer deaths in nonsmokers each year.

Symptoms of lung cancer do not usually appear until the disease has advanced to the invasive stage. Signals such as a persistent cough, chest pain, or recurring bronchitis may be the first indication of a tumor's presence. Lung cancer is most often treated by some combination of surgery, radiation, and chemotherapy; if all the tumor cells can be removed or killed, a cure is possible. Lung cancer is usually detected only after it has begun to spread, however, and only about 15% of lung cancer patients are alive 5 years after diagnosis.

Colon and Rectal Cancer

Another common cancer in the United States is colon and rectal cancer (also called colorectal cancer). It is the second leading cause of cancer death, after lung cancer, for men and women combined. Age is a key risk factor, with more than 90% of cases diagnosed in people age 50 and older. Many cancers arise from preexisting polyps, small

cancer Abnormal, uncontrolled cellular growth.

tumor A mass of tissue that serves no physiological purpose.

benign tumor A tumor that is not cancerous.

malignant tumor A tumor that is cancerous and capable of spreading.

lymphatic system A system of vessels that returns proteins, lipids, and other substances from fluid in the tissues to the circulatory system.

metastasis The spread of cancer cells from one part of the body to another.

carcinogen Any substance that causes cancer.

growths on the wall of the colon that may gradually develop into malignancies. About 15–30% of colon cancers may be due to inherited gene mutations.

Lifestyle also affects colon cancer risk. Regular physical activity reduces risk; obesity increases risk. Although the mechanisms are unclear, high intake of red meat, smoked meat and fish, or simple sugars appears to increase risk, as does excessive alcohol consumption and smoking. Protective lifestyle factors may include a diet rich in fruits, vegetables, and whole grains; adequate intake of folic acid, calcium, magnesium, and vitamin D; regular use of nonsteroidal anti-inflammatory drugs such as aspirin and ibuprofen; and, in women, use of oral contraceptives.

Young polyps and early-stage cancers can be removed before they spread. Because polyps may bleed, the standard warning signs of colon cancer are bleeding from the rectum and a change in bowel habits. The American Cancer Society (ACS) recommends that regular screening be started at age 50. A stool blood test can detect traces of blood in the stool long before obvious bleeding can be noticed. Another test is the colonoscopy, in which a flexible fiber-optic device is inserted through the rectum, allowing the colon to be examined and polyps to be removed (Figure 12.3). Studies show that screening could reduce the occurrence of colorectal cancer by 80%, but only about half of adults undergo these tests.

Surgery is the primary method of treatment. Colon and rectal cancer is more curable than lung cancer, particularly if caught before it spreads.

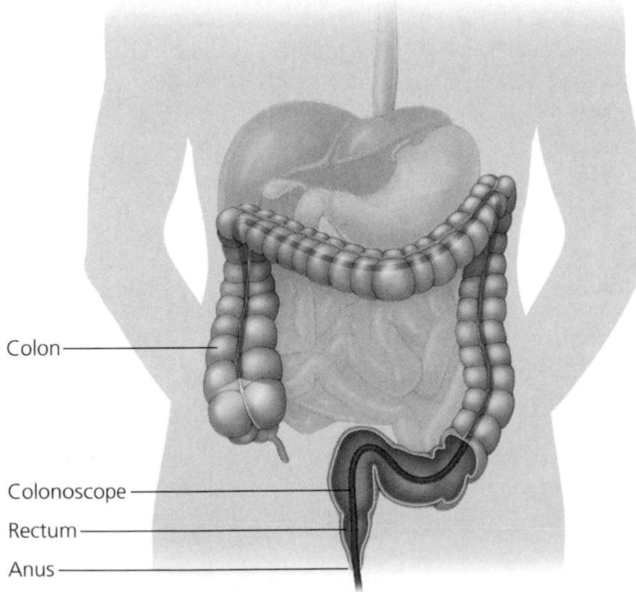

FIGURE 12.3 Colonoscopy. A colonoscopy allows the entire colon to be examined and facilitates the removal of growths, such as polyps, that may become cancerous.

Breast Cancer

Breast cancer is the most common cancer in women, but it kills fewer women than lung cancer. In the United States, about 1 in 8 women will get breast cancer. Breast cancer occurs only rarely in men.

Risk Factors There is a strong genetic factor in breast cancer. A woman who has a first-degree relative (mother, sister, or daughter) with breast cancer is twice as likely to develop the disease as a woman with no first-degree relative with breast cancer. However, only about 15% of breast cancers occur in women with a family history of the disease.

Other risk factors include these:

- Experiencing early-onset menstruation or late-onset menopause
- Having no children or having a first child after age 30
- Currently receiving hormone replacement therapy
- Being obese
- Using alcohol

The female hormone estrogen may be a common element in some of these risk factors. Estrogen promotes cell growth in responsive tissues, such as the breast and uterus, so any factor that increases estrogen exposure may raise the risk of breast cancer. Fat cells also produce estrogen, and estrogen levels are higher in obese women. Alcohol can increase estrogen in the blood as well.

Prevention Although some risk factors cannot be changed, lifestyle modifications may reduce the chance of developing breast cancer. Exercise is extremely important because it helps control body weight and may reduce estrogen levels. Diet is another key factor; experts suggest eating plenty of vegetables and favoring monounsaturated over polyunsaturated fats.

Detection The ACS stresses early detection of breast cancer through a three-part approach:

- ***Mammography.*** A **mammogram** is a low-dose breast X-ray, which can spot breast abnormalities before physical symptoms arise. A newer type of mammography, called digital mammography, may provide more accurate results in some women, as may magnetic resonance imaging (MRI). Experts recommend that women over 40 get a mammogram every year.
- ***Clinical breast exams.*** Women between the ages of 20 and 39 should have a clinical breast exam about every 3 years. Women over 40 should have one every year.
- ***Breast self-exams.*** By doing breast self-exams (BSEs), a woman can become familiar with her breasts and alert her physician to any changes (see the box "Breast Self-Examination"). Women who choose to do self-exams should begin at age 20.

If any of these methods detects a lump in the breast, it can be **biopsied** or scanned by **ultrasonography** to

TAKE CHARGE

Breast Self-Examination

The best time for a woman to examine her breasts is when the breasts are not tender or swollen. Women who are pregnant or breastfeeding or have breast implants can also choose to examine their breasts regularly. Women who examine their breasts should have their technique reviewed by their health care professional during their clinical breast exams (CBEs). It is acceptable for women to choose not to do BSE or to do BSE occasionally. Women who choose not to do BSE should still be aware of their breasts and report any changes to their health care professional without delay.

How to Examine Your Breasts

- Lie down and place your right arm behind your head. The exam is done while lying down, not standing up. This is because when lying down the breast tissue spreads evenly over the chest wall and it is as thin as possible, making it much easier to feel all the breast tissue.
- Use the finger pads of the three middle fingers on your left hand to feel for lumps in the right breast. Use overlapping dime-size circular motions of the finger pads to feel the breast tissue.

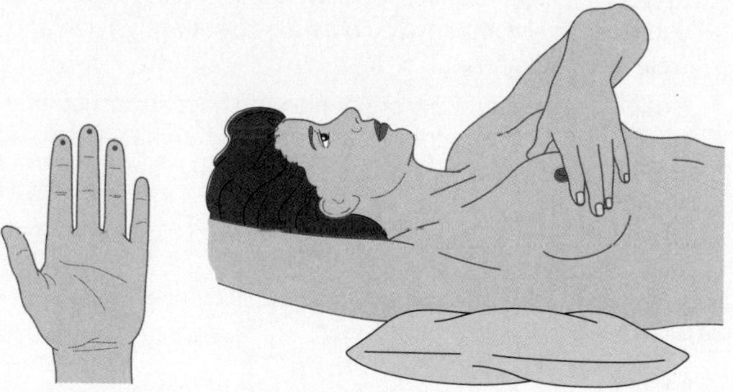

- Use three different levels of pressure to feel all the breast tissue. Light pressure is needed to feel the tissue closest to the skin; medium pressure to feel a little deeper; and firm pressure to feel the tissue closest to the chest and ribs. A firm ridge in the lower curve of each breast is normal. If you're not sure how hard to press, talk with your doctor or nurse. Use each pressure level to feel the breast tissue before moving on to the next spot.
- Move around the breast in an up-and-down pattern starting at an imaginary line drawn straight down your side from the underarm and moving across the breast to the middle of the chest bone (the sternum, or breastbone). Be sure to check the entire breast area, going down until you feel only ribs and to the neck or collar bone (clavicle).
- There is some evidence to suggest that the up-and-down pattern (sometimes called the vertical pattern) is the most effective pattern for covering the entire breast, without missing any breast tissue.

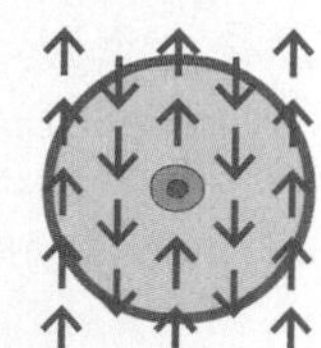

- Repeat the exam on your left breast, using the finger pads of the right hand.
- While standing in front of a mirror with your hands pressing firmly down on your hips, look at your breasts for any changes of size, shape, contour, dimpling, pulling, or redness or scaliness of the nipple or breast skin. (Pressing down on the hips contracts the chest wall muscles and enhances any breast changes.) Continue to look for changes with your arms down at your sides and then with your arms raised up over your head with your palms pressed together.
- Examine each underarm while sitting up or standing and with your arm only slightly raised so you can easily feel in this area. Raising your arm straight up tightens the tissue in this area and makes it difficult to examine.

SOURCE: American Cancer Society's Web site, www.cancer.org, 2006.

determine whether it is cancerous. In 90% of all cases, lumps are found to be harmless.

Treatment If a lump is cancerous, one of several surgical treatments may be used, ranging from a lumpectomy (removal of the lump and surrounding tissue) to a mastectomy (removal of the breast). Chemotherapy or radiation treatment may also be used to eradicate as many cancerous cells as possible.

Several drugs have been developed for preventing and treating breast cancer. These include selective estrogen-receptor modulators (SERMs), which act like estrogen in some tissues but block estrogen's effects in others. The two best-known SERMs are tamoxifen and raloxifene. Another category of drug, called trastuzumab (Herceptin), is a special type of antibody that binds to a specific cancer-related target in the body.

Regardless of the treatments used, social support can also affect a patient's psychological and physical wellness (see the box "Coping with Cancer").

If the tumor is discovered early, before it has spread to the adjacent lymph nodes, the patient with breast cancer has about a 97% chance of surviving more than 5 years.

TERMS

mammogram A low-dose X-ray of the breasts used for the early detection of breast cancer.

biopsy The removal and examination of a small piece of body tissue for the purpose of diagnosis.

ultrasonography An imaging method in which inaudible high-pitched sound (ultrasound) is bounced off body structures to create an image on a monitor.

Coping with Cancer

Visiting a Cancer Patient

- Before you visit, call to ask if it's a good time. Don't overstay your welcome.
- Be a good listener. Let the person express his or her feelings; don't discount fears or minimize the situation. Let the patient decide whether to talk about the illness. It's human to want to discuss other things sometimes.
- Ask "What can I get you?" or "How can I help?" instead of saying "Let me know if I can help." Make specific offers: to clean the bathroom, go shopping, do laundry, or give caregivers a break.
- Refrain from offering advice. Unless you are asked for suggestions, keep them to yourself.
- If you want to take food, ask about dietary restrictions ahead of time. Use a disposable container so the patient doesn't have to return it.
- Don't be put off if you get a lukewarm reception. Many cancer victims are on an emotional roller coaster; their feelings and needs will change over time.

If You Are the Patient

- Remember that cancer doesn't always mean death. Many cancers are curable or controllable for long periods, and survivors may return to a normal, healthy life. Hope and optimism can be important elements in cancer survival.
- Work toward having a positive attitude, but don't feel guilty if you can't keep a positive attitude all the time. Having cancer is difficult, and low moods will occur no matter how good you are at coping. If they become frequent or severe, seek help.

- Use any strategies that have helped you solve problems and manage your emotions in the past. Some people respond to information gathering, talking with others, and prayer or meditation. Physical activity, music, art, and sharing stories all reduce stress.
- Find a physician you trust and with whom you can communicate well. Ask questions and be a partner in your treatment.
- Confide your worries to someone close to you. Don't bottle up your feelings to spare your loved ones. Ask someone you trust to accompany you on visits to your physician and treatment sessions.
- Explore support groups for people who have cancer or who have survived it. Support group participation has been shown to reduce anxiety and depression and enhance quality of life.

SOURCES: National Cancer Institute. 2006. Facing Forward: Life After Cancer Treatment (http://www.cancer.gov/cancertopics/life-after-treatment; retrieved June 6, 2007). Daneker, B. B. 2007. *The Compassionate Caregiver's Guide to Caring for Someone with Cancer.* Bloomington, Ind.: AuthorHouse.

Prostate Cancer

The prostate gland is situated at the base of the bladder in men. It produces seminal fluid; if enlarged, it can block the flow of urine. Prostate cancer is the most common cancer in men and the second leading cause of cancer death in men. Nearly 220,000 new cases of prostate cancer are diagnosed in the United States each year.

Age is the strongest predictor of the risk of prostate cancer, with about two-thirds of cases diagnosed in men over age 65. Inherited genetic predisposition may be responsible for 5–10% of cases; men with a family history of the disease should be vigilant about screening. Diets high in calories, dairy products, refined grains, and animal fats and low in plant foods (especially vegetable fiber) have been implicated as possible culprits, as have obesity, inactivity, and a history of sexually transmitted diseases. Type 2 diabetes and insulin resistance are also associated with prostate cancer. Diet may be an important means of preventing prostate cancer. Soy foods, tomatoes, and cruciferous vegetables are being investigated for their possible protective effects.

Some cases are first detected by rectal examination during a routine physical exam. During this exam, a physician feels the prostate through the rectum to determine if the gland is enlarged or if lumps are present. Ultrasound and biopsy may also be used to detect and diagnose prostate cancer. The **PSA blood test,** which measures the amount of prostate-specific antigen (PSA) in the blood, can also be used to help diagnose prostate cancer. An elevated level or a rapid increase in PSA can signal trouble. The ACS suggests that all men have a rectal exam and a PSA test annually, starting at age 50. Men at high risk for the disease (such as African American men and men with a first-degree relative who has been diagnosed with prostate cancer) should start annual testing at age 45.

If the tumor is malignant, the prostate is usually removed surgically. However, a small, slow-growing tumor in an older man may be treated with watchful waiting because he is more likely to die from another cause before his cancer becomes life-threatening. A less invasive treatment involves radiation of the tumor by surgically implanting radioactive seeds in the prostate gland. The 5-year survival rate for all stages of prostate cancer is now nearly 100%.

Cancers of the Female Reproductive Tract

Because the uterus, cervix, and ovaries are subject to similar hormonal influences, the cancers of these organs can be discussed as a group.

Cervical Cancer Cervical cancer is at least in part a sexually transmitted disease. Most cases of cervical cancer stem from infection by the human papillomavirus (HPV), which causes genital warts and is transmitted during unprotected sex (see Chapter 14). Smoking and prior infection with the STDs herpes and chlamydia may also be risk factors for cervical cancer.

Cervical cancer can be prevented by avoiding infection with HPV; sexual abstinence, mutually monogamous sex with an uninfected partner, or regular use of condoms can reduce the risk of HPV infection (see Chapter 14 for more on HPV and other STDs).

There is also an FDA-approved vaccine (Gardasil) that protects against four types of HPV viruses. The vaccine can help prevent cervical cancer as well as cancers of the vagina and vulva. The vaccine is recommended for all girls age 11 12; the recommendation also allows vaccination of girls as young as 9 and women up to age 26.

Screening for the changes in cervical cells that precede cancer is done chiefly by means of the **Pap test.** During a pelvic exam, loose cells are scraped from the cervix and examined. If cells are abnormal, a condition referred to as *cervical dysplasia,* the Pap test is repeated at intervals. In about one-third of cases, the cellular changes progress toward malignancy. If this happens, the abnormal cells must be removed, either surgically or by destroying them with an ultracold (cryoscopic) probe or localized laser treatment. In more advanced cases, treatment may involve chemotherapy, radiation, or hysterectomy (surgical removal of the uterus).

Uterine or Endometrial Cancer Cancer of the lining of the uterus, or endometrium, most often occurs after age 55. The risk factors are similar to those for breast cancer. The use of oral contraceptives, which combine estrogen and progestin, appears to provide protection. Endometrial cancer is usually detectable by pelvic examination. It is treated surgically, commonly by hysterectomy. Radiation and chemotherapy may be used as well.

Ovarian Cancer Although ovarian cancer is rare compared with cervical or uterine cancer, it is the fifth most deadly cancer among women. There are no screening tests to detect it, so it is often diagnosed late in its development. The risk factors are similar to those for breast and endometrial cancer. Anything that lowers a woman's lifetime number of ovulation cycles—pregnancy, breastfeeding, or use of oral contraceptives—reduces the risk of ovarian cancer. A diet rich in fruits and vegetables may also reduce risk.

In 2007, the Gynecologic Cancer Foundation announced that scientists had reached a consensus on symptoms of ovarian cancer: bloating, pelvic or abdominal pain, difficulty eating or feeling full quickly, and urinary problems (urgency or frequency). Women who experience these symptoms almost daily for a few weeks should see their physician. Some ovarian cancers are also detected through regular pelvic exams, sometimes with ultrasound imaging of the ovaries. Ovarian cancer is treated by surgical removal of one or both ovaries, the fallopian tubes, and the uterus.

Other Female Reproductive Tract Cancers Daughters born to women who took DES (diethylstilbestrol) to prevent miscarriage have an increased risk, about 1 in 1000, of a vaginal or cervical cancer called clear cell cancer. (There is also some risk to DES sons, who may have an increased risk for undescended testicles, a risk factor for testicular cancer.) A DES daughter should find a physician who is familiar with the problems of DES exposure; more frequent and more thorough pelvic exams may be recommended.

Skin Cancer

Skin cancer is the most common cancer of all when cases of the highly curable forms are included in the count. Almost all cases of skin cancer can be traced to excessive exposure to **ultraviolet (UV) radiation** from the sun, including longer-wavelength ultraviolet A (UVA) and shorter-wavelength ultraviolet B (UVB) radiation. UVB radiation causes sunburns and can damage the eyes and immune system. UVA is less likely to cause a sunburn, but it damages connective tissue and leads to premature aging of the skin. Tanning lamps and tanning salon beds emit mostly UVA radiation. Both solar and artificial sources of UVA and UVB radiation are human carcinogens that cause skin cancer.

Both severe, acute sun reactions (sunburns) and chronic low-level sun reactions (suntans) can lead to skin

TERMS

PSA blood test A diagnostic test for prostate cancer that measures blood levels of prostate-specific antigen (PSA)

Pap test A scraping of cells from the cervix for examination under a microscope to detect cancer; also called *Pap smear.*

ultraviolet (UV) radiation Light rays of a specific wavelength, emitted by the sun; most UV rays are blocked by the ozone layer in the upper atmosphere.

cancer. According to the American Academy of Dermatology, the risk of skin cancer doubles in people who have had five or more sunburns in their lifetime. People with fair skin have less natural protection against skin damage from the sun and a higher risk of skin cancer than people with naturally dark skin. Severe sunburns in childhood have been linked to a greatly increased risk of skin cancer in later life, so children in particular should be protected. Other risk factors include having many moles (particularly large ones), spending time at high altitudes, and having a family history of the disease.

There are three main types of skin cancer, named for the types of skin cell from which they develop. **Basal cell** and **squamous cell carcinomas** together account for about 95% of the skin cancers diagnosed each year. They are usually found in chronically sun-exposed areas, such as the face, neck, hands, and arms. They usually appear as pale, waxlike, pearly nodules, or red, scaly, sharply outlined patches. These cancers are often painless, although they may bleed, crust, and form an open sore.

Melanoma is by far the most dangerous skin cancer because it spreads so rapidly. It is the most common cancer among women age 25–29. It can occur anywhere on the body, but the most common sites are the back, chest, abdomen, and lower legs. A melanoma usually appears at the site of a preexisting mole. The mole may begin to enlarge, become mottled or varied in color (colors can include blue, pink, and white), or develop an irregular surface or irregular borders. Tissue invaded by melanoma may also itch, burn, or bleed easily.

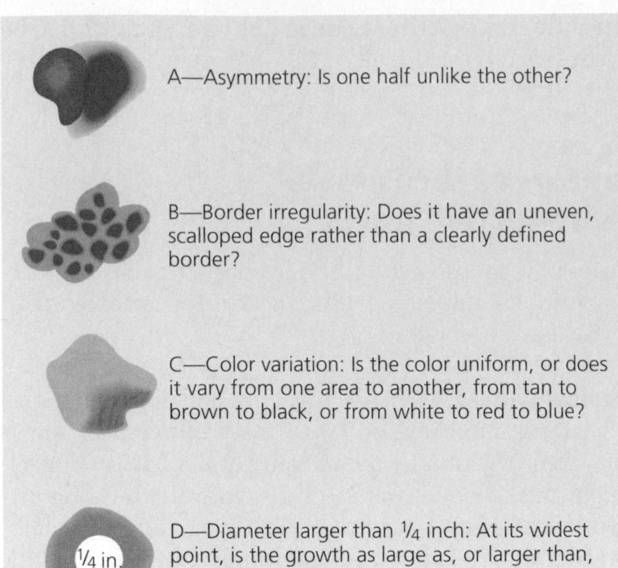

A—Asymmetry: Is one half unlike the other?
B—Border irregularity: Does it have an uneven, scalloped edge rather than a clearly defined border?
C—Color variation: Is the color uniform, or does it vary from one area to another, from tan to brown to black, or from white to red to blue?
D—Diameter larger than 1/4 inch: At its widest point, is the growth as large as, or larger than, a pencil eraser?
1/4 in.

FIGURE 12.4 The ABCD test for melanoma. To see a variety of photos of melanoma and benign moles, visit the National Cancer Institute's Visuals Online site (http://visualsonline.cancer.gov).

To protect yourself against skin cancer, avoid overexposure to UV radiation. People of every age, including babies and children, need to be protected from the sun (see the box "Choosing and Using Sunscreens and Sun-Protective Clothing"). You can help with early detection by examining your skin regularly. Most of the spots, freckles, moles, and blemishes on your body are normal, but if you notice an unusual growth, discoloration, or sore that does not heal, see your physician or a dermatologist immediately. The characteristics that may signal that a skin lesion is a melanoma are illustrated in Figure 12.4.

If you have an unusual skin lesion, your physician will examine it and possibly perform a biopsy. If the lesion is cancerous, it is usually removed surgically, a procedure that can almost always be performed in the physician's office using a local anesthetic. Treatment is usually simple and successful when the cancer is caught early.

Oral Cancer

Oral cancer—cancers of the lip, tongue, mouth, and throat—can be traced principally to cigarette, cigar, or pipe smoking; the use of smokeless (spit) tobacco; and excessive consumption of alcohol. These risk factors work together to compound a person's risk of oral cancer. The incidence of oral cancer is more than twice as great in men as in women and most frequent in men over 40. Oral cancers are fairly easy to detect but often hard to cure. Treatment usually includes surgery and radiation.

MOTIVATION BOOSTER

Use dramatic photos. Nearly half of all college students report having used tanning lamps within the past year, and more than 90% of tanning lamp users are aware that their use causes premature aging of the skin and skin cancer. These statistics show that knowledge alone isn't enough to motivate people. To increase your motivation, try using visual images. Place photos of people whose skin has become wrinkled and leathery through sun exposure on your refrigerator. Seeing how UV radiation permanently damages skin may remind you to slap on the sunscreen whenever you're outside. The immediacy of dramatic visual images can be more motivating than words.

TERMS

basal cell carcinoma Cancer of the deepest layers of the skin.

squamous cell carcinoma Cancer of the surface layers of the skin.

melanoma A malignant tumor of the skin that arises from pigmented cells, usually a mole.

Choosing and Using Sunscreens and Sun-Protective Clothing

With consistent use of the proper clothing, sunscreens, and common sense, you can lead an active outdoor life *and* protect your skin against most sun-induced damage.

Clothing

- Wear long-sleeved shirts and long pants. Dark-colored, tightly woven fabrics provide reasonable protection from the sun. Another good choice is clothing made from special sun-protective fabrics; these garments have an ultraviolet protection factor (UPF) rating, similar to the SPF for sunscreens. For example, a fabric with a UPF rating of 20 allows only one-twentieth of the sun's UV radiation to pass through. There are three categories of UPF protection: A UPF of 15–24 provides "good" UV protection; a UPF of 25–39 provides "very good" protection; and a UPF of 40–50 provides "excellent" protection. By comparison, typical shirts provide a UPF of only 5–9, a value that drops when clothing is wet.
- Consider washing some extra sun protection into your clothes. A new laundry additive adds UV protection to ordinary fabrics; it is recommended by the Skin Cancer Foundation.
- Wear a hat. Your face, ears, neck, and scalp are especially vulnerable to the sun's harmful effects, making hats an essential weapon in the battle against sun damage. A good choice is a broad-brimmed hat or a legionnaire-style cap that covers the ears and neck. Wear sunscreen on your face even if you are wearing a hat.
- Wear sunglasses. Exposure to UV rays can damage the eyes and cause cataracts.

Sunscreen

- Use a sunscreen and lip balm with a sun protection factor (SPF) of 15 or higher. (An SPF rating refers to the amount of time you can stay out in the sun before you burn, compared with not using sunscreen. For example, a product with an SPF of 15 would allow you to remain in the sun without burning 15 times longer, on average, than if you didn't apply sunscreen.) If you're fair-skinned, have a family history of skin cancer, are at high altitude, or will be outdoors for many hours, use a sunscreen with a high SPF (30+).
- Choose a broad-spectrum sunscreen that protects against both UVA and UVB radiation. The SPF rating of a sunscreen currently applies only to UVB, but a number of ingredients, especially titanium dioxide and zinc oxide, are effective at blocking most UVA radiation. In 2006, the FDA approved a product called Anthelios SX that protects against both UVA and UVB radiation. Use a water-resistant sunscreen if you swim or sweat a great deal. If you have acne, look for a sunscreen that is labeled "noncomedogenic," which means that it will not cause pimples.
- In late 2007, the FDA proposed new regulations that would require more stringent testing and labeling of commercial sunscreen products. The new system would require products to be tested for UVA protection and would implement a 4-star rating system based on those tests. The higher a product's rating in stars, the more protection it would provide against UVA radiation. The FDA also proposed placing caps on SPF ratings (which indicate how well a product protects against UVB radiation), to make those ratings more consistent and meaningful to consumers.
- Shake sunscreen before applying. Apply it 30 minutes before exposure to allow it time to bond to the skin. Reapply sunscreen frequently and generously to all sun-exposed areas (many people overlook their temples, ears, and sides and backs of their necks). Most people use less than half as much as they need to attain the full SPF rating. One ounce of sunscreen is enough to cover an average-size adult in a swimsuit. Reapply sunscreen 15–30 minutes after sun exposure begins and then every 2 hours after that and/or following activities, such as swimming, that could remove sunscreen.
- If you're taking medications, ask your physician or pharmacist about possible reactions to sunlight or interactions with sunscreens. Medications for acne, allergies, and diabetes are just a few of the products that can trigger reactions. If you're using sunscreen and an insect repellent containing DEET, use extra sunscreen (DEET may decrease sunscreen effectiveness).
- Don't let sunscreens give you a false sense of security. Most of the sunscreens currently on the market allow considerable UVA radiation to penetrate the skin, with the potential for causing skin cancers (especially melanoma), as well as wrinkles and other forms of skin damage.

Time of Day and Location

- Avoid sun exposure between 10 A.M. and 4 P.M., when the sun's rays are most intense. Clouds allow as much as 80% of UV rays to reach your skin. Stay in the shade when you can.
- Consult the day's UV Index, which predicts UV levels on a 0–10+ scale, to get a sense of the amount of sun protection you'll need; take special care on days with a rating of 5 or above. UV Index ratings are available in local newspapers, from the weather bureau, or from certain Web sites.
- Be aware that UV rays can penetrate at least 3 feet in water. Thus swimmers should wear water-resistant sunscreens. Snow, sand, water, concrete, and white-painted surfaces are also highly reflective.

Tanning Salons and Sunless Tanning Products

- Stay away from tanning salons! Despite advertising claims to the contrary, the lights used in tanning parlors are damaging to your skin. Tanning beds and lamps emit mostly UVA radiation, increasing your risk of premature skin aging (such as wrinkles) and skin cancer.
- If you really want a tan, consider using a sunless tanning product. Lotions, creams, and sprays containing the color additive dihydroxyacetone (DHA) are approved by the FDA for tanning. (The FDA has not approved so-called tanning accelerators and tanning pills because these products have not been proven to be safe or effective.) DHA is for external use only and should not be inhaled, swallowed, or used around the eyes. Tanning salons that offer spraying or misting with DHA need to ensure that customers are protected from exposure to the eyes, lips, and mucous membranes as well as internal exposure. Most sunless tanning products do not contain sunscreen, so if you use them in the sun, be sure to wear sunscreen.

TAKE CHARGE

Testicle Self-Examination

The best time to perform a testicular self-exam is after a warm shower or bath, when the scrotum is relaxed. First, stand in front of a mirror and look for any swelling of the scrotum. Then, examine each testicle with both hands. Place the index and middle fingers under the testicle and the thumbs on top; roll the testicle gently between the fingers and thumbs. Don't worry if one testicle seems slightly larger than the other—that's common. Also, expect to feel the epididymis, the soft, sperm-carrying tube at the rear of the testicle .

Perform the self-exam each month. If you find a lump, swelling, or nodule, consult a physician right away. The abnormality may not be cancer, but only a physician can make a diagnosis. Other possible signs of testicular cancer include a change in the way a testicle feels, a sudden collection of fluid in the scrotum, a dull ache in the lower abdomen or groin, a feeling of heaviness in the scrotum, or pain in a testicle or the scrotum.

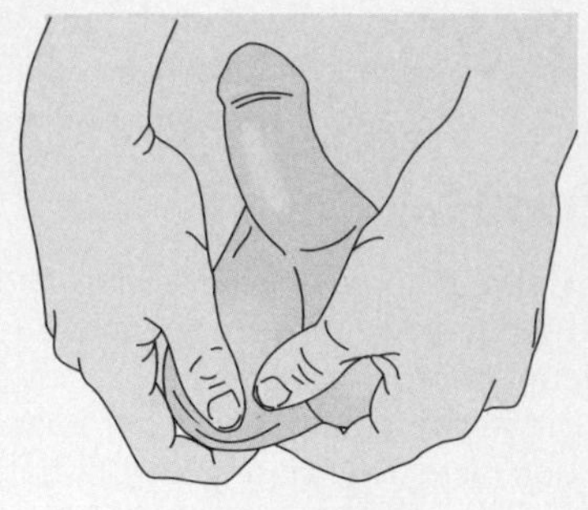

SOURCES: Testicular Cancer Resource Center. 2006. *How to Do a Testicular Self Examination* (http://tcrc.acor.org/tcexam.html; retrieved December 1, 2007). National Cancer Institute. 2005. *Testicular Cancer: Questions and Answers* (http://www.cancer.gov/cancertopics/factsheet/sites-types/testicular; retrieved December 1, 2007).

Testicular Cancer

Testicular cancer is relatively rare, accounting for only 1% of cancers in men, but it is the most common cancer in men age 20–35. Testicular cancer is much more common among white Americans than Latinos, Asian Americans, or African Americans. Men with undescended testicles are at increased risk for testicular cancer, and for this reason the condition should be corrected in early childhood. Self-examination may help in the early detection of testicular cancer (see the box "Testicle Self-Examination"). Tumors are treated by surgical removal of the testicle and, if the tumor has spread, by chemotherapy.

Other Cancers

Several other cancers affect thousands of people each year. Some have identifiable risk factors, but the causes of others are still under investigation.

- ***Pancreatic cancer*** is the fifth leading cause of cancer death in the United States. The disease is usually well advanced before symptoms become noticeable, and no effective cure is available. About 3 out of 10 cases are linked to smoking. Other risk factors include being male, African American, or over age 60; having a family history of pancreatic cancer; having diabetes; being inactive and obese; and eating a diet high in fat and meat and low in vegetables.

QUESTIONS FOR CRITICAL THINKING AND REFLECTION

Has anyone you know had cancer? If so, what type of cancer was it? What were its symptoms? Based on the information presented so far in this chapter, did the person have any of the known risk factors for the disease?

- ***Bladder cancer*** is twice as common in men as in women, and smoking is the key risk factor. The first symptoms are likely to be blood in the urine and/or increased frequency of urination. These symptoms can also signal a urinary tract infection but should trigger a visit to a physician, who can evaluate the possibility of cancer.
- ***Kidney cancer*** usually occurs in people over 50; smoking and obesity are mild risk factors, as is a family history of the disease. Symptoms may include fatigue, pain in the side, and blood in the urine.
- ***Brain cancer*** commonly develops for no apparent reason and can arise from most of the cell types that are found in the brain. One of the few established risk factors for brain cancer is ionizing radiation, such as X-rays of the head. Symptoms are often nonspecific and include headaches, fatigue, behavioral changes, and sometimes seizures. Some brain tumors are curable by surgery or by radiation and chemotherapy, but most are not.
- ***Leukemia,*** cancer of the white blood cells, starts in the bone marrow but can then spread to the lymph nodes, spleen, liver, other organs, and central nervous system. Most people with leukemia have no known risk factors. About 20% of cases of adult leukemia are related to smoking; other possible risk factors include radiation and certain chemicals and infections. Most symptoms occur because leukemia cells crowd out the production of normal blood cells; the result can be fatigue, anemia, weight loss, and increased risk of infection.
- ***Lymphoma*** is a form of cancer that begins in the lymph nodes and then may spread to almost any part of the body. There are two types: Hodgkin's disease and non-Hodgkin's lymphoma (NHL). NHL is the more common and more deadly form of the disease; risk factors for NHL are not well understood but may include genetic factors, radiation, and certain chemicals and infections.

DIMENSIONS OF DIVERSITY

Ethnicity, Poverty, and Cancer

Rates of cancer have declined among all U.S. ethnic groups in recent years, but significant disparities still exist.

- Among U.S. ethnic groups, African Americans have the highest incidence of and death rates from cancer.
- White women have a higher incidence of breast cancer, but African American women have the highest death rate. Black women are less likely to receive regular mammograms and more likely to experience delays in follow-up.
- African American men have a higher rate of prostate cancer than any other U.S. group and more than twice the death rate of other groups. However, black men are less likely than white men to undergo PSA testing for prostate cancer.
- Latinas have the highest incidence of cervical cancer, but African American women have the highest death rate. Language and cultural barriers and problems accessing screening services are thought to particularly affect Latinas, who have relatively low rates of Pap testing.
- Asian Americans and Pacific Islander Americans have the highest rates of liver and stomach cancers. Recent immigration helps explain these higher rates, as these cancers are usually caused by infections that are more prevalent in the recent immigrant's country of origin.

Some disparities in cancer risks and rates may be influenced by genetic or cultural factors. For example, certain genetic/molecular features of aggressive breast cancer are more common among African American women; they are more likely to be diagnosed at a later stage and with more aggressive tumors. Genetic factors may also help explain the high rate of prostate cancer among black men. Women from cultures where early marriage and motherhood is common are likely to have a lower risk of breast cancer. People who don't smoke or who are vegetarians may have lower rates of many cancers.

Most of the differences in cancer rates and deaths, however, are thought to be the result of socioeconomic inequities. People of low socioeconomic status are more likely to smoke, abuse alcohol, eat unhealthy foods, and be sedentary and overweight—all of which are associated with cancer. High levels of stress associated with poverty may impair the immune system, the body's first line of defense against cancer.

People with low incomes also are more likely to live in unhealthy environments. For example, Latinos and Asian and Pacific Islander Americans are more likely than other groups to live in areas that do not meet federal air quality standards. Low-income people may also have jobs in which they come into daily contact with carcinogenic chemicals. They may face similar risks in their homes and schools, where they may be exposed to asbestos or other carcinogens.

People with low incomes also have less exposure to information about cancer, are less aware of the early warning signs of cancer, and are less likely to seek medical care when they have such symptoms. Lack of health insurance is a key factor explaining higher death rates among people with low incomes. A study comparing low-income Americans and Canadians found that the Canadians were more likely to survive cancer, possibly due to Canada's system of universal health care, which ensures access to treatment regardless of income.

Public education campaigns that encourage healthy lifestyle habits, routine cancer screening, and participation in clinical trials may be one helpful strategy to reduce cancer disparities. But the effects of poverty are more difficult to overcome. Some medical scientists look to policymakers for solutions and maintain that living and working conditions in the inner cities must be improved and that access to quality health care must be assured for all Americans. Then, even without new miracle drugs or medical breakthroughs, the United States could see a real decrease in cancer rates in low-income populations.

SOURCES: American Cancer Society. 2007. *Cancer Facts and Figures 2007*. Atlanta: American Cancer Society. Chlebowski, R. T., et al. 2005. Ethnicity and breast cancer: Factors influencing differences in incidence and outcome. *Journal of the National Cancer Institute* 97(6): 439–448. CDC Office of Minority Health and Health Disparities. 2007. *Eliminate Disparities in Cancer Screening and Management* (http://www.cdc.gov/omhd/AMH/factsheets/cancer.htm; retrieved December 1, 2007). National Cancer Institute. 2007. *Cancer Health Disparities* (http://www.cancer.gov/cancertopics/types/disparities; retrieved June 6, 2007).

THE CAUSES OF CANCER

Although scientists do not know everything about what causes cancer, they have identified genetic, environmental, and lifestyle factors. Typically, these factors work together (see the box "Ethnicity, Poverty, and Cancer").

The Role of DNA

Heredity and genetics are important factors in a person's risk of cancer. Certain genes may predispose some people to cancer, and specific gene mutations have been associated with cancer.

DNA Basics The nucleus of each cell in your body contains 23 pairs of **chromosomes,** which are made up of tightly packed coils of **DNA** (deoxyribonucleic acid). Each chromosome contains thousands of **genes;** you have

TERMS

chromosomes The threadlike bodies in a cell nucleus that contain molecules of DNA; most human cells contain 23 pairs of chromosomes.

DNA Deoxyribonucleic acid, a chemical substance that carries genetic information.

gene A section of a chromosome that contains the instructions for making a particular protein; the basic unit of heredity.

about 25,000 genes in all. Each of your genes controls the production of a particular protein. By making different proteins at different times, genes can act as switches to alter the ways a cell works. Some genes are responsible for controlling the rate of cell division.

DNA Mutations and Cancer A *mutation* is any change in the makeup of a gene. Some mutations are inherited; others are caused by environmental agents known as mutagens. Mutagens include radiation, certain viruses, and chemical substances in the air we breathe. (When a mutagen also causes cancer, it is called a carcinogen.) Some mutations are the result of copying errors that occur when DNA replicates itself as part of cell division.

A mutated gene no longer contains the proper code for producing its protein. It usually takes several mutational changes before a normal cell takes on the properties of a cancer cell. Genes in which mutations are associated with the conversion of a normal cell into a cancer cell are known as **oncogenes.** In their undamaged form, many oncogenes play a role in controlling or restricting cell growth; they are called suppressor genes. Mutational damage to suppressor genes releases the brake on growth and leads to rapid and uncontrolled cell division—a precondition for the development of cancer.

An example of an inherited mutated oncogene is BRCA1 (breast cancer gene 1): Women who inherit a damaged copy of this suppressor gene face a significantly increased risk of breast and ovarian cancer.

In most cases, however, mutational damage occurs after birth. For example, only about 5–10% of breast cancer cases can be traced to inherited copies of a damaged BRCA1 gene. In addition, lifestyle factors are important even for those who have inherited a damaged suppressor gene. Testing and identification of hereditary cancer risks can be helpful for some people, especially if it leads to increased attention to controllable risk factors and better medical screening.

Cancer Promoters Substances known as *cancer promoters* make up another important piece of the cancer puzzle. They don't directly produce DNA mutations, but they accelerate the growth of cells, which means less time for a cell to repair DNA damage caused by other factors. Estrogen, which stimulates cellular growth in the female reproductive organs, is an example of a cancer promoter. Although much still needs to be learned about the role of genetics in cancer, it's clear that minimizing mutation damage to our DNA will lower our risk of many cancers. Unfortunately, a great many substances produce cancer-causing mutations, and we can't escape them all. By identifying the important carcinogens and understanding how they produce their effects, we can help keep our DNA intact and avoid activating "sleeping" oncogenes.

TERMS

oncogene A gene involved in the transformation of a normal cell into a cancer cell.

carotenoid Any of a group of yellow-to-red plant pigments; some can be converted to vitamin A by the liver, and many act as antioxidants or have other anticancer effects. The carotenoids include beta-carotene, lutein, lycopene, and zeaxanthin.

phytochemical A naturally occurring substance found in plant foods that may help prevent chronic diseases such as cancer and heart disease; *phyto* means "plant."

Dietary Factors

Diet is one of the most important factors in cancer prevention, but it is also one of the most complex and controversial. Your food choices affect your cancer risk by both exposing you to potentially dangerous compounds and depriving you of potentially protective ones. The following sections examine some of the dietary factors that may affect cancer risk.

Dietary Fat and Meat The 2006 American Cancer Society (ACS) Nutrition and Physical Activity Guidelines for Cancer Prevention encourage individuals to limit consumption of processed and red meats. Diets high in fat and meat appear to contribute to certain cancers, including colon, stomach, and prostate. As is true with heart disease, certain types of fats may be riskier than others. Diets favoring omega-6 polyunsaturated fats are associated with a higher risk of certain cancers than are diets favoring the omega-3 forms commonly found in fish and canola oil. (See Chapter 8 for more information on types of fatty acids.)

Alcohol Alcohol is a known human carcinogen and is associated with an increased incidence of several cancers. For example, an average alcohol intake of three drinks a day is associated with a doubling in the risk of breast cancer. Alcohol and tobacco interact as risk factors for oral cancer. Heavy users of both alcohol and tobacco have a risk for oral cancer up to 15 times greater than that of people who don't drink or use tobacco.

Fried Foods Scientists have found high levels of the chemical acrylamide (a probable human carcinogen) in starch-based foods that have been fried or baked at high temperatures, including french fries and certain types of snack chips and crackers. Studies are ongoing, but, in 2005, the World Health Organization urged food companies to work to lower the acrylamide content of foods to reduce any risk to public health. Acrylamide levels vary widely in foods, and there are currently no warnings against eating specific foods. The wisest course may be to consume a variety of foods and avoid overindulging in any single class of foods, particularly items like french fries and potato chips, which may contain other unhealthy substances such as saturated and trans fats. You can also limit your exposure to acrylamide by not smoking—you get much more of the chemical from smoking than from food.

Fiber Various potential cancer-fighting actions have been proposed for fiber, but none has been firmly established. Although further study is needed to clarify the relationship between fiber intake and cancer risk, experts still recommend a high-fiber diet for its overall positive effect on health.

Fruits and Vegetables The 2006 ACS guidelines encourage individuals to eat a plant-based diet containing five or more servings of a variety of vegetables and fruits every day and to choose whole grains over processed grains. A massive number of epidemiological studies provide evidence that high consumption of fruits and vegetables reduces the risk of many cancers. Exactly which constituents of fruits and vegetables are responsible for this reduction in risk is less certain.

Some essential nutrients have been found to act against cancer. For example, vitamin C, vitamin E, selenium, and the **carotenoids** (vitamin A precursors) may help block the initiation of cancer by acting as antioxidants. Antioxidants prevent free radicals from damaging DNA. Vitamin C may also block the conversion of nitrates (food preservatives) into cancer-causing agents. Folic acid may inhibit the transformation of normal cells into malignant cells and strengthen immune function. Calcium inhibits the growth of cells in the colon and may slow the spread of potentially cancerous cells.

Many other anticancer agents in the diet fall under the broader heading of **phytochemicals,** substances in plants that help protect against chronic diseases (see Table 12.1). One of the first to be identified was sulforaphane, a compound found in broccoli.

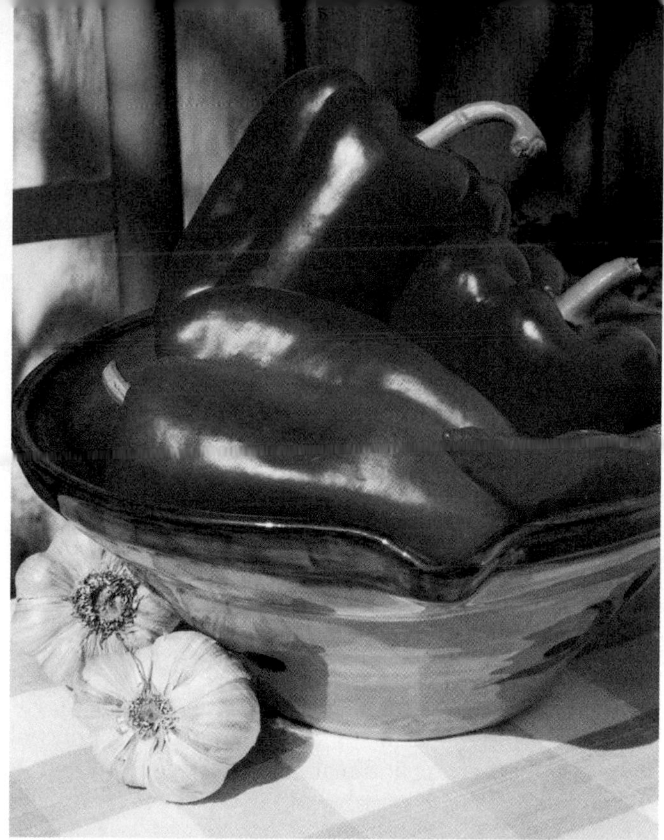

Your food choices significantly affect your risk of cancer. Red bell peppers, chili peppers, and garlic are just a few of the foods containing cancer-fighting phytochemicals.

To increase your intake of potential cancer fighters, eat a wide variety of fruits, vegetables, legumes, and grains (see Lab 12.1). Don't rely on supplements. Isolated phytochemicals may be harmful if taken in high doses, and it is likely that the anticancer effects of many

Table 12.1 Foods with Phytochemicals

Food	Phytochemical	Potential Anticancer Effects
Chili peppers (*Note:* Hotter peppers contain more capsaicin.)	Capsaicin	Neutralizes effect of nitrosamines; may block carcinogens in cigarette smoke from acting on cells
Oranges, lemons, limes, onions, apples, berries, eggplant	Flavonoids	Act as antioxidants; block access of carcinogens to cells; suppress malignant changes in cells; prevent cancer cells from multiplying
Citrus fruits, cherries	Monoterpenes	Help detoxify carcinogens; inhibit spread of cancer cells
Cruciferous vegetables (broccoli, cabbage, bok choy, cauliflower, kale, brussels sprouts, collards)	Isothiocyanates	Boost production of cancer-fighting enzymes; suppress tumor growth; block effects of estrogen on cell growth
Garlic, onions, leeks, shallots, chives	Allyl sulfides	Increase levels of enzymes that break down potential carcinogens; boost activity of cancer-fighting immune cells
Grapes, red wine, peanuts	Resveratrol	Acts as an antioxidant; suppresses tumor growth
Green, oolong, and black teas (*Note:* Drinking burning hot tea may *increase* cancer risk.)	Polyphenols	Increase antioxidant activity; prevent cancer cells from multiplying; help speed excretion of carcinogens from body
Orange, deep yellow, red, pink, and dark green vegetables; some fruits	Carotenoids	Act as antioxidants; reduce levels of cancer-promoting enzymes; inhibit spread of cancer cells
Soy foods, whole grains, flax seeds, nuts	Phytoestrogens	Block effects of estrogen on cell growth; lower blood levels of estrogen
Whole grains, legumes	Phytic acid	Binds iron, which may prevent it from creating cell-damaging free radicals

MOTIVATION BOOSTER

Carry lists. Healthy food choices are key in many behavior change plans, but changing long-term eating habits is a challenge. Look through the lists of recommended foods in this chapter and in Lab 12.1, and choose 10 foods that you enjoy and can see yourself eating on a regular basis. Write them down and carry the list with you when you shop for food or eat out. It will remind you that there are many healthy options available in your environment.

foods are the result of many chemical substances working in combination.

Obesity and Inactivity

The ACS recommends maintaining a healthy weight throughout life by balancing caloric intake with physical activity and achieving and maintaining a healthy weight if currently overweight or obese. Being overweight or obese is linked with increased risk of several kinds of cancer, including breast and colon cancer (Figure 12.5). The ACS guidelines encourage everyone to adopt a physically active lifestyle. For adults, at least 30 minutes of moderate-to-vigorous physical activity, above usual activities, on 5 or more days per week are recommended; 45–60 minutes of intentional physical activity are preferable. For children and adolescents, at least 60 minutes of moderate-to-vigorous physical activity at least 5 days per week are recommended.

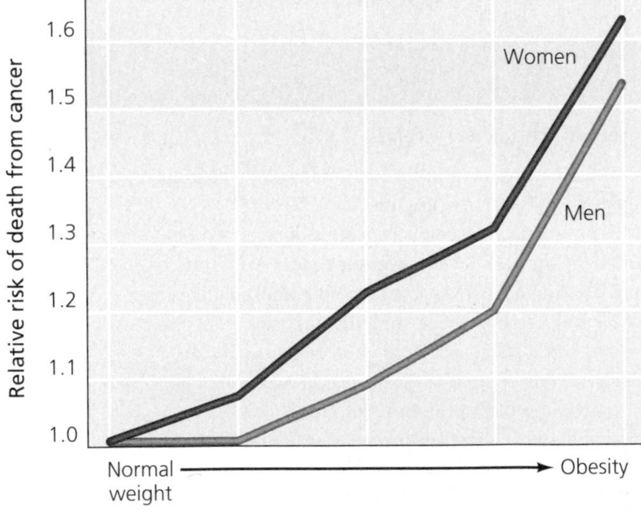

FIGURE 12.5 Body weight and cancer mortality. For both men and women, overweight and obesity are associated with significantly higher rates of death from cancer.

SOURCE: Calle, E. E., et al. 2003. Overweight, obesity, and mortality from cancer in a prospectively studied cohort of U.S. adults. *New England Journal of Medicine* 348(17): 1625–1638.

Carcinogens in the Environment

Some carcinogens occur naturally in the environment, like the sun's UV rays. Others are synthetic substances that show up occasionally in the general environment but more often in the work environments of specific industries.

Ingested Chemicals The food industry uses preservatives and other additives to prevent food from becoming spoiled or stale. Some of these compounds are antioxidants and may actually decrease any cancer-causing properties the food might have.

Other compounds, like the nitrates and nitrites found in hot dogs, ham, bacon, lunch meats, and beer and ale, are potentially more dangerous. Although nitrates and nitrites are not themselves carcinogenic, they can combine with dietary substances in the stomach and be converted to nitrosamines, which are highly potent carcinogens. Foods cured with nitrites, as well as those cured by salt or smoke, have been linked to esophageal and stomach cancer, and they should be eaten only in modest amounts.

Environmental and Industrial Pollution The best available data indicate that less than 2% of cancer deaths are caused by general environmental pollution, such as substances in our air and water. Exposure to carcinogenic materials in the workplace is a more serious problem. Occupational exposure to specific carcinogens may account for up to 5% of cancer deaths. With increasing industry and government regulations, industrial sources of cancer risk should continue to diminish.

Radiation All sources of radiation are potentially carcinogenic, including medical X-rays, radioactive substances (radioisotopes), and UV radiation from the sun, sunlamps, and tanning beds. Most physicians and dentists are quite aware of the risk of radiation, and successful efforts have been made to reduce the amount of radiation needed for mammography, dental X-rays, and other necessary medical X-rays.

Another source of environmental radiation is radon gas. Radon is a radioactive decomposition product of radium, which is found in small quantities in some rocks and soils. Fortunately, in most of our homes and classrooms, radon is rapidly dissipated into the atmosphere, and very low levels of radon do not appear to significantly increase cancer risk. However, in certain kinds of enclosed spaces, such as mines, some basements, and airtight buildings, it can rise to dangerous levels.

Microbes About 15% of the world's cancers are caused by microbes, including viruses, bacteria, and parasites, although the percentage is much lower in developed countries like the United States. As discussed earlier, certain types of HPV cause many cases of cervical cancer.

QUESTIONS FOR CRITICAL THINKING AND REFLECTION

What do you think your risks for cancer are? Do you have a family history of cancer, or have you been exposed to carcinogens? How about your diet and exercise patterns? What can you do to reduce your risks?

Other microbes linked to cancer include the *Helicobacter pylori* bacterium, which can cause both stomach ulcers and stomach cancer. The Epstein-Barr virus, best known for causing mononucleosis, is also suspected of contributing to Hodgkin's disease, cancer of the pharynx, and some stomach cancers. Human herpesvirus 8 has been linked to Kaposi's sarcoma and certain types of lymphoma. Hepatitis virus B and C together cause as many as 80% of the world's liver cancers.

PREVENTING CANCER

Your lifestyle choices can radically lower your cancer risks, so you *can* take a practical approach to cancer prevention. Here are some guidelines:

- ***Avoid tobacco.*** Smoking is responsible for 80–90% of lung cancers and for about 30% of all cancer deaths. The carcinogenic chemicals in smoke are transported throughout the body in the bloodstream, making smoking a carcinogen for many forms of cancer other than lung cancer. The use of spit tobacco increases the risk of cancers of the mouth, larynx, throat, and esophagus. It's also important to avoid exposure to ETS.
- ***Control diet and weight.*** About one-third of all cancers are in some way linked to what we eat. Choose a low-fat, plant-based diet containing a wide variety of fruits, vegetables, and whole grains rich in phytochemicals. Drink alcohol only in moderation, if at all. Maintain a healthy weight.
- ***Exercise regularly.*** Regular exercise is linked to lower rates of colon and other cancers. It also helps control weight.
- ***Protect skin from the sun.*** Almost all cases of skin cancer are sun-related. Wear protective clothing when you're out in the sun, and use a sunscreen with an SPF rating of 15 or higher. Don't go to tanning salons.
- ***Avoid environmental and occupational carcinogens.*** Try to avoid occupational exposure to carcinogens and don't smoke; the cancer risks of many of these agents increase greatly when combined with smoking.

Your first line of defense against cancer involves the lifestyle changes described in this chapter. Your second line of defense against cancer is early detection. The American Cancer Society recommends that you stay alert for any of the seven major warning signs illustrated in Figure 12.6; you can remember these with the acronym CAUTION. The appearance of any of these warning signs, although not a sure indication of cancer, should send you to your physician. The ACS also recommends routine tests to screen for common cancers. In addition to the screening guidelines listed in Table 12.2 (p. 366), some experts recommend regular skin self-exams and, for men, monthly testicular self-exams. Discuss appropriate screening tests with your physician.

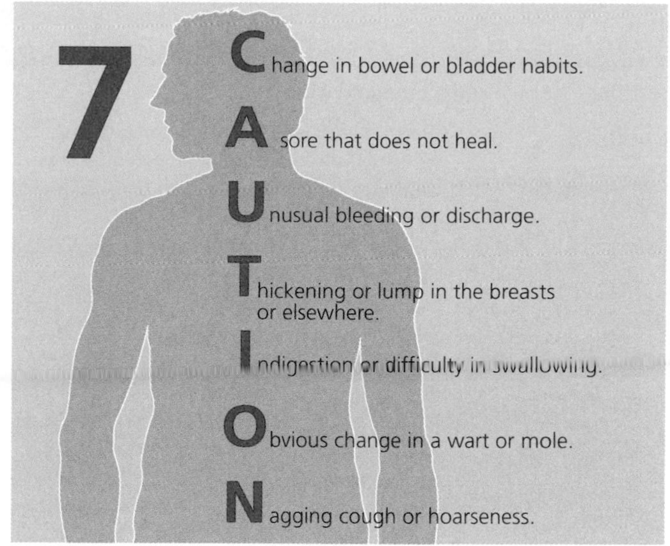

FIGURE 12.6 The seven major warning signs of cancer.

TIPS FOR TODAY AND THE FUTURE

A growing body of research suggests that we can take an active role in preventing many cancers by adopting a wellness lifestyle.

RIGHT NOW YOU CAN

- If you are a woman, do a breast self-exam; if you are a man, do a testicular self-exam.
- Buy multiple bottles of sunscreen and put them in places where you will most likely need them, such as your backpack, gym bag, or car.
- Check the cancer screening guidelines on p. 366, and make sure you are up to date on your screenings.

IN THE FUTURE YOU CAN

- Learn where to find information about daily UV radiation levels in your area, and learn how to interpret the information. Many local newspapers and television stations (and their Web sites) report current UV levels every day.
- Gradually add foods with abundant phytochemicals to your diet, choosing from the list shown in Table 12.1.

Table 12.2	Screening Guidelines for the Early Detection of Cancer in Asymptomatic People
Site	**Recommendation**
Breast	• Yearly mammograms are recommended starting at age 40. The age at which screening should be stopped should be individualized by considering the potential risks and benefits of screening in the context of overall health status and longevity. • Clinical breast exam should be part of a periodic health exam, about every 3 years for women in their 20s and 30s, and every year for women 40 and older. • Women should know how their breasts normally feel and report any breast change promptly to their health care provider. Breast self-exam is an option for women starting in their 20s. • Women at increased risk (e.g., family history, genetic tendency, past breast cancer) should talk with their doctors about the benefits and limitations of starting mammography screening earlier, having additional tests (i.e., breast ultrasound and MRI), or having more frequent exams.
Colon and rectum	Beginning at age 50, men and women should begin screening with one of the examination schedules below. • A fecal occult blood test (FOBT) or fecal immunochemical test (FIT) every year • A flexible sigmoidoscopy (FSIG) every 5 years • Annual FOBT or FIT and flexible sigmoidoscopy every 5 years* • A double-contrast barium enema every 5 years • A colonoscopy every 10 years **Combined testing is preferred over either annual FOBT or FIT, or FSIG every 5 years, alone. People who are at moderate or high risk for colorectal cancer should talk with a doctor about a different testing schedule.*
Prostate	The PSA test and the digital rectal examination should be offered annually, beginning at age 50, to men who have a life expectancy of at least 10 years. Men at high risk (African American men and men with a strong family history of one or more first-degree relatives diagnosed with prostate cancer at an early age) should begin testing at age 45. For men at both average risk and high risk, information should be provided about what is known and what is uncertain about the benefits and limitations of early detection and treatment of prostate cancer so that they can make an informed decision about testing.
Uterus	***Cervix:*** Screening should begin approximately 3 years after a woman begins having vaginal intercourse, but no later than age 21. Screening should be done every year with regular Pap tests or every 2 years using liquid-based tests. At or after age 30, women who have had three normal test results in a row may get screened every 2 to 3 years. Alternatively, cervical cancer screening with HPV DNA testing and conventional or liquid-based cytology could be performed every 3 years. However, doctors may suggest a woman get screened more often if she has certain risk factors, such as HIV infection or a weak immune system. Women aged 70 years and older who have had three or more consecutive normal Pap tests in the past 10 years may choose to stop cervical cancer screening. Screening after total hysterectomy (with removal of the cervix) is not necessary unless the surgery was done as a treatment for cervical cancer. ***Endometrium:*** The American Cancer Society recommends that at the time of menopause all women should be informed about the risks and symptoms of endometrial cancer and strongly encouraged to report any unexpected bleeding or spotting to their physicians. Annual screening for endometrial cancer with endometrial biopsy beginning at age 35 should be offered to women with or at risk for hereditary nonpolyposis colon cancer (HNPCC).
Cancer-related checkup	For individuals undergoing periodic health examinations, a cancer-related checkup should include health counseling and, depending on a person's age and gender, might include examinations for cancers of the thyroid, oral cavity, skin, lymph nodes, testes, and ovaries, as well as for some nonmalignant diseases.

SOURCE: American Cancer Society's *Cancer Facts and Figures 2007*.

SUMMARY

• Cancer is an abnormal and uncontrollable growth of cells or tissue; cancer cells can metastasize.

• Lung cancer kills more people than any other type of cancer; tobacco smoke is the primary cause.

• Colon and rectal cancer is linked to age, heredity, and a diet with low intake of fruits and vegetables.

• Breast cancer has a genetic component, but lifestyle and hormones are also factors. Prostate cancer is chiefly a disease of aging; diet, heredity, and ethnicity are other risk factors.

• Cancers of the female reproductive tract include cervical, uterine, and ovarian cancer. Cervical cancer is linked to HPV infection; the Pap test is an effective screening test. Vaccination with Gardasil is recommended for girls and women age 9–26.

• Melanoma is the most serious form of skin cancer; excessive exposure to UV radiation in sunlight is the primary cause.

• Oral cancer is caused primarily by smoking, excess alcohol consumption, and use of spit tobacco.

• Testicular cancer can be detected early through self-examination.

• The genetic basis of some cancers appears to be mutational damage to suppressor genes, which normally limit cell division.

Q What is a biopsy?

A A biopsy is the removal and examination of a small piece of body tissue. Biopsies enable cancer specialists to carefully examine cells that are suspected of having turned cancerous. Some biopsies are fairly simple to perform, such as those on tissue from moles or skin sores. Other biopsies may require the use of a needle or probe to remove tissue from inside the body, such as in the breast or stomach.

Q How is cancer treated?

A The ideal cancer therapy would kill or remove all cancer cells while leaving normal tissue untouched. Sometimes this is almost possible, as when a surgeon removes a small superficial tumor of the skin. Usually a tumor is less accessible, and some combination of treatments is necessary. Current treatments for cancer are based primarily on the following:

- ***Surgery.*** Sometimes the organ containing the tumor is not essential for life and can be partially or completely removed. Surgery is less effective when cancer involves widely distributed cells (such as in the case of leukemia) or when the cancer has already metastasized.
- ***Chemotherapy.*** Cancer cells can be killed by administering drugs that interfere chemically with their growth. Although chemotherapy is targeted at rapidly dividing cancer cells, it can also affect cells in normal tissue, leading to unpleasant side effects.
- ***Radiation.*** In radiation therapy, a beam of X-rays or gamma rays is directed at the tumor, killing the cancer cells. Radiation destroys both normal and cancerous cells but can usually be precisely directed at the tumor.

Some experimental techniques that show promise for some particular types of cancer include the following:

- ***Bone marrow transplants.*** Healthy bone marrow cells from a compatible donor are transplanted following the elimination of the patient's bone marrow by radiation or chemotherapy. Transplants of stem cells may provide a solution to the problem of donor incompatibility. These unspecialized cells can divide and produce many specialized cell types, including bone marrow cells. Stem cells can be grown outside the body and then transplanted back into the cancer patient, allowing safe repopulation of bone marrow.
- ***Vaccines and genetically modified immune cells.*** These enhance the reaction of a patient's own immune system.
- ***Anti-angiogenesis agents.*** These starve tumors by blocking their blood supply.
- ***Proteasome inhibitors.*** Proteasomes help control the cell cycle—the process through which cells divide. If proteasomes malfunction, as is often the case in cancer cells, then cells may begin multiplying out of control. Proteasome inhibitors block the action of proteasomes, halting cell division and killing the cells. One proteasome inhibitor is now being used against certain cancers, and other such drugs are in development.
- ***Enzyme activators/blockers.*** Normal cells die after dividing a given number of times. Scientists believe that the enzyme caspase triggers the death of normally functioning cells. In cancer cells, caspase activity may be blocked. Conversely, if the enzyme telomerase becomes active in cancer cells, the life/death cycle stops and the cells duplicate indefinitely. In effect, inactive caspase or active telomerase may make cancer cells "immortal." Researchers are studying compounds that can either activate caspase or deactivate telomerase; either type of drug might lead cancer cells to self-destruct. No such drugs are now in clinical use.

In the future, gene sequencing techniques may allow treatments to be targeted at specific cancer subtypes, much as specific antibiotics are now used to treat specific bacterial diseases.

For more Common Questions Answered about cancer, visit the Online Learning Center.

- Cancer-promoting dietary factors include meat, certain types of fat, and alcohol. Dietary elements that may protect against cancer include antioxidants and phytochemicals. An inactive lifestyle is associated with some cancers.
- Some carcinogens occur naturally in the environment; others are manufactured substances. Occupational exposure is a risk for some workers.
- All sources of radiation are potentially carcinogenic, including X-rays, UV rays of the sun, and radon gas.
- Strategies for preventing cancer include avoiding tobacco; eating a varied, moderate diet and controlling weight; exercising regularly; protecting skin from the sun; avoiding exposure to environmental and occupational carcinogens; staying alert for cancer warning signs; and getting recommended cancer-screening tests.

FOR FURTHER EXPLORATION

BOOKS

American Cancer Society. 2007. *Cancer Caregiving A–Z.* Atlanta: American Cancer Society. *Written for the layperson who must care for someone with cancer; covers a wide range of cancer-related topics in easy-to-understand language.*

American Institute for Cancer Research. 2005. *The New American Plate Cookbook.* Berkeley: University of California Berkeley Press. *Provides guidelines and recipes for healthy eating to prevent cancer and other chronic diseases.*

McKinnell, R. G., et al. 2006. *The Biological Basis of Cancer,* 2nd ed. Boston: Cambridge University Press. *Examines the underlying causes of cancer and discusses actual cases of the disease and its impact on patients and families.*

Rosenbaum, E., et al. 2007. *Everyone's Guide to Cancer Therapy*, rev. 5th ed. Riverside, N.J.: Andrews McMeel. *Reviewed by a panel of more than 100 oncologists; provides articles on the known causes, diagnoses, and treatments for many types of cancer.*

Turkington, C., and W. LiPera. 2005. *The Encyclopedia of Cancer.* New York: Facts on File. *Includes entries on a variety of topics relating to cancer causes, prevention, diagnosis, and treatment.*

ORGANIZATIONS, HOTLINES, AND WEB SITES

American Academy of Dermatology. Provides information on skin cancer prevention.
866-503-SKIN
http://www.aad.org

American Cancer Society. Provides a wide range of free materials on the prevention and treatment of cancer.
800-ACS-2345
http://www.cancer.org

American Institute for Cancer Research. Provides information on lifestyle and cancer prevention, especially nutrition.
800-843-8114
http://www.aicr.org

CureSearch National Childhood Cancer Foundation. Offers information on childhood cancers and initiatives to raise awareness and funds for research.
800-458-6223
http://www.curesearch.org

EPA/Sunwise. Provides information about the UV Index and the effects of sun exposure, with links to sites with daily UV Index ratings for U.S. and international cities.
http://www.epa.gov/sunwise/uvindex.html

Washington University School of Medicine: Your Disease Risk. Includes interactive risk assessments as well as tips for preventing common cancers.
http://www.yourdiseaserisk.wustl.edu

LiveStrong (The Lance Armstrong Foundation). Provides resources on cancer and cancer support.
512-236-8820
http://www.livestrong.org

MedlinePlus: Cancers. Provides links to reliable cancer information.
http://www.nlm.nih.gov/medlineplus/cancers.html

National Cancer Institute. Provides information on treatment options, screening, clinical trials, and newly approved drugs.
800-4-CANCER
http://www.cancer.gov

Skin Cancer Foundation. Provides information on all types of skin cancers, their prevention, and treatment.
800-SKIN-490
http://www.skincancer.org

Susan G. Komen for the Cure. Provides information and resources on breast cancer.
877-465-6636
http://cms.komen.org/komen/index.htm

World Health Organization: Cancer. Home page of WHO's worldwide anticancer initiative.
http://www.who.int/cancer/en

SELECTED BIBLIOGRAPHY

American Cancer Society. 2007. *Cancer Facts and Figures, 2007.* Atlanta: American Cancer Society.

Betts, K. S. 2007. Secondhand suspicions: Breast cancer and passive smoking. *Environmental Health Perspectives* 115(3): A136–A143.

Centers for Disease Control and Prevention. 2005. Breast cancer screening and socioeconomic status. *Morbidity and Mortality Weekly Report* 54(39): 981–984.

Chan, J. M., F. Wang, and E. A. Holly. 2005. Vegetable and fruit intake and pancreatic cancer in a population-based case-control study in the San Francisco Bay Area. *Cancer, Epidemiology, Biomarkers and Prevention* 14(9): 2093–2097.

Chao, A., et al. 2005. Meat consumption and risk of colorectal cancer. *Journal of the American Medical Association* 293(2): 172–182.

Chia, K. S., et al. 2005. Profound changes in breast cancer incidence may reflect changes into a Westernized lifestyle: A comparative population-based study in Singapore and Sweden. *International Journal of Cancer* 113(2): 302–306.

Chiu, B. C., et al. 2007. Obesity and risk of non-Hodgkin lymphoma (United States). *Cancer Causes and Control* 18(6): 677–685.

Danforth, K. N., et al. 2007. Breastfeeding and risk of ovarian cancer in two prospective cohorts. *Cancer Causes and Control* 18(5): 517–523.

Exon, J. H. 2006. A review of the toxicology of acrylamide. *Journal of Toxicology and Environmental Health: Part B, Critical Reviews* 9(5): 397–412.

Flood, A., et al. 2005. Calcium from diet and supplements is associated with reduced risk of colorectal cancer in a prospective cohort of women. *Cancer Epidemiology, Biomarkers and Prevention* 14(1): 126–132.

Flora, S. J. 2007. Role of free radicals and antioxidants in health and disease. *Cellular and Molecular Biology* 53(1): 1–2.

International Agency for Research on Cancer Working Group on Artificial Ultraviolet (UV) Light and Skin Cancer. 2007. The association of use of sunbeds with cutaneous malignant melanoma and other skin cancers: A systematic review. *International Journal of Cancer* 120(5): 1116–1122.

Kim, D. H., et al. 2007. Computed tomographic colonography for colorectal screening. *Endoscopy* 39(6): 545–549.

Li, C. I., K. E. Malone, and J. R. Daling. 2005. The relationship between various measures of cigarette smoking and risk of breast cancer among older women 65–79 years of age (United States). *Cancer Causes Control* 16(8): 975–985.

Martinez, M. E. 2005. Primary prevention of colorectal cancer: Lifestyle, nutrition, exercise. *Recent Results in Cancer Research* 166: 177–211.

National Toxicology Program. 2005. *Report on Carcinogens*, 11th ed. Research Triangle Park, N.C.: National Toxicology Program.

Pisano, E. D., et al. 2005. Diagnostic performance of digital versus film mammography for breast-cancer screening. *New England Journal of Medicine* 353(17): 1773–1783.

Ravdin, M., et al. 2007. The decrease in breast cancer incidence in 2003 in the United States. *New England Journal of Medicine* 356(16): 1670–1674.

Romond, E. H., et al. 2005. Trastuzumab plus adjuvant chemotherapy for operable HER2-positive breast cancer. *New England Journal of Medicine* 353(16): 1673–1684.

Schatzkin, A., et al. 2007. Dietary fiber and whole-grain consumption in relation to colorectal cancer in the NIH-AARP Diet and Health Study. *American Journal of Clinical Nutrition* 85(5): 1353–1360.

Swaen, G. M., et al. 2007. Mortality study update of acrylamide workers. *Occupational and Environmental Medicine* 64(6): 396–401.

Trimble, C. L., et al. 2005. Active and passive cigarette smoking and the risk of cervical neoplasia. *Obstetrics and Gynecology* 105(1): 174–181.

Troisi, R., et al. 2007. Cancer risk in women prenatally exposed to diethylstilbestrol. *International Journal of Cancer* 121(2): 356–360.

Valko, M., et al. 2007. Free radicals and antioxidants in normal physiological functions and human disease. *International Journal of Biochemistry and Cellular Biology* 39(1): 44–84.

Van Gils, C. H., et al. 2005. Consumption of vegetables and fruits and risk of breast cancer. *Journal of the American Medical Association* 293(3): 183–193.

Walter, M., et al. 2005. Dietary patterns and risk of prostate cancer in Ontario, Canada. *International Journal of Cancer* 116(4): 592–598.

Name ______________________ Section ______________ Date ______________

LAB 12.1 Cancer Prevention

This lab looks at two areas of cancer prevention over which you have a great deal of individual control—diet and sun exposure. For a detailed personal risk profile for many specific types of cancer, complete the assessments at the Harvard University Center for Cancer Prevention's "Your Disease Risk" site (http://www.yourdiseaserisk.harvard.edu).

Part I Diet and Cancer

Track your diet for 3 days, recording the number of servings from each of the following groups that you consume.

Day 1	Day 2	Day 3	Potential Cancer Fighters
____	____	____	Orange, deep yellow, pink, and red vegetables and some fruits (for example, apricots, cantaloupe, carrots, corn, grapefruit, mangoes, nectarines, papayas, red and yellow bell peppers, sweet potatoes, pumpkin, tomatoes and tomato sauce, watermelon, winter squash such as acorn or butternut)
____	____	____	Dark green leafy vegetables (for example, broccoli rabe, chard, kale, romaine and other dark lettuces, spinach; beet, collard, dandelion, mustard, and turnip greens)
____	____	____	Cruciferous vegetables (bok choy, broccoli, brussels sprouts, cabbage, cauliflower, kohlrabi, turnips)
____	____	____	Citrus fruits (for example, grapefruit, lemons, limes, oranges, tangerines)
____	____	____	Whole grains (for example, whole-grain bread, cereal, and pasta; brown rice; oatmeal; whole-grain corn; barley; popcorn; bulgur)
____	____	____	Legumes (peas, lentils, and beans, including fava, navy, kidney, pinto, black, and lima beans)
____	____	____	Berries (for example, strawberries, raspberries, blackberries, blueberries)
____	____	____	Garlic and other allium vegetables (onions, leeks, chives, scallions, shallots)
____	____	____	Soy products (for example, tofu, tempeh, soy milk, miso, soybeans)
____	____	____	Other cancer-fighting fruits (apples, cherries, cranberries or juice, grapes, kiwifruit, pears, plums, prunes, raisins)
____	____	____	Other cancer-fighting vegetables (asparagus, beets, chili peppers, eggplant, green peppers, radishes)
____	____	____	**Daily totals (average for three days: ____)**

The goal is to eat at least 7 (women) or 9 (men) servings of cancer-fighting fruits and vegetables each day; the more servings, the better. (Research is ongoing, and this list of cancer fighters is not comprehensive. Remember, nearly all fruits, vegetables, and grains are healthy choices.)

Part II Skin Cancer Risk Assessment

Your risk of skin cancer from the ultraviolet radiation in sunlight depends on several factors. Take the quiz that follows to see how sensitive you are. The higher your UV-risk score, the greater your risk of skin cancer—and the greater your need to take precautions against too much sun. Score 1 point for each true statement:

____ 1. I have blond or red hair.
____ 2. I have light-colored eyes (blue, gray, green).
____ 3. I freckle easily.
____ 4. I have many moles.
____ 5. I had two or more blistering sunburns as a child.
____ 6. I spent lots of time in a tropical climate as a child.
____ 7. I have a family history of skin cancer.
____ 8. I work outdoors.
____ 9. I spend a lot of time in outdoor activities.
____ 10. I like to spend as much time in the sun as I can.
____ 11. I sometimes go to a tanning parlor or use a sunlamp.
____ **Total score**

Score	Risk of skin cancer from UV radiation
0	Low
1–3	Moderate
4–7	High
8–11	Very high

Using Your Results

How did you score? (1) How close did you come to the goal of eating 7–9 or more servings of cancer fighters each day? Are you surprised by your results?

Are you satisfied with your diet in terms of cancer prevention? If not, set a specific goal for a target number of servings of cancer-fighting fruits and vegetables:

(2) What is your skin cancer risk assessment score? Are you surprised by the result? Does it indicate that you are at high or very high risk? Do you feel you need to take action because of your risk level?

What should you do next? Enter the results of this lab in the Preprogram Assessment column in Appendix D. (1) If you've set a goal for the diet and cancer portion of the lab, select a target number of additional cancer fighters from the list to try over the next few days; list the foods below, along with your plan for incorporating them into your diet (as a side dish, as a snack, on a salad, as a substitute for another food, etc.).

Cancer fighter to try:	Plan for trying:
____________________	____________________
____________________	____________________
____________________	____________________
____________________	____________________

(2) You cannot control all of your risk factors for skin cancer, but you can control your behavior with regard to sun exposure. Keep a journal to track your behavior on days when you are outdoors in the sun for a significant period of time. Compare your behavior with the recommendations for skin cancer prevention described in the chapter. Record such information as time of day, total duration of exposure, UV index for the day, clothing worn, type and amount of sunscreen used, frequency of sunscreen applications, and so on. From this record, identify ways to improve your behavior to lower your risk of skin cancer. Put together a behavior change plan.

Next, begin to put your strategies into action. After several weeks of a program to improve your diet or reduce your UV exposure, do this lab again and enter the results in the Postprogram Assessment column of Appendix D. How do the results compare?

SOURCE: Part II: Skin Cancer Risk Assessment adapted from Shear, N. 1996. "What's Your UV-risk Score?" Copyright © 1996 by the Consumers Union of the United States, Inc., Yonkers, NY 10703-1057, a nonprofit organization. Reprinted with permission from the author.

LOOKING AHEAD>>>>>

AFTER READING THIS CHAPTER, YOU SHOULD BE ABLE TO:

- Define and discuss the concepts of addictive behavior, substance abuse, and substance dependence
- Describe the major categories of psychoactive drugs, and discuss how drug abuse can be prevented and treated
- Explain the short-term and long-term effects of alcohol use
- Describe strategies for drinking alcohol responsibly and in moderation
- List the health hazards associated with tobacco use and exposure to environmental tobacco smoke, and discuss quitting strategies

SUBSTANCE USE AND ABUSE 13

TEST YOUR KNOWLEDGE

1. Which of the following is the most widely used illegal drug among college students?

a. cocaine
b. hallucinogens
c. marijuana
d. heroin

2. If a man and a woman of the same weight drink the same amount of alcohol, the woman will become intoxicated more quickly than the man.

True or false?

3. Every day in the United States, about 4000 children and adolescents start smoking.

True or false?

ANSWERS

1. **c.** Marijuana ranks first, followed (in order) by cocaine, hallucinogens, and heroin. Alcohol remains by far the most popular drug among college students.
2. **TRUE.** Women usually have a higher percentage of body fat than men and a less active form of a stomach enzyme that breaks down alcohol. Both factors cause them to become intoxicated more quickly and to a greater degree.
3. **TRUE.** The average age of a first-time smoker is 13.

FIT AND WELL ONLINE LEARNING CENTER www.mhhe.com/fahey

Visit the *Fit and Well* Online Learning Center for resources that will help you get the most out of your course!

- Study and review aids include practice quizzes, glossary flashcards, chapter summaries, learning objectives, PowerPoint presentations, Common Questions Answered, student handouts, crossword puzzles, Internet activities, and links to wellness Web sites.
- Behavior change tools include a daily fitness and nutrition journal, a behavior change workbook, sample behavior change plans, and blank behavior change logs to print and use.

The use of **drugs** for both medical and social purposes is widespread in America (Table 13.1). Many people believe that every problem, no matter how large or small, has or should have chemical solutions. Advertisements, social pressures, and the human desire for quick fixes to life's difficult problems all contribute to the prevailing attitude that drugs can ease all pain. Unfortunately, using drugs can—and often does—have negative consequences.

The most serious consequences are abuse and addiction. The drugs most often associated with abuse are **psychoactive drugs**—those that alter a person's state of mind or consciousness. In the short term, many psychoactive drugs can cause **intoxication**, an altered state in which physical and emotional changes occur. In the long term, recurrent drug use can have profound physical, emotional, and social effects.

This chapter examines the use of psychoactive drugs, including alcohol and tobacco, and explains their short- and long-term effects and their potential for abuse and addiction. The information provided is designed to help you make healthy, informed decisions about the role of drugs in your life. Before turning to the specific types of drugs, we look first at addictive behavior in general.

ADDICTIVE BEHAVIOR

Although addiction is most often associated with drug use, many experts now extend the concept of addiction to other areas. **Addictive behaviors** are habits that have gotten out of control, with resulting negative effects on a person's health and life.

What Is Addiction?

Historically, the term *addiction* was applied only when the habitual use of a drug produced chemical changes in the user's body. One such change is physical tolerance, in which the body adapts to a drug so that the initial dose no longer produces the same emotional or psychological effects. This process, caused by chemical changes in the brain, means the user has to take larger and larger doses of the drug to achieve the same high.

TERMS

drug Any chemical other than food intended to affect the structure or function of the body.

psychoactive drug A drug that can alter a person's state of mind or consciousness.

intoxication The state of being mentally affected by a chemical (literally, a state of being poisoned).

addictive behavior Any habit that has gotten out of control, resulting in a negative effect on one's health.

VITAL STATISTICS

Table 13.1 Nonmedical Drug Use Among Americans

Substance	Percentage Using Substance in the Past 30 Days: College Students (age 18–25)	All Americans (age 12 and over)
Any illicit drug	20.1	8.1
Tobacco (all forms)	44.3	29.4
Cigarettes	39.0	24.9
Smokeless tobacco	5.1	3.2
Cigars	12.2	5.6
Pipe tobacco	1.5	0.9
Alcohol	60.9	51.8
Binge alcohol use	41.2	22.7
Marijuana/hashish	16.6	6.0
Cocaine	2.6	1.0
Crack	0.3	0.3
Heroin	0.2	0.1
Hallucinogens	1.5	0.4
LSD	0.2	0.0
Ecstasy	0.8	0.2
Inhalants	0.5	0.3
Psychotherapeutics*	6.3	2.6
Pain relievers	4.7	1.9
Tranquilizers	1.9	0.7
Stimulants	1.3	0.4
Methamphetamine	0.6	0.2
Sedatives	0.2	0.1

*Nonmedical use of prescription-type pain relievers, tranquilizers, stimulants, or sedatives.

SOURCE: Office of Applied Studies, Substance Abuse and Mental Health Services Administration. 2006. *Results from the 2005 National Survey on Drug Use and Health: National Findings.* April 2007 Update (http://oas.samhsa.gov/nhsda.htm; retrieved June 8, 2007).

Some scientists think that other behaviors may share some of the brain chemistry of drug addiction. They suggest that activities like gambling, eating, and exercise trigger the release of brain chemicals that cause a pleasurable rush in much the same way that psychoactive drugs do. The brain's chemicals thus become the "drug" that causes addiction. However, the view that addiction is based in our brain chemistry does *not* imply that a person bears no responsibility for his or her addictive behavior. Lifestyle, personality traits, and other factors also play key roles in the development of addictive behavior.

It is sometimes difficult to distinguish between a healthy habit and one that has become an addiction. Experts have identified some general characteristics typically associated with addictive behaviors.

- ***Reinforcement.*** Some aspect of the behavior produces pleasurable physical and/or emotional states or relieves negative ones.

- ***Compulsion or craving.*** The individual feels a compelling need to engage in the behavior.
- ***Loss of control.*** The individual loses control over the behavior and cannot block the impulse to engage in it.
- ***Escalation.*** More and more of the substance or activity is required to produce its desired effects.
- ***Negative consequences.*** The behavior continues despite serious negative consequences, such as problems with academic or job performance, difficulties with personal relationships, or health problems.

The Development of Addiction

Many common behaviors are potentially addictive, but most people who engage in them do not develop problems. If a person does something that brings pleasure or dulls pain—drinking a beer or going shopping, for example—he or she is likely to repeat the behavior. When done appropriately and in moderation, most such behaviors can be harmless. But if the person becomes increasingly dependent on the behavior and tolerance develops, the behavior is likely to become a central focus in her or his life.

There is no single cause of addiction. Characteristics of the individual, of the environment in which the person lives, and of the substance or behavior he or she abuses combine in an addictive behavior. Many people with addictions use the substance or activity as a substitute for healthier coping strategies. People vary in their ability to manage their lives, and those who have the most trouble dealing with stress and painful emotions may be more susceptible to addiction. Some research studies have found that genetic factors play a role in risk for drug abuse, and some people may have a genetic predisposition for addiction to a particular drug.

Examples of Addictive Behaviors

Besides the use and abuse of alcohol, tobacco, and other psychoactive drugs, a number of behaviors can become addictive for some people.

Compulsive or Pathological Gambling Compulsive gamblers are unable to resist the urge to gamble, even in the face of financial ruin. Most say they are seeking excitement more than money, and a recent study of university students confirms that excessive gamblers are significantly greater risk takers than social gamblers are. Compulsive gambling often occurs with other disorders, particularly substance abuse.

The consequences of compulsive gambling are not just financial: The suicide rate among compulsive gamblers is 20 times higher than that of the general population. Compulsive gambling is an increasing problem because of the spread of legalized gambling, both on Native American tribal lands and on the Internet. In the United States, an estimated 1% of adults are compulsive (pathological) gamblers, and another 2–3% are "problem gamblers." As many as 4% of adults who live within 50 miles of a casino may be compulsive gamblers.

Because the Internet is so easy to access and offers a nearly endless variety of content, millions of users find themselves spending far too much of their time online. Many Americans have become addicted to Internet use.

Compulsive Buying or Shopping A compulsive buyer repeatedly gives in to the impulse to buy more than he or she needs or can afford. Compulsive buyers are usually distressed by their behavior and its social, personal, and financial consequences. Compulsive spenders usually buy luxury items rather than daily necessities. Some experts link compulsive shopping with neglect or abuse during childhood; it also seems to be associated with eating disorders, depression, and bipolar disorder.

Internet Addiction Research has indicated that surfing the Internet can also be addictive. To spend more time online, Internet addicts skip important school, social, or recreational activities. Despite negative financial, social, or academic consequences, they don't feel able to stop. The Internet addicts identified in one study averaged 38 online hours per week. As with other addictive behaviors, online addicts may be using their behavior to alleviate stress or avoid painful emotions. There is some concern that widespread access to the Internet may expose many more people to other potentially addictive behaviors, including gambling and shopping. According to a 2006 study, 5–10% of the U.S. population may experience Internet addiction.

QUESTIONS FOR CRITICAL THINKING AND REFLECTION

Have you ever repeatedly or compulsively engaged in a behavior that had negative consequences? What was the behavior, and why did you continue? Did you ever worry that you were losing control? How were you able to bring the behavior under control?

Other behaviors that can become addictive include exercising, eating, watching TV, and working. Any substance or activity that becomes the focus of one's life at the expense of other needs can be damaging to health.

PSYCHOACTIVE DRUGS

Psychoactive drugs include legal compounds such as caffeine, tobacco, and alcohol as well as illegal substances such as heroin, cocaine, and LSD (Figure 13.1). In this section, we examine general issues that apply to the use of any psychoactive drug. Later in the chapter, we take a close look at two commonly used and abused psychoactive drugs: alcohol and tobacco.

Drug Use, Abuse, and Dependence

The American Psychiatric Association's (APA) *Diagnostic and Statistical Manual of Mental Disorders* is the authoritative reference for defining mental and behavioral disorders, including those related to drugs. The APA has chosen not to use the term *addiction,* in part because it is so broad and has so many connotations. Instead, the APA refers to two forms of substance (drug) disorders: substance abuse and substance dependence. Both are maladaptive patterns of substance use that lead to significant impairment or distress. Although the APA's definitions are more precise and more directly related to drug use, they clearly encompass the general characteristics of addictive behavior described in the previous section.

Drug Abuse As defined by the APA, **substance abuse** involves one or more of the following factors:

- Recurrent drug use, resulting in a failure to fulfill major responsibilities at work, school, or home
- Recurrent drug use in situations in which it is physically hazardous, such as before driving a car
- Recurrent drug-related legal problems
- Continued drug use despite persistent social or interpersonal problems caused by or worsened by the effects of the drug

The pattern of use may be constant or intermittent, and **physical dependence** may or may not be present. For example, a person who smokes marijuana once a week and cuts classes because he or she is high is abusing marijuana, even though he or she is not physically dependent.

Drug Dependence **Substance dependence** is a more complex disorder and is what many people associate with addiction. The seven specific criteria the APA uses to diagnose substance dependence are listed below. The first two are associated with physical dependence; the final five are associated with compulsive use. To be considered dependent, an individual must experience a cluster of three or more of these seven symptoms during a 12-month period.

1. *Developing tolerance to the substance.* When a person requires increased amounts of a substance to achieve the desired effect or notices a markedly diminished effect with continued use of the same amount, he or she has developed **tolerance.** For example, heavy heroin users may need to take 10 times the amount they took at the beginning to achieve the desired effect.
2. *Experiencing withdrawal.* In an individual who has maintained prolonged, heavy use of a substance, a drop in its concentration within the body can result in unpleasant physical and cognitive **withdrawal** symptoms. For example, nausea, vomiting, and tremors are common withdrawal symptoms in people dependent on alcohol, opioids, or sedatives.
3. *Taking the substance in larger amounts or over a longer period than was originally intended.*
4. *Expressing a persistent desire to cut down on or regulate substance use.* This desire is often accompanied by many unsuccessful efforts to reduce or discontinue use of the substance.
5. *Spending a great deal of time obtaining the substance, using the substance, or recovering from its effects.*
6. *Giving up or reducing important school, work, or recreational activities because of substance use.* A dependent

TERMS

substance abuse A maladaptive pattern of use of any substance that persists despite adverse social, psychological, or medical consequences; the pattern may be intermittent, with or without tolerance and physical dependence.

physical dependence The result of physiological adaptation that occurs in response to the frequent presence of a drug; typically associated with tolerance and withdrawal.

substance dependence A cluster of cognitive, behavioral, and physiological symptoms that occur in an individual who continues to use a substance despite suffering significant substance-related problems, leading to significant impairment or distress; also known as *addiction.*

tolerance Lower sensitivity to a drug so that a given dose no longer exerts the usual effect and larger doses are needed.

withdrawal Physical and psychological symptoms that follow the interrupted use of a drug on which a user is physically dependent; symptoms may be mild or life-threatening.

Category	Representative drugs	Street names	Potential short-term effects	Potential long-term effects
Opioids	Heroin	Dope, H, junk, brown sugar, smack	Relief of anxiety and pain; euphoria; lethargy, apathy, drowsiness, confusion, inability to concentrate; nausea and vomiting, constipation, respiratory depression, lowered responsiveness to sexual stimulation, overdose and death	• Dependence, tolerance, and withdrawal; symptoms of withdrawal can include cramps, chills, nausea, tremors, feelings of panic • Injection drug use can spread HIV and hepatitis and cause skin infections
	Opium	Big O, black stuff, hop		
	Morphine	M, Miss Emma, monkey, white stuff		
	Oxycodone, codeine, hydrocodone	Oxy, O.C., killer, Captain Cody, schoolboy, vike		
Central nervous system depressants	Barbiturates	Barbs, reds, red birds, yellows, yellow jackets	Reduced anxiety, mood changes, (irritability, abusiveness), lowered inhibitions, impaired muscle coordination, reduced pulse rate, drowsiness, loss of consciousness, respiratory depression, death	• Dependence, tolerance, and withdrawal; symptoms of withdrawal may include anxiety, weakness, convulsions, cardiovascular collapse, and death • Brain damage, impaired ability to reason and make judgments • Overdose, especially when combined with alcohol or another depressant • Some are prescribed for insomnia and anxiety, to control seizures, and to calm patients before medical procedures; prescription depressants can also be abused
	Benzodiazepines (e.g., Valium, Xanax, Rohypnol)	Candy, downers, tranks, roofies, forget-me pill		
	Methaqualone	Ludes, quad, quay		
	Gamma hydroxy butyrate (GHB)	G, Georgia home boy, grievous bodily harm		
Central nervous system stimulants	Amphetamine, methamphet-amine	Bennies, speed, black beauties, uppers, chalk, crank, crystal, ice, meth	Increased heart rate, blood pressure, metabolism; increased mental alertness and energy; nervousness, insomnia, impulsive behavior; reduced appetite, disturbed sleep; high doses can cause death	• Dependence, tolerance, and withdrawal • Severe behavioral disturbances, including delusions of persecution and unprovoked violence • Brain damage, impaired judgment, and crashing (extreme sleepiness) when effects of a dose wear off • Prenatal effects—miscarrriage, premature labor, stillbirth, birth defects
	Cocaine, crack cocaine	Blow, C, candy, coke, flake, rock, toot		
	Ritalin	JIF, MPH, R-ball, Skippy		
Marijuana and other cannabis products	Marijuana	Dope, grass, joints, Mary Jane, reefer, skunk, weed	Euphoria, slowed thinking and reaction time, confusion, anxiety, impaired balance and coordination, increased heart rate, dilation of blood vessels in the eyes	• Throat and lung irritation, reduced lung function, precancerous changes in the lungs • Decreased testosterone levels and sperm counts; increased sperm abnormalities • Memory impairment, temporarily reduced IQ • Prenatal effects—impaired growth and development of fetus
	Hashish	Hash, hemp, boom, gangster		
Hallucinogens	LSD	Acid, boomers, blotter, yellow sunshines	Altered states of perception and feeling; nausea; increased heart rate, blood pressure; delirium; impaired motor function; numbness; weakness; panic; depersonalization	• Rapidly developing tolerance • Unpredictable effects, including panic reactions and psychological disturbances
	Mescaline (peyote)	Buttons, cactus, mesc		
	Psilocybin	Shrooms, magic mushrooms		
	Ketamine	K, special K, cat Valium, vitamin K		
	PCP	Angel dust, hog, love boat, peace pill		
	MDMA (ecstasy)	X, peace, clarity, Adam		
Inhalants	Solvents, aerosols, nitrites, anesthetics	Laughing gas, poppers, snappers, whippets	Stimulation, loss of inhibition, slurred speech, loss of motor coordination, loss of consciousness, death	• Damage to central nervous system, liver, kidneys, bone marrow, hearing • Increased risk of cancer

FIGURE 13.1 Commonly abused drugs and their effects.

SOURCES: U.S. Drug Enforcement Agency. 2005. *Drug Information* (http://www.usdoj.gov/dea/concern/concern.htm; retrieved June 8, 2007). National Institute on Drug Abuse 2007. *Commonly Abused Drugs* (http://www.drugabuse.gov/drugpages/drugsofabuse.html; retrieved June 8, 2007).

person may withdraw from family activities and hobbies to use the substance or to spend more time with substance-using friends.

7. *Continuing to use the substance in spite of recognizing that it is contributing to a psychological or physical problem.*

If a drug-dependent person experiences either tolerance or withdrawal, he or she is considered physically dependent. However, dependence can occur without a physical component, based solely on compulsive use.

Who Uses (and Abuses) Drugs?

The use and abuse of drugs occurs at all income and education levels, among all ethnic groups, and at all ages. Society is concerned with the casual or recreational use of illegal drugs because it is not possible to know when drug use will lead to abuse or dependence. Some casual users develop substance-related problems; others do not. Some psychoactive drugs, however, are more likely than others to lead to dependence (Table 13.2).

Characteristics that place people at higher-than-average risk for trying illegal drugs include being male, being young, having frequent exposure to drugs through family members or peers, being disinterested in school, and having a risk-taking personality. Drug use is less common among young people who attend school regularly, get good grades, have strong personal identities, are religious, have a good relationship with their parents, and are independent thinkers whose actions are not controlled by peer pressure. Coming from a family that has a clear policy on drug use and deals with conflicts constructively is also associated with not using drugs.

Why do some people use psychoactive drugs without becoming dependent, while others aren't as lucky? The answer seems to be a combination of physical, psychological, and social factors. Some people may be born with certain characteristics of brain chemistry or metabolism that make them more vulnerable to drug dependence. Psychological risk factors include having difficulty controlling impulses and having a strong need for excitement and immediate gratification. People may turn to drugs to numb emotional pain or to deal with difficult experiences or feelings such as rejection, hostility, or depression. Social factors that may increase the risk for dependence include exposure to drug-using family members or peers, poverty, and easy access to drugs (see the box "Club Drugs").

Table 13.2 Psychoactive Drugs and Their Potential for Producing Dependence

	Potential for Dependence	
Drug	**Physical**	**Psychological**
Alcohol	Possible	Possible
Amphetamine	Possible	High
Barbiturates	High	Moderate
Chloral hydrate	Moderate	Moderate
Cocaine	Possible	High
Codeine	Moderate	Moderate
Crack cocaine	High	High
Hashish	Unknown	Moderate
Heroin	High	High
Ice (smoked methamphetamine)	High	High
LSD	None	Unknown
Marijuana	Unknown	Moderate
Methaqualone	High	High
Opium	High	High
PCP	Unknown	High
Psilocybin	None	Unknown

SOURCES: U.S. Department of Health and Human Services, Substance Abuse and Mental Health Services Administration. 2007. Drugs of Abuse (http://ncadi.samhsa.gov/govpubs/rop926; retrieved June 8, 2007). Beers, M. H., et al. 2006. *The Merck Manual of Diagnosis and Therapy*, 18th ed. New York: Wiley.

MOTIVATION BOOSTER

Use professional resources. Outside help is sometimes needed to change behaviors or conditions that are too serious for a self-management approach. If you have a problem with alcohol, tobacco, or other drugs, don't let the seriousness of the situation block your desire to change. Professional help is widely available and can help you develop, start, and stick with a program to change substance abuse or dependence problems.

Treatment for Drug Abuse and Dependence

Different types of programs are available to help people break their drug habits, but there is no single best method of treatment. The relapse rate is high for all types of treatment, but being treated is better than not being treated. Professional treatment programs usually take the form of drug substitution programs or treatment centers; nonprofessional self-help groups and peer counseling are also available. To be successful, a treatment program must deal with the reasons behind users' drug abuse and help them develop behaviors, attitudes, and a social support system that will help them remain drug-free. See For Further Exploration at the end of the chapter for resources related to treatment.

Young people with drug problems are often unable to seek help on their own. In such cases, friends and family members may need to act on their behalf. The following signals suggest drug dependence:

- Sudden withdrawal or emotional distance
- Rebellious or unusually irritable behavior

Club Drugs

Club drugs are part of the popular dance culture of clubs and raves. Some people refer to club drugs as soft drugs because they see them as recreational—more for the casual, weekend user—rather than addictive. But club drugs have many negative effects and are particularly potent and unpredictable when mixed with alcohol. Substitute drugs are often sold in place of club drugs, putting users at risk for taking dangerous combinations of unknown substances.

MDMA (Ecstasy)

Taken in pill form, MDMA (methylenedioxymethamphetamine) is a stimulant with mildly hallucinogenic and amphetamine-like effects. It can produce dangerously high body temperature and potentially fatal dehydration; some users experience confusion, depression, anxiety, paranoia, muscle tension, involuntary teeth clenching, blurred vision, and seizures. Even low doses may affect concentration and driving ability; use during pregnancy is linked to increased risk of birth defects. Chronic use of MDMA may produce long-lasting, perhaps permanent, damage to the neurons that release serotonin; this may explain why heavy use is associated with persistent problems with learning and verbal and visual memory. MDMA users perform worse than nonusers on complex cognitive tasks of memory, attention, and general intelligence.

Methamphetamine

A potent stimulant, methamphetamine is available in many forms and can be swallowed, smoked, snorted, or injected. It causes the release of high levels of the neurotransmitter dopamine, which enhances mood and body movement; other effects include insomnia, anxiety, irritability, paranoia, and aggressiveness. High doses can cause convulsions and death. Methamphetamine is highly addictive and may damage brain cells.

LSD

A potent hallucinogen, LSD (lysergic acid diethylamide) is sold in tablets or capsules, in liquid form, or on small squares of paper called blotters. LSD increases heart rate and body temperature and may cause nausea, tremors, sweating, numbness, and weakness.

Ketamine

A veterinary anesthetic that can be taken in powdered or liquid form, ketamine may cause hallucinations and impaired attention and memory. At higher doses, ketamine can cause delirium, amnesia, high blood pressure, and potentially fatal respiratory problems. Tolerance to ketamine develops rapidly.

GHB

GHB (gamma hydroxybutyrate) can be produced in clear liquid, white powder, tablet, and capsule form; it is often made in basement chemistry labs, where toxic substances may unintentionally be added or produced. GHB is a central nervous system (CNS) depressant that in large doses can cause sedation, loss of consciousness, respiratory arrest, and death. Evidence suggests that GHB is addictive and that it may cause prolonged and potentially life-threatening withdrawal symptoms. Some dietary supplements contain the chemically similar compounds GBL (gamma butyrolactone) or BD (butanediol); the FDA is working to remove these dangerous products from the market.

Rohypnol

Taken in tablet form, Rohypnol (flunitrazepam) is a sedative 10 times more potent than Valium. Its effects, which are magnified by alcohol, include reduced blood pressure, dizziness, confusion, gastrointestinal disturbances, and loss of consciousness. Users of Rohypnol may develop physical and psychological dependence on the drug.

Rohypnol, GHB, and several other club drugs are sometimes used as date-rape drugs. They can be surreptitiously added to beverages and unknowingly consumed by intended rape victims. In addition to depressant effects, some drugs also cause anterograde amnesia, the loss of memory of things occurring while under the influence of the drug. Because of concern about Rohypnol, GHB, and other similarly abused drugs, Congress passed the Drug-Induced Rape Prevention and Punishment Act, which increased penalties for use of any controlled substance to aid in sexual assault.

- Loss of interest in usual activities or hobbies
- A decline in school performance
- A sudden change in group of friends
- Changes in sleeping or eating habits
- Frequent borrowing of money

Preventing Drug Abuse and Dependence

The best solution to drug abuse is prevention. Government attempts at controlling the drug problem tend to focus on stopping the production, importation, and distribution of illegal drugs. Creative efforts are also being made to stop the demand for drugs. Approaches include building young people's self-esteem, improving their academic skills, increasing their recreational opportunities, providing them with honest information about the effects of drugs, and teaching them strategies for resisting peer pressure.

The Role of Drugs in Your Life

Whatever your experience has been up to now, it's likely that you will encounter drugs at some point in your life. To make sure you'll have the inner resources to resist peer pressure and make your own decision, cultivate a variety of

QUESTIONS FOR CRITICAL THINKING AND REFLECTION

Have you ever tried a psychoactive drug for fun? What were your reasons for trying it? Who were you with, and what were the circumstances? What was your experience like? What would you tell someone else who was thinking about trying the drug?

activities you enjoy doing, realize that you are entitled to have your own opinion, and keep your self-esteem high.

Before you try a psychoactive drug, consider the following questions:

- ***What are the risks involved?*** Many drugs carry an immediate risk of injury or death or legal consequences. Most carry long-term risk of abuse and dependence.
- ***Is using the drug compatible with your goals?*** Consider how drug use will affect your education and career objectives, your relationships, your future happiness, and the happiness of those who love you.
- ***What are your ethical beliefs about drug use?*** Consider whether using a drug would cause you to go against your personal ethics, religious beliefs, social values, or family responsibilities.
- ***What are the financial costs?*** Many drugs are expensive, especially if you become dependent on them. Many companies drug test prospective and/or current employees, so drug use can seriously impact job opportunities.
- ***Are you trying to solve a deeper problem?*** Drugs will not make emotional pain go away; in the long run, they will only make it worse. If you are feeling depressed or anxious, seek help from a mental health professional instead of self-medicating with drugs.

ALCOHOL

More than 65% of Americans over age 12 drink alcohol in some form. Many people think of alcohol the way it's portrayed in advertisements, on television, and in movies—as part of a good time, an integral ingredient of celebrations and special events. However, like other drugs, alcohol can impair functioning in the short term and cause devastating damage in the long term. According to the CDC, there were more than 20,000 alcohol-induced deaths in the United States in 2004.

Ethyl alcohol is the common psychoactive drug in all alcoholic beverages. One drink—a 12-ounce beer, a 1.5-ounce cocktail, or a 5-ounce glass of wine—contains about 0.5–0.6 ounce of ethyl alcohol.

Chemistry and Metabolism

Ethyl alcohol is the common psychoactive ingredient in all alcoholic beverages. The concentration of alcohol varies with the type of beverage; it is indicated by the proof value, which is two times the percentage concentration. For example, if a beverage is 80 proof, it contains 40% alcohol. When alcohol consumption is discussed, "one drink" refers to a 12-ounce bottle of beer, a 5-ounce glass of table wine, or a cocktail with 1.5 ounces of 80-proof liquor. Each of these drinks contains approximately the same amount of alcohol: 0.5–0.6 ounce.

When consumed, alcohol is absorbed into the bloodstream from the stomach and small intestine. Once in the bloodstream, alcohol is distributed throughout the body's tissues, affecting nearly every body system (Figure 13.2). The main site of alcohol metabolism is the liver, which transforms alcohol into energy and other products.

Immediate Effects of Alcohol

Blood alcohol concentration (BAC) is a primary factor determining the effects of alcohol. BAC is determined by the amount of alcohol consumed and by individual factors such as heredity, body weight, and amount of body fat. Compared with a man who drinks the same

TERMS

ethyl alcohol The intoxicating ingredient in fermented liquors; a colorless, pungent liquid.

blood alcohol concentration (BAC) The amount of alcohol in the blood in terms of weight per unit volume; used as a measure of intoxication.

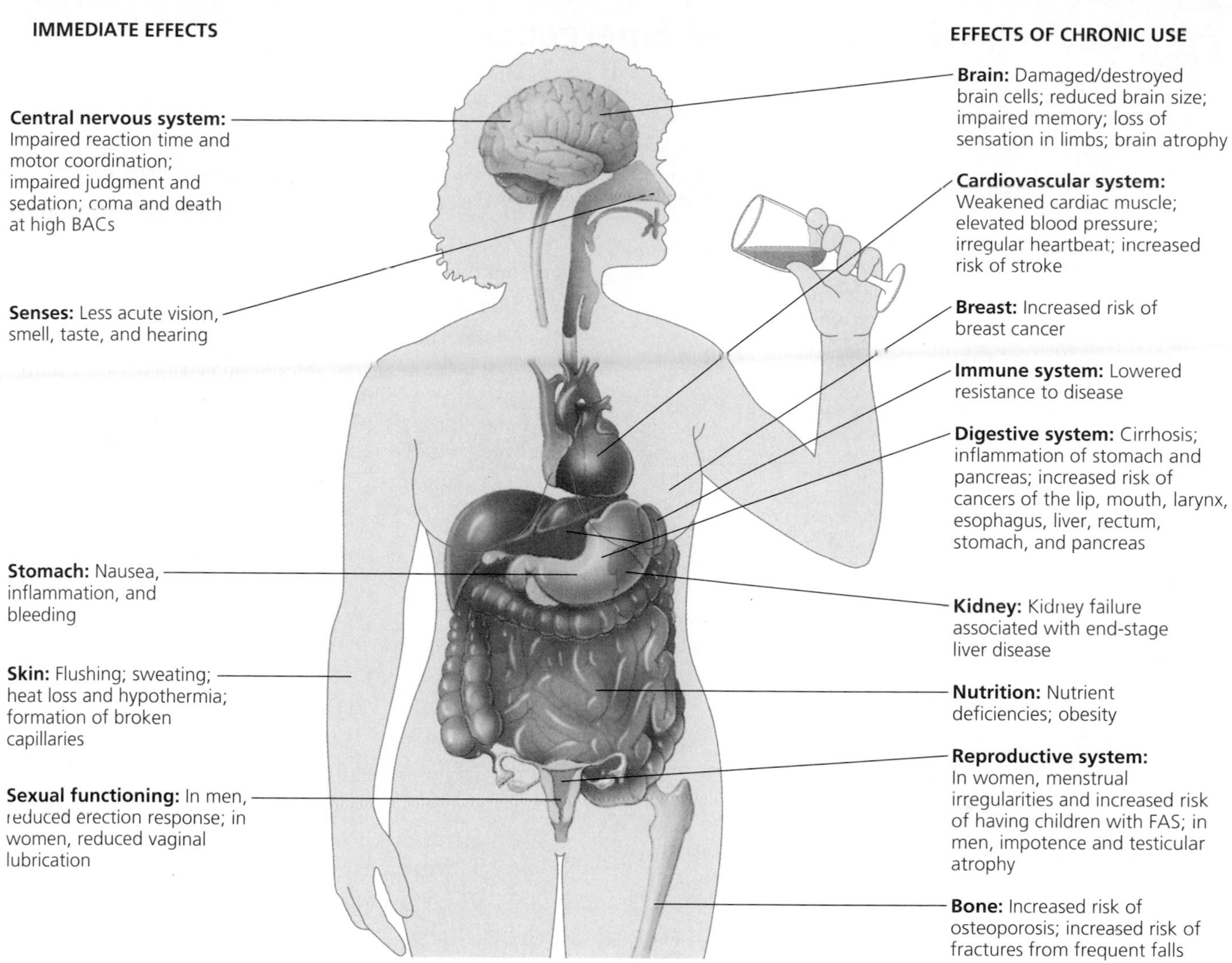

FIGURE 13.2 The immediate and long-term effects of alcohol use.

amount of alcohol, a woman will typically have a higher BAC because of her smaller size, greater percentage of body fat, and less-active alcohol-metabolizing stomach enzymes. The body can typically metabolize about half a drink in an hour. If a person drinks slightly less than that each hour, BAC remains low. People can drink large amounts of alcohol this way over a long period of time without becoming noticeably intoxicated; however, they do run the risk of significant long-term health problems. But if more alcohol is consumed than is metabolized, the BAC will steadily increase, as will the level of intoxication.

Low doses of alcohol induce relaxation and release inhibitions; higher doses lead to less pleasant effects, including flushing and sweating; disturbed sleep; and hangover, characterized by headache, nausea, and generalized discomfort (Table 13.3). The combination of impaired judgment, weakened sensory perception, reduced inhibitions, impaired motor coordination, and, often, increased aggressiveness and hostility that characterizes alcohol intoxication can be dangerous or even deadly. People are much more likely to be perpetrators or victims of crimes, including sexual assaults of all types and date rape in particular, if they have been drinking. One study found that banning alcohol at college football games reduced the number of arrests, assaults, and ejections from the stadium by over 50%. Through homicide, suicide, car crashes, and other incidents, alcohol use was linked to more than 75,000 American deaths in 2001. Alcohol poisoning is also a risk: Drinking large amounts of alcohol over a short time can rapidly raise the BAC into the lethal range (see the box "Dealing with an Alcohol Emergency").

Drinking and Driving

In addition to increasing the risk of injury and death, driving while intoxicated can have serious legal consequences. The legal limit for BAC in all states is 0.08%; however, alcohol impairs the user even at much lower

TAKE CHARGE

Dealing with an Alcohol Emergency

Being very drunk is potentially life-threatening. Helping a drunken friend could save a life.

- Be firm but calm. Don't engage the person in an argument or discuss her drinking behavior while she is intoxicated.
- Get the person out of harm's way; don't let him drive or wander outside. Don't let him drink any more alcohol.
- If the person is unconscious, don't assume she is just "sleeping it off." Place her on her side with her knees up. This position will help prevent choking if she should vomit.
- Stay with the person; you need to be ready to help if he vomits or stops breathing.
- Don't try to give the person anything to eat or drink, including coffee or other drugs. Don't give cold showers or try to make her walk around. None of these things help sober someone up, and they can be dangerous.

Call 911 immediately in any of the following instances:

- You can't wake the person up even by shouting or shaking.
- The person is taking fewer than 8 breaths per minute, or his breathing seems shallow or irregular.
- You think the person took other drugs in addition to alcohol.
- The person has had an injury, especially a blow to the head.
- The person drank a large amount of alcohol within a short time and then became unconscious. Death from alcohol poisoning most often occurs when the blood alcohol level rises very quickly due to rapid ingestion of alcohol.

If you aren't sure what to do, call 911. You may save a life.

BACs (Figure 13.3). States now also have zero-tolerance laws regarding alcohol use by drivers under age 21. Under these laws, a young driver who has consumed any alcohol can have his or her license suspended. There are stiff penalties for drunk driving, including fines, loss of license, confiscation of vehicle, and jail time.

People who drink and drive are unable to drive safely because their judgment is impaired, their reaction time is slower, and their coordination is reduced. If you are out drinking, find an alternative means of transportation or follow the practice of having a designated driver, an individual who refrains from drinking in order to provide safe transportation home for others in the group.

It's more difficult to protect yourself against a drunk driver. Learn to be alert to the erratic driving that signals an impaired driver. Warning signs include making wide, abrupt, and illegal turns; straddling the center line or lane marker; driving against traffic; driving on the shoulder; weaving, swerving, or nearly striking an object or another vehicle; following too closely; maintaining erratic speed; driving with headlights off at night; and driving with the window down in very cold weather. If you see any of these signs, try the following strategies:

- If the driver is ahead of you, maintain a safe following distance. Don't try to pass.
- If the driver is behind you, pull off the road when you can do so safely, and let the driver pass.
- If the driver is approaching your car, move to the shoulder and stop. Avoid a head-on collision by sounding your horn or flashing your lights.
- When approaching an intersection, slow down and watch for vehicles that don't appear to be slowing in preparation for stopping at a stop sign or red light.

Table 13.3 Effects of Alcohol

Blood Alcohol Concentration (%)	Common Behavioral Effects	Hours Required to Metabolize Alcohol
0.00–0.05	Slight change in feelings, usually relaxation and euphoria; decreased alertness.	2–3
0.05–0.10	Emotional instability with exaggerated feelings and behavior; reduced social inhibitions; impairment of reaction time and fine motor coordination; increasing impairment while driving. Legally drunk at 0.08% in all states.	3–6
0.10–0.15	Unsteadiness in standing and walking; loss of peripheral vision. Driving is extremely dangerous.	6–10
0.15–0.30	Staggering gait; slurred speech; impairment of pain perception and other sensory perceptions.	10–24
More than 0.30	Stupor or unconsciousness; anesthesia. Can result from rapid or binge drinking with few earlier effects. Death possible at 0.35% and above.	More than 24

BAC Zones: 90–109 lb | 110–129 lb | 130–149 lb | 150–169 lb | 170–189 lb | 190–209 lb | 210 lb & Over

Time from First Drink | Total Drinks 1 2 3 4 5 6 7 8 (for each weight zone)

1 hr
2 hr
3 hr
4 hr

(0.00%) Not impaired

(0.01–0.04%) Sometimes impaired

(0.05–0.07%) Usually impaired

(0.08% and up) Always impaired

FIGURE 13.3 Approximate blood alcohol concentration and body weight. This chart shows the BAC an average person of a given weight would reach after drinking the specified number of drinks in the time shown. The legal limit for BAC is 0.08%. For drivers under 21 years of age, many states have zero-tolerance laws that set BAC limits of 0.01% or 0.02%.

- Make sure your safety belt is fastened and young children are in approved safety seats.
- Report suspected impaired drivers to the nearest police station by phone. Give a description of the vehicle, license number, location, and direction the vehicle is headed.

Effects of Chronic Alcohol Use

The average life span of alcohol abusers is 15 years shorter than that of nonabusers. **Cirrhosis,** a major cause of death in the United States, is one result of continued alcohol use. In this condition, liver cells are destroyed and replaced with fibrous scar tissue. Alcohol can also inflame the pancreas, causing nausea, vomiting, abnormal digestion, and severe abdominal pain. Although moderate doses of alcohol (one or two drinks a day) may slightly reduce the chances of heart attack in some people, high doses are associated with cardiovascular problems, including high blood pressure and a weakening of the heart muscle. Alcohol is a known human carcinogen and is causally related to oral cancer; cancers of the esophagus, liver, stomach, and pancreas; and possibly breast cancer. Chronic alcohol abuse has also been linked to asthma, gout, diabetes, recurrent infections, nutritional deficiencies, and nervous system diseases. Psychiatric problems associated with excessive alcohol use include paranoia and memory gaps. Heavy drinking—100 or more drinks per month for men, 80 or more for women—causes brain damage and impaired mental functioning.

Maternal drinking during pregnancy can result in miscarriage, stillbirth, or **fetal alcohol syndrome (FAS).** Children with this syndrome are small at birth, are likely to have heart defects, and often have abnormal features such as small, wide-set eyes. Many are mentally impaired; others exhibit more subtle problems with learning and fine motor coordination. FAS is the most common preventable cause of mental impairment in the Western world; its incidence in the United States is estimated to be 1 or 2 out of every 1000 live births. Many more babies are born with alcohol-related neurodevelopmental disorder (ARND). These children appear physically normal but often have learning and behavioral problems and are more likely as adults to develop substance abuse and legal problems. Getting drunk just one time during the final three months of pregnancy, when the fetus's brain cells are developing rapidly, can cause fetal brain damage. The safest course of action is abstinence from alcohol during pregnancy.

Alcohol Abuse

Alcohol abuse is defined as recurrent alcohol use that has negative consequences, such as drinking in dangerous situations (such as before driving), or drinking patterns that result in academic, professional, interpersonal, or legal difficulties. **Alcohol dependence,** or **alcoholism,** involves more extensive problems with alcohol use, usually

TERMS

cirrhosis A disease in which the liver is severely damaged by alcohol, other toxins, or infection.

fetal alcohol syndrome (FAS) A characteristic group of birth defects caused by excessive alcohol consumption by the mother, including facial deformities, heart defects, and physical and mental impairments.

alcohol abuse The use of alcohol to a degree that causes physical damage, impairs functioning, or results in behavior harmful to others.

alcohol dependence A pathological use of alcohol, or impairment in functioning due to alcohol; characterized by tolerance and withdrawal symptoms; alcoholism.

alcoholism A chronic psychological disorder characterized by excessive and compulsive drinking.

including physical tolerance and withdrawal. Various experts use different definitions to describe problems associated with drinking. The important point is that one does not have to be an alcoholic to have problems with alcohol. The person who drinks only once a month, perhaps after an exam, but then drives while intoxicated is an alcohol abuser. (Lab 13.1 includes an assessment to help you determine if alcohol is a problem in your life.)

How can you tell if you are beginning to have a problem with alcohol or if someone you know is? Look for the following warning signs:

- Drinking alone or secretively
- Using alcohol deliberately and repeatedly to perform or get through difficult situations
- Feeling uncomfortable on certain occasions when alcohol is not available
- Escalating alcohol consumption beyond an already established drinking pattern
- Consuming alcohol heavily in risky situations, such as before driving
- Getting drunk regularly or more frequently than in the past
- Drinking in the morning or at other unusual times

It's also important to remember that alcohol use can be an expensive habit. As a group, college students currently spend $5.5 billion a year on alcohol. That's more than they spend on textbooks, soft drinks, tea, milk, juice, and coffee combined.

OLC VITAL STATISTICS

Table 13.4 Effects of Binge Drinking on College Students

	Percentage of Students Experiencing Problems	
Alcohol-Related Problem	**Nonbinge Drinkers**	**Frequent Binge Drinkers**
Drove after drinking alcohol	18	58
Did something they regretted	17	62
Argued with friends	10	43
Missed a class	9	60
Got behind in schoolwork	9	42
Got hurt or injured	4	28
Had unprotected sex	4	21
Got into trouble with police	2	14
Had five or more of these problems since school year began	4	48

SOURCE: Wechsler, H., and B. Wuethrich. 2003. *Dying to Drink: Confronting Binge Drinking on College Campuses*, reprint ed. Emmaus, Pa.: Rodale.

Binge Drinking

A common form of alcohol abuse on college campuses is **binge drinking.** In surveys of students on more than 100 college campuses, 44% reported binge drinking, defined as having five drinks in a row for men or four in a row for women on at least one occasion in the 2 weeks prior to the survey. Some 23% of all students were found to be frequent binge drinkers, defined as having at least three binges during the 2-week period. Students who lived in fraternity and sorority houses had the highest rate of binge drinking. Men were more likely to binge than women, and white students had higher rates of binge drinking than students of other races and ethnicities. Only 19% of students abstained from alcohol.

Binge drinking has a profound effect on students' lives. Frequent binge drinkers were found to be 3–7 times more likely than nonbinge drinkers to engage in unplanned or unprotected sex, to drive after drinking, and to get hurt or injured (Table 13.4). Binge drinkers were also more likely to miss classes, get behind in schoolwork, and argue with their friends. The more frequent the binges, the more problems the students encountered. Despite their experiences, fewer than 1% of the binge drinkers identified themselves as problem drinkers.

Binge drinking also affects nonbinge drinkers. At schools with high rates of binge drinking, the nonbinge-drinking students were up to twice as likely to report being bothered by the drinking-related behaviors of others than were students at schools with lower rates of binge drinking. These problems included having sleep or studying disrupted; having to take care of a drunken student; experiencing unwanted sexual advances; and being pushed, hit, or assaulted. Overall, it is estimated that alcohol use contributes to 1700 deaths, 100,000 cases of sexual assault, and 500,000 injuries among college students each year.

Alcoholism

As described earlier, alcoholism is usually characterized by tolerance and withdrawal. Everyone who drinks—even nonalcoholics—develops tolerance to alcohol after repeated use. When alcoholics stop drinking or cut their intake significantly, they have withdrawal symptoms, which can range from unpleasant to serious and even life-threatening distress. Symptoms of alcohol withdrawal include trembling hands (shakes, or jitters), a rapid pulse and breathing rate, insomnia, nightmares, anxiety, and gastrointestinal upset. Less common are seizures and the severe reaction known as the **DTs (delirium tremens)**, characterized by confusion and vivid, usually unpleasant, hallucinations.

The lifetime risk of alcoholism in the United States is about 10% for men and 3% for women. However, women tend to experience the adverse physical effects of chronic drinking sooner and at lower levels of alcohol consumption

TAKE CHARGE

Drinking Behavior and Responsibility

The responsible use of alcohol includes understanding your own attitudes and behaviors, managing your behavior, and encouraging responsible behavior in others.

Examine Your Attitudes and Behavior

- ***Consider your feelings about alcohol and drinking.*** Do you care if alcohol is available at activities where people are having fun? Do you consider it essential, or are you indifferent to its presence or absence? How do you feel about people who don't drink?
- ***Consider where your attitudes toward drinking and alcohol come from.*** How was alcohol used in your family when you were growing up? How is it used—or how do you think it's used—on your campus? How is it portrayed in ads you see? In other words, what influences might be shaping your alcohol use?
- ***Consider your own drinking behavior.*** If you drink, what are your reasons for doing so? Is your drinking moderate and responsible? Or do you drink too much and experience negative consequences?

Drink Moderately and Responsibly

- ***Drink slowly and space your drinks.*** Sip your drinks and alternate them with nonalcoholic choices. Don't drink alcoholic beverages to quench your thirst. Avoid drinks made with carbonated mixers. Watch your drinks being poured or mixed so that you can be sure of what you're drinking.
- ***Eat before and while drinking.*** Don't drink on an empty stomach. Food in your stomach will slow the rate at which alcohol is absorbed and thus often lower the peak BAC.
- ***Know your limits and your drinks.*** Learn how different BACs affect you and how to keep your BAC and behavior under control.
- ***Be aware of the setting.*** In dangerous situations, such as driving or operating complicated machinery, abstinence is the only appropriate choice.
- ***Use designated drivers.*** Arrange carpools to and from parties or events where alcohol will be served. Rotate the responsibility for acting as a designated driver.
- ***Learn to enjoy activities without alcohol.*** If you can't have fun without drinking, you may have a problem with alcohol.

Encourage Responsible Drinking in Others

- ***Encourage responsible attitudes.*** Learn to express disapproval about someone who has drunk too much. Don't treat the choice to abstain as strange. The majority of American adults drink moderately or not at all.
- ***Be a responsible host.*** Serve only enough alcohol for each guest to have a moderate number of drinks, and offer lots of nonalcoholic choices. Always serve food along with alcohol. Stop serving alcohol an hour or more before people will leave. Insist that a guest who drank too much take a taxi, ride with someone else, or stay overnight rather than drive.
- ***Hold drinkers fully responsible for their behavior.*** Pardoning unacceptable behavior fosters the attitude that the behavior is due to the drug rather than the person.
- ***Take community action.*** Find out about prevention programs on your campus or in your community. Consider joining an action group such as Students Against Destructive Decisions (SADD) or Mothers Against Drunk Driving (MADD).

than men. Female alcoholics also have death rates 50–100% higher than those of male alcoholics. The cost of alcoholism to society and to the personal well-being of its citizens is inestimable. Despite media attention on cocaine, heroin, and marijuana, alcohol causes more problems than illegal drugs.

Some alcoholics recover without professional help, but the majority do not. Treatment is difficult. However, many different kinds of programs exist, including those that emphasize group and buddy support, those that stress lifestyle management, and those that use drugs and chemical substitutes as therapy. Although not all alcoholics can be treated successfully, considerable optimism has replaced the older view that nothing can be done.

Drinking and Responsibility

The responsible use of alcohol means drinking in a way that keeps your BAC low and your behavior under control. Suggestions are given in the box "Drinking Behavior and Responsibility."

MOTIVATION BOOSTER

Plan ahead. Have you ever found yourself doing something you didn't plan to do because of environmental influences, whether people, places, or situations? Plan ahead and practice assertive communication when you know you're going to be in a challenging situation. For example, say, "No thanks, I've had enough for now," or "I'm switching to water—I have to get up early tomorrow." Being aware of how others may influence you can help you keep your behavior change program on track.

TERMS

binge drinking Periodically drinking alcohol to the point of severe intoxication.

DTs (delirium tremens) A state of confusion brought on by the reduction of alcohol intake in an alcohol-dependent person; other symptoms are sweating, trembling, anxiety, hallucinations, and seizures.

QUESTIONS FOR CRITICAL THINKING AND REFLECTION

Do you know anyone with a serious alcohol problem? From what you have read in this chapter, would you say that person abuses alcohol (uses alcohol recurrently despite negative consequences) or is dependent on alcohol (has developed tolerance, experiences withdrawal symptoms when trying to quit, has lost control of use)? What effects, if any, has this person's problem had on your life? Have you thought about getting support or help?

TOBACCO

According to the U.S. Surgeon General, smoking is the leading preventable cause of illness and death in the United States. Each year, 440,000 Americans die prematurely from smoking-related causes, and millions of Americans suffer chronic illnesses (such as cancer and heart disease) as a result of smoking. Tobacco in any form—cigarettes, cigars, pipes, chewing tobacco, clove cigarettes, or snuff—is unsafe. Despite its well-known hazards, tobacco use is still widespread in our society, particularly among certain groups (Table 13.5). About 70 million Americans, including nearly 4 million adolescents, use tobacco. Surveys indicate that many smokers underestimate the dangers of smoking and are misinformed about smoking cessation tools and success rates.

WEB VITAL STATISTICS

Table 13.5 Who Smokes?

	Percentage of Smokers		
	Men	Women	Total
Ethnic Group (age ≥ 18)			
White	24.0	20.0	21.9
Black	26.7	17.3	21.5
Asian	20.6	6.1	13.3
American Indian/ Alaska Native	37.5	26.8	32.0
Latino	21.1	11.1	16.2
Education (age ≥ 25)			
≤8 years	21.0	13.4	17.1
9–11 years	36.8	29.0	32.6
12 years (no diploma)	30.2	22.2	26.0
GED diploma	47.5	38.8	43.2
12 years (diploma)	28.8	20.7	24.6
Associate degree	26.1	17.1	20.9
Undergraduate degree	11.9	9.6	10.7
Graduate degree	6.9	7.4	7.1
Total	23.9	18.1	20.9

SOURCE: Centers for Disease Control and Prevention. 2006. Tobacco use among adults—United States, 2005. *Morbidity and Mortality Weekly Report* 55(42): 1145–1148.

Nicotine Addiction

Regular tobacco use, and especially cigarette smoking, is not just a habit but an addiction, involving physical dependence on the psychoactive drug **nicotine.** Nicotine addiction can start after just a few cigarettes. Addicted tobacco users must keep a steady amount of nicotine circulating in the blood and going to the brain. If that amount falls below a certain level, they experience withdrawal symptoms including muscular pains, headaches, nausea, insomnia, and irritability. Many heavy smokers continue to smoke not for pleasure but to avoid the unpleasantness of withdrawal.

Health Hazards of Cigarette Smoking

Cigarette smoking has negative effects on nearly every part of the body and increases the risk of many life-threatening diseases. Some of the many damaging chemicals in tobacco are carcinogens and cocarcinogens (agents that can combine with other chemicals to promote cancer). Others irritate the tissues of the respiratory system. Carbon monoxide, the deadly gas in automobile exhaust, is present in cigarette smoke in concentrations 400 times greater than the safety threshold set in workplaces. Low-tar and low-nicotine cigarettes deliver just as dangerous a dose of these chemicals as regular cigarettes because smokers inhale more deeply and frequently.

The effects of nicotine on smokers vary, depending on the size of the dose and the smoker's past smoking behavior. Nicotine can either excite or tranquilize the nervous system, generally resulting in stimulation that gives way to tranquility and then depression. Figure 13.4 summarizes the immediate effects of smoking.

In the short term, smoking interferes with the functions of the respiratory system and often leads rapidly to shortness of breath and the conditions known as smoker's throat, smoker's cough, and smoker's bronchitis. Other common short-term complaints are loss of appetite, diarrhea, fatigue, hoarseness, weight loss, stomach pains, insomnia, and impaired visual acuity, especially at night.

Long-term effects fall into two general categories. The first is reduced life expectancy: On average, smokers live 10–15 years less than nonsmokers. The second category of long-term effects involves quality of life. Smokers have higher rates of acute and chronic diseases than those who have never smoked. The more people smoke, and the

TERMS

nicotine A poisonous, addictive substance found in tobacco and responsible for many of the effects of tobacco.

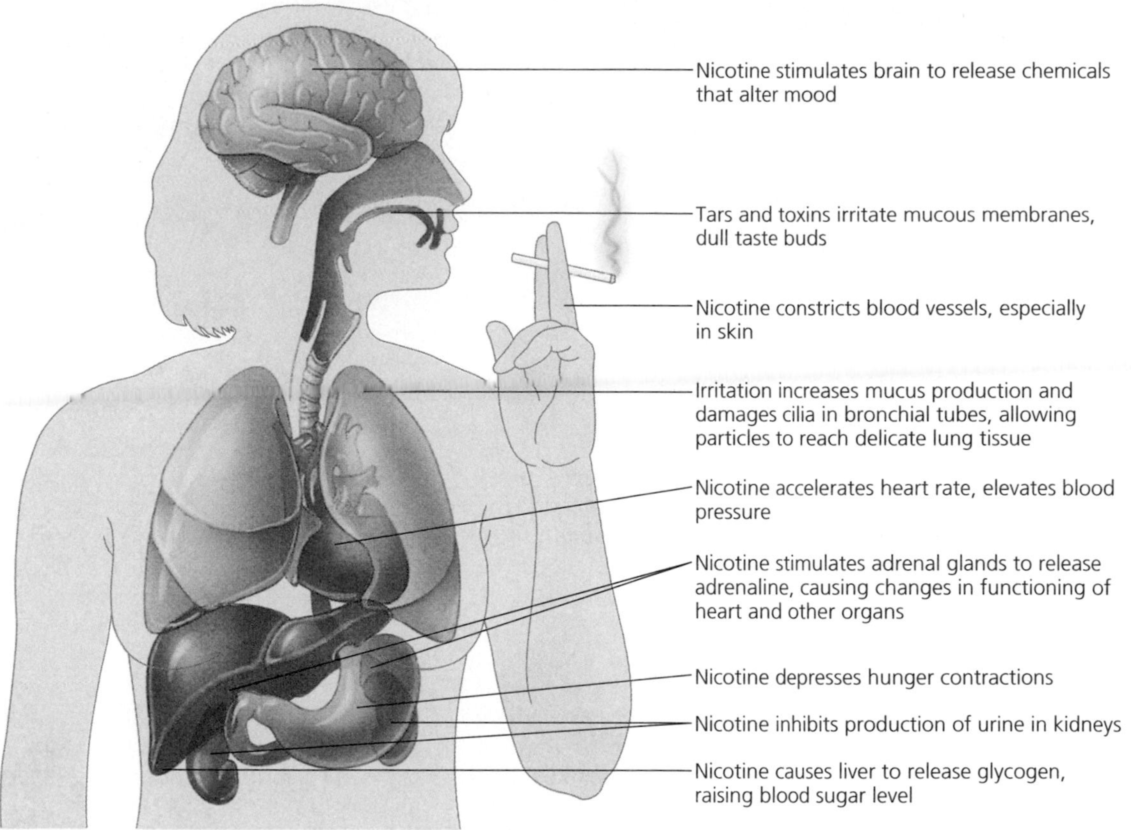

Nicotine stimulates brain to release chemicals that alter mood
Tars and toxins irritate mucous membranes, dull taste buds
Nicotine constricts blood vessels, especially in skin
Irritation increases mucus production and damages cilia in bronchial tubes, allowing particles to reach delicate lung tissue
Nicotine accelerates heart rate, elevates blood pressure
Nicotine stimulates adrenal glands to release adrenaline, causing changes in functioning of heart and other organs
Nicotine depresses hunger contractions
Nicotine inhibits production of urine in kidneys
Nicotine causes liver to release glycogen, raising blood sugar level

FIGURE 13.4 The short-term effects of smoking a cigarette.

deeper and more often they inhale, the greater the risk of disease and other complications. Cigarette smoking increases risk for all the following:

- Cardiovascular disease (heart attack, stroke, hypertension, high cholesterol levels), lung disease (emphysema, chronic bronchitis), osteoporosis, diabetes, and many types of cancer (lung, trachea, mouth, pharynx, esophagus, larynx, pancreas, bladder, kidney, cervix, stomach, liver, colon)
- Tooth decay, gum disease, bad breath, colds, ulcers, hair loss, facial wrinkling, and discolored teeth and fingers
- Menstrual disorders, early menopause, impotence, infertility, stillbirth, and low birth weight (see the box "Gender and Tobacco Use," p. 386)
- Motor vehicle crashes and fire-related injuries

In addition, smoking is expensive. A pack-a-day habit costs an average of $1500 a year. Other financial costs include higher health and home insurance premiums; more frequent cleaning of clothes, teeth, home, office, and car; and repairs of burnt clothing, upholstery, and carpeting—for a total cost of about $3000 per year. Employees who smoke take more sick days and may be less productive than other workers.

When smokers quit, health improvements begin almost immediately. The younger people are when they stop smoking, the more pronounced are these improvements (see the box "Benefits of Quitting Smoking," p. 387).

Other Forms of Tobacco Use

Many smokers have switched from cigarettes to other forms of tobacco, such as cigars, pipes, clove cigarettes, and spit (smokeless) tobacco. However, these alternatives are far from safe.

Cigars and Pipes Cigar and pipe smokers are at increased risk for many health problems, including cardiovascular and respiratory diseases and many types of cancer. Cigars contain more tobacco than cigarettes and so contain more nicotine and produce more tar when smoked. Cigar smokers who don't inhale have a six-times greater risk of throat cancer than nonsmokers; their risk of heart and lung disease approaches that of cigarette smokers. The risks are even higher for cigar smokers who inhale. Regular cigar smokers also have an increased risk for several other cancers.

Clove Cigarettes and Bidis Clove cigarettes, imported from Indonesia and Pakistan, are made of tobacco mixed with chopped cloves. Also known as *kreteks,* they contain almost twice as much tar, nicotine, and carbon monoxide as conventional cigarettes. Clove cigarettes are considered "trainer cigarettes" because cloves impart a sweet taste

DIMENSIONS OF DIVERSITY

Gender and Tobacco Use

American men are currently more likely than women to smoke, but as the rate of smoking among women approaches that of men, so do rates of tobacco-related illness and death. Lung cancer, emphysema, and cardiovascular diseases sicken and kill both men and women who smoke, and more American women now die each year from lung cancer than from breast cancer.

Although overall risks for tobacco-related illness are similar for women and men, sex appears to make a difference in some diseases. Women, for example, are more at risk for smoking-related blood clots and strokes than are men, and the risk is even greater for women using oral contraceptives. Among men and women with the same smoking history, the odds of developing three major types of cancer, including lung cancer, are 1.2–1.7 times higher for women than men. One possible explanation for this difference is that women are more likely to use low-tar cigarettes and thus engage in compensatory behaviors such as deep inhalation, which is linked to increased respiratory damage. Women may also have a greater biological vulnerability to lung cancer.

Tobacco use also is associated with sex-specific health problems. Men who smoke increase their risk of erectile dysfunction and infertility. Women who smoke have higher rates of osteoporosis (a bone-thinning disease that can lead to fractures), thyroid-related diseases, and depression.

Women who smoke also have risks associated with reproduction and the reproductive organs. Smoking is associated with greater menstrual bleeding, greater duration of painful menstrual cramps, and more variability in menstrual cycle length. Smokers have a more difficult time becoming pregnant, and they reach menopause on average a year or two earlier than nonsmokers. When women smokers become pregnant, they face increased chances of miscarriage, placental disorders, premature delivery, ectopic pregnancy, preeclampsia, and stillbirth. Smoking is a risk factor for cervical cancer, too.

Women are less successful than man in quitting. Women report more severe withdrawal symptoms when they stop smoking and are more likely than men to report cravings in response to social and behavioral cues associated with smoking. For men, relapse to smoking is often associated with work or social pressure; women are more likely to relapse when sad or depressed or concerned about weight gain. Women and men also respond differently to medications: Nicotine replacement therapy appears to work better for men, whereas the non-nicotine medication bupropion appears to work better for women.

and numb the mouth. Some chemical constituents of cloves can be dangerous, and there have been a number of respiratory injuries and deaths from smoking clove cigarettes.

Bidis, or "beadies," are small cigarettes imported from India that contain a type of tobacco different from that used in U.S. cigarettes; they are rolled in ebony leaves and often flavored. Bidis contain up to four times more nicotine and twice as much tar as U.S. cigarettes.

Spit (Smokeless) Tobacco Spit tobacco comes in two main forms: snuff and chewing tobacco. Both forms have high levels of nicotine, and use can lead to nicotine addiction. Snuff is tobacco in the form of a coarse, moist powder, mixed with flavorings. The user places a pinch of tobacco between the lower lip or cheek and gum and sucks it. Long-term snuff use may increase the risk of cancer of the cheek and gums by as much as 50 times.

Spit (or chewing) tobacco is in the form of shredded leaves, pressed into bricks or cakes or twisted into rope-like strands. The user places a wad of tobacco in the mouth and chews or sucks it, spitting out or swallowing the tobacco juice. Spit tobacco causes bad breath, tooth decay, and gum disease. One of the most serious effects of chewing tobacco is the increased risk of oral cancer—cancers of the lip, tongue, cheek, throat, gums, roof and floor of the mouth, and larynx.

Environmental Tobacco Smoke

Environmental tobacco smoke (ETS), commonly called *secondhand smoke,* consists of **mainstream smoke**, the smoke exhaled by smokers, and **sidestream smoke**, the smoke that enters the atmosphere from the burning end of the cigarette, cigar, or pipe. Undiluted sidestream smoke is unfiltered by a cigarette filter or a smoker's lungs, so it contains significantly higher concentrations of toxic and carcinogenic compounds than mainstream smoke.

Nearly 85% of the smoke in a room where someone is smoking is sidestream smoke. Even though such smoke is diffuse, the concentrations can be considerable. In rooms where people are smoking, levels of carbon monoxide, for instance, can exceed those permitted by Federal Air Quality Standards for outside air.

Effects of ETS ETS is a known human carcinogen. The EPA estimates that people who live or work among smokers face a 24–50% increase in lung cancer risk. ETS is responsible for about 35,000 deaths each year, including 3000 deaths from lung cancer. ETS also contributes to heart disease and aggravates respiratory conditions such as allergies and asthma.

Scientists have been able to measure changes capable of contributing to lung tissue damage, coronary artery damage, and tumor promotion in the bloodstreams of

Benefits of Quitting Smoking

Within 20 minutes of your last cigarette:

- Blood pressure drops
- Pulse rate drops
- Temperature of hands and feet increases

At 8 hours:

- Carbon monoxide level in blood drops to normal
- Oxygen level in blood increases to normal

At 24 hours:

- Chance of heart attack decreases

At 48 hours:

- Nerve endings start regrowing
- Ability to smell and taste is enhanced

At 2 weeks–3 months:

- Circulation improves
- Walking becomes easier
- Lung function increases

At 1–9 months:

- Coughing, sinus congestion, fatigue, and shortness of breath all decrease

At 1 year:

- Heart disease risk declines to half that of smokers

At 5 years:

- Stroke risk drops to that of nonsmokers

At 10 years:

- Lung cancer risk drops to 50% of that of continuing smokers
- Risk of other cancers (mouth, throat, larynx, esophagus, bladder, kidney, and pancreas) decreases
- Risk of ulcer decreases

At 15 years:

- Risk of death drops to about that of people who have never smoked
- Risk of heart disease is close to that of nonsmokers

SOURCE: American Lung Association. 2007. *Quit Smoking: What Are the Benefits of Quitting Smoking?* (http://www.lungusa.org/site/apps/s/content.asp?c=dvLUK9O0E&b=34706&ct=66747; retrieved June 8, 2007).

healthy young test subjects who spent just 30 minutes to 3 hours in a smoke-filled room. Up to 25% of nonsmokers subjected to ETS develop coughs, 30% develop headaches and nasal discomfort, and 70% develop eye irritation. Other symptoms range from breathlessness to sinus problems. Tobacco odor, which clings to the skin and clothes, is another unpleasant effect of ETS.

Children and ETS Infants and children are particularly vulnerable to the harmful effects of ETS. Because they breathe faster than adults, they inhale more air—and more of the pollutants in the air. Because they weigh less than adults, children inhale proportionately more pollutants per unit of body weight.

The EPA estimates that secondhand smoke triggers 150,000–300,000 cases of bronchitis, pneumonia, and other respiratory infections in infants and toddlers each year. Older children suffer, too. ETS can induce asthma in children and exacerbate symptoms in children who already have asthma. Approximately 19 million American infants and children are regularly exposed to ETS, usually in the home.

Avoiding ETS As a nonsmoker, you have the right to breathe clean air, free from tobacco smoke. Try these strategies to keep the air around you safe:

- ***Speak up tactfully.*** Try something like, "Would you mind putting your cigarette out or moving to another spot? The smoke is bothering me."
- ***Don't allow smoking in your home or room.*** Get rid of ashtrays and ask smokers to light up outside.
- ***Open a window.*** If you cannot avoid being in a room with smokers, at least try to provide some ventilation.
- ***Sit in the nonsmoking section in restaurants and other public areas.*** Complain to the manager if none exists.
- ***Fight for a smoke-free work environment.*** For your sake and that of your coworkers, join with others either to eliminate all smoking indoors or to confine it to certain areas.
- ***Discuss quitting strategies.*** Social pressure is a major factor in many former smokers' decision to quit.

Smoking and Pregnancy

Smoking almost doubles a pregnant woman's chance of having a miscarriage, and women who smoke also face an increased risk of **ectopic pregnancy.** Maternal

TERMS

environmental tobacco smoke (ETS) Smoke that enters the atmosphere from the burning end of a cigarette, cigar, or pipe, as well as smoke that is exhaled by smokers; also called *secondhand smoke.*

mainstream smoke Smoke that is inhaled by a smoker and then exhaled into the atmosphere.

sidestream smoke Smoke that enters the atmosphere from the burning end of a cigarette, cigar, or pipe.

ectopic pregnancy A pregnancy in which the fertilized egg implants itself in an oviduct rather than in the uterus; the embryo must be surgically removed.

smoking causes an estimated 4600 infant deaths in the United States each year, primarily due to premature delivery and smoking-related problems with the placenta, the organ that delivers blood, oxygen, and nutrients to the fetus. Infants whose mothers smoked during pregnancy are also more likely to die from sudden infant death syndrome (SIDS). Maternal smoking is a major factor in low birth weight, which puts newborns at high risk for infections and other potentially fatal problems.

Babies born to mothers who smoke more than two packs a day perform poorly on developmental tests in the first hours after birth when compared with babies of nonsmoking mothers. Children born to women who smoked during pregnancy are at a much higher risk of ear infection as well. Later in life, hyperactivity, short attention span, and lower scores on spelling and reading tests all occur more frequently in children whose mothers smoked throughout pregnancy than in those born to nonsmoking mothers. Nevertheless, about 11% of pregnant women smoke throughout pregnancy.

Action Against Tobacco

Individuals and communities have taken action against this major health threat. Thousands of local ordinances have been passed across the country banning or restricting smoking in restaurants, stores, and other public places. Communities are also restricting many forms of tobacco advertising, such as billboards.

Action at the state level can have a significant effect. For example, California has one of the nation's most aggressive tobacco control programs, combining taxes on cigarettes, graphic ads, and bans on smoking in bars and restaurants. In the past decade, per capita cigarette consumption fell by 50% in California, which now has the second lowest rate of smoking in the United States (Utah has the lowest rate). Both lung cancer cases and heart disease deaths have also declined in California.

Many states, as well as the federal government, have filed lawsuits against the tobacco industry to reclaim money spent on tobacco-related health care. A 1998 agreement requires the tobacco companies to pay states $206 billion over 25 years. For these and other reasons, tobacco consumption in the United States is declining among some groups. In response, the U.S. tobacco industry has increased its efforts to sell in foreign markets, especially in developing nations with few restrictions on tobacco advertising.

Giving Up Tobacco

Giving up tobacco is a long-term, difficult process, usually accompanied by psychological craving and physical withdrawal. Research shows that most tobacco users move through predictable stages—from being uninterested in stopping, to thinking about change, to making a concerted effort to stop, to finally maintaining abstinence. Most attempt to quit several times before they finally succeed. Relapse is a normal part of the process, as with most behavior change plans.

Quitting requires a strategy for success. Some people quit cold turkey, while others taper off more slowly. There are over-the-counter and prescription products that help many people (see the box "Smoking Cessation Products"). Behavioral factors that have been shown to increase the chances of a smoker's permanent smoking cessation are support from others and regular exercise. Support can come from friends and family, Web sites, and/or formal group programs sponsored by organizations such as the American Cancer Society, the American Lung Association, and the Seventh-Day Adventist Church or by a college health center or community hospital.

Most smokers in the process of quitting experience both physical and psychological effects of nicotine withdrawal, and exercise can help with both. For many smokers, tobacco use is associated with certain times and places—following a meal, for example. Resolving to walk after dinner instead of lighting up provides a distraction from cravings and eliminates the cues that trigger a desire to smoke. (Lab 13.2 can help identify your smoking triggers.) In addition, many people worry about weight gain associated with quitting. Although most ex-smokers gain a few pounds, at least temporarily, incorporating exercise into a new, tobacco-free routine lays the foundation for healthy weight management. The health risks of adding a few pounds are far outweighed by the risks of continued smoking; it's estimated that a smoker would have to gain 75–100 pounds to equal the health risks of smoking a pack a day.

As with any significant change in health-related behavior, giving up tobacco requires planning, sustained effort, and support. It is an ongoing process, not a one-time event. Tracking and controlling urges make relapses less likely. Keeping track of them in a health journal helps you deal with them. When you have an urge to use tobacco, use a relaxation technique, take a brisk walk, chew gum, or substitute some other activity. Practice time management so you don't get overwhelmed at school or work. Exercise regularly, eat sensibly, and get enough sleep.

MOTIVATION BOOSTER

Find a role model. Find someone who successfully quit smoking, overcame drug or alcohol dependency, or enjoys social events without drinking or using drugs. Interview that person about her or his methods, and identify strategies you can apply to your own situation.

Smoking Cessation Products

Each year, millions of Americans visit their doctors in the hope of finding a drug that will help them stop smoking. Although pharmacological options are limited, the few available drugs have proved successful.

Chantix (Varinicline)

The newest smoking cessation drug, marketed under the name Chantix, received approval from the FDA in May 2006. The active ingredient in Chantix, varinicline tartrate, works in two ways: It reduces nicotine cravings, easing the withdrawal process, and it blocks the pleasant effects of nicotine. The drug acts on neurotransmitter receptors in the brain.

Unlike most smoking cessation products currently on the market, Chantix is not a nicotine replacement. For this reason, smokers may be advised to continue smoking for the first few days of treatment, to avoid withdrawal and to allow the drug to build up in their system. The approved course of treatment is 12 weeks, but the duration and recommended dosage depend on several factors, including the smoker's general health and the length and severity of his or her nicotine addiction.

Side effects reported with Chantix include nausea, headache, vomiting, sleep disruptions, and changes in taste perception. People with kidney problems or who take certain medications should not take Chantix, and it is not recommended for women who are pregnant or nursing.

Zyban (Bupropion)

Bupropion is an antidepressant (prescribed under the name Wellbutrin) as well as a smoking cessation aid (prescribed under the name Zyban). As a smoking cessation aid, bupropion eases the symptoms of nicotine withdrawal and reduces the urge to smoke. Like Chantix, it acts on neurotransmitter receptors in the brain.

Because the drug is not a nicotine replacement, the user may need to continue smoking for the first few days of treatment. A nicotine replacement product, such as a patch or gum, may be recommended to further ease withdrawal symptoms after the user stops smoking.

Bupropion users have reported an array of side effects, but they are rare. Side effects may be reduced by changing the dosage, taking the medicine at a different time of day, or taking it with or without food. Bupropion is not recommended for people with specific physical conditions or who take certain drugs. Zyban and Wellbutrin should not be taken together.

Nicotine Replacement Products

The most widely used smoking cessation products replace the nicotine that the user would normally get from tobacco. The user continues to get nicotine, so withdrawal symptoms and cravings are reduced. Although still harmful, nicotine replacement products provide a cleaner form of nicotine, without the thousands of poisons and tars produced by burning tobacco. Less of the product is used over time, as the need for nicotine decreases.

Nicotine replacement products come in several forms, including patches, gum, lozenges, nasal sprays, and inhalers. They are available in a variety of strengths and can be worked into many different smoking cessation strategies. Most are available without a prescription.

The nicotine patch is popular because it can be applied and forgotten until it needs to be removed or changed, usually every 16 or 24 hours. Placed on the upper arm or torso, it releases a steady stream of nicotine, which is absorbed through the skin. The main side effects are skin irritation and redness. Nicotine gum and nicotine lozenges have the advantage of allowing the smoker to use them whenever he or she craves nicotine. Side effects of nicotine gum include mouth sores and headaches; nicotine lozenges can cause nausea and heartburn. Nicotine nasal sprays and inhalers are available only by prescription.

Although all these products have proved to be effective in helping users stop smoking, experts recommend them only as one part of a complete smoking cessation program. Such a program should include regular professional counseling and physician monitoring.

QUESTIONS FOR CRITICAL THINKING AND REFLECTION

Despite all the information available about the dangers of tobacco use, one-fifth of Americans still smoke. Why do you think this is the case? In your experience, what role do you think is played by advertising, movies, music, peers, family members, and other influences in a person's decision to start smoking?

TIPS FOR TODAY AND THE FUTURE

The best treatment for dependence is prevention—not starting in the first place—but it's never too late to regain control of your life.

RIGHT NOW YOU CAN

- Carefully consider your use of drugs, alcohol, or tobacco—if any—and decide whether this is the time for you to stop. If it is, throw away the offending products.
- List five things you can do instead of giving in to the temptation to use a drug, alcohol, or tobacco.

IN THE FUTURE YOU CAN

- Look for local resources that can help you stop using drugs, alcohol, or tobacco. Your school may offer counseling or support services, such as a smoking cessation program. It can also be informative and inspiring to attend an Alcoholics Anonymous (AA) meeting.
- Track your progress toward quitting for good. Use a journal to record your cravings or urges and to describe the tactics you used to overcome them.

Q Is there anything I can do for someone I know who has a drug problem?

A If you believe a friend or family member has a drug problem, obtain information about resources for drug treatment available on your campus or in your community. Communicate your concern, provide information about treatment options, and offer your support during treatment.

If the person continues to deny having a problem, you may want to talk with an experienced counselor about setting up an intervention—a formal, structured confrontation designed to end denial by having family, friends, and other caring individuals present their concerns to the drug user. Participants in an intervention point out the ways in which the abuser is hurting others as well as him- or herself. If your friend or family member agrees to treatment, encourage him or her to attend a support group such as Narcotics Anonymous or Alcoholics Anonymous.

In addition, examine your relationship with the abuser for signs of codependency. A codependent is someone whose actions help or enable a person to remain dependent on a drug by removing or softening the effects of the drug use on the user. Common actions by codependents include making excuses or lying for someone, loaning money to someone to continue drug use, and not confronting someone who is obviously intoxicated or high on a drug.

People often become enablers spontaneously and naturally because they want to help their friend or loved one. Unfortunately, the habit of enabling can inhibit a drug-dependent person's recovery because the person never has to experience the consequences of her or his behavior. If you see yourself developing a codependent relationship, get help for yourself; friends and family of drug users can often benefit from counseling. Al-Anon and Alateen are organizations dedicated to helping people who are affected by someone else's drinking.

Q Does drinking benefit health?

A Drinking in moderation—defined as one drink a day for women and two drinks a day for men—may lower the risk of coronary heart disease among some men over 45 and women over 55. For younger people, alcohol consumption confers little, if any, health benefit. Moderate drinking in older adults appears to lower the risk for heart attack and some strokes by raising blood levels of HDL, the beneficial form of cholesterol, and by making blood platelets less likely to stick together to form clots.

Moderate drinking is not without risk, however. Even one drink a day can slightly raise the risk of breast cancer, and people with medical conditions that are worsened by alcohol use (such as peptic ulcer, diabetes, or depression) should avoid drinking. Some people should not drink at all, including people who cannot restrict their drinking to a moderate level, women who are pregnant or who may become pregnant, and people taking certain medications that can interact with alcohol. Overall, the window of benefit is a narrow one, and it shouldn't be used to justify inappropriate or excessive drinking.

Q Does drinking coffee help an intoxicated person sober up more quickly?

A No. Once alcohol is absorbed into the body, there are no ways of appreciably accelerating its breakdown. The rate of alcohol metabolism varies among individuals, largely as a result of heredity, but it is not affected by caffeine, exercise, fresh air, or other stimulants. It is the same whether a person is asleep or awake. To sober up, you simply have to wait until your body has had sufficient time to metabolize all the alcohol you have consumed.

Q Is it true that marijuana can be used medically?

A Yes, although its use is restricted. Even though marijuana is considered an illegal drug in the United States and some other countries, there is a growing movement to make it legally available to treat certain illnesses and medical conditions. A report issued in 1999 by the National Academy of Sciences' Institute of Medicine found that marijuana appears to be helpful in treating pain, nausea, AIDS-related weight loss, muscle spasms in multiple sclerosis, and other problems. Many cancer patients and people with AIDS use marijuana, often illegally, because they find it effective in relieving nausea and restoring appetite. Research is under way to find methods of administering the drug that don't subject the user to the hazards of cancer, lung damage, and emphysema.

For more Common Questions Answered about tobacco, alcohol, and other drugs, visit the Online Learning Center.

SUMMARY

- Addictive behaviors are habits that have gotten out of control and have a negative impact on a person's health. Characteristics of addictive behaviors include reinforcement, craving, loss of control, escalation, and negative consequences.
- Drug abuse is a maladaptive pattern of drug use that persists despite adverse social, psychological, or medical consequences. Drug dependence involves taking a drug compulsively; tolerance and withdrawal symptoms are often present.
- Factors to consider when deciding whether to try a psychoactive drug include short- and long-term risks of drug use, one's

future goals and ethical beliefs, the financial cost of the drug, and one's reasons for drug use.

• At low doses, alcohol causes relaxation; at higher doses, it interferes with motor and mental functioning and is associated with injuries; at very high doses, alcohol poisoning, coma, and death can occur.

• Continued alcohol use has negative effects on the digestive and cardiovascular systems and increases cancer risk and overall mortality. Women who drink while pregnant risk giving birth to children with fetal alcohol syndrome.

• Alcohol abuse involves drinking in dangerous situations or drinking to a degree that causes academic, professional, interpersonal, or legal difficulties.

• Alcohol dependence, or alcoholism, is characterized by more extensive problems with alcohol, usually involving tolerance and withdrawal.

• Binge drinking is a common form of alcohol abuse on college campuses that has negative effects on both drinking and nondrinking students.

• Nicotine is the addictive psychoactive drug in tobacco products.

• In the short term, smoking can either excite or tranquilize the nervous system; it also interferes with the functions of the respiratory system. Long-term effects of smoking include higher rates of acute and chronic diseases and reduced life expectancy.

• Other forms of tobacco use—cigars, pipes, clove cigarettes, and spit tobacco—also have serious associated health risks.

• Environmental tobacco smoke contains toxic and carcinogenic compounds in high concentrations. It causes health problems, including cancer and heart disease, in nonsmokers exposed to it; infants and children are especially at risk.

• Many approaches and products are available to aid people in quitting smoking.

FOR FURTHER EXPLORATION

BOOKS

Brandt, A. M. 2007. *The Cigarette Century: The Rise, Fall, and Deadly Persistence of the Product That Defined America.* New York: Basic Books. *A detailed study of the cigarette's impact on American history and Americans' efforts to overcome the addictive power of smoking.*

Dean, M. 2007. *Empty Cribs: The Impact of Smoking on Child Health.* New York: Arts & Sciences. *Examines the effects of smoking on children, both before and after delivery, with a special focus on SIDS.*

Gilman, S. L., et al. 2004. *Smoke: A Global History of Smoking.* London: Reaktion Books. *A look at smoking and its effects, including history and issues related to culture, art, and gender.*

Herrick, C. 2006. *100 Questions & Answers About Alcoholism & Drug Addiction.* Boston: Jones and Bartlett. *Answers a range of specific questions about alcohol abuse, dependence, and treatment options.*

Karch, S. B. 2006. *Drug Abuse Handbook,* 2nd ed. London: CRC Press. *Explores drug abuse from a variety of perspectives, including clinical and criminological.*

Kinney, J. 2009. *Loosening the Grip: A Handbook of Alcohol Information,* 9th ed. New York: McGraw-Hill. *A fascinating book about alcohol, including information on physical effects, abuse, alcoholism, and cultural aspects of alcohol use.*

Ksir, C., C. L. Hart, and O. S. Ray. 2008. *Drugs, Society, and Human Behavior,* 12th ed. New York: McGraw-Hill. *Examines drugs from the behavioral, pharmacological, historical, social, legal, and clinical perspectives.*

Seaman, B. 2006. *Binge: Campus Life in an Age of Disconnection and Excess.* New York: Wiley. *An exploration of campus life at 12 residential colleges and universities, with discussions on the effects of student isolation, peer pressure, and drinking on today's students.*

U.S. Institute of Medicine. 2007. *Ending the Tobacco Problem: A Blueprint for the Nation.* Washington, D.C.: National Academies Press. *Reviews tobacco policy and public approaches to stopping smoking.*

Wilson, H. T. 2008. *Annual Editions: Drugs, Society and Behavior.* New York: McGraw-Hill. *An annually updated collection of articles reflecting the most current thought on the drug problem in American culture.*

ORGANIZATIONS, HOTLINES, AND WEB SITES

Action on Smoking and Health (ASH). Provides statistics, news briefs, and other information about smoking.
http://www.ash.org

Al-Anon Family Group Headquarters. Provides information and referrals to local Al-Anon and Alateen groups.
888-4AL-ANON
http://www.al-anon.org

Alcoholics Anonymous (AA) World Services. Provides information on AA, literature on alcoholism, and information about AA meetings.
http://www.aa.org

American Cancer Society (ACS). Sponsor of the annual Great American Smokeout; provides information on the dangers of tobacco, as well as tools for preventing and stopping the use of tobacco products.
800-ACS-2345
http://www.cancer.org

American Lung Association. Provides information on lung diseases, tobacco control, and environmental health.
800-LUNG-USA; 212-315-8700
http://www.lungusa.org

American Psychiatric Association: College Mental Health. Covers a variety of mental health issues affecting college students, including alcohol abuse and treatment.
http://www.healthyminds.org/collegementalhealth.cfm

BACCHUS Network. An association of college- and university-based peer education programs that focus on the prevention of alcohol abuse.
http://www.bacchusgamma.org

CDC: Smoking and Tobacco Use. Provides educational materials and tips on how to quit smoking.
http://www.cdc.gov/tobacco

College Alcohol Study. Harvard School of Public Health. Provides information about and results from recent studies of binge drinking on college campuses.
http://www.hsph.harvard.edu/cas

Facts on Tap. Provides information about alcohol and college life, and sex and alcohol, as well as tips for students who have been negatively affected by other students' alcohol use.
http://www.factsontap.org

Higher Education Center for Alcohol and Other Drug Abuse and Violence Prevention. Provides information about alcohol and drug abuse on campus and links to related sites.
http://www.higheredcenter.org

National Clearinghouse for Alcohol and Drug Information. Provides statistics, information, and publications on substance abuse, including resources for people who want to help friends and family members overcome substance-abuse problems.
800-729-6686
http://ncadi.samhsa.gov

National Institute on Alcohol Abuse and Alcoholism (NIAAA). Provides booklets and other publications on a variety of alcohol-related topics, including fetal alcohol syndrome, alcoholism treatment, and alcohol use and minorities.
http://www.niaaa.nih.gov

National Institute on Drug Abuse. Develops and supports research on drug abuse prevention programs; fact sheets on drugs of abuse are available on the Web site.
http://www.drugabuse.gov

Quitnet. Provides interactive tools and questionnaires, support groups, a library, and the latest news on tobacco issues.
http://www.quitnet.org

Smokefree.gov. Provides step-by-step strategies for quitting as well as expert support via telephone or instant messaging.
http://www.smokefree.gov
1-800-QUITNOW (1-800-784-8669)
http://www.cancer.gov (additional information)

Substance Abuse and Mental Health Services Administration (SAMHSA). Provides statistics, information, and other resources related to substance abuse, prevention, and treatment.
http://www.samhsa.gov

The following hotlines provide support and referrals:
800-ALCOHOL; 800-662-HELP

SELECTED BIBLIOGRAPHY

American Cancer Society. 2007. *Cancer Facts & Figures 2007.* Atlanta: American Cancer Society.

American Psychiatric Association. 2001. *Diagnostic and Statistical Manual of Mental Disorders,* 4th ed., Text Revision (DSM-IV-TR). Washington, D.C.: American Psychiatric Association.

Bjartveit, K., and A. Tverdal. 2005. Health consequences of smoking 1–4 cigarettes per day. *Tobacco Control* 14(5): 315–320.

Brodbeck, J., et al. 2007. Motives for cannabis use as a moderator variable of distress among young adults. *Addictive Behaviors* 32(8): 1537–1545.

Centers for Disease Control and Prevention. 2005. Annual smoking-attributable mortality, years of potential life lost, and productivity losses—United States. *Morbidity and Mortality Weekly Report* 54(25): 625–628.

Centers for Disease Control and Prevention. 2007. Surveillance of certain health behaviors among states and selected local areas: United States, 2005. *Morbidity and Mortality Weekly Report Surveillance Summaries* 56(4): 1–160.

Cox, R. G., et al. 2007. Academic performance and substance use: Findings from a state survey of public high school students. *The Journal of School Health* 77(3): 109–115.

de la Chica, R. A., et al. 2005. Chromosomal instability in amniocytes from fetuses of mothers who smoke. *Journal of the American Medical Association* 293(10): 1212–1222.

Doiron, J. P., and R. M. Nicki. 2007. Prevention of pathological gambling: A randomized controlled trial. *Cognitive Behavior Therapy* 36(2): 74–84.

Ford, J. A. 2007. Substance use among college athletes: A comparison based on sport/team affiliation. *Journal of American College Health* 55(6): 367–373.

Gades, N. M., et al. 2005. Association between smoking and erectile dysfunction: A population-based study. *American Journal of Epidemiology* 161(4): 346–351.

Hingson, R., et al. 2005. Magnitude of alcohol-related mortality and morbidity among U.S. college students ages 18–24. *Annual Review of Public Health* 26: 259–279.

Hurd, Y. L., et al. 2005. Marijuana impairs growth in mid-gestation fetuses. *Neurotoxicology and Teratology* 27(2): 221–229.

Insurance Institute for Highway Safety. 2007. *DUI/DWI Laws as of March 2007* (http://www.iihs.org/laws/dui.aspx; retrieved January 17, 2008).

Klatsky, A. L. 2007. Alcohol, cardiovascular disease and diabetes mellitus. *Pharmacological Research* 55(3): 237–247.

Lee, C. M., et al. 2007. Marijuana motives: Young adults' reasons for using marijuana. *Addictive Behaviors* 32(7): 1384–1394.

Linnet, K. M., et al. 2005. Smoking during pregnancy and the risk for hyperkinetic disorder in offspring. *Pediatrics* 116(2): 462–467.

Maglione, M., et al. 2005. Psychiatric effects of ephedra use. *American Journal of Psychiatry* 162(1): 189–191.

Martins, S. S., et al. 2007. Pathways between ecstasy initiation and other drug use. *Addictive Behaviors* 32(7): 1511–1518.

Mukamal, K. J., et al. 2005. Alcohol and risk for ischemic stroke in men: The role of drinking patterns and usual beverage. *Annals of Internal Medicine* 142(1): 11–19.

Mukamal, K. J., et al. 2005. Alcohol consumption and risk of atrial fibrillation in men and women: The Copenhagen City Heart Study. *Circulation* 112(12): 1736–1742.

Parrott, A. C. 2005. Chronic tolerance to recreational MDMA or ecstasy. *Journal of Psychopharmacology* 19(1): 71–83.

Pletcher, M. J., et al. 2005. Alcohol consumption, binge drinking, and early coronary calcification. *American Journal of Epidemiology* 161(5): 423–433.

Reid, R. D., et al. 2007. Smoking cessation: Lessons learned from clinical trial evidence. *Current Opinions in Cardiology* 22(4): 280–285.

Renna, F. 2007. The economic cost of teen drinking: Late graduation and lowered earnings. *Health Economics* 16(4): 407–419.

Shiffman, S., M. E. Di Marino, and J. L. Pillitteri. 2005. The effectiveness of nicotine patch and nicotine lozenge in very heavy smokers. *Journal of Substance Abuse Treatment* 28(1): 49–55.

Slutske, W. S. 2005. Alcohol use disorders among U.S. college students and their non-college-attending peers. *Archives of General Psychiatry* 62(3): 321–327.

Staten, R. R., et al. 2007. Social influences on cigarette initiation among college students. *American Journal of Health Behavior* 31(4): 353–362.

Trimble, C. L., et al. 2005. Active and passive cigarette smoking and the risk of cervical neoplasia. *Obstetrics and Gynecology* 105(1): 174–181.

Wareing, M., et al. 2005. Visuo-spatial working memory deficits in current and former users of MDMA ('ecstasy'). *Human Psychopharmacology* 20(2): 115–123.

Name ______________________ Section ______________ Date ______________

LAB 13.1 Is Alcohol a Problem in Your Life?

Part I Do You Have a Problem with Alcohol?

For each question, choose the answer that best describes your behavior. Then total your scores.

Questions	Points: 0	1	2	3	4	Your Score
1. How often do you have a drink containing alcohol?	Never	Monthly or less	2 to 4 times a month	2 to 3 times a week	4 or more times a week	____
2. How many drinks containing alcohol do you have on a typical day when you are drinking?	1 or 2	3 or 4	5 or 6	7 to 9	10 or more	____
3. How often do you have six or more drinks on one occasion?	Never	Less than monthly	Monthly	Weekly	Daily or almost daily	____
4. How often during the past year have you found that you were not able to stop drinking once you had started?	Never	Less than monthly	Monthly	Weekly	Daily or almost daily	____
5. How often during the past year have you failed to do what was normally expected from you because of drinking?	Never	Less than monthly	Monthly	Weekly	Daily or almost daily	____
6. How often during the past year have you needed a first drink in the morning to get yourself going after a heavy drinking session?	Never	Less than monthly	Monthly	Weekly	Daily or almost daily	____
7. How often during the past year have you had a feeling of guilt or remorse after drinking?	Never	Less than monthly	Monthly	Weekly	Daily or almost daily	____
8. How often during the past year have you been unable to remember what happened the night before because you had been drinking?	Never	Less than monthly	Monthly	Weekly	Daily or almost daily	____
9. Have you or has someone else been injured as a result of your drinking?	No	Yes, but not in the past year (2 points)		Yes, during the past year (4 points)		____
10. Has a relative or friend or a doctor or other health worker been concerned about your drinking or suggested you cut down?	No	Yes, but not in the past year (2 points)		Yes, during the past year (4 points)		____

Total ____

A total score of 8 or more indicates a strong likelihood of hazardous or harmful alcohol consumption.

Part II Are You Troubled by Someone's Drinking?

Millions of people are affected by the excessive drinking of someone close to them. The following questions are designed to help you decide whether you need Al-Anon. If you answer yes to any question, put a check next to it.

____ 1. Do you worry about how much someone else drinks?
____ 2. Do you have money problems because of someone else's drinking?
____ 3. Do you tell lies to cover up for someone else's drinking?
____ 4. Do you feel that if the drinker cared about you, he or she would stop drinking to please you?
____ 5. Do you blame the drinker's behavior on his or her companions?
____ 6. Are plans frequently upset or canceled or meals delayed because of the drinker?
____ 7. Do you make threats, such as, "If you don't stop drinking, I'll leave you"?
____ 8. Do you secretly try to smell the drinker's breath?
____ 9. Are you afraid to upset someone for fear it will set off a drinking bout?
____10. Have you been hurt or embarrassed by a drinker's behavior?
____11. Are holidays and gatherings spoiled because of drinking?
____12. Have you considered calling the police for help in fear of abuse?
____13. Do you search for hidden alcohol?
____14. Do you often ride in a car with a driver who has been drinking?
____15. Have you refused social invitations out of fear or anxiety?
____16. Do you feel like a failure because you can't control the drinker?
____17. Do you think that if the drinker stopped drinking, your other problems would be solved?
____18. Do you ever threaten to hurt yourself to scare the drinker?
____19. Do you feel angry, confused, or depressed most of the time?
____20. Do you feel there is no one who understands your problems?

If you answered yes to three or more of these questions, Al-Anon or Alateen may be able to help.

Using Your Results

How did you score? (1) What is your alcohol use assessment score from Part I? Are you surprised by your score? Does your score indicate a problem?

(2) Did the Al-Anon quiz indicate that you are affected by someone else's excessive drinking? Are you surprised by the result?

What should you do next? If your alcohol use assessment score indicates hazardous or harmful alcohol consumption, or if you are encountering drinking-related problems with your academic performance, job, relationships, or health, or with the law, you should consider seeking help. Check for campus or community resources, including counseling, self-help groups, AA, and formal treatment programs.

If you are troubled by someone else's drinking, you can contact Al-Anon or Alateen by looking in your local telephone directory or contacting Al-Anon's main office (1600 Corporate Landing Parkway, Virginia Beach, VA 23454; 800-344-2666; http://www.al-anon.org).

SOURCES: Part I from Saunders, J. B., et al. 1993. Development of the Alcohol Use Disorders Identification Test (AUDIT): WHO Collaborative Project on Early Detection of Persons with Harmful Alcohol Consumption—II. *Addiction* 88: 791–804, June. Carfax Publishing Ltd. Reprinted with permission from Blackwell Publishing. Part II from Are You Troubled by Someone's Drinking? (http://www.al-anon.alateen.org/quiz.html). Copyright © 1980 Al-Anon Family Group Headquarters, Inc. Reprinted by permission of Al-Anon Family Group Headquarters, Inc.

Name ______________________ Section ______________ Date ______________

LAB 13.2 For Smokers Only: Why Do You Smoke?

Although smoking cigarettes is physiologically addictive, people smoke for reasons other than nicotine craving. What kind of smoker are you? Knowing what your motivations and satisfactions are can ultimately help you quit. This test is designed to provide you with a score on each of six factors that describe many people's smoking. Read the statements and then circle the number that represents how *often* you feel this way when you smoke cigarettes. Be sure to answer each question.

		Always	Frequently	Occasionally	Seldom	Never
A.	I smoke cigarettes to keep myself from slowing down.	5	4	3	2	1
B.	Handling a cigarette is part of the enjoyment of smoking it.	5	4	3	2	1
C.	Smoking cigarettes is pleasant and relaxing.	5	4	3	2	1
D.	I light up a cigarette when I feel angry about something.	5	4	3	2	1
E.	When I have run out of cigarettes, I find it almost unbearable until I can get them.	5	4	3	2	1
F.	I smoke cigarettes automatically without even being aware of it.	5	4	3	2	1
G.	I smoke cigarettes for stimulation, to perk myself up.	5	4	3	2	1
H.	Part of the enjoyment of smoking a cigarette comes from the steps I take to light up.	5	4	3	2	1
I.	I find cigarettes pleasurable.	5	4	3	2	1
J.	When I feel uncomfortable or upset about something, I light up a cigarette.	5	4	3	2	1
K.	I am very much aware of the fact when I am not smoking a cigarette.	5	4	3	2	1
L.	I light up a cigarette without realizing I still have one burning in the ashtray.	5	4	3	2	1
M.	I smoke cigarettes to get a "lift."	5	4	3	2	1
N.	When I smoke a cigarette, part of the enjoyment is watching the smoke as I exhale it.	5	4	3	2	1
O.	I want a cigarette most when I am comfortable and relaxed.	5	4	3	2	1
P.	When I feel "blue" or want to take my mind off cares and worries, I smoke cigarettes.	5	4	3	2	1
Q.	I get a real gnawing hunger for a cigarette when I haven't smoked for a while.	5	4	3	2	1
R.	I've found a cigarette in my mouth and didn't remember putting it there.	5	4	3	2	1

How to Score

Enter the numbers you have circled in the spaces provided. Total the scores on each line. Total scores can range from 3 to 15. Any score of 11 or above is high; any score of 7 or below is low.

							Totals
______ A	+	______ G	+	______ M	=	______	Stimulation
______ B	+	______ H	+	______ N	=	______	Handling
______ C	+	______ I	+	______ O	=	______	Pleasurable relaxation
______ D	+	______ J	+	______ P	=	______	Crutch: tension reduction
______ E	+	______ K	+	______ Q	=	______	Craving: strong physiological or psychological addiction
______ F	+	______ L	+	______ R	=	______	Habit

Using Your Results

How did you score? For which factors did you score the highest? Are you surprised by the results of the assessment?

What should you do next? Use the information from this assessment to help plan a successful approach for quitting. The six factors measured by this test describe ways of experiencing or managing certain kinds of feelings. The higher your score on a particular factor, the more important that factor is in your smoking, and the more useful the tips below will be in your attempt to quit. Highlight or make a list of the strategies that seem most helpful to you and post the list in a prominent place.

Stimulation: If you score high on this factor, it means you are stimulated by a cigarette—you feel that it helps wake you up, organize your energies, and keep you going. If you try to give up smoking, you may want a safe substitute—a brisk walk or moderate exercise, for example—whenever you feel the urge to smoke.

Handling: Handling things can be satisfying, but there are many ways to keep your hands busy without lighting up or playing with a cigarette. Try doodling or toying with a pen, pencil, or other small object.

Pleasurable relaxation: Those who do get real pleasure from smoking often find that an honest consideration of the harmful effects of their habit is enough to help them quit. They substitute social or physical activities and find they do not seriously miss their cigarettes.

Crutch: Many smokers use cigarettes as a kind of crutch in moments of stress or discomfort, and occasionally it may work; but heavy smokers are apt to discover that cigarettes do not help them deal with their problems effectively. When it comes to quitting, this kind of smoker may find it easy to stop when everything is going well but may be tempted to start again in a time of crisis. Physical exertion or social activity may serve as a useful substitute for cigarettes.

Craving: Quitting smoking is difficult for people who score high on this factor. It may be helpful for them to smoke more than usual for a day or two, so that the taste for cigarettes is spoiled, and then isolate themselves completely from cigarettes until the craving is gone.

Habit: These smokers light up frequently without even realizing it; they no longer get much satisfaction. They may find it easy to quit and stay off if they can break the habit patterns they have built up. The key to success is becoming aware of each cigarette when it's smoked. Ask, "Do I really want this cigarette?"

SOURCE: National Institutes of Health. 1990. *Why Do You Smoke?* NIH Pub. no. 90-1822. U.S. Department of Health and Human Services. Public Health Service.

LOOKING AHEAD>>>>>

AFTER READING THIS CHAPTER, YOU SHOULD BE ABLE TO:

- Explain how HIV infection affects the body and how it is transmitted, diagnosed, and treated
- Discuss the symptoms, risks, and treatments of other major STDs
- List strategies for protecting yourself from STDs

SEXUALLY TRANSMITTED DISEASES 14

TEST YOUR KNOWLEDGE

1. About _____ Americans are believed to be infected with HIV, the virus that causes AIDS.

a. 10,000
b. 100,000
c. 1 million

2. A man with an STD is more likely to transmit the infection to a woman than vice versa.

True or false?

3. After you have had an STD once, you become immune to that disease and cannot get it again.

True or false?

ANSWERS

1. **c.** By 2006, the Centers for Disease Control and Prevention (CDC) estimated that about 1 million Americans were living with HIV infection. An estimated one-quarter of them are unaware they are infected.
2. **TRUE.** Infected men are at least twice as likely as infected women to transmit an STD to their partner. Many STDs are more physically damaging to women than to men.
3. **FALSE.** Reinfection with STDs is very common. For example, if you are treated for and cured of chlamydia and then you have sex with your untreated partner, the chances are very good that you will be infected again.

FIT AND WELL ONLINE LEARNING CENTER www.mhhe.com/fahey

Visit the *Fit and Well* Online Learning Center for resources that will help you get the most out of your course!

- Study and review aids include practice quizzes, glossary flashcards, chapter summaries, learning objectives, PowerPoint presentations, Common Questions Answered, student handouts, crossword puzzles, Internet activities, and links to wellness Web sites.
- Behavior change tools include a daily fitness and nutrition journal, a behavior change workbook, sample behavior change plans, and blank behavior change logs to print and use.

Acquired immunodeficiency syndrome (AIDS) is a leading cause of death worldwide. Of the approximately 40 million people who are infected with the virus that causes AIDS—**human immunodeficiency virus (HIV)**—most will probably die within 10 years. The death rate from AIDS began to decline in the United States in 1996, but AIDS remains a major killer of Americans. Since the global AIDS epidemic's inception in 1981, more than 500,000 of the approximately 1.5 million Americans who have been infected with HIV have died from the disease. Worldwide, AIDS is the leading cause of death for people age 15–59.

Although recent public education programs have focused primarily on HIV infection, all **sexually transmitted diseases (STDs)** continue to have a high incidence among Americans (Table 14.1). In fact, the United States has the highest rate of STDs of any developed nation, with nearly 19 million new cases each year; at current rates, half of all young people will aquire an STD by age 25. Worldwide, STDs affect more than 400 million people each year.

STDs can be prevented. Many can also be cured if they are treated early and properly. This chapter provides information about healthy, safer sexual behavior and about what you can do to reduce the risk of contributing to the further spread of these diseases.

VITAL STATISTICS

Table 14.1 Estimated Incidence and Prevalence of STDs in the United States

	Estimated Annual Incidence (New Cases)	Estimated Prevalence* (Currently Infected People)
Trichomoniasis	7,400,000	n/a
HPV infection	6,200,000	20,000,000
Chlamydia	2,800,000	1,900,000
Genital herpes	1,600,000	45,000,000
Gonorrhea	718,000	n/a
Hepatitis B**	81,000	1,250,000
Syphilis (all stages)†	61,000	n/a
HIV infection**	40,000	1,000,000

n/a = not available

*Because the viral STDs are persistent and incurable, the number of currently infected people capable of transmitting the infection (prevalence) greatly exceeds the annual number of new cases (incidence) of the viral STDs. Chlamydia prevalence remains high because most cases are asymptomatic and undiagnosed.

**Hepatitis B and HIV infection can be transmitted in a variety of ways; about half of HIV cases and 30–60% of hepatitis B cases are transmitted sexually.

†Total includes about 8000 cases of primary- and secondary-stage syphilis, the stages of the disease during which it can be easily transmitted to others.

SOURCES: Weinstock, H., S. Berman, and W. Cates. 2004. Sexually transmitted diseases among American youth: Incidence and prevalence estimates, 2000. *Perspectives on Sexual and Reproductive Health* 36(1): 6–10. Additional data from the Centers for Disease Control and Prevention and the Kaiser Family Foundation.

THE MAJOR STDs

In general, seven different STDs pose major health threats: HIV/AIDS, chlamydia, gonorrhea, human papillomavirus (HPV) infection (genital warts), genital herpes, hepatitis B, and syphilis. These diseases are considered major because they are serious in themselves, cause serious complications if left untreated, and/or pose risks to a fetus or newborn. In addition, pelvic inflammatory disease (PID), a common complication of gonorrhea and chlamydia, merits discussion as a separate disease. Lab 14.1 will help you evaluate your risk of contracting an STD.

The bacterial STDs, including chlamydia, gonorrhea, and syphilis, can be cured with antibiotics. However, many people do not know they are infected and need treatment. Further, previous infection does not confer immunity, so a person can be reinfected despite treatment.

The viral STDs—herpes, genital warts, hepatitis, and HIV infection—cannot be cured with current therapies. Although antiviral drugs and other medications can reduce the effects of these STDs, the virus may remain in the body and cause chronic or recurrent infection. All STDs can cause sores and inflammation that allow HIV to pass more easily from person to person.

HIV Infection and AIDS

HIV infection is one of the most serious and challenging problems facing the United States and the world today. The Centers for Disease Control and Prevention (CDC) now estimates that about 40,000 Americans become infected with HIV every year. About 1 million Americans are believed to currently be living with HIV, including approximately 1 in 500 college students. Women account for 26% of reported cases in the United States, and African Americans and Hispanics account for about 70% of new cases. About one-quarter of HIV-infected Americans are unaware they are infected.

Worldwide, the World Health Organization (WHO) estimates that 10 people are infected with HIV every minute—nearly 6 million per year—and half of these new infections are in people age 15–24. Despite the intense efforts of health professionals all around the world, HIV infection continues to spread.

What Is HIV Infection? **HIV infection** is a chronic disease that progressively damages the body's immune system, making an otherwise healthy person less able to resist a variety of infections and disorders. Normally,

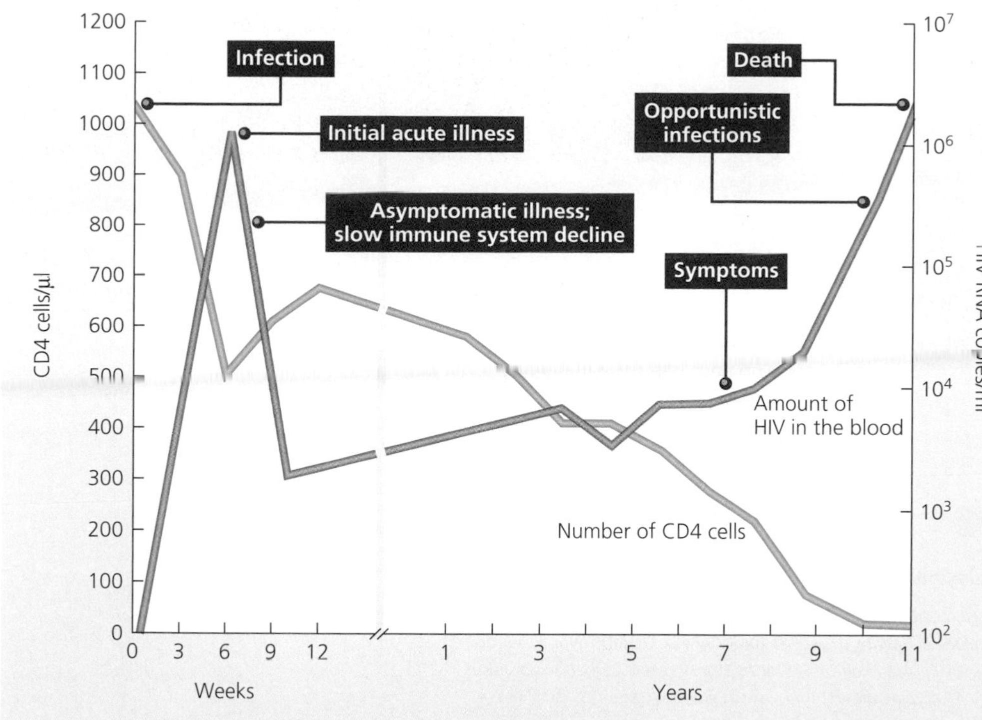
1200
1100
1000
900
800
700
600
500
400
300
200
100
0
CD4 cells/μl
Infection
Initial acute illness
Asymptomatic illness; slow immune system decline
Death
Opportunistic infections
Symptoms
Amount of HIV in the blood
Number of CD4 cells
10^7
10^6
10^5
10^4
10^3
10^2
HIV RNA copies/ml
0 3 6 9 12
Weeks
1 3 5 7 9 11
Years
During the initial acute illness, CD4 levels fall sharply and HIV RNA levels increase; more than 50% of infected people experience flulike symptoms during this period. Antibodies to HIV usually appear 2–12 weeks after the initial infection. During the asymptomatic phase that follows, CD4 levels gradually decline, and HIV RNA levels again increase. Due to declines in immunity, infected individuals eventually begin to experience symptoms; when CD4 levels drop very low, people become vulnerable to serious opportunistic infections characteristic of full-blown AIDS. Chronic or recurrent illnesses continue until the immune system fails and death results.

FIGURE 14.1 The general pattern of untreated HIV infection. The blue line represents the number of CD4 cells in the blood, a marker for the status of the immune system. The orange line shows the amount of HIV RNA in the blood.

SOURCE: Adapted from Fauci, A. S., et al. 1996. Immunopathogenic mechanisms of HIV infection. *Annals of Internal Medicine* 124: 654–663. Reprinted with permission of the American College of Physicians—American Society of Internal Medicine.

when a virus or other pathogen enters the body, it is targeted and destroyed by the immune system. But HIV attacks the immune system itself, taking over immune system cells and forcing them to produce new copies of HIV. It also makes them incapable of performing their immune functions.

The destruction of the immune system is signaled by the loss of **CD4 T cells** (Figure 14.1). As the number of CD4 T cells declines, an infected person may begin to experience mild to moderately severe symptoms. A person is diagnosed with AIDS when he or she develops one of the conditions defined as a marker for AIDS or when the number of CD4 T cells in the blood drops below a certain level (200/μl). People with AIDS are vulnerable to a number of serious—often fatal—secondary, or opportunistic, infections.

The asymptomatic period of HIV—the time between the initial viral infection and the onset of disease symptoms—may range from 2 to 20 years, with an average of 11 years in untreated adults. More than 50% of infected people experience flulike symptoms shortly after the initial infection, but most remain generally healthy for years. During this time, however, the virus is progressively infecting and destroying the cells of the immune system. People infected with HIV can pass the virus to others—even if they have no symptoms and even if they do not know they have been infected.

Transmitting the Virus HIV lives only within cells and body fluids, not outside the body. It is transmitted by blood and blood products, semen, vaginal and cervical

TERMS
WEB

acquired immunodeficiency syndrome (AIDS) A generally fatal, incurable, sexually transmitted viral disease.

human immunodeficiency virus (HIV) The virus that causes HIV infection and AIDS.

sexually transmitted disease (STD) A disease that can be transmitted by sexual contact; some STDs can also be transmitted by other means.

HIV infection A chronic, progressive disease that damages the immune system.

CD4 T cell type of white blood cell that helps coordinate the activity of the immune system; the primary target for HIV infection. A decrease in the number of these cells correlates with the risk and severity of HIV-related illness.

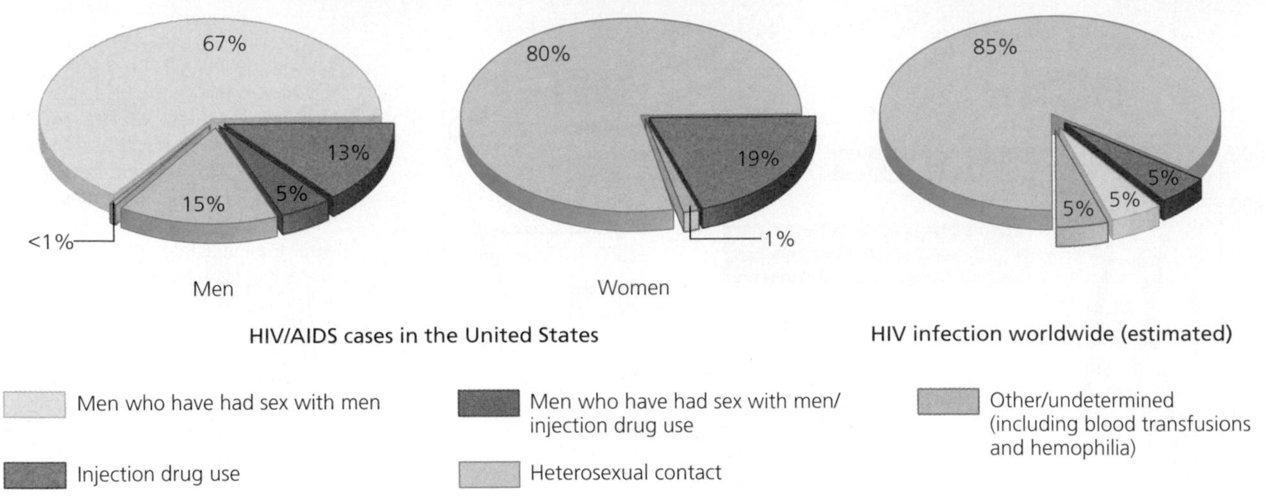

FIGURE 14.2 Routes of HIV transmission among adults.

SOURCES: Centers for Disease Control and Prevention. 2006. *HIV/AIDS Surveillance Report* 17. Joint United Nations Programme on HIV/AIDS (UNAIDS), 2006. *AIDS Epidemic Update, December 2006.* Geneva: UNAIDS. World Health Organization. 2001. Global AIDS surveillance. *Weekly Epidemiological Record* 76(50): 389–400. Centers for Disease Control and Prevention. 2007. *A Glance at the HIV AIDS Epidemic* (http://www.cdc.gov/hiv/resources/factsheets/at-a-glance.htm; retrieved December 2, 2007).

secretions, and breast milk (Figure 14.2). It cannot live in air, in water, or on objects or surfaces such as toilet seats, eating utensils, or telephones.

There are three main routes of HIV transmission:

- Specific kinds of sexual contact
- Direct exposure to infected blood
- Contact between an HIV-infected woman and her child during pregnancy, childbirth, or breastfeeding

Levels of HIV in the blood are very high during the first weeks following infection, and researchers believe that many cases of HIV are acquired from people who have recently been infected.

SEXUAL CONTACT HIV is more likely to be transmitted through unprotected vaginal or anal intercourse than by other sexual activities. Any trauma or irritation of tissues, such as those that can occur through rough or unwanted intercourse or through the overuse of spermicides, increase the risk of HIV transmission. The presence of lesions or blisters from other STDs also makes it easier for the virus to be passed. During vaginal intercourse, male-to-female transmission is more likely to occur than female-to-male transmission. HIV has been found in preejaculatory fluid, so transmission can also occur before ejaculation.

Oral-genital contact carries some risk of transmission, although less than vaginal or anal intercourse. The risk of HIV transmission during oral sex increases if a participant has oral sores, has poor oral hygiene practices, or brushes or flosses just before or after oral sex. Some evidence suggests that drinking alcohol before oral sex may make the cells that line the mouth more susceptible to infection with HIV.

CONTACT WITH INFECTED BLOOD Direct contact with infected blood is another major route of HIV transmission. Needles used to inject drugs (including heroin, cocaine, and anabolic steroids) are routinely contaminated by the blood of the user. If needles are shared, small amounts of one person's blood are injected into another person's bloodstream. HIV may be transmitted through subcutaneous and intramuscular injection as well, from needles or blades used in acupuncture, tattooing, ritual scarring, and piercing of any body part.

HIV has been transmitted in blood and blood products used in the medical treatment of injuries and illnesses, resulting in about 14,000 cases of AIDS. The blood supply in all licensed blood banks and plasma centers in the United States is now screened for HIV. The American Blood Bank Association estimates that fewer than 1 in 2 million units of blood products is capable of transmitting HIV.

CONTACT BETWEEN MOTHER AND CHILD The final major route of HIV transmission is mother-to-child, also called *vertical* or *perinatal* transmission, which can occur during pregnancy, childbirth, or breastfeeding. The number of new cases of HIV/AIDS among American infants has declined more than 90% since 1992 because of testing and treatment of infected women with anti-HIV drugs. Treatment is expensive, however, and vertical transmission continues to be a major threat worldwide, with 600,000 infants infected each year (see the box "HIV Infection Around the World"). Cesarean delivery further reduces

HIV Infection Around the World

In 2006, the world marked the twenty-fifth year since AIDS, a previously unknown disease, was diagnosed in five young gay men in Los Angeles. We now know that HIV originated in Africa about five decades earlier. HIV is now a worldwide scourge, with 65 million people infected and 25 million deaths since the epidemic began. Although some developments in efforts to address the epidemic have been promising, the number of people living with AIDS increased in every region of the world between 2004 and 2006.

The vast majority of cases—95%—have occurred in developing countries, where heterosexual contact is the primary means of transmission, responsible for 85% of all adult infections. In the developed world, HIV is increasingly becoming a disease that disproportionately affects the poor and ethnic minorities. Worldwide, women are the fastest-growing group of newly infected people; nearly half (48%) of adults living with HIV in 2006 were women. In addition, an estimated 2.3 million children are living with HIV infection, and about 15 million children are AIDS orphans.

Sub-Saharan Africa remains the hardest hit of all areas of the world. Two-thirds of all adults and children with HIV live in this region, and three-quarters of all deaths due to AIDS in 2006 occurred here. However, because the epidemic started about 10 years later in Asia than in Africa, experts expect an explosion of new cases in Asia. And because Asia accounts for more than 50% of the world's population, the pool of people at risk is much larger than in Africa. India has overtaken South Africa as the country with the largest number of people living with HIV infection. HIV is also spreading rapidly in eastern Europe, and former Soviet countries have seen a 50-fold increase in HIV infection in 8 years.

Efforts to combat AIDS are complicated by political, economic, and cultural barriers. Education and prevention programs are often hampered by resistance from social and religious institutions and by the taboo on openly discussing sexual issues. Condoms are uncommon in many countries, and women in many societies do not have sufficient control over their lives to demand that men use condoms during sex. Prevention approaches that have had success include STD treatment and education, public education campaigns about safer sex, and syringe exchange programs for injection drug users.

In countries where there is a substantial imbalance in the social power of men and women, empowering women is a crucial priority in reducing the spread of HIV. In particular, reducing sexual violence against women, allowing women property and inheritance rights, and increasing women's access to education and employment are essential.

International efforts are under way to make condoms more available by lowering their price and to develop effective antiviral creams that women can use without the knowledge of their partners. Other potential strategies for fighting the spread of HIV include the widespread use of drugs to suppress genital herpes simplex, an extremely common STD that can dramatically increase transmission of HIV. Also, the practice of male circumcision might be useful in reducing the spread of HIV (and chlamydia, discussed later in this chapter). Recent research has shown a 60% reduction in HIV transmission among circumcised men compared with uncircumcised men, even when controlling for other factors.

In developed nations such as the United States, new drugs are easing AIDS symptoms and lowering viral levels dramatically for some patients. In the past few years, a small but growing number of people in poor countries have gained access to antiviral drugs because of the introduction of inexpensive generic drugs and increasing international funding for HIV treatment. Still, the vast majority of people with HIV remain untreated. Until vaccines or a low-cost cure is developed, efforts must continue to focus on prevention through educational campaigns and behavior change.

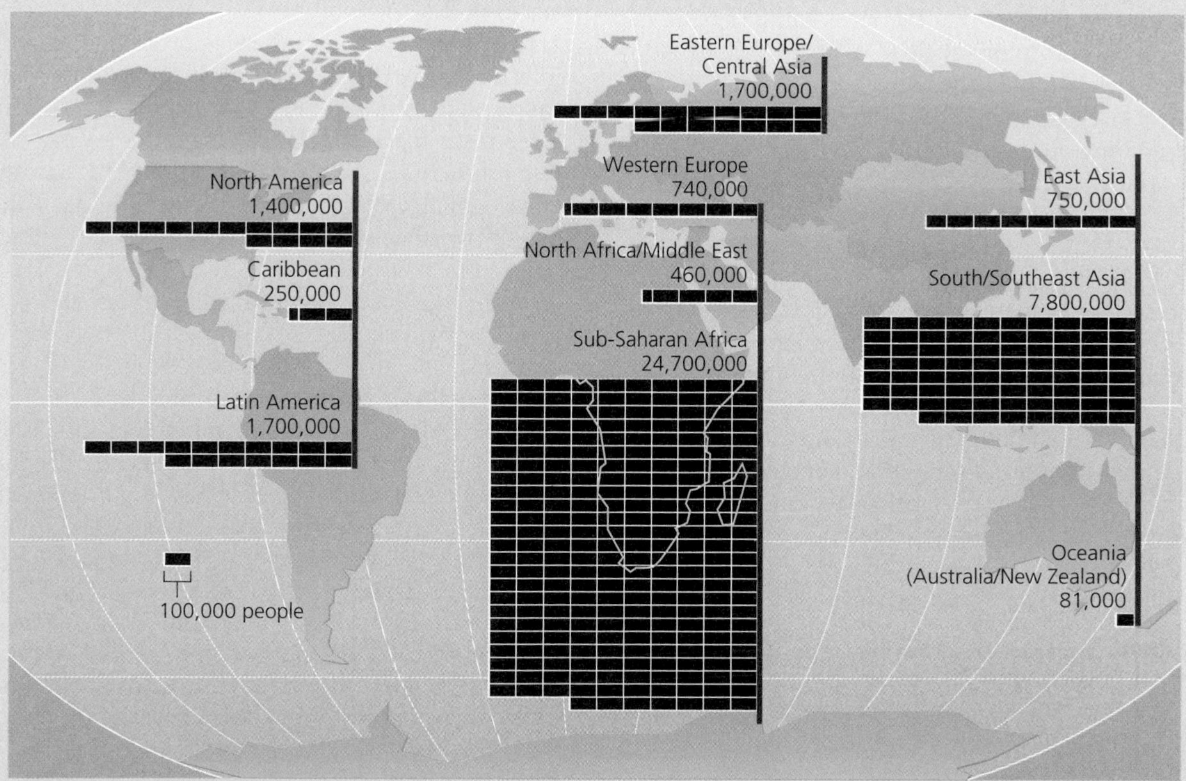

Approximate number of people living with HIV/AIDS in 2006. SOURCE: Joint United Nations Programme on HIV/AIDS (UNAIDS). 2006. *AIDS Epidemic Update: December 2006*. Geneva: UNAIDS.

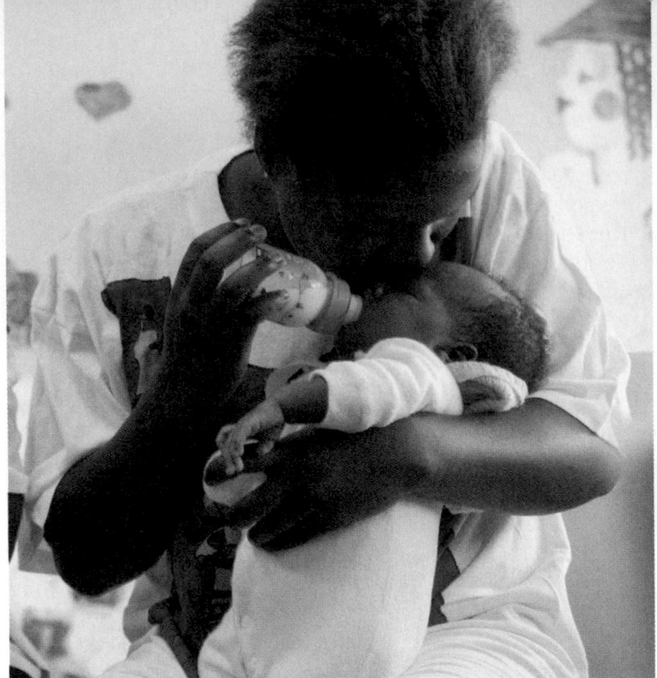

Early diagnosis and treatment of HIV infection are important for everyone, but particularly so for pregnant women. Currently available treatments can significantly increase the chance that this baby, born to an HIV-infected mother, will be free of the virus.

the risk of HIV transmission in women with high blood levels of HIV.

OTHER TYPES OF CONTACT Trace amounts of HIV have been found in the saliva and tears of some infected people. Researchers believe, however, that these fluids do not carry enough of the virus to infect another person. HIV has been found in urine and feces, and contact with the urine or feces of an infected person may carry some risk. An infected person's sweat is not believed to carry any risk. There is no evidence that the virus can be spread by insects such as mosquitoes or fleas.

HIV is not transmitted through casual contact. A person is not at risk of getting HIV infection by being in the same classroom, dining room, or even household with someone who is infected.

Symptoms Within a few days or weeks of infection with HIV, about half of victims develop symptoms of *primary HIV infection*. These can include fever, fatigue, rashes, headache, swollen lymph nodes, body aches, night sweats, sore throat, nausea, and diarrhea. Because the symptoms of primary HIV infection are similar to those of many common viral illnesses, the condition often goes undiagnosed.

Because the immune system is weakened, people with HIV infection are highly susceptible to other infections, both common and uncommon. The infection most often seen among people with HIV is *Pneumocystis carinii* pneumonia, a protozoal infection. Kaposi's sarcoma, a once-rare form of cancer, is common in HIV-infected men. Women with HIV infection often have frequent and difficult-to-treat vaginal yeast infections. Cases of tuberculosis are also increasingly being reported in people with HIV.

Diagnosis Early diagnosis of HIV infection is important to minimize the effects of the disease—medically, psychologically, and socially. The most commonly used screening blood test for HIV is the HIV antibody test. This procedure consists of an initial screening called an ELISA test and a more specific confirmation test called the Western blot. These tests determine whether a person has antibodies to HIV circulating in the bloodstream, a sign that the virus is present in the body (see the box "Getting an HIV Test").

If a person is diagnosed as **HIV-positive,** the next step is to determine the current severity of the disease in order to plan appropriate treatment. The status of the immune system can be gauged by taking CD4 T-cell measurements every few months. The infection itself can be monitored by tracking the amount of virus in the body (the viral load) through a test that measures the amount of HIV RNA in a blood sample. This HIV RNA assay can also be used to detect HIV infection in its very earliest stages, before antibodies appear.

The CDC's criteria for a diagnosis of AIDS reflect the stage of HIV infection at which a person's immune system becomes dangerously compromised. A diagnosis of AIDS is made if a person is HIV-positive and either has developed an infection or condition defined as an AIDS indicator or has a severely damaged immune system, as measured by CD4 T-cell counts.

Treatment Although there is no known cure for HIV infection or AIDS, recently developed drugs can significantly alter the course of the disease and extend life. The three main types of antiviral drugs are reverse transcriptase inhibitors, protease inhibitors, and fusion inhibitors, all of which block HIV from replicating itself. Research has shown that using combinations of antiviral drugs—referred to as drug cocktails—can sometimes reduce HIV levels in the blood to undetectable levels. However, people on antiviral drugs can still pass the infection on, and concerns are growing that even these very aggressive treatments are starting to fail and that drug-resistant strains of HIV are developing rapidly. In addition to antiviral drugs, most patients with low CD4 T-cell counts take a variety of antibiotics to help prevent opportunistic infections such as pneumonia and tuberculosis.

The cost of treatment for HIV infection—$14,000–$35,000 per year in the United States—is much too high for the vast majority of people around the world who are infected with HIV. For those who can afford the drugs, toxicity is a key concern. Long-term use of antivirals can cause a number of serious side effects, and the treatment

TERMS

HIV-positive A diagnosis resulting from the presence of HIV antibodies in the bloodstream; also referred to as *seropositive*.

Getting an HIV Test

The CDC recommends that everyone age 13–64 be tested for HIV at least once as part of routine medical care. You should strongly consider being tested if any of the following apply to you or to any past or current sexual partner: You have had unprotected sex (vaginal, anal, or oral) with more than one partner or with a partner who was not in a mutually monogamous relationship with you; you have used or shared needles, syringes, or other paraphernalia for injecting drugs (including steroids); you received a transfusion of blood or blood products between 1978 and 1985; you have been diagnosed with an STD; or you are pregnant.

If you decide to get an HIV test, you can either visit a physician or health clinic or take a home test.

Physician or Clinic Testing

Your physician, student health clinic, Planned Parenthood, public health department, or local AIDS association can arrange your HIV test. It usually costs $50–$100, but public clinics often charge little or nothing. The standard test involves drawing a sample of blood that is sent to a laboratory to check for the presence of antibodies; if the first stage of testing is positive, a confirmatory test is done. This standard test takes 1–2 weeks, and you'll be asked to phone or come in personally to obtain your results, which should also include appropriate counseling.

Alternative tests are available at some clinics. The Orasure test uses oral fluid, which is collected by placing a treated cotton pad in the mouth; urine tests are also available. Oral fluid and urine tests may be helpful for people who avoid blood tests due to fear of needles. If you suspect that you have been recently exposed to HIV and might be in a very early stage of infection, see your physician and ask about an HIV RNA test.

New rapid tests are also available at some locations. These tests involve the use of blood or oral fluid and can provide results in as little as 20 minutes. If a rapid test is positive for HIV infection, a confirmatory test will be performed.

Before you get a test, be sure you understand what will be done with the results. Results from confidential tests may still become part of your medical record and/or reported to state and federal public health agencies. If you decide you want to be tested anonymously, check with your physician or counselor about how to obtain an anonymous test or use a home test.

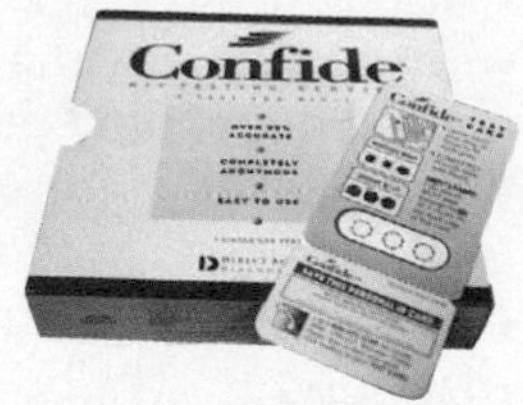

Home Testing

Home test kits for HIV are available and cost about $40. (Take care to avoid testing kits that are not FDA-approved; many such unapproved kits are being sold over the Internet.) To use a home test, you prick a finger with a supplied lancet, blot a few drops of blood onto blotting paper, and mail it to the company's laboratory. In about a week, you call a toll-free number to find out your results. Anyone testing positive is routed to a trained counselor, who can provide emotional and medical support. The results of home test kits are completely anonymous.

Understanding the Results

A negative test result means that no antibodies were found in your sample. However, it usually takes at least a month (and possibly as long as 6 months in some people) after exposure to HIV for antibodies to appear, a process called seroconversion. Therefore, an infected person may get a false-negative result. If you think you've been exposed to HIV, get a test immediately; if it's negative but your risk of infection is high, ask about obtaining an HIV RNA assay, which allows very early diagnosis.

A positive result means that you are infected. It is important to seek medical care and counseling immediately. Rapid progress is being made in treating HIV, and treatments are potentially much more successful when begun early.

For more information on testing, visit the National HIV Testing Resources Web site (http://www.hivtest.org).

guidelines issued by the National Institutes of Health in 2001 recommend that asymptomatic patients hold off on treatment until they are at a more advanced stage of the disease. However, immediate treatment is still recommended for anyone who is experiencing symptoms and is considered for anyone who has very recent primary HIV infection. For people with primary infection, treatment may reduce the initial spike in viral level (see Figure 14.1) and slow the progress of the disease; it may also reduce the risk of transmitting the virus to others.

In some cases, people may be treated within hours after exposure in an attempt to prevent infection. The CDC has long recommended post-exposure prophylaxis (PEP) for health care workers exposed to HIV on the job through needle sticks and other mishaps; PEP is also often recommended for victims of sexual assault. In 2005, the CDC for the first time recommended PEP for people who are at risk for HIV infection from recent nonoccupational exposure—for example, after unprotected sex or contact with a contaminated needle. PEP consists of 28 days of antiviral drugs, which should begin as soon as possible after exposure but always within 72 hours.

Even for people who have access to the drugs and can tolerate the side effects, treatment is difficult and may involve taking dozens of pills every day at precise times. Medications that combine drugs are under development to simplify treatment; one such drug, Atripla, approved by the FDA in 2006, combines three medicines in one pill. No medication eliminates the virus from the body, however, and it is unclear to what extent a damaged immune system can rebound with treatment.

The best hope for preventing the spread of HIV worldwide rests with the development of a safe, effective, and inexpensive vaccine. Many different approaches to the development of an AIDS vaccine are currently under investigation, and human trials have begun on several vaccines. However, no vaccine is likely to be ready for widespread use within the next 5 years. Researchers are making more rapid progress in producing a microbicide that could be used to prevent HIV and other STDs. A microbicide in the form of a cream, gel, sponge, or suppository could function as a kind of chemical condom.

Prevention Although AIDS is currently incurable, it is preventable. You can protect yourself by avoiding behaviors that may bring you into contact with HIV. This means making careful choices about sexual activity and not sharing needles if you inject drugs (Figure 14.3).

Surveys of college students indicate that the majority are not engaging in safer sex even though most know that condom use can protect against HIV infection. Many students also report a willingness to lie about past sexual activity to obtain sex. Many students believe their risk of contracting HIV depends on "who they are" rather than on their sexual behavior. These attitudes and behaviors place college students at continued high risk for contracting HIV.

High Risk

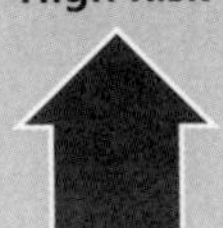

Unprotected anal sex is the riskiest sexual behavior, especially for the receptive partner.

Unprotected vaginal intercourse is the next riskiest, especially for women, who are much more likely to be infected by an infected male partner than vice versa.

Oral sex is probably considerably less risky than anal and vaginal intercourse but can still result in HIV transmission.

Sharing of sex toys can be risky because they can carry blood, semen, or vaginal fluid.

Use of a condom reduces risk considerably but not completely for any type of intercourse. Anal sex with a condom is riskier than vaginal sex with a condom; oral sex with a condom is less risky, especially if the man does not ejaculate.

Hand-genital contact and deep kissing are less risky but could still theoretically transmit HIV; the presence of cuts or sores increases risk.

Sex with only one uninfected and totally faithful partner is without risk but effective only if both partners are uninfected and completely monogamous.

Activities that don't involve the exchange of body fluids carry no risk: hugging, massage, closed-mouth kissing, masturbation, phone sex, and fantasy.

Abstinence is completely without risk. For many people, it can be an effective and reasonable method of avoiding HIV infection and other STDs during certain periods of life.

No Risk

FIGURE 14.3 What's risky and what's not: The approximate relative risk of HIV transmission of various sexual activities. Safer sex strategies that reduce the risk of HIV infection will also help protect you against other STDs. The main point to remember is that any activity that involves contact with blood, semen, or vaginal fluid can transmit HIV.

Chlamydia

Chlamydia trachomatis causes **chlamydia,** the most prevalent bacterial STD in the United States, with about 3 million new cases occurring every year. An estimated 5–15% of all sexually active young American women are infected with chlamydia; rates among men are similar. The highest rates of infection occur in single people between ages 15 and 24; African American men and women have higher rates of infection than other groups for both chlamydia and gonorrhea.

Both men and women are susceptible to chlamydia, but women bear the greater burden because of possible complications from and consequences of the disease. If left untreated, chlamydia can lead to pelvic inflammatory disease (PID), a serious infection that can cause infertility.

Chlamydia can also lead to infertility in men, although not as often as in women. In men under age 35, chlamydia is the most common cause of epididymitis—inflammation of the sperm-carrying ducts (refer to Figures 14.4 and 14.5 for basic information about human sexual anatomy). Up to half of all cases of urethritis—inflammation of the urethra—in men are caused by chlamydia.

Symptoms Most people experience few or no symptoms from chlamydia infection, increasing the likelihood that they will inadvertently spread the infection to their partners. In men, symptoms can include painful urination, a slight watery discharge from the penis, and sometimes pain around the testicles. Women may notice increased vaginal discharge, burning with urination, pain or bleeding with intercourse, and lower-abdominal pain.

MOTIVATION BOOSTER

Plan ahead and practice what you'll say. Do you feel nervous or intimidated about having a conversation about safer sex with a potential partner? As for other challenging situations relating to behavior change, practice and planning can boost your confidence and make you more successful in your efforts to stick with your goals. Practice in a mirror or with a friend until you feel comfortable. Getting the conversation started may be the most difficult part; try something like "It seems as if we're getting to a point in our relationship where we should talk about STDs and safer sex" or "I think always using condoms is part of being a responsible person. What do you think?"

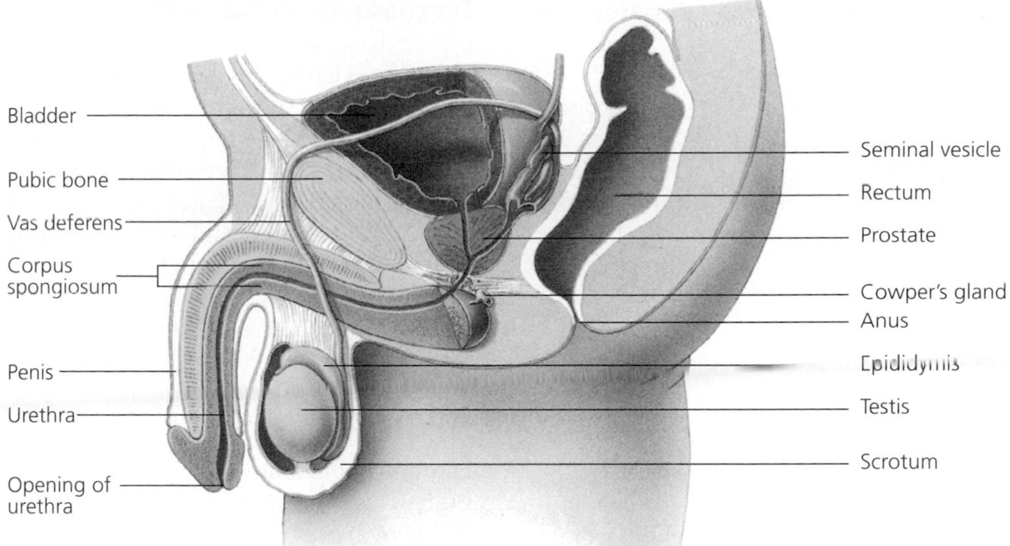

FIGURE 14.4 Male sexual anatomy.

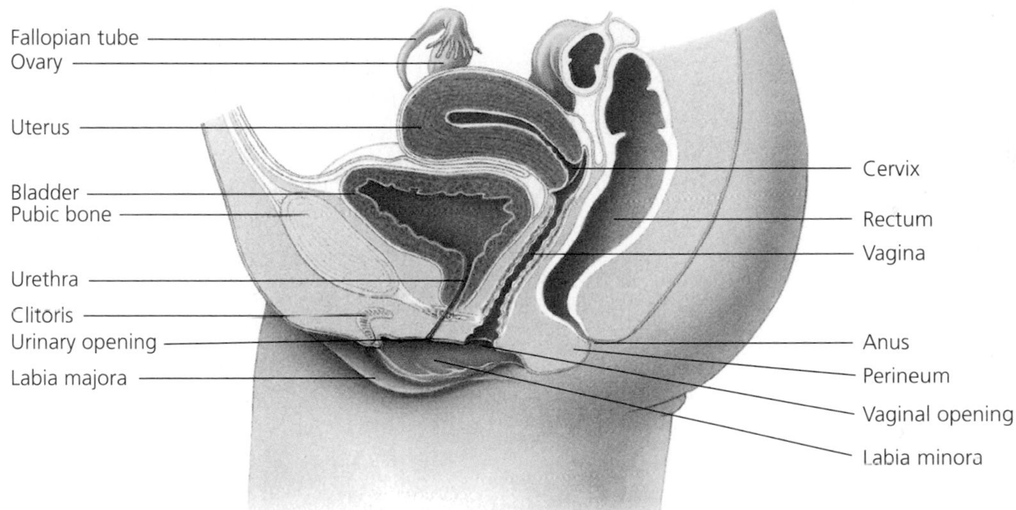

FIGURE 14.5 Female sexual anatomy.

Because infection rates are high and most women are asymptomatic, annual screening is recommended for sexually active young women.

Diagnosis and Treatment Chlamydia is diagnosed through a urine test or laboratory examination of fluid from the urethra or cervix. Once chlamydia has been diagnosed, the infected person and his or her partner(s) are given antibiotics, usually doxycycline, erythromycin, or a newer drug, azithromycin, which cures chlamydia in a single dose.

Gonorrhea

In the United States, an estimated 700,000 new cases of **gonorrhea** occur every year. The highest incidence is among 15- to 24-year-olds. Like chlamydia, untreated gonorrhea can cause PID in women and urethritis and epididymitis in men. It can also cause arthritis and rashes, and it occasionally involves internal organs. An infant passing through the birth canal of an infected mother may contract *gonococcal conjunctivitis,* an infection in the eyes that can cause blindness if not treated. Gonorrhea is caused by the bacterium *Neisseria gonorrhoeae,* which

TERMS

chlamydia An STD transmitted by the bacterium *Chlamydia trachomatis.*

gonorrhea An STD transmitted by the bacterium *Neisseria gonorrhoeae.*

flourishes in mucous membranes; it cannot thrive outside the human body.

Symptoms In males, the incubation period for gonorrhea is brief, generally 2–7 days. The first symptoms are due to urethritis, which causes urinary discomfort and a thick, yellowish-white or yellowish-green discharge from the penis. The lips of the urethral opening may become inflamed and swollen. In some cases, the lymph glands in the groin become enlarged and swollen. Many males have very minor symptoms or none at all.

Most females with gonorrhea are asymptomatic. Those who have symptoms often experience urinary pain, increased vaginal discharge, and severe menstrual cramps. Women may also develop painful abscesses in the Bartholin's glands, a pair of glands located on either side of the opening of the vagina.

Gonorrhea can also infect the throat or rectum of people who engage in oral or anal sex. Gonorrhea symptoms in the throat may be a sore throat or pus on the tonsils, and those in the rectum may be pus or blood in the feces or rectal pain and itching.

Diagnosis and Treatment Several tests—gram stain, detection of bacterial genes or DNA, or culture—may be performed. Samples of urine or cervical, urethral, throat, or rectal fluids may be collected.

A variety of new and relatively expensive antibiotics are usually effective in curing gonorrhea. Older, less expensive antibiotics such as penicillin and tetracycline are not currently recommended for treating gonorrhea because of widespread and increasing drug resistance.

Pelvic Inflammatory Disease

A major complication in 10–40% of women who have been infected with either chlamydia or gonorrhea and have not received treatment is **pelvic inflammatory disease (PID).** PID occurs when the initial infection travels upward, often along with other bacteria, beyond the cervix into the uterus, oviducts, ovaries, and pelvic cavity. PID is often serious enough to require hospitalization and sometimes surgery. Even if the disease is treated successfully, about 25% of affected women will have long-term problems such as a continuing susceptibility to infection, ectopic pregnancy, infertility, and chronic pelvic pain. PID is the leading cause of infertility in young women.

Symptoms Symptoms of PID vary greatly. Some women, especially those with PID from chlamydia, may be asymptomatic; others may feel very ill with abdominal pain, fever, chills, nausea, and vomiting. Early symptoms are essentially the same as those described for chlamydia and gonorrhea. Symptoms often begin or worsen during or soon after a woman's menstrual period. Many women have abnormal vaginal bleeding—either bleeding between periods or heavy and painful menstrual bleeding.

Diagnosis and Treatment Diagnosis of PID is made on the basis of symptoms, physical examination, ultrasound, and laboratory tests. **Laparoscopy** may be used to confirm the diagnosis and obtain material for cultures.

Treatment should begin as quickly as possible to minimize damage to the reproductive organs. Antibiotics are usually started immediately; in severe cases, the woman may be hospitalized and antibiotics given intravenously. It is especially important that an infected woman's partners be treated. As many as 60% of the male contacts of women with PID are infected but asymptomatic.

Human Papillomavirus Infection

Human papillomavirus (HPV) infection causes several human diseases, including common warts, **genital warts,** and genital cancers. HPV also causes virtually all cervical cancer, as well as penile cancer and some forms of anal cancer. Genital HPV is usually spread through sexual activity. Research also links some oral cancers with HPV, leading to greater concern about oral sex among HPV-infected persons.

HPV is one of the most common STDs in the United States; more than 80% of sexually active people will have been infected with HPV by age 50. HPV is especially common in young people, with some of the highest infection rates among college students.

In 2006, the FDA approved a vaccine for HPV (Gardasil), and other vaccines are in development. Gardasil protects against 4 types of HPV virus that account for 90% of genital warts and 70% of cervical cancers. Vaccination is recommended for girls and women age 9–26.

Symptoms HPV-infected tissue often appears normal; it may also look like anything from a small bump on the skin to a large warty growth. Untreated warts can grow together to form a cauliflower-like mass. In males, they appear on the penis and often involve the urethra, appearing first at the opening and then spreading inside. The growths may cause irritation and bleeding, leading to painful urination and a urethral discharge. Warts may also appear around the anus or within the rectum.

In women, warts may appear on the labia or vulva and may spread to the *perineum,* the area between the vagina and the anus. If warts occur only on the cervix, the woman will generally have no symptoms or awareness that she has HPV.

The incubation period ranges from 1 month to 2 years from the time of contact. People can be infected with the virus and be capable of transmitting it to their sex partners without having any symptoms at all. The vast majority of people with HPV infection have no visible warts or symptoms of any kind.

Diagnosis and Treatment Genital warts are usually diagnosed based on the appearance of the lesions. Frequently,

TAKE CHARGE

Using Male Condoms

Although they're not 100% effective as a contraceptive or as protection from STDs—only abstinence is—condoms improve your chances on both counts. Use them properly:

- ***Buy latex condoms.*** If you're allergic to latex, use a polyurethane condom or wear a lambskin condom under a latex one.
- ***Buy and use condoms while they are fresh.*** Packages have an expiration date or a manufacturing date. Don't use condoms beyond the expiration date or more than 5 years after the manufacturing date (2 years if it contains spermicide).
- ***Try different styles and sizes.*** Male condoms come in a variety of textures, colors, shapes, lubricants, and sizes. Shop around until you find a brand that's right for you. Condom widths and lengths vary by about 10–20%. A condom that is too tight may be uncomfortable and more likely to break; one that is too loose may slip off.
- ***Don't remove the condom from an individual, sealed wrapper until you're ready to use it.*** Open the packet carefully. Don't use a condom if it's gummy, dried out, or discolored.
- ***Store condoms correctly.*** Don't leave condoms in extreme heat or cold, and don't carry them in a pocket or wallet.
- ***Use only water-based lubricants such as K-Y Jelly.*** Never use oil-based lubricants like Vaseline or hand lotion; they may cause the condom to break. Avoid oil-based vaginal products.

- ***Avoid condoms with lubricants containing the spermicide nonoxynol-9 (N-9).*** N-9 has been found to cause tissue irritation that increases the risk of STD transmission.
- ***Use condoms correctly.*** Roll the condom down over the penis as soon as it's erect. Squeeze the air out of the reservoir tip or the top quarter-inch of the condom as you unroll it to leave room for semen. Make sure there are no air bubbles. Remove it after ejaculation but before the penis becomes flaccid. Use a new condom every time you have intercourse.
- ***Practice.*** Condoms aren't hard to use, but practice helps. Take one out of the wrapper; examine it and stretch it to see how strong it is. Practice by yourself and with your partner.

Open the discussion of using condoms with your partner *before* you have sex. Despite the embarrassment most people feel at bringing up the subject at all, a study showed that even if you have to *insist* on using condoms, your partner will like you more, respect you more, be more likely to want a long-term relationship with you, and feel that the sexual encounter was more intimate and meaningful.

HPV infection of the cervix is detected on routine Pap tests. Because of the relationship between HPV and cervical cancer, women who have had genital warts should have Pap tests at least every 12 months.

Treatment of genital warts focuses on reducing the number and size of warts. The currently available treatments do not eradicate HPV infection. Warts may be removed by cryosurgery (freezing), electrocautery (burning), or laser surgery. Direct applications of podophyllin or other cytotoxic acids may be used, and there are treatments that patients can use at home.

Even after treatment and the disappearance of visible warts, the individual may continue to carry HPV in healthy-looking tissue and can probably still infect others. Anyone who has ever had HPV should inform all partners. Condoms should be used, even though they do not provide total protection (see the box " Using Male Condoms").

Genital Herpes

Genital herpes affects about 45 million people in the United States. Two herpes simplex viruses are of greatest concern: HSV-1 and HSV-2. The HSV-1 virus usually causes oral-labial herpes (cold sores); HSV-2 typically causes genital herpes. Both viruses, however, can cause either oral-labial or genital lesions (blisterlike sores). Many people wrongly assume that they are unlikely to pick up an STD if they limit their sexual activity to oral sex, but this is not true, particularly in the case of genital herpes. HSV can also cause rectal lesions, usually transmitted through anal sex. Infection with HSV is generally lifelong; after infection, the virus lies dormant in nerve cells and can reactivate at any time.

HSV-1 infection is so common that 50–80% of adults have antibodies to HSV-1 (indicating previous exposure to the virus). Most people are exposed to HSV-1 during childhood. HSV-2 infection usually occurs during adolescence and early adulthood, most commonly between ages 18 and 25. About 22% of adults have antibodies to HSV-2, but most do not know they are infected and contagious.

HSV-2 is almost always sexually transmitted. The infection spreads readily whether people have active sores or are completely asymptomatic. If you have ever had an outbreak of genital herpes (that is, the appearance of genital

TERMS

pelvic inflammatory disease (PID) An infection that progresses from the vagina and cervix to the uterus, oviducts, and pelvic cavity.

laparoscopy A method of examining the internal organs by inserting a tube containing a small light through an abdominal incision.

human papillomavirus (HPV) The virus that causes human warts, including genital warts.

genital warts A sexually transmitted viral infection characterized by growths on the genitals, caused by HPV.

genital herpes A sexually transmitted infection caused by the herpes simplex virus.

Stress and Genital Herpes

Having genital herpes is stressful for most people—but can being under stress *cause* an outbreak in a person with herpes infection? A study of women with genital herpes found that persistent stressors (those lasting more than a week) and persistent high levels of anxiety were associated with increased genital herpes outbreaks. Short-term stress, mood changes, and brief negative life experiences did not influence the rate of herpes outbreaks.

Experts suspect that stress has a negative impact on the immune system. Studies show that cell-mediated immune function and antibody levels may drop in response to psychological stress. Perhaps herpesviruses that are usually dormant in nervous system tissue become activated when immune function declines due to stress.

The next logical step is to investigate whether stress-reduction techniques such as meditation or exercise result in reduced rates of herpes outbreaks. Until such research becomes available, it makes sense for people who suffer recurrent genital herpes outbreaks to do what they can to reduce stress, especially long-term stress and anxiety.

If you have herpes, a support group may help reduce your stress and improve your ability to cope with the disease. If you have more than six outbreaks a year, consider taking an antiviral medication. Keep in mind that genital herpes outbreaks naturally tend to become less and less frequent over time. Knowing that your outbreaks are likely to diminish can in itself help reduce your feelings of stress.

sores), you should consider yourself always contagious and inform your partners. Avoid intimate contact when any sores are present, and use condoms during all sexual contact, including times when you have no symptoms.

Newborns can occasionally be infected with HSV, usually during passage through the birth canal of an infected mother. Without treatment, 65% of newborns with HSV will die, and most who survive will have some degree of brain damage. Pregnant women who have ever been exposed to genital herpes should inform their physician so that appropriate precautions can be taken to protect the baby from infection.

Symptoms Most people who are infected with HSV have no symptoms. Those who develop symptoms often first notice them within 2–20 days of having sex with an infected partner. The first episode of genital herpes frequently causes flulike symptoms in addition to genital lesions. The lesions usually heal within 3 weeks, but the virus remains alive in an inactive state within nerve cells. A new outbreak of herpes can occur at any time. On average, newly diagnosed people will experience five to eight outbreaks a year, with a decrease in the frequency of outbreaks over time. Outbreaks can be triggered by stress, illness, fatigue, sun exposure, sexual intercourse, and menstruation (see the box "Stress and Genital Herpes").

Diagnosis and Treatment Genital herpes can be diagnosed on the basis of symptoms; a sample of fluid from the lesions may also be sent to a laboratory for evaluation. A new blood test that can determine if a person is infected with HSV-1 or HSV-2 is now available and may alert many asymptomatic people to the fact that they are infected.

There is no cure for herpes. Once infected, a person carries the virus for life. Antiviral drugs such as acyclovir can be taken at the beginning of an outbreak to shorten the severity and duration of symptoms. Support groups are available to help people learn to cope with herpes.

Hepatitis B

Hepatitis (inflammation of the liver) can cause serious and sometimes permanent damage to the liver, which can result in death in severe cases. One of the many types of hepatitis is caused by hepatitis B virus (HBV). Hepatitis B virus is somewhat similar to HIV, but it is much more contagious than HIV, and it can also be spread through nonsexual close contact.

HBV is found in all body fluids, including blood and blood products, semen, saliva, urine, and vaginal secretions. It is easily transmitted through any sexual activity that involves the exchange of body fluids, the use of contaminated needles, and any blood-to-blood contact, including the use of contaminated razor blades, toothbrushes, and eating utensils. The primary risk factors for acquiring hepatitis B are sexual exposure and injection drug use; having multiple partners greatly increases risk. (Information about hepatitis A and hepatitis C is available in Common Questions Answered on the Online Learning Center.)

Symptoms Many people infected with HBV never develop symptoms; they have what is known as a silent infection. The normal incubation period is about 30–180 days. Mild cases of hepatitis cause flulike symptoms; as the illness progresses, there may be nausea, vomiting, dark-colored urine, abdominal pain, and jaundice.

People with hepatitis B sometimes recover completely, but they can also become chronic carriers of the virus, capable of infecting others for the rest of their lives. Some chronic carriers remain asymptomatic; others develop chronic liver disease. Chronic hepatitis can cause cirrhosis, liver failure, and a deadly form of liver cancer. Hepatitis kills some 5000 Americans each year; worldwide, the annual death toll exceeds 600,000.

Diagnosis and Treatment Blood tests can be used to diagnose hepatitis through analysis of liver function and detection of the specific organism causing the infection. There is no cure for HBV and no specific treatment for acute infections; antiviral drugs may be used for chronic HBV infection. For people exposed to HBV, treatment with hepatitis B immunoglobulin can provide protection against the virus.

The vaccine for hepatitis B is safe and effective. Immunization is recommended for everyone under age 19 and for all adults at increased risk, including people who have more than one sex partner in 6 months, men who have sex with other men, those who inject illegal drugs, and health care workers who are exposed to blood and body fluids.

Syphilis

Syphilis, a disease that once caused death and disability for millions, can now be effectively treated with antibiotics. About 7,000–10,000 new cases of early syphilis are reported in the United States each year, and about 70,000 people are diagnosed at all stages of the disease.

Syphilis is caused by a corkscrew-shaped bacterium called *Treponema pallidum.* It requires warmth and moisture to survive and dies very quickly outside the human body. The bacterium passes through any break or opening in the skin or mucous membranes and can be transmitted by kissing, vaginal or anal intercourse, or oral genital contact.

Symptoms Syphilis progresses through several stages. *Primary syphilis* is characterized by an ulcer called a **chancre** that appears within about 10–90 days after exposure. The chancre is usually found at the site where the organism entered the body, such as the genital area, but it may also appear in other sites such as the mouth, breasts, or fingers. Chancres contain large numbers of bacteria and make the disease highly contagious when present; they are often painless and typically heal on their own within a few weeks. If the disease is not treated during the primary stage, about a third of infected individuals progress to chronic stages of infection.

Secondary syphilis is usually marked by mild, flulike symptoms and a skin rash that appears 3–6 weeks after the chancre. The rash may cover the entire body or only a few areas, but the palms of the hands and soles of the feet are usually involved. Areas of skin affected by the rash are highly contagious but usually heal within several weeks or months. If the disease remains untreated, the symptoms of secondary syphilis may recur over a period of several years; affected individuals may then lapse into an asymptomatic latent stage in which they experience no further consequences of infection. In about a third of cases of untreated secondary syphilis, however, the individual develops *late,* or *tertiary, syphilis.* Late syphilis can damage many organs of the body, possibly causing severe dementia, cardiovascular damage, blindness, and death.

In infected pregnant women, the syphilis bacterium can cross the placenta. If the mother is not treated, the probable result is stillbirth, prematurity, or congenital deformity. In many cases, the infant is born infected (congenital syphilis) and requires treatment.

Diagnosis and Treatment Syphilis is diagnosed by examination of infected tissues and with blood tests. All stages can be treated with antibiotics, but damage from late syphilis can be permanent.

Other STDs

A few other diseases are transmitted sexually and require responsible sexual behavior.

Trichomoniasis, often called *trich,* is a common STD. The single-celled organism that causes trich, *Trichomonas vaginalis,* thrives in warm, moist conditions, making women particularly susceptible to these infections in the vagina. Women who become symptomatic with trich develop a greenish, foul-smelling vaginal discharge and severe itching and pain in the vagina. Prompt treatment with metronidazole (Flagyl) is important because studies suggest that trich may increase the risk of HIV transmission and, in pregnant women, premature delivery.

Bacterial vaginosis (BV) is the most common cause of abnormal vaginal discharge in women of reproductive age. BV occurs when healthy bacteria that normally inhabit the vagina become displaced by unhealthy species. BV is clearly associated with sexual activity and often occurs after a change in partners. Symptoms of BV include vaginal discharge with a fishy odor and sometimes vaginal irritation. BV is treated with topical and oral antibiotics.

Pubic lice (commonly known as *crabs*) and **scabies** are highly contagious parasitic infections. Treatment is generally easy, although lice infestation can require repeated applications of medications.

TERMS

hepatitis Inflammation of the liver, which can be caused by infection, drugs, or toxins; some forms of infectious hepatitis can be transmitted sexually.

syphilis A sexually transmitted bacterial infection caused by the spirochete *Treponema pallidum*.

chancre The sore produced by syphilis in its earliest stage.

trichomoniasis A protozoal infection caused by *Trichomonas vaginalis*, transmitted sexually and externally.

bacterial vaginosis (BV) A condition caused by an overgrowth of certain bacteria inhabiting the vagina.

pubic lice Parasites that infest the hair of the pubic region; commonly called *crabs*.

scabies A contagious skin disease caused by burrowing parasitic mites.

QUESTIONS FOR CRITICAL THINKING AND REFLECTION

Have you ever engaged in sexual activities you regretted later? If so, what were the circumstances, and what influenced you to act the way you did? Were there any negative consequences? What preventive strategies can you use in the future to make sure it doesn't happen again?

WHAT YOU CAN DO ABOUT STDs

You can take responsibility for your health and help reduce the incidence of STDs.

Education

Many schools have STD counseling and education programs. These programs allow students to practice communicating with potential sex partners and negotiating safer sex, to engage in role-playing to build self-confidence, and to learn how to use condoms.

You can find free pamphlets and other literature about STDs at public health departments, health clinics, physicians' offices, student health centers, and Planned Parenthood; easy-to-understand books are available in libraries and bookstores. National hotlines provide free, confidential information and referral services to callers anywhere in the country (see For Further Exploration at the end of the chapter).

Diagnosis and Treatment

Early diagnosis and treatment of STDs can help you avoid complications and can also help prevent the spread of STDs. If you are sexually active, be alert and seek treatment for any sign or symptom of disease, such as a rash, a discharge, sores, or unusual pain. Many STDs are often asymptomatic, however, so a professional examination and testing are recommended following any risky sexual encounter—even in the absence of symptoms.

If you are diagnosed as having an STD, begin treatment as quickly as possible. Inform your partner(s) and avoid any sexual activity until your treatment is complete. Follow instructions for treatment carefully and complete all the medication as prescribed.

Prevention

The only sure way to avoid exposure to STDs is to abstain from sexual activity. If you choose to be sexually active, think about prevention before you have a sexual encounter or find yourself in the "heat of the moment." Plan ahead for safer sex. For tips and strategies, see the box "Protecting Yourself from STDs." Remember that asking questions and being aware of signs and symptoms show that you care about yourself and your partner. Concern about STDs is an essential and mutually beneficial part of a sexual relationship.

TIPS FOR TODAY AND THE FUTURE

Because STDs can have serious, long-term effects, it's important to be vigilant about exposure, treatment, and prevention.

RIGHT NOW YOU CAN

- Make an appointment with your health care provider if you are worried about possible STD infection.
- Resolve to discuss condom use with your partner if you are sexually active and are not already using condoms.

IN THE FUTURE YOU CAN

- Learn how to communicate effectively with a partner who resists safer sex practices or is reluctant to discuss sexual history. Support groups and educational classes can help.
- Make sure all your vaccinations are up to date; ask your doctor if you should be vaccinated against hepatitis B or any other STDs.

SUMMARY

- HIV damages the immune system and causes AIDS. People with AIDS are vulnerable to often-fatal opportunistic infections.
- HIV is carried in blood and blood products, semen, vaginal and cervical secretions, and breast milk; it is transmitted through the exchange of these fluids.
- Drugs have been developed to slow the course of HIV infection and to prevent or treat certain secondary infections, but there is no cure.
- HIV infection can be prevented by making careful choices about sexual activity, not sharing drug needles, and learning how to protect oneself.
- Chlamydia is a bacterial infection that causes epididymitis and urethritis in men and can lead to PID in women.
- Untreated, gonorrhea can cause PID in women and epididymitis in men, leading to infertility. In infants, untreated gonorrhea can cause blindness.
- Pelvic inflammatory disease (PID), a complication of untreated chlamydia or gonorrhea, is an infection of the uterus and oviducts that may extend to the ovaries and pelvic cavity. It can lead to infertility, ectopic pregnancy, and chronic pelvic pain.
- Genital warts, caused by the human papillomavirus (HPV), are associated with cervical cancer. Treatment does not eradicate the virus, but a vaccine is available, recommended for girls and women age 9–26.

TAKE CHARGE

Protecting Yourself from STDs

• ***Abstinence.*** The only truly foolproof way to protect yourself from STDs is abstinence—abstaining from sexual relations with other people. Remember that it is OK to say no to sex.

• ***Monogamy.*** Next to abstinence, the most effective way to protect yourself is monogamy—having sex exclusively with one partner, who engages in sex with no one else but you and who does not have an STD.

• ***Communication.*** If you choose to be sexually active, protect yourself by practicing open and honest communication and insisting on the same from your partner. Be truthful about your past, and ask your partner to do the same. Remember that you are indirectly exposing yourself to all of your partner's prior sexual contacts.

• ***Safer sexual activities.*** Know what sexual activities are risky (see Figure 14.3). Safer alternatives to intercourse include fantasy, hugging, massage, rubbing clothed bodies together, mutual mastrubation, and closed-mouth kissing.

• ***Condoms.*** Always use latex condoms during every act of vaginal intercourse, anal intercourse, and oral sex. Condoms do not provide absolute protection, but they greatly reduce your risk of contracting an STD. Multiple studies show that regular condom use can reduce the risk of several diseases, including HIV, chlamydia, and genital herpes. Make sure you know how to use condoms correctly—see the box "Using Male Condoms."

• ***Activities to avoid.*** Don't drink or use drugs in sexual situations. Mood-altering drugs can affect your judgment and make you more likely to engage in risky behaviors. Limit the number of sexual partners; having multiple partners is associated with increased risk of STDs. Avoid sexual contact with partners who have an STD or have had unprotected sex in the past. Avoid sexual contact that could cause tears or cuts in the skin or tissue. Don't inject drugs; don't share needles, syringes, or anything that might have blood on it. Decontaminate needles and syringes with household bleach and water. If you are at risk for HIV infection, don't donate blood, sperm, or organs.

• ***Other preventive measures.*** Get tested for HIV during your next routine medical examination. Have periodic screenings for STDs if you are at risk. Make sure all your vaccinations are up to date. Girls and women age 9–26 should be vaccinated against HPV, unless there are medical reasons to avoid the vaccination. Ask your physician if it is appropriate for you to be vaccinated against hepatitis B.

• Genital herpes is a common incurable viral infection characterized by outbreaks of lesions and periods of latency.

• Hepatitis B is a viral infection of the liver transmitted through sexual and nonsexual contact. Some people become chronic carriers of the virus and may develop serious, potentially fatal, complications.

• Syphilis is a highly contagious bacterial infection that can be treated with antibiotics. If left untreated, it can lead to deterioration of the central nervous system and death.

• Other common STDs include trichomoniasis, bacterial vaginosis, and pubic lice and scabies.

• Successful diagnosis and treatment of STDs involves being alert for symptoms, getting tested, informing partners, and following treatment instructions.

• All STDs are preventable; the key is practicing responsible sexual behaviors.

FOR FURTHER EXPLORATION

BOOKS

Engel, J. 2007. *The Epidemic: A Global History of AIDS.* New York: Collins. *A historical, social, and cultural perspective on the AIDS epidemic, from its beginning in 1981 to the present day, from a medical historian.*

Hyde, J. S., and J. D. DeLamater. 2006. *Understanding Human Sexuality,* 9th ed. New York: McGraw-Hill. *A comprehensive, multidisciplinary introduction to human sexuality; includes material on STDs.*

Klausner, J. D., and E. W. Hook. 2007. *Current Diagnosis and Treatment of Sexually Transmitted Diseases.* New York: McGraw-Hill. *Written for the clinician; provides an easy-to-use reference of the latest diagnostic and treatment information available on STDs.*

Marr, L. 2007. *Sexually Transmitted Diseases: A Physician Tells You What You Need to Know.* Baltimore, Md.: Johns Hopkins University Press. *Practical, up-to-date information on the diagnosis, treatment, and prevention of sexually transmitted diseases of all types.*

McIlvenna, T. 2005. *The Complete Guide to Safer Sex.* Fort Lee, N.J.: Barricade Books. *Provides practical advice for STD prevention.*

Moore, E. A. 2004. *Encyclopedia of Sexually Transmitted Diseases.* Jefferson, N.C.: McFarland. *Includes a variety of information on STDs in an easy-to-use format.*

ORGANIZATIONS, HOTLINES, AND WEB SITES

American College Health Association. Offers free brochures on STDs, alcohol use, acquaintance rape, and other health issues.
http://www.acha.org

American Social Health Association (ASHA). Provides written information and referrals on STDs; sponsors support groups for people with herpes and HPV.
800-227-8922
http://www.ashastd.org

The Body: The Complete HIV/AIDS Resource. Provides information about prevention, testing, and treatment, and includes an online risk assessment.
http://www.thebody.com

Q Why do young people, including college students, have high rates of STDs?

A Half of young Americans will have an STD by age 25. Contributing factors may include the following:

- ***College students underestimate their risk of STDs and HIV.*** Although students may know about STDs, they often feel the risks do not apply to them. One study of students with a history of STDs showed that more than half had unprotected sex while they were infected, and 25% of them continued to have sex without ever informing their partner(s).
- ***Risky sexual behavior is common.*** One study of college students found that fewer than half used condoms consistently and one-third had had 10 or more sex partners. Another study found that 19% of male students and 33% of female students had consented to sexual intercourse simply because they felt awkward refusing. Nearly half of young adults are sexually active by age 18 (more than 95% by age 25), but they are not yet in long-term monogamous relationships; they are more likely to have more than one partner over time and to have a partner with an STD. Low self-esteem and emotional distress are linked to risky sexual behaviors. Among young women, having an older sex partner, lacking control in a romantic relationship, and fearing to discuss condom use increase the risk of STDs.
- ***Alcohol and drug use plays an important role.*** Between one-third and one-half of college students report participating in sexual activity as a direct result of being intoxicated. Students who binge-drink are more likely to have multiple partners, use condoms inconsistently, and delay seeking treatment for STDs than students who drink little or no alcohol. Sexual assaults occur more frequently when either the perpetrator or the victim has been drinking.
- ***Young women are biologically more vulnerable to STDs than older women.*** The less-mature cervix is more easily infected. As a woman ages, the type of cells at the opening of the cervix gradually changes so that the tissue becomes tougher and more resistant to infection. If an 18-year-old woman and a 30-year-old woman are exposed to the same pathogen, the younger woman is far more likely to develop a serious STD.

Q Does the success of the new AIDS drugs mean that I don't need to worry about HIV infection anymore?

A No. The new combination drug therapy has had dramatic effects for some people infected with HIV. In the United States, the number of HIV-infected people who progress to AIDS each year is declining, as is the death rate from AIDS. But the new drugs are expensive, can have serious side effects, and are not effective for everyone. Scientists do not yet know how long the drugs will keep HIV at bay, and no treatment has yet been shown to permanently eradicate HIV from the body. AIDS is still an incurable, fatal disease, and everyone needs to take preventive measures.

Q Which contraceptive methods protect best against STDs?

A Latex male condoms are the best known protection against HIV and other STDs. Condoms are not foolproof, however, and they do not protect against the transmission of diseases from sores that they do not cover.

You can increase the effectiveness of condoms by using them properly. Breakage is most often caused by inadequate lubrication, use of an improper (oil-based) lubricant, and failure to smooth out air bubbles, which may pop and break the condom during sexual activity. Condoms slipping off during withdrawal is another common cause of failure. Refer to the box on p. 407 for more information on proper condom use.

CDC National Prevention Information Network. Provides extensive information and links on AIDS and other STDs.
800-458-5231
http://www.cdcnpin.org

CDC National STD and AIDS Hotlines. Callers can obtain information, counseling, and referrals for testing and treatment. The hotlines offer information on more than 20 STDs and include Spanish and TTY service.
800-342-AIDS or 800-227-8922
800-344-SIDA (Spanish); 800-243-7889 (TTY, deaf access)

HIV InSite: Gateway to AIDS Knowledge. Provides information about prevention, education, treatment, statistics, clinical trials, and new developments.
http://hivinsite.ucsf.edu

Joint United Nations Programme on HIV/AIDS (UNAIDS). Provides statistics and information on the international HIV/AIDS situation.
http://www.unaids.org

MedlinePlus: Sexually Transmitted Diseases. Maintained by the CDC; a clearinghouse of links and information on STDs.
http://www.nlm.nih.gov/medlineplus/sexuallytransmitteddiseases.html

Planned Parenthood Federation of America. Provides information on STDs, family planning, and contraception.
800-230-PLAN
http://www.plannedparenthood.org

Smarter Sex. Designed for college students; provides tips and information on safer sex practices, relationships, STDs, and more.
http://www.smartersex.org

SELECTED BIBLIOGRAPHY

Aspy, C. B., et al. 2007. Parental communication and youth sexual behavior. *Journal of Adolescence* 30(3): 449–466.

Some other contraceptive methods may provide some protection against certain STDs. The diaphragm and cervical cap cover the cervix and may offer some protection against diseases that involve the infection of cervical cells. Combining these barrier methods with a condom can provide even greater protection.

Hormonal methods such as oral contraceptives do not protect against STDs in the lower reproductive tract but do provide some protection against PID. If vaginal irritation occurs from the use of spermicides, the risk of infection with HIV and other STDs may actually increase.

Q Why are women hit harder by STDs than men?

A Sexually transmitted diseases cause suffering for all who are infected, but in many ways, women and girls are the hardest hit, for both biological and social reasons:

- ***Male-to-female transmission of many infections is more likely to occur than female-to-male transmission.*** This is particularly true of HIV.
- ***Young women are even more vulnerable to STDs than older women because the less-mature cervix is more susceptible to injury and infection.*** As a woman ages, the type of cells at the opening of the cervix gradually changes so that the tissue becomes more resistant to infection. Young women are also more vulnerable for social and emotional reasons: Lack of control in relationships, fear of discussing condom use, and having an older sex partner are all linked to increased STD risk.
- ***Once infected, women tend to suffer more consequences of STDs than men.*** For example, gonorrhea and chlamydia can cause PID and permanent damage to the oviducts in women, while these infections tend to have less serious effects in men. HPV infection causes nearly all cases of cervical cancer. HPV infection is also associated with penile cancer in men, but penile cancer is much less common than cervical cancer. Women also have the added concern of the potential effects of STDs during pregnancy.
- ***Women with HIV infection often face tremendous challenges when they are ill.*** Women may become sicker at lower viral loads compared to men. Women and men with HIV do about as well if they have the similar access to treatment, but in many cases women are diagnosed later in the course of HIV infection, receive less treatment, and die sooner. In addition, they may be caring for family members who are also infected and ill. The proportion of new AIDS cases in women is increasing both in the United States and worldwide.
- ***Worldwide, social and economic factors play a large role in the transmission and consequences of AIDS and other STDs for women.*** Such practices as very early marriage for women, often to much older men who have had many sexual partners, places women at risk for infection. Cultural gender norms that promote premarital and extramarital relationships for men, combined with women's lack of power to negotiate safe sex, make infection a risk even for women who are married and monogamous. In some parts of the world, the stigma of AIDS hits women harder. In addition, lack of education and limited economic opportunities can force women into commercial sex work, placing them at high risk for all STDs.

Solutions to the STD crisis in women include greater access to health care as well as empowerment in the social sphere.

For more Common Questions Answered about STDs, visit the Online Learning Center. 

Brown, D. R., et al. 2005. A longitudinal study of genital human papillomavirus infection in a cohort of closely followed adolescent women. *Journal of Infectious Diseases* 191(2): 182–192.

Centers for Disease Control and Prevention. 2005. Antiretroviral postexposure prophylaxis after sexual, injection-drug use, or other nonoccupational exposure to HIV in the United States. *MMWR Recommendations and Reports* 54(RR02): 1–20.

Centers for Disease Control and Prevention. 2005. HIV testing in the United States, 2002. *Advance Data from Vital and Health Statistics* No. 363.

Centers for Disease Control and Prevention. 2005. *Trends in Reportable Sexually Transmitted Diseases in the United States, 2004*. Atlanta: Centers for Disease Control and Prevention.

Centers for Disease Control and Prevention. 2006. Sexually Transmitted Diseases Treatment Guidelines 2006. *MMWR Recommendations and Reports* 55(RR-11).

Centers for Disease Control and Prevention. 2007. Quadrivalent human papillomavirus vaccine: Recommendations of the Advisory Committee on Immunization Practices (ACIP). *Morbidity and Mortality Weekly Report Recommendations and Reports* 56(RR-2): 1–24.

Erbelding, E. J., and J. M. Zenilman. 2005. Toward better control of sexually transmitted diseases. *New England Journal of Medicine* 352(7): 720–721.

Ginige, S., et al. 2007. Interventions for increasing Chlamydia screening in primary care: A review. *BMC Public Health* 7(1): 95.

Hightow, L. B., et al. 2005. The unexpected movement of the HIV epidemic in the Southeastern United States: Transmission among college students. *Journal of Acquired Immune Deficiency Syndrome* 38(5): 531–537.

Kennedy, S. B., et al. 2007. A quantitative study on the condom-use behaviors of 18- to 24-year-old urban African American males. *AIDS Patient Care and STDs* 21(5): 306–320.

Kushner, M., and Solorio, M. R. 2007. The STI and HIV testing practices of primary care providers. *Journal of the National Medical Association* 99(3): 258–263.

Marrazzo, J. 2007. Syphilis and other sexually transmitted diseases in HIV infection. *Topics in HIV Medicine* 15(1): 11–16.

McCarthy, M. Drug-resistant gonorrhoeae spread in the USA. *The Lancet* 369(9573): 1592.

Niccolai, L. M., et al. 2005. Condom effectiveness for prevention of *Chlamydia trachomatis* infection. *Sexually Transmitted Infections* 81(4): 323–325.

NIMH Collaborative HIV/STD Prevention Trial Group. 2007. Sexually transmitted disease and HIV prevalence and risk factors in concentrated and generalized HIV epidemic settings. *AIDS* 21(Suppl. 2): S81–S90.

Patinkin, M., et al. 2007. An investigation of the practice of unsafe sex yet repeated HIV testing. *Social Work in Health Care* 44(1–2): 73–90.

Sanders, G. D., et al. 2005. Cost-effectiveness of screening for HIV in the era of highly active antiretroviral therapy. *New England Journal of Medicine* 352(6): 570–585.

Shafii, T., et al. 2007. Association between condom use at sexual debut and subsequent sexual trajectories: A longitudinal study using biomarkers. *American Journal of Public Health* 97(6): 1090–1095.

U.S. Preventive Services Task Force. 2005. Screening for HIV: Recommendation statement. *Annals of Internal Medicine* 143(1): 32–37.

Wald, A., et al. 2005. The relationship between condom use and herpes simplex virus acquisition. *Annals of Internal Medicine* 143(10): 707–713.

Weiss, H. A. 2007. Male circumcision as a preventive measure against HIV and other sexually transmitted diseases. *Current Opinion in Infectious Diseases* 20(1): 66–72.

Name ______________________ Section ______________ Date ______________

LAB 14.1 Behaviors and Attitudes Related to STDs

Part I Risk Assessment

To identify your risk factors for STDs, read the following list of statements and mark whether they're true or false for you. *Note:* The statements in this assessment are worded in a way that assumes current sexual activity. If you have never been sexually active, you are not now at risk for STDs. Respond to the statements in the quiz based on how you realistically believe you would act. If you are currently in a mutually monogamous relationship with an uninfected partner or are not currently sexually active (but have been in the past), you are at low risk for STDs at this time. Respond to the statements in the quiz according to your attitudes and past behaviors. (For more on your risk factors for STDs, take the online assessment available at www.thebody.com.)

True	False	
____	____	1. I have only one sex partner.
____	____	2. I always use a latex condom for each act of intercourse, even if I am fairly certain my partner has no infections.
____	____	3. I do not use oil-based lubricants with condoms.
____	____	4. I discuss STDs and prevention with new partners before having sex.
____	____	5. I do not use alcohol or another mood-altering drug in sexual situations.
____	____	6. I would tell my partner if I thought I had been exposed to an STD.
____	____	7. I am familiar with the signs and symptoms of STDs.
____	____	8. I regularly perform genital self-examination to check for signs and symptoms of STDs.
____	____	9. When I notice any sign or symptom of any STD, I consult my physician immediately.
____	____	10. I have been tested for HIV or plan to be tested at my next routine medical exam.
____	____	11. I obtain screenings for STDs regularly. In addition (if female), I obtain yearly pelvic exams and Pap tests.
____	____	12. I have been vaccinated for hepatitis B. In addition (if female), I have been vaccinated or plan to be vaccinated for HPV.
____	____	13. When diagnosed with an STD, I inform all recent partners.
____	____	14. When I have a sign or symptom of an STD that goes away on its own, I still consult my physician.
____	____	15. I do not use drugs prescribed for friends or partners or left over from other illnesses to treat STDs.
____	____	16. I do not share syringes or needles to inject drugs.

Using Your Results

How did you score? False responses indicate attitudes and behaviors that may put you at risk for contracting STDs or for suffering serious medical consequences from them. How many false responses did you give? Are you satisfied that you're doing everything you can to protect yourself from STDs?

What should you do next? Any false reponse indicates a factor that you could change to reduce your risk for STDs. Choose one as the focus of a behavior change program.

Part II Communication

Good communication with sex partners or potential sex partners is a critical component of STD prevention. Regardless of your responses to the risk assessment, complete this communication exercise to help build your communication skills.

1. List three ways to bring up the subject of STDs with a new partner. How would you ask whether he or she has been exposed to any STDs or engaged in any risky behaviors? (Remember that because many STDs can be asymptomatic it is important to know about past behaviors even if no STD was diagnosed.)

   a. ______________________________

   ____

   b. ______________________________

   ____

   c. ______________________________

   ____

2. List three ways to bring up the subject of condom use with your partner. How might you convince someone who does not want to use a condom?

   a. ______________________________

   ____

   b. ______________________________

   ____

   c. ______________________________

   ____

3. If you have had an STD in the past that you might possibly still pass on (e.g., herpes, genital warts), how would you tell your partner(s)?

   ____

   ____

   ____

4. If you were diagnosed with an STD that you believe was given to you by your current partner, how would you begin a discussion of STDs with her or him?

   ____

   ____

   ____

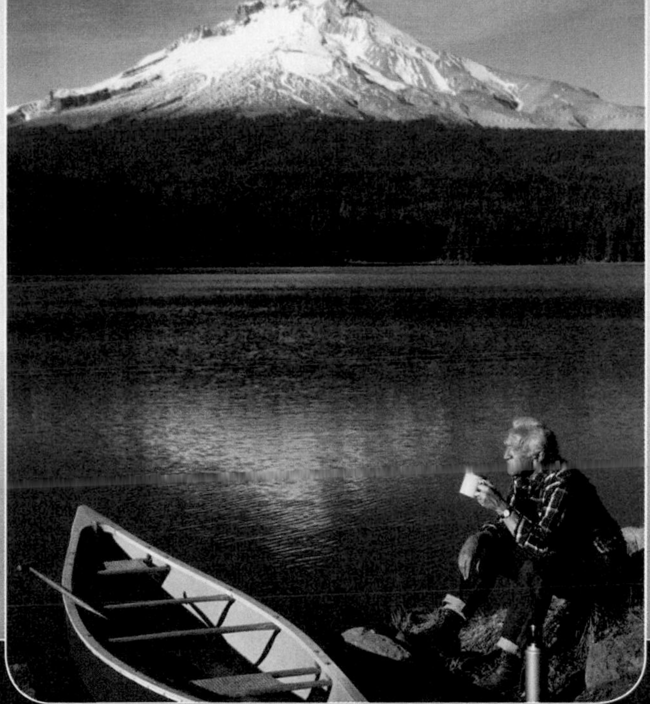

LOOKING AHEAD>>>>>

AFTER READING THIS CHAPTER, YOU SHOULD BE ABLE TO:

- List the characteristics, skills, and behaviors that support successful relationships and families
- Explain what individuals can do to promote healthy aging
- Discuss strategies for effective self-care and effective use of the health care system
- Describe the role that the environment plays in personal wellness and the steps individuals can take to preserve and restore the environment
- List the steps for creating and maintaining an effective behavior change program

15 WELLNESS FOR LIFE

TEST YOUR KNOWLEDGE

1. **Married people tend to be healthier and to live longer than unmarried people.**

   True or false?

2. **Approximately how many Americans have no health insurance?**

   a. 4 million
   b. 14 million
   c. 40 million

3. **Most of the energy used by a standard incandescent lightbulb is converted into light.**

   True or false?

ANSWERS

1. **TRUE.** One explanation is that marriage encourages healthy behaviors. Surveys have found that married people are more likely to wear safety belts, be physically active, and not smoke.
2. **c.** According to the National Center for Health Statistics, nearly 42 million Americans (including 10% of all children) have no health insurance coverage. Some private estimates are as high as 50 million.
3. **FALSE.** About 90% of the energy used by a standard bulb is wasted because it is given off as heat, not light. If each American replaced one incandescent bulb with a compact fluorescent, the yearly energy savings would equal the total production of four nuclear power plants.

FIT AND WELL ONLINE LEARNING CENTER www.mhhe.com/fahey

Visit the *Fit and Well* Online Learning Center for resources that will help you get the most out of your course!

- Study and review aids include practice quizzes, glossary flashcards, chapter summaries, learning objectives, PowerPoint presentations, Common Questions Answered, student handouts, crossword puzzles, Internet activities, and links to wellness Web sites.
- Behavior change tools include a daily fitness and nutrition journal, a behavior change workbook, sample behavior change plans, and blank behavior change logs to print and use.

The goal of this book has been to introduce the concept of wellness and to provide the knowledge and skills you need to attain fitness and lifelong wellness. Knowing the effects of your actions on your health enables you to make informed choices. Using behavioral self-management enables you to make important lifestyle changes. This chapter briefly addresses some other skills that are important for a lifetime of wellness: developing and maintaining meaningful interpersonal relationships, meeting the challenges of aging, using the health care system intelligently, and understanding environmental health.

DEVELOPING SUCCESSFUL INTERPERSONAL RELATIONSHIPS

Human beings need social relationships; we cannot thrive as solitary creatures (see the box "Intimate Relationships Are Good for Your Health"). Nor could the human species survive if as adults we didn't cherish and support each other, if we didn't form strong mutual attachments with our infants, and if we didn't create families in which to raise children. Simply put, people need people.

Although people are held together in relationships by a variety of factors, the foundation of many relationships is love. Love in its many forms—romantic, passionate, platonic, parental—is the wellspring from which much of life's meaning and delight flows. In our culture, it binds us together as partners, parents, children, and friends. People devote tremendous energy to seeking mates, nurturing intimate relationships, keeping up friendships, and maintaining marriages—all for the pleasure of loving and being loved.

Forming Relationships

Intimate relationships satisfy many human needs, including the need for approval and affirmation, for companionship, for a sense of belonging, and for sexual expression. Many of society's needs are also fulfilled by relationships, particularly the need to nurture and socialize children within that society.

Self-Concept and Self-Esteem To have successful relationships, we must first accept and feel good about ourselves. A positive self-concept and a healthy level of self-esteem are rooted in childhood, in the relationships we had with our parents and other family members. As adults, we probably have a sense that we're basically lovable, worthwhile people if, as children, we felt loved, valued, and respected. Our ways of relating to each other—that is, our adult styles of loving—may also be rooted in childhood. People who are secure in their intimate relationships probably had a secure, trusting attachment to their mother, father, or other parenting figure.

Even if people's earliest experiences and relationships were less than ideal, they can still establish satisfying relationships in adulthood. That's because humans are resilient and flexible; they have the capacity to change their ideas, beliefs, and behavior patterns. They can learn how to improve their self-esteem, communicate better, and resolve interpersonal conflicts. Although it helps to have a good start in life, it may be even more important to begin again, right from where you are.

Friendship The first relationships we form outside the family are friendships. With members of either the same or the other sex, friendships give people the opportunity to share themselves and discover others. Friendships usually include these characteristics:

- ***Companionship.*** Friends are relaxed and happy in each other's company. They have common values and interests and spend time together.
- ***Respect.*** Good friends respect each other's feelings and opinions and work to resolve their differences without demeaning or insulting each other. They are honest with one another.
- ***Acceptance.*** Friends feel free to be themselves and express their feelings spontaneously without fear of ridicule or criticism.
- ***Help.*** Sharing time, energy, and even material goods is important to friendship. Friends know they can rely on each other in times of need.
- ***Trust.*** Friends are secure in the knowledge that they will not intentionally hurt each other.
- ***Loyalty.*** Friends can count on each other. They stand up for each other in both word and deed.
- ***Mutuality.*** Friends retain their individual identities, but they share the ups and downs in each other's lives—"what affects you affects me."
- ***Reciprocity.*** There is give-and-take between friends, along with the feeling that both share joys and burdens more or less equally over time.

Friendships are often more stable and longer lasting than intimate partnerships. Friends are often more accepting and less critical than lovers, probably because their expectations are different. Like love relationships, friendships bind society together, providing people with emotional support and buffering them from stress.

Love and Intimacy Intimate love relationships are among the most profound human experiences. They may not give people perfect happiness, but they do tend to give life much of its meaning. For most adults, love, sex, and commitment are closely linked ideals in intimate relationships. Love reflects the positive factors that draw people together and sustain them in a relationship—trust, caring, respect, loyalty, interest in the other, and concern for the other's well-being. Sex brings excitement and

Intimate Relationships Are Good for Your Health

Research studies consistently underscore the importance of strengthening your family and social ties to help maintain emotional and physical wellness. Living alone, or simply feeling alone, can have a negative effect on both your state of mind and your physical health. Married people, on average, live longer than unmarried people—whether single, divorced, or widowed—and they score higher on measures of mental health. Findings suggest that there are intrinsic benefits to marriage.

People with strong social ties are less likely to become ill and tend to recover more quickly if they do. The benefits of intimate relationships have been demonstrated for a range of conditions: People with strong social support are less likely to catch colds. They recover better from heart attacks and live longer with heart disease. Men with prostate cancer who are married live significantly longer than those who are single, divorced, or widowed.

What is it about social relationships that supports wellness? Friends and partners may encourage and reinforce healthy habits, such as exercising, eating right, and seeing a physician when needed. In times of illness, a loving partner can provide both practical help and emotional support. Feeling loved, esteemed, and valued brings comfort at a time of vulnerability, reduces anxiety, and mitigates the damaging effects of stress.

Although good relationships may help the sick get better, bad relationships may have the opposite effect. The impact of relationship quality on the course of illness may be partly explained by effects on the immune system: A study of married couples whose fighting went beyond normal conflict and into criticism and name-calling found them to have weaker immune responses than couples whose arguments were more civil.

Marriage, of course, isn't the only support system available. Whether married or single, if you have supportive people in your life, you are likely to enjoy better physical and emotional health than if you feel isolated and alone. So when you start planning lifestyle changes to improve your health and well-being, don't forget to nurture your relationships with family and friends. Relationships are powerful medicine.

passion to the relationship, adding fascination and pleasure. Commitment, the determination to continue, reflects the stable factors that help maintain the relationship—responsibility, reliability, and faithfulness. Although love, sex, and commitment are related, they are not necessarily connected. One can exist without the others. Despite the various permutations of the three, most people long for a special relationship that contains them all.

When two people fall in love, their relationship at first is likely to be characterized by high levels of passion and rapidly increasing intimacy. In time, passion decreases as the partners become familiar with each other. The diminishing of passionate love is often experienced as a crisis in a relationship. If a quieter, more lasting love fails to emerge, the relationship will likely break up, and each person will search for another who will once again ignite his or her passion.

But love does not necessarily have to be passionate. When intensity diminishes, partners often discover a more enduring love. They can now move from absorption in each other to a relationship that includes external goals and projects, friends, and family. In this kind of more secure love, satisfaction comes not just from the relationship but also from achieving other creative objectives, such as work or child rearing. The key to successful relationships isn't in maintaining intensity but in transforming passion into an intimate love, based on closeness, caring, and the promise of a shared future.

Choosing a Partner Although the pool of potential partners for a relationship may appear huge, most people pair with someone who lives in the same geographic area and who is similar in ethnic and socioeconomic background, educational level, lifestyle, physical appearance, and other traits. In simple terms, people select partners like themselves.

Although differences add interest to a relationship, similarities increase the chances of a relationship's success. Perhaps the most important question two people can ask is, "How much do we have in common?" If there are major differences, partners should ask first, "How accepting of differences are we?" and second, "How well do we communicate?" Acceptance and communication skills go a long way toward making a relationship work, no matter how different the partners.

Because the Internet is a good tool for locating others who share hobbies and interests, people are increasingly looking to cyberspace to find friends and even intimate partners. Most Americans, however, find romantic partners through some form of dating. They narrow the field through a process of getting to know each other. Dating often revolves around a mutually enjoyable activity, such as seeing a movie or having dinner. In the traditional male-female dating pattern, the man takes the lead, initiating the date, while the woman waits to be called. In this pattern, casual dating might evolve into steady or exclusive dating, then engagement, and finally marriage.

For many young people today, traditional dating has given way to a more casual form of getting together in groups. Greater equality between the sexes is at the root of this change. People go out in groups rather than strictly as couples, and each person pays his or her way. A man and woman may begin to spend more time together, but often in the group context. If sexual involvement develops, it is more likely to be based on friendship, respect, and

For many young people today, group activities have replaced dating as a way to meet and get to know potential partners.

common interests than on expectations related to gender roles. In this model, mate selection may progress from getting together to living together to marrying.

Communication

The key to developing and maintaining any type of intimate relationship is good communication. Most of the time, we don't think about communicating; we simply behave naturally. But when problems arise—when we feel other people don't understand us or when someone accuses us of not listening—we become aware of our limitations or, more commonly, what we think are other people's limitations. Miscommunication creates frustration and distances us from our friends and partners.

As much as 65% of face-to-face communication is nonverbal. Even when we're silent, we're communicating. We send messages when we look at someone or look away, lean forward or sit back, smile or frown. Especially important forms of nonverbal communication are touch, eye contact, and proximity. If someone we're talking to touches our hand or arm, looks into our eyes, and leans toward us when we talk, we get the message that the person is interested in us and cares about what we're saying. If a person keeps looking around the room while we're talking or takes a step backward, we get the impression the person is uninterested or wants to end the conversation. It's important, when sending messages, to make sure our body language agrees with our words. When our verbal and nonverbal messages don't correspond, we send a mixed message.

Communication Skills Three keys to good communication in relationships are self-disclosure, listening, and feedback.

- ***Self-disclosure*** involves revealing personal information that we ordinarily wouldn't reveal because of the risk involved. It usually increases feelings of closeness and moves the relationship to a deeper level of intimacy.
- ***Listening*** is a rare skill. Good listening skills require that we spend more time and energy trying to fully understand another person's "story" and less time judging, evaluating, blaming, advising, analyzing, or trying to control. Empathy, warmth, respect, and genuineness are qualities of skillful listeners. Attentive listening encourages friends or partners to share more and, in turn, to be attentive listeners. To connect with other people and develop real emotional intimacy, listening is essential.
- ***Feedback,*** a constructive response to another's self-disclosure, is the third key to good communication. Giving positive feedback means acknowledging that the friend's or partner's feelings are valid—no matter how upsetting or troubling—and offering self-disclosure in response. Self-disclosure and feedback can open the door to change, whereas other responses block communication and change.

For tips on improving your skills, see the box "Guidelines for Effective Communication."

Conflict and Conflict Resolution Conflict is natural in intimate relationships. No matter how close two people become, they still remain separate individuals with their own needs, desires, past experiences, and ways of seeing the world. Conflict itself isn't dangerous to a relationship; it may simply indicate that the relationship is growing. But if it isn't handled in a constructive way, it will damage—and ultimately destroy—the relationship.

Conflict is often accompanied by anger—a natural emotion, but one that can be difficult to handle. If we express anger, we run the risk of creating distrust, fear, and distance. If we act it out without thinking things through, we can cause the conflict to escalate. If we suppress it, it turns into resentment and hostility. The best way to handle anger in a relationship is to recognize it as a symptom of something that requires attention and needs to be changed. When angry, partners should back off until they calm down and then come back to the issue later and try to resolve it rationally. Negotiation will help dissipate the anger so the conflict can be resolved. (See Chapter 10 for additional strategies for managing anger.) Some basic strategies are useful in successfully negotiating with a partner:

1. ***Clarify the issue.*** Take responsibility for thinking through your feelings and discovering what's really bothering you. Agree that one partner will speak

Guidelines for Effective Communication

TAKE CHARGE

Getting Started

- When you want to have a serious discussion with your partner, choose an appropriate time and place. Find a time when you will not be interrupted and a private place.
- Face your partner and maintain eye contact. Use nonverbal feedback to show that you are interested and involved in the communication process.

Being an Effective Speaker

- State your concern or issue as clearly as you can.
- Use "I" statements—statements about how *you* feel—rather than statements beginning with "You," which tell another person how you think he or she feels. When you use "I" statements, you are taking responsibility for your feelings. "You" statements are often blaming or accusatory and will probably get a defensive or resentful response. The statement "I feel unloved," for example, sends a clearer, less blaming message than the statement "You don't love me."
- Focus on a specific behavior rather than on the whole person. Be specific about the behavior you like or don't like. Avoid generalizations beginning with "You always" or "You never." Such statements make people feel defensive.
- Make constructive requests. Opening your request with "I would like" keeps the focus on your needs rather than your partner's supposed deficiencies.
- Avoid blaming, accusing, and belittling. Even if you are right, you have little to gain by putting your partner down. Studies have shown that when people feel criticized or attacked, they are less able to think rationally or solve problems constructively.
- Ask for action ahead of time. Tell your partner what you would like to have happen in the future; don't wait for him or her to blow it and then express anger or disappointment.

Being an Effective Listener

- Provide appropriate nonverbal feedback (nodding, smiling and so on).
- Don't interrupt.
- Develop the skill of reflective listening. Don't judge, evaluate, analyze, or offer solutions (unless asked to do so). Your partner may just need to have you there in order to sort out feelings. By jumping in right away to "fix" the problem, you may actually be cutting off communication.
- Don't give unsolicited advice. Giving advice implies that you know more about what a person needs to do than he or she does; therefore, it often evokes anger or resentment.
- Clarify your understanding of what your partner is saying by restating it in your own words and asking if your understanding is correct.
- Be sure you are really listening, not off somewhere in your mind rehearsing your reply. Try to tune in to your partner's feelings as well as the words.
- Let your partner know that you value what she or he is saying and want to understand. Respect for the other person is the cornerstone of effective communication.

first and have the chance to speak fully while the other listens. Then reverse the roles. Try to understand the other partner's position fully by repeating what you've heard and asking questions to clarify or elicit more information.

2. ***Find out what each person wants.*** Ask your partner to express her or his desires. Don't assume you know what your partner wants and speak for her or him. Clarify and summarize.
3. ***Identify alternatives for getting each person what he or she wants.*** Practice brainstorming to generate a variety of options.
4. ***Decide how to negotiate.*** Work out some agreements or plans for change. For example, agree that one partner will do one task and the other will do another task or that one partner will do a task in exchange for something she or he wants.
5. ***Solidify the agreements.*** Go over the plan verbally and write it down, if necessary, to ensure that you both understand and agree to it.
6. ***Review and renegotiate.*** Decide on a time frame for trying out the new plan and set a time to discuss how it's working. Make adjustments as needed.

Marriage

The primary functions and benefits of marriage are those of any intimate adult relationship, including affection, personal affirmation, companionship, sexual fulfillment, and emotional growth. Marriage also provides a setting in which to raise children, and it affords some provision for the future. By committing themselves to their relationship, people establish themselves with lifelong companions and some insurance for their later years.

Although we might like to believe otherwise, love is not enough to make a successful marriage. Couples have to be strong and successful in their relationship before marriage. The following relationship characteristics appear to be the best predictors of a happy marriage:

- The partners have realistic expectations about their relationship.
- Each feels good about the personality of the other.
- They communicate well.
- They have effective ways of resolving conflicts.
- They agree on religious/ethical values.
- They have an egalitarian role relationship.

TAKE CHARGE

Strategies for Enhancing Support in Relationships

- ***Be aware of the importance of support.*** Time and energy spent on support will help both you and your partner deal with stress and create a positive atmosphere that will help when differences or conflicts occur.
- ***Learn to ask for help from your partner.*** Try different ways of asking for help and support from your partner, and note which approaches work best for your relationship.
- ***Help your partner the way she or he would like to be helped.*** Some people prefer empathy and emotional support; others like more practical help with problems.
- ***Avoid negativity, especially when being asked for help.*** Asking for help puts a person in a vulnerable position. If your partner asks for your aid, be gracious and supportive; don't use phrases like "I told you so" or "You should have just . . ." Otherwise, your partner may learn not to ask for your help or support at all.
- ***Make positive attributions.*** If you're unsure about the reasons for your partner's behavior, give her or him the benefit of the doubt. For example, if your partner arrives for a date 30 minutes late and in a bad mood, assume it's because she or he had a bad day rather than attributing it to a character flaw or relationship problem. Offer appropriate support.
- ***Help yourself.*** Develop coping strategies for times your partner won't be available. These might include things you can do for yourself, such as going for a walk, or other people you can turn to for support.
- ***Keep relationship problems separate.*** Avoid bringing up relationship problems when you are offering or asking for help.
- ***Avoid giving advice.*** Immediately offering advice when asked for help implies that you are smarter or more capable than your partner at solving your partner's difficulty. Begin by providing emotional support and validating your partner's feelings. Then, if asked, help brainstorm solutions.

SOURCE: Plante, T., and K. Sullivan. 2000. *Getting Together and Staying Together: The Stanford Course on Intimate Relationships.* Bloomington, Ind.: AuthorHouse.

- They have a good balance of individual versus joint interests and leisure activities.

Coping with the challenges of marriage requires that couples be committed to remaining married through the inevitable ups and downs of the relationship. They need to be tolerant of each other's imperfections, keep their sense of perspective and their sense of humor, and be willing and able to put energy into providing and sustaining mutually sufficient levels of intimacy, sexual satisfaction, and commitment (see the box "Strategies for Enhancing Support in Relationships").

Successful Families

Family relationships are another important part of a healthy life. Researchers have proposed that six major qualities or themes appear in strong families.

1. ***Commitment.*** The family is very important to its members; sexual fidelity between partners is included in commitment.
2. ***Appreciation.*** People care about one another and express that caring. The home is a positive place to be.
3. ***Communication.*** Family members listen to one another and enjoy one another's company. They talk about disagreements and try to solve problems.
4. ***Time together.*** People do things together, often simple activities that don't cost money.
5. ***Spiritual wellness.*** The family promotes sharing, love, and compassion for other human beings.
6. ***Coping with stress and crisis.*** When faced with illness, death, marital conflict, or other crises, family members pull together, seek help, and use other coping strategies to meet the challenge.

Partners in committed relationships and members of strong families often go to counseling centers. They know that the smartest thing to do in some situations is to get help. Many counseling resources are available, including marriage and family counselors, clergy, psychologists, and other trained professionals.

QUESTIONS FOR CRITICAL THINKING AND REFLECTION

How do you handle conflict in your relationships? Do you fight intensely and then make up? Discuss, negotiate, and compromise? Avoid conflict altogether? Whatever your pattern of conflict resolution (or avoidance), where do you think you learned it? How effective is it for you? If it isn't working well, what ideas do you have for improvement?

MEETING THE CHALLENGES OF AGING

Aging is a normal process of development that occurs over the entire life span. Although youth is not entirely a state of mind, your attitude toward life and your attention to your health significantly influence the satisfaction you derive from life, especially when new physical and mental challenges occur in later years. If you take charge of your health during young adulthood, you can exert greater control over the physical and mental aspects of aging, and you can respond better to events that might be out of your control. With foresight and energy, you can shape a creative, graceful, and even triumphant old age.

What Happens as You Age?

Aging results from biochemical processes that aren't fully understood. Physiological changes stem from a combination of gradual aging, injury, and disease. Because most organ systems have an excess capacity for performing their functions, the body's ability to function is not affected until damage is fairly extensive. Studies of healthy people indicate that general functioning remains essentially constant until after age 70.

Some of the physical changes that accompany aging are these:

- Skin becomes looser, drier, and less elastic.
- The ability to hear high-pitched and certain other sounds declines in most people.
- Presbyopia, the inability of the eyes to focus sharply on nearby objects, occurs gradually in most people beginning in their forties. The eyes require more time to adapt to dark conditions, and depth perception may become distorted.
- The sensations of taste and smell diminish somewhat.
- Cells at the base of hair follicles produce progressively less pigment and eventually die. (Hair is thickest at age 20; individual hair shafts shrink after that.)
- Bone mass is lost and muscles become weaker, although both of these changes can be minimized significantly through regular exercise, a proper diet, and other measures.
- The heart pumps less blood with each beat, and maximum heart rate drops. Most of the other changes in the cardiovascular system that are associated with aging can be largely controlled through lifestyle.
- Sexual response slows, but an active and satisfying sex life can continue for both men and women throughout life.

Table 15.1 lists some of the most prevalent health issues facing older Americans.

VITAL STATISTICS

Table 15.1 Percentage Prevalence of Chronic Health Conditions Among Americans Age 65+

Condition	Men	Women
Hypertension	44.6	51.1
Arthritis	40.4	51.4
Chronic joint pain/stiffness	39.7	47.7
Heart disease (all types)	33.1	25.9
Coronary heart disease	24.3	16.5
Cancer (any type)	23.2	17.5
Diabetes	16.9	14.7
Ulcers	13.1	10.4
Stroke	8.9	8.2
Asthma	8.6	10.6

SOURCE: Centers for Disease Control and Prevention. 2007. *Trends in Health and Aging: Prevalence of Selected Chronic Conditions by Age, Sex, and Race/Ethnicity: United States, 1997–2005.* (http://209.217.72.34/aging/ReportFolders/ReportFolders.aspx; retrieved June 12, 2007).

Life-Enhancing Measures

Many of the characteristics associated with aging aren't due to aging at all. They are the result of neglect and abuse of our bodies and minds. These assaults lay the foundation for later mental problems and chronic conditions. You can prevent, delay, lessen, or even reverse some of the changes associated with aging through good health habits. A few simple things you can do every day will make a vast difference to your health, appearance, energy, and vitality.

- ***Challenge your mind.*** Creativity and intelligence remain stable in healthy individuals. Staying involved in learning as a lifelong process can help you stay sharp and retain all your mental abilities.
- ***Plan for social changes.*** Social roles change over time and require a period of adjustment. Retirement and an empty nest confer the advantage of increased leisure time, but many people do not know how to enjoy it. Throughout life, cultivate interests and hobbies you enjoy, both alone and with others, so that you can continue to live an active and rewarding life in your later years. Volunteering in your community can enhance self-esteem and allow you to be a contributing member of society (see the box "Help Yourself by Helping Others").
- ***Develop physical fitness.*** Exercise enhances both psychological and physical health. A 2006 study showed that elderly people who burned extra calories through daily activity had a much lower mortality rate than their peers who did not exercise. Even in people over 80, endurance and strength training can improve balance, flexibility, and physical functioning and reduce the potential for dangerous falls.

MOTIVATION BOOSTER

Keep at it. Remember that modest changes in lifestyle maintained over the long term are more beneficial than dramatic changes that last only a few weeks. Long-term maintenance of behavior change is challenging. If your motivation lags and your lapses increase, try some of the strategies described earlier in the text (see especially Chapters 1 and 7). If something specific is causing problems—a high stress level or a significant change in your daily schedule—develop specific strategies to address the issue.

WELLNESS CONNECTION

Help Yourself by Helping Others

Volunteering can enhance emotional, social, spiritual, and physical wellness. Surveys and studies indicate that the sense of purpose and service and the feelings of generosity and kindness that go with helping others may be as important a consideration for wellness as good nutrition and regular exercise. A 2006 study followed sedentary older people who joined a volunteer group called Experience Corps. The subjects' volunteer activities resulted in many of the same benefits as regular exercise, such as increased energy and vitality. Older adults who volunteer have higher levels of emotional and social wellness and lower rates of death. In a national survey of volunteers from all fields, helpers reported the following benefits:

- "Helper's high"—physical and emotional sensations such as sudden warmth, a surge of energy, and a feeling of euphoria
- Feelings of increased self-worth, calm, and relaxation
- A perception of being healthier
- Fewer colds and headaches, improved eating and sleeping habits, and some relief from the pain of chronic diseases such as asthma and arthritis.

In helping others, we focus on things other than our own problems, and we get a special kind of attention from the people we help. Helping others can also expand our perspective and enhance our appreciation for our own lives. Helping improves mood, banishes the blues, and may benefit physical health by providing a temporary boost to the immune system and by combating stress and hostile feelings linked to the development of chronic disease.

No matter what your age, to get the most out of helping, keep the following guidelines in mind:

- Remember that helping others doesn't require a huge time commitment or a change of career.
- Choose an activity that involves personal contact. Work with a group to form bonds with other helpers who support your interests and efforts.
- Focus on the process, not the outcome. We can't always measure or know the results of our actions.
- Practice random acts of kindness. Smile, let people go ahead of you in line, pick up litter, and so on.
- Adopt a pet. Several studies suggest that pet owners enjoy better health, perhaps by feeling needed or by having a source of unconditional love.
- Avoid burnout. Recognize your limits, pace yourself, and try not to feel guilty or discouraged. Take pride in being a volunteer or caregiver.

In addition to benefiting you, volunteering has the added bonus of increasing the well-being of others. It fosters a sense of community and can provide some practical help for many of the problems facing our society today.

- ***Eat wisely.*** A varied diet with special attention to calorie intake and nutrient density improves health at every age. (See Chapter 8 for detailed information on nutrition.)
- ***Maintain a healthy body composition.*** Sensible eating habits and an active lifestyle can help you maintain a healthy body composition throughout your life.
- ***Control drinking and overdependence on medications.*** Alcohol abuse ranks with depression as a common hidden mental health problem, affecting 10% of older adults. The problem is often not identified because the effects of alcohol or drug addiction can mimic disease, such as Alzheimer's disease. Don't use alcohol to relieve anxiety or emotional pain; don't take medications when safer forms of treatment are available.
- ***Don't smoke.*** The average pack-a-day smoker can expect to live as much as 15 years less than a nonsmoker and to be susceptible to disabilities that affect the quality of life. Premature balding, skin wrinkling, and osteoporosis are also associated with smoking.
- ***Recognize and reduce stress.*** Don't wear yourself out through lack of sleep, abuse of drugs, or overwork. Practice relaxation and stress management using the techniques described in Chapter 10.

Other strategies for successful aging include getting regular physical examinations to detect treatable diseases, protecting your skin and eyes from the sun, and avoiding extremely loud noises to protect your hearing.

QUESTIONS FOR CRITICAL THINKING AND REFLECTION

How do you envision your old age? Do you want it to resemble the old age of older adults you know now, or do you want it to be different? What specific attributes and abilities will make your old age happy and productive? What are you doing now to ensure that you will be able to reach your goals?

USING THE HEALTH CARE SYSTEM INTELLIGENTLY

Just as people can prevent many illnesses through healthy lifestyle choices, they can also avoid many visits to the medical clinic by managing their own health care—by gathering information, soliciting advice, making their own decisions, and taking responsibility for following through. People who manage their own health care are informed partners in medical care; they also practice safe, effective self-care.

How can you develop this self-care attitude and take a more active role in your own health care? First, you have

to learn to identify and manage medical problems. Second, you have to learn how to make the health care system work for you. This section will help you become more competent in both of these areas.

Managing Medical Problems

The first step in managing medical problems is observing your body and assessing your symptoms. Symptoms—pain, fever, coughing, diarrhea, and so on—are signals that something isn't working right. Many self-tests are available to help you evaluate medical problems at home: blood pressure monitoring equipment, blood sugar tests for those with diabetes, pregnancy tests, self-tests for urinary tract infections, and more than a dozen other do-it-yourself kits and devices. Careful self-observation and the selective use of self-tests can help provide you with the type of information you need to make informed self-care decisions and participate more actively in your care.

Knowing When to See a Physician In most cases, and with sufficient time and rest, the body heals itself. The decision to seek professional assistance for a symptom is generally guided by the nature of the symptom and by your own history of medical problems. If you're unsure about a symptom, call your physician; you may be able to obtain medical advice over the telephone or, in some cases, via e-mail.

Seek professional assistance for any symptom that is severe, unusual, persistent, or recurrent. Medical emergencies requiring a trip to the emergency room include broken bones, severe burns, deep wounds, uncontrollable bleeding, chest pain, loss of consciousness, poisoning, drug overdose, and difficulty breathing.

Self-Treatment In most cases, your body can itself relieve your symptoms and heal a disorder. The prescriptions filled by your body's internal pharmacy are frequently the safest and most effective treatment. Patience and careful self-observation (watchful waiting) are often the best choices in self-treatment.

Nondrug options are often highly effective. For example, massage, ice packs, and neck exercises may at times be more helpful than drugs in relieving headaches and other pains. Adequate rest and a new chair are just two of the many nondrug options for preventing or relieving many common health problems. For a variety of disorders caused or aggravated by stress, the treatment of choice may be relaxation, visualization, or some other stress-management strategies (see Chapter 10). Before reaching for medications, consider all of your nondrug options.

Nonprescription or **over-the-counter (OTC) medications** play an important part in our health care system. Many OTC drugs are highly effective in relieving symptoms and sometimes curing illnesses. Common OTC drugs include antihistamines, expectorants, cough suppressants, pain relievers, bandages, and other products.

Stress management is one of the challenges of aging. Activities such as painting and gardening can be both relaxing and gratifying.

Any drug can have side effects. These guidelines will help you use medicines safely and effectively:

- Always read drug labels and follow directions.
- Do not exceed the recommended dosage or length of treatment unless your physician approves.
- Because OTC drugs, prescription drugs, and herbal remedies can interact, let your physician or pharmacist know before taking more than one type of drug or health remedy at the same time.
- Select medications with one active ingredient rather than combination products. Using single-ingredient products allows you to adjust the dosage of each medication separately for optimal symptom relief; you'll also avoid potential side effects from drugs you don't really need.
- Never take or give a drug from an unlabeled container or in the dark when you can't read the label.
- If you are pregnant, are nursing, or have a chronic medical condition, consult your physician before self-medicating.
- Store medications in a safe place out of the reach of children; avoid locations where dampness or heat might ruin them. Dispose of all expired medications.

TERMS

over-the-counter (OTC) medication A medication or medical product that a consumer can purchase without a prescription.

VITAL STATISTICS

Table 15.2 Percentage of Uninsured Americans Under Age 65

Age		Ethnicity		Income (percent of poverty level)	
Under 18	9.8	White	16.0	Below 100%	31.1
18–24	30.1	Asian American	18.2	100–149%	31.9
25–34	25.4	African American	18.4	150–199%	27.6
35–44	17.0	Latino	34.7	200% or more	10.0
45–54	13.6	American Indian/ Alaska Native	35.0		
55–64	10.9				

SOURCE: National Center for Health Statistics. 2006. *Health, United States, 2006.* Hyattsville, Md.; National Center for Health Statistics.

- Use special caution with aspirin. Because of an association with a rare but serious problem known as Reye's syndrome, aspirin should not be used for children or adolescents who may have the flu, chicken pox, or any other viral illness.

Getting the Most out of Medical Care

Although many health problems can be self-treated, many others require treatment by trained professionals. The key to using the health care system effectively is good communication with your physician and other members of the health care team.

Communicating with Your Physician When interacting with health care providers, you should be assertive in a firm but not aggressive manner. Feel free to ask questions, express your concerns, and be persistent. Strategies for good communication include the following:

- ***Before the visit.*** Make a list of your questions and concerns; include notes about your symptoms. Bring a list of all medications and supplements you are taking, or bring them with you to the office.
- ***During the visit.*** Present your major concerns at the beginning of the visit. Be specific and concise. Try to be as open and honest as you can in sharing your thoughts, feelings, and fears. If you're not sure about something your physician has said, ask to go over it again. If appropriate, ask your physician to write down her or his instructions or to recommend reading material.
- ***At the end of the visit.*** In your own words, briefly state what you understood the physician to say about your problem and what you're supposed to do. Make sure you understand what the next steps are.

Obtaining Appropriate Screening Tests Another important part of preventive health care is regular screening for various conditions and diseases. Be sure to follow the cholesterol and blood pressure testing recommendations provided in Chapter 11, the cancer screening guidelines given in Chapter 12, and the STD screening and testing recommendations given in Chapter 14. If you have symptoms, or if you are at risk for a particular disease, see your physician to discuss your needs.

Paying for Health Care Health care in the United States is currently financed by a combination of patient out-of-pocket payments, private and public insurance plans, and government assistance. However, this system of financing does not cover everyone. Nearly 42 million people have no health insurance at all (Table 15.2), and people without insurance are more likely to receive care that is inadequate. Health insurance enables people to budget in advance for health care costs that might otherwise be unpredictable and ruinously high. Most people are insured through a group policy obtained through their place of employment or through their parents' or spouse's employer. Others are covered by government programs such as Medicare and Medicaid.

If you work for a large company, you may be given a choice of several types of plans, some with a traditional framework and some offering managed care. In a traditional plan, you pay a premium up front, a fixed deductible, and a percentage of expenses thereafter. In a managed-care plan, you (or your employer) pay just the premium and usually a small per-visit fee. When services are used, the fixed fees remain the same, regardless of the amount or level of services provided. Managed-care plans tend to cost consumers less money, but they have restrictions governing which physicians, facilities, tests, and treatments are available to patients.

When you are choosing among several health insurance plans, obtain a copy of each policy that sounds suitable, and read it carefully. Ask the following questions about each plan:

- ***Does the plan include the doctors and hospitals you want?*** If you are happy with your current physician or hospital, find out which plans they accept.
- ***Does the plan provide the benefits you need?*** Determine which health care services are most important to you and your family, and then check to see if the plan covers them. Examples of services include physician office

visits, prescription medications, preventive care, physical therapy, prenatal care, mental health services, and care for preexisting or chronic conditions.

- ***Do the physicians, pharmacies, and other services in the plan have convenient times and locations?*** Check in advance about such things as after-hours care and parking.
- ***Does the plan fit your budget?*** Consider all the costs: monthly premiums, annual deductibles, and co-payments. Also ask how much more you will need to pay if you go outside the health plan's network of physicians, hospitals, and other providers, and if there is a maximum limit on services.
- ***How is the plan rated for quality? Is the plan accredited?*** A variety of consumer and professional organizations rate health plans. Ask the health plan to provide data, or contact your state health insurance commissioner (check the phone book).

Using Complementary and Alternative Medicine

Complementary and alternative medicine (CAM) is defined as those therapies or practices that do not form part of conventional, or mainstream, health care and medical practice as taught in most U.S. medical schools and offered in most U.S. hospitals. The inclusion of the term *complementary* indicates that most people use such approaches in addition to conventional medical treatments rather than in their place.

Consumer surveys show that more and more people in the United States are using various forms of CAM (Table 15.3). Despite their growing popularity, many CAM practices remain controversial, and you need to be critically aware of safety issues (see the box "Avoiding Health Care Fraud and Quackery," p. 428).

Because there is less information available about CAM therapies, as well as less regulation of associated products and providers, it is important for consumers to take an active role. The National Center for Complementary and Alternative Medicine (NCCAM), which is a part of the National Institutes of Health, advises consumers not to seek CAM therapies without first visiting a conventional health care provider for an evaluation and diagnosis of their symptoms. It's usually best to try conventional treatments that have been shown to be beneficial for your condition. If you are thinking of trying any alternative therapies, it is critically important to talk with your physician or pharmacist to avoid any dangerous interactions. For example, some dietary supplements block or enhance the actions of prescription and OTC drugs. Areas to discuss with your physician include the following:

- ***Safety.*** Is there anything unsafe about the treatment in general or for you specifically? Are there safety issues you should be aware of?
- ***Effectiveness.*** Is there any research about the use of the therapy for your condition?
- ***Timing.*** Is the immediate use of a conventional treatment indicated?
- ***Cost.*** Is the therapy likely to be very expensive, especially in light of the potential benefits?

VITAL STATISTICS

Table 15.3 Use of Complementary and Alternative Therapies in the United States

Therapy	Percentage Who Ever Used Therapy
Prayer	55.3
Natural products (nonvitamin, nonmineral)	25.0
Chiropractic care	19.9
Deep breathing exercises	14.6
Meditation	10.2
Massage	9.3
Yoga	7.5
Diet-based therapies	6.8
Progressive relaxation	4.2
Acupuncture	4.0
Megavitamin therapy	3.9
Homeopathic treatment	3.6
Guided imagery	3.0
Taijiquan	2.5
Hypnosis	1.8
Energy healing therapy/Reiki	1.1
Biofeedback	1.0
Any therapy	**74.6**

SOURCE: Barnes, P. M., et al. 2004. Complementary and alternative medicine use among adults: United States, 2002. *Advance Data from Vital and Health Statistics* No. 343. Hyattsville, Md.: National Center for Health Statistics.

MOTIVATION BOOSTER

Outsmart ads. Advertisements—for food, alcohol, tobacco, dietary supplements, fitness equipment, medications, and so on—are one of the environmental factors that can influence your behavior and derail your motivation to change. What ads do you find most memorable and difficult to resist? Examine each one carefully. What are the obvious and subtle verbal and visual messages in the ad and what do they convey? Who do you think is being targeted by the ad? Becoming more aware of the influence of ads is the first step to resisting their appeal.

TERMS

complementary and alternative medicine (CAM) Therapies or practices that are not part of conventional or mainstream health care and medical practice as taught in most U.S. medical schools and available at most U.S. health care facilities.

Avoiding Health Care Fraud and Quackery

CRITICAL CONSUMER

According to the Federal Trade Commission, consumers waste billions of dollars on unproven, fraudulently marketed, and sometimes useless or even harmful health care products and treatments. In addition, people with serious medical problems may waste valuable time before seeking proper treatment. Health fraud is a business that sells false hope. It preys on people who are victims of diseases that have no cure and on people who want shortcuts to weight loss or improvements to personal appearance.

The first rule of thumb for evaluating any health claim is that if it sounds too good to be true, it probably is. Also, be on the lookout for the typical phrases and marketing techniques fraudulent promoters use to deceive consumers:

- The product is advertised as a quick and effective cure-all for a wide range of ailments.
- The promoters use words like *scientific breakthrough, miraculous cure, secret ingredient,* or *ancient remedy.* Also remember that just because a product is described as "natural" or unprocessed does not necessarily mean it's safe.
- The promoter claims the government or the medical profession has conspired to suppress the product.
- The advertisement includes undocumented case histories claiming amazing results.
- The product is advertised as available from only one source, and payment is required in advance.
- The promoter promises a no-risk "money-back guarantee." Be aware that many fly-by-night operators are not around to respond to your request for a refund.

To check out a particular product, talk to a physician or another health care professional and to family members and friends. Be wary of treatments offered by people who tell you to avoid talking to others. Check with the Better Business Bureau or local attorney general's office to see whether other consumers have lodged complaints about the product or the product's marketer. You can also check with the appropriate health professional group. For example, check with the American Diabetes Association or the National Arthritis Foundation if the products are promoted for diabetes or arthritis. Take special care with products and devices sold online; the broad reach of the Internet, combined with the ease of setting up and removing Web sites, makes online sellers particularly difficult to regulate.

If you think you have been a victim of health fraud or if you have an adverse reaction that you think is related to a particular supplement, you can report it to the appropriate agency:

- ***False advertising claims.*** Contact the FTC by phone (877-FTC-HELP), by mail (Consumer Response Center, Federal Trade Commission, Washington, DC 20580), or online (http://www.ftc.gov; click on File a Complaint). You can also contact your state attorney general's office, your state department of health, or the local consumer protection agency (check your local telephone directory).
- ***False labeling on a product.*** Contact the FDA district office consumer complaint coordinator for your area. (The FDA regulates safety, manufacturing, and product labeling.)
- ***Adverse reaction to a supplement.*** Call a doctor or other health care provider immediately. You may also report your adverse reaction to FDA MedWatch by calling 800-FDA-1088 or by visiting the MedWatch Web site (http://www.fda.gov/medwatch).
- ***Unlawful Internet sales.*** If you find a Web site that you think is illegally selling drugs, medical devices, dietary supplements, or cosmetics, report it to the FDA. Problems can be reported to MedWatch or on the FDA Web site (http://www.fda.gov/oc/buyonline/buyonlineform.htm).

You can also get information from individual CAM practitioners and from schools, professional organizations, and state licensing boards. Ask about education, training, licensing, and certification. When talking with a CAM practitioner, ask for a full description of the therapy and any potential side effects, the time the therapy should continue before it can be determined if it is beneficial, and the cost. Tell the practitioner about any conventional treatments you are receiving. If anything a CAM practitioner recommends directly conflicts with advice from your physician, discuss it with your physician before making any major changes in any current treatment regimen or in your lifestyle.

You can investigate CAM therapies on your own by going to the library or doing research online, although caution is in order when using Web sites for the various forms of CAM. A good place to start are the Web sites of government agencies like the FDA or NCCAM and of universities and hospitals that conduct government-sponsored research on CAM approaches (see For Further Exploration at the end of the chapter).

QUESTIONS FOR CRITICAL THINKING AND REFLECTION

Drug manufacturers use television and magazine advertising to sell their products directly to consumers, telling them, "Ask your doctor about . . ." Has such an ad ever led you to believe you had a condition you didn't know you had? Or informed you about a treatment you didn't know existed? What do you think are the advantages and disadvantages of direct-to-consumer advertising?

ENVIRONMENTAL HEALTH

Because of the close relationship between human beings and the environment, even the healthiest lifestyle can't protect a person from the effects of polluted air, contaminated water, or a nuclear power plant mishap. Environmental health encompasses all the interactions between humans and the environment, as well as the health consequences of these interactions.

Environmental health still focuses on such long-standing concerns as clean air and water, food inspection, and waste disposal, but in recent years, its focus has expanded and become more complex. Many of the health challenges of the twenty-first century will involve protecting the environment from the by-products of human activity. Technological advances and rapid population growth have increased the ability of humans to affect and damage the environment. Water supplies are being depleted, landfills are filling up, toxic wastes contaminate both soil and water, and air pollution is altering the Earth's atmosphere and climate. Today there is a growing recognition that we hold the world in trust for future generations and for other forms of life. Our responsibility is to pass on an environment no worse—and preferably better—than the one we enjoy today.

Population Growth

The rapid expansion of the human population, particularly during the past 50 years, is generally believed to be responsible for most of the stress humans put on the environment. At the beginning of the first century A.D., there were about 300 million people alive. By the seventeenth century, the world's population had gradually increased to 500 million. But then it started to rise exponentially, zooming to 1 billion by about 1800, to 2 billion by 1950, and then doubling again in just 40 years. The world's population, currently at about 6.5 billion, is increasing at a rate of about 76 million per year—150 per minute. The United Nations now projects that world population will continue to increase dramatically until it levels off above 10 billion people in 2200. Most of this growth will take place in the developing world, where population growth rates remain high. With so many people consuming and competing for the Earth's resources, it is difficult for societies to provide such basics as clean air and water and to work toward a better environment.

Although population trends are difficult to influence, many countries recognize the importance of population management. A key goal of population management is to improve the conditions of people's lives so they feel less pressure to have large families. Research indicates that improved health, better education, and increased opportunities for women in the economic, political, and social realms work together with family planning and improved access to effective contraception to cut fertility rates and uncontrolled population growth.

Pollution

Many modern environmental problems are problems of pollution—contaminants in the environment that may pose a health risk. Air pollution is not a human invention—it can be caused by a forest fire, a dust storm, a pollen bloom, or the eruption of a volcano—but it is magnified

A key strategy for reducing air pollution and greenhouse gas emissions is to reduce energy consumption. Most people drive alone to commute to work or school; try to cut back on your solo driving time by riding your bike, walking, carpooling, or using public transportation.

by human activities, particularly the burning of fossil fuels like coal and gasoline. Air pollution can cause illness and death if pollutants become concentrated for several days or weeks. Increased amounts of carbon monoxide and other pollutants and decreased amounts of oxygen in the air put extra strain on people suffering from heart or respiratory illnesses.

Three atmospheric problems have surfaced in recent years that may have long-range effects on human health.

The Greenhouse Effect, or Global Warming The gradual raising of the temperature of the lower atmosphere of the Earth is called the greenhouse effect. Warming occurs as a result of the burning of fossil fuels, which releases "greenhouse gases." Experts differ in their estimates of how much temperatures will rise in the near future but agree that continuing temperature change could melt polar ice caps, raise the level of the sea, and change weather patterns. The full health implications of such an increase are unknown.

Thinning of the Ozone Layer The ozone layer in the Earth's atmosphere is being destroyed primarily by chlorofluorocarbons (CFCs), industrial chemicals used in coolants, propellants, solvents, and foaming agents. The ozone layer absorbs ultraviolet (UV) radiation from the sun. As this layer becomes too thin or disappears in spots, increased exposure to UV light may cause more cases of skin cancer, increase the incidence of cataracts and blindness, and impair immune system functioning. It may also interfere with photosynthesis and cause lower crop yields.

What You Can Do for the Environment

- Ride your bike, walk, use public transportation, or carpool in a fuel-efficient vehicle instead of driving.
- Keep your car tuned up and well maintained.
- Make sure your residence is well insulated.
- Use compact fluorescent lightbulbs instead of incandescent bulbs to save energy.
- Buy energy-efficient appliances and use them only when necessary.
- Run the washing machine or dishwasher only when they have full loads.
- Buy products with the least amount of packaging you can, or buy products in bulk. Avoid disposable products. Buy recycled or recyclable products.
- Recycle newspapers, glass, cans, paper, and other recyclable items.
- Store food in glass jars and reusable plastic containers rather than plastic wrap.
- Take your own bag along when you go shopping.
- Dispose of household hazardous wastes according to instructions.
- Take showers rather than baths to save water.
- Install sink faucet aerators, water-efficient showerheads, and water-displacement devices in toilets.
- Don't let the water run when you're brushing your teeth, shaving, or hand-washing clothes or dishes.
- Buy products and services from environmentally responsible corporations. Don't buy products made from endangered species.
- Join or support organizations working on environmental causes.
- Vote for political candidates who support environmentally sound practices. Communicate with your elected representatives about environmental issues.

Acid Precipitation When certain atmospheric pollutants, most of which are produced by coal-burning electric power plants, combine with moisture in the air, they fall to Earth as highly acidic rain or snow. Acid precipitation has damaged trees and aquatic life in many parts of the world, including the northeastern United States, Canada, and northern Europe.

Other forms of pollution pose problems as well. Chemical substances, including lead, asbestos, pesticides, and hundreds of other products, can cause illness and death. Radiation, whether from the sun, X-rays, nuclear power plants, or other sources, can cause cancer, chromosome damage, sterility, and other health problems. Even noise pollution—loud or persistent noise in the environment—can cause hearing loss and stress.

What Can You Do?

Faced with an array of complex and confusing environmental issues, you may feel overwhelmed and conclude that there isn't anything you can do. This isn't true. People can take many actions to limit their negative impact on the environment and to promote environmentally sound practices in the social and political arenas. If everyone made individual changes in his or her life, the impact would be tremendous. Refer to the box "What You Can Do for the Environment" for actions you can take.

Assuming responsibility for your actions in relation to the environment isn't very different from assuming responsibility for your own health behaviors. It involves knowledge, awareness, insight, motivation, and commitment. The same strategies that work to change personal health behaviors can be used to change environment-related behaviors.

QUESTIONS FOR CRITICAL THINKING AND REFLECTION

Do you consider environmental issues during your daily activities—for example, when using water or electricity, choosing means of transportation, or disposing of trash or hazardous waste? If not, what would it take to get you to become more environmentally aware and conscientious? How can you increase your knowledge and motivation?

FIT AND WELL FOR LIFE

Adopting a wellness lifestyle is the most important thing you can do to ensure a high quality of life for yourself, now and in the future. The first chapter of this book described a behavior change program that can be used to change problem behaviors and move toward wellness. Subsequent chapters have provided information on important areas of wellness—physical fitness, nutrition, weight management, stress management, cardiovascular health, cancer, substance use and abuse, and sexually transmitted diseases. As you learned about these aspects of wellness and assessed your own status in relation to each of them, you probably identified personal behaviors that fell short of the ideal. Take the opportunity now (if you haven't already) to consider which of these behaviors you can begin to change. As you do so, let's review the basics of behavior change.

- Choose one behavior to change at a time. Begin with something simple.
- Make sure your motivation and commitment are sufficient to carry you through to success. If they're

not, review the health consequences of not changing this behavior.

- Follow the five-step program outlined in Chapter 1: (1) Monitor your behavior and gather data; (2) analyze the data and identify patterns; (3) set realistic, specific goals; (4) devise a strategy or plan of action; and (5) make a personal contract. The Behavior Change Workbook at the end of the text contains a blank contract and program plan, which you can adapt to fit most behavior change programs. Once your plan is in place, put it into action.
- Build rewards into the plan.
- Make sure the new behavior is enjoyable and fits into your routine.
- Get support from family and friends.
- Forgive yourself when you slip. Don't blame yourself or others or undermine yourself by feeling guilty.
- Expect to succeed. Use positive self-talk to create a new self-image—one that includes your new behavior.

You live in a world in which your own choices and actions have a tremendous impact on your health. Don't let the broad scope of wellness be an excuse for apathy; instead, let it be a call to action. The time to start making changes in your lifestyle—to start becoming fit and well—is right now!

TIPS FOR TODAY AND THE FUTURE

On every level, from personal to planetary, we can all take an active role in shaping our environment and our level of wellness—now and in the future.

RIGHT NOW YOU CAN

- Call someone you care about and let her or him know how important the relationship is to you. (Don't wait for a special occasion or a crisis!)
- Contact a nonprofit group in your community and offer your time and talent; choose a cause that fits your values and would benefit most from your specific talents.
- Research any alternative or complementary practice or product you are using to find out if it is considered safe.
- Turn the lights off in any unoccupied rooms. Turn the heat down a few degrees and put on a sweater, or turn the air conditioner off and change into shorts.

IN THE FUTURE YOU CAN

- Stay mentally challenged by taking up a new hobby (such as chess) or learning a new language.
- As your existing lightbulbs burn out, replace them with compact fluorescent bulbs, which last longer and use much less electricity than standard incandescent bulbs.
- Have your car checked to make sure it runs as efficiently and produces the least amount of emissions possible.

SUMMARY

- Individual and social needs are fulfilled by interpersonal relationships. Self-esteem, trust, and communication skills are the essential elements for building and maintaining good relationships.
- Friendships are characterized by companionship, respect, acceptance, help, trust, loyalty, and reciprocity.
- Intimate love relationships encompass love, sex, and long-term commitment. Passion normally decreases with time and is replaced by closeness, caring, shared goals, and family activities.
- Communication skills and conflict resolution are especially important to successful relationships.
- Strong families are characterized by commitment, appreciation, communication, time spent together, spiritual wellness, and the ability to cope with stress and crisis.
- Many of the changes associated with aging are the result of an unhealthy lifestyle. There are many things that people can do to prevent, delay, lessen, or reverse these changes.
- Managing one's own health care involves identifying and managing medical problems and making the best use of the existing health care system.
- Self-care means knowing which symptoms need professional attention and understanding how to self-treat responsibly, with or without over-the-counter and prescription drugs.
- The best use of the health care system requires good communication with physicians and regular medical screenings. Consumers need to use critical thinking skills when considering complementary and alternative therapies.
- Today's environmental health challenges include protecting the environment from the by-products of human activity. Overpopulation contributes to environmental problems, including pollution. Individual actions to minimize negative environmental effects can have a tremendous impact.

FOR FURTHER EXPLORATION

BOOKS

Gore, Al. 2006. *An Inconvenient Truth: The Planetary Emergency of Global Warming and What We Can Do About It.* New York: Rodale Books. *An introduction to global warming by a former vice president, with practical advice for everyone on how to slow the pace of global warming.*

Katz, M. 2007. *LifeTips 101 Health Insurance Tips.* Charlestown, Mass.: LifeTips. *An easy-to-read overview of how health insurance works, with tips for selecting a plan that is affordable and meets your needs.*

Mayo Clinic. 2007. *Mayo Clinic Book of Alternative Medicine: The New Approach to Using the Best of Natural Therapies and Conventional Medicine.* New York: Time. *The latest information on a wide range of complementary and alternative practices, with explanations of which approaches work best, and under what circumstances.*

Olson, D., and J. DeFrain. 2006. *Marriages and Families: Intimacy, Diversity, and Strengths,* 5th ed. New York: McGraw-Hill. *A comprehensive introduction to relationships and families.*

Weil, A. 2007. *Healthy Aging: A Lifelong Guide to Your Well-Being.* New York: Knopf. *One of America's best-known experts on complementary and alternative medicine offers advice on staying well throughout life.*

Wright, R. T., and B. J. Nebel. 2007. *Environmental Science: Toward a Sustainable Future,* 10th ed. New York: Prentice-Hall. *Presents environmental concerns from scientific, political, and historical perspectives, and discusses current efforts to deal with environmental issues.*

ORGANIZATIONS, HOTLINES, AND WEB SITES

American Association of Retired Persons (AARP). Provides information on all aspects of aging, including health promotion, health care, and retirement planning.
888-OUR-AARP (888-687-2277)
http://www.aarp.org

American Medical Association (AMA). Provides information about physicians, including their training, licensure, and board certification; the Web site includes recent medical news, advice for consumers, and links to related sites.
http://www.ama-assn.org

FuelEconomy.gov Provides information on the fuel economy of cars made since 1985 and tips on improving gas mileage.
http://www.fueleconomy.gov

Go Ask Alice. Answers from professional and peer educators to questions on many topics relating to interpersonal relationships and communication.
http://www.goaskalice.columbia.edu

National Center for Complementary and Alternative Medicine (NCCAM). Provides general information, consumer advice, research abstracts, and other resources.
888-644-6226
http://nccam.nih.gov

Student Counseling Virtual Pamphlet Collection. Provides links to more than 400 pamphlets by different student counseling centers; topics include relationships, family issues, and sexual orientation.
http://www.dr-bob.org/vpc

Student Environmental Action Coalition (SEAC). A coalition of student and youth environmental groups; Web site has contact information for local groups.
304-414-0143
http://www.seac.org

USA.gov: Senior Citizens' Resources. A gateway to government resources on the Internet for older Americans.
http://www.usa.gov/topics/seniors.shtml

U.S. Environmental Protection Agency (EPA). Provides many consumer-oriented materials.
http://www.epa.gov

U.S. Food and Drug Administration (FDA). Provides information on FDA activities and publishes *FDA Consumer* magazine, which frequently includes helpful strategies for evaluating health products and services.
888-INFO-FDA (888-463-6332)
http://www.fda.gov

Many national and international organizations work on environmental health problems. A few of the largest and best known are listed below.

Greenpeace: 800-326-0959;
http://www.greenpeace.org

National Wildlife Federation: 800-822-9919;
http://www.nwf.org

The Nature Conservancy: 800-628-6860;
http://www.nature.org

Sierra Club: 415-977-5500;
http://www.sierraclub.org

World Wildlife Fund: 202-293-4800;
http://www.worldwildlife.org

SELECTED BIBLIOGRAPHY

Anderson, K., et al. 2005. Depression and the risk of Alzheimer's disease. *Epidemiology* 16(2): 233–238.

Bookwala, J. 2005. The role of marital quality in physical health during the mature years. *Journal of Aging and Health* 17(1): 85–104.

Curtis, L. H., et al. 2004. Inappropriate prescribing for elderly Americans in a large outpatient population. *Archives of Internal Medicine* 164(15): 1621–1625.

DeGenova, M. K., and F. P. Rice. 2005. *Intimate Relationships, Marriages, and Families,* 6th ed. New York: McGraw-Hill.

Gottman, J. M. 2004. *The Seven Principles for Making Marriage Work.* New York: Three Rivers Press.

Hadley, J. 2007. Insurance coverage, medical care use, and short-term health changes following an unintentional injury or the onset of a chronic condition. *Journal of the American Medical Association* 297(10): 1073–1084.

Houle, C., et al. 2007. What women want from their physicians: A qualitative analysis. *Journal of Women's Health* 16(4): 543–550.

Karasu, S. R. 2007. The institution of marriage: terminable or interminable? *American Journal of Psychotherapy* 61(1): 1–16.

Kunzli, N., et al. 2005. Ambient air pollution and atherosclerosis in Los Angeles. *Environmental Health Perspectives* 113(2): 201–266.

Low, G., and A. E. Molzahn. 2007. Predictors of quality of life in old age: A cross-validation study. *Research in Nursing and Health* 30(2): 141–150.

Meadows, M. 2005. Use caution buying medical products online. *FDA Consumer,* January/February.

National Center for Complementary and Alternative Medicine. 2007. *Are You Considering Using Complementary and Alternative Medicine (CAM)?* (http://nccam.nih.gov/health/decisions/index.htm; retrieved June 13, 2007).

NASA Goddard Institute for Space Studies. 2007. *Global Temperature Trends: 2004 Summation* (http://data.giss.nasa.gov/gistemp; retrieved June 13, 2007).

Olson, D., and J. DeFrain. 2006. *Marriages and Families: Intimacy, Diversity, and Strengths,* 5th ed. New York: McGraw-Hill.

Robinson, J. G., and A. E. Molzahn. 2007. Sexuality and quality of life. *Journal of Gerontological Nursing* 33(3): 19–27.

Slingerland, A. S., et al. 2007. Aging, retirement, and changes in physical activity: Prospective cohort findings from the GLOBE study. *American Journal of Epidemiology* 165(12): 1356–1363.

Tsang, W. W., and C. W. Hui-Chan. 2005. Comparison of muscle torque, balance, and confidence in older tai chi and healthy adults. *Medicine and Science in Sports and Exercise* 37(2): 280–289.

United Nations. 2005. *United Nations Convention on Climate Change: Essential Background* (http://unfccc.int/essential_background/items/2877.php; retrieved June 13, 2007).

United Nations Population Division. 2007. *World Population Prospects: The 2006 Revision.* New York: United Nations.

Name ____________________ Section ____________________ Date ____________________

LAB 15.1 Looking to the Future: Your Values, Goals, and Lifestyle

Your Values

1. List the personality traits or characteristics that you most value—for example, friendly, patient, successful, outgoing, cooperative, loyal to family and friends, or respectful of diversity. List characteristics of your own or of others.

2. List the activities and accomplishments that you most value—for example, making lots of money, getting good grades, spending time with friends, making your own decisions, or helping others. List accomplishments of your own or of others, or goals you have for the future.

Your Goals and Aspirations

1. Describe the person you want to become. What is the purpose of your life? What is its meaning? What are you trying to accomplish?

2. What significant goals have you yet to realize? These can be creating something or having a particular experience.

3. What can you do to help reach these goals and become the person you want to become? What would you most like to change about yourself?

4. What do you want your life to be like in 5 years? In 10 years? In 20 years?

Your Lifestyle

1. Keeping your values and goals in mind—along with what you've learned from this text about the effects of lifestyle on wellness—examine your current lifestyle. Are you doing everything you can to enhance the quality of your life in the future? Does your current lifestyle reflect your values and goals? List 10 positive behaviors you engage in now that will help you maintain wellness throughout your life and achieve your goals; examples might include exercising regularly, taking a yoga class to manage stress, maintaining close relationships with family and friends, drinking alcohol moderately or not at all, not smoking, and always wearing a safety belt. Next to each behavior, list how it helps you achieve wellness and your long-term goals.

2. Next, list your current habits and behaviors that detract from wellness and may keep you from acting in accordance with your values and achieving your goals. For example, if you smoke, you may not be able to participate in your favorite recreational activities as you get older. You may also find that smoking goes against your values because the habit has a significant amount of control over your daily routine (loss of control and freedom), and you negatively affect the health of those you care about by exposing them to environmental tobacco smoke.

Lifestyle Management: Now and in the Future

1. Briefly describe the behavior change plan(s) you worked on during this course. What behavior(s) did you target? How successful was your program for behavior change? Do you think you'll be able to maintain your healthier behavior(s) in the future?

2. How would you rate your wellness status now? Has it improved in recent weeks or months? Are you more aware of your behavior and its effect on your level of wellness? Look back at the lab activities you completed for Chapter 1. Has your lifestyle improved? Have you moved up the wellness continuum? If you haven't already retaken some of the assessment lab activities, do so now to check your progress (see Appendix D).

3. List several behaviors that could be targets for behavior change in the future (see the list you prepared under item 2 in the previous section). Think about which of these behaviors you might want to try to change now. Begin working through the steps in Chapter 1 (and the Behavior Change Workbook). Every positive change is a step toward wellness.

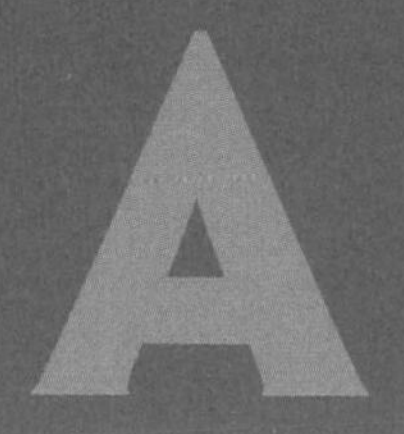

APPENDIX A

INJURY PREVENTION AND PERSONAL SAFETY

Unintentional injuries are the fifth leading cause of death among Americans overall and the leading killer of young people. Injuries affect all segments of the population, but they are particularly common among minorities and people with low incomes, primarily due to social, environmental, and economic factors. The economic cost of injuries in the United States is high, with nearly $600 billion spent each year for medical care and rehabilitation of injured people.

Injuries are generally classified into four categories, based on where they occur: motor vehicle injuries, home injuries, leisure injuries, and work injuries.

MOTOR VEHICLE INJURIES

According to the CDC, more than 37,000 Americans were killed and 3 million injured in motor vehicle crashes in 2004. Motor vehicle accidents are a leading cause of paralysis due to spinal injury and the leading cause of severe brain injury.

Factors in Motor Vehicle Injuries

Driving Habits Nearly two-thirds of motor vehicle injuries are caused by bad driving, especially speeding. As speed increases, momentum and force of impact increase and the time available for the driver to react decreases. Speed limits are posted to establish the safest *maximum* speed limit for a given area under *ideal* conditions. Aggressive driving—characterized by speeding, frequent and abrupt lane changes, tailgating, and passing on the shoulder—also increases the risk of crashes.

Anything that distracts a driver—sleepiness, bad mood, children or pets in the car, use of a cell phone—can increase the risk of a crash. Sleepiness reduces reaction time, coordination, and speed of information processing and can be as dangerous as drug and alcohol use. Even mild sleep deprivation causes a deterioration in driving ability comparable to that caused by a 0.05% blood alcohol concentration.

Cell phone users respond to hazards about 20% slower than undistracted drivers and are about twice as likely to rear-end a braking car in front of them. A 2006 study showed that drivers who use cell phones are nearly six times as likely to be involved in a crash as drivers who don't. Hands-free devices do not help significantly; the mental distraction of talking is the factor in crashes rather than holding a phone.

Safety Belts and Air Bags A person who doesn't wear a safety belt is twice as likely to be injured in a crash as a person who does wear a safety belt. Safety belts not only prevent occupants from being thrown from the car at the time of the crash but also provide protection from the "second collision," which occurs when the occupant of the car hits something inside the car, such as the steering column or windshield. The safety belt also spreads the stopping force of a collision over the body.

Since 1998, all new cars have been equipped with dual air bags—one for the driver and one for the front passenger seat. Air bags provide supplemental protection in a collision but are most useful in head-on collisions. (Many newer vehicles feature side air bags to offer protection in a side-impact crash.) They also deflate immediately after inflating and so do not provide protection in collisions involving multiple impacts. To ensure that air bags work as intended, follow these guidelines:

- Place infants in rear-facing infant seats in the backseat.
- Transport children age 12 and under in the backseat.
- Always use safety belts or appropriate safety seats.
- Keep at least 10 inches between the air bag cover and the breastbone of the driver or passenger.

A person who cannot comply with these guidelines, can apply to the National Highway Traffic Safety Administration for permission to install an on-off switch that temporarily disables the air bag.

Alcohol and Other Drugs Alcohol is involved in about 40% of all fatal crashes. Alcohol-impaired driving, defined by blood alcohol concentration (BAC), is illegal. The legal BAC limit is 0.08% in all states, but driving ability is impaired at much lower BACs. All psychoactive drugs have the potential to impair driving ability.

Preventing Motor Vehicle Injuries

About 75% of all motor vehicle collisions occur within 25 miles of home and at speeds lower than 40 mph. These crashes often occur because the driver believes safety measures are not necessary for short trips. Clearly, the statistics prove otherwise.

To prevent motor vehicle injuries:

- Obey the speed limit. If you have to speed to get to your destination on time, you're not allowing enough time.
- Always wear a safety belt and ask passengers to do the same. Strap infants and toddlers into government-approved car seats in the backseat. Children who have outgrown child safety seats but who are still too small for adult safety belts alone (usually age 4–8) should be secured using booster seats. All children under 12 should ride in the backseat.
- Never drive under the influence of alcohol or other drugs with a driver who is.

- Do not drive when you are sleepy or have been awake for 18 or more hours.
- Avoid using your cell phone while driving—your primary obligation is to pay attention to the road. If you do make calls, follow laws set by your city or state. Place calls when you are at a stop, and keep them short. Pull over if the conversation is stressful or emotional.
- Keep your car in good working order. Regularly inspect tires, oil and fluid levels, windshield wipers, spare tire, and so on.
- Always allow enough following distance. Follow the "3-second rule": When the vehicle ahead passes a reference point, count out 3 seconds. If you pass the reference point before you finish counting, drop back and allow more following distance.
- Always increase following distance and slow down if weather or road conditions are poor.
- Choose interstate highways rather than rural roads. Highways are much safer because of better visibility, wider lanes, fewer surprises, and other factors.
- Always signal before turning or changing lanes.
- Stop completely at stop signs. Follow all traffic laws.
- Take special care at intersections. Always look left, right, and then left again. Make sure you have plenty of time to complete your maneuver in the intersection.
- Don't pass on two-lane roads unless you're in a designated passing area and have a clear view ahead.

Motorcycles and Mopeds

About 1 out of every 10 traffic fatalities among people age 15–34 involves someone riding a motorcycle. Injuries from motorcycle collisions are generally more severe than those involving automobiles because motorcycles provide little, if any, protection. Moped riders face additional challenges. Mopeds usually have a maximum speed of 30–35 mph and have less power for maneuverability.

To prevent motorcycle and moped injuries:

- Make yourself easier to see by wearing light-colored clothing, driving with your headlights on, and correctly positioning yourself in traffic.
- Develop the necessary skills. Lack of skill, especially when evasive action is needed to avoid a collision, is a major factor in motorcycle and moped injuries. Skidding from improper braking is the most common cause of loss of control.
- Wear a close-fitting helmet, one marked with the symbol DOT (for Department of Transportation).
- Protect your eyes with goggles, a face shield, or a windshield.
- Drive defensively and never assume that other drivers see you.

Pedestrians and Bicycles

Injuries to pedestrians and bicyclists are considered motor vehicle–related because they are usually caused by motor vehicles. About 1 in 8 motor vehicle deaths each year involves a pedestrian; more than 80,000 pedestrians are injured each year.

To prevent injuries when walking or jogging:

- Walk or jog in daylight.
- Make yourself easier to see by wearing light-colored, reflective clothing.
- Face traffic when walking or jogging along a roadway, and follow traffic laws.
- Avoid busy roads or roads with poor visibility.
- Cross only at marked crosswalks and intersections.
- Don't use headphones while walking or jogging.
- Don't hitchhike; it places you in a potentially dangerous situation.

Bicycle injuries result primarily from not knowing or understanding the rules of the road, failing to follow traffic laws, and not having sufficient skill or experience to handle traffic conditions. Bicycles are considered vehicles; bicycle riders must obey all traffic laws that apply to automobile drivers, including stopping at traffic lights and stop signs.

To prevent injuries when riding a bike:

- Wear safety equipment, including a helmet, eye protection, gloves, and proper footwear. Secure the bottom of your pant legs with clips and secure your shoelaces so they don't get tangled in the chain.
- Make yourself easier to see by wearing light-colored, reflective clothing. Equip your bike with reflectors and use lights, especially at night or when riding in wooded or other dark areas.
- Ride with the flow of traffic, not against it, and follow traffic laws. Use bike paths when they are available.
- Ride defensively; never assume that drivers see you. Be especially careful when turning or crossing at corners and intersections. Watch for cars turning right.
- Stop at all traffic lights and stop signs. Know and use hand signals.
- Continue pedaling at all times when moving (don't coast) to help keep the bike stable and to maintain your balance.
- Properly maintain your bike.

Aggressive Driving

Aggressive driving, known as *road rage,* has increased more than 50% since 1990. Aggressive drivers increase the risk of crashes for themselves and others. They further increase the risk of injuries if they stop their vehicles and confront each other. Even if you are successful at controlling your own aggressive driving impulses, you may still encounter an aggressive driver.

To avoid being the victim of an aggressive driver:

- Always keep distance between your car and others. If you are behind a very slow driver and can't pass, slow down to increase distance in case that driver does something unexpected. If you are being tailgated, do not increase your speed; instead, let the other driver pass you. If you are in the left lane when being tailgated, signal and pull over to let the other driver go by, even if you are traveling at the speed limit. When you are merging, make sure you have plenty of room. If you are cut off by a merging driver, slow down to make room.

- Be courteous, even if the other driver is not. Use your horn rarely, if ever. Avoid making gestures of irritation, even shaking your head. When parking, let the other driver have the space that you both found.
- Refuse to join in a fight. Avoid eye contact with an angry driver. If someone makes a rude gesture, ignore it. If you think another car is following you and you have a cell phone, call the police. Otherwise, drive to a public place and honk your horn to get someone's attention.
- If you make a mistake while driving, apologize. Raise or wave your hand or touch or knock your head with the palm of your hand to indicate "What was I thinking?" You can also mouth the words "I'm sorry."

HOME INJURIES

Contrary to popular belief, home is one of the most dangerous places to be. The most common fatal home injuries are caused by falls, poisoning, fires, suffocation and choking, and incidents involving firearms.

Falls

Falls are second only to motor vehicle injuries in terms of causing deaths. They are a significant cause of unintentional death for people under age 25. Most deaths occurring from falls involve falling on stairs or steps or from one level to another. Falls also occur on the same level, from tripping, slipping, or stumbling. Alcohol is a contributing factor in many falls.

To prevent injuries from falls:

- Install handrails and nonslip surfaces in the shower and bathtub. Place skidproof backing on rugs and carpets.
- Keep floors clear of objects or conditions that could cause slipping or tripping, such as heavy wax coating, electrical cords, and toys.
- Put a light switch by the door of every room so that no one has to walk across a room to turn on a light. Use night-lights in bedrooms, halls, and bathrooms.
- Outside the house, clear dangerous surfaces created by ice, snow, fallen leaves, or rough ground.
- Install handrails on stairs. Keep stairs well lit and clear of objects.
- When climbing a ladder, use both hands. Never stand higher than the third step from the top. When using a stepladder, make sure the spreader brace is in the locked position. With straight ladders, set the base 1 foot out for every 4 feet of height. Don't stand on chairs to reach things.
- If there are small children in the home, place gates at the top and bottom of stairs. Never leave a baby unattended on a bed or table.

Poisoning

More than 2.4 million poisonings occur every year in the United States.

To prevent poisoning:

- Store all medicines out of the reach of children. Use medicines only as directed on the label or by a physician.
- Use cleaners, pesticides, and other dangerous substances only in areas with proper ventilation. Store them out of the reach of children.
- Never operate a vehicle in an enclosed space. Have your furnace inspected yearly. Use caution with any substance that produces potentially toxic fumes, such as kerosene. If appropriate, install carbon monoxide detectors.
- Keep poisonous plants out of the reach of children. These include azalea, oleander, rhododendron, wild mushrooms, daffodil and hyacinth bulbs, mistletoe berries, apple seeds, morning glory seeds, wisteria seeds, and the leaves and stems of potato, rhubarb, and tomato plants.

To be prepared in case of poisoning:

- Keep the number of the nearest Poison Control Center (or emergency room) in an accessible location. A call to the national poison control hotline (800-222-1222) will be routed to a local center.

Emergency first aid for poisonings:

1. Remove the poison from contact with eyes, skin, or mouth, or remove the victim from contact with poisonous fumes or gases.
2. Call the Poison Control Center immediately for instructions. Have the container with you.
3. Do not follow emergency instructions on labels. Some may be out-of-date and carry incorrect treatment information.
4. If you are instructed to go to an emergency room, take the poisonous substance or its container with you.

Guidelines for specific types of poisons:

- *Swallowed poisons.* If the person is awake and able to swallow, give water only; then call the Poison Control Center or a physician for advice.
- *Poisons on the skin.* Remove any affected clothing. Flood affected parts of the skin with warm water, wash with soap and water, and rinse. Then call for advice.
- *Poisons in the eye.* For children, flood the eye with lukewarm water poured from a pitcher held 3–4 inches above the eye for 15 minutes; alternatively, irrigate the eye under a faucet. For adults, get in the shower and flood the eye with a gentle stream of lukewarm water for 15 minutes. Then call for advice.
- *Inhaled poisons.* Immediately carry or drag the person to fresh air and, if necessary, give rescue breaths (Figure A.1). If the victim is not breathing easily, call 911 for help. Ventilate the area. Then call the Poison Control Center for advice.

Fires

Each year, about 80% of fire deaths and 65% of fire injuries occur in the home. Careless smoking is the leading cause of fire deaths.

To prevent fires:

- Dispose of all cigarettes in ashtrays. Never smoke in bed.
- Do not overload electrical outlets. Do not place extension cords under rugs or where people walk. Replace worn or frayed extension cords.

EMERGENCY CARE FOR CHOKING

- If the victim is coughing, encourage the coughing to clear the object from the airway.
- If the victim is not coughing, follow the steps in "Choking Care for Responsive Adult or Child."

Choking Care for Responsive Adult or Child

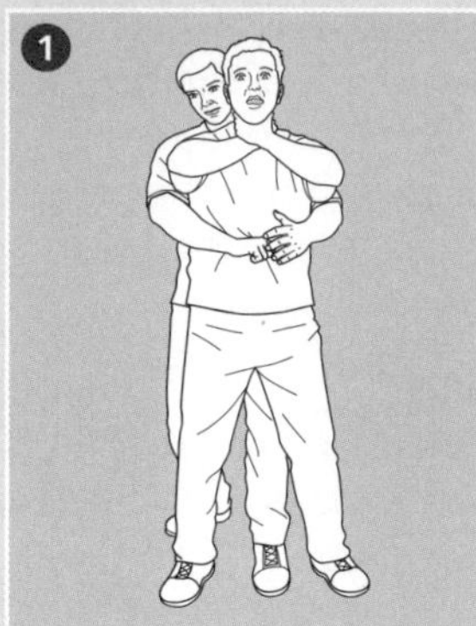

Stand behind an adult victim with one leg forward between the victim's legs. (With a child, kneel behind the victim.) Keep your head slightly to one side. Reach around the abdomen with both arms. Make a fist with one hand and place the thumb side of the fist against the abdomen just above the navel.

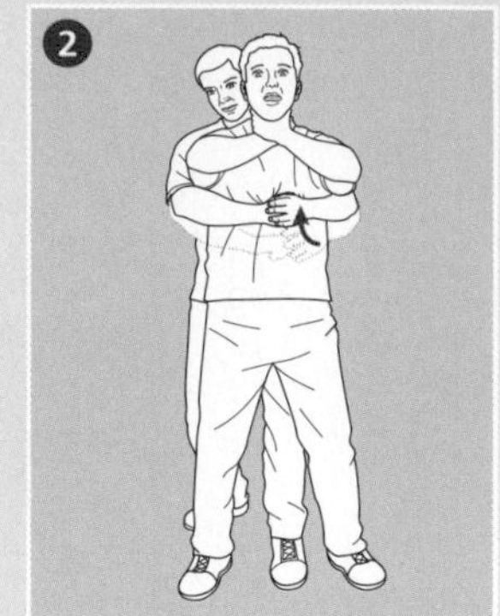

Grasp your fist with your other hand and thrust inward and up-ward into the victim's abdomen with quick jerks. Continue abdominal thrusts until the victim expels the object or becomes unresponsive. If the victim becomes unresponsive while you are administering abdominal thrusts, lower the victim to the floor onto his or her back, and follow the steps in "Choking Care for Unresponsive Adult or Child."

Choking Care for Unresponsive Adult or Child: CPR

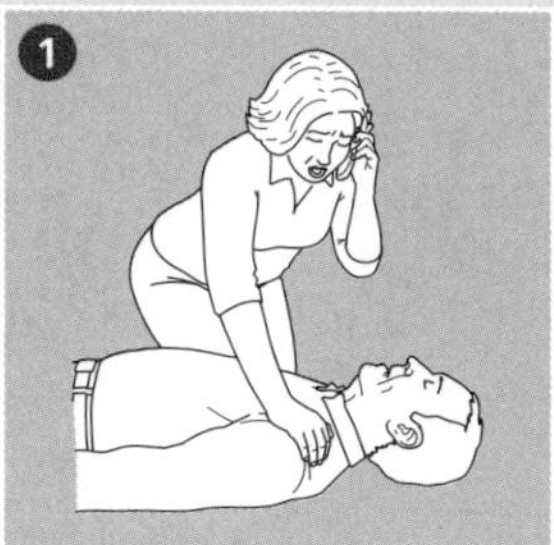

Call 911 and begin CPR.

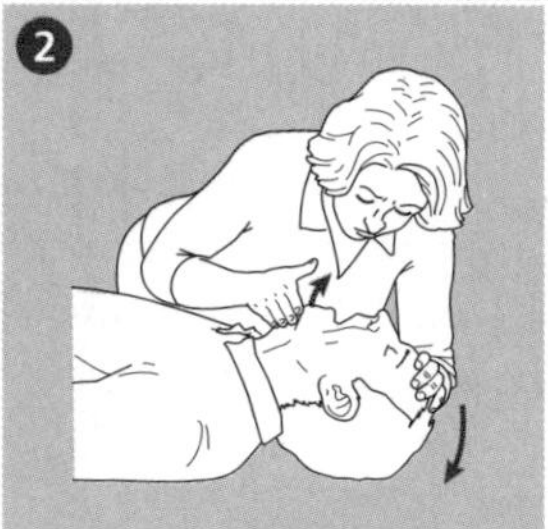

Open the airway to see if the victim is breathing. Use the "head tilt–chin lift" maneuver to open the airway: Push down on the forehead and lift the chin.

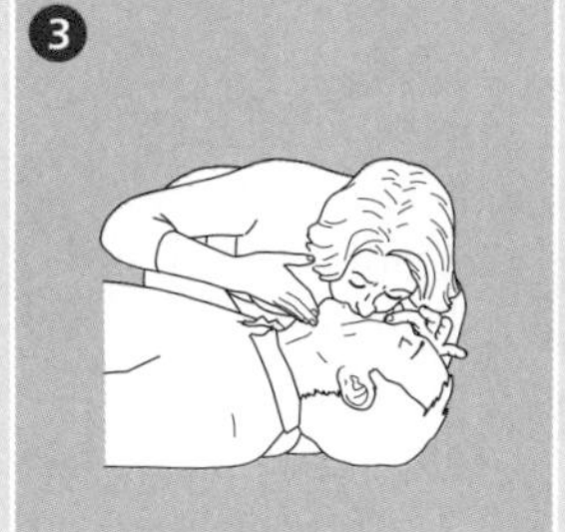

If the victim is not breathing, give two rescue breaths, each lasting 1 second. Pinch the victim's nose shut and blow a normal breath into the victim's mouth. If the first breath does not go in (the chest does not rise), reposition the head to open the airway and try again. Each time you give a rescue breath, look for an object in the victim's mouth and remove it if present.

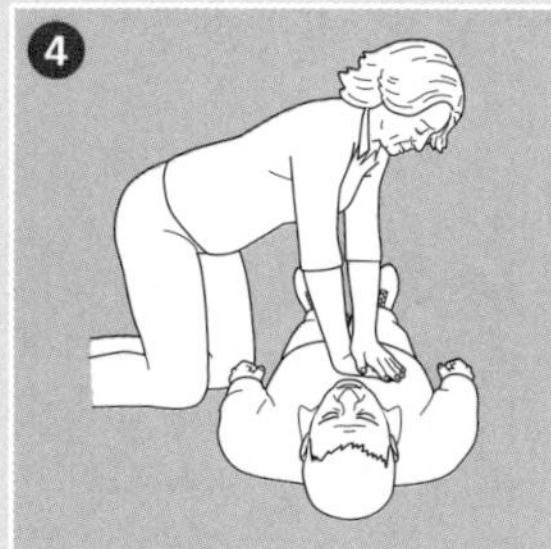

If the obstruction remains, begin chest compressions. Place the heel of one hand in the center of the chest between the nipples and the other hand on top of the first. Position your shoulders over your hands and lock your elbows. Give 30 chest compressions at a rate of 100 per minute. The chest should go down by 1½ to 2 inches. Then give two breaths, looking in the mouth for an expelled object. Continue chest compressions until help arrives. **Remember: Push hard and push fast at a rate of 100 compressions per minute.**

EMERGENCY CARE FOR CARDIAC ARREST

For cardiac arrest, the American Heart Association's revised (2005) Emergency Cardiac Care guidelines are as follows:

1. Call 911.
2. Start CPR (100 compressions per minute, stopping every 30 to 60 seconds to give two rescue breaths).
3. If an automatic external defibrillator (AED) is available, or when one arrives, give one shock to restart the victim's heart.
4. Go back to CPR immediately after the shock.

Don't wait for an emergency to learn how to use an AED or perform CPR.
To find a course in your area, contact the American Heart Association (800 242-8721) or the American Red Cross (202 303-4498).

FIGURE A.1 Emergency care for choking and for cardiac arrest.

SOURCES: Adapted from National Safety Council, 2007. *First Aid: Taking Action.* New York: McGraw-Hill, American Heart Association, 2005. Adult basic life support. *Circulation* 112: 19–34. New CPR guidelines. Simplicity to the rescue, 2006. *Harvard Health Letter,* March. Streamlined CPR guidelines a life-taking move, 2006. *Harvard Heart Letter,* February.

- Place a wire screen in front of fireplaces and woodstoves. Remove ashes carefully and store them in airtight metal containers, not paper bags.
- Properly maintain electrical appliances, kerosene heaters, and furnaces. Clean flues and chimneys annually.
- Keep portable heaters at least 3 feet away from curtains, bedding, towels, or anything that might catch fire. Never leave heaters on when you're out of the room or sleeping.

To be prepared for a fire:

- Plan at least two escape routes out of each room. Designate a location outside the home as a meeting place. Stage a home fire drill.
- Install a smoke detection device on every level of your home. Clean the detectors and test batteries once a month, and replace the batteries at least once a year.
- Keep a fire extinguisher in your home and know how to use it.

To prevent injuries from fire:

- Get out as quickly as possible and go to the designated meeting place. Don't stop for a keepsake or a pet. Never hide in a closet or under a bed. Once outside, count heads to see if everyone is out. If you think someone is still inside the burning building, tell the firefighters. Never go back inside a burning building.
- If you're trapped in a room, feel the door. If it is hot or if smoke is coming in through the cracks, don't open it; use the alternative escape route. If you can't get out of a room, go to the window and shout or wave for help.
- Avoid inhaling smoke. Smoke inhalation is the largest cause of death and injury in fires. To avoid inhaling smoke, crawl along the floor away from the heat and smoke. Cover your mouth and nose, ideally with a wet cloth, and take short, shallow breaths.
- If your clothes catch fire, don't run. Drop to the ground, cover your face, and roll back and forth to smother the flames. Remember: Stop-drop-roll.

Suffocation and Choking

Suffocation accounts for about 4000 deaths annually in the United States. Young children account for nearly half of these deaths. Children can suffocate if they put small items in their mouths, get tangled in their crib bedding, or get trapped in airtight appliances like old refrigerators. Keep small objects out of reach of children under age 3, and don't give them raw carrots, hot dogs, popcorn, peanuts, or hard candy. Examine toys carefully for small parts that could come loose; don't give plastic bags or balloons to small children.

Adults can also become choking victims, especially if they fail to chew food properly, eat hurriedly, or try to talk and eat at the same time. Many choking victims can be saved with abdominal thrusts, also called the Heimlich maneuver (see Figure A.1). Infants who are choking can be saved with blows to the upper back, followed by chest thrusts if necessary.

Incidents Involving Firearms

Firearms pose a significant threat of unintentional injury, especially to people between ages 5 and 29.

To prevent firearm injuries:

- Never point a loaded gun at something you do not intend to shoot.
- Always unload a firearm before storing it. Store unloaded firearms under lock and key in a place separate from ammunition.
- Inspect firearms carefully before handling them.
- If you ever plan to handle a gun, take a firearms safety course first.

LEISURE INJURIES

Leisure injuries take place in public places (but do not involve motor vehicles) and include recreational, sports, and transportation injuries. Many injuries in this category involve such recreational activities as boating and swimming, playground activities, in-line skating, and sports.

Drowning and Boating Injuries

Although most drownings are reported in lakes, ponds, rivers, and oceans, more than half the drownings of young children take place in residential pools. Among adolescents and adults, alcohol plays a significant role in many boating injuries and drownings.

To prevent drowning and boating injuries:

- Develop adequate swimming skill and make sure children learn to swim.
- Make sure residential pools are fenced and that children are never allowed to swim without supervision.
- Don't swim alone or in unsupervised places.
- Use caution when swimming in unfamiliar surroundings or for an unusual length of time. To avoid being chilled, don't swim in water colder than 70°F.
- Don't swim or boat under the influence of alcohol or other drugs. Don't chew gum or eat while in the water.
- Check the depth of water before diving.
- When on a boat, use a life jacket (personal flotation device).

In-Line Skating and Scooter Injuries

Most in-line skating injuries occur because users are not familiar with the equipment and do not wear appropriate safety gear. Injuries to the wrist and head are the most common. To reduce your risk of being injured while skating, wear a helmet, elbow and knee pads, wrist guards, a long-sleeved shirt, and long pants.

Wearing a helmet and knee and elbow pads is also important for preventing scooter injuries. The rise in popularity of lightweight scooters has seen a corresponding increase in associated injuries. Scooters should not be viewed as toys, and young children should be closely supervised. Be sure that handlebars, steering column, and all nuts and bolts are securely fastened. Ride on smooth, paved surfaces away from motor vehicle traffic. Avoid streets and surfaces with water, sand, gravel, or dirt.

Sports Injuries

Since more people have begun exercising to improve their health, there has been an increase in sports-related injuries.

To prevent sports injuries:

- Develop the skills required for the activity. Recognize and guard against the hazards associated with it.
- Always warm up and cool down.
- Make sure facilities are safe.
- Follow the rules and practice good sportsmanship.
- Use proper safety equipment, including, where appropriate, helmets, eye protection, knee and elbow pads, and wrist guards. Wear correct footwear.
- When it is excessively hot and humid, avoid heat stress by following the guidelines given in the box "Exercising in Hot Weather" in Chapter 3.

WORK INJURIES

Many aspects of workplace safety are monitored by the Occupational Safety and Health Administration (OSHA), a federal agency. The highest rate of work-related injuries occurs among laborers, whose jobs usually involve extensive manual labor and lifting—two areas not addressed by OSHA safety standards. Back injuries are the most common work injury.

To protect your back when lifting:

- Don't try to lift beyond your strength. If you need it, get help.
- Get a firm footing, with your feet shoulder-width apart. Get a firm grip on the object.
- Keep your torso in a relatively upright position and crouch down, bending at the knees and hips. Avoid bending at the waist. To lift, stand up or push up with your leg muscles. Lift gradually, keeping your arms straight. Keep the object close to your body.
- Don't twist. If you have to turn with an object, change the position of your feet.
- Put the object down gently, reversing the rules for lifting.

Another type of work-related injury is damage to the musculoskeletal system from repeated strain on the hand, arm, wrist, or other part of the body. Such repetitive-strain injuries are proliferating due to increased use of computers. One type, carpal tunnel syndrome, is characterized by pain and swelling in the tendons of the wrists and sometimes numbness and weakness.

To prevent carpal tunnel syndrome:

- Maintain good posture at the computer. Use a chair that provides back support and place the feet flat on the floor or on a footrest.
- Position the screen at eye level and the keyboard so the hands and wrists are straight.
- Take breaks periodically to stretch and flex your wrists and hands to lessen the cumulative effects of stress.

VIOLENCE AND INTENTIONAL INJURIES

According to the Federal Bureau of Investigation (FBI), nearly 1.4 million violent crimes occurred in the United States in 2005. Violence includes assault, sexual assault, homicide, domestic violence, suicide, and child abuse. Compared with rates of violence in other industrialized countries, U.S. rates are unusually high in two areas: homicide and firearm-related deaths.

Assault

Assault is the use of physical force to inflict injury or death on another person. Most assaults occur during arguments or in connection with another crime, such as robbery. Poverty, urban settings, and the use of alcohol and drugs are associated with higher rates of assault. The FBI estimates that more than 16,500 Americans were murdered in 2005. Homicide victims are most likely to be male, between ages 19 and 24, and members of minority groups. Most homicides are committed with a firearm; the murderer and the victim usually know each other.

To protect yourself at home:

- Secure your home with good lighting and effective locks, preferably deadbolts. Make sure that all doors and windows are securely locked.
- Get a dog or post "Beware of Dog" signs.
- Don't hide keys in obvious places, and don't give anyone the chance to duplicate your keys.
- Install a peephole in your front door. Don't open your door to people you don't know.
- If you or a family member owns a weapon, store it securely. Store guns and ammunition separately.
- If you are a woman living alone, use your initials rather than your full name in the phone directory. Don't use a greeting on your answering machine that implies you live alone or are not home.
- Teach everyone in the household how to get emergency assistance.
- Know your neighbors. Work out a system for alerting each other in case of an emergency.
- Establish a neighborhood watch program.

To protect yourself on the street:

- Avoid walking alone, especially at night. Stay where people can see and hear you.
- Walk on the outside of the sidewalk, facing traffic. Walk purposefully. Act alert and confident. If possible, keep at least two arm lengths between yourself and a stranger.
- Know where you are going. Appearing to be lost increases your vulnerability.
- Carry valuables in a fanny pack, pants pocket, or shoulder bag strapped diagonally across the chest.
- Always have your keys ready as you approach your vehicle or home.
- Carry a whistle to blow if you are attacked or harassed. If you feel threatened, run and/or yell. Go into a store or knock on the door of a home. If someone grabs you, yell, "Help!" or "Fire!"

To protect yourself in your car:

- Keep your car in good working condition, carry emergency supplies, and keep the gas tank at least half full.
- When driving, keep doors locked and windows rolled up at least three-quarters of the way.
- Park your car in well-lighted areas or parking garages, preferably those with an attendant or a security guard.
- Lock your car when you leave it, and check the interior before opening the door when you return.

- Don't pick up strangers. Don't stop for vehicles in distress; drive on and call for help.
- Note the location of emergency call boxes along highways and in public facilities. Carry a cell phone.
- If your car breaks down, raise the hood and tie a white cloth to the antenna or door handle. Wait in the car with the doors locked and windows rolled up. If someone approaches to offer help, open a window only a crack and ask the person to call the police or a towing service.
- When you stop at a light or stop sign, leave enough room to maneuver if you need an escape route.
- If you are involved in a minor automobile crash and you think you have been bumped intentionally, don't leave your car. Motion to the other driver to follow you to the nearest police station. If confronted by a person with a weapon, give up your car.

To protect yourself on public transportation:

- While waiting, stand in a populated, well-lighted area.
- Make sure that the bus, subway, or train is bound for your destination before you board it. Sit near the driver or conductor in a single seat or an outside seat.
- If you flag down a taxi, make sure that it's from a legitimate service. When you reach your destination, ask the driver to wait until you are safely inside the building.

To protect yourself on campus:

- Make sure that door and window locks are secure and that halls and stairwells have adequate lighting.
- Don't give dorm or residence keys to anybody.
- Don't leave your door unlocked or allow strangers into your room.
- Avoid solitary late-night trips to the library or laundry room. Take advantage of on-campus escort services.
- Don't exercise outside alone at night. Don't take shortcuts across campus that are unfamiliar or seem unsafe.
- If security guards patrol the campus, know the areas they cover and stay where they can see or hear you.

Sexual Assault—Rape and Date Rape

The use of force and coercion in sexual relationships is one of the most serious problems in human interactions. The most extreme manifestation of sexual coercion—forcing a person to submit to another's sexual desires—is rape. Taking advantage of circumstances that render a person incapable of giving consent (such as when drunk) is also considered sexual assault or rape. Coerced sexual activity in which the victim knows or is dating the rapist is often referred to as date rape.

Nearly 700,000 females are raped annually in the United States, and some males—perhaps 10,000 annually—are raped each year by other males. Rape victims suffer both physical and psychological injury. The psychological pain can be substantial and long-lasting.

To protect yourself against rape:

- Follow the guidelines listed earlier for protecting yourself against assault.
- Trust your gut feeling. If you feel you are in danger, don't hesitate to run and scream.
- Think out in advance what you would do if you were threatened with rape. However, no one knows what he or she will do when scared to death. Trust that you will make the best decision at the time—whether to scream, run, fight, or give in to avoid being injured or killed.

To protect yourself against date rape:

- Believe in your right to control what you do. Set limits and communicate them clearly, firmly, and early. Be assertive; men often interpret passivity as permission.
- If you are unsure of a new acquaintance, go on a group date or double date. If possible, provide your own transportation.
- Remember that some men think flirtatious behavior or sexy clothing indicates an interest in having sex.
- Remember that alcohol and drugs interfere with judgment, perception, and communication about sex. In a bar or at a party, don't leave your drink unattended, and don't accept opened beverages; watch your drinks being poured. At a party or club, check on friends and ask them to check on you.
- Use the statement that has proven most effective in stopping date rape: "This is rape and I'm calling the cops!"

If you are raped:

- Tell what happened to the first friendly person you meet.
- Call the police. Tell them you were raped and give your location.
- Try to remember everything you can about your attacker and write it down.
- Don't wash or douche before the medical exam. Don't change your clothes, but bring a new set with you if you can.
- Be aware that at the hospital you will have a complete exam. Show the physician any bruises or scratches.
- Tell the police exactly what happened. Be honest and stick to your story.
- If you do not want to report the rape to the police, see a physician as soon as possible. Be sure you are checked for pregnancy and STDs.
- Contact an organization with skilled counselors so you can talk about the experience. Look in the telephone directory under "Rape" or "Rape Crisis Center" for a hotline number.

Guidelines for men:

- Be aware of social pressure. It's OK not to score.
- Understand that "No" means "No." Stop making advances when your date says to stop. Remember that she has the right to refuse sex.
- Don't assume that flirtatious behavior or sexy clothing means a woman is interested in having sex, that previous permission for sex applies to the current situation, or that your date's relationships with other men constitute sexual permission for you.
- Remember that alcohol and drugs interfere with judgment, perception, and communication about sex.

Stalking and Cyberstalking

Stalking is characterized by harassing behaviors such as following or spying on a person and making verbal, written, or implied threats. It is estimated that 1 million U.S. women and 400,000 men are stalked each year; most stalkers are men.

Cyberstalking, the use of electronic communications devices to stalk another person, is becoming more common. Cyberstalkers may send harassing or threatening e-mails or chat room messages to the victim, or they may encourage others to harass the victim by posting inflammatory messages and personal information on bulletin boards or chat rooms.

To protect yourself online:

- Never use your real name as an e-mail user name or chat room nickname. Select an age- and gender-neutral identity.
- Avoid filling out profiles for accounts related to e-mail use or chat room activities with information that could be used to identify you.
- Do not share personal information in public spaces anywhere online or give it to strangers.
- Learn how to filter unwanted e-mail messages.
- If you experience harassment online, do not respond to the harasser. Log off or surf elsewhere. Save all communications for evidence. If harassment continues, report it to the harasser's Internet service provider, your Internet service provider, and the local police.
- Don't agree to meet someone you've met online face-to-face unless you feel completely comfortable about it. Schedule a series of phone conversations first. Meet initially in a very public place and bring along a friend to increase your safety.

Coping After Terrorism, Mass Violence, or Natural Disasters

Certain areas of the United States are prone to natural disasters like Hurricane Katrina, which devastated the Gulf Coast in 2005. Other natural disasters include tornadoes, floods, and earthquakes. Less frequent in the United States are episodes of mass violence or terrorist events such as those that occurred in Oklahoma in April 1995 and on September 11, 2001. When such events occur, some people suffer direct physical harm and/or the loss of relatives, friends, or possessions; many others experience emotional distress and are robbed of their sense of security.

Each person reacts differently to traumatic disaster, and it is normal to experience a variety of responses. Reactions may include disbelief and shock, fear, anger and resentment, anxiety about the future, difficulty concentrating or making decisions, mood swings, irritability, sadness and depression, panic, guilt, apathy, feelings of isolation or powerlessness, and many of the behaviorial signs such as headaches or insomnia that are associated with excess stress (see Chapter 10). Reactions may occur immediately or may be delayed until weeks or months after the event.

Taking positive steps can help you cope with powerful emotions. Consider the following strategies:

- Share your experiences and emotions with friends and family members. Be a supportive listener. Reassure children and encourage them to talk about what they are feeling.
- Take care of your mind and body. Choose a healthy diet, exercise regularly, get plenty of sleep, and practice relaxation techniques. Don't turn to unhealthy coping techniques such as using alcohol or other drugs.
- Take a break from media reports and images, and try not to develop nightmare scenarios for possible future events.
- Reestablish your routines at home, school, and work.
- Find ways to help others. Donating money, blood, food, clothes, or time can ease difficult emotions and give you a greater sense of control.

Everyone copes with tragedy in a different way and recovers at a different pace. If you feel overwhelmed by your emotions, seek professional help. Additional information about coping with terrorism and violence is available from the Federal Emergency Management Agency (www.fema.gov), the U.S. Department of Justice (www.usdoj.gov), and the National Mental Health Association (www.nmha.org).

Emergency Preparedness

Most prevention and coping activities related to terrorism, mass violence, and natural disasters occur at the federal, state, and community levels. However, one step individuals can take is to put together an emergency plan and kit for their family or household that can serve for any type of emergency or disaster.

Emergency Supplies Your kit of emergency supplies should include everything you'll need to make it on your own for at least 3 days. You'll need nonperishable food, water, first aid and sanitation supplies, a battery-powered radio, clothing, a flashlight, cash, keys, copies of important documents, and supplies for sleeping outdoors in any weather. Remember special-needs items for infants, seniors, and pets. Supplies for a basic emergency kit are listed in Figure A.2; add to your kit based on your family situation and the type of problems most likely to occur in your area.

You may want to create several kinds of emergency kits. The primary one would contain supplies for home use. Put together a smaller, lightweight version that you can take with you if you are forced to evacuate your residence. Smaller kits for your car and your workplace are also recommended.

A Family or Household Plan You and your family or household members should have a plan about where to meet and how to communicate. Choose at least two potential meeting places—one in your neighborhood and one or more in other areas. Your community may also have set locations for community shelters. Where you go may depend on the circumstances of the emergency situation. Use your common sense, and listen to the radio or television to obtain instructions from emergency officials about whether to evacuate or stay in place. In addition, know all the transportation options in the vicinity of your home, school, and workplace; roadways and public transit may be affected, so a sturdy pair of walking shoes is a good item to keep in your emergency kit.

Everyone in the family or household should also have the same emergency contact person to call, preferably someone who lives outside the immediate area and won't be affected by the same local disaster. Local phone service may be significantly disrupted, so long-distance calls may be more likely to go through. Everyone should carry the relevant phone numbers and addresses at all times.

A

Basic emergency supplies

- Map of the area for locating evacuation routes or shelters
- Cash, coins, and credit cards
- Copies of important documents stored in watertight container
- Emergency contact list and phone numbers
- Extra sets of house and car keys
- Flashlights or lightsticks
- Battery- or solar-powered radio
- Battery-powered alarm clock
- Extra batteries and bulbs
- Cell phone or prepaid phone card
- Signal flares
- Fire extinguisher (small A-B-C type)
- Whistle
- Ladder
- Tube tent and rope
- Sleeping bags or warm blankets
- Foam pads, pillows, baby bed
- Complete change of warm clothing, footwear, outerware (jacket or coat, long pants, long-sleeved shirt, sturdy shoes, hat, gloves, raingear, extra socks and underwear, sunglasses)
- Work gloves
- Shutoff wrench for gas and water supplies
- Shovel, hammer, pliers, screwdriver, and other tools
- Compass
- Matches in a waterproof container
- Aluminum foil
- Plastic storage containers, bucket
- Duct tape, utility knife, and scissors
- Paper, pens, pencils
- Needles and thread

First aid kit

- First aid manual
- Thermometer
- Scissors
- Tweezers
- Safety pins, safety razor blades
- Needle
- Latex or other sterile gloves
- Sterile gauze pads
- Cleansing agents (soap, isopropyl alcohol, antiseptic towelettes)
- Sunscreen
- Insect repellent
- Antibiotic ointment
- Burn ointment
- Petroleum jelly or another lubricant
- Sterile adhesive bandages, several sizes
- Sterile rolled bandages and triangular bandages
- Cotton balls
- Eyewash solution
- Chemical heat and cold packs
- Aspirin or nonaspirin pain reliever
- Anti-diarrhea medication
- Laxative
- Antacid
- Activated charcoal (use if advised by Poison Control Center)
- Potassium iodide (use following radiation exposure if advised by local health authorities)
- Prescription medications and prescribed medical supplies
- List of medications, dosages, and any allergies
- Medicine dropper

Special needs items

- Infant care needs (formula, bottles, diapers, powdered milk, diaper rash ointment)
- Books or toys
- Extra eyeglasses, contact lenses and supplies
- Feminine hygiene supplies
- Denture needs
- Hearing aid or wheelchair batteries; other special equipment
- Pet care supplies, including leash, pet carrier, copy of vaccination history, and tie-out stakes
- Other (list)

Food and related supplies

- Manual (nonelectric) can opener
- Utility knife
- Paper towels
- Eating utensils: Mess kits, or paper cups and plates and utensils
- Plastic garbage bags and resealing bags
- Small cooking stove and cooking fuel (if food must be cooked)
- Water purification tablets

Water: Three-day-supply, at least 1 gallon of water per person per day, stored in plastic containers:

Number of people: ______ x 1 gallon x 3 days = ______ total minimum gallons of water

Store additional water if you live in a hot climate or if your household includes infants, pregnant women, or people with special health needs. Don't forget to store water for pets. Containers can be sterilized by rinsing them with a diluted bleach solution (one part bleach to ten parts water). Replace your water supply every six months.

Food: At least a three-day supply of nonperishable foods—those requiring no refrigeration, preparation, or cooking and little or no water. Choose foods from the following list and add foods that members of your household will eat. Replace items in your food supply every six months.

- Ready-to-eat canned meats, fruits, soups, and vegetables
- Protein or fruit bars
- Dry cereal or granola
- Peanut butter
- Sugar, salt, pepper
- Dried fruit
- Nuts
- Crackers
- Canned, powdered, or boxed juices
- Nonperishable pasteurized milk or powered milk
- Coffee, tea, sodas
- High-energy foods
- Comfort/stress foods
- MREs (military rations)
- Infant formula and baby foods
- Pet foods

Sanitation

- Plastic garbage bags (and ties)
- Toilet paper
- Moist towelettes or hand soap
- Washcloth and towel
- Personal hygiene items (toothbrush, shampoo, deodorant, comb, shaving cream, and so on)
- Plastic bucket with tight lid
- Household chlorine bleach, disinfectant
- Powdered lime
- Small shovel for digging latrine

For a clean air supply

Face masks or several layers of dense-weave cotton material (handkerchiefs, t-shirts, towels) that fit snugly over your nose and mouth.

Shelter-in-place supplies, to be used in an interior room to create a barrier between you and potentially contaminated air outside: Heavyweight plastic garbage bags or plastic sheeting; duct tape; scissors; and if possible, a portable air purifier with a HEPA filter.

Family emergency plan

Plan places where your family will meet; choose one location near your home and one outside your neighborhood.

Local ______________________ Outside neighborhood ______________________

Have one local and one out-of-state contact person for family members to call if separated during a disaster. (It may be easier to make long-distance calls than local calls.)

Local ______________________ Out-of state ______________________

FIGURE A.2 Sample emergency preparedness kit and plan.

It is also important to check into the emergency plans at any location where you or family members spend time, including schools and workplaces. For each location, know the safest place to be for different types of emergencies—for example, near load-bearing interior walls during an earthquake or in the basement during a tornado. Also know how to turn off water, gas, and electricity in case of damaged utility lines; keep the needed tools next to the shutoff valves.

Other steps you can take to help prepare for emergencies include taking a first aid class and setting up an emergency response group in your neighborhood, residential building, or office. Talk with your neighbors: Who has specialized equipment (for example, a power generator) or expertise that might help in a crisis? Do older or disabled neighbors have someone to help them? More complete information about emergency preparedness is available from local government agencies and from the following:

American Academy of Pediatrics (www.aap.org)
American Red Cross (www.redcross.org)
Federal Emergency Management Agency (www.fema.gov)
U.S. Department of Homeland Security (www.ready.gov)

PROVIDING EMERGENCY CARE

You can improve someone else's chances of surviving if you are prepared to provide emergency help. A course in first aid offered by the American Red Cross and on many college campuses can teach you to respond appropriately when someone needs help. Emergency rescue techniques can save the lives of people who have stopped breathing, who are choking, or whose hearts have stopped beating. Pulmonary resuscitation (also known as rescue breathing, artificial respiration, or mouth-to-mouth resuscitation) is used when a person is not breathing (see Figure A.1). Cardiopulmonary resuscitation (CPR) is used when a pulse can't be found. Training is required before a person can perform CPR. Significant changes were made to the guidelines for lay rescue CPR in 2005. Courses are offered by the American Red Cross and the American Heart Association.

When You Have to Provide Emergency Care

Remain calm and act sensibly. The basic pattern for providing emergency care is *check-call-care:*

1. ***Check the situation.*** Make sure the scene is safe for both you and the injured person. Don't put yourself in danger; if you get hurt too, you will be of little help to the injured person.
2. ***Check the victim.*** Conduct a quick head-to-toe examination. Assess the victim's signs and symptoms, such as level of responsiveness, pulse, and breathing rate. Look for bleeding and any indications of broken bones or paralysis.
3. ***Call for help.*** Call 911 or a local emergency number. Identify yourself and give as much information as you can about the condition of the victim and what happened.
4. ***Care for the victim.*** If the situation requires immediate action (no pulse, shock, etc.), provide first aid if you are trained to do so (see Figure A.1).

SELECTED BIBLIOGRAPHY

Bren, L. 2005. Prevent your child from choking. *FDA Consumer,* September/October.

Central Intelligence Agency. 2007. *The World Factbook.* Washington, D.C.: Central Intelligence Agency.

Federal Bureau of Investigation. 2006. *Hate Crime Statistics, 2005.* Washington, D.C.: U.S. Department of Justice.

Federal Bureau of Investigation. 2007. *Crime in the United States: Preliminary Annual Uniform Crime Reports, 2006.* Washington, D.C.: U.S. Department of Justice.

Insurance Information Institute. 2007. *Road Rage* (http://www.iii.org/individuals/auto/lifesaving/roadrage; retrieved June 14, 2007).

Iudice, A., et al. 2005. Effects of prolonged wakefulness combined with alcohol and hands-free cell phone divided attention tasks on simulated driving. *Human Psychopharmacology* 20(2): 125–132.

National Center for Health Statistics. 2006. Deaths: Preliminary Data for 2004. *National Vital Statistics Reports* 54(19).

National Center for Health Statistics. 2006. *Health, United States, 2006, with Chartbook on Trends in the Health of Americans.* Hyattsville, Md.: National Center for Health Statistics.

National Center for Injury Prevention and Control. 2006. *Intimate Partner Violence Fact Sheet* (http://www.cdc.gov/ncipc/factsheets/ipvfacts.htm; retrieved June 14, 2007).

National Center for Injury Prevention and Control. 2007. *Fire Deaths and Injuries Fact Sheet* (http://www.cdc.gov/ncipc/factsheets/fire.htm; retrieved June 14, 2007).

National Center for Injury Prevention and Control. 2007. *Sexual Violence Fact Sheet* (http://www.cdc.gov/ncipc/factsheets/svfacts.htm; retrieved June 14, 2007).

National Institute on Drug Abuse. 2005. NIDA *InfoFacts: Drugged Driving* (http://www.nida.nih.gov/Infofacts/driving.html; retrieved August 5, 2005).

National Safety Council. 2007. *Injury Facts 2007 Edition Kit.* Itasca, Ill.: National Safety Council.

National Traffic Safety Administration. 2005. *Traffic Safety Facts Research Note: Driver Cell Phone Use in 2004—Overall Results.* Washington, D.C.: National Traffic Safety Administration.

U.S. Department of Homeland Security. 2005. *Ready America* (www.ready.gov/index.html; retrieved March 4, 2005).

B APPENDIX B
NUTRITIONAL CONTENT OF COMMON FOODS

For this food composition table, foods are listed within the following groups, corresponding to MyPyramid: (1) breads, cereals, rice, and pasta; (2) vegetables; (3) fruit; (4) milk, yogurt, and cheese; (5) meat, poultry, fish, dry beans, eggs, and nuts; and (6) fats, oils, sweets, and alcoholic beverages.

Data are provided for a variety of nutrients. For planning and easy reference, complete the following chart with your approximate daily goals or limits; refer to Chapter 8 and the Nutrition Resources section that follows Chapter 8. Fill in the daily totals that apply to your approximate daily calorie intake, sex, and age.

TOTAL DAILY GOAL OR LIMIT			
Total energy	________ calories	**Cholesterol**	300 mg
Protein	________ grams	**Sodium**	________ mg
Carbohydrate	________ grams	**Vitamin A**	________ RE
Dietary fiber	________ grams	**Vitamin C**	________ mg
Total fat	________ grams	**Calcium**	________ mg
Saturated fat	________ grams	**Iron**	________ mg

This appendix contains information on the same nutrients found on most food labels, so you can make easy comparisons. On food labels, percent Daily Values without corresponding units are usually provided for vitamins and minerals. For reference, the Daily Values are as follows: 5000 IU of vitamin A, 60 mg of vitamin C, 1000 mg of calcium, and 18 mg of iron.

BREADS, CEREALS, RICE, AND PASTA

MyPyramid recommends a range of daily servings of grains based on caloric intake; for someone consuming a 2000-calorie diet, 6 ounce-equivalents are recommended, half of them whole grains. Each of the following counts as 1 ounce-equivalent: a slice of bread, a small muffin, I cup ready-to-eat cereal flakes, or ½ cup cooked cereal, rice, grains, or pasta.

Name	Amount	Weight g	Energy calories	Protein g	Carb. g	Fiber g	Total fat g	Sat. fat g	Chol. mg	Sod. mg	Vit. A RE	Vit. C mg	Calc. mg	Iron mg
Bagel, plain	1 bagel, 40″ dia.	89	229	8.9	45.0	2.0	1.4	0.4	0	399	0	1	79	5.4
Barley, pearled, cooked	½ cup	79	97	1.8	22.2	3.0	0.4	0.1	0	2	0	0	9	1.0
Bulgur, cooked	½ cup	91	76	2.8	16.9	4.1	0.2	0	0	5	0	0	9	0.9
Biscuit	1 biscuit, 2½″ dia.	35	128	2.2	17.0	0.5	5.8	0.9	0	368	0	0	17	1.2
Bread, corn	1 piece	60	188	4.3	28.9	1.4	6.0	1.6	37	467	26	0	44	1.1
Bread, French	1 slice	64	185	7.5	36.2	1.5	1.2	0.3	0	416	0	0	28	2.3
Bread, oatmeal	1 slice	27	73	2.3	13.1	1.1	1.2	0.2	0	162	1	0	18	0.73
Bread, pita, white	1 pita, 6½″ dia.	60	165	5.5	33.4	1.3	0.7	0.1	0	322	0	0	52	1.6
Bread, pita, whole wheat	1 pita, 6½″ dia.	64	170	6.3	35.2	4.7	1.7	0.3	0	340	0	0	10	2.0
Bread, pumpernickel	1 slice	26	65	2.3	12.4	1.7	0.8	0.1	0	174	0	0	18	0.8
Bread, raisin	1 slice	32	88	2.5	16.7	1.4	1.4	0.3	0	125	0	0	21	0.9
Bread, rye	1 slice	32	83	2.7	15.5	1.9	1.1	0.2	0	211	0	0.1	23	0.9
Bread sticks	2 sticks, 7⅝″ × ⅝″	20	82	2.4	13.7	0.6	1.9	0.3	0	131	0	0	4	0.9
Bread stuffing	½ cup	100	177	3.2	21.7	2.9	8.6	1.7	0	543	118	0	32	1.1
Bread, white	1 slice	30	80	2.3	15.2	0.7	1.0	0.2	0	204	0	0	45	1.1

Name	Amount	Weight g	Energy calories	Protein g	Carb. g	Fiber g	Total fat g	Sat. fat g	Chol. mg	Sod. mg	Vit. A RE	Vit. C mg	Calc. mg	Iron mg
Bread, whole wheat	1 slice	28	69	3.6	11.6	1.9	0.9	0.2	0	132	0	0	30	0.7
Buckwheat groats, cooked	½ cup	84	77	2.8	16.8	2.3	0.5	0.1	0	3	0	0	6	0.7
Cake, angelfood	1/12 of 10″ cake	50	128	3.1	29.4	0.1	0.2	0	0	254	0	0	42	0.1
Cake, chocolate w/frosting	1/8 of 18 oz cake	64	235	2.6	34.9	1.8	10.5	3.1	27	214	17	0.1	28	1.4
Cake, yellow w/frosting	1/8 of 18 oz cake	64	243	2.4	35.5	1.2	11.1	3.0	35	216	21	0	24	1.3
Cereal, All-Bran	½ cup	31	81	4.1	23.0	9.1	1.5	0.2	0	75	163	6.2	121	5.5
Cereal, Cheerios	1 cup	30	110	3.0	22.8	2.8	1.8	0.4	0	210	150	6.0	100	8.4
Cereal, corn flakes	1 cup	28	101	1.9	24.3	0.7	0	0	0	202	128	6.2	1	8.1
Cereal, Cream of Wheat	½ cup	125.5	65	1.9	13.8	0.6	0.3	0	0	69	0	0	58	5.2
Cereal, Frosted Flakes	¾ cup	31	114	1.0	28.0	1.0	0.2	0.1	0	148	160	6.2	2	4.5
Cereal, granola, low fat	½ cup	55	209	9.5	44.0	3.4	2.8	0.6	0	135	262	2.8	23	2.0
Cereal, raisin bran	1 cup	61	195	5.2	46.5	7.3	1.5	0.3	0	362	155	0.4	29	4.6
Cereal, Total	¾ cup	30	160	2.0	23.1	2.7	0.5	0.1	0	190	150	60.0	1000	18
Cereal, Wheat Chex	1 cup	50	180	5.0	40.55	5.4	1.0	0.1	0	420	150	6.0	100	14.4
Cereal, Wheaties	1 cup	30	110	3.0	24.2	3.0	1.0	0.2	0	210	150	6.0	20	8.4
Coffeecake w/topping	1 piece	56	178	3.1	30.0	0.7	5.4	1.0	27	236	20	0.1	76	0.8
Cookie, chocolate chip	1 medium cookie	15	69	0.5	8.9	0.5	3.4	1.1	0	49	0	0	2	0.4
Cookie, fig bar	1 cookie	16	56	0.6	11.3	0.7	1.2	0.2	0	56	1	0	10	0.5
Cookie, fortune	1 cookie	8	30	0.3	6.7	0.1	0.2	0.1	0	22	0	0	1	0.1
Cookie, oatmeal	1 large cookie	18	81	1.1	12.4	0.5	3.3	0.8	0	69	1	0.1	7	0.5
Cookie, sandwich	1 cookie	10	48	0.5	7.2	0.1	0.2	0.3	0	35	0	0	3	0.2
Corn meal, dry	¼ cup	35	126	2.9	26.8	2.6	0.6	0.1	0	1	0	0	2	1.4
Corn grits, cooked	½ cup	121	71	1.7	15.6	0.4	0.2	0	0	2	0	0	4	0.7
Couscous, cooked	½ cup	79	88	3.0	18.2	1.1	0.1	0	0	4	0	0	0	0.3
Cracker, crispbread, rye	3 crispbreads	30	110	2.4	24.7	5.0	0.4	0	0	79	0	0	9	0.7
Cracker, graham	3 squares	28	119	2.0	21.3	1.0	2.8	0.4	0	185	0	0	22	1.2
Cracker, matzo	1 matzo	28	111	2.8	23.4	0.8	0.4	0.1	0	1	0	0	4	0.9
Cracker, melba toast	6 pieces	30	117	3.6	23.0	1.9	1.0	0.1	0	249	0	0	28	1.1
Cracker, Ritz	5 crackers	16	79	1.2	10.3	0.3	3.7	0.6	0	124	0	0	24	0.6
Cracker, saltine	10 squares	30	128	2.8	21.3	0.9	3.4	0.5	0	322	0	0	20	1.7
Cracker, whole wheat	6 crackers	24	106	2.1	16.5	2.5	4.1	0.8	0	158	0	0	12	0.7
Croissant, butter	1 medium	57	231	4.7	26.1	1.5	12.0	6.6	38	424	117	0.1	21	1.2
Danish pastry, cheese	1 pastry	71	266	5.7	26.4	0.7	15.5	4.8	11	320	25	0.1	25	1.1
Doughnut, glazed	1 medium	45	192	2.3	22.9	0.7	10.3	2.7	14	181	1	0	27	0.5
English muffin, plain	½ muffin	29	67	2.2	13.1	0.8	0.5	0.1	0	132	0	0	50	0.3
French toast	1 slice	65	149	5.0	16.3	0	7.0	1.8	75	311	81	0.2	65	1.1
Macaroni, cooked	½ cup	70	111	4.1	21.6	1.3	0.7	0.1	0	1	0	0	5	1.0
Muffin, blueberry	2″ by 2¾″	57	162	3.71	23.2	0	6.2	1.2	21	251	22	0.9	108	1.3
Muffin, oat bran	1 small	66	178	4.6	31.9	3.0	4.9	0.7	0	259	0	0	42	2.8
Noodles, chow mein	½ cup	23	119	1.9	12.9	0.9	6.9	1.0	0	99	0	0	4	1.1
Noodles, egg, cooked	½ cup	80	110	3.6	20.0	1.0	1.7	0.3	23	4	5	0	10	1.2
Noodles, Japanese soba	½ cup	57	56	2.9	12.2	0	0.1	0	0	34	0	0	2	0.3
Oat bran, raw	¼ cup	24	58	4.1	15.6	3.6	1.7	0.3	0	1	0	0	14	1.3
Oatmeal, instant	1 packet	28	102	3.6	18.8	2.7	2.0	0.3	0	78	330	0	110	8.2
Pancake	4″ pancake	38	74	2.0	13.9	0.5	1.0	0.2	5	239	4	0.1	48	0.6
Pasta, cooked	2 oz.	57	75	2.9	14.2	0	0.6	0.1	19	3	3	0	3	0.7
Popcorn, air-popped	2 cups	16	62	2.0	12.4	2.3	0.7	0.1	0	1	2	0	1	0.5
Popcorn, oil-popped	2 cups	22	110	2.0	12.6	2.2	6.2	1.1	0	194	0	0.1	2	0.6
Pretzels, hard, salted	10 twists	60	228	6.2	47.9	1.8	1.6	0.2	0	814	0	0	11	3.1
Quinoa, uncooked	¼ cup	43	159	5.6	29.3	2.5	2.5	0.3	0	9	0	0	26	3.9
Rice, brown, cooked	½ cup	98	108	2.5	22.4	1.8	0.9	0.2	0	5	0	0	10	0.4
Rice cake	1 cake	9	35	0.7	7.3	0.4	0.3	0	0	29	0	0	1	0.1
Rice, white, cooked	½ cup	79	103	2.1	22.3	0.3	0.2	0	0	1	0	0	8	0.9
Rice, wild, cooked	½ cup	82	83	3.3	17.5	1.5	0.3	0	0	3	0	0	2	0.5
Roll, dinner	1 roll, 2″ square	28	87	3.0	14.6	0.6	1.8	0.4	0	150	0	0	50	1.0
Spaghetti, cooked	½ cup	70	110	4.0	21.4	1.3	0.6	0.1	0	90	0	0	5	0.9
Taco shell	1 medium	13	59	0.9	8.0	0.6	2.7	0.6	0	49	0	0	13	0.2
Tortilla chips	1 oz.	28	137	2.2	18.3	1.5	6.5	0.7	0	119	1	0	49	0.7
Tortilla, corn	1 medium	24	52	1.4	10.7	1.5	0.6	0.1	0	11	0	0	19	0.3
Tortilla, flour	8″ tortilla	51	146	4.4	25.3	0	3.1	0.4	0	249	0	0	97	1.0
Wheat germ, toasted	¼ cup	28	108	8.3	14.1	4.3	3.0	0.5	0	1	1	1.7	13	2.6

VEGETABLES

MyPyramid recommends a range of daily servings of vegetables based on caloric intake; for someone consuming a 2000-calorie diet, 2½ cups are recommended. Each of the following counts as ½ cup or equivalent: ½ cup raw or cooked vegetables, ½ cup vegetable juice, or 1 cup raw leafy salad greens.

Name	Amount	Weight g	Energy calories	Protein g	Carb. g	Fiber g	Total fat g	Sat. fat g	Chol. mg	Sod. mg	Vit. A RE	Vit. C mg	Calc. mg	Iron mg
Alfalfa sprouts	½ cup	17	4	0.7	0.4	0.3	0.1	0	0	1	1	1.4	5	0.2
Artichoke, cooked	1 medium	120	60	4.2	13.4	6.5	0.2	0	0	114	11	12.0	54	1.5
Arugula, raw	1 cup	20	5	0.5	0.7	0.3	0.1	0	0	5	24	3.0	32	0.3
Asparagus, cooked	6 spears	90	20	2.2	3.7	1.8	0.2	0.1	0	13	45	6.9	21	0.8
Bamboo shoots, canned	½ cup	66	12	1.1	2.1	0.9	0.3	0.1	0	5	1	0.7	5	0.2
*Beans, baked (plain)	½ cup	127	119	6.0	26.9	5.2	0.5	0.1	0	428	6	0	43	1.5
*Beans, black, cooked	½ cup	86	114	7.6	20.4	7.5	0.5	0.1	0	1	0	0	23	1.8
*Beans, fava, raw	½ cup	63	55	4.9	11.1	0	0.5	0.1	0	16	11	2.3	23	0.9
Beans, green snap, cooked	½ cup	63	22	1.2	4.9	2.0	0.2	0	0	1	22	6.1	28	0.4
*Beans, kidney, cooked	½ cup	89	112	7.7	20.2	5.7	0.4	0.1	0	1	0	1.1	31	2.0
*Beans, lentils, cooked	½ cup	99	115	8.9	19.9	7.8	0.4	0.1	0	2	0	1.5	19	3.3
*Beans, lima, cooked	½ cup	94	108	7.3	19.6	6.6	0.4	0.1	0	2	0	0	16	2.2
*Beans, navy, cooked	½ cup	91	127	7.5	23.7	9.6	0.5	0.1	0	0	0	0.8	63	2.2
*Beans, pinto, cooked	½ cup	85.5	122	7.7	22.4	7.7	0.6	0.1	0	1	0	0.7	39	1.8
*Beans, refried	½ cup	126	118	6.9	19.6	6.7	1.6	0.6	10	377	0	7.6	44	2.1
Beans, yellow snap, cooked	½ cup	63	22	1.2	4.9	2.1	0.2	0	0	2	2	6.1	29	0.8
Beet greens, cooked	½ cup	72	19	1.9	3.9	2.1	0.1	0	0	174	276	17.9	82	1.4
Beets, cooked	½ cup	85	37	1.4	8.5	1.7	0.2	0	0	65	2	3.1	14	0.7
Broccoli spears, cooked	2 spears	74	21	2.2	3.7	2.4	0.3	0	0	30	73	31.0	30	1.0
Brussels sprouts, cooked	4 sprouts	84	34	2.1	7.3	2.2	0.4	0.1	0	18	33	52.1	30	1.0
Cabbage, cooked	½ cup	75	17	1.0	4.1	1.4	0	0	0	6	3	28.1	36	0.1
Cabbage, raw	½ cup	45	11	0.6	2.6	1.1	0	0	0	8	2	16.3	18	0.2
Carrot, juice	¾ cup	177	71	1.7	16.4	1.4	0.3	0	0	51	1692	15.0	42	0.8
Carrots, cooked	½ cup	78	27	0.6	6.4	2.3	0.1	0	0	236	671	2.8	23	0.3
Carrots, raw	1 medium	61	25	0.6	5.8	1.7	0.2	0	0	42	513	3.6	20	0.2
Cauliflower, cooked	½ cup	62	14	1.1	2.5	1.7	0.3	0	0	9	1	27.5	10	0.2
Celery, raw	8 sticks	32	5	0.2	1.0	0.5	0	0	0	26	7	1.0	13	0.1
Chard, cooked	½ cup	88	18	1.6	3.6	1.8	0.1	0	0	157	268	15.8	51	2.0
Coleslaw, homemade	½ cup	60	47	0.8	7.4	0.9	1.6	0.2	5	14	32	19.6	27	0.4
Collards, cooked	½ cup	95	25	2.0	4.7	2.7	0.3	0	0	9	386	17.3	133	1.1
Corn, yellow, cooked	½ cup	82	89	2.7	20.6	2.3	1.1	0.2	0	14	11	5.1	2	0.5
Cucumber, raw	½ cup	52	8	0.3	1.9	0.3	0.1	0	0	1	3	1.5	8	0.2
Eggplant, cooked	½ cup	50	17	0.4	4.3	1.2	0.1	0	0	0	1	0.6	3	0.1
Endive, raw	½ cup	25	4	0.3	0.8	0.8	0.1	0	0	6	27	1.6	13	0.2
Hominy, canned	½ cup	83	59	1.2	11.8	2.1	0.7	0.1	0	173	0	0	8	0.5
Kale, cooked	½ cup	65	18	1.2	3.6	1.3	0.3	0	0	15	443	26.6	47	0.6
Kohlrabi, cooked	½ cup	83	24	1.5	5.5	0.9	0.1	0	0	17	2	44.5	21	0.3
Leeks, raw	½ cup	45	27	0.7	6.3	0.8	0.1	0	0	9	37	5.3	26	0.9
Lettuce, green leaf, shredded	1 cup	36	5	0.5	1.0	0.5	0.1	0	0	10	133	6.5	13	0.3
Lettuce, iceberg, shredded	1 cup	72	10	0.7	2.1	0.9	0.1	0	0	7	18	2.0	13	0.3
Lettuce, romaine, shredded	1 cup	47	8	0.6	1.5	1.0	0.1	0	0	4	136	11.3	16	0.5
Mushrooms, raw	½ cup	35	8	1.1	1.1	0.3	0.1	0	0	2	0	0.7	1	0.2
Mushrooms, cooked	½ cup	78	22	1.7	4.1	1.7	0.3	0	0	2	0	3.1	5	1.4
Mustard greens, cooked	½ cup	70	10	1.6	1.5	1.4	0.2	0	0	11	221	17.7	52	0.5
Okra, cooked	½ cup	80	18	1.5	3.6	2.0	0.1	0	0	5	11	13.0	62	0.2
Onion, raw	½ cup	80	32	0.9	7.5	1.4	0.1	0	0	3	0	5.9	18	0.2
Parsley, raw	2 tablespoons	8	3	0.2	0.5	0.3	0.1	0	0	4	32	10.1	10	0.5
Parsnip, raw	½ cup	67	50	0.8	12.0	3.3	0.2	0	0	7	0	11.3	24	0.4
*Peas, chickpeas (garbanzos)	½ cup	82	134	7.3	22.5	6.2	2.1	0.2	0	6	1	1.1	40	2.4
Peas, edible, podded	10 pea pods	34	14	1.0	2.6	0.9	0.1	0	0	1	18	20.4	15	0.7
Peas, green	½ cup	80	67	4.3	12.5	4.4	0.2	0	0	2	32	11.4	22	1.2
*Peas, split, cooked	½ cup	98	116	8.2	20.6	8.1	0.4	0.1	0	2	0	0.4	14	1.3
Pepper, green chili, canned	½ cup	70	15	0.5	3.2	1.2	0.2	0	0	276	4	23.8	25	0.9
Pepper, sweet green, raw	1 small	74	15	0.6	3.4	1.3	0.1	0	0	2	13	59.5	7	0.3
Pepper, sweet red, raw	1 small	74	19	0.7	4.5	1.5	0.2	0	0	1	116	140.6	7	0.3

Name	Amount	Weight g	Energy calories	Protein g	Carb. g	Fiber g	Total fat g	Sat. fat g	Chol. mg	Sod. mg	Vit. A RE	Vit. C mg	Calc. mg	Iron mg
Pickle, dill	1 medium	65	8	0.4	1.7	0.7	0.1	0	0	569	6	0.5	27	0.2
Potato, mashed w/milk	½ cup	105	87	2.0	18.4	1.6	0.6	0.3	2	317	4	7.0	25	0.3
Potato salad	½ cup	125	179	3.4	14.0	1.6	10.3	1.8	85	661	40	12.5	24	0.8
Potato, baked w/skin	1 medium	173	161	4.3	36.6	3.8	0.1	0	0	17	2	16.6	26	1.9
Potato, boiled	1 potato, 2 ½″ dia.	136	118	2.5	27.4	2.4	0.1	0	0	5	0	17.7	7	0.4
Potato, french fries	10 fries	50	109	1.7	17.0	1.6	4.1	1.9	0	22	0	4.8	5	0.7
Pumpkin, canned	½ cup	123	42	1.3	9.9	3.6	0.3	0.2	0	6	953	5.1	32	1.7
Radish, raw	13 medium	59	9	0.4	2.0	0.9	0	0	0	23	0	8.7	15	0.2
Rutabaga, mashed	½ cup	120	47	1.5	10.5	2.2	0.3	0	0	24	0	22.6	58	0.6
Sauerkraut, canned	½ cup	71	13	0.6	3.0	1.8	0.1	0	0	469	1	10.4	21	1.0
Soybeans, green, boiled	½ cup	90	127	11.1	9.9	3.8	5.8	0.7	0	13	7	15.3	131	2.3
Spinach, raw	1 cup	30	7	0.9	1.1	0.7	0.1	0	0	24	141	8.4	30	0.8
Spinach, cooked	½ cup	90	21	2.7	3.4	2.2	0.2	0	0	63	472	8.8	122	3.2
Squash, summer, raw	½ small squash	59	9	0.7	2.0	0.6	0.1	0	0	1	6	10.0	9	0.2
Squash, summer, cooked	½ cup	90	18	0.8	3.9	1.3	0.3	0	0	1	10	5.0	24	0.3
Squash, winter	½ cup	103	38	0.9	9.1	2.9	0.4	0.1	0	1	268	9.8	23	0.5
Sweet potato, baked	½ cup	100	90	2.0	20.7	3.3	0.2	0	0	36	961	19.6	38	0.7
Sweet potato, canned w/syrup	½ cup	114	101	1.1	23.7	2.9	0.2	0.1	0	50	430	12.0	17	0.9
Tomato, red, raw	1 medium	123	22	1.1	4.8	1.8	0.2	0	0	13	21	16.0	17	0.9
Tomato sauce	½ cup	122	29	1.6	6.6	1.8	0.2	0	0	642	21	8.6	16	1.3
Tomato juice	¾ cup	182	31	1.4	7.7	0.7	0.1	0	0	18	42	33.4	18	0.8
Turnip, cooked, mashed	½ cup	115	25	0.8	5.8	2.3	0.1	0	0	118	0	13.3	38	0.2
Vegetable juice	¾ cup	182	34	1.1	8.3	1.5	0.2	0	0	490	142	50.3	20	0.8
Vegetables, mixed	½ cup	91	59	2.6	11.9	4.0	0.1	0	0	32	195	2.9	23	0.7
Vegetable soup	1 cup	241	72	2.1	12.0	0.5	1.9	0.3	0	822	116	1.4	22	1.1
Waterchestnuts	½ cup	62	60	0.9	14.8	1.9	0.1	0	0	9	0	2.5	7	0

*Dry beans and peas (legumes) can be counted as servings of vegetables or as servings from the meat, poultry, fish, dry beans, eggs, and nuts group. They are listed here and marked with an asterisk.

FRUIT MyPyramid recommends a range of daily servings of fruit based on caloric intake; for someone consuming a 2000-calorie diet, 2 cups are recommended. Each of the following counts as ½ cup or equivalent: ½ cup fresh, canned, or frozen fruit, ½ cup fruit juice, 1 small whole fruit, or ¼ cup dried fruit.

Name	Amount	Weight g	Energy calories	Protein g	Carb. g	Fiber g	Total fat g	Sat. fat g	Chol. mg	Sod. mg	Vit. A RE	Vit. C mg	Calc. mg	Iron mg
Apple, raw, w/skin	1 medium	138	72	0.4	19.1	3.3	0.2	0	0	1	4	6.3	8	0.2
Apple juice	¾ cup	179	84	0.3	20.7	0.2	0.2	0	0	13	0	44.8	11	0.5
Apple sauce, unsweetened	½ cup	122	52	0.2	13.8	1.5	0.1	0	0	2	1	25.9	4	0.1
Apricots	2 medium	70	34	1.0	7.8	1.4	0.3	0	0	1	67	7.0	10	0.3
Apricots, dried	9 halves	32	76	1.1	19.7	2.3	0.1	0	0	3	57	0.3	17	0.8
Avocado	1 medium	201	322	4.0	17.1	13.5	29.5	4.3	0	14	14	20.1	24	1.1
Banana	1 medium	118	105	1.3	27.0	3.1	0.4	0.1	0	1	4	10.3	6	0.3
Blackberries, raw	½ cup	72	31	1.0	6.9	3.8	0.4	0	0	1	8	15.1	21	0.5
Blueberries	½ cup	74	42	0.6	10.7	1.8	0.2	0	0	1	2	7.2	4	0.2
Cantaloupe	¼ melon, 5″ dia.	138	47	1.2	11.3	1.2	0.3	0.1	0	22	233	50.6	12	0.3
Carambola (starfruit)	1 small	70	22	0.7	4.7	1.2	0.2	0	0	1	2	24.1	2	0.1
Cherries, sweet, raw	11 cherries	75	47	0.8	12.0	1.6	0.2	0	0	0	2	5.2	10	0.3
Cherries, canned in syrup	½ cup	127	105	0.8	26.9	1.9	0.2	0	0	4	10	4.6	11	0.4
Cranberries, raw	½ cup	48	22	0.2	6.0	2.2	0.1	0	0	1	1	6.3	4	0.1
Cranberry juice cocktail	¾ cup	190	102	0	25.6	0	0.2	0	0	4	0	80.3	6	0.2
Cranberry sauce	¼ cup	69	105	0.1	26.9	0.7	0.1	0	0	20	1	1.4	3	0.2
Currants, dried	¼ cup	36	102	1.5	26.7	2.4	0.1	0	0	3	1	1.7	31	1.2
Dates, dried	¼ cup	45	125	1.1	33.4	3.6	0.2	0	0	1	0	0.2	17	0.5
Figs, raw	2 medium	100	74	0.8	19.2	2.9	0.3	0.1	0	1	7	2.0	35	0.4
Fruit cocktail, heavy syrup	½ cup	124	91	0.5	23.4	1.2	0.1	0	0	7	12	2.4	7	0.4
Fruit cocktail, light syrup	½ cup	121	69	0.5	18.1	1.2	0.1	0	0	7	12	2.3	7	0.4
Fruit cocktail, juice	½ cup	119	55	0.5	14.1	1.2	0	0	0	5	18	3.2	9	0.3
Grapefruit	½ medium	123	37	0.7	9.2	1.4	0.1	0	0	0	16	45.5	18	0.2
Grapefruit juice	¾ cup	185	72	1.0	17.0	0	0.2	0	0	2	41	70.4	17	0.4
Grapes	10 grapes	49	34	0.4	8.9	0.4	0.1	0	0	1	1	5.3	5	0.2

Name	Amount	Weight g	Energy calories	Protein g	Carb. g	Fiber g	Total fat g	Sat. fat g	Chol. mg	Sod. mg	Vit. A RE	Vit. C mg	Calc. mg	Iron mg
Guava	1 fruit	55	37	1.4	7.9	3.0	0.5	0.2	0	1	17	125.6	10	0.3
Honeydew	⅛ melon, 5¼″ dia.	125	45	0.7	11.4	1.0	0.1	0	0	22	4	22.5	8	0.2
Kiwifruit	1 large	91	56	0.9	13.5	3.1	0.4	0	0	5	8	68.2	24	0.4
Kumquats	5 fruits	95	67	1.8	15.1	6.2	0.8	0.1	0	10	14	41.7	59	0.8
Lemon, with peel	1 fruit	108	22	1.3	11.6	5.1	0.3	0	0	3	2	83.2	66	0.8
Lemon juice	2 tablespoons	30	6	0.1	1.9	0.1	0.1	0	0	6	0	7.4	3	0
Mango	½ medium	103	67	0.5	17.0	1.9	0.3	0.1	0	2	39	28.7	10	0.1
Nectarine	1 fruit	142	62	1.5	15	2.4	0.5	0	0	0	24	7.7	9	0.4
Olives, ripe	10 large	44	51	0.4	2.8	1.4	4.7	0.6	0	384	9	0.4	39	1.5
Orange	1 medium	131	62	1.2	15.4	3.1	0.2	0	0	0	14	69.7	52	0.1
Orange juice	¾ cup	186	84	1.3	19.3	0.4	0.4	0	0	2	19	93	20	0.4
Papaya	½ medium	152	59	0.9	14.0	2.7	0.2	0.1	0	5	84	93.9	36	0.2
Peach, raw	1 medium	150	58	1.4	14.3	2.2	0.4	0	0	0	24	9.9	6	0.4
Peach, canned in juice	½ cup	125	55	0.8	14.3	1.6	0	0	0	5	24	4.5	7	0.3
Pear, raw	1 medium	178	103	0.7	27.5	5.5	0.2	0	0	2	2	7.5	16	0.3
Pear, canned	½ cup	124	62	0.4	16	2.0	0.1	0	0	5	0	2.0	11	0.4
Persimmon, raw	1 fruit	25	32	0.2	8.4	0	0.1	0	0	0	0	16.5	7	0.6
Pineapple, canned in juice	½ cup	125	75	0.5	19.5	1.0	0.1	0	0	1	2	11.8	17	0.3
Pineapple, raw	1 slice, 3½″ × ¾″	84	40	0.5	10.6	1.2	0.1	0	0	1	3	30.4	11	0.2
Plantain, raw	1 medium	179	218	2.3	57.1	4.1	0.6	0.3	0	7	100	32.9	5	1.1
Plums	1½ medium	99	46	0.7	11.3	1.4	0.3	0	0	0	17	9.4	6	0.2
Prune juice	¾ cup	192	136	1.2	33.5	1.9	0.1	0	0	8	0	7.9	23	2.3
Prunes (dried plums)	5 prunes	48	114	1.0	30.3	3.4	0.2	0	0	1	19	0.3	20	0.4
Raisins	¼ cup	41	125	1.4	32.8	1.6	0.2	0	0	5	0	1.3	22	0.7
Raspberries	½ cup	62	32	0.7	7.3	4.0	0.4	0	0	1	1	16.1	15	0.4
Rhubarb, raw	1 stalk	51	11	0.5	2.3	0.9	0.1	0	0	2	3	4.1	44	0.1
Strawberries	5 large	90	29	0.6	6.9	2.1	0.3	0	0	1	1	52.9	14	0.4
Tangerine	1 medium	88	47	0.7	11.7	1.6	0.3	0	0	2	30	23.5	33	0.1
Watermelon	1⁄16 melon	283	85	1.7	21.3	1.1	0.4	0	0	3	79	22.9	20	0.7

MILK, YOGURT, AND CHEESE MyPyramid recommends a range of daily servings of milk products based on caloric intake; for someone consuming a 2000-calorie diet, 3 cups of milk or the equivalent are recommended. Each of the following counts as 1 cup: 1 cup milk or yogurt, ½ cup ricotta cheese, 1½ ounces natural cheese, or 2 ounces processed cheese.

Name	Amount	Weight g	Energy calories	Protein g	Carb. g	Fiber g	Total fat g	Sat. fat g	Chol. mg	Sod. mg	Vit. A RE	Vit. C mg	Calc. mg	Iron mg
Buttermilk, lowfat	1 cup	245	98	8.1	11.7	0	2.2	1.3	10	257	17	2.5	284	0.1
Cheese, American	2 oz.	57	188	11.1	4.7	0	13.9	8.7	36	548	90	0	282	0.5
Cheese, blue	1½ oz.	43	150	9.1	1.0	0	12.2	7.9	32	593	84	0	225	0.1
Cheese, cheddar	1½ oz.	43	171	10.6	0.5	0	14.1	9.0	45	264	113	0	307	0.3
Cheese, cottage, creamed	1 cup	210	216	26.2	5.6	0	9.5	6.0	32	850	92	0	126	0.3
Cheese, cottage, lowfat (1%)	1 cup	226	163	28.0	6.1	0	2.3	1.5	9	918	25	0	138	0.3
Cheese, cottage, non-fat	1 cup	145	123	25.0	2.7	0	0.6	0.4	10	19	13	0	46	0.3
Cheese, cream	2 oz.	57	198	4.3	1.5	0	19.8	12.5	62	168	208	0	45	0.7
Cheese, cream, fat free	2 oz.	57	55	8.2	3.3	0	0.8	0.5	5	311	159	0	105	0.1
Cheese, feta	1½ oz.	43	112	6.0	1.7	0	9.0	6.4	38	475	53	0	210	0.3
Cheese, Mexican	1½ oz.	43	151	9.6	1.2	0	12.0	7.6	45	279	23	0	281	0.2
Cheese, Monterey	1½ oz.	43	159	10.4	0.3	0	12.9	8.1	38	228	84	0	317	0.3
Cheese, mozzarella (part skim)	1½ oz.	43	108	10.3	1.2	0	6.8	4.3	27	263	54	0	333	0.1
Cheese, Parmesan, grated	2 tablespoons	10	43	3.9	0.4	0	2.9	1.7	9	153	12	0	111	0.1
Cheese, process spread	2 oz.	56	170	9.1	5.5	0	12.3	8.1	45	839	100	0.1	261	0.1
Cheese, provolone	1½ oz.	43	149	10.9	0.9	0	11.3	7.3	29	373	100	0	321	0.2
Cheese, ricotta, part skim	½ cup	123	170	14.0	6.3	0	9.7	6.1	38	154	132	0	335	0.5
Cheese, Swiss	1½ oz.	43	162	11.5	2.3	0	11.8	7.6	39	82	94	0	336	0.1
Ice cream, chocolate	1 cup	132	285	5.0	37.2	1.6	14.2	9.0	45	100	156	0.9	144	1.2
Ice cream, vanilla, rich	1 cup	214	533	7.5	47.7	0	34.7	22.1	197	131	389	0	250	0.7
Ice cream, vanilla, light	1 cup	152	251	7.3	39.2	0.5	7.3	4.4	41	12	195	1.8	245	0.3
Ice cream, vanilla, soft-serve	1 cup	172	382	7.0	38.2	1.2	22.4	12.9	157	105	279	1.4	225	0.4
Milk, chocolate	1 cup	250	208	7.9	25.9	2.0	8.5	5.3	30	150	65	2.2	280	0.6
Milk, fat free (nonfat)	1 cup	245	83	8.3	12.1	0	0.2	0.3	5	103	149	0	306	0.1
Milk, lowfat (1%)	1 cup	244	102	8.2	12.2	0	2.4	1.6	12	107	142	0	290	0.1

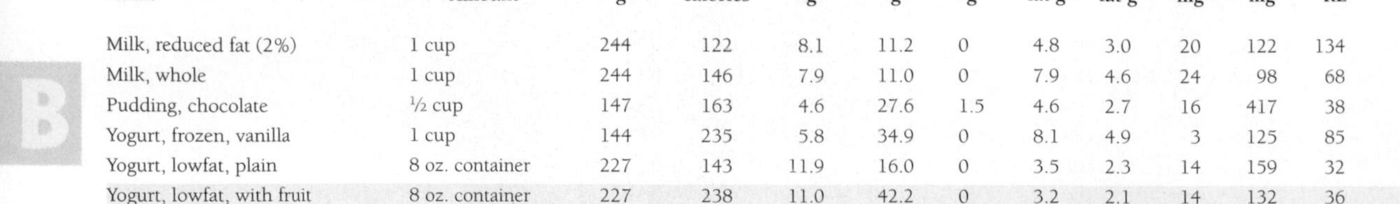

Name	Amount	Weight g	Energy calories	Protein g	Carb. g	Fiber g	Total fat g	Sat. fat g	Chol. mg	Sod. mg	Vit. A RE	Vit. C mg	Calc. mg	Iron mg
Milk, reduced fat (2%)	1 cup	244	122	8.1	11.2	0	4.8	3.0	20	122	134	0.5	285	0.1
Milk, whole	1 cup	244	146	7.9	11.0	0	7.9	4.6	24	98	68	0	276	0.1
Pudding, chocolate	½ cup	147	163	4.6	27.6	1.5	4.6	2.7	16	417	38	1.3	150	0.4
Yogurt, frozen, vanilla	1 cup	144	235	5.8	34.9	0	8.1	4.9	3	125	85	1.2	206	0.4
Yogurt, lowfat, plain	8 oz. container	227	143	11.9	16.0	0	3.5	2.3	14	159	32	1.8	415	0.2
Yogurt, lowfat, with fruit	8 oz. container	227	238	11.0	42.2	0	3.2	2.1	14	132	36	1.6	345	0.2
Yogurt, nonfat, plain	8 oz. container	227	127	13.0	17.4	0	0.4	0.3	5	175	5	2.0	452	0.2

MEAT, POULTRY, FISH, DRY BEANS, EGGS, AND NUTS

MyPyramid recommends a range of daily servings of meat and beans based on caloric intake; for someone consuming a 2000-calorie diet, 5.5 ounce-equivalents are recommended. Each of the following counts as 1 ounce-equivalent: 1 ounce cooked lean meat, poultry, or fish; ¼ cup cooked dry beans or tofu; 1 egg; 1 tablespoon peanut butter; or ½ ounce nuts or seeds.

Name	Amount	Weight g	Energy calories	Protein g	Carb. g	Fiber g	Total fat g	Sat. fat g	Chol. mg	Sod. mg	Vit. A RE	Vit. C mg	Calc. mg	Iron mg
Bacon, Canadian	2 slices	47	87	11.3	0.6	0	3.9	1.3	27	727	0	0	5	0.4
Beef, lean, fat trimmed	3 oz.	85	179	25.4	0	0	7.9	3.0	73	56	0	0	7	2.5
Beef, corned	3 oz.	85	213	15.4	0	0	16.1	5.3	83	964	0	0	7	1.6
Beef, ground, 95% lean, broiled	3 oz.	85	145	22.4	0	0	5.6	2.5	65	55	0	0	6	2.4
Beef, ground, 85% lean, broiled	3 oz.	85	212	22.0	0	0	13.2	5.0	76	61	0	0	15	2.2
Beef, ground, 70% lean, broiled	3 oz.	85	232	21.6	0	0	15.5	6.3	70	69	0	0	30	1.9
Beef liver, braised	1 slice	68	130	19.8	0	0	3.6	1.2	269	54	6421	1.3	4	4.5
Beef ribs, broiled	3 oz.	85	309	20.1	0	0	24.8	10.5	71	53	0	0	11	1.8
Chicken breast, w/skin, rst	½ breast	98	193	29.2	0	0	7.6	2.1	82	70	27	0	14	1.0
Chicken, dk mt, w/skin, rst	3 oz.	85	215	22.1	0	0	13.4	3.7	77	74	51	0	13	1.2
Chicken, dk mt, w/o skin, rst	3 oz.	85	205	27.4	0	0	9.7	2.7	93	93	22	0	15	1.3
Chicken, dk mt, w/skin, fried	3 oz.	85	253	18.6	8.0	0	15.8	4.2	76	251	26	0	18	1.2
Chicken, drumstick, w/skin, rst	1 drumstick	52	112	14.1	0	0	5.8	1.6	47	47	16	0	6	0.7
Chicken, lt mt, w/skin, rst	3 oz.	85	189	24.7	0	0	9.2	2.6	71	64	28	0	13	1.0
Chicken, lt mt, w/o skin, rst	3 oz.	85	147	26.3	0	0	3.8	1.1	72	65	8	0	13	0.9
Chicken, lt mt, w/skin, fried	3 oz.	85	235	20.0	8.1	0	13.1	3.5	71	244	20	0	17	1.1
Chicken, thigh, w/skin, rst	1 thigh	62	153	15.5	0	0	9.6	2.7	58	52	31	0	7	0.8
Chicken, wing, w/skin, rst	1 wing	34	99	9.1	0	0	6.6	1.9	29	28	16	0	5	0.4
Chicken liver, pan-fried	3 oz.	100	172	25.8	1.1	0	6.4	1.7	564	92	4296	2.7	10	12.9
Egg white, large	1 egg white	33	17	3.6	0.2	0	0	0	0	55	0	0	2	0
Egg, whole, large	1 egg	50	74	6.3	0.4	0	5.0	1.6	212	70	70	0	26	0.9
Egg yolk, large	1 yolk	17	55	2.7	0.6	0	4.5	1.6	210	8	65	0	22	0.5
Fish, catfish, baked/broiled	3 oz.	85	129	15.9	0	0	6.8	1.5	54	68	13	0.7	8	0.7
Fish, cod, baked/broiled	3 oz.	85	89	19.4	0	0	0.7	0.1	47	66	12	0.8	0.2	0.4
Fish, halibut, baked/broiled	3 oz.	85	119	22.7	0	0	2.5	0.4	35	59	46	0	51	0.9
Fish, salmon, baked/broiled	3 oz.	85	175	18.8	0	0	10.5	2.1	54	52	13	3.1	13	0.3
Fish, salmon, canned, w/o salt	3 oz.	85	130	17.4	0	0	6.2	1.4	37	64	45	0	203	0.9
Fish, salmon, smoked	3 oz.	85	99	15.5	0	0	3.7	0.8	20	666	22	0	9	0.7
Fish, sardine, canned in oil	1 can (3.75 oz.)	92	191	22.7	0	0	10.5	1.4	131	465	29	0	351	2.7
Fish, snapper, baked/broiled	3 oz.	85	109	22.3	0	0	1.5	0.3	40	48	30	1.4	34	0.2
Fish sticks	3 sticks	84	209	9.3	17.8	1.2	11.1	1.7	27	354	26	0	22	0.9
Fish, swordfish, baked/broiled	3 oz.	85	132	21.6	0	0	4.4	1.2	42	98	35	0.9	5	0.9
Fish, trout, baked/broiled	3 oz.	85	162	22.6	0	0	7.2	1.3	63	57	16	0.4	47	1.6
Fish, tuna, canned in oil	3 oz.	85	158	22.6	0	0	6.9	1.2	26	337	4	0	3	0.6
Fish, tuna, canned in water	3 oz.	85	109	20.1	0	0	2.5	0.7	36	320	5	0	12	0.8
Ham, extra lean	3 oz.	85	116	18.0	0.4	0	4.1	1.4	26	965	0	0	5	0.8
Ham, regular	3 oz.	85	137	13.9	3.2	1.1	7.2	2.5	48	1095	0	3.4	20	0.9
Lamb, trimmed	3 oz.	85	218	20.8	0	0	14.3	6.7	74	65	0	0	14	1.6
Lunch meat, beef pastrami, cured	3 oz.	84	123	18.3	0	0	4.9	2.3	57	743	28	1.1	8	1.9
Lunch meat, beef, sliced	3 oz.	85	127	16.2	0.8	0	6.0	2.5	60	1201	0	0	9	1.8
Lunch meat, bologna (beef)	3 slices	84	261	8.6	3.3	0	23.7	9.4	47	907	11	12.8	26	0.9
Lunch meat, bologna (turkey)	3 slices	84	176	9.6	3.9	0.4	13.5	3.7	63	1052	8	11.2	103	2.5
Lunch meat, chicken breast, fat-free	3 oz.	85	67	14.3	1.8	0	0.3	0.1	31	924	0	0	5	0.3
Lunch meat, franks (beef)	1 frank	56	162	7.0	1.2	0	14.4	5.9	38	557	2	11.2	8	1.0
Lunch meat, franks (chicken)	1 frank	45	116	5.8	3.1	0	8.8	2.5	45	616	18	0	43	0.9

Name	Amount	Weight g	Energy calories	Protein g	Carb. g	Fiber g	Total fat g	Sat. fat g	Chol. mg	Sod. mg	Vit. A RE	Vit. C mg	Calc mg	Iron mg
Lunch meat, liverwurst	3 oz.	85	277	12.0	1.9	0	24.2	9.0	134	731	7066	0	22	5.4
Lunch meat, salami, dry	8 slices	80	326	18.1	1.2	0	27.0	9.5	63	1808	0	0	10	1.0
Lunch meat, turkey, smoked	3 oz.	85	85	15.0	2.0	0	2.0	0.5	36	781	0	0	8	0.6
Luncheon slices, meatless	3 oz.	85	161	15.1	3.8	0	9.4	1.1	0	604	0	0	35	1.5
Meatloaf (80% lean meat)	3 oz.	85	216	21.5	0	0	13.7	5.2	76	57	0	0	20	2.2
Nuts, almonds	⅓ cup	47	273	10.0	9.3	5.6	23.9	1.8	0	0	0	0	117	2.0
Nuts, cashews, dry roasted, w/o salt	⅓ cup	46	262	7.0	14.9	1.4	21.2	4.2	0	7	0	0	21	2.7
Nuts, chestnuts, roasted	⅓ cup	48	117	1.5	25.2	2.4	1.0	0.2	0	1	1	12.4	14	0.4
Nuts, macadamia, dry roasted	⅓ cup	45	321	3.5	6.0	3.6	34.0	5.3	0	2	0	0.3	31	1.2
Nuts, pecans	⅓ cup	36	249	3.3	5.0	3.5	25.9	2.2	0	0	1	0.4	25	0.9
Nuts, pine	⅓ cup	45	300	6.1	5.8	1.6	30.5	2.2	0	1	0	0.4	7	2.5
Nuts, pistachios, dry roasted	⅓ cup	41	234	8.8	11.3	1.2	18.9	2.3	0	4	5	0.9	45	1.7
Nuts, walnuts	⅓ cup	40	261	6.1	5.5	2.7	26.1	2.5	0	1	0	0.5	39	1.2
Peanut butter, chunky	2 tablespoons	32	188	7.7	6.9	2.6	16.0	2.6	0	156	0	0	14	0.6
Peanut butter, smooth	2 tablespoons	32	188	8.0	6.3	1.9	16.1	3.3	0	147	0	0	14	0.6
Peanuts, dry roasted	⅓ cup	48	281	11.4	10.4	3.9	23.9	3.3	0	3	0	0	26	1.1
Pork chop, pan fried	3 oz.	85	205	21.0	0	0	12.8	4.4	70	66	2	0.7	19	0.9
Pork ribs, braised	3 oz.	85	252	20.3	0	0	18.3	6.8	74	50	2	0.6	25	1.0
Pork roast	3 oz.	85	214	22.9	0	0	12.9	4.5	69	41	3	0	5	0.8
Pumpkin seeds, roasted	¼ cup	57	296	18.7	7.6	2.2	23.9	4.5	0	10	22	1.0	24	8.5
Sausage, beef	1 sausage	43	134	6.1	1.0	0	11.6	4.9	29	486	0	0	3	0.8
Sausage, pork	1 link	68	265	15.1	1.4	0	21.6	7.7	46	1020	0	1.4	20	0.8
Sausage, smoked links	3 2″ links	48	150	6.4	0.9	0	13.3	4.7	31	563	0	0	20	0.7
Shellfish, clams, canned	3 oz.	85	126	21.7	4.4	0	1.7	0.2	57	95	154	18.8	78	23.8
Shellfish, clams, steamed	10 clams	95	141	24.3	4.9	0	1.9	0.2	64	106	162	21.0	87	26.6
Shellfish, crab, steamed	3 oz.	85	82	16.4	0	0	1.3	0.1	45	911	8	6.5	50	0.6
Shellfish, oysters, fried	6 medium	88	173	7.7	10.2	0	11.1	2.8	71	367	80	3.3	55	6.1
Shellfish, shrimp, canned	3 oz.	85	85	17.4	0	0	1.2	0.2	214	660	0	3.5	123	1.8
Shellfish, shrimp, fried	4 large	30	73	6.4	3.4	0.1	3.7	0.6	53	103	17	0.5	20	0.4
Sunflower seeds, dry roasted	¼ cup	32	186	6.2	7.7	2.9	15.9	1.7	0	1	0	0.4	22	1.2
Tempeh	½ cup	83	160	15.4	7.8	0	9.0	1.8	0	7	0	0	92	2.2
Tofu, firm	½ cup	126	183	19.9	5.4	2.9	11.0	1.6	0	18	10	0.3	861	3.4
Turkey, dk mt, w/o skin, rst	3 oz.	85	138	24.5	0	0	3.7	1.2	95	67	0	0	22	2.0
Turkey, dk mt, w/skin, rst	3 oz.	85	155	23.5	0	0	6.0	1.8	99	65	0	0	23	2.0
Turkey, lt mt, w/o skin, rst	3 oz.	85	119	25.7	0	0	1.0	0.3	73	48	0	0	13	1.3
Turkey, lt mt, w/skin, rst	3 oz.	85	139	24.5	0	0	3.9	1.1	81	48	0	0	15	1.4
Veal, sirloin, roasted	3 oz.	85	172	21.4	0	0	8.9	3.8	87	71	0	0	11	0.8
Vegetarian bacon, cooked	1 oz.	16	50	1.7	1.0	0.4	4.7	0.7	0	234	1	0	4	0.4
Vegetarian franks	1 link	51	495	12.1	1.5	1.5	7.1	0.7	0	224	0	0	16	1.0
Vegetarian patties (burger)	1 patty	71	117	12.6	10.2	3.1	2.9	0.4	1	370	22	3.1	42	1.6
Vegetarian sausage	1 patty	38	98	7.0	3.7	1.1	6.9	1.1	0	337	0	0	24	1.4

FATS, OILS, SWEETS, AND ALCOHOLIC BEVERAGES

If nutrient-dense forms are selected from each of the basic food groups in MyPyramid, a small amount of additional calories can be consumed from solid fats and added sugars (see Chapter 8). Foods in this category should not replace foods from the other groups because they tend to provide calories but few nutrients.

Name	Amount	Weight g	Energy calories	Protein g	Carb. g	Fiber g	Total fat g	Sat. fat g	Chol. mg	Sod. mg	Vit. A RE	Vit. C mg	Calc mg	Iron mg
Alcoholic beverage, beer	1 can or bottle	356	153	1.6	12.6	0	0	0	0	14	0	0	14	0.1
Alcoholic beverage, wine	5 oz.	148	124	0.1	4.0	0	0	0	0	7	0	0	12	0.6
Bacon	3 slices	24	133	8.7	0.3	0	10.5	3.4	26	533	3	0	2	0.4
Beverage, fruit punch	1 cup	247	114	0.2	28.8	0.2	0	0	0	10	0	108.2	10	0.2
Beverage, cola	1 can	368	136	0.3	35.2	0	0	0	0	15	0	0	7	0.4
Beverage, lemon-lime soda	1 can	369	148	0.2	37.4	0	0.1	0	0	33	0	0	7	0.4
Beverage, tea, bottled, sweetened	1 bottle	518	186	0	47.1	0	0	0	0	109	0	0	16	0
Butter	1 tablespoon	14	102	0.1	0	0	11.5	7.3	31	82	97	0	3	0
Candy, caramels	1 piece	10	39	0.5	7.8	0	0.8	0.3	1	25	1	0	14	0
Candy, fudge	1 piece	17	70	0.4	13	0.3	1.8	1.0	2	8	7	0	8	0.3

Name	Amount	Weight g	Energy calories	Protein g	Carb. g	Fiber g	Total fat g	Sat. fat g	Chol. mg	Sod. mg	Vit. A RE	Vit. C mg	Calc. mg	Iron mg
Candy, jelly beans	10 large	28	105	0	26.4	0	0.1	0	0	14	0	0	1	0
Candy, milk chocolate	1 bar	44	235	3.4	26.1	1.5	13.1	6.3	10	35	22	0	83	1.0
Chocolate syrup	2 tablespoons	39	109	0.8	25.4	1.0	0.4	0.2	0	28	0	0.1	5	0.8
Cream, half and half	2 tablespoons	30	39	0.9	1.3	0	3.5	2.1	11	12	29	0.3	32	0
Cream, whipped	½ cup	60	207	1.2	1.7	0	22.2	13.8	82	23	247	0.4	39	0
Cream, sour	1 tablespoon	12	26	0.4	0.5	0	2.5	1.6	5	6	21	0.1	14	0
Frosting, chocolate	2 tablespoons	41	163	0.5	25.9	0.4	7.2	2.3	0	75	0	0	3	0.6
Honey	1 tablespoon	21	64	0.1	17.3	0	0	0	0	1	0	0.1	1	0.1
Jam/preserves	1 tablespoon	20	56	0.1	13.8	0.2	0	0	0	6	0	1.8	4	0.1
Juice bar	1 bar	92	80	1.1	18.6	0.9	0.1	0	0	4	1	8.7	5	0.2
Lard	1 tablespoon	13	115	0	0	0	12.8	5.0	12	0	0	0	0	0
Marmalade, orange	1 tablespoon	20	49	0.1	13.3	0	0	0	0	11	1	1.0	8	0
Margarine, regular stick	1 tablespoon	14	101	0.1	0.1	0	11.4	2.0	0	133	115	0	4	0
Margarine, liquid	1 tablespoon	14	102	0.3	0	0	11.4	1.9	0	111	116	0	9	0
Margarine-like spread (40% fat)	1 tablespoon	14	46	0.3	0.3	0	4.9	1.0	0	88	115	0	7	0
Mayonnaise, regular	1 tablespoon	15	57	0.1	3.5	0	4.9	0.7	4	105	3	0	2	0
Mayonnaise, fat free	1 tablespoon	16	11	0	2.0	0.3	0.4	0	2	120	1	0	1	0
Oil, canola	1 tablespoon	14	124	0	0	0	14.0	1.0	0	0	0	0	0	0
Oil, corn	1 tablespoon	14	120	0	0	0	13.6	1.7	0	0	0	0	0	0
Oil, olive	1 tablespoon	14	119	0	0	0	13.5	1.8	0	0	0	0	0	0.1
Salad dressing, blue cheese	2 tablespoons	30	151	1.4	2.2	0	15.7	3.0	5	328	20	0.6	24	0.1
Salad dressing, French	2 tablespoons	32	146	0.3	5.0	0	14.3	1.8	0	268	7	0	8	0.3
Salad dressing, Italian	2 tablespoons	29	86	0.1	3.1	0	8.3	1.3	0	486	1	0	2	0.2
Salad dressing, Italian, reduced fat	2 tablespoons	30	22	0.1	1.4	0	1.9	0.1	0	410	0	0	3	0.2
Sherbet	½ cup	74	107	0.8	22.5	0	1.5	0.9	0	34	7	2.3	40	0.1
Shortening, vegetable	1 tablespoon	13	113	0	0	0	12.8	3.2	0	1	0	0	0	0
Sugar, brown	1 tablespoon	14	52	0	13.4	0	0	0	0	5	0	0	12	0.3
Sugar, white	1 tablespoon	13	49	0	12.6	0	0	0	0	0	0	0	0	0
Syrup, corn	1 tablespoon	20	57	0	15.5	0	0	0	0	0	31	0	0	0.1
Syrup, maple	¼ cup	80	210	0	54.0	0	0.2	0	0	7	0	0	53	1.0

DATA SOURCE: U.S. Department of Agriculture, Agricultural Research Service. 2006. *USDA National Nutrient Database for Standard Reference, Release 19* (http://www.nal.usda.gov/fnic/foodcomp).

APPENDIX C

NUTRITIONAL CONTENT OF POPULAR ITEMS FROM FAST-FOOD RESTAURANTS

Arby's

	Serving size (g)	Calories	Protein (g)	Total fat (g)	Saturated fat (g)	Trans fat (g)	Total carbohydrate (g)	Sugars (g)	Fiber (g)	Cholesterol (mg)	Sodium (mg)	Vitamin A (% Daily Value)	Vitamin C (% Daily Value)	Calcium (% Daily Value)	Iron (% Daily Value)	% calories from fat
Regular roast beef	154	320	21	14	5	-	34	5	2	44	953	0	0	6	20	34
Super roast beef	198	398	21	19	6	-	40	10	2	44	1060	7	10	7	25	44
Junior roast beef	125	272	16	10	4	-	34	5	2	29	740	0	0	6	15	33
Market Fresh® Ultimate BLT	294	779	23	45	11	0.5	75	18	6	51	1571	16	28	17	27	52
Market Fresh® Roast Turkey & Swiss	359	725	45	30	8	0.5	75	17	5	91	1788	13	17	36	29	37
Market Fresh® Low Carbys™ Southwest chicken wrap	254	567	36	29	9	1	42	3	4	88	1451	12	13	24	24	47
Chicken Breast Fillet (grilled)	233	414	32	17	3	-	36	7	3	9	913	13	18	9	15	37
Martha's Vineyard™ salad (w/o dressing)	330	277	26	8	4	0	24	17	4	72	451	61	55	19	9	26
Raspberry vinaigrette	64	194	0	14	2	0	18	16	0	0	387	-	4	-	-	63
Santa Fe™ salad (w/o dressing)	365	477	29	21	6	0.5	42	6	42	53	1131	128	58	36	20	40
Curly fries (medium)	125	397	5	24	4	0	46	0	4	0	928	8	10	5	11	53
Jalapeno Bites®, regular (5)	110	305	5	21	9	1	29	3	2	28	526	14	1	3	5	63
Chocolate shake, regular	397	507	13	13	8	-	83	81	0	34	357	8	9	51	2	24

SOURCE: Arby's © 2007, Arby's, Inc. (http://www.arbysrestaurant.com). Used with permission of Arby's, Inc.

Burger King

	Serving size (g)	Calories	Protein (g)	Total fat (g)	Saturated fat (g)	Trans fat (g)	Total carbohydrate (g)	Sugars (g)	Fiber (g)	Cholesterol (mg)	Sodium (mg)	Vitamin A (% Daily Value)	Vitamin C (% Daily Value)	Calcium (% Daily Value)	Iron (% Daily Value)	% calories from fat
Original Whopper®	290	670	28	39	11	1.5	51	11	3	51	1020	10	15	15	30	32
Original Whopper® w/o mayonnaise	269	510	28	22	9	1	51	11	3	80	880	10	15	15	30	39
Original Double Whopper® w/cheese	398	990	52	64	24	2.5	52	11	3	195	1520	15	15	30	45	59
Original Whopper Jr.®	158	370	15	21	6	0.5	31	6	2	50	570	4	6	8	15	51
Original Chicken Sandwich	219	660	24	40	8	2.5	52	5	4	70	1440	2	2	10	20	55
Chicken Tenders® (8 pieces)	123	340	19	20	5	3	21	1	<1	55	960	2	0	2	6	50
French fries (medium, salted)	116	360	4	220	4.5	4.5	41	1	4	0	590	0	15	2	4	45
Onion rings (medium)	91	320	4	16	4	3.5	40	5	3	0	460	0	0	6	6	45
Tendergrill™ Chicken Garden Salad	292	240	33	9	3.5	0	8	1	4	80	720	200	60	15	15	33
Ken's® Border Ranch Dressing	57	190	1	20	3	0	2	1	0	20	560	2	2	4	2	64
Croissan'wich® w/bacon, egg & cheese	115	300	12	17	6	2	26	5	<1	145	740	10	0	15	15	50
Hershey®'s sundae pie	79	310	3	19	12	0	32	22	1	0	220	2	0	4	6	53
Vanilla shake (medium)	412	560	11	21	13	0.5	79	77	0	85	330	15	6	50	2	34

SOURCE: BURGER KING® nutritional information used with permission from Burger King Brands, Inc.

Domino's Pizza

(1/8 of Pizza)

	Serving size	Calories	Protein	Carbohydrates	Fiber	Sugars	Total fat	Saturated fat	Trans fat	Cholesterol	Vitamin A	Vitamin C	Calcium	Iron	Sodium	Calories from fat
	g	Kcal	g	g	g	g	g	g	g	mg	% Daily Value				mg	Kcal
Medium Hand Tossed Cheese	88	190	8	27	1	2	6	2.5	0	10	6	6	8	10	370	50
Medium Thin Crust Cheese	55	140	5	14	1	1	7	2.5	0	10	6	4	10	2	240	60
Medium Deep Dish Cheese	95	220	8	27	3	1	10	3.5	0	10	8	4	10	10	530	90
Large Hand Tossed Cheese	122	260	11	38	2	3	8	3	0	10	10	8	10	15	510	70
Large Thin Crust Cheese	75	180	7	19	1	2	10	3.5	0	15	10	6	15	2	340	90
Large Deep Dish Cheese	137	320	12	41	5	2	14	5	0	15	10	4	15	15	750	130
Large Hand Tossed Pepperoni	132	310	13	38	2	3	12	5	0	20	10	8	10	15	700	110
Large Hand Tossed Pepperoni & Sausage	145	350	14	39	2	3	16	6	0	30	10	8	15	15	830	140
Large Hand Tossed Ham & Pineapple	145	280	12	40	2	5	8	3.5	0	15	10	10	10	15	620	80
Large Hand Tossed ExtravaganZZa	183	390	18	41	3	3	18	7	0	35	10	15	20	20	970	160
Large Hand Tossed Hawiian Feast	157	310	15	41	2	5	11	5	0	25	10	10	15	15	740	100
Large Hand Tossed Vegi Feast	155	300	13	40	2	3	11	4.5	0	20	10	15	20	15	670	100
Large Hand Tossed MeatZZa	163	380	17	39	2	3	18	7	0	35	10	8	20	15	940	160
Barbeque Buffalo Wings (2 per serving)	87	230	17	6	0	4	14	3.5	0	50	4	2	2	6	410	130
Domino's Pizza Chicken Kickers (2 per serving)	50	100	9	7	1	0	4.5	0.5	0	20	0	0	0	2	280	40
Blue Cheese Dipping Cup (one cup)	43	210	1	2	0	2	22	4	0	20	2	0	2	0	390	200
Breadsticks (1 of 8 average size pieces)	33	120	2	12	0	1	6	1.5	0	0	0	2	0	4	105	60
Brownie Squares	40	160	2	22	1	12	7	1.5	0	15	2	0	2	10	95	38

SOURCE: Domino's Pizza, 2007 (http://www.dominos.com). © Domino's Pizza, 2007. Reproduced with permission from Domino's Pizza LLC.

KFC

	Serving size	Calories	Protein	Total fat	Saturated fat	Trans fat	Total carbohydrate	Sugars	Fiber	Cholesterol	Sodium	Vitamin A	Vitamin C	Calcium	Iron	% calories from fat
	g		g	g	g	g	g	g	g	mg	mg	% Daily Value				
Original Recipe® Chicken breast	161	360	37	21	5	0	7	0	0	115	1020	2	2	8	6	53
Original Recipe® Chicken thigh	126	330	20	24	6	0	8	0	0	110	870	4	2	4	8	67
Extra Crispy™ Chicken breast	162	440	34	27	6	0	15	0	0	105	970	2	2	6	6	57
Extra Crispy™ thigh	114	370	18	28	6	0	12	0	0	85	850	2	0	2	6	68
Tender Roast® sandwich w/sauce	236	430	37	18	3.5	0	29	4	2	80	1180	6	15	8	15	37
Tender Roast® sandwich w/o sauce	217	300	37	4.5	1.5	0	28	3	2	70	1060	6	15	8	15	13
Hot Wings™ (5 pieces)	112	350	20	24	5	0	14	0	2	105	740	4	0	4	8	63
Popcorn chicken (large)	160	550	29	35	6	0	30	0	3	80	1600	4	2	4	10	58
Chicken pot pie	423	770	33	40	15	14	70	2	5	115	1680	200	0	0	20	47
Roasted Caesar Salad w/o dressing and croutons	301	220	30	8	4.5	0	6	3	3	70	830	45	35	25	10	36
KFC® creamy parmesan caesar dressing	57	260	2	26	5	0	4	2	0	15	540	2	0	6	2	88
Corn on the cob (5.5")	162	150	5	3	1	0	26	10	7	0	10	0	10	6	6	17
Mashed potatoes w/gravy	151	140	2	5	1	0.5	20	1	1	0	560	2	2	4	8	32
Baked beans	136	220	8	1	0	0	45	28	7	0	730	6	2	10	15	5
Cole slaw	130	180	1	10	1.5	0	22	18	3	5	270	10	20	4	4	50
Biscuit (1)	57	220	4	11	2.5	3.5	24	2	1	0	640	2	0	4	10	45
Potato salad	128	180	2	9	1.5	0	22	6	2	5	470	2	10	0	2	45

SOURCE: KFC Corporation, 2007. Nutritional information provided by KFC Corporation from its web site (www.kfc.com) as of July 30, 2007 and subject to the conditions listed therein. KFC and related marks are registered trademarks of KFC Corporation. Reproduced with permission from Kentucky Fried Chicken Corporation.

McDonald's

	Serving size	Calories	Protein	Total fat	Saturated fat	Trans fat	Total carbohydrate	Sugars	Fiber	Cholesterol	Sodium	Vitamin A	Vitamin C	Calcium	Iron	% calories from fat
	g		g	g	g	g	g	g	g	mg	mg	% Daily Value				
Hamburger	100	250	12	9	3.5	0.5	31	6	2	25	528	0	2	10	15	40
Quarter Pounder®	169	410	24	19	7	1	37	8	3	65	730	2	4	15	20	41
Quarter Pounder® w/cheese	198	510	29	26	12	1.5	40	9	3	90	1190	10	4	30	25	45
Big Mac®	214	540	25	29	10	1.5	45	9	3	75	1040	6	2	25	25	48
Big N' Tasty®	206	460	24	24	8	1.5	37	8	3	70	720	6	8	15	25	47
Filet-O-Fish®	143	380	15	18	4	1	38	5	2	35	660	2	0	15	10	42
McChicken®	147	360	14	16	3.5	1	40	5	1	40	790	0	2	10	15	42
Medium French Fries	114	380	4	20	4	5	47	0	5	0	220	0	10	2	0	47
Chicken McNuggets® (6 pieces)	96	250	15	15	3	1.5	15	0	0	35	670	2	2	2	4	52
Chicken Select® Premium Breast Strips (5 pieces)	221	630	39	33	6	4.5	46	0	0	90	1550	0	6	4	8	48
Tangy Honey Mustard Sauce	43	70	1	2.5	0	0	13	9	0	5	170	0	0	0	1	29
Bacon Ranch Salad w/Grilled Chicken (w/o dressing)	321	260	33	9	4	0	12	5	3	90	1010	130	50	15	10	35
Caesar Salad w/Crispy Chicken (w/o dressing)	313	300	25	13	4	1.5	22	4	3	55	1020	130	50	20	10	40
Newman's Own® Ranch Dressing (2 oz)	59	170	1	15	2.5	0	9	4	0	20	530	0	0	4	0	76
Egg McMuffin®	139	300	18	12	5	0	30	3	2	260	820	10	2	30	20	37
Sausage Biscuit w/Egg	156	490	17	32	10	5	34	2	1	250	1110	6	0	8	20	57
Hotcakes (2 pats margarine & syrup)	223	610	9	18	4	4	105	47	3	20	680	2	0	15	15	26
Fruit 'n Yogurt Parfait	149	160	4	2	1	0	31	21	1	5	85	0	15	15	4	13
Chocolate Triple Thick® Shake (16 oz)	444	580	13	14	8	1	102	84	1	50	250	20	0	45	10	21

SOURCE: McDonald's Corporation, 2007 (http://www.mcdonalds.com). Used with permission from McDonald's Corporation. For the most current information, visit the McDonald's Web site.

Subway

Based on standard formulas with 6-inch subs on Italian or wheat bread

	Serving size	Calories	Protein	Total fat	Saturated fat	Trans fat	Total carbohydrate	Sugars	Fiber	Cholesterol	Sodium	Vitamin A	Vitamin C	Calcium	Iron	% calories from fat
	g		g	g	g	g	g	g	g	mg	mg	% Daily Value				
6" Italian BMT®	243	450	23	21	8	0	47	8	4	55	1770	10	35	15	25	42
6" Meatball marinara	377	560	24	24	11	1	63	13	7	45	1690	15	60	20	40	39
6" Steak & cheese	278	400	29	12	6	0.5	48	9	5	60	1110	10	40	15	40	27
Subway Melt®	254	380	25	12	5	0	48	8	4	45	1600	10	35	15	25	29
Tuna	250	530	22	31	7	0.5	44	7	4	45	1010	10	35	15	30	53
Sweet onion chicken teriyaki	281	370	26	5	1.5	0	59	19	5	50	1200	8	40	8	25	12
Roast beef	224	290	19	5	2	0	45	8	4	20	900	8	30	5	35	16
Turkey breast	224	280	18	4.5	1.5	0	46	7	4	20	1000	8	35	6	25	14
Veggie Delite®	167	230	9	3	1	0	44	7	4	0	500	8	35	6	25	13
Turkey Breast salad(w/o dressing)	378	110	12	2.5	0.5	0	13	6	4	20	580	60	50	6	10	20
New England style clam chowder	310	150	6	5	1	0	20	2	4	10	990	0	-	4	6	30
Chili con carne	310	290	19	8	3.5	0	35	13	12	25	990	15	20	8	20	25
Chocolate Chip Cookie	45	210	2	10	6	0	30	18	1	15	150	6	0	0	6	43

SOURCE: Subway U.S. Nutrition Info as found on http://www.subway.com, 6/30/2007. Reprinted by permission of Subway.®

Taco Bell

	Serving size	Calories	Protein	Total fat	Saturated fat	Trans fat	Total carbohydrate	Sugars	Fiber	Cholesterol	Sodium	Vitamin A	Vitamin C	Calcium	Iron	% calories from fat
	g		g	g	g	g	g	g	g	mg	mg	% Daily Value				
Crunchy Taco	78	170	8	10	3.5	0	13	1	3	25	350	4	2	8	6	47
Crunchy Taco Supreme®	113	210	9	13	6	0	15	2	3	40	370	10	6	10	6	57
Soft taco, beef	99	200	10	9	4	0	21	2	3	25	630	4	2	10	10	40
Gordita Supreme®, steak	153	290	15	13	5	0	28	6	2	40	530	6	6	10	15	41
Grilled steak soft taco, Fresco style	128	160	10	4.5	1.5	0	20	3	2	20	550	4	10	8	10	25
Gordita Baja®, chicken	153	320	17	16	3.5	0	28	6	3	40	800	8	6	10	10	44
Chalupa Supreme, beef	153	380	14	23	7	0.5	30	4	3	40	620	8	6	15	15	55
Chalupa Supreme, chicken	153	380	17	20	5	0	29	4	2	45	650	6	8	10	15	49
1/2 lb. Beef combo burrito	241	430	21	18	8	1	51	4	8	45	1630	15	6	20	30	38
Bean burrito	198	340	13	9	3.5	0.5	54	4	8	5	1190	10	8	20	25	24
Burrito Supreme®, chicken	248	390	20	13	6	0.5	49	5	6	45	1380	15	15	20	25	31
Grilled stuffed burrito, beef	325	680	27	30	10	1	76	6	9	55	2120	15	4	30	40	40
Tostada	170	230	11	10	3.5	0.5	27	2	7	15	730	10	8	20	10	39
Zesty Chicken Border Bowl™ w/dressing	418	640	22	35	6	1	60	4	10	30	1800	15	15	15	25	37
Express taco salad	479	610	25	32	10	1.5	56	8	14	65	1420	20	20	30	25	48
Steak quesadilla	184	520	26	28	13	1	39	4	3	70	1300	10	0	45	20	50
Nachos Supreme	195	450	12	25	7	1.5	41	3	7	35	800	8	8	10	10	51
Nachos BellGrande®	308	770	19	44	9	3	77	5	12	12	1280	8	8	20	20	50
Pintos 'n cheese	128	150	9	6	3	0.5	19	1	7	15	670	10	6	15	8	33
Mexican rice	131	170	6	7	3	0	23	1	1	15	740	15	6	10	8	35

SOURCE: Taco Bell Corporation, 2007 (http://www.tacobell.com). Reproduced courtesy of Taco Bell Corporation.

Wendy's

	Serving size	Calories	Protein	Total fat	Saturated fat	Trans fat	Total carbohydrate	Sugars	Fiber	Cholesterol	Sodium	Vitamin A	Vitamin C	Calcium	Iron	% calories from fat
	g		g	g	g	g	g	g	g	mg	mg	% Daily Value				
Classic Single® w/everything	218	430	25	20	7	1	37	9	2	65	900	8	8	4	25	42
Jr. Hamburger	117	280	15	9	3.5	0.5	34	7	1	30	590	0	0	2	20	29
Jr. Bacon Cheeseburger	161	370	19	18	7	0.5	34	6	2	50	790	10	6	10	20	46
Ultimate Chicken Grill Sandwich	227	370	28	7	1.5	0	36	8	2	70	950	6	10	4	20	19
Spicy Chicken Fillet Sandwich	231	440	28	16	2.5	0	46	6	3	60	1320	6	8	4	15	32
Homestyle Chicken Fillet Sandwich	228	430	25	16	2.5	0	48	6	2	45	1140	6	8	4	15	31
Homestyle Chicken Strips	159	410	28	21	3.5	0	33	0	0	60	1470	0	0	2	6	39
Caesar Side Salad (no toppings or dressing)	99	80	6	4.5	2	0	6	1	2	10	240	100	35	10	6	57
Mandarin Chicken® Salad (no toppings or dressing)	348	170	21	2.5	0.5	0	16	12	3	60	520	70	50	6	10	9
Southwest Taco Salad (no toppings or dressing	501	430	30	22	12	1	30	9	8	80	1090	80	35	45	20	45
Creamy ranch dressing	64	200	1	20	3.5	0	4	2	0	15	400	0	0	4	2	87
Reduced fat creamy ranch dressing	64	90	1	7	1.5	0	6	3	1	10	400	0	0	6	2	70
Large French Fries	190	520	7	24	3.5	1	69	0	7	0	560	4	15	2	10	44
Sour Cream & Chive Baked Potato	312	320	9	4	2.5	0	63	4	7	10	55	4	60	8	15	11
Low Fat Strawberry Flavored Yogurt w/Granola	163	250	8	6	1.5	0	42	30	1	5	90	2	2	22	6	33
Chili, small, plain	227	220	17	6	2.5	0	23	6	5	35	780	4	4	8	15	27
Crispy Chicken Nuggets™ (5)	75	230	12	15	3	0	12	0	0	35	520	0	0	0	2	59
Barbecue sauce (1 packet)	28	45	1	0	0	0	10	8	0	0	170	0	0	0	4	0
Frosty,™ medium	298	430	10	11	7	0	74	55	0	45	200	20	0	40	20	23

SOURCE: Wendy's International, Inc., 2007 (http://www.wendys.com). Reproduced with permission from Wendy's International, Inc. The information contained in Wendy's International Information is effective as of May 2007. Wendy's International, Inc., its subsidiaries, affiliates, franchises, and employees do not assume responsibility for a particular sensitivity or allergy (including peanuts, nuts or other allergies) to any food product provided in our restaurants. We encourage anyone with food sensitivities, allergies, or special dietary needs to check on a regular basis with Wendy's Consumer Relations Department to obtain the most up-to-date information.

Information on additional foods and restaurants is available online; see the Web sites listed in this appendix and the following additional sites: **Hardees:** http://www.hardees.com; **White Castle:** http://www.whitecastle.com

APPENDIX D

MONITORING YOUR PROGRESS

NAME ______________________ **SECTION** ____________ **DATE** ____________

As you completed the labs listed below, you entered the results in the Preprogram Assessment column of this lab. Now that you have been involved in a fitness and wellness program for some time, do the labs again and enter your new results in the Postprogram Assessment column. You will probably notice improvement in several areas. Congratulations! If you are not satisfied with your progress thus far, refer to the tips for successful behavior change in Chapter 1 and throughout this book. Remember—fitness and wellness are forever. The time you invest now in developing a comprehensive, individualized program will pay off in a richer, more vital life in the years to come.

	Preprogram Assessment	Postprogram Assessment
LAB 2.3 Pedometer	Daily steps: _____	Daily steps: _____
LAB 3.1 Cardiorespiratory Endurance		
1-mile walk test	$\dot{V}O_{2max}$: _____ Rating: _______	$\dot{V}O_{2max}$: _____ Rating: _______
3-minute step test	$\dot{V}O_{2max}$: _____ Rating: _______	$\dot{V}O_{2max}$: _____ Rating: _______
1.5-mile run-walk test	$\dot{V}O_{2max}$: _____ Rating: _______	$\dot{V}O_{2max}$: _____ Rating: _______
LAB 4.1 Muscular Strength		
Maximum bench press test	Weight: _____ lb Rating: _______	Weight: _____ lb Rating: _______
LAB 4.2 Muscular Endurance		
Curl-up test	Number: _____ Rating: _______	Number: _____ Rating: _______
Push-up test	Number: _____ Rating: _______	Number: _____ Rating: _______
Squat endurance test	Number: _____ Rating: _______	Number: _____ Rating: _______
LAB 5.1 Flexibility		
Sit-and-reach test	Score: _____ cm Rating: _______	Score: _____ cm Rating: _______
LAB 5.3 Low-Back Muscular Endurance		
Side bridge endurance test	Right: _____ sec Rating: _______	Right: _____ sec Rating: _______
	Left: _____ sec Rating: _______	Left: _____ sec Rating: _______
Trunk flexors endurance test	Trunk flexors: _____ sec Rating: _____	Trunk flexors: _____ sec Rating: _____
Back extensors endurance test	Back extensors: _____ sec Rating: _____	Back extensors: _____ sec Rating: _____

	Preprogram Assessment	Postprogram Assessment
LAB 6.1 Body Composition		
Body mass index	BMI: ____ kg/m^2 Rating: ______	BMI: ____ kg/m^2 Rating: ______
Skinfold measurements (or other method for determining percent body fat)	Sum of 3 skinfolds: ____ mm % body fat: ____ % Rating: ______	Sum of 3 skinfolds: ____ mm % body fat: ____ % Rating: ______
Waist circumference	Circumf.: ______ Rating: ______	Circumf.: ______ Rating: ______
Waist-to-hip-circumference ratio	Ratio: ____ Rating: ______	Ratio: ____ Rating: ______
LAB 8.1 Daily Diet		
Number of oz-eq	Grains: ______	Grains: ______
Number of cups	Vegetables: ______	Vegetables: ______
Number of cups	Fruits: ______	Fruits: ______
Number of cups	Milk: ______	Milk: ______
Number of oz-eq	Meat and beans: ______	Meat and beans: ______
Number of tsp	Oils: ______	Oils: ______
Number of g	Solid fats: ______	Solid fats: ______
Number of g or tsp	Added sugars: ______	Added sugars: ______
LAB 8.2 Dietary Analysis		
Percentage of calories	From protein: ______ %	From protein: ______ %
Percentage of calories	From fat: ______ %	From fat: ______ %
Percentage of calories	From saturated fat: ______ %	From saturated fat: ______ %
Percentage of calories	From carbohydrate: ______ %	From carbohydrate: ______ %
LAB 9.1 Daily Energy Needs	Daily energy needs: ______ cal/day	Daily energy needs: ______ cal/day
LAB 10.1 Identifying Stressors	Average weekly stress score: ______	Average weekly stress score: ______
LAB 11.1 Cardiovascular Health		
CVD risk assessment	Score: ____ Estimated risk: ____	Score: ____ Estimated risk: ____
Hostility assessment	Score: ______ Rating: ______	Score: ______ Rating: ______
LAB 12.1 Cancer Prevention		
Diet: Number of servings	Fruits/vegetables: ______	Fruits/vegetables: ______
Skin cancer	Score: ______ Risk: ______	Score: ______ Risk: ______

BEHAVIOR CHANGE WORKBOOK

This workbook is designed to take you step by step through a behavior change program. The first eight activities in the workbook will help you develop a successful plan—beginning with choosing a target behavior, moving through the planning steps described in Chapter 1, and completing and signing a behavior change contract. The final seven activities will help you work through common obstacles to behavior change and maximize your program's chances of success.

Part 1 Developing a Plan for Behavior Change and Completing a Contract

1. Choosing a Target Behavior
2. Gathering Information About Your Target Behavior
3. Monitoring Your Current Patterns of Behavior
4. Setting Goals
5. Examining Your Attitudes About Your Target Behavior
6. Choosing Rewards
7. Breaking Behavior Chains
8. Completing a Contract for Behavior Change

Part 2 Overcoming Obstacles to Behavior Change

9. Building Motivation and Commitment
10. Managing Your Time Successfully
11. Developing Realistic Self-Talk
12. Involving the People Around You
13. Dealing with Feelings
14. Overcoming Peer Pressure: Communicating Assertively
15. Maintaining Your Program over Time

ACTIVITY 1 CHOOSING A TARGET BEHAVIOR

Use your knowledge of yourself and the results of Lab 1.2 (Lifestyle Evaluation) to identify five behaviors that you could change to improve your level of wellness. Examples of target behaviors include smoking cigarettes, not exercising regularly, eating candy bars every night, not getting enough sleep, getting drunk frequently on weekends, and not wearing a safety belt when driving or riding in a car. List your five behaviors below.

1. ______________________________
2. ______________________________
3. ______________________________
4. ______________________________
5. ______________________________

For successful behavior change, it's best to focus on one behavior at a time. Review your list of behaviors and select one to start with. Choose a behavior that is important to you and that you are strongly motivated to change. If this will be your first attempt at behavior change, start with a simple change, such as wearing your bicycle helmet regularly, before tackling a more difficult change, such as quitting smoking. Circle the behavior on your list that you've chosen to start with; this will be your target behavior throughout this workbook.

ACTIVITY 2 GATHERING INFORMATION ABOUT YOUR TARGET BEHAVIOR

Take a close look at what your target behavior means to your health, now and in the future. How is it affecting your level of wellness? What diseases or conditions does this behavior place you at risk for? What will changing this behavior mean to you? To evaluate your behavior, use information from this text, from the resources listed in the For Further Exploration section at the end of each chapter, and from other reliable sources.

Health behaviors have short-term and long-term benefits and costs associated with them. For example, in the short term, an inactive lifestyle allows for more time to watch TV and hang out with friends but leaves a person less able to participate in recreational activities. In the long term, it increases risk for cardiovascular disease, cancer, and premature death. Fill in the blanks below with the benefits and costs of continuing your current behavior and of changing to a new, healthier behavior. Pay close attention to the short-term benefits of the new behavior—these are an important motivating force behind successful behavior change programs.

Target (current) behavior ______________________________

Benefits *Short-Term* | *Long-Term*

______________________ | ______________________

______________________ | ______________________

______________________ | ______________________

Costs *Short-Term* | *Long-Term*

______________________ | ______________________

______________________ | ______________________

______________________ | ______________________

New behavior ______________________________

Benefits *Short-Term* | *Long-Term*

______________________ | ______________________

______________________ | ______________________

______________________ | ______________________

Costs *Short-Term* | *Long-Term*

______________________ | ______________________

______________________ | ______________________

______________________ | ______________________

ACTIVITY 3 MONITORING YOUR CURRENT PATTERNS OF BEHAVIOR

To develop a successful behavior change program, you need detailed information about your current behavior patterns. You can obtain this information by developing a system of record keeping geared toward your target behavior. Depending on your target behavior, you may want to monitor a single behavior, such as your diet, or you may want to keep daily activity records to determine how you could make time for exercise or another new behavior. Consider tracking factors such as the following:

- What the behavior was
- When and for how long it occurred
- Where it occurred
- What else you were doing at the time
- What other people you were with and how they influenced you
- What your thoughts and feelings were
- How strong your urge for the behavior was (for example, how hungry you were or how much you wanted to watch TV)

Figure 1.7 shows a sample log for tracking daily diet. Additional sample logs are available under Behavior Change Tools on the Online Learning Center. Below, create a format for a sample daily log for monitoring the behavior patterns relating to your target behavior. Then use the log to monitor your behavior for a day. Evaluate your log as you use it. Ask yourself if you are tracking all the key factors that influence your behavior; make any necessary adjustments to the format of your log. Once you've developed an appropriate format, use a separate notebook (your health journal) to keep records of your behavior for a week or two. These records will provide solid information about your behavior that will help you develop a successful behavior change program. Later activities in this workbook will ask you to analyze your records.

ACTIVITY 4 SETTING GOALS

For your behavior change program to succeed, you must set meaningful, realistic goals. In addition to an ultimate goal, set some intermediate goals—milestones that you can strive for on the way to your final objective. For example, if your overall goal is to run a 5K road race, an intermediate goal might be to successfully complete 2 weeks of your fitness program. If you set a final goal of eating 7 servings of fruits and vegetables every day, an intermediate goal would be to increase your daily intake from 3 to 4 servings. List your intermediate and final goals below. Don't strive for immediate perfection. Allow an adequate amount of time to reach each of your goals.

Intermediate Goals	**Target Date**
______________________	____________
______________________	____________
______________________	____________
______________________	____________
______________________	____________

Final Goal

______________________	____________

ACTIVITY 5 EXAMINING YOUR ATTITUDES ABOUT YOUR TARGET BEHAVIOR

Your attitudes toward your target behavior can determine whether your behavior change program will be successful. Consider your attitudes carefully by completing the following statements about how you think and feel about your current behavior and your goal.

1. I like ______________ (current behavior) because ______________
2. I don't like ______________ (current behavior) because ______________
3. I like ______________ (behavior goal) because ______________
4. I don't like ______________ (behavior goal) because ______________
5. I don't ______________ (behavior goal) now because ______________
6. I would be more likely to ______________ (behavior goal) if ______________

If your statements indicate that you have major reservations about changing your behavior, work to build your motivation and commitment before you begin your program. Look carefully at your objections to changing your behavior. How valid and important are they? What can you do to overcome them? Can you adopt any of the strategies you listed under statement 6? Review the facts about your current behavior and your goals.

ACTIVITY 6 CHOOSING REWARDS

Make a list of objects, activities, and events you can use as rewards for achieving the goals of your behavior change program. Rewards should be special, relatively inexpensive, and preferably unrelated to food or alcohol—for example, tickets to a ball game, a CD, or a long-distance phone call to a family member or friend—whatever is meaningful for you. Write down a variety of rewards you can use when you reach milestones in your program and your final goal.

Many people also find it helpful to give themselves small rewards daily or weekly for sticking with their behavior change program. These could be things like a study break, a movie, or a Saturday morning bike ride. Make a list of rewards for maintaining your program in the short term.

And don't forget to congratulate yourself regularly during your behavior change program. Notice how much better you feel. Savor how far you've come and how you've gained control of your behavior.

ACTIVITY 7 BREAKING BEHAVIOR CHAINS

Use the records you collected about your target behavior in Activity 3 and in your health journal to identify what leads up to your target behavior and what follows it. By tracing these chains of events, you'll be able to identify points in the chain where you can make a change that will lead to your new behavior. The sample behavior chain on the next page shows a sequence of events for a person who wants to add exercise to her daily routine—but who winds up snacking and watching TV instead. By examining the chain carefully, you can identify ways to break it at every step. After you review the sample, go through the same process for a typical chain of events involving your target behavior. Use the blank behavior chain on the following page.

Some general strategies for breaking behavior chains include the following.

- ***Control or eliminate environmental cues that provoke the behavior.*** Stay out of the room where your television is located. Go out for an ice cream cone instead of keeping a half gallon of ice cream in your freezer.
- ***Change behaviors or habits that are linked to your target behavior.*** If you always smoke in your car when you drive to school, try taking public transportation instead.
- ***Add new cues to your environment to trigger your new behavior.*** Prepare easy-to-grab healthy snacks and carry them with you to class or work. Keep your exercise clothes and equipment in a visible location.

See also the suggestions in Chapter 1.

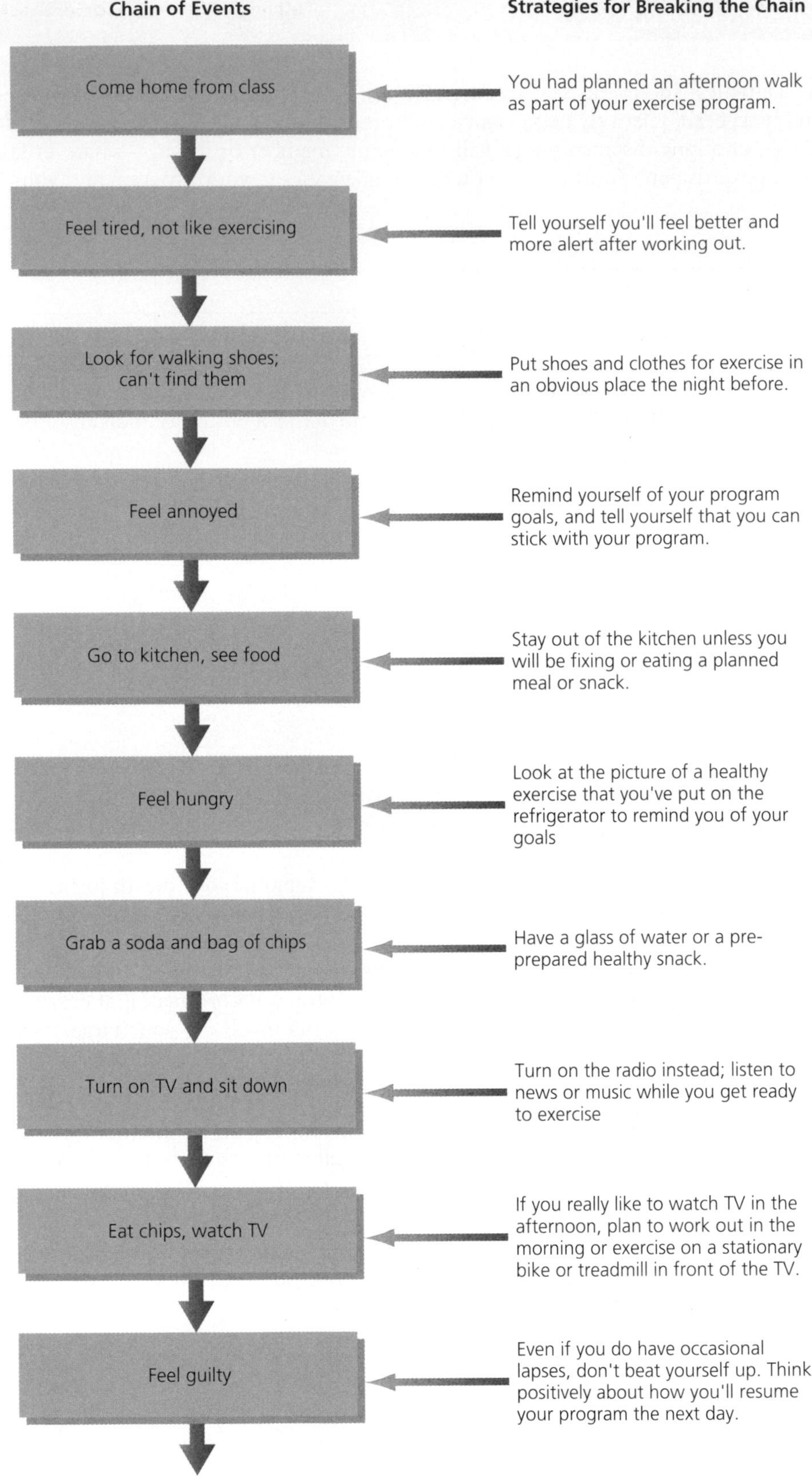
Chain of Events
Strategies for Breaking the Chain
Come home from class
You had planned an afternoon walk as part of your exercise program.
Feel tired, not like exercising
Tell yourself you'll feel better and more alert after working out.
Look for walking shoes; can't find them
Put shoes and clothes for exercise in an obvious place the night before.
Feel annoyed
Remind yourself of your program goals, and tell yourself that you can stick with your program.
Go to kitchen, see food
Stay out of the kitchen unless you will be fixing or eating a planned meal or snack.
Feel hungry
Look at the picture of a healthy exercise that you've put on the refrigerator to remind you of your goals
Grab a soda and bag of chips
Have a glass of water or a pre-prepared healthy snack.
Turn on TV and sit down
Turn on the radio instead; listen to news or music while you get ready to exercise
Eat chips, watch TV
If you really like to watch TV in the afternoon, plan to work out in the morning or exercise on a stationary bike or treadmill in front of the TV.
Feel guilty
Even if you do have occasional lapses, don't beat yourself up. Think positively about how you'll resume your program the next day.

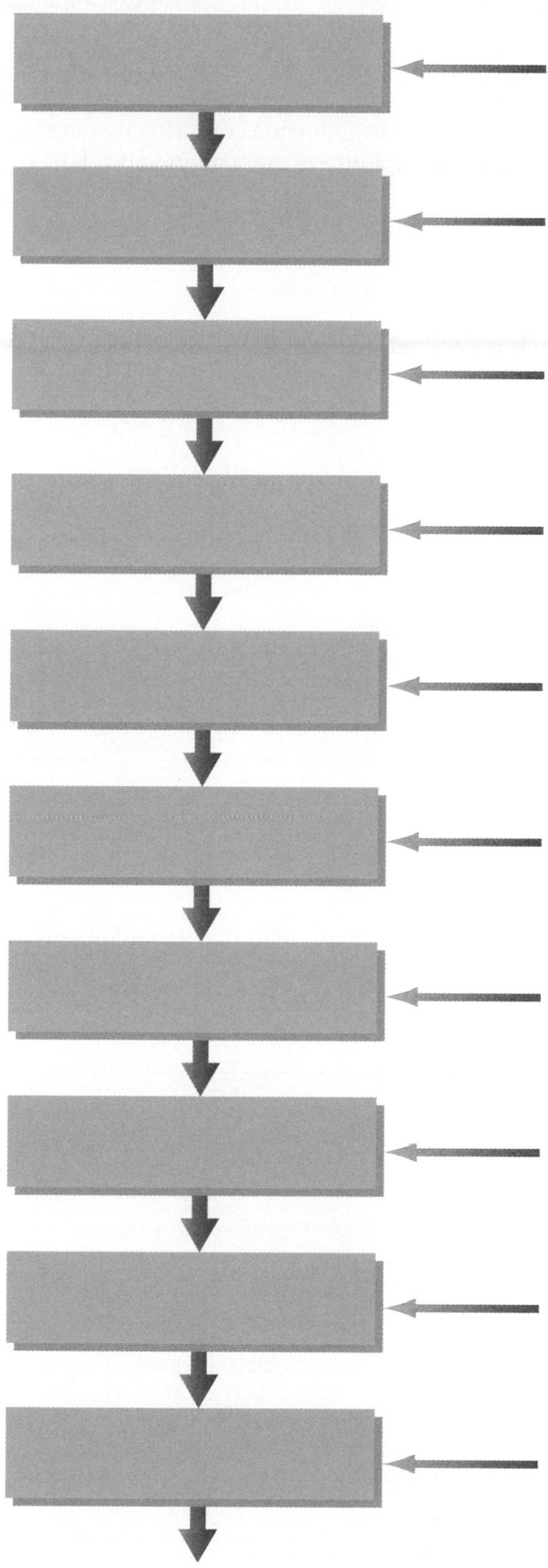

Strategies for Breaking the Chain

ACTIVITY 8 COMPLETING A CONTRACT FOR BEHAVIOR CHANGE

Your next step in creating a successful behavior change program is to complete and sign a behavior change contract. Your contract should include details of your program and indicate your commitment to changing your behavior. Use the information from previous activities in this workbook to complete the following contract. (If your target behavior relates to exercise, you may want to use the program plan and contract for a fitness program in Lab 7.1.)

1. I, ______________________ (name), agree to ______________________ (specify behavior you want to change)

   ____

2. I will begin on __________ (start date) and plan to reach my goal of ______________________ (specify final goal)

   ______________________ by __________

3. To reach my final goal, I have devised the following schedule of mini-goals. For each step in my program, I will give myself the reward listed.

______ (mini-goal 1)	______ (target date)	______ (reward)
______ (mini-goal 2)	______ (target date)	______ (reward)
______ (mini-goal 3)	______ (target date)	______ (reward)
______ (mini-goal 4)	______ (target date)	______ (reward)
______ (mini-goal 5)	______ (target date)	______ (reward)

   My overall reward for reaching my final goal will be ______________________

4. I have gathered and analyzed data on my target behavior and have identified the following strategies for changing my behavior: ______________________

   ____

   ____

5. I will use the following tools to monitor my progress toward reaching my final goal:

   ______________________ (list any charts, graphs, or journals you plan to use)

   ____

   I sign this contract as an indication of my personal commitment to reach my goal.

   ______________________ (you signature) __________ (date)

   I have recruited a helper who will witness my contract and ______________________

   ______________________ (list any way in which your helper will participate in your program)

   ______________________ (helper's signature) __________ (date)

Describe in detail any special strategies you will use to help change your behavior (refer to Activity 7).

Create a plan below for any charts, graphs, or journals you will use to monitor your progress. The log format you developed in Activity 3 may be appropriate, or you may need to develop a more detailed or specific record-keeping system. Examples of journal formats are included in Labs 3.2, 4.3, 5.2, 8.1, and 10.1. You might also want to develop a graph to show your progress; posting such a graph in a prominent location can help keep your motivation strong and your program on track. Depending on your target behavior, you could graph the number of push-ups you can do, the number of servings of vegetables you eat each day, or your average daily stress level.

ACTIVITY 9 BUILDING MOTIVATION AND COMMITMENT

Complete the following checklist to determine whether you are motivated and committed to changing your behavior. Check the statements that are true for you.

_______ I feel responsible for my own behavior and capable of managing it.

_______ I am not easily discouraged.

_______ I enjoy setting goals and then working to achieve them.

_______ I am good at keeping promises to myself.

_______ I like having a structure and schedule for my activities.

_______ I view my new behavior as a necessity, not an optional activity.

_______ Compared with previous attempts to change my behavior, I am more motivated now.

_______ My goals are realistic.

_______ I have a positive mental picture of the new behavior.

_______ Considering the stresses in my life, I feel confident that I can stick to my program.

_______ I feel prepared for lapses and ups-and-downs in my behavior change program.

_______ I feel that my plan for behavior change is enjoyable.

_______ I feel comfortable telling other people about the change I am making in my behavior.

Did you check most of these statements? If not, you need to boost your motivation and commitment. Consider these strategies:

- Review the potential benefits of changing your behavior and the costs of not changing it (see Activity 2). Pay special attention to the short-term benefits of changing your behavior, including feelings of accomplishment and self-confidence. Post a list of these benefits in a prominent location.
- Visualize yourself achieving your goal and enjoying its benefits. For example, if you want to manage time more effectively, picture yourself as a confident, organized person who systematically tackles important tasks and sets aside time each day for relaxation, exercise, and friends. Practice this type of visualization regularly.
- Put aside obstacles and objections to change. Counter thoughts such as "I'll never have time to exercise" with thoughts like "Lots of other people do it and so can I."
- Bombard yourself with propaganda. Take a class dealing with the change you want to make. Read books and watch television shows on the subject. Post motivational phrases or pictures on your refrigerator or over your desk. Talk to people who have already made the change.
- Build up your confidence. Remind yourself of other goals you've achieved. At the end of each day, mentally review your good decisions and actions. See yourself as a capable person, as being in charge of your behavior.

List two strategies for boosting your motivation and commitment; choose from the list above or develop your own. Try each strategy, and then describe how well it worked for you.

Strategy 1: ____

How well it worked: ____

____

Strategy 2: ____

How well it worked: ____

____

ACTIVITY 10 MANAGING YOUR TIME SUCCESSFULLY

"Too little time" is a common excuse for not exercising or engaging in other healthy behaviors. Learning to manage your time successfully is crucial if you are to maintain a wellness lifestyle. The first step is to examine how you are currently spending your time; use the following grid to track your activities.

Time	Activity	Time	Activity
6:00 A.M.		6:00 P.M.	
6:30 A.M.		6:30 P.M.	
7:00 A.M.		7:00 P.M.	
8:00 A.M.		8:00 P.M.	
9:00 A.M.		9:00 P.M.	
10:00 A.M.		10:00 P.M.	
11:00 A.M.		11:00 P.M.	
12:00 P.M.		12:00 A.M.	
1:00 P.M.		1:00 A.M.	
2:00 P.M.		2:00 A.M.	
3:00 P.M.		3:00 A.M.	
4:00 P.M.		4:00 A.M.	
5:00 P.M.		5:00 A.M.	

Next, list each type of activity and the total time you engaged in it on a given day in the chart below (for example, sleeping, 7 hours; eating, 1.5 hours; studying, 3 hours; working, 3 hours; and so on). Take a close look at your list of activities. Successful time management is based on prioritization. Assign a priority to each of your activities according to how important it is to you: essential (A), somewhat important (B), or not important (C). Based on these priority rankings, make changes in your schedule by adding and subtracting hours from different categories of activities; enter a duration goal for each activity. Add your new activities to the list and assign a priority and duration goal to each.

Activity	Current Total Duration	Priority (A, B, or C)	Goal Total Duration

Prioritizing in this manner will involve trade-offs. For example, you may choose to reduce the amount of time you spend watching television, listening to music, and chatting on the telephone while you increase the amount of time spent sleeping, studying, and exercising. Don't feel that you have to miss out on anything you enjoy. You can get more from less time by focusing on what you are doing. Strategies for managing time more productively and creatively are described in Chapter 10.

ACTIVITY 11 DEVELOPING REALISTIC SELF-TALK

Self-talk is the ongoing internal dialogue we have with ourselves throughout much of the day. Our thoughts can be accurate, positive, and supportive, or they can be exaggerated and negative. Self-talk is closely related to self-esteem and self-concept. Realistic self-talk can help maintain positive self-esteem, the belief that one is a good and competent person, worthy of friendship and love. A negative internal dialogue can reinforce negative self-esteem and can make behavior change difficult. Substituting realistic self-talk for negative self-talk can help you build and maintain self-esteem and cope better with the challenges in your life.

First, take a closer look at your current pattern of self-talk. Use your health journal to track self-talk, especially as it relates to your target behavior. Does any of your self-talk fall into the common patterns of distorted, negative self-talk shown in Chapter 10 (p. 318)? If so, use the examples of realistic self-talk from Chapter 10 to develop more accurate and rational responses. Write your current negative thoughts in the left-hand column, and then record more realistic thoughts in the right-hand column.

Current Self-Talk About Target Behavior	More Realistic Self-Talk

ACTIVITY 12 INVOLVING THE PEOPLE AROUND YOU

Your behavior change program will be more successful if the people around you are supportive and involved—or at least are not sabotaging your efforts. Use your health journal to track how other people influence your target behavior and your efforts to change it. For example, do you always skip exercising when you're with certain people? Do you always drink or eat too much when you socialize with certain friends? Are friends and family members offering you enthusiastic support for your efforts to change your behavior, or do they make jokes about your program? Have they even noticed your efforts? Summarize the reactions of those around you in the chart below.

Target behavior ______________________________

Person	Typical Effect on Target Behavior	Involvement in/Reaction to Program

It may be difficult to change the actions and reactions of the people who are close to you. For them to be involved in your program, you may need to develop new ways of interacting with them (for example, taking a walk rather than going out to dinner as a means of socializing). Most of your friends and family members will want to help you—if they know how. Ask for exactly the type of help or involvement you want. Do you want feedback, praise, or just cooperation? Would you like someone to witness your contract or to be involved more directly in your program? Do you want someone to stop sabotaging your efforts by inviting you to watch TV, eat rich desserts, and so on? Look for ways that the people who are close to you can share in your behavior change program. They can help to motivate you and to maintain your commitment to your program. Develop a way that each individual you listed above can become involved in your program in a positive way.

Person	Target Involvement in Behavior Change Program

Choose one person on your list to tackle first. Talk to that person about her or his current behavior and how you would like her or him to be involved in your behavior change program. Below, describe this person's reaction to your talk and her or his subsequent behavior. Did this individual become a positive participant in your behavior change program?

____

____

____

____

ACTIVITY 13 DEALING WITH FEELINGS

Long-standing habits are difficult to change in part because many represent ways people have developed to cope with certain feelings. For example, people may overeat when bored, skip their exercise sessions when frustrated, or drink alcoholic beverages when anxious. Developing new ways to deal with feelings can help improve the chance that a behavior change program will succeed.

Review the records on your target behavior that you kept in your health journal. Identify the feelings that are interfering with the success of your program, and develop new strategies for coping with them. Some common problematic feelings are listed below, along with one possible coping strategy for each. Put a check mark next to those that are influencing your target behavior, and fill in additional strategies. Add the other feelings that are significant roadblocks in your program to the bottom of the chart, along with coping strategies for each.

✔	Feeling	Coping Strategies
	Stressed out	Go for a 10-minute walk.
	Anxious	Do one of the relaxation exercises described in Chapter 10.
	Bored	Call a friend for a chat.
	Tired	Take a 20-minute nap.
	Frustrated	Identify the source of the feeling and deal with it constructively.

- Julia is trying to give up smoking; her friend Marie continues to offer her cigarettes whenever they are together.
- Emilio is planning to exercise in the morning; his roommates tell him he's being antisocial by not having brunch with them.
- Tracy's boyfriend told her that in high school he once experimented with drugs and shared needles; she wants him to have an HIV test, but he says he's sure the people he shared needles with were not infected.

Peer pressure is the common ingredient in these situations. To successfully maintain your behavior change program, you must develop effective strategies for resisting peer pressure. Assertive communication is one such strategy. By communicating assertively—firmly, but not aggressively—you can stick with your program even in the face of pressure from others.

Review your health journal to determine how other people affect your target behavior. If you find that you often do give in to peer pressure, try the following strategies for communicating more assertively:

- Collect your thoughts, and plan in advance what you will say. You might try out your response on a friend to get some feedback.
- State your case—how you feel and what you want—as clearly as you can.
- Use "I" messages—statements about how you feel—rather than "you" statements.
- Focus on the behavior rather than the person. Suggest a solution, such as asking the other person to change his or her behavior toward you. Avoid generalizations. Be specific about what you want.
- Make clear, constructive requests. Focus on your needs ("I would like . . .") rather than the mistakes of others ("You always . . .").
- Avoid blaming, accusing, and belittling. Treat others with the same respect you'd like to receive yourself.
- Ask for action ahead of time. Tell others what you would like to have happen; don't wait for them to do the wrong thing and then get angry at them.
- Ask for a response to what you have proposed. Wait for an answer and listen carefully to it. Try to understand other people's points of view, just as you would hope that others would understand yours.

With these strategies in mind, review your health journal and identify three instances in which peer pressure interfered with your behavior change program. For each instance, write out what you might have said to deal with the situation more assertively. (If you can't think of three situations from your experiences, choose one or more of the three scenarios described at the beginning of this activity.)

1. ______________________________

____

____

2. ______________________________

____

____

3. ______________________________

____

____

Assertive communication can help you achieve your behavior change goals in a direct way by helping you keep your program on track. It can also provide a boost for your self-image and increase your confidence in your ability to successfully manage your behavior.

ACTIVITY 15 MAINTAINING YOUR PROGRAM OVER TIME

If you maintain your new behavior for at least 6 months, you've reached the maintenance stage, and your chances of lifetime success are greatly increased. However, you may find yourself sliding back into old habits at some point. If this happens, there are some things you can do to help maintain your new behavior.

- Remind yourself of the goals of your program (list them here).

___

___

___

___

___

- Pay attention to how your new pattern of behavior has improved your wellness status. List the major benefits of changing your behavior, both now and in the future.

___

___

___

___

___

- Consider the things you enjoy most about your new pattern of behavior. List your favorite aspects.

___

___

___

___

___

- Think of yourself as a problem solver. If something begins to interfere with your program, devise strategies for dealing with it. Take time out now to list things that have the potential to derail your program and develop possible coping mechanisms.

Problem	**Solution**
___	___
	___
___	___
	___
___	___
	___
___	___
	___

- Remember the basics of behavior change. If your program runs into trouble, go back to keeping records of your behavior to pinpoint problem areas. Make adjustments in your program to deal with new disruptions. And don't feel defeated if you lapse. The best thing you can do is renew your commitment and continue with your program.

INDEX

Boldface numbers indicate pages on which glossary definitions appear.

Recognizing Quackery: Becoming an Informed Consumer

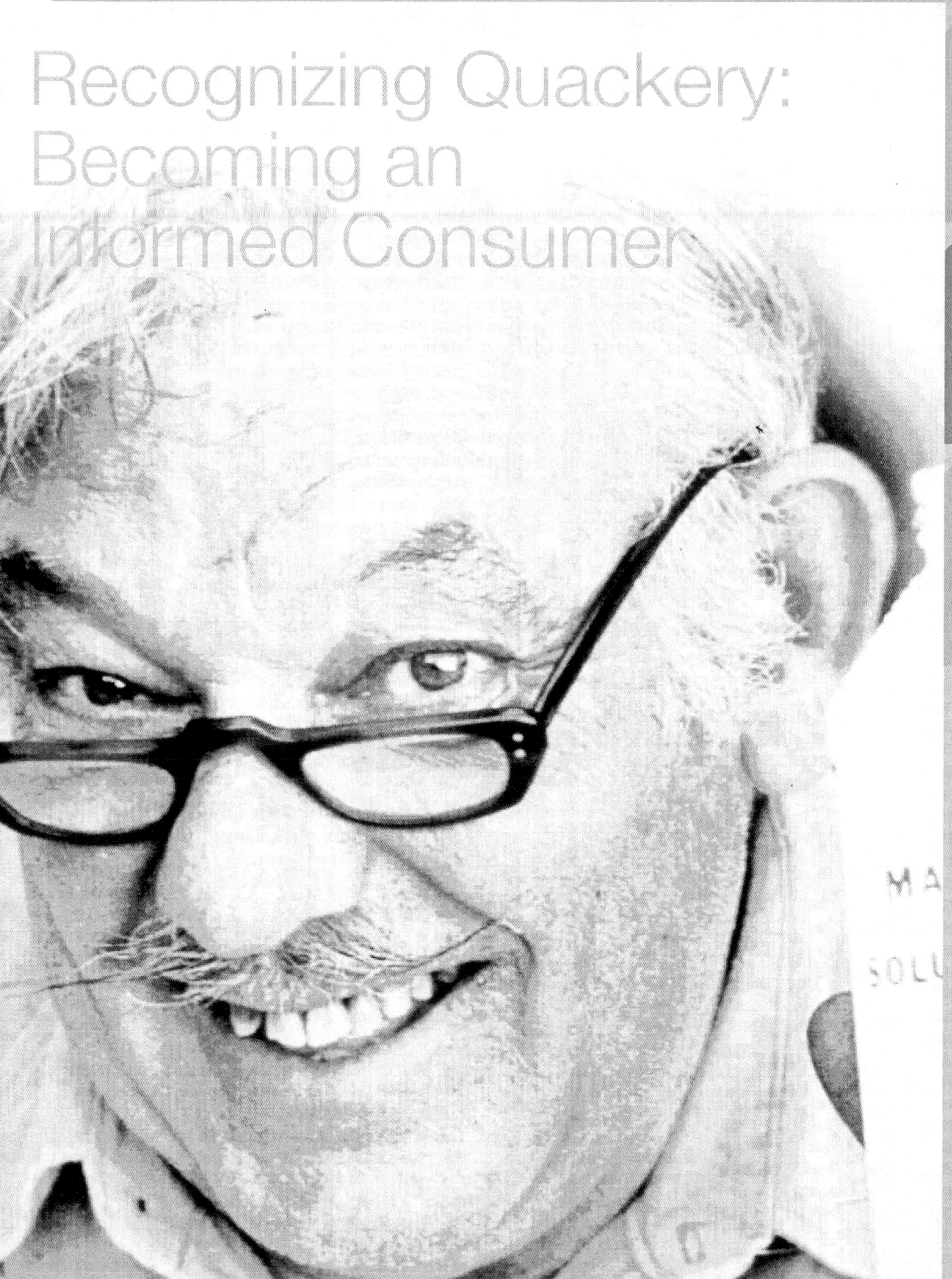

"Let the buyer beware" is a good motto for the consumer seeking advice or planning a program for developing or maintaining fitness, health, or wellness.

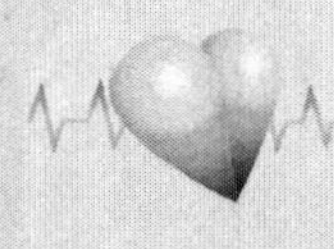

Health Goals

for the year 2010

- Increase number of college and university students who receive information on priority health-risk behaviors.
- Improve health literacy and increase access to public health information.
- Increase health communication activities that include research and evaluation.
- Increase adoption and maintenance of appropriate daily physical activity.
- Increase proportion of people who meet national dietary guidelines.
- Promote healthy and safe communities.

People have always searched for the fountain of youth and the easy, quick, and miraculous route to health and happiness. In current society, this search often focuses on fitness, nutrition, weight loss, or appearance. A variety of products are available that promise weight loss, improved health, or improved fitness with little or no effort. Sale of these products can typically be classified as either quackery or fraud, since in nearly all cases they do not work.

The dictionary definition of *quack* is "a pretender of medical skill" or "one who talks pretentiously without sound knowledge of the subject discussed." These definitions imply that the promotion of quackery involves deliberate deception, but quacks often believe in what they are doing. A consumer watchdog group called Quackwatch defines quackery more broadly as "anything involving overpromotion in the field of health." This definition encompasses questionable ideas as well as questionable products and services. The word *fraud* is reserved for situations in which deliberate deception is involved. This concept discusses common myths and provides important guidelines to help you be a more informed consumer of health, fitness, and nutrition products.

Common Myths about Exercise, Nutrition, and Health

There is no easy way to get the benefits from physical activity. Contrary to the hype from some fitness commercials and products, the benefits associated with regular activity require real effort maintained over time. Advertisements for some fitness devices claim that 10 minutes on their product is as good as 30 minutes on another product—this is simply not true. The benefits of any activity depend on the relative intensity and duration, not on the equipment. Some products promise to enhance the metabolism in the same way as exercise and these are just stimulants that have little or no effect on energy expenditure and certainly no effect on fitness.

It is NOT true that if a little of something is "good" more is "better." Marketing of nutrition products often relies on convincing people that additional vitamins, minerals, or enzymes are beneficial. It is true that deficiency of certain compounds may be harmful but extra amounts don't always provide added protection or improved health. The myth that vitamin C can cure the common cold is based on the fact that deficiencies of vitamin C can lead to scurvy. The same hype is used to sell consumers many unnecessary exercise, diet, and nutrition supplements. For example, protein supplements are marketed with convincing (and honest) claims that the body needs amino acids to form muscle. The hidden truth is that the body cannot store or use more than it needs.

Getting rid of cellulite does not require a special exercise, diet, cream, or device, as some books and advertisements insist. Cellulite is ordinary fat with a fancy name. You do not need a special treatment or device to get rid of it. In fact, it has no special remedy. Fat is fat. To decrease fat, reduce calories and do more physical activity.

Spot-reducing, or losing fat from a specific location on the body, is not possible. It is a fallacy. When you do physical activity, calories are burned and fat is recruited from all over the body in a genetically determined pattern. You cannot selectively exercise, bump, vibrate, or squeeze the fat from a particular spot. If you were flabby to begin with, local exercise could strengthen the local muscles, causing a change in the contour and the girth of that body part. But exercise affects the muscles, not the fat on that body part. General aerobic exercises are the most effective for burning fat, but you cannot control where the fat comes off.

Surgically sculpting the body with implants and liposuction to acquire physical beauty will not give you physical fitness and may be harmful. Rather than doing it the hard way, an increasing number of people are having their love handles removed surgically and fake calf and pectoral muscles implanted to improve their physique. Liposuction is not a weight loss technique but, rather, a contouring procedure. Like any surgery, it is not without risks. There have been fatalities and there is a risk for infection, hematoma, skin slough, and other conditions.

Muscle implants give a muscular appearance, but they do not make you stronger or more fit. The implants are not really muscle tissue but, rather, silicon gel or saline such as that used in breast implants or a hard substitute. Some complications can occur, such as infection and bleeding, and some physicians believe that calf implants may put pressure on the calf muscles and cause them to atrophy. A better way to improve physique and fitness is proper exercise.

The use of hand weights and wrist weights while walking, running, dancing, or bench-stepping can increase the energy expended but requires caution. Various devices have been marketed for increasing the energy expenditure in activities such as walking, running, and other forms of aerobic exercise. Examples include wrist, arm, or ankle weights and small hand-held weights. Step benches are another device that can be used to increase energy expenditure for aerobic exercise.

The practice of carrying weights is controversial. Carrying weights (not more than 1 to 3 pounds) while doing aerobic dance, walking, and other aerobic activities has been shown to increase energy expenditure, but the effect is negligible unless the arms are pumped (bending the elbow and raising the weight to shoulder height and then extending the elbow as the arm swings down). When the arms are pumped, the energy output is comparable to a slow jog. Some experts caution that pumping the arms using weight can increase the risk for injury and suggest that the benefit of added energy expenditure is not worth the added risk for injury. Also, gripping weights while exercising can cause an increase in blood pressure.

Those who choose to use weights while doing aerobic activity are at less risk for injury if they use wrist weights rather than hand-held weights. Arm movements should be limited to a range of motion below the shoulder level. Coronary patients and people with shoulder or elbow joint problems, such as arthritis, are advised not to use hand or wrist weights. Ankle weights are not recommended because they may alter your gait pattern in a way that is stressful to the knees.

Herbal products are often assumed to be safer or better than other products and this isn't true. A number of herbal products contain no useful ingredients, and some even lack the principal ingredient for which people buy them. Herbs may seem safe because they are purported to be "natural." However, it is important to recognize that a large percentage of medicines are extracted from plants. The fact that it comes from nature does not imply that it is safe. Improper use of herbs may lead to a number of harmful side effects and even death.

Claims for many forms of exercise are overstated or unsubstantiated. New exercise programs or routines are often promoted as the complete answer for total fitness or a **panacea** for health. Claims for Hatha Yoga suggest it will help you lose weight, trim inches, strengthen glands and organs, or cure health problems, such as the common cold or arthritis. Hatha yoga can be useful in reducing stress, promoting relaxation, and improving flexibility but the other claims are overstated.

Similar hype may be used for promoting new pieces of exercise equipment. Each piece of equipment claims to be fun, easy to use, and more effective than other forms of exercise. The benefits from exercise are dependent on the relative intensity and duration of the activity—and whether it is done regularly over time. The best form of exercise is clearly the one that you are willing and able to do!

Contrary to claims, passive exercises do not provide any benefits for fitness or weight loss. For exercise to be beneficial the actual work must be done by contracting skeletal muscles. A variety of **passive exercise** forms have been promoted to try to reduce the effort required to perform regular exercise. These devices employ a variety of approaches to convince people of possible benefits, but without active involvement of muscles in the movement they cannot be of any real value. The fallacies associated with many past forms of passive exercise such as fat rolling machines (purported to break up and redistribute fat) would seem obvious today but new approaches come out all the time with different marketing and promotions. The list that follows highlights some of the common forms of passive exercise.

Panacea A cure-all; a remedy for all ills.

Passive Exercise Exercise in which no voluntary muscle contraction occurs; an outside force moves the body part with no effort by the person.

- *Vibrating belts*. These wide canvas or leather belts may be designed for the chin, hips, thighs, or abdomen. Driven by an electric motor, they jerk back and forth, causing loose tissue of the body part to shake. They have no beneficial effect on fitness, fat, or figure, and they are potentially harmful if used on the abdomen (especially if used by women during pregnancy, during menstruation, or while an IUD is in place). They might also aggravate a back problem.
- *Vibrating tables and pillows*. Some of these quack devices are actually called toning tables. Contrary to advertisements, these passive devices will not improve posture, trim the body, reduce weight, or develop muscle **tonus.**
- *Continuous passive motion (CPM) tables*. The motor-driven CPM table, unlike the vibrating table, moves body parts repeatedly through a range of motion. Tables are designed to do such things as passively extend the leg at the hip joint or raise the upper trunk in a sit-up-like motion. Many of the same false claims are made for it as for the vibrating table. It also claims to remove cellulite, increase circulation and oxygen flow, and eliminate excess water retention. All of these claims are false, but the table might be justified in claiming to maintain the range of motion in certain body parts for people who cannot move themselves. Hospitals and rehabilitation centers use a similar machine to maintain range of motion in the legs of knee surgery patients, maintain integrity of the cartilage, and decrease the incidence of blood clots. Certainly, the normal, healthy person has nothing to gain from using such a device.
- *Motor-driven cycles and rowing machines*. Like all mechanical devices that do the work for the individual, these motor-driven machines are not effective in a fitness program. They may help increase circulation, and some may even help maintain flexibility, but they are not as effective as active exercise. *Nonmotorized cycles and rowing machines* are good equipment for use in a fitness program.
- *Massage*. Whether done by a masseur/masseuse or by a mechanical device, massage is passive, requiring no effort on the part of the individual. It can help increase circulation, induce relaxation, prevent or loosen adhesions, retard muscle atrophy, and serve other therapeutic uses when administered in the clinical setting for medical reasons. However, massage has no useful role in a physical fitness program and will not alter your shape. There is no scientific evidence that it can hasten nerve growth, remove subcutaneous fat, or increase athletic performance. Some athletes (e.g., cyclists) find that it aids in recovery from exercise.
- *Magnets*. The law requires magnets marketed with medical claims to obtain clearance from the **Food and Drug Administration (FDA).** To date, the FDA has not approved the marketing of any magnets for medical use, and sellers making medical claims for magnets are in violation of the law.
- *Electrical muscle stimulators*. Neuromuscular electrical stimulators cause the muscle to contract involuntarily. In the hands of qualified medical personnel, muscle stimulators are valuable therapeutic devices. They can increase muscle strength and endurance selectively and aid in the treatment of edema. They can also help prevent atrophy in a patient who is unable to move, and they may decrease muscle spasms, but in a healthy person they do not have the same value as exercise. The Federal Trade Commission (FTC) recently filed a false advertising complaint against three firms that market exercise stimulators that promise to build six-pack abs and tone muscles without exercise. These devices, worn over the abdomen, are heavily advertised in infomercials and have been shown to be ineffective and potentially hazardous to health. Electrical stimulators placed on the chest, back, or abdomen can interfere with the normal rhythm of the heart, even for normally healthy people. For those with heart, gastrointestinal, orthopedic, kidney, and other health problems, such as epilepsy, hernia, and varicose veins, they can be especially dangerous. These devices are ineffective and potentially harmful for personal use. Also beware of spas and clinics that use these devices and make claims of fitness enhancement for normally healthy people.
- *Weighted belts*. Claims have been made that these belts reduce waists, thighs, and hips when worn for several hours under the clothing. In reality, they do none of these things and have been reported to cause physical harm. However, when used in a progressive resistance program, wristlet, anklet, or laced-on weights can help produce an overload and, therefore, develop strength or endurance.
- *Inflated, constricting, or nonporous garments*. These garments include rubberized inflated devices (sauna belts and sauna shorts) and paraphernalia that are airtight plastic or rubberized. Evidence indicates that their girth-reducing claims are *unwarranted*. If exercise is performed while wearing such garments, the exercise, not the garment, may be beneficial. You cannot squeeze fat out of the pores, nor can you melt it.
- *Body wrapping*. Some reducing salons, gyms, or clubs advertise that wrapping the body in bandages soaked in a magic solution will cause a permanent reduction in body girth. This so-called treatment is pure quackery. Tight, constricting bands can temporarily indent the skin and squeeze body fluids into other parts of the body, but the skin or body will regain its original size within minutes or hours. The solution is usually similar to epsom salts, which can cause fluid to be drawn from tissue. The fluid is water, not fat, and is quickly replaced. Body wrapping may be dangerous to your health; at least one fatality has been documented.

Having a good tan is often associated with being fit and looking good, but getting tanned can be risky business. **www.mhhe.com/fit_well/web25 Click 01.** Tanning salons may claim their lamps are safe because they emit only UV-A rays, but these rays can age the skin prematurely and make it look wrinkled and leathery. They may also increase the cancer-producing potential of UV-B rays and cause eye damage. Since there is no warning sign of redness, overdosing can occur. Thirty minutes of exposure to UV-A can suppress the immune system. Tanning devices can also aggravate certain skin diseases. The Food and Drug Administration (FDA) advises against the use of any suntan lamp. It is dangerous to use tanning accelerator lotions with the lamps because they can promote burning of the skin. Tanning pills are an even worse choice. They can cause itching, welts, hives, stomach cramps, and diarrhea and can decrease night vision. Tanning in the sun is also hazardous because it damages the skin, making it age prematurely. It may cause skin cancer. It is best to use products with sun blockers if you must spend long periods in the sun (SPF 15 or higher).

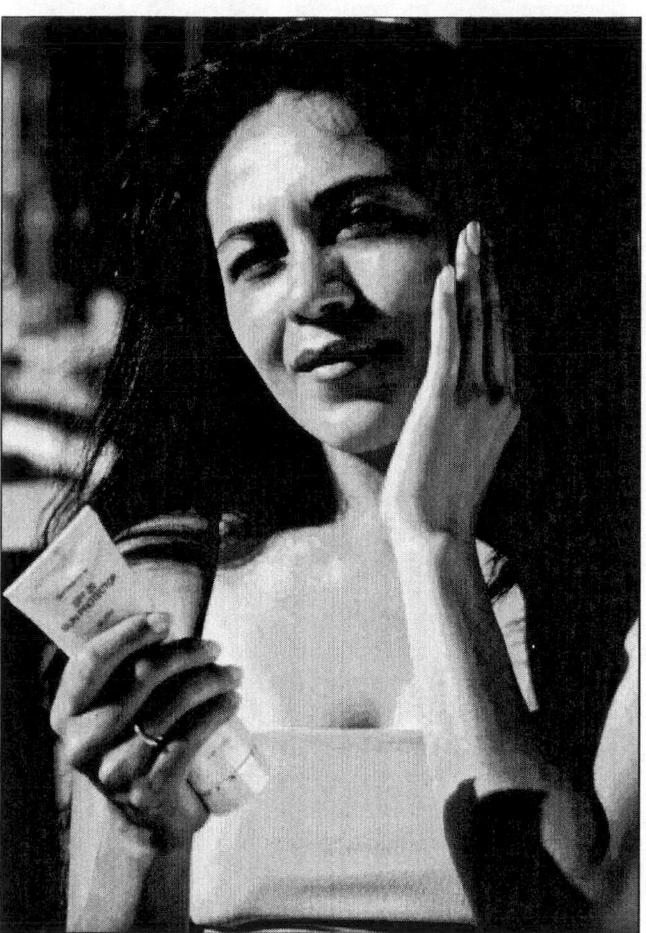

Wearing sunscreen (SPF 15 or higher) is recommended by the American Cancer Society.

Saunas, steam baths, whirlpools, and hot tubs provide no significant health benefits, and guidelines must be followed to ensure safety. Baths do not melt off fat; fat must be metabolized. The heat and humidity from baths may make you perspire, but it is water, not fat, oozing from the pores.

The effect of such baths is largely psychological, although some temporary relief from aches and pains may result from the heat. The same relief can be had by sitting in a tub of hot water in your bathroom. The following guidelines/precautions should be considered when using a sauna, steam bath, whirlpool, or hot tub:

- Take a soap shower before and after entering the bath.
- Do not wear makeup or skin lotion/oil.
- Wait at least an hour after eating before bathing.
- Cool down after exercise before entering the bath to avoid overheating.
- Drink plenty of water before or during the bath to avoid dehydration.
- Do not wear jewelry.
- Do not sit on a metal stool; do sit on a towel in the steam or sauna bath.
- Do not bathe alone.
- Do not drink alcohol before bathing.
- Get out immediately if you become dizzy; feel hot, chilled, or nauseous; or get a headache.
- Get approval from your physician if you have heart disease, low or high blood pressure, a fever, kidney disease, or diabetes; are obese; are pregnant or think you might be pregnant; or are on medications (especially anticoagulants, stimulants, or tranquilizers).
- Limit use for the elderly and for children.
- Do not exercise in a sauna or steam bath.
- Skin infections can be spread in a bath; make certain it is cleaned regularly and that the hot tub or whirlpool has proper pH and chlorination.
- Follow appropriate guidelines:

  Sauna: should not exceed 190°F (88°C) and duration should not exceed 10 to 15 minutes

  Steam bath: should not exceed 120°F (49°C) and duration should not exceed 6 to 12 minutes

  Whirlpool/hot tub: should not exceed 100°F (37°C) and duration should not exceed 5 to 10 minutes

Tonus Tonus (or tone) is the most frequently misused and abused term in fitness vocabularies. Tonus is the tension developed in a muscle as a result of passive muscle stretch. Tonus cannot be determined by feeling or inspecting a muscle. It has little or nothing to do with the strength of a muscle.

Food and Drug Administration (FDA) The federal agency that recommends and enforces government regulations regarding certain foods and drugs.

Beware of energy drinks with "boosts" sold at health bars in fitness clubs. Many health bars that sell food and drinks of various types. Some drinks contain "boosts" consisting of a tablespoon or two of a food supplement. Pharmacies were developed to prevent medical practioners from selling their own medicines rather than the best available medicine. Health clubs that sell drinks with supplements are susceptible to the claim that they are selling products for financial gain rather than the best interest of clients. Even if supplements are effecitve, which most are not, taking one dose in a drink would be ineffective and a waste of money.

Quacks

You can usually tell the difference between an expert and a quack because a quack does not use scientific methods. **www.mhhe.com/fit_well/web25 Click 02.** A good example of this fact is seen in a study that attempted to obtain documentation for products claiming to enhance athletic performance. The study found that no published scientific evidence existed to support the promotional claims of 42 percent of the products. Thirty-two percent had some scientific documentation but were marketed in a misleading manner, and 21 percent were without any human clinical trials.

Some of the ways to identify quacks, frauds, and rip-offs are to look for these clues:

- They do not use the scientific method of controlled experimentation that can be verified by other scientists.
- To a large extent, they use testimonials and anecdotes to support their claims rather than scientific methods. There is no such thing as a valid testimonial. Anecdotal evidence is no evidence at all.
- They advise you to buy something you would not otherwise have bought.
- They have something to sell.

Changing your lifestyle, rather than quick solutions, is the key to health, fitness, and wellness.

- They claim everyone can benefit from the product or service they are selling. There is no such thing as a simple, quick, easy, painless remedy/tonic or other concoction that is effective for ailments or conditions for which medical science has not yet found a remedy.
- They promise quick, miraculous results. A perfect, no-risk treatment does not exist.
- The claims for benefits are broad, covering a wide variety of conditions.
- They may offer a money-back guarantee. A guarantee is only as good as the company.
- They may claim the treatment or product is approved by the FDA. Note: Federal law does not permit the mention of the FDA in any way that suggests marketing approval.
- They may claim the support of experts, but the experts are not identified.
- The ingredients or materials in the product may not be identified.
- They may claim there is a conspiracy against them by "bureaucrats," "organized medicine," the FDA, the American Medical Association (AMA), and other experts and governmental bodies. Never believe a doctor who claims the medical community is persecuting him or her or that the government is suppressing a wonderful discovery.
- Their credentials may be irrelevant to the area in which they claim expertise.
- They use scare tactics, such as "If you don't do this, you will die of a heart attack."
- They may appear to be a sympathetic friend who wants to share a new discovery with you.
- They may quote from a scientific journal or another legitimate source, but they misquote or quote out of context to mislead you; they may also mix a little bit of truth with a lot of fiction.
- They may cite research or quote from individuals or institutions that have questionable reputations for scientific truth.
- They may claim it is a new discovery (usually it is said to have originated in Europe). There is never a great medical breakthrough that debuts in an obscure magazine or tabloid. No secret cures or magic formulas have been recognized by the scientific community, a picture on the cover of *Time* magazine, nomination for a Nobel Prize, and so on.
- The product or organization named is often similar to that of a famous person or creditable institution (e.g., the Mayo diet had no connection with the Mayo Clinic).
- They often sell products through the mail, which does not allow you to examine the product personally. There are no miracle products available only by mail order or from a single source.

You can reduce your susceptibility to quackers by being an informed consumer. The three key characteristics that predispose people to health-related quackery are a concern about appearance, health, or performance; a lack of knowledge; and a desire for immediate results. Understanding the principles of exercise and nutrition presented in this book will help you know when something sounds "too good to be true."

When evaluating health-related products or information, carefully consider the quality of your source. Common sources of misinformation are magazines, health food stores, and TV infomercials. These entities all have an economic incentive in promoting the purchase and use of exercise, diet, and weight loss products. Because of freedom of speech laws, it is legal to state opinion through these media. Note, however, that few companies make claims on product labels, since this is false advertising. Follow these additional guidelines to avoid being a victim of quackery:

- Read the ad carefully, especially the small print.
- Do not send cash; use a check, money order, or credit card so you will have a receipt.
- Do not order from a company with only a post office box, unless you know the company.
- Do not let high-pressure sales tactics make you rush into a decision.
- When in doubt, check out the company through your Better Business Bureau (BBB).

Equipment

Home exercise equipment can be helpful, but care should be used when selecting and purchasing equipment. There are many types of home exercise equipment available on the market. Because they are often expensive, care should be used when making a decision. To determine if a piece of equipment is worthwhile, ask yourself the following four questions. *Do you need it? Will you use it? Does it work? Does it work for you?* For it to be a worthwhile purchase, the answer to all four questions should be yes. Many people wonder about the relative advantages and disadvantages of different pieces of equipment. The answer to the question "What is the best piece of exercise equipment?" is the one that you will use.

It is best to buy your equipment from reputable dealers or companies. When considering several models of the same type of device, remember that you get what you pay for. Higher-end models may last longer and may promote more use, since they may be quieter or feel better to use than lower-priced models. Consult an expert if you want to know more about the quality and effectiveness of different products. Individuals with a college degree in physical education, physical therapy, or kinesiology should be able to give you good advice.

Health Clubs

Health and fitness clubs provide access to equipment and support but it is important to consider a number of factors before deciding to join. The first question to ask yourself is whether access to the facility is essential for you to begin or maintain your exercise program. The second question is whether the facility is convenient enough for you to access regularly. The distance of the gym from home or work will greatly influence your potential use of the facility. If you are serious about joining a club, consider the following points:

- Determine the qualifications of the personnel, especially of the individual responsible for your program. Is he or she an expert, as defined previously?
- Check to see if your membership can be sold or transferred to another person if you move. Check to see if you can cancel the contract if you prove you are moving outside the community.
- Choose a no-contract or monthly payment option if it is available so you can change your mind. Be prepared to resist options for long-term contracts.
- Check for hidden costs associated with membership (e.g., costs for testing, use of personal training).
- Do not be swayed by promises of quick results.
- Check the equipment to be sure that it is up to date and well maintained.
- Check to see that towels are provided to wipe machines after use and that weights are replaced after use. If not, it is good indication that supervision is not adequate.
- Check to see if rules are posted. For example, is there a time limit for using machines and is there a dress code?
- Speak with other members to get an insider's perspective regarding how they have been treated.
- Make a trial visit to the establishment during the hours when you would normally expect to use the facility to determine if it is open, if it is overcrowded, and if you would enjoy the company of the other patrons.

Visit a health club before you join.

- Make certain the club is a well-established facility that will not disappear overnight.
- Check its reputation with the Better Business Bureau. Be aware, however, that the BBB can only tell you if complaints have been made against a company. It does not endorse companies and may lack information on new companies.
- Investigate programs offered by the YMCA/YWCA, local colleges and universities, and municipal park and recreation departments. These agencies often have excellent fitness classes at lower prices than commercial establishments and usually employ qualified personnel.

Dietary Supplements

The burden of proof about the effectiveness of food supplements rests with the consumer. **www.mhhe.com/fit_well/web25 Click 03.** The passage of the Dietary Supplements Health and Education Act in 1994 shifted the burden of providing assurances of product effectiveness from the FDA to the food supplement industry, which really means it shifted to you—the consumer. Food supplements are typically not considered to be drugs, so they are not regulated. Unlike drugs and medicines, food supplements need not be proven effective or even safe to be sold in stores. To be removed from stores, they must be proven ineffective or unsafe. This leaves consumers vulnerable to false claims. Many experts suggest that quackery has increased significantly since 1994, when the act was passed.

The act had at least one positive effect. Food supplement labeling must now be truthful and not misleading. Claims concerning disease prevention, treatment, or diagnosis must be substantiated in order to appear on the product. Unfortunately, the act did not limit false claims if they are not on the product label. The result has been the removal of claims from labels in favor of claims on separate literature, often called third-party literature, because the label makes no claims, and the seller makes no written claims (second party). Rather, the seller provides claims in literature by other people (third party). The literature is distributed separately from the product, thus allowing sellers to make unsubstantiated claims for products. Also, the law does not prohibit unproven verbal claims by salespeople. A highly respected medical journal indicates that "alternative treatments should be subjected to scientific testing no less rigorous than that required for advocating unproven and potentially harmful treatments." However, as things currently stand, it is up to the consumer to make decisions about the safety and effectiveness of food supplements, so it is especially important to be well informed.

Current legislation does not provide protection to food supplement customers. **www.mhhe.com/fit_well/web25 Click 04.** Since the Dietary Supplements Health and Education Act was passed in 1994, food supplement sales have doubled (from $8 billion to more than $16 billion a year). A wide variety of supplements include ergogenic aids, vitamins and minerals, and herbals and botanicals. Ergogenic aids associated with muscle fitness are discussed in other concepts. Vitamin and mineral supplements are discussed in the nutrition concept, and herbals and botanicals are discussed here.

Recently, the sales of supplements has leveled off, primarily because of the increasing evidence of the danger of some supplements and the evidence showing the ineffectiveness of others. Evidence supports the value of some supplements. As noted earlier in this book, folic acid, calcium, vitamin E, and a daily multiple vitamin supplement can be beneficial for many people. Also, aspirin can be important for the prevention of heart disease and some forms of cancer, and evidence shows that glucosomine supplements can relieve joint pain for some people. On the other hand, over the past few years, the FDA has received thousands of complaints of adverse events (resulting in approximately 200 deaths). An editorial in a leading national newspaper suggests that "troubling side effects mount" and that "putting customers' health at risk is a high price to pay for a free market in diet supplements." Some of the problems associated with supplements are described in Table 1. Among the adverse effects reported are lead poisoning, nausea, vomiting, diarrhea, abnormal heart rhythm, fainting, impotence, and lethargy. Over a 6-year period, 2,621 adverse events were reported to the FDA and 184 resulted in death. Also, one study showed that 15 to 20 percent of over 1,600 supplements tested included substances that would cause a positive test for drugs banned by sports organizations.

More than one-half of American adults are unaware that food supplements are unregulated by the FDA or any governmental agency. Because they are unregulated, there is no guarantee that a supplement contains the ingredients it claims to contain. Further, many have been shown to contain contaminants. Even when a supplement is what it claims to be, the effects can vary widely from one person to another. Many supplements have dangerous interactions with prescribed and over-the-counter medicines and can be very dangerous.

In spite of the problems associated with lack of supplement regulations, a recent study indicates that nearly half of Americans routinely take supplements and slightly more than half believe in the value of the supplements. Interestingly, 44 percent believe that physicians know little or nothing about supplements.

Most adults (80 percent) believe that the FDA should review supplements before they are offered for sale. More than 60 percent believe that there are not enough

Table 1 ▶ Problems Associated with Supplements
Postsurgical problems, including bleeding, irregular heartbeat, and stroke. Examples: echinacea, ephedra, ginkgo, kava, St. John's wort, ginseng.
Dangerous interactions with medicines. Examples: ephedra, St. John's wort (interact with birth control pills and HIV pills).
FDA warnings concerning unsubstantiated claims about herbs added to foods, such as energy bars and water. Examples: ginkgo, ginseng, echinacea.
Allergic and other physiological reactions; negative effect on decision making. Example: GHB.
Known ill effects to health. Examples: comfrey (kidneys), kava (liver), ephedra (54 deaths associated with use).
Possible slow bone mending. Example: Vioxx.
Recall because of dangerous effects associated with contamination. Examples: PC SPES, Lipokinetix.
Action by the FTC because of deceptive advertisements. Examples: Exercise in a Bottle, Fat Trapper.
Banned by several sporting groups, including the International Olympic Committee, NCAA, and NFL. Examples: steroids, androstendione, ephedra, THC.
Contents may not be what they appear to be and dosage information is unknown. Example: The government does not guarantee contents of supplements and there is little evidence concerning dosage for most supplements.

rules to ensure purity and accurate dosage. A similar number of adults want more regulation on advertising claims. More than a few critics point out that self-regulation within the industry has not worked well. They suggest that the public will have more confidence in supplements if the FDA was watching out for their best interest. Table 2 presents some questions that should be asked about food supplements.

Fitness Books, Magazines, and Articles

Not all fitness books provide scientifically sound, accurate, and reliable information. Because publishers are motivated by profit and publishing is a highly competitive field, the choice of material to be printed is often selected on the basis of how popular, famous, or attractive the author is or how sensational or unusual his or her ideas are. Movie stars, models, TV personalities, and even Olympic athletes are rarely experts in biomechanics, anatomy and physiology, exercise, and other foundations of physical fitness. Having a good figure/physique, being fit, or having gone through a training program does not, in itself, qualify a person to advise others.

After reading the facts presented in this book you should be able to evaluate whether or not a book, a magazine, or an article on exercise and fitness is valid, reliable, and scientifically sound. To assist you further, however, ten guidelines are listed in Lab 25A.

Health Information on the Internet

Not all Internet websites provide scientifically sound, accurate, and reliable information. **www.mhhe.com/fit_well/web25 Click 05.** The development of the Internet (World Wide Web) has made information more and more accessible to the masses. Since 1995, Internet saturation has increased from 9 percent to 66 percent. Nearly three-fourths of teens and young adult computer users seek health information on the Web. Leading topics of information are cancer, diabetes, sexually transmitted diseases, and weight control. A health goal for the nation—as outlined in *Healthy People 2010*—is to increase the proportion of households with access to the Internet with the intent of making reliable health information available to as many people as possible. The Internet has made an almost unlimited amount of health information accessible, it has also been the source of much misinformation and even fraud.

The FTC is a federal government agency charged with making sure that advertising claims for products are not false or misleading. In an effort to clean up websites, the FTC initiated "Operation Cure-All." As part of this operation, the FTC conducted two "Health Claim Surf Days," during which they identified 800 websites and usenet newsgroups with questionable content. The FTC sent mailers to these sites, and 28 percent either removed the claims or the website completely. In spite of the FTC efforts, there is still much health misinformation on the Web, leading one FTC official to suggest that "miracle cures, once thought to have been laughed out of existence, have now found a new medium . . . on the Internet" (see *Web Resources*).

Another research study randomly selected 400 websites from 27,000 available on four different well-known search engines for a study of cancer. Nearly half had unverified information and 6 percent had major inaccuracies. Clearly, Internet users must be careful in selecting websites for obtaining fitness, health, and wellness information. One of the most useful rules is always get a second opinion. Consult at least two or more sources to confirm information. Getting confirmation of information from non-Web sources is also a good idea.

You can follow some general rules to help when you use the Web to obtain fitness, health, and wellness information. In general, government websites are good sources that contain sound information prepared by experts and based on scientific research. Government sites typically include "gov" as part of the address. Professional organizations and

Table 2 ▶ Questions and Comments about Food Supplements

Questions	Comments
Does the government regulate this product to be sure that it is safe and effective?	Since 1994, food supplements can be sold without proof that they are effective. The government does not test food supplements to ensure effectiveness or safety. The FDA must prove the product to be harmful or ineffective to remove it from the market. It is much harder to prove a product ineffective than to provide evidence that it is effective.
Do claims for the supplement have supporting evidence?	The evidence should be based on research with normal people, not evidence based on a population of subjects who have medical problems or nutritional deficiencies. Third-party information often cites research out-of-context or refers to weak studies that use inappropriate research techniques.
What are the active ingredients?	If the active ingredient really works, research will show its effectiveness. Of course, if it works, then it is much like a medicine and has similar side effects. Sellers of supplements often suggest the product works but that it has no side effects that are associated with medicines. Both cannot be true. For example, Cholestin is a variety of red yeast—a natural product. It contains lovastatin, the same active ingredients in medicines for lowering cholesterol. Though the product works, it has now been banned by the FDA as an over-the-counter supplement because it has the same active ingredient as medicine and has the same side effects. The regulation of this product by the FDA has been challenged in the courts by the supplement industry. The decision of the courts will have consequences for future regulation of supplements.
What are the possible side effects and risks of taking the supplement?	As noted above, if a product works as well as a medicine, it probably has the same side effects. If you know the active ingredient, you will know more about the side effects.
Are there possible interactions associated with taking the supplement?	When you take a medicine, you consult a physician or pharmacist about drug interactions. Supplements may interact with other supplements or medicines.
What are the long-term effects of taking the supplement?	Because supplements are not regulated, there has been little research about long-term effects of products. For example, melatonin is a hormone that is used for insomnia. Hormones have strong effects on the body and little is known about melatonin's long-term effects. Consider alternative solutions to long-term use of an unstudied supplement.
Are you sure the product is what it claims to be and that the size of the dose is appropriate?	U.S. Pharmacopeia (USP) is a private nonprofit organization that tests vitamins, minerals, and other supplements, to assure quality and purity as well as appropriate size and strength of a standard unit of the product (dose size and strength). The USP label ensures that the product is what it says it is. As many as two or three dozen herbal products are currently being evaluated to determine appropriate dose size. Products with the USP label that fail to meet standards will be removed from stores. Without the USP label, you are at the mercy of the company that produces the product. The deaths associated with L-tryptophan, an amino acid supplement, occurred because of contaminants (Peak-X) in the unregulated product.
Who makes the product?	In the absence of regulations, the reputation of the company that makes the product is crucial. Have complaints been made against the company? Have there been health problems with their products? How long has the company been in business? Large pharmaceutical companies are now beginning to sell supplements because of the high profit margin. Using a product from a large drug company is more likely to ensure that a product is what it is supposed to be, but it does not ensure that the product is effective.
Is the cost worth the potential benefits?	The costs of dietary supplements are typically quite high. For example, protein supplements may cost as much as $1.00 a gram. The cost per gram in good food, such as protein in a chicken breast, is typically a few cents per gram. Most experts suggest that even the most effective supplements have relatively small effects at a high cost.
Is the source of your information about the supplement reliable and accurate?	Avoid verbal information about products, especially information from the seller. Be wary of third-party literature or research in obscure journals. Be wary of those who discredit sound medical advice or information from regulatory agencies, such as the FDA.

universities can also be good sources of information. Organizations typically have "org" and universities typically have "edu" as part of the address. However, caution should still be used with organizations because it is easy to start an organization and obtain an "org" Web address. Your greatest trust can be placed in the sites of stable organizations of long standing, such as the AMA, the American Cancer Society, the American Heart Association, the American College of Sports Medicine, the National Council against Health Fraud, and the American Alliance for Health, Physical Education, Recreation and Dance, among others listed in this text. The AMA has recently developed extensive guidelines for health information on the Web (see *Suggested Readings*). The great majority of websites promoting health products have "com" in the title because these are commercial sites that are in business to make a profit. Because they are in business to make a profit, they are more inclined to contain information that is suspect or totally incorrect. Some "com" sites contain good information—for example, those listed at the end of each concept of this book. Nevertheless, it is important to evaluate, with special care, information found at "com" sites. The Tufts University School of Nutrition Science and Policy has developed a website that rates diet and health sites on the Internet. You may want to consult this website (http://navigator.tufts.edu). In Lab 25A, you can rate a website, using a checklist.

When selecting websites for inclusion at the end of each concept of the book, we used the same checklist as in Lab 25A. You will see that a majority of the sites listed are governmental and organizational sites. We do include some commercial sites but with some reservation. What we see when we evaluate a site may not be what you see when you use the site at a later date. It is important that you evaluate all websites, using the criteria suggested here.

Technology Update

Medwatch

Medwatch is a website of the FDA. This website provides a variety of consumer information, including safety alerts for drugs, product recall advisories, changes in drug safety labeling, warnings and safety information concerning dietary supplements, and health advisories concerning medical devices. This is an excellent source relating to quackery (**www.fda.gov/medwatch**).

Strategies for Action

Being a good consumer requires time, information, and effort. **www.mhhe.com/fit_well/web25 Click 06.** With time and effort, you can gain the information you need to make good decisions about products and services that you purchase. In Lab 25A, you will evaluate an exercise device, a food supplement, a magazine article, or a website. In Lab 25B, you will evaluate a health/wellness or fitness club. Taking the time to investigate a product will help you save money and help you avoid making poor decisions that affect your health, fitness, and wellness. When you are making decisions about products or services, it is a good idea to begin your investigation well in advance of the day when a decision is to be made. Salespeople often suggest that "this offer is only good today." They know that people often make poor decisions when under time pressure, and they want you to make a decision today so that they will not lose a sale.

Study Resources

Check out additional online study resources for this concept in the Student Edition of the Online Learning Center at www.mhhe.com/corbin6e.

Web Resources

Agency for Health Care Policy and Research **www.ahcpr.gov**
American Dietetics Association **www.eatright.org**
AMA Health Insight **www.ama-assn.org**
Center for Science in the Public Interest **www.cspinet.org**
Federal Trade Commission **www.ftc.gov**
Food and Drug Administration **www.fda.gov**
Healthfinder **www.healthfinder.gov**
Medwatch **www.fda.gov/medwatch/**
National Council against Health Fraud **www.ncahf.org**
Office of Dietary Supplements **http://ods.od.nih.gov**
Quackwatch **www.familyinternet.com/quackwatch/**
Tufts University Nutrition Navigator **http://navigator.tufts.edu**
U.S. Consumer Information Center **www.pueblo.gsa.gov**

Suggested Readings

Additional reference materials for Concept 20 are available at **www.mhhe.com/fit_well/web25 Click 07.**

Blendon, R. J., et al. 2001. Americans' views on the use and regulation of dietary supplements. *Archives of Internal Medicine* 161(6):805–810.

Catlin, D. H., et al. 2000. Trace contamination of over-the-counter androstenedione and positive urine test results for a nandrolone metabolite. *Journal of the American Medical Association* 284(20):2618–2621.

Consumer Reports. June 2003. Regular reports on exercise machines. For example treadmills and heart rate monitors.

Drazen, J. M. 2003. Inappropriate advertising of dietary supplements. *New England Journal of Medicine* 348(9):777–778.

Ernst, E., and K. Schmidt. 2002. Alternative cancer cures via the Internet. *British Journal of Cancer* 87(5):479–480.

Fairfield, K. M., and R. H. Fletcher. 2002. Vitamins for chronic disease prevention in adults: Scientific review. *Journal of the American Medical Association* 287(23): 3116–3126.

Fletcher, R. H., and K. M. Fairfield. 2002. Vitamins for chronic disease prevention in adults: Clinical applications. *Journal of the American Medical Association* 287(23):3127–3129.

Fontanarosa, P. B., et al. 2003. The need for regulation of dietary supplements—lessons from ephedra. *Journal of the American Medical Association* 289(12):1568–1570.

Krone, C. 2004. Nutritional supplements: Friend or foe? *New Zealand Medical Journal* 117(1196):U937–U945.

National Council against Health Fraud Newsletter. Published every other month, it contains articles about health products and food supplements. NCAHF, P.O. Box 1276, Loma Linda, CA 92354.

Park, R. L. 2000. *Voodoo Science: The Road from Foolishness to Fraud.* New York: Oxford University Press.

Soloman, P. R., et al. 2002. Ginkgo for memory enhancement: A randomized controlled trial. *Journal of the American Medical Association* 288(7):835–840.

Tekin, K. A., and L. Kravitz. 2004. The growing trend of ergogenic aids and supplements. *ACSM's Health and Fitness Journal* 8(2):15–18.

USA Today. April 15, 2002. Dietary supplement use: Troubling side effects. *USA Today* 11A.

USA Today. May 10, 2001. Herbal drug bust. *USA Today* A14.

Winker, M. A., et al. 2000. Guidelines for medical and health information sites on the Internet: Principles governing AMA web sites. *Journal of the American Medical Association* 283(12):1600–1606.

In the News

Increased Regulation of Dietary Supplements

There are over 29,000 dietary supplements available to consumers and sales have topped $16 billion. Because the Dietary Supplement Health and Education Act (DSHEA) shifted the burden of proof to the FDA, there has been rampant quackery and fraud in this industry. Recent efforts by a number of organizations is aiming to address the problem. The following list summarizes some of the recent initiatives.

- The FDA recently published regulations that would strengthen the manufacturing requirements of dietary supplements. If finalized, this rule would give consumers greater confidence that the dietary supplements they choose to use will have the purity, strength, quality, and potency claimed on the label. This will help to reduce problems such as superpotency, subpotency, contamination, and improper packaging that have been reported in recent years.
- The Federal Trade Commission (FTC) and the FDA have tightened links that will help to detect and deter health fraud. The FDA is responsible for the safety, manufacturing, and labeling of supplements. The FTC is responsible for regulating the advertising of the products. The revised arrangements will improve communication and provide a clearer jurisdiction of authority between the two organizations.
- The Institute of Medicine released a recent report (*Dietary Supplements: A Framework for Evaluating Safety*), which proposes solutions to the loopholes that were created after the release of the 1994 Dietary Supplement Health and Education Act (DSHEA). The document highlights ways in which the FDA can set priorities for evaluating potentially harmful products. For additional information, visit **http://nap.edu.**
- The *Consumer Health Information for Better Nutrition Initiative* of the FDA is designed to provide more science-based, FDA-regulated information on food labels. The idea is to provide information on the product that will allow the consumer to know the level of agreement of scientists concerning various claims. The following are the new informational labels:
  - A, significant scientific agreement for the claim
  - B, good scientific evidence but not entirely conclusive
  - C, evidence is limited and inconclusive
  - D, there is little scientific evidence support the claim

By providing clearer information about the health consequences of foods and dietary supplements the FDA hopes that consumers can make better nutritional choices. The initiative ultimately hopes that consumer demand for healthier products will stimulate changes in the food service industry. A system in which companies have to compete to provide healthier products to Americans would greatly improve the quality of products available to consumers. For additional information, visit the website at **www.fda.gov/oc/mcclellan/chbn.html.**